THE PUNISHER

OFFICIAL INDEX TO THE
MARVEL UNIVERSE

W9-ATB-525

HEAD WRITERS/COORDINATORS
Daron Jensen, Stuart Vandal & Jeph York

WRITERS
Paul Bourcier, Chris Buchner, Russ Chappell, Chris McCarver, Jacob Rougemont, Al Sjoerdsma, Robert J. Sodaro & Kevin Wasser

EDITOR
Jeff Youngquist

EDITORS, SPECIAL PROJECTS
Jennifer Grünwald & Mark D. Beazley

ASSISTANT EDITORS
Alex Starbuck & Nelson Ribeiro

SENIOR VICE PRESIDENT OF SALES
David Gabriel

SVP OF BRAND PLANNING & COMMUNICATIONS
Michael Pasciullo

BOOK DESIGN
Spring Hoteling

PRODUCTION
Joe Frontirre

EDITOR IN CHIEF
Axel Alonso

CHIEF CREATIVE OFFICER
Joe Quesada

PUBLISHER
Dan Buckley

EXECUTIVE PRODUCER
Alan Fine

Special thanks to George Olshevsky for starting it all and setting the standard so high, the folks at the Marvel Chronology Project for appreciating what we get right and pointing out what we get wrong, Spiderfan.org, the Marvel Appendix, Mile High Comics' Chuck Rozanski & Chris Boyd, Mike Hansen, Jesse Herndon, Sarah Jensen, Harvey Johnston, Andy Nystrom, Sidney Osinga, Jeff Christiansen, and the rest of the Handbook team.

In loving memory of Medusa Jensen, 2006-2011

Welcome to the new *Official Index to the Marvel Universe*'s eighth collected edition, featuring the Punisher!

Entry format: Credits include all the known creators. Where the cover artists are different from those handling the interior, we credit them separately. Pencilers and inkers are separate credits, unless the same person did both, whereby they are credited for "art." Feature Characters are the lead, often title, characters in the comic. Supporting Cast are the regular cast. Villains should be obvious. Guest Stars cover other heroes and major characters who turn up in the story, while Other Characters covers everyone else. When multiple characters have used a given codename, we identify which version the character is the first time they appear in a given title; thereafter, unless otherwise stated, all subsequent appearances can be assumed to be the same version. Locations/Items serves to list places plus unusual, unique, or significant equipment. The Synopsis covers the events depicted in the story. Flashbacks are placed in their own section for ease of reference and divided into four types (fb, dfb, pfb, & rfb) described in the Abbreviation Key. The Note section covers interesting information and anomalies that don't fit the other headings. **Chronologies:** Along with telling you which characters turn up in which issues, we also try to let you know where they were beforehand, and where they go afterwards. After so many years of flashbacks and retroactive continuity (retcons), this can become a tricky process. For Feature Characters, we list, in order, all appearances between the issue being covered and the character's next appearance in the series. For all other reoccurring characters, we list their last and next appearances. However, so that readers can enjoy tracking a character's appearances both in the genuine historical order, and in the revised order created by the insertions of flashbacks over the years, we distinguish between real world and flashback-revised "chronologically" last and next appearances. We omit "next in" if the subsequent issue is that character's next appearance (or if the issue in question is their final appearance to date), and, for Supporting Cast, we omit "last in" if the previous appearance is within the last five issues of the same series. We also include characters' next and last "behind-the-scenes" appearances, if applicable. As confusion has arisen in the past over volume numbers, we distinguish between different volumes sharing the same cover title by including the publication year. Issue numbers with a slash and extra digit indicate later stories in the same issue; for example, 50/3 is the third story in issue 50.

FRANCIS CASTIGLIONE, FRANK CASTLE AND THE PUNISHER - Before Punisher #1 (January 1986)

Mario Lorenzo Castiglione leaves Sicily for America with his wife Louisa, who is pregnant with their son, Francis (PWJ #25, '90 fb). Francis "Frank" Castiglione grows up in Queens, New York (Pun #18, '97 fb, Pun #1, '98 fb & PWJ #18, '90 fb) and studies for the priesthood, but leaves the seminary to join the Marines (Pun:Int, '89 fb). Trained at Camp Lejeune (PWJ #3, '07 fb), Pvt. Castiglione is initially stationed at Big Nothing (Pun:RBN, '89 fb) before his first tour of duty in Vietnam where he encounters Col. No-Name (TheNam #67-69, '92 fb), is stationed at Marble Mountain Airbase (Pun #1, '87 fb), romances Angela Wynoski (PunBl, '91 fb) and battles the North Vietnamese Army (Pun #1, '98 fb). Frank marries Maria Elizabeth (Pun #100, '95 fb), battles in Vietnam (Pun #59, '92 fb, Pun #18, '97 fb, Pun:AG, '88 fb & PWJ #21, '90 fb) and returns home (Pun:AG, '88 fb) for the birth of his daughter, Lisa Castiglione (Pun Ann #4, '91 fb & Pun:AG, '88 fb). In Vietnam, Burt Kenyon rescues Sgt. Castiglione, but is later discharged as mentally unfit for duty (ASM #175, '77 fb). In Cambodia, Sgt. Castiglione battles other Marines who are trafficking drugs (Pun:RBN, '89 fb). At the end of his first tour (TheNam #69, '92 fb) Frank celebrates the birth of his son, Frank Castiglione, Jr (Pun:AG, '88 fb). In his second tour, Sgt. Castiglione serves with MACV SOG Special Ops with DX Hanrahan (PWZ #20-21, '93 fb). In his third tour with 1st Marine Division in Da Nang, Sgt. Castiglione learns he can't reenlist (PunTheNam, '94 fb).

Unable to adjust to normal life, Frank changes his and his family's name to Castle, enlists in the Marines again (PunTheNam, '94 fb) and goes through basic training at Fort Dix (Pun #1, '98 fb, PunTheNam, '94 fb, Pun:OM #1, '93 & Pun:Int, '89 fb) and advanced training at Fort Benning where he's awarded Green Beret status (PunTheNam, '94 fb) and dispatched to Vietnam (Pun:OM #1, '93) where he serves with the 5th Civilian Indigenous Defense Group (Pun:BSS #3, '94 fb) and encounters the Death Doctor and kills Col. No-Name in Saigon (PunTheNam, '94 fb). When Castle's friend Roger Wong is arrested for a black market weapons operation, Frank is put on recruitment duty in the States for a month (Pun:OM #1, '93). Phan Bighawk trains Frank in wilderness survival (Pun #77, '93 fb). In Vietnam, Sgt. Castle is observed by the demon Olivier (Pun #3, '99 fb) and captured by the Monkey; Sgt. Castle usurps the Monkey's skull symbol, paints it on his chest and kills the Monkey (TheNam #52-53, '91). After 2nd Lt. Castle's platoon is slaughtered on Christmas (PunHol #2, '94 fb), Lt. Castle battles in Vietnam (Pun #1, '86 fb), encounters another Marine drug smuggling operation (PWJ #4, '89 fb) and meets Sgt. Joe Perrett (Pun #6, '02 fb). After one of Capt. Castle's men triggers a land mine (Pun/Cap #3, '92 fb), Capt. Castle receives the Distinguished Service Cross, returns home (Pun Ann #4, '91 & Pun #1, '98 fb), works for a security firm (Pun:OM #1, '93) and trains Special Forces (Pun Ann #4, '91). After DX Hanrahan visits the Castle family on Halloween (PWZ #21, '93 fb), the Castle family celebrates Christmas (Pun Ann #4, '91, PunHol #2, '94 fb & Pun:XMas #1, '07 fb). After spending time with childhood friend Lucy Mellace (Pun #1, '98 fb) and his family (PWZ #24, '94 fb, Pun #100, '95 fb & Pun #10, '09 fb), Frank learns he'll be receiving the Presidential Freedom Award (Pun Ann #4, '91) and plans to picnic in Central Park (Pun:RBN, '89 fb).

As an aide with the San Lorenzo embassy in New York, Hector Montoya works with an embassy courier and Forest Hunt to exchange narcotics for funds to buy weapons for neighboring Santo Angelo's contras. Congress resumes aid to Santo Angelo and, sensing that the idealistic Montoya would stop the drug trade, Hunt and his mob connections scheme to eliminate Montoya. Montoya learns of Hunt's treachery and replaces his latest drug shipment with fake drugs. Bruno Costa and his mobsters turn on Hunt when they discover the fake drugs (PWJ #3, '89 fb). The Castle family arrives in Central Park (MP #2, '75 fb) and set up a picnic while unknowingly being observed by Costa family mobsters (PWJ #1, '88 fb). The Castle family eats (PWZ #25, '94 fb) and mobsters continue to watch (Pun #17, '97 fb). As the Castle children play with a Frisbee (Pun #4, '99 fb) and a kite (PWJ #1, '88 fb, Pun Ann #4, '91, PunBl, '91 fb & DE:A, '95 fb), the Costa mobsters prepare to kill Forest Hunt (PWJ #3, '89 fb). The kite gets away from Frank and his son (Pun/Cap #3, '92 fb) as Hunt is shot (DE:A, '95 fb). Frank Jr. notices movement behind some trees, and the Castle family sees the Costa mobsters hanging Hunt from a tree (Pun #4, '99 fb, PWJ #1, '88 fb & MP #2, '75 fb). The Castle family tries to run away (MP #2, '75 fb), but the Costa mobsters take aim (PWJ #1, '88 fb) and shoot the Castle family (MP #2, '75 fb). Frank lunges at the mobsters in a rage, but is shot (Pun Ann #4, '91). Frank tries to protect his family but is shot again (Pun #4, '99 fb, PWJ #1, '88 fb & PWJ #3, '89 fb). Covered in his family's blood (Pun/Cap #3, '92 fb), Frank falls and the Costa mobsters escape (Pun Ann #4, '91). As Maria, Lisa and Frank Jr. lay dead (DE:A, '95 fb & PWJ #1, '88 fb), Frank awakens (PWJ #1, '88 fb) and finds Maria dead (MP #2, '75 fb) and his children's bodies (PWJ #1, '88 fb). Frank weeps for his dead family (PWJ #3, '89 fb & Pun #1 '86 fb). Det. Johnny Laviano investigates the Castle family murders, discovers the unconscious Frank Castle and Forest Hunt are not dead and takes them to Mount Sinai hospital where Frank is treated by Miles Warren (Pun:YO #1, '94). Frank confirms his family is dead (Pun:AG, '88 fb), Hunt dies (PWJ #3, '89 fb) and Frank survives a mob assassination attempt (Pun:YO #1-2, '94-95). Laviano tells Frank the Costas killed his family (Pun Ann #4, '91). Later, as Frank buries his family, Laviano tells Frank the Costas will go free (MSA Mag #1, '76 fb). Unable to commit suicide, Frank gathers evidence to have the Costas arrested. The Costas send Billy Russo to kill Frank (Pun:YO #2-4, '95).

Surviving his home's destruction, Frank Castle becomes the Punisher, records his first War Journal entry and destroys Billy Russo's face, turning it into a jigsaw (Pun:YO #4, '95). Punisher hunts down and kills the Costa mobsters (MSA Mag #1, '76 fb) and their leader, Frank Costa (Pun #4, '99 fb). With his family avenged, Punisher begins his war on crime (Pun #1, '86 fb, Pun #17, '97 fb & Pun:AG, '88 fb) by battling the Ramone Drug Cartel (PunBl, '91), Lorenzo Jacobi (ASM #202, '80 fb), terrorists, druglords and mobsters (Pun:OM #2, '93). Alongside the time-traveling Killpower, Punisher fights the Huns and Street Amazons (Kill:EY #3, '93). Miles Warren, now the villainous Jackal, hires Punisher to kill Spider-Man and kills the Mechanic, Punisher's arms supplier (ASM #129, '74). Later, Punisher teams up with Spider-Man to battle the Tarantula (ASM #134-135, '74), hires Roger Wong to be his new weapons supplier but Wong is killed, and recruits Microchip into his war on crime (Pun:OM #2, '93). After Punisher and Spider-Man battle Moses Magnum (GSSM #4, '75), Punisher destroys Mark Christianson's International Industrial Alliance (MP #2, '75), kills mob assassin Audrey (MSA Mag #1, '76), battles Bullseye in Nicaragua (Bull:GH #3, '05 fb) and destroys Oswald Zinn's bank robbery network (W/Pun #1, '04 fb). Punisher again teams with Spider-Man to battle Billy Russo, now the mobster Jigsaw (ASM #161-162, '76) and Burt Kenyon now the mercenary Hitman (ASM #174-175, '77). Continuing his war against the mob (CoH #2, '97), Punisher runs afoul of Captain America (Cap #241, '80), with Spider-Man battles Lorenzo Jacobi (ASM #201-202, '80) and slaughters a mobster's bachelor party (PunvBull #1, '06 fb). After battling Dr. Octopus with Spider-Man (ASM Ann #15, '81), Punisher attacks more mobsters (U #3, '06 fb & Pun #80, '93 fb), trains (Pun Ann #2/3, '89 fb & Pun Ann #3/2, '90 fb), is shot by Daredevil (DD #181-184, '82) and imprisoned at Dannemora State Prison (PPSSM #78-79, '83), where cook Martini drugs his food to make him psychotic (Pun #1, '86 bts). Punisher escapes by coercing fellow inmate Boomerang's help, vowing to kill the Kingpin (PPSSM #81, '83) but also targets minor offenders. Kingpin overpowers him, and Spider-Man hands Punisher over to the police (PPSSM #82, '83). At his arraignment, Punisher has a breakdown (PPSSM #83, '83), but recovers and is sent to Ryker's Island prison (PWJ #2, '88 fb) until his trial…

PUNISHER #1 (January 1986)

"Circle of Blood!" (40 pages)

CREDITS: Steven Grant (writer), Michael Zeck (pencils, colors), John Beatty (inks), Ken Bruzenak (letters), Carl Potts (editor), Phil Zemelman (c inks)
FEATURE CHARACTER: Punisher (Francis G. "Frank" Castle, born "Castiglione," vigilante, also as Lt. Castle in fb2 between PunHol #2, '94 fb & PWJ #4, '89 fb; also as Frank Castle in fb3 between PWJ #3, '89 fb & Pun:YO #1, '94; also in fb1&4 between Pun #4, '99 fb & Pun #17, '97 fb; last in PPSSM #83, '83, chr last in PWJ #2, '88 fb)
SUPPORTING CAST: Maria Elizabeth Castle (Frank's murdered wife), Frank David "Frank Jr." Castle, Lisa Barbara "Christie" Castle (Frank's two murdered children) (all in fb between PWJ #3, '88 fb & Pun:YO #1, '94)
VILLAINS: The Trust: Jerome Gerty (Rykers Island Warden, 1st), his aide Tommy (1st) (both next in Pun #4, '86), other Trust members (bts); Jigsaw (Billy Russo, crimelord scarred by Punisher, last in ASM #188, '79, next in Pun #4, '86), Don "the Brain" Cervello (prison crime boss, 1st, next in Pun #56, '91 fb) & Gregario (his right-hand man, 1st, chr next bts in Pun #56, '91 fb, next in Pun #55, '91), Ryker's Island prisoners inc Alroy, Gold, O'Brien, Pladenas & "the Mule"; Charlie Siciliano (mob boss, 1st) & his men, Frisky "Martini" Martin (corrupt prison cook), corrupt prison guards
OTHER CHARACTERS: Tony Massera (murdered mob boss Mickey Massera's son, 1st), prison guards inc Mitch, riot police, Frannie (mentioned, corrupt prison guard's woman)
LOCATIONS/ITEMS: Central Park, Vietnam jungle (both photos only), Ryker's Island, Manhattan streets / Punisher's Kevlar armor, skull uniform, & utility belt (see NOTE), guns, lead pipes, Mitch's poisoned coffee, soda bottle silencer, Tommy's Punisher file (see NOTE)
FLASHBACKS: The Punisher fires his pistols (1), Frank jumps away from an explosion while firing his machine gun in Vietnam (2), Frank kneels crying over the corpses of his slain family (3), the Punisher carrying a shotgun (4).
SYNOPSIS: Returned to Ryker's Island following his escape from prison during a psychotic rampage, Punisher confronts prison cook Martini, revealing he knows Martini drugged him to induce the madness. Later trailing Martini to find who ordered the drugging, Frank discovers his old enemy Jigsaw is the culprit. Jigsaw's followers attack Frank, eventually overwhelming him, but the brawl ends when senior crime lord Don Cervello intervenes, fearing guards will clamp down if an inmate is killed. Punisher and Cervello pretend to call a truce until a prison break can be launched. A few nights later, as the breakout commences, Punisher fakes his death to draw attention from himself, and heads to a security tower to prevent the criminals from escaping. He alerts tower guards to the fleeing criminals, with the guards in turn gunning down the escapees. Cervello and Jigsaw flee to the Warden's office, taking the Warden hostage, but the Punisher disables Jigsaw and bluffs Cervillo into surrendering. The Warden and his aide Tommy then offer an alliance to the Punisher, revealing they are part of "the Trust," an organization devoted to destroying criminals. The Punisher agrees to their aid. Outside Ryker's, mob boss Charlie Siciliano convinces the peaceful Tony Massera to avenge the Punisher's slaying of Tony's father...
NOTE: Frank's file here states his family name was changed from "Castiglione" to "Castle" by Frank's parents when he was age six, but PunTheNam, '94 reveals Frank changed the name to Castle after both his children were born; his parents were originally named Mario and Louisa Castiglione. His formal first name is confirmed in PWZ #21,'90; his middle initial "G" is revealed by his dog tag in TheNam #69, '92. Pun #11, '88, reveals Maria Castle's first name, and Pun #1, '04, her middle name; though this last comic was subsequently confirmed to feature an alternate reality (Earth-200111) Punisher, the names revealed therein hold for the mainstream (Earth-616) Castles too. Lisa Castle's first name is revealed in ST #14, '88, her middle in Pun #11, '88, her nickname "Christie" in PunTheNam, '94. Frank Jr.'s first name and nickname "Frankie" are revealed in Pun #11, '88 and his middle name in Pun #1, '04. Punisher's armor, uniform and belt are considered part of his standard equipment and will not be listed hereafter except when their status changes. Jerome Gerty's full name is revealed in OHMUHC #9, '09. Punisher's drugging prior to this issue retroactively explains his mentally unbalanced depiction in PPSSM #81-83, '83.

PUNISHER #2 (February 1986)

"Back to the War" (24 pages)

CREDITS: Steven Grant (writer), Michael Zeck (pencils), John Beatty (inks), Ken Bruzenak (letters), Bob Sharen (colors), Carl Potts (editor), Phil Zemelman (c inks)
FEATURE CHARACTER: Punisher
VILLAINS: The Trust: Alex Alaric (high ranking Trust member, 1st), Angela (Alaric's lover, 1st) & other Trust members (bts); crime bosses: Kingpin (Wilson Fisk, crimelord king, bts, last in PPSSM #109, '85, next bts in Pun #4, '86), Bo Barrigan (last in Daz #5, '81, dies), George "Georgie Porgy" Ovani (crime boss, dies), Injun Joe (last in DD #180, '82, dies), Happy Jack Turner (crime boss, dies), "Killer" Croesus (last in DD #135, '76, dies), Morgan (last in MTU #88, '79, next in BP #16, '00), Tomas Santiago, "Joisey" Joe Simon Ejszaka (last in DD #148, '77), other crime bosses (several die), Nolo Contendre (hitman, dies), Charlie Siciliano & his men
OTHER CHARACTERS: Ben Urich (Daily Bugle reporter, bts on phone, last in ASM #262, '85, next in DD #221, '85), Tony Massera, Kingpin body double (dead), fisherman, priest (mentioned on newspaper headline as slain in mob violence), reporter (on TV screen only), subway bystanders, Alaric's dog
LOCATIONS/ITEMS: Alaric's mansion, Angela's house, Georgy Porgy's house, Grand Central Station, Kingpin's highrise, Hudson Park, Riverside Park (both mentioned as near Angela's house) / Angela's bed, phone, Kingpin's bomb, chair, desk, Nolo Contendre's gun, Punisher Battle Van (destroyed), Daily Bugle newspaper, dump truck, grappling hook, grenade, knife, Chinese food, city bus (mentioned as caught in gang battle), subway car
SYNOPSIS: Secretly freed from prison by the Trust, the Punisher scales the Kingpin's highrise to confront the villain, but is caught by a body double left by the Kingpin, triggering a bomb and sending him falling from the building. Barely breaking his fall, Punisher passes out from his wounds, awakening in the home of Angela, who tells him she recognized his uniform and wants to aid his war on crime, claiming criminals murdered her family. Learning Kingpin has faked his death, Frank spreads word to the newspapers, hoping to ignite a gang war that will take out many of the crime lords. As the war heats up, Charlie Siciliano calls for a cease-fire, holding a meeting at Grand Central Station that the Punisher spies on. When assassin Nolo Contendre fires on the mobsters, Punisher chases the shooter onto a subway car, eventually killing Nolo, but not before other passengers are wounded. Frank departs the subway remorseful for his role in starting the gang war. Upon arriving back at his van, the vehicle explodes from a planted bomb. Frank calls his Trust contact Alaric for assistance, unaware Alaric and Angela are lovers...
NOTE: In this issue, the Punisher records War Journal entry 1053.

PUNISHER #3 (March 1986)

"Slaughterday" (23 pages)

CREDITS: Steven Grant (writer), Michael Zeck (pencils), John Beatty (inks), Ken Bruzenak (letters), Bob Sharen (colors), Carl Potts (editor), Phil Zemelman (c inks)
FEATURE CHARACTER: Punisher
VILLAINS: The Trust: Alex Alaric, Angela, Markus Coriander (1st, dies), Texas (1st) & other Trust members (bts); Punishment Squad (brainwashed Ryker's criminals), Charlie Siciliano (dies, last app), Carlos & Emmanuel & Tomas Santiago (prev 3 crime boss brothers, only app, die), & their men, Luis (Santiago driver, bts, replaced by the Punisher), "Joisey" Joe Simon Ejszaka (next in Dline #1, '02), and his men
OTHER CHARACTERS: Tony Massera, bystanders (1 girl killed), Vietnamese peasants (in Frank's mind only)
LOCATIONS/ITEMS: Alaric's mansion, Angela's house, Cafe San Juan, Markus Coriander's office at Park & 27th / Santiago's car, guns, hidden microphone, speakers
SYNOPSIS: The Punisher rescues Tomas Santiago from a mob hit, pledging to let him live if he'll set up another meeting to end the gang war. Santiago agrees. Later, at Angela's house, Angela tries to convince Frank to join the Trust, while Alaric and fellow Trust member "Texas" listen over a hidden microphone. Frank goes outside to investigate a parked car spying on Angela's house, discovering Tony Massera inside. Massera explains he intends to kill the Punisher to avenge his father's death, but is waiting till Frank ends the gang war. Frank warns Massera to stay away. Later, as the mob bosses begin a phone conference, figures dressed as the Punisher appear, killing each mobster. The real Punisher arrives in time to slay the "Punisher" who shot Santiago. Believing remaining mob boss Markus Coriander is behind the shootings, Frank goes to confront him. Coriander escapes, ordering his "Punishment Squad" to cover his escape. Frank defeats the copycats and chases Coriander. In his flight, Coriander accidentally kills a child. In shock, Markus stops running, revealing to Frank that he's a member of the Trust. Angela appears and kills Markus, before shooting Frank and leaving him for dead.

PUNISHER #4 (April 1986)

"Final Solution" (23 pages)

CREDITS: Steven Grant (writer), Michael Zeck (pencils), John Beatty (inks), Ken Bruzenak (letters), Bob Sharen (colors), Carl Potts (editor), Phil Zemelman (c inks)
FEATURE CHARACTER: Punisher
VILLAINS: Kingpin (bts, last bts in Pun #2, '86, next in DD #227, '86), the Trust: Alex Alaric, Angela, Jerome Gerty, Texas, Tommy, helicopter pilot (prev 4 die) & other Trust members (bts); Punishment Squad: Jigsaw (last in Pun #1, '86), Joey Sabo (only app)
OTHER CHARACTERS: Tony Massera, police (Dave named, dies), Alaric's bloodhound
LOCATIONS/ITEMS: Alaric's mansion inc pressurized gas chamber, Manhattan, Ryker's Island, Tommy's apartment, Warden's apartment / Alaric's monitor screens, Jigsaw's grenade launcher, Texas' helicopter, Tommy's address rolodex, Tony Massera's car, Warden's address book, police car, handcuffs
SYNOPSIS: The Punisher breaks into the apartment of Tommy, the Warden's aide, but finds him slain by a Punishment Squad member. Frank races to Warden Gerty's apartment, killing the Punisher copycat before he can slay Gerty. The Warden reveals Alaric's address to the Punisher, but refuses to go to prison, taking his own life with a gun instead. The police arrive and arrest Frank, who warns them the Trust is out for him. A Punishment Squad soon attacks, killing one officer; uncuffed by the other officer, Frank slays the Squad then flees. He confronts Tony Massera, forcing Tony to drive him to Alaric's home. Trust member Texas warns Alaric the rest of the Trust are growing doubtful of Alaric's plan. Arriving at Alaric's home, Frank pushes Tony out the car and storms the mansion. Jigsaw is among the brainwashed Punishment Squad guards, but seeing Frank jolts his memory. Texas accuses Alaric of failure; Alaric kills him in response. Alaric asks Angela to leave, insisting he must confront the Punisher alone, then traps the Punisher in their reconditioning gas chamber, beginning the process to brainwash Frank.

PUNISHER #5 (May 1986)

"Final Solution Part 2" (22 pages)

CREDITS: Steven Grant (plot), Jo Duffy (script), Mike Vosburg (pencils), John Beatty (inks), Ken Bruzenak (letters), Bob Sharen (colors), Carl Potts (editor), Michael Zeck (c pencils), Phil Zemelman (c inks)
FEATURE CHARACTER: Punisher (next in ASM #284-285 & 288, Pun #1, all '87)
VILLAINS: The Trust: Alex Alaric (next in PWJ #75, '95), Angela (next in PWJ #68, '94 bts, next in PWJ #69, '94); Punishment Squad (others next in PWJ #75, '95) inc Jigsaw (next in Pun #35, '90)
OTHER CHARACTERS: Tony Massera (last app), Alaric's bloodhound
LOCATIONS/ITEMS: Alaric's mansion inc pressurized gas chamber, bedroom / Alaric's luggage, Angela's jeep, gas, guns, knife, helicopter wreckage
SYNOPSIS: The Punisher clogs a gas vent, causing pressure to build and exploding a wall of the gas chamber. Exiting, he is attacked by Jigsaw as the Punishment Squad watches. When Punisher defeats Jigsaw, the other Punishment Squad members break their conditioning and flee. A panicking Alaric catches the Punisher off guard but flees before finishing him off. Pursuing, the Punisher finds Alaric in his room packing his luggage to escape. Realizing Alaric is a coward without the Trust and Punishment Squad to back him, Frank orders Alaric to call reporter Ben Urich and give a full account of the Trust's activities, leaving Alaric quivering in fear. As Frank is leaving, Tony Massera confronts him and threatens to shoot Frank for killing his father. Frank reminds Tony his father was a criminal, and warns Tony against entering the cycle of vengeance. Tony relents and lets Frank leave. Waiting outside the mansion, Angela sees Frank exit and realizes he's defeated Alaric. She tries to run over Frank with her jeep, but he shoots the vehicle, leaving her teetering on the edge of the bridge leading to Alaric's mansion. When she calls for help, he walks away.
NOTE: Tony Massera is mistakenly referred to as Tony Siciliano here. Alaric either fails to expose the Trust, or his exposing of the organization results in a leadership vacuum he exploits, as he is the Trust's leader by his next appearance in PWJ #75, '95.

PUNISHER #1 (July 1987)

"Marching Powder" (23 pages)

CREDITS: Mike Baron (writer), Klaus Janson (art, colors), James Novak (letters), Carl Potts (editor)
FEATURE CHARACTER: Punisher (also as Bill Messina, also in pfb, also as Pvt. Castiglione in fb1 between TheNam #69, '92 fb & PunBl, '91)
VILLAINS: General Buktir van Tranh aka "The General" (drug cartel leader, 1st, voice only), Wilfrid Sobel (head of Tranh's NYC drug trafficking, only app, dies), Belinda Foster (model, Sobel's lover, only app), Hector Gomez (former pro boxer, Sobel's enforcer, only app, dies), Damasco (Bolivian torturer, only app, dies), Lt. Curtis Hoyle (Vietnam vet turned drug trafficker, 1st), Vado brothers (Chicago-based criminals, mentioned only), Pink Lady bouncer, Sobel's drug dealers & guards (die), drug addict mugger
OTHER CHARACTERS: Bruce Ayres (Vietnam vet, 1st, also in pfb & photo fb, dies bts), Sheriff Walters (on phone only), hot dog vendor, Pink Lady patrons, bystanders; pigeons
LOCATIONS/ITEMS: Lower East Side inc Lasalle St inc rock house (drug den), hotel, New Jersey inc Punisher's hideout, Soho inc the Pink Lady club, Sobel's penthouse, Washington DC inc Vietnam Memorial, New York Public Library / drug addict's knife, electric cables ("Bolivian telephone"), Gomez's brass knuckles, Damasco's rubber gloves, Wilfrid's answer phone, hot dog vendor cart, kilo of cocaine, locked Dumpster, park bench, payphone, photo of Frank and Ayres, cash filled strongbox, Punisher's crossbow, hat, diamond tip fingernails, grappling line, knife, machine gun, rocket launcher, trench coat, tuxedo, wallet
FLASHBACKS: Frank and Bruce Ayres pose together for a photo at Marble Mountain Air-base in 1968 (1). Visiting the Vietnam Memorial, Frank runs into old friend and fellow veteran Bruce Ayres. Bruce reveals corrupt veteran Curtis Hoyle has offered him a job flying narcotics from Bolivia. Frank urges Bruce to turn down the offer. The next day, Frank checks on Bruce, but learns Bruce is dead (p).
SYNOPSIS: After allowing a crack addict to mug him, Punisher follows the addict back to a drug house. Frank assaults the building, killing those within; before dying the last dealer reveals he answers to local drug lord Wilfrid Sobel. The next night, Punisher visits Sobel's lounge, the Pink Lady. Pretending to be an ambitious dealer, he warns Sobel that Curtis Hoyle is responsible for the drug house attack, and that Hoyle wants Sobel's job. Not believing him, Sobel's men knock out Frank. He awakens in Sobel's penthouse, where Sobel's enforcers torture him for info. Breaking free, Frank kills Sobel and his men. Using Sobel's answer phone, Frank contact's Sobel's Bolivian supplier, "the General," pretending he killed Sobel to prove he's capable of taking Sobel's job. Told to wait on the library steps the next day, Frank is met by Curtis Hoyle, sent to take Frank to Bolivia.
NOTE: The Punisher notes the date as "March 1987" in his War Journal. As with all such dates in subsequent issues, the sliding timescale of Marvel's present day has invalidated it, and it is considered only a topical reference.

PUNISHER #2 (August 1987)

"Bolivia" (22 pages)

CREDITS: Mike Baron (writer), Klaus Janson (art, colors), Ken Bruzenak (letters), Carl Potts (editor)
FEATURE CHARACTER: Punisher (also in photo)
VILLAINS: General Buktir van Tranh (former South Vietnamese Army General turned drug lord, 1st on panel app, dies), & his men (75 soldiers, many die) inc Fernando (dies), Lt. Curtis Hoyle (last app, dies)
OTHER CHARACTERS: Senor Valencia (Bolivian DEA, dies), Bruce Ayres (in photo only)
LOCATIONS/ITEMS: Bolivia inc General's base inc barracks, lab, mansion; jungle, Washington DC inc Vietnam Memorial / Apache helicopter, ammo crates, bandolier, duffel bag, Fernando's pistol, knife, soldiers' Kalashnikovs, grenades, Lear jet, jeep, Peruvian Air Force jet, plastique & detonators, photo of Frank and Ayres, Punisher's diamond tip fingernails, body armor, automatic shotguns, South African Striker, surface to air rocket, two million dollars, Valencia's cigarettes
SYNOPSIS: Frank and Hoyle travel to the General's base in the Bolivian jungle. Frank is escorted into the mansion only to discover he knows the General from his time in Vietnam. General Tranh considers Frank's false offer to join their cartel, asking Frank to execute honest Bolivian drug enforcement agent Valencia to prove his loyalty. Instead, Frank turns the gun on Valencia's guard, freeing Valencia and escaping into the jungle. The two break into the base's armory and gather weapons, attacking the General's men. Hoyle arrives in an Apache helicopter and attacks Frank, but Frank jumps from a rooftop and climbs aboard, killing the pilot and Hoyle. After using the chopper's rockets to destroy the coke factory and General's jet, Frank leaps into the jungle canopy below seconds before a surface to air rocket destroys the helicopter. Sneaking back towards the base, Frank witnesses General Tranh execute a recaptured Valencia. Frank storms the compound, killing Tranh and destroying the base. Days later, Frank pays another visit to the Vietnam memorial in Washington, tearing up the photo of himself and Ayres, sick of the long-ended war that has just claimed another friend.
NOTE: Features "Creative Support Team" page featuring bios of Carl Potts, Klaus Janson, & Mike Baron, with design artwork by Carl Potts.

PUNISHER #3 (October 1987)

"The Devil Came From Kansas!" (22 pages)

CREDITS: Mike Baron (writer), Klaus Janson (art, colors), Ken Bruzenak (letters), Joanne Spaldo (asst editor), Carl Potts (editor)
FEATURE CHARACTER: Punisher (also as Arnold Groetsch & FBI Special Agent Peterson)
VILLAINS: New American Revolution inc Col. Joseph Fryer (leader & retired US soldier, only app, dies) & bank robbers (Tulie named, most die)
OTHER CHARACTERS: Mr. Blandings (Marion realtor), woman & her son (Tommy), police, raccoon, Diamondback rattlesnakes; Microchip (1st mention)
LOCATIONS/ITEMS: Marion, Missouri inc real estate office, Sherrill, Kansas inc Fryer's office & landfill / Punisher's new Battle Van (modified Ford V-6 with twin turbo chargers & bullet-proof windows, destroyed), motorcycle, dart gun, handgun, knife & gold-plated lighter; robbers' automatic handguns, shotgun & car; pick-up truck, grenades, sniper rifle, light plane, Uzis, Caterpillar Wheel Loader, headlight shell, gasoline
SYNOPSIS: Posing as Arnold Groetsch, Frank's efforts to take a break from his war are interrupted when he spots robbers entering a bank across the street from the real estate office he's in. The robbers exit the bank firing, gunning down a cop before Punisher can intervene. As they

flee in their getaway car, he pursues in his van; when a police car joins the chase, Punisher tells them via radio that he is FBI Agent Peterson, seconds before an unexpected backup vehicle destroys the patrol car with a grenade. Punisher runs the backup off the road, and follows the robbers as they turn off the highway. Forced to stop when an explosion drops a tree across the dirt road, Punisher is shot at by a sniper, but the vigilante circles round and captures him. Interrogating his prisoner, Punisher learns he belongs to retired US Colonel Fryer's New American Revolution, which desires the restoration of "white Christian supremacy" in America. Told Fryer is based out of a real estate office in Sherill, Kansas, Frank goes undercover under the premise of looking for commercial real estate to get close to the colonel. Fryer takes him to a landfill where Punisher plays to Fryer's prejudices, earning an invitation into the group before revealing who he really is. However, Fryer's men intervene, and Punisher is injured in the resulting fracas. Taking out Fryer's men, Punisher punctures the gas tank of a Wheel Loader and lures Fryer to it. Punisher lights the gas, resulting in southern-fried colonel.

NOTE: War Journal dates the story July 1987.

PUNISHER #4 (November 1987)

"The Rev" (22 pages)

CREDITS: Mike Baron (writer), Klaus Janson (art, colors), Ken Bruzenak (letters), Marc McLaurin (asst editor), Carl Potts (editor)
FEATURE CHARACTER: Punisher (also as Joe Rainey & Frank Loomis)
SUPPORTING CAST: Microchip (David Linus Lieberman, Punisher's tech support, 1st actual app but chr last in Pun:OM #2, '93, next in Pun #6, '88), Microchip Jr. (Louis Frohike, Microchip's son & student at Cal Tech, 1st but chr last in Pun:OM #2, '93, next in Pun #6, '88)
VILLAINS: Church of the Saved (1 dies, some in pfb): the Rev (Samuel "Sammy" Smith, 1st, Satanist with healing powers, also in pfb), Byron Gresham (Rev's right hand, 1st), Keena (Church muscle, 1st)
OTHER CHARACTERS: Ray White (cop, 1st), Vickie White (Ray's wife, 1st) & Melissa White (her daughter, bts), Homer (Church member, in pfb, dies), Lagodney (reporter, only app, dies), Martin (Punisher's supply sergeant, dies), bar patrons, junkies, parishioners, kids; Joe Rainey (mentioned, dead Marine whose identity Punisher uses as cover)
LOCATIONS/ITEMS: Microchip's workshop, Pig's Poke bar, Church of the Saved inc the Rev's office, Lagodney's apartment, subway, Guiana (pfb) / Punisher's 9mm handgun, lock pick & glass cutter; Martin's car, Church of the Saved flier, computers, White's shotgun, baseball bat, Lagodney's Uzi, video tapes, Rev's revolver (pfb)
FLASHBACK: In Guiana, the Rev kills a follower for going against him and seeing his family, while another reports they've secured plutonium (p).
SYNOPSIS: Visiting Microchip to arrange the construction of a new Battle Van, Frank is introduced to Microchip's computer programmer son. Frank next goes to meet Martin, one of his weapon suppliers, but as Martin begins telling Frank that the Church of the Saved is bulk-buying weapons, a gunman shoots him. Killing the attacker, Punisher finds a Church flier on his body. Microchip puts Frank in touch with Ray White, a cop whose wife left him for the Church, and Frank convinces him to help. Frank goes into the church as a transient and "protects" it from Ray, who comes in with a shotgun. The plan succeeds, and after the Microchips set up his false identity Frank meets the Rev, whose touch Frank likens to electricity. The Rev sends Frank out with two of his men, Byron and Keena, to take a negative documentary about the Church away from a reporter. They find the reporter crazed and heavily armed. He kills Byron and mortally wounds Frank before Frank takes him down. Evacuating Frank and Byron, Keena takes them to the Rev. Frank passes out, waking to find the Rev has healed him. Learning no one found the tapes where he stashed them during the confusion, Frank retrieves them to see what is making the Rev so anxious to relocate to Guiana, and learns of the Rev's plutonium acquisition.
NOTE: Though fatally shot by Lagodney, Byron appears next issue alive, presumably resurrected by the Rev. The source of the Rev's healing power remains unrevealed; he may be a mutant. War Journal dates the story July 1987. Melissa is named next issue.

PUNISHER #5 (January 1988)

"Ministry of Death" (22 pages)

CREDITS: Mike Baron (writer), Klaus Janson (art, colors), Ken Bruzenak (letters), Marc McLaurin (asst editor), Carl Potts (editor)
FEATURE CHARACTER: Punisher (also as Joe Rainey)
VILLAINS: Church of the Saved (some die): Sadie Smith (Rev's sister, only app), the Rev (next in Pun #35, '90), Byron Gresham (dies), Keena (last app), Phil (only app, dies) & others
OTHER CHARACTERS: Representative Richard Fryer (Harlem congressman, only app), Ray & Vickie White (both last app), Melissa White (only actual app), Louis (disenchanted Church member, dies), Fryer's aide, congregation (some die), party guests inc Guiana Deputy Prime Minister Umberto
LOCATIONS/ITEMS: Guiana inc Georgetown & jungle w/Church of the Saved compound inc Rev's dwelling & women's dorm, Ray's building / cargo ship, M-16s, Beretta M-12s, assault rifle, school buses, stinger, Byron's revolver, Punisher's handgun, cooking pots, potassium cyanide
SYNOPSIS: As the congregation travel to Guiana by boat, Frank is tasked to teach them weapon usage; he considers killing the Rev immediately, before he can cause further bloodshed, but hesitates, troubled by old feelings woken by the Rev's healing touch. Once at the compound, the Rev asks Frank to teach Keena to use a stinger ground-to-air missile, intended to slay US Congressman Richard Fryer, who the Rev insists is a CIA operative planning to assassinate him, when Fryer flies in on a "fact-finding mission." His reward is a night with Vickie White. The Rev's sister Sadie, who claims to have a different version of "the touch," arrives at the camp to confirm Fryer's impending arrival. The Rev rallies his troops, but one of his followers tries to kill him upon realizing what a fraud he is. Frank stops him, not knowing why, and attempts to let the man escape but Byron shoots him. Later, Frank discovers the Rev is preparing cyanide for a "revolutionary suicide." The next morning, after donning his uniform, Frank finds the Rev's soldiers are murdering more "traitors" who have tried to leave. Shooting one of them, Frank races into the Rev's house, where he tries to force the Rev to order their surrender, but Sadie's interference causes an accidental discharge, leaving the Rev badly wounded. Using the PA system, Punisher announces to the Rev's flock that Rev's last words were to stop fighting and return home. With Sadie fled, Frank declines Rev's plea to be taken to a hospital, but doesn't finish the Rev off as repayment for the Rev having saved his life. Fryer arrives and Frank passes himself off as a CIA agent in order to claim Vickie and her kid and take them back to Ray.
NOTE: Vickie's name is spelled Vicki here. War Journal dates the story September 1987.

PUNISHER #6 (February 1988)

"Garbage" (22 pages)

CREDITS: Mike Baron (writer), David Ross (pencils), Kevin Nowlan (inks), Ken Bruzenak (letters), John Wellington (colors), Marc McLaurin (asst editor), Carl Potts (editor), Mike Mignola (c pencils)
FEATURE CHARACTER: Punisher
SUPPORTING CAST: Microchip Jr. (next in Pun #8, '88), Microchip
VILLAINS: Harold Magary (Mecozzi crime family member, CEO of Unisym, only app, dies), Magary's men: Hassan Ibn Mohamet (only app, dies), Mannuel "Manny" Herrera (ex-CIA now working for Mecozzi mob, 1st), others (some die); Yasir (Revolutionary Jihad terrorist, 1st but chr last in Pun #7, '88 fb), Ahmad "Mountain" Rasfanjani (Revolutionary Jihad enforcer, 1st); Rosetti mobsters
OTHER CHARACTERS: Rosetti Brothers' garbage men (bodies), guard dogs; Rose Kugel (1st bts but chr last in Pun:EQ, '94 fb)
LOCATIONS/ITEMS: Punisher's New Jersey warehouse, Microchip's workshop, Unisym compound in North Patterson, landfill / Rosetti's garbage truck, Punisher's rubber blanket, blow gun, knife, new Battle Van, pole, handgun & Geiger counter; dump truck, Harold's revolver, Hassan's machine gun, Yasir's car (destroyed), oil drums, skulls, plutonium, suitcase of money, handguns, Uzis, grenades, rifles, infra-red anti-tank rocket launcher, jeeps
SYNOPSIS: The Punisher's peaceful Saturday morning is interrupted when he hears the sound of the garbage truck outside his warehouse home interrupted by soft pops; checking, Punisher finds the garbage men murdered, their corpses left in the back of their truck. Frank has Micro Jr. investigate who might be muscling in on the Rosettis' business, learning that the Mecozzi mob's Unisym Systems is trying to control waste management statewide. He breaks into Unisym's compound, and, after killing the men there, discovers the area is radioactive, before intercepting a call that leads him to a landfill. There, he finds bodies hidden in oil drums and learns the Mecozzi mob is selling plutonium to Arab terrorists. Punisher crashes the buy, finding and using their own cache of weapons against them; noting military grade hardware, he vows to find out where they are getting their weapons. While the Punisher is evading the mobsters, the terrorists leave. Capturing and interrogating a mobster, Punisher learns the terrorists intend to detonate a nuclear bomb in the US in a week's time. Punisher takes a rocket launcher, but as he sets up near the main gate intending to blow up the armory, the Rosettis arrive in force, looking for payback, with Frank caught in the crossfire
NOTE: A flier mentions the upcoming Liberty Bell Celebration on October 30th. Ahmad's surname and nickname are revealed next issue.

PUNISHER #7 (March 1988)

"Wild Rose" (23 pages)

CREDITS: Mike Baron (writer), David Ross (pencils), John Beatty (inks), Ken Bruzenak (letters), John Wellington (colors), Marc McLaurin (asst editor), Carl Potts (editor)
FEATURE CHARACTER: Punisher (next in Pun:AG, '88)
SUPPORTING CAST: Microchip
VILLAINS: Yasir (also in fb to chr 1st prior to Pun #6, '88), Manuel Herrera, Ahmad Rasfanjani (prev 3 die, last app), Mecozzi mobsters (Lou named), Mr. Mecozzi, Rosetti mobsters, Philadelphia gunman
OTHER CHARACTERS: Javier Pérez de Cuéllar (UN Secretary-General, bts, attends theatrical premiere, only app), Ed Koch (New York mayor, bts, attends theatrical premiere, last in WoSM #21, '86 fb, next in Av #291, '88), Rose Kugel (alleged Mossad agent, called "Wild Rose" by Punisher, 1st actual app, next in Pun #48, '91), FBI receptionist (voice only, on phone), David Merrick (theatrical producer), Scotti Brothers (garbage collection company), Unisym (prev 3 mentioned only), TV news reporter (voice only, on TV), bartender, bystanders, guard dogs, New York City & Philadelphia police, theatergoers
LOCATIONS/ITEMS: New Jersey inc landfill, Unisym's North Paterson collection station & Punisher's warehouse, Philadelphia inc Liberty Hall, Manhattan inc I-95 & Times Square inc Kubert Theater & Gallagher Plaza w/ elevator / Yasir's assault rifle (in pfb) & LAWs rocket, Ahmad's knife, bucket of plutonium, fence, Rose Kugel's drill, tracer (both bts), crossbow, gun, ID card, knife & rhino tranquilizer darts, Lou's knife, mobsters' guns, jeeps & telephone, photo of Gallagher Plaza, pipes, police van, Punisher's assault rifle, Battle Van, computer, pistol, rocket launcher & television, RBG boom crane, telephone booth at Texaco gas station, traffic, videotape
FLASHBACK: Yasir denounces the West in a videotaped message intended for playing after a terrorist attack.
SYNOPSIS: Punisher launches a rocket at the warring Rosettis and Mecozzis and returns to his warehouse, where Microchip gives him more information about the link between the Mecozzis and the Arab terrorists, the Revolutionary Jihad. Believing the Jihad is targeting the Liberty Bell celebration in Philadelphia, Frank alerts the FBI and returns to his warehouse, which he finds has been breached by Rose Kugel, a self-proclaimed Mossad agent who has been tracking Yasir. Castle and Kugel head to Philadelphia, but the terrorists do not strike there. They return to New Jersey and pump Manuel Herrera for information. Punisher concludes that the Jihad's true targets are the attendees of a Manhattan theater premiere and that Ahmad, a former crane operator, plans to dump the plutonium on the crowd from a boom crane atop nearby Gallagher Plaza. Castle and Kugel make their way to the plaza's rooftop, where Punisher guns down Yasir and Ahmad throws Rose from the boom crane to her apparent death. Castle dispatches Rasfanjani and prevents the plutonium drop. Punisher later learns that Mossad has no record of Kugel.
NOTE: Kubert Theater is probably based on the real-life Schubert Theatre but named after comic book artist, Joe Kubert. This story features the opening of a revival of the musical, "1776."

MARVEL GRAPHIC NOVEL: THE PUNISHER, ASSASSIN'S GUILD (1988)

"The Punisher in Assassin's Guild" (62 pages)

CREDITS: Jo Duffy (writer), Jorge Zaffino (art), Jim Novak (letters), Julie Michel (colors), Marc McLaurin (asst editor), Carl Potts (editor, title design)
FEATURE CHARACTER: Punisher (also as James Maxwell, also in rfb, also as Pvt. Castiglione in fb1 between Pun #18, '97 fb & PWJ #21, '90 fb, also as Frank Castiglione in fb2 between PWJ #21, '90 fb & Pun Ann #4, '91 fb, also as Frank Castiglione in fb3 between Pun Ann #4, '91 fb & ASM #175, '77 fb, also as Frank Castiglione in fb4 between TheNam #69, '92 fb & PWZ #20, '93 fb, also as Frank Castle in fb5 during Pun:YO #1, '94, also in fb6 between Pun #17, '97 fb & PunBl, '91 fb; next in ST #12-14, '88, Pun #8, '88)

SUPPORTING CAST: Maria Castiglione (in fb2 between Pun #59, '92 fb & bts in Pun Ann #4, '91 fb, in fb3 between bts in Pun Ann #4, '91 fb & bts in Pun:RBN, '89 fb, in fb4 between bts in Pun:RBN, '89 fb & Pun Ann #4, '91), Lisa Castiglione (in fb3 & fb4 between bts in Pun Ann #4, '91 fb & off-panel in Pun Ann #4, '91), Frank Castiglione, Jr. (in fb4 to 1st chr app before Pun Ann #4, '91) (all also as Castle in rfb)

VILLAINS: Favors Network (blackmail business) inc Robert Abbey (attorney & blackmailer, dies), Wendell Pine (attorney & blackmailer), Richard Fletcher (leader, dies) & his security team (some die); Kevin Reynolds (spoiled rich kid, dies), Stanley Reynolds (Kevin's father), Castillo, Platzer (both rapists, die), Mr. DiTomassio (rapists' lawyer, dies), Arsene Jourdan III & associates (acclaimed thieves, die), North Vietnamese Army (in fb1), criminals (in fb6, die)

OTHER CHARACTERS: Assassin's Guild (assassin business) inc Reiko (also as Mrs. Akina Maxwell), Masumi (Reiko's cousin, also as Toshi Umezaki, dies) & Daryl; Grace Williams (Reiko's friend, dies), Cathy Williams (Grace's sister), Mr. Williams (Grace & Cathy's father), Jane (Grace & Cathy's friend), Michele Reynolds (Kevin's mother), Caroline Linnet (teenager), her family & her friends; Timmy Mulvey (troubled teen), Kay (Abbey's secretary, voice only), US Marines (in fb1), doctor (in fb5), jewelry store guard (dies), hotdog vendor, reporters, police, bystanders; D. Marrow Levy (realtor, mentioned, Assassin's Guild assignment), Timmy's mother (mentioned, government employee)

LOCATIONS/ITEMS: Vietnam (in fb1), Castiglione home (in fb3), hospital (in fb5), New York inc Central Park (in rfb), Thousand Autumns restaurant, jewelry store, Punisher's apartment, Abbey's office, Grace's apartment, Pine's office & 6th Ave. office building w/Fletcher's office / Castiglione's assault rifle & knife (both in fb1), Punisher's Uzi, gun, sniper rifle, impact grenades & police radio; Masumi's throwing knives, impact grenades, guns & remote zapper; Reiko's stilettos, Kevin's revolver, thieves' guns, jewelry store guard's gun, security team's guns, criminals' guns (in fb6)

FLASHBACKS: Frank Castiglione battles in Vietnam (1). Frank returns home to Maria (2), plays with the newborn Lisa (3) and the newborn Frank Jr. (4). The Castle family is killed in Central Park (MP #2, '75 fb). A doctor tells Frank his family is dead (5). Frank begins his war on crime as the Punisher (6).

SYNOPSIS: Punisher kills a group of internationally wanted thieves. Four days later, Grace Williams and Kevin Reynolds are involved in a minor car accident. Kevin flies into a rage and police detain him. The next day, Assassin's Guild member Reiko kills two recently released rapists before returning to the Thousand Autumns where her cousin Masumi kills the rapists' lawyer. The Thousand Autumns owner and Assassin's Guild leader arrives and assigns the Guild's newest assassination to Daryl. Punisher listens to police reports. Attorney Robert Abbey considers erasing Timmy Mulvey's record, but only if his parents are rich enough. Blaming Grace for ruining his life, Kevin murders Grace and takes her friend hostage while her sister escapes. Hearing of the incident on the police radio, Punisher shoots and kills Kevin. Investigating, Punisher learns that Abbey is part of the Favors Network and erased Kevin's criminal record. Grace's father hires the Assassin's Guild to kill Abbey. Punisher spots Reiko following Abbey, recognizes her from the crowd outside Grace's building and tails her to the Thousand Autumns. Having heard of the Assassin's Guild, Punisher begins a relationship with Reiko. Punisher later confronts Abbey, learning his boss is Richard Fletcher before Masumi kills Abbey. Punisher confronts Reiko who confesses to being a member of the Assassin's Guild. Punisher points out the Favors Network will continue without Abbey and forms a temporary alliance with the Assassin's Guild to destroy the Favors Network. Punisher, Reiko and Masumi, posing as a family wanting to erase a criminal record, arrange a meeting with Fletcher through Wendell Pine, Abbey's replacement. The three attack Fletcher's office but Masumi is captured. Fletcher tortures Masumi as Punisher and Reiko kill Fletcher's security team. Punisher kills Fletcher, but Masumi dies in the crossfire. Reiko incinerates the scene and Masumi's body to hide evidence of the Assassin's Guild. Later, Stanley Reynolds attempts to hire the Assassin's Guild to kill Punisher, but they refuse. Punisher decides not to destroy the Assassin's Guild.

NOTE: Includes title/credits page (2 pages). Back cover features art by Jorge Zaffino of & brief biographies on Jo Duffy, Jorge Zaffino & Julie Michel. The title is given as Assassin's Guild on cover & title page, but Assassins' Guild in the indicia.

PUNISHER #8 (May 1988)

"The Ghost of Wall Street" (22 pages)

CREDITS: Mike Baron (writer), Whilce Portacio (pencils), Scott Williams (inks), Thomas Orzechowski (letters), John Wellington (colors), Marc McLaurin (asst editor), Carl Potts (editor)

FEATURE CHARACTER: Punisher (also as Mr. McRook)

SUPPORTING CAST: Microchip Jr., Microchip

VILLAINS: Billionaire Boys' Club: Arnold Hansen (Hanset CEO, corrupt Wall Street tycoon), Roky Vance (corrupt Wall Street broker & Skidrow Slasher); Mr. Tokegura & his bodyguards: Sijo (Tokegura's bodyguard & Skidrow Slasher) & Kiyami, 3 street punks (Skidrow Slasher copycats, 2 die)

OTHER CHARACTERS: Quentin O'Toole (former Wall Street broker, now vagrant), Wall Street bystanders, diner patrons & waitress

LOCATIONS/ITEMS: Diner, Punisher's warehouse, Wall Street, Warrick County, Connecticut inc Criston Hills Shopping Mall parking lot, Microcorp corporate house, Praxdord HQ skyscraper, bowery / cars inc Blue Chrysler, Quentin's breakfast & coffee, morphine needle, Punisher's boot knife, business suit, fake mustache & glasses, infrared scope, 9mm gun & van, Micro Jr's taser, .45 revolver, $2000, Roky's knife & limo, Wall Street Journal newspaper, Sijo's camera

SYNOPSIS: Frank sets his sights on taking down corrupt Wall Street billionaires Arnold Hansen and Roky Vance, starting with a visit to street bum Quentin O'Toole, his Wall Street contact. Quentin asks Frank for a gun to protect himself, fearful of a serial killer targeting the homeless whom the media have dubbed the Skidrow Slasher. Later, Frank and Microchip Jr. tail Roky Vance on a trip to a secluded corporate house in Connecticut. Spying on the house from a nearby hilltop, Frank sees Hansen and Vance meeting with Japanese businessman Tokegura. Tokegura's bodyguard Sijo catches him unawares, choking him, but Microchip Jr attacks Sijo with a taser. Sijo smashes Jr away in retaliation but the distraction gives Frank a chance to fight back, and he knocks Sijo out, then retreats, taking the unconscious Micro Jr. with him. The next day, Frank provides Quentin with a revolver. That night, Frank pretends to be a homeless man, attracting the attention of street thugs copycatting the Skidrow Slasher; he kills two of them. Meanwhile, in another alley, Quentin encounters the real Skidrow Slasher – Roky. When he tries to defend himself with his gun, Sijo attacks from the shadows, disarming him, then stands back to take photos as Roky moves in with his knife for the kill!

NOTE: Cover title: "No Way Out of the Graveyard!" The Punisher notes the date in his War Journal entry as "March 28" but his Wall Street Journal is dated January 12th 1988. Arnold Hansen is also called Arnold Ansen here. Kiyami is named next issue.

PUNISHER #9 (June 1988)

"Insider Trading" (21 pages)

CREDITS: Mike Baron (writer), Whilce Portacio (pencils), Scott Williams (inks), Bill Oakley (letters), John Wellington (colors), Marc McLaurin (asst editor), Carl Potts (editor)
FEATURE CHARACTER: Punisher
SUPPORTING CAST: Microchip (next in Pun Ann #1/2, '88), Microchip Jr. (dies, next in Pun #10, '09)
VILLAINS: Arnold Hansen & his men (Carl, Ollie & Mitch named), Mr. Takegura & his men, inc Kiyami & Sijo, Roky Vance (all die)
OTHER CHARACTERS: Peggy Snow (WNEX news anchor, on TV screen only), Quentin O'Toole (news broadcast picture only)
LOCATIONS/ITEMS: Connecticut inc Microcorp Corporate house, rock quarry, Punisher's warehouse / motorized skate platform w/armor-piercing tear gas dispenser; body bag, Microchip Jr's automatic pistol, neck brace & body bag, Punisher's Battle Van, machine gun, "tear gas delight" concoction & TV, Tokegura's limousine, Sijo's katana, rock grinder
SYNOPSIS: Punisher listens to a news report detailing Quentin O'Toole's murder by the Skidrow Slasher. Having discovered Quentin's body before the police, Frank notes that Quentin wrote the message "Roky" in his own blood, alerting Frank that Roky Vance is the Slasher. Later that night, Punisher disables Mr. Tokegura's limo and captures the Japanese businessman. Frank explains he wants to take down Hansen and Roky and suggests Tokegura leaves the country, ending his takeover of the American stock market. Bringing Micro Jr. to watch his back, Frank sets up a trade with Tokegura's men, with the men bringing a resistant Roky to an exchange site at a nearby rock quarry; a suspicious Hansen covertly follows. While in the middle of the exchange, Sijo, now dressed as a ninja, attacks Frank and slays the now expendable Roky. Punisher fights a running battle with Sijo, stumbling across Micro Jr.'s body, murdered by Sijo, during the fight. Frank eventually defeats Sijo, tossing him into the quarry's rock grinder. Frank kills Tokegura in retaliation for the Slasher's victims, and Hansen kills himself when Frank reveals he's informed the authorities about Hansen's criminal enterprises. Frank returns Micro Jr.'s body to Microchip.
NOTE: Roky Vance called Roky Erikson here. Tokegura called Takegura here.

PUNISHER #10 (August 1988)

"The Creep" (22 pages)

CREDITS: Mike Baron (writer), Whilce Portacio (pencils), Scott Williams (inks), Ken Bruzenak (letters), John Wellington (colors), Marc McLaurin (asst editor), Carl Potts (editor)
FEATURE CHARACTER: Punisher (also as Tony Knowlen Ross, also in DD #257, '88 & Pun #7, '12 fb, next in Pun Ann #1, '88)
GUEST STAR: Daredevil (Matthew "Matt" Murdock, blind crimefighter w/enhanced senses, last in DD #256, '88, also in Pun #7, '12 fb, also & next in DD #257, '88)
VILLAIN: Alfred Coppersmith (disgruntled ex-Zum corporation employee, 1st, also in Pun #7, '12 fb, also & next in DD #257, '88)
OTHER CHARACTERS: Cindy (Alfred's neighbor, 1st, next in Pun #7, '12 fb), Mr. Bates (bts, neighbor bothered by Alfred's noise), Mrs. Fielding (dies) & her son, pharmacy clerk, Mr. Ablanap (Jehovah's Witness congregation leader) & his congregation, TV news reporter (on TV), three alleged drug dealers (mentioned, apprehended by Daredevil)
LOCATIONS/ITEMS: Alfred Coppersmith's apartment, Cindy's apartment, Jehovah's Witness' church, Mr. Bates apartment (door only), Mrs. Fielding's apartment, pharmacy, Punisher's hideout / Alfred's knife & weightlifting equipment, Jehovah's Witness' files, Metro Plumbing Van, Punisher's computer, clock, fake federal ID, phone, & plumber outfit, Zumatrin pain reliever pills (tampered with cyanide) & Zum "Sparklene Mouthwash"
SYNOPSIS: A mother dies taking poisoned Zum pain relief medicine. Later, as the news broadcasts about the string of poisonings occurring in Queens, the Punisher, whose check on disgruntled Zum ex-employees has provided an excessively large suspect list, contacts a local Jehovah's Witnesses Church, asking for help identifying any suspicious individuals in the neighborhood. Alfred Coppersmith, the poisoner, works out in his apartment, upsetting the next-door neighbor with his racket. When infatuated neighbor Cindy asks Alfred to be nice to the neighbor, he dismisses her. Punisher and Alfred separately watch a news broadcast in which Daredevil calls for the poisoner to surrender himself to authorities. The church calls Frank back, informing him of Alfred being a hostile person nearby that they've encountered. Disguising himself as a plumber Frank heads to Alfred's apartment. Cindy greets him, letting him know Alfred's not home and asking him to fix her sink. Frank stops her from drinking poisoned mouthwash just as Alfred arrives home. Confused, Cindy warns Alfred of Frank's presence and tries to help him when Frank attacks. Frank chases the fleeing Alfred out a window and across rooftops, but Daredevil intervenes, defeating the Punisher and apprehending Alfred. Daredevil warns Punisher to change his ways and departs with Alfred, while the Punisher backtracks to inform a disbelieving Cindy that Alfred was the poisoner.
NOTE: This story is told from Daredevil's perspective in DD #257, '88 & the police's perspective in Pun #7, '12 fb.

PUNISHER ANNUAL #1 (1988)

"Evolutionary Jihad" (30 pages)

CREDITS: Mike Baron (writer), Mark Texeira (pencils), Scott Williams (inks), James Novak (letters), Janet Jackson (colors), Carl Potts (editor)
FEATURE CHARACTER: Punisher (next in Pun #11, '88)
VILLAINS: High Evolutionary (Herbert Wyndham, genius geneticist, bts, sent Eliminators, last in XFac Ann #3, '88, next in SS Ann #1, '88), el Caiman ("the Great White," coke dealer) & his men (some die) inc Claudio (dies) & Julio, Eliminators (armored HE agents, all die)
OTHER CHARACTERS: Lucinda (el Caiman's daughter), bystanders, piranha, caiman crocodile
LOCATIONS/ITEMS: Bogota inc el Caiman's drug lab, Little Caesar hill inc Caiman's safe house , village inc "the tank" / Punisher's 5.66mm Korean assault rifle, Claudio's gun, Eliminator armor & ship, el Caiman's shotgun & helicopter, el Caiman's men's guns, Uzi, ammo crates, armor-piercing rounds, stinger, incendiary rounds, HK, Teflon rounds, ammo clips
SYNOPSIS: In Bogota, the Punisher is waiting for bystanders to clear the street so he can attack local drug lord el Caiman's main coke lab when

armored Eliminators attack it, uncaring of civilian casualties. Punisher rescues a girl from one of them, who turns out to be Lucinda, el Caiman's daughter, and learns the Eliminators plan to weed out the "junkies and the crazies" and that he is on their list. Punisher and Lucinda head for Caiman's safe house on Little Caesar, where Punisher explains his intent to take Caiman down, despite all the good Caiman claims to do for the people of his town. With the Eliminators intent on killing them both, Caiman and Punisher call a truce to fend off the attacking Eliminators. Outgunned and with Caiman's men all dead, they retreat to Caiman's village, home of the aquarium that houses his trademarked crocodile. Caiman shows Punisher his extensive armory before watching as a captured Eliminator is fed to the crocodile. Figuring Teflon-coated bullets will work against the Eliminators' armor, Punisher and Caiman have Lucinda load while they fire. The final Eliminator, staying back out of the line of fire, explains the High Evolutionary's intent to advance the human race after removing the scum like Punisher and Caiman, but Punisher shoots through the tank to kill the Eliminator instead. Caiman turns on Punisher but Punisher fires on the aquarium, shattering the glass, and in the resultant flood the corpse of his own crocodile crushes Caiman. Punisher saves Lucinda again, and as they begin their trek out of the jungle he's left to wonder if she plans to shoot him in the back.

NOTE: Part of the "Evolutionary War" crossover which continues from XFac Ann #3, '88, and into SS Ann #1, '88. A special thanks is given to Archie Goodwin at the end of the story. Features a 2-page schematic of the Punisher's Battle Van and 1-page schematic of the Punisher's warehouse.

2ND STORY: "3 Hearts" (16 pages)
CREDITS: Roger Salick (writer), Mike Vosburg (art), Ken Bruzenak (letters), Christi Scheele (colors)
FEATURE CHARACTER: Microchip (next in Pun #12, '88)
VILLAINS: James "Jim" Nugent (Felicia's 2nd husband & hitman, only app), Tommy & their boss (all die), Kafdrah (Jim's Aqirian employer, bts)
OTHER CHARACTERS: Felicia Nugent (Micro's friend, only app), hotel cashier, 2 police (die), news anchor, reporters, bystanders (all on TV), Senator Mills (picture on TV, victim of Jim's), Rudy (Micro's godson, photo), Senator Alan Borsuk, Sewer Commissioner David Weiss (both mentioned, recent assassination victims), Sally (Micro's late wife, mentioned), Ben (Felicia's late husband)
LOCATIONS/ITEMS: Microchip's warehouse, Felicia's duplex (destroyed), Advanced Exports, dive hotel / armored Lamborghini, Uzi, Micro's armored Plymouth Fury (destroyed), explosives detector, suitcases, fake beard, telescope, microphone shooter, recorder, anti-tank gun, handgun, & thermite device with remote detonator; C-4 bomb, Jim's Uzi, police car
SYNOPSIS: Felicia, an old friend of Microchip's, calls him for help after learning her husband is a hitman assassinating politicians for Aqirian money, who has threatened to kill her if she goes to the authorities. Noticing a suspicious "gas man" working outside, Micro sweeps Felicia's duplex and finds a bomb, escaping just before it goes off. Micro takes Felicia back to his place and proceeds to stake out Jim and his associates. After getting incriminating evidence on tape, Micro blows up their office, killing all but Jim. Jim steals a police car and Micro chases him down. Micro tells him if either he or Felicia die, his tape gets released. Micro offers his car to allow Jim to just get away. Jim takes it, and Micro remotely detonates the explosives hidden inside.
NOTE: Aqiria is a Middle Eastern nation first seen in FF #308, '87; Aqirian spelled Aquiran here.

3RD STORY: "The High Evolutionary Chapter Two: The Pet Project" (6 pages)
CREDITS: Mark Gruenwald (writer), Paris Cullins (pencils), Tony DeZuniga (inks), Ken Lopez (letters), Gregory Wright (colors), Ralph Macchio (editor)
FEATURE CHARACTER: High Evolutionary (as Herbert Edgar Wyndham, also in symbolic image, also in Thor #135, '66 fb & SW #1, '78 fb, last in UXM #380, '00 fb, next in SS Ann #1/4, '88)
OTHER CHARACTERS: Jonathan Drew, Merriam Drew (both also in SW #1, '78 fb, last in XFac Ann #3/3, '88, next in SS Ann #1/4, '88), Jessica Drew (last bts in SW:O #1, '06, next in SW #1, '78 fb), Dempsey (mutated Dalmatian, dies, also in Thor #135, '66 fb, last in XFac Ann #3/3, '88), Professor Reardon, professor, hunters (Rolly named), students, Wyndham's mother & aunt (bts)
LOCATIONS/ITEMS: Oxford University inc physics lab, Wyndham home, Drew home, Transia inc Wundagore Mountain / microscope, genetic accelerator, gene sketches, hazard suit, hunters' guns
SYNOPSIS: In 1930, Wyndham's grades threaten to get him removed from Oxford. Wyndham bargains with his professors to let him set his own curriculum after showing the success of his genetics experiments. But their shortsighted thinking causes him to lose his temper and get expelled. Several months later in his lab at home, he mutates his Dalmatian Dempsey into humanoid form. Dempsey runs out of the lab and is shot by hunters, mistaken for a dear. Realizing he needs a more secluded place to work, he approaches the Drews about pooling their resources to develop their own facilities. They agree and set their sights on Wundagore Mountain in Transia.
NOTE: This story forms part of a series covering the High Evolutionary's history; this segment incorporates his appearances in Thor #135, '66 fb & SW #1, '78 fb with new information.

PUNISHER #11 (September 1988)

"Second Sight" (22 pages)

CREDITS: Mike Baron (writer), Whilce Portacio (pencils), Scott Williams (inks), Ken Bruzenak (letters), John Wellington (colors), Marc McLaurin (asst editor), Carl Potts (editor)
FEATURE CHARACTER: Punisher
VILLAINS: Illegal immigrant smugglers inc Carlo, Hector, Luis, Manuel, Martinez & Roberto (all die)
OTHER CHARACTERS: Maria (illegal immigrant, only app), Pepe (a brujo/spiritual wise man, only app), 29 illegal immigrants (dead, mentioned on news broadcast only), other illegal immigrants (bts), Rosinante (Pepe's burro), Lupe (Pepe's pet snake), buzzards, moth (in Punisher's vision only), mouse; Frank Jr. Castle, Lisa Castle, Maria Castle, mobsters (prev 4 hallucinations only)
LOCATIONS/ITEMS: Northern Mexico desert & ravine, Pepe's house / Pepe's bandoleer, cannon, keg of gun powder, satchel (filled with rocks), Punisher's knife & infrared scope
SYNOPSIS: After hearing of illegal immigrants left to die by uncaring smugglers in the Texas desert, Frank travels to the Mexican desert to kill the smugglers. He observes a truck stopping in a ravine. When a couple of smugglers pull a woman out of the back and prepare to rape her, the Punisher intervenes. When more smugglers emerge, Frank is temporarily blinded by a stray bullet, and the woman is grazed as well, sending them toppling over the edge of the small ravine, and the smugglers leave them, thinking them dead. The Punisher wakes in the house of desert hermit Pepe, who guides Frank on a spiritual vision, encouraging him to leave behind his life of violence. His vision is interrupted as the woman warns the smugglers have returned. The Punisher and Pepe prepare to fire Pepe's antique cannon, and try to lure the smugglers out from behind their cover. Frank suddenly senses his wife warning him of smugglers sneaking up behind them, turning the cannon and firing upon them. The resulting battle ends with Lupe injured, but the woman kills the last of the smugglers. When Frank asks for her name, he comments that it's Maria, the same name as his deceased wife.
NOTE: Punisher notes that his family was killed in May. Frank's hallucination of his family's murder is not a true flashback, as the details are inconsistent with previous depictions of their murder. However the names of Frank's family, as revealed here, can be considered correct.

PUNISHER #12 (October 1988)

"Castle Technique" (21 pages)

CREDITS: Mike Baron (writer), Whilce Portacio (pencils), Scott Williams (inks), Ken Bruzenak (letters), John Wellington (colors), Marc McLaurin (asst editor), Carl Potts (editor)
FEATURE CHARACTER: Punisher (also as Rubber Rook)
SUPPORTING CAST: Microchip (last in Pun Ann #1/2, '88, next in PWJ #1, '88)
VILLAINS: Gary Saunders (serial killer, also in photos, dies), Underground Liberation Army inc Bishop, Lydia Spoto ("Samson Family" member, murderer, 1st), Arnold Porter (serial killer, bts, on death row), prostitute, 2 truck hijackers
OTHER CHARACTERS: Ortiz (Vietnam veteran & prison guard, 1st), Annie Overdrive (trucker, voice only), diner patrons & waitress, prison guards, Judy Knoefler (Saunder's victim) & her parents (both mentioned), police (in photos)
LOCATIONS/ITEMS: Lyla's truck stop on State HWY 18, Nebraska inc I-80, Utah State Maximum Security Facility / Punisher's knife, helicopter & Peterbilt truck w/weapons armory; Ortiz's jeep, semi trucks
SYNOPSIS: Convicted serial killer Gary Saunders is languishing on Death Row in Utah, evading his final sentence with endless appeals. Finding out the Feds have learned that Samson family member Lydia Spoto, herself in prison for trying to assassinate the president, has been plotting using her Underground Liberation Army to arrange a dual jailbreak, Punisher plans to break Gary Saunders out himself, torture him to find where the still-missing bodies of some of his victims are, then kill him. Frank transports a miniature helicopter in a semi-truck across country to Saunder's prison in Utah. When he stops at a Nebraskan truck stop to rest, two men attempt to hijack his truck; overpowering them, he learns the Underground Liberation Army paid them to hijack his vehicle. Traveling to Utah, his prison contact signal's Frank that it's time. Launching the helicopter, Frank picks up Saunders while he is let out of his cell to walk in the yard. However, when they land in the mountains nearby, Saunders pummels Frank from behind, revealing his rescuer didn't state the password. Spoto arrives with the Liberation Army, having tailed Frank from Nebraska hoping to steal his helicopter. Having only wanted Saunders for his legal expertise, Spoto kills Saunders when he gets into an argument with another Liberation Army member. They take off with Frank's semi-truck full of weapons, leaving him for dead. Frank's contact, a prison guard named Ortiz, arrives and picks up Frank.
NOTE: Gary Saunders is also called Gary Gilmore. The Underground Liberation Army's password is "Queen's Knight."

PUNISHER #13 (November 1988)

"Sacrifice Play" (21 pages)

CREDITS: Mike Baron (writer), Whilce Portacio (pencils), Scott Williams (inks), Ken Bruzenak (letters), Mark Chiarello (colors), Marc McLaurin (asst editor), Carl Potts (editor)
FEATURE CHARACTER: Punisher (next in PPSSM #140-143, '88, PWJ #1-3, '88-89)
VILLAINS: Charles Samson (cult leader & murderer, only app, dies), his "Samson Family" inc Lydia Spoto (dies, last app), Underground Liberation Army inc Bishop & Ernie (all die, last apps)
OTHER CHARACTERS: Ortiz (dies, last app), Conchita Ortiz (his wife, 1st, next in Pun #15, '89), police (Thomason named, many die), Ranch farm owner (possibly named "Conner," body only), 2 teenage girls
LOCATIONS/ITEMS: Nevada inc Santa Clara mountains inc Conner Movie ranch, Utah wilderness inc Ortiz's friend's shack, Ortiz's home (in nearby town) / police cars, motorcycles and prison transport bus, Liberation Army's motorcycles, Ortiz's guns, jeep & station wagon, Punisher's stolen helicopter & Peterbilt semi-truck
SYNOPSIS: Frank awakens in a remote shack with Ortiz watching over him. Ortiz, who knew Frank in Vietnam, reveals he knows Frank is the Punisher; he and his like-minded wife, Conchita, want to kill criminals. They track down the Liberation Army to their old hangout at the Conner Movie Ranch. As they do surveillance, Conchita propositions Frank, but he turns her down. The next day, they follow the Liberation Army as they ambush a police prison transport carrying their leader Charles Samson. Samson escapes, ungratefully killing the Liberation Army members who shot the guards since they know about his hideouts. Lydia Spoto arrives in Frank's helicopter and carries Samson away. Frank and his allies attack, with Frank chasing after the helicopter on motorcycle. In an effort to make the helicopter go faster, Samson pushes Lydia out. When Punisher shoots the chopper's pilot, it crashes and Frank finishes the mortally wounded Samson off. As more police arrive, Ortiz blows up Frank's semi-truck with himself next to it, rather than face the law. Frank departs, leaving Conchita to mourn.
NOTE: Punisher's license plate on his semi-truck reads "PUN-18F." Charles Samson and the Samson Family represent convicted murders Charles Manson and the Manson Family. Ortiz refers to the Punisher as "Captain," revealing Castle held that rank at one point in the Vietnam War.

PUNISHER #14 (December 1988)

"Social Studies" (21 pages)

CREDITS: Mike Baron (writer), Whilce Portacio (pencils), Scott Williams (inks), Ken Bruzenak (letters), Glynis Oliver (colors), Marc McLaurin (asst editor), Carl Potts (editor)
FEATURE CHARACTER: Punisher (also as Mr. Melchior)
VILLAINS: Kingpin (bts, last in PWJ #1, '88), Hassad (Libyan or Syrian terrorist, bts; see Pun #15, '89 NOTE); Winston Piper (career criminal, dies), Kelton Rhodes (1st), Rusty, Tully, Spud, Nazi (prev 5 gang members), 3 unruly Malcolm Shabazz students inc Lopez & Moogie (1st)
OTHER CHARACTERS: Malcolm Shabazz High School students inc Reese McDowell (1st), Bruce Atterly, Roxanne, Robert, Bernard, & the 5th hour social studies class; Vernon Brooks (chemistry teacher, 1st), Malcolm Shabazz principal; Cecil Ashford (mentioned, absent student)
LOCATIONS/ITEMS: NYC, Malcolm Shabazz High School inc classroom, utility closet, furnace room; sewers / chain, knives, boom box, briefcase, roll book, school books, handguns inc .38, paper airplane, H&K MP53a assault rifle, enrollment sheet, concussion grenade, rubber bullets
SYNOPSIS: Finding evidence linking Kingpin to high school gangs, Castle goes undercover in Malcolm Shabazz High School as a substitute teacher hunting Winston Piper, a 29-year-old career criminal pretending to be a student that the Kingpin has installed to organize the local gang. Posing as Mr. Melchior, Castle establishes his authority by throwing a large, abusive student who challenges him out the first floor class' window. The class settles down until gang member Tully comes in and pulls Kelton Rhodes out. When Castle puts another student, Roxanne, in charge, intending to follow, another student,

McDowell, reveals he is armed and offers to help; though Castle declines the aid, McDowell lends him the gun. Castle follows the gang into the furnace and overhears Piper telling the gang he has struck a deal with Libyan terrorists to blow up the school in exchange for $1.5 million. Another teacher and McDowell, who ignored Frank's instructions to stay in class, arrive offering their help, but Tully spots them and a brief gun battle breaks out as the gang retreats into the sewer. Sending his erstwhile allies back upstairs, Frank changes into costume and reenters sewer four blocks uptown. Locating the gang, Frank stuns them with a concussion grenade, causing Piper to fall into the water and drown. Returning to class, Frank finds Roxanne is still teaching.

NOTE: The story credits appear as names written on blackboard. Malcolm Shabazz is a tribute to slain Civil Rights leader, Malcolm X. In 1996 actor Tom Berenger stared in a film entitled The Substitute where he played a mercenary who took a job substitute teaching in a Miami school to stop a gang calling themselves the Kings of Destruction. Brooks' name and McDowell's first name are revealed next issue.

PUNISHER #15 (January 1989)

"To Topple the Kingpin" (22 pages)

CREDITS: Mike Baron (writer), Whilce Portacio (layouts), Scott Williams (finished art), Ken Bruzenak (letters), Marc McLaurin (asst editor), Carl Potts (editor)
FEATURE CHARACTER: Punisher (also as Mr. Melchior)
SUPPORTING CAST: Microchip (last in PWJ #3, '89)
VILLAINS: Kingpin & his thugs (many die) inc Bill & Wesley; Soyasset (Kingpin's secretary, dies), Mr. Emerson (Soyasset's replacement), Syrian terrorists (bts), Mr. Kliegg (freelance mercenary, 1st), Kelton Rhodes
OTHER CHARACTERS: Conchita Ortiz (last in Pun #13, '88), Reese McDowell, Vernon Brooks, pigeon
LOCATIONS/ITEMS: NYC inc Fisk Tower (Kingpin's skyscraper), Vernon Brooks' apartment, Punisher's warehouse & Microchip's warehouse (both destroyed); dome house, freight yard, phonebooth, Conchita's house, Provo Utah; camp outside Mirisch, FL / Punisher's new Battle Van, Ruger Mini-14 w/sniper scope & silencer, Ingram MAC-10 (M10), beeper, engine block, deadfall, weaponized "dalek" anti-personnel robot, anti-tank rocket launchers, elevator, carbon-compound dagger, carbon-fibre .44 Magnum Derringer, pigeon coup, grenades, M16 & War Journal

SYNOPSIS: Apprised of Punisher's recent interference at Malcolm Shabazz High School, the Kingpin decides it is time to deal with the vigilante. Soon after, Microchip calls Punisher to inform him a gang is breaking into his warehouse home, and Punisher rushes to his aid. Between Frank and Micro's traps, the invaders are soon eliminated. The last surviving thug reveals that backup outside have an anti-tank rocket trained on the building, and Microchip and Punisher hastily evacuate via the sewers just before the warehouse is destroyed. They head out of town to Microchip's domed backup hideout, where Micro prepares a virus designed to erase Kingpin's records, crippling his business. Meanwhile Kingpin brings in Mr. Klieg, a specialist. After Microchip uploads the virus, Punisher recruits Reese McDowell, Vernon Brooks and Conchita Ortiz, bringing them to an abandoned camp in Florida for training. He boobytraps his warehouse, which blows up when Kingpin's men find and invade it. However, Kliegg tracks Punisher to the camp and prepares to move in.

NOTE: Last issue Winston Piper mentioned dealing with Libyan terrorists, but Soyasset here describes the deal as being with Syrians.

PUNISHER #16 (February 1989)

"Escalation" (22 pages)

CREDITS: Mike Baron (writer), Whilce Portacio (layouts), Scott Williams (finished art), Ken Bruzenak (letters), Janet Jackson (colors), Marc McLaurin (asst editor), Carl Potts (editor)
FEATURE CHARACTER: Punisher
SUPPORTING CAST: Microchip
VILLAINS: Kingpin, Kliegg (dies), Chalmers (Kingpin henchman, only app), the Board (Jeremy Wilson, 14 year old computer hacker, 1st), Kingpin's thugs (some killed)
OTHER CHARACTERS: Reese McDowell, Vernon Brooks, Conchita Ortiz, Disneyworld security employees (guard, computer room manager, both only app), bystanders, jaguar
LOCATIONS/ITEMS: Florida Everglades, Disneyworld; NYC inc Fisk Tower, house in Bucks County, PA, King's Inn casino, Atlantic City; Kingpin's collection house in Naragansett (mentioned) / tiger trap w/punji sticks, Kliegg's AK47, handguns, grenade, spring trap, knife, crossbow, quarrel, motorboat, car, skateboard, intercom, computers, photos, bulletin board, RPG, grappling hook, Tech 9s, briefcase, money, dynamite, duffle bag, Punisher's Battle Van & boots with carbon-fibre plated soles, Kingpin's battlebus, machine gun

SYNOPSIS: In the Florida Everglades with Reese McDowell, Punisher demonstrates his tracking skills by sneaking up and tapping a jaguar on the nose. However, seconds later a sniper shot kills McDowell. Punisher returns fire, pursuing the killer, who turns out to be Kliegg. They fight, and Kliegg eventually gets the drop on Punisher, only to be slain by a quarrel shot by Conchita Ortiz. Disguised as computer repairmen, Punisher and Microchip make their way through the glades to Disneyworld where they bluff their way into the computer room, using Disney's computers to check up on Kingpin's holdings, before heading to Pennsylvania. Kingpin is informed of the computer virus and the botched hit on Punisher, so he calls in the Board, a young hacker, to combat the virus and plan a trap on Punisher. In Bucks County, Punisher and his team plan to hit Kingpin's King's Inn casino in Atlantic City. At the Inn, Punisher and Conchita blow a hole in the building, stage an assault, steal all the cash, pitching some into the street to create a diversion, then escape. They rendezvous with Microchip and Vernon Brooks in the Battle Van, but are chased by Kingpin's men, as well as Kingpin in a battlebus.

PUNISHER #17 (March 1989)

"Computer War" (21 pages)

CREDITS: Mike Baron (writer), Whilce Portacio (pencils), Scott Williams (inks), Ken Bruzenak (letters), Janet Jackson (colors), Marc McLaurin (asst editor), Carl Potts (editor)
FEATURE CHARACTER: Punisher
SUPPORTING: Microchip
VILLAINS: Board, Kingpin, Kingpin's driver, Triad Counters: Mr. Tam (criminal accountant), George Tam Wong (Tam's nephew w/photographic memory) (both 1st), Mr. Lem (Wong's personal assassin, dies, only app)
OTHER CHARACTERS: Conchita Ortiz (dies), Vernon Brooks, pizza delivery boy (bts), police, bystanders
LOCATIONS/ITEMS: Fisk Tower, Atlantic City streets, river, Punisher's New Jersey safe house / Board's skateboard, bystander's cars, Conchita's cigarettes & gun, Kingpin's battlebus inc laser defense, Mr. Lem's

machine gun, pizza box, police cars, Punisher's Battle Van inc steering wheel, scuba gear, Microchip & Board's computers, safe house's fridge inc milk & yogurt, Texacorp tanker

SYNOPSIS: The Kingpin's battlebus chases the Punisher's van across Atlantic City. Microchip attempts to hack into Kingpin's computer system, but Board counters with his own hack. Punisher crashes his van into the river before Board can shut down the vehicle. Retreating to their safe house, the Punisher and his crew plan their next move. Conchita wants to go after the Kingpin himself, while Microchip urges they stick to restricting the Kingpin's ability to run criminal enterprises. At his highrise, Kingpin welcomes Triad gang members to act as money counters until his computer systems are operational again. When Board refuses to escort the counters around, the Kingpin allows young Triad member George to assault the hacker. Triad member Mr. Lem's psychic powers locates Punisher's safe house, and he breaks in, murdering Conchita when she goes downstairs for a snack after sleeping with Frank. Frank hears the silenced shots and kills Lem, then vows to go after Kingpin.

NOTE: The letters page announces the production of the 1989 Punisher movie starring Dolph Lundgren.

PUNISHER #18 (April 1989)

"Face Off" (23 pages)

CREDITS: Mike Baron (writer), Whilce Portacio (pencils), Scott Williams (inks), Ken Bruzenak (letters), John Wellington (colors), Marc McLaurin (asst editor), Carl Potts (editor)
FEATURE CHARACTER: Punisher (next in PWJ #4-5, '89)
GUEST STARS: X-Men: Colossus, Dazzler, Havok, Longshot, Rogue, Storm, Wolverine (all last in UXM #245, '89, next in X Ann #13, '89)
SUPPORTING CAST: Microchip (next bts in PWJ #4, '89, next in PWJ #5, '89)
VILLAINS: Board (dies, last app), Kingpin (chr next in TM:BB '95, next in WoSM #48, '89) & his helicopter pilot, money handler, & security guards (some die, Wildech named, on monitor screen only), George Wong (next in Pun #53, '91), Mr. Wong (last app)
OTHER CHARACTERS: Vernon Brooks (last app), street bystanders, Nightcrawler (see NOTE)

LOCATIONS/ITEMS: Central Park inc Roof of 617 Central Park West, Kingpin's highrise inc private elevator, Punisher's New Jersey safe house / Board's skateboard, George's skateboard & knife, coffee, floor plans to highrise, Kingpin's helicopter & gas mask, Micro's gas canister, gas mask & satchel bomb, Punisher's gas mask & experimental communications laser, Vernon's machine gun, rifle & two-way radio

SYNOPSIS: Microchip receives a message from Board, offering to sell info on the Kingpin. A meeting is set for Central Park, with Vernon covering them with a rifle from a nearby rooftop. The Board meets with Microchip in the park, offering a code that will disable Fisk Tower's security systems in return for one million dollars. As the Board starts to skate away, George Wong rides up on another skateboard and kills him. Vernon refuses to fire on the young George, earning a rebuke from Frank. Later that night, the Punisher, Microchip, and Vern plot an assault on the Kingpin's highrise. Punisher demands Vern stay out of it, no longer trusting him. Frank and Microchip take over one of Kingpin's helicopters, flying it onto the roof. On his own initiative, Vernon infiltrates the building as a repairman. Frank and Microchip blast into Kingpin's penthouse, but the Kingpin knocks out Microchip and overcomes Frank in battle. Before the villain can kill him though, Vernon arrives, ordering Kingpin at gunpoint to release Frank, and in exchange they'll leave. The wounded Punisher can't believe Vernon and Microchip are letting Kingpin live, but they point out that the resulting gang war to fill his title will claim innocent bystander's lives.

NOTE: Cover title reads "Face Off With the Kingpin." Nightcrawler's tail is visible in the X-Men cameo, but is an art error, as at this time he was in England with Excalibur and believed the other X-Men to be dead.

PUNISHER #19 (May 1989)

"The Spider" (22 pages)

CREDITS: Mike Baron (writer), Larry Stroman (pencils), Randy Emberlin (inks), Ken Bruzenak (letters), John Wellington (colors), Marc McLaurin (asst editor), Carl Potts (editor), Tom Mandrake (c inks)
FEATURE CHARACTER: Punisher (also as weapons buyer Eastman & drug supplier Mr. Yousoufian, next in PP #46, '89, PWJ #6-7, '89)
SUPPORTING CAST: Microchip (between PWJ #5-6, '89)
VILLAINS: Mr. Kenton (drug dealer), Spider Roque (drug dealer, Australian army veteran) & his men, Jackie & Mick (all only apps, die), unnamed drug dealer
OTHER CHARACTERS: Laird (Australian arms seller), Tran Thi (young girl) & her mother (dies), Qantas Airways Limited receptionist (bts, on phone), camel renter, drug buyer, TV news reporter, bystanders, camel, cat, crabs, spider

LOCATIONS/ITEMS: Australia inc King's Cross, Sydney & Cooterman's Creek w/ Spider Roque's base at former opal mine, New Jersey inc Punisher's warehouse, New York inc Hotel Broslin, apartment building, comic store & Manhattan's Lower East Side inc Vets House / P-49 (designer drug, mentioned only), Kenton's pistol, silencer & briefcase of money, kilo of heroin, Laird's car, prop plane, Punisher's book ("The Natural History of the Mediterranean"), brass knuckles, computer, Kevlar body armor, knife, money, printout, silencer, telephone, television w/ remote control, throwing star & firearms inc Uzi pistol & 9mm Beretta, Spider Roque's jeep, knife, pistol, satellite dish & shoe box, Qantas Airways Limited jet

SYNOPSIS: Using fake drug deals, the Punisher has been luring dealers to ambushes in a variety of hotels. While waiting in the latest one for former ANZAC turned dealer Spider Roque, a young neighbor comes looking for help for her choking mom. Frank administers the Heimlich maneuver, saving her, but the grateful woman subsequently interrupts Punisher's deal with the paranoid Roque, who murders her, knocks Castle out with a glancing head shot, and makes off with his heroin. After learning that the spooked Roque rushed back to his base in the Australian desert, Punisher flies to Australia, buys some weapons, and travels by camel to Cooterman's Creek. There he attacks Roque and his men but falls into a mineshaft. Believing that Castle was hired by the survivors of a village where he massacred eleven people, Roque is tricked by Punisher into accepting what he thinks is Castle's payment of a valuable opal, only to be bit by a poisonous spider that Punisher collected. Castle climbs out of the shaft, collects Roque's blood money and, once back home, instructs Microchip to use the money to help the orphaned girl.

NOTE: Punisher's War Journal notes that it's Tuesday, September 6, 1988. Punisher's pseudonym of Eastman is an homage to writer Kevin Eastman and the character Laird is an homage to artist Peter Laird.

PUNISHER #20 (June 1989)

"Bad Tip" (22 pages)

CREDITS: Mike Baron (writer), Shea Anton Pensa (pencils), Gerry Talaoc (inks), Ken Bruzenak (letters), Christine Scheele (colors), Marc McLaurin (asst editor), Carl Potts (editor), Whilce Portacio (c pencils), Ron Randall (c inks)
FEATURE CHARACTER: Punisher
SUPPORTING CAST: Microchip (bts, last in PWJ #6, '89)
VILLAINS: Belzer (cross-dressing assassin, also as Christine Barnes, only app, dies), 2 muggers (Charlie Sexton named, both die), unnamed mobster (hires Belzer)
OTHER CHARACTERS: Big Louis Amato (designer of the Royal Palms hotel, murdered, mentioned only), Magnusson (private investigator, only app), Otis Offenbach (key mobster prosecution witness, dies bts), Sidney Schwab (defense lawyer, hires Magnusson to find Belzer, mentioned only), middle aged couple (targeted by muggers), cab driver, Royal Palms valet driver, security guards, Black Jack dealer, bystanders (Howard named) inc female waitress/hostage
LOCATIONS/ITEMS: Las Vegas inc Alhambra Hotel inc Room 274B, Royal Palms casino / blackjack cards, poker chips, cars, Las Vegas Voice newspaper, Magnusson's black jack & knife, muggers' car & cigarette, Punisher's ankle holster, brass knuckles, gambler disguise, 9 mm & .22 with silencer, Belzer's bomb & gun
SYNOPSIS: The Punisher has come to Las Vegas to intercept the assassin "Belzer," who has been hired to kill a witness in a trial combating Vegas' organized crime. Scoring big in disguise at a roulette table, he is flirted with by a Christine Barnes, but turns down her advances and leaves for the parking lot instead, where he overpowers two would-be muggers, interrogating them for word on Belzer, a known gambler. Learning nothing, he moves on, but later spies the two muggers following other possible targets at the Royal Palms, the witness' hotel. When he confronts them in the parking lot, they attack him, but he dispatches them, getting a possible location for Belzer out of them before finishing them off. Frank heads to the hotel room he believes belongs to Belzer, but instead finds Magnusson, a private eye hired to look for Belzer. Defeating Magnusson, Frank realizes that Belzer put out word on Magnusson as a distraction. He races back to the Royal Palms in time to see Christine Barnes, who he realizes is a disguised Belzer, detonate a bomb killing the witness. Belzer flees, grabbing a hostage, but Frank kills him before he can escape.
NOTE: Cover title reads "Las Vegas Nights." The Punisher notes his wife and children were murdered "10 years ago." The address in mugger Charlie Sexton's wallet is 419 Knox Place.

PUNISHER #21 (July 1989)

"The Boxer" (22 pages)

CREDITS: Mike Baron (writer), Erik Larsen (pencils), Scott Williams (inks), Ken Bruzenak (letters), John Wellington (colors), Marc McLaurin (asst editor), Carl Potts (editor)
FEATURE CHARACTER: Punisher
SUPPORTING CAST: Microchip (next in Pun Ann #2, '89)
VILLAINS: Les Daniels (BJ's manager, dies), Iris Green (toxicology expert, Eternal Sun section chief, 1st, next in Pun #24, '89, see NOTE)
OTHER CHARACTERS: BJ Johnson (boxer, also on TV), Derek Mullen (ex-Penn State boxing champ), Derek Simpson (BJ's opponent, on TV), Buck Engle (BJ's sparring partner), gym manager, BJ's trainer (also on TV), boxers in training, bartender, bar patrons, Daniels' bodyguards, ninjas (on TV), fight attendees (on TV), ring announcer (on TV), St. Mary's nurse (voice on phone only)
LOCATIONS/ITEMS: Philadelphia inc Cobb's Gym w/locker room, bar, apartment building w/Iris' condo, & boxing arena (on TV), Newark, NJ, inc Punisher's warehouse / Frank's gym bag, boxing gloves, assault rifle, laxative vial, antitoxic stimulant, & suction cups; lockers, boxing ring, BJ's boxing gloves, Buck's boxing gloves, jump rope, speed bag, Microchip's PC, Iris' medical kit & paralytic syringe, Daniels' syringe & wallet, Scully's Ninja Training Camp brochure
SYNOPSIS: Investigating crooked boxing promoter Les Daniels, Frank Castle visits a Philadelphia boxing gym where Daniels' new championship prospect, BJ Johnson, is training. Frank accepts Daniels' offer to spar with BJ for cash, and provokes BJ into knocking him out in the first round. Impressed by Frank, BJ invites Frank for drinks at a bar, where Frank meets Iris Green, BJ's girlfriend. Frank insults the pair into leaving by suggesting Daniels could benefit from BJ losing his upcoming title fight. At Frank's warehouse, Microchip's research determines that Iris has a toxicology background and attended a "ninja training camp." After failing to stop the fight by drugging BJ's water supply during a sparring session, Frank, in Punisher garb, breaks into Iris' condo. Iris subdues him with a paralytic then departs for the fight, leaving the TV on for Frank to watch. BJ is defeated in Round 6 after his trainer gives him a drugged water bottle. Daniels arrives to kill Frank with a poison syringe, but Frank ingests an antidote and the two fight. Frank kills Daniels with his own syringe, then, after notifying BJ's hospital to check him for poisoning, finds a brochure in Iris' belongings for the ninja training camp Micro mentioned.
NOTE: This story is dedicated to ex-Marvel writer/editor Denny O'Neil. Iris' affiliation with Eternal Sun, a right-wing militia, is revealed in Pun #24, '89, as her ulterior motive of fixing BJ's fight as a means of financing Eternal Sun's activities. Frank's narration mentions this is his third Jersey warehouse; he presumably abandoned the one Rose Kugel compromised in Pun #7, '88, and he blew up the second in Pun #15, '89.

PUNISHER #22 (August 1989)

"Ninja Training Camp" (21 pages)

CREDITS: Mike Baron (writer), Erik Larsen (pencils), Scott Williams (inks), Ken Bruzenak (letters), Gregory Wright (colors), Marc McLaurin (asst editor), Carl Potts (editor)
FEATURE CHARACTER: Punisher (also as Fred D'amato)
VILLAINS: Chester Scully (Ninja Camp founder, also as "Joe," 1st), Daryl, Wayne (both 1st, Ninja Camp's top instructors), Tanto (Scully's dog, 1st)
OTHER CHARACTERS: Katherine Yakamoto (daughter of famed ninja Hatsu Yakamoto, 1st), ninja students inc Higganbotham (Merc Magazine reporter, 1st), Saracen (Muzzafar Lambert, Free Armenian army member, 1st), Sykes (only app) & Phillips (1st), Yael Mishikov (Israeli Intelligence member, mentioned only, vouched for "D'amato"), ninjas (in traditional & modern uniforms, in Punisher's mind only), Chester's wife Janeen (mentioned only), Abe Hargreaves (U.S. Congressman, mentioned as trained at Ninja Camp), raccoon

LOCATIONS/ITEMS: Sloman, Kansas inc Antler Inn, Ninja Camp inc Scully's house, training hall, dining hall, furnace & trainee bunkhouse / Daryl & Wayne's motorcycles, Scully's crowbar, driver's license & truck, file cabinet inc Iris Green's file, Punisher's knife, makeshift bola (rock & shoelaces), pistol, kerosene cans, Gravy Train dogfood bags, greyhound bus, tripwire

SYNOPSIS: Trailing Iris Green, an assassin trained at a "Ninja Training Camp," the disguised Punisher signs up for the camp, meeting its owner Scully at a bar in Sloman, Kansas. After being shown to the bunkhouse on Scully's ranch, the Punisher spies a ninja woman exiting, smiling at him as she leaves. The next morning, their training begins, with Merc Magazine reporter Higganbotham questioning if this is truly ninja training. Frank further challenges their credibility by defeating hand-to-hand instructor Wayne with a cheap shot. Later on that night, instructor Daryl drops each of the students off into the countryside, asking they prove they can survive in the wilderness alone. Frank uses the opportunity to sneak into Scully's house, finding a file on Iris Green inside. He is confronted by the female ninja, who identifies herself as Katherine Yakamoto, daughter of famed ninja master Hatsu Yakamoto, whom Scully falsely claims to have trained under. She asks for Frank's help as the instructors burst into the home. Yakamoto slips away, while Frank sets the house on fire and leaves. Scully retrieves his files as the house burns, vowing to make whoever did this pay.

NOTE: Cover title reads "Ninja Training Camp." Tanto, Phillips and Janeen named next issue. Saracen's real name is revealed in OHMU #1, '10. Higganbotham's name also spelled Higgenbotham.

PUNISHER #23 (September 1989)

"Capture the Flag" (21 pages)

CREDITS: Mike Baron (writer), Erik Larsen (pencils), Scott Williams (inks), Ken Bruzenak (letters), John Wright (colors), Marc McLaurin (asst editor), Carl Potts (editor)
FEATURE CHARACTER: Punisher (also as Fred D'amato, next in Pun Ann #2, '89)
VILLAINS: Chester Scully, Daryl & Wayne, Tanto (all die, last apps)
OTHER CHARACTERS: Higganbotham (corpse only), Katherine Yakamoto, Phillips (dies), Saracen (next in PWJ #25, '90), cows
LOCATIONS/ITEMS: Kansas inc Ninja Camp inc Scully's house, Grain elevator / Iris Green's file, Phillips' gun, Punisher's knife, Scully's ballistic knife & machine gun, Daryl's H&K 93 machine gun, Katherine's note, manrikigusari & flare, Saracen's javelin, Wayne's shuriken, katana & truck

SYNOPSIS: Unsure who is to blame, Scully and his instructors decide to hunt down each of the students and start over with their camp. Wayne soon catches up with Frank, but Frank defeats the instructor in combat. Frank leaves Wayne alive, taking the instructor's sword and severing his hamstring. Frank finds Higganbotham shot dead, and spies fellow student Phillips being killed by sniper fire. Stumbling across other student Saracen, the two team up to keep from being picked off, with Saracen admitting he attended the camp to track an assassin his Free Armenian Army believes trained there. As they fan out again, Saracen is wounded, with Scully tracking him down while Punisher gets in a gun battle with Daryl. Wayne reappears, having dragged himself to his truck. He attempts to run over Frank, but crashes, with his vehicle exploding when struck by Daryl's bullets. Frank uses the smoke cover to sneak up and dispatch Daryl. He then finds the wounded Saracen at a nearby grain elevator. Scully confronts Frank, but Katherine intervenes, stating she has a score to settle with Scully and ordering Frank to leave. Frank flees with the wounded Saracen as the grain elevator explodes. He finds Iris Green's file left for him, along with a letter from Katherine inviting Frank to meet her father in Japan.

NOTE: Cover title reads "Fire Fight!"

PUNISHER ANNUAL #2 (1989)

"Knight Fight" (24 pages)

CREDITS: Mike Baron (writer), Bill Reinhold (art), Janice Chiang (letters), Gregory Wright (colors), Marc McLaurin (asst editor), Carl Potts (editor)
FEATURE CHARACTER: Punisher (next in Pun Ann #2/3, '89)
GUEST STAR: Moon Knight (Marc Spector, wealthy urban vigilante, between MK #3-4, '89)
SUPPORTING CAST: Microchip (next in Pun Ann #2/3, '89)
VILLAINS: Viper (Ophelia Sarkissian, terrorist ex-Hydra agent, also as Leona Hiss, last in ASM Ann #23, '89, next in DD Ann #5, '89) & her snake-like mutates (some die) inc Ralph Newton (junkie murderer turned mutate, also as Helmut Snead & Morton), Smalto (dies), 3 drug dealers (2 die)
OTHER CHARACTERS: Jean-Paul "Frenchie" DuChamp (Moon Knight's pilot & confidante, between MK #3-4, '89), pet shop owner (voice only) & customer, dog, bird, gerbils (die), pedestrians, sleeping junkie, junkies (Sammy named), comatose black mamba, rabbits (one dies), hamsters, police (bts in cars)
LOCATIONS/ITEMS: Long Island inc Long Island Pet Salon, Borgwardt Estate (Save Our Society HQ), Moon Knight's mansion w/war room & bedroom, Save our Society rehab clinic / Frank's guns, grappling hook launcher; dealers' guns, Micro's computer, Moon Knight's helicopter, nunchaku, glider cape & crescent darts; Newton's syringe & gun, Snead's credit card, Viper's bullwhip & escape rocket, map of Borgwardt Estate, pet cages, hang-glider, thermal packs

SYNOPSIS: Moon Knight's probe of a pet store customer he, as Marc Spector, saw eating a live gerbil and the Punisher's hunt for drug peddler Ralph Newton lead them both to Save Our Society, an anti-drug charity. The two meet during Frank's stakeout of their rehab clinic and join forces; comparing notes, Punisher realizes Newton was the man Moon Knight saw. Breaking into the clinic, they confront Newton just after he has injected a junkie. Newton suddenly takes on reptilian features and attacks Frank, while Moon Knight is attacked by a group of other snakelike assailants. Frank and Moon Knight emerge victorious, and Moon Knight invites Frank to his mansion to research SOS, finding links to the terrorist Viper, recently broken out of prison by Dr. Tyrone. Frank and Moon Knight attack the estate where SOS is housed and are attacked by Viper's snake-men. Viper injects Frank with the drug she used to transform her minions, but Frank unexpectedly goes on a drug-crazed killing spree. Moon Knight dispatches the last of the snake-men, but Viper escapes. Moon Knight tries to hypnotize Frank out of his affliction, but goes into convulsions, and Moon Knight rushes him back to the mansion, where he sweats the drug his system over the next two days.

NOTE: Includes table of contents page (1 page) w/art taken from page 18, panel 1. Part 5 of the "Atlantis Attacks" event running through Marvel's 1989 annuals. Continued from ASM Ann #23, '89 and into PPSSM Ann #9, '89. The unseen Tyrone is really the Roman villain Tyrannus. Frenchie mentions the Washington, DC snake riot, a reported mass hallucination where people thought they were turning into snakes. This was a whitewash of Viper's biological attack on the city that actually did transform its citizens into reptilian creatures, as seen in Cap #344, '88.

2ND STORY: "Dark Seeker" (15 pages)

CREDITS: Roger Salick (writer), Tod Smith (pencils), John Beatty (inks), Ken Bruzenak (letters), Gregory Wright (colors), Carl Potts (editor)
FEATURE CHARACTER: Microchip (last in Pun Ann #2/3, '89, next bts in PWJ #8, '89, next in PWJ #10, '89)
VILLAINS: Cannibal (Tran Du Thong, runs protection racket, dies, also in pfb), Dinh (Tran's enforcer, dies), Tran's 2 henchmen (both die)
OTHER CHARACTERS: Pham (restaurant owner), Hue (Pham's wife), Danny (Micro's courier, voice on phone only), Vietnamese boat people (all in pfb, some die in pfb), freighter crew (in pfb), Tran's nephew (in pfb only, dies)
LOCATIONS/ITEMS: New York inc Micro's warehouse, Pham's Restaurant w/dining room & kitchen, Truc Giang, Vietnam w/harbor (in pfb), South China Sea (in pfb), Tran's warehouse & adjoining docks / "Wolf's Ears" audio enhancers, night optic goggles, silenced Ingram MAC-11, Battle Van, junk w/inoperative engine (in pfb), 2 freighters (both in pfb), clubs (in pfb), explosive charge, Kevlar briefcase, Tran & his men's guns, Pham's ropes, stock pot of water, V-40 mini-grenade, Tran's speedboat, tranquilizer gun w/paralytic dart
FLASHBACK: Tran and his men ferry a group of Vietnamese immigrants, including Pham and Hue, to Malaysia. The boat breaks down before they reach their destination, and the hardship and hunger prompt Tran to drown and eat Pham and Hue's nephew (p).
SYNOPSIS: On his way to send a package of new equipment to the Punisher, Microchip stops by his favorite Vietnamese restaurant. The owner, Pham, is assaulted by a gangster nicknamed "the Cannibal," to whom Pham owes protection money. Micro tries to save him but is beaten unconscious. Pham's wife Hue tells Micro about the Cannibal, and Micro vows to help Pham. With Hue outside ready to detonate an explosive on the power lines, Micro travels to the Cannibal's warehouse ostensibly to deliver the money Pham owes him. Hue blows the power out and Micro rescues Pham. Micro stalks the Cannibal and shoots him with a paralytic that knocks him in the water and will leave him awake as he drowns.

3RD STORY: "Punisher's Fighting Techniques" (6 pages)
CREDITS: Roger Salick (writer), Jim Lee (pencils), Scott Williams (inks), Ken Lopez (letters), Gregory Wright (colors), Carl Potts (editor)
FEATURE CHARACTER: Punisher (also in fb1 between Pun #80, '93 fb & Pun Ann #3/2, '90 fb, also in fb2-5, next in PWJ #8-9, '89)
SUPPORTING CAST: Microchip (last in Pun Ann #2, '89, next in Pun Ann #2/3, '89)
VILLAINS: Saz (inmate, in fb1, dies), Harvey Moy (drug dealer, in fb2, dies), Big Mike (would-be rapist, in fb3), James Metzger (serial killer, in fb4, dies), Leroy "Tiger" Tibbs (gangster, in fb5, dies)
OTHER CHARACTERS: Bar patrons (in fb3), Mike's prospective victim (in fb3), Leroy's 3 friends (all in fb5)
LOCATIONS/ITEMS: Punisher's warehouse w/exercise area, New York inc Ryker's Island (in fb1), bar (in fb3), park (in fb5) / Punisher & Micro's gis, Micro's headgear, Saz's broken bottle (in fb1), Moy's Lamborghini Countach (in fb2), Mike's pool cue, Punisher's makeshift escrima sticks (prev 2 in fb3), Metzger's knife (in fb4)
FLASHBACKS: The Punisher kills Saz, a fellow Ryker's inmate (1). The Punisher defeats and kills drug dealer and martial artist Harvey Moy (2). The Punisher dispatches a would-be rapist named Big Mike in a bar (3). The Punisher kills serial killer James Metzger (4). The Punisher kills career criminal Leroy Tibbs in a park (5).
SYNOPSIS: The Punisher and Microchip introduce a series of vignettes demonstrating the Punisher's unarmed combat techniques.
NOTE: First page contains a disclaimer advising not to attempt the maneuvers depicted in the story.

4TH STORY: "Saga of the Serpent Crown: Heirs Apparent" (6 pages)
CREDITS: Peter Sanderson (writer), Mark Bagley (pencils), Keith Williams (inks, see NOTE), Jade Moede (letters), Mister Adam (colors), Gregory Wright (managing editor), Mark Gruenwald (editor)
FEATURE CHARACTER: Uatu the Watcher (last in ASM Ann #23/7, '89, next in PPSSM #9/5, '89)
VILLAINS: Grog (god-slayer, in 1st chr app in fb before Thor #390, '88), Set (serpentine elder god, in fb between Conan #147, '83 & PPSSM Ann #9/5, '89), Seth (Heliopolitan death god, in fb between Thor #240, '75 fb & IHulk #257, '81 fb)
OTHER CHARACTERS: Conan (Cimmerian barbarian), Conn (Conan's son), Ferdrugo (King of Zingara), Thoth-Amon (Stygian wizard), Duke Villagro (prev 5 in rfb), Zingarans (all in rfb), Conan's soldiers (all in rfb), 5 serpent-men (all in rfb, 3 as corpses), 2 Egyptian priests (both in rfb)
LOCATIONS/ITEMS: Ferdrugo's palace, Aquilonia (prev 2 in rfb), Egypt w/Seth's pyramid / Cobra Crown, abdication scroll, Conan's swords, soldiers' swords & shields, Conn's sword, priest's sceptres
FLASHBACKS: Thoth-Amon and Villagro scheme to use the Cobra Crown to compel Zingara's King Ferdrugo to install Villagro as the new king, but Thoth-Amon betrays Villagro and makes himself king. Conan arrives and warns the Zingarans of the magic at work, and Thoth-Amon kills Villagro, which unfortunately burns out the crown's power (SSwConan #41-43, '79). Thoth-Amon and his Serpent-Men war with Conan and his son Conn for decades (KConan #1-55, '80-89). Seth passes himself off as the personification of Set to a pair of priests, angering Set.
SYNOPSIS: The Watcher continues his tale of the Serpent Crown's history.
NOTE: Part 5 of the Watcher's oral history of the Serpent Crown, which runs as a series of backup stories in all of the "Atlantis Attacks" annuals. The contents page lists Keith Williams as this story's inker, whereas the credits on the story's first page credits inks to "the Dudes." 3rd & 4th stories bookend a pair of pinups, one of the Punisher by Tod Smith and Scott Williams (1 page) and the other of the Punisher and Wolverine by Jon Bogdanove (2 pages).

PUNISHER #24 (October 1989)

"Land of the Eternal Sun" (21 pages)

CREDITS: Mike Baron (writer), Erik Larsen (pencils), Scott Williams (inks), Ken Bruzenak (letters), John Wellington (colors), Marc McLaurin (asst editor), Carl Potts (editor)
FEATURE CHARACTER: Punisher
GUEST STARS: Shadowmasters (ninja clan): Manzo, Yuriko Ezaki, Philip Richards (all last in PWJ #9, '89)
VILLAINS: Iris Green (last in Pun #21, '89), Eternal Sun assassins (some die) & helicopter pilot (dies)
OTHER CHARACTERS: Hatsu Yakamoto (ninja master, Katherine's father, last in PWJ #8, '89), Katherine Yakamoto (also as elderly villager), Morgenstern (Abe Hargreaves' representative, bts, intercepted & possibly killed by Shadowmasters), villagers, Eternal Sun guard
LOCATIONS/ITEMS: Mt. Yakashin, Hokkaido inc Yakamotos' house, nearby forest, hotel, & Eternal Sun's coastal base / Frank's rental car, 9mm handgun, & night-vision scope; Katherine's mask & rifle; Eternal Sun assassins' swords, flash powder, garrote, knife, rifles, mortar launcher; Hatsu's longbow, arrows, & revolver; Philip's rifle, Yuriko's rifle, Manzo's Belgian armor-piercing rocket launcher & rockets, Eternal Sun helicopter gunship (destroyed)

SYNOPSIS: Arriving in a Hokkaido village in response to Hatsu Yakamoto's invitation, Frank Castle is directed by an elderly villager to Yakamoto's mountaintop home. On the way, a sword-wielding assassin attacks Frank. Yakamoto chases off the assassin with a fired arrow and greets Frank. While sharing tea, Yakamoto asks Frank to officially represent his ninjitsu style in the States, but Frank politely refuses. Yakamoto nevertheless asks Frank to stay at least a day and meet his new students, the Shadowmasters, who soon arrive and are recognized by Frank. Yakamoto tells Frank about the assassin's employer, a fanatical right-wing Japanese super-patriot militia called Eternal Sun. A team of Eternal Sun assassins suddenly attacks. Frank and his allies defeat the assassins, but Yakamoto's home is destroyed. The elderly woman from the village emerges and reveals herself as a disguised Katherine Yakamoto. The next day, Frank and the others plan to infiltrate Eternal Sun's coastal headquarters, substituting Philip Richards and Yuriko Ezaki for representatives of Congressman Abe Hargreaves, a name Frank recognizes from Scully's camp. That night, Frank and Katherine watch from afar as Philip and Yuriko arrive at the base, but Frank is stunned to see that the Eternal Sun representative meeting them is Iris Green.

NOTE: Frank previously fought alongside the Shadowmasters in PWJ #9, '89. Morgenstern's name is revealed next issue. Katherine spelled Katherine here. Yuriko and Manzo are mistakenly identified as one another.

PUNISHER #25 (November 1989)

"Sunset in Kansas" (40 pages)

CREDITS: Mike Baron (writer), Erik Larsen (pencils), Al Williamson (inks), Ken Bruzenak (letters), John Wellington (colors), Hilary Barta (c inks), Marc McLaurin (asst editor), Carl Potts (editor)
FEATURE CHARACTER: Punisher (next in Pun Ann #3, '90, Pun:RBN, '89)
GUEST STARS: Shadowmasters: Yuriko Ezaki, Manzo, Philip Richards (also as "Mr. Morgenstern") (all last chr app)
VILLAINS: Iris Green (apparently dies, last app), Congressman Abe Hargreaves (gun-happy politician, also in photo, apparently dies, only app)
OTHER CHARACTERS: Hatsu Yakamoto (dies, last app), Katherine Yakamoto (also as "Ms. Yakamura," last app), Foley (Hargreaves' aide), Eternal Sun guards (some die), Iris' motorcyclist (dies), commuters, party guests, Faxtech guards, Ronald Reagan (in photo)
LOCATIONS/ITEMS: Eternal Sun's Hokkaido base (destroyed) w/conference room, restroom, helipad, computer room & pier; Washington, DC w/Hargreaves' office, Iris' hotel room; Tokyo w/Yakamoto's safe house w/Frank's bedroom & balcony; Topeka, Kansas inc Hilton Hotel w/Hargreaves' suite & Faxtech Aerospace w/security checkpoint, presentation room, & hangar (destroyed) / helicopter (destroyed); Punisher's night-vision scope, Uzi, grenade, & clip-on tie; Philip's plastique-filled briefcase, trade bill paperwork, hidden explosive charge, detonator pen, & smoke bomb; Katherine's rifle, manrikigusari, Uzi, & shuriken; Iris' handgun, bandage, bow, arrows, security pass, & poisoned ring; dessert plate; guards' guns & machine-gun nest (destroyed); Manzo's rocket launcher & timed explosive; Yuriko's rifle, speedboat; Hatsu's junk, longbow, & arrows; Hargreaves' rifle & handgun; motorcycle, Faxtech flex-wing fighter (destroyed), fireproof canvas
SYNOPSIS: As the Punisher and Katherine Yakamoto watch, Philip Richards and Yuriko Ezaki are escorted into Eternal Sun's base. Philip and Yuriko attend a meeting with Iris, during which Philip excuses himself to use the restroom, where he plants a bomb. Philip returns and detonates the bomb, blowing away a corner of the building and signaling Frank, Katherine, Hatsu Yakamoto, and Manzo to attack. Frank and his allies assault the base and plant a bomb in its computer room, then escape by speedboat. The bomb destroys the base, but Iris survives. The next day, Iris notifies Abe Hargreaves of the base's destruction and his envoy's likely death. At a Tokyo safe house, Frank and the others celebrate their victory, but Frank feigns drunkenness and retires. That night, Frank and Hatsu take a walk, during which Hatsu tells Frank more about Eternal Sun, and reveals he taught Iris about poisons. Iris then fatally shoots Hatsu with an arrow. Frank fires back with Hatsu's bow, killing the motorcyclist chauffeuring Iris, but Iris escapes nonetheless. Divided between fighting Eternal Sun and stopping Iris and Hargreaves, the Shadowmasters respectfully part ways with Frank and Katherine. Iris arrives in Topeka to meet with Hargreaves and shocks him by saying they have run afoul of the Punisher. Frank and Katherine infiltrate an aerospace company's unveiling party featuring a prototype aircraft bankrolled by Hargreaves and Eternal Sun. In the plane's hangar, Iris unsuccessfully tries to kill Frank, then Hargreaves and Katherine arrive. As a battle ensues, the Shadowmasters subdue the company's security guards. Katherine and Frank wrap themselves in fireproof canvas, then Katherine shoots the plane's fuel pods, destroying the hangar. Protected by the canvas, Katherine and Frank emerge and see the Shadowmasters waving. Frank turns to speak to Katherine, but she has vanished.
NOTE: Though the Shadowmasters have no further chronological appearances, they have one final outing in a flashback story in MCP #162/4, '94.

EPIC GRAPHIC NOVEL: THE PUNISHER - RETURN TO BIG NOTHING (1989)

"Return to Big Nothing" (62 pages)

CREDITS: Steven Grant (writer), Mike Zeck (pencils, co-colors, c art), John Beatty (inks), Ken Bruzenak (letters), Ian Tetrault (colors), Phil Zimelman (colors, c colors), Robbin Brosterman (design), Margaret Clark (editor), Carl Potts (consulting editor)
FEATURE CHARACTER: Punisher (also as Lee Costa, also as Pvt. Castiglione in fb1 between PWJ #3, '07 fb & TheNam #67, '92 fb, also as Sgt. Castiglione in fb2 & fb4 between ASM #175, '77 fb & TheNam #69, '92 fb, also as Frank Castle in fb3 between Pun Ann #4, '91 & MP #2, '75 fb; next in PWJ #10, '89, Pun #26, '89)
SUPPORTING CAST: Maria Castle (bts as Castiglione, pregnant, in fb2 during Pun:AG, '88 fb, in fb3 between Pun Ann #4, '91 & MP #2, '75 fb), Lisa Castle, Frank Castle Jr. (both in fb3 between Pun #10, '09 fb & MP #2, '75 fb)
VILLAINS: Sgt. Cleve Gorman (smuggler, also in fb1, 2&4), Mr. Snow (casino owner, also in fb2&4), Khieu Dap (smuggler, also in fb4) & his men (some in fb4) inc Harry, Lenny, Jess, Hok, Wat Phu, gunrunners inc Jimmy Troun, Rodney, Oscar (all die)
OTHER CHARACTERS: Verta Mae (cathouse owner), Lee Costa, Thom (both FBI agents, die); Col. Janss (Pendleton base commander), Janss' secretary (bts), reporter (on TV), dealers inc Henry, cathouse customers, Marines, prison guards inc Arch, prostitutes inc Carly, Snow's security; casino staff & patrons; Big Nothing soldiers (in fb1, die), North Vietnamese soldiers (corpses, in fb2), Owens (Fisk Spices International agent, in fb4), US marines (in fb2&4, those in fb2 die), Burt Kenyon (in fb4 to 1st chr app before ASM #175, '77 fb; see NOTE)
LOCATIONS/ITEMS: "Big Nothing" (isolated army camp, also in fb1), Camp Pendleton, CA inc Gorman's supply hut; Snow's casino; Cambodia inc Siem Pang (fb2), Vietnamese city (fb4), Verta Mae's cathouse, Goodspring, Nevada; Las Vegas inc Golden Ram casino, San Joaquin prison / Punisher's mini-flashlight, rifle, handgun, knife; gunrunners' truck w/weapons crates inc grenades (all destroyed), agents' handguns, gunrunners' handguns, rifles & Uzis; Costa's ID, Dap's men's weapons, cars, bomb & detonator; Verta Mae matchbook, Lenny's handguns & cowboy hat,

money case, Snow's Camaro, Arch's nightstick, helicopters (fb4), Gorman's handgun (also in fb4) & bazooka, "Big Nothing" banner (also in fb1)

FLASHBACKS: Stationed at a camp nicknamed "Big Nothing" before his first deployment, Pvt. Frank Castiglione talks big to fellow recruits about facing the Vietcong, until combat veteran Gorman beats him, nicknaming Frank a "Big Nothing" too (1). Having entered Cambodia to "cut off enemy supply lines," Gorman and Snow send Sgt. Castiglione ahead on point, then kill their own men to use their corpses to transport drugs. They claim the enemy attacked, blaming Frank's ineptitude, and though Frank realizes the truth, he keeps quiet, wanting to live to return home to his pregnant wife (2). The night before their planned park trip, Frank checks on his kids before going to bed with Maria (3). As US forces evacuates a Vietnamese city, Frank finds Gorman taking Cambodians out on a helicopter. Gorman shoots Frank and takes off (4).

SYNOPSIS: Punisher hides in the back of a gunrunners' truck, planning an ambush when they meet their buyers, but two FBI agents crash the sale, triggering a firefight. Joining in, Punisher kills the dealers and destroys the weapons. One agent, Lee Costa, is still alive but fatally wounded; before dying, he tells Frank they plan a Cambodian gang, were working with a marine, Cleve Gorman, and a surprised Frank recalls his first encounter with Gorman at the "Big Nothing." With his army discharge imminent, Gorman frets when he hears about the bust and Punisher's involvement, until he learns the vigilante's identity, remembering Frank with derision. Using Costa's ID, Punisher enters Camp Pendleton to confront Gorman, but finds Gorman and his Cambodian allies expecting him. They knock him out and Gorman, not wanting to explain a corpse, tells the Cambodians to kill Punisher in the desert in a car explosion. Escaping just prior to detonation, Punisher finds a discarded matchbook; with Gorman gone by the time Punisher walks out the desert, the matchbook leads him to Verta Mae's cathouse, where he waits for Gorman's men until the Cambodians loudly arrive. Punisher kills most of them, and gets the final gangster to divulge the location of Gorman's partner, Snow: the Golden Ram casino. Posing as a gambler, Punisher visits the casino, then confronts and interrogates a terrified Snow. Told Khieu Dup, the Cambodian gang's leader, operates out of San Joaquin prison, Punisher uses a stolen guard uniform to reach Khieu Dap, who says Gorman is at Big Nothing before Frank kills him. Waiting for Punisher's attack at the abandoned army base, Gorman watches Punisher arrive, and fires a rocket at him. Approaching the crippled Punisher to finish him, Gorman discovers his victim is Snow, dressed as the Punisher and sent on point to draw Gorman out. Punisher shoots Gorman, who surrenders, certain Frank Castle would never shoot an unarmed prisoner. Punisher kills him and drapes the "Big Nothing" banner over him.

NOTE: Released both as a softcover and a hardcover with dustjacket, each with different covers. Includes title/credits page (2 pages) w/art taken from page 6, panel 2. Back cover image taken from page 61, panel 1. In the fbs, Frank's fellow soldiers call him Castle, but his surname was Castiglione during his first tour of duty; PunTheNam, '94 clarifies that he changed his name later to circumvent rules limiting the number of tours a single soldier could do. Burt Kenyon, identified here only by surname, will become Spider-Man foe, the Hitman.

PUNISHER #26 (November 1989)

"The Whistle Blower" (21 pages)

CREDITS: Mike Baron (writer), Russ Heath (art), Ken Bruzenak (letters), John Wellington (colors), Marc McLaurin (asst editor), Carl Potts (editor)
FEATURE CHARACTER: Punisher
VILLAINS: Adm. Fairfax (North Atlantic Fleet commander, 1st), Robert Morse (Underwater Boat CEO, 1st), Weise's assailants (Bob named, 2 die)
OTHER CHARACTERS: Herman Weise (Underwater Boat fluid dynamics engineer, 1st), Barry Fishbein (Morse's lawyer), Jerry (Fairfax's aide), Cdr. Suggs (Percival's CO, on phone, see NOTE), protesters (all on TV), reporters (all on TV), Senators, hearing attendees, security guards, police (on monitor), businessman, Pt. Klug communications officer (in shadow), recon pilot (callsign "Babyhawk 2")
LOCATIONS/ITEMS: Buford, Ct. headquarters of Underwater Boat (naval manufacturer, also on TV) w/security checkpoint (also on monitor) & submarine dock; Newark, NJ, inc Punisher's warehouse, docks, Washington, DC inc Capitol building (also on TV) w/hearing room, Morse's Virginia mansion, Long Island Sound / computer, lighter, dollar bill (destroyed), Battle Van's bus-style door release, assailants' guns; Punisher's sub-machine gun, court order, car, & blackjack; Morse's limo, copy of Playboy magazine, Piranha (experimental submarine) w/cockpit, torpedo, periscope, & transceiver balloon; Navy recon planes, Fairfax's "black bag" phone, USS Percival (nuclear submarine)

SYNOPSIS: The Punisher watches a news report on Senate investigations into Underwater Boat, a naval contractor suspected of corporate corruption, something he himself is investigating. He drives out to meet with company engineer Herman Weise, who unsuccessfully attempted to provide proof of the company's graft and finds him being assaulted by three men. Frank injures one and kills the others, then rescues Weise. After the next round of hearings, Underwater Boat's CEO Robert Morse is told that his agents failed to silence Weise. Seeking the only remaining copy of Weise's evidence, Frank and Weise break into Underwater Boat and steal the Piranha, the experimental sub where Weise hides his notes. Frank calls Morse to demand he answer for his crimes. Adm. Fairfax, Morse's military ally, orders the submarine Percival to destroy the Piranha. Frank and Weise try to escape, but the Percival finds them.

NOTE: Fairfax's position in the Navy, Weise's area of expertise, and the location of Morse's house are all revealed next issue. The Percival's commander is renamed Capt. Daniel Lustig next issue. USS Percival registry changes from "087" in this issue to "616" in the next. The new number may be an in-joke referencing the Marvel Universe's Earth's designation of Earth-616.

PUNISHER #27 (December 1989)

"Your Tax Dollar$ at Work" (21 pages)

CREDITS: Mike Baron (writer), Russ Heath (art), Ken Bruzenak (letters), John Wellington (colors), Marc McLaurin (asst editor), Carl Potts (editor)
FEATURE CHARACTER: Punisher (also as "Dmitri Velikoff," next in PWJ #11, '89, CPun #1/3, '89)
VILLAINS: Adm. Fairfax (dies off-panel), Robert Morse (last app)
OTHER CHARACTERS: Capt. Daniel Lustig (Percival's CO), Barry Fishbein, Jerry (prev 3 last app), Sen. Ron Power (only app), George Bush (in shadow, chr last in MK:Div, '92, next bts in DC2 #1, '89), presidential aides (all in shadow), Casey's commander, helicopter pilot (both voice only), Percival officers & crew inc XO, radio officer, & boarding party; prostitutes (Sheila named)
LOCATIONS/ITEMS: Long Island Sound, Morse's Virginia mansion w/war room, Washington, DC inc White

House w/Oval Office, Buford, Conn. inc docks, parking lot, & bridge / USS Percival w/bridge, Piranha w/cockpit (destroyed); Weise's printout of his evidence, limousines, sea charts, Morse's radio & surveillance equipment; boarding party's Uzis, raft, & wetsuits; Lustig's binoculars, Fairfax's gun, 2 underwater scooters

SYNOPSIS: In communication with the Percival, the Punisher pretends to be a Soviet defector intending to defect and names Herman Weise as his prisoner as a ploy to get aboard the Percival. While entertaining a group of high-powered friends, Robert Morse is notified that the Percival has found the Piranha. Adm. Fairfax says he has an agent aboard the Percival that will kill Weise and his ally once aboard. A boarding party from the Percival arrives to take Frank and Wiese in, but Frank overpowers them and strands them on the Piranha. Frank forces his and Weise's way onto the Percival at gunpoint so Weise can broadcast his findings to the press, but Fairfax orders a jam on all radio broadcasts in the area. Frank instructs the Percival's captain to submerge so Weise can transmit his message to the Navy via underwater communications, but another sub arrives, sent by Fairfax to sink the Percival. Frank orders missiles aimed at Morse's home, prompting the President to issue stand-down orders through Fairfax. Defeated, Morse's friends flee the house and Fairfax shoots himself. Frank and Weise leave the Percival via SCUBA sleds and destroy the Piranha via remote self-destruct, then Frank offers to relocate Weise with a new identity.

NOTE: Frank's alias, "Dmitri Velikoff," may be a real person or an alias Frank has previously used, since Fairfax says that Velikoff is a KGB colonel the government has tracked for months. Underwater Boat is misnamed multiple times as "Electric Boat."

CLASSIC PUNISHER #1 (December 1989)

"Death Sentence" (32 pages)

CREDITS: Carl Potts (reprint editor designer), Marcus McLaurin (asst editor), Larry Stroman (c art), Frank Cirocco (c colors)
NOTE: Reprints MP #2, '75. Cover printed between p12 &13 of story, ensuring two page spreads near the start and end of the story are properly presented.

2ND STORY: "Accounts Settled…Accounts Due!" (20 pages)
NOTE: Reprints MSA Mag #1, '76.

3RD STORY: "Kites" (8 pages)
CREDITS: Mike Baron (writer), Mike Vosburg (art), Ken Bruzenak (letters), Carl Potts (editor)
FEATURE CHARACTER: Punisher (also in own thoughts as Mr. McRook, next in Pun:Int, '89)
SUPPORTING CAST: Microchip (last in PWJ #11, '89, next in Pun:Int, '89)
OTHER CHARACTERS: Spider Roque, Micro Jr. (both in rfb), Jigsaw, Sijo Kanaka, Kingpin (prev 3 on computer screens), Iris Green, Congressman Abe Hargreaves (both in Punisher's thoughts)
LOCATIONS/ITEMS: Central Park, Microchip's warehouse, Punisher's bedroom, Spider-Roque's base at Cooterman's Creek (rfb), Japan (in thoughts) / Kites inc Punisher's razor-tipped Malaysian war kite & Microchip's kite, Punisher's book & gun, Broken Hill Australian lager 6-pack, Narragansett beer 6-pack, Miller beer 6-pack, Sopporo Japanese beer case, Microchip's van & computers, fighter jet, Japanese house (both in thoughts), Micro Jr.'s broken glasses (rfb)
FLASHBACKS: Punisher fights Spider Roque (Pun #19, '89). Micro Jr. is slain (Pun #9, '88)
SYNOPSIS: Punisher is taking a break from the war to fly his kite in the park on Sunday, but another kite, controlled by a user on the other side of the hill, attacks his; Punisher severs the attacker's line, then races to confront the other flier, but finds only Australian beer and a note: "Next Friday." Checks into old foes with Australian connections turns up no leads, so Punisher returns on Friday to fly his kite again, this time letting the other kite win, but again his unseen opponent evades him, leaving behind more beer. Stumped, Frank asks Microchip to covertly photograph his foe when they have their next kite-fight. The next Friday Micro drops Punisher off at the park, and this time the kites become entangled. Pulling them in, Punisher discovers the attacker's kite has the same skull motif as his own; realizing his attacker's identity, he runs over the hill to confront Micro, who is waiting with more beer. Micro reminds Frank it is the anniversary of Micro Jr.'s death, and they drink a toast in his memory.
NOTE: Features a wrap-around cover with black & white interior. Inside front page has Punisher art by Bret Blevins. Credits page incorrectly lists Rick Heath as artist. MSA Mag #1 cover reprinted after 3rd story. Punisher incorrectly states "Sato" killed Micro Jr.; the killer was Sijo.

PUNISHER: INTRUDER (1989)

"The Punisher in Intruder" (60 pages)

CREDITS: Mike Baron (writer), Bill Reinhold (art), Willie Schubert (letters), Linda Lessman (colors), Marc McLaurin (asst editor), Carl Potts (editor, title design), Kevin Nowlan (logo design)
FEATURE CHARACTER: Punisher (also as Father Angus McFee & DEA Agent Bruce Ayers, also as Frank Castiglione in fb1&3 between PWJ #18, '90 fb & PWJ #3, '07 fb, also as Frank Castle in fb2 between Pun:OM #1, '93 & PunTheNam, '94 fb; next in MK #8-9, '89, Pun #28, '89)
SUPPORTING CAST: Microchip (last in CPun #1/3, '89, next in Pun #28, '89)
VILLAINS: Col. Ross Whittaker (rogue CIA agent) & his men inc Swain, C. Potts & Slovic (all die), Reverend Moon Teck-Yo & his men inc Col. Kim & Mr. Soon (dies), Flaco Moldinaro (smuggler, also on TV), Juanita Moldinaro (Flaco's wife, bts) (as Mr. & Mrs. Lorenzo DiPatti, both also in photo)
OTHER CHARACTERS: Greg Pulowski & his wife (both die, also in photo), Margaret Pulowski (7-year-old, also in photo), Father Angus McFee (also in fb1&3), Mother Superior, nuns inc Sister Esmerelda, Lt. Manuel Herrera (pilot), reporter (on TV); Sgt. Gus Culpepper (in fb2); Raggedy Annie (doll), Richard Nixon (photo), Tactical Battlepod, Optimus Prime (both on TV)
LOCATIONS/ITEMS: Vaporville, Illinois inc water tower, DiPatti house (5980 Cedar Drive) & Pulowski house (5978 Cedar), Microchip's warehouse; Global Systems world HQ (atop a Utah mesa); Saint Bianca convent, Romida O'Hare hotel in Chicago, seminary (in fb1) / Punisher's binoculars, rifle, zip line, bazooka, handgun, Battle Van, rock climbing gear, explosives, blow dart gun, handgun; Whittaker's men's cars, van & various weapons; Greg's shotgun, Micro's computers, Bicardi bottle (broken), milk carton w/Maggie's photo, A-7 & F-14 fighter jets, helicopters, forged documents, flight simulator (also in fb), Air Force F-5 (destroyed), lab equipment & Bunsen burner, handcuffs, plastic bag, strap, IV of urine, flight helmets, missiles, parachute
FLASHBACKS: Frank Castiglione, plagued with doubts about why God would permit so much suffering in the world, tells Father Angus McFee

he is quitting the seminary (1). In the flight simulator, Sgt. Culpepper instructs Frank how to fly using faith and a light touch (2). Frank tells Father Angus he feels he could do more outside the seminary, perhaps as a cop, and admits to becoming enraged when he witnesses wrongdoing. Angus tells him there is evil in the world, and they must fight it (3).

SYNOPSIS: Punisher spies on the house of a smuggler who is living under an assumed identity in the suburbs when he witnesses armed men arrive and storm the neighboring house, then depart almost as swiftly as they came. Suspecting they hit the wrong house, Punisher checks inside, find the occupants dead, except for their young daughter, Maggie. Finding unusual, military cartridge shells, Punisher concludes the attackers were a top secret anti-drugs organization, and that they will come back to silence Maggie once they realize she's a witness, so Punisher takes her to Microchip's warehouse. Micro does some online research, finding evidence tying a $200 million CIA naval weapons research appropriation to ex-agent Col. Whittaker, now head of private think tank Global Security, Inc., who in turn has ties to the Korean CIA and Reverend Moon Teck-Yo. Elsewhere, Whittaker demonstrates his proficiency in Korean martial arts to Teck-Yo's men, Col. Kim and Mr. Soon, by effortlessly knocking Kim out. As Kim recovers, Mr. Soon expresses concern over Whittaker's men hitting the wrong house, but Whittaker blames computer error and faulty information from the Koreans. He reveals his men returned and found an unknown individual's observation post, but promises to find both this watcher and the girl. After Micro locates Global System's base, Punisher takes Maggie to a nunnery, Saint Bianca's, using forged orders from the Holy See to convince them to hide and care for the girl. Meanwhile, Whittaker arranges for an F-5 to lose power and crash into a hotel to kill Senator Orrin Kelsey, the leading candidate for the Attorney General's office, who Reverend Yo feared would allow Communism to spread to America. Whittaker is informed that the latest cocaine shipment to Moldarino's house has been intercepted and brought to the base, something Whittaker keeps from his zealously anti-drug partners. That night, Punisher infiltrates the base and looks around via the ventilation shafts, finding a coke lab and aircraft hangar. After setting explosives and stealing a sentry's uniform, Punisher learns they plan to assassinate Leslie Hooks, another Attorney General candidate, but is captured moments later. Left alone with Whittaker, Punisher attacks, but with his hands cuffed together, he is swiftly defeated, and given to Mr. Soon, who tortures him to learn Maggie's whereabouts. Feigning being broken, Punisher claims to be a DEA agent, telling Soon the base is about to be raided, and offers to help Yo and Soon avoid arrest and scandal. Convinced, Soon releases Punisher, who immediately kills him, arms his hidden explosives, then gets to the hangar, just as Whittaker launches and the bomb detonates. Stealing a a plane, Punisher uses it to destroy the rest of the base, then engages Whittaker in a dogfight and takes him down. Returning to the convent to check on Maggie, Punisher finds Father McFee waiting, and is informed Maggie was placed with a family she knows and trusts: the DiPattis.

NOTE: Released both as a softcover and a hardcover with dustjacket, each with different covers. Includes title/credits page (2 pages). Followed by brief creator bios with drawn "mug shots" (1 page). Maggie watches Robotech and Transformers, two 1980's cartoons. Global System's base resembles an aircraft carrier carved atop a mesa. Punisher's alias Bruce Ayers is the name of his friend from Pun #1, '87. C. Potts' name is revealed on the side of a jet, referencing editor Carl Potts.

PUNISHER #28 (Mid December 1989)

"Change Partners and Dance" (22 pages)

CREDITS: Mike Baron (writer), Bill Reinhold (pencils), Mark Farmer (inks), Ken Lopez (letters), John Wellington (colors), Rob Tokar (asst editor), Don Daley (editor)
FEATURE CHARACTER: Punisher
SUPPORTING CAST: Microchip (last in Pun:Int, '89)
VILLAINS: "Acts of Vengeance" conspirators (aka Prime Movers): Dr. Doom (Victor von Doom, scientist, deposed Latverian dictator, also bts posing as Joe Spiff, last in Cap #366, '89, also in DD #275, '89, W #19, '89, WoSM #60, '90, ASM #328, '90 bts, PPSSM #160, '90, WoSM #61, '90, next in PP #53, '90 fb), Kingpin (last in Cap #366, '89, also in W #19, '89, WoSM #60, '90, ASM #328, '90 bts, PPSSM #160, '90, WoSM #61, '90, MGN:RMA, '89, next bts in PP #53, '90 fb, next in Av #312, '89); Kristoff Vernard (as Dr. Doom, Latverian ruler, last in Thor #410, '89), 2 of Dr. Doom's flying squad
OTHER CHARACTERS: Joe Spiff (Quebec-based gun runner, mentioned only), Cynthia von Doom, Werner von Doom (Dr. Doom's parents, both in painting only), Sheila (telephone operator, voice only, on phone), Athena (as statue only), Latverian guards
LOCATIONS/ITEMS: Punisher's New Jersey warehouse (see NOTE), Asgard's Isle of Silence inc Loki's conference chamber, farm, Latveria inc Rietzhorn & Royal Palace w/ National Museum & storm drain, Maine inc bait shop, quarry & Colonial Motel inc Punisher's cabin, Manhattan inc Fisk Tower w/ Kingpin's office / backpacks, bottle of Mountain mineral water, Doombots, Dr. Doom's bombers w/ bombs, Dr. Doom's soldier's guns & jet packs, fire truck, Kingpin's cigars, Kristoff's giant robot, Latverian soldiers' rifles, hashish cigarette & lighter, Latverian National Museum display case & collections inc Athena statue, Fabergé egg, medieval suit of armor & painting of Dr. Doom's parents, Latverian Wiesel tank w/ 90mm cannon, Microchip's car, laptop & scrambler, pay phone, police car, Prime Movers' conference table, chairs & globe, Punisher's flashlight, knife, rocket pack w/ satellite gyroscope, smoke cap & Battle Van w/ radio & roof-mounted mini-gun w/ remote control, railroad track, trail mix, walking sticks
SYNOPSIS: Having agreed to participate in a conspiracy to eliminate super heroes, Kingpin and Dr. Doom encounter each other in the conference chamber of Loki, Asgardian god of evil and secret orchestrator of the villainous plot. Seeking to discredit Kingpin, Doom resolves to eradicate the crime lord's enduring adversary, Punisher. Posing as a gunrunner, Doom lures Frank Castle to a Maine quarry to face an attack by a Doombot, a pair of flying soldiers and a tank that destroys Punisher's Battle Van. Castle escapes and meets with Microchip, who proposes that he convince Doom to back off by stealing and threatening to destroy a valued Fabergé egg, housed at the National Museum in Doom's homeland of Latveria. Doom learns of Punisher's New Jersey warehouse and bombs it, believing his target to be there. Meanwhile, Castle and Microchip arrive in Latveria, where Punisher sneaks into the Royal Palace, fights a giant robot, kills a guard and grabs the egg from a museum display case. Suddenly, "Dr. Doom" appears and demands an explanation. When Punisher mentions the earlier ambush, "Doom" claims Frank's opponent is a rogue robot, and unexpectedly invites him to dinner.
NOTE: An "Acts of Vengeance" tie-in. Credits for this issue are given in Pun #30, '90. Punisher uses the code name "Rook" and notes that Microchip's code name is "Bishop." Punisher's current New Jersey warehouse is revealed to be one of five warehouses he maintains and is composed of 24 interconnected U-Rent mini-warehouses on a property that also houses facilities of Wow Chemical and O'Connell Steel. The narration mentions the Austrian/Latverian border, but Austria and Latveria are not adjacent nations, as revealed in OHMU #4, '83. At this time the real Doom is deposed, and has been replaced by his young brainwashed protégé Kristoff Vernard; Kristoff genuinely believes himself the true Doom, and that the real Doom is a renegade Doombot.

PUNISHER #29 (January 1990)

"Too Many Dooms" (21 pages)

CREDITS: Mike Baron (writer), Bill Reinhold (pencils), Mark Farmer (inks), Ken Lopez (letters), Gregory Wright (colors), Rob Tokar (asst editor), Don Daley (editor)
FEATURE CHARACTER: Punisher (next in PWJ #12-13, '89, DC2 #2, '89, DC2 #4, '90)
GUEST STARS: Avengers: Captain America (Steve Rogers, living legend of WWII, last in Cap #367, '90, next in DC2 #2, '89), Namor the Sub-Mariner (Atlantean monarch, last in Cap #367, '90, next in Av #19/3, '90 fb), Thor (Asgardian thunder god, last in C&D #9, '89, next in Thor #413, '90); Nick Fury (Col. Nicholas Joseph Fury, head of SHIELD spy agency, last in MGN:RMA, '89, next in DC2 #3, '90)
SUPPORTING CAST: Microchip (next in PWJ #12, '89)
VILLAINS: Prime Movers: Loki (Asgardian god of evil), Dr. Doom, Kingpin (all last in Av #312, '89, next in PWJ #12, '89); Freedom Force (superhuman US government agents): Avalanche (Dominic Petros, generates vibrations), Blob (Frederick J. "Fred" Dukes, obese mutant able to become immovable), Pyro (St. John Allerdyce, flame manipulator) (prev 3 last in Av #312, '89, next in IHulk #369, '90 fb); Kristoff Vernard (as Dr. Doom, next in FF #350, '91)
OTHER CHARACTERS: Cynthia von Doom, Werner von Doom (both in painting only), Eric Nesheim (deceased artist, mentioned only as painter of Dr. Doom's parents' portrait), Renée Brandt (art forger), Quasar (Wendell Vaughn, Avenger, only on cover), bystanders, Kingpin's security officers, Latverian guards, New York City police, News 2 TV reporter, protesters, SHIELD agents & pilot, West German Air Force pilot
LOCATIONS/ITEMS: West Germany inc Stackheim Air Force Base (last bts), Asgard's Isle of Silence inc Loki's conference chamber, Latveria's Royal Palace inc dining room, helicopter pad, National Museum, Punisher's guest room, turret & war room, Manhattan inc Chased Gallery, Guggenheim Museum, Trump Plaza, dock, water tower & Fisk Tower w/ Kingpin's office, Paris's Orly Airport inc SHIELD office / Punisher's Battle Van (see NOTE), Captain America's shield, Concorde passenger airliner, Doombots, Dr. Doom's spherical hovercraft, fire extinguisher, Kingpin's cigar & monitors, Kristoff's dining table, chairs, dinner & tea services, guest bed & helicopter, Latverian guards' guns, Latverian National Museum display case & collections inc Chan Dynasty vase, Fabergé egg, medieval suit of armor, painting of Dr. Doom's parents & Persian tapestries, Microchip's duffle bag & monocular, News 2 van, nightstick, picket signs, police cars & barricades, Prime Movers' conference table, chairs, globe & machinery, Punisher's gun, lighter, tube case, wristwatch & Battle Van w/ monitor, police scanner & jamming device, Pyro's flamethrower, replica of painting of Dr. Doom's parents, SHIELD aircraft, guns & holographic projector, taxi cabs, traffic, TV camera, West German Air Force jet
SYNOPSIS: The brainwashed "Dr. Doom" (Kristoff Vernard) identifies the Dr. Doom who attacked Punisher as a rogue Doombot and invites Castle to be his guest at the Latverian Royal Palace. In New York, as Kingpin and Dr. Doom bicker in Fisk Tower, Captain America prevents Kingpin's security forces from breaking up a protest against Kingpin and the proposed Super Powers Registration Act. Punisher steals a portrait of Dr. Doom's parents from the Latverian National Museum and escapes in a Latverian helicopter. The SHIELD spy agency intercepts him and Microchip after Castle uses a classified SHIELD code to travel unimpeded, but SHIELD Director Nick Fury lets them go and they return to New York, where they have an art forger create a replica of the stolen portrait. Punisher tapes the forgery to the top of his Battle Van hoping to attract Doom's attention. After encountering a battle between the Avengers and Freedom Force, Castle draws Doom out. Punisher returns the real painting in exchange for Doom's vow to leave him alone. Doom informs Castle that he is the true Doom and that Kristoff is a pretender, then departs convinced Kristoff will kill Punisher to avenge his honor.
NOTE: An Acts of Vengeance tie-in. The Battle Van shown here is a quick replacement for the one destroyed last issue and lasts only 124 miles before its electrical system is fried. Punisher mistakenly notes that Latveria is a Baltic country. The Super Powers Registration Act mentioned here is introduced as the Super Hero Registration Act in FF #334, '89.

PUNISHER #30 (February 1990)

"Confession" (22 pages)

CREDITS: Mike Baron (writer), Bill Reinhold (pencils), Mark Farmer (inks), Ken Lopez (letters), John Wellington (colors), Rob Tokar (asst editor), Don Daley (editor)
FEATURE CHARACTER: Punisher
SUPPORTING CAST: Microchip (between PWJ #13-14, '89-90)
VILLAINS: Bayside Butcher (serial killer, dies)
OTHER CHARACTERS: Father Bernard (priest), Emory Neese (dentist accused of sexual assault, also in photo), Det. Sgt. Smith (lead investigator on Bayside Butcher case), Christmas tree cutter, raccoon, Bayside butcher's 7th victim (as corpse), bartender, bar patron, prostitutes, john (in shadows), Navy seamen, drug dealers (one, hands only), drug seeker (hands only), confessors (in photos), pedestrians, Dr. Osterhaus (Butcher's psychiatrist, mentioned)
LOCATIONS/ITEMS: New York inc St. Luke's Church w/confessional; the Bronx inc Bronx Museum of Popular Culture w/ Butcher's studio, wax smelter, & basement; Newark, NJ, inc Punisher's warehouse w/garage, bathroom, & bedroom; forest in Bucks County, Pa. inc bar, motel, & Smith's house / Father Bernard's crucifix & rosary, wax statues (many containing parts of Bayside Butcher's victims, in images of Jesus Christ, Dracula, a mummy, Frankenstein's monster, Joan of Arc), 2 Battle Vans (one with engine removed & in repair), Micro's computer, Smith's car, drug vials, microfiche camera, photos of Neese & confessors, Neese's BMW, Punisher's handgun & rosary, Butcher's sword & gun, statue & body parts
SYNOPSIS: While confessing at St. Luke's church, Frank Castle is told by a priest of another confessor who admitted to killing, whom he has deduced from news reports is the serial killer called the Bayside Butcher. Frank returns home and has Microchip put the church under surveillance. After the seventh victim is found in Pennsylvania, Frank visits Det. Sgt. Smith, the case's lead detective, and learns geltrate, a substance used in dental molds, was found on the body. Microchip points Frank to Emory Neese, a dentist with a criminal background who was seen at St. Luke's. Frank finds and interrogates Neese, but Neese has an alibi. Frank then sees a poster for a wax museum exhibit and, realizing geltrate is used in wax statues, goes to the museum and overhears their modelmaker speaking to his latest creation about using actual body parts in his statues. The modelmaker catches Frank off guard with a sword, but Frank pursues him through the museum's basement and kills him. After calling Smith, Frank goes home and unsuccessfully tries to say his evening prayer. The next day at St. Luke's, Frank learns the priest left the priesthood, and the sight of the church's wax Jesus statue, left by an anonymous donor, unsettles him into leaving.

PUNISHER #31 (March 1990)

"Crankin'" (22 pages)

CREDITS: Mike Baron (writer), Bill Reinhold (pencils), Mark Farmer (inks), Ken Lopez (letters), John Wellington (colors), Rob Tokar (asst editor), Don Daley (editor)
FEATURE CHARACTER: Punisher (also as "Freewheelin' Frank")
VILLAINS: Hector "Hec" Birch (biker, environmental fanatic, 1st), Wild Bill Gannon (Hec's chief rival, 1st), Austin Lang (real estate developer, 1st), Satan's Lords (Hec's biker gang, Baxter, Gashog, Snaggletooth named, named members all die), Galloping Geese (Gannon's biker gang)
OTHER CHARACTERS: Holly Lang (Hec's girlfriend, Lang's ex-wife), Esmerelda (farmer), Esmerelda's husband
LOCATIONS/ITEMS: Soda Springs, Ariz. inc Lords' camp, Esmerelda's house, Yuma, Ariz. inc Holly's house & ranch w/Austin's trophy room & adjoining shed / Frank's bike & meth supply; Lords' truck, bikes, guns, meth lab trailer (destroyed), & delivery truck; Hec's trailer & binoculars, Gashog's binoculars, 2 trail bikes, Geese's truck, bikes, & mortar launcher, Esmerelda's truck, Holly's Rolls Royce, meth lab equipment & chemicals, Lang's Ithaca .37 shotgun, gun collection, totem poles, stuffed eagle, & animal head mountings (stag, buffalo, bear, boar, & deer)
SYNOPSIS: Investigating the methamphetamine ("crank") trade in the Southwest US, Frank Castle meets with the Satan's Lords motorcycle gang and introduces himself to Lords leader Hec Birch as "Freewheelin' Frank," a biker and crank cook. Just as Hec takes Frank to show him their mobile lab, the Galloping Geese, a rival gang attacks the Lords. Frank and Hec escape on trail bikes, then stop at a farmhouse for water, where Frank learns from the lady of the house that Hec helps the downtrodden in addition to his criminal activities. Buying the farmers' truck, Frank and Hec travel to the home of Hec's girlfriend Holly, and Frank learns Hec funnels all proceeds from his meth business to an ecological group fighting against over development. After Frank cooks a batch of crank to prove himself, he learns that Hec becomes erratic and maddened when high on it. Frank helps Hec and his friends load a truck, but Austin Lang, Holly's developer ex-husband, ambushes Frank. The two fight, but the drugged Hec, wrongly thinking Frank is in league with Austin, kills his two friends, locks Frank and Lang in the truck and forces Holly into the cab, thinking her Lang's accomplice as well.

PUNISHER #32 (April 1990)

"Speedy Solution" (22 pages)

CREDITS: Mike Baron (writer), Bill Reinhold (pencils), Mark Farmer (inks), Ken Lopez (letters), Gregory Wright (colors), Rob Tokar (asst editor), Don Daley (editor)
FEATURE CHARACTER: Punisher (next in PWJ #14-15, ASM #330-331, PWJ #16, all '90)
VILLAINS: Hec Birch, Wild Bill Gannon, Austin Lang (dies), Galloping Geese (Loser & Ropeman named & die)
OTHER CHARACTERS: Holly Lang (last app), rattlesnake
LOCATIONS/ITEMS: Santa Ynez Mountains inc highway; Yuma, Ariz. inc Holly's ranch (destroyed) w/trophy room & shed / delivery truck (destroyed) w/cargo chains, crowbar, meth crates, chemical drums, Frank's piano wire, gloves, drawstring bag, knife, Geese's bikes, Beretta 9mm handgun, Gannon & Ropeman's guns, Hec's gun, motorcycle (destroyed)
SYNOPSIS: Holly Lang fails to reason with the drug-addled Hec Birch, who is intent on killing Austin Lang and Frank Castle. In the back of Hec's truck, Austin and Frank pry the chemical drums loose, causing them to roll backwards and break open the doors. Frank jumps out, but Austin smashes the cab's back window and attacks Hec, giving Holly a chance to jump out. The truck jumps a cliff and explodes. Frank and Holly make their way back, but see the Galloping Geese approaching. Frank sets a tripwire trap as a delaying tactic that kills one of the Geese, then captures a rattlesnake in the desert. As Frank and Holly walk back to the ranch, they argue over Hec's use of drugs to fund his ecological endeavors. Seeing two Geese bikes at the ranch, Frank breaks in but runs afoul of Wild Bill Gannon. Frank escapes, using the rattlesnake to fend them off, and rigs the meth lab to explode despite Holly's objections. The lab explodes, injuring Gannon and killing fellow Goose Ropeman. Hec then reappears, aiming a gun at Frank, but Lang runs Hec over with a motorcycle and careens into the burning ranch. Frank holds Holly as she laments the loss of her ranch.

PUNISHER #33 (May 1990)

"Reaver Fever" (22 pages)

CREDITS: Mike Baron (writer), Bill Reinhold (pencils), Mark Farmer (inks), Ken Lopez (letters), John Wellington (colors), Rob Tokar (asst editor), Don Daley (editor)
FEATURE CHARACTER: Punisher
SUPPORTING CAST: Microchip (last in PWJ #16, '90)
VILLAINS: Reavers (anti-mutant cyborgs): Bonebreaker (tank-like lower body, also in schematic), Pretty Boy (extendable arms & data-manipulating eye filaments), Murray Reese (ex-Hellfire Club soldier) (all last in UXM #255, '89), Lady Deathstrike (Yuriko Oyama, Adamantium-taloned samurai), Donald Pierce (Reavers' leader, cybernetic limbs) (prev 2 last in UXM #261, '90)
OTHER CHARACTERS: Gateway (Aborigine mutant teleporter, bts, last in UXM #252, '89, next in UXM #269, '90), police (in shadows), vagrants
LOCATIONS/ITEMS: Newark, NJ, inc Punisher's warehouse (destroyed) w/shooting range, garage, roof, boiler room, catwalks, & main storm sewer; Reavers' outback HQ (Cooterman's Creek, Northern Territory, Australia) w/computer room, shooting range, & hangar / Microchip's computer (destroyed) & remote, Punisher's guns, schematic of Bonebreaker's cybernetics, Reavers' computers, guns, & supersonic aircraft; Bonebreaker's computerized sighting device, "Bang!" flag, rocket launcher, & laser; forklift, equipment crates, plastique demolition charges, motion detectors, Micro's Dalek w/new extendable turret (also on monitor, destroyed), raft w/paddles (destroyed), 2 disposable body gloves w/ face masks, trap door w/toe trigger, Pretty Boy's 2 spare hands & tracer, acetylene torch, sewer grate
SYNOPSIS: Microchip intercepts a pirate data transmission and unwittingly attracts the attention of the Reavers. The Reavers' respond by uploading a virus into Micro's system and sending a strike team to the Punisher's location. Frank and Micro spend four hours emptying their equipment out of the warehouse

and boobytrapping the building with explosives. Micro finds and deploys his Dalek, and sets up an escape route in the adjoining sewer. Frank goes to the roof and encounters Murray Reese. Frank drops back inside, evading Reese's gunfire, then helps out the Dalek against Pretty Boy before rejoining Micro. Bonebreaker breaks through the warehouse's wall and destroys the Dalek. As Frank and Micro escape in the sewer, Bonebreaker notices their absence and orders the Reavers out, just before the warehouse explodes. As Bonebreaker trades fire with the arriving police, Pretty Boy's extendable hand plants a tracer on Frank & Micro's raft that transmits an image of Frank and Micro to Donald Pierce, who orders their deaths. Pretty Boy shoots up the raft as it falls out of the sewer drain, and neither Frank or Micro appear to surface.
NOTE: The Reavers mistake the data intrusion to be the work of the X-Men, particularly Wolverine, while the Punisher and Microchip believe the Reavers are agents of Kristoff Vernard. Working unwillingly for the Reavers, Gateway is not considered a villain.

PUNISHER #34 (June 1990)

"Exo-Skeleton" (22 pages)

CREDITS: Mike Baron (writer), Bill Reinhold (pencils), Mark Farmer (inks), Ken Lopez (letters), Gregory Wright (colors), Rob Tokar (asst editor), Don Daley (editor)
FEATURE CHARACTER: Punisher (next in Pun Ann #3/3, '90)
SUPPORTING CAST: Microchip (next in Pun Ann #3/4, '90)
VILLAINS: Reavers: Bonebreaker, Lady Deathstrike, Donald Pierce, Pretty Boy, Murray Reese (all next in UXM #262, '90)
OTHER CHARACTERS: Elliot (Micro's arms-dealing cousin, dies), Simba (Elliot's dog), NW Public Works employee, lingerie model (on calendar)
LOCATIONS/ITEMS: Newark, NJ, inc sewer drain; Reavers' Australian outback HQ w/communications room, Queens, NY w/Queensboro, Bridge & Elliot's Auto Salvage w/office shack & underground weapons storage w/Winnebago entrance, Manhattan w/Pierce's penthouse / Reavers' guns & helicopter, shredded Punisher shirt, wrecked car, Public Works car, Frank & Micro's body gloves & SCUBA gear, Micro's CD-ROM backup & gun, Frank's bullpup assault rifle & knife, Simba's leash; Elliot's arsenal, computer, explosive R/C trucks (destroyed) & handgun; powered exoskeleton (destroyed) w/rocket launchers, machine gun, & sword; Pierce's computer, box of grenades; Bonebreaker's parachute, swords, & tank chassis (destroyed); Reese's spare legs, Pretty Boy's spare hands (destroyed)
SYNOPSIS: As the Reavers search the river for Punisher and Microchip and call in a progress report to Donald Pierce, Frank and Micro emerge elsewhere and steal a Public Works car. Micro suggests to Frank that they go to a junkyard owned by his cousin Elliot, who deals illegal arms. Once there, Elliot shows Frank and Micro his weapons cache, including a giant powered exoskeleton. Since Micro ran across the Reavers' transmission while researching a hack into an aerospace company, he tries it again using a different method in order to learn the identity of their attackers. Unfortunately, the Reavers again catch him hacking into Pierce's Manhattan computer and trace their location. With Frank in the exoskeleton and Elliot and Micro armed, they lie in wait as the Reavers arrive and open fire. As the firefight rages, Bonebreaker ambushes Frank after he saves Micro from Pretty Boy, but Frank escapes the exoskeleton as the Reavers pile onto it and detonate it by remote. The damaged Reavers flee the junkyard, but Elliot is found killed. Frank and a stunned Micro leave.
NOTE: Cover tagline, "Part man... part machine... all vigilate!" is a play on the tagline "Part man, part machine, all cop" tagline from the "RoboCop" film franchise. Punisher's exo-skeleton, redubbed his exo-armor, is rebuilt, used again, and destroyed again in PWJ #56, '93.

PUNISHER ANNUAL #3 (1990)

"The Progamma Strain!" (25 pages)

CREDITS: Mike Baron (writer), Neil Hansen (art), Rick Parker (letters), Pat Redding (colors), Rob Tokar (asst editor), Don Daley (editor)
FEATURE CHARACTER: Punisher (last in Pun #25, '89, next in Pun Ann #3/2, '90 fb)
VILLAINS: Jethro Prufrock (right-wing politician, 1st but chr last in IHulk Ann #16, '90 fb, dies), Lifeform (George Prufrock, Jethro's germ-mutated son, AIM agent, 1st but chr last in IHulk Ann #16, '90 fb, next in DD Ann #6, '90), AIM agent (dies)
OTHER CHARACTERS: Martha Prufrock (Jethro's daughter, 1st but chr last in IHulk Ann #16, '90 fb), Simba (Prufrocks' dog, dies), security guards (some die)
LOCATIONS/ITEMS: Upstate New York inc Progamma (biotechnology company) w/viral storage & communications room, & Prufrock's mansion w/security gate & armory / bolt cutters, glass cutter, guards' guns, viral samples, George's knife & crowbar; Frank's muffled motorcycle, rifle, AIM uniform & handgun; Prufrock's pipe, gun, & weapons stockpile, Martha's shotgun, rocket launcher
SYNOPSIS: AIM agent George Prufrock breaks into a biotech company called Progamma to steal virus samples, and becomes exposed to one while fighting a security guard. The Punisher, investigating a tip that AIM is producing bioweapons, travels to Progamma and learns from another AIM agent in the building that Jethro Prufrock, George's politician father, ordered the creation of the virus and its theft. George, now hideously mutated from the virus he contracted, attacks Frank and kills the other agent. Frank escapes, trades fire with Progamma's security guards, then heads for Prufrock's house. Frank questions Prufrock about the virus, but George breaks into the house and kills his father. Prufrock's daughter Martha tries to shoot him, but George is unfazed. Frank obtains a rocket launcher from Prufrock's personal weapons cache and shoots George, causing him to fall into a nearby lake and apparently die. Martha mourns her father and promises to continue his work, and Frank leaves.
NOTE: Includes table of contents page (1 page) w/art taken from page 18. Story continued in DD Ann #6, '90.

2ND STORY: "Punisher's Fighting Techniques" (6 pages)
CREDITS: Roger Salick (writer), Mark Texeira (art), Chris Eliopoulos (letters), Heidi Goodhue (colors), Rob Tokar (asst editor), Don Daley (editor)
FEATURE CHARACTER: Punisher (also in fb4 between Pun Ann #2/3, '89 & DD #181, '82, also in fb1-3 & fb5, next in Pun:RBN, '89)
VILLAINS: Eric & Lars Hels (Norwegian twin assassins, in fb1 only, both die), Tomasini (hitman, in fb2 only, dies), mugger (in fb3 only), Ryker's inmate (in fb4 only), Sperino's 2 enforcers (both in fb5 only)
OTHER CHARACTERS: Mugger's victim (in fb3 only), Sperino (mob boss, mentioned in fb5)
LOCATIONS/ITEMS: Punisher's gym, New York inc Chinatown (in fb2) & Ryker's Island (in fb4) / Hels brothers' guns (both in fb1), Tomasini's balisong knife (in fb2), mugger's knife, subway car (prev 2 in fb3), inmate's pipe (in fb4), enforcers' car (in fb5)
FLASHBACKS: The Punisher kills Lars & Eric Hels (1), dispatches an amateur hitman named Tomasini (2), saves an elderly woman from a

subway mugger (3), subdues an inmate during a Ryker's stay (4), and beats up a pair of mob enforcers (5).
SYNOPSIS: The Punisher introduces a series of vignettes demonstrating his unarmed combat techniques.
NOTE: Published with a disclaimer advising readers against attempting any of the depicted maneuvers. 2nd & 3rd stories bookend a four-page "Punisher Arsenal" segment written and drawn by Eliot R. Brown, which features the Davis D-23 derringer, the Intratec Tec-9, a magazine modification kit for the Colt Model 1911 A1, and a custom holster for the Beretta 92-F/M.

3RD STORY: "Forewarned or Foretold?" (6 pages)
CREDITS: Gregory Wright (writer), Lee Sullivan (pencils), Kim DeMulder (inks), Rick Parker (letters), Evan Skolnick (colors), Rob Tokar (asst editor), Don Daley (editor)
FEATURE CHARACTER: Punisher (also in own dream, next in WoSM Ann #6/2, PWJ #17-24, Pun:NE, all '90)
OTHER CHARACTERS: Kingpin (as demon) & his minions, guide, Punisher's victims (all in Punisher's dream)
LOCATIONS/ITEMS: Punisher's bedroom; Hell (in dream) w/cells & Kingpin's throne room / guide's torch, Kingpin's throne of human bones, minions' clubs & guns (prev 3 in dream)
SYNOPSIS: The Punisher has a nightmare wherein he is led through Hell past many of the criminals he has killed into a throne room occupied by a giant Kingpin. He orders his minions to kill him and he awakens. Frank resigns himself to the spiritual consequences of his war on crime.

4TH STORY: "Philanthropy" (9 pages)
CREDITS: Mike Baron (writer), Mark Texeira (layouts), Dwayne Turner (finishes), Rick Parker (letters), Brad Vancata (colors), Rob Tokar (asst editor), Don Daley (editor)
FEATURE CHARACTER: Microchip (last in Pun #34, '90, next in PWJ #17, '90)
VILLAIN: Roger Boelter (crooked philanthropist)
OTHER CHARACTERS: Roger Bontrager (Boelter's employee), Linda (Boelter's secretary), Mrs. Rosen (Micro's neighbor), Yodelin' Sam (country singer, on TV), New Yorkers, businessmen, hardware store owner, security guards, factory manager, angry husband of one of Boelter's contributors
LOCATIONS/ITEMS: New Jersey inc Microchip's new home (227 Fenster St.), Mrs. Rosen's apartment, Houston inc Save our Children (Boelter's fraudulent charity), Metamoros, Mexico inc Boelter's tape factory w/security gate & motel / Mrs. Rosen's door locks, electromagnet, Boelter's computers & gun, tape duplication equipment, husband's rifle, recording of Boelter's confession, cat food can
SYNOPSIS: While moving into his new residence, Micro sees his elderly neighbor pass out through her window. After helping her, he learns she has been fleeced for her savings by a children's charity. Micro researches the charity and its head, Roger Boelter, a con man with a history of mail fraud charges. Posing as a computer repairman, Micro sabotages his computers, bugs his office and uses Boelters' side business, distributing cassettes of singer Yodelin' Sam, to distribute recordings of Boelter candidly discussing his crimes to his charity's contributors. He then arranges for a large refund to Mrs. Rosen.
NOTE: Boelter misidentifies his secretary as Lisa.

THE PUNISHER: NO ESCAPE (1990)

"No Escape" (48 pages)

CREDITS: Gregory Wright (writer, colors), Tod Smith (breakdowns), Danny Bulanadi (finishes), Ken Lopez (letters), Steve White (colors), Rob Tokar (asst editor), Don Daley (editor), Joseph Jusko (c art)
FEATURE CHARACTER: Punisher (also in dfb2, next in Pun:Prize, '90)
GUEST STARS: Paladin (last in MK #15, '90, next in Cap #381, '91), USAgent (also in rfb as Captain America, last in AvS #34/2, '90, next in AWC Ann #5/4, '90)
SUPPORTING CAST: Microchip (last in PWJ #20, '90 fb, next in Pun: Prize, '90)
VILLAINS: Maggia (many die, 1 also in dfb2) inc John Bartoli (narcotics supplier, dies), Vincent Mangano (Maggia godfather, dies), Bobby Peculo (low level Maggia member, dies), Ralph Parlini (also on computer screen & dfb1, drug trafficker), Joseph (low-level Maggia thug)
OTHER CHARACTERS: Commission on Superhuman Activities (CSA): Raymond Sikorsky (chr last in SSS #1, '92, last in Cap #355, '89, next in ASM #326, '89), Adrian Sammish, Orville Sanderson (both last in Cap #354, '89), Henry Peter Gyrich (last in DC #4, '90, next in Nomad #1, '90), Valerie Cooper (last in AFlt #88, '90, next in Nomad #1, '90), Gen. Lewis Hayerth (last in Cap #382, '91, last bts in AvS #31/2, '90, next in Nomad #1, '90), George Mathers (last in Cap #352, '89); Rosa Bartoli, Rob Bartoli (John Bartoli's wife & son, both die), firemen, cameraman, reporter, train passengers, guards, guard dogs, teen couple, police officer, Agora Dance Club patrons, Caleb & Emily Walker (USAgent's parents, in fb), Mrs. Parlini & her daughter (Ralph Parlini's family, also in dfb1), Parlini's driver (in dfb1), State Representative Macchio (Maggia target, mentioned only)
LOCATIONS/ITEMS: Manhattan inc Bartoli's townhouse (destroyed) on Central Park West, Punisher's warehouse, Mangano's Long Island mansion, Peculo's restaurant in Little Italy, Ryker's Maximum Security Prison (on computer screen only), Agora Dance Club, Brooklyn Heights; Washington, DC inc CSA building; New Jersey inc Punisher's New Jersey hideout, 7 Eleven, 252 Charles Lido Beach home / Punisher's Battlevan, motorbike & sports car inc onboard headset computer link, Paladin's Stun Gun & bulletproof costume, USAgent's shield, Maggia agents' guns, commuter train, Mangano's car, Peculo's car (wrecked)
FLASHBACK: Released from Ryker's, Parilini is met by his wife and daughter (d1). USAgent witnesses his parents' murder (Cap #345, '88). Punisher forces a Maggia agent at gunpoint to wear the Punisher costume and confront Mangano (d2).
SYNOPSIS: After Maggia godfather Vincent Mangano bombs the home of his own nephew, John Bartoli, killing Bartoli's family as well, the Punisher decides to take down the Maggia crime family. He catches low-level Maggia operative Bobby Peculo, but Peculo commits suicide, because squealing will get his family killed. Mangano hires the mercenary Paladin to kill the Punisher, while the CSA order USAgent to arrest Punisher. While investigating Peculo's restaurant, Punisher is attacked by Paladin but escapes into the nearby river. Punisher tracks Peculo's business partner Ralph Parlini to the Agora Dance Club, witnessing Parlini meet Mangano, but when he follows them out, he is ambushed by Paladin, Mangano and Parlini. USAgent arrives, and Paladin and the two Maggia men flee, thinking he is Captain America. Following a brief battle, USAgent agrees to help Punisher take down the Maggia on the condition Punisher surrenders to the Agent afterwards. Shortly thereafter, Paladin kidnaps Microchip. Mangano orders Parlini to plant a state representative, then bombs Parlini's home; watching Parlini hoping he would lead them to Mangano, Punisher and USAgent save Parlini's family. Sending USAgent to intercept Parlini, Punisher takes Parlini's family to Micro's warehouse to hide, but finds a note from Paladin, informing him where to go if he wants Micro back. Punisher calls USAgent to tell

him of Paladin's message, then rushes to Mangano's mansion, battling Paladin again in the mansion grounds. USAgent intervenes, breaking Paladin's legs, then follows Punisher inside Mangano's darkened mansion. Separated from USAgent, Punisher captures a guard, promising him a chance to survive if he does as he is told. Moments later Punisher, silhouetted in a doorway, confronts Mangano, who shoots him in the face, but the distraction allows Micro to escape and snatch a grenade from a guard's corpse. USAgent arrives to witness Punisher's corpse collapse to the floor, moments before the grenade explodes, slaying Mangano and setting the mansion aflame. Later, as USAgent reports Punisher's death to the CSA, Microchip and Punisher celebrate Punisher faking his own demise.
NOTE: Includes title/credits page (inside front cover). Followed by brief creator bios with drawn "mug shots" (inside back cover).

PUNISHER: THE PRIZE (1990)

"The Prize" (62 pages)

CREDITS: Chris Henderson (writer), Mike Harris (art), John A. Wilcox (colors), Janice Chiang (letters), Kelly P. Corvese (asst editor), Terry Kavanagh (editor)
FEATURE CHARACTER: Punisher (also as Frank Cecolini, also in photo, also in pfb & dfb, next in ImpSVS #1/5, MCP #59/4, GR #5-6, Pun:KG, all '90)
SUPPORTING CAST: Microchip (last in Pun: NE, '90, next in Pun: KG, '90)
VILLAINS: Rivera drug family, auction envelope sellers (both in pfb, most die), Mossad agents (also in pfb) inc "Cashmere" (also on video camera), KGB agents (most die), LA gangsters inc Fernando (most die), Spanish mob inc "Junior," Hector, Raymond Gonzalez, Ramirez (thug wearing old Iron Man armor), Jimmy (some as corpses only, most others die)
OTHER CHARACTERS: Vincent Martinelli (Stane International security agent, last in IM #234, '88, next bts in NThr #10, '94), Jessica Bradley (reporter, also in dfb), Jessica's LA contacts (corpses), bystanders inc Carlos & Larry, Lisa Castle, Frank Castle Jr, Maria Castle (prev 3 in Punisher's thoughts only), Franklin Schmidt (dead arms dealer, mentioned), airport users, Mexico customs officer, television audience, talk show presenter
LOCATIONS/ITEMS: Manhattan inc Rivera warehouse, Central Park (both pfb), Israeli Consulate, E 38th St, Washington Square Park, expressway, Microchip's warehouse, "Cecolini's" house inc bathroom & exercise room; Newark Airport; Los Angeles inc the Barrio, Westin Comino hotel inc Punisher's room; Mexico City inc Stark Safe House, Mayan temple (destroyed) / Punisher's Battlevan, Mercedes car (wrecked), auction invitation, Punisher's M-16 & knife; Ma Deuce .50-caliber, rocket launcher, Jessica's LA car (damaged) & video camera, Martinelli's car (license plate # NUD 339), knock-out gas & smoke gas grenade; KGB car (crashes), mobsters' cars (many destroyed) & guns, jeep, Mark 1 Iron Man armor (destroyed)
FLASHBACKS: Surveilling the Rivera drug family, the Punisher overhears their desire to gain a super-weapon, and follows them to a meeting where they pay heavily to purchase an envelope. As Punisher watches, another group murder the mobsters, taking the envelope but leaving the money. Punisher trails them to New York's Israeli Consulate and realizes the killers were Mossad (p). Frank spots Martinelli at Newark Airport (d).
SYNOPSIS: Bugging the Israeli Consulate, Punisher overhears the Israelis talking to Russians about the weapon and watches a rogue Mossad agent sell the envelope. Killing the buyers, Punisher finds it contains a year-old auction invitation. Microchip tells him of a reporter, Jessica Bradley, investigating a super-weapons auction, and Punisher, disguised as mercenary Frank Cecolini, meets her. She tells him she has a contact in LA with a lead, and asks him to protect her during the investigation; realizing she will proceed regardless, Frank agrees. In LA they find Jessica's contacts recently murdered and are attacked by mobsters. Killing all but one, Punisher learns the Spanish mob is also after the super-weapon. Growing close to Jessica in their travels, Frank reveals his family's murder to her. As they travel to Mexico City, Punisher recognizes a bald man on their flight as having been at Newark when they flew out to LA. In Mexico the KGB try to kidnap Frank, and as he takes them down he spots the bald man following him again. Challenging him, Punisher learns the man is Stane International security chief Vincent Martinelli, who explains the super-weapon everyone is after was part of a cache stolen from Stark International around the time Stane bought the company; the thief planned to auction the stolen weapons, but accidentally killed himself with one of the devices. Now one of his gang has resurfaced, and everyone is competing to buy the remaining weapon. Martinelli agrees to work with Punisher and Jessica, and they accompany him when he meets with some of the seller's gang to buy the weapon. Punisher stops the gangsters, who planned to kill Martinelli and take his money, and they learn the gang has the weapon hidden in the jungle in a Mayan temple. With his two compatriots, Punisher launches a surprise attack on the temple, which goes well until the weapon itself confronts them, an old Iron Man armor worn by one of the gang. Nothing Punisher brings to bear works against the armor, until Punisher hurls a knife into the helmet's eye slit. The fatally wounded gangster fires blindly, killing his fellow mobsters and bringing down the temple around them. Two weeks later, Punisher joins Jessica at a studio recording of a chat show and thinks to himself that someday he'll earn the prize of a normal life again.
NOTE: Includes a statement from the Punisher, and a quote from Leonardo da Vinci: "He who does not punish evil commands it to be done" (inside front cover) & title/credits page (2 pages). Followed by brief creator bios with drawn "mug shots" (inside back cover).

THE PUNISHER, KINGDOM GONE (August 1990)

"Kingdome Gone" (60 pages)

CREDITS: Chuck Dixon (writer), Jorge Zaffino (art), Ken Lopez (letters), John Wellington (c colors), colors), Nick Jainschigg (colors), Carl Potts (editor, title design), Marc McLaurin (mng editor), Kevin Nowlan (logo design)
FEATURE CHARACTER: Punisher (next in Pun #35, '90)
SUPPORTING CAST: Microchip (last in Pun:Prize, '90, next in Pun #35, '90)
VILLAINS: Hamilton "Bo" Greaves (1st, white collar crime boss, dies) & his men (some die) inc Richie (computer expert), Donald, Harley, Kingsley, Marzianni (prev 5 die), Dave, Landau; Calvin Mellon (smuggler) & his boys; crack supplier (dies)
OTHER CHARACTERS: Dan Blazer, Adam Wilson (both reporters, on TV), Esperanza (Greaves' girl) & her father (both die), Phillipe (Puerto Salvaje president), Mr. Stewart (dies) & his secretary, Greaves' lawyer, nurse, cameramen (2 bts), Randy Stern (anchorman, voice only), federal agents, State Department officials, US Marines (also on TV) inc General Leo Besserman (on TV), Macrae & Tellinger; Puerto Salvaje residents (one on TV), Butcher (guard dog, dies), guard dogs (bts, heard by Punisher), crack supplier's girlfriend
LOCATIONS/ITEMS: Stewart's office, Atlanta skyscraper inc Greaves' penthouse, Microchip's Jersey warehouse, Puerto Salvaje (Caribbean republic) inc Greaves' mansion, Mellon Air Freight in Hepple Forge, Indiana, Albany Airport / Stewart's handgun, Punisher's climbing equipment,

Uzi, Battle Van, automatic rifle, parachute, Marines uniform & grenade; Greaves' men's weapons, computer, suitcases, money, & phone, Richie's note w/computer passwords & codes, marines' weapons, Mellon's plane, Greaves' handgun, helicopter, apple, knife & gym equipment; supply crates, jeep, Marine helicopter, Heineken, US Marshals' bus & uniforms

SYNOPSIS: When federal agents visit Mr. Stevens' office, he commits suicide. In Atlanta, Punisher goes after Hamilton Greaves, a top-level embezzler and money launderer for the mob, before he runs with his stolen millions or ends up in a federal "resort." Greaves prepares to skip the country, covering his trail electronically before having his hacker killed. Punisher breaches Greaves' penthouse, but his rushed planning means he is slowed fighting Greaves' men, allowing Greaves to escape without a trace. Punisher stews in the interim, wanting to get vengeance for the innocents who lost their money and the criminals who profit from Greaves' actions. Meanwhile, Greaves strong-arms the president of Puerto Salvaje out of his family's bank, effectively taking control of the small country, but doing so allows Micro to locate him and report to Punisher, while Phillipe tricks the US State Department into invading his country by letting them believe Greaves is preparing the island for a Cuban invasion force. With the island closed off, Punisher forces a smuggler to fly him close enough to parachute in, disguised in a Marines uniform. Later, the father of Esperanza, a girl Greaves has seduced, asks Greaves to let her go. Greaves refuses and insults the girl's virtue, causing the father to attack and Greaves to kill him. Esperanza, having seen her father, begs to go home, but Greaves lies and informs Esperanza has sold her. After finding Greaves' mansion too heavily guarded to sneak in, Punisher poses as a Colonel and orders recruits some Marines to accompany him to the mansion, giving the illusion of an inspection. Leaving the Marines outside, Punisher is escorted in, then kills his guide and begins hunting Greaves; the discovery of his victims alerts Greaves to his presence. Greaves' men shoot at the Marines, believing them part of the ambush, and they return fire. Meanwhile, Punisher finds Greaves, but is attacked by Greaves' enforcer Harvey; though Punisher kills Harvey, the delay allows Greaves to escape into the custody of the arriving Marines responding to the firefight. Esperanza is slain by the Marines as she tries to kill Greaves with his own gun. The Marines pull out of the country while Greaves gets a cushy jail sentence for giving up some minor mobsters. However, Punisher and Micro pick him up disguised as US Marshals and give him a more fitting sentence.

NOTE: Hardcover with dust jacket. Includes title/credits page (2 pages). Followed by brief bios on the creators with drawn portraits (1 page).

PUNISHER #35 (July 1990)

"Jigsaw Puzzle" (22 pages)

CREDITS: Mike Baron (writer), Bill Reinhold (pencils), Mark Farmer (inks), Ken Lopez (letters), Brad Vancata (colors), Rob Tokar (asst editor), Don Daley (editor)
FEATURE CHARACTER: Punisher (also as Guillermo Marzol & phone company employee)
SUPPORTING CAST: Microchip (last in Pun:KG, '90, next in MK #21, '90)
VILLAINS: Rev (last in Pun #5, '88), Jigsaw (last in Pun #5, '86) & their henchmen (Guillermo Marzol named), Belasco (sorcerer turned demon, bts as "Lucifer," last in FF #314, '88)
OTHER CHARACTERS: Dr. Miller (scientist), family (mother, father, son, all die), Westchester police (all die)
LOCATIONS/ITEMS: New York inc Rico Bros. warehouse (destroyed), docks, Microchip's warehouse & Pandrake Labs; New Jersey Turnpike, Westchester inc family's home w/bedrooms / Punisher's 9mm gun & Ingram submachine gun; Marzol's gun, Micro's computer & video game project, sterilizing poison, Rev's semi truck w/mobile base trailer & knife, Jigsaw's Porsche, Miller's lab equipment, boy's Ninja Turtle action figures

SYNOPSIS: Punisher stakes out a cocaine warehouse, frustrated that Microchip doesn't return his calls. Punisher kills a guard and disguises himself as the guard to gain entry. Once inside, Punisher attacks, but is surprised that Jigsaw is running the operation. After taking some coke for analysis, Punisher blows up the warehouse and returns to Micro's warehouse, where the two argue over Micro's declining interest in Punisher's war on crime. Jigsaw meets with Rev, who became a follower of "Lucifer" after Punisher left him for dead, and has agreed to heal Jigsaw's face in return for his services. Micro and Punisher discover the "coke" is actually a sterilizing poison derived from a Venezuelan plant. Micro refuses to go with Punisher to Venezuela. Rev slaughters a suburban family to appease Lucifer. Jigsaw watches and kills police when they spot him. Punisher sees Jigsaw's fleeing car and gives chase.

NOTE: Cover labeled "Jigsaw Puzzle, Part 1 of 6." Series begins biweekly publication until Pun #40, '90. Frank has taken residence at Micro's warehouse since the destruction of his own warehouse last issue.

PUNISHER #36 (Early August 1990)

"The Neighborhood Defense Fund" (22 pages)

CREDITS: Mike Baron (writer), Mark Texeira (art), Ken Lopez (letters), Bob Budiansky (colors), Rob Tokar (asst editor), Don Daley (editor)
FEATURE CHARACTER: Punisher
VILLAINS: Pegs, Cubes (both street gangs, many die) inc Vargas (dies) & Lopez, Jigsaw, Rev, Belasco (bts)
OTHER CHARACTERS: Sam Canaday (Neighborhood Defense Fund (NDF) founder), Priscilla Canady (Sam's wife), Priscilla's son, NDF members inc Terrence, school children, automobile driver
LOCATIONS/ITEMS: Grocery store; Oakley Square; Saddlebrook Regional Airport / Punisher's Battle Van inc bulletproof windshields & fire retardant foam sprayer, & motorcycle inc front-mounted gun; Jigsaw's Porsche inc trunk-mounted gun, tanker truck (destroyed), incendiary clip, stolen Chevy

SYNOPSIS: To evade the pursuing Punisher, Jigsaw destroys a tanker truck; the explosion launches his Porsche off an overpass. Punisher follows, spots Jigsaw's wrecked car and asks some nearby men where the driver went. The men demand money at gunpoint for the NDF. Punisher drives away, ignoring the men as their shots bounce off the bulletproof van, but stops to pick up Priscilla Canaday and her child, who are being chased by hoodlums. Priscilla tells Punisher that two local gangs, Pegs and Cubes, are warring within their neighborhood and her husband Sam set up the real NDF to oppose the gangs. Punisher evades Cubes while learning Jigsaw has allied himself with them. Punisher takes Priscilla to Sam and agrees to help while Jigsaw contacts the Rev, who gives Jigsaw twelve hours to meet at their rendezvous point. Punisher sends Sam in the Battle Van to lure Pegs to Oakley Square then plows through Cubes territory on his motorbike. The survivors pursue Punisher to Oakley Square where a massive firefight erupts between the rival gangs. Jigsaw follows Punisher to the roofs, engages Punisher in a firefight and flees when Punisher takes out his gang allies. Punisher allows the NDF to keep the $20,000 raided from Cubes and use it to defend their neighborhood. Jigsaw meets with the Rev and they depart on a plane to Venezuela.

NOTE: Cover labeled "Jigsaw Puzzle: Part 2 of 6." The kids in the gang-ridden zone normally attend Pun #14, '88's Malcolm Shabazz school.

"Perilous Passage" (22 pages)

CREDITS: Mike Baron (writer), Mark Texeira (art), Ken Lopez (letters), Bob Budiansky (colors), Rob Tokar (asst editor), Carl Potts (editor), Tom Morgan (c art)
FEATURE CHARACTER: Punisher
VILLAINS: The Rev, Jigsaw, gang bangers (most die) inc Duwayne, Stacker (both only as corpses, killed by Microchip's automatic defenses), Jamal; Diego (Medellin cartel man, 1st), Belasco (bts)
OTHER CHARACTERS: Paco (drug dealer), Joy Adams (1st, hotel activities director) the Rev's gatherers inc Fredo (dies), concierge, bystanders, horses inc Nugget
LOCATIONS/ITEMS: Punisher's New Jersey warehouse, Tepuis region of SE Venezuela inc Rev's pyramid, Club Maracca inc stables / gang's knives & guns, Gunny Bear (Microchip's Dalek, destroyed), Punisher's bazooka, Battle Van, German car/plane, gun case & books (Wilhelm Reich's "Listen Little Man" & Collier's "Ellington"; Jigsaw's gun, Peña flowers, Paco's truck, spark plugs, Joy's compact, Mai Tai inc straw, Club Sandwich inc toothpicks, extra hot salsa
SYNOPSIS: Punisher returns to New Jersey to find the warehouse infested by gangbangers. After taking some of them down, he sneaks into the warehouse to retrieve his gear. He destroys Micro's defensive robot and uses the remote control on the Battle Van to clear out the last of the riffraff before taking off in a car/plane. Meanwhile in Venezuela, the Rev learns the other drug lords have grown suspicious of his operation and are getting information from his men. The Rev hopes to have all the Peña flower he'll need in two weeks, and gives Jigsaw one last chance to kill Punisher. Punisher eventually reaches the Tepuis region and checks into Club Maracca. He meets Joy who knows where a patch of Peña flower grows. After he disables a tail from the local cartel using a makeshift blowgun formed from his sandwich's toothpicks dipped in salsa and fired through his drink's straw into the observer's ear, Joy takes him to the patch only to find it picked clean and Jigsaw waiting.
NOTE: Cover labeled "Jigsaw Puzzle: Part 3 of 6." Nugget is named next issue.

"Basuco" (22 pages)

CREDITS: Mike Baron (writer), William Reinhold (pencils), Mark Farmer (inks), Ken Lopez (letters), Linda Lessmann (colors), Rob Tokar (asst editor), Don Daley (editor)
FEATURE CHARACTER: Punisher
VILLAINS: Rev, Belasco (both bts), Jigsaw, Diego & his men (most die), drug dealers (some die)
OTHER CHARACTERS: Eva (Joy's friend), Tomás (Eva's son) (both only app), Joy Adams, bystanders, horses inc Nugget
LOCATIONS/ITEMS: Tepuis region of SE Venezuela inc town, Eva's house, Diego's mansion / Punisher's knife, handgun & bag inc ammo, handgun & rifle; Jigsaw's Uzi, machine gun & knife; dealers' guns, Diego's men's guns, jeeps, bazooka
SYNOPSIS: Joy's gets her horse, Nugget, to rear up at Jigsaw with a whistle, distracting him while she and Punisher escape down a cliff side, though Joy is distraught that she scars her face doing so. They head to a nearby town where local dealers accost them. Punisher kills one, making the others back off, and the pair hastily head to stay with Eva, a friend of Joy. Punisher asks Eva's son run back to the hotel for his bag while he consoles Joy over her face, assuring her she's still attractive. While they make love, elsewhere Jigsaw approaches drug lord Diego, who Frank injured with his salsa blowgun earlier that day, for help in killing Punisher, citing him as a danger to his operation. Diego agrees and goes out with a contingent of men and Jigsaw. Now armed, Punisher and Joy attempt to get past Diego's men. Diego double crosses Jigsaw, ordering some of his men to kill him, but Jigsaw kills them. Diego and his men corner Punisher and Joy, wounding Frank. Diego has him in his sights when Jigsaw blasts the drug lord with a bazooka looted from Diego's men, knocking Punisher out in the process. Jigsaw takes the opportunity to cut up Punisher's face before taking Joy away with him.
NOTE: Cover labeled "Jigsaw Puzzle: Part 4 of 6."

"A Man of Wealth and Taste" (22 pages)

CREDITS: Mike Baron (writer), Jack Slamn (pencils), James Sherman (inks, colors), Ken Lopez (letters), Rob Tokar (asst editor), Don Daley (editor), Denys Cowan (c art)
FEATURE CHARACTER: Punisher
VILLAINS: Belasco (as "Lucifer"), Jigsaw (dies), Rev, drug dealers (some die)
OTHER CHARACTERS: Joy Adams, farmer, Rev's gatherers, Microchip's contacts (bts, gathers Punisher's intel), bystanders, goat, pigs
LOCATIONS/ITEMS: Tepuis region of SE Venezuela inc the Rev's pyramid & farmer's hut, Diego's mansion, town / Rev's machete, Punisher's machete, mirror, dental floss, kayak, oars, Range Rover, machine guns, handguns, rifles, Uzis, rocket launchers, Peña flowers, axe, Jigsaw's Uzi & knife
SYNOPSIS: The Rev cuts off his hand for his lord Lucifer and it reforms as Jigsaw enters with Joy. The Rev takes an interest in Joy as she reminds him of his sister. Elsewhere, Punisher hacks his way through the jungle until the blood loss catches up with him. He wakes up two days later with a farmer who found and patched him up. All he asks in return is for Frank to kill everyone involved with the local drugs trade. Breaking into the late Diego's mansion, Frank kills Diego's would-be heirs and steals weapons and transportation, then heads towards where Microchip's sources say the Peña flower grows. Meanwhile, the Rev shows Joy around his operation, explains his beliefs, and heals her face, covertly watched by Jigsaw, who grows angry over not receiving the same treatment. That night as the Rev cuts off a foot in worship, Jigsaw barges in and demands his face be fixed. The Rev complies, but moments later Punisher shows up, and shoots Jigsaw dead. With Joy backing him up, Punisher demands the Rev fix his face in return for a head start. Telling Punisher he needs to believe in Lucifer before the healing can work, the Rev calls on his infernal master, who unexpectedly appears in response.
NOTE: Cover labeled "Jigsaw Puzzle: Part 5 of 6." The Rev's appearance changes here, going from a bearded, robed redhead to brunette with a goatee and tribal attire. Jigsaw also loses his Hawaiian shirt vest and neckerchief in favor of a sleeveless tee.

PUNISHER #40 (Early October 1990)

"End of the Game" (22 pages)

CREDITS: Mike Baron (writer), Bill Reinhold (pencils), Mark Farmer (inks), Chris Eliopoulos, Ken Lopez (letters), Sloat, Gregory Wright (colors), Rob Tokar (asst editor), Don Daley (editor)
FEATURE CHARACTER: Punisher (next in MK #19-21, '90)
VILLAINS: Belasco (next bts in AFlt #123, '93, next in AFlt #124, '93), Jigsaw (resurrected, next in Pun #55, '91), Rev (dies)
OTHER CHARACTERS: Joy Adams (next in PWJ #28, '91), villagers, 3 drug dealers (as corpses)
LOCATIONS/ITEMS: Venezuela inc temple, surrounding jungle, & tribal village / Frank's gun & machete, Joy's gun, Peña flowers, villagers' spears, dealers' guns; Jigsaw's assault rifle, grenades, rocket launcher, knife & detonator, winch-drawn basket, drums containing Peña extract, spiny plant, helicopter
SYNOPSIS: The Punisher refuses to believe that "Lucifer," in fact the demon Belasco, is the true Devil, but fires on Belasco when the Rev asks him to resurrect Jigsaw. Unharmed, Belasco blinds Frank and Joy Adams with a flash of light, enabling the Rev to disarm them. Belasco and the Rev give Frank and Joy a 15-minute headstart before he resurrects and re-arms Jigsaw to hunt them, saying that whoever survives will become the Rev's servant. As Frank and Joy travel to a nearby village, Belasco tells Rev that the Peña extract is to be dumped into the Gulf Stream in order to poison Earth's oceans. The Rev then revives Jigsaw. At the village, Frank and Joy ask for help against the Rev, and the villagers point them to a crashed drug plane in the jungle, where Frank and Joy find weapons. Jigsaw finds the plane and blows it up, but is ambushed by Joy and Frank. Frank beats Jigsaw and rams his face into a spiny plant, disfiguring him again. Frank catches the Rev attempting to escape via helicopter and forces him to heal his face. He allows the Rev to leave, but blows up his helicopter with planted explosives when the Rev attempts to kill him. As Frank, Joy, and a now bored Belasco respectively depart, Jigsaw awakens and swears revenge.
NOTE: Cover labeled "Jigsaw Puzzle: Part 6 of 6.

PUNISHER #41 (Late October 1990)

"Should a Gentleman Offer a Tiparillo to a Lady?" (22 pages)

CREDITS: Mike Baron (writer), Bill Reinhold (pencils, c art), John Nyberg, Michael Ritter, Tony DeZuniga, José Marzan Jr. (inks), Ed Lazellari (colors), Ken Lopez (letters), Rob Tokar (asst editor), Don Daley (editor)
FEATURE CHARACTER: Punisher (also as Rook)
GUEST STAR: Nick Fury (last bts in UXM #268, '90, last in NF:AoS #14, '90, next in Dlk #2, '91)
SUPPORTING CAST: Microchip (also as Bishop, last in MK #21, '90)
VILLAINS: Waterboys: Delores (rape victim), Janet, Ruth (prev 2 sisters); drug dealer
OTHER CHARACTERS: Chief Lewis, federal agent, TV newsreader, Mayor of New York, police (some die), SHIELD agents inc Al MacKenzie (last in NF:AoS #14, '90, next in Dlk #3, '91), bystanders
LOCATIONS/ITEMS: Badger Park, Microchip's apartment & cabin, Gracie Mansion, Ashokan Reservoir, Jacobson's Hotel, Kensico Pumping Station (mentioned, site of explosion), Bronx pumping station / drugs, New York Post, Punisher's blade, brass knuckles & Uzi; payphone, ransom note, helicopter, the Tiparillo (mini-sub), machine gun, handgun, mineral water, schematics, bombs
SYNOPSIS: Through a coded personal ad, Microchip invites Punisher to his new place and announces his intentions to rejoin Frank's crusade. Soon after New York's water supply is temporarily cut off following an explosion at a pumping station; the Mayor receives a letter from "the Waterboys" claiming responsibility and demanding $20 million from the city. SHIELD is assigned to stop them, and Punisher informs SHIELD's Nick Fury he too is investigating. Meanwhile the Waterboys, sisters Janet and Ruth who feel the city's management wronged their father, and Delores, a rape survivor seeking revenge against the city because her assailant was only given probation, plot their next attack. While Delores is checking on their ransom demand, the sisters invade the Bronx pumping station, prompting Nick Fury to ask Frank for help since SHIELD doesn't have adequate manpower. Punisher enters the pumping station in a mini-sub and engages Janet and Ruth. Capturing Janet, he escapes before their bombs go off, but Ruth is lost in the confusion; Punisher turns Janet over to Fury.
NOTE: Janet's hair is miscolored red on the cover.

PUNISHER #42 (November 1990)

"St. Paradine's" (22 pages)

CREDITS: Mike Baron (writer), Mark Texeira (art), Bob Budiansky (colors), Ken Lopez (letters), Rob Tokar (asst editor), Don Daley (editor) Ron Wagner (c pencils), Andy Kubert (c inks)
FEATURE CHARACTER: Punisher (also as Mr. Chaloner, Knight & FBI agent Arnold Holtzman, next in PWJ #25-27, '90-91)
SUPPORTING CAST: Microchip (also as Bishop, next in PWJ #25, '90)
VILLAINS: Col. Herbert Fedenia (Vietnam vet & St. Paradine's headmaster) & his men (some die) inc Pete, Pudpadnoy Tooboothokoot (former Muay Thai champion & St. Paradine's instructor, dies), Stokely (gun dealer), buyer (both die)
OTHER CHARACTERS: Gloria (St. Paradine's receptions secretary), St. Paradine's cadets & instructors, bystanders; Richard Nixon, Ronald Reagan (both in photo)
LOCATIONS/ITEMS: Stokely's apartment, Microchip's apartment, St. Paradine's in Virginia inc Fedenia's office & communications building / case of AR-15s & ammo, VCRs, porn videos, Punisher's machine gun, binoculars, knife & throwing stars coated w/ blowfish toxin, handgun; rifles, movie camera, lights, bullhorn
SYNOPSIS: A raid on an arms dealer uncovers child porn videos from St. Paradine's in Virginia, a school with a regime based on military structure. Posing as a parent interested in enrolling his son, Punisher meets the headmaster, Col. Fedenia, then returns that night and sneaks into the campus. He interrupts the latest video shoot, but Fedenia flees while Punisher is occupied fighting the school's martial-arts instructor. After taking him down, Punisher finds a bullhorn and announces Fedenia's crimes to the campus. As the students turn on Fedenia, Punisher overpowers the headmaster, then entrusts the cadets to guard him until the police arrive.
NOTE: St. Paradine's exterior is a photo of New York's City Hall.

PUNISHER #43 (December 1990)

"Border Run" (22 pages)

CREDITS: Mike Baron (writer), Bill Reinhold (art, c pencils), Ken Lopez (letters), Linda Lessmann (colors), Rob Tokar (asst editor), Don Daley (editor), Josef Rubenstein (c inks)
FEATURE CHARACTER: Punisher (next in UXM #272, '91, FF #349, '91)
VILLAINS: Dr. Alonzo Garcia (drug lord associate), Hector Balboa (drug lord) & his men (some die) inc Bill, Carlos, Eduardo, Elmo, Felipe, Juan, Ruiz (prev 7 die) & Gomez; Tomas (airstrip owner, betrays Punisher, dies), border runners (one dies)
OTHER CHARACTERS: Mrs. Horowitz (DEA agent's widow), Garcia's girl, rancher, Mexican Air Force pilot, bystanders, horses, mule
LOCATIONS/ITEMS: Tehultepec, Mexico inc La Valencia restaurant, ranch, Balboa's ranch, Tijuana, Mexico; King's Inn motel in San Ysidro, Horowitz apartment / Garcia's limo, tracking device & Huey Cobra helicopter w/ rocket packs & miniguns; dirtbikes, Uzis, Punisher's Uzi & sniper rifle; limo antenna, car, Cessna, Balboa's helicopter, Balboa's handgun, French Mirage jet & Harrier jump jet, handcuffs, binoculars, Balboa's men's rifles & machine guns, surface-to-air missile, Mexican Air Force jet, Among Madmen novel
SYNOPSIS: In Mexico Punisher kidnaps Dr. Alonzo Garcia, who repeatedly revived captured DEA agent Allen Horowitz so drug lord Hector Balboa could continue to torture him; Frank intends to deliver Garcia to Horowitz's widow, so she can decide Garcia's fate. Balboa's men swiftly find them thanks to a hidden tracking device on Garcia. After slaying them, Punisher ditches the tracker and takes Garcia to his waiting plane, but finds the fuel lines cut, as his local contact, Tomas, has sold him out. More of Balboa's men attack, seemingly prepared to let Garcia die. Garcia directs Punisher to Balboa's ranch where more aircraft are stored, and, after eliminating the guards there, they take off in Garcia's helicopter, with Garcia piloting. Balboa's men give chase in his jet, but Garcia takes them out. Instead of finishing off Balboa, Punisher has them head north. After evading the Mexican Air Force and almost being swindled by runners taking them across the border, Punisher gets Garcia to Horowitz's widow. He tells her it's her right to decide Garcia's fate. Appalled, she tells Punisher to let Garcia go, not wanting his death on her conscience. Punisher complies, but promises to kill Garcia next time they meet.
NOTE: Punisher's corner box image is dressed up like Clint Eastwood's Man With No Name character.

PUNISHER #44 (January 1991)

"Flag Burner" (22 pages)

CREDITS: Mike Baron (writer), Neil Hanson (art), Jade Moede, Ken Lopez (letters), Linda Lessmann (colors), Kevin Kobasic (asst editor), Don Daley (editor), Andy Kubert (c pencils)
FEATURE CHARACTER: Punisher (next in NW #7-9, '91, PWJ #48, '92 fb)
VILLAINS: Harold Meecham (bank president) & his men inc Arn, Ben, Bob, Karl & Terry, Brian (Meecham's nephew), Matthew (Brian's partner) (all die)
OTHER CHARACTERS: Arc Light (rap musician & protester), Sheriff Bob, Harlan (deputy) (both die), Sally (Meecham's secretary), Sally (dispatcher), Wilson (deputy) (both voice only), Phipps (deputy, mentioned), Sheriff Bob's brother (mentioned, beat Meecham for State Legislature position), gas station attendant, bystanders, statue of Col. Hans Christian Heg & his horse, Arc Light's flag & boom box, Meecham's limo & boat,
LOCATIONS/ITEMS: River City Iowa inc town square, Hartley's Gas, park, Meecham Mercantile Farmer's Bank, Babcock farm & American Automobile Company factory (destroyed), Bailey's Tavern (mentioned, site of race riot) / Punisher's Battle Van & gun, statue of Col. Hans Christian Heg & his horse, Arc Light's flag & boom box, Meecham's limo & boat, sheriff's gun, patrol car & radio, acetone barrels, Arn, Karl, Brian & Matthew's guns, bomb
SYNOPSIS: While vacationing in Iowa, Frank rescues a flag-burning protester, Arc Light, when onlookers Arn, Ben, Bob and Terry assault him. Arn and his friends inform banker Harold Meecham, who takes Karl with him to the car factory, and sends the others out to find Arc Light. Alerted by Meecham's secretary, Sheriff Bob and his deputy head to town to search for Meecham, but stop to investigate a light in the derelict factory. Meanwhile, Brian and Matthew interrupt Frank's lunch with Arc Light and try to steal Frank's van. Frank shoots and injures Matthew, then he and Arc Light retreat as Brian returns fire. Unable to get into the van, Brian finishes Matthew off, then leaves to report to Meecham. Finding that Meecham has been manufacturing amphetamines at the factory, Bob and Harlan arrest Meecham and Karl, but Brian surprises them, and Meecham has Karl and Brian kill the two lawmen. Having followed Brian, Punisher sneaks into the factory, but Brian sees him and knocks him out. Karl sets a bomb to blow up the factory and Punisher, and Brian kills Karl. Arc Light draws Meecham's other men to the back of the factory, where they discover Meecham and Brian trying to escape in a boat. Punisher warns them the factory will explode soon, but the men are eager to recover Meecham's money. Punisher and Arc Light leave in the boat, just as the factory explodes.

PUNISHER #45 (February 1991)

"One Way Fare" (20 pages)

CREDITS: Chuck Dixon (writer), Tod Smith (pencils), Dan Bulanadi (inks), Ken Lopez (letters), John Wellington (colors), Kevin Kobasic (asst editor), Don Daley (editor), Ron Wagner (c art)
FEATURE CHARACTER: Punisher
SUPPORTING CAST: Microchip (last in PWJ #26, '91)
VILLAINS: Delbert Rogofsky (drug dealer) & his gang, cabbie killer (dies), cab robber
OTHER CHARACTERS: Ricky Delmarra (mentioned, boy killed by Rogofsky), Winslow (New York City Taxi & Limousine Commission officer), cab driver (dies), Delbert Rogofsky's lawyer, Action News TV reporter, bystanders, cab passengers, reporters
LOCATIONS/ITEMS: New York inc Queens College (mentioned only), Brooklyn-Battery Tunnel, Brooklyn Bridge, courthouse, Jolly Burger restaurant & Brooklyn & Manhattan streets (Brooklyn-Queens Expressway, 4th Ave, Gowanus Expressway, 8th St, 9th St, Prospect St., St. Johns Ave), Punisher's base w/ garage / ambulance, cab robber's .32 revolver,

cabbie killer's .44 Magnum, drug dealers' semi-automatic firearms, French fries, hamburger, Microchip's Brooklyn map, computer, transceiver & welder, money, police cars, press microphones, Punisher's taxi cab 10A7 (w/ AM-FM cassette player, Lexan windows, plate steel shielding, roll bar, seat-mounted shotgun w/ pull ring, strobe light, transceiver, 450 V8 engine & supercharger) & television w/ remote control, reporters' microphones, Rogofsky's Chevy Blazer 4x4, taxi cab, traffic, Winslow's wallet & ID card

SYNOPSIS: After watching a TV news report about Delbert Rogofsky, a drug dealer who made bail after allegedly shooting a young boy, Frank Castle poses as a taxi driver to flush out a killer who has gunned down five cabbies. Driving a taxi tricked out by Microchip, Punisher picks up a number of fares, thwarts a would-be robber, and encounters a crooked hack bureau officer in Brooklyn. While driving a female passenger, Castle receives a call from Microchip that Rogofsky has been spotted in the area. Punisher finds and pursues the drug dealer's vehicle as Rogofsky's gang fire at him. After causing Rogofsky to crash, Castle learns his passenger is the cabbie murderer, motivated by a rape she blames on taxi drivers who refused to give her a ride. Punisher kills the woman with a shotgun hidden under her seat.

NOTE: Story followed by pinups (2 pages) featuring Punisher (Whilce Portacio, art) & Punisher & armed thugs (Cooper Smith & Michael Ritter, art). Letters page includes LoC from future comics writer Jan C. Childress.

PUNISHER #46 (March 1991)

"Cold Cache" (21 pages)

CREDITS: Mike Baron (writer), Hugh Haynes (pencils), Vince Evans, Ed Lazellari, Ariane Lenshoek, Santiago Oliveras, James Palmiotti, Rodney Ramos, Bob Wiacek (inks), Kevin Kobasic (inks, asst editor), Bud LaRosa (inks, c inks), Ken Lopez (letters), John Wellington (colors), Don Daley (editor)
FEATURE CHARACTER: Punisher (also as oil cartel representative Mr. Rook, next in PWJ #28, '91)
SUPPORTING CAST: Microchip (also as pilot Lester Lute)
VILLAINS: Mr. Connaught (Rolwell International Aircraft executive), New Model Army (neo-Nazi group) (all die)
OTHER CHARACTERS: Amalgamated Aerospace technicians, US Defense Dept procuring agents (both mentioned as paid off by Connaught), Rudolf Brunner (former German Luftwaffe lieutenant & intelligence operative, also in pfb), Richard Bruce "Dick" Cheney (US Secretary of Defense, bts, stuck in Saudi Arabia, 1st, next in IM #74, '04), Dr. Lieberman (Microchip's father, German scientist), Microchip's sister (Ft. Lauderdale housewife) (both mentioned only), Brunner's Luftwaffe crew (die bts in fb), Miller (Rolwell employee, bts, on phone), Greenland fishermen (bts in fb), huskies (in fb), bystanders
LOCATIONS/ITEMS: Canada, Nazi base in Iceland (both in fb), Greenland glacier (also in fb), Iraq, Newfoundland (both mentioned only), Trondheim, Norway (bts, New Model Army's departure point), Manhattan inc Central Park, 5th Ave & Punisher's apartment w/ living room, Rolwell International Aircraft Co headquarters inc Connaught's office, rural New Jersey airfield inc hangar / Dornier bomber (also in fb) w/ hydraulic system & tailguns, Dr. Lieberman's notebooks (mentioned only), Odinbolt (Nazi particle-beam prototype), Whirlitzer (Microchip's remote-controlled toy helicopter), airplane, binoculars, bomb w/ timer, cables, Connaught's pilot helmet, electric blankets, gelignite, generator, heating coils, helicopters, igniter, inflatable raft, parachutes, parkas, Punisher's briefcase, radio headsets, Rolwell experimental aircraft, screwdriver, sleeping bags, Soviet assault transport, Stinger missile launcher, torches, transmitter, US Defense Dept papers, walkie talkie, winch, New Model Army's automatic firearms & snowmobiles
FLASHBACK: During World War II, Luftwaffe officer Rudolf Brunner flies a bomber on a mission to destroy New York with the Odinbolt, a particle-beam prototype developed by Microchip's father, but a storm forces him to land on a glacier in Greenland and abandon the mission. (p).
SYNOPSIS: A reformed Rudolf Brunner asks Microchip and Punisher to help him retrieve the Odinbolt from his bomber in a Greenland glacier before a Neo-Nazi group called the New Model Army seizes it. Frank Castle goes to an aircraft company to buy a helicopter for the journey to Greenland and is forced to blackmail its corrupt executive, Connaught, to obtain it. Punisher, Microchip and Brunner arrive at the glacier, and as they extract the bomber from the ice, the New Model Army attacks. An air battle ensues, and Microchip blows up the Neo-Nazis' aircraft with explosives packed into his remote control toy helicopter. Suddenly, Connaught arrives in one of his company's planes and insists on taking the Odinbolt for himself. Microchip activates the Odinbolt and Punisher aims the bomber at Connaught's plane. The bomber's occupants parachute to safety as Connaught's aircraft explodes. As Castle, Microchip and Brunner float away on a raft, Brunner reveals that a second bomber is frozen in the glacier.
NOTE: The inkers are collectively credited as "the Inking Squad of Death." This issue reveals Microchip's father's background as a German scientist. A reference is made to the Persian Gulf War. Rolwell is also spelled "Rollwell."

PUNISHER #47 (April 1991)

"The Brattle Gun Part One" (22 pages)

CREDITS: Mike Baron (writer), Hugh Haynes (pencils, c art), José Marzan Jr. (inks), John Wellington (colors), Ken Lopez (letters), Kevin Kobasic (asst editor), Don Daley (editor), John Romita Sr., Terry Kevin Austin, KK (c art)
FEATURE CHARACTER: Punisher
SUPPORTING CAST: Microchip
VILLAINS: Saracen (as Col. Hawk, new Trafian chief of security, last in PWJ #27, '91), "John Mack Schenectady" (Mossad assassin), Col. Razir (Trafian general) (both die), Watban (Trafian interrogator), President Jekohadeem (Trafian president), Trafian soldiers, gun dealer
OTHER CHARACTERS: Rose Kugel (chr last in Pun #48, '91 fb, last in Pun #7, '88), Morris Brattle (gun designer, 1st), Pasha Shakbander (Zuki spy), Immam Mullah (Zuki leader) & his aides inc Sukjeesh, flight crew, pilots (bts), plane passengers, bystanders
LOCATIONS/ITEMS: Brattle's apartment building & apartment, Microchip's apartment, Trafia (Middle Eastern nation) inc airport, market & supergun site, Zukistan (rival Middle Eastern nation) inc Zukistan City / Punisher's handgun, body armor (Specter shield hybrid armor), fake mustache, diamond-tipped fingernails & knife; Brattle's hat, coat & briefcase; Brattle Gun & schematic, Air Trafia plane, Razir's limo, motorcycles, SP-70 tanks, gun dealer's guns inc AK-47, soldier's clubs, Sikorsky flyby drone, jeeps, Hawk's sword & gun
SYNOPSIS: Punisher saves Morris Brattle, a gun designer, from a would-be assassin. Brattle provided the nation of Trafia with a powerful gun against their enemy Zukistan. Initially wanting to kill him for it, Microchip instead offers him a bribe to sabotage it – a job Brattle claims may be half done already, thanks to inferior parts he was forced to use to meet deadlines. He and Frank travel to Trafia, with Frank secretly applying diamond

tips to his fingernails during the flight. Met at the airport, Brattle is given a tour by Col. Razir, witnessing the Colonel fatally wound an already tortured Zuki spy and looking in on an imprisoned second, female, spy, before checking out the gun. Meanwhile, a disguised Frank tries to buy guns in the town but is sold out by the merchant and arrested. At the same time, Micro convinces the Zuki leaders to mobilize against Trafia. For allowing the Zukis to launch a surprise attack, the president kills Razir, then appoints Col. Hawk in his place. Hawk, secretly Saracen, recognizes the captured Punisher, and, as the Brattle Gun is aimed at Zuki City, Saracen straps Frank across the end of the barrel.

NOTE: Jekohadeem and Immam Mullah resemble Saddam Hussein and the Ayatollah Khomeini respectively. Includes two Punisher posters, one by Brad Vancata, one by David Ross and Josef Rubinstein.

PUNISHER #48 (May 1991)

"The Brattle Gun Part Two" (20 pages)

CREDITS: Mike Baron (writer), Hugh Haynes (pencils), Jimmy Palmiotti (inks), Ken Lopez (letters), Greg Wright (colors), Kevin Kobasic (asst editor), Don Daley (editor), Terry Austin (c inks)
FEATURE CHARACTER: Punisher (next in W/Pun #1-3, '93, DC #4, '91, Pun Ann #4/2, '91)
SUPPORTING CAST: Microchip (chr next in W/Pun #1, '93 fb, next in Pun Ann #4/3, '91)
VILLAINS: Saracen (next in PWJ #33, '91), Trafian soldiers
OTHER CHARACTERS: Rose Kugel (next in Pun:EQ, '94), Morris Brattle (dies), Immam Mullah (dies), other mullahs, Zuki general & soldiers inc Fastnir (named), Zuki citizens, bystanders
LOCATIONS/ITEMS: Trafia inc Rose's prison cell & military encampment w/bunker; Zukistan City; outside Brattle's New York brownhouse / Brattle Gun w/muzzle & shells, Trafian & Zuki tanks, Zuki artillery & assault rifles, Punisher's diamond-tipped fingernails & assault rifle, Saracen's gun & knife, Microchip's gun

SYNOPSIS: With Punisher lashed to its muzzle, Saracen prepares to fire the Brattle Gun. Outside the encampment, the Zuki tank brigade, led by Microchip, launches its attack. Punisher frees himself with his diamond-tipped fingernails and breaks into the female spy's cell, finding Rose. She tells him her mission is to kill Brattle. In the turret, Brattle assures Jekohadeem that the cannon is safe. Outside, Punisher and Rose argue: Punisher wants to save Brattle and kill Saracen, while Rose wants the opposite. Saracen appears and tells Rose their orders have changed, that Brattle lives and Punisher dies. While Punisher and Brattle fight, Rose leaves to finish her mission. Suffering from dehydration, Frank falls to Saracen, but is saved when Microchip arrives in a tank. Microchip prevents Frank from killing Saracen, saying it was a term of the deal he made with Immam Mullah. In the turret, Brattle leaves with Punisher, but reminds Jekohadeem the cannon is safe. The President fires the Brattle Gun, but it explodes. Jekohadeem survives the explosion, but is killed by Rose. In Zukistan City, Immam Mullah informs Microchip that Brattle has agreed to build a bigger gun for Zukistan. Two weeks later, in New York, Punisher kills Brattle.
NOTE: Cover titled "Next stop: Baghdad," further acknowledging the similarity of Trafia and Zukistan to Iraq and Iran. This issue includes a pin-up of Punisher by André Smith Coates and Keith Williams, and a pin-up of Punisher and two thugs by Mark Pacella and Al Williamson.

PUNISHER ANNUAL #4 (1991)

"Genesis of a Vigilante" (3 pages)

CREDITS: Mike Baron (writer), Tom Morgan (art), Jim Novak (letters), Paul Mounts (colors), Kevin Kobasic (asst editor), Don Daley (editor), Michael Golden (c pencils), Klaus Janson (c inks), Joe Rosas (c colors)
FEATURE CHARACTER: Punisher (also as Frank Castiglione in fb during Pun:AG, '88 fb, last in Pun/Cap #3, '92 fb, also in Pun #1, '98 fb, Pun:OM #1, '93, PWZ #21, '93 fb, PunHol #2, '94 fb, Pun:XMas #1, '07 fb, PWZ #24, '94 fb, Pun #100, '95 fb, Pun #10, '09 fb, Pun:RBG, '89 fb, MP #2, '75 fb, PWJ #1, '88 fb, PWZ #25, '94 fb, Pun #17, '97 fb, Pun #4, '99 fb, PunBl, '91 fb, DE:A, '95 fb, Pun/Cap #3, '92 fb, PWJ #3, '89 fb, Pun:YO #1, '94, Pun:AG, '88 fb & Pun:YO #2, '95, next in Pun:YO #2, '95)
SUPPORTING CAST: Maria Castle (also as Castiglione bts in fb during Pun:AG, '88 fb; last in Pun:AG, '88 fb, also in Pun #1, '98 fb, PWZ #21, '93 fb, PunHol #2, '94 fb, Pun:Xmas #1, '07 fb, PWZ #24, '94 fb, Pun #100, '95 fb, Pun #10, '09 fb, Pun:RBN, '89 fb, MP #2, '75 fb, PWJ #1, '88 fb, PWZ #25, '94 fb, Pun #17, '97 fb, DE:A, '95 fb & Pun/Cap #3, '92 fb, next in Pun #4, '99 fb), Lisa Castle (also as Castiglione bts in fb to 1st chr app before Pun:AG, '88 fb), Frank Castle, Jr. (both last in Pun:AG, '88 fb, also in Pun #1, '98 fb, PWZ #21, '93 fb, Pun:Xmas #1, '07 fb, PWZ #24, '94 fb, Pun #100, '95 fb, Pun #10, '09 fb, Pun:RBN, '89 fb, MP #2, '75 fb, PWJ #1, '88 fb, PWZ #25, '94 fb, Pun #17, '97 fb, Pun #4, '99 fb, PunBl, '91 fb, DE:A, '95 fb & Pun/Cap #3, '92 fb, next in Pun #4, '99 fb)
VILLAINS: Bruno Costa (last in MP #2, '75 fb, also in Pun #4, '99 fb & PWJ #3, '89 fb, next in Pun:YO #3, '95), Luis Allegre, Leon Kolsky (both last in MP #2, '75 fb, also in PWJ #3, '89 fb, next in MSA Mag #1, '76 fb), Byron Hannigan, Matt Skinner (both last in MP #2, '75 fb, also in Pun #4, '99 fb & PWJ #3, '89 fb, next in MSA Mag #1, '76 fb),
OTHER CHARACTERS: Det. Johnny Laviano (last in Pun:YO #4, '95, next in MSA Mag #1, '76 fb), nurses (in fb), US Marines
LOCATIONS/ITEMS: Aircraft carrier, train station, Castle house, hospital maternity ward, Central Park, Mercy General hospital / mobster's guns, Punisher's machine guns
FLASHBACK: Frank waits while Lisa is born.
SYNOPSIS: Frank Castle receives the Distinguished Service Cross, returns home to his family and takes a job training recruits upstate. The Castle family celebrates Christmas. Frank learns he'll be receiving the Presidential Freedom Award. On their way to DC, the Castle family picnic in Central Park where mobsters gun down Frank's family (MP #2, '75 fb). Frank lunges at them in a rage, but is shot. In the hospital, Frank learns the Costa crime family killed his family. He leaves the hospital and embarks on his mission of vengeance as the Punisher.
NOTE: Cover labeled "The Von Strucker Gambit Part 2." Includes table of contents/credits page (2 pages) w/art taken from page 7. This is a recounting of Punisher's origin. Followed by PWJ #31, '90 preview (1 page).

2ND STORY: "The Cutting Edge" (25 pages)
CREDITS: Greg Wright (co-writer, co-colors), Dan Chichester (co-writer), John Herbert (pencils), Jimmy Palmiotti, Don Hudson, Jim Reddington (inks), Jade Moede (letters), Ed Lazellari, Sarra Mossoff (colors), Kevin Kobasic (asst editor), Don Daley (editor)
FEATURE CHARACTER: Punisher
GUEST STAR: Nick Fury (last in DD Ann #7/2, '91, next in Cap Ann #10/2, '91)

VILLAINS: Baron (Wolfgang) von Strucker (Nazi war criminal, head of Hydra terrorist organization), Dakini (Hydra assassin) (both last in DD Ann #7/2, '91, next in Cap Ann #10/2, '91), Guillotine (genetically-modified assassin, last in DD Ann #7/2, '91, next in NF:AoS #27, '91), Ron Takimoto (Hydra assassin, last in DD Ann #7/2, '91, dies), Jimmy Sabini's men, Magon (drug dealer), Nori Okun (former Yakuza boss) (prev 3 die) & his men (some die), Hydra agents

OTHER CHARACTERS: Alexander Pierce (SHIELD agent, last in DD Ann #7/2, '91, next in Pun:POV #3, '91), other SHIELD agents, Nigerians (drug mules, die), drug lords' bodies; Clive Bronkowitz (mentioned, drug shipment buyer)

LOCATIONS/ITEMS: Docks, drug lab, Sloat Plaza inc Gentili suite, Okun's warehouse / Okun's men's Uzis, heroin bags, Takimoto's swords, Dakini's blades, Punisher's machine gun, knives, automatic rifle, Kevlar, Battle Van (destroyed) & Uzi; Magon's handgun, SHIELD weapons, medkit & hovercar; Hydra implant, submarine & rifles, helicopter, manacles

SYNOPSIS: On the docks, Yakuza boss Nori Okun has his newest man, Guillotine, slaughter Jimmy Sabini's men and their drug mules to get the heroin inside them. Later, Hydra hunters Ron Takimoto and Dakini find the site, respectively tracking escaped Hydra experiments Guillotine and Romulus. Ron suggests they work together, but Dakini has other ideas. Elsewhere, Punisher interrogates a dealer, leading him to the man's suppliers, but finds Ron has already slain the dealers, and is waiting, hoping to enlist his help in hunting Guillotine. Nick Fury bursts in, intending to arrest Ron, but he escapes with Punisher's help. Meanwhile, Guillotine takes over Okun's business, convincing Okun's own men to slay their boss. As they prepare their next shipment, Punisher and Ron attack. When Guillotine is about to kill Punisher, Ron sacrifices himself to save his ally. Punisher pursues Guillotine as he flees in a helicopter. Their mid-air duel ends when Punisher tricks Guillotine into severing his own arm, causing him to fall into the water. Fury arrives and scours the water for Guillotine, but Hydra has already snatched him.

NOTE: Part 2 of 3 of the Von Strucker Gambit, continued from DD Ann #7/2, '91 & in Cap Ann #10/2, '91. includes Punisher/Nick Fury: Rules of the Game GN preview (2 pages); advertised as by Greg Wright (co-writer) & Jim Lee (co-writer & art) at 64 pages with a late '91 release date. War Journal entry dated April 9th.

3RD STORY: "Fat Farm" (11 pages)

CREDITS: Mike Baron (writer), Tom Morgan (art), Mike Heisler (letters), Brad Vancata (colors), Kevin Kobasic (asst editor), Don Daley (editor)

FEATURE CHARACTER: Microchip (last in Pun #48, '91, last bts in W/Pun #2, '93, next in PWJ #29, '91)

SUPPORTING CAST: Punisher

VILLAINS: Camp Slimline: Rudy Thurston (head nutritionist), Eddie Lewis (ex-con, also as Elmo Sorenson, assistant nutritionist), Pam (liaison); Cherelle Timmons (crooked deputy)

OTHER CHARACTERS: Clients (Tom Courney named, dies), paramedics

LOCATIONS/ITEMS: Microchip's apartment, Camp Slimline, 227 Blackbird Lane, Raleigh, North Carolina inc Micro's room, Cherelle's room, auditorium, nutritionist office, administration office, gym & basement / scale, Camp Slimline business card, Micro's bag, M&Ms & handgun, bottle of appetite suppressants, alarm clock, copy machine, fax machine, computer, ambulance, Cherelle's handgun, Elmo's handgun, syringe of sodium pentathol

SYNOPSIS: Deciding it's time to lose weight, Micro visits a fat farm, but becomes suspicious when "nutritionist" Elmo offers him drugs to lose weight. Breaking into the administration office, Micro discovers the farm's clients either have money or history of drug abuse. After a client dies of an apparent stroke, Micro teams up with Cherelle, a deputy sheriff from Georgia, to get proof of clients being turned into addicts or blackmailed upon release. They split up, but Elmo and his boss Rudy catch Micro, and take him to the drug-filled basement for interrogation. Cherelle intervenes, knocking them out, but then sedates Micro. When Micro wakes, he finds the drugs and Cherelle gone. Checking Cherelle's fat farm file, Micro learns she was a dirty cop suspected of stealing evidence and drug dealing. He deletes the files, calls the police and returns home.

4TH STORY: "A Public Service Message" (3 pages)

CREDITS: George Caragonne (writer), Mike Harris (pencils), Stan Drake (inks), Joe Rosas (colors), Kevin Kobasic (asst editor), Don Daley (editor)

FEATURE CHARACTER: Punisher (next in DD #292-293, '91, Pun/Cap #1-3, '92, Namor #16 & 18-20, PWJ #29-30, Pun:POV #1-4, PWJ #31-34, all '91, ASM #353-356, '91-92, Dhawk #9, '91, PWJ #35-36, '91, Dlk #6-7, '91-92, PunSS #1, '91, PWJ #48, '92 fb, PWJ #37, '91, GR/W/ Pun, '91, MCP #101/4, '92, Pun:Blood, '91)

VILLAINS: Drug dealers, punk (dies)

LOCATIONS/ITEMS: West 79th Street Boat Basin, Henry Hudson Parkway / Punisher's binoculars & rocket launcher, punk's gun & 1957 Chevy Bel Air

SYNOPSIS: Before he can stop a drug deal, Punisher is caught by surprise by a punk who plans to sell him to the Kingpin. The punk makes Punisher drive his car while he holds his gun on him. Punisher crashes the car, sending the punk through the windshield. As he walks from the wreck, Punisher notes that seat belts save lives.

NOTE: Followed by Punisher pin-up by Michael Golden (1 page) & 3 pin-ups of Punisher taking down criminals by Niel Hansen, Val Mayerik & Tod Smith and Jack Abel, respectively (1 page each).

PUNISHER: BLOODLINES (1991)

"Bloodlines" (64 pages)

CREDITS: Gerry Conway (writer), Dave Cockrum (pencils), Jeff Albrecht (inks), Phil Felix (letters), Paty Cockrum (colors), Mark Powers (asst editor), Terry Kavanagh (editor)

FEATURE CHARACTER: Punisher (also in own thoughts, rfb & pfb, also as Pvt. Castiglione in fb1 between Pun #1, '87 fb & Pun #1, '98 fb; last in Pun #17, '97 fb, next in ASM #202, '80 fb, Pun:OM #1, '93, Kill:EY #3, '93, ASM #129, '74)

VILLAINS: Captain Manuel Flores de Ortega (corrupt head of San Domingo Security police force, dies) & his soldiers (most die), Hector Ramone (also in pfb, druglord, dies) & his goons (some in pfb, most die) inc Juan & Rodriguez (both die)

OTHER CHARACTERS: Quincy Jefferson (also in pfb, Vietnam vet turned DEA agent, dies), Angela Wynoski Jefferson (also in fb1, Quincy's wife, dies), Laura Jefferson (Quincy & Angela's daughter), Estaban Ramone (also in pfb, Hector Ramone's son); US Embassy soldier (possibly also in pfb, see NOTE), jaguar (dies), Maria Castle, Frank Castle Jr, Lisa Castle, Bruno Costa, mobsters, mob victim (prev 6 in rfb only), criminals (in Punisher's thoughts only), Saigon marketplace visitors (in fb1 only), Estella Ramone (Estaban's mother, dies), Los Angeles bar patrons, wedding guests, Estaban's friends (prev 4 in pfb only)

LOCATIONS/ITEMS: San Domingo inc US Embassy, Jefferson home, Hector Ramone's airfield inc warehouse (destroyed), mountains & Hector Ramone's plantation w/Ramone's house (destroyed); Los Angeles inc bar, church & Ramone home; Saigon marketplace (fb1), Central Park (rfb) / Punisher's Armalite AR-180 sporter carbine rifle w/sight, scope &mount, .357 automag, MBA gyrojet pistol, universal enforcer autocarbine & satchel w/C-4 explosives & timer; Jefferson family silverware, Ortega's limo, Ortega's men's guns, Hector's goons' guns, 2 cargo planes (destroyed), Hector Ramone's cocaine & helicopters (1 destroyed)

FLASHBACKS: Marine Frank Castiglione visits Saigon marketplace with Angela Wynoski (1). In LA Hector Ramone charms and marries the youthful and naïve Estella, but abuses both her and their son, Estaban. Estella flees to Miami with the boy, but six years later, Hector finds them. He kills Estella and takes Estaban to San Domingo. The boy eventually escapes, and makes it to the US embassy, where he meets Quincy Jefferson. Later, Punisher learns of Captain de Ortega (p). Frank Castle plays with his family in Central Park before Bruno Costa's mobsters gun them down (MP #2, '75).

SYNOPSIS: After tracing a drug ring to the small South American country of San Domingo, Punisher witnesses his old friend Quincy Jefferson angrily accuse San Domingo's security police commander, Captain de Ortega, of being corrupt. Later visiting Quincy, Frank learns his friend has married Frank's former lover Angela Wynoski and taken in Estaban Ramone, druglord Hector Ramone' runaway son. Captain de Ortega's goons attack the house, murdering Quincy and Angela and kidnap their daughter, Laura, but Punisher gets Estaban out and captures Ortega, who informs him that Laura has been sent to Hector's mountain plantation before Punisher slays him. Accompanied by Estaban, Punisher raids Hector's plantation, rescuing Laura before blowing Hector's house up with C-4. Escaping alive, Hector pursues Punisher and the children in a helicopter; cornered on a cliff, Punisher pretends to surrender to lure Hector closer, then commandeers the helicopter, throwing Hector out. Hanging to the cliff by his fingertips, Hector begs Estaban to save him, but the boy lets Hector fall to his death. Escaping San Domingo in Hector's helicopter, Punisher tells Laura she will have to spend some time with her aunt, while Estaban worries what kind of son he has become.

NOTE: Followed by title/credits page (interior back cover). Back cover image taken from page 56. The story is inconsistent as to whether colonels or generals control San Domingo. The US embassy soldier seen in the pfb when Estaban flees there may be the same one working at San Domingo's US embassy when Punisher covertly observes Quincy meeting Ortega. Laura Jefferson's stuffed animals include a tiger (an homage to comic strip Calvin & Hobbes) and penguin (an homage to comic strip Opus & Bill).

THE PUNISHER: BLOOD ON THE MOORS (December 1991)

"Blood on the Moors" (62 pages)

CREDITS: Alan Grant, John Wagner (writers), Cam Kennedy (art, colors), Jim Novak (letters), Joseph Kaufman (design), Richard Ashford (asst editor), Nelson Yomtov (editor)

FEATURE CHARACTER: Punisher (also as Mr. Trump, also in pfb, next in PWZ #37, '95, Pun #49, '91)

SUPPORTING CAST: Microchip (last in ASM #354, '91, next in Pun #50, '91)

VILLAINS: Bruno Zanussi (major drug dealer) & his men, Hans-Dieter-Flurgen (cocaine distributor), Mingus Strathcoe (whiskey distiller) & his men inc Adolf, Archie, Gemmill, Gaffer & Greg; Christophe Marat (French smuggler), "Moscow" Eddie Yarkov (Russian smuggler) & his men inc Ivan, Murdoch (Glasgow crimelord) & his men inc Chib (all also in pfb, die), Foster (drug dealer, in pfb), 4 drug dealers (3 bts, in pfb, all probably die), Clan Campbell (as spirits), corrupt docks customs officers, Foster (owes Murdoch money, mentioned), Punjab Charlie (drug dealer, mentioned)

OTHER CHARACTERS: Mrs. Brechin (lodging house owner), Japanese tourist, Edinburgh Castle tour guide, police inc Chick, Rangers & Hearts of Midlothian football players, Rangers & Hearts supporters, British soldiers, rabbits (1 dies), chip shop staff, bystanders (all in pfb); Clansman (Det. Sgt. Duncan Ferguson, possessed by "Red" Ian Og, also in pfb1), Angus Strathcoe (Mingus' father); Clan MacDonald (as spirits, all die)

LOCATIONS/ITEMS: Scotland, Edinburgh inc Castle Rock w/Edinburgh Castle, Zanussi's hotel room, lodging house, police station, pub, Steamy Washeteria launderette, Foster's Royal Mile apartment & Waverly railway station; Glasgow inc Queen's Street Station, chip shop, docks & Ibrox Park inc Murdoch's private box; Microchips' New Jersey warehouse (all in pfb), Glencoe inc Clan MacDonald farmland (also in pfb1), Castle Coe Distillery (also in pfb) & Ian Og's memorial; Clansman's crofthouse, Loch Leven inc Eilean Munde w/Ian Og's grave / Punisher's Uzi, motorcycle, binoculars; tourist's camera, Zanussi's men's handguns, battle axe, soldiers' rifles, notepad, plate of haggis, rope, police car, fire axe, Murdoch's men's sawed-off shotgun & knife, Murdoch's revolver, fish & chips, Evening Times newspaper, ticker tape machine, Andrew Duggan cargo ship, Zanussi's car & truck, crates of cocaine, Ferguson's binoculars, Strathcoe's men's Uzis, Yarkov's limo, handgun & cigar; vats of whiskey, broken bottles (used as daggers), Zanussi's handgun, Angus' bagpipes (all in pfb), glasses, bowl of herbs, cannon, Strathcoe's handgun, Marat's throwing knife, fire tender, andiron (used as club), whiskey barrels; Clansman's Sword of Scotia (also in pfb), Clan Campbell's swords, muskets & pistols

FLASHBACK: Visiting Scotland, Punisher follows drug dealer Bruno Zanussi around Edinburgh hoping to learn about a major cocaine operation, but at Edinburgh Castle the ghostly Clansman attacks Zanussi. Forced to intervene, Punisher fights him until arriving soldiers cause Clansman to withdraw rather than harm innocents. Punisher finds Zanussi has cleared out of his hotel, but a notepad provides a name, Andrew Duggan. After his boarding house landlady tells him the Clansman is alleged to be "Red" Ian Og's ghost, Punisher calls Microchip to run a search on Og and Andrew Duggan. Meanwhile, the police review tourist footage of the fight and identify Punisher. They figure he's there for Zanussi, but wonder why Interpol didn't warn them about the dealer's arrival, until they discover someone at the station hid Interpol's dispatch. Punisher interrogates several dealers looking for Zanussi, but one is under police surveillance, and Sgt. Duncan Ferguson catches Punisher. Frank informs the police about Zanussi's big deal before escaping. Neither Micro nor another dealer, Murdoch, provide further leads, but by chance Punisher notices a newspaper listing cargo vessel Andrew Duggan in the shipping arrivals. Elsewhere, Ferguson learns European drug dealer Hans-Dieter-Flurgen is flying into Glasgow, but tells his partner they will follow this up themselves, in case there is a departmental leak. Locating Zanussi collecting merchandise from the Duggan, Punisher follows him to Castle Coe Distillery. Unaware someone is watching him, Punisher infiltrates, observing distillery owner Mingus Strathcoe explain to gathered international criminals his plan to ship cocaine distilled undetectably into whiskey. Punisher attacks but is overpowered, and the crooks dunk him in the tainted whiskey until he passes out, then dump him in the wilderness, trusting the weather to finish him. Witnessing the unconscious Punisher being carried out, the person who had watched Frank earlier picks up the Sword of Scotia and transforms into the Clansman (p).

SYNOPSIS: A drugged Punisher collapses in the snow, oblivious to a spectral echo of events long past playing out around him, showing Clan Campbell massacring Clan MacDonald, and "Red" Ian Og dying when he intervenes, stabbed with his own claymore, cursing the Campbells'

kith and kin with his final breath. Forcing himself to keep moving, Punisher reaches Ian Og's memorial, where he witnesses a vision of Og's body being found and a local crone imbuing Og's claymore with his restless spirit, destined to rise when Scotland needs him. As the criminals listen to Mingus' disapproving father, Angus, tell the Clansman's legend, Clansman finds Punisher, takes him to shelter and gives him herbs to purge the drugs from his system. Telling Punisher he's a regular man who shares his body with Ian Og, Clansman departs to slay the criminals, and Punisher forces himself to follow and help. Attacking simultaneously via different routes, they slaughter their way through the criminals until Angus intervenes, trying to order Clansman to depart. Mingus uses the distraction to shoot Clansman, but the dying specter impales him. After Punisher finishes off the remaining crooks, Clansman asks him to return the sword to its resting place, then changes back into Ferguson. Later, Punisher delivers the sword to Eilean Munde, where Og is buried, to wait for the next time Scotland needs its hero.

NOTE: Hardcover with a wraparound cover dust jacket. Includes title/credits page (2 pages). The 1692 Glencoe Massacre is a real historical event, still infamous in Scotland today. Eilean Munde (Island of Munde) is misspelled Ailean Munde.

PUNISHER #49 (June 1991)

"Death Below Zero" (22 pages)

CREDITS: Chuck Dixon (writer), Ron Wagner (art, c pencils), Chris Eliopoulos (letters), John Wellington (colors), Kevin Kobasic (asst editor), Don Daley (editor), Andy Kubert (c inks)
FEATURE CHARACTER: Punisher (next in Pun #50/2, '91 fb)
VILLAINS: Kidnappers inc Hennings, Lukens, Meglin & Meyer (all die)
OTHER CHARACTERS: Carla Summerville & her husband (both department store chain owners), pilot
LOCATIONS/ITEMS: Western Pennsylvania woods inc kidnappers' cabin / Punisher's car, G-3 battle rifle, handgun, grenades & shotgun mike, kidnappers' Jeep, guns & snowmobiles, Summerville's plane, tripwire, fallen tree
SYNOPSIS: Punisher leaves his car and stalks through the snow, seeking Carla Summerville & her kidnappers. He finds their cabin and watches three of them leave in a Jeep to pick up the ransom. When Frank breaks into the cabin he finds six more men. He helps Carla escape, killing four of them. He sends Carla to the car to wait for him, but she panics and leaves in the car. The men in the Jeep return with the ransom money and shoot Frank, but he escapes by stealing the Jeep, along with the money. When the Jeep runs off the road, Punisher sets a trap, killing Lukens with a grenade. The remaining four kidnappers track him on snowmobiles. Finding shelter, Frank burns some of the money to keep warm and sets out again the next morning. Furious over the burnt money, Meglin is decapitated when he carelessly crosses a tripwire on his snowmobile. The seventh kidnapper dies when his snowmobile plunges into a frozen river. Succumbing to his injury, Punisher finally collapses on the ice. Hennings and Meyer arrive and demand the money. Punisher gives them the money bag, but their combined weight cracks the ice and they fall beneath the surface and plummet over a waterfall.

PUNISHER #50 (July 1991)

"Yo Yo" (33 pages)

CREDITS: Mike Baron (writer), Hugh Haynes (pencils), Jimmy Palmiotti (inks), Ken Lopez (letters), Kevin Kobasic (asst editor), Don Daley (editor), Michael Golden (c art)
FEATURE CHARACTER: Punisher
SUPPORTING CAST: Microchip (last in Pun:Blood, '91)
VILLAINS: Yo-Yo Ng (designer/engineer) & his scientists (Barnes, Schultz, Woitz named, all die), Dolly (Ng's girlfriend)
OTHER CHARACTERS: Grand Couree Dam employees (Manuel Corona, Juan Gutierrez named) inc engineer (all deceased, mentioned only) & his mother, NASA (National Aeronautics & Space Administration, bts, believes Ng is doing space research), Colorado police (voice only, on radio), Schultz's father (bts, dying), WNEX-TV pilot (bts) & field crew, Arizona firefighters, police & EMTs, Astrex security guards, dam tour guide & visitors, disgruntled Colorado rancher, priest, waitress
LOCATIONS/ITEMS: Astrex Biosphere, Hubris, Arizona, inc control room, cryogenics chamber, hydroponics/oxygen generation lab & underground service entrance, southern Colorado inc Koala Color photo developing store & Grand Couree Dam w/ flood control gate, museum gift shop & turbine room, Manhattan inc diner, Punisher's apartment & church w/ confessional / AT&T Comsat satellite (bts), ambulance, Astrex Biosphere model, satellite uplink, sign & turbines, cryogenic container, documents, fire truck, forklift, Grand Couree Dam ladder & aqueduct diagram, Microchip's computer & telescope w/ case, Ng's razor-spiked yo-yo & sonic disruptor, police cars, priest's rosary, prop plane, Punisher's binoculars, knife, pistol, semi-automatic firearm, skateboard & grappling hook w/ launcher, radio headsets, rancher's tractor trailer cab, receipt, Schultz's journal, scuba suit, WNEX news van
SYNOPSIS: After confessing his sins to a priest, Frank Castle is approached by a woman who wants him to stop Yo-Yo Ng, the unscrupulous engineer who designed and built the Grand Couree Dam with substandard materials, with whom she invested her money and whom she suspects of being responsible for the death of her son, an engineer on the dam. Punisher and Microchip tour the dam and learn that Ng is holed up in a nearby biosphere. Castle sneaks into the dam's control room and finds evidence against Ng. When Ng learns of the break-in, he beheads Schultz, the scientist who left the evidence at the dam. Microchip informs Punisher that Ng is using the dam's power and the biosphere's uplink to access communications satellites to break the financial community's codes. Castle infiltrates the biosphere and mercy kills Schultz, whose head is cryogenically preserved. Ng orders all the biosphere's turbines activated, putting a strain on the dam, and as Punisher fights Ng, the dam breaks. Castle escapes and Ng is nowhere to be found.
NOTE: Colorist is uncredited.

2ND STORY: "Bark Like a Dog" (6 pages)
CREDITS: Marc McLaurin (writer), Roderick Delgado (pencils), Pat Redding (inks, colors), Jade Moede (letters), Kevin Kobasic (asst editor), Don Daley (editor)
FEATURE CHARACTER: Punisher (also in Azalee Martin's story, in fb between Pun #49-50, '91)
VILLAINS: Azalee Martin (gang leader, also in fb & his story) & his gang (all die in fb), Ryker's Island inmates
OTHER CHARACTERS: Rape victim (in fb & Martin's story), Ryker's Island Prison guards
LOCATIONS/ITEMS: Manhattan park (in fb & Martin's story), Ryker's Island Penitentiary / Azalee Martin's car, Punisher's Battle Van, tree (all in fb),

Martin's & Punisher's guns (in fb & Martin's story), Azalee Martin's gang's guns, Punisher's "death car" (both in Martin's story), prison barbells & bench press
FLASHBACK: When the Punisher appears in a Manhattan park to stop a gang leader and rapist named Azalee Martin, Martin panics and shoots his men before fleeing in a car that he crashes into a tree.
SYNOPSIS: Newly admitted to Ryker's Island Prison, Azalee Martin tries to impress fellow inmates with a fabricated story about how he survived an attack by the Punisher. Another inmate calls Martin on his lies and supplies the true story of the circumstances leading to Martin's arrest, based on police and coroner's reports and eyewitness accounts.

PUNISHER #51 (August 1991)

"Golden Buddha" (20 pages)

CREDITS: Mike Baron (writer), Tom Morgan (art), Ed Lazellari, Paul Mounts (colors), Kevin Kobasic (asst editor), Don Daley (editor)
FEATURE CHARACTER: Punisher (also as Richard Rook)
SUPPORTING CAST: Microchip (chr next in Pun #64, '92, next in Pun #53, '91)
VILLAINS: Camden Leung (Chinese colonel, also as cook Charlie Leung, dies) & his men (Chin named), Li Pung (Chinese general & restaurant owner), Royal Cobras (Vietnamese gang) inc Rupert Duc (Muay Thai fighter) & Terry Fong, Savage Tigers (Chinatown gang, branch of Hong Kong's White Lotus Society) inc sentry (dies), Harry & Marty Siu
OTHER CHARACTERS: Li Pung's employees inc Chin, FBI (bts, conducting racketeering investigations), Gloria Swanson (actress, on TV), bystanders, Chinatown residents, club & restaurant patrons
LOCATIONS/ITEMS: Manhattan inc Punisher's apartment, Savage Tigers' Pier 61 warehouse, Battery w/ Pearl of Shadowed Enlightenment warehouse & Chinatown w/ Khieu Gardens (Viet club), Golden Buddha restaurant, grocery store & subway entrance / Golden Buddha (Laotian statue), barrels & crates, chopsticks used as weapons by Punisher, Rupert Duc's pack of Lucky Strike cigarettes, Terry Fong's throwing star, forklift, Camden Leung's gun, Microchip's computer & TV, police cars w/ sirens, popcorn, Punisher's mini-Uzi, rope used to bind Leung, Royal Cobras' guns, Savage Tigers' guns, sentry's MAC-10 machine pistol, Marty Siu's blowtorch & lighter
SYNOPSIS: The Chinese Savage Tigers gang holds up a Chinatown restaurant and kidnaps its cook, Charlie Leung. The restaurant's owner, Li Pung, tells Frank Castle that the gang is extorting money from Leung, an illegal alien from Hong Kong. Punisher seeks assistance from a rival gang, the Vietnamese Royal Cobras. After proving himself in combat with the Cobras' Rupert Duc, Castle learns about a golden Buddha statue stolen by Chinese troops from a Laotian temple and brought to Manhattan. Knowing Leung's identity as a former Chinese colonel, the Tigers force him to show them the location of the Buddha in a Battery warehouse. Punisher and the Cobras follow and a firefight ensues. Duc kills Leung and Castle reports to Li Pung, aware now that the restaurant owner is the former Chinese general responsible for the Buddha's theft. Punisher threatens Li Pung into returning the statue to Laos.
NOTE: No credits are listed in the issue. Microchip watches the 1950 film, "Sunset Boulevard" and reveals he has repetitive motion stress syndrome. Story followed by pinups (2 pages) featuring Punisher & armed thugs in Punisher War Journal entry dated 1/11/91 (José Massaroli, art) & Punisher & Captain America in Punisher War Journal entry dated 3/28/91 (Scott Williams, art).

PUNISHER #52 (September 1991)

"Lupe" (22 pages)

CREDITS: Mike Baron (writer), Paul Guinan (pencils), Jimmy Palmiotti (inks), Ken Lopez (letters), Ed Lazellari (colors), Kevin Kobasic (asst editor), Don Daley (editor), Ron Harris (c pencils), Rodney Ramos (c inks)
FEATURE CHARACTER: Punisher (next in Pun #64-70, '92, Pun:GI #1-2, '93)
VILLAINS: Lupe Gutierrez (baby snatcher, former Mexican wrestler, dies), drug distributors
OTHER CHARACTERS: Bob & Margo Lynn Bartlett (see NOTE), Elinora (Bob Bartlett's assistant, voice only), Curtis Hoover (good Samaritan), Yolanda Juarez (new mother), Graciela Munoz (mother) (both die), Loreto Pinto (former drug dealer) & his friends, Rafe (boy), Ricardo (Juarez's & Pinto's baby, adoptive name Eric Kent Bartlett), Sanford Mandelbaum (Bartletts' attorney), Ruben Blades (Panamanian musician, on radio), hospital doctors & nurses inc Nurse Holly, Munoz's baby & family, graffitist, bystanders, bird
LOCATIONS/ITEMS: Manhattan inc Bartletts' 5th Ave home, Punisher's apartment, uptown hospital (see NOTE), alley, burned out building on 151st St, grocery store, rooftop, tenements & Lupe Gutierrez's apartment w/fire escape / Bob Bartlett's crib & lighter, drug distributors' guns, Lupe Gutierrez's pack of cigarettes, purse & revolver, Curtis Hoover's shotgun, Jolanda Juarez's baby medication & prescription form, Mercedes sedan w/ radio, Microchip's computer & modem, Graciela Munoz's baby stroller, playing cards, Punisher's concussion grenades, 9mm pistol, MAC-10 machine pistol, motorcycle & motorcycle helmet, release form, taxi cab, wallet w/ stolen cash & credit cards
SYNOPSIS: Shortly after being discharged from the hospital with her newborn son, Yolanda Juarez is killed and her baby stolen by Lupe Gutierrez, who sells the child to the Bartletts, a wealthy couple. While fighting drug distributors in uptown Manhattan, Frank Castle discovers Yolanda's corpse and sets out to find her missing baby. As he checks on the infant's father, a former drug dealer named Loreto Pinto, they learn of another baby snatching nearby. An eyewitness helps Punisher trace Lupe to her apartment, where she tends to the newly stolen child. Castle fights Lupe until she falls from a nearby rooftop. After returning the baby to his family, Punisher takes Yolanda's son from the Bartletts and delivers him to Pinto, who promises to look after him.
NOTE: Letters page includes LoC from future fiction writer Marcus Pelegrimas. Bartlett's wife is called both "Margo" and "Lynn." Named "Edgewater Hospital" on a sign, the hospital is called "St. Mary's" in dialog. The drug distributors deal in "Tango & Cash," designer smack named after the 1989 Sylvester Stallone/Kurt Russell action-comedy film.

PUNISHER #53 (October 1991)

"The Finger" (22 pages)

CREDITS: Mike Baron (writer), Hugh Haynes (pencils), Jim Palmiotti (inks), Chris Eliopoulos (letters), Marie Javins (colors), Kevin Kobasic (asst editor), Don Daley (editor)
FEATURE CHARACTER: Punisher (also in photo)
SUPPORTING CAST: Microchip (also in photo, last in Pun #51, '91, chr last in Pun:GI #2, '93)
VILLAINS: Kingpin (last in Sleep #6, '91, chr last in TM:BB #1, '95) & his employees inc Archie & Maureen, Howard Nees (Miami racketeer, also in photo, 1st) & his gang (Lyle named, some last in PWJ #34, '91), George Wong (now Kingpin's accountant & advisor, last in Pun #18, '89), synthetic smack manufacturers
OTHER CHARACTERS: Ishmael DeLeon (Howard Nees' front man), Mike Wallace (journalist) (all mentioned only), Doors (rock band, on poster), Hulk (as mask), Madonna (entertainer, in newspaper photo), Nakoma front desk clerk, New York City police, Toy Fair attendees, Robot B-9 (Lost in Space robot, as toy), bystanders
LOCATIONS/ITEMS: Manhattan inc dockside drug lab, Fisk Tower & Punisher's apartment / bed, cleaver, Kingpin's brain-zapping helmet, cigars, note, sub-freezing storage box & tea service, Kingpin's men's guns & missile launchers, manhole, Microchip's computer, newspaper clippings & poster, morphine, Howard Nees' transceiver, Nees's men's binoculars & guns, police cars & barricade tape, Punisher's Battle Van, machine pistol, missile launcher, pistol, sparring dummy, sticks, telephone, throwing knives & welding gloves & mask, smack manufacturers' barbecue fork, drug equipment & guns, George Wong's cigarette & valise w/ brass knuckles, photos, pistol, scissors, sticks of Big Red chewing gum & Perfect Fantasy Massage Parlor matches, New York Toy Fair displays inc dinosaur, inflatable clown, "Lost in Space" Robot, model aircraft, radio-controlled Bigfoot toy vehicle, toy motorcycle & video arcade w/ Frog Boil, Scud Busters & Tanks for the Memories video games
SYNOPSIS: Frank Castle busts a synthetic smack lab and learns racketeer Howard Nees supplied it. Concerned about Nees's encroachment on his business, Kingpin calls on George Wong, whose college education Kingpin funded. Wong suggests forcing Punisher to deal with Nees by threatening Microchip. Kingpin's employees kidnap Microchip from the New York Toy Fair, sever one of his fingers and deliver it to Castle with a note to report to the Fisk Building that night. Punisher creates a distraction by directing his auto-piloted Battle Van to smash the tower and lead Kingpin's men on a chase. Castle confronts Kingpin, who convinces him to smash Nees's rackets for Microchip's safety. Nees and his men spot Punisher sneaking out of Fisk Tower and decide to attack him.
NOTE: Cover labeled "The Final Days, Part One of Seven." Series published semi-monthly October 1991-January 1992. This issue reveals Microchip anonymously runs a legitimate business on the side and that one of his inventions ("Tank Fight," re-titled "Tanks for the Memories") is nominated for Best New Video Game at Toy Fair. One of the Toy Fair booth signs advertises "Waiting for Godot" action figures from Beckett Industries, a reference to the absurdist play by Irish writer, Samuel Beckett.

PUNISHER #54 (Early November 1991)

"The Squeeze" (22 pages)

CREDITS: Mike Baron (writer), Hugh Haynes (pencils), Jimmy Palmiotti (inks), Ken Lopez (letters), Marcus David (colors), Kevin Kobasic (asst editor), Don Daley (editor)
FEATURE CHARACTER: Punisher (next in Pun #57, '91 fb)
SUPPORTING CAST: Microchip
VILLAINS: Howard Nees (dies) & his men (Eddie, Gino & Spike named, all 3 die), Kingpin, George Wong
OTHER CHARACTERS: Max (Rottweiler, Punisher's guard dog, 1st but chr last in PWZ #37, '95, next in Pun #57, '91), New York City police
LOCATIONS/ITEMS: Central Park West inc Punisher's apartment (destroyed), Queens inc Aberg Trucking Company building & Punisher's safe house at 1708 Rush St (see NOTE) / Max's automatic feeder, sandbox (both bts), Punisher's remote control for Metzler electronic security system (see NOTE), knife, mini-Uzi, parachute, rope, Claymore mines w/ remote detonator & "unlimited freeway fighter" ($8 million assault vehicle, destroyed) w/ rocket, rocket launcher & transceiver, bone & dog bowl, armored car, Kingpin's ashtray, chess set, cigar, telephone & monitors, Microchip's bandage, sling, removable guitar & gold records, milk truck, Howard Nees's pistol, LAWS rocket, rocket launcher & pencil used as a weapon, Howard Nees's men's guns, police cars, guns & helicopters, semi-truck
SYNOPSIS: Spying Howard Nees's men waiting for him in his apartment, Frank Castle destroys the place by detonating a stash of Claymore mines he planted there. George Wong reports the explosion to Kingpin to the dismay of Microchip, who is playing chess with his captor. Both Wong and Punisher correctly surmise that Nees will attack Kingpin's trucking operation in Queens next. Castle heads to Queens, kills Nees's men, and slays Nees. As he attempts to flee the scene, Castle is cornered by police and forced to surrender.
NOTE: Cover labeled "The Final Days, Part Two of Seven." Story followed by pinups (2 pages) of Punisher & armed thugs (Tod Smith & Andrew Pepoy, art) & Punisher (Roderick Delgado, art). One of Microchip's gold records is revealed to be for "Gonna Cut You Down to Size," by Big Bore and the Blowhards. The Queens location of Kingpin's trucking company is referred to as Brooklyn in Pun #55, '91. The address of Punisher's Queens safe house and the name of its security system are revealed in Pun #56, '91.

PUNISHER #55 (Late November 1991)

"Plea Bargain" (21 pages)

CREDITS: Mike Baron (writer), Hugh Haynes (pencils), Jim Palmiotti (inks), Ken Lopez (letters), Marcus David (colors), Kevin Kobasic (asst editor), Don Daley (editor), Joe Quesada (c pencils)
FEATURE CHARACTER: Punisher (also in drawing)
SUPPORTING CAST: Microchip
VILLAINS: Kingpin, George Wong (both next in Pun #57, '91), Gregario (last in Pun #1, '86, chr last in Pun #56, '91 fb, now Ryker's Nubian Nation leader), Jigsaw (last in Pun #40, '90), Urso Merrick (head of Aryan Nation at Ryker's Island Penitentiary, 1st, bts, in prison), Tice (1st) & other Ryker's Island inmates inc Aryan Nation & Nubian Nation members, criminal detainees inc Bill
OTHER CHARACTERS: Pappy New Guinea (Ryker's Island inmate, 1st), Otto (Microchip's Zurich friend, voice

only), Mr. Creighton (lawyer from New York City District Attorney's Office), Duane Pritchard (public defender), Father Coughlin (priest), Charlene (prostitute, bts, working at SMD Club), news reporter (voice only), TV-8 cameraman & journalist, bailiff, court stenographer, judge, police, Ryker's Island Prison guards, Thai citizens inc Po, demonstrators, bystanders, oxen, rats; Max, Trust (both mentioned)

LOCATIONS/ITEMS: SMD Club (New York brothel), Brooklyn inc NYPD Precinct 13 & Men's Detention Center w/ holding cell, New York courthouse w/ judge's chamber, Ryker's Island Penitentiary inc cells & shower, Thailand inc Pak Chong, farm fields & rural lading strip / extradition request from Dade County, FL, Kingpin's cigars & limousine, Microchip's bag & bandage, Po's motorcycle, police monitors, prisoner transport vehicle, Duane Pritchard's briefcase, pencil & drawings, prop plane, Tice's knife, TV-8 news van

SYNOPSIS: Deposited by George Wong in rural Thailand, Microchip makes his way to a local village, where he calls a friend for help. Secretly paid off by Kingpin, public defender Duane Pritchard meets with the incarcerated Frank Castle while the vigilante's supporters picket the New York police station where he is held. The police turn a blind eye when Punisher fights detainees in the station's holding cell. At Castle's arraignment, Pritchard gets Punisher's first degree murder charges reduced to manslaughter and the judge, also under Kingpin's influence, sentences him to three consecutive ten-year sentences at Ryker's Island Penitentiary. Castle is admitted to Ryker's, gets into a fight with another inmate, and meets old foe Jigsaw and the head of the prison's Nubian Nation, Gregario.

NOTE: Cover labeled "The Final Days, Part Three of Seven." Story followed by pinup (1 page) of Punisher & armed thugs (Mark Pacella & M.M. Ritter, art). Punisher's Ryker's Island prisoner number is 64110958. This issue reveals that he has a 32-inch waist and a 34 inseam and wears size 12 shoes. Ryker's is spelled Rikers here and in some subsequent issues.

PUNISHER #56 (Early December 1991)

"The Jailhouse Rock" (22 pages)

CREDITS: Mike Baron (writer), Hugh Haynes (pencils), Jim Palmiotti (inks), Ken Lopez (letters), Marcus David (colors), Kevin Kobasic (asst editor), Don Daley (editor), Joe Quesada (c pencils)

FEATURE CHARACTER: Punisher

SUPPORTING CAST: Microchip

VILLAINS: Don Carlo Cervello (bts, in hospital, last in Pun #1, '86, last app), Jigsaw (next in PWJ #61, '93), Urso "Hog" Merrick (1st actual app, nickname revealed), Pike's 2 associates inc Manny (see NOTE), Tice (last app), Gregario, Ryker's Island corrupt prison guard & inmates inc Aryan Nation & Nubian Nation members

OTHER CHARACTERS: Derek "Cannibal" Pike (Ryker's Island inmate), Max, Otto (both mentioned only), Pappy New Guinea, Bangkok residents inc children, hair stylist, store owners & travel agent

LOCATIONS/ITEMS: Bangkok inc Bangkok Travel Agency, Concepts Unlimited Hair Salon & store w/ American Express desk, Ryker's Island Penitentiary inc cells, infirmary, mess hall, utility room & visiting room / video arcade games (see NOTE), briefcase w/cash & passport, knives, Microchip's Rolex & disguise inc colored contact lenses, fake beard & hairpiece, morphine, Pike's men's boat & rocket launcher

SYNOPSIS: In Ryker's Island Penitentiary, Jigsaw, Gregario and his men gang up on Frank Castle until fellow inmate, Hog Merrick, interrupts the fight. Punisher declines Hog's invitation to join Aryan Nation and makes another enemy. In Bangkok, Microchip picks up money sent to him by a friend and adopts a disguise before flying back to New York. He visits Castle and agrees to look after Punisher's safe house guard dog, Max. Wishing to help Castle, inmate Cannibal Pike slips him a knife, which comes in handy when Jigsaw, Gregario and company ambush Punisher again. Jigsaw carves up Castle's face and Punisher ends up in the prison infirmary, joined by the badly burned Pike, who was attacked because he helped Castle. Pike tells Punisher to take his place in a prison break he arranged earlier. Castle escapes the prison and swims to a getaway boat piloted by Pike's associates, who mistake the bandaged vigilante for Pike himself.

NOTE: Cover labeled "The Final Days, Part Four of Seven." Creators and editor in chief Tom DeFalco are drawn in credits. Manny's name is revealed next issue. Microchip's video game is here re-titled "Tank Attack."

PUNISHER #57 (Late December 1991)

"America's Most Hunted" (22 pages)

CREDITS: Mike Baron (writer), Hugh Haynes (pencils), Jimmy Palmiotti (inks), Ken Lopez (letters), Marie Javins (colors), Kevin Kobasic (asst editor), Don Daley (editor), Eliot R. Brown (c art)

FEATURE CHARACTER: Punisher (also on TV, also in fb Pun #54-55, '91)

SUPPORTING CAST: Microchip

VILLAINS: Kingpin (bts, has George Wong follow Microchip), George Wong (both last in Pun #55, '91), Derek Pike's 2 associates inc Manny, Queens gang bangers (die), drug dealer, mugger

OTHER CHARACTERS: Max (last in Pun #54, '91, next in PWJ #59, '93), host of TV's "America's Most Wanted" show, TV cameraman, bystanders

LOCATIONS/ITEMS: Brooklyn's Red Hook section inc Pike's associates' base w/ bedroom & fire escape, Queens inc Punisher's weapons warehouse / Punisher's automatic pistols (also on TV), assault rifle, assault vehicle, bandages, grenade, knife & Metzler electronic security system w/ camera, lock & monitor, beer bottle used as weapon by Punisher, Microchip's car, disguise & pistol, mirror shard, mugger's crack pipe & knife, Pike's associates' gun & television, George Wong's butterfly knife, car, pistol & spectrographic scanner, TV camera

FLASHBACK: Punisher poses for his mug shot following his arrest.

SYNOPSIS: Frank Castle flees from his rescuers' Brooklyn base when they discover he's not Derek Pike. Badly injured, Punisher is barely able to defeat a drug dealer before he removes his bandages and sees his horribly scarred face. Microchip arrives at Punisher's secret safe house in Queens but is forced to fetch his equipment when he cannot unscramble the lock. After watching Microchip from nearby, George Wong gains entry into the safe house. Punisher's guard dog Max attacks Wong, who is forced to flee after wounding the dog. Castle arrives at the safe house, and as he tends to Max, gangbangers enter and help themselves to Punisher's weapons. The enraged Castle retaliates, slaying the trespassers before collapsing at Microchip's feet.

NOTE: Cover labeled "The Final Days, Part Five of Seven." Issue also appears w/ photo cover & outer cover w/ Punisher wanted poster on back. No credits are listed in the issue. Story followed by pinups (2 pages) of Punisher & Reavers (Bonebreaker, Skullbuster & Pretty Boy; Ed Lazellari & Bud LaRosa, art) & Punisher & armed thugs (Mark Bagley & Donald C. Hudson, art).

PUNISHER #58 (Early January 1992)

"The Noose Tightens" (22 pages)

CREDITS: Mike Baron (writer), Hugh Haynes (pencils), Jim Palmiotti (inks), Ken Lopez (letters), Marie Javins (colors), Kevin Kobasic (asst editor), Don Daley (editor), Michael Golden (c art)
FEATURE CHARACTER: Punisher (also in photo)
SUPPORTING CAST: Microchip
VILLAINS: Miltion Melchior, Screwtop (Jacques Delacroix's representatives, both 1st), Byron Ballymor (Kingpin's operative, dies), Mr. Deems (Kingpin's operative, bts, in SUV, 1st), Fleet Street Maulers (New York gang), Kingpin, George Wong, Kingpin's men, New York criminals
OTHER CHARACTERS: Art (George Wong's accountant uncle), Dr. Melinda Brewer (junkie plastic surgeon, 1st), Jacques Delacroix (leader of Red Hares Jamaican posse, bts, writes letter, 1st), Reeves (George's chauffeur, 1st), Sting (rock musician, on poster), Art's assistant, bystanders, homeless people
LOCATIONS/ITEMS: New York inc Mulberry Park (abandoned Queens amusement park), Alcatraz Bar, Bowery, Chinatown, Harlem, New York Public Library, apartment #3413 used by Jacques Delacroix's men & Fisk Tower w/ Kingpin's office, putting green & training room / Punisher's assault rifles & automatic pistols (also in photo), criminal's Armani suit, Jacques Delacroix's letter, Fleet Street Maulers' automatic firearms, garbage truck, homeless people's shopping cart & tent, Kingpin's cigars, damaged desk & golf bag, clubs & ball, Kingpin's men's SUV, Microchip's disguise & gun, morphine, Mulberry Park rides, ticket booth & funhouse w/ car, dummies, props & track, photo of Punisher, posters, Punisher's MAC-10 machine pistols, George Wong's arm sling, butterfly knife, car, cigar & limousine
SYNOPSIS: Kingpin spreads the word among New York's lowlifes to find and kill the injured Frank Castle. George Wong ignores his uncle's plea to stop working for the crime lord and meets with representatives of Jacques Delacroix, the leader of a Jamaican posse with whom Kingpin wishes to do business. Gang members find Punisher holed up in the funhouse of an abandoned amusement park and a gunfight ensues. Castle defeats his attackers with the help of Microchip, who arranges for him to undergo plastic surgery to repair his disfigured face. When Punisher meets with surgeon and drug addict Melinda Brewer, Kingpin's men attack.
NOTE: Cover labeled "The Final Days, Part Six of Seven." Story followed by pinups (2 pages) of Punisher & armed divers (Michael Ritter, art) & Punisher & tribal warriors (Michael Ritter & Bob McLeod, art). Reeves' name is revealed in Pun #59, '92.

PUNISHER #59 (Late January 1992)

"Changes" (21 pages)

CREDITS: Mike Baron (writer), Hugh Haynes (pencils), Jim Palmiotti (inks, c pencils), Ken Lopez (letters), Marie Javins (colors), Kevin Kobasic (asst editor), Don Daley (editor), Mark Texeira (c inks)
FEATURE CHARACTER: Punisher (also in own dream, also as Frank Castiglione in fb between Pun #100, '95 fb & Pun #18, '97 fb)
SUPPORTING CAST: Microchip (next in PWJ #39, '92), Maria Castiglione (in Punisher's dream; in fb between Pun #100, '95 fb & Pun:AG, '88 fb)
VILLAINS: Kingpin (also in dream, next in DD #297, '91) & his men, Mr. Deems (dies), George Wong (next in Pun #61, '92), Scooter, Ziggy (both drug addicts)
OTHER CHARACTERS: Reeves, Dr. Melinda Brewer, US Marines (in fb); Gregario, Jigsaw, guards (prev 3 in Punisher's dream)
LOCATIONS/ITEMS: DuWayne Corp's upstate New York chemical plant inc infirmary, Manhattan inc Central Park (in dream), dock (in fb), highway, New York Public Library, Chrysler Building w/ gargoyle & Fisk Tower w/ airshaft & Kingpin's office / chains, guard's guns, Jigsaw's knife (all in dream), Marines' duffle bags & ship (in fb), medical equipment & instruments (inc clamps, scalpels, syringes & anesthetic canister & mask), bottle of pills, car, cooler, cot, Kingpin's abacus & cigar, Kingpin's men's SUV, Microchip's bubble gum, cleaning cloth, disguise, receiver, transmitter & surveillance device w/ headset & laser, mirror, morphine, Punisher's assault rifles & bandages, scrubs, George Wong's $5 bill & limousine, Ziggy's pistol
FLASHBACK: A pregnant Maria Castiglione bids her husband Frank goodbye as he leaves for a tour of duty with the Marines.
SYNOPSIS: Frank Castle kills Kingpin's men and Dr. Brewer drives him to a deserted infirmary in upstate New York. Microchip eavesdrops on Kingpin and George Wong and plants a transmitter on Wong's limousine as he leaves to continue his deal with the Jamaican posse. As Brewer prepares for surgery on Punisher's face, two drug addicts break into the infirmary and the doctor is forced to kill them with Castle's rifle. At Punisher's request, she applies her experiments with tissue regeneration and melanin to change his appearance. After five days of delirious dreaming, Castle wakes to discover his face is healed and his skin is now black.
NOTE: Cover labeled "The Final Days, Part Seven of Seven." Story followed by pinup (1 page) of Punisher & Asian opponents (Michael Ritter, art). The scenes from Punisher's dream are based on events from his past, but altered by his delirium, and thus are not considered true flashbacks. Wong is called "Mr. Tam" in this issue; Tam may be an alias, a middle name, or non-Anglicized first name.

PUNISHER #60 (February 1992)

"Escape from New York" (19 pages)

CREDITS: Mike Baron (plot, script), Marcus McLaurin (script), Val Mayerik (pencils), Al Williamson (inks), Dave Sharpe (letters), Marie Javins (colors), Kevin Kobasic (asst editor), Don Daley (editor)
FEATURE CHARACTER: Punisher (also in rfb, as Frank Rook)
GUEST STAR: Luke Cage (Carl Lucas, Hero for Hire, last in Cage #2, '92)
VILLAINS: El Rukens (Chicago street gang, 1st), Rinaldo (drug dealer)
OTHER CHARACTERS: Gregario, Jigsaw, Kingpin & his men, Microchip, Howard Nees & one of his men, "Cannibal" Pike's associates, George Wong, inmates, judge, police (all in rfb), Spike Johansen, Mojo Murchison (both smack dealers), Little Billy Higgins (Chicago vigilante) (prev 3 mentioned only), Dr. Melinda Brewer (also in rfb, next in Pun #62, '92), Aisha (Chicago girl, 1st), Illinois Auxiliary Police, Chicago boy & homeless men, rats
LOCATIONS/ITEMS: New York City inc courthouse, Fisk Tower, Queens & Ryker's Island Penitentiary (all in rfb), DuWayne Corp's upstate New York chemical plant inc infirmary (also in rfb), New York State Thruway, Chicago inc highway ramps, Sears Tower & South Side inc Cage's apartment w/ bedroom & Royal Tuck Hotel w/ basement, elevator & lobby / inmates' knives, judge's gavel, Kingpin's cigar, Kingpin's men's

guns, Microchip's disguise, mirror, Pike's men's boat, police guns (all in rfb), Punisher's assault rifles (also in rfb), basketball, bottle of Dexedrine, Cage's rental car, corporate fleet car, El Rukens' baseball bat, knife, pistols & rifles, police cars, gun & nightsticks, Punisher's firearms, safe & weapons cabinet
FLASHBACK: When Kingpin forces Frank Castle to kill Howard Nees, Punisher is arrested and sentenced to prison, where Jigsaw carves up his face. After Castle escapes, Microchip hooks him up with a surgeon who fixes his face and changes his skin color (Pun #53-59, '91-92).
SYNOPSIS: Eager to leave New York, the transformed Frank Castle drives to Chicago to retrieve weapons and cash from a safe stash he has in the basement of a Chicago hotel. In Chicago, bigoted police pull him over and provoke him into fighting them. Local hero for hire Luke Cage encounters the melee and rescues Punisher. Going by the name Frank Rook, Castle tricks Cage into helping him access his stash. After fighting a street gang called El Rukens, the duo discovers that the money is gone but the weapons are still present. Realizing that Rook scammed him, Cage persuades Punisher to repay him by helping him expel El Rukens from the local neighborhood.
NOTE: Story followed by pinup (1 page) of Punisher & Luke Cage in his Power Man costume (Mark D. Bright & Daniel Panosian, art). Erroneously called "El Rubens" once by Cage, El Rukens is based on the real-life Chicago gang, El Rukn.

PUNISHER #61 (March 1992)

"Crackdown" (20 pages)

CREDITS: Mike Baron (plot), Marcus McLaurin (script), Val Mayerik (pencils), Al Williamson (inks), Dave Sharpe (letters), Marie Javins (colors), Tim Tuohy (asst editor), Don Daley (editor)
FEATURE CHARACTER: Punisher (as Frank Rook)
GUEST STAR: Luke Cage
VILLAINS: George Wong (last in Pun #59, '92), Mr. Rudy (smack dealer, dies), El Rukens inc Wrench (dies) & Zig, Elio "Angel" Angelopoulos III (Chicago crime lord, last in Cage #1, '92) & his men
OTHER CHARACTERS: Chicago South Side residents inc Aisha (last app to date), Keisha & Melva (both 1st)
LOCATIONS/ITEMS: Elio Angelopoulos' conference room on Chicago's Gold Coast, Chicago's South Side inc apartment building, Bensley Park playground, Bird's Tavern / basketball hoop, mannequins, phone booth, playground equipment, Punisher's assault rifle & revolver, Rudy's conference table & surveillance monitors, El Rukens' guns & knives, smoke grenade, stick used as a weapon, Wrench's wrench
SYNOPSIS: Aiming to purge El Rukens from the South Side apartment building of innocent Chicago residents, the black "Frank Rook" poses as a drug client and meets the gang's smack supplier, Mr. Rudy. The infiltration goes poorly and Punisher is forced to retreat. Gang members assault the women who hired Luke Cage to oppose them, but Cage and Rook fight them off. That night, Punisher and Cage raid the apartment building and protect the remaining residents during the ensuing firefight. To Cage's dismay, Rook kills Rudy and a gangbanger named Wrench. George Wong meets with Elio Angelopoulos III, a Chicago crime lord upset about El Rukens' defeat. Wong offers his services to retaliate.
NOTE: Wong is a free agent following Kingpin's fall from power in DD #300, '92.

PUNISHER #62 (April 1992)

"Fade…to White" (23 pages)

CREDITS: Mike Baron (plot), Marcus McLaurin (script), Val Mayerik (pencils), Al Williamson (inks), Dave Sharpe (letters), Marie Javins (colors), Tim Tuohy (asst editor), Don Daley (editor), Joe Quesada (c pencils)
FEATURE CHARACTER: Punisher (as Frank Rook, also in rfb, next in Cage #3-4, '92, PunHol #1/3, '93, MHol, '91/3, PWJ #38-41, '92, Pun:GF, '92)
GUEST STAR: Luke Cage (next in Cage #3, '92)
VILLAINS: George Wong (dies), Elio Angelopoulos III (dies) & his men inc Spike, South Side criminals
OTHER CHARACTERS: Frank Castle Jr., Lisa Castle, Maria Castle (all in rfb), Dr. Melinda Brewer (last in Pun #60, '92, next in PWJ #68, '94), Chicago South Side residents inc Keisha & Melva, chauffeur (bts, driving limousine), female decoy
LOCATIONS/ITEMS: Central Park (in rfb), Elio Angelopoulos' headquarters on Chicago's Gold Coast inc conference room & shipping room, Chicago's South Side inc Cage's apartment & Harkness rug store / bullets, kite (both in rfb), crime lord's baseball bat, spot lamps & media console w/ monitors, Angelopoulos's men's assault rifles, automatic pistols, plastic net, rocket launcher & truck, criminals' knives & pistol, Punisher's revolver, ropes used to bind Punisher, George Wong's knife & limousine
FLASHBACK: Frank Castle's family is gunned down (MP #2, '75).
SYNOPSIS: George Wong tells Elio Angelopoulos the black Frank Rook is really the Punisher and accepts funding from the gangster to prove it. In return for shelter, Rook helps Luke Cage as an unarmed crime fighter on Chicago's South Side. Wong tracks down Rook and forces Melinda Brewer, whom he's located and drugged, to identify him as Punisher. Lured by a staged mugging planned by Wong, Rook is subdued and driven to Angelopoulos's headquarters, where Wong tries to force him to admit he's Frank Castle. Rook pulls out a revolver and shoots Wong in the head. As Brewer's injections wear off, turning Punisher's skin back to white, Cage bursts on the scene. Punisher breaks free of his bonds and helps Cage defeat Angelopoulos and his men. Upset at Castle's deception, Cage insists that Punisher owes him again, but Castle leaves, convinced that he needs to resume his ruthless brand of justice.
NOTE: Story followed by pinup (1 page) of Punisher, Luke Cage in his Power Man costume & bar patrons (Mark D. Bright, art).

THE PUNISHER: G FORCE (1992)

"G Force" (46 pages)

CREDITS: Mike Baron (writer), Hugh Haynes (pencils), Jimmy Palmiotti (inks), Ken Branch (bg inks), Ken Lopez (letters), Gregory Wright, Marie Javins (colors), Joe Kaufman (book designs), Tim Tuohy (asst editor), Don Daley (editor), Stephanie Fogle (manufacturing), Mark A. Nelson (c art)
FEATURE CHARACTER: Punisher (also as Carlo, next in PWZ #1-11, '92-93, PunSS #2, '92, MK #35-37, '92, Pun #63, '92)
SUPPORTING CAST: Microchip (last in PWJ #39, '92, next in PWZ #1, '92)
VILLAINS: Willie Chauvin (also on computer screen, drug-smuggling astronaut, dies) & his goons (some die) inc Gerard (dies), Uncle Snake (pimp, dies)
OTHER CHARACTERS: Janelle (Willie Chauvin's fling, dies), Julius (Microchip's friend), waiter, party guests, prostitutes, reporter, policemen, Francostar employees (prev 3 TV only), Gruber Massingal, Jean Disecle, Farouk

Daoud (all also on computer screen, astronauts), D'Azur bar patrons & barman, Ramona (French prostitute, dies), French hotel clerk, French Guyanan bystanders, Francostar security personnel, Murgtroid (60-pound boa constrictor), astronauts inc Bertrand

LOCATIONS/ITEMS: New York inc Francostar party penthouse, Punisher's HQ; Marseilles, France inc D'Azur bar, Pensiones building, Federal Express building, Willie Chauvin's mansion, Francostar building; Belizon, French Guyana inc Francostar Launch Facility, Francostar space station (destroyed) w/laser; North African desert / Uncle Snake's car (license plate SNAKE 1), gun & chains, Punisher's knife & motorcycle, Gerard's drugs & car, Microchip's anti-accelerant pills, Chauvin family armor & pike, Francostar centrifuge, personnel carrier & space shuttle, Willie Chauvin's Mirage jet, pressure suit, rivet gun, astronauts' space suits, oxygen bottle, butane lighter

SYNOPSIS: At a penthouse party French astronaut Willie Chauvin introduces partygoer Janelle to cocaine, while in the street down below Punisher attacks pimp Uncle Snake, who proves unexpectedly strong, nearly shooting Punisher before Janelle lands on Snake's car, killing both herself and the pimp. Learning from Microchip that Janelle was attending a Francostar aerospace party, and that astronaut Willie is heir to Marseilles' Chauvin crime family, Punisher travels to France to investigate. As "Carlo," he buys cocaine from local drug pusher Gerard, which Micro analyzes, finding traces of rocket fuel. Punisher follows Gerard to Willie's mansion, but is captured while breaking in. Wanting to find out who Punisher is, Willie leaves Gerard to interrogate him, using the centrifuge machine as a torture device, but Punisher frees himself using the emergency release lever and learns from Gerard that Willie has gone to French Guyana for an impending shuttle launch. Racing there in Willie's stolen jet, Punisher sneaks on to the launch site, knocks out astronaut Gruber Massingal and takes his place onboard the space shuttle. Once onboard the Francostar space station, Punisher fights Willie, who takes refuge inside the station's hub. Punisher reveals to the other astronauts that Chauvin is processing drugs at the launch site and using his diplomatic immunity to smuggle the drugs, and they realize he has been using the space station's laser to fry rival druglords' facilities on Earth. As Chauvin attempts to vent the rest of the station's oxygen and turn the laser on California, Punisher confronts him and ignites an oxygen tank, killing Chauvin. Punisher targets Chauvin's mansion with the laser, then escapes the station with the astronauts just before the fire he started reaches the other oxygen tanks. Hijacking the shuttle, Punisher has it land in the North African desert, where he is picked up by Microchip's friend Julius.

NOTE: Includes credits page (interior front cover) & title page (2 pages) w/art taken from page 34. Back cover art taken from page 29, panel 5.

PUNISHER #63 (May 1992)

"The Big Check-Out" (20 pages)

CREDITS: Chuck Dixon (writer), Tod Smith (pencils), Joe Rubinstein & Co. (inks), Jim Novak (letters), Marie Javins (colors), Tim Tuohy (asst editor), Don Daley (editor), Mark Texeira (c art)
FEATURE CHARACTER: Punisher (next in MK #38, '92, PWJ #42-44, '92, Pun:Easy, '92)
VILLAINS: Junkie thieves: Fred, Leon, Mike, Ralph (all die)
OTHER CHARACTERS: Shoppers, bystanders, child shoplifters, Goliath supermarket employees inc Lurlene, Mr. Wolff (store manager) & security guard, police officers, lobsters
LOCATIONS/ITEMS: Junkie's apartment, Goliath Supermarket inc manager's office / junkie's masks (2 pantyhose, 1 hockey mask & 1 balaclava), van & shotguns, Punisher's bandana, shopping trolleys, Rock magazine, Casa del Pizza pizza box, Ramco toys (inc Army Soldiers & Farm Animals), Hershey's Bar, cereals inc Cheerios, Beasties & Totalled

SYNOPSIS: While junkies prepare to rob a local business for drug money, Punisher is shopping at a nearby Goliath Supermarket. He deters some young shoplifters before the junkies invade the store. Alerted by the sound of them gunning down the security guard, Punisher covertly assesses the situation. When the junkies take the manager into the back safe, Punisher tells an employee to evacuate people out the fire exit, then sneaks up on and fatally stabs Leon, the crook with the manager. Firing Leon's shotgun, Punisher lures two of the junkies away from the hostages at the front of store, and tricks them into shooting a trolley full of ammonia and chlorine bleach, which combine to produce phosgene gas, then guns them down. The last junkie, their leader, Mike, takes an employee, Lurlene, hostage but Punisher tricks Mike by handing him a bag containing a live lobster instead of the back safe's cash. When Mike reaches into the bag it attacks him, and he lets go of his hostage. Punisher guns Mike down, and escapes just before the police arrive.

NOTE: This issue includes a Punisher pinup by Han Nguyen (pencils) & Bob McLeod (inks).

THE PUNISHER: DIE HARD IN THE BIG EASY (1992)

"Die Hard in the Big Easy" (46 pages)

CREDITS: John Wagner (writer), Phil Gascoine (art), Mike Heisler, Jon Babcock (letters), Steve Buccellato (colors), Joe Kaufman, Kevin Somers (designers), Paula Foye (asst editor), Marie Javins (editor), Carl Potts (exec editor)
FEATURE CHARACTER: Punisher (also in pfb, next in Pun/BW, '92)
SUPPORTING CAST: Microchip (last in PWJ #43, '92, next in Pun #71, '92; also in pfb)
VILLAINS: Mortician (Toussaint Murrow, voodoo leader, dies) & his followers (most die) (both also in pfb), Silk (pair of cocaine dealers, both die), drug dealers (all die), Roach (J. C. "Rocky" Rochechouart, drug-running driver, dies), Harold James Monsarrat ("Mr M," New Orleans druglord socialite, dies) & his lackeys (some die) inc Hank, Kleever, Wilt, Curly (prev 4 die), Kenny (prev 10 pfb only) & Billy (also in pfb, dies)
OTHER CHARACTERS: NYPD officers, Carnival partygoers, Gwendoline Monsarrat (Harold's daughter) (all pfb only), Jonas Jackson (New Orleans resident), Andy (Jonas' dog), trucker, New Orleans policeman, Monsarrat's party guests inc "General" (also bts in pfb), alligator, corpses
LOCATIONS/ITEMS: New York inc warehouse (in pfb only), Microchip's warehouse (also in pfb); New Orleans inc Punisher's hotel, Cajun Kitchens building (both pfb only), Harold Monsarrat's plantation (also in pfb), Baron Cemetery building (also in pfb, Mortician's HQ) / Silk's cocaine, Roach's driver's license, Punisher's Battle Van, chicken gumbo cans (all pfb only), police car, truck, Monsarrat's riverboat, Monsarrat's men's vehicles & guns (some in pfb), Mortician's men's shovels (in pfb) & guns, Silk's guns (in pfb), Monsarrat dummy, coffins (1 in pfb), Andy's shovel, Mortician's staff (shoots paralyzing darts) w/hidden blade, voodoo paraphernalia inc Punisher doll
FLASHBACK: After killing Silk, a duo of drug traffickers, the Punisher finds their dead driver, J. C. Rochechouart, came from New Orleans. Going there, Punisher searches Rochechouart's hotel rooms, but the clerk, Kenny, is working for Rochechouart's boss, New Orleans socialite Harold Monsarrat, and sends Punisher into an ambush in an abandoned Cajun Kitchens factory. He kills his attackers, prompting Monsarrat to

hire voodoo assassin and undertaker the Mortician, who finds Punisher back at the hotel getting Monsarrat's name out of a terrified Kenny. The Mortician drugs Punisher and prepares him to be buried alive, intending to raise him as a zombie (p).

SYNOPSIS: The Mortician and his followers bury the Punisher alive, unaware New Orleans resident Jonas Jackson is watching. Jackson digs Punisher up, and the Punisher has Microchip research Monsarrat, learning he is has political ambitions for a failing family business, and so has turned to drug dealing for easy financing. Visiting Monsarrat's plantation Punisher finds Monsarrat throwing a gambling themed costume party aboard a riverboat, and crashes the party to shoot Monsarrat dead in front of his guests. Punisher next captures the Mortician, and buries the terrified man alive at the same spot where Mortician interred him earlier. Jonas Jackson again secretly observes the burial, but decides not to unearth this coffin.

NOTE: Includes title/credits page (2 pages). Mortician's real name is revealed in MEnc #5, '04.

PUNISHER #64 (June 1992)

"Eurohit, 1 of 7: Arrivals" (20 pages)

CREDITS: Dan Abnett, Andy Lanning (writers), Doug Braithwaite (pencils), Al Williamson (inks), Ken Lopez (letters), Christie Scheele (colors), Tim Tuohy (asst editor), Don Daley (editor)
FEATURE CHARACTER: Punisher (also in photos, chr last in Pun #52, '91, see NOTE)
SUPPORTING CAST: Microchip (last in Pun #51, '91)
VILLAINS: Kingpin (in pfb, last in Sleep #6, '91), Miles Bentley (Kingpin's UK representative, in pfb, 1st), Snakebite (Aaron Cashin, contract killer, 1st), smugglers employed by Clippers (shady international haulage company) inc Arthur ("Arfur"), Den (both die) & bookkeeper
OTHER CHARACTERS: Interpol agents: Superintendent Coldstream (next in Pun #70, '92) & Magpies One, Two & Three; Outlaw (Nigel Higgins, vigilante, 1st), Morgan Sinclair (TransMarche Link engineering supervisor, 1st), news reporter (voice only, on TV), TML engineers inc Richards (dies), air travelers, customs official, bystanders
LOCATIONS/ITEMS: Brussels, Belgium, Gander, Newfoundland, New York, Oslo, Norway, Reykjavik, Iceland (all mentioned as places Punisher has just been), Cheriton, Kent, England & Coquelles, France inc Chunnel (Channel Tunnel) service tunnel, London inc Heathrow Airport (in pfb), London Docklands Airport, Battersea w/ Outlaw's base & Holborn w/ Smithfield's Meat Market / Outlaw's security system (inc halogen dazzler array, high-pressure hoses, sting-ball grenades & taser, all bts, & perimeter alarm), Heckler & Koch assault rifle, computer, motorcycle, helmet, pistol, 686 revolver, target dummy, television & photos of Punisher; Space Invaders (video game, mentioned only), baggage carousel & carts, bookkeeper's personal organizer, Chunnel tram, Clippers assault rifles, rocket launcher & truck, entrance gate, forklift, Interpol agents' earpiece transceivers & revolvers, jet airliner, Kawasaki KLR motorcycle, luggage, Microchip's assault gear, rental van & rifle, press microphones, Punisher's briefcase, Snakebite's car, tear gas grenades
FLASHBACK: When Wilson Fisk arrives in London to chair a meeting about the construction of the Chunnel, his UK representative, Miles Bentley, holds a press conference.
SYNOPSIS: When Frank Castle arrives in London in pursuit of an assassin named Snakebite, he is intercepted by Interpol agents but is rescued by Outlaw, a Punisher-idolizing vigilante targeted by Snakebite. Microchip follows Punisher to Outlaw's base, where the three men learn that Kingpin is in England for a meeting of Chunnel business interests. That night, Outlaw leads Castle and Microchip to an illegal arms shipment conducted by a shady international haulage company. After a gun battle, Punisher and Outlaw hijack the smugglers' truck and, with Microchip following behind, track Snakebite to the Chunnel, the site of the next shipment. After wounding Outlaw, Snakebite flees and takes Morgan Sinclair, a Chunnel engineer, hostage. He rides a tram through a service tunnel to France, with Punisher pursuing on a motorcycle.
NOTE: Story followed by pinup (1 page) of Punisher and Typhoid (John Czop, art). The Eurohit story arc (Pun #64-70, '92) occurs out of sequence with other issues of this title, before Pun #53, '91. Snakebite's name revealed in OHMU:U #3, '10. The real Chunnel was completed in 1994.

PUNISHER #65 (Early July 1992)

"Eurohit, 2 of 7: French Connections" (20 pages)

CREDITS: Dan Abnett, Andy Lanning (writers), Dougie Braithwaite (pencils), Al Williamson (inks), Ken Lopez (letters), Ian Laughlin (colors), Tim Tuohy (asst editor), Don Daley (editor)
FEATURE CHARACTER: Punisher
SUPPORTING CAST: Microchip
VILLAINS: Batroc (Georges Batroc, French mercenary & savate master, last in MCP #97/4, '92), Armand Chauffard (French computer hacker & pilot, 1st), Rapido (Roussel Dupont, French weaponsmith, 1st), Miles Bentley, Kingpin, Snakebite, Interpol cell guard
OTHER CHARACTERS: Philippe Delon (French construction executive) & his associates (all as corpses), Outlaw, Morgan Sinclair
LOCATIONS/ITEMS: Battersea, London inc Outlaw's base, Coquelles, France inc Chunnel service tunnel, Paris inc Eiffel Tower, Kingpin's office, meeting room, rooftops & Interpol holding station w/ cell, Vosges, France inc Philippe Delon's villa / Miles Bentley's briefcase, CD player, cot, Armand Chauffard's assault helicopter w/ missile, Philippe Delon's security camera & monitor, handcuffs w/ key, headsets, helicopter, hit list, Kawasaki KLR motorcycle, Kingpin's cigar, Outlaw's arm sling, computer & Heckler & Koch assault rifle, Punisher's bandages, Rapido's rotary cannon, Batroc's Kevlar costume, searchlight, smugglers' firearms, Snakebite's automatic pistols, revolver & wrist pistols, speaker phones
SYNOPSIS: Frank Castle assaults Snakebite but is taken by surprise when the assassin shoots him with hidden wrist pistols. Snakebite gets away, and Interpol arrests Morgan Sinclair and the injured Punisher. Snakebite attends a meeting with mercenaries Batroc, Armand Chauffard and Rapido, and Kingpin, who is upset that Sinclair managed to get Snakebite's hit list during the scuffle at the Chunnel. Kingpin instructs a crooked Interpol guard to kill his prisoners, but Castle subdues the guard and escapes with Sinclair. They proceed to the home of the nearest person on the hit list, a French construction executive, and find him slain. Suddenly, Snakebite, Rapido and Batroc attack. Commandeering a helicopter, Punisher and Sinclair flee, but Chauffard shoots their helicopter down.
NOTE: Story followed by pinup (1 page) of Punisher & armed skiers (unknown artist). Series published semi-monthly July-September 1992. MAtlas #1, '08 reveals Chauffard's first name. Rapido's name revealed in MEnc, '04.

"Eurohit, 3 of 7: Black Forest, Black Bear" (22 pages)

CREDITS: Dan Abnett, Andy Lanning (writers), Dougie Braithwaite (pencils), Al Williamson (inks), Ken Lopez (letters), Christie Scheele (colors), Tim Tuohy (asst editor), Don Daley (editor)
FEATURE CHARACTER: Punisher (also as Mr. Fort)
SUPPORTING CAST: Microchip
VILLAINS: Klaus Baumer (German racketeer), Jurgen Muller (Baumer's assistant), Bear (Romanian racketeer) & his thugs (all die), Miles Bentley (next in Pun #69, '92), Dieter (German racketeer, bts, in London, 1st, next in Pun #69, '92), Batroc, Armand Chauffard, Kingpin, Rapido, Snakebite
OTHER CHARACTERS: Morgan Sinclair (also as Mrs. Fort), Herr Weiss (hotel manager), Outlaw, 2 hunting dogs
LOCATIONS/ITEMS: London inc Outlaw's Battersea base & Kingpin's office, Rottweil, Germany inc mercenaries' base & Swartzberg Hunting Lodge w/ dining room, guest room, reception desk & fireplace / Batroc's surveillance equipment & transceiver, Bear's bottle of liquor, Bear's men's hunting knife, rifles, bear trap, Striker auto shotgun & transceiver, computers, dishes, hotel telephone, Outlaw's computer & telephone, Rapido's rotary cannon, ropes used to bind Morgan Sinclair, Snakebite's bombs, cigars, headset & revolver, sword, table used as weapon by Punisher, train
SYNOPSIS: A Romanian racketeer named Bear unexpectedly arrives with his men at a German hunting lodge run by Klaus Baumer, a fellow smuggler targeted by Kingpin. Batroc secretly watches as Bear refuses to go along with Baumer's plan to join a nascent European cartel in league with American gangsters. Bear kills Baumer and his assistant and takes over the lodge. When Kingpin learns of Bear's interference, he orders the Romanian killed. Following through on Snakebite's hit list, Frank Castle and Morgan Sinclair arrive at the lodge in search of Baumer and find themselves guests of Bear. After Punisher calls Microchip to get more intelligence about the people on the hit list, Bear becomes suspicious of Castle and releases him into the woods to be hunted down by his men. Snakebite storms the lodge and leaves a ticking bomb behind. Punisher kills Bear's men and returns to the lodge, where he slays Bear and disposes of the bomb with seconds to spare. Sinclair tells Castle that Snakebite mentioned that he works for Kingpin, her boss as the main backer of the Chunnel project.
NOTE: Story followed by pinup (1 page) of Punisher & armed thugs in car (Andre Coates & Michael Ritter, art).

"Eurohit, 4 of 7: Swiss Timing" (22 pages)

CREDITS: Dan Abnett, Andy Lanning (writers), Dougie Braithwaite (pencils), Al Williamson (inks), Ken Lopez (letters), Christie Scheele (colors), Tim Tuohy (asst editor), Don Daley (editor)
FEATURE CHARACTER: Punisher
SUPPORTING CAST: Microchip (next in Pun #69, '92)
VILLAINS: Kingpin (bts, sends mercenaries to Geneva), Armand Chauffard (next in Pun #70, '92), Tarantula (Luis Alvarez, Delvadian mercenary, last in MCP #88/3, '91), Ginelli (1st) & other Italian mobsters, Batroc, Rapido, Snakebite, Spanish mobsters, Swiss mobsters
OTHER CHARACTERS: Outlaw (next in Pun #69, '92), Morgan Sinclair, birds
LOCATIONS/ITEMS: Outlaw's London base, Swiss ski lodge, Geneva, Switzerland inc clock tower & Punisher's hotel w/ guest room / Batroc's motorcycle, binoculars, Armand Chauffard's helicopter w/ gun & ladder, gangsters' firearms, hotel telephone, 3 Italian coupes, Outlaw's computer & telephone, parachutes, Punisher's rental Jaguar & Steyr assault rifle w/ scope, Rapido's rotary cannon & van, Snakebite's assault rifle & headset, Spanish mobsters' firearms, streetcar
SYNOPSIS: Planning to intercept Snakebite's next hit, Frank Castle and Morgan Sinclair spy on a meeting of Swiss and Italian mobsters in Geneva. Microchip calls and tells Punisher he's deduced that Kingpin owns controlling interest in the Chunnel through dummy companies and plans to murder key men in Europe's major crime cartels to unify the continent's underworld under his control. Snakebite emerges from a nearby clock tower and starts shooting his targets, and Castle fires at him from his hotel room. The Italian mobsters flee the city, pursued by Rapido in a van and Snakebite and Armand Chauffard in a helicopter. Punisher and Sinclair cause Rapido to crash and fend off an assault by Batroc. Castle shoots down the mercenaries' chopper and forces a surviving mobster to take him and Sinclair to the ski lodge where he was due to meet his backup. There, they encounter Tarantula and Spanish mobsters.

"Eurohit, 5 of 7: Seeing Red" (22 pages)

CREDITS: Dan Abnett, Andy Lanning (writers), Dougie Braithwaite (pencils), Al Williamson (inks), Ken Lopez (letters), Christie Scheele (colors), Tim Tuohy (asst editor), Don Daley (editor)
FEATURE CHARACTER: Punisher
VILLAINS: Paco Cardenas (Spanish racketeer), Miguel (matador, Paco Cardenas's nephew) (both die), Kingpin (bts, tells mercenaries to return to London), Batroc, Ginelli, Rapido, Snakebite, Tarantula, Spanish mobsters, Spanish gunmen inc Jorge & Manuel
OTHER CHARACTERS: Morgan Sinclair, chickens, Spanish fighting bulls
LOCATIONS/ITEMS: Northern Spain inc Paco Cardenas' ranch w/ house, paddocks & bull pen barn / chair, Paco Cardenas' cigar & prop plane, handcuffs & ropes used to bind Punisher & Morgan Sinclair, Manuel's banderillas, cape & sword, Rapido's rotary cannon, Morgan Sinclair's pistol, Snakebite's revolver & transceiver, Spanish gunmen's guns, knife & flash grenades, Spanish mobsters' firearms
SYNOPSIS: Tarantula brings Frank Castle and Morgan Sinclair to the Spanish ranch of racketeer Paco Cardenas, another mobster on Snakebite's hit list and an old friend of Sinclair's father. Cardenas tells Sinclair that her father was killed because he too was a criminal. Punisher informs Cardenas about Kingpin's plot to kill underworld deputies across Europe before slaying cartel heads gathered in London. Suddenly, local gunmen raid the ranch and Castle launches a counterattack. Suspecting that Tarantula tipped off the gunmen, Cardenas prepares to kill him, but the true traitor, his nephew, the matador Miguel, murders the Spanish racketeer. As Punisher fights Miguel, Batroc, Rapido and Snakebite arrive at the ranch, but their assault is

interrupted by a stampede of bulls enraged by the explosion of flash grenades set off by Castle. The rushing bulls gore Miguel and Punisher barely escapes their fury. Tarantula and Sinclair pick up Castle and fly away in a plane. Kingpin orders his mercenaries back to London.
NOTE: Story followed by unused page from PWZ #6, '92 featuring Punisher.

PUNISHER #69 (Early September 1992)

"Eurohit, 6 of 7: Seeing Red" (23 pages)

CREDITS: Dan Abnett, Andy Lanning (writers), Doug Braithwaite (pencils), Al Williamson (inks), Ken Lopez (letters), Christie Scheele (colors), Tim Tuohy (asst editor), Don Daley (editor)
FEATURE CHARACTER: Punisher
SUPPORTING CAST: Microchip (last in Pun #67, '92)
VILLAINS: Miles Bentley (last in Pun #66, '92), Dieter (last bts in Pun #66, '92), Batroc, Kingpin, Rapido, Snakebite, Tarantula, European crime bosses
OTHER CHARACTERS: Outlaw (last in Pun #67, '92), Transmanche (British-French construction consortium, mentioned only), Morgan Sinclair, London Special Branch police, Special Air Service officers, bystanders, financiers
LOCATIONS/ITEMS: London inc Outlaw's Battersea base & Omni Tower w/ corridor, elevators, floodgate 4, rooftop garden, 80th-floor conference room, stairwell & ventilation shaft / crime bosses' guns, electronic key, Kingpin's cane & cigar, Omni Inc. computers, electronic lock, security desk, security uniforms, conference table & chairs, headsets, Outlaw's computers, flashlight, guns & rope, poster for Notting Hill Carnival '87, Punisher's assault rifle & knife, Rapido's rotary cannon, Morgan Sinclair's pistol, Snakebite's assault pistol, tack board w/ photos of Omni Tower, Tarantula's nunchaku & shuriken, van, window cleaning cradle
SYNOPSIS: Frank Castle meets with Microchip, Outlaw, Tarantula and Morgan Sinclair at Outlaw's base to plan to stop Kingpin from assassinating Europe's crime bosses and replacing them with his own men, who have infiltrated the bosses' syndicates. The next day, Kingpin excuses himself from a legitimate conference with fellow Chunnel financiers on the rooftop of London's Omni Tower to meet with his targeted gang leaders inside the building. Posing as an executive, Sinclair sneaks into the tower's security substation and with Microchip's help hacks into the facility's computers to allow Punisher, Outlaw and Tarantula in. Instructed by Kingpin to slay the crime bosses, Snakebite discovers that Castle has entered the meeting room through the window and has informed the gathered hoodlums of Kingpin's plans. Elsewhere in the building, Tarantula attacks Batroc while Rapido assaults Outlaw. Snakebite flees Punisher, only to be confronted by the armed Sinclair. As Castle tries to find Snakebite, he encounters Kingpin.

PUNISHER #70 (Late September 1992)

"Eurohit 7 of 7: Tunnel Vision" (22 pages)

CREDITS: Dan Abnett, Andy Lanning (writers), Doug Braithwaite (pencils), Al Williamson (inks), Ken Lopez (letters), Christie Scheele (colors), Tim Tuohy (asst editor), Don Daley (editor)
FEATURE CHARACTER: Punisher (next in Pun:GI #1-2, '93, Pun #53, '91)
SUPPORTING CAST: Microchip (next in Pun:GI #1, '93)
VILLAINS: Batroc (next in Cap #411, '93), Armand Chauffard (last in Pun #67, '92, next in PWJ #61, '93), Kingpin (also on TV, next in Pun:GI #1, '93), Rapido (next in PWJ #61, '93), Snakebite (dies)
OTHER CHARACTERS: Outlaw (next in Pun #86, '93), Tarantula (next in Cap #411, '93), Morgan Sinclair (next in Pun Ann #7, '94), Superintendent Coldstream (last in Pun #64, '92), Interpol agents, Special Air Service troops inc Team One & Team Two, financiers, government minister, reporters (on TV)
LOCATIONS/ITEMS: Omni Corporation building inc offices & safety net, hospital, Chunnel (on TV), Heathrow International airport / Tarantula's blades, Batroc's throwing stars, Snakebite's wrist pistols, guns & knife, Rapido's rotary cannon, pipe (used by Snakebite as weapon), SAS guns, gas grenades, gas masks & equipment, parachute suits, Battle Van inc inflatable crash bags, handguns
SYNOPSIS: Batroc and Tarantula fight, and though Batroc gets the upper hand, leaving Tarantula hanging out of a window, Tarantula nicks Batroc with his poisoned toe blades. Racing off in search of an antidote, Batroc accidentally collides with Punisher, giving Kingpin the opportunity to slip away. Punisher rescues Tarantula and goes after Fisk. Tarantula finds Outlaw just after the British vigilante has tricked Rapido into shooting the floor out from under himself, and they flee as the SAS arrive. Snakebite guns down Morgan seconds before Punisher finds and attacks him. The assassin attempts to board Fisk's helicopter, but Fisk leaves him for Punisher. Snakebite knocks Punisher off the roof, but he lands on a safety net; Snakebite tries to cut it loose, but Morgan, wounded but not dead, knocks him off instead. Outlaw and Tarantula arrive, and they and Punisher don parachute suits and escape as the SAS arrive, leaving Morgan, who had a legitimate reason to be there, behind to be taken to the hospital. Later, Outlaw checks on Morgan at the hospital, and they watch TV footage of Fisk at the Chunnel dedication. At the airport, Tarantula parts ways with Frank and Micro. Interpol agents stop them, but with the British government not wanting the problems that come with incarcerating the Punisher, all they can do is order Frank and Micro to leave Europe.
NOTE: Cover labeled "Eurohit 7 of 7: the Final Conflict." The SAS are erroneously described as the "Strategic" Air Service.

PUNISHER/BLACK WIDOW: SPINNING DOOMSDAY'S WEB (December 1992)

(untitled, 48 pages)

CREDITS: Daniel G. Chichester (writer), Larry Stroman (pencils), Mark Farmer (inks), Michael Heisler, Chris Eliopoulos (letters), Gloria Vasquez (colors), J.K. (design), Richard Ashford (asst editor), Nelson Yomtov (editor), Earl Norem (c art), Gregory Wright, Suzanne Dell'orto, John Lewandowski (special thanks)
FEATURE CHARACTERS: Black Widow (also as sailor & in rfb, last in IM #284, '92 fb, next in Cap #408/3, '92), Punisher (last in Pun:Easy, '92, next in Motor #3-6, '92, Pun #71, '92)
GUEST STAR: Nick Fury (last in Dlk #21, '93, next in Cap #411, '93)
VILLAINS: Peter Malum (insane nuclear engineer, also in photos & pfb) & his men inc Cassaday & Jerry (all die)
OTHER CHARACTERS: Alexander Pierce (SHIELD agent, last in Dlk #21, '93, next in NF:AoS #46, '93), other SHIELD agents, FBI agents inc Charlie, Gabe & Kenny (prev 3 die), air traffic controllers inc Mr. Kensington, American & Russian Naval officers,

Lepton (Mallum's former engineering assistant), Shore Patrolman, reporter (on TV), hangar guard (dies), helicopter pilot (corpse), Malum's victims (die in pfb, also in photos as corpses); Red Guardian, KGB agents (both in rfb)

LOCATIONS/ITEMS: FBI safe house, SHIELD installation, Malum's lab, Treasure Island naval base, Anchorage International Airport / Black Widow's Widow's Bite, parachute & binoculars; Punisher's Battle Van, assault rifle & machine pistol; SHIELD plane, jeep, hover jeep & communicator; Malum's firepoker (in pfb), knife (also in pfb), bear trap & blow torch; Malum's men's guns, helicopter & gunship (destroyed) w/ tear gas bombs; FBI agents' revolvers, Naval cruiser; Russian ship, jetliner 22 (converted into SLAM), nuclear reactor, SLAM (Supersonic Low-Altitude Missile) prototype

FLASHBACKS: Malum kills two men (p). The KGB uses Red Guardian's "death" to recruit Black Widow (Av #44, '67 fb).

SYNOPSIS: Peter Malum is liberated from FBI custody. When Black Widow fails to stop his escape she feels she's losing her edge. Nick Fury retrieves Black Widow and tells her that while Malum was head of the US military's Project Pluto, he created the SLAM, a nuclear reactor powered ramjet that leaves a wake of radiation behind it. When Project Pluto was cancelled, Malum went on a killing spree. Fury assigns Black Widow to apprehend Malum before he can build and use another SLAM, and warns her that Punisher is after Malum for being a murderer. Elsewhere, Malum oversees the creation of his new SLAM, intent on using it to destroy the world. In San Francisco on a Naval cruiser, Black Widow interviews Lepton, who was Malum's engineering assistant on Project Pluto. Suddenly, Malum attacks by helicopter and steals a nuclear reactor. Black Widow battles Malum but is forced to defend him when the Punisher arrives and shoots at Malum. Malum escapes with the reactor, but Black Widow uses her Russian contacts to track Malum to Alaska, where Malum has commandeered a passenger jetliner and converted it into a SLAM. Black Widow and Punisher board the plane as it takes off. Punisher kills Malum's men and pilots the plane as Black Widow kills Malum. Later, SHIELD stores the converted SLAM alongside the prototype and Black Widow is satisfied she still has her edge.

NOTE: Includes credits page (interior front cover) featuring Punisher's skull & indicia page (interior back cover) featuring Black Widow's spider. Back cover image is taken from page 39, panel 1.

PUNISHER #71 (October 1992)

"Loose Ends" (22 pages)

CREDITS: Dan Abnett, Andy Lanning (writers), Doug Braithwaite (pencils), Jimmy Palmiotti (inks), Ken Lopez (letters), Marie Javins (colors), Tim Tuohy (asst editor), Don Daley (editor)
FEATURE CHARACTER: Punisher (also in photo, next in Pun Ann #5, '92)
SUPPORTING CAST: Microchip (last in Pun:Easy, next in Pun Ann #5, '92)
VILLAINS: Tommy Deruss (narcotics dealer) & his men, Willis Brunster (trafficker) & his men, Auto Eddie (mob soldier), Pete Lorenza (wheel man), drug suppliers inc Hector Wintle, drug dealers, other criminals (all die) Recoil (psychotic agent of MC, 1st), MC (bts, sends Recoil)
OTHER CHARACTERS: Paramedics, police, reporters, bystanders
LOCATIONS/ITEMS: JFK airport, Microchip's apartment, Brunster's greenhouse (destroyed), shooting range, Derusi's meat freezer / Daily Bugle newspaper, Micro & Frank's luggage, drugs, Recoil's magnum, laser sight & Corvette, dealers' guns & van, car (stolen by Micro, used to ram dealers' van), Polaroids, computer, Punisher's machine gun, knife & handgun; criminal names list, trimming shears, various guns, Lorenza's armored cab

SYNOPSIS: While searching for their car in airport parking, Frank comes across a drug sale where teenage dealers have tried to rob their suppliers and been gunned down by the enforcer Recoil. Frank and Micro kill the suppliers, but Recoil escapes. Frank recognizes one of the suppliers as a formerly minor crook he let live once. Realizing things have gotten out of hand in his absence, Frank decides to go after other loose ends he left. Systematically, Punisher goes throughout the city taking down criminals of various levels, sending the city a message that he's back, and the war goes on.

PUNISHER ANNUAL #5 (1992)

"Byte by Byte (The System Bytes Part 1)" (29 pages)

CREDITS: Peter David (writer), Steven Butler (pencils), Dan Panosian (inks, c inks), Michael Higgins (letters), Kevin Tinsley (colors), Tim Tuohy (managing editor), Don Daley (editor), Mark Pacella (c pencils)
FEATURE CHARACTER: Punisher
SUPPORTING CAST: Microchip
VILLAINS: Raycom Industries: Ray Fortuna (president, dies) & his men (Mr. Smith named, most die), Mr. Waters (Fortuna's assistant, dies); Ampersand Communications: Mazzilli (president) & his men (some die)
OTHER CHARACTERS: Max E. Mumm (Maxwell Edward Mummford, computer hacker, 1st, next in DD Ann #8, '92), gate guard
LOCATIONS/ITEMS: Punisher's warehouse, Raycom Industries inc computer room & Fortuna's office, Ampersand Communications inc Mazzilli's office, Max's apartment / Micro's computers, Punisher's handgun, rifle, sniper rifle & bomb; Ultra-Max computer virus, various weapons, cocaine, Fortuna's pool cue gun, shotgun & machine gun

SYNOPSIS: While trying to get shipping manifests related to Raycom's drug smuggling, Micro's computer becomes infected with a virus in Raycom's systems, forcing Micro and Punisher to infiltrate Raycom as computer techs. Hearing about them and assuming they're from competitor Mazzilli, Fortuna orders them killed. Elsewhere, Max E. Mumm is ejected from Mazzilli's company after asking about his missing files related to the most powerful virus ever created. Max returns home to find Punisher and Micro waiting to ask him about the same thing. That night, Punisher breaks up an attempt by Mazilli's men to steal Fortuna's drugs while Max and Micro try to get into Raycom's servers to shut down the virus. Punisher follows Mr. Smith to Fortuna. Fortuna manages to get Punisher on the run, but Punisher escapes through the computer room while leaving a bomb behind, destroying Raycom. The result breaks Max and Micro's connection, but unless Ultra-Max could jump systems Micro is convinced it's dead. Unfortunately, he's wrong...

NOTE: Cover labeled "The System Bytes Part 1." Includes table of contents/credits page (1 page) w/art taken from page 22, panel 2. Story continues in DD Ann #8, '92. Ultra-Max's greeting is taken from the 1983 movie War Games.

2ND STORY: "The Vengeance Routine" (8 pages)
CREDITS: Rob Tokar (writer), Vince Evans (pencils), Al Williamson (inks), Phil Felix (letters), Linda Lessman (colors), Tim Tuohy (managing editor), Don Daley (editor)

FEATURE CHARACTER: Punisher
SUPPORTING CAST: Microchip (also as Linus Schultz: reporter, construction worker, repairman & laundry worker, next in PWJ #45, '92)
VILLAINS: Jamal Jones (crack dealer, dies), Dr. Stephan Evanski (drug dealer, dies)
OTHER CHARACTERS: Doctor, desk nurse, nurse, Keith, Paul (both reporters), police (prev 3 on TV), bystanders
LOCATIONS/ITEMS: Punisher's warehouse, Beth Israel hospital inc Jamal's room & Evanski's office / Punisher's Uzi, machine gun, rifle & handgun; fake reporter ID, tool belt, headphones, "Let's Scare Jamal to Death starring the Punisher" video tape, VCR, "Frank's Cleaners" van
SYNOPSIS: When one of Punisher's targets survives and is placed under police protection in hospital, Micro uses a series of disguises to gain access. He patches a video into Jamal's room of the Punisher demanding information for his life. Instead, Jamal calls his boss, who turns out to be the doctor treating him, unaware Micro has tapped the line. Micro fixed Jamal's prescription to a fatal medication, getting Evanski indicted for murder and killed by his associates in retribution for Jamal's death.
NOTE: Micro plays the Super Mario Bros video game.

3RD STORY: "Icecapade" (10 pages)
CREDITS: Roger Salick (writer), Val Mayerik (art), Phil Felix (letters), Linda Lessman (colors), Tim Tuohy (managing editor), Don Daley (editor)
FEATURE CHARACTER: Punisher (next in PWJ #45-46, Nomad #5, DD #308-309, Nomad #6, PWJ #47, Pun #72, all '92)
VILLAINS: Vandals (Weegee named, all die)
OTHER CHARACTER: Security guard
LOCATIONS/ITEMS: Ice house / ice sculptures, Punisher's handgun, handgun, crowbar, ice tongs, knife, stun gun, tank of brine, ice block
SYNOPSIS: Punisher comes across vandals wrecking ice sculptures for the city's ice festival. A sneak attack leaves Punisher unarmed, so he uses what he finds to hand to take them down, including ice tongs, a tank of super-cooled brine, a door, their knife and a block of ice.
NOTE: On p.41 panel 4, Punisher and the vandal's hands are miscolored and their weapons are switched.

4TH STORY: "Punisher's Top 10 Villains" (3 pages)
CREDITS: George Caragonne (writer), Art Nichols (art), Richard Starkings (letters), Paul Becton (colors), Tim Tuohy (managing editor), Don Daley (editor)
FEATURE CHARACTER: Punisher
VILLAINS: Criminals
OTHER CHARACTERS: Bruno Costa, Daredevil, Sgt. Cleve Gorman, Gregario, Jigsaw, Kingpin, Klosky, the Rev, Saracen, Skinner, Spider-Man, Reavers: Bonebreaker, Pretty Boy, Reese; prisoners
SYNOPSIS: Punisher recounts his top 10 villains to the reader.
NOTE: Followed by pin-ups of Punisher by Jae Lee & Bob Wiacek, Punisher shooting a biker by Kevin Hopgood & Ken Branch, Punisher with his criminal file by Sean Chen & Robert McLeod, and Punisher disrupting a jailbreak by Roderick Delgado & Ken Branch.

PUNISHER #72 (November 1992)

"Life During Wartime" (22 pages)

CREDITS: Dan Abnett, Andy Lanning (writers), Doug Braithwaite (pencils), Jimmy Palmiotti, Mike McKenna, Al Williamson, Sean Hardy (inks), Ken Lopez (letters), Marie Javins (colors), Tim Tuohy (asst editor), Don Daley (editor), Mark Farmer (c inks)
FEATURE CHARACTER: Punisher (next in Q #42, '93, IHulk #395-396, '92, TInc #6-7, '92-'93, PWJ #48-49, '92, PWJ #51, '93, PWJ #50, '93, Dhold #4-5, '93, Pun:BSS #1, '92)
SUPPORTING CAST: Microchip (last in PWJ #50, '93, next bts in Pun #73, '92, next in Pun #74, '93)
VILLAINS: Gang members inc Santos (all die) & Ennio Setara (1st), MC (voice only), Recoil
OTHER CHARACTERS: Mr. Fontana (corpse only), bystanders, Mr. Thornton (speech giver), Congressman Bernard Modine (1st, politician, next in Pun #74, '93), security officers, Tim Bowens (television reporter, on TV only)
LOCATIONS/ITEMS: Brezzia's TV & Audio store; Freeburg Mall (inc Parking Level B & Thornton Gallery) / Budwiezel beer, gang's van w/radio & guns, Punisher's bulletproofed Plymouth, Recoil's magnum, laser sight & Corvette w/ car phone
SYNOPSIS: When a gang of drug dealers realizes Punisher is observing them, they flee in a van, with Punisher in hot pursuit. As Punisher guns down the men in the back, one of the others radios their boss, who sends their killer Recoil to aid the gang. The three-vehicle chase ends in the nearby Freeburg Mall, where the van and Recoil both crash. Surviving the accident, Recoil gets up and stumbles away while the Punisher focuses his attention on the gang members, soon gunning one down. Chasing the last one, Ennio, into Thornton Gallery, Punisher's battle with the gang member interrupts a speech by Congressman Bernard Modine, whose wrist is broken when Punisher tackles him out of the path of a bullet. After interrogating Ennio and leaving him for dead, Punisher meets with Microchip and the two watch on television as Congressman Modine announces the formation of VIGIL, an anti-vigilante squad.
NOTE: Includes a Punisher pinup by Ken Branch (pencils) & Temujin (inks). Pun #73, '92 reveals Ennio's last name.

PUNISHER #73 (December 1992)

"Police Action: Part 1 of 3" (22 pages)

CREDITS: Dan Abnett, Andy Lanning (writers), Doug Braithwaite (pencils), Rodney Ramos, Sean Hardy, Jimmy Palmiotti, Mike McKenna, Al Williamson (inks), Ken Lopez (letters), Marie Javins (colors), Tim Tuohy (asst editor), Don Daley (editor), Mark Farmer (c inks)
FEATURE CHARACTER: Punisher
SUPPORTING CAST: Microchip (bts, built robot drones, last in PWJ #50, '93)
VILLAINS: MC (rising drug lord, 1st full app), Recoil, Capriski (employee of MC), Ennio Setara (dies), MC's gang, Lt. Taylor Blackwell (1st, VIGIL 2nd-in-command), the Trust (bts, last in Pun #59, '86, see NOTE)
OTHER CHARACTERS: VIGIL (Vigilante Infraction General Interdiction and Limitation, anti-vigilante taskforce): Captain Mike "Rusty" Nails (VIGIL leader), Brady, Riggs, Nails' pilot (all 1st), others; Speedo (Federico Wantaugh, motorcycle-riding vigilante)
LOCATIONS/ITEMS: MC's Warehouse (giant, heavily defended crack house) inc points of sale, labs, penthouse, elevator & landing pad, VIGIL HQ / Warehouse's chain-guns, Battle Van, VIGIL helicopters, body armor & batons, MC's helicopter, Speedo's bike, Daily Bugle newspapers,

Microchip's robot remotes

SYNOPSIS: While the vigilante-hunting VIGIL group apprehends the motorcycle-riding Speedo, with Lt Taylor taking visible pleasure from pounding the downed target until his superior, Captain Nails, stops him, Punisher goes undercover at the "Warehouse," MC's giant, fortified crack house base, to learn more about his setup and security. While Punisher is downstairs, in the penthouse MC welcomes Recoil, returning via helicopter having snatched Ennio Setara from the hospital; on MC's orders, Recoil slays Ennio. Meanwhile VIGIL figures out Punisher is likely to go after MC, and goes on stand-by alert, with Nails hoping they might destroy the Warehouse as a bonus while stopping the Punisher. Two days later, Punisher launches his assault, using Microchip's robot remote drones to keep the guards and automatic defenses occupied. Alerted by the heavy gunfire, VIGIL boards their helicopters and makes their way towards the Warehouse.

NOTE: Followed by an uncredited Punisher pin-up (1 page). The psychopathic Blackwell is considered a villain, unlike his fellow VIGIL members. Brady and Riggs are named in Pun #83, '93. PWJ #75, '95 reveals the Trust fund and covertly direct VIGIL; they can be considered bts in all VIGIL's appearances.

PUNISHER #74 (January 1993)

"Police Action: Part 2 of 3" (22 pages)

CREDITS: Dan Abnett, Andy Lanning (writers), Doug Braithwaite (pencils), Joe Rubinstein, Jimmy Palmiotti, Al Williamson (inks), Ken Lopez, Michael Higgins (letters), Marie Javins, Kevin Somers (colors), Tim Tuohy (asst editor), Don Daley (editor)
FEATURE CHARACTER: Punisher
SUPPORTING CAST: Microchip (last in PWJ #50, '93, last bts in Pun #73, '93, next in MHol '92/4, '92)
VILLAINS: MC, Recoil, Capriski, Warehouse criminals inc Reynolds & Roberto; Lt. Blackwell
OTHER CHARACTERS: VIGIL: Captain Nails, Nails' pilot, Riggs, Brady (prev 2 bts), others; Congressman Bernard Modine (last in Pun#72, '92, next in Pun#85, '93), Marsha (Congressman Modine's secretary)
LOCATIONS/ITEMS: MC's Warehouse inc penthouse, labs; Modine's office / Microchip's robot remotes, Punisher's boot knife, crowbar, drill, high-tension weather balloon, maximum pressure helium can, radio headphones; chain guns, Micro's remote control, radio headphones & car, VIGIL's helicopters, body armor & guns, Recoil's magnum, gang's Uzis, M16s inc grenades, AKs, Macs; coffee crates (used for smuggling drugs)

SYNOPSIS: As Punisher fights his way towards the Warehouse's penthouse, Microchip warns him VIGIL is on their way. MC sends Recoil to stop the Punisher and the two engage in brutal combat. Meanwhile VIGIL leader, Captain Nails, calls Congressman Modine to inform him VIGIL is closing in on the Punisher. Having defeated Recoil, Punisher is about to execute MC when VIGIL arrives, demanding he throw down his weapons.

NOTE: Capriski's name is misspelled as "Kapriski" in this issue.

PUNISHER #75 (February 1993)

"Police Action Part Three of Three" (30 pages)

CREDITS: Dan Abnett, Andy Lanning (writers), Doug Braithwaite (pencils), Josef Rubinstein (inks), Kevin Tinsley (colors), Michael Higgins (letters), Tim Tuohy (asst editor), Don Daley (editor), Steve Geiger (c art)
FEATURE CHARACTER: Punisher
VILLAINS: MC Crack & his men, Recoil (all die), Lt. Taylor Blackwell (next in Pun #83, '93)
OTHER CHARACTERS: VIGIL: Riggs, Brady (both bts), Captain Nails (all next in Pun #83, '93), Nails' pilot (dies), others (some presumably die); bystanders
LOCATIONS/ITEMS: MC's Warehouse (destroyed), the Lake in Central Park / Vigil helicopters (2 destroyed) & machine guns, Punisher's machine gun, knife & Derringer; Recoil's machine gun & armed autogyro ("Tweety Pie," destroyed), MC's helicopter (destroyed), MC's men's guns, wrench (used by MC to hit Punisher), Nail's gun

SYNOPSIS: Surrounded by VIGIL, Punisher is about to surrender, unwilling to fight honest cops, but Recoil bursts onto the scene, shooting at them. In the confusion MC gets to his own helicopter, which takes off with Punisher hanging on, and VIGIL in pursuit. Recoil downs a VIGIL helicopter, then readies his personal autogyro. Climbing into the helicopter, Punisher grapples with one of MC's thugs, and both fall out, catching a rope hanging from the helicopter to stop them falling to their deaths. As Recoil catches up, shooting down the VIGIL copter before opening fire on Punisher, the vigilante cuts the line below himself, sending the thug falling into Recoil's autogyro blades, causing the vehicle to crash explosively. Shooting MC's helicopter, Punisher forces it to crash land in Central Park; he is about to kill MC when Nails arrives. As Nails won't let Punisher kill MC, the vigilante tosses his gun to MC, forcing Nails to kill the crook to stop him from murdering Punisher. Nails tries to take Punisher in, but he's wobbly from blood loss. Punisher disarms him and gives him a field dressing until paramedics arrive. Nails asks him why he does it, and Punisher responds "Because I have to."

NOTE: Issue has a foil-stamped embossed cover.

2ND STORY: "Bar Wars" (6 pages)
CREDITS: Roger Salick (writer), Val Mayerik (art), Linda Lessman (colors), Phil Felix (letters), Tim Tuohy (asst editor), Don Daley (editor)
FEATURE CHARACTER: Punisher
VILLAINS: Longshoremen inc Raffles, Ziggy (informant, bts, set Punisher up)
OTHER CHARACTERS: Bartender
LOCATIONS/ITEMS: Benny's Dockside Café / Punisher's Battle Van, bottle (tossed at Punisher), table, chair, windshield wiper (prev 3 used as weapons)
SYNOPSIS: Ziggy, an informant, calls Punisher down to a seaside bar, but it proves to be a set-up, payback for Punisher breaking Ziggy's nose in Ryker's Island years ago. Punisher fights his way out and leaves, promising to remember the ambush next time he meets Ziggy.

3RD STORY "Flare Up" (4 pages)
CREDITS: Mike Lackey (writer), Simon Bisley (art), Marie Javins (colors), Phil Felix (letters), Tim Tuohy (asst editor), Don Daley (editor)

FEATURE CHARACTER: Punisher (next in PunHol #1, '93, MHol, '92/4, PWZ #12-16, SSWP #10, SM #32-34, SecDef #4-5, all '93)
VILLAINS: Drug dealers (all die)
OTHER CHARACTERS: Police (some bts)
LOCATIONS/ITEMS: Crack lab / lab equipment, doorman's gun, Punisher's Battle Van, police motorcycle & helicopters
SYNOPSIS: Punisher raids a crack lab, methodically rubbing out the men there. He uses the drugs to set one on fire and rescues their money from being burned, intending to use it to fund his war. He escapes the burning lab and gets into his Battle Van. A police officer passes by and asks if he has seen the Punisher around.

PUNISHER #76 (March 1993)

"Lava" (21 pages)

CREDITS: Mark Baron (writer), Larry Stroman (pencils pages 1-8), Kevin Kobasic (pencils, pages 9-21), Al Milgrom (inks), Ken Lopez (letters), Marie Javins (colors), Tim Tuohy (asst editor), Don Daley (editor), Darick Robertson (c pencils), Ron Boyd (c inks)
FEATURE CHARACTER: Punisher (as Frank Hut)
VILLAINS: Jerry Lewis Lee ("Uncle Jerry", owner of Paradise Acres), Ramón, Steve (both Jerry's men) (all die)
OTHER CHARACTERS: Pele (Hawaiian goddess of fire, bts or as Mama Lihune, see NOTE, next in XFor #81, '98), Mama Lihune (owner of Lihune Realty, see NOTE) & her dog, Bonita (Jerry's girlfriend), Holtzman (Jerry's debtor, dies), Kamapua'a (Hawaiian fertility demi-god, as wild hog, see NOTE), Paula Kilauea (Mama Lihune's client & resident of Kona Estates, see NOTE), nightclub host & customers, stewardess, Pocahontas (Native American princess), Frank Sinatra Jr. (singer) (prev 2 mentioned)
LOCATIONS/ITEMS: Hawaii inc Kona Coast, nightclub, forest preserve, Jerry's house, Kona Estates, airport, Lihune Realty, Paradise Acres subdivision & volcano w/lava field / Punisher's brass knuckles, truck & gun, Jerry's rifles & bomb, Ramon & Steve's guns, ropes
SYNOPSIS: Uncle Jerry meets with Holtzman. When Holtzman can't pay the money he owes, Jerry kills him, claiming his blood is a sacrifice to Pele. He also shoots at an elderly lady and her dog who witness his crime, but they seem to vanish. Later, outside Jerry's nightclub, Frank saves a young woman, who introduces herself as Paula. She tells Frank that Jerry plans to set off a bomb near a volcano, destroying Kona Estates, a competing development to his failing Paradise Acres. Stopping at a forest preserve, they spend the night together, while outside a wild hog with red eyes watches, seemingly jealous, but the next morning Frank wakes to find Paula gone. Later, Punisher is on a hillside overlooking Jerry's house, when an old woman with a dog appears and offers advice on approaching the house. He encounters Bonita, who knocks him out when his back is turned. When he wakes up, he is tied to the side of the volcano, near Jerry's bomb. He breaks free and uses Steve's gun to kill Ramón. Steve shoots Punisher with Ramón's gun, but before Jerry can deliver the killing blow, a lava vent spontaneously erupts, killing Jerry. On the flight home, a stewardess explains that Pele is the Hawaiian volcano goddess, who appears sometimes as a young woman, at other times as an old woman with a dog, leaving Frank to wonder if one or both of the women was Pele.
NOTE: The story hints that either or both Mama Lihune and Paula Kilauea may be different aspects of Pele, though they appear together in one scene. Similarly hinted at but unconfirmed is that the wild hog that watches Frank when he is with Paula is Pele's jealous lover Kamapua'a.

PUNISHER #77 (April 1993)

"Survival Part 1" (23 pages)

CREDITS: Roger Salick (writer), Val Mayerik (plot, art), Matthew Hollingsworth (colors), Michael Higgins (letters), Tim Tuohy (asst editor), Don Daley (editor)
FEATURE CHARACTER: Punisher (also as Frank Castle in fb between Pun:OM #1, '93 & Pun #3, '99 fb)
VILLAINS: Bikers inc Tank (some die)
OTHER CHARACTERS: Sammy (Punisher's pilot & friend, 1st); grizzly bear, deer, rabbits, fish (prev 3 die); Phan Bighawk (Indian Scout, in fb)
LOCATIONS/ITEMS: Mikey's bar in Kratinka, Alaska, Sammy's lake cabin, Alaskan wilderness / ashtray, stuffed bear's head, bottle, pool cue, pool table (prev 4 all used as weapons), bikers' guns, Sammy's truck & sea plane, gas barrels, flare gun, helicopters, Punisher's automatic rifle & shoelace, twigs & branches, flint (used to make an axe), bones (used to make a spear), spikes, rock
FLASHBACK: Bighawk shows Frank how to survive in the wild.
SYNOPSIS: Sammy calls Punisher to Alaska to investigate a strange base he spotted in the mountains. Their conversation is interrupted by bikers in the bar causing trouble. Sammy and Punisher fight their way out, and as the bikers open fire and prepare to pursue, Punisher dumps gas off the back of Sammy's truck, the lights it and the bikers on fire with a flare. Later, when Sammy takes Punisher up in his plane, helicopters attack them. Punisher is knocked out of the plane, surviving the fall thanks to landing in snow, and he watches Sammy's plane go down in the distance. Alone in the wilderness with a busted shoulder and leg, Punisher recalls his survival training, fashioning shelter and tools out of surrounding materials. While hunting a deer for food, Punisher is forced to chase down the wounded animal, but is challenged for his kill by an angry grizzly. Unable to stop it, as it begins to maul him, Punisher dives off a nearby cliff to escape.

PUNISHER #78 (May 1993)

"Survival Part 2" (22 pages)

CREDITS: Roger Salick (writer), Val Mayerik (plot, art), Matthew Hollingsworth (colors), Michael Higgins (letters), Tim Tuohy (asst editor), Don Daley (editor)
FEATURE CHARACTER: Punisher
VILLAINS: Ishenko (Russian investor), Pablo (Colombian investor), Yoshi (Japanese investor, 1st), General Trask (mercenary) (all 1st) & his men (some die)
OTHER CHARACTERS: Chagee (Native American, 1st), Sammy, grizzly (dies), deer (remains), 2nd deer (dies)
LOCATIONS/ITEMS: Alaskan wilderness, private army compound inc General's office & brig / flint, wood, Clovis spear, cedar fiber rope, deadfall trap w/spiked tree trunk, spring-trap, helicopters, bear-claw tipped club, bear-skin poncho, Sno-Cat (destroyed), various guns, food tray, thermos of coffee
SYNOPSIS: After surviving the fall, Punisher sets up a series of traps for the bear, lures it in and kills it. After skinning it to make a poncho for warmth and disguise himself from intermittent helicopter patrols, Punisher heads on towards his original target. At a private army compound, three big investors land and are greeted by General Trask, who discusses their plans to forcibly seize Kamchatka's mineral rights using his private army. Meanwhile, Sammy gets to know his fellow prisoner in the brig, a local Native American who believes the spirit of the shape-shifter will exact retribution for his family, murdered by Trask's men. Punisher commandeers a Sno-Cat and takes it as close to the base as he dares before ditching it over a cliff, having rigged it to explode. Trask's men investigate, and Punisher picks off an outlier before letting the others catch sight of him in the distance, leaving them unsure if they have seen a bear or a man. Punisher backs off, ready to play some mind games with them.

PUNISHER #79 (June 1993)

"Survival Part 3" (22 pages)

CREDITS: Roger Salick (writer), Val Mayerik (plot, art), Matthew Hollingsworth (colors), Michael Higgins (letters), Tim Tuohy (asst editor), Don Daley (editor)
FEATURE CHARACTER: Punisher (next in PWJ #52-56, Ns #5-6, SMPunSabre, all '93)
VILLAINS: Ishenko, Pablo, Yoshi, General Trask & his men (many die)
OTHER CHARACTERS: Sammy, Chagee
LOCATIONS/ITEMS: Private army compound inc power station (destroyed), brig & General's office / Punisher's bear poncho & clawed-club, gas cans, various automatic rifles & machine guns, helicopters, jets (both destroyed), crates of ammo & C-4, lanterns, flashlights, Sammy's knife
SYNOPSIS: Punisher returns to the compound and begins systematically striking at it, first blowing up their power station, then their satellite dish to cut them off from outside communication, and then destroying their weapons cache and vehicles. All the while he sticks to the shadows, letting his bear suit play with their imaginations. Suspecting the prisoners know something, Trask sends for Sammy and Chagee, but when they are taken from their cell, Punisher kills their escort, having slipped inside the darkened compound. When Chagee informs Punisher the valley only has one way in, Frank decides to blow up the base, then exit the valley and blow the pass behind them, trapping the mercenaries within to freeze to death. However, the heavy resistance they face forces them to leave the building intact and head out the pass. Realizing it would be easy for their opponents to pick them off in the pass, the soldiers back off and head back for the building. Chagee states they'll be burning their gunpowder for heat in no time, and Punisher proceeds with his plan to blow the pass and lock them in.

SPIDER-MAN/PUNISHER/SABRETOOTH: DESIGNER GENES (1993)

"Designer Genes" (62 pages)

CREDITS: Terry Kavanagh (writer), Scott McDaniel (pencils), Keith Williams (inks), Joe Rosen (letters), Tom Smith (colors), Mike Lackey (assist editor), Danny Fingeroth (editor)
FEATURE CHARACTERS: Punisher (also as homeless man, next in Pun #80, '93), Spider-Man (last in SecDef #8, '93, next in MSUn #3, '93), Sabretooth (also in own thoughts, last in MCP #136/2, '93, next in Sabre #1, '93)
SUPPORTING CAST: Microchip (last in PWJ #56, '93, next bts in PunSS #3/2, '93, next in PWZ #17, '94)
VILLAINS: Dr. Phillip Chambers (former Dept. K scientist, dies), Brandon Chambers (Phillip's brother & Roxxon executive), Mr. Greycrest (mobster, voice only), Mitchell Chambers (Phillip's brother, mutated w/bear, coyote & wolf traits), Scorchers (pyrotechnic mercenaries), F. Hopkins (corrupt realtor, bts, hired Scorchers), Roxxon guards
OTHER CHARACTERS: Lynch (ESU security guard), homeless people (some as corpses) inc Barry, Gert & Pixie, Dr. Chambers' mutated test subjects, police, nurse, bystanders, ESU lab animals (corpses), lions; Silver Fox, Wolverine, Dept. K scientists (prev 3 in Sabretooth's thoughts)
LOCATIONS/ITEMS: New York inc Empire State University, Alphabet City, Bronx Zoo, 59th St. Bridge, sewers, Dr. Chambers' lab, Roxxon riverfront corporate HQ & East River / Punisher's motorcycle, thermite grenades, directional microphone, infrared binoculars, concussion grenades, plastique explosives, gas grenades, gas mask, pulse tracer, knife & assault rifles; Microchip's helicopter, Pixie's knife, Roxxon robots, Roxxon guards' guns, police guns
SYNOPSIS: Peter Parker discovers mutilated lab animals at Empire State University and investigates as Spider-Man. Punisher stops the Scorchers from killing some homeless people, who tell Punisher about a series of recent homeless mutilations. After Punisher leaves to investigate in the sewers, Sabretooth passes through. Elsewhere, Dr. Phillip Chambers finalizes a working prototype of his "Designer Genes" mutating serum. Spider-Man interrogates an ESU security guard, who gives Spider-Man an address for a lab. Roxxon executive Brandon Chambers prepares to sell Designer Genes to the mob. Sabretooth arrives at Dr. Chambers' lab, sees how the animals are being treated and flies into a berserker rage. Spider-Man and Punisher both arrive at the lab and battle the delirious Sabretooth. The fight ends at the Bronx Zoo when Sabretooth calms down, explains he's searching for a Department K scientist from his past who now works for Roxxon, and escapes. Spider-Man and Punisher separately search for Roxxon HQ. Brandon argues with his brother Dr. Chambers about Designer Genes' use until

Punisher arrives. Spider-Man stops Punisher from killing Dr. Chambers, who unleashes his other brother Mitchell, mutated with animal traits, on them, and reveals Mitchell killed the homeless people and ESU lab animals. Spider-Man and Punisher defeat Mitchell while Sabretooth kills Dr. Chambers. Punisher escapes as the police arrive. Before his trial, Brandon donates his brother's research to fight cancer.
NOTE: Includes title page (w/art taken from page 59, panel 2) & credits page (2 pages). Back cover image is taken from page 13 (Sabretooth) & page 35 (Punisher & Spider-Man).

PUNISHER #80 (July 1993)

"Last Confession" (22 pages)

CREDITS: Steven Grant (writer), Dave Hoover (art), Matthew Hollingsworth (colors), Ken Lopez (letters), Tim Tuohy (asst editor), Don Daley (editor)
FEATURE CHARACTER: Punisher (also in fb between in U #3, '06 fb bts & Pun Ann #2/3, '89 fb, next in PunSS #3, '93, PWZ #17-19, '93)
VILLAINS: Mr. McKay (crime lord) & his men inc Aguilar, McKay's woman, bank robbers inc Jared, Braden & Vinson, Mr. Scala (St. Louis criminal), Mr. Kroh (Scala's bodyguard), Welsh (Scala's contact), Cusmano's men (all die), Mr. Cusmano (Nebraska crime boss) (all in fb), Mike Quillan (criminal posing as priest Jack Gotch, also in fb)
OTHER CHARACTERS: Parishioners; Jack Gotch, Father Estrada, Davey (bartender) (prev 3 die), bank tellers, police, bystanders (1 dies) (all in fb)
LOCATIONS/ITEMS: St. Patrick's Cathedral, Commerce Bank, McKay's boat, wayward house, Nebraska Pipe and Supply co. / robbers' sawed-off shotguns, motorcycles & truck; suitcase of money, Aguilar's handgun, McKay's men's guns, Punisher's boat, automatic rifle & handgun; stolen car, Cusmano's men's revolvers, pipe, Quillan's revolver (in pfb), handgun & crucifix
FLASHBACK: During a bank robbery Mike Quillan murders a man who gets in his way. Later, he and his associates go to local crimelord Mr. McKay to give him a cut of their $12,000 take, payment for permission to operate on his territory, but he informs them that the unauthorized killing means they need to pay him $40,000 instead, and kills one of them to make a point. Their meeting is interrupted by Punisher's arrival, and Quillan and his pals murder McKay while the guards are distracted fighting the vigilante. However, Punisher kills everyone on the boat except Quillan, who is overlooked purely by chance. Scared to death and convinced the Punisher is coming for him, Quillan steals a car and flees, but eventually passes out and crashes the car. Waking, he learns he is in Nebraska, in the care of Jack Gotch, a priest-to-be, who suggests he stay on to help Father Estrada when Jack goes to the seminary. Instead, Quillan seeks out the local crime boss, Cusmano, and takes a job. He and Cusmano's men raid a pick-up at a local bar, but when one of crooks carelessly reveals Quillan's name to the bartender, Quillan chases the bartender outside and kills him. As he returns to the bar, he hears shots, then spots the Punisher emerging from the bar. In panic, Quillan returns to Gotch's house looking for money and kills Jack and Estrada. Finding Jack's seminary invitation, Quillan takes his identity and looks to change his life.
SYNOPSIS: With his current target out of town, Punisher decides to hang out in a church where good people will surround him. Seeing Punisher enter, a priest, the former Mike Quillan, hides in the confessionals. Though the other booth is empty, he admits his sinful past, then fatally shoots himself to escape Punisher. Having heard the shot, Punisher checks on the dying priest, who states "I knew you'd find me" before expiring. None the wiser as to who the priest was, Punisher leaves before the police arrive.

PUNISHER #81 (August 1993)

"Bodies of Evidence" (22 pages)

CREDITS: Steven Grant (writer), Hoang Nguyen (art), Matthew Hollingsworth (colors), Ken Lopez (letters), Tim Tuohy (asst editor), Don Daley (editor)
FEATURE CHARACTER: Punisher (also in pfb, next in Venom:FP #1-3, PWZ Ann #1, PWJ #57-60, Pun Ann #6, all '93)
VILLAINS: Det. Sgt. Cordover (dies), Lorga (crime boss, dies) & his men (2 die in pfb), Winters (Lorga's enforcer, also in pfb, dies), Brancato (Lorga's accountant, also in pfb), "Lolita" (Lucille Stander, hooker, also in pfb), "Stolly" (Stolarz, in pfb, mugger, dies)
OTHER CHARACTERS: Police inc Luis Generes, SWAT, motel manager, bystanders (some in pfb)
LOCATIONS/ITEMS: Motel inc Punisher's room, police precinct, hospital, Brancato's office, Lorga's tower / Punisher's guns, rifle, fresh orange juice, sandbags, raw meat wrapper, vitamin & protein powders & psyllium husks; police guns, Cordover's shotgun, Generes' revolver, Stolly's gun (in pfb)
FLASHBACK: Lolita lures Punisher into an alley where her partner, Stolly, tries to rob him. Punisher kills Stolly and tells Lolita to tell Lorga that Punisher is coming. Lorga's accountant Brancato hears Punisher is in town, panics and clears out his office. Lorga's enforcer Winters roughs Brancanto up for his disloyalty. Punisher arrives, kills Winters' men, lets Winters live and takes Brancato to the hospital (p).
SYNOPSIS: Following an anonymous tip, Detective Sgt. Cordover leads a raid on Punisher's motel room, unaware Punisher is observing from a nearby rooftop. Afterwards, by-the-book novice cop Luis Generes, assigned to observe and learn from Cordover, joins the detective in questioning Lolita and then Brancato about their Punisher encounters, and realize Punisher is targeting Lorga. Discovering a floppy disk containing blueprints for Lorga's heavily defended tower amongst Punisher's confiscated possessions, they conclude Punisher is already there. The police storm the building, prompting Lorga and Winters to flee, and Cordover realizes Punisher used them to smoke Lorga out. Punisher runs Lorga's car off the road, but before he can kill Lorga, Cordover and Generes arrive. Lorga reveals Cordover is on his payroll and shoots Generes, while Cordover guns down Punisher. Saved by his bulletproof vest, Punisher kills Lorga and Cordover. Checking the wounded Generes will survive, and ignoring the honest cop's insistence that he is under arrest, Punisher leaves, promising to call Generes medical help.

PUNISHER ANNUAL #6 (1993)

"Death Metal" (26 pages)

CREDITS: Pat Mills, Tony Skinner (writers), Dave Hoover (art), Ken Lopez (letters), Daisy DePuthod (colors), Tim Tuohy (asst editor), Don Daley (editor)
FEATURE CHARACTER: Punisher
VILLAINS: Eradikator 4 (robot assassin, destroyed), Hiram Jones (Industrial Skills PLC CEO, dies), Lenny the Weasel (crack dealer), Pavicci Brothers (criminals)
OTHER CHARACTERS: Bill Neville (Neville Robotics owner, dies), Carlyle Neville (Bill's daughter) & her guards, Hiram's secretary (voice only), club goers inc Cindy (Carlyle's friend), party guests, Neville Robotics guards, human combat testers (in pfb), Spencer Neville (Bill's brother, mentioned, killed by Eradikator)
LOCATIONS/ITEMS: Neville Robotics, Carlyle Neville's yacht, The Joint (nightclub), Industrial Skills PLC inc Hiram Jones' office / $100.00 bill, $200 shirt (destroyed), cocaine, mirrors, chair (used against Eradikator), nightclub lasers, Neural Particle Beam Gun (anti-robot gun), Punisher's jet-ski, grenade launcher, 9mm & .45-caliber guns, sheet of ¼ metal plate, electronic magnet & crane, acid bath, Eradikator's photo-sensors & mechanical spider legs, Carlyle Neville's sports car, Eradikator prototypes (in pfb)
FLASHBACK: Eradikator robots are tested in combat against human opponents.
SYNOPSIS: After an Eradikator 4 kills Bill Neville, Frank Castle, who served with Bill in Vietnam, learns Bill's brother was also recently slain, and figures Neville's daughter, Carlyle, will be targeted next. He goes to her yacht, defeats her ineffectual bodyguards, and becomes her new protector. Asked who her father's enemies were, Carlyle suggests their competitor, Industrial Skills PLC, explaining that Neville Robotics built a Neural Particle Beam to counter Industrial Skills' Eradikator robots. Carlyle goes to a nightclub, where Punisher angers her by literally blowing away her cocaine. Moments later an Eradikator enters and attacks. Using the club's light show lasers, Punisher temporarily scrambles the robot's brain, giving them time to retreat. They drive to Neville Robotics, where the Eradikator catches up with them. After scrambling it with the Neural Particle Beam, Punisher drops it in an acid bath. Later, Punisher confronts Industrial Skills CEO Hiram Jones with the Eradikator's remains, and kills him when he tries to pull a gun. Returning to Carlyle, he tells her to grow up and become a daughter Bill could be proud of.
NOTE: All of Marvel's 1993 Annuals were bagged with trading cards featuring a new character introduced in each issue. This issue's card, #25 in the series, featured Eradikator 6 art by Dave Hoover; however, the story identifies the robot as Eradikator 4. Includes table of contents/credits page (1 page) w/art taken from page 19, panel 3.

2ND STORY "Preacher" (8 pages)
CREDITS: Steven Grant (writer), Shawn McManus (art), Ken Lopez (letters), John Kalisz (colors), Tim Tuohy (asst editor), Don Daley (editor)
FEATURE CHARACTER: Punisher
VILLAINS: Lorenz (weapons designer, dies), Danny Pizano (Houston mob Capo, dies), Pizano's men inc Tommy (many killed)
LOCATIONS/ITEMS: Texas desert / Preacher (prototype non-magnetic polymer handgun, takes any clip size & ammo caliber), Preacher design plans (destroyed), Punisher's ammo belt (destroyed) & grenades, cars, .45-caliber guns
SYNOPSIS: In the Texas desert, gun designer Lorenz is killed by mobster Danny Pizano after handing over a high-tech handgun, "the Preacher." Having observed the exchange, Punisher attacks, killing most of Pizano's men before a lucky shot by Pizano blows up Punisher's ammo belt. When Pizano moves in too close to deliver the killing shot, Punisher snaps his neck, takes the Preacher, and walks away.

3RD STORY "Tracers" (15 pages)
CREDITS: Chuck Dixon (writer), Dale Eaglesham (pencils), Pat Redding (inks, colors), Richard Starkings (letters), Tim Tuohy (asst editor), Don Daley (editor)
FEATURE CHARACTER: Punisher (next in PunBSS #2/1-4, '92, Pun #82, '93)
VILLAINS: Chicago & Jersey gangsters (several die), paramilitary muscle (many die), Ducky (helicopter pilot, dies)
OTHER CHARACTERS: Firefighters inc Haycroft & Jimmy, dogs
LOCATIONS/ITEMS: Poconos inc Vegas crooner's home, woods & stream / Semtex ball packed w/ball bearings packed round it, RPG, flashlights, automatic weapons, rifles, handguns, helicopter w/search light (both destroyed), bulldozer, shovels,
SYNOPSIS: After blowing up Vegas and New Jersey gangsters meeting in an isolated Poconos house, Punisher is pursued through the woods by their hired guns. Scaling down a cliff, a helicopter spotlights him, and he jumps into the trees below to evade gunfire. He kills some pursuers at the river, so their blood will break his scent trail, but is again spotlighted by the chopper. Racing towards approaching ground forces blinded by the chopper's spotlight, Punisher kills them, then shoots out the chopper's spotlight, causing the pilot to crash, starting a forest fire. The next morning the battered and bruised Punisher walks past firefighters cleaning up after the fire, who take one look at him and give him a wide berth.
NOTE: Followed by five pinups: Punisher w/machine gun by Andrew Wildman (pencils) & George Wildman (inks); two thugs interrogating a captured Punisher by Ken Branch (pencils) & Jason Temujin (inks); Punisher holding a guy by his necktie by Ken Branch (art); Punisher w/ bazooka by Scott Kolins (pencils) & Ken Branch (inks); all colored by Sue McTeigue; & Punisher & Black Widow by McDuffy (pencils), Josef Rubinstein (inks) & Kevin Somers (colors).

PUNISHER #82 (September 1993)

"Firefight Part One" (21 pages)

CREDITS: Dan Abnett, Andy Lanning (writers), Hugh Haynes (pencils), Mick Gray, Mark McKenna (inks), Michael Higgins (letters), John Kalisz (colors), Tim Tuohy (asst editor), Don Daley (editor)
FEATURE CHARACTER: Punisher
VILLAINS: Ramsey Sutherland III (also as "Little Ramsey", corrupt real estate tycoon, 1st, also chr 1st in fb prior to Pun #83, '93 fb), Raymond "Ray" F. Sutherland (arsonist, 1st, also in fb prior to main story), weapon smugglers (some die) inc Louis, Miguel, Pablo (prev 3 1st)
OTHER CHARACTERS: Mary-Lynn (Ramsey's secretary, voice only), Ramsey Sutherland II (Ramsey Sutherland III's father, 1st, in fb) & his wife (bts in fb, dies), Raul (Ramsey's limo driver), hospital guard, WMAR jock (voice only, on radio broadcast), firefighters (some in fb), ambulance driver (dies), tenement residents (many die), pick-up truck driver, car drivers & passengers, distraught mother, her 2 daughters (1st)
LOCATIONS/ITEMS: State Hospital for the Criminally Insane, Manhattan inc Twin Towers, Ramsey Sutherland's penthouse, Manhattan Bridge, tenement (destroyed), textile mill (in fb, destroyed), Wharf 18 / Punisher's Striker w/ CS gas shells, cannon w/rubber-nose slugs, scuba gear; Ramsey Sutherland III's cigar, chilled moet, phone, limousine; Ray Sutherland's remote control detonator; United Nations crates & weapons inc grenades & Uzis; weapon smuggler's truck; ambulance, boat, firetruck, Lanning Linen's truck, pick-up truck, tenement oil tank, incendiary device
FLASHBACK: Ramsey Sutherland II arrives with his son at the textile mill he owns to find it engulfed in flames. As firefighters try to put out the flames, the older Ramsey confronts his brother Ray for starting the fire.
SYNOPSIS: Ramsey Sutherland III pulls strings and frees his arsonist uncle Ray from a state institution. Ramsey threatens to return Ray there if he doesn't perform a job for him. Later, the Punisher attacks weapon smugglers at a wharf, but three escape in a munitions filled van; Punisher steals a pick-up truck and pursues, chancing to drive past a tenement just as Ray detonates a bomb inside. The blast wave knocks Punisher's truck over, and as he climbs out of the wreckage, he hears a woman screaming that her daughters are still inside the burning building. Racing inside, he finds the girls on the roof, but spots a bomb attached to a rooftop oil tank. Grabbing the girls in his arms, he leaps off the roof as the bomb explodes behind him. Meanwhile, as the street fills with police and emergency vehicles, the smugglers hijack an ambulance, while, blocks away, Ramsey watches the fires from his penthouse with mounting glee.
NOTE: Followed by an uncredited pin-up of Punisher battling a street gang (1 page).

PUNISHER #83 (October 1993)

"Firefight Part Two" (23 pages)

CREDITS: Dan Abnett & Andy Lanning (writers), Hugh Haynes (pencils), Mick Gray, Mark McKenna (inks), Michael Higgins (letters), John Kalisz (colors), Tim Tuohy (asst editor), Don Daley (editor)
FEATURE CHARACTER: Punisher
SUPPORTING CAST: Microchip (last in Pun:BSS #2, '93)
VILLAINS: Ramsey Sutherland III (also in fb between Pun #82, '93 fb & Pun #82, '93), Ray Sutherland (also on computer screen), Louis, Miguel, Pablo
OTHER CHARACTERS: VIGIL inc Commander Blackwell (last in Pun #75, '93, next in Pun #85, '93), Brady, Rigg (both last in Pun #73, '92, last bts in Pun #75, '93, next in Pun #85, '93), Letz (1st, next in PWJ #63, '94), Dawkins, Blue Squad members; Ramsey Sutherland II (in fb, dies), firefighters inc Chief Russell (1st), Jonesey (dies), police inc Officer Cruikshank, 2 tenement girls, bystanders
LOCATIONS/ITEMS: Ramsey Sutherland's penthouse, Manhattan inc Twin Towers, Brooklyn Bridge; VIGIL command headquarters, tenements (in flames), Microchip's warehouse / Micro's computer, VIGIL's machine guns & nightsticks, Punisher's scuba gear & machine gun, firetrucks inc cherry picker, CB radio, firefighter's hoses, oxygen tanks, & jump cushion, Cruikshank's handcuffs & street map, police cars, Ray's radio headset & firebombs (bts), Ramsey's radio, stolen ambulance, Louis' automatic weapon
FLASHBACK: Ramsey Sutherland II stands on the edge of his high-rise balcony screaming at the city, blaming it for stealing his fortune. As his son watches, the elder Ramsey leaps to his death.
SYNOPSIS: Punisher and the two girls land in a jump cushion placed by firefighters. Frank blacks out, waking to find himself handcuffed to a firetruck while a police officer and firefighter argue over whether to arrest Punisher in the midst of a blaze spreading through the neighborhood. Punisher contacts Microchip on the firetruck's CB, asking for leads on who could've started the fires. At VIGIL headquarters, Commander Blackwell is informed of a possible Punisher sighting. He orders his men into action. Back at the blaze, fire chief Russell races into the burning building to rescue a trapped firefighter. Frank frees himself and takes control of the firetruck's ladder and hose, rescuing Russell, though the firefighter Russell tried to save dies. With Russell's permission, Frank contacts Microchip again, and is told that arsonist Ray Sutherland was released from a secure facility two days ago. Punisher and Russell study maps, realizing the bombings are in a pattern leading towards a chemical plant. VIGIL arrives and tries to arrest Frank, but he escapes with Russell's help. Nearby the smugglers open fire on pedestrians, trying to clear a path for their stolen ambulance, only to be confronted by the Punisher standing in their way.

PUNISHER #84 (November 1993)

"Firefight Part Three" (23 pages)

CREDITS: Dan Abnett, Andy Lanning (writers), Hugh Haynes (pencils), Mick Gray (co-inks), Mark McKenna (co-inks, c inks), Michael Higgins (letters), John Kalisz (colors), Tim Tuohy (asst editor), Don Daley (editor)
FEATURE CHARACTER: Punisher (next in Kill:EY #2-3, PWZ #20-22, SSol #8, all '93, PunHol #2, '94, Tstrike #3, '93)
SUPPORTING CAST: Microchip (next in PWZ #20, '93)
VILLAINS: Ramsey Sutherland III (also on computer screen), Ray Sutherland, Louis, Miguel, Pablo (all die)
OTHER CHARACTERS: Firefighters inc Chief Russell, TV reporter & cameraman, police, protesters, bystanders
LOCATIONS/ITEMS: Manhattan inc Twin Towers, chemical plant, buildings (on fire) / Microchip's computers; Punisher's machine gun; Ray's cigar & match, ambulance, bomb, cars, CB radio, firetrucks inc TV set, plastique
SYNOPSIS: Punisher guns down the weapons smugglers, with the last one fleeing into a nearby burning building and

getting caught in a backdraft. Commandeering the ambulance, the Punisher speeds to the chemical plant. He contacts Microchip, who has figured out that Ramsey Sutherland released his arsonist uncle Ray so he would set fires allowing Ramsey to cheaply buy back the land Ramsey's family lost when he was a kid. Frank confronts Ray inside the chemical plant, defusing the bomb before Ray can set it off, but Ray douses himself with gasoline, ignites it and tries to jump into the chemical vats. Punisher knocks both of them out of a window instead, landing in the harbor behind the plant. Fire Chief Russell arrives as Frank clambers out the water, warning him the flames from the building fires are spreading towards the chemical plant. Russell thinks there is no way to stop the plant from exploding, but Punisher crashes the ambulance filled with the smuggler's plastique into the fire, and when it explodes it creates a firebreak, saving the chemical plant. Frank helps Russell's men fight the fire for several hours, but as they finally get things under control, they see on the firetruck's TV that the police have arrested Ramsey, anonymously tipped off by Micro, who thought Frank was dead. Convinced Ramsey will evade justice, Frank borrows a firetruck from Russell; minutes later, when the arresting officers leave Ramsey handcuffed but unattended in the back of a police cruiser, Frank drives the heavy firetruck over the smaller vehicle, crushing it and its occupant, then escapes.

PUNISHER #85 (December 1993)

"Smoke & Fire" (22 pages)

CREDITS: Steven Grant (writer), Hoang Nguyen (art), Matthew Hollingsworth (colors), Ken Lopez (letters), Tim Tuohy (asst editor), Don Daley (editor)
FEATURE CHARACTER: Punisher (next in PunTheNam, '94, see NOTE)
VILLAINS: Lt. Blackwell (last in Pun #83, '93), Mondo Pain (Edmondo Paina, psychotic hit man, 1st, next in PWJ #73, '94), Ballard & his men (most die) inc Arn, Ricky, Smitty & Tex (prev 4 die)
OTHER CHARACTERS: Bernard Modine (last in Pun #74, '93, next bts in PWJ #65, '94), VIGIL inc Capt. Nails (last in Pun #75, '93), Brady, Riggs (both last in Pun #83, '93), Harold Jessup (1st), Gabriella; Ballard's woman, waitress, security guard (dies), reporters inc WTIM 2 reporter
LOCATIONS/ITEMS: US/Canadian border, VIGIL HQ, warehouse, Ballard's mansion inc bedroom, Oasis 76, motel / stolen trucks (2 destroyed), Uzis, Punisher's Uzis, rifle, match & handguns; VIGIL's guns, boxes of cigarettes, guard's gun, Mondo's cigarette, Blackwell & Jessup's guns & motorcycles, explosive thermos, VIGIL helicopter
SYNOPSIS: Punisher stops a stolen truck carrying contraband running across the border. Meanwhile Congressman Bodine informs VIGIL their budget is being cut, out of favor after failing to make a major arrest, enraging Blackwell. He drags Jessup along on his personal vendetta to take down Punisher. Elsewhere, an unlucky security guard catches Ballard's men robbing his warehouse, and is brutally killed by Ballard's enforcer, Mondo Pain. Since Ballard was robbing his own warehouse for the insurance, he doesn't take kindly to the death, but he and his men are too terrified to discipline Mondo. Blackwell and Jessup, watching Ballard in anticipation of Punisher striking, run down Mondo and demand information. Posing as a trucker, Punisher kills two of Ballard's hijackers, then anonymously calls Ballard, telling him Mondo is about to steal Ballard's shipment, and Blackwell, informing him Ballard is moving earlier than Mondo claimed; Blackwell confronts Mondo, who assumes Ballard has double-crossed him. Delivering his cargo to a quiet border crossing where Ballard's men are waiting, Punisher claims he is meant to meet Mondo, convincing Ballard of Mondo's betrayal. Ballard's men shoot Punisher, but his bulletproof vest saves him, and he blows fire on Ballard's men, just before Blackwell arrives with guns blazing. Mondo forces Jessup to crash VIGIL's helicopter, but as he tries to escape across the border Punisher shoots him. News helicopters and vans arrive, called by Punisher, allowing the vigilante to escape Blackwell in the confusion. Stopping the smuggling earns VIGIL a new lease on life, but all Blackwell can focus on is killing Punisher.
NOTE: Cover labeled "Suicide Run: 0" and continues in PWJ #61, '93. Continuity issues necessitate a considerable gap between this issue and Suicide Run: 1, resulting in Pun #86-88, '94 taking place out of published sequence and after Pun #93, '93. Nails' hair is miscolored white here.

PUNISHER INVADES THE 'NAM: FINAL INVASION (February 1994)

"Chapter 1: Rolling Thunder" (22 pages)
"Chapter 2: Death Hole" (22 pages)
"Chapter 3: Retribution" (22 pages)

CREDITS: Don Lomax (writer), Alberto Saichann (art), Steve Dutro (letters), John Kalisz (colors), Tim Tuohy (asst editor), Don Daley (editor), Joe Kubert (c art)
FEATURE CHARACTER: Frank Castle (also as Frank Castiglione in fb1 between PWZ #21, '93 fb & Pun:OM #1, '93, also in Pun #1, '98 fb, Pun:OM #1, '93, Pun:Int, '89 fb, Pun:OM #1, '93 & Pun:BSS #3, '94 fb, becomes Frank Castle; next in PWZ #25/2, PWJ #64/2, PWZ #26-30, Pun #89, all '94)
VILLAINS: Colonel No-Name (traitorous US Marine Colonel, in fb1, last in TheNam #69, '92 fb, dies, next in TheNam #69, '92 as corpse) & his helicopter crew (die); Death Doctor (Chinese surgeon working on remote-control "puppet soldier" program, in fb2 & fb1), his Cuban soldiers (in fb2 & fb1some die) & mercenaries (in fb2 & fb1, some die); North Vietnamese Army (NVA) (in fb1, several die)
OTHER CHARACTERS: 5th Civilian Indigenous Defense Group (5th CIDG) inc Junior (also in fb2); US Marines (some die, others on TV) inc Col. Stoner, Green Berets, drill instructors & a Sgt.; 6 US Air Force airmen (2 die) inc Maj. Roger Pouran; Military Police inc a Sgt. & a Cpl.; US Air Calvary, Death Hole prisoners (many die, others a corpses, others in fb2), Hotel Parisian staff, bartender, bar patrons, news anchor (on TV), scorpions, snakes (both also in fb2), rats (all in fb1), war veteran, bystanders, dog; Richard M. Nixon (mentioned in fb1, current US President); Maria Castle (mentioned in fb1, also changed name)
LOCATIONS/ITEMS: Da Nang inc US Marine base & 5th Special Forces Group HQ, C-Det; Laos inc 5th CIDG's base camp & Death Hole (also in fb2) inc Death Doctor's cave laboratory; Quang Tri Province inc Highway 9; Saigon inc Hotel Parisian; Brooklyn inc bar; Fort Benning (all in fb1), Washington, DC inc Vietnam Memorial & Washington Monument / Sgt. Castiglione's grenade w/tripwire, Sgt. Castle's assault rifle, knife, M60, machete, RPG & sniper rifle; Junior's assault rifle (also in fb2), machete & crossbow; 5th CIDG's assault rifles & RPG; NVA's assault rifles & anti-aircraft missiles; Colonel No-Name's helicopter & opium (both destroyed); Death Doctor's revolver & lab equipment; mercenaries' cages (also in fb2), Cuban soldiers' assault rifles (also in fb2), Military Police's assault rifles, US Marines' explosives, US Air Force B-52 (destroyed) (all in fb1)
FLASHBACKS: At the end of his third tour in Da Nang, Sgt. Castiglione learns his request for extending for another tour has been denied. In Brooklyn, Frank Castiglione finds that he can't adjust to normal life. He changes his name to Frank Castle and re-enlists. Going through basic training

again under his new name, he's accepted into the Green Berets and eventually stationed in Laos advising the 5th Civilian Indigenous Defense Group. Sgt. Castle and the 5th CIDG ambush a North Vietnamese Army patrol, and Junior, Castle's 5th CIDG counterpart, interrogates the survivor. Meanwhile, a US Air Force B-52 is shot down; two of the crew die and four are captured. Junior tells Castle he learned an American officer is scheduled to pick up an opium shipment from the NVA. They ambush the pickup and Castle recognizes the officer as Colonel No-Name, who also recognizes Castiglione. The opium is destroyed, but the Colonel escapes. Castle prepares to pursue the Colonel, but Junior tells him about the captured B-52 crew, and that they're likely at Death Hole. Junior accompanies Castle in a rescue mission to Death Hole. Meanwhile the Colonel makes his way to a US base. Castle and Junior infiltrate Death Hole and Castle frees the airmen. Junior and the airmen escape but Castle is captured. Later at 5th Special Forces Group HQ, the airmen are interrogated by Colonel No-Name about Sgt. Castle. At Death Hole, Castle is tortured. Colonel No-Name threatens the airmen with treason charges until base Commanding Officer Colonel Stoner interrupts. Death Doctor readies Castle for his experiments, explaining he's working on a way to control soldiers remotely. Castle breaks free and kills the guards but Death Doctor escapes. Junior returns and the two kill more guards. Colonel No-Name runs out a window and Colonel Stoner arranges a rescue mission for Castle. Junior and Castle escape, but Junior is injured. The rescue mission finds them, Junior is tended to and Death Hole is demolished. Later, Colonel Stoner tells Sgt. Castle who Colonel No-Name is. In Saigon at the Hotel Parisian, Castle kills Colonel No-Name (1). On patrol with the 5th CIDG, Junior is captured and brought to the Death Hole where Death Doctor tortures and experiments on his compatriots. Junior eventually escapes (2).
SYNOPSIS: Frank Castle visits the Vietnam War Memorial and meets a paralyzed veteran. After finding Colonel No-Name on the Wall, Castle gives the veteran his Congressional Medal of Honor and leaves.
NOTE: Includes title page (1 page), table of contents/credits page (1 page) & forward by Tim Tuohy (1 page) which explains this story was intended to be TheNam #84-86 until that book's cancellation, and how TheNam #52-53, '91 & #67-69, '92 fit chronologically with this story. Features 3 Chapter Start pin-ups by Joe Kubert (1 page each); Chapter 1 End art (1 page) taken from page 9, panel 3 (reversed), Chapter 2 End art (1 page) taken from page 37, panel 1 & Chapter 3 End art (1 page) taken from page 64, panel 6. Followed by Cover Gallery (5 pages) featuring covers of TheNam #52-53, '91 & #67-69, '92. Back cover art taken from page 60, panel 3.

PUNISHER #86 (January 1994)

"Deadline" (30 pages)

CREDITS: Steven Grant (writer), Hugh Haynes (pencils), Mark McKenna, Mick Gray, Jon Holdredge (inks), Michael Higgins (letters), Lia Pelosi, Joe Andreani (colors), Tim Tuohy (asst editor), Don Daley (editor), Michael Golden (c art)
FEATURE CHARACTER: Punisher (next in PWZ #24, '94)
SUPPORTING CAST: Microchip (last in PWZ #23, '94, next in PWJ #62, '94), Mickey Fondozzi (minor crook, Punisher's unwilling informant, last in PWZ #23, '94, next in PWJ #64, '94), Lynn Michaels (cop turned vigilante, last in PWJ #61, '93, next in PWJ #62, '94 as "Lady" Punisher)
VILLAINS: Lt. Blackwell (next in PWJ #62, '94), Dean Swaybrick (entrepreneur, 1st, next as "Yup" Punisher), Tommy "Peach" Cullen (mob boss, 1st, next in PWZ #24, '94), Louis Cullen, Alfie Cullen, Dirk Cullen (prev 3 1st, mobsters, next in Pun #88, '94)
OTHER CHARACTERS: Outlaw (last in Pun #70, '92, next in PWZ #24, '94), Payback (retired vigilante, last in PWJ #51, '93, next in PWJ #62, '94), Jimmy Pierce (former vigilante, 1st, next as "Hitman" Punisher), Tess Clay (TV reporter, 1st), VIGIL inc Capt. Nails (next in PWJ #62, '94), Jessup, Brady, Riggs; Carson, Wills (FBI agents, both 1st, next in PWJ #62, '94), Punisher's "corpse" (1st, next in PWJ #62, '94), Barnes (Dean's butler), Dean's girl, diner cook, excavation crew, firefighters (some on TV), police, pub patrons & waitress, reporters (some on TV), bystanders; Jackie-Dee (mobster, on TV)
LOCATIONS/ITEMS: Manhattan Tower building (rubble), diner, Dean's penthouse, Lynn's apartment, London inc Pippo's pub, Cullen warehouse, police impound yard, Payback's warehouse, Lincoln Tunnel / Micro's detonator, fake ConEd van, Dean's Punisher suit & weapons, VIGIL helicopters & machine guns, Lynn's binoculars, motorcycle & machine gun; Outlaw's motorcycle, Cullen' guns, portable TV, Punisher suit, gas grenades, police guns; Payback's revolver, Blackwell's handgun
SYNOPSIS: Top mobsters meet at Manhattan Tower to discuss solving the Punisher problem, while Punisher's vigilante cop ally Lynn Michaels quits the force, tired of the ineffective justice system (PWJ #61, '93). Despite the meet being watched by several law enforcement agencies and Micro's insistence it's a trap, Punisher crashes the meet, killing several mobsters before the explosives he rigged bring the building down on all of them (PWZ #23, '93). In the aftermath of Manhattan Tower's collapse, VIGIL and the FBI fight over jurisdiction. In a diner Micro and Mickey Fondozzi see news reports and hear that the fake ConEd truck has been reported to the police; leaving the diner intending to ditch the van, they spot police already gathered round the parked van. Micro refuses to risk police lives by detonating it, prompting Mickey to flee. Elsewhere, Dean Swaybrick is overjoyed to hear of Punisher's death, as he has his own plans for the identity. Meanwhile, VIGIL's Blackwell and Jessup raid Lynn Michaels' apartment, but find she has already left. In England, Outlaw learns of Punisher's death and decides to go to America to either find Punisher or avenge him. As rescue work begins up top, Punisher, pinned by rubble far below, tries to free himself before blacking out. Meanwhile, the Cullen crime family recruit family black sheep and ex-cop Jimmy Pierce to be their Punisher, wanting to exploit his reputation. FBI Agent Carson visits the impound yard to look at the captured van, but it's stolen from the yard as he watches. Blackwell and Jessup raid retired vigilante Payback's warehouse, wanting info on Punisher, but Lynn rescues him. Blackwell and Jessup chase them to the Lincoln Tunnel until Nails calls with a report of body heat found in the rubble, needing Blackwell's helicopter to help with clearing rubble. Instead Blackwell bombs it. VIGIL heads into the resultant hole and finds Punisher's body.
NOTE: Cover labeled "Suicide Run: 3"; interior credits title the story "Deadline Pt.3." Continues from PWJ #61, '93 & PWZ #23, '93, and into PWJ #62, '94 & PWZ #24, '94. The first 3 parts of the story featured embossed foil-stamped covers. The cover image is grayscaled on 2 pgs, with credits superimposed over one. Michaels, Pierce & Swaybrick all assume the Punisher name. Promotional material identified them as Lady Punisher, Hitman Punisher & Yuppunisher respectively to distinguish them from the other copycats, though none were identified as such within the story. Pierce, revealed in PWJ #69, '94 to only be working for the Cullens because he believes they are holding his mother hostage, is not considered a villain. The issue features pin-ups of Punisher in Chinatown by Kelly Krantz & Klaus Janson, Punisher crashing through a window by Darick Robertson & Ron Boyd, Punisher in a prison fight by Roderick Delgado & Michael Higgins, and Punisher in the sewer by Shawn McManus. Pun #88, '94 hints that Dean's uncle initially suggested Dean become the Punisher and provided guidelines for spinning this to the media; Pun:Anniv, '94 reveals this uncle is Alex Alaric of the Trust (last in Pun #5, '86, next in PWJ #76, '95). Alaric is not considered bts here, as he apparently made this suggestion some time earlier.

PUNISHER #87 (February 1994)

"False Moves Pt. 6" (22 pages)

CREDITS: Steven Grant (writer), Hugh Haynes (pencils), Mark McKenna, Mick Gray (inks), Michael Higgins (letters), John Kalisz (colors), Tim Tuohy (asst editor), Don Daley (editor), Michael Golden (c art)
FEATURE CHARACTER: Punisher (next in PWJ #63, '94, PWZ #25, '94)
SUPPORTING CAST: Lynn Michaels (between PWJ #62-63, '94)
VILLAINS: Lt. Blackwell (last in PWZ #24, '94, next in PWJ #63, '94), "Yup" Punisher ("New Punisher", also on TV) & his private army, Tommy Cullen (next in PWJ #69/2, '94), Kaska (bts on phone) & his men, criminals (die)
OTHER CHARACTERS: Payback (between PWJ #62-63, '94), "Hitman" Punisher (next in PWJ #63, '94), Sheriff Harry Bendix (Laastekist sheriff) & his deputy (both last in PWZ #24, '94, next in PWJ #63, '94), VIGIL inc Capt. Nails (last in PWZ #24, '94), Jessup (dies), Brady & Riggs; Tess Clay (also on TV), Elliot (Dean's associate, 1st), Al Clooney (talk show host, on TV), Trish (Al's guest, on TV), camera operator, gamblers, Al's audience (bts on TV)
LOCATIONS/ITEMS: Kaska's rolling casino (destroyed), Al Clooney Show set (on TV), VIGIL HQ inc interrogation room, Alphabet City, Laastekist sheriff department / Pierce's Uzis, Punisher costume & skull mask; Dean's Punisher costume & weapons, Blackwell's handgun, Jessup's gun
SYNOPSIS: Lynn Michaels convinces Payback to help her continue the Punisher's war against crime. When they hit a mob bank for some capital, VIGIL swarms in and captures them (PWJ #63, '94). The FBI learns the body they found wasn't Frank Castle's. Outlaw purchases weapons to begin his quest to avenge Punisher. An injured and weakened Punisher hitches a ride upstate where he's cared for by Amy Bendix. Her father, the town sheriff, finds him and beats him senseless (PWZ #24, '94). Dressed as Punisher, Pierce robs and destroys Kaska's rolling casino. On the Al Clooney Show, Swaybrick, as the Punisher, promotes his book about Frank Castle and pushes his idea that an army of Punishers working within the law would eliminate crime. Elsewhere, Nails catches Blackwell's overly violent interrogation of Lynn and Payback, and tells him Jessup is replacing him on guard duty. Meanwhile, Pierce delivers the stolen money to his uncle, Tommy Cullen, and attempts to quit, but Tommy refuses, intent on using the Punisher name to garner further power. The next day, as Swaybrick televises live the start of his campaign against crime, and his men prepare to attack a crack house, in VIGIL HQ Blackwell resumes his brutal interrogation, but is caught by Jessup. At the same time, the crack house chances to be where Pierce has been sent to rub out more of the Cullen's competition, and he is caught on camera. The Punisher's apparent return steals Swaybrick's limelight, and he swears vengeance. Blackwell attempts to go after Pierce, but Jessup tries to arrest him for his brutality; while they are preoccupied, the prisoners escape. Blackwell murders Jessup and blames the escapees when Nails arrives. Upstate in Laastekist, Punisher lays unconscious in a cell while the sheriff department waits for the FBI to process his fingerprints.
NOTE: Cover labeled "Suicide Run: 6," continuing from PWJ #62, '94 & PWZ #24, '94, and into PWJ #63, '94 & PWZ #25, '94. The credits are run over a grayscaled copy of the cover image.

PUNISHER #88 (March 1994)

"Past the Point of Rescue Pt. 9" (23 pages)

CREDITS: Steven Grant (writer), Hugh Haynes (pencils), Mark McKenna, Mick Gray (inks), Michael Higgins (letters), John Kalisz (colors), Freddy Mendez (asst editor), Don Daley (editor), Liam Sharp (c pencils), Mark Farmer (c inks)
FEATURE CHARACTER: Punisher (next in PWJ #64-69, Pun #94, all '94)
SUPPORTING CAST: Lynn Michaels (last in PWZ #25, '94, next in PWJ #64, '94)
VILLAINS: Lt. Blackwell (last in PWZ #25, '94, next in PWJ #64, '94), Louis Cullen, Dirk Cullen, Alfie Cullen & his associates (prev 4 die), "Yup" Punisher (dies) & his private army, Righteous Ones (motorcycle gang), various criminals
OTHER CHARACTERS: Payback, Sheriff Harry Bendix (both last in PWZ #25, '94, next in PWJ #64, '94), "Hitman" Punisher (last in PWJ #63, '94, next in PWJ #67/2, '94), Outlaw (between PWJ #63-64, '94), Amy Bendix (last in PWZ #25, '94), FBI agents inc Carson (last in PWZ #24, '94), Elliot (dies), VIGIL inc Capt. Nails (next in PWJ #65, '94), Brady (next in PWJ #68, '94), Riggs (next in PWJ #70, '94); Laastekist residents, doctor; Tess Clay (bts, en route to Laastekist, next in PWJ #64, '94), governor (approved FBI's lockdown plan)
LOCATIONS/ITEMS: Cullen warehouse, Laastekist inc sheriff department, Bendix property, doctor's office / Swaybrick's automatic rifles & guns, Cullen' Uzis, FBI weapons, Outlaw's motorcycle & handgun, Righteous Ones' motorcycles & pipe, Blackwell's handgun & nightstick
SYNOPSIS: Sheriff Bendix's checking Punisher's prints draws multiple law enforcement agencies and crooks to Laastekist, turning the town into a war zone. Punisher tries to convince the sheriff to let him out to help (PWJ #64, '94). Punisher is freed and begins killing the invading criminals, rescuing Bendix's daughter from Blackwell in the process. Meanwhile, Lynn and Payback head for Laastekist (PWZ #25, '94). Swaybrick leads a raid on a Cullen business to track down their Punisher, discovering the joy of killing in the process, learning Pierce has been sent to Laastekist. Arriving in Laastekist, Lynn and Payback are gunned down by the Cullens, upsetting Jimmy Pierce, who has been trying to avoid killing innocents. Checking their bodies, he falsely claims they are dead; after the Cullens depart, Payback wakes, and Bendix, having watched from the shadows unwilling to intervene lest he endanger his unconscious daughter, directs them to the doctor and informs them they're under arrest. Bendix tries to phone out of town for help, but learns the FBI decided that since crooks and vigilantes have already invaded the town, they will continue to let more in, trapping them together before moving in. In town, Outlaw confronts the Righteous Ones biker gang, but is overpowered. Bendix returns to his property and is ambushed by a delusional Blackwell, who then attacks the town doctor, having spotted an unconscious Lynn through the window; he leaves to hunt the Punisher unaware Payback was hiding within. Swaybrick finds the Cullens and Pierce; his men gun down the Cullens, but flee when Swaybrick prepares to murder the unarmed and surrendered Pierce, distracting Swaybrick long enough for Pierce to grab a gun and kill him. Blackwell then shoots Pierce, believing he was the Punisher. The real Punisher attacks Blackwell, but Blackwell's gunshots are heard by the Righteous Ones, who abandon the unconscious Outlaw to investigate. Punisher knocks Blackwell out, then looks up to find himself surrounded.
NOTE: Cover labeled "Suicide Run: 9," continuing from PWJ #63 & PWZ #25, and into PWJ #64, all '94. The credits are run over a grayscaled copy of the cover image. Nails' hair is miscolored white. Eliot mentions "Yup" Punisher's uncle; see Pun #86, '94 note.

PUNISHER #89 (April 1994)

"Fortress: Miami" (20 pages)

CREDITS: Chuck Dixon (writer), Russ Heath (art), Jim Novak (letters), Phil Felix (colors), Freddy Mendez (asst editor), Don Daley (editor), Elman Brown (c art)
FEATURE CHARACTER: Punisher (last in PWZ #30, '94)
SUPPORTING CAST: Microchip (last in PWZ #30, '94)
VILLAINS: Gen. Hector Carranza (1st) & his men (some also as National Guardsmen) inc Lupo (1st), Solomon Garland (1st, drug dealer, aka "Solly Wise" & "Bottle Jake") & his thugs (some die), Bosqueverdan soldier (dies), Miami drug gangsters (some die)
OTHER CHARACTERS: Felicia McBride (1st, Solomon's mistress), Aaron (Microchip's uncle, mentioned), Navy Seal squadron, sailors, Solomon's customer, Carranza's mistress & attorney, Imperial Motor Lodge clerk, Florida's governor (calls out the National Guard bts), reporters (one on television), cameramen, federal marshals, police, truck driver, snitch (bts, dies), pilot, stewardesses, Florida national guardsman (some also bts on television), bystanders (some die), dog
LOCATIONS/ITEMS: Bosqueverde (a Caribbean island) inc presidential palace; Newark inc highway, airport & Imperial Motor Lodge; Miami inc federal courthouse, Garland's Rivo Alto home & Dade County jail w/Carranza's cell; Carranza's attorney's office, Microchip's home, Aaron's Fort Lauderdale home / Navy plane & submarine, Seals' guns, knives & inflatable rafts, Punisher's van, gun & binoculars, Garland's thugs' guns, reporters' microphones, cameramen's cameras, marshals', police & drug gangsters' guns, transfer truck, Garland's trademarked "Toro" drug packets, National Guard humvee (on television)
SYNOPSIS: Late one night, a squadron of Navy Seals storm Gen. Carranza's Bosqueverdan presidential palace and arrest him. Meanwhile, in Newark, Punisher raids a seedy hotel seeking Solomon Garland, a drug trader. Garland escapes but Punisher interrogates his mistress and discovers that Garland is marketing his product with the brand name "Toro." Days later, from his Dade County jail cell, Carranza instructs Lupo to find a way to free him. Over the next few days, a drug war breaks out in Miami, and the police are helpless to stop the destruction. The governor calls out the National Guard and declares martial law, cordoning off the city. When Punisher discovers a shipment of Garland's drugs in a truck from Florida, he tracks down Felicia and takes her to Fort Lauderdale. She tells Micro and him that Garland has a place in Rivo Alto, a sandbar in Biscayne Bay. Leaving her to be watched by Micro, late that night Frank bypasses the roadblocks by snorkeling across the bay. Watching the house from the beach, he is shocked to see Garland socializing with National Guardsmen, including Lupo.
NOTE: Carranza's first name is revealed in Pun #91, '94.

PUNISHER #90 (May 1994)

"Hammered" (20 pages)

CREDITS: Chuck Dixon (writer), Russ Heath (art), Jim Novak (letters), Phil Felix (colors), Freddy Mendez (asst editor), Don Daley (editor), Elman Brown (c art)
FEATURE CHARACTER: Punisher
SUPPORTING CAST: Microchip (next in PunSS #4/2, '94)
VILLAINS: Gen. Carranza & his men inc Lupo (some also as National Guardsmen, some die), Solomon Garland (dies) & his thugs (some die), drug gang
OTHER CHARACTERS: Felicia McBride, Carranza's attorney, Garland's women, jail guard (dies), National guardsmen, police
LOCATIONS/ITEMS: Garland's Rivo Alto home, Aaron's Fort Lauderdale home, Miami inc Morningside Park; Dade County jail w/conference room & Carranza's cell, Reavers nightclub, Coral Springs Municipal Airport / Punisher's binoculars, car & gun, National Guard guns, drug gang's bazooka & guns, frying pan (swung by Felicia), Garland & his men's guns, Lupo's gun & humvees, police car (destroyed), Carranza's military transport plane
SYNOPSIS: A squad of real National Guardsmen encounters Punisher, but he escapes by diving into the bay. The next day, Frank radios Microchip and instructs him to find a National Guard officer's uniform, along with travel papers. While Micro is distracted, Felicia knocks him out with a frying pan and flees. Meanwhile, Carranza rejoices when he learns the escape plans are all in place. That night, Punisher revives Microchip and is disappointed to learn that Microchip has not been able to acquire the supplies. Felicia goes to Reavers nightclub and warns Garland that Punisher is looking for him. Enraged that Felicia might have led the vigilante to him, Garland points his gun at Felicia, but Frank, following up an earlier lead from Felicia, arrives and kills Garland's men. Grabbing a gun during the firefight, Felicia kills Garland, but not before he reveals that Carranza's men are breaking him out of jail at that moment. Lupo frees Carranza from jail, but on the way to the airport, Punisher intercepts them. Frank chases them to airport and kills several of Carranza's men, but Carranza reaches his plane and escapes.
NOTE: This issue includes a two-page entry in Microchip's journal, written & drawn by Eliot R. Brown. The entry describes his portable Faraday room and Punisher's new Flyer's Immersion Coverall.

PUNISHER #91 (June 1994)

"Fortress: Miami Part 3 The Silk Noose" (22 pages)

CREDITS: Chuck Dixon (writer), Russ Heath (art), Jim Novak (letters), Phil Felix (colors), Freddy Mendez (asst editor), Don Daley (editor), Elman Brown (c art)
FEATURE CHARACTER: Punisher (also as "the Colonel")
VILLAINS: Gen. Carranza (also in pfb on television), Porquito (1st, Carranza's government liaison), Red Condors (all 1st, elite Bosqueverdan army squad): Carlos, Jorgito, Manuel, Rabio, Reynardo, Tico; Bosqueverdan soldiers (many die) inc Fernando, the Lhosa brothers (prev 3 die), Rafito; "Little Bo" Bojarsky (federally protected witness), 2 drug smugglers (prev 3 die)
OTHER CHARACTERS: Federal marshals, Carranza's mistresses, snake, Bosqueverdan dignitaries (in pfb on television)
LOCATIONS/ITEMS: Bojarsky's motel room, Bosqueverde inc Verdenoches Airport (in pfb on television), Red Condors' camp & Carranza's Sierra Angeles prison compound w/nearby jungle / Punisher's guns, taser, parachute, grenades, microphone, crossbow, knife, map, telescope & GSP receiver, marshals' guns, smugglers' plane (destroyed), soldiers'

guns & machetes, Red Condors' helicopter, guns, night goggles, knives & grenade

FLASHBACK: Carranza arrives to a hero's welcome at Verdenoches Airport after escaping US custody (p).

SYNOPSIS: After killing a mobster in the witness protection program, Punisher learns that Carranza has been placed under arrest in Bosqueverde, and imprisoned in a secluded compound. Carranza is actually living in luxury, until the heat of international attention dies down. Punisher hires drug smugglers to drop him by parachute from their plane near the compound, leaving behind a grenade that destroys the plane. After Frank kills several of Carranza's men, the dictator calls in the elite Red Condors to kill Punisher, offering them a multi-million dollar reward. The Condors drop from a helicopter and pursue Frank. As Punisher crosses a ravine on a fallen tree, one Condor tosses a grenade, which explodes nearby and sends Frank cascading into the river below. Frank stumbles to the shore, deafened from the blast, with the Condors close behind.

NOTE: Carranza's first name, Hector, is revealed here. Carlos, Jorgito, Reynardo, Tico & Manuel's names are revealed in Pun #92, '94.

PUNISHER #92 (July 1994)

"Fortress: Miami Part 4 Razor's Edge" (22 pages)

CREDITS: Chuck Dixon (writer), Russ Heath (art, colors), Jim Novak (letters), Freddy Mendez (asst editor), Don Daley (editor), Elman Brown (c art)
FEATURE CHARACTER: Punisher (next in PunSS #4, PWZ Ann #2, Pun:BSS #3, all '94)
VILLAINS: Gen. Carranza (dies), Porquito, Red Condors: Carlos, Jorgito, Manuel, Rabio (also as Condor Uno), Reynardo, Tico; helicopter pilot & copilot (prev 8 die), Bosqueverdan soldiers
OTHER CHARACTERS: Carranza's mistresses
LOCATIONS/ITEMS: Carranza's Sierra Angeles prison compound w/nearby jungle / Punisher's knife & club, Red Condors' helicopter, radio & guns (all commandeered by Punisher), Carranza's guns
SYNOPSIS: Carlos and Manuel search for Punisher in the river, but he rises from the water behind them and kills Carlos, then escapes with Carlos' gun before Manuel can shoot him. When Rabio reports to Carranza, the dictator recognizes Punisher's skull emblem. After briefly panicking, he reassures himself that the Condors can defeat Punisher. In the jungle outside, Punisher doubles back and abducts Reynardo, tying him to the base of a tree as bait. He uses Reynardo's radio to taunt the other Condors. Tico finds Reynardo, but realizes he cannot save him without putting his own life at risk. When Punisher shoots Reynardo in the leg, Tico disobeys Rabio's orders and leaves his shelter to aid Reynardo, only to be killed by Punisher. Moments later, Frank bushwhacks Jorgito and kills him. With Reynardo's usefulness exhausted, Punisher kills him. When Punisher shoots and kills Manuel from a distance, Rabio calls for extraction from the helicopter. Believing this signals Punisher's defeat, Carranza celebrates, but Punisher kills Rabio and commandeers the chopper. Flying the helicopter, Punisher attacks Carranza's compound and kills the dictator, then flies away.

NOTE: Carlos, Reynardo, Jorgito, Tico & Manuel's names are revealed here. Reynardo, perhaps delirious from pain, refers to Tico as Manuel. A note at the start of the issue confirms this story takes place prior to the earlier published Suicide Run. On p6 one of Carranza's mistresses' midriffs is miscolored, turning her bikini into a swimsuit.

PUNISHER: A MAN NAMED FRANK (June 1994)

"A Man Named Frank" (45 pages)

CREDITS: Chuck Dixon (writer), John Buscema (art), Jim Novak (letters), Christie Scheele (colors), Melisa Danon, Cindy Emmert, Johnny Greene (production), Comicolor (separator), Freddy Mendez (asst editor/young gun), Don Daley (editor/regulator), Bob Larkin (c art, c colors), Scott "Pondscum" Elder (special thanks)
FEATURE CHARACTER: Frank (retired cavalryman & farmer)
VILLAINS: William Tyrone "Billy" Simms, Tuck "Swede" Jurgenson, "the Breed," "Pig Eyes" (killers of Frank's family); Simms' pals, Angus MacCauley (crooked Texan rancher) (all die); rustlers (some die) inc Liam Dunn (dies) & Liam's brother (bts, dies); General Zuvalo (Mexican insurgent) & his men (some die)
OTHER CHARACTERS: Maria (bts), Frank's unnamed son & daughter; Baxters (mentioned, Frank's closest neighbors), Father Domingo (priest), nuns, Augustus ("Gus," Frank's war buddy), saloon patrons, Taos Chinaman, Pueblo rail detective (both mentioned, provide leads), Denver police; MacCauley ranch hands inc Silas, Boetticer saloon patrons & barman, MacCauley's New York friends, bystanders, restaurant staff, NYPD, cattle
LOCATIONS/ITEMS: New Mexico inc Frank's farmhouse w/graves, cave, Gallup inc saloon, San Carlos mission (mentioned); Denver inc Sheehan's hotel, Texas inc Angus MacCauley's ranch w/ranchhouse, Boetticher (border town) inc saloon, Mesa Gordo near Mexican border, Mexico inc railroad tracks (destroyed), New York City inc restaurant / wagon wheel, crucifijo, horses, Frank's guns, double eagle coins, arrest warrants & Lewis gun, Gus' armory, train, MacCauley's truck
SYNOPSIS: In New Mexico on December 23rd 1910, a farmer named Frank memorizes the faces of the men who have attacked his farmhouse and killed his family; the worst of the group remains hidden in shadows beneath a sombrero, but Frank sees the man has taken his wife Maria's crucifijo as a trophy. Having found nothing of value, they depart, leaving Frank bound to a wagon wheel, figuring he will die a slow, lingering death, but driven by hatred Frank carries the massive wheel on his back across the desert until he collapses. He is saved by a priest and nuns on their way to a mission, and the priest stays with Frank to nurse him back to health, sheltering in a cave out of the desert sun, where Frank notices a skull-faced painting on the cave wall. After burying his family, Frank marks his shirts with the cave's skull symbol and becomes a bounty hunter, searching for clues to his family's killers. Finally putting a name to one of them, Billy Simms, Frank tracks him to Denver and kills him. On Simms' corpse he finds a letter signed by "S" telling Simms that Texas cattleman Angus MacCauley needs gun hands. Frank heads to Texas and signs on as one of MacCauley's regulators, agreeing to his new employer's demand not to just discourage rustlers, but to punish them. Frank spends months guarding MacCauley's north range, killing rustlers and looking for S, but none of the farmhands fit the bill. Eventually a rustler tells Frank that Mexicans are stealing cattle from the south range, which the other regulator, Tuck Jurgenson, patrols. Staking out a pass near the border, Frank witnesses Tuck deliver cattle to Mexican bandits, whose members include two of the men Frank has been hunting. Frank ambushes the train the bandits are using to transport the cattle, disabling the tracks as it passes over a gorge, then guns down his two targets. Frank returns to MacCauley's ranch to warn him of Tuck's involvement with Mexican rustlers, but MacCauley already knows, as he ordered it. As Tuck holds Frank at gunpoint, Frank spots Maria's crucifijo round his neck, and realizes Tuck is the final killer. However, the vengeful Mexicans attack the ranch, blaming MacCauley for the ambush; using the distraction, Frank retrieves his Lewis gun and slaughters the bandits. After the battle he finds MacCauley has fled, leaving a wounded Tuck behind. Tuck admits to being S, his nickname being "Swede," and Frank kills him,

then reclaims Maria's crucifijo. After visiting his family's graves to leave the crucifijo on Maria's grave marker, Frank tracks MacCauley to New York and executes him, having decided to continue riding where the law cannot reach, and punish those who trespass.
NOTE: Prestige format. Includes credits page (1 page). Back cover art taken from page 5, panel 1. MWOFiles, '06 confirms Frank to be part of Earth-616 (the main Marvel Earth)'s history, rather than an alternate reality version of Punisher.

PUNISHER #93 (August 1994)

"Killing Streets" (21 pages)

CREDITS: Chuck Dixon (writer), Todd Fox (art), Enrique Villagran (inks), Janice Chiang (letters), Glynis Oliver (colors), Freddy Mendez (asst editor), Don Daley (editor), Michael Golden (c colors), Bill Sienkiewicz (c art), George Roussos (c colors)
FEATURE CHARACTER: Punisher (also as Fat Franny, next in PWZ #31-36 & 38-40, '94-95, PunHol #3, '95, GR/W/Pun, '94, PWJ #61, '93, PWZ #23, '94, Pun #86, '94)
VILLAINS: Razors (a drug gang, some also in pfb), drug dealers, street criminals (all die)
OTHER CHARACTERS: Gonzalo (young boy) & his mother (both also in pfb), Soong (produce store owner) & his employee (both in pfb), Hernandez (sandwich store owner), Fat Franny (newsstand owner, vacationing bts in Ocean City), tie store owner (dies), Gonzalo's friends, police, bystanders (some also in pfb); Mrs. Clark (candyshop owner, mentioned, opinion of Punisher quoted by Gonzalo), Mr. Getzel (local business owner, mentioned), Franny's sister (mentioned)
LOCATIONS/ITEMS: New York City inc East Tenth neighborhood (also in pfb), Hernandez's sandwich shop, Gonzalo's bedroom, Gonzalo's mother's flower shop, Clark's Candyshop, Fat Franny's newsstand, Family of Ties (tie store), Razor's drug den (formerly Dunrite Dryclean, also in pfb), Soong's store (in pfb), Time Goes By (vintage clothing store, replaces drug den) / Punisher's gun, Razors' guns, tie store owner's broom
FLASHBACK: The Razors set up a drug den in an empty drycleaners. When residents ask for police help, the Razors beat up Soong, then seek protection money from the shop owners, including Gonzalo's mother (p).
SYNOPSIS: Punisher discovers a young boy, Gonzalo, posting flyers asking for his help. Gonzalo is distraught over a drug gang who have taken control of his neighborhood and established a protection racket, and asks Punisher to "punish them." Frank agrees, but cautions Gonzalo to hide when things go down. Meanwhile, the Razors terrorize the neighborhood, including Fat Franny and Gonzalo's mother. When a former Marine opens up a store in the neighborhood and rallies the other owners into fighting back, Gonzalo is convinced the newcomer is Punisher in disguise. However, to Gonzalo's shock, the Razors gun the Marine down in the street. When the deadline for delivering their protection money arrives, Fat Franny is the first owner to show up. The Razors are caught flat-footed when Franny reveals himself as Punisher, and the vigilante wipes out the gang. When Gonzalo shows up, Frank warns him that it's not over yet, and to go home. That night, Punisher kills the dealers who show up to deliver the drugs, then disappears. Weeks later, life is better for Gonzalo. While he sometimes wishes he could meet Punisher again to thank him, other times, he is glad he never will.

PUNISHER #94 (September 1994)

Untitled (24 pages)

CREDITS: Dan Abnett, Andy Lanning (writers), Frank Teran (art), Susan Crespi (letters), Christie Scheele (colors), Freddy Mendez (asst editor), Don Daley (editor), Michael Golden (c colors)
FEATURE CHARACTER: Punisher (last in PWJ #69, '94)
VILLAINS: Grisholm (1st, inhumanly strong gangster), Irish Joe (Tourney Bar owner, 1st bts), Tourney Bar patrons & contestants
OTHER CHARACTER: Train conductor (in shadow)
LOCATIONS/ITEMS: Brooklyn inc East River train trestle & Tourney Bar w/fight cage (chain link fence topped w/ barb wire) / spiked clubs, pipes, knives, sledgehammer, pipe wrench, baseball bats, pickaxe, scythes, axe, sword, chain, guns (all wielded by Tourney Bar patrons & contestants)
SYNOPSIS: Punisher chases Grisholm down on the East River trestle. As they trade blows, Frank recognizes the rumble of the Brooklyn train. Punisher and Grisholm leap off the tracks, barely avoiding the train, and the chase continues across the rooftops. When Grisholm charges Punisher, they plunge through a skylight into the Tourney Bar fightclub. They land in the middle of the cage, interrupting a fight. A hush falls over the heavily-armed crowd, and Punisher and Grisholm realize they must team up if they are to survive. They quickly dispatch the two contestants, but the crowd erupts and charges the ring. In the midst of the melee, one thug shoots at Frank, but he uses an unconscious foe's body and his Kevlar to block the shots. When the thug aims at Punisher's head, Grisholm saves him, but the violent mob quickly overruns them.
NOTE: The story has no title, but "No Rules Part I" appears on the cover. Irish Joe's name is revealed in Pun #95, '94.

PUNISHER #95 (October 1994)

"No Rules Round Two No Mercy" (23 pages)

CREDITS: Dan Abnett, Andy Lanning (writers), Frank Teran (art), Susan Crespi (letters), Christie Scheele (colors), Freddy Mendez (asst editor), Don Daley (editor), Michael Golden (c colors)
FEATURE CHARACTER: Punisher (next in PWJ #71-72, Pun:EQ fb, PWJ #73, Pun:EQ, all '94)
VILLAINS: Grisholm, Irish Joe & his thugs, Knucklebone, Krush (both Emporium pit champions) (all die), Grisholm's associate (bts on phone) & mercenaries, fight spectators, ring announcer
LOCATIONS/ITEMS: Irish Joe's Emporium, Grisholm's mansion / chains, crane, spectators & Irish Joe's thugs' guns, Grisholm's mercenaries' grenades & chain guns, lighting wires, Punisher's gun
SYNOPSIS: Punisher and Grisholm wake to find themselves captives of Irish Joe. Joe tells them they will fight in his Emporium to reimburse him for lost revenue when they wrecked his bar. That night, a large crowd gathers to witness the fight between two teams: Punisher and Grisholm against Emporium champions, the massive Knucklebone and Krush. After a brutal fight Grisholm stuns Knucklebone, then turns to aid the struggling Punisher, who temporarily disables

Krush by ripping out his earring, providing Grisholm an opening to knock Krush down. Enraged, Joe grabs a gun from one of his men and shoots wildly into the ring. In a last-ditch effort to stop Joe, Grisholm hoists Punisher to the platform above. Punisher wrests the gun from Joe and kills his henchmen. He shoots out the lighting rig, which collapses, then kills Joe. In the ring, Krush gets back up, and chokes Grisholm, but Punisher guns down Knucklebone and wounds Krush; he releases his grip on Grisholm, who kills Krush with a punch that drives Krush's nasal cartilage into his brain. The crowd opens fire, blasting out the side of the staging, and letting the East River flood in, just before Grisholm's mercenaries charge in. The mercenaries hesitate to kill Punisher when they notice he's holding live wires over the water they're standing in. Grisholm orders his men to let Punisher go, but that night Punisher visits Grisholm at his mansion and kills him.
NOTE: Irish Joe is named in this story.

PUNISHER: EMPTY QUARTER (November 1994)

"Empty Quarter" (62 pages)

CREDITS: Mike Baron (writer), Bill Reinhold (art), Willie Schubert (letters), Mark Badger (colors/separator), Cindy Emmert, Jim Hoston, Jon Babcock, Melisa Danon (production), Freddy Mendez (asst editor), Don Daley (editor)
FEATURE CHARACTER: Punisher (also as Rook & Saracen, also in rfb & pfb, also in fb1 between PWJ #72-73, '95, next in Pun Ann #7, '94)
VILLAINS: Saracen (also in pfb1 & 2, last in PWJ #33, '91), Jackal (terrorist leader) (both die) & his men (in pfb1, 1 in rfb1), Raul Rawdah (terrorist, dies), terrorists (some die) inc IRA, Hezbollah, Shining Path (also in pfb2) inc Quetzl (in pfb2), AIM, Khmer Rouge, Tamil Militia, KGB inc Major Kulyin (dies), Humans Off Planet, animal rights extremists, Olsen, Lars, Ms. Goldwomyn, Selim, Larry, Dom (prev 3 die), Yasir; Chicago gun-runners (in fb1)
OTHER CHARACTERS: Rose Kugel (last in Pun #48, '91), "Rolf Ganzi" (Mossad agent, corpse), Brenda (Raul's lover), passengers, pilots (prev 3 die), airport check-in staff, barman, ticket agent, Jackal's servants, young boy, sheep, bystanders, camels; Bolivian DEA Agent, Federales (both in pfb1); Truby (in rfb1), Rocco & Esmeralda Castiglione (in rfb2)
LOCATIONS/ITEMS: Germany inc Frankfurt International Airport; Cyprus inc Nicosia Airport; Hama village, Ran-al-Khali (Empty Quarter) desert inc terrorist fort, Chicago (in fb1), Bolivian jungle inc prison (in pfb1 & 2) / Brenda's suitcase bomb, airplanes, Raul's Mercedes, taxi, fishing boat, small plane, Raul's binoculars & canteens, Raul's International Freedom Fighter's Convention invite (Mansell's freeze-dried ear), Saracen's invite (another freeze-dried ear, in pfb1), other invites (freeze-dried ears), terrorists' guns, explosives & Humvee, Saracen's sword, Punisher's fake nose, sword, spiked ball, Uzi, handgun (prev 2 in rfb1), rifle, machete, baseball bat (prev 3 in pfb1), scuba gear (rfb2); tents (pfb1), ship (rfb2), helicopter (pfb1), hookah pipe, Rose's rifle, Semtex & knife, Jackal's jeep, Rollwell jetpacks, jeep & tow chain
FLASHBACKS: Punisher kills gunrunners in Chicago (1; see NOTE), which leads him to crooks in Reno (PWJ #73, '94). In the Bolivian jungle, Punisher comes across Saracen's camp. Finding Saracen's invitation to the terrorist convention, Punisher arranges for the Bolivian DEA to capture Saracen, then takes his place at the convention while Saracen is in prison (p1). Saracen kills Rocco & Esmeralda Castiglione (PWJ #27, '91). Saracen is freed by Shining Path and given transport out of the country (p2).
SYNOPSIS: Raul sees his pregnant lover off on a flight, having secretly given his unwitting girlfriend a bomb that goes off shortly after take-off. Changing his appearance, Raul heads along the terrorist railroad until he reaches the terrorist convention in the Ran-al-Khali, the "Empty Quarter." He arrives to find Saracen challenging him for a supposed betrayal in an earlier encounter, but just before killing Raul, Saracen quietly reveals it is revenge for the bombing. Back in his quarters Punisher briefly removes his disguise, and recalls how he came to take Saracen's place at the convention. At the fort, experts teach others how to be effective terrorists under the Jackal's notion for a unified terror front against their enemies. Jackal grants "Saracen" an audience,considering him the world's second-most important "freedom fighter" after himself, and offers him a choice of lovers to keep his bed warm. Knowing refusing will offend and possibly blow his cover, Punisher chooses the woman, who turns out to be his old ally, undercover Mossad agent Rose Kugel. She tells him about an arsenal the Iraqis dumped in the fort, and with his help plans to take it out. As Punisher and Rose make their way to the armory, Saracen makes his way across the desert to the convention, finding the corpse of Rose's missing partner in the desert. Saracen reaches the fort just as Punisher and Rose find the arsenal. Just as they finish setting explosives, Jackal and his men storm the arsenal. Punisher and Rose fight them long enough to ensure most of them are present for the blast, before escaping through a ventilation shaft. After the arsenal blows, Saracen takes Rose captive and confronts Punisher, challenging him to a duel for Rose's life. After a brutal fight, Punisher kills Saracen, and he and Rose head away from the Empty Quarter in a purloined jeep.
NOTE: Prestige format. Maintaining his Saracen cover, Punisher calls Raul "Hakim," Arabic for "leader." Fb1 is intended to show events from "Cold Steel," an upcoming story arc in PWZ, but the series was cancelled before the story came out.

PUNISHER ANNUAL #7 (1994)

"Unfinished Business" (6 pages)
"Eurohit '94" (52 pages)

CREDITS: Dan Abnett, Andy Lanning (writers), Andrew Currie (pencils p1-6), Doug Braithwaite (pencils p7-58, c pencils), Art Nichols (inks), Fred Fredericks, Al Williamson (inks p7-58), Bill Oakley (letters p1-6), Ken Lopez (letters p7-58), Joe Andreani (colors p1-6), Christie Scheele (colors p7-58), Freddy Mendez (asst editor), Tim Tuohy (consulting editor), Don Daley (editor)
FEATURE CHARACTER: Punisher (also as Snakebite, also in dfb, next in Pun #96, '94)
SUPPORTING CAST: Microchip (last in PWJ #68, '94, chr next in Pun #100/2, '95, next in Pun #97, '95)
VILLAINS: Rapido (last in PWZ #23, '94, next in CW:BDR, '07, also in rfb), Armand Chauffard (last in Pun #68, '92, last bts in PWJ #61, '93, dies; also in rfb), Architect (Orville Nugent, criminal planner, last in PWZ #19, '93, last bts in PWJ #61, '93, dies; also in rfb), mobsters (many die, some also in rfb), Jerry (Architect's assistant), European mob bosses, Mr. Cooly (American mob boss, dies), Architect's staff
OTHER CHARACTERS: Outlaw (last in PWJ #64, '94, also in rfb & dfb), Morgan Sinclair (last in Pun #70, '92, also in rfb), Jack Oonuk (Inuit troubleshooter, last in PWZ #19, '93, also in rfb & dfb), NYPD cops (2 die), Major "Tiger" Timms (SAS commander, dies) & his men (die), Interpol agents inc Superintendent Coldstream (last in Pun #70, '92), French government minister, surgeons, TV newsreader (on TV), Tunnel opening ceremony attendees; Batroc, Kingpin, Microchip, Snakebite, Tarantula (prev 5 in rfb)

LOCATIONS/ITEMS: Manhattan Towers ruins (also in rfb), Architect's European base, British end of Channel Tunnel (also in rfb); Amaldo Observatory, Pyranees, Catalan, Spain; Beauvais Rail Terminal, France; TML HQ, Dover; hospital room / Rapido's chain gun (also in rfb), cybernetic arm & laser-sight, Architect's limo, jet & gun, Daily Express newspaper, snowmobiles, scuba gear (bts), Oonuk's rocket launcher, Intercontinental Bullet Trains w/concealed contraband compartments inc Pod 6, Punisher's guns, knife & Snakebite disguise; Outlaw's guns, glass cutter & remote-controlled van (destroyed) Sinclair's gun, Oonuk's gun & Kevlar vest

FLASHBACKS: Punisher and Microchip pursue Snakebite to Europe, and thwart Kingpin's plans to expand there (Pun #64-70, '92). Punisher works with Jack Oonuk to prevent the Architect from maiming the Northern Territories (PWJ #17-19, '93). Punisher blows up a mob boss meeting in Manhattan Towers, nearly killing himself and Rapido in the process (PWZ #23, '93). "Snakebite" and his men raid one of the Architect's contraband shipments (d).

SYNOPSIS: Punisher reviews his past battles with Rapido and the Architect, leading up to the destruction of Manhattan Towers. Surviving that building's collapse, an injured Rapido digs himself from the rubble, and is spotted by Architect and Chauffard, both of whom were invited to attend the mob meeting at the Towers, but were delayed, saving their lives. The Architect enlists them in his plot to resurrect the Kingpin's plan to unite Europe's mobs, and arranges for Rapido's medical care and cybernetic upgrade of his rail gun arm to a more versatile weapons platform. At a European mob boss meeting, Architect outlines his plans to use the Channel Tunnel as a way of uniting their organizations, then dispatches Rapido to execute Morgan Sinclair, CEO of the tunnel operators, TML, so she won't interfere; during the resulting firefight in the tunnel, Sinclair shoots out a valve seal, flooding the area and seemingly drowning. Learning his old nemesis Jack Oonuk has been tapping into his Pyranees communications center, Architect sends Rapido to eliminate Oonuk too; their battle ends with Oonuk swept into a ravine by an avalanche and seemingly killed. A few days later the Architect test runs his smuggling system, using hidden compartments built into the Channel Tunnel's high-speed Intercontinental Bullet Trains; however, one of the smuggling pods is attacked, and the men within slain. Video footage shows Snakebite, who Rapido believed slain by the Punisher long ago, is behind the raid. Learning Outlaw is investigating Morgan's death, Architect instructs Rapido to stop him; when Outlaw flees their confrontation in a van, Rapido shoots it off the road, and it explodes. Meanwhile Snakebite has contacted Architect, demanding to be cut into the Tunnel deal and threatening sabotage otherwise. Architect agrees to a meeting on the day the Tunnel opens, intending to have Rapido and his men kill Snakebite instead. However, "Snakebite" turns out to be Punisher, and his entourage includes Morgan, Outlaw and Oonuk; having caught wind of Architect's deal, Punisher anticipated Architect would see them as threats, and forewarned them, allowing them to fake their deaths. Morgan shoots Chauffard dead while Oonuk kills the Architect, and Rapido's fight with Punisher ends when a train strikes him. Surviving but arrested, Rapido recuperates in hospital, vowing he will get revenge.

NOTE: Includes table of contents/credits page (1 page) w/art taken from page 14, panel 4.

PUNISHER #96 (November 1994)

"Raving Beauty" (22 pages)

CREDITS: Richard Rainey (writer), Isaac M. Del Rivero (art), Ken Lopez (letters), Kevin Tinsley (colors), Freddy Mendez (asst editor), Don Daley (editor), Dave Eaglesham (c pencils), Scott Koblish (c inks), Michael Golden (c colors)
FEATURE CHARACTER: Punisher (next in PWJ #74, '95)
VILLAINS: Redmond (gangster), Lucas (his security chief), Redmond's hit men & bodyguards (some also in photo) (all die)
OTHER CHARACTERS: Raving Beauty (Cheryl, vigilante & Redmond's former mistress, also in pfb, in movie poster in pfb & in police composite sketch), Mike Lourdes (Hollywood Examiner reporter), Gil Tremaine (Las Vegas high roller, also in photo, dies), hotel customers, doorman, desk clerk & other staff, limo driver, helicopter pilot, bystanders, photographers, Miss USA announcer, contestants & spectators (prev 4 in fb), Andros (mentioned, Cheryl's LA victim), Hermit Beach Monster (in movie poster in fb)
LOCATIONS/ITEMS: Las Vegas inc Tremaine's honeymoon suite; San Francisco inc hotel w/Cheryl's 10th floor room, 2nd hotel's poolside, Redmond's compound; auditorium (in fb) / hit men's gun & knife, Punisher's grenade, guns & binoculars, Cheryl's gun, purse, shoe & poison lipstick ("Toxic Titillation"); San Fran Tour Craft helicopter, Lourdes' press pass & camera, Redmond's bodyguards' guns & trucks, Redmond's gun, motion sensors & spotlights, Horror of Hermit Beach movie poster

FLASHBACK: After coming in second at the Miss USA pageant, Cheryl works as an actress in a horror film. Redmond, her producer, encourages her to star in porn movies, and the drug habit she starts there eventually leads her to prostitution (p).

SYNOPSIS: Cheryl uses poison lipstick to kill Tremaine in his suite. The next day, Lucas alerts Redmond that Cheryl is systematically killing his former associates. Meanwhile, en route home from a recent mission, Punisher is about to check into a hotel when he notices two hit men following Cheryl. Punisher helps Cheryl kill the assassins, and they leave for a lower profile location. Later, reporter Mike Lourdes arrives at the hotel and bribes the clerk for information. After learning the hit men worked for Redmond, Lourdes hires a tour helicopter to fly him over the compound. The helicopter shows up just as Punisher and Cheryl are launching their attack. Gunfire from the compound forces the chopper down, but Punisher and Cheryl kill the guards who come to investigate. While other guards step into an explosive ambush laid by Lourdes, Punisher and Cheryl assault the compound, ultimately killing Redmond. Lourdes reports that Cheryl was killed in the battle, leaving her free to restart her life.

NOTE: Frank's narration describes his hideout with Cheryl as a low-profile hotel in downtown Houston, rather than San Francisco.

PUNISHER #97 (December 1994)

"The Devil's Secret Name" (22 pages)

CREDITS: Chuck Dixon (writer), Rod Whigham (pencils), Rudy D. Nebres (inks), James Novak (letters), Chia-Chi Wang (colors), Freddy Mendez (asst editor), Don Daley (editor), Frank Teran (c art), Michael Golden (c colors)
FEATURE CHARACTER: Punisher
SUPPORTING CAST: Microchip (last in Pun Ann #7, '94, chr last in Pun #100/2, '95; also on computer screen as Cringe), Mickey Fondozzi (last in PWZ #31, '94)
VILLAINS: Nasty E (Norton Bussels, MIT chemistry grad turned drug dealer, dies), TeeVee (top drug dealer, mentioned), terrorists (die), muggers, drug dealers & other criminals (many killed)
OTHER CHARACTERS: Carlos Cruz (1st, aka C.C., former Navy SEAL), "A" Train passengers, TV newsman, TV newswoman, Moe's Tavern bartender, newsstand owner, Punjab Darjeeling (cab driver), CNBC analyst, talk show host, Jennie (talk show interviewee), bystanders
LOCATIONS/ITEMS: "A" Eighth Avenue Express train inc. train station, TV studio, Moe's Tavern Mick's Auto Parts (blown up), newsstand,

Nasty E's tenement building, outdoor basketball court, Punisher's Weehawken motel / Punisher's laser-sited handguns; plastic explosive, "Love Machine" car, Honda auto parts, explosive timer, muggers' guns, Micro's wallet, gun & computer-generated Cringe mask (on screen), Cruz's baseball bat, newspapers & magazines (all carrying anti-Punisher headlines), taxi cab, machine gun, computer, basketball, soda, drugs

SYNOPSIS: On an "A" Train full of innocent bystanders, Punisher guns down terrorists en route to a bombing, kicking the final, booby trapped one off the train as it pulls into an empty station before opening fire, so that the resultant explosion only kills the bomber. In a bar in another part of town, Microchip listens with concern to news reports claiming Punisher's actions endangered innocent lives. Intent on making sure the city's lowlifes know he is back, and rebuilding his own network, Punisher visits Mick's Auto Parts, roughing Mick up for information on Micro's whereabouts and who has risen to lead the underworld since the Manhattan Tower Massacre; Mick claims he hasn't seen Micro in weeks, but identifies Cringe as a new drug lord. Punisher tells Mick to find out more, then blows up Mick's place. Across town, muggers attack Micro, but he is saved by self-appointed neighborhood watchman Carlos Cruz. As the media's anti-Punisher hype escalates, Punisher slaughters his way through lowlife crooks, looking for a lead on Cringe; they all deny knowledge of him, but Punisher finally finds a lead in drug dealer Nasty E's files. Meanwhile Micro, having run a background check on Carlos and learned he is a former Navy SEAL, tells his new friend he might have a job for him.

NOTE: Pun #99, '95 reveals Cringe is Microchip. Mickey calls Punisher "Johnny;" Castle was using the name Johnny Tower when they met.

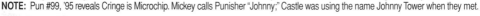

PUNISHER #98 (January 1995)

"Armies of the Night" (22 pages)

CREDITS: Chuck Dixon (writer), Rod Whigham (pencils), Elman Brown, Rudy D. Nebres (inks), Vickie Williams (letters), Ian Laughlin, Chia-Chi Wang (colors), Freddy Mendez (asst editor), Don Daley (editor), Frank Teran (c art), Michael Golden (c colors)
FEATURE CHARACTER: Punisher (also in rfb)
SUPPORTING CAST: Microchip (also on computer screen as Cringe), Mouse (Hal Flynt) & Ponygirl (Wendy Christiansen, aka Pony) (both 1st, teenage computer hackers), Mickey Fondozzi
VILLAINS: Vaducci mobsters (all die), gangbangers (some die), drug dealers, Teevee (drug dealer, 1st), Teevee's guards & chemists (all die), Shining Condors (Vietnamese gang, 1st, next in Pun #101, '95)
OTHER CHARACTERS: Carlos Cruz, Randy (Carlos' nephew, dies), Luis (Carlos' uncle) (both 1st, next in Pun #101, '95), Christina (Carlos' sister, 1st bts, next in Pun #101, '95), Gomez (grocery store owner), police, detectives, EMS workers, TV reporters, pizza chef, paramedics, bystanders; Nasty E (in rfb), Stimpy (cartoon character, as toy), glamour models (on posters)
LOCATIONS/ITEMS: Manhattan, East New York section of Brooklyn, Vaducci Clan skyscraper inc computer room, Mickey's trailer, pizza place, Microchip's warehouse, Teevee's Brooklyn crackhouse; restaurant, Gomez's store / Mouse & Ponygirl's computers; Punisher's rappel line, guns, flash bang grenade & night-vision goggles; Vaducci Clan machine guns & hand guns; Gomez Bodega, Stimpy plush doll, TV cameras, Microchip's van & computer-generated Cringe mask (also in rfb), Punisher uniform (for Carlos), propane, alcohol, drug-making paraphernalia, ambulance
FLASHBACK: Punisher finds info about Cringe on Nasty E's computer (Pun #97, '94).
SYNOPSIS: Seeking information on Cringe, Punisher invades a Vaducci Clan skyscraper, slaughtering his way to the computer room. He finds a pair of youthful hackers, Mouse and Ponygirl, keeping Vaducci's records, but, on an impulse and knowing his own computer skills are lacking, recruits their services as replacements for the absent Microchip. Meanwhile, Micro, worried Punisher no longer knows where to draw the line, works on convincing a dubious Carlos to become a new Punisher. Punisher, Mouse and Ponygirl set up shop in Mickey's trailer, but when Mickey goes out for pizza, he calls someone, warning them about Punisher's activities. While Mouse and Ponygirl cyber-track Cringe, Carlos' young nephew, Randy, is killed when he inadvertently gets caught between rival gangs involved in a drive-by. Following a lead provided by Mouse and Ponygirl, Punisher raids a Brooklyn crackhouse run by Teevee, a crack dealer; while he is doing so, Cringe reverse hacks into Mouse and Ponygirl's computers, warning them to stay out of his way or die. Moments later, as Teevee desperately denies knowing Cringe to Punisher, Cringe interrupts the signal to Teevee's TVs, to taunt Punisher. Upon learning of his nephew's death, Carlos goes to Microchip, and agrees to become the new Punisher.
NOTE: The Shining Condors are identified in Pun #101, '95.

PUNISHER #99 (February 1995)

"Bury Me Deep" (22 pages)

CREDITS: Chuck Dixon (writer), Rod Whigham (pencils), Elman Brown, Rudy D. Nebres (inks), Vickie Williams (letters), Ian Laughlin, Chia-Chi Wang (colors), Freddy Mendez (asst editor), Don Daley (editor), Frank Teran (c art)
FEATURE CHARACTER: Punisher
SUPPORTING CAST: Microchip (also as Cringe), Mouse, Ponygirl, Mickey Fondozzi
VILLAINS: Teevee (dies), drug dealers (die)
OTHER CHARACTERS: Carlos Cruz (1st as new Punisher), Ed Wychak, (WANX DJ, Talkbeat host, 1st, next in Pun #101, '95) & his technician, bystanders, Nicky (voice only, caller from Yonkers), Helen (voice only, caller from White Plains), Rosalie Carbone, Maria Castle, Lisa Castle, Frank Castle Jr (prev 4 photos)
LOCATIONS/ITEMS: Teevee's Brooklyn crackhouse, Mickey's trailer, 24 hour diner, WANX radio station, Microchip's warehouse, drug dealers' hideout (destroyed); Cringelli Manufacturing factory, Newark, NJ, inc recreation of Castle family home on Flatbush Ave, Brooklyn / Mouse & Ponygirl's computers, Punisher's car, box of M67 fragmentation grenades & radio, Microchip's van, guns & computer; C-4 explosives (taped to Teevee's chest) & remote detonator, children's toys inc squeaky turtle, Castle family photos, Captain America action figure, Carlos' Punisher costume inc skull helmet & guns
SYNOPSIS: A terrified Teevee swears he doesn't know Cringe, but promises to help find him if Punisher lets him live. He bundles Teevee into the trunk of his car, then calls Mouse and Ponygirl, telling them to keep looking for Cringe. Going out on the pretext of getting breakfast, Mickey calls his mysterious contact, leaving a message that their plan has Punisher running round in circles. At his warehouse, Microchip briefs Carlos on how to operate as the new Punisher; Carlos remains doubtful, but feels fate is pushing him into the role. After strapping a listening device and C4 explosives to Teevee's chest, Punisher sends him into another drug dealer's house looking for information about Cringe, but when it becomes clear those inside don't know anything, Punisher detonates the bomb. Mouse and Ponygirl tell Punisher they have found a Cringelli Manufacturing in Newark, which appears to have mob connections, prompting Punisher to investigate Cringelli Manufacturing's abandoned and out-of-the-way factory. Stalking his way through the building, Punisher follows a child's voice into the basement, anticipating a trap, but instead of the expected ambush, a metal door seals him into a recreation of his family's old house, complete with photos of his family. Meanwhile

Microchip tells Carlos, now decked out as the Punisher, that his first assignment is to kill mob capo Rosalie Carbone. Back in the Castle home reconstruction, a recording of Cringe unmasks to reveal he is Microchip, who tells Punisher he has been imprisoned to save him from himself.

PUNISHER #100 (March 1995)

"The Cage" (48 pages)

CREDITS: Chuck Dixon (writer), Rod Whigham (pencils), Elman Brown (p27, 29, 32, 38-39, 42, 45-46, 49-50, 52-54 inks), Scott Elmer (p30, 37, 40-41, 42-44 inks), Mick Gray (p47-48, 51 inks), Michael Higgins (p28, 33, 35-36 inks; letters), Rudy D. Nebres (p2-26 inks), Phil Sheehy (p31 inks), Timothy Tuohy (p34 inks), Ian Laughlin, Chia-Chi Wang (colors), Freddy Mendez (asst editor), Don Daley (editor), Bobbie Chase (group editor), Frank Teran (c art)

FEATURE CHARACTER: Punisher (also as Frank Castiglione in fb1 between Pun #1, '98 fb & Pun #59, '92 fb, also as Frank Castle in fb2 between PWZ #24, '94 fb & Pun #10, '09 fb; next in PWJ #75, '95)

SUPPORTING CAST: Maria Castle (as Castiglione in fb1 to 1st chr app before Pun:AG, '88 fb), Lisa Castle, Frank Castle, Jr. (all in fb2 between PWZ #24, '94 fb & Pun #10, '09 fb; also in photos), Mickey Fondozzi (next in PWJ #78, '95), Microchip, Mouse, Ponygirl

VILLAINS: Rosalie Carbone (Carbone mob capo, last in PWJ #75, '95; also in portrait), Hog (1st, Carbone's on-call security), Carbone family mobsters (many die) inc Dion (dies), Hog's gang, Rosalie's bodyguard, Vito Vaducci (mobster, last in PWJ #61, '93), Rocco & Sticks (Vito's bodyguards), Vito's hit squad inc Pauly (many die), Fat Tony (1st bts), senior mob family leaders

OTHER CHARACTERS: Carlos Cruz (also as Punisher), Rusty (Castle family dog, in fb2 & photo), Dion's girlfriend; Punisher's sister-in-law (mentioned, her photos used to reconstruct Castle home)

LOCATIONS/ITEMS: Microchip's HQ, Castle family home reconstruction in Cringelli Manufacturing sub-basement, Microchip's surveillance trailer; Rosalie Carbone's estate, 18 Southampton Commons; Motel 9, Mickey's trailer, Ocean Empress (cruise ship) in international waters / TVs (some destroyed), Punisher's shotgun, Castle family photos, children's toys; Carlos' sniper rifle w/scope, radio mike, Punisher costume inc skull helmet, scuba gear, inflatable dinghy & ballistic knife; Microchip's service van, w/surveillance equipment, explosives, Hog's Gatling gun, tug boat, helicopter, Rosalie's thigh holster & pistol

FLASHBACKS: Frank and Maria Castiglione are married (1). The Castle family chase their dog, Rusty, round the yard, trying to give Rusty a bath, while Frank tries to read the paper (2).

SYNOPSIS: In Cringelli Manufacturing's sub-basement, Punisher is trapped in a reconstruction of his family's old home; a video of Microchip explains he feels Punisher is out of control. Punisher destroys the TV and wrecks the room. Once he stops, a second monitor hidden in the wall appears, and Micro's next pre-recorded message tells Punisher there are months of provisions for him; Micro understands Punisher will be angry now, but hopes he will eventually understand and thank him. Punisher destroys the new monitor, but another activates, playing home movies of the Castle family together, trying to remind Frank of his old life. He watches the videos of happier times with mounting depression. Meanwhile Carlos, directed over radio by Micro and garbed as the Punisher, invades mobster Rosalie Carbone's estate, killing the guards and setting off an alarm alerting on-call security, a gang led by Hog. Reaching Rosalie's bedroom, Carlos finds one of the guard's girlfriends there instead of Rosalie. Back at Mickey's trailer, Mouse and Ponygirl wonder what happened to Frank. At the Carbone estate, Carlos fights his way past Hog's arriving men with the girl in tow, his only lead to Rosalie's whereabouts, but Hog gets the drop on him, until Micro runs Hog over with his surveillance van. After they escape, the girl tells Carlos that Rosalie is on a cruise. On the Ocean Empress cruise ship, Rosalie is attending a mob family meeting called by Vito Vaducci, before leaving the ship. Carlos reaches Rosalie's suite just ahead of the assassins, and a running firefight ensues, which escalates when Hog arrives, pursuing Carlos. Carlos stabs Hog in the eye, and kills the assassins, but as he is about to slay Rosalie, Hog tackles him over the ship's side. Fearing he has gotten Carlos killed, Microchip frantically calls Punisher, but hears a shotgun blast go off on the other side of the line.

2ND STORY "Computers to Kill by" (7 pages)

CREDITS: Richard Ashford (writer), John Herbert (pencils), Fred Fredericks (inks), Susan Crespi (letters), Anibal Rodriguez (colors), Freddy Mendez (asst editor), Don Daley (editor), Bobbie Chase (group editor)

FEATURE CHARACTER: Microchip (also as "Mr. Doran," last in Pun Ann #7, '94, next in Pun #97, '95)

VILLAINS: Computer Killers (2 hackers, both killed)

OTHER CHARACTERS: Police, Bob (detective), CSI, Wall St. executive, ad agency executive (both killed), Punisher (monitor picture only)

LOCATIONS/ITEMS: Wall St. office, Madison Avenue ad agency office / computers, lab equipment, padded bomb suit, bomb

SYNOPSIS: When exploding computers begin killing company executives, the lead detective, Bob, calls Microchip in to help. Figuring out that a virus caused weakened vacuum tubes inside the monitors to explode, Micro traces the assassins and poses as a businessman wanting to hire them to kill an employee, but secretly rigs the hackers' computer to explode, and reroutes their killer signal back at them.

NOTE: Issue has a variant foil-enhanced cover.

PUNISHER #101 (April 1995)

"Dead Tomorrows" (22 pages)

CREDITS: Chuck Dixon (writer), Rod Whigham (pencils), Elman Brown, Michael Higgins, Jay Oliveras, Tim Tuohy (inks), Michael Higgins (letters), Ian Laughlin, Chia-Chi Wang (colors), Freddy Mendez (asst editor), Don Daley (editor), Bobbie Chase (group editor), Frank Teran (c art)

FEATURE CHARACTER: Punisher

SUPPORTING CAST: Microchip, Mouse, Ponygirl

VILLAINS: Rosalie Carbone, Hog (dies), Fat Tony (Carbone mobster), Vito Vaducci, Shining Condors (last in Pun #98, '95, many die), Bullseye (Lester, assassin w/perfect throwing aim, last in DD #290, '91)

OTHER CHARACTERS: Carlos Cruz, Luis, Randy (corpse) (both last in Pun #98, '95), Christina (last in Pun #98, '95 bts, 1st actual app), Randy's sisters, Ed Wychak (last in Pun #99, '95), Edith from Queens, Salvatore in

Seagate (both voice only, calling Wychak's show), sharks

LOCATIONS/ITEMS: Castle family home reconstruction in Cringelli Manufacturing sub-basement, Microchip's warehouse, Shining Condors clubhouse on East 8th (destroyed), funeral home, cemetery, WANX radio station, Rosalie Carbone's NYC penthouse, Ocean Empress / Microchip's surveillance trailer & computer, Randy's machine gun, Vito's helicopter, ballistic knife, Carlos' grenades, guns & Punisher costume inc skull helmet, Ponygirl's radio mike, Bullseye's knife

SYNOPSIS: Grappling underwater, Carlos notices Hog still has the ballistic knife Carlos stabbed him with sticking out of his bandaged eye socket; Carlos headbutts it further into Hog's skull, killing him. Meanwhile a panic-stricken Micro tries unsuccessfully to get Punisher to respond to his call; fearing Frank has committed suicide, Micro apologizes for trapping him, explaining he felt Frank had lost himself in the daily violence, and needed to remember the reasons for the war. Rosalie's men rush to her side as Vito Vaducci's helicopter returns to the ship, and Carlos swims for shore. When Vaducci lands, he feigns surprise at the assault, and Rosalie pretends to believe him. Later, after Micro finds Carlos emerging from the sea at their prearranged rendezvous, Carlos attends his nephew, Randy's, memorial, then goes after the gang who killed him, slaughtering them. After Randy's funeral Micro asks Carlos to check on the Punisher. Out hunting for the missing Castle, Mouse and Ponygirl visit Cringelli Manufacturing, and spot the Punisher-garbed Carlos entering. Carlos opens up the sealed sub-basement, and is ambushed by a very angry Punisher, while back in her Manhattan penthouse, Rosalie hires Bullseye to kill Vaducci and Punisher.

PUNISHER #102 (May 1995)

"Under the Gun" (22 pages)

CREDITS: Chuck Dixon (writer), Rod Whigham (pencils), Pam Eklund (inks), Vickie William (letters), Chia-Chi Wang (colors), Chris Cooper (editor), Bobbie Chase (group editor), Frank Teran (c art)
FEATURE CHARACTER: Punisher (next in PWJ #78, '95)
SUPPORTING CAST: Mouse, Ponygirl (both next in PWJ #78, '95), Mickey Fondozzi (between PWJ #77-78, '95), Microchip
VILLAINS: Stone Cold (Derek Smalls, killer of vigilantes, between PWJ #77-78, '95) Rosalie Carbone, Vito Vaducci, Bullseye; Rosalie's bodyguards, Vito's security force (many die), senior mobsters (all die; see NOTE)
OTHER CHARACTERS: Phalanx (Cord Mather, armored vigilante, last in PWZ Ann #1, '93), Carlos Cruz (also as Punisher), Neil (Shamrock bartender), Liz (Nevadan gas station owner)
LOCATIONS/ITEMS: Castle family home reconstruction in Cringelli Manufacturing sub-basement, Microchip's warehouse, Nevada inc Rancho Pacifica (Vito's ranch) & isolated gas station, Shamrock bar / Punisher's shotgun, Micro's computer, Mouse's laptop, Carlos' guns & Punisher costume inc skull helmet, Phalanx's jeep, guns & armor; security forces' jeeps, guns & motorbikes, Bullseye's guns, keypad

SYNOPSIS: As Punisher holds his shotgun to Carlos' head, Micro triggers jets of knock-out gas. Carlos dives away, and Micro remotely activates the room's heavy, metal door, imprisoning the Punisher again. Unaware Mouse and Ponygirl are watching, Carlos leaves, and the hackers begin working on the keypad, trying to free Punisher. In another part of town, the slayer of vigilantes, Stone Cold, abducts Mickey Fondozzi. Wanting to finish off Rosalie Carbone, Carlos follows her to Nevada, where she is attending another mob boss meeting, at Vito Vaducci's ranch. Asking for directions to what the locals dub "Rancho Mafia" leads to an encounter with local mechanic Cole Mather, who initially suspects Carlos of being a mobster. Upon learning otherwise, Cole reveals he is the reluctant vigilante Phalanx, taking the fight to the mob who are hunting him for the armor he invented. As they mount a joint assault, inside the ranch house Vito plans to eliminate Rosalie, but her assassin, Bullseye, makes his move first, killing the other mob bosses. Rosalie tells Bullseye to slay Vito too, but before he can, the wall explodes and Carlos and Phalanx enter.
NOTE: Bullseye identifies one of his mob victims as "Sally the Gimp;" it is unclear if this was the mobster's actual nickname, or whether Bullseye was just being insulting. The African-American Stone Cold is miscolored as Caucasian here.

PUNISHER #103 (June 1995)

"Countdown 4: The Butcher's Block" (23 pages)

CREDITS: Chuck Dixon (writer), Rod Whigham (pencils), Enrique Villagrán (inks), Vickie Williams (letters), Chia-Chi Wang (colors), Chris Cooper (editor), Bobbie Chase (group editor), Jae Lee (c art)
FEATURE CHARACTER: Punisher (next in PWJ #79, CD #7, GR #61, Blaze #10-12, SM:PoT #2-4, PWZ #41, all '95)
SUPPORTING CAST: Mouse, Ponygirl (both last in PWJ #78, '95, next in PWJ #79, '95), Microchip (next in PWJ #79, '95)
VILLAIN: Rosalie Carbone (next in PWJ #79, '95), Vito Vaducci (dies), Bullseye (next in PWJ #79, '95), Stone Cold (between PWJ #78-79, '95), Vito's men (die), Rosalie's men inc Jerry & Tank
OTHER CHARACTERS: Carlos Cruz (also as Punisher, next in PWJ #79, '95; see NOTE), Phalanx (dies), senior mobsters (corpses)
LOCATIONS/ITEMS: Cringelli Manufacturing, Microchip's warehouse, Rancho Pacifica, Nevada; Stone Cold's apartment, Punisher's motel room / Carlos' guns, knives & Punisher costume inc skull helmet, Phalanx's guns & armor, Bullseye's guns & knives; grenade, Punisher's shotgun

SYNOPSIS: Mouse and Ponygirl finally free Punisher, and they hide out in a motel; Castle tells the hackers to locate Microchip; elsewhere in the New York, Stone Cold tortures his captive, Mickey Fondozzi, also seeking Micro. Meanwhile, in Nevada, Bullseye battles Carlos and Phalanx; though Phalanx's armor is bulletproof, Bullseye wounds Phalanx with a knife thrown through the eye slot. Forgotten by the fighters as the combat moves on, Rosalie Carbone shoots Vito Vaducci dead. When some surviving mob guards attack, Phalanx, struggling to keep going with his head wound, shields Carlos from a grenade, and though his armor is undamaged, the concussive force transmits through and kills him. Bullseye rejoins the combat, slaying the mobsters so he and Carlos can continue their fight uninterrupted. Meanwhile Rosalie and her men evacuate the ranch, taking Phalanx's corpse so Rosalie can claim his armor. After working together to kill all the remaining guards, Bullseye and Carlos try to shoot one another point blank in the head, but find they are both out of ammunition. Finding this amusing, and having realized Carlos is not Frank Castle, Bullseye walks away, ending the fight. The next day Micro is in his warehouse; hearing someone behind him, he assumes that it is Carlos, until Castle points a shotgun at his head.
NOTE: Story continues in PWJ #79, '95 ("Countdown: 3"), where Mouse and Ponygirl flee the USA, while Stone Cold kills Microchip, and Carlos wrongly blames the Punisher. The Hood resurrects Micro in Pun #4, '09. Stone Cold kills Carlos, and Punisher accidentally kills the innocent Dreyer family while they are out picnicking in PWZ #41, '95 (the final issue of that series, and "Countdown: 2"), the resonance with his own family's demise leading to the events of next issue.

PUNISHER #104 (July 1995)

"The Murder Men" (22 pages)

CREDITS: Chuck Dixon (writer), Rod Whigham (pencils), Enrique Villagrán (inks), Vickie Williams (letters), Chia-Chi Wang (colors), Chris Cooper (editor), Bobbie Chase (group editor), Jae Lee (c art)
FEATURE CHARACTER: Punisher (next in PWJ #80, DE:A, MaxC:A, WoSM #127, DD #344, IHulk #433, DrS #81 bts, DE:Ω, Pun #1, all '95)
GUEST STAR: Nick Fury (last in GR #65, '95, next in PWJ #80, '95)
SUPPORTING CAST: Mickey Fondozzi (last in PWJ #41, '95, next in MKn #5, '00)
VILLAIN: Rosalie Carbone (last in PWJ #79, '95, next in DE:A, '95), Bullseye (last in PWZ #41, '95, next in PWJ #80, '95), Stone Cold (last in PWZ #41, '95, next in PWJ #80, '95), Kingpin (last in PWZ #41, '95, next in DCvM #1, '96 bts, DCvM #2, '96), Kingpin's men; Ho Brothers (Chinese mob bosses, as corpses), Stasi Gromyko, "Minky" Kolyma, Molina mob (prev 3 Russian mob, bts, all dead), "Snowman" Henry (East Manhattan's top crack dealer, as corpse), Jimmy Chama, Jimmy's friend (both Medellin mob, as corpses), Lou, Lou's two associates (mobsters, all 3 die), Lou's men (as corpses), Pauly (Rosalie's guard, voice only, dies), Max Silk (top heroine dealer, dies), Silks' guards, driver (bts) & guard escort (prev 3 die), Rosalie's guards (bts), Rosalie's boyfriend
OTHER CHARACTERS: SHIELD agents (1 dies), police detectives & uniform cops, hobo; Microchip, Steven Dreyer, Lisa Dreyer (prev 3 as corpses in rfb)
LOCATIONS/ITEMS: Police station, Kingpin's hideout, Stone Cold's apartment, Chinatown, Gulag Room (Russian mob base), sewers, truck park, Rosalie's 21st floor apartment, Oahu beach / Kingpin's weapons stash inc guns, automatic weapons, grenades; Phalanx's armor, Kingpin's mobster files, Ho Brother's shot-up car, noose, Bullseye's automatic weapon, laser-sighted rocket launcher, Rosalie's cell phone, SHIELD Helicarrier, jets & helicopters, SHIELD agents' guns & body armor, Silk's limo & escort vehicles, Punisher's truck
FLASHBACKS: Steven and Lisa Dreyer lie dead (PWZ #41, '95). Microchip lies dead (PWJ #79, '95).
SYNOPSIS: Haunted by recent events, an unarmed Punisher tries to walk into a police station to surrender himself, but is intercepted by Kingpin's thugs. The deposed crimelord offers Frank a chance of redemption via an arsenal of weapons, and files identifying the city's top criminals and their weaknesses, crooks Punisher had never been able to get to before, all rivals Kingpin wants eliminated so he can rise to power again. Castle accepts, but tells Kingpin he will be next. Elsewhere, Stone Cold finds Mickey Fondozzi, tied up by Bullseye, and takes him prisoner again. Mickey is saved by chance when SHIELD agents intercept Stone Cold's car trying to capture the assassin. After Stone Cold evades them, Nick Fury debriefs the agents, who admit to their superior that Stone Cold is a rogue SHIELD operative. Punisher slaughters his way through the Kingpin's list, killing all his targets bar Rosalie Carbone, who escapes only because she is on vacation when he blows up her apartment, then prepares to go after Kingpin.
NOTE: Final issue of this volume. Cover label denotes this story as Countdown: 1. The Punisher's battles against Bullseye and Stone Cold end in PWJ #80, '95 (the final issue of that series, and "Countdown: 0"). Nick Fury assigns the mercenary Shotgun to stop Stone Cold, and he apprehends Frank, bringing the last of Punisher's ongoing titles to an end with Frank in SHIELD custody. In DE:A, '95 Frank is brainwashed into believing Nick Fury caused his family's death, prompting him to seemingly kill Fury in DE:Ω, '95, and the story is continued in Pun #1, '95. Before Pun #1, '95, the Index is presenting Punisher War Journal #1-80, '88-95 & Punisher War Zone #1-41, '92-95, both published concurrently with Punisher #1-104, '87-95. Since Punisher's full chronology has already been presented in Pun #1-104, '87-95, only his immediate before and after appearances will be given in PWJ #1-80, '88-95 & PWZ #1-41, '92-95. Full chronologies will resume in Pun #1, '95, which is on page 115.

PUNISHER WAR JOURNAL #1 (November 1988)

"An Eye for an Eye, Chapter One: Sunday in the Park" (29 pages)

CREDITS: Carl Potts (writer, layouts, c pencils), Jim Lee (finished art), Jim Novak (letters), John Wellington (colors), Don Daley (editor), Scott Williams (c inks)
FEATURE CHARACTER: Punisher (also as Frank Castle in fb between MP #2, '75 fb & PWJ #3, '89 fb, also in PWZ #25, '94 fb, Pun #17, '97 fb, Pun #4, '99 fb, Pun Ann #4, '91, PunBl, '91 fb, DE:A, '95 fb, Pun/Cap #3, '92 fb & MP #2, '75 fb; last in SpSM #143, '88)
GUEST STARS: Matt Murdock (last in DD #265, '89), Shadowmasters (ninja clan): Philip Richards (next in PWJ #3, '89), Yuriko Ezaki (both 1st but chr last in Shadow #4, '90), Rikichi (1st)
SUPPORTING CAST: Maria Castle, Lisa Castle, Frank Castle, Jr. (all in fb between MP #2, '75 fb & PWJ #3, '89 fb, also in PWZ #25, '94 fb, Pun #17, '97 fb, Pun #4, '99 fb, Pun Ann #4, '91, PunBl, '91 fb, DE:A, '95 fb, Pun/Cap #3, '92 fb & MP #2, '75 fb, die), Microchip (last in Pun #12, '88)
VILLAINS: Kingpin (last in SpSM #143, '88, next bts in Pun #14, '88, next in Pun #15, '89), Forest Hunt (in fb between Pun #4, '99 fb & PWJ #3, '89 fb, also in MP #2, '75 fb & PWJ #3, '89 fb), Maggia: Bruno Costa (in fb between Pun #4, '99 fb & MP #2, '75 fb, also in MP #2, '75 fb), Luis Allegre (in fb between DE:A, '95 fb & MP #2, '75 fb, also in MP #2, '75 fb), Byron Hannigan, Leon Kolsky, Matt Skinner (prev 3 in fb between Pun #4, '99 fb & MP #2, '75 fb); Hector Montoya (ex-Santo Angelo embassy official, poisons expert, 1st in pfb but chr last in PWJ #3, '89 fb, also in photo), Mark Scotti (gangster, dies) & his henchmen (2 die) inc Lenny, Rick, John, Sal & Mario; inmates (in pfb) inc Raymond (1st in pfb but chr last in PWJ #2, '88 fb) & Big Mac; French Foreign Legion soldiers
OTHER CHARACTERS: Mokele-Mbembe (mythical African dinosaur), Scotti's wife & her son, Steven (Scotti's wife's boyfriend), Alex (Scotti's wife's mentally disabled nephew), New Yorkers inc cab driver, prison guards (in pfb), twin schoolchildren, peasant farmers, Amazon villagers (die), factory workers, swimmer, hammerhead shark, Microchip Jr. (as corpse in Microchip's thoughts), Raymond's half-sister (mentioned), Angela Montoya (Montoya's wife), Montoya's son (both in photo), Tony Orlando (musician, voice on radio), Spider-Man (image on Frank Jr.'s shirt)
LOCATIONS/ITEMS: New Jersey inc Microchip's warehouse; George Washington Bridge, New York inc Upper West Side w/Punisher's Manhattan safehouse, Winning Deli (Shadowmasters' cover business, located below Punisher's safehouse), Ryker's Island (in pfb) inc Raymond & Montoya's cells, Central Park (also in fb), Scotti's mansion w/bathroom, Washington Monument (in picture) / Microchip's 9mm submachinegun, Daily Bugle newspaper, Robert Frost poetry book & computer; Punisher's Goncz 9 w/extra magazines, Battle Van & motorcycle, 3 kites (one in fb, another destroyed), Montoya's Walkman (in pfb), Stingball riot grenade, voice stress detector;

Scotti's limousine, gun, & radio; Scotti's henchmen's guns, guard's truncheon (in pfb), picnic hamper, Maggia's guns (both in fb)
FLASHBACKS: One week ago on Ryker's Island: Raymond and Big Mac try to provoke Hector Montoya into a fight to blow his impending parole for good behavior, but a guard stops them (p).Frank and Maria Castle take their children to Central Park for a picnic. Frank sets up his children's kite and flies it with them, but runs across five Maggia interrogating Forest Hunt. They gun the Castles down, and the children's kite lands on Lisa and Frank Jr's bodies to soak in their blood. Frank wakes to find to his horror that his family is dead. The kite floats away, the blood spatter forming a skull pattern.
SYNOPSIS: After testing his Kevlar body armor against a new gun, Frank drives to the deli located under his as yet unused Manhattan safehouse, where he buys lunch and a wrapped item. Once he leaves, the elderly shopkeeper and his young employee discuss their landlord's harassment attempts. Frank spots two armed men ushering a young couple with a baby into a car, and notices the driver tapping an SOS with the brake lights. Frank subdues the hoods, but his item is smashed. The women explains that her friend is helping her flee her abusive husband, gangster Mark Scotti; when Scotti agreed to let her leave but demanded he keep his son, the woman abducted her similarly-aged mentally disabled nephew and switched the infants, rationalizing that Scotti would pay for the child's medical care, but Scotti realized the ruse. Frank hides the couple in his safehouse, then assaults Scotti's mansion. Finding Scotti taking a bath, Frank kicks a radio into the tub, fatally electrocuting Scotti. After sending the couple safely on their way, Frank replaces the items lost in the initial fight, then goes to Central Park to have lunch and fly a kite in remembrance of his last moments with his family.
NOTE: Next issue reveals Montoya's first name and former occupation. Rikichi's name and Philip and Yuriko's first names are revealed in PWJ #8, '89; the latter pair's last names are revealed in Shadow #2, '90. This issue's fbs are spread across the story's bottom panels. The last page shows single panels depicting events leading up to future Pun and PWJ storylines, including the Mokele-Mbembe (PWJ #6-7, '89), Kingpin plotting (Pun #15-18, '89), a gang-ridden high school (Pun #14, '88), peasants tending poppy fields (PWJ #22-24, '90), a private army slaughtering Amazonian villagers (PWJ #20, '90), Al Levin's wheelchair being manufactured (PWJ #4, '89), and a shark in the Philippine Sea (PWJ #21, '90). A Daily Bugle newspaper displays stories about murders Punisher will investigate in the next two issues, Alpha Flight's disbanding (AFlt #61, '88), and a Mokele-Mbembe sighting. Rikichi consults with Matt Murdock regarding his landlord's gentrification tactics, prompting Murdock's appearance as Daredevil in the next two issues. Ryker's is called Riker's in this and some subsequent issues; while the real world prison is Riker's Island, the Marvel Universe version is named Ryker's.

PUNISHER WAR JOURNAL #2 (December 1988)

"An Eye for an Eye, Chapter Two: Tie a Yellow Ribbon" (26 pages)

CREDITS: Carl Potts (writer, layout pencils, c inks), Jim Lee (finished art, c pencils), Jim Novak (letters), Gregory Wright (colors), Don Daley (editor)
FEATURE CHARACTER: Punisher (also in own thoughts & rfb, also in fb between PPSSM #83, '83 & Pun #1, '86)
GUEST STARS: Daredevil, Shadowmasters: Yuriko Ezaki, Rikichi
SUPPORTING CAST: Microchip
VILLAINS: Hector Montoya (also in fb1 between PWJ #3, '89 fb & PWJ #1, '88 fb, also in photo), inmates (some in fb1) inc Raymond (dies; also in 1st chr app in fb1 before PWJ #1, '88 fb), 3 crackheads (all 1st) inc Rex & Gomez
OTHER CHARACTERS: Gen. Jose Accardo (Santo Angelo contra leader, 1st but chr last in PWJ #3, '89 fb, dies), Jason Hunt (Forest Hunt's son, 1st but chr last in PWJ #3, '89 fb), Angela Montoya, Montoya's son (both 1st actual app, also in photo), postman, Accardo's cat, gangsters, police, prison guards, Montoya's parents (both 1st), newscaster (as voice on radio); Frank Castle Jr., Lisa Castle, Maria Castle, Forest Hunt; Maggia: Luis Allegre, Bruno Costa, Byron Hannigan, Leon Kolsky, Matt Skinner (prev 9 in rfb), Spider-Man (as image on Frank Jr.'s shirt)
LOCATIONS/ITEMS: Queens, NY inc Accardo's house w/kitchen, Manhattan inc Central Park (also in rfb), Punisher's safehouse, New York Harbor w/Pier 3, Montoyas' house, factory, New Jersey inc Microchip's warehouse, Ryker's Island (also in fb1) inc Montoya's cell & dock, Brooklyn inc Jason's house / Accardo's gun, poisoned letter, Punisher's kite, Battle Van, supply boxes, ballistic knife, & Goncz 9; Maggia's guns (all in rfb), inmates' shivs & pipes (all in fb1), Jason's motorcycle, gun & wallet; Microchip's computer, radio & Robert Frost poetry book; Daredevil's billy club; Montoya's Walkman, gun w/silencer & poison bottle, crackheads' knife & pipe, garbage can lid
FLASHBACKS: Frank Castle stumbles onto Forest Hunt's interrogation (r1). Maria, Lisa and Frank Castle Jr. are shot (r2). Forest hangs from a tree (r3) (r1-3 all PWJ #1, '88 fb). During Frank's first stay in Ryker's, inmates ambush both him and Hector Montoya; the two men defeat them, then go their separate ways, silently acknowledging one another (1).
SYNOPSIS: In Queens, a poisoned letter sent by Hector Montoya kills contra leader Jose Accardo. While flying his kite in Central Park, Frank Castle finds Forest Hunt's son Jason shadowing him. Claiming Hector Montoya ordered his father's death and thus caused Frank's family's deaths, Jason tells Frank he intends to kill Hector upon his impending release. Frank advises him against seeking revenge, but Jason brands Frank a coward and leaves. After consulting Microchip for intel on Montoya and Jason, Frank stocks his safehouse. Spotting him, Daredevil tells Frank about his deli-owning neighbors' landlord troubles, but Frank dismisses him. Frank travels to Brooklyn to shadow Jason, unaware Daredevil has hitched a ride atop his van. Montoya departs Ryker's, leaving behind a poison-coated Walkman to kill Raymond. Tailing Jason, Frank falls behind when he stops to covertly take down crackheads intending to mug the boy. Seeing Montoya with his family, Jason begins to reconsider his plan, but as he leaves, Montoya sports him, follows, and demands answers at gunpoint. Frank intervenes, but Jason flees and Montoya splashes Frank with poison and escapes with Jason's dropped wallet, leaving a disoriented Frank vulnerable to the crackheads he beat up earlier.
NOTE: Forest Hunt, 1st seen in MP #2, '75 fb, is finally named here. Rex and Gomez are named next issue. Issue includes Eliot R. Brown equipment pinup featuring two Goncz 143 submachine guns, later reprinted in PunArm #1, '90. Though blonde in other issues and a photograph herein, Angela is brunette in this issue. Microchip says Hector has two children, but only one is seen here.

PUNISHER WAR JOURNAL #3 (February 1989)

"An Eye for an Eye, Chapter 3: A Dish Best Served Cold" (24 pages)

CREDITS: Carl Potts (writer, layout pencils, c inks), Jim Lee (finished art, c pencils), Jim Novak (letters), Gregory Wright (colors), Don Daley (editor)
FEATURE CHARACTER: Punisher (also in rfb & symbolic image, also as Frank Castle in fb1 between PWJ #1, '88 fb & Pun/Cap #3, '92 fb, also in fb4 between PWJ #1, '88 fb & Pun #1, '86 fb; next in Pun #14, '88)
GUEST STARS: Daredevil (next in DD #264, '89, also in rfb); Shadowmasters: Yuriko Ezaki, Rikichi (both next in PWJ #6, '89); Philip Richards (last in PWJ #1, '88, next in PWJ #6, '89)
SUPPORTING CAST: Maria Castle, Lisa Castle, Frank Castle Jr. (all in fb1 between Pun #4, '99 fb & DE:A, '95 fb, also in fb4 between PWJ #1, '88 fb & Pun #1, '86 fb), Microchip (next in Pun #15, '89, also in rfb)
VILLAINS: Forest Hunt (in fb2&3 to 1st chr app before Pun/Cap #3, '92 fb, in fb1 during PWJ #1, '88 fb, in fb4 between PWJ #1, '88 fb & Pun:YO #1, '94, in fb5 after Pun:YO #1, '94) & his 3 mob associates (in fb2), Maggia: Bruno Costa (in fb2 to 1st chr app before Pun #17, '97 fb, in fb3 between Pun #17, '97 fb & DE:A, '95 fb, in fb1 between Pun #4, '99 fb & Pun Ann #4, '91), Luis Allegre, Leon Kolsky (both in fb3 to 1st chr app before Pun/Cap #3, '92 fb, fb1 during Pun Ann #4, '91), Byron Hannigan (in 1st chr app in fb3 before Pun/Cap #3, '91 fb, in fb1 between Pun #4, '99 & Pun Ann #4, '91), Matt Skinner (in fb3 between Pun #17, '97 fb & Pun/Cap #3, '92 fb, in fb1 between Pun #4, '99 fb & Pun Ann #4, '91); Hector Montoya (also in 1st chr app in fb2&6 before PWJ #2, '88 fb, & in fb7 between PWJ #1, '88 fb & PWJ #1, '88 fb), embassy courier (in fb2&6), crackheads inc Rex & Gomez, Raymond (as corpse, also in rfb)
OTHER CHARACTERS: Jason Hunt (next in PWJ #12, '89 bts; also in 1st chr app in fb5 before PWJ #2, '88, also in rfb), Angela Montoya, Montoya's son (also in 1st chr app in fb2 before PWJ #2, '88), Nazz (Jason's dog), Montoya's parents, 3 criminals (in symbolic image, one as gun muzzle-flash only, one dies), cab driver, security guard, Santo Angelo contras (both in fb2) inc Jose Accardo (in 1st chr app in fb2 before PWJ #2, '88), 2 paramedics (in fb5), Jason's mother, doctor (both in fb5), police inc Det. Stone & Ricco, New Yorkers inc van driver & elderly pedestrian, Laurie (Jason's fiancée, bts on phone, also in photo)
LOCATIONS/ITEMS: Manhattan inc Central Park (in fb1, 3, 4 & rfb), Punisher's safehouse (also in rfb); Montoyas' house (also in fb2) inc dining room, Hector & Angela's bedroom & bathroom; San Lorenzo Embassy inc Hector's office (in fb2); hospital room (in fb5), subway station, police interview room (both in fb5) & Winning Deli; Microchip's warehouse (also in rfb), Brooklyn inc Jason Hunt's house; Santo Angelo (in fb5), Ryker's Island (also in fb5 & rfb) inc prison clinic (also in fb5) & Montoya's cell (in fb7) / Punisher's Goncz 9, ballistic knife, Battle Van & taser; Maggia's guns (in fb1&3 & rfb), criminal's guns (in symbolic image), Daredevil's billy club (in rfb), taxi, Microchip's Frost poetry book, Jason's wallet & driver's license, Montoya's handgun w/silencer & poison vials, drug shipments, contras' guns & helicopter (prev 3 in fb2), police officers' guns
FLASHBACKS: The Castles go on a picnic in Central Park (PWJ #1, '88 fb), but stumble upon a Maggia execution and are shot by the gangsters (1). Frank meets Jason Hunt, consults with Microchip about Hector Montoya and Jason, and is visited by Daredevil (PWJ #2, '88). As an aide with the San Lorenzo embassy in New York, Hector Montoya worked with an embassy courier and Forest Hunt to exchange narcotics for funds to buy weapons for neighboring Santo Angelo's contras. Congress resumes aid to Santo Angelo and, sensing that the idealistic Montoya would stop the drug trade, Hunt and his mob connections scheme to eliminate Montoya. Montoya learns of Hunt's treachery and replaces his latest drug shipment with fake drugs (2). Hunt's mob allies turn on him at a meeting in Central Park (3). The Castles stumble upon Hunt's interrogation (PWJ #1, '88 fb). Frank weeps near the bodies of his wife and children (4). On his deathbed, Hunt lies to his wife and son, claiming Montoya engineered the drug trade and that he was trying to stop it. He also makes Jason promise not to seek revenge (5). Montoya tries to push his courier in front of a subway train, but the courier evades the train and a witness sees the murder attempt. His diplomatic immunity nullified by marriage to an American citizen, Montoya pleads not guilty to safeguard the contras. In prison, Montoya works as a clinic intern and teaches himself how to make poisons (6). Montoya and Frank Castle battle a gang of inmates (PWJ #2, '88 fb). Montoya begins sending poison-treated letters to his former allies (7). Raymond dies (PWJ #2, '88).
SYNOPSIS: The crackheads take Punisher's weapons but two injure themselves with his ballistic knife and flee. The third shoots Frank and also flees, unaware of Frank's body armor. Daredevil arrives and helps an ungrateful Frank get back to his safehouse. Meanwhile Hector Montoya decides to eliminate Jason, determined to protect his family at all costs. NYPD detective Stone investigates Raymond's death and deduces Montoya is responsible. As Montoya breaks into Jason's house, Stone searches Montoya's home and finds Jason's wallet. Despite his injuries, Frank travels to Jason's home and finds Montoya wrestling with Jason's attacking dog. Unaware that the dog ripped Montoya's surgical gloves, the two men struggle, causing Montoya's poison vials to leak onto his hands. Desperate to spend his last moments with his family, Montoya flees, but runs into arriving cops led by Stone, who, upon seeing Montoya's gun, shoot him dead.
NOTE: Issue includes Punisher's taser equipment pinup by Eliot R. Brown, later reprinted in PunArm #1, '90. Forest Hunt is spelled Forrest here.

PUNISHER WAR JOURNAL #4 (March 1989)

"Sniper" (23 pages)

CREDITS: Carl Potts (co-plot, script, c inks), John Wellington (co-plot), Jim Lee (pencils), Don Hudson (background inks), Scott Williams (figure inks), Ken Lopez (letters), Gregory Wright (colors), Don Daley (editor)
FEATURE CHARACTER: Punisher (also as Lt. Castle in fb1&2 between PunHol #2, '94 fb & Pun #6, '00 fb voice-only, also bts in PWJ #5, '89 fb; last in Pun #18, '89)
SUPPORTING CAST: Microchip (voice only, last in Pun #17, '89)
VILLAINS: Col. Ray Schoonover (ex-Marine/politician, dies), Sniper (Rich Von Burian, ex-Marine sharpshooter) (both 1st but chr last in fb2, also in 1st chr apps in fb1&2 before main story)
OTHER CHARACTERS: USMC 3rd Company (Punisher's former Marine unit): Lee Inoguchi, Dr. William "Doc" Pope (medic), Barry "Red" Thorne (machine gunner) (prev 3 1st, also in 1st chr apps in fb1 prior to main story, all die), Al Levin (Defense Espionage Agency operative, 1st but chr last in PWJ #5, '89 fb, also in 1st chr app in fb1 before PWJ #5, '89 fb), Walter Chin (mentioned by Shaw as killed prior to main story), Taylor, Wilson (both die in fb1); Helen Shaw (drug-addicted KMAR Channel 7 reporter), David (Helen's cameraman) (both 1st), New Yorkers, NVA soldiers (in fb1, some die in fb1, some as corpses as fb2), mules (in fb1), TV announcer (voice only), Lee's 2 bodyguards, police (2 die), hotel guests, waitress, family of 4 (killed bts, see NOTE)
LOCATIONS/ITEMS: New York inc 42nd St.; JFK International Airport inc parking garage & Gate 23 terminal; Indochina (in fb1); Westchester inc Rye Town Resort (hotel) w/banquet room & Schoonover's suite, Marine barracks (in fb2), KMAR news offices w/ladies' restroom / Sniper's

2 sniper rifles (one in fb1&2), briefcase w/MAC-10, gas grenade & armored Mercedes w/oil slick dispenser, rear-mounted machine guns, mines & surface-to-air heat-seeking missile; Marines' assault rifles (all in fb1); Punisher's radio, knife (both in fb1), Beretta handgun; Battle Van w/dashboard TV, targeting helmet, minigun, built-in jack, remote control & LCD panels; false wig, glasses & beard; grenade & bomb-equipped RC car; Red's M60 machine gun (in fb1), Marine helicopters w/mounted machine guns (in fb1&2, 1 destroyed in fb1), NVA soldiers' rifles & bayonets (in fb1), Schoonover's handgun (also in fb1), Levin's wheelchair, officers' guns, Helen's cocaine vial, decoy dummy, police helicopter (destroyed), SUV (as wreckage)

FLASHBACKS: Indochina: Lt. Frank Castle's platoon is pinned down by NVA fire while holding a landing zone for an incoming mule train supposedly carrying dead soldiers' bodies. On an incoming helicopter, Frank's CO, Col. Ray Schoonover, rejects Frank's extraction request, prioritizing protecting the mule train, but when the NVA fire on the helicopters, Schoonover orders clearing fire without regard for the lives of Frank's team. Schoonover lands and, after arguing with Frank, orders him and his team onto the helicopters on top of the body bags. Barry "Red" Thorne, one of the wounded, sees his teammate Al Levin taken prisoner as he is airlifted away (1). Richard Von Burian shoots an NVA soldier (PWJ #4, '89 fb, see NOTE). Aboard the evac helicopter, Von Burian notices the bodybags contain drug-filled remains of dead NVA soldiers, dressed in American uniforms. Schoonover, the leader of the smuggling operation, recruits Von Burian (2).

SYNOPSIS: A sniper shoots Red Thorne, a former squadmate of the Punisher's; among the witnesses to Thorne's death is a wheelchair-bound man. Frank Castle goes to JFK to meet another squadmate, William Pope, arriving in town for a reunion, only to see him gunned down. Police mistake Frank for the shooter, forcing him to abandon pursuit of Pope's killer. Microchip alerts Frank to a news report about the murders of his ex-squadmates and an interview between reporter Helen Shaw and Ray Schoonover, his self-serving former CO. Frank travels to the reunion and finds Helen interviewing Marine Lee Inoguchi. The pair head outside to chat privately, secretly shadowed by Frank, but Lee is infuriated when Helen offers him cocaine. Lee is then killed, and Frank trades fire with the assassin. Frank chases the assassin in the Battle Van, but the assassin's car drops mines that blow his tire, and as he affects repairs, Sniper, an ex-squadmate who is exterminating the unit in case any of them discovered Schoonover's drug-smuggling scheme in Indochina, subdues him. Frank gets the drop on Sniper and flees as the police arrive, but one of Sniper's mines has destroyed a passing SUV. Frank returns to the hotel and forces Schoonover to telephone a confession to Helen and then to shoot himself. As a shaken Helen flushes her cocaine, Frank departs, unaware he is in Sniper's crosshairs.

NOTE: Microchip informs Frank that a family of four was in the SUV destroyed by Sniper's mine. The rfb depicting Von Burian's shooting of an NVA soldier repeats a panel from fb1. Issue includes Punisher's ballistic knife equipment pinup by Eliot R. Brown, later reprinted in PunArm #1, '90. "Punisher War Journal Entries" lettercol begins. The hotel's name, Al Levin's occupation and Helen's station's call letters are revealed next issue.

PUNISHER WAR JOURNAL #5 (April 1989)

"Crucible" (22 pages)

CREDITS: Carl Potts (writer), Jim Lee (pencils), Scott Williams (inks, see NOTE), Ken Lopez (letters), Gregory Wright (colors), Kelly Corvese (asst editor), Don Daley (editor)
FEATURE CHARACTER: Punisher (also bts as Lt. Castle in fb during PWJ #4, '89 fb; next in Pun #19, '89)
SUPPORTING CAST: Microchip (on live video, next in Pun #19, '89)
VILLAINS: Ray Schoonover (as corpse, also bts in PWJ #4, '89 fb and PWJ #4, '89 fb, also as recorded voice), Sniper (next in PWJ #10, '89)
OTHER CHARACTERS: Al Levin (also in fb between PWJ #4, '89 fb & PWJ #4, '89), Helen Shaw, David (cameraman, dies), NVA soldiers (all in fb, some die), anti-Red Hill tribespeople (all in fb), 2 DEA operatives (both in fb), newsroom employee, news helicopter pilot (see NOTE)
LOCATIONS/ITEMS: Westchester inc Rye Town Resort w/Schoonover's room & Sniper's house w/library & office; Indochina (in fb) inc village / Schoonover's handgun, Sniper's sniper rifle, triangular blade, Mercedes, revolver w/scope & house's security traps inc road mines, tripwire grenades, motion detectors, automated machine guns, bullet-mines & automated crossbow; Levin's electricity-generating "talon glove," Marine helicopters (in fb), NVA soldiers' rifles (in fb), tribes' rifles (in fb), Punisher's Battle Van w/minigun & "big ear" parabolic microphone, Goncz auto-pistol, M-16 w/underslung shotgun, grenades, ballistic knife, rocket launcher, fishing weight, knuckle-guarded combat knife, news helicopter, David's camera
FLASHBACK: Indochina: Al Levin escapes from his NVA captors and is rescued by anti-Red Hill tribespeople who welcome him into their village and culture. Shortly thereafter, the DEA recruits Levin.
SYNOPSIS: As Helen Shaw reports on Schoonover's phone confession, Sniper prepares to shoot the Punisher, but Al Levin, previously feigning wheelchair-necessary paralysis, stops him. After Levin explains how he survived Indochina, Sniper subdues him and inflicts a fatal blade wound. Coercing Schoonover for Sniper's home address, Frank travels there and navigates Sniper's booby traps, then summons Helen intending to give her the story on the assassinations, but Sniper drives a car through the room, surprising Frank. The two battle until Helen arrives aboard a news helicopter. Sniper kills Helen's cameraman and holds her at knifepoint, keeping Frank at bay long enough for Sniper to board the helicopter and escapes, coercing the pilot to fly him away.
NOTE: Other uncredited inkers assisted Scott Williams; inks on this issue are credited to "Scott Williams & Co." PWJ #10, '89 reveals Sniper killed the pilot shortly after his escape. Includes a Barret .50 caliber sniper rifle equipment pinup by Eliot R. Brown, later reprinted in PunArm #1, '90.

PUNISHER WAR JOURNAL #6 (June 1989)

"On the Track of Unknown Animals" (22 pages)

CREDITS: Carl Potts (writer, pencil layouts), Jim Lee (layouts, finished art, c art), Jim Novak (letters), Gregory Wright (colors), Kelly Corvese (asst editor), Don Daley (editor)
FEATURE CHARACTER: Punisher (last in PP #46, '89, also as "Charles 'Chuck' Fort")
GUEST STARS: Shadowmasters: Yuriko Ezaki, Philip Richards (prev 2 last in PWJ #3, '89, next in PWJ #8, '89), Rikichi (last in PWJ #3, '89); Wolverine (also as "Patch," last in UXM Ann #13/2, '89)
SUPPORTING CAST: Microchip (last in Pun #19, '89, next in Pun #20, '89 bts, Pun #21, '89)
VILLAINS: Cpl. Ebambe (corrupt Congolese security officer), Otis C. Roberts (oil tycoon, Norma's employer), Norma Wyeth (illegal game hunter) (all 1st), illegal furs dealer
OTHER CHARACTERS: Lt. Bokenga (Congolese security officer), Bill Lim (anthropologist/entomologist), Chief Victor Obiang, Jacques Tsolo (prev 2 pygmy guides), Kurt Reader (geomorphologist/paleontologist), Prof. Richard

Wyeth (expedition leader, Norma's husband) (all 1st), Jean N'dosa (pygmy guide, dies), Father Murray (mission leader), Mokele-Mbembe, Maj. Kinami (corrupt Congolese security officer, mentioned, dies off-panel), African villagers, bar patrons, bartender, pygmy guides, commuters, 3 black mambas (one bts, 2 die), deer (2 die), gorillas (some as skulls, some as corpses, one dies), fruit bats, moths, chimpanzee, alligator

LOCATIONS/ITEMS: Microchip's warehouse; San Antonio inc Roberts' office & San Antonio International Airport, Madripoor inc Princess Bar, Shadowmasters' apartment w/kitchen, Congo Basin inc airfield, Impfondo (village), Father Murray's mission, Lake Tele / Microchip's first-aid kit w/antiseptic, sponge, bandages & surgical scissors; Roberts' empty Mokele-Mbembe head plaque, fur dealer's cheetah-pelt coat (later used by Wolverine as bush camouflage) & knife, commuter airplane, expedition members' equipment packs, Norma's camera, Bokenga's rifle, Ebambe's rifle w/silencer, Punisher's assault rifle w/underslung shotgun & knife, medical supplies inc aspirin, fungicides, & antivenom, guides' machetes, Jacques' & Obiang's crossbows, Wyeth's book of animal silhouettes

SYNOPSIS: After Punisher gets wounded again, Microchip insists he take a break. In Madripoor, Wolverine interrogates a man dealing in illegal furs for a corrupt Congolese Security officer. At Microchip's urging, Frank takes a security job for an African expedition seeking a mythical species of modern dinosaur. Meanwhile Rikichi's meditation visions prompt him to visit Texas. In the Congo one of the expedition's younger guides, Jean N'dosa, begins to hero-worship Frank. After offloading medical supplies to the local mission, the expedition visit a village whose residents have seen the dinosaur. Norma Wyeth, the expedition leader's wife, and her bodyguard, Cpl. Ebambe, distract Jean while they hunt native gorillas for their skulls. Norma notices Jean's suspicion upon his return. Norma and Ebambe return to the village claiming the gorillas took Jean, and Frank and another guide find him mortally wounded. Wolverine arrives in search of the fur-smuggling ring. Frank investigates Jean's death, but is attacked by a surviving gorilla and forced to kill him. Mistaking Frank for a poacher, Wolverine attacks Frank, slashing him and leaving him in a river as an alligator approaches.

NOTE: Microchip's alias for Frank, Charles Fort, is taken from the unexplained-phenomena researcher of the same name. Roberts' name and connection to Norma are revealed next issue. Includes a Model 452 Stingball riot grenade, the Model 429 stun grenade, and the Thunder Strip stun device equipment pinup by Eliot R. Brown, later reprinted in PunArm #1, '90.

PUNISHER WAR JOURNAL #7 (July 1989)

"Endangered Species" (22 pages)

CREDITS: Carl Potts (writer, co-pencil layouts, c inks), Jim Lee (co-layouts finished art, c pencils), Jim Novak (letters), Gregory Wright (colors), Kelly Corvese (asst editor), Don Daley (editor)
FEATURE CHARACTERS: Punisher (also as "Chuck Fort," next in Pun #20 '89)
GUEST STAR: Wolverine (next in W #4, '89), Rikichi
VILLAINS: Cpl. Ebambe, Norma Wyeth (both die), Otis C. Roberts
OTHER CHARACTERS: Lt. Bokenga, Bill Lim, Kurt Reader, Jacques Tsolo, Prof. Richard Wyeth, "Pumpkin" (rabbit), alligator, snake (both die), deer (one dies), leopard, guard dogs, villagers inc chief, 2 Mokele-Mbembe
LOCATIONS/ITEMS: Congo Basin inc village, San Antonio inc Roberts' ranch w/office, New York's Upper West Side inc corridor outside Punisher's safehouse / Punisher's tree branch, assault rifle w/underslung shotgun, Wolverine's cheetah pelt, Roberts' computer, expedition's equipment packs, Jacques' crossbow, Bokenga's rifle, Ebambe's rifle & aquatic mines, Norma's gold bracelet, copy of the Wall St. Journal, six-pack of Lone Star beer, Roberts' empty head plaque, Rikichi's note

SYNOPSIS: The Punisher kills the alligator with a broken tree branch, then reclaims his rifle and hunts for Wolverine. In San Antonio, Rikichi sneaks into Otis Roberts' ranch and hacks his computer. Back in Africa, Richard Wyeth sends Jacques to find "Fort" and interviews more villagers about the Mokele-Mbembe, but the villagers claim ignorance. Norma Wyeth and Ebambe bribe a female villager with Norma's gold bracelet into leading them to two of the dinosaurs, then send her away. Wyeth recognizes Norma's bracelet on the girl, and her chief orders her to explain herself. Frank tracks Wolverine down, and they battle near Norma and Ebambe. Norma orders them killed, but an arriving Lt. Bokenga shoots Ebambe. Norma tries to herd the dinosaurs towards mines she and Ebambe planted, but Frank shoots her and herds them away with gunfire. As Norma confesses her crimes to Wyeth, Wolverine hunts the fleeing Ebambe to finish him off, but decides otherwise when Frank approaches. Frank binds Ebambe with Wolverine's lost cheetah pelt and leaves him to a pack of approaching gorillas. Days later, Frank finds a newspaper on his doorstep and an anonymous note from Rikichi directing him to an article about Roberts emptying his investment portfolio into a wildlife charity.
NOTE: Includes an XM-174 rocket launcher and two Striker automatic shotguns "Punisher's Arsenal" pinup by Eliot R. Brown, later reprinted in PunArm #1, '90.

PUNISHER WAR JOURNAL #8 (September 1989)

"Damage" (22 pages)

CREDITS: Carl Potts (writer), Jim Lee (art), Jim Novak (letters), Gregory Wright (colors), Kelly Corvese (asst editor), Don Daley (editor), Klaus Janson (c inks)
FEATURE CHARACTER: Punisher (last in Pun Ann #2/3, '89)
GUEST STARS: Shadowmasters: Yuriko Ezaki, Philip Richards (both last in PWJ #6, '89), Manzo (1st), Rikichi
SUPPORTING CAST: Microchip (bts, last in Pun Ann #2/2, '89, next in PWJ #10, '89)
VILLAINS: Bunsen Burners (street gang) inc Damage (Jaime Ortiz, leader, 1st, next in PWJ #18, '90 bts, PWJ #19, '90), Ron Salazar (1st, next in PWJ #11, '89), Egghead, Davey, Ramone (some die); Sunrise Society clone assassin (dies)
OTHER CHARACTERS: Sam Bryan (newsstand owner, also in photo), Edna (Sam's neighbor) & her son, Larry (taxi driver) (all die), Isabelle Salazar (Ron's infirm sister), Ron's grandmother (both 1st, next in PWJ #11, '89), Hatsu Yakomoto (ninja master, mentioned by Manzo)

LOCATIONS/ITEMS: New York inc Sam's Newsstand, Winning Deli w/Shadowmasters' apartment, Salazars' apartment w/Isabelle's bedroom, Lazzaro Warehouse (Bunsen Burners' HQ) / Bunsen Burners' guns, van, sledgehammers, bats, crowbars, concussion grenade; Larry's taxi (destroyed), Punisher's parabolic microphone, thermal imager, gas & smoke grenades, rappelling line, gas mask, Uzi, Goncz auto-pistol, ballistic knife & Battle Van w/sonic pain generators, tear gas dispensers, Stingball riot grenades, hubcap plasma generators, minigun w/plastic rounds & memory-metal capture coils; Ron's grandmother's cane, wooden table, power line, assassin's battle-suit, Rikichi's shoulder bag w/flash powder

SYNOPSIS: Damage, leader of the Bunsen Burners street gang, kills civic-minded business owner Sam Bryan and several of his neighbors. At Winning Deli, Manzo, one of the Shadowmasters, reunites happily with Yuriko, Phillip and Rikichi, but they notice he is wounded. The Punisher coerces the Bunsen Burners' hideout location from member Ron Salazar, but Ron's grandmother's arrival stops Frank from killing Ron. As Manzo explains to the Shadowmasters that he has found them a ninpo grandmaster from which to learn and that he was attacked upon arrival in New York, the wall of their

apartment is blown apart. Damage calls Ron, who tells him Punisher's Battle Van is parked nearby. Damage and some of the gang attempt to steal the van, unaware Frank is laying waste to the rest of the gang at their warehouse hideout. Damage and his gang fall victim to the van's security systems until only Damage and gang member Egghead remain, and Egghead flees after Damage is ensnared by the van's capture coils. The Shadowmasters defeat their attacker, but Yuriko is horrified to see his face is that of her father. Frank returns to find Damage horribly mangled by the coils, and drives him to a hospital.
NOTE: Ron's family name is revealed in PWJ #11. The Punisher encounters Hatsu Yakamoto alongside the Shadowmasters in Pun #24-25, '89. The Shadowmasters' origins and enmity with the Sunrise Society, a group of Japanese militants, is detailed in Shadow #1-4, '89-90, promoted in an editorial footnote herein. The Sunrise Society began amassing clones of Yuriko's father, Shigeru Ezaki, in Shadow #2, '89. Damage's real name is revealed in MEnc #4, '04. Goncz is misspelled Goenz. The Bunsen Burners' warehouse is located on 185th St. Includes a FN Herstal PN90 submachine gun "Punisher's Arsenal" pinup by Eliot R. Brown, later reprinted in PunArm #1, '90.

PUNISHER WAR JOURNAL #9 (October 1989)

"Guilt Trip" (22 pages)

CREDITS: Carl Potts (writer), Jim Lee (art), Jim Novak (letters), Gregory Wright (colors), Kelly Corvese (asst editor), Don Daley (editor)
FEATURE CHARACTER: Punisher (next in Pun #24, '89)
GUEST STARS: Black Widow (last in FF Ann #22, '89, next in AvS #27/2, '89; also as spider in symbolic images), Shadowmasters: Yuriko Ezaki (also in rfb3-5), Philip Richards (also in rfb3-4), Manzo (prev 3 next in Pun #24, '89), Rikichi (next in PWJ #17, '90)
VILLAINS: 4 Sunrise Society clone assassins (all die, one also in rfb5, see NOTE; also in symbolic image), 3 home invaders
OTHER CHARACTERS: Frank Castle Jr., Lisa Castle, Maria Castle (all in rfb1), Forest Hunt; Maggia: Luis Allegre, Bruno Costa, Byron Hannigan, Leon Kolsky, Matt Skinner (prev 6 bts in rfb1); Tengu (Shigeru Ezaki, Shadowmaster, in fb1 during Shadow #1, '89, also in rfb3-4), Kantaro Umezu (Sunrise Society founder, in fb2&4 & symbolic image), Yuriko's mother (in rfb3)
LOCATIONS/ITEMS: Manhattan inc west side condo, Winning Deli w/Shadowmasters' apartment / Black Widow's line & Bite (electrical stinger); home invaders' guns & knives, assassins' battle-suits; Punisher's Battle Van (destroyed) w/minigun
FLASHBACKS: Frank and his family go to the park, stumble across the Maggia interrogating Forest Hunt, and are gunned down (PWJ #1, '89). Post war, Tengu hunts Japanese renegades, including Kantaro Umezu (Shadow #1, '89; see NOTE). He trains his children as they grow, but eventually the Sunrise Society attack, blowing up Shigeru's home (Shadow #2, '89). Yuriko and Philip attack the Sunrise Society's base, discovering Shigeru, believed slain in the explosion, has been the Society's prisoner. She witnesses Umezu slay him and kills Umezu in turn (Shadow #4, '89). Yuriko kicks the Sunrise Society assassin out the window, then sees he is a clone of her father (PWJ #8, '89).
SYNOPSIS: Black Widow swings across Manhattan's rooftops towards the Winning Deli, having promised Daredevil she will keep watch on it, pausing en route to stop a home invasion. At the Widow's destination, Yuriko is shocked to see the Sunrise Society assassin is a clone of her father. Grabbing supplies, the Shadowmasters quickly flee the apartment, but come under fire from a second armored attacker; they split up, but the assassin is about to slay Manzo and Yuriko when the Punisher, using his Battle Van's minigun, guns him down. To Yuriko's distress, this assassin also proves to be her father, and she faints. As Punisher exits his van, it is blown up by a third assassin. With Punisher stunned, Manzo and Philip lead the assassin into the park, while Rikichi uses meditative techniques to let Yuriko and Castle share one another's memories: Castle recalls his family's murder, imagining himself as their killer as he blames himself for not saving them, and remembers his guilt transforming him into the Punisher, while Yuriko recalls her father's war with the Shadow Society. As Widow arrives, Rikichi merges their memories so they view their enemies as a common foe, and they witness a vision of their armored attacker being destroyed by a giant spider. The assassin returns as they wake, and together they take him down. As the other Shadowmasters return from the park, a fourth assassin attacks, but Black Widow intervenes, slaying him. Rikichi thanks Punisher, and the Shadowmasters depart, heading for Japan to end things with the Sunrise Society, but promising to see Frank again.
NOTE: Includes a Colt XM-177E1 "Punisher's Arsenal" pinup by Eliot R. Brown, later reprinted in PunArm #1, '90. The end of the Shadowmasters' fight with the first assassin briefly overlaps the scenes from last issue. The flashbacks contain minor inaccuracies – Yuriko was not born when her father fought Kantaro Umezu; having only been told about the fight, she imagines Umezu wearing an eye-patch that he only wore later, as a result of injuries Shigeru inflicted. Additionally, it was her dying father who slew Umezu, not Yuriko

PUNISHER WAR JOURNAL #10 (November 1989)

"Second Shot" (22 pages)

CREDITS: Carl Potts (writer, c inks), Jim Lee (pencils), Scott Williams (inks), Jim Novak (letters), Gregory Wright (colors), Rob Tokar (asst editor), Don Daley (editor)
FEATURE CHARACTER: Punisher (last in Pun:RBN, '89, next in Pun #26, '89; also as Lt. Wohl)
SUPPORTING CAST: Microchip (last bts in PWJ #8, '89; also as Captain Siry)
VILLAIN: Sniper (last in PWJ #5, '89, next in PWJ #21, '90; also in rfb)
OTHER CHARACTERS: US soldiers (some die) inc Lt. Curtis, Reeves, Brown; Helga (waitress), French soldiers, military show attendees, hotel guests & staff, East German border guards; Helen Shaw, David (prev 2 in rfb)
LOCATIONS/ITEMS: West Germany inc military show, NATO base & hotel w/Punisher & Microchip's rooms, French NATO base, East German border w/Grenze watch tower / M1A1 Abrams Main Battle Tanks (some destroyed) w/infrared scopes, target tanks; Vulcan anti-aircraft vehicle, 2 Bradley infantry fighting vehicles, scout helicopter (destroyed), Simnet simulator; Sniper's rifle (also in rfb), gun w/silencer, knife, pole vault & flashlight; Microchip's portable computer; Apache helicopters; Frank & Microchip's stolen uniforms
FLASHBACK: Von Burian was the Marine Corps' top sniper, but he became a drug rings' assassin. Punisher fought him, but he took hostages, forcing Frank to let him go (PWJ #5, '89).
SYNOPSIS: Punisher and Microchip attend a military show in West Germany, suspecting Sniper is in the area, as someone with his signature MO has recently been breaking into high security bases. As Microchip hacks into computer systems looking for leads, Sniper sneaks onto a US base to steal weapons systems data for his East German clients; as he is raiding the computer files, he and Microchip cross virtual paths and spar inconclusively. Leaving that base, Sniper steals an Apache helicopter from a French NATO base just before dawn, intending to use

it to cross the border. Hearing of the theft when they arrive at the military show, and figuring Sniper will take a direct route to East Germany and so pass over the show, Frank and Micro steal Army uniforms and commandeer the soldiers and vehicles due to perform at the show. As anticipated, Sniper's path takes him over their location, and a grueling battle ensues, ending with Sniper's helicopter crashing and exploding on the other side of the East German border.
NOTE: Includes a Glock 19 "Punisher's Arsenal" pinup by Eliot R. Brown, later reprinted in PunArm #1, '90.

PUNISHER WAR JOURNAL #11 (Mid-November 1989)

"Shock Treatment" (19 pages)

CREDITS (BOTH STORIES): Carl Potts (writer), Jim Lee (pencils), Klaus Janson (inks), Jim Novak (letters), Gregory Wright (colors), Rob Tokar (asst editor), Don Daley (editor)
FEATURE CHARACTER: Punisher (last in Pun #27, '89, also in 2nd story, next in CPun #3/3, '89)
SUPPORTING CAST: Microchip (next in CPun #3/3, '89)
VILLAINS: Drug dealers (some die), gang members inc basketball players (also in 2nd story)
OTHER CHARACTERS: Police (some also in 2nd story), Ron Salazar (last in PWJ #88, '89; also in 2nd story & on TV), Ron's grandma, Isabelle (Ron's sister), Cujo (pit bull), drug addicts (1 also in 2nd story) inc Shaky; Vincent Hayes (TV reporter, on TV), camp inmates (on TV), camp sergeant (on TV), Ron's parole officer, Phillipe (Ron's uncle, mentioned), undercover cops (next in 2nd story, some die off panel) inc Mick & Steve (both next in 2nd story)
LOCATIONS/ITEMS: New Jersey inc Microchip's warehouse, Upper Manhattan inc basketball court, crack houses (one damaged), Salazar apartment; Upstate New York inc Camp Newton (on TV, young offenders boot camp) / drug dealers' guns & knives; Punisher's gun, H&K G-11, disguise, 2x4 w/wire & nails, Battle Van w/remote, "Big Ear" microphone, sniper rifle & motorbike, police cars & guns; crack cocaine, National Enquirer newspaper
SYNOPSIS: In Upper Manhattan police crash an informal basketball game, and when one player goes for his bag, they gun him down and take him away, warning the other players to get straight and stay straight. Elsewhere the Punisher attacks a drugs den and kills the dealers. The next morning, Ron Salazar apologizes to his grandmother for not helping with the bills; he's gone straight since his encounter with Punisher, but nobody wants to hire a dropout ex-gang member, and his bedridden sister needs expensive medicine, so he reluctantly decides to go back to dealing crack. Meanwhile Punisher stakes out another crack house while reading a newspaper about cops being killed and wounded by a drug gang. He raids the house, leaving only the addicts alive, and wonders if he is going soft and should kill them too, before they hurt innocents to feed their habits. Traveling across the roofs he spots Ron dealing, recognizes him as the member of Damage's gang he let live, and is about to shoot him when police show up and arrest Ron as part of a general round-up looking for the cop killer. A few weeks later Punisher is angered to learn Ron got a light sentence, and has enrolled in a new boot camp program that will make him eligible for parole in six months. Four months later Microchip watches a news report about the boot camp, which depicts Ron as one of the program's successes. Microchip returns to finishing a remote for Punisher's van. A month later, Ron has been released, and Punisher has learned he is leaving for Texas to work on a relative's farm; convinced Ron will re-offend, Punisher plans to kill Ron, but Microchip remotely disables the van. Unfortunately Frank has his motorbike in the van, and still reaches Ron's apartment building before Ron departs; listening on a radio mike to Ron saying goodbye to his parole officer and grandma, Frank has second thoughts, and lets Ron live, deciding Microchip can keep tabs on him and report if he falls back into crime. As he rides off, Punisher notices two gangs fighting, but decides to let them kill one another.
NOTE: Includes an AUG (Army Universal Geweher) "Punisher's Arsenal" pinup by Eliot R. Brown. The issue's 2nd story largely overlaps this one, identifying Mick and showing a different perspective on several scenes.

2ND STORY: "Scared Straight" (3 pages)
FEATURE CHARACTER: Punisher (during 1st story)
VILLAINS: Gang members inc basketball players (during 1st story)
OTHER CHARACTERS: Police (some during 1st story), Ron Salazar (during 1st story), drug addict (during 1st story), undercover cops (also in 2nd story, some die off panel) inc Mick & Steve (both during 1st story)
LOCATIONS/ITEMS: Upper Manhattan inc basketball court, Queens inc undercover cop's home / drug dealers' guns & knives; Punisher's H&K G-11, disguise, police cars & guns; National Enquirer newspaper, crack cocaine, beers
SYNOPSIS: In Upper Manhattan police crash an informal basketball game, and when one player goes for his bag, they gun him down and take him away, warning the other players to get straight and stay straight. They go to a Queens house, where the cops congratulate one another, especially their "victim," undercover cop Mick, for scaring the players' straight, though Mick points out they should have waited for the gang to actually commit a crime. At the same time, the gang angrily discusses Mick's "murder"; having recognized some of the cops from a nearby precinct, they decide to follow them home after their shift is over and get payback. Later, Punisher reads a newspaper about cops being killed and wounded by a drug gang. The police round up known gang members for the surviving cops to identify, including Ron Salazar, inadvertently saving him from Punisher. No-one is successfully charged with the cop killings, emboldening the gang, who begin a turf war to expand their territory.

PUNISHER WAR JOURNAL #12 (December 1989)

"Contrast in Sin" (22 pages)

CREDITS: Carl Potts (writer), Jim Lee (pencils, c art), Al Milgrom (inks), Don Hudson (background inks), Jim Novak (letters), Gregory Wright (colors), Rob Tokar (asst editor), Don Daley (editor)
FEATURE CHARACTER: Punisher (last in Pun #29, '90, also in photo)
SUPPORTING CAST: Microchip (last in Pun #29, '90)
VILLAINS: Dr. Doom, Kingpin, Loki (all last in Pun #29, '90), Bushwacker (Carl Burbank, assassin w/bionic gun arm, last in DD #260, '88), drug runners (some die) inc Hernando Brothers (die) & Freddie; Marauders (bts, see NOTE)
OTHER CHARACTERS: Maria Castle, Frank Castle, Jr., Lisa Castle (prev 3 in photo), CMN TV news anchor, radio news reporter (both voice only), Marilyn Burbank (Bushwacker's wife, last in DD #249, '87), Gretchen Carrenna (sculptor, dies), Jason Hunt (also in photos; bts, killed by Bushwacker, last in PWJ #3, '89), Simon Winston (CMN TV news commentator, 1st, also on TV), artists (some die), bystanders
LOCATIONS/ITEMS: CMN offices inc Simon Winston's office; Cresskill, New Jersey inc Bushwacker's home w/kitchen & living room; Isle of Silence inc Loki's conference chamber; Manhattan inc art studio, Central Park, George Washington Bridge & pier; Microchip's New Jersey

warehouse inc closet / Bushwacker's bionic firearms, motorcycle, television & John Steinbeck's "The Acts of King Arthur and His Noble Knights" book; briefcase of cash, drug smugglers' automatic firearms, file w/photographs, Kingpin's computer, Microchip's automatic door opener, newspaper clipping, paintings, packages of cocaine, radio, ship, Simon Winston's cigarette & computer; Punisher's automatic rifle, ballistic knife, Battle Van, gas grenade, Goncz automatic pistol, Harley Davidson motorcycle, headset, Kevlar motorcycle helmet & revolvers

SYNOPSIS: Frank Castle busts drug runners on a Manhattan pier and frightens a survivor into providing information about their smuggling operation. Meanwhile, Bushwacker murders a sculptor whose mutant nature unwittingly gives her artistic talent. The gun-armed assassin returns home, where his wife nags him about his mercenary life. He becomes enraged by a TV news editorial comparing Punisher favorably to him, unaware the disguised Loki paid the commentator for his incendiary remarks, working under Kingpin's instruction. Loki hires Bushwacker to kill Castle, and points him towards Jason Hunt as a possible information source. Weeks later, Bushwacker shows up in Central Park on the anniversary of the Castle family's deaths, having tortured and then killed Jason Hunt to learn Punisher returns there every year to commemorate the tragedy. Bushwacker follows his quarry back to Microchip's warehouse and attacks him.

NOTE: This issue and the next are part of the Acts of Vengeance crossover, where a villain cabal arranges for foes to fight heroes other than their traditional opponents. Bushwacker has been hired by the Marauders to kill mutant savants; since it remains unrevealed which specific Marauders employ Bushwacker, no chronologies can be supplied. Issue includes Automag III .30 cal. semiautomatic handgun "Punisher's Arsenal" pin-up by Eliot R. Brown.

PUNISHER WAR JOURNAL #13 (Mid December 1989)

"Confession" (22 pages)

CREDITS: Carl Potts (writer), Jim Lee (pencils, c art), Dan Bulanadi (inks), Jim Novak (letters), Gregory Wright (colors), Rob Tokar (asst editor), Don Daley (editor)
FEATURE CHARACTER: Punisher (next in DC2 #2, '89)
SUPPORTING CAST: Microchip (next in Pun #30, '90)
VILLAINS: Bushwacker (next in DD #334, '94), Dr. Doom (next in Av #313, '90 bts, C&D #13, '90), Kingpin (next in Av #313, '90), Loki (next in AWC #54, '90)
OTHER CHARACTERS: Maria Castle (in Punisher's thoughts), Marilyn Burbank, Simon Winston (on TV)
LOCATIONS/ITEMS: Cresskill, New Jersey inc bridge, river & Bushwacker's home w/garage & living room; Isle of Silence inc Loki's conference chamber; Manhattan; Microchip's home & New Jersey warehouse / Bushwacker's television (bts), aquarium, bionic firearms, mailbox, motorcycle & wall mirror; Marilyn Burbank's car, Kingpin's computer & desk; Punisher's automatic rifle, ballistic knife, Battle Van, "Big Ear" microphone & gas grenades

SYNOPSIS: Bushwacker beats Frank Castle to within an inch of his life but leaves the scene, convinced Punisher's death needs to be more artistic and public. Microchip revives Castle and takes him to his home, where he gathers intelligence on Bushwacker, including the assassin's home address. Loki reports Bushwacker's actions to Kingpin, whose rival and ally Dr. Doom derides the crime boss for his failure. Punisher assaults Bushwacker at his house and when Bushwacker's wife sees him about to kill Castle in the ensuing melee, she smashes a mirror over her husband and storms away in her car, disgusted that Bushwacker is no better than his adversary. Bushwacker pursues his wife and Punisher follows. Castle attacks the injured and rejected Bushwacker and allows him to fall off a bridge. The next day, Doom gloats as he, Kingpin and Loki watch a TV news report about Punisher's victory and his subsequent drug busts.

NOTE: Includes Blackhawk Superbow, the Browning compound bow and Magnus II arrows "Punisher's Arsenal" pin-up by Eliot R. Brown. The issue credits David Ross and Russ Heath for pencils and inks; PWJ #20, '90 corrects this to Lee and Bulanadi.

PUNISHER WAR JOURNAL #14 (January 1990)

"Blind Faith" (23 pages)

CREDITS: Carl Potts (writer), David Ross (pencils), Russ Heath (inks), Jim Novak (letters), Gregory Wright (colors), Rob Tokar (asst editor), Don Daley (editor), Jim Lee (c art)
FEATURE CHARACTER: Punisher (last in Pun #32, '90)
GUEST STAR: Spider-Man (last in ASM #330, '90)
SUPPORTING CAST: Microchip (last in Pun #30, '90)
VILLAINS: Eric Hartmann (neo-Nazi, 1st, also in fb to chr 1st prior to PWJ #15, '90 fb) & his men inc Rick Turner (blind neo-Nazi), Dunn (wheelchair-bound neo-Nazi), Gordon, Miller (all 1st, prev 3 named next issue), Nazi nurses (1 next in PWJ #15, '90 fb), Nazi soldiers (both in pfb)
OTHER CHARACTERS: Kate Cushing (last in WoSM #60, '90), J. Jonah Jameson (last in SpSM #160, '90), Mary Jane Watson-Parker (last in ASM #330, '90), Mr. Watkins & his family, Daily Bugle staff, police, bystanders, turkey (dies); Adolf Hitler, Eva Braun, Otto Gunschie (bts) (prev 3 in rfb), concentration camp inmates, Allied soldiers, German infants, Russian soldiers (prev 4 in pfb); Hartmann's sisters (in hallucination as angels, also bts in fb prior to PWJ #15, '90 fb)
LOCATIONS/ITEMS: Concentration camp, Nazi baby ward (both pfb), Hitler's bunker (in rfb), New Jersey inc Microchip's warehouse, Washington Square Park, Daily Bugle, Hartmann's ranch, Watkins house / tank, bomber planes, various WWII weapons (all in pfb), Hitler's Luger, Eva's poisoned drink (both in rfb), Punisher's Battle Van w/mini gun, M40 advanced combat shotgun, handgun; targets; Spider-Man's camera & web-shooters; payphone, bottles (thrown), Jonah's pad & pencil, Rick's crossbow, bolts & cane; Dunn's wheelchair & binoculars; Daily Bugle newspaper, Micro's computer, Hartmann's men's rifles, grenades, cars & flatbed truck w/cannon; lamp (used as club), wheelchair-accessible van
FLASHBACK: Hitler attempts suicide (WI? #4, '77). Nazis send Jews to concentration camps, and babies deemed to fit the Aryan ideal are taken to be raised by the state. As the Russians secure Berlin, a nurse escapes with three of her charges.

SYNOPSIS: In Washington Park, Peter Parker witnesses Eric Hartmann honoring the anniversary of Hitler's death with a neo-Nazi rally that devolves into a brawl between his followers and others in the area. The next day, two of Hartmann's followers, the blind Rick Turner and wheelchair-bound Dunn, practice their crossbow marksmanship, compensating for one another's disabilities. Hartmann angrily reads the Daily Bugle's report of events and heads up to a cliff top to confer with the angels, who tell him it's time to take a bold stroke. Meanwhile, Punisher, curious about Hartmann, has Microchip hack Hartmann's computer. Micro discovers lists of names; one is of witnesses set to testify against Hartmann's men for the park brawl, but older lists prove to be people who have unexplained violent deaths or gone missing. Micro calls to warn the ones on the first list, but the Watkins family dismisses him as another threatening phone call. Having learned of the Watkins' receiving threatening calls via the police, the Bugle sends Peter to photograph them. Both he and Punisher arrive at the Watkins just as Hartmann's men attack, and together they stop them, with Spidey trying to keep Punisher from killing. Spidey accompanies Punisher to Hartmann's ranch but they find the road blocked by his men and hear a report that the Daily Bugle is under siege. Punisher gives Spidey a choice: risk the Bugle hostages, including Mary Jane, by taking their enemies alive, or kill them and get to the Bugle faster.

PUNISHER WAR JOURNAL #15 (February 1990)

"Headlines!" (24 pages)

CREDITS: Carl Potts (writer), David Ross (pencils), Russ Heath (inks), Jim Novak (letters), Gregory Wright (colors), Rob Tokar (asst editor), Don Daley (editor), Jim Lee (c art)
FEATURE CHARACTER: Punisher (also in rfb, next in ASM #330, '90)
GUEST STAR: Spider-Man (next in SpSM #161, '90)
SUPPORTING CAST: Microchip (voice only, next in ASM #330, '90)
VILLAINS: Eric Hartmann (also in fb between PWJ #14, '90 fb & PWJ #14, '90) & his men (some die) inc Rick Turner, Gordon, Miller (prev 3 die) & Dunn
OTHER CHARACTERS: Kate Cushing, J. Jonah Jameson, Mary Jane Watson-Parker (all next in SpSM #161, '90), Glory Grant (last in WoSM #60, '90, next in SpSM #168, '90), Betty Leeds (last in SpSM #156, '89, next in WoSM #63, '90), Daily Bugle staff (some die) & security guards (3 die), police, SWAT (some die); Adolf Hitler, Jewish bodies, Nazis, Eva Braun, Otto Gunsche (both bts); Maria Castle, Lisa Castle, Frank Castle Jr, Bruno Costa, Byron Hannigan, Leon Klosky, Matt Skinner (prev 12 in rfb); Hartmann's sisters (in fb & hallucination as angels)
LOCATIONS/ITEMS: Daily Bugle inc Jonah's office, printing room & loading dock, concentration camp, Hitler's bunker (both in rfb), sewers / Hartmann's men's rifles, Uzis, knives, radios, cars, flatbed truck w/cannon, rocket launcher; guards' night sticks & key card, Punisher's Battle Van w/pain field disruptor, crowbar, bazooka & Uzi; Spider-Man's web-shooters, Jonah's computer, Hitler's luger (in rfb), Rick's crossbow & bolts, Dunn's wheelchair & handgun, SWAT helicopter w/machine gun (destroyed), police cars & rifles, Hartmann's handgun, extension cord (used to tie up Hartmann)
FLASHBACK: Hitler attempts suicide (WI? #4, '77). Punisher's family is killed (MPr #2, '75 fb). Hartmann's nurse whisks him and his sisters away (PWJ #14, '90 fb) and raises them for 10 years with Nazi ideals before she dies. Hartmann does odd jobs to support his family, but one day they disappear. He goes to America where he eventually has a vision of angels, who tell him he's destined to finish Hitler's work. Hartmann recruits like-minded followers.
SYNOPSIS: Eric Hartmann and his men invade the Daily Bugle and take Jonah and the staff hostage, as well as Mary Jane, there picking up Peter's check. In upstate New York, where more of Hartmann's men have waylaid Punisher's Battle Van, Spider-Man insists on using non-lethal force to stop them, despite this taking longer than Punisher's methods. At the Bugle, Jonah reluctantly agrees to run Hartmann's article to save the hostages' lives. Meanwhile, the police try to retake the building, but are met with heavy resistance. To dissuade further attempts, Hartmann has a staff member thrown out a window. Punisher and Spidey arrive and split up; Punisher hitting the sewers and Spidey going high. Microchip informs Punisher of Hartmann's "contactee" syndrome, believing he has been visited by beings accompanied by a bright light. Punisher enters via the loading dock and kills the neo-Nazis there, then informs Hartmann over the radio that he's coming. Believing the police prevented his message from getting out, Hartmann sends Rick and Dunn out to continue to spread his word, posing as hostages freed because of their disabilities. Spidey bursts in, and Hartmann throws Mary Jane out the window to distract him. Spidey saves her and Jonah takes Hartmann down, just as his angels, who he now believes are revealed to be his sisters, appear and inform him he's a failure. Punisher catches Rick and Dunn in the lobby and sees through their ruse when he spots Rick's crossbow bolts. Dunn fires on Frank but accidentally kills Rick, and Punisher disarms him with shots to the shoulder, then departs through the sewers.
NOTE: The beginning of the issue takes place during PWJ #14, '90.

PUNISHER WAR JOURNAL #16 (March 1990)

"Panhandle" (21 pages)

CREDITS: Mike Baron (writer), Neil Hansen (pencils), Mark Texeira (inks, c art), Steve Biasi, Kenneth Rubenoff (background inks), Ken Bruzenak (letters), John Wellington (colors), Rob Tokar (asst editor), Don Daley (editor)
FEATURE CHARACTER: Punisher (last in ASM #331, '90, next in Pun #33, '90)
SUPPORTING CAST: Microchip (last in ASM #330, '90, next in Pun #33, '90)
VILLAINS: "Big" Reese Kelleher (Texan swindler & drug-runner), Barry Swindell (Reese's lawyer) (both die), Reese's men (some die) inc Ramon
OTHER CHARACTERS: Amos Lockhart (fraud victim, dies), bank staff inc Bill (dies), Cicero Roosevelt Pike, Flaco (both Houston homeless), reporters (2 on TV), Carlotta (Reese's woman), Reese's driver, Elsinor police, Houston police, bystanders; Felipe (Carlotta's brother, dies)
LOCATIONS/ITEMS: Texas inc Elsinor w/South Texas Savings & Loan, Houston, Reece's ranch inc house w/office & kitchen, Gila Point; New Jersey inc Microchip's warehouse / Amos' shotgun, police cars & sniper rifle; Punisher's disguise, radio equipment, bug, sponge, motorbike, knife & infrared goggles; Reece's limo, Lamborghini Cheetah, gun, grenade, jet & accounts book; rosary, frying pan
SYNOPSIS: In Elsinor, Texas, an enraged Amos Lockhart takes the local bank hostage after his money is lost to a crooked investment scheme set up by Reese Kelleher; a police marksman kills him after he shoots one of the staff dead. News reports of the incident prompt Punisher to investigate. In Houston a disguised Punisher befriends panhandler Cicero, who used to work for Reese before being wiped out by one of Reese's fraudulent schemes, and as Reese leaves a court hearing Frank plants a bug on Reese's limo, learning Reese is expecting a drugs shipment from across the border. Reese and his lawyer, Barry, return to Reese's ranch, where Reese rebuffs his lover Carlotta's attentions; Barry tries to comfort her, telling her Reese is smuggling her brother Felipe into the country that night. With intel from Cicero, Punisher stakes out the river crossing on the border where Felipe is bringing Reese's drugs across, but Felipe loses the drugs to the current, managing only to hang on to a rosary he brought for Carlotta. Reese guns Felipe down, then races back to the ranch when his men radio him that the Feds are planning to raid it. Reese tells Carlotta her brother never showed, but Barry gives her the rosary and she realizes the truth. Having followed Reese home, Punisher attacks the ranch and corners Reese, but promises to let him live if he gives up his Swiss bank account numbers. Reese stuns him with a grenade and guns down Barry when he intervenes, but before he can slay Punisher, Carlotta attacks with a frying pan and beats Reese to death. After Punisher finds Reese's accounts book, the pair escape the ranch, and return to Houston, where Punisher entrusts Cicero with some of the stolen money to distribute to those Reese robbed, promising to check in a few months to make sure he has done as asked.
NOTE: Issue includes a b&w poster of Captain America & Punisher by Scott Williams.

PUNISHER WAR JOURNAL #17 (April 1990)

"Tropical Trouble" (22 pages)

CREDITS: Carl Potts (writer), Jim Lee (pencils, c art), Al Milgrom (inks), Don Hudson (background inks), Rick Parker (letters), Gregory Wright (colors), Rob Tokar (asst editor), Don Daley (editor)
FEATURE CHARACTER: Punisher (last in WoSM Ann #6/2, '90)
GUEST STAR: Rikichi (last in PWJ #9, '89)
SUPPORTING CAST: Microchip (last in Pun Ann #3/4, '90)
VILLAINS: Drug runners inc Stevie, Roger, Hank (all die); Kingpin (last in DC2 #2, '90, next in PWJ #20, '90 bts, GR #1, '90), Arranger (Oswald Silkworth, Kingpin's aide, last in WoSM #5, '85, chr last in X23 #3, '05); Hawaiian dope growers (some bts, some in dfb, some die) inc Jessie (leader, also in dfb), Bud, Dirk, Mitch, Rosco, Lenny, Ralphie, Squid, Henson, Winston (both die)
OTHER CHARACTERS: Andy Wiggins (dies), Helen Wiggins (next in PWJ #19, '90), Tracy Wiggins (all 1st, also in dfb), Edith (1st, Hawaiian Kahuna magician), airplane passengers inc Chris, air stewardess, alligators; operator (voice only, on phone), Captain James Cook, Hawaiian natives (both in fb)
LOCATIONS/ITEMS: Florida everglades, New Jersey inc Microchip's warehouse w/answering machine & phone, JFK airport, Fisk Tower, northern Japan inc Rikichi's home village, Hawaii inc Maui & Honolulu airport / Punisher's heat-seeking anti-aircraft missile, knife & plastic crossbow, Microchip's gun & rental jeep, drug runners' plane (damaged) & guns, dope growers' booby traps, radios, sniper rifle & H&Ks; "Hawaii Off the Beaten Track" guide books, Wiggins' car, payphone, airport metal detectors, jumbo jets, helicopter
FLASHBACKS: Tracy flees to her car, but finds the crooks guarding it. Hiding all night, she makes her way down the mountain the next morning, and finds a payphone (d). Captain Cook discovers Hawaii and is worshipped as a god. When the natives learn he is mortal, they dismember and eat him.
SYNOPSIS: In Florida Punisher shoots down a drug-runners' plane and kills the survivors. Meanwhile, in Hawaii, the holidaying Wiggins family stumbles into dope growers' territory; the father, Andy, is gunned down, and his wife, Helen, is captured, but their daughter, Tracy, flees. Reaching a phone, she calls her "uncle" Bart, an alias of Microchip, desperately informing him of events before gang member Dirk catches her. He demands a ransom to lure "Bart" to Hawaii, intending to silence him. Unable to reach Punisher, Microchip catches a plane to Hawaii. Meanwhile, in Japan, Rikichi meditates on his fellow Shadowmasters' news that the last true ninja master has died, and concludes Punisher might achieve that role if he can lose his focus on revenge; Rikichi's vision prompts him to go to Hawaii. In NYC, Kingpin orders Arranger to establish a stable of assassins. Meanwhile Punisher returns home to learn of Tracy's call, and hastily follows Microchip, though flying over the ocean triggers a phobic nightmare of being blown out the plane into the water. He tries to calm himself by reading about Hawaii's history, learning Captain Cook's fate. In Hawaii, Rikichi's vision leads him to a local Kahuna (Hawaiian magician), Edith. Having also reached Hawaii, Punisher hires a helicopter to get him to the "ransom drop" ahead of Microchip, and begins killing the dope growers, who are spread out waiting to ambush "Bart." Moments later Microchip arrives, just as a crook gets Punisher in his sniper sight.
NOTE: Issue includes Grendel's P-10 "Punisher's Arsenal" pin-up by Eliot R. Brown. Mitch, Ralphie, Lenny, Squid and Bud are named this issue. The last ninja master, Hatsu Yakamoto, died in Pun #25, '89. Next issue reveals Punisher has a childhood phobia of the ocean.

PUNISHER WAR JOURNAL #18 (May 1990)

"Kahuna" (22 pages)

CREDITS: Carl Potts (writer), Jim Lee (pencils, c art), Al Milgrom (inks), Don Hudson (background inks), Rick Parker (letters), Gregory Wright (colors), Rob Tokar (asst editor), Don Daley (editor)
FEATURE CHARACTER: Punisher (also as Frank Castiglione in fb between Pun #1, '99 fb & Pun:Int, '89 fb)
GUEST STAR: Rikichi
SUPPORTING CAST: Microchip
VILLAINS: Arranger; Hawaiian dope growers (some bts, some die) inc Jessie, Dirk, Mitch, Roscoe Bud, Lenny, Squid, Ralphie (prev 4 die); Damage (bts, last in PWJ #8, '89; also as picture)
OTHER CHARACTERS: Coast guard, Frank's childhood friends inc Helen & Myron (all in fb) Tracy Wiggins; Edith, shark; Bullseye (pictures)
LOCATIONS/ITEMS: Hawaii inc Edith's house & beach, unidentified beach (in fb) / Microchip's gun; dope growers' H&Ks, radios & sniper rifle; Punisher's plastic crossbow, Edith's jeep, shark-tooth club, miniature blow-gun, Captain Cook's flintlock, Myron's raft, coast guard boat (both in fb)
FLASHBACK: To impress Helen at the beach, young teen Frank Castiglione steals Myron's raft and heads out into the sea, but falls asleep and wakes up miles out to sea. A coast guard ship, alerted by Myron, rescues him.
SYNOPSIS: Microchip shoots the sniper before he can kill Punisher, unaware who the target was but having overheard the crooks' radio chatter that their target is trying to rescue Tracy. Reaching the cliff top where gang leader Jessie, his lieutenant Dirk and Tracy are, Punisher wounds Dirk's hand and snatches Tracy, but Jessie tackles them, sending all three off the cliff and into the sea. The waves separate them, and Jessie makes it to shore, ordering his men to fetch a boat and retrieve Tracy. Outnumbered and out of ammo, Microchip retreats to figure out a plan. Tracy has reached some rocks, and tries to help the stunned Punisher as he floats nearby, deliriously recalling his childhood rafting mishap. He wakes to find himself once more floating out in the ocean, miles from anywhere, but spots a fin approaching; recalling tales of dolphins rescuing people, he hangs on, and is taken back to the shore, where Edith is waiting, Rikichi having absented himself to avoid being seen. Edith welcomes Frank back to land, and surprises him by identifying Frank's rescuer as a shark, then offers to remove his fear of open water. To get a ride from the isolated beach, Frank humors her and agrees, and she takes him back to her home. She casts her spell and Frank is about to leave when she senses the dope growers approaching, and lends him the handful of archaic weapons she owns. Meanwhile, in NYC, Arranger reads of Damage, and wonders if the hospitalized gang boss might be rebuilt as an assassin. Back in Hawaii, Frank kills one gang member, and plays dead to lure a second in, but the wary crook decides to shoot him from a safe distance.
NOTE: Jessie is called Jesse here and next issue.

PUNISHER WAR JOURNAL #19 (June 1990)

"Trauma in Paradise" (22 pages)

CREDITS: Carl Potts (writer), Jim Lee (pencils), Al Milgrom (inks), Don Hudson (background inks), Rick Parker (letters), Gregory Wright (colors), Rob Tokar (asst editor), Don Daley (editor), Klaus Janson (c inks)
FEATURE CHARACTER: Punisher
GUEST STAR: Rikichi
SUPPORTING CAST: Microchip (also as Detective Joe Fields)
VILLAINS: Drug growers inc Jessie, Dirk (all die), Ralphie (corpse); Damage, Arranger
OTHER CHARACTERS: Helen Wiggins (last in PWJ #17, '90), Tracy Wiggins, Edith, Hawaiian cops inc Detective Joe Fields, doctor, nurse, Rick Meloni (jet-ski renter), NYC cop
LOCATIONS/ITEMS: New York hospital inc Damage's room, Hawaii inc Edith's home, hospital, sporting goods store / Shark-tooth club; drug growers' H&Ks & speedboat, Edith's jeep, Joe Fields' ID, jet-ski, Arranger's anesthetic spray; Microchip's gunpowder & coconut bomb, boogie board
SYNOPSIS: The dope grower carelessly moves too close, and Punisher kills him with Edith's shark-tooth club. With the immediate threat over, Edith comes out her house, and explains that gang leader Jessie was once her student, and now protects the gang from her powers. She tells the dubious Frank that the spirits say both Tracy and Microchip are in immediate danger. Meanwhile Microchip visits the hospital, figuring some of the gang might go there if they were wounded; sure enough, he locates Dirk getting his wounded hand treated, and trails him when he leaves, hoping to be led to Tracy. At the same time Edith drops Punisher off at a sporting goods store, where he rents a jet-ski, narrowly missing Rikichi buying a boogie board. Having found the gang's hideout and confirmed Helen is there, Microchip notes the gang seems to be into local magic, and decides to play on their superstitions. Using the jet-ski, Punisher gets back to where he last saw Tracy, rescuing her from some gang members trying to recapture her, and discovering Edith's treatment to remove her open-water phobia has worked. In a New York hospital Arranger visits the crippled Damage. Back in Hawaii, Tracy shows Punisher and Edith where the gang's hideout is; they arrive moments after Microchip terrifies the gang by impersonating the Hawaiian death god using explosives, gunfire and skull-face make-up. The gang panic, and when they try to flee, abandoning the wounded Dirk, he guns all but Jessie down; Jessie kills Dirk in turn and escapes. As Microchip frees Helen, Punisher, Edith and Tracy arrive, and Punisher pursues Jessie. Catching up with him, they grapple and Frank eventually throws Jessie off a cliff. The next day Punisher relaxes at a local hotel, until someone sneaks on to his balcony and leaves a boogie board as a present. Figuring it is from Edith, Frank decides to go down to the beach and use it, unaware Rikichi is watching, happy to see his gift being accepted.

PUNISHER WAR JOURNAL #20 (July 1990)

"The Debt" (22 pages)

CREDITS: Carl Potts (writer), Todd Smith (pencils), Al Milgrom (inks), Jim Novak (letters), Gregory Wright (colors), Rob Tokar (asst editor), Don Daley (editor), Tom Morgan (c art)
FEATURE CHARACTER: Punisher (also as Charles Fort & Major Bateman, also in pfb)
GUEST STAR: Rikichi
SUPPORTING CAST: Microchip (in pfb)
VILLAINS: Damage (next in W/Pun #1, '93), Arranger, Sgt. Spaldo (Legionnaire leader, dies), rebels (some die) inc Charles (dies), Kingpin (bts, last in PWJ #17, '90)
OTHER CHARACTERS: US ambassador (dies), Remy (dies), Jaques (both Triji government officials), French Foreign Legion (some die) inc Gomez (dies), doctors, plane passengers (some die), bar patrons inc drunk, pilots (bts), rebel villagers (some die)
LOCATIONS/ITEMS: Triji inc Jaques' house, bar, hotel & rebel village; Hawaii hotel (in pfb), New York medical clinic / Jaques' gun, rebels' guns & anti-aircraft gun; airplane, Legionnaires' guns & trucks; mugs of beer, medical monitoring equipment, surgical tools, Punisher's suitcase (fb) & knife (also in fb), postcard, pencil
FLASHBACK: Punisher tells Microchip he's taking a vacation from the war, but Micro insists he's unable to keep from looking for trouble (p).
SYNOPSIS: On Triji, rebels kill a government official, but one of them dies in the process. The next day, Punisher, going to visit an old friend in the Philippines, is on a plane shot down by the rebels because it is carrying the US ambassador. Surviving the crash, Punisher retaliates, luring them away from the plane and passengers, until the French Foreign Legion arrive to finish the rebels. As they pull bodies from the wreckage, one of which is Rikichi feigning death, Sgt. Spaldo explains that when France gave Triji independence, the people couldn't agree on a government and things escalated to violence, until the government asked for the Legion's support. In a bar that night, Spaldo tells Punisher that he was raised to be ruthless by an Italian fascist father who joined the Legion after WWII to evade being tried as a war criminal. In New York, Arranger oversees Damage being bionically augmented. Punisher follows Spaldo's next patrol and witnesses his group slaughter an entire village that only contained a single armed rebel. Punisher saves the last survivor, a young boy, claiming to be as Legion Internal Affairs, and is forced to kill Spaldo when he tries to kill the boy again. Unaware Rikichi is watching, Punisher writes to Micro, then heads on his way, while the violence continues on Triji.

PUNISHER WAR JOURNAL #21 (August 1990)

"Deep Water" (22 pages)

CREDITS: Carl Potts (writer), Tod Smith (pencils), Tony DeZuniga (inks), Jim Novak (letters), John Wellington (colors), Rob Tokar (asst editor), Don Daley (editor), Tom Morgan (c art)
FEATURE CHARACTER: Punisher (also as Frank Fort, also in rfb, also as Pvt. Castiglione in fb1 during Pun:AG, '88 fb)
SUPPORTING CAST: Microchip (in rfb, next in Pun:NE, '90)
VILLAINS: Arranger (next in GR #3, '90 bts, SpSM #164, '90), Kingpin (bts, next in GR #1, '90), Sniper (last in PWJ #10, '89, next in W/Pun #1, '93), David Keeton (Frank's war buddy, also in fb1 to chr 1st app, also in pfb), pirates (many die, 1 on wanted poster, some also in fb2) inc Juan (dies), communist rebels (in fb2, die)
OTHER CHARACTERS: Virgilio (Philippine resident), Maria Keeton (David's wife, also in fb1 to chr 1st app, also

in pfb), David & Maria's 2 sons, Virgilio's cousin (bts, in militia, supplies Virgilio w/weapons), fishermen inc Carlos, ferry passengers, refugees, sharks inc hammerheads, Philippine residents

LOCATIONS/ITEMS: Philippines inc Keeton house & mangrove swamps, Philippine sea, East Germany inc Sniper's house, Hawaii (in rfb), Vietnam (in fb1) / ferryboat, refugee boat; pirate boats, guns & chains; coast guard boats, Virgilio's motorbike, grenades & fishing boat; Arranger's briefcase full of money, Punisher's M-16 & knife, Sniper's handgun, David's boat (in pfb) & knife

FLASHBACKS: Punisher tells Microchip he's taking a vacation from the war, but Micro insists he's unable to keep from looking for trouble (PWJ #20, '90). David Keeton fights alongside Frank Castiglione in Vietnam, but the killing takes its toll. While on R&R in the Philippines with Frank he falls in love with Maria. Communist rebels try to take them hostage, but Frank and David kill them. Vowing never to kill again, David deserts to live with Maria (1). Pirates take David prisoner (p).

SYNOPSIS: A ferryboat traversing between Philippine islands stops to give a refugee boat from Indochina food and water, but pirates attack both vessels until the coast guard intervenes. Punisher, on another ferry which comes to the first's aid, spots a passenger fighting back, but he and the pirate fall overboard and a shark closes in, so Punisher dives in, helping the passenger out the water and throwing the pirate back to distract the shark. When they reach land the passenger, Virgilio, gives Frank a lift to his friend David Keeton's house, but David's wife Maria reveals that pirates abducted David six months ago. Frank and Virgilio use themselves as bait for the pirates, hoping to find David alive, but when the pirates attack, Virgilio is captured. Frank commandeers the hindmost pirate boat and follows the others back to base. Meanwhile, in East Germany, the Arranger visits a healing Sniper with a job offer. In the Philippines Frank sees the pirates chain captured fisherman in a lagoon to wait for the rising tide to let sharks in. Frank comes to the rescue, slaughtering the pirates, but finds the last pirate is David, who bought his survival by joining them. Disgusted, Frank throws the wounded and bleeding David into water to distract the sharks while he frees the captives.

PUNISHER WAR JOURNAL #22 (September 1990)

"Snowstorm" (22 pages)

CREDITS: Carl Potts (writer), Tod Smith (breakdowns), Kim DeMulder (finishes), Jim Novak (letters), Gregory Wright (colors), Rob Tokar (asst editor), Don Daley (editor), Andy Kubert (c art)
FEATURE CHARACTER: Punisher
VILLAINS: Victorio Santiago (1st, cartel boss, also on TV & in photo) & his assassins (some die) inc Eduardo (dies), Vincente Moroto (drug trafficker), corrupt orphanage administrator
OTHER CHARACTERS: Airport passengers & security (some die), José Santos (bystander & terrorist victim, dies), Angela Santos (José's widow), Angela (José's daughter), José's son, Judge Santos, television reporter (on TV), San Lorenzo jail guard (shadow only), Santiago's serving girl, orphan girls (1 as corpse), San Lorenzo holding pen inmates, newsstand owner
LOCATIONS/ITEMS: Lima inc airport, Frank Castle's hotel room & Victorio Santiago's offices; San Lorenzo inc Vincente Moroto's home, police station holding pen & orphanage; San Gabriel inc Victorio Santiago's estate (1800 Via Catherine) & Eduardo's home / Victorio Santiago's Mayan artifacts, security guards' guns, Santiago's men's guns, facemasks, cars & grenades; Eduardo's cocaine, newspaper

SYNOPSIS: At Lima airport returning home to the USA, Frank Castle witnesses gunmen attack Judge Santos, heedless of bystanders. Unarmed, Frank tries to protect a family caught in the firing line, saving a baby but not, unfortunately, its father, José Santos. The gunmen leave the judge alive, but warn him to make the right decision the following day. Returning the baby to his mother, Angela, Frank steals one of the dead guards' guns. The next day the judge declares a mistrial in the case against cartel boss Victorio Santiago, and Santiago, posing as a legitimate businessman and concerned citizen, offers money to victims of the attack. Punisher stakes out Santiago's offices until he sees Angela Santos leaving the office. Breaking in, Punisher overhears Santiago's croney Eduardo on the phone to Santiago, telling his boss he has tricked Angela into becoming an unwitting drug courier in exchange for money to feed her children, sending her to deliver to San Lorenzo trafficker Vincente Moroto. Visiting Moroto, Punisher learns Angela has been arrested en route and beats Santiago's address out of him. He visits the local jail's holding pen, and learns from Angela that her daughter has been placed in an orphanage because of her arrest, and her infant will be taken too as soon as he is old enough. Promising to save the girl, Punisher visits the orphanage to learn Eduardo has "adopted" the girl. He storms Santiago's estate, taking out numerous guards before confronting Santiago himself behind a wall of bulletproof glass. Taking out the remaining guards, Punisher intimidates Santiago into giving up Eduardo's address, then surrendering into police custody and clearing Angela's name. After making sure Santiago holds up his end of the deal, Punisher raids Eduardo's home, finding him about to stuff the corpse of a murdered child with drugs to smuggle, with Angela and another child his next intended victims. Punisher kills Eduardo and rescues the surviving children. The next morning Angela is freed and reunited with her daughter but Punisher sees a newspaper reporting on Santiago's release, and Punisher decides it isn't time for him to go home yet.
NOTE: Moroto is also called Maroto.

PUNISHER WAR JOURNAL #23 (October 1990)

"Firepower Among The Ruins: Part I" (22 pages)

CREDITS: Carl Potts (writer), Tod Smith (pencils), Kim DeMulder (inks), Jim Novak (letters), Gregory Wright (colors), Rob Tokar (asst editor), Don Daley (editor), Andy Kubert (c art)
FEATURE CHARACTER: Punisher (also as Charles Fort)
VILLAINS: Victorio Santiago, Santiago's drug traffickers (some die) inc José, Ramon (both die), Hector, Raymond & Diaz (1st), Guatemalan rebels & soldiers (most die), Hernandez (crooked archaeologist)
OTHER CHARACTERS: Captain James Wesley (British army officer, 1st), Gurkha soldiers (some die) inc Sgt. Thapa (1st), Milissa Jones (archaeologist, 1st), Santiago's charter pilot (mentioned), Belize Defense Force (mentioned); Caradol's kin (in fb, dies), Caradol & Tikur citizens (in fb, most die)
LOCATIONS/ITEMS: Belize inc jungle, Santiago's cocaine refining operation, Caradol (also in fb) & Tikur (in fb) / automatic shotgun, drug traffickers' guns, Wesley's pistol, Gurkhas' rifles, tents & kukris (specialized knives), Mayan artifact reproductions (hollow, used to smuggle cocaine), stretcher, archaeological expedition's tents, Altar of Skulls (in fb), 2 Mayan books (mentioned)
FLASHBACK: Centuries ago, the Tikur army conquers Caradol, kills only its king and rules over the city's enslaved inhabitants for hundreds of years before Caradol rises up and kills the Tikur people, ushering in a period of stagnation in Mayan culture.
SYNOPSIS: Punisher has trailed Santiago to Belize, where he is now engaged in a jungle firefight with drug runners who were guarding Santiago's private airstrip and waiting to ambush the Belize Defense Force and their British advisors. Arriving Gurkhas led by a British officer

strikes terror into the criminals, and all but one are shot down; begging to be spared from the Gurkha's, the last man divulges Santiago's location to Punisher. Frank kicks him to break his neck, then flees the Gurkhas. Nearby, Santiago bemoans Punisher's disruption of his Peruvian operations and arranges to buy some ancient Mayan books found at the nearby ancient ruins of Caradol from a crooked member of the archaeological expedition digging there. Meanwhile the Gurkhas halt their pursuit of Frank to deal with Guatemalan rebels who have crossed the border pursued by the Guatemalan army, which turns into a three-way firefight. Frank intervenes to help the Gurkhas, saving Sgt. Thapa's life, and afterwards accompanies them to their camp at Caradol, which they are protecting as part of their duties. At Caradol Punisher meets chief archaeologist Milissa Jones, who tells him something of Caradol's brutal history. The next day Santiago is told security at Caradol is too tight for his agents to retrieve the Mayan books; enraged, he sends men to talk to the Guatemalan rebels and soldiers, arranging an ambush for the Gurkha patrol, and assembles his own forces to seize Caradol from the small force left defending it, which includes the Punisher.
NOTE: Diaz named next issue. Punisher disrupted Santiago's Peruvian operation between last issue and this.

PUNISHER WAR JOURNAL #24 (November 1990)

"Firepower Among the Ruins: Part II" (22 pages)

CREDITS: Carl Potts (writer), Tod Smith (pencils), Al Milgrom (inks), Jim Novak (letters), Gregory Wright (colors), Rob Tokar (asst editor), Don Daley (editor), Rod Ramos (c pencils), Brad Vancata (c inks)
FEATURE CHARACTER: Punisher (also in rfb; also as Charles Fort; next in Pun:NE, '90)
VILLAINS: Victorio Santiago (dies) & his men (some die) inc Diaz (dies), Guatemalan rebels & soldiers (some die)
OTHER CHARACTERS: Tikur army, Caradol's king & residents (all in rfb2), Gurkha soldiers inc Sgt. Thapa (also in rfb1) & Captain Wesley, guards (die), Milissa Jones (see NOTE), Belizians, archaeologists inc Henry
LOCATIONS/ITEMS: Belize inc airport (in rfb1) & Caradol (also in rfb2) inc tomb / Punisher's rifle (in rfb1), Altar of Carved Skulls (in rfb2), bazooka, guards' guns, Guatemalan rebels' & soldiers' rifles, Gurkhas' helicopter, kukris & rifles; Santiago's men's grenade, pistols & rifles; airplane, archaeologists' tents, box of Mayan antiquities, chisels, mallet, packets of cocaine, Punisher's pistol & rifle, reproduction Mayan sculptures, Wesley's pistol
FLASHBACKS: Punisher and British Gurkha troops wipe out Victor Santiago's airport security (PWJ #23, '90). Centuries ago, the Tikur army conquers Caradol, kills only its king and rules over the city's enslaved inhabitants for hundreds of years before Caradol rises up and kills the Tikur people, ushering in a period of stagnation in Mayan culture (PWJ #23, '90).
SYNOPSIS: Victor Santiago learns Punisher is in Belize and resolves to kill him as local workers pack reproduction Mayan sculptures with cocaine for Santiago's drug smuggling operation. As Charles Fort, Frank Castle works with archaeologists at the Caradol Mayan site and recalls the story of its ancient inhabitants. Set up by Santiago, Guatemalan rebels and soldiers converge on the site and fight Gurkha soldiers determined to protect it. Santiago infiltrates the site, steals valuable Mayan antiquities and bombs a tomb, injuring Milissa Jones. Punisher sets up an ambush and lets Gurkha Sgt. Thapa decapitate Santiago, intimidating his remaining men into surrendering. The next day, Castle departs with a kukri knife as a gift of appreciation from the Gurkhas.
NOTE: Thapa erroneously refers to Capt. Wesley as Lt. Wesley. Milissa is called Melissa here.

PUNISHER WAR JOURNAL #25 (December 1990)

"Get Out of Town" (21 pages)

CREDITS: Mike Baron (writer), Tex (art, see NOTE), George Roberts (letters), Gregory Wright (colors), Kevin Kobasic (asst editor, see NOTE), Don Daley (editor), Michael Golden (c art)
FEATURE CHARACTER: Punisher (also bts in fb to 1st chr app before Pun #18, '97 fb; last in Pun #42, '90)
SUPPORTING CAST: Microchip (last in Pun #42, '90)
VILLAINS: Saracen (last in Pun #23, '89), Senator Stan Ori (1st, voice only, corrupt politician), Don Elio Bessucho (1st, Sicilian crime lord) & his men (3 die), telephone employee (voice only, informant for Bessuchos), Oliveras & his partner (dirty cops, both die, see NOTE)
OTHER CHARACTERS: Rocco Castiglione (Punisher's uncle, also in fb), Esmeralda Giovanni (Rocco's fiancée) (both 1st), Alfredo (Esmeralda's nephew), antiques dealer (sells illicit guns), Miami police, SWAT team, pilots (bts); Mario Lorenzo "Renzo" Castiglione (Punisher's father, also in photo), Louisa Castiglione (Frank's mother), Fredo Castiglione (Frank's uncle, dies) & Don Feruccio Bessucho (dies) & his men, horses (prev 6 in fb), Pierluigi Bessucho (mentioned, Las Vegas criminal), Frank's aunt (in photo)
LOCATIONS/ITEMS: Florida shack & motel, Microchip's NJ warehouse: Sicily inc Palermo w/antique shop, Brasery village inc cemetery, Alfredo's house, telephone company & Bessucho compound / Punisher's Uzi, handgun, Battle Van (destroyed) w/remote, Beretta & sawed-off Ithaca pump-action shotgun; cocaine, money, police cars, SWAT van, police guns, payphone, Micro's computer, rented Porsche, Feruccio's men's guns, fishing boat, fishing net, Elio's men's guns & Uzis, Rocco's gun & boat
FLASHBACK: Fredo and Lorenzo overrule their brother Rocco and inform Don Bessucho they won't allow him to use their fishing boats to ship his drugs. Having had enough of local corruption, Lorenzo leaves for America with his pregnant wife. While fishing, Rocco dives into the water to free their snagged net when the boat explodes, killing Fredo. Rocco kills Bessucho, escapes Bessucho's men and disappears.
SYNOPSIS: In Florida, Punisher takes out a pair of dirty cops who kill dealers to get their hands on their drugs and money for their own purposes. Later, Microchip calls him to warn him that one of the cops was Senator Stan Ori's nephew, and the police have tracked him down. Punisher escapes, and with various agencies after him, decides to visit Sicily, where his father came from, until things quiet down. Punisher visits the local cemetery and find his family's gravestones shattered. A local woman, Esmeralda, tells him about the Bessuchos that run the area, and came into conflict with the Castigliones, until three men attempt to take her away. Punisher kills them, and Esmeralda takes him to her nephew's to finish the story of his family's struggle. Hearing enough, he contacts Micro for a weapons drop. Hearing men are looking for him, Punisher and Esmeralda buy a truck and take off to wait for the ammo dump, which will be guided by the tracking device embedded in Punisher's neck. Meanwhile, concerned about their operation, Ori sends Saracen to his cousin Elio. Elsewhere, Esmeralda reveals she was engaged to Rocco, just as Punisher is signaled that his weapons have arrived. They go down to meet the ship carrying them, which turns out to be captained by Rocco himself.
NOTE: Cover labeled "The Sicilian Saga Part One of Three." Art is credited to Tex; the letters page plays this as a mystery until PWJ #28, '90, which reveals Tex is Mark Texeira and "his loyal band of java junkies" Vince Evans, Mike Harris, Ariane Lenshoek, Santiago Oliveras, Jimmy

Palmiotti and assistant editor Kevin Kobasic, "often with the help of Ed Lazellari, and Ed Murr"; since it is thus problematic as to whether all of them worked on each issue where Tex is credited, this index will list them as Tex. One of the dirty cops Frank kills is Senator Ori's nephew; it is presumably Oliveras, the youngest of the two.

PUNISHER WAR JOURNAL #26 (January 1991)

"Cry Uncle" (22 pages)

CREDITS: Mike Baron (writer), Tex (art), Jim Novak (letters), Gregory Wright (colors), Kevin Kobasic (asst editor), Don Daley (editor), Michael Golden (c art)
FEATURE CHARACTER: Punisher (also in photo)
SUPPORTING CAST: Microchip (voice only, next in Pun #45, '91)
VILLAINS: Hakim Abdullah (Jurgen Hohne, PLO officer) & his men (all die), Saracen, Senator Stan Ori, Don Elio Bessucho & his men
OTHER CHARACTERS: Rocco Castiglione, Esmeralda Giovanni, sharks (cover only), Abdul Abismah (slain PLO officer, mentioned)
LOCATIONS/ITEMS: Sicily inc Brasery village & Bessucho compound, Rocco's island cave hideout / Rocco's boat, computer (both destroyed), scuba gear, water sled, telescope & weapons cache inc Herstal P-90 & Barrett machine gun; Punisher's harpoon gun, Libyans' helicopter (bts), patrol boat, scuba gear, harpoon guns, H&K MSPA rifle & knives; Esmeralda's Mac-10, Saracen's knife; winch & cable; Abdullah's gunship, .50-caliber sniper rifle, Punisher's Ryker's file
SYNOPSIS: Rocco reveals to Punisher that he and Microchip connected over the computer when he played Micro's game "Tank," and Rocco has since been running projects for Micro, supplying PLO officer Abdul Abismah to help him kill his rival Hakim Abdullah, encouraging the PLO's self-destruction. Rocco leads Punisher to his hidden weapons cache hidden in a cave on an isolated island, but are interrupted by Libyans working for Hakim, who have come looking for Abdul's supplier. They leave the ammo and kill the advance party, but know others will likely follow. After calling Micro to get info about Abdullah, and learning he is an associate of Saracen, they return to the ammo dump. Meanwhile, hearing Hakim's men have found the ammo dump, Elio asks Saracen to ensure Hakim doesn't get it, wanting to take over the weapon supplies trade. At the dump, Hakim arrives with his men on a gunship and the Castigliones are forced on the defensive, splitting up while Punisher deals with the landing party. Meanwhile, Ori arrives at Elio's compound and informs Elio that his recent troubles were caused by Punisher, a Castiglione. Back on the island, Punisher returns to his allies, but finds Rocco wounded and is knocked out by Saracen.
NOTE: Cover labeled "The Sicilian Saga Part Two of Three." Rocco erroneously speaks Punisher's dialogue on p8 panel 4. Microchip claims Hakim is German, but Saracen says he is French.

PUNISHER WAR JOURNAL #27 (February 1991)

"Saracen With the Clock!" (20 pages)

CREDITS: Mike Baron (writer), Tex (art), Jim Novak (letters), Gregory Wright (colors), Kevin Kobasic (asst editor), Don Daley (editor), Michael Golden (c art)
FEATURE CHARACTER: Punisher (also as Saracen, next in Pun #43, '90)
VILLAINS: Saracen (next in Pun #47, '91) & his men inc Jerath (dies), Senator Stan Ori (dies), Don Elio Bessucho (next in PWJ #36, '91) & his men
OTHER CHARACTERS: Rocco Castiglione, Esmeralda Giovanni (both die), Elio's driver (bts), reporter (voice only), ticket agent, bystanders
LOCATIONS/ITEMS: Sicily inc Brasery village & Bessucho compound; Rocco's island cave hideout, Messina airport / Saracen's sword, knife, rope, handcuffs, handcuff keys, gunship, scuba gear & water sled; Rocco's winch & crane, chain, weapons cache inc harpoon gun, bombs & detonator; Uzi, Punisher's handgun & Saracen mask, car
SYNOPSIS: Punisher wakes to find Saracen standing over him. Frank figures out Saracen's affiliation with Ori and offers up the weapons cache to save Rocco's life. To ensure his honesty, Saracen lowers Punisher down a volcanic chimney using Rocco's winch, intending for Frank to slowly suffocate under the weight of his own body. After Saracen departs to use the cave's underwater entrance, Esmeralda returns to aid Rocco and lower Punisher into the cave. Saracen reports in to Ori and Elio, who instruct him to bring Punisher in alive. Saracen and one of his man dive down to the cave but find Punisher waiting. He kills Saracen's man and threatens to use planted bombs to blow up the cave if Saracen doesn't face him without a gun. They fight until Saracen grabs an Uzi, and Punisher flees using Saracen's underwater sled. He hits the bomb's detonator and blows the cache. Saracen escapes to his boat and, spotting Rocco and Esmeralda on the island's summit, has his boat open fire on them, killing them. Believing Punisher dead too, Saracen returns to Elio's compound, accepts his payment from Ori, and departs. Ori sets off to return to Miami, but at the airport, Saracen guns Ori down in front of dozens of witnesses. "Saracen" drives down the road listening to the radio report the killing and resulting manhunt for Saracen, and unmasks, revealing himself to be Punisher.
NOTE: Cover labeled "The Sicilian Saga Part Three of Three." Includes 2 bonus pin-ups, one of Punisher using a rocket-launcher on a tank by Herb Trimpe, and one of Punisher firing a gun from a subway entrance by Mark Bagley and Don Hudson.

PUNISHER WAR JOURNAL #28 (March 1991)

"Meat" (20 pages)

CREDITS: Mike Baron (writer), Tex (art), Jim Novak (letters), Gregory Wright (colors), Kevin Kobasic (asst editor), Don Daley (editor), Michael Golden (c art)
FEATURE CHARACTER: Punisher (between Pun #46-47, '91)
VILLAINS: Cole Grist (meatpacking magnate, dies), Animal Liberation Army terrorists inc Wallace Weist
OTHER CHARACTERS: Joy Adams (last in Pun #40, '90), Len Levan (Pupkin Investments representative), Davis (country club employee), Raskewicz (union official, dies), Marcus Roberts (jazz pianist, mentioned), North Salem police inc Rupert Delaney; mailman (bts, dies), bystander, country club attendees, music band, policeman, calf, protesters inc Arnie
LOCATIONS/ITEMS: Bronx inc Bedford Park Boulevard & Bruno's Steak House; Grist meatpacking plant inc meat locker; Mill Run Country Club; North Salem, New York inc Cole Grist's home / Joy's car, cell phone, diamond ring, fur coat & Master Class credit card; Cole Grist's mailbox, mail bomb (both bts), anvil, Rupert Delaney's pipe

& lighter; Cole Grist's assault pistol, cigarette, lighter & water pipe; bag of crack cocaine, beef carcasses, bucket of red paint, conveyor switch, dinner check, freebasing equipment, knife, meat hooks, picket signs, prime rib, Raskewicz's cigarette, sledgehammer, terrorist's pistol, veal cage; Punisher's Battle Van, hybrid vest & pistol; Wallace Weist's club & wallet w/identification card

SYNOPSIS: Frank Castle catches up with Joy Adams, who announces that she's in love with Cole Grist, a meatpacking executive whose company is targeted by animal rights activists. After protesters assault Joy and a mail bomb meant for Grist kills a mailman, Punisher agrees to guard the businessman. When Castle accompanies Grist and Joy to Grist's plant, he gets suspicious of the meatpacker. Punisher subdues an animal rights terrorist and Grist guns another one down before his and Joy's eyes. High on crack, Grist attacks Castle, thinking that he's having an affair with Joy. Punisher discovers that Grist killed a union official, and after Grist threatens Joy's life, she assists Punisher in killing him.

NOTE: Michael Golden's credit is given in PWJ #27, '91's letters page. This issue's letters page lists all the artists collectively credited as "Tex" (see PWJ #25, '90). Includes 1 page promo for next issue.

PUNISHER WAR JOURNAL #29 (April 1993)

"Crash and Burn" (21 pages)

CREDITS: Mike Baron (writer), Tex (art), Jim Novak (letters), Gregory Wright (colors), Kevin Kobasic (asst editor), Don Daley (editor), Michael Golden (c art)
FEATURE CHARACTER: Punisher (last in Namor #20, '91)
GUEST STAR: Ghost Rider (Dan Ketch, last in Q #24, '91)
SUPPORTING CAST: Microchip (last in Pun Ann #4/3, '91)
VILLAINS: Straker (spin creator, bts), Manion (Straker's courier), Roaring Island crew, Manion's backup cars' crews
OTHER CHARACTERS: Hovelhaus (Aerostar lead singer), Noble Kale (last in Q #24, '91, spirit controlling the Ghost Rider), biker (dies), police (some die), roadie, security guards (1 dies), concert attendees; Road Runner (on TV)
LOCATIONS/ITEMS: Long Island Expressway, Micro's apartment, Long Island Coliseum / Punisher's motorcycle, skull-helmet, riding gear & handgun; suicide biker's helmet, bike & lighter, Ghost Rider's motorcycle & chain, Micro's computer, anti-accelerant pills, courier's motorcycle & MAC-10, Spin, money, police cars & guns, Roaring Island, Island crew's rifles, cars & concussion grenade

SYNOPSIS: While testing his new motorcycle, Punisher witnesses a speeding biker light himself on fire. As he examines the remains, Ghost Rider arrives and informs Frank the biker came from the Roaring Island, a massive vehicle composed of dozens of smaller ones, and Punisher in turn informs the Rider of a new drug, Spin, made in the Roaring Island. Punisher offers to team up and investigate, but Ghost Rider rebuffs him. Later, Micro gives Punisher a visor capable of seeing the camouflaged Roaring Island if he can get within a half mile. That night, Punisher awakens to find anti-accelerants left by Micro to combat the effects of Spin. Punisher heads to the Aerostar concert, having heard their lead singer often uses Spin. Punisher spots and tails the courier, but is attacked on the highway by cars working with the courier. Ghost Rider enters the fray to protect innocents caught in the crossfire and leaves Punisher to the pursuing police. Suddenly, all electrical objects go out as the Roaring Island speeds through. It kills the cops and Punisher attempts to get his rocket launcher from the bike, but a concussion grenade thrown from the Island knocks him out.

NOTE: Followed by an uncredited pin-up of Punisher over a wounded village boy (1 page). The courier's bike is named Kobasic, after this issue's assistant editor; another vehicle is a Palmiotti, named for artist Jimmy Palmiotti. Manion is named next issue.

PUNISHER WAR JOURNAL #30 (May 1991)

"Spin Cycle" (21 pages)

CREDITS: Mike Baron (writer), Tex (art), Jim Novak (letters), Gregory Wright (colors), Kevin Kobasic (asst editor), Don Daley (editor), Michael Golden (c art)
FEATURE CHARACTER: Punisher (also as Frank Rook, next in Pun:POV #1, '91)
GUEST STAR: Ghost Rider (next in GR #18, '91)
SUPPORTING CAST: Microchip (also as Lester Lute, next in Pun:POV #1, '91)
VILLAINS: Straker & his men, thugs
OTHER CHARACTERS: Noble Kale (next in GR #18, '91), police (bts), bystanders
LOCATIONS/ITEMS: New York inc bridge, West Side Highway, Greenwich Village w/Rigby Arms apartment building (see NOTE) & Queens w/Branch Flowers Etc. floral shop / Spin (designer drug), motorcycle helmet & motorcycles w/gas turbine engine, onboard gyro & stealth hardware (prev 3 invented by Straker, see NOTE); homeostasis capsules (mentioned), Ghost Rider's motorcycle, Roaring Island w/monitor & rocket launcher; Microchip's compact disc; Punisher's motorcycle & motorcycle helmet; remote-control explosive wristband, Ritz coffee mug; Straker's cigarette, pipe & weapons computer; shackles used to bind Punisher, sports car, thugs' knives, hypodermic needle w/sodium pentathol

SYNOPSIS: Straker forces Frank Castle to take his designer drug, Spin, and sends him off on a mission to test his worthiness to join his gang. Wearing a remote-control explosive wristband, Punisher uses a Straker-designed motorcycle to deliver the drug to Lester Lute, who is actually an undercover Microchip. He gives Castle a compact disc with a program designed to destroy Straker's Rolling Island. Punisher seeks out Ghost Rider's help and, after Castle plants the disc, Ghost Rider attacks the island, tricking Straker into activating it. The island is destroyed, and Straker flees his demolished juggernaut.

NOTE: Includes 1 page Punisher's Arsenal feature about listening devices by Eliot R. Brown. The Straker-designed motorcycle bears the surnames of artists Ariane Lenshoek & Santiago Oliveras. Graffiti at the Rigby Arms includes names of comic strip character Betty Boop, rock bands The Cure & Queensryche and comics creators Ron Aikens, Darren Auck, Karl Bollers, Ken Branch, Steve Bunche, Christopher Eliopoulos, Vince Evans, Frank Frazetta, Manny Galan, Mark Gruenwald, Mike Harris, Kevin Kobasic, Ed Lazellari, Ariane Lenshoek, Joe Madureira, Ed Murr, Santiago Oliveras, Jimmy Palmiotti, Rod Ramos, Joe Rosas & Christine Slusarz.

"Pipe Line" (20 pages)

CREDITS: Mike Baron (writer), Andy Kubert (pencils), Joe Kubert (inks), Jim Novak (letters), Gregory Wright (colors), Kevin Kobasic (asst editor), Don Daley (editor), Joe Jusko (c art)
FEATURE CHARACTER: Punisher (also as Charles Fort & Chuck, last in Pun:POV #4, '91)
SUPPORTING CAST: Microchip (also as Wolfgang, last in Pun:POV #4, '91)
VILLAINS: Gen. Xandiaong Urt (1st, former Soviet soldier) & his men inc Chang, Humans Off Planet (some die) inc Alphonse, Crips inc Guttierez (prev 3 die)
OTHER CHARACTERS: Alice Hoffman ("Hanoi Alice," actress & activist, 1st), concierge, bartender, pilot, security guard, tour guide, police, bystanders
LOCATIONS/ITEMS: Fairbanks, Alaska inc hotel, Mt. Kisco geothermal station, Ray's Trading Post, Old Timberland Road & Trans-Alaskan pipeline; Microchip's NYC apartment / Punisher's suitcase, handgun, rented car, Uzi, Beretta, Steyr, concussion grenades; Guttierez's handgun, payphones, Micro's computer, parachute & binoculars; HOP members' skis & Uzis, snowmobile, cargo plane, crate w/parachute, tanks
SYNOPSIS: Punisher comes to Fairbanks, Alaska to stop the Crips and Bloods from spreading their crack trade. Spotting a suspect, Punisher follows the man to a meeting with Chang; arguing over an arms deal, the first man pulls a gun, and Chang kills him. Punisher follows Chang to the geothermal station and into their hot springs room. Two Crips burst in looking for Chang, and Punisher takes them down, informing Chang that Chang's boss sent him as backup. Chang reveals his employer General Urt is supplying the Crips and Humans off Planet with weapons to attack the Trans-Alaskan pipeline, something Urt plans to exploit for his own ends. Punisher calls Micro for information and returns to the hotel to find a HOP agent, Alice Hoffman, waiting for him. Pretending to be Urt's man, Punisher arranges to meet her associates later to deliver their weapons. Micro calls Punisher to tell him Urt is an ex-Soviet general now dealing in drugs and weapons. Punisher goes to his HOP rendezvous, but is attacked by HOP members, as Chang and Alice have compared notes and realized his deception; Frank kills them all. The next day, Micro parachutes in with Punisher's weapons and Micro informs Punisher that Urt has taken over a refinery at Kronski as they head to HOP's staging area, where they find Urt with a veritable army by the pipeline, complete with tanks aimed right at it.
NOTE: Cover labeled "The Kamchatkan Konspiracy Part 1 of 3." Features two Punisher pin-ups by JB & Al, and José Massaroli.

"Blow Out" (21 pages)

CREDITS: Mike Baron (writer), Ron Wagner (pencils), Mark Pennington (inks), Jim Novak (letters), Gregory Wright (colors), Kevin Kobasic (asst editor), Don Daley (editor), Joe Jusko (c art)
FEATURE CHARACTER: Punisher (also as Charles Fort)
SUPPORTING CAST: Microchip
VILLAINS: Humans Off Planet eco-terrorists (some next in PWJ #37, '91), Gen. Xandiaong Urt & his men inc guard, helicopter pilot & Chang
OTHER CHARACTERS: John Threepoles (dies), Alice Hoffman
LOCATIONS/ITEMS: Alaska inc Trans-Alaskan Pipeline, canning factory & geothermal station w/R&D wing & steam bath / Alice's binoculars, pistol, rifle & vehicle; assault helicopters w/machine guns; bath towels, Buddha statuette, candles, Humans Off Planet rocket launcher & snowmobile; Microchip's automatic pistol, binoculars, M-16 rifle, pot & spoon; map, model of Kamchatka's Borska Refinery, 1934 Ford Tri-Star plane, oil company helicopters, tarp, Trans-Alaska oil pipeline, truck; Punisher's AT-4 antitank weapon, camping tent, rocket launcher & snowmobile; Gen. Urt's tanks, Gen. Urt's men's rifles
SYNOPSIS: Frank Castle fires an antitank weapon at General Urt and his men, but the assault doesn't prevent them from rupturing the oil pipeline. While their fellow eco-activists pursue Punisher and Microchip, John Threepoles tells Alice Hoffman he distrusts Urt, but Hoffman insists on maintaining their alliance with Urt at a nearby geothermal station, and when Threepoles defies Urt, the general drowns him in a steam bath. Alice learns that Urt plans to destroy Alaskan oil flow to drive up the value of his own Kamchatkan crude and allow him to fund secession from the Soviet Union. She decks Urt's right-hand man, Chang, and escapes. Alice assists Castle against an assault by Urt's assault helicopters and shoots Chang as he and Urt's men evacuate the geothermal station. Alice leads Punisher and Microchip to her Tri-Star plane, which Castle plans to use to take the fight to Kamchatka.
NOTE: Cover labeled "The Kamchatkan Konspiracy Part 2 of 3." Includes pinup of Punisher and his criminal victims by Ernie Colon (1 page). This issue mentions fictional movies "Barefoot by the River," "The Meltdown Syndrome" and "The Swine."

"Fire in the Hole" (21 pages)

CREDITS: Mike Baron (writer), Ron Wagner (pencils), Dan Green (inks), Jim Novak (letters), Gregory Wright (colors), Kevin Kobasic (asst editor), Don Daley (editor), Tom Palmer (c art)
FEATURE CHARACTER: Punisher (also in photo; see NOTE)
SUPPORTING CAST: Microchip (next in PWJ #36, '91)
VILLAINS: Saracen (last in Pun #48, '91, next in Pun:EQ, '94), Gen. Xandiaong Urt & his men inc Mr. Irkuk
OTHER CHARACTERS: Saracen's wife (mentioned), Alice Hoffman (also as Bambistar in fb to 1st chr app prior to PWJ #31, '91), Kylif (dancer), actor (in fb), airstrip employee, Kamchatkan resistance fighters inc Grandithkit
LOCATIONS/ITEMS: Kamchatka inc airstrip, Borska Refinery & resistance base / 1934 Ford Tri-Star plane, Army surplus M-16 rifles, "Bambistar" film reel, film projector, hashish, hookahs, M-60 machine guns, photo of Punisher; resistance's AK-47 assault rifles, binoculars, communications equipment, computer & M-72 light antitank weapons (LAWS rockets); Russian Apex air-to-ground rocket, Saracen's rifle, snow tractor; Gen. Urt's binoculars, helicopter, pistol & surface-to-air missile launchers; Gen. Urt's men's rifles
FLASHBACK: Alice Hoffman performs in the sci-fi soft porn film, "Bambistar."

SYNOPSIS: Frank Castle, Microchip and Alice Hoffman arrive at the anti-General Urt Kamchatkan resistance fighters' base. As the rebels watch one of Alice's old movies, the actress-turned-activist gets intimate with Punisher. At the seized Kamchatkan oil refinery, Urt meets his prospective high-tech arms supplier, Saracen, who convinces him he'll get more money from the Soviets by threatening to dump the refinery's oil into the sea than by selling the oil to other nations. Saracen is alarmed to learn Castle has opposed Urt's plans, and when the resistance assaults the refinery Saracen anticipates Punisher's strategy and rushes to an undefended side of the site. He scrambles for safety when he sees Castle launch an Apex rocket from Alice's plane. Punisher destroys the refinery but runs out of ammunition before he can kill Saracen and is forced to leave as soldiers open fire on their plane.

NOTE: Cover labeled "The Kamchatkan Konspiracy Part 3 of 3." Alice refers to Punisher as "Mr. Rook" even though he is going by the name Charles Fort. She makes a reference to the film "The Power and the Glory."

PUNISHER WAR JOURNAL #34 (September 1991)

"Blackout" (21 pages)

CREDITS: Mike Baron (writer), Ron Wagner (pencils), Michael Bair, Don Hudson, Bud LaRosa, Ed Lazellari, Ariane Lenshoek, Jimmy Palmiotti, Rodney Ramos (inks), Jim Novak (letters), Gregory Wright (colors), Kevin Kobasic (asst editor), Don Daley (editor), John Beatty (c art)
FEATURE CHARACTER: Punisher (next in PWJ #48, '92 fb, ASM #353, '91)
VILLAINS: Howard Nees' gang (some die, some next in Pun #53, '91, see NOTE), muggers inc Cosmo (die)
OTHER CHARACTERS: Edna (store shopper), Hildy (Barrett's ex), Whittaker (Barrett's acquaintance) (all mentioned), Soon Oh Kim & his cousin Roland (electronics store owners), Barrett Browning (ex-Wall Street bond trader), New York Mayor Driscoll (bts, planning to meet community leaders, see NOTE), Ed (TV weatherman, on TV), TV news reporters inc Ethel (on TV), African American & Korean Queens residents, driver, vagrants
LOCATIONS/ITEMS: Manhattan inc George Washington Bridge; Microchip's New Jersey warehouse; Queens inc Blunt Street, Kim Electronics store, Korean Video store, Prima Pizza parlor, Kon-Edison office building & power station & subway tunnel w/ construction shed / Barrett Browning's dynamite bombs & lock pick; drug dealers' assault pistol, automatic rifles, Chevy van, knife, limousine & pickup truck; muggers' knife, lighter & lock pick; Punisher's assault pistols, beret, binoculars, computer, pistol, 30-mm machine gun, targeting helmet, headphone w/scope & $8 million urban assault vehicle w/hellfire missiles, machine gun & water cannon; ice (drug), aluminum "cap," baseball bats, crowbar, drum barrel, flashlights, liquor bottles, picket signs, streetlight, televisions, TV remote control, weather map
SYNOPSIS: Barrett Browning, a mentally ill ex-bond trader, blows up Queens power stations, believing them to be transmission towers for invading Martians. Howard Nees' uncontrolled drug dealers take advantage of the ensuing blackout, looting businesses and murdering local residents. As Frank Castle fights the thugs and tries to solve the mystery of the bombings, the violence and mayhem exacerbate racial tensions between African Americans and Koreans in Queens. The tensions come to a head and as the two groups square off, Nees' men interrupt the melee and try to rob everyone present. The African Americans and Koreans team up to battle the criminals and Punisher joins the fray. Castle encounters Browning, learns that he's responsible for the bombings and humors him upon realizing his mental condition. Punisher makes Browning show him the source of his explosives and kills two muggers who threaten the ill man. Taking pity on Browning, Castle resolves to help him get treatment.
NOTE: Michael Blair's name is misspelled in the credits. Includes pinup of Punisher riding a skeletal horse by Mark Pacella & John Beatty (1 page). This issue features the earliest reference to Miami racketeer Howard Nees, who 1st appears in Pun #53, '91. Mayor Driscoll must have replaced Mayor Dinkins, who is last noted in NW 16, '91.

PUNISHER WAR JOURNAL #35 (October 1991)

"Motivation" (20 pages)

CREDITS: Mike Baron (writer), Ron Wagner (pencils), Jimmy Palmiotti, Michael Witherby (inks), Jim Novak (letters), Gregory Wright (colors), Kevin Kobasic (asst editor), Don Daley (editor), Steve Geiger (c pencils), Bob McLeod (c inks)
FEATURE CHARACTER: Punisher (last in Dhawk #9, '91, also as Charles Fort & "Retaliator")
VILLAINS: C.B. Bissel (motion picture director, dies), Ace Kromberg (actor, dies)
OTHER CHARACTERS: Barry (publicist), Dino (motion picture executive, bts, provides reference for Charles Fort), Luann (C.B. Bissel's production assistant), Retaliator (Fyodor "Mac" Tesla, actor, former Hungarian circus strongman, dies), stuntman (as "Romulus," dies), Golden Harvest (film company, mentioned), bats, seagulls, film crew inc videographer; Rio Ricans inc female captive
LOCATIONS/ITEMS: Rio Rico (Central American nation) inc bar, city street, cliff & C.B. Bissel's penthouse / C.B. Bissel's .32-caliber revolver, limousine, safe, Sony camcorder, videotape & television w/remote control; beer can, boom microphone, bottle of Manle Aiban mezcal, cocaine, film crew's headsets, gag, helicopters, Ace Kromberg's knife, lamps, MAC-10 machine pistol, motion picture camera, produce stand, Retaliator's pistols, safety harness, trailers, train w/boxcars & steam locomotive; Punisher's automatic pistol, flashlight, grappling hook, lock pick & motorcycle
SYNOPSIS: Posing as stuntman Charles Fort, Frank Castle goes to Rio Rico to investigate the filming of an action movie by C.B. Bissel, a reckless film director whose productions have resulted in the deaths of actors and stuntmen. While filming a scene as the Retaliator, the feature character inspired by Punisher, Castle witnesses the careless destruction of two occupied helicopters and discovers blood in a boxcar outfitted for a scene not in the movie. Punisher breaks into Bissel's penthouse safe and learns that he's been making violent, exploitative, underground films involving actual murders. Castle follows Bissel and actor Ace Kromberg back to the boxcar, where they are filming a captive woman. Actor Fyodor Tesla, who fancies himself as a real-life Retaliator, interrupts the filming and Kromberg kills him. Punisher in turn slays Kromberg and Bissel.
NOTE: Includes pinups of Punisher riding a speedboat by Cooper Smith & M.M. Ritter (1 page) and fighting an aquatic battle by Tom Morgan (1 page). One of the films on Punisher's fake resume is "Blood Punch" (originally titled "Tiger's Paw, Drunken Fist in a Quart of Booze-Ridden Pig").

PUNISHER WAR JOURNAL #36 (November 1991)

"Let Them Eat Cake" (20 pages)

CREDITS: Mike Baron (writer), Steven Butler (pencils), Kim DeMulder (inks), Jim Novak (letters), Gregory Wright (colors), Kevin Kobasic (asst editor), Don Daley (editor, c pencils), Eliot Brown (c inks)
FEATURE CHARACTER: Punisher (also as caterer Mr. Effel; next in Dlk #6, '91)
SUPPORTING CAST: Microchip (also as caterer's assistant Lester Lute; next in ASM #354, '91)
VILLAINS: Elio Bessucho (last in PWJ #27, '91) & his men (some die) inc Oliver (dies); James "Jimmy the Shrimp" Cappadonna (smack distributor, dies) & his men (some die) inc Bruno, Fabio & Tony; Angelo Presto (mob boss, rapist, dies) & his men inc Barry; "Goose" & his men (mentioned only)
OTHER CHARACTERS: Katherine "Kathy" Cappadonna (Jimmy's daughter), Ramona Cappadonna (Jimmy's wife), Mr. & Mrs. Frederico Presto (Angelo's parents, bts, attend wedding), Spewing Vomit (punk band), FBI task force (bts, investigating Jimmy Cappadonna), catering staff, chef, cocktail waitress, minister, photographer, wedding guests
LOCATIONS/ITEMS: Las Vegas' Burning Sands Country Club inc Sandtrap Room (bts), chapel, golf course, guest house, Horseshoe Room & kitchen w/walk-in freezer / Punisher's Armani suit, grenades, LAWs rocket, machine gun, padlock, pistol, rapier & automatic pistol w/silencer; airplane, banquet tables, bed, bottle of scotch, camera, candelabra, catering van, cooler, Microchip's pistol, mobsters' firearms & grenades, "mousse chest," piano, seafood blintzes, service carts, Swedish meatballs, wedding cake; Spewing Vomit's drums, guitars & microphones
SYNOPSIS: Posing as caterers, Frank Castle and Microchip infiltrate the wedding of a mob boss/rapist to the daughter of smack distributor, Jimmy Cappadonna. They smuggle weapons into the freezer of the country club where the wedding is held and eliminate the few mob goons who uncover their ruse. At the reception, Punisher emerges from the wedding cake, kills the groom and Cappadonna and mows his way through their men. He and Microchip flee the scene before Castle has the chance to kill Elio Bessucho, who entered the country illegally to attend the nuptials.
NOTE: Includes pinups of Punisher fighting assailants by Ron Wagner (1 page) and shaving by Ed Sheng & Joe Rubenstein (1 page). Bussucho's name is also spelled "Bessucco."

PUNISHER WAR JOURNAL #37 (December 1991)

"Controversy" (22 pages)

CREDITS: Mike Baron (writer), Mike Harris (pencils), Art Nichols (inks), Jim Novak (letters), Gregory Wright (colors), Kevin Kobasic (asst editor), Don Daley (editor)
FEATURE CHARACTER: Punisher (last in PunSS #1/3, '91, chr last in PWJ #48, '92 fb, next in GR/W/Pun, '91)
VILLAINS: Humans Off Planet eco-terrorists (some last in PWJ #31, '91, die), gunman (dies), 3 rapists
OTHER CHARACTERS: Percy Baxter (conservative radio talk show host), Brad (radio listener, voice only), Jose (Percy Baxter's chauffeur), Wally South (Trafia/Contra conspirator, bts, attends roast, see NOTE), Elle Watson (Baxter's executive secretary), meatpacker (bts, disposes of gunman's corpse), news reporter (voice only), Hulk (noted on picket sign), Percy Baxter's bodyguard, bystanders, police, protesters, radio producer
LOCATIONS/ITEMS: Percy Baxter's home, auditorium, eco-terrorist's Manhattan base, radio studio, Wampanaug State Park / Percy Baxter's bar, limousine & telephone; eco-terrorists' automatic pistol, car & pistol; gunman's money clip & Webley automatic pistol; glass of iced tea, picket signs, police barricades, protest banner; Punisher's assault rifle, automatic pistols, knife, motorcycle, motorcycle helmet, telephone bug, tracer & tracking device; rapists' knife & pistol; Elle Watson's business card & car; rope & chair used to bind Percy Baxter; broadcast studio equipment inc microphone
SYNOPSIS: Frank Castle rescues assault victim Elle Watson, secretary of conservative radio talk show host, Percy Baxter, whose controversial views have sparked angry protests from a variety of liberal activists. Concerned for Baxter's safety and wanting to defend his right to free speech, Punisher checks on him and silently kills a gunman who tries to murder the broadcaster. When Baxter receives a death threat at home, Castle puts a tracer on him. That night, Humans Off Planet kidnaps Baxter at a public event. Punisher tracks the talk show host to the eco-terrorists' base and kills Baxter's abductors.
NOTE: PWJ #38, '92 provides this issue's credits. Wally South parodies Iran-Contra figure Oliver North. The Arab nation of Trafia was introduced in Pun #47, '91. A sponsor of Baxter's show is Werner's Weedkiller. Graffiti includes the names of this issue's creators Daley, Harris and Nichols.

PUNISHER WAR JOURNAL #38 (January 1992)

"Terminal Velocity" (23 pages)

CREDITS: Chuck Dixon (writer), Ron Wagner (pencils), Mike Witherby (inks), Jim Novak (letters), Gregory Wright (colors), Kevin Kobasic (asst editor, c inks), Don Daley (editor)
FEATURE CHARACTER: Punisher (last in MHol, '91/3, also in pfb)
VILLAINS: Drug suppliers, scientist (all also in pfb, die), drug dealers (in fb, die)
OTHER CHARACTERS: Bystanders, birds
LOCATIONS/ITEMS: Bronx, I-95, Stamford, Connecticut inc Benny's diner, cluster development w/scientist's home, strip mall w/Wright's pizza parlor & industrial park w/Biosphere Ltd. facility & gravel service road (all in pfb) / Punisher's binoculars, telescope, van & rifle w/scope; drug dealers' rifle & bag of cash; high rollers' briefcase, Mercedes, rocket launcher & watch; scientist's car; fence (all in pfb), Thermos canister of genetically altered coca seeds, high rollers' airplane, automatic pistols & parachutes (prev 4 also in pfb), Punisher's knife, scientist's refrigerator & sink w/garbage disposal
FLASHBACK: Frank Castle follows a group of drug suppliers from the Bronx to Connecticut as they gun down drug dealers, steal their cash and give their money to a scientist for a mysterious canister. The suppliers spot Punisher and subdue him. Castle awakens on a plane with the drug suppliers who jump out at their drop zone, leaving Punisher behind in the empty aircraft with no fuel (p).
SYNOPSIS: Castle jumps from the plane without a parachute, catches up to and kills the drug suppliers in mid-air and uses their chutes to land safely with the canister. Punisher tracks down the scientist, who reveals that the canister contains genetically altered coca seeds designed to grow anywhere. Castle kills the scientist, disposes of the seeds and seizes the money.
NOTE: Includes 1 page next issue preview.

PUNISHER WAR JOURNAL #39 (February 1992)

"Slay Ride" (20 pages)

CREDITS: Chuck Dixon (writer), Ron Wagner (pencils, c art), Rodney Ramos (inks), Jim Novak (letters), Phil Hugh Felix, Renee Witterstaetter (colors), Kevin Kobasic (asst editor), Don Daley (editor)
FEATURE CHARACTER: Punisher
SUPPORTING CAST: Microchip (last in Pun #59, '92, next in Pun:GF, '92)
VILLAIN: Cataleptic murderer
OTHER CHARACTERS: Jimmy Stewart (actor, recorded voice only, on TV), bus driver (dies), radio news reporter (voice only, on radio), bus riders (some die) inc Randy (dies), Cindy, Jeffrey (boy) & his mother; rescue workers
LOCATIONS/ITEMS: Microchip's home; Paradise Valley, Montana inc Mountain State Home for the Criminally Insane, ski lodge (both bts) & mountain road / Jeffrey's Baxter Bunny flashlight; Punisher's Glock pistol, luggage (both bts, on bus) & revolver; Microchip's couch, television & Christmas lights & tree; bus, cans of beer, Cindy's radio, ski pole, stretcher, murderer's knife & medic alert bracelet
SYNOPSIS: Frank Castle heads to a Montana ski lodge for Christmas but his bus is rammed by an avalanche and is buried under ten feet of snow. With the bus driver dead and one passenger apparently so, Punisher tries to calm the other passengers and befriends a boy and his mother who remind him of his own lost family. A radio report notes the escape of a psychotic murderer from a nearby mental health facility and when a passenger is knifed to death in the dark bus, everyone becomes paranoid. After more passengers are murdered, Castle deduces that the killer is the first apparently deceased passenger, who suffers from catalepsy. Punisher skewers the murderer with a ski pole and digs a tunnel to safety. As a rescue crew arrives, Castle asks the mother to tell authorities that the killer died at the hands of one of his victims.
NOTE: Includes pinups of Punisher in action on a jeep by Mike Harris & Vincent Evans (1 page) and on a motorcycle by Cooper Smith & M.M. Ritter (1 page). Punisher watches the movie, "It's a Wonderful Life."

PUNISHER WAR JOURNAL #40 (March 1992)

"Good Money After Bad" (22 pages)

CREDITS: Chuck Dixon (writer), Steven Butler (pencils), Mike Barreiro, Kim DeMulder (inks), Jim Novak (letters), Steve Buccellato (colors), Tim Tuohy (asst editor), Don Daley (editor), Joe Jusko (c art)
FEATURE CHARACTER: Punisher
VILLAINS: Earlene (also as Julie), Big, Mule (armored car robbers), 3 unnamed robbers, Eddie Prince & his men (all die)
OTHER CHARACTERS: 2 armored car drivers, auto mechanic, restaurant customers & workers, 2 truck drivers inc Leo
LOCATIONS/ITEMS: Davenport, Iowa; Canada, Milwaukee, Mississippi River (all mentioned), Michigan's Upper Peninsula inc Allenville, Sault Ste. Marie (both mentioned) & Schoolcraft County inc fire road, Route 642 & Tolliver w/gas station, Lake Pomus Lodge & Tolliver Motel / Big's mask, revolver & rifle; Earlene's backpack & pistol; motel mirror, television & toilet; Eddie Prince's cigarette, lighter & luxury car; Punisher's automatic pistol, automatic rifle, bandages, knife & pistol; armored car, bags of money, junk food containers, oil drum, phone booth, telephones, tractor trailer; robbers' automatic pistol, can of beer, rental muscle car & 9 mm revolver
SYNOPSIS: Frank Castle pursues three murderous robbers to Michigan's Upper Peninsula, where he kills them and takes their car. Not far away, three more criminals rob an armored car. One of them, Earlene, shoots the other two to keep the cash for herself. She hikes to a nearby town, encounters Punisher and persuades him to give her a ride. One of Earlene's victims, Big, survives and rendezvouses with Eddie Prince and his men. Together, they pursue Castle and Earlene and all but Big die in a car accident. When Earlene kills Big, Punisher realizes she's no innocent and guns her down. Castle takes her stolen money and leaves.
NOTE: Letters page includes a LoC by future novelist Stephen L. Shrewsbury. Punisher mentions Motel 6 and GM's Mr. Goodwrench brand.

PUNISHER WAR JOURNAL #41 (April 1992)

"Armageddon Express" (20 pages)

CREDITS: Chuck Dixon (writer), Gary Kwapisz (art), Jim Novak (letters), Glynis Oliver (colors), Tim Tuohy (asst editor), Don Daley (editor), John Romita Jr. (c art)
FEATURE CHARACTER: Punisher (next in Pun:GF, '92)
VILLAINS: Green Planet (eco-terrorist group) inc Dr. Artemus Greel (leader), Calvin, Gig, Hudson & Mitch (all die)
OTHER CHARACTERS: College students (inc Wendy) & their faculty advisor, 2 trainmen
LOCATIONS/ITEMS: Rocky Mountains between Albuquerque & Denver inc Gunnison Pass / Dr. Greel's cigarette; Green Planet's handcuffs, knife, M1 carbines, masks, remote-control explosive, sword & device for defeating dead man switch; Punisher's taser (bts), coat, concussion grenade, knife, machine gun, pistol, rappelling gear & 12 gauge shotgun in scabbard; balloons, boom box, cans of beer, confetti, railroad switch; Silver Snowbird (train) inc dead man passenger cars & locomotive w/dead man rig; US Army train carrying plutonium waste
SYNOPSIS: Frank Castle infiltrates Green Planet, an eco-terrorist group, and learns of their plot to crash a Rocky Mountain passenger train into a US Army train carrying plutonium waste. He steals aboard the passenger train and discovers one car is occupied by partying college students on break. Punisher uncouples their car to protect them from the violent radicals but to his dismay a curious student named Wendy joins him. Punisher saves Wendy from falling from the train and tells her to hide as he kills one terrorist after another on his way to the locomotive. Castle throws the dead man switch and foils Green Planet's plot while the Army train slams into the radicals' leader, Dr. Greel.
NOTE: Letters page includes a LoC by future novelist Stephen L. Shrewsbury.

PUNISHER WAR JOURNAL #42 (May 1992)

"Ten-to-One" (20 pages)

CREDITS: Chuck Dixon (writer), Todd Fox (pencils), Fred Fredericks (inks), Jim Novak (letters), Glynis Oliver (colors), Tim Tuohy (asst editor), Don Daley (editor), John Romita Jr. (c art)
FEATURE CHARACTER: Punisher (last in MK #38, '92)
VILLAINS: Tommy Flynn (Black Cullens mobster, see NOTE) & his men inc Rourke (all die); Kim Rhee (Korean mob boss) & his men (all die)
OTHER CHARACTERS: Antonelli, Nelson (both NYPD officers), Nathan (boy), Larry (Nathan's uncle), Moe Dee (rapper, name in graffiti), informant (bts, waiting to meet Punisher), Queens youth, bystanders
LOCATIONS/ITEMS: Queens inc Blue Sky Deli, building at 1026 Northern Blvd, Jeb's Bar, Uncle Larry's apartment & Woodside inc Queens Blvd / Nathan's Jordan sneakers (bts), Punisher's armored taxi cab (see NOTE), Antonelli's & Nelson's pistols, Tommy Flynn's car & pistol, Tommy Flynn's men's guns; Kim Rhee's pistol, Kim Rhee's men's pistols & assault weapons; cigarettes, police car, traffic, Uncle Larry's dresser & revolver; Punisher's machine gun, pistol & ammunition inc double aught shotgun shells, rifled slugs, special effects rounds & "bats" rounds (buckshot in liquid Teflon)
SYNOPSIS: While on his way to see an informant, Frank Castle spies Irish mobster Tommy Flynn in a car and follows him to the site in Queens where Flynn and his men are to meet rival Korean mobster Kim Rhee and his men to discuss mutual enemies. Local boy Nathan enters the scene with his uncle's revolver to reclaim his stolen sneakers from a group of youths. When Nathan fires his gun, both mobs think the other is attacking and a full-blown firefight ensues. Punisher and two police officers are drawn into the battle. In the end, all of mobsters are killed, the cops survive and Castle tells Nathan to drop his weapon and go home.
NOTE: Includes pin-up of Punisher in a subway station by John Hebert & Josef Rubinstein (1 page). The leaders of the Irish Black Cullens mob first appear in Pun #86, '94. Punisher's taxi, introduced and last seen in Pun #45, '91, has a new medallion number and ceramic-coated steel body.

PUNISHER WAR JOURNAL #43 (June 1992)

"Adirondack Haunts" (22 pages)

CREDITS: Rich Rainey (writer), Val Mayerik (pencils), Fred Fredericks (inks), Jim Novak (letters), Glynis Oliver (colors), Tim Tuohy (asst editor), Don Daley (editor), John Romita Jr. (c art)
FEATURE CHARACTER: Punisher
SUPPORTING CAST: Microchip (last in MK #38, '92, next in Pun:Easy, '92)
VILLAINS: Giovanni Monk (aka Johnny the Monk, mobster, dies), Novus Ordo capos (in fb), Adam Shockley (aka Doc Shock, surgeon, also in fb, dies) & his assistants (die); Don Stilicho (mobster, dies) & his men inc Nicky (die); Don Valerian (mobster, dies) & his men; organ traffickers
OTHER CHARACTERS: Adam Shockley's female companions (in fb), Tom L. Garlani (mountain climber), Don Valerian's nurse, bartender, bar patrons inc Paulie, hospital staff inc nurse
LOCATIONS/ITEMS: Cannes, Nice (both mentioned); La Spezia, Italy inc restaurant (in fb), Adirondacks of upstate New York inc Ausable River, bar, Gray Hall Gorge, hospital, White Rapids & Shockley Research Clinic w/operating room; Don Valerian's Cape Cod residence / champagne, glass of wine, patio table (all in fb); Don Stilicho's cigarette & limousine; bar phone, billiard balls, cue sticks, gurneys, helicopter, hospital bed, intravenous drip, medical files, mobsters' handguns, pay phone, pickup trucks, pool table, thermometer, US Air Force jets, water pitcher & glasses, surgical tools inc scalpels; Microchip's computer & speaker phone; Punisher's binoculars, borescope, car, land mines, micro bugs, MP5 submachine gun, pinhole drill, satellite communications unit, starflash shell, thermite grenades, tranquilizer darts & 30-mm disruptor gun w/scope
FLASHBACK: Adam Shockley's illegal medical activities bring him to the attention of European mobsters who fund a clinic in the Adirondacks where crime bosses can get organ transplants.
SYNOPSIS: Mountain climber Tom Garlani is kidnapped and taken to Shockley's medical clinic, where the surgeon transplants his kidney into mobster Don Valerian. Frank Castle follows Don Stilicho to the clinic, where the crime boss is to receive Garlani's heart in a second operation. Punisher sees Valerian leave and acquires information from Microchip about Shockley. After a local resident tells Castle about recent missing persons reports, Punisher returns to the clinic, kills Shockley and the mobsters inside and rescues Garlani. Castle deposits Garlani at a local hospital, retrieves Valerian and delivers him to the hospital so Garlani can get his kidney back. Punisher shoots Valerian in the head and departs.

PUNISHER WAR JOURNAL #44 (June 1992)

"Barbarians" (21 pages)

CREDITS: Chuck Dixon (writer), Val Mayerik (pencils), Fred Fredericks (inks), Jim Novak (letters), Glynis Oliver (colors), Tim Tuohy (asst editor), Don Daley (editor), John Romita Jr. (c pencils), Klaus Janson (c inks)
FEATURE CHARACTER: Punisher (also as Francis Stronghold; next in Pun:Easy, '92)
VILLAINS: Brandeis (insurance scammer), child pornographer, home invaders inc Hector & his brother (all die)
OTHER CHARACTERS: Achilles (hero of Greek mythology, mentioned), Julia (Brandeis' babysitter), Brandeis' baby boy, Brandeis' secretary, Julia's boyfriend
LOCATIONS/ITEMS: New York City inc Brandeis' office; Brandeis estate in Tarrytown, New York / Brandeis' candlestick, fence, kitchen knives, safe, utility box & wine bottles; home invaders' battering ram, club, duffel bags, flashlight, knife, rifles, rope, screwdriver, sledgehammer & auger drill w/diamond bit; Julia's boyfriend's car; Punisher's assault rifle, briefcase, Colt pistol, rifle & van
SYNOPSIS: Frank Castle kills a child pornographer after getting a tip from him that home invaders are planning to rob the estate of a man named Brandeis. Punisher arrives at the home, dispatches one of the burglars and turns off the power. He loans his pistol to the babysitter and gets her and Brandeis' baby boy to safety. As Castle takes down the remaining home invaders he learns that Brandeis hired them in an insurance fraud scheme. Punisher goes to Brandeis' office and shoots him.

PUNISHER WAR JOURNAL #45 (August 1992)

"The Vegas Idea" (22 pages)

CREDITS: Chuck Dixon (writer), John Hebert (pencils), Fred Fredericks (inks), Jim Novak (letters), Glynis Oliver (colors), Tim Tuohy (asst editor), Don Daley (editor), John Romita Jr. (c pencils), Klaus Janson (c inks)
FEATURE CHARACTER: Punisher (also as Johnny Tower & in photo, last in Pun Ann #5/2, '92)
SUPPORTING CAST: Microchip (last in Pun Ann #5/2, '92), Mickey Fondozzi (last in PWZ #10)
VILLAINS: Silvermane, Werner von Strucker (both last in DD #307, '92) & his men, Pit-Viper (subversive agent & double for Viper, 1st), Secret Empire inc Number 3 (last in Nomad #4, '92), Pretorians inc Chainsaw (chainsaw-wielding biker gang leader, last in MK #23, '91), Forchard & his men (Secret Empire hit squad, all die), 3 bikers (die)
OTHER CHARACTERS: Bucky (Julia Winter, Nomad's baby "partner," last in Nomad #4, '92), Eddie (Mickey's employee), Mickey's bimbo, casino staff & patrons; Tombstone, Deadpool, other criminals (prev 3 in photos)
LOCATIONS/ITEMS: Long Island Expressway overpass, Mickey's warehouse, the Palentine hotel & casino, Mojave Motor Lodge inc Room 109 / bikers' push dagger & bike chain, Punisher's Battle Van, shotgun, stun baton & government model Colts; shipping van, cigarette cartons, suitcase containing $100,000, rental car, hit squad's Uzis, Silvermane's "Ironhorse Shipping" big rig, hat & coat; Chainsaw's chainsaw & motorcycle, Pretorian's motorcycles, camper vans & cars
SYNOPSIS: A phone call from a woman lures Punisher to under the Long Island Expressway, where bikers attack him. After he kills them, Viper reveals her presence, having confirmed that he lives up to his reputation, and tells him about a Las Vegas gathering of major criminals. Punisher considers shooting her, but instead visits Mickey Fondozzi, instructing him to set himself up as a high roller in Vegas. The next day, Microchip and Punisher meet Mickey in the Palentine hotel to hear what he's learned, but Punisher is recognized and a squad of hitmen attack. Once the assassins are slain, Punisher, Micro and Mickey relocate to a motel, not realizing Silvermane is staying there too. Hearing of their hit squad's failure, the Secret Empire's Number 3 sends the Pretorians to kill Punisher. Mickey and Micro return to the Palentine, where Micro spots Werner von Strucker and follows him. Viper turns up in Punisher's room and gives him a file with all the hoods in town, just before the Pretorians strike.
NOTE: Cover labeled "Dead Man's Hand Part III," with story continuing from DD #307, '92 & Nomad #4, '92 and into Nomad #5, '92 & DD #308, '92. DD #307 shows criminal leaders gathering in Vegas to divvy up the fallen Kingpin's empire, and Daredevil becoming involved in the story, while Nomad #4 had Nomad hunting the crimelord Slug, and running into Bushwacker, who kidnaps Nomad's unofficially adopted child Bucky, only for her to fall into Pretorian hands.

PUNISHER WAR JOURNAL #46 (September 1992)

"Hot Chrome and Cold Blood" (21 pages)

CREDITS: Chuck Dixon (writer), John Hebert (pencils), Fred Fredericks (inks), Jim Novak (letters), Glynis Oliver (colors), Tim Tuohy (asst editor), Don Daley (editor), John Romita Jr. (c pencils), Mike Manley (c inks)
FEATURE CHARACTER: Punisher (also in Nomad #5 & DD #308, next in DD #309, all '92)
GUEST STAR: Daredevil (last in DD #307, '92, also in DD #308, '92, next in DD #309, '92)
SUPPORTING CAST: Microchip (also as Number Four), Mickey Fondozzi (also as Number Eight)
VILLAINS: Silvermane (also in DD #308, '92, next in IHulk #404, '93), Werner von Strucker (also in Nomad #5, '92, next in DD #309, '92) & his men (Hydra agents, 3 as security guards), Baron Strucker (as Snakeskin, also in DD #308, last in DD #307, next in DD #309, all '92), Secret Empire inc Number 3 (also in DD #308, '92, next in DD #309, '92), Number 6 (also in DD #308, '92, last in Nomad #4, '92, next in DD #309, '92), Agent Zero (as Hydra agent) & 1 other; Pretorians inc Chainsaw (also in Nomad #5, '92), Pit-Viper, Yakuza, the Hand
OTHER CHARACTERS: Bucky (also in Nomad #5, '92, next in Nomad #8, '92), police (bts), bystanders
LOCATIONS/ITEMS: Mojave Motor Lodge inc Room 109, Palentine hotel & casino / Punisher's government model Colts, extendable staff, assault rifle, grenade; Viper's specialized gun, Chainsaw's chainsaw & "Big Joe" shotgun w/explosive shells, Pretorian's guns, motorcycles, cars & van; Silvermane's hat, coat & rifle; Hydra agents' handguns & rings, armored car; rented car, Yakuza guns, Hand swords
SYNOPSIS: The Pretorians blast the motel, and Punisher and Viper respond in kind. Two Pretorians attempt to flee when the tide turns, but run into Silvermane, who throttles them, believing the assault is meant for him. Punisher stuns Chainsaw and snatches Bucky, and the Pretorians retreat right into Silvermane's waiting hands. Meanwhile, Micro and Mickey follow Strucker to his room, only to be captured by Hydra agents. Punisher returns to Vegas (see NOTE). Punisher returns to his rental car to retrieve additional weapons, but Hydra agents disguised as security guards confront him. Punisher kills them and takes off, using a grenade to take out an armored Hydra vehicle that follows. Meanwhile, Micro claims he and Mickey are members of the Secret Empire's Circle of Ten, preventing Hydra from executing them for fear of breaking the truce. The Empire's spy in Hydra alerts his superiors to the claim; unable to verify or disprove Micro's claim, they conclude their fellow Circle of Ten members are plotting against them, and decide to send the Pretorians to eliminate them. Elsewhere, Punisher comes across the Hand and Yakuza fighting. He joins in and chases the Hand into Circus Circus, where he finds Daredevil amid the spoils of his own battle with the Hand and Silvermane.
NOTE: Cover labeled "Dead Man's Hand Part VI." Story interweaves with Nomad #5, '92 & DD #308, '92, '92 and into DD #309, '92 & Nomad #6, '92. The letters page of DD #308 explains parts 4 & 5 were mistakenly switched. Nomad #5 starts the same way as this issue, but the fight is shorter with a different ending. Nomad #5 also shows that Punisher encounters Nomad on his return to Vegas and gives him Bucky. This issue's ending runs directly into DD #308's ending. Issue includes pin-up of Punisher under fire by Andrew Wildman & Sue McTiegue, credited in PWJ #50, '93's letters page. The Pretorians are spelled Praetorians here; while the latter is the correct spelling of the word, it isn't how the gang spells their name. Bushwacker is spelled Bushwhacker here.

PUNISHER WAR JOURNAL #47 (October 1992)

"Say Goodbye to Vegas" (22 pages)

CREDITS: Chuck Dixon (writer), John Hebert (pencils), Fred Fredericks (inks), Jim Novak (letters), Glynis Oliver (colors), Tim Tuohy (asst editor), Don Daley (editor)
FEATURE CHARACTER: Punisher (last in Nomad #6, '92, next in Pun #72, '92)
GUEST STARS: Daredevil (last in Nomad #6, '92, next in DD Ann #8, '92), Nomad (between Nomad #6-7, '92)
SUPPORTING CAST: Microchip (next in PWJ #51, '93), Mickey Fondozzi (next in PWJ #60, '93)
VILLAINS: Pit-Viper (next in NF:AoS #45, '93 bts, SSWP #15, '93), Tombstone (Lonnie Lincoln, superstrong albino) (both last in DD #309, '92, next in Cap #411, '93), Fenris: Andrea Strucker, Andreas Strucker (Baron Strucker's twin children, both last in DD #309, '92, next in AFlt #121, '93), Secret Empire inc Number 3, Number 6 (both last in DD #309, '92, die), Pretorians inc Chainsaw (next in MCP #152/4, '94), thugs
LOCATIONS/ITEMS: Nevada inc freeway & airfield / rented car, Nomad's shotgun & stun discs, Viper's helicopter, specialized gun & Camaro; Hammerhead's limo & handgun, Tombstone's handgun, Number 3's blaster, Daredevil's Billy clubs, helicopter, Punisher's assault rifle, oil drums, Pretorians' motorcycles & guns, Chainsaw's chainsaw
SYNOPSIS: Viper gives the heroes a helicopter ride to the airfield where the remaining crime bosses are about to depart, and a firefight ensues. Hammerhead and Tombstone kill Number 3 and his compatriots when they try to steal Hammerhead's limo. Fenris shoot down Viper's helicopter, but Nomad knocks them out, only to be struck by Hammerhead's car as he and Tombstone escape together. Daredevil boards a helicopter trying to leave while Punisher and Viper take out the last of the Empire. As the Pretorians attack, Daredevil crashes the helicopter near them, taking them out. Viper escapes as Mickey and Micro arrive in a car to pick the heroes up and take them away before the police arrive.
NOTE: Cover labeled "Dead Man's Hand Part IX," continuing from DD #309, '92 & Nomad #6, '92. In DD #309 Daredevil reluctantly teams up with Punisher and Tombstone to stop the Hand, and Baron Strucker, disguised as Snakeskin, creates internal dissent between the crime lords. In Nomad #6, Daredevil and Punisher help Nomad catch up to Slug, but Nomad can't bring himself to kill the crimelord. Features pin-up of Punisher killing a thug by John Czopppp & Ken Branch. This issue's credits are given in PWJ #49, '92. Nomad and Punisher on the cover are taken and recolored from p15 panel 2, with Daredevil replacing Viper.

PUNISHER WAR JOURNAL #48 (November 1992)

"Walk Through Fire, Part One: Backs to the Wall" (21 pages)

CREDITS: Chuck Dixon (writer), Todd Fox (pencils), Fred Fredericks (inks), Jim Novak (letters), Glynis Oliver (colors), Tim Tuohy (asst editor), Don Daley (editor), Doug Braithwaite (c pencils), Paul Neary (c inks)
FEATURE CHARACTER: Punisher (last in TInc #7, '93, also in fb1 between NW #9, '91 & Pun #45, '91; also in fb2 between PunSS #1/4, '91 & PWJ #37, '91)
VILLAINS: Drug hit men (die), arsonists, bank robbers, racketeers (prev 4 in fb1); crooked cops (in fb2), mobsters (also in fb2, die)
OTHER CHARACTERS: Payback (Edward "Eddie" Dyson, ex-cop vigilante, 1st, also in fb1-2 prior to this issue), Dorry Dyson (Payback's wife), Eddie Dyson's 2 daughters inc Cindy (prev 3 die), NYPD internal affairs investigators, bar patrons, bartender, bystanders, construction workers & contractors, medical staff, TV news cameraman & reporter (all in fb2); David Dinkins (in fb1, last in Pun #41, '90), NYPD police, arrestees (both in fb1), Tony Bennett (singer, on stereo in fb2), doctor, motel owner
LOCATIONS/ITEMS: New York City inc Midtown South police station, Brooklyn's Bedford-Stuyvesant neighborhood inc tenement (all in fb1), alley, bar, bridge, federal courthouse, police station & construction site (prev 6 in fb2), Eddie Dyson's Riverdale, Bronx home (also in fb1), hospital (also in fb2) & mobsters' house; Stopp Inn motel / Eddie Dyson's gold shield commendation, lawn mower & revolver; Eddie Dyson's children's ball, Punisher's Colt pistols, briefcase of cash, drug hit men's handguns, press cameras; police car, files, revolvers, van & walkie talkie; racketeer's headset & tape recorder (all in fb1); ashtray, construction trailer, glass of liquor, gurney, internal affairs tape recorder, oxygen mask, pay phone; Eddie Dyson's cigarettes & money; Eddie Dyson's wife's purse; mobsters' cars, guns, rifle, tape recorder, transceiver & keg of C-4 & roofing nails; Punisher's Barrett semi-automatic rifle, "bloop gun" grenade launcher & remote listening device (prev 19 in fb2), Eddie Dyson's leg cast & wheelchair; hospital bed & telephone; mobsters' telephone; motel ice & soda machines; Payback's car, Colt pistol, knife, leg splint & shotgun; Punisher's pistol, rifle & van
FLASHBACKS: After Frank Castle kills hit men in Brooklyn, he gets caught by police rookie Eddie Dyson and offers to let the officer take credit for the bust in exchange for his freedom. Dyson accepts, receives a commendation and works his way up to the NYPD major crimes unit busting bank robbers, arsonists and racketeers (1). Dyson informs Punisher that mobsters are extorting money from city contractors and fellow officers are being paid to look the other way. Castle kills the extortionists and convinces Dyson to help internal affairs nail the crooked cops. The sting earns Dyson a place in homicide and the hatred of other officers. Surviving mobsters bomb Dyson's home, killing his family. Dyson survives with an injured leg (2).
SYNOPSIS: Punisher calls Dyson at the hospital to let him know he's killed the men responsible for his family's deaths, but Dyson blames Castle for his fate and swears revenge. Dyson holes up in a motel and adopts the vigilante identity of Payback.
NOTE: Includes pinup of Punisher & Kingpin by Kerry Gammill (1 page). Payback's first name is revealed in PWJ #75, '95; his surname is revealed in PWJ #77, '95.

PUNISHER WAR JOURNAL #49 (December 1992)

"Walk Through Fire, Part II: A Gunfight" (20 pages)

CREDITS: Chuck Dixon (writer), Todd Fox (pencils), Fred Fredericks (inks), Steve Dutro (letters), Glynis Oliver (colors), Tim Tuohy (asst editor), Don Daley (editor), Greg Land (c pencils), Dan Panosian (c inks)
FEATURE CHARACTER: Punisher (next in Pun #51, '93, see NOTE)
VILLAINS: Bino Luchesi (mob-connected cement contractor, dies), Jimmy, Marty (Luchesi's men, die), Steve Venture's men inc Charlie (1st, most die)
OTHER CHARACTERS: Payback (next in PWJ #51, '93), Arnold Bryce (informant, dies), football player (on TV), porn actor, sports announcer (both voices only, on TV), Bob (bts on TV)
LOCATIONS/ITEMS: Brooklyn (mentioned), Luchesi Cement facility, highway, mall parking lot; Steve Venture's home at 10 Hickory Run, Morristown, New Jersey inc billiards room, kitchen & living room / Bino Luchesi's Rolodex (bts) & television, Luchesi's men's pistols, Luchesi Cement trucks, crushing truck & fence; Payback's automatic rifle, car, Colt pistol, garrote, knife, leg splint & shotgun; Punisher's Colt pistols, lock pick, rifle, van & rounds w/ball bearings & Semtex; Steve Venture's pool cues & table & television; Steve Venture's men's handguns & rifles; beer bottle & cans, pizza; chain & ropes used to bind Luchesi
SYNOPSIS: After arranging for an informant to tell Frank Castle about mob-connected cement contractor Bino Luchesi, Payback shoots the snitch and flees. Punisher raids Luchesi's business and forces him to reveal the name of the racketeer with whom he works, Steve Venture. Castle heads for Venture's home, followed discretely by Payback. Punisher assaults Venture's men and is shot in the foot during the melee. As Castle struggles to maintain consciousness, Payback arrives and kills the remaining mobsters before turning his gun on Punisher.
NOTE: Story continues in Pun #51, '93, with PWJ #50 telling a stand-alone story. Includes Kevin Branch pinup of Punisher drowning a victim (1 page) and 1 page next issue promo.

PUNISHER WAR JOURNAL #50 (January 1993)

"The Unfriendly Skies" (21 pages)

CREDITS: Chuck Dixon (writer), Mark Texeira (art, back c art), Richard Starkings (letters), Steve Buccellato (colors), Tim Tuohy (asst editor), Don Daley (editor), Steve Geiger (c art)
FEATURE CHARACTER: Punisher (last in PWJ #50, '93)
SUPPORTING CAST: Microchip (last in PWJ #51, '93, next in Pun #72, '92)
VILLAINS: Raven (Roberto Aviar, terrorist for hire) & his men inc Kamal (all die)
OTHER CHARACTERS: Lois (flight attendant), Phil (navigator), pilot, co-pilot, janitor, ticket agent, baggage handlers, paramedics, police, security guards, bystanders
LOCATIONS/ITEMS: JFK Airport inc security desk, ticket desk, lockers, baggage claim, concourse & runways / Raven's walker w/explosive device, airplane (Toronto flight) inc luggage hold, Kamal's suitcase, fiberglass dagger, Punisher's handgun, tool kit & Battle Van; Micro's suitcases
SYNOPSIS: While waiting for Microchip at the airport, Punisher recognizes known terrorist "the Raven" and figures by his inconsistent limp that his walker contains some kind of explosive. Sneaking on to the plane, Punisher waits until one of Raven's men heads his way and kills him, taking his fiberglass knife. When Raven's other man goes with the flight attendant to check on his partner's disappearance, Punisher ambushes and kills him. Identifying himself as an air marshal, he has the plane turned back to JFK but Raven gets wise and uses his explosive device to hold the attendant and plane hostage. Punisher kills the lights and attacks, but Raven releases the device and it blows a hole in the side of the plane. As the plane depressurizes Punisher sends Raven out the hole. The pressure stabilizes and the plane makes an emergency landing. During the resultant confusion at the airport, Punisher picks up Micro and they slip away.
NOTE: Features embossed cover, frontispiece by John Hinkleton, contents page (1 page), pin-ups of Punisher in the sewer by John Czop & Temujin Minor, Punisher killing criminals in the street by Donald C. Hudson, and a preview of Pun 2099 #1, '93 (5 pages).

2ND STORY: "Trespassers" (8 pages)
CREDITS: Steven Grant (writer), Shawn McManus (art), Jim Novak (letters), Matt Hollingsworth (colors), Tim Tuohy (asst editor), Don Daley (editor)
FEATURE CHARACTER: Punisher (next in Dhold #4, '93)
VILLAINS: Jack Starker, Jake Starker (bounty-hunting brothers), Kenny (swamp dweller) (all die)
OTHER CHARACTERS: Susie (Kenny's abused wife), Janie (mentioned, Kenny's 1st wife, murdered by him), Janie's "boyfriend" (mentioned, victim of Kenny's suspicions, murdered by him)
LOCATIONS/ITEMS: Swamp inc Susie & Kenny's shack / Punisher's Kevlar vest, rifle & shotgun, Kenny's shotgun
SYNOPSIS: Sent out to check the traps by her abusive husband Kenny, Susie finds Punisher unconscious in the water. She pulls him into the basement to tend to him, but her being down there makes Kenny suspicious, and he is about to beat her when the Starker boys arrive, tracking the Punisher, and open fire on the house with guns they took from their prey. Irrationally concluding Susie has been cheating on him, Kenny gets his shotgun and shoots Jack, while Punisher revives and kills Jake, retrieving his gun. Kenny is about to kill Susie for her "betrayal" when Punisher confronts him. Kenny shoots, but Punisher is saved by his Kevlar and kills Kenny. Susie begs Punisher to take her with him, but he tells her she wouldn't like where he's going.

PUNISHER WAR JOURNAL #51 (February 1993)

"Walk Through Fire, Part III: Sidewinder" (22 pages)

CREDITS: Chuck Dixon (writer), Todd Fox (pencils), Fred Fredericks (inks), Jim Novak (letters), Glynis Oliver (colors), Tim Tuohy (asst editor), Don Daley (editor), Ron Garney (c pencils), Klaus Janson (c inks)
FEATURE CHARACTER: Punisher (last in PWJ #49, '92, next in PWJ #50, '93)
SUPPORTING CAST: Microchip (last in PWJ #47, '92, next in PWJ #50, '93)
VILLAINS: Steve Venture (racketeer) & his men inc Cammy, Cheech, Nicky, Phil & Vic (all die)
OTHER CHARACTERS: Payback (next in Pun #86, '94), Gina Venture (Steve Venture's daughter), American Express customer service representative (bts, on phone), rummies (bts, at marina bar)
LOCATIONS/ITEMS: Daytona, Florida; Miami; Newark, New Jersey (all mentioned), Boca Raton, Florida inc marina bar (bts) & beach; Microchip's warehouse, Stop Inn motel; Steve Venture's Morristown, New Jersey home inc billiards room /

Microchip's computer & tahini & raisin sandwich on health bread; Payback's automatic rifle, car, Colt pistol, leg splint, revolver & shotgun; Punisher's beach chair, binoculars, cooler, crutch, fishing rods, leg cast, machine gun, rifle, van, splint made from chopped .410 shotgun & camper w/swivel mounted Vulcan 20mm anti-aircraft gun w/high explosive and armor piercing rounds; Steve Venture's cell phone, pistol & yacht; Steve Venture's men's pistols & rifle; bucket of plaster of Paris, cans of Grizzly soda, motel ice & soda machines & telephone, pizza box

SYNOPSIS: Payback tells Frank Castle that he lured him into raiding Steve Venture's house and spares Punisher's life when he learns that Venture wasn't home. Castle goes to Microchip's warehouse to get his broken ankle set. Payback returns to his motel and learns that Venture flew to Florida. After Microchip discovers that Venture is in Boca Raton, Punisher travels there in his camper. Venture notices Castle watching his yacht from the beach and sends two of his men to check him out. Punisher kills the men with a shotgun hidden in his leg splint. Payback steals aboard the boat and shoots Venture in front his young daughter as Castle bombards the yacht with rounds from an anti-aircraft gun. Payback arrives on shore with the girl and calls a truce with Punisher, who realizes that Payback is the cop who swore vengeance on him.

NOTE: Story concludes from PWJ #49, '92. Includes pinup of Punisher shooting down a helicopter by D. Nguyen & Al Williamson (1 page). Punisher mistakenly notes that he was shot in the leg instead of the foot. He refers to Payback as Payday. The license plate on Punisher's camper reads "I'd rather be bassin'."

PUNISHER WAR JOURNAL #52 (March 1993)

"Heart of Ice" (20 pages)

CREDITS: Chuck Dixon (writer), Gary Kwapisz (art), Jim Novak (letters), Glynis Oliver (colors), Tim Tuohy (asst editor), Don Daley (editor)
FEATURE CHARACTER: Punisher (last in Pun #79, '93)
GUEST STAR: Mike "Ice" Phillips (Vietnam veteran, 1st, see NOTE)
VILLAINS: Sword of Liberty (paramilitary crazies, some die) inc Armstrong (leader), Deena Hammond (both 1st) & Rover One (patrol group) inc Jake (1st); Arms seller
OTHER CHARACTERS: Mr. Hammond (Houston businessman), FBI agents, Treasury agents, Redding police, bank customers & staff (prev 2 die), dogs
LOCATIONS/ITEMS: Arms dealer's cabin, California inc Golden State Savings, Redding, Cascades w/Valhalla (Sword of Liberty camp) inc Quonset hut; Houston inc Hammond's office / police cars & shotguns, Sword Liberty's guns, explosives, radios, camouflage gear, trip wires, Claymore mines & Huey helicopter; Armstrong's sword; Punisher's shotgun, star-lite scope, knife, camping gear, garrote & Barnett crossbow; Ice's knife, camping gear, Taser & Ruger Match pistol w/homemade suppressor
SYNOPSIS: In Redding, California, three members of the Swords of Liberty try to rob a bank, and then blow themselves and their hostages up when the police arrive. Punisher interrogates a local arms dealer and learns the Swords' main encampment, Valhalla, is in Cascades. The Sword's leader, Armstrong, is a delusional paranoid who believes only his constant vigilance protects America from an army of enemies, but his lover, Deena, remains besotted with him even when he executes one of his own men for a perceived infraction. Meanwhile Deena's worried father, Houston businessman Mr. Hammond, hires Vietnam Special Forces vet "Ice" Phillips to retrieve his daughter. Frank and Ice run into one another as both hike to Valhalla, and, after a brief scuffle, they recognize one another from the war. Although each thinks the other's mission foolish, with Ice only wanting to extract his target while Punisher intending to destroy Valhalla, together they take out Valhalla's outlying sentries. However, Ice then tasers Punisher, and when he comes to a patrol has moved in.
NOTE: Jake is named next issue. Ice Phillips is the Earth-616 (mainstream Marvel Earth) counterpart to The 'Nam (Earth-85101) Ice Phillips. Though this issue is 616 Ice's 1st, the other Ice last appeared in The 'Nam #69, '92; presumably 616 Ice's life includes similar events to those depicted in The 'Nam, but in a conflict other than Vietnam and a world containing superhumans.

PUNISHER WAR JOURNAL #53 (March 1993)

"Heart of Stone" (21 pages)

CREDITS: Chuck Dixon (writer), Gary Kwapisz (art), Richard Starkings (letters), Glynis Oliver (colors), Tim Tuohy (asst editor), Don Daley (editor)
FEATURE CHARACTER: Punisher
GUEST STAR: Ice Phillips (next in PWZ #27, '94)
VILLAINS: Sword of Liberty (most die) inc Armstrong, Clark, Rover One patrol inc Jake (prev 4 die), Deena Hammond, Rover Two patrol & Rover Three patrol
OTHER CHARACTERS: Dogs
LOCATIONS/ITEMS: California inc Cascades w/Valhalla / Sword Liberty's guns, grenades, radios, tanglefoot wire, trip flares, Claymore mines, jeeps & Huey helicopter; Armstrong's sword; Punisher's binoculars
SYNOPSIS: The patrol receives radioed instructions to bring Frank in for interrogation alongside the other intruder, and realizes Ice has also been caught. One of the patrol moves carelessly close to Punisher, allowing him to seize their weapon and kill the entire patrol. Armstrong questions Ice, but refuses to believe that he is simply there to rescue Deena, sure a greater conspiracy must be involved. Punisher meanwhile scouts around the camp, planning to attack after nightfall. Left alone with Deena, Ice tries to convince her to go with him, but she remains enamored of Armstrong. Shortly before nightfall, Punisher ambushes some of the men patrolling; soon after a man races into the perimeter defenses and is gunned down. Armstrong, aware of where all the booby-traps are hidden, goes out to check the corpse, but finds it is one of the missing patrolmen, Clark, forced to charge the base by Punisher. As alarms go off on the other side of camp, Armstrong concludes Clark was a diversion and leads his men to defend the base, not realizing that too is another of the captured patrolmen. Meanwhile Punisher slips by Clark's corpse into the base, using Armstrong's own footprints to navigate the traps. He frees Ice and suggests they commandeer the Swords' own helicopter and blow the camp up from the air, but Ice is still focused on getting paid for retrieving Deena. They storm Armstrong's cabin and have a stand-off over her, but put aside differences when Armstrong arrives and attacks. Fighting their way out, they reach the helicopter; Punisher guns down the pursuing Armstrong, then orders the grieving Deena on board.

PUNISHER WAR JOURNAL #54 (May 1993)

"Surface Thrill" (22 pages)

CREDITS: Chuck Dixon (writer), Gary Kwapisz (art), Janice Chiang (letters), Glynis Oliver (colors), Tim Tuohy (asst editor), Don Daley (editor)
FEATURE CHARACTER: Punisher
VILLAINS: Family (criminal family): Bosephus, Gig, Maw, Mitch, Paw; Killer B (Anton Bigelow, Baltimore crimelord), Killer B's girlfriend, Bad Boyz (Killer B's gang) inc container ship scuba patrol (die) (all 1st); drug user, "guy who heard it from a guy who had heard it from a guy" (mentioned, Punisher beat him for info)
OTHER CHARACTERS: Baltimore police (some die) inc Charlie Bash, Sam "the Clam" (both narcotics division, partners), Maw's dog (1st, next in PWJ #56, '93)
LOCATIONS/ITEMS: Baltimore inc Dundalk in Baltimore Harbor, liquor store, Killer B's Pimlico high rise w/Killer B's penthouse, Family's house / Punisher's rebreather rig, spring-loaded knives, shaped charges, sniper rifle, binoculars, radio mike, Battle Van & guns; Marcella (container ship carrying heroin), container ship patrol's scuba gear, knives & spear guns; Charlie's shotgun, police cars & guns, drug user's axe, Killer B's gun & limo, Bad Boyz cars, Family's guns & Angel Dust, Charlie & Sam's car
SYNOPSIS: In Baltimore Harbor Punisher blows up a container ship carrying local druglord Killer B's cocaine. Meanwhile local cops try to subdue a PCP addict, who kills several of them with an axe before narcotic cop Charlie Bash guns him down. Using a radio mike, Punisher listens in on Killer B's penthouse, and learns another outfit is moving in on the crook's territory; Punisher decides to take down both groups. Meanwhile Maw, matriarch of the rival gang, orders her sons to slay Killer B. Punisher tails Killer B when his entourage leaves the penthouse, unaware he in turn has been spotted by Charlie Bash and his taciturn partner, Sam the Clam. As they watch, one of Maw's sons, Bosephus attacks Killer B's car with Angel Dust-induced superhuman strength and rage, while his brothers Gig and Mitch gun down Killer B's soldiers. Punisher moves in, thinking this an opportunity to eliminate both gangs, killing several of Killer B's men; Gig and Mitch flee, and Bosephus is engulfed in flames when one of the cars ignites. Thinking the fight all but over, Punisher is about to slay Killer B when the burning Bosephus grabs him from behind.

PUNISHER WAR JOURNAL #55 (June 1993)

"Bad Boyz" (22 pages)

CREDITS: Chuck Dixon (writer), Gary Kwapisz (art), Janice Chiang (letters), Glynis Oliver (colors), Tim Tuohy (asst editor), Don Daley (editor)
FEATURE CHARACTER: Punisher (also in picture)
SUPPORTING CAST: Microchip (last in PWZ #16, '93)
VILLAINS: Family: Bosephus, Gig, Maw, Mitch, Paw; Killer B, Wizard (1st, designer drug maker)
OTHER CHARACTERS: Baltimore police inc Charlie Bash, Sam the Clam, Officer Skeets; nurse, patients, pizza delivery boy, pizza buyer, reporter (on TV), bystanders, guard dogs, rabbits
LOCATIONS/ITEMS: Baltimore inc Rye Street, Family's house inc kitchen, Wizard's lab, police station, motel, hospital & Diamandaras' towing & salvage yard; Microchip's warehouse / Punisher's submachine gun, Battle Van & handgun; Charlie & Sam's car, Charlie's shotgun w/CS gas pellets, Sam's revolver, police guns, pizza van, pizzas, Maw's knife, Micro's computer, IV bag, bandages, needle of PCP, medication tray, patient's wheelchair, Gig's truck & submachine gun, gas grenade
SYNOPSIS: Bash and Sam ram their car into Bosephus, freeing Punisher, who retreats as he hears approaching sirens. As Bosephus turns on the newly arrived cops, Bash calls in for more backup and impounds Punisher's van. Soon after, an angry Maw listens to Gig and Mitch's excuses, and sends them to free Bosephus, who has survived and is now being held under guard in the hospital, so heavily bandaged he looks like a mummy. Meanwhile Killer B turns to drug designer Wizard for help; recognizing from Killer B's description that his attacker was on PCP, Wizard suggests stealing the other gang's clientele by producing a PCP variant which will have fewer side effect. Bash and Sam identify the Punisher, while Punisher phones Micro to bring him armament and his exo-armor. Mitch sneaks into the hospital and loads more PCP into Bosephus' IV, sending him in another unstoppable rage, and they escape the hospital. Punisher sneaks into the commercial yard where his van has been sent, but Bash and Sam ambush him, and Bash offers him a job.

PUNISHER WAR JOURNAL #56 (July 1993)

"24 Hours of Power!" (23 pages)

CREDITS: Chuck Dixon (writer), Gary Kwapisz (art), Janice Chiang (letters), Glynis Oliver (colors), Tim Tuohy (asst editor), Don Daley (editor)
FEATURE CHARACTER: Punisher (next in Ns #5, '93)
SUPPORTING CAST: Microchip (next in PunSS #3/2, '93 bts, PWZ #17, '93)
VILLAINS: Killer B; Bad Boyz inc Biv & Lester (all die); Wizard (on video); Family: Maw, Bosephus, Gig, Mitch, Paw (prev 4 die)
OTHER CHARACTERS: Charlie Bash, Sam the Clam; Wizard's 4 dogs (on video, die); Maw's dog (last in PWJ #54, '93); family in tailed car (voices only)
LOCATIONS/ITEMS: Baltimore inc salvage yard, Killer B's Pimlico high rise w/Killer B's penthouse & airspace, Vista Pines motel, Family's house inc garage & kitchen / Charlie's shotgun, Sam's revolver, Sam & Charlie's car & tracking device; Punisher's boot knife, .357 mag wrist Derringer, Battle Van, exo-armor w/Vulcan mini-gun, shaped charges & .50 cal supermag; Wizard's videotape & PCP variant, Killer B's TV & VCR; Microchip's rental van, family saloon
SYNOPSIS: Bash gives Punisher blueprints for Killer B's condo and lets Punisher leave with his van in return for agreeing to permanently remove Killer B, though the suspicious cop makes it clear he and his partner Sam will be watching Punisher to ensure he upholds his end of the deal, rightly distrusting the pair, who plan to arrest him as soon as Killer B is dead. Meanwhile Killer B receives a sample of Wizard's new drug with an instructional video; Killer B has already swallowed three tablets before the recording of Wizard explains the drugs massively heighten strength and aggression, and no more than half a tablet should be consumed. Across town Punisher meets with Microchip, collects the exo-armor, and asks Micro to sweep the van for anything Sam and Bash may have planted. At the same time Maw orders her sons to dose Bosephus up on PCP again and eliminate Killer B. Soon after this, Sam and Bash trail Punisher's Battle Van, unaware Micro is driving it as a decoy. Bosephus attacks Killer B's penthouse, battling the equally drug-fueled Killer B,

joined moments later by the armored Punisher, who climbed up the airspace that runs up the entire building. Killer B's men flee down the stairs, but find Gig and Mitch waiting and are gunned down. Punisher throws Bosephus down the airspace, but Killer B tosses Punisher in turn down the stairs, inadvertently crushing Mitch and Gig to death beneath his armored foe. Punisher slays Killer B with his Vulcan mini-gun, then ditches the wrecked armor, and pursues Bosephus, who has survived a ten-story drop back home. The vigilante shoots the weakening Bosephus dead, and Maw hastily claims Paw led her children into crime, feigning innocence. Falling for her deception, Punisher executes Paw but leaves her alive. Meanwhile Bash and Sam continue following the tracker they hid on the Battle Van, unaware Microchip has attached it to a random car heading to Albany.

PUNISHER WAR JOURNAL #57 (August 1993)

"Blood Money" (22 pages)

CREDITS: Chuck Dixon (writer), Gary Kwapisz (art), Janice Chiang (letters), Glynis Oliver (colors), Tim Tuohy (asst editor), Don Daley (editor)
FEATURE CHARACTER: Punisher (last in PWZ Ann #1/3, '93)
GUEST STARS: Daredevil (last in IC #6, '93), Ghost Rider (last in FF #374, '93)
SUPPORTING CAST: Microchip (last in PWZ Ann #1, '93, next bts in PWJ #59, '93), Lynn Michaels (last in PWZ #10, '92)
VILLAINS: Mr. Sandeen (black market blood dealer, 1st, bts, sends men to kill nuns) & his men (some die), meth dealers (die) & customers
OTHER CHARACTERS: Noble Kale (last in FF #374, '93), medical examiner (bts, performs autopsies), nuns (die), bystanders, cats, NYPD police & detectives inc Len
LOCATIONS/ITEMS: Manhattan's Lower East Side inc Hari Krishna temple on Rivington St., Hasidic temple on Delancy St., Kingdom Hall (all mentioned), bar, chicken restaurant, Joe's Deli, killers' base, meth lab on roof of East 11th St. tenement, Roy's Pawn Shop, Seward Park, Taco Pete's Restaurant & Blessed Saint Agnes Order of Mercy convent w/chapel; Lynn Michaels' apartment / Daredevil's billy club; Ghost Rider's chain & motorcycle; Lynn Michaels' bed, pistol, teddy bear & telephone; Microchip's computer; Punisher's pistol, taxi cab, telephone, Manville grenade launcher w/20-mm grenades & "bloop gun" grenade launcher w/40-mm round w/Semtex; Sandeen's men's blood extractor, handcart, pistols, rifles & attack helicopter w/machine gun, missile launcher & hellfire missile; convent pews & votive candles, hot dog cart, meth dealers' pulley, nun's rosary, pay phones, police cars, sign for 87th Ave. Storage
SYNOPSIS: After Frank Castle destroys a meth lab, he follows a scream to a nearby convent where he faces a squad of paramilitary killers. Ghost Rider bursts in and helps Punisher fight the murderers but some of them get away in an attack helicopter with blood they drained from the convent's nuns. As the police investigate this latest in a series of attacks on religious organizations dubbed the "vampire killings," Castle calls officer Lynn Michaels for information and he and Ghost Rider search the streets for any sign of the killers. Daredevil investigates independently and tracks the murderers to their base. Meanwhile, the attack helicopter resurfaces and fires an incendiary missile at Ghost Rider.
NOTE: Includes pinup of Punisher on a motorcycle by Scott McDaniel (1 page).

PUNISHER WAR JOURNAL #58 (September 1993)

"Blood Red Moon" (22 pages)

CREDITS: Chuck Dixon (writer), Gary Kwapisz (art), Janice Chiang (letters), Glynis Oliver (colors), Tim Tuohy (asst editor), Don Daley (editor)
FEATURE CHARACTER: Punisher
GUEST STARS: Daredevil (next in DD #317, '93), Ghost Rider (next in TInc #13, '93)
SUPPORTING CAST: Lynn Michaels
VILLAINS: Mr. Sandeen (1st actual app, dies) & his men (some die)
OTHER CHARACTERS: Carbones, FBI, Kingpin (all mentioned), Noble Kale (next in TInc #13, '93), NYPD police dispatcher (voice only, on radio), truck driver
LOCATIONS/ITEMS: Manhattan's Lower East Side inc Army Navy store, Blue Nite strip club, killers' base & Seward Park; Lynn Michaels' apartment / Ghost Rider's chain & motorcycle; Lynn Michaels' bed, car, notepad, pistol, police radio, rifle & teddy bear; Punisher's Manville grenade launcher w/20-mm grenades; Sandeen's men's attack helicopter, automatic pistols, blood extractor, handcart, machine gun, rifles & storage tanks; phone booth, truck; chains & rope used to bind Daredevil
SYNOPSIS: Ghost Rider survives the attack and downs the helicopter. When Lynn Michaels doesn't receive an expected phone call from Frank Castle, she decides to help. Daredevil infiltrates the killers' base but is knocked out. When he comes to, he meets the murderers' boss, Mr. Sandeen, who explains that he's collecting the blood of the innocent to sell on the black market. As Sandeen prepares to extract Daredevil's blood, Punisher and Ghost Rider burst in and assault Sandeen's men. Daredevil breaks free and attacks Sandeen, but when Castle and Ghost Rider arrive, he lets Sandeen go to save the criminal's life. Ghost Rider stops Castle from killing Sandeen, who returns with a machine gun. Sandeen is shot dead by Michaels, who realizes she's stepped over the line by assisting Punisher. Castle reprimands her and tells her he doesn't need her.
NOTE: This issue reveals that Daredevil's blood type is AB negative.

PUNISHER WAR JOURNAL #59 (October 1993)

"The House That Hate Built" (22 pages)

CREDITS: Chuck Dixon (writer), Gary Kwapisz (art), Janice Chiang (letters), Glynis Oliver (colors), Tim Tuohy (asst editor), Don Daley (editor)
FEATURE CHARACTER: Punisher
SUPPORTING CAST: Microchip (bts, last in PWJ #57, '93, next in Pun:BSS #2, '93), Lynn Michaels
VILLAINS: Bigg (Projects gangster, 1st), Ghetto Rangers (Bigg's gang, some die) inc Carlo, Parnell, Sidney, Squeak (prev 4 die); Clyde Allen Durkin (aka Ryerson, child killer, 1st)
OTHER CHARACTERS: Max (last in Pun #57, '91), police inc Stan Townsend, 2 homeless men
LOCATIONS/ITEMS: Queens inc Punisher's safehouse (destroyed) / Lynn Michael's car & gun, Bigg's gang's guns & cars; Carlo's Air Jordans (destroyed), unmarked police car, Durkin's knife & stolen goods; police's guns;

children's shoes, Claymore mines

SYNOPSIS: With his own ride trashed, Punisher reluctantly has Lynn Michaels drive him to his Queens safehouse, carefully directing her through the building's traps and introducing her to the guard dog, Max. They depart after Punisher calls Microchip to arrange to be picked up, unaware some local down and outs spotted them. One informs a local gang, the Ghetto Rangers, who arrive in force hoping to kill the Punisher, only for several of them to be slain by the Punisher's traps and the remainder attacked by Max. The gang's leader finally knocks Max out, and, impressed by the animal's ferocity, decides to retrain Max as his own attack dog. Meanwhile Lynn returns to work, joining her partner Stan Townsend and another cop carrying out a robbery warrant on a suspected thief. The suspect attacks them when they enter his apartment, and after they subdue him Lynn discovers pictures of young children who have gone missing recently, and shoes belonging to same. Soon afterwards Punisher finds his safehouse has been compromised and Max taken, and swears to kill those who took the dog.

NOTE: Durkin is called Ryerson here. Lynn calls Townsend "Stan" but another cop calls him "Blake." It is possible that the word balloon was misplaced, and the cops who capture Ryerson with Lynn are Stan Townsend and Blake.

PUNISHER WAR JOURNAL #60 (November 1993)

"Dogged" (22 pages)

CREDITS: Chuck Dixon (writer), Gary Kwapisz (art), Janice Chiang (letters), Glynis Oliver (colors), Tim Tuohy (asst editor), Don Daley (editor)
FEATURE CHARACTER: Punisher (next in Pun Ann #6, '93)
SUPPORTING CAST: Mickey Fondozzi (last in PWJ #47, '92, next in PWZ #31, '93)
VILLAINS: Bigg (dies), Ghetto Rangers (some die), Ty Fetters (dog fight trainer, dies), Ty's men (some die) inc Billy; Carter (dog-fighting enthusiast, dies) & his 2 pals (die), Clyde Durkin (on TV, next in PWJ #62, '94), dog fighting fans (most die)
OTHER CHARACTERS: Max, cops (some on TV) inc Blackleigh (1st, Lynn's superior), Stan Townsend, roadhouse waitress & patrons, District Attorney, reporters (on TV, 1 voice only), fighting dogs, Ren & Stimpy (cartoon characters, on TV)

LOCATIONS/ITEMS: Ghetto Rangers' base, Mickey's office, Central Pine Barrens inc Ty's farm w/house & barn, roadhouse, Blue Moon Motel / Punisher's Semtex, guns, pick-up truck; Mickey's VCRs, TVs & machine gun; Ty's Taser, Carter's friends' gun & baseball bat, Carter's car, Lynn's gun & TV

SYNOPSIS: Punisher raids the Ghetto Rangers headquarters, killing the entire gang, but learns they found Max untrainable and so sold him to a Buddtown dog fighting promoter, Ty Fetters. Punisher enlists Mickey Fondozzi to accompany him to Buddtown and assist him tracking down Fetters, insisting it isn't about Max. Meanwhile Lynn is informed that the DA is cutting their child-killing suspect Clyde Durkin a deal, since the warrant to search his apartment, given out on suspicion of robbery, makes the murder evidence they found inadmissible. In the Buddtown area Punisher and Mickey track down Fetters' location and learn there is a dog fight scheduled for that night. At his farm, Fetters oversees mistreating Max, getting him angry in preparation for the fight. With Punisher still telling himself he's not doing this because he cares about his dog, they raid the fight, just as Max kills his opponent after a brutal fight; Punisher wings Fetters, who falls into the dog fight pit for Max to finish off. When Punisher goes into the pit, Max calms down, recognizing his friend, and they depart with Mickey to get Max some medical treatment.

NOTE: Includes 16 page insert promoting the Midnight Sons crossover "Siege of Darkness."

PUNISHER WAR JOURNAL #61 (December 1993)

"Terminal Objectives Pt. 1" (29 pages)

CREDITS: Chuck Dixon (writer), Gary Kwapisz (art), Joe Andreani (colors), Janice Chiang (letters), Tim Tuohy (asst editor), Don Daley (editor), Michael Golden (c art)
FEATURE CHARACTER: Punisher (last in GR/W/Pun, '94, next in PWZ #23, '94)
SUPPORTING CAST: Microchip (last in PunHol #3/2, '93, next in PWZ #23, '94), Lynn Michaels (next in Pun #86, '93), Mickey Fondozzi (last in PWZ #31, '94, next in PWZ #23, '94)
VILLAINS: Jackie Dee (mob boss), Flynn Cullen (Black Cullens), Vlad Slozchk (Russian Molina), Vito Vaducci (racketeer) & his men, Buck Wrango (Tallahassee mobster), "Tiger" Tanner Wilson (controls northern Manhattan), Turk (the Righteous Ones), Bruce Lam (August Dragon clan), Pike (the Outfit in Chicago), Tony Rhee (Korean Mafia), Bruce & all their men (all 1st, next in PWZ #23, '94), Rosalie Carbone (last in PWZ #11, '93, next in PWJ #63, '94) & her men (3 die), Jigsaw (last in Pun #56, '91, next in Pun #2, '95), Rapido (last in Pun #70, '92, next in PWZ #23, '94), mobsters (5 die), money launderer

OTHER CHARACTERS: Bruno (Rosalie's boy toy), Blackleigh, Stan Townsend, ATF agents, FBI agents
LOCATIONS/ITEMS: Warehouse, Carbone mansion inc swimming pool, Jackie Dee's mansion, Microchip's warehouse, police station, Manhattan Tower / Punisher's Uzis, silenced .380, rappel-o-matic, shotgun, night vision goggles & detonator; mobsters' various weapons, chair, rope, piece of tape, FBI's surveillance equipment & van, Manhattan Tower blueprints, Lynn's badge, Excalibur vintage wine truck w/Semtex, hand truck, boxes of wine, ultra-lite glider, Manhattan dummy w/dynamite (both destroyed), detonator

SYNOPSIS: After killing some mobster Punisher captures their accountant / money launderer, who informs him of a big crime family meet going down in Manhattan Tower soon. Punisher breaks into Rosalie Carbone's place, holding her at gunpoint to get her boy toy to talk; he confirms that mobster Jackie Dee has arranged the gathering for a few weeks before Thanksgiving. Meanwhile, Jackie Dee holds a meeting with various mob representatives, discussing how they plan to use the meeting as a lure to kill Punisher. One attendee, Jigsaw, believes it will go badly and leaves, wanting no part of it, while outside the FBI listen in. Elsewhere, Microchip tries unsuccessfully to talk Punisher out of attacking the Tower, suspecting the meeting it a trap. Lynn Michaels turns in her gun and badge, quitting because of child-killer Clyde Durkin's inadequate sentence. On the day of the meet, Punisher has Mickey deliver champagne, then abandon his stalled truck in the loading dock. Micro guides in an ultra-lite with explosives to the roof, detonating it to cause a distraction. Punisher emerges from a compartment in Mickey's truck, blasts the guards, and works his way up the elevator shaft and into the building, only to be faced by an army of mobsters ready and waiting for him. However, Punisher isn't expecting any of them, himself included, to get out alive, and reveals the truck in the basement is full of Semtex, ready to bring down the entire skyscraper if he releases his deadman switch.

NOTE: Cover labeled "Suicide Run: 1", continuing from Pun #85, '93 and into PWZ #23, '94 & Pun #87, '94. The first 3 parts of the story featured embossed foil-stamped covers. The first 2 interior pages show grayscaled versions of the cover, with credits superimposed over the 2nd. The issue features Punisher armory entry about ascender/descender kit for climbing elevator shafts (1 page) and a pin-up of Punisher mowing through gangsters by Henry Flint & Jimmy Palmiotti.

2ND STORY: "Clock's Ticking" (4 pages)

CREDITS: Mike Lackey (writer), Phil Gosier (pencils), Frank Percy (inks), Lia Pelosi (colors), Dave Sharpe (letters), Tim Tuohy (asst editor), Don Daley (editor)

FEATURE CHARACTER: Punisher

VILLAIN: Pedophile (dies)

LOCATIONS/ITEMS: Pedophile's apartment / Pedophile's handgun, refrigerator, TV

SYNOPSIS: Punisher forcibly interrogates a pedophile for the location of his latest victim, whom he believes to still be alive for now based on prior MO. Punisher succeeds when he dangles the pedophile out his window, getting the location of the little girl under the Brooklyn Bridge. The pedophile begs for his life, blaming porn and TV for his addiction. Punisher reels him back in, only to kill him by shoving his head through the TV. Whether the girl lives or dies, Punisher is assured the criminal's been punished.

PUNISHER WAR JOURNAL #62 (January 1994)

"Standing in the Shadows Pt. 4" (19 pages)

CREDITS: Chuck Dixon (writer), Gary Kwapisz (art), Glynis Oliver (colors), Janice Chiang (letters), Tim Tuohy (asst editor), Don Daley (editor), Michael Golden (c art)

SUPPORTING CAST: Lynn Michaels (between Pun #86-87, '94), Microchip (last in Pun #86, '94, next in PWJ #64, '94)

VILLAINS: Lt. Blackwell (last in Pun #86, '94, next in PWZ #24, '94), Clyde Allen Durkin (last in PWJ #60, '93, dies), meatpackers (black market bankers, all die)

OTHER CHARACTERS: Payback (last in PWJ #51, next in Pun #87, '94), Desmond Kline (Punisher-idolizing postal worker, 1st), VIGIL inc Capt. Nails (last in Pun #86, '94, next in PWZ #24, '94); Carson, Wills (both last in Pun #86, '94, next in PWZ #24, '94), Winnow (Treasury agent), Fenders (Organized crime agent), prison guard, reporter (on TV), ATF agents, FBI agents, paramedics, police, postal workers, Punisher's "body" (last in Pun #86, '94), bystanders, Kline's dog; gun babe (on poster)

LOCATIONS/ITEMS: Manhattan Tower ruins, the Tombs, Kline's apartment, Microchip's warehouse (destroyed), post office, VIGIL HQ, meatpacking plant / Gurnies, Lynn's sniper rifle, motorcycle & handgun; carton of cigarettes, pizza, gun magazines, bus, Micro's laptop & anesthetic gas spray, C-4, Payback's shotgun, handgun & car; meatpackers' various guns, VIGIL's tanks, helicopters & guns

SYNOPSIS: Paramedics remove Punisher's body from the rubble, his faced smashed by a beam, but the government agents present wonder if there might have been more than one Punisher, and if not, how long before those he inspired step up to fill his void. In jail awaiting transfer to prison, Clyde Durkin is given a carton of cigarettes by an apparently sympathetic guard, who tells him to look out the window to see who sent them; when Durkin does, Lynn Michaels shoots him dead with a sniper rifle. Punisher fan Desmond Kline hears of his hero's death on TV. On the bus to Scranton, Microchip remotely actives the New Jersey warehouse's defenses just as the ATF moves in on it. When they attempt to blow their way in, the entire building is leveled. Later, Payback meets Lynn, who convinces him to partner with her until they take down VIGIL. The next day, Kline's co-workers tease him about Punisher's death. Kline, convinced Punisher is still alive, proclaims that as long as the city needs him Punisher will be there. Nails chastises Blackwell over his impetuousness, and offers him a second chance, instructing him to take down Lynn and Payback. Lynn takes Payback to a black market bank hidden in a meatpacking plant to drum up some capital for their war. They secure $250 grand when VIGIL arrives, just as Lynn was counting on.

NOTE: Cover labeled "Suicide Run: 4," continuing from Pun #86, '94 and into PWZ #24, '94 & Pun #87, '94. The credits are run over a grayscaled copy of the cover image. Letters page includes note explaining Max's appearance in PWJ #59, '93 after the dog's apparent demise in Pun #57, '91. Michaels assumes the Punisher name. Promotional material identified her as Lady Punisher to distinguish her from the other copycats, though she was not identified as such within the story.

PUNISHER WAR JOURNAL #63 (February 1994)

"Known Associates Pt. 7" (20 pages)

CREDITS: Chuck Dixon (writer), Gary Kwapisz (art), Glynis Oliver (colors), Janice Chiang (letters), Tim Tuohy (asst editor), Don Daley (editor)

FEATURE CHARACTER: Punisher (last in Pun #87, '94, next in PWZ #25, '94)

SUPPORTING CAST: Lynn Michaels (last in Pun #87, '94, next in PWZ #25, '94)

VILLAINS: Lt. Blackwell (last in Pun #87, '94, next in PWZ #25, '94), Rosalie Carbone (last in PWJ #61, '93, next in PWJ #73, '95) & her men, gangsters (all die), carjackers, August Dragon Clan, the Righteous Ones, Vaducci family

OTHER CHARACTERS: Payback, Sheriff Harry Bendix & his deputies inc Mose & Reed (dies), Amy Bendix (all last in Pun #87, '94, next in PWZ #25, '94), Marge (Amy's babysitter, last in PWZ #24, '94, next in PWJ #68, '94), "Hitman" Punisher (Jimmy Pierce, between Pun #87-88, '94), Outlaw (last in PWZ #24, '94, next in Pun #88, '94), Desmond Kline (dies), gas station attendant, FBI agents, VIGIL inc Dutton (1st, next in PWJ #73, '94), police inc Tommy; cowboys (on TV)

LOCATIONS/ITEMS: Laastekist inc sheriff's office, gas station, relay station & Bendix house; VIGIL HQ, motel, police station, Kline's apartment / Blackwell's radio & pick-up truck, beer, sponge, Kline's revolver, handgun, shotgun & knife; Outlaw's motorcycle & handgun, gangsters' limo & various guns, Dragons' jeep, Righteous Ones' motorcycles & map, FBI's car, Vaducci's private plane & limo, explosives & detonator, "Hitman" Punisher's car, bazooka, Uzi, police car (destroyed)

SYNOPSIS: Punisher wakes up in a jail cell with fingerprint ink on his fingers. He tries and fails to get an urgent audience with the sheriff, knowing putting his prints in the system will bring a whole world of trouble. VIGIL receives the hit and Blackwell is notified, prompting him to abandon his stakeout of Lynn and Payback's motel. Meanwhile Lynn contacts a police friend to check on her own status since she broke out of VIGIL custody, and is also informed that Punisher might be alive. Rosalie's men report the news to her, but she refuses to send anyone after Punisher. Elsewhere, Desmond Kline fashions himself a Punisher outfit and arms himself, preparing to take up the mantle. Outlaw takes down a group of gangsters, who reveal to him the news. In Laastekist, Sheriff Bendix is dubious when Punisher tries to warn him of impending trouble, but finally agrees to check why he hasn't gotten the fingerprints results yet. When he gets the runaround, Bendix grows worried. Meanwhile, several gangs and crime families make their way towards Laastekist. Back in the city, Kline confronts some carjackers, but stumbles, dropping his weapons, and is killed. As "Hitman" Punisher rolls into town, Blackwell blows the power plant to prevent anyone from getting in his way. As the lights go out, Bendix's deputies radio him to say they are under attack, moments before being slain by a rocket launcher, and another radio message informs him his daughter Amy has been taken hostage, in return for Punisher being handed over. Punisher tells him the only way to save her let him out and give him a gun.

NOTE: Cover labeled "Suicide Run: 7," continuing from Pun #87, '94 and into PWZ #25, '94 & Pun #88, '94. The credits are run over a grayscaled copy of the cover image. Pierce's criminal relatives blackmailed him into assuming the Punisher name, and so he is not considered a villain. Promotional material identified him as Hitman Punisher and Kline as "Idiot" Punisher to distinguish them from the other copycats, though they were not identified as such within the story.

PUNISHER WAR JOURNAL #64 (March 1994)

"Everything Changes Pt. 10" (30 pages)

CREDITS: Chuck Dixon (writer), Gary Kwapisz (art), Glynis Oliver (colors), Janice Chiang (letters), Freddy Mendez (asst editor), Don Daley (editor)
FEATURE CHARACTER: Punisher (last in Pun #88, '94)
SUPPORTING CAST: Microchip (last in PWJ #62, next in PWJ #68, '94), Lynn Michaels (last in Pun #88, '94, next in PWJ #68, '94), Mickey Fondozzi (last in PunSS #4/2, '94, next in PWJ #68, '94)
VILLAINS: Lt. Blackwell (last in Pun #88, '94), August Dragon Clan, the Righteous Ones, mugger (all die), Vaducci family inc Trevor
OTHER CHARACTERS: Payback (last in Pun #88, '94, next in PWJ #68, '94), Outlaw (last in Pun #88, '94, next in Pun Ann #7, '94), Sheriff Harry Bendix (last in Pun #88, '94, next in PWJ #67, '94), Tess Clay (last bts in Pun #88, '94), Vince, cameraman, doctor, doctor's friend, pilot, waitress, police, state troopers, bystanders

LOCATIONS/ITEMS: Laastekist inc gas station (destroyed), doctor's office, Tamanac ski lodge (destroyed); Lou's fine dining / various criminals' guns, police car, Vaducci's limo, pizza box, Punisher's shotgun & Mac-10, Bendix's assault rifle, news copter, TV camera, coffin, Micro's handgun, Mickey's handgun, troopers' cars, hearse, police barricades, Outlaw's motorcycle & Mac-10, various police guns, propane tanks, lighter
SYNOPSIS: Crooks corner Punisher and his captive Blackwell at a gas station until Sheriff Bendix comes to the rescue in his car. As they drive off and the police arrive, Vaducci's men convince him to withdraw. Elsewhere, Microchip convinces Mickey to join him in continuing the war on crime. With the town doctor's help, Payback smuggles the recuperating Lynn out of town inside a coffin, escaping a police roadblock when Outlaw blasts through it on his bike, providing a diversion. Bendix, Punisher and Blackwell abandon the car to hike to a ski lodge, but Blackwell refuses to go. Punisher sends Bendix on ahead, moments before Tess Clay arrives in a news helicopter; despite these witnesses, Punisher kills Blackwell. As the criminals follow, Punisher and Bendix reach the lodge, set up open propane tanks and take cover in the freezer box. One of the thugs uses a lighter to see and the place explodes. With all his pursuers dead or fled, Punisher leaves. Bendix lets Punisher go and tells police that Punisher died in the blast. Back in New York, Punisher resumes the war with a vengeance.
NOTE: Cover labeled "Suicide Run: 10," continuing from Pun #88, '94. This issue has a variant cover, the direct edition being a die-cut cover over the newsstand cover. Features a frontispiece of the grayscaled direct edition cover, with the credits run over an inverted color version.

2ND STORY: "Tunnel Vision" (6 pages)
CREDITS: Roger Salick (writer), Bill Wylie (pencils), Jay Oliveras (inks), Mike Thomas (colors), Jeffrey Powell (letters), Freddy Mendez (asst editor), Don Daley (editor)
FEATURE CHARACTER: Punisher (next in PWZ #26-30, Pun #89-92, PunSS #4, PWZ Ann #2, Pun:BSS #3, Pun #93, all '94, PWZ #31-40, '94-95, PunHol #3, '95, GR/W/P, '94, PWJ#61, '93)
VILLAINS: Subway gangbangers (2 die)
OTHER CHARACTERS: Conductor, bystanders (all bts)
LOCATIONS/ITEMS: Subway tunnel / subway train, Punisher's bottle, coat, staff, handgun & combat knife; bangers' knives
SYNOPSIS: A violent gang roams the subway tunnels, and Punisher disguises himself as a bum to flush them out. They take the bait and he toys with them before taking two out. He leaves one alive to spread the word to his friends: if they come down into the subway, they belong to Punisher.

PUNISHER WAR JOURNAL #65 (April 1994)

"Pariah!" (20 pages)

CREDITS: Steven Grant (writer), Hugh Haynes (pencils), Mark McKenna, Mike Gray, Scott Koblish (inks), Michael Higgins (letters), Jon Kalisz, Scott Marshall (colors), Freddy Mendez (asst editor), Don Daley (editor), Bill Sienkiewicz (c art)
FEATURE CHARACTER: Punisher (also news footage on TV)
GUEST STAR: Captain America (last in Av #375, '94)
VILLAINS: Derek Sternes (1st, VIGIL's new commander & secret Trust agent, next in PWJ #67, '94), Ermin (Machette's lackey, dies), Machette (bts on phone to Ermin), Rudger (crooked cop, dies), drug dealers, Machette's helicopter pilot (dies)
OTHER CHARACTERS: VIGIL inc Capt. Nails (last in Pun #88, '94, next in PWJ #67, '94), John Lowe (1st, Justice Department, VIGIL's new field commander); Bernard Modine (bts, last in Pun '85, '93), Tess Clay, Tony (1st, Tess' cameraman), Tess' helicopter pilot (bts), Bill Clinton (last bts in Nova #9, '94, next in PWJ #73, '94), Hilary Clinton (last in Wlk&IW #22, '93, next bts in IHulk #463, '98), Attorney General Janet Reno (bts), Eddie (corpse, Ermin's victim), NYPD inc Recon One, Jacobs & Rudger; homeless Brooklynites, bar patrons, government hearing attendees, cop's family, Secret Service, White House aides, Lt. Taylor Blackwell (news footage)
LOCATIONS/ITEMS: East New York inc Brooklyn w/Brooklyn Bridge & drugs lab; bar, hearing room, family home / VIGIL guns, body armor & buses; tanks, NYPD riot gear, cars, guns, radios, shotgun & flares; Eddie's suitcase w/cocaine & cash, Machette's "police" helicopter (destroyed), news helicopter, Tony's TV camera
SYNOPSIS: As news footage of Punisher killing Blackwell shocks the nation, the President appoints Derek Sternes the new head of VIGIL, and tasks him with Punisher's capture. In turn, Sternes appoints Derek Lowe VIGIL's new field commander, sidelining Captain Nails to a desk job. Having tracked the vigilante to the crime-ridden East New York, they cordon off the area and send in a massive taskforce of police and VIGIL agents, unaware Punisher deliberately let himself be tracked there, intending to trick the forces pursuing him into cleaning out the gangs and

drug labs. Ermin, a small-time crook working for crimelord Machette, finds himself trapped within the cordon having just killed a man to retrieve a briefcase full of cocaine stolen from his boss, and runs right by Punisher. After overpowering some pursuing cops, Punisher sees Ermin about to climb aboard a fake police helicopter sent by Machette to retrieve him, and shoots it down with a flare gun. Ermin runs into a crooked cop he knows, Rudger, and offers to make a deal to get out, showing him the cocaine, but Rudger kills him, intending to take the drugs for himself. Punisher witnesses this and guns Rudger down, his actions caught by a helicopter news crew once again, reconfirming his new reputation as a cop killer. Lowe arrives and orders the forces holding the perimeter to enter the neighborhood, irregardless of anyone in their way, and not to bother taking the Punisher alive, but his order is countermanded by another new arrival, Captain America, who insists he will bring Punisher in.
NOTE: Cover labeled "Pariah Part One." Includes armory page on Carleton COBRA (Closed-Circuit Oxygen Breathing Apparatus).

PUNISHER WAR JOURNAL #66 (May 1994)

"Last Exit" (20 pages)

CREDITS: Steven Grant (writer), Hugh Haynes (pencils), Mark McKenna, Mike Gray, Scott Koblish (inks), Michael Higgins (inks, letters), Jon Kalisz (colors), Freddy Mendez (asst editor), Don Daley (editor), Brent Eric Anderson (c art)
FEATURE CHARACTER: Punisher
GUEST STAR: Captain America (next in Cap #428, '94)
VILLAINS: Machette (East New York crimelord, next in PWJ #68, '94) & his men inc Willy (Eddie's brother, dies), kidnapper (dies)
OTHER CHARACTERS: Tess Clay, Tony, Tess' helicopter pilot, VIGIL inc John Lowe, NYPD inc Lou, kidnapped women, East New York family, homeless people
LOCATIONS/ITEMS: East New York inc Brooklyn, kidnapper's den, family apartment / NYPD's riot armor, radios, guns, rocket launcher, Eddie's suitcase w/cocaine & cash, Captain America's shield, Machette's blades, news helicopter, Tony's TV camera, water tower
SYNOPSIS: Punisher continues to evade pursuing cops, running through an alleyway full of vagrants then blocking the path behind him by throwing the cocaine he took off Rudger into the air, so that the down and outs start a free-for-all trying to get it, but he is intercepted by Captain America. Meanwhile Machette executes the man whose brother stole Machette's cocaine and who then hired Ermin to retrieve it, then orders his men to capture whoever has his drugs and bring them to him to be made an example of. Punisher and Cap brawl, but a degenerative disease is weakening Cap and Punisher makes a break, reaching the rooftops. As police helicopters with snipers close in, Tess Clay's news helicopter moves closer to capture the action; with Cap moments behind him, Punisher moves next to a water tower. The snipers take their shot, but Punisher hunches, taking some hits on his Kevlar and letting the rest strike the tower. It breaks open, and Cap blocks the water torrenting towards him with his shield. Punisher jumps onto the shield, and uses it to spring aboard Tess' helicopter, hijacking it to make his getaway. As the news helicopter heads for Manhattan, Cap stops John Lowe from having it shot down.
NOTE: Cover labeled "Pariah Part Two." Includes armory page on trapshooting clay & Sturm Ruger SP-101 pistol (1 page) and GI folding shovel & Atlas Snowshoe Company snow shoes (1 page). Cap's weakness here relates to a storyline in his own comic.

PUNISHER WAR JOURNAL #67 (June 1994)

"Nailed" (15 pages)

CREDITS: Steven Grant (writer), Hugh Haynes (pencils), Mark McKenna, Mike Gray, Scott Koblish (inks), Michael Higgins (letters), Jon Kalisz (colors), Freddy Mendez (asst editor), Don Daley (editor), Elman Brown (c art), Justin F. Gabrie (c color)
FEATURE CHARACTER: Punisher
GUEST STAR: Spider-Man (last in BCat #4, '94, chr last in SMU #11/2, '96)
VILLAIN: Derek Sternes (last in PWJ #65, '94)
OTHER CHARACTERS: Sheriff Harry Bendix (last in PWJ #64, '94), VIGIL inc Capt. Nails (last in PWJ #65, '94), John Lowe & Hal (bts, see NOTE); Tess Clay, Tony, Tess' helicopter pilot; Barry Crease (WENO-3 reporter), Barry's cameraman, Barry's helicopter pilot (bts), "Punisher's" corpse (last in PWZ #24, '94), Joseph Highland (prev 2 bts, see NOTE), NYPD snipers & divers, Roosevelt Island tram users, reporter (on TV), diners, bystanders
LOCATIONS/ITEMS: Sterne's Washington office, VIGIL HQ inc Nails' office, Laastekist inc sheriff's office, New York City inc East River, Queensboro Bridge, 24 Hour Mail Boxes, restaurant / news helicopters, Tony's TV camera, Barry Crease's TV camera, Nails' TV, armor, radio & guns, Sternes' TV, NYPD helicopters, rifles, boats & scuba gear; Punisher's mailbox & guns, parachutes, Roosevelt Island tram, kitchen knives, Spider-Man's webshooters & Spider-signal
SYNOPSIS: With police helicopters in hot pursuit of Punisher's hijacked new helicopter, Punisher orders everyone else to parachute out as they cross the East River; only seconds later, once the police are sure Punisher is alone on board, they shoot his helicopter out the sky, but he bails out unnoticed and clings on to the side of the Roosevelt Island tram. Meanwhile, two VIGIL agents arrive in Laastekist and arrest Sheriff Bendix for aiding and abetting the Punisher, and back in New York Spider-Man learns of the Punisher pursuit from a TV report. Having also seen that Punisher was heading into Manhattan, Captain Nails leaves the VIGIL offices and goes hunting. Punisher retrieves fresh armor and weapons from one of his drop-boxes, but Nails is waiting, as VIGIL had located the drop box some time earlier. They fight a running battle, with Nails determined to stop the man he believes is a cop-killer, but Punisher finally gets the drop on him, then departs without slaying him. As the vigilante runs outside, he is caught in the beam of Spider-Man's spider-signal.
NOTE: Cover labeled "Pariah Part Three." Includes page displaying letters between NYC deputy coroner Joseph Highland & Hal at VIGIL forensic division discussing Punisher's survival when Manhattan Tower was destroyed.

2ND STORY: "Trouble Part I" (5 pages)
CREDITS: Steven Grant (writer), Elman Brown (pencils), Scott Koblish (inks), Susan Crespi (letters), Joe Andreani (colors), Freddy Mendez (asst editor), Don Daley (editor)
FEATURE CHARACTER: Jimmy Pierce (last as "Hitman" Punisher in Pun #88, '94)
VILLAINS: Lori Pierce (Jimmy's sister), Duke Cullen, Davey-Boy Cullen (members of Cullen crime family) (all 1st)
LOCATIONS/ITEMS: Manhattan inc 12th Ave, 2nd Ave w/Lori Pierce's apartment / stolen car (destroyed), Jimmy's Punisher outfit & guns
SYNOPSIS: Two joyriding Cullens, members of the Cullen crime family, are run off the road by a man dressed like Punisher, and forced to

give up family head Tommy "Peach" Cullen's location. Shortly thereafter Lori Pierce returns to her apartment to be confronted by her brother, Jimmy, still dressed as the Punisher. He explains the outfit was their uncle Peach's idea, and that he is back to make Peach pay for the trouble he has caused.

PUNISHER WAR JOURNAL #68 (July 1994)

"Pariah Part 4: Bad Turn" (15 pages)

CREDITS: Steven Grant (writer), Hugh Haynes (pencils), Mark McKenna, Mick Gray (inks), Scott Koblish (inks, c pencils), Michael Higgins (letters), John Kalisz (colors), Freddy Mendez (asst editor), Don Daley (editor), Elman Brown (c inks)
FEATURE CHARACTER: Punisher
GUEST STAR: Spider-Man (next in SM #47, '94)
SUPPORTING CAST: Microchip (last in PWJ #64, '94, next in Pun Ann #7, '94), Mickey Fondozzi (also as Tower, last in PWJ #64, '94, next in PWZ #41, '95)
VILLAINS: Derek Sternes (next in PWJ #70, '94), Machette (last in PWJ #66, '94) & his men inc Boone (disguised as VIGIL agent), Angela (bts, last in Pun #5, '86) & her 2 technicians (1st), Brown
OTHER CHARACTERS: Sheriff Harry Bendix (next in PWJ #70, '94), Amy Bendix (last in PWZ #25, '94), Dr. Melinda Brewer (last in Pun #62, '92, next in PWJ #70, '94), Marge (last in PWJ #63, '94, next bts in PWJ #73, '94), Lynn Michaels, Payback (both last in PWJ #64, '94, next in PWJ #70, '94), Tess Clay, producer, cameraman, assistant, VIGIL inc Capt. Nails, John Lowe (both next in PWJ #70, '94), Brady (last in Pun #88, '94, next in PWJ #70, '94)
LOCATIONS/ITEMS: Factory, TV studio, Bendix house, VIGIL HQ, Brewer's basement, Vietnam War memorial, Machette's slaughterhouse / Punisher's Battle Van; Spider-Man's web-shooters & spider-signal, "VIGIL" van, Machette's men's guns, Brewer's flashlight, Micro's specialized Walkman, envelope of money, Machette's sword
SYNOPSIS: Two men wheel Punisher's van into a factory and try to get past its defenses and break in. Elsewhere, Spider-Man, believing Punisher a cop-killer, overpowers him and leaves him for arriving VIGIL agents. However, the agents are actually Machettes' disguised men. Meanwhile real VIGIL agents brutally interrogate Sheriff Bendix on Sternes' orders. In Melinda Brewer's basement, where Payback has brought the unconscious Lynn Michaels for medical help following the battle in Laastekist, Lynn finally wakes and weakly calls out for Punisher. Upset, Payback leaves. Meanwhile, Micro and Mickey purchase something illegal from a criminal. At Machette's slaughterhouse, Machette's men check on the unmoving Punisher, who attacks them and escapes into the ventilation system. Informed of this, Machette demands Punisher be recaptured so he can torture the location of his money out of Punisher.
NOTE: Cover labeled "Pariah Part Four." Features armory pages on DOS500-T2 optical surveillance system (1 page) & portable ballistic shielding for car doors (1 page). The fake VIGIL van is disguised as a "Bobbit Plumbing" van, with a logo showing a tap with the end sliced off. The operation Micro and Mickey were conducting here is never followed up on.

2ND STORY: "Trouble Part Two: Family Values" (5 pages)
CREDITS: Steven Grant (writer), Kevin Kobasic (breakdowns), Elman Brown (pencils, inks), Susan Crespi (letters), Joe Andreani (colors), Freddy Mendez (asst editor), Don Daley (editor)
FEATURE CHARACTER: Jimmy Pierce
VILLAINS: Lori Pierce (next in PWJ #70, '94), Davey-Boy Cullen, Duke Cullen (dies)
OTHER CHARACTER: Philip (medical student, friend of Lori's)
LOCATIONS/ITEMS: Lori's apartment / Philip's medical bag, Dave & Duke's handguns, frying pan, handcuffs, shower curtain
SYNOPSIS: Lori's friend Philip patches Jimmy up, but as he is about to leave Lori's apartment, Davey-Boy and Duke burst in. Jimmy stuns Duke with a frying pan and takes his gun, then uses Duke as a shield to force Davey-Boy to surrender. Jimmy handcuffs Duke to the shower, but Lori wants to shoot Davey-Boy, hating them for the family's treatment of her while Jimmy was away. Jimmy takes Davey-Boy with him, intending to use him to get to Tommy Cullen, but after they leave, Lori suffocates Duke with the shower curtain, swearing that once Jimmy kills the hated Cullens, she will kill Jimmy in turn for abandoning her.

PUNISHER WAR JOURNAL #69 (August 1994)

"Pariah, the Conclusion: Strict Time!" (15 pages)

CREDITS: Steven Grant (writer), Hugh Haynes (pencils, c art), Mark McKenna, Mike Gray, Scott Koblish (inks), Michael Higgins (letters), Karl Bollers (colors), Freddy Mendez (asst editor), Don Daley (editor)
FEATURE CHARACTER: Punisher (next in Pun #94, '94)
VILLAINS: Machette (dies) & his men (most die) inc Boone (dies) & Zafiro (1st, next in PWJ #74, '95); Angela (next in PWJ #71, '95), Clarence (Angela's muscle), Angela's 2 technicians (1 dies, other next in PWJ #74, '95)
LOCATIONS/ITEMS: Machette's slaughterhouse / Machette's men's guns & stun dart; Machette's swords & skull-shaped glasses, Punisher's Battle Van & War Journal, Clarence's gun
SYNOPSIS: Punisher fights his way out of the slaughterhouse but finds himself trapped atop a cliff, and is recaptured. Meanwhile the two men who have been trying to breach Punisher's Battle Van manage to retrieve his War Journal from the vehicle's wreckage. Soon afterwards their employer, Angela of the Trust, arrives; she claims the book and has her bodyguard, Clarence, gun both men down. Back at the slaughterhouse Machette sends one of his men away to deal with urgent business, then challenges Punisher to a sword duel in front of the rest of his men. Punisher agrees, but goes unarmed, knowing Machette will be the superior swordsman; instead, Punisher cheats, elbowing one of the armed spectators in the throat, snatching his gun and shooting Machette dead. He then retrieves Machette's sword and turns on the rest of the drug lord's men. A short while later he walks out of Machette's home carrying the bloodstained blade and wearing Machette's skull-shaped sunglasses.
NOTE: Cover labeled "Pariah Part Five." Includes armory pages on stun guns & Paralyser batons (1 page) and IR lasers & N/BIS-3 Night Multi-Purpose Commander Binocular (1 page), both by Eliot R. Brown (art) & John Wellington (colors).

2ND STORY: "Homecoming: Trouble Part 3" (5 pages)
CREDITS: Steven Grant (writer), Kevin Kobasic (breakdowns), Elman Brown (pencils), Scott Koblish (inks), Susan Crespi (letters), Joe Andreani (colors), Freddy Mendez (asst editor), Don Daley (editor)
FEATURE CHARACTER: Jimmy Pierce
VILLAINS: Cullens inc Davey-Boy & Lyle, Tommy "Peach" Cullen (last in Pun #87, '94), Midge Cullen (Jimmy's mother, 1st but chr last in PWJ #70/2, '94 fb)
LOCATIONS/ITEMS: Cullen Park Avenue Penthouse / Cullen guns, coffee pot, Jimmy's rope
SYNOPSIS: As the Cullens gather for a war council chaired by Tommy Cullen, Jimmy Pierce spots his mother, Midge Cullen, standing by the window of an adjoining room. Tommy threatened to kill Midge to make him become the family's ersatz Punisher, so Jimmy breaks in to rescue her. He knocks out Lyle Cullen, who is guarding her, and tells his surprised mother he is there to get her out, but as he prepares to crash the family meeting, she stuns him with a coffee pot, telling him he is no better than his father. As Jimmy struggles to rise, he sees his mother standing alongside the other Cullens, while Tommy leans over him, chastising him for not going against the family.

PUNISHER WAR JOURNAL #70 (September 1994)

"Warm Bodies: Last Entry Prelude" (17 pages)

CREDITS: Steven Grant (writer), Hugh Haynes (pencils), Scott Koblish (inks), Lia Pelosi, Jon Kalisz (letters), Jade Moede (colors), Freddy Mendez (asst editor), Don Daley (editor)
FEATURE CHARACTER: Punisher (also in pictures, last in Pun #95, '94)
SUPPORTING CAST: Lynn Michaels (last in PWJ #68, '94, next in PWJ #73, '94)
VILLAIN: Derek Sternes (last in PWJ #68, '94, next in PWJ #73, '94)
OTHER CHARACTERS: Payback (last in PWJ #68, '94, next in PWJ #75, '95), Sheriff Harry Bendix (last in PWJ #68, '94, next in PWJ #73, '94), Amy Bendix, Marge (both in video recordings); Dr. Melinda Brewer (last in PWJ #68, '94), VIGIL inc Rigg (last in Pun #88, '94, next in PWJ #75, '95), Capt. Nail, John Lowe, Brady (prev 3 last in PWJ #68, '94, next in PWJ #73, '94); NYPD, Bob's Bar patrons & bartender, car salesman
LOCATIONS/ITEMS: VIGIL HQ, Bendix house (on video), Bob's Bar, Melinda Brewer's basement / Punisher wanted posters, Nails' guns & armor, police cars, Greyhound bus, 2nd hand car
SYNOPSIS: Derek Sterns oversees Harry Bendix's interrogation, tormenting him with threats against his daughter Amy, and demanding to know about the Punisher's organization, sure Bendix was part of it. Meanwhile Nails responds to a police call for assistance, as they think they may have Punisher cornered in a bar. It proves to be Payback, drowning his sorrows over his family's deaths and because Lynn, who he has fallen for, apparently loves Punisher and may be dying. Nails and Payback fight, but after knocking Nails down, Payback leaves him to return to his drink, giving Nails time to recover. Believing Payback and Lynn murdered VIGIL agent Jessup, Nails pummels Payback, who surrenders, still too badly injured from when corrupt VIGIL agent tortured him. Payback's surprise at hearing of Jessup's death, makes Nails begin to reconsider what he thought he knew, and he realizes Blackwell might have crossed the line and then murdered Jessup to cover it up, which in turn might explain why Punisher killed Blackwell. Nevertheless, Nails takes Payback into custody. Meanwhile, an incognito Punisher buys himself a second hand car. Back in New York City, Nails finds Melinda Brewer's name in Payback's address book, and goes there intending to apprehend Lynn. However, Lynn is gone, and is now watching VIGIL HQ, planning to attack it and kill Blackwell, unaware he is already dead.

2ND STORY: "Trouble Part 4: Tough Love" (5 pages)
CREDITS: Steven Grant (writer), Kevin Kobasic, Elman Brown (pencils), Frank Percy (inks), Susan Crespi (letters), Joe Andreani (colors), Freddy Mendez (asst editor), Don Daley (editor)
FEATURE CHARACTER: Jimmy Pierce
VILLAINS: Cullens inc Tommy Cullen, Midge Cullen (next in PWJ #72, '94, also in fb to chr 1st prior to PWJ #69, '94)
OTHER CHARACTERS: Jack Pierce (Jimmy's father, in fb), Lori Pierce (last in PWJ #68, '94)
LOCATIONS/ITEMS: Cullens' Park Avenue Penthouse, New York (in fb) / Cullen guns & knives, Lori's gun, Jack's motorbike, plane (both in fb)
FLASHBACKS: Midge Cullen fell in love with wild boy Jack Pierce. Though this angered her close-knit family, he was allowed to live for her sake, and offered a place in the family business, but he refused to kill for them. However, he was willing to kill for his country when conscripted, leaving behind his pregnant and angry wife.
SYNOPSIS: Midge Cullen taunts her son, telling him how she came to hate his father for spurning the Cullen family. Since Jimmy has also rejected the family, Tommy Cullen orders his demise, but Lori interrupts, crashing into the room with a gun, and she and Jimmy make a break for it.

PUNISHER WAR JOURNAL #71 (October 1994)

"Last Entry – Part One: Road to Death" (17 pages)

CREDITS: Steven Grant (writer), Hugh Haynes (pencils), Scott Koblish (inks, c inks), Mick Gray (inks), Mike Higgins (letters), Jon Kalisz (colors), Freddy Mendez (asst editor), Don Daley (editor)
FEATURE CHARACTER: Punisher
VILLAINS: Viva Paina (assassin, Mondo Paine's sister), Goose (assassin, dies), Angela (last in PWJ #69, '94, next in PWJ #75, '95)
OTHER CHARACTERS: Lu Vincent (reporter), Dave (bts, Lu's editor), janitor, bystanders
LOCATIONS/ITEMS: Gas stations, Angela's house, Verona inc town hall, Rexburg / welding torch & mask, 2nd hand car, Lu's car (destroyed), bomb, Viva & Goose's car, Goose's binoculars, gun & knife, Viva's knife, Punisher's War Journal, payphone, Punisher's skull-shaped glasses
SYNOPSIS: As the Punisher finishes fixing up his second-hand car at a gas station, a woman, reporter Lu Vincent, pulls up, and, mistaking him for a mechanic, asks him to check her car, since the newly installed battery seems to have conked out. When he checks under the bonnet, he sees a bomb, and tackles the woman away from the vehicle just before it explodes. The assassins who planted the device, the assassins Viva and Goose, watch the detonation through binoculars, angrily noting their target's survival, and pursue as Punisher bundles the woman into his car and races away. While Goose drives, Viva calls their employer, Angela, to update her on the situation;

Angela insists they keep the kill discrete, so it can't be traced back to her. Reaching the small town of Verona, Punisher drops Lu off at the town hall, but it is virtually deserted, and as she is about to leave the two killers confront her and drag her into the basement. Having spotted the killers following Lu into the building, Punisher intervenes, and Lu flees. Goose gets a lucky shot in, knocking Punisher out, but Viva stops Goose from finishing him, since there's no money in it. They follow Lu into the street, and while Viva holds bystanders at gunpoint to stop them interfering, Goose chases Lu down. Just before he reaches her, Punisher's car runs him down, and Punisher orders Lu to get in while Viva is still in shock at her partner's demise. Punisher drops Lu off at a payphone and departs, but as Lu calls her editor, she suddenly realizes who her savior was, and she tells her editor to scrap the political book she was working on, as she plans to write one about the Punisher.

2ND STORY: "Trouble Part 5: Father's Day" (5 pages)
CREDITS: Steven Grant (writer), Elman Brown (pencils), Frank Percy (inks), Susan Crespi (letters), Joe Andreani (colors), Freddy Mendez (asst editor), Don Daley (editor)
FEATURE CHARACTER: Jimmy Pierce (also as baby in photo)
GUEST STAR: Punisher
VILLAINS: Cullens inc Tommy Cullen
OTHER CHARACTERS: Lori Pierce, Jack Pierce (photo), Jack's girlfriend (mentioned)
LOCATIONS/ITEMS: Storage facility inc Lori's locker / Jack's diary, Lori's flashlight, Punisher's second hand car
SYNOPSIS: Telling Jimmy about how terrible it was for her, left with their abusive mother, Midge, while Jimmy was on the road, and how she dreamed he would come back and rescue her, Lori takes Jimmy to a storage facility, where she shows him a locker of their father's things that she retrieved after Midge threw them out. It includes their father's diary, which reveals he brought a woman home with him from the war; the diary, finished by Jack Pierce's lover after he died, explains that Midge and Tommy murdered him for this. However, even this revelation can't convince Jimmy to kill, and he departs, telling the rage-filled Lori she is on her own. Lori keeps screaming at him long after he has gone, right up until Tommy and some of the Cullen boys find her. A short while later Jimmy is hitchhiking, looking to go anywhere but the place he currently is. A car stops and he climbs in, not realizing the driver is the Punisher.

PUNISHER WAR JOURNAL #72 (November 1994)

"Last Entry Pt2: Truck Stop Women!" (22 pages)

CREDITS: Steven Grant (writer), Melvin Rubi (pencils), Scott Koblish (inks, c inks), Frank Percy (inks), Vickie Williams (letters), Jon Kalisz (colors), Freddy Mendez (asst editor), Don Daley (editor)
FEATURE CHARACTER: Punisher (next in Pun:EQ, '94 fb)
GUEST STAR: Jimmy Pierce
VILLAINS: Cullens inc Huey, Bobo, Quince (prev 3 Tommy's sons), Chalky, Sid, Tommy Cullen, Midge Cullen (last in PWJ #70, '94); Lori Pierce
LOCATIONS/ITEMS: Rust belt, Haji's Truck Stop / Punisher's guns, shotgun, skull-shaped glasses & second hand car, Cullens' car & guns, Tommy Cullen's limo
SYNOPSIS: A car full of Cullens attacks the Punisher's vehicle on the road, but he shoots their tire out, causing them to crash. A few minutes later Tommy Cullen's limo arrives; he chastises his sons for failing to catch Jimmy Pierce, and tells them to get in the limo, which is already full with Midge Cullen, various Cullen girls, and their prisoner, Lori Pierce. Punisher stops at an abandoned truck stop, and, not realizing the mobsters were actually after his passenger, lends Jimmy a gun and tells him to hide. Punisher watches from the truck stop's roof as the Cullens arrive and spread out to hunt their prey, and he begins picking them off one by one. With all the men and her mother inside, Lori makes a break from the limo, pursued by the Cullen girls. While Punisher kills all the younger Cullen men, Jimmy confronts Midge and Tommy, holding them at gunpoint and trying to reason with them. When Lori arrives and demands the Punisher slay their father, Jimmy angrily points out that her birth date means she was conceived while Jack Pierce was in Vietnam. Promising to leave forever, and pointing out that Tommy can always replace the sons he has lost, so long as he survives this encounter, Jimmy convinces Tommy there is nothing left to gain with continuing the feud, but Lori grabs Jimmy's gun and shoots both Midge and Tommy. Jimmy snatches the gun off her, but she promises to tell the Cullens that he is the killer, ensuring they will never stop hunting him. Jimmy opens the door to be confronted by Punisher. As he flees, Punisher hears Lori calling Jimmy a Cullen, but lets him go, unconcerned by the possibility that one criminal killed another. Once he departs the Cullen girls corner Lori, but Tommy, clinging to life, tells the women to accept Lori as their new leader, feeling she has proven herself a true Cullen. As Jimmy flees through the night, Lori promises to modernize the gang and make it more powerful than ever.

PUNISHER WAR JOURNAL #73 (December 1994)

"Final Entry Part 3: A Journal of the Plague Years" (22 pages)

CREDITS: Steven Grant (writer), Melvin Rubi (pencils), Scott Koblish (inks), Frank Percy (inks, c inks), Vickie Williams (letters), Jon Kalisz (colors), Freddy Mendez (asst editor), Don Daley (editor)
FEATURE CHARACTER: Punisher (next in Pun:EQ, '94)
GUEST STAR: Lynn Michaels (last in PWJ #70, '94, becomes Punisher)
VILLAINS: Cussler (Luminoso's courier, dies), Truby & his 2 compatriots (Reno crooks, die), Sendero Luminoso (drug lord, mentioned, see NOTE), Rosalie Carbone (last in PWJ #63, '94), Mondo Paine (last in Pun #85, '93), Derek Sternes (last in PWJ #70, '94, next in PWJ #75, '95)
OTHER CHARACTERS: VIGIL inc Capt. Nails, John Lowe, (both last in PWJ #70, '94), Dutton (last in PWJ #63, '94), Einhorn, Letz (both 1st) (all next in PWJ #75, '95), Brady (last in PWJ #70, '94); Sheriff Harry Bendix (last in PWJ #70, '94), Marge, Amy Bendix (both bts, last in PWJ #68, '94), Bill Clinton (last in PWJ #65, '94, next in Cap #444, '95), Luigi (Rosalie's butler), Sandy (bts, Rosalie's friend, on phone), Secret Service man
LOCATIONS/ITEMS: Reno inc casino, Central Park, VIGIL HQ inc holding cells & chapel, Washington inc Capitol Building w/Sternes' office, Rosalie's mansion / Punisher's gun & skull-shaped glasses, Truby's car & gun, Cussler's briefcase w/money, passport & ticket to Peru, VIGIL flier, Lynn's rifle
SYNOPSIS: In Reno, Punisher kills some mobsters who have just murdered another criminal's courier, and retrieves the courier's package, which includes a ticket to Peru. Intrigued, he decides to follow the trail to South America. In Washington DC, Derek Sternes tries to convince the president

to expand VIGIL's powers, turning them into a national police force; the president agrees to consider the proposal. Back in Manhattan, Lynn Michaels shoots down a VIGIL flier as it flies over Central Park during the night. Meanwhile, in VIGIL's headquarters, agent Einhorn is on guard duty, monitoring the cells where Harry Bendix and Payback are being held. He is shocked to learn from Nails that Bendix has been held without charge for weeks, but is overheard by John Lowe, who angrily tells him not to worry about the prisoners' rights. Lynn uses the commandeered flier to get into VIGIL, and begins fighting her way through the building looking for Blackwell, only to discover he is already dead. When a call goes out for all available personnel to assist in her capture, Einhorn takes the opportunity to let Bendix out his cell, giving him a chance to escape. With the odds against her mounting, Lynn tries to escape, but is caught by agent Dutton, who intends to shoot her, seeing this as balancing the scales for Blackwell's death. However, Bendix tackles him, and joins Lynn. They run into Nails, but he makes no attempt to stop them, and the pair exit the building. Harry quickly calls home to tell his babysitter to get his daughter Amy somewhere safe. In the aftermath of Lynn's raid, Lowe suspends Einhorn, but Nails is impressed with him, and decides to take Einhorn into his confidence. Meanwhile Rosalie Carbone instructs Mondo Paine to find Lynn and kill her.

NOTE: Punisher going to Peru leads him into the events of Pun:EQ, '94, which reveals Luminoso's 1st name.

PUNISHER WAR JOURNAL #74 (January 1995)

"Final Entry Part 4: Deadstop!" (22 pages)

CREDITS: Steven Grant (writer), Melvin Rubi (pencils), Frank Percy (inks), Vickie Williams (letters), Ian Laughlin (colors), Freddy Mendez (asst editor), Don Daley (editor)
FEATURE CHARACTER: Punisher (also in photo, between Pun #96-97, '94)
GUEST STAR: Lynn Michaels (as Punisher)
VILLAINS: Mondo Paine, Rosalie Carbone, Zafiro (last in PWJ #69, '95) & his men; Paine's men, drug dealers (die), Blind Joe Death (as Sammy, assassin posing as newsstand owner, 1st)
OTHER CHARACTERS: Harry Bendix, undercover cops (1 dies) inc Jody Coyle (last in PWZ #1, '92), Detective Sagrada (1st), Stew (cop), Angela's technician (last in PWJ #69, '94), Philadelphia bystanders, criminals & victim (prev 2 in photo)
LOCATIONS/ITEMS: Philadelphia inc newsstand, Manhattan inc drug dealers' apartment, Lynn's riverside hideout & factory / newspaper, Zafiro's van & gun; Paine's knife, cops' guns, radio mike, Rosalie's yacht, Zafiro & Paine's men's guns, police cars
SYNOPSIS: Back in the USA, Punisher sees newspaper reports of a new, female Punisher, but is unbothered by this, glad to still be considered dead. Soon after, Mondo Paine and Zafiro, former lieutenant of the late Machette and now a drug lord in his own right, strike a deal to work together to take down the female Punisher. A few weeks later a drug deal goes wrong when the dealers realize their buyers are undercover cops. They gun down one officer, but Lynn Michaels crashes into the apartment and kills the dealers down before they can slay the other cop, Jody Coyle, then flees as other police arrive. She returns to the riverside hideout she and Harry Bendix are sharing, unaware Carbone's men have tracked them down. The mobsters attack, and Mondo battles Lynn, their fight taking them down under the house, next to the river. Getting the upper hand, Mondo prepares to shoot Lynn. Meanwhile police find the technicians who broke into Punisher's Battle Van for Angela; one is still alive, and tells the detectives that Angela has Punisher's War Journal, containing all the vigilante's secrets.

PUNISHER WAR JOURNAL #75 (February 1995)

"Final Entry: Conclusion!" (37 pages)

CREDITS: Steven Grant, Chuck Dixon (writers), Hugh Haynes (pencils), Scott Koblish, Peter Palmiotti, Don Hudson, Rod Ramos (inks), Vickie Williams (letters), John Kalisz, Chia Chi Wang, Ian Laughlin, Colin Jorgensen (colors), Freddy Mendez (asst editor), Don Daley (editor), Bobbie Chase (group editor), Mark Texeira (c art)
FEATURE CHARACTER: Lynn Michaels
GUEST STAR: Punisher (between Pun #100-101, '95)
VILLAINS: Rosalie Carbone (next in Pun #100, '95), Angela (last in PWJ #71, '94), Blind Joe Death, Heathen (mercenary, 1st), Mondo Pain, Derek Sternes (last in PWJ #73, '94), Punishment Squad (others last in Pun #5, '86, some die, some or others next in PWJ #77, '95), Ricky (gang member, dies)
OTHER CHARACTERS: Payback (last in PWJ #70, '94), Sheriff Harry Bendix, VIGIL inc Capt. Nails, John Lowe, Einhorn, Dutton, Letz (prev 5 last in PWJ #73, '94), Rigg (last in PWJ #70, '94), Bancroft, West (both 1st); homeless people, police (some die) inc Sgt. Galas, waiters, bystanders
LOCATIONS/ITEMS: Sternes' office in Washington, DC; VIGIL HQ, subway station, Heathen's museum, Manhattan Tower II construction site, Payback's apartment, Lynn's riverside hideout & apartment (bts), Castle family home reconstruction in Cringelli Manufacturing sub-basement / Punisher's War Journal, journal replicas, Blind Joe's cane gun/knife & rifle, Lynn's handgun & motorcycle; police guns & boat, VIGIL radios, jets & guns; Dutton's Uzi, Letz's handgun, oil drum, cruise ship, ship phone, Payback's gear & shotgun, Punisher's rifle
SYNOPSIS: A gang member carrying Punisher's War Journal is killed by sightless assassin Blind Joe Death, who takes the book. Meanwhile, river police interrupt Mondo and Lynn's confrontation; Mondo kills one and Lynn stops Mondo from slaying the other, then flees. In the floors above, police arrest Bendix. Elsewhere, Angela tells Sternes to have VIGIL pursue the missing war journal. These new orders pull VIGIL's surveillance team off Lynn's apartment; Lynn overhears and follows. Meanwhile, the Punishment Squad spots Blind Joe and pursues him to a museum, but scatter as VIGIL arrives. Lynn races to the museum; Lentz and Dutton pursue. Joe leads Lynn to his employer, Heathen, who now has the book. Dutton and Letz burst in and Heathen escapes, dropping the journal. Letz follows Heathen while Lynn takes the journal and escapes from Dutton. Joe and Heathen ambush and murder Letz while Lynn escapes. Mondo watches, then spots the journal, seemingly dropped during the confusion. Later, Lowe chastises VIGIL for their failure until Einhorn reveals he found the journal in the rubble. Sternes gives it to the arriving Angela. Lynn reads the journal she found and dismayed at its cold, psychopathic tone, burns it and decides to find her own way. Mondo negotiates selling the journal to Rosalie Carbone. Angela confronts Heathen, having realized her copy is a phony. Angela produces the real War Journal and then disposes of it, explaining he had forgeries created to sow disinformation, noting Castle never knew about him, despite being so useful to Heathen for so long. Lynn recruits Payback. Meanwhile, Punisher sits alone, trapped in a wrecked replica of his family home.

NOTE: This issue's inkers and colorists are credited on the letters page. Part of Lynn's caption is obscured on p37 panel 2. The Punishment Squad call themselves the Terminal here, presumably to prevent them being tied back to the Trust. Heathen's comments suggest he manipulated Punisher to his own ends for some time, but exactly how is not revealed before Heathen is slain in PWJ #78, '95. The final panel references events taking place in Pun #100-101, '95.

PUNISHER WAR JOURNAL #76 (March 1995)

"Stone Dead" (21 pages)

CREDITS: Chuck Dixon (writer), Mel Rubi (pencils), Frank Percy, Reggie Jones (inks), Vickie Williams (letters), John Kalisz (colors), Chris Cooper (editor), Bobbie Chase (group editor), Hugh Haynes (c pencils), Scott Koblish (c inks)
FEATURE CHARACTER: Lynn Michaels
VILLAINS: Alex Alaric (last in Pun #5, '88), Stone Cold (Derek Smalls, 1st, assassin), Derek Sternes, Blind Joe Death, Heathen, Angela, muggers (die), gang (shadows only)
OTHER CHARACTERS: VIGIL inc Capt. Nails, John Lowe, Alvarez, Einhorn, Dutton, West, Dave, Bancroft (all die); Payback, Mr. Jeffries (Justice Department agent), Lynn's father (1st), reporter (on TV)
LOCATIONS/ITEMS: Derelict building inc basement, Lynn's safe house, Sternes' office in Washington, DC; Angela & Alaric's Hudson Valley home / Stone Cold's handgun, trigger & car; Lynn's binoculars, VIGIL helicopters & Humvees (both destroyed), missiles, Lynn's handgun, Angela's revolver & TV, muggers' knives, Joe's cane gun
SYNOPSIS: Having taken Dutton and Bancroft prisoner, Stone Cold kills Dutton to convince Bancroft to lure VIGIL into a trap in return for his life. VIGIL comes in force to rescue Bancroft, but Stone Cold slaughters them with a missile attack. Meanwhile, Lynn's father turns up at her safehouse, looking for his daughter. In Washington, Mr. Jeffries informs Sternes that VIGIL is to be dismantled in light of its recent activity and losses, with Sternes to take the blame for the debacle and resign. Angela is upset to learn of this after working so hard to place Sternes in VIGIL, but Alaric assures her they have other tools. Elsewhere, Stone keeps his promise not to kill Bancroft, instead abandoning him unarmed and handcuffed in the crime-ridden neighborhood, where a gang swiftly moves on him. Lynn's father tries to convince her to escape her problems by returning to the family farm, but nearby Blind Joe picks up Lynn's scent and starts to track her down for Heathen.
NOTE: Angela and Alaric look significantly different from prior appearances.

PUNISHER WAR JOURNAL #77 (April 1995)

"Bound by Blood" (22 pages)

CREDITS: Chuck Dixon (writer), Mel Rubi (pencils), Steve Moncuse, M. Peter Keating (inks), Mike Kraiger (inks, c inks), Vickie Williams (letters), John Kalisz (colors), Chris Cooper (editor), Bobbie Chase (group editor), Doug Wheatley (c pencils)
FEATURE CHARACTER: Lynn Michaels (as Punisher)
SUPPORTING CAST: Payback, Lynn's father
VILLAINS: Angela, Heathen, Stone Cold (next in Pun #102, '95), Blind Joe (dies), Alex Alaric (also on video screen), Trust agents, Punishment Squad, assassins (die)
OTHER CHARACTERS: "Little Jimmy" Ronkin (junkie, corpse), bar patrons (die), Mr. Jeffries, Punisher (in Lynn's dream)
LOCATIONS/ITEMS: Ronkin's apartment, Lynn's safehouse, Mr. Jeffries' house, airport motel, bar, Alaric's penthouse inc hot tub / Lynn's guns, Joe's cane gun, Lynn's father's shotgun & camper van, Trust guns & video screen, Payback's guns, police cars, Punishment Squad's guns & rifles, Mr. Jeffries' car, Punisher's guns (in dream)
SYNOPSIS: Visiting an informant who sent word of a hot tip, Lynn finds him dead and is ambushed by two assassins; she kills them, but wonders how many more will die before she too is slain. Back at her safe house, her father again tries to convince her to return home, but as she tells him she can't run from her problems an alarm goes off, alerting her to Blind Joe and Heathen's imminent arrival. They find only Lynn's father, but his claim that he lives alone doesn't fool them, and he opens fire with a concealed shotgun. Blind Joe returns fire, and Lynn and Payback enter the room, guns blazing. Heathen uses Blind Joe as a human shield and leaps from the window, escaping at the cost of his ally's life. Meanwhile Trust agents waylay Justice Department official Mr. Jeffries, and their boss Alex Alaric demands he hand over files on New York City's vigilantes, intending to eliminate these wild cards who might interfere with his plans. Elsewhere Stone Cold hunts for Punisher's old associates, forcing some unfortunate bar patrons to give up Mickey Fondozzi's name. Payback, Lynn and her father relocate to an airport motel, where a nightmare of Punisher killing her for failing him makes Lynn finally decide to go back to Iowa. However, Lynn's father has charged the room to his credit card, unwittingly giving away their location to Alaric, and as the trio prepares to leave, the Punishment Squad attack.

PUNISHER WAR JOURNAL #78 (May 1995)

"Bound by Blood" (22 pages)

CREDITS: Chuck Dixon (writer), Mel Rubi, Paul Martin (pencils), Steve Moncuse (inks, c inks), John Lowe, Mike Kraiger, Pam Eklund (inks), Vickie Williams (letters), Bob Sharpen (colors), Chris Cooper (editor), Bobbie Chase (group editor), Doug Wheatley (c pencils)
FEATURE CHARACTER: Punisher (between Pun #102-103, '95)
SUPPORTING CAST: Lynn Michaels (next in PWJ #80, '95), Mickey Fondozzi (last in Pun #100, '95), Mouse, Ponygirl (both between Pun #102-103, '95)
VILLAINS: Angela, Alex Alaric, Heathen, Punishment Squad (all die), Stone Cold (between Pun #102-103, '95), gang members (on train, die), Alaric's servant
OTHER CHARACTERS: Payback, Lynn's father (both next in PWJ #80, '95), commuters, train driver
LOCATIONS/ITEMS: Airport motel, Alaric's penthouse inc gym, Stone Cold's house, subway maintenance tunnels, Cringelli Manufacturing sub-basement / Lynn's guns & flash-bang grenade, Payback's guns & mask w/night-vision, Lynn's father's gun & camper van, Punishment Squad's guns & night-vision goggles, subway train, train to Iowa, Heathen's gun, Stone Cold's gun
SYNOPSIS: After a brief firefight Payback, Lynn and her father slay the Punishment Squad members. Noticing that their camper van's gas tank had been hit during the battle, the trio head for the subway. Meanwhile Alaric waits impatiently for news on the hit, until he receives a call from Heathen, who informs him of the trio's location for his own reasons. Elsewhere, Mickey Fondozzi asks Stone Cold to release him, claiming to have told him everything he knows about Punisher and Microchip. Stone Cold declines, instead gagging Mickey before heading out on an

errand. Several Punishment Squad members attack the train, but Payback, Lynn and her father kill them all, then quit the train, heading down a maintenance tunnel to avoid the transit police, only to find Alaric and Angela waiting for them. Lynn tries to bargain, admitting she and Payback are leaving town, but the two Trust members decide to shoot them anyway. However, Heathen has been observing, and shoots Angela and Alaric dead, satisfied that Payback and Lynn are out of the game. Moments after Payback, Lynn and her father have left, Stone Cold catches Heathen by surprise and kills him, noting that only leaves two more targets, Castle and Microchip. On a train to Iowa, Lynn finally relaxes, realizing her ordeal is finally over. However, while her nightmare has ended, others continue, as back in the city the teenage hackers Mouse and Ponygirl free Punisher from the prison Microchip has been holding him in.

PUNISHER WAR JOURNAL #79 (June 1995)

"Countdown: 3. House of the Dead" (22 pages)

CREDITS: Chuck Dixon (writer), Douglas T. Wheatley (pencils), Steve Moncuse (inks), Vickie Williams (letters), John Kalisz (colors), Chris Cooper (editor), Bobbie Chase (group editor), Jae Lee (c art)
FEATURE CHARACTER: Punisher (last in Pun #103, '95, next in CD #7, '95)
SUPPORTING CAST: Microchip (last in Pun #103, '95, next in Pun #3, '09), Mickey Fondozzi (last in Pun #103, '95, next in PWZ #41, '95), Mouse, Ponygirl (both last in Pun #103, '95)
VILLAINS: Stone Cold, Bullseye (both last in Pun #103, '95, next in PWZ #41, '95), Rosalie Carbone (between Pun #103-104, '95), White Jihad (neo-Nazis, die)
OTHER CHARACTERS: Carlos Cruz (also as Punisher, last in Pun #103, '95, next in PWZ #41, '95), Rosalie's lover (corpse), firefighters, ambulance men, Skip, Dee-Dee, Butchie (prev 3 mentioned, Mickey's friends)
LOCATIONS/ITEMS: Sheepshead Bay inc Microchip's garage, Stone Cold's home, Mickey's trailer, Rosalie's home, White Jihad's base / Microchip's computer, Battle Van w/robot driver & gun; Punisher's gun, starlite glasses, rocket launchers & grenades, robot gun ("Artie-Dootie"), Mouse & Ponygirl's VW Beetle, Bullseye's dagger, Rosalie's gun, Stone Cold's rocket launcher, Phalanx's armor, White Jihad's arsenal
SYNOPSIS: Punisher confronts Microchip at gunpoint over Micro trapping and confining him, but Micro uses a voice-activated code to switch the warehouse lights off, and flees in the ensuing darkness. Each man quickly arms himself from the warehouse's equipment, and Punisher begins hunting his former friend. Meanwhile Stone Cold has beaten the location of Microchip's new garage hideout out of Mickey Fondozzi, and leaves his captive tied to a chair while he goes to check the information out. As soon as he leaves, Mickey rocks the chair back so that it falls over and breaks under him, knocking him out in the process. Waking up, he walks out of Stone Cold's basement, planning to get out of town. Back at Mickey's trailer, Mouse and Ponygirl help themselves to Punisher's cash reserve and flee the country, fearing that one of Punisher's enemies will kill them if they stay. In the garage, Punisher doggedly pursues Micro, until Micro finally accepts the inevitable and surrenders, offering up the back of his head to shoot and asking only that Punisher makes his death quick. Before Punisher can pull the trigger however, the room explodes, as Stone Cold takes out the building with a rocket launcher. Over at Rosalie Carbone's home, the crime heiress points a gun at an unconcerned Bullseye, less angry that he has invaded her bedroom and killed her lover than that he missed Punisher after she hired him to kill the vigilante. Annoyed by this slur to his reputation, Bullseye offers to finish off the new Punisher wannabe, and she gives him the bulletproof Phalanx armor in lieu of an advance. Meanwhile Punisher pulls himself from the garage rubble, having survived the explosion because Microchip's body shielded him. A short while later Micro's ally, Punisher replacement Carlos Cruz, arrives to see Micro's corpse being removed from the ruins by ambulance men, the body still gripping a scrap of fabric adorned with a skull. Thinking Punisher has slain Micro, Carlos swears to find and kill him. Needing to restock his dwindling weapons supply, Punisher wipes out a faction of the neo-Nazi White Jihad and steals their arsenal.
NOTE: Cover labeled "Countdown: 3." Story continues from Pun #103, '95 ("Countdown: 4") and into PWZ #41, '95 ("Countdown: 2").

PUNISHER WAR JOURNAL #80 (July 1995)

"Countdown: 0. The Last Bad Man" (22 pages)

CREDITS: Chuck Dixon (writer), Douglas T. Wheatley (pencils), Steve Moncuse (inks), Vickie Williams (letters), John Kalisz (colors), Chris Cooper (editor), Bobbie Chase (group editor), Jae Lee (c art)
FEATURE CHARACTER: Punisher (last in Pun #104, '95, next in DE:A, '95)
GUEST STARS: Nick Fury (last in Pun #104, '95, next in DE:A, '95)
SUPPORTING CAST: Lynn Michaels (last in PWJ #78, '95, next in CW:BDR, '07 bts, PWJ #11, '07)
VILLAINS: Stone Cold (last in Pun #104, '95, dies), Bullseye (last in Pun #104, '95, next in Pun #1, '95), Blanco gang & drug manufacturers (most die)
OTHER CHARACTERS: Payback (last in PWJ #78, '95), Lynn's father (last in PWJ #78, '95), Shotgun (J.R. "Jr" Walker, government agent, last in PWZ #6, '92, next in SM Ann '97), SHIELD agents inc doctor, Steven Dreyer, Lisa Dreyer (both corpses in rfb), Kingpin, Maria Castle, Lisa Castle, Frank Castle Jr, Microchip, Microchip Jr (prev 6 in Punisher's thoughts)
LOCATIONS/ITEMS: Coney Island inc amusement pier, Central Park (in Punisher's thoughts), Michael's farm, Iowa / Phalanx's armor, Punisher's guns, explosives & night vision goggles, Fed Ex truck, SHIELD airships & Helicarrier, Stone Cold's 50 caliber Magnum, Bullseye's machine guns, Shotgun's customized shotgun
FLASHBACKS: Steven and Lisa Dreyer lie dead (PWZ #41, '95). Microchip lies dead (PWJ #79, '95).
SYNOPSIS: Unable to sleep without seeing memories of Microchip's corpse or the bodies of two dead children he recently killed accidentally, Punisher assaults a drug lab hidden on an abandoned Coney Island pier. As Stone Cold arrives and heads in kill Punisher, Frank finds Bullseye waiting for him, wearing the late vigilante Phalanx's bulletproof armor. As they battle, SHIELD airships fly over the pier, but SHIELD commander Nick Fury declines to send his men in, aware of just how dangerous the combatants are, preferring to wait for the arrival of the one man he feels might be able to come back out alive. On the pier Bullseye taunts the vigilante with the names of the tourist family he killed, and is preparing to finish Punisher off when Stone Cold opens fire; though his shots can't penetrate the Phalanx armor, the impacts send Bullseye over the pier's edge. Stone Cold turns to kill Punisher, but is gunned down from behind by Fury's agent, Frank's old friend Shotgun. Spotting Bullseye hanging on to the pier by one hand and starting to pull himself up, Punisher shoots away the piece of pier the assassin is clinging to, sending him falling into the water. Punisher surrenders, expecting Shotgun to kill him, but finds Fury merely wants him taken in. He goes quietly, and once in custody becomes almost catatonic, lost in a dream of a better world where his family and friends are happy and well … and alive.

NOTE: Final issue. Cover labeled "Countdown: 0," continuing from Pun #104, '95, the final issue of that series. Punisher believes he accidentally killed the innocent Dreyer family while they were out picnicking (PWZ #41, '95), and will not learn the real culprit was Bullseye until Pun #1, '95.

PUNISHER: WAR ZONE #1 (March 1992)

"Only The Dead Know Brooklyn" (24 pages)

CREDITS: Chuck Dixon (writer), John Romita Jr. (pencils, c art), Klaus Janson (inks), James Novak (letters), Gregory Wright (colors), Tim Tuohy (asst editor), Don Daley (editor)
FEATURE CHARACTER: Punisher (also as Johnny Tower, last in Pun:GF '92)
SUPPORTING CAST: Microchip (also in Punisher's thoughts, last in Pun:GF '92, next in PWZ #7, '92), Mickey Fondozzi (Carbone family turncoat, 1st)
VILLAINS: Julius Carbone (Carbone family boss) & his soldiers inc Arnie, Freddie, Nico & Tony the Tuna (prev 4 die), Salvatore "Sal" Carbone (Julius' brother), Andy Calabrese (Carbone family lieutenant, next in PWZ #4, '92) (all 1st), Delbert (junkie informant), Triad gang members, Republic of Yaritagua's El Presidente (in pfb) & his Democratic Guard (in pfb, 1 also in pfb)
OTHER CHARACTERS: Shotgun (J.R. "Junior" Walker, government hitman, last in DD #273, '89) & Gary, Microchip's psychiatrist, reporters (voice only), Delbert's children, bystanders; Microchip Jr., Maria Castle, Lisa Castle, Frank Castle, Jr. (prev 4 in Punisher's thoughts)
LOCATIONS/ITEMS: Republic of Yaratagua (also in pfb), Carbone estate, Bushwick inc Delbert's tenement; Brooklyn inc Punisher's safe house; New York inc Frankie's Rec Room, Quon Luck restaurant, Mickey's apartment, Mulberry St., parking garage, psychiatrist's office, parking garage & subway / Punisher's Uzi, assault rifle, gun w/laser sight, acetylene torch, steak & popsicle; Shotgun's guns, Delbert's gun, Coyle's revolver, Carbone soldiers' guns, Democratic Guard's assault rifles (in pfb)
FLASHBACK: In the Republic of Yaritagua, Shotgun kills El Presidente and slaughters his Presidential Guard (p).
SYNOPSIS: When Punisher finds his informant Delbert high and holding two police officers hostage, Punisher kills Delbert. Officer Coyle decides not to arrest Punisher, but refuses to speak with reporters. Later, Punisher follows Microchip across town and watches Microchip secretly meet with someone. When Microchip returns to the safe house, Punisher accuses Microchip of conspiracy. Microchip reveals he's seeing a psychiatrist and leaves in disgust. In the Republic of Yaritagua, Shotgun kills the General to stop him from becoming El Presidente. Punisher interrupts a gang fight between Carbone family soldiers and Triad gang members, killing everyone involved but Mickey Fondozzi, a low-level Carbone soldier. Punisher "tortures" Mickey by poking him with a popsicle while implying it's an acetylene torch. Later, Mickey introduces the Carbone family to Punisher as "Johnny Tower," Mickey's cousin from Kansas.
NOTE: Includes interior front cover (2 pages) w/art taken from page 12, panel 3 & PWZ #2, '92, page 7, panel 2. Followed by Punisher pin-up (interior back cover) by John Romita Jr. (pencils) & Klaus Janson (inks). PWZ #3, '92 reveals Sal's full 1st name. PWJ #74, '95 reveals Coyle's 1st name.

PUNISHER: WAR ZONE #2 (April 1992)

"Blood in the Water" (22 pages)

CREDITS: Chuck Dixon (writer), John Romita Jr. (pencils), Klaus Janson (inks), James Novak (letters), Gregory Wright (colors), Tim Tuohy (asst editor), Don Daley (editor)
FEATURE CHARACTER: Punisher (also as Johnny Tower, also in photo)
SUPPORTING CAST: Mickey Fondozzi (also in photo)
VILLAINS: Julius Carbone & his soldiers (die) inc Marco (dies), Sal Carbone, Depanini family (die) inc Oscar Depanini, Vinnie & Art (prev 3 die)
OTHER CHARACTERS: Rosalie Carbone (Julius Carbone's daughter, 1st), Shotgun & his government liaison (1st), European mobsters (in photos)
LOCATIONS/ITEMS: Carbone estate, Depanini hideout, Shotgun's motel room, Punisher's safe house, Mickey's apartment w/Punisher's room; Rockaway inc Horan Liquor w/Carbone numbers bank / Punisher's machine gun, assault rifle, grenade & motorcycle; Shotgun's guns, Carbone soldiers' machine guns, Depanini family's guns
SYNOPSIS: "Johnny Tower" leads a Carbone assault on the rival Depanini crime family. After killing all of the rival gang, Punisher kills the Carbone soldiers except for Mickey. Salvatore Carbone warns Julius Carbone that Mickey and Johnny screwed up in letting so many of their men get killed, but Julius instead hails the duo as heroes. Julius appoints Mickey and Johnny to head a numbers bank in Rockaway. Elsewhere, Shotgun receives a contract to go after the Carbone Family. While looking through surveillance photos of the criminals, Shotgun recognizes Punisher. After failing to contact Microchip, Punisher destroys the Rockaway numbers bank and takes all of the money. Julius orders Mickey and Johnny to find out who destroyed the numbers bank. Punisher notices that Julius' daughter Rosalie has become infatuated with Johnny Tower.
NOTE: Series' letters page "War Correspondence" debuts this issue.

PUNISHER: WAR ZONE #3 (May 1992)

"The Frame" (23 pages)

CREDITS: Chuck Dixon (writer), John Romita Jr. (pencils), Klaus Janson (inks), James Novak (letters), Gregory Wright (colors), Tim Tuohy (asst editor), Don Daley (editor)
FEATURE CHARACTER: Punisher (also as Johnny Tower, also in photo)
SUPPORTING CAST: Mickey Fondozzi
VILLAINS: Julius Carbone & his soldiers (some die) inc Butchie, Dukey & Geese; Sal Carbone (also in photo), Asian mobsters (some also in photos, die off-panel)
OTHER CHARACTERS: Rosalie Carbone & her wedding organizers, Shotgun & his government liaison, paramedics, police, bystanders
LOCATIONS/ITEMS: Carbone estate, shooting range, New York inc Girico's restaurant, Aldo's Northern Italian Cuisine & mechanics garage, New Jersey inc Pine Barrens & Amonte Storage / Shotgun's guns, Mickey's tranquilizer & camera; Carbone soldiers' guns, car buffer & wrenches; Johnny Tower's car, Asian mobsters' teddy bears stuffed with heroin

SYNOPSIS: "Johnny Tower" and Mickey Fondozzi interrogate several Carbone soldiers, pretending to seek out who assaulted the Carbone numbers bank. They decide to pin the blame on Salvatore Carbone. Elsewhere, Shotgun practices with his new weapons. Johnny and Mickey secretly tail Sal and witness Sal engaging in deals with the Asian mob at a storage lot. Later, Punisher later breaks into the storage garage and finds teddy bears stuffed with heroin. Mickey tells Julius that his brother Sal is behind the troubles they've been having lately. Mickey and Johnny take Julius to the storage lot and interrogate captured members of the Asian mob. Julius orders Mickey and Johnny to kill Sal. Johnny and Mickey take Sal to the New Jersey Pine Barrens. Sal escapes only to fall into a frozen lake. Mickey takes a picture of Sal as proof of his death for Julius. Hours later, paramedics get Sal out of the lake.

PUNISHER: WAR ZONE #4 (June 1992)

"Closer to the Flame" (22 pages)

CREDITS: Chuck Dixon (writer), John Romita Jr. (pencils), Klaus Janson (inks), James Novak (letters), Gregory Wright (colors), Tim Tuohy (asst editor), Don Daley (editor)
FEATURE CHARACTER: Punisher (also as Johnny Tower, also in photo & Sal's hallucination)
SUPPORTING CAST: Mickey Fondozzi (also in Sal's hallucination)
VILLAINS: Julius Carbone (also in Sal's hallucination) & his soldiers (many die) inc a Ryker's prison guard, Sal Carbone, Andy Calabrese (last in PWZ #1, '92), Ryker's inmates inc Stiles
OTHER CHARACTERS: Rosalie Carbone, Shotgun, doctors (also in Sal's hallucination)
LOCATIONS/ITEMS: Carbone estate, Ryker's Island prison, New Jersey inc hospital; New York inc Mickey's apartment; Brooklyn inc Punisher's safe house; Queens inc Crank laboratory / Punisher's machine pistol, guns w/ laser sights & explosive satchels w/remote detonator; Carbone soldiers' Crank, baseball bats, C4 bomb & chains
SYNOPSIS: Punisher destroys a crank lab in Queens. Meanwhile, Sal Carbone slowly recovers in the hospital. At the Carbone estate, Julius Carbone promotes Mickey while "Johnny Tower" has some fun with Rosalie. At Ryker's Island, Shotgun interrogates a prisoner who identifies Johnny Tower as the Punisher. Unable to remember who he is, Sal leaves the hospital. A Ryker's guard tells the Carbone family who Johnny Tower is. Punisher returns to Mickey's apartment where Carbone enforcers attack. They quickly overwhelm Punisher, knocking him unconscious. Punisher awakens to find himself chained to the steering wheel of a car with a bomb on the passenger seat. Punisher drives to his safe house hoping Microchip is there to defuse the bomb, but Microchip isn't there.

PUNISHER: WAR ZONE #5 (July 1992)

"Feeding Frenzy" (22 pages)

CREDITS: Chuck Dixon (writer), John Romita Jr. (pencils), Klaus Janson (inks), James Novak (letters), Gregory Wright (colors), Tim Tuohy (asst editor), Don Daley (editor)
FEATURE CHARACTER: Punisher
SUPPORTING CAST: Mickey Fondozzi
VILLAINS: Julius Carbone & his soldiers (die), Sal Carbone (also in pfb, becomes Thorn), Andy Calabrese, Italian mobsters inc Don Marco & his son Enrico (both 1st)
OTHER CHARACTERS: Rosalie Carbone, Shotgun, Sal's victim (in pfb, dies), truck driver, taxi driver, plane passenger, sharks
LOCATIONS/ITEMS: Carbone estate, Brooklyn inc Punisher's safe house (Auto Body Detail Shop, destroyed); la Isla de Tiburones Durimientes (Island of the Sleeping Sharks) inc Carbone compound / Punisher's assault rifles, Shotgun's guns, scatterguns, grenade launcher, thermal glasses & jet; Mickey's gun, box cutter, ice pick & pizza cutter; Carbone soldiers' guns, machine pistols, C4 bomb & chains; Julius' jet
FLASHBACK: Sal Carbone kills a man for his coat (p).
SYNOPSIS: Shotgun frees Punisher before the bomb explodes, but Punisher's safe house is destroyed. Punisher recognizes Shotgun from Vietnam, and the two decide to team up against the Carbone family. Meanwhile, the Carbones fly to a Caribbean island to meet with a Sicilian crime family. Elsewhere, Sal Carbone hitchhikes to New York. Unable to remember his name, Sal calls himself Thorn. Punisher and Shotgun rescue Mickey Fondozzi from Carbone family soldiers, then assault the Carbone estate, learning that the Carbone family has flown to the Island of Sharks. As Punisher, Shotgun and Mickey leave, Thorn arrives and learns of the Caribbean meeting. On the island, Julius meets with Sicilian mob boss Marco, introducing his daughter Rosalie to her fiancé, Marco's son Enrico. Meanwhile, Punisher and his allies fly to the island, while Thorn flies on a commercial airliner.

PUNISHER: WAR ZONE #6 (August 1992)

"The Carrion Eaters" (24 pages)

CREDITS: Chuck Dixon (writer), John Romita Jr. (pencils), Klaus Janson (inks), James Novak (letters), Gregory Wright (colors), Tim Tuohy (asst editor), Don Daley (editor)
FEATURE CHARACTER: Punisher
SUPPORTING CAST: Mickey Fondozzi (next in PWZ #9, '92)
VILLAINS: Julius Carbone & his soldiers inc Len & Lar; Andy Calabrese, Don Marco, Enrico (all die), Thorn (next in PWZ Ann #2, '94)
OTHER CHARACTERS: Rosalie Carbone, Shotgun (next in PWJ #80, '95), boat driver, sharks (die)
LOCATIONS/ITEMS: La Isla de Tiburones Durimientes inc Carbone compound & grotto / Punisher's gun, assault rifle & machine pistols; Shotgun's jet, parachutes, sword, guns, shredder rounds & warhead bullets; Julius' communication satellite & bracelet stiletto; Carbone soldiers' guns
SYNOPSIS: Punisher, Shotgun and Mickey parachute onto the Island of Sharks and make their way to the Carbones on the other side of the island. Meanwhile, Thorn hires a boat captain to take him to the island. Julius Carbone unveils his communications satellite to the Sicilian

mobsters, explaining they can be the most coordinated crime organization in the world. Thorn arrives on the island and encounters Rosalie and Enrico. Thorn kills Enrico and attacks the guards. Punisher and Shotgun arrive and begin their assault on the mobsters. When Marco learns that his son has been killed, Marco ends their partnership. Julius kills Marco, and the two crime families start killing each other. Punisher chases Julius and Rosalie to a grotto and battles Julius. Rosalie falls into shark infested water. Punisher rescues Rosalie while Thorn arrives and kills Julius. Punisher shoots Thorn and leaves him for dead. Later, Thorn climbs back onto his boat and collapses, vowing to hunt again another day.

PUNISHER: WAR ZONE #7 (September 1992)

"Mugger's Picnic" (22 pages)

CREDITS: Chuck Dixon (writer), John Romita Jr. (pencils), Klaus Janson (co-inks, c inks), Mike Manley (co-inks), James Novak (letters), Kevin Tinsley (colors), Tim Tuohy (asst editor), Don Daley (editor)
FEATURE CHARACTER: Punisher (also in photo)
SUPPORTING CAST: Microchip (as "The Stop Inn" bartender, last in PWZ #1, '92), Lynn Michaels (police officer, 1st)
VILLAINS: Rosalie Carbone, her lieutenants (one dies) & soldiers, rapist (1st), child abductor, muggers, drug dealers (prev 3 die)
OTHER CHARACTERS: Central Park attendees inc Brent & his girlfriend, Cory & his parents & mugging victims inc Danny; "Stop Inn" bar patron; Maria Castle, Lisa Castle, Frank Castle Jr. (prev 3 in Punisher's thoughts)
LOCATIONS/ITEMS: New York inc Carbone family hideout & Central Park; Key West, FL inc The Stop Inn / Punisher's hunting perch, binocular, knife, 10mm rifle, gun w/laser sight & sniper rifle w/sight, silencer & incendiary rounds; drug dealer's money, narcotics & guns; muggers' knives, Lynn's revolver
SYNOPSIS: Rosalie Carbone attends a meeting of the remaining Carbone family lieutenants. She takes control of the organization after having her soldiers kill the one lieutenant who voices opposition to her. As her first order of business, she puts a bounty on the Punisher. In Central Park, Punisher patrols the area looking for a reported rapist. As he surveys the area, he kills muggers, drug dealers, and a child abductor. In Florida, Microchip hears about Punisher killing the Carbone family and considers returning to New York. Punisher eventually spots the rapist attacking a lone female jogger. Punisher tackles the rapist to break him away from the jogger, but the rapist rolls away and flees. Punisher prepares to shoot the rapist, but the jogger reveals herself as a police officer and tells Punisher he's under arrest.
NOTE: PWJ #58, '93 reveals Lynn's 1st name & PWJ #57, '93 reveals her surname; her badge number is 8709.

PUNISHER: WAR ZONE #8 (October 1992)

"The Hunting Ground" (22 pages)

CREDITS: Chuck Dixon (writer), John Romita Jr. (pencils), Mike Manley (co-inks, c inks), Jimmy Palmiotti, Josef Rubinstein (co-inks), James Novak (letters), Kevin Tinsley (colors), Tim Tuohy (asst editor), Don Daley (editor)
FEATURE CHARACTER: Punisher (also in photo)
SUPPORTING CAST: Microchip, Lynn Michaels
VILLAINS: Cane (cane w/hidden guns & sword), Combat (guns), Garotte (garotte), Roc (brute strength), Silence (ninja), Stiletto (knives), Tequila (poison) (all assassins, 1st), Rosalie Carbone (next in PWZ #10, '92) & her guards, Madripoor criminals (die), rapist
OTHER CHARACTERS: Central Park attendees inc drunk teenagers & rape victim; Stiletto's victims (1 dies, others as corpses), Garotte's victim, Cane's victims, Roc's victims, Tequila's victim (prev 4 die), Combat's victims, Rosalie's masseur, bystanders, Tequila's scorpion; Maria Castle, Lisa Castle, Frank Castle, Jr. (prev 3 in Punisher's thoughts)
LOCATIONS/ITEMS: Brasilla inc government office; New York inc assassin meeting place, Central Park & diner; London inc street corner; Madrid, Spain, Madripoor, Marseilles, France inc mansion; Vera Cruz, Mexico inc mansion; Waco, TX inc bar / Punisher's 10mm handgun & knife; Lynn's revolver, Cane's cane gun, Garotte's garrote, Silence's blowgun & blow darts, Stiletto's stiletto; rapist's Mac-10 machine gun
SYNOPSIS: The female officer reveals she's off duty and trying to capture the rapist on her own time. Punisher convinces her to work with him and they agree to meet tomorrow night in the park. Rosalie Carbone is informed that seven world class assassins are now after the bounty Rosalie put on the Punisher. Meanwhile, Stiletto, Garotte, Combat, Silence, Cane, Roc and Tequila each complete separate assassinations across the world. Punisher meets with the female officer and the two go hunting through Central Park for the rapist, eventually finding him assaulting another woman. The rapist sees them and shoots at them. Punisher fires back and wounds the rapist, but the rapist escapes. Meanwhile, Microchip makes his way back to New York. Rosalie meets with the seven assassins and announces the bounty on the Punisher is worth five million dollars.
NOTE: Punisher notes his CompuServe e-mail box is "1996 R. Castillo."

PUNISHER: WAR ZONE #9 (November 1992)

"Goners" (22 pages)

CREDITS: Chuck Dixon (writer), Mike Harris (pencils), Mike Manley (co-inks, c art), Jimmy Palmiotti (co-inks), Michael Higgins (letters), Kevin Tinsley (colors), Tim Tuohy (asst editor), Don Daley (editor)
FEATURE CHARACTER: Punisher
SUPPORTING CAST: Mickey Fondozzi (last in PWZ #6, '92), Microchip, Lynn Michaels
VILLAINS: Cane, Combat, Garotte, Silence, Stiletto, Roc, Tequila; rapist (dies), carjackers, drug addict
OTHER CHARACTERS: Guardian Angels (1 dies), bartender, bar patron, taxi driver, subway passengers, bystanders
LOCATIONS/ITEMS: New York inc 47th street subway station & bar; Brooklyn inc Punisher's safe house (wreckage); Chinatown / Punisher's 10 mm handgun, Lynn's revolver, Cane's cane, Garotte's garrote, Silence's

blowgun, bartender's shotgun, rapist's shotgun

SYNOPSIS: Roc, Combat and Cane capture Mickey Fondozzi and demand to know where they can find the Punisher. Meanwhile, Punisher and the female officer track the rapist to his apartment. Punisher chases the rapist onto a passing subway car. Garrote and Tequila hear about the chase on the radio and get on the subway at the next stop. Meanwhile, Microchip returns to Punisher's destroyed safe house, unaware Silence is watching him. Stiletto begins following the female officer. Mickey tells Roc, Combat, and Cane that Punisher's "address" is in Chinatown. Tequila, secretly holding the rapist hostage but posing as the rapist's hostage, distracts Punisher while Garotte attacks Punisher from behind. Punisher kills the rapist, but Garrote continues to strangle Punisher.

NOTE: Microchip is a fan of Hawaiian Luau music, revealed here.

PUNISHER: WAR ZONE #10 (December 1992)

"Tight Spot" (22 pages)

CREDITS: Chuck Dixon (writer), Mike Harris (pencils), Mike Manley (co-inks, c art), J.J. Birch (co-inks), Michael Higgins (letters), Kevin Tinsley (colors), Tim Tuohy (asst editor), Don Daley (editor)
FEATURE CHARACTER: Punisher
SUPPORTING CAST: Mickey Fondozzi (next in PWJ #45, '92), Lynn Michaels (next in PWJ #57, '93), Microchip
VILLAINS: Rosalie Carbone (last in PWZ #8, '92) & her guards inc Vinnie & Philly (both die), Garotte, Silence, Stiletto (prev 3 die), Cane, Combat, Roc, Tequila; Asian gangsters, carjackers
OTHER CHARACTERS: Steve (news anchor), meteorologist (both on TV)
LOCATIONS/ITEMS: New York inc Lynn's apartment, bar & subway; Chinatown inc Asian gang hideout; Brooklyn inc Punisher's safe house (wreckage) / Punisher's assault rifle & 10mm handgun; Microchip's gun, Lynn's revolver, Garotte's garotte, Silence's sai, Stiletto's stiletto, Vinnie's gun, Asian gangsters' guns

SYNOPSIS: Punisher manages to grab the subway's emergency stop cord; the sudden stop throws Garotte and Tequila off their feet. Punisher kills Garotte but Tequila escapes. At Punisher's destroyed safe house, Microchip kills Silence. Roc, Combat and Cane break into the address Mickey gave them, but find themselves facing the Asian mob. Meanwhile, carjackers steal the car Mickey is tied up inside. Punisher arrives at the female officer's apartment and she dresses his wounds. Stiletto sneaks in and attacks, but Punisher kills Stiletto. The female officer kisses Punisher. The carjackers wreck the car and abandon it, never realizing Mickey was in the trunk. The surviving assassins meet and decide to pool their resources against the Punisher. Outside a shopping mall, Punisher kills Rosalie Carbone's bodyguards and tells Rosalie he needs to have to talk with her.

NOTE: Microchip is a Neil Diamond fan, revealed here.

PUNISHER: WAR ZONE #11 (January 1993)

"In a Deadly Place" (24 pages)

CREDITS: Chuck Dixon (writer), Mike Harris (pencils), Mike Manley (co-inks, c art), J.J. Birch, Mike Harris (co-inks), Michael Higgins (letters), Kevin Tinsley (colors), Tim Tuohy (asst editor), Don Daley (editor)
FEATURE CHARACTER: Punisher (next in PunSS #2, '92, MK #35-37, '92, Pun #63, '92)
SUPPORTING CAST: Microchip (next in MK #36, '92)
VILLAINS: Rosalie Carbone (next in Pun #100, '95) & her soldiers (die), Cane, Combat, Tequila (prev 3 die), Roc (next in PWZ Ann #2/2, '94)
LOCATIONS/ITEMS: Bradford County, PA inc Punisher's cabin; Carbone estate, Microchip's hideout / Punisher's highshot standard Derringer, assault rifle & Claymore mines; Microchip's computer & rifle; Tequila's knives & revolver; Cane's cane, Carbone soldiers' guns

SYNOPSIS: Punisher throws Rosalie Carbone into the trunk of her car and drives away. Microchip searches through Punisher's various safe houses' security records to find out where Punisher is. Cane, Combat, Roc and Tequila return to the Carbone estate where they learn Rosalie is missing. Punisher calls the Carbone soldiers, reveals he has Rosalie and tells them where to find him. Punisher takes Rosalie to his safe house in rural Bradford County, Pennsylvania. When Punisher enters the cabin, Microchip is alerted to Punisher's location. When the assassins and Carbone soldiers arrive at the cabin, Punisher attacks. Roc almost crushes Punisher with a boulder, but Microchip arrives and shoots Roc. Punisher kills the remaining assassins. Microchip says he thought he could leave the war against crime, but couldn't stay away. Punisher leaves Rosalie to fend for herself in the woods.

PUNISHER: WAR ZONE #12 (February 1993)

"Psychoville USA Part 1 of 5, Family Ties" (22 pages)

CREDITS: Dan Abnett, Andy Lanning (writers), Mike McKone (pencils), Mark McKenna, Mick Gray (inks), Richard Starkings (letters), Kevin Tinsley (colors), Tim Tuohy (asst editor), Don Daley (editor)
FEATURE CHARACTER: Punisher (last in MHol, '92/4, also in PWZ #15, '93 fb)
VILLAINS: Dr. Erwin Shane (brain-washing NSA agent, chr last in PWZ #15, '93 fb) & his Caretakers (also in PWZ #15, '93 fb) inc Eight (Norm Lenski), Da Rosa (mobster, also as "Vincent Rose"), Chicane "citizens" (brain-washed criminals) inc Saul, Laura, George Beddoes, Alice Beddoes & the "Castle family": Mary-Louise Snoffer (as Frank's wife "Kim"), Donna (daughter) & Mikey (son, next in PWZ #14, '93) (all 1st)
OTHER CHARACTER: Walters (Shane's technician, in Punisher's dream as gunman)
LOCATIONS/ITEMS: New York, Chicane, WV inc Castle family home, George's home, Norm's home & Arkin's Timber & Lumber Inc w/Shane's office / Punisher's assault rifle & gun; Da Rosa's gun, George's shotgun

SYNOPSIS: In New York, Punisher chases and captures mobster Da Rosa. Punisher prepares to kill Da Rosa, but a crowd surrounds them and knocks Punisher out. Frank Castle wakes up confused, not quite recognizing his wife Kim, daughter Donna and son Mikey. Frank gets a ride from his neighbor Norm and goes to work at the lumber mill. Fellow worker Vinnie Rose freaks out and Frank quickly subdues him. Not knowing where he learned how to fight, Frank visits Dr. Erwin Shane, the mill's doctor. Dr. Shane tells Frank not to worry about it. Later, Frank wakes from a nightmare and hears screams from across the street. Frank breaks into his neighbor's house and stops the husband and wife from killing each other. Meanwhile, Norm makes a phone call and says they may have a problem with Frank.

NOTE: Includes frontispiece (1 page) labeled "Psychoville Part 1." PWZ #15, '93 names the Caretakers & reveals Norm's surname & Caretaker number. PWZ #16, '93 reveals Da Rosa is a mobster, Walters is the gunman Punisher sees in his thoughts, Mary-Louise butchered her kindergarten class, Mikey vivisected his parents & Donna murdered four of her foster siblings. PWZ #13, '93 reveals the Beddoes' surname.

PUNISHER: WAR ZONE #13 (March 1993)

"Psychoville USA Part 2 of 5, Happy Days" (23 pages)

CREDITS: Dan Abnett, Andy Lanning (writers), Mike McKone (pencils), Mark McKenna, Mick Gray (inks), Richard Starkings (letters), Kevin Tinsley (colors), Tim Tuohy (asst editor), Don Daley (editor)
FEATURE CHARACTER: Punisher (also in own thoughts)
SUPPORTING CAST: Microchip (last in MHol, '92/4, chr last in PWZ #14, '93 fb)
VILLAINS: Dr. Erwin Shane, his technicians & his Caretakers (1 also in Punisher's thoughts) inc Eight, Sheamur (NSA agent, 1st), Da Rosa (as "Vincent Rose"), Chicane "citizens" inc police, George Beddoes, Alice Beddoes, Lenny, Saul, Francine, Chuck Mohen, Kyle Reese (mentioned, Donna's boyfriend) & the "Castle family": Mary-Louise Snoffer (as "Kim") & Donna
LOCATIONS/ITEMS: Chicane, WV inc Castle family home, K-Mart, police station, Arkin's Timber & Lumber Inc & Shane's lab / Microchip's binoculars & van; Caretakers' incapacitation equipment, Alice's knife

SYNOPSIS: Men in hazmat suits storm Frank's neighbor's house and subdue Frank and his murderous neighbors. Frank wakes up confused. He checks his neighbor's house but no one is home. Norm tells Frank they're on vacation. Frank checks with the police to see if there was anything reported from last night, but there was nothing. Police bring in a man screaming about people messing with his head. When he breaks free, Frank subdues him and wanders off in a daze. Frank drives to the edge of town, but decides not to leave. In a lab, Dr. Shane and his government liaison Sheamur discuss programming Punisher to assassinate a politician. At the mill, Vinnie returns to work, but no one but Frank remembers Vinnie going crazy. Norm becomes suspicious of Frank's stability and makes a phone call. Outside of town, Microchip spots Frank with his binoculars and wonders what Frank's doing.

NOTE: Mick Gray is credited in PWZ #14's "War Correspondence."

PUNISHER: WAR ZONE #14 (April 1993)

"Part 3 of 5, My Two Dads" (20 pages)

CREDITS: Dan Abnett, Andy Lanning (writers), Mike McKone (pencils), Mark McKenna, Mick Gray (inks), Richard Starkings (letters), Kevin Tinsley (colors), Tim Tuohy (asst editor), Don Daley (editor)
FEATURE CHARACTER: Punisher (also in photo & own dream)
SUPPORTING CAST: Microchip (also in fb between MHol, '92/4 & PWZ #13, '93)
VILLAINS: Dr. Erwin Shane (also in photo), Caretaker Eight, Chicane "citizens" inc police (die) & the "Castle family": Mary-Louise Snoffer (as "Kim," also in photo & as Fox's wife in Punisher's dream), Mikey (last in PWZ #12, '93) & Donna (prev 3 next in PWZ #16, '93)
OTHER CHARACTERS: Bearstead librarian, Fox (politician, on TV & in Punisher's dream), Walters (in Punisher's dream as gunman), bystanders (others in Punisher's dream); Kingpin, Maria Castle, Lisa Castle, Frank Castle, Jr. (prev 4 in dream)

LOCATIONS/ITEMS: New York (in fb), Bearstead inc library; Chicane, WV inc Castle family home & park / Microchip's trip line, binoculars, camera, computer & van; police chainsaw & guns; license plate (in fb)
FLASHBACK: Microchip finds a Chicane, WV license plate where Punisher was last seen.
SYNOPSIS: Punisher dreams of killing a politician. Microchip continues to watch Frank until Chicane police try to kill him. Microchip kills the policemen and escapes. Frank takes his family to the park where his son Mikey "attacks" him with a toy gun. Frank has a seizure and wakes up in his house, where Dr. Shane assures Kim that Frank will be fine. In the nearby town Bearstead, Microchip researches Chicane, learning it's an abandoned logging town recently purchased by Pineridge Holdings. Microchip finds that Dr. Erwin Shane is Pineridge's director, and was involved with the NSA's Project Artichoke, a brainwashing initiative designed to create assassins. Microchip races back to Chicane. That night, Frank watches TV until images of his past as the Punisher flash across the screen.

PUNISHER: WAR ZONE #15 (May 1993)

"Part 4 of 5, Father Knows Best" (20 pages)

CREDITS: Dan Abnett, Andy Lanning (writers), Mike McKone (pencils), Mark McKenna, Mick Gray (inks), Richard Starkings (letters), Kevin Tinsley (colors), Tim Tuohy (asst editor), Don Daley (editor)
FEATURE CHARACTER: Punisher (also in own dream, photo & rfb, also in fb during PWZ #12, '93)
SUPPORTING CAST: Microchip (bts, sends image of Punisher to Frank's TV)
VILLAINS: Dr. Erwin Shane (also in fb to 1st chr app before PWZ #12, '93), his technicians (some in fb) inc Walters (1st full app) & Caretakers (some in Punisher's dream & rfb, others in fb during PWZ #12, '93, some die) inc Eight (dies), Five, Twelve, Sixteen & Twenty-Three, Sheamur, Chicane "citizens" (some also in Punisher's dream)
OTHER CHARACTERS: Mary-Louise Snoffer (as "Kim"), Donna, Mikey (all in Punisher's dream), Da Rosa (in rfb), Fox (in photo)

LOCATIONS/ITEMS: New York (in fb), Chicane, WV inc Castle family home & Shane's lab / Punisher's 9mm Beretta, shotgun & propane tank (destroyed); Caretakers' handguns; Norm's file
FLASHBACK: Punisher chases Da Rosa (PWZ #12, '93). Caretakers overpower and capture Punisher, but the vigilante knocks a license plate off their van. Dr. Shane reprograms Punisher to live in Chicane.
SYNOPSIS: Frank dreams of skull-faced gunmen killing Kim, Donna and Mikey in the park until Norm knocks on the door. Norm's pleasant façade quickly fades as he gives Frank an assignment to kill a politician in Portland. When Norm gives Frank a gun, the TV flashes an image

of the Punisher. His personality restored, Frank kills Norm. In the lab, Dr. Shane learns that Norm is dead. Sheamur takes control of the lab and sends a Caretaker squad to the Castle home. Punisher kills the attacking Caretakers and drives into town. The lab gets reports of Chicane citizens reverting to their true personalities and wreaking havoc all over town. Sheamur orders everyone in town killed. Chicane falls into chaos.
NOTE: Followed by an uncredited Punisher pin-up (1 page). The cover is signed as the Three Stooges: McMoe, McLarry & McCurly.

PUNISHER: WAR ZONE #16 (May 1993)

"Part 5 of 5, Empty Nest" (23 pages)

CREDITS: Dan Abnett, Andy Lanning (writers), Mike McKone (pencils), Mark McKenna, Mick Gray (inks), Richard Starkings (letters), Kevin Tinsley (colors), Tim Tuohy (asst editor), Don Daley (editor)
FEATURE CHARACTER: Punisher (next in SSWP #10, SM #32-34, SecDef #4-5, Pun #76, all '93)
SUPPORTING CAST: Microchip (next in PWJ #55, '93)
VILLAINS: Dr. Erwin Shane, his technicians inc Walters & Caretakers inc Thirty-Four, Da Rosa (also as "Vincent Rose"), Chicane "citizens" inc the "Castle family": Mary-Louise Snoffer (as "Kim"), Donna & Mikey (prev 3 last in PWZ #14, '93) (all die), Sheamur & his men
LOCATIONS/ITEMS: Chicane, WV inc Shane's lab (destroyed) / Punisher's shotgun, machine gun, handguns & Battle Van; Microchip's gun, Caretakers' vans, handguns & Uzis; Sheamur's Uzi, Da Rosa's revolver, Walters' Uzi, technicians' Uzis
SYNOPSIS: Punisher wades through the rioting Chicane citizens, killing Caretakers as he finds them. Punisher finds and kills Da Rosa. Microchip finds Punisher and tells him everyone in town are reprogrammed killers. They drive to Dr. Shane's lab where Shane has Punisher's "family" hostage. Shane's technician Walters issues Punisher's trigger code, subduing the vigilante. Shane activates Donna and orders her to kill her "family," but she fights her conditioning and shoots Shane instead. The technicians kill Punisher's "family" when they use their bodies to shield Punisher from the technician's bullets. Punisher kills the technicians. Shane escapes only to be lynched by the Chicane citizens. Punisher and Microchip escape before Sheamur, who has salvaged Shane's research, destroys Chicane.
NOTE: Punisher's trigger code is "Ain't that touching? Ain't that sweet... Say goodbye love-birds..."

PUNISHER: WAR ZONE #17 (July 1993)

"The Jericho Syndrome" (20 pages)

CREDITS: Dan Abnett, Andy Lanning (writers), Hugh Haynes (pencils, c art), Rodney Ramos (inks), Michael Higgins (letters), Kevin Tinsley (colors), Tim Tuohy (asst editor), Don Daley (editor)
FEATURE CHARACTER: Punisher (last in PunSS #3/3, '93)
SUPPORTING CAST: Microchip (last in SMPunSabre, '93, last bts in PunSS #3/2, '93)
VILLAINS: Architect (Orville Nugent, criminal planner, 1st) & his men (1 as policeman, dies), Luka (criminal, die) & his associates (die)
OTHER CHARACTERS: Jack Oonuk (troubleshooter, 1st), Marty (Jack's partner, dies), Pan-Allied Industries executives, Coodie's staff & patrons, Eat Truck Stop staff & patrons, police (some die), bystanders (some die)
LOCATIONS/ITEMS: Grand Straight inc Coodie's, Eat Truck Stop & dam (destroyed); Architect's office, Pan Allied Industries corporate HQ / Punisher's shotgun, gun, knife, M60 & Battle Van; Jack's Uzi & binoculars; Luka's Uzi, Luka's associate's gun, Architect's vibration charge, Architect's man's gun w/silencer
SYNOPSIS: As Microchip eavesdrops on a criminal transaction in Grand Straight, troubleshooters Jack Oonuk and Marty search for a bomb; the Architect is threatening to destroy the town's dam if Pan-Allied doesn't pay his ransom. Microchip tells Punisher the criminal transaction has taken place and Punisher attacks as the dam is destroyed. Punisher kills the criminals as several people die in the dam's destruction, including Marty. As they leave town, Microchip begs Punisher to do something about the disaster, but there's no one for Punisher to shoot. Jack escapes from Architect's men and jumps in Punisher's Battle Van. A helicopter chases them and Punisher shoots it down. Punisher knocks Jack out. Architect tells his men they'll hold another landmark hostage until Pan-Allied pays the ransom. Jack explains his situation to Punisher, who agrees to help kill Architect. Later, the Pan-Allied executives tell Jack they're paying Architect's ransom, and Jack will deliver it.
NOTE: Pun Ann #7, '94 reveals Architect's real name.

PUNISHER: WAR ZONE #18 (August 1993)

"The Jericho Syndrome Part 2" (20 pages)

CREDITS: Dan Abnett, Andy Lanning (writers), Hugh Haynes (pencils, c art), Rodney Ramos (inks), Michael Higgins (letters), Kevin Tinsley (colors), Tim Tuohy (asst editor), Don Daley (editor)
FEATURE CHARACTER: Punisher
SUPPORTING CAST: Microchip (next in Venom:FP #3, '93)
VILLAINS: Architect & his men (some also as construction workers, others as oil rig crew, some die), Wrench (amphetamine dealer, also in photo, 1st)
OTHER CHARACTERS: Jack Oonuk, Pan-Allied Industries Caretakers (1 dies), oil rig crew, bystanders
LOCATIONS/ITEMS: San Jerome suspension bridge, Architect's office, Canada inc Whale Sound oil platform, Northwest Territories / Punisher's sniper rifle w/tracer round & Battle Van; Microchip's tracker drone, Architect's compass, Architect's men's vibration charges, chains & guns; Caretaker's gun, Wrench's wrench & amphetamines
SYNOPSIS: Punisher waits on top of the San Jerome suspension bridge for Jack Oonuk to deliver Pan-Allied's ransom money to the Architect's men. Posing as construction workers, Architect's men meet with Jack. Punisher prepares to fire a tracer round at their vehicle to track them, but Pan-Allied's Caretakers notice Punisher and shoot at him. Architect abandons the mission and activates vibration charges which begin to shake the bridge apart. Microchip attaches a tracker drone to the escaping Architect's men's vehicle as Punisher and Jack disable the vibration charges. Architect is presented with his ransom money, but he's upset the suspension bridge survived. Architect announces he'll destroy the Whale Sound oil platform, this time without a ransom. Punisher, Microchip and Jack follow Architect's men to Canada and sign up to work on

the oil platform after them. Later, as Jack is attacked by Architect's men, Punisher stumbles across Wrench, the platform's amphetamine dealer. Wrench attacks Punisher, thinking he's the police.
NOTE: Followed by Punisher in a strip club pin-up (1 page) by Jonathan Holdredge.

PUNISHER: WAR ZONE #19 (September 1993)

"The Jericho Syndrome Part 3" (21 pages)

CREDITS: Dan Abnett, Andy Lanning (writers), Hugh Haynes (pencils, c art), Rodney Ramos (inks), Michael Higgins (letters), Kevin Tinsley (colors), Tim Tuohy (asst editor), Don Daley (editor)
FEATURE CHARACTER: Punisher (next in Pun #81, '93 & fb)
GUEST STAR: Wolverine (last in W #74, '93, next in W:Kill, '93)
VILLAINS: Architect (next bts in PWJ #61, '93, next in Pun Ann #7, '94) & his men (as oil rig crew) inc Brody, Larry & Mike; Wrench (dies)
OTHER CHARACTERS: Jack Oonuk (next in Pun Ann #7, '94), oil rig crew
LOCATIONS/ITEMS: Architect's office; Canada inc diner & Whale Sound oil platform, Northwest Territories / Punisher's hazmat suit, Architect's architectural plans for Big Ben clock tower, Eiffel Tower, Empire State Building, Sydney Opera House, US Capitol, Whale Sound oil platform & White House; Architect's men's automatic pistols, explosive charges & pistols; Wrench's wrench
SYNOPSIS: Wrench inadvertently throws Punisher into Architect's men, saving Jack Oonuk. Architect's men finish setting their charges, which Punisher learns are meant not only to destroy the rig but also to blow-back and ignite the seabed oil reserves, causing an ecological disaster. Wrench assaults Punisher again but suddenly falls; Wolverine has stabbed him from behind. Wolverine explains his old Canadian government colleague, Oonuk, called him in to return a favor. Architect's men escape the burning rig by helicopter, but Logan hurls Wrench's wrench at his fleeing helicopter and downs it. As the rig crew evacuates, the heroes fight more of Architect's men and realize they don't have time to save the rig. Punisher dons a hazmat suit and, joined by Wolverine, caps the wellhead to inhibit the blow-back and save the oil field. Punisher, Logan and Oonuk escape the rig just before it explodes. Later, the trio regrets that Architect got away. Elsewhere, the extortionist contemplates his next plan.
NOTE: Followed by Punisher & Wolverine pin-up (1 page) by Hoang Nguyen & Bud LaRosa.

PUNISHER: WAR ZONE ANNUAL #1 (1993)

"Bulletproof" (30 pages)

CREDITS: Chuck Dixon (writer), John Buscema (art), Michael Higgins (letters), Kevin Tinsley, Ericka T. Moran (colors), Tim Tuohy (asst editor), Don Daley (editor), Michael Golden (c art)
FEATURE CHARACTER: Punisher (last in Venom:FP #3, '93)
SUPPORTING CAST: Microchip (last in Venom:FP #3, '93, next in PWJ #57, '93), Mickey Fondozzi (last in PWJ #47, '92, next in PWJ #60, '93)
GUEST STAR: Phalanx (Cord Mather, armor inventor, 1st, next in Pun #102, '95)
VILLAINS: Dr. Blanchard (criminal financier, dies) & his men inc Ace; Manuel Llosa (Bosqueverde cocaine caesar, also in photo), Russian mobsters inc Dink (dies), Korean mobsters (some die), Sicilian mobsters (some die), Triad mobsters (some die), Yakuza (some die), other mobsters (some die), Latin American drug cartel bosses (some die), terrorists (some die)
OTHER CHARACTERS: Ellen Mather (Cord's wife), Brad Mather (Cord's son), Ellen's father, Rodeo Casino staff, bus driver, commuters, bystanders; Carmine Valdocchi, Mike Leling (both mentioned, mob bosses)
LOCATIONS/ITEMS: New York inc illegal casino, pool hall, Davor Meats building, Blanchard's compound & Microchip's warehouse; Atlantic City inc Rodeo Casino; Mather home, Ellen's father's home / Punisher's shotgun, gun, assault rifle, machine pistol, MAC 10, Maadi-Griffin P-50 semi-automatic, binoculars & Battle Van; Blanchard's men's machine guns, guns, .45-cal. hollowpoint bullets, .45-cal. Magnum revolver & .50-cal. Nitro Express rounds; mobsters' meat cleaver, guns, sword & machine guns; Microchip's computer, Blanchard's machine pistol, Phalanx armor (also in schematic)
SYNOPSIS: Frank Castle attacks Yakuza mobsters at an illegal casino. Elsewhere, Cord Mather and his financier Dr. Blanchard tests Cord's experimental Phalanx armor, which is bulletproof. Castle visits his informant, Mickey Fondozzi, at a mob butchery. When Russian mobsters attack them, Castle and Mickey escape. Mickey tells Castle about an upcoming mob auction. Cord tells his wife they soon won't have to worry about money; his Phalanx armor is being sold to the US government. Punisher, Microchip and Mickey learn the mob auction will be held at the Rodeo Casino in Atlantic City. Cord recognizes a possible Phalanx buyer, but can't place him. Castle and Mickey stake out the Rodeo Casino. Cord realizes the buyer is Manuel Llosa, a cocaine trafficker. Punisher prepares to attack the Rodeo Casino. Inside, Cord confronts Dr. Blanchard about Llosa. Blanchard reveals he never had a government contract for the Phalanx armor, all the buyers are criminals and threatens Cord's family. Punisher watches as Phalanx kills Blanchard and attacks the other gathered criminals. Punisher joins the slaughter and demands the Phalanx armor when the criminals are dead. Phalanx refuses. Punisher warns Phalanx the mob will want him dead for his vigilante actions. Cord phones his wife, claims that he has found someone else and leaves her to protect her.
NOTE: All of Marvel's 1993 Annuals were bagged with trading cards featuring a new character introduced in each issue. This issue's card, #17 in the series, featured Phalanx art by Mike Harris (pencils), Bob McLeod (inks) & Paul Mounts (colors) which shows a different Phalanx design: a muscular man w/no armor, a crew cut and a belt-fed Gatling gun; his name given on the card is Dick Johnson. Includes table of contents/credits page (1 page) w/art taken from 1st story, page 20. Phalanx's surname is revealed in Pun #102, '95.

2ND STORY: "Unfinished Business" (10 pages)
CREDITS: Steven Grant (writer), Bill Marimon (pencils), Matt Banning (inks), Janice Chiang (letters), Kevin Tinsley (colors), Tim Tuohy (asst editor), Don Daley (editor)
FEATURE CHARACTER: Punisher
VILLAINS: Sammy Maggs (mobster, formerly of Costa family), Bobo (Sammy's driver), Dolly (mob boss) (all die)
LOCATIONS/ITEMS: New York, interstate, cemetery w/Castle family grave / Punisher's gun & motorcycle; Sammy's revolver & car; Bobo's shotgun

SYNOPSIS: Mobster Sammy Maggs kidnaps his boss Dolly in a plan to take Dolly's place. Dolly taunts Sammy for being a failure since his first job as a lookout for the Costa mob years ago. Sammy kills Dolly, but his driver Bobo notices they're being followed. Punisher chases them into a cemetery, causing them to crash which kills Bobo. Punisher confronts Sammy, who realizes that he was the lookout for the Costa mob on the day the Castle family was killed. Punisher kills Sammy in front of his family's tombstone.

3RD STORY: "Professionals" (9 pages)
CREDITS: George Caragonne (writer), Louis Williams (pencils), Joe Rubinstein (inks), Richard Starkings (letters), Kevin Tinsley (colors), Tim Tuohy (asst editor), Don Daley (editor)
FEATURE CHARACTER: Punisher (next in PWJ #57-60, '93, Pun Ann #6, '93)
VILLAINS: Black Jack Giancomo & his mobsters (all die)
OTHER CHARACTER: Theresa ("Tracy," prostitute, stewardess; Senator Josh Bridge (voice only), Kat (Tracy's prostitute friend, voice only), Hiro Yamashito (Yakuza, voice only), Gino (mentioned, Black Jack's cousin), Raul (mentioned, Kat's pimp), Mr. Matshuska (mentioned, Yakuza)
LOCATIONS/ITEMS: New York inc Tracy's apartment & Xanadu w/Punisher's suite; Bensonhurst, Brooklyn inc Giancomo family compound / Punisher's shotguns & Battle Van; Tracy's motorcycle
SYNOPSIS: Prostitute Tracy listens to her messages then meets with Frank at the Xanadu. She gives Frank information about her criminal clients then tries to seduce him, having fallen for Frank over the past year of their relationship, despite knowing nothing about him. Frank pays her and leaves. Tracy follows Frank to the Giancomo family compound and is terrified to discover he's the Punisher. Punisher kills the mobsters and notices Tracy's presence. He gives her money and tells her to get out of town, or he'll kill her for being a criminal. A heartbroken Tracy later boards a plane.
NOTE: Followed by Punisher fighting men in hazmat suits pin-up (1 page) by Chuck Wojtkiewicz (pencils), Ken Branch (inks) & Sue McTeigue (colors), Punisher fighting goons in a pool hall pin-up (1 page) by Luke McDonnell (art) & Sue McTeigue (colors), Punisher shooting guns pin-up (1 page) by Anthony Williams (pencils), Jeff Albrecht (inks) & Sue McTeigue (colors), Punisher fighting man in burning building pin-up (1 page) by Ed Murr (pencils), Jack Abel (inks) & Sue McTeigue (colors), & Punisher fighting man in mech suit pin-up (1 page) by Rike DaSilva (pencils), Ken Branch (inks) & Sue McTeigue (colors).

PUNISHER: WAR ZONE #20 (October 1993)

"Numbah One Boom Boom" (22 pages)

CREDITS: Larry Hama (writer), Hoang Nguyen (art), John Workman (letters), Kevin Tinsley, Ericka Moran (colors), Tim Tuohy (asst editor), Don Daley (editor)
FEATURE CHARACTER: Punisher (last in Kill:EY #3, '93, also as Sgt. Castiglione in fb between Pun:AG, '88 fb & PWZ #21, '93 fb)
SUPPORTING CAST: Microchip (last in Pun #84, '93)
VILLAINS: Dennis Xavier "D.X." Hanrahan (US Marine, in fb, 1st), Pretty Legs Gambello (dies) & his men (some as corpses, 1st but chr last in PWZ #21, '93 fb, others die), the DeStefani brothers (die), Joey the Pooch (dies) & his men (die) inc Jelly & 2-Tall (both die); carjackers (die), North Vietnamese Army officer & soldiers (in fb, some die)
OTHER CHARACTERS: MACV-SOG (Military Assistance Command, Vietnam, Studies and Observation Group) soldiers inc Bong (in fb, dies), strippers, bystander (voice only)
LOCATIONS/ITEMS: Cambodia (in fb), Red Hook inc Joey's building; Gambello estate / Castle, Hanrahan & North Vietnamese Army's AK-47s, Hanrahan's gun (all in fb) & C4 explosive (also in fb), Punisher's M60, K-Bar, gun, grenade launcher, concussion grenades & Battle Van w/ Claymore mines; Microchip's Merry & Pippin (recon robots), Joey's Uzi, Joey's men's guns, carjackers' shotguns
FLASHBACK: In Cambodia, Frank Castiglione and D.X. Hanrahan battle North Vietnamese Army soldiers alongside MACV-SOG. When their interpreter Bong is injured, D.X. kills Bong so they won't be slowed down. D.X. then suddenly kills his prisoners with C4 explosives.
SYNOPSIS: Punisher ambushes Joey the Pooch and his men. Meanwhile outside, Microchip is carjacked. As Punisher kills Joey's men and interrogates Joey, Microchip activates the Battle Van's Claymore mines and kills the carjackers. Acting on Joey's information, Punisher and Microchip drive to Pretty Legs Gambello's estate, finding Gambello's men dead inside. Punisher looks around, finds more of Gambello's men and kills them. Punisher finds Gambello tied up with C4 explosives. Punisher recognizes it as D.X. Hanrahan's work before Gambello explodes.

PUNISHER: WAR ZONE #21 (October 1993)

"2 Mean 2 Die" (22 pages)

CREDITS: Larry Hama (writer), Hoang Nguyen (art), John Workman (letters), Kevin Tinsley (colors), Tim Tuohy (asst editor), Don Daley (editor)
FEATURE CHARACTER: Punisher (also in photo, also as Sgt. Castiglione in fb2 between PWZ #20, '93 fb & PunTheNam, '94 fb; also as Frank Castle in fb3 during Pun Ann #4, '91)
SUPPORTING CAST: Maria Castle (in fb3 during Pun Ann #4, '91), Lisa Castle, Frank Castle, Jr. (both in fb3 between Pun #1, '98 fb & Pun Ann #4, '91) (all also in photo), Microchip (next in PunHol #2, '94)
VILLAINS: D.X. Hanrahan (mercenary, also in photo, also in fbs 2, 3 & 1 following PWZ #20, '93 fb), Tony the Banker (bagman, Pretty Legs Gambello's brother-in-law, dies) & his men (die) inc Augie, Paulie & Sal (prev 3 die); Pretty Legs Gambello's men (in fb1 to 1st chr app before PWZ #20, '93, die), Patricia Gambello (Pretty Legs' wife, 1st), North Vietnamese Army officer & soldiers (both in fb2, die)
OTHER CHARACTERS: MACV-SOG soldiers (in fb2), US Army intelligence major (bts in fb3, provides Hanrahan w/Castles' address), trick-or-treaters (in fb3), Augie Gambello (mobster), Gambello lieutenant, Pretty Boy Gambello's sons (prev 3 mentioned, killed by D.X. Hanrahan), DeStafani mobster (in photo)
LOCATIONS/ITEMS: Cambodia (in fb2), Castle family home (in fb3), Gambello estate (also in fb1), Microchip's warehouse, T&G Wholesalers building in Manhattan's Meatpacking District / Hanrahan's AK-47 rifles, High Standard .22-cal. pistol & K-Bar knife, North Vietnamese Army officer's AK-47 & Tokarev pistol, North Vietnamese Army soldiers' AK-47s & field mine placement map (all in fb2), Gambello's men's guns (in fb1), Punisher's assault rifle, bandolier, machine gun, medal of valor, pistol & Battle Van; Microchip's computer w/crime families database; Hanrahan's Glock pistols (also in

fb1), grenades & knife; Patricia's automatic pistol & Kevlar vest; Tony the Banker's revolver, Tony the Banker's men's pistols & rifles

FLASHBACKS: D.X. Hanrahan kills Pretty Legs Gambello's men (1). In Cambodia, Hanrahan saves Frank Castiglione from an ambush, then starts a firefight with a nearby North Vietnamese Army patrol. Frank discovers that Hanrahan's actions inadvertently spared them from death on a land-mined trail (2). One Halloween after the war, Hanrahan visits the Castle family and asks Frank to join him on a lucrative job in Southeast Asia. Frank kicks Hanrahan out when D.X. taunts Frank's children (3).

SYNOPSIS: Punisher recovers from the explosion only for Pretty Legs' wife Patricia to shoot at him. Punisher smacks Patricia around and leaves. When Punisher reviews the Gambello estate's security tape with Microchip, he confirms that the mobsters' killer was his fellow former Marine, the ruthless D.X. Hanrahan. Punisher and Microchip learn that D.X. has been murdering other members of the Gambello and DeStefani crime families, who are distributors for a drug pipeline that originates in Madripoor, a place where Hanrahan has done business. Guessing that D.X.'s next victim is Pretty Legs' brother-in-law Tony the Banker, Punisher raids Tony's meatpacking facility in Manhattan at the same time as Hanrahan. D.X. kills Tony, tells Trish that he killed her sons and shoots Trish. Trish's Kevlar vest saves her, but D.X. creates a distraction with grenades and escapes. Punisher resolves to kill Hanrahan.

NOTE: Cover is homage to W #67, '93. PWZ #22, '93 reveals Patricia's full 1st name.

PUNISHER: WAR ZONE #22 (December 1993)

"Taking Tiger Mountain" (22 pages)

CREDITS: Larry Hama (writer), Hoang Nguyen (pencils, co-inks, c art), Han Nguyen (co-inks), John Workman, Michael Higgins (letters), Kevin Tinsley (colors), Tim Tuohy (asst editor), Don Daley (editor)
FEATURE CHARACTER: Punisher (also in own dream & as Mr. Schloss, next in SSol #8, '93, PunHol #2, '94, Ts #3, '93, Pun #85, '93)
VILLAINS: D.X. Hanrahan (also in Punisher's dream, dies) & his mercenaries (die), General Nguyen Ngoc Coy (crimelord, last in MCP #92, '91, next in W #98, '96) & his soldiers (some die), Madripoor criminals (some die) inc Dog-Meat Charlie (arms dealer), Patricia Gambello (also in photo)
OTHER CHARACTERS: Tyger Tiger (Jessan Hoan, Madripoor crimelord, last in NThr #4, '93, next in MCP #152, '94), Police Chief Tai (last in W #17, '89, next in W #87, '94) & his men, South Seas Skyways pilot, Princess bar bartender, Madripoor citizens

LOCATIONS/ITEMS: Madripoor inc Princess Bar, Gen. Coy's hangar & Tiger Mountain / Punisher's assault rifle, C4 explosives, Claymore mine & aluminum-covered asbestos fire suit; Hanrahan's RPG & gun; Coy's men's guns, assault rifles, helicopter & AH-1 Douglas Sky Raider w/Napalm; criminals' guns

SYNOPSIS: Posing as "Mr. Schloss," Punisher arrives in Madripoor and is greeted by Inspector Tai. Punisher fails to bribe Tai, but is eventually released. Punisher asks for D.X. Hanrahan at the Princess Bar. Tyger Tiger tells Punisher D.X. is on Tiger Mountain. Punisher tries to buy some weapons, but Patricia Gambello, who is also after Hanrahan, already bought all the good stuff. General Coy arrives and announces he doesn't believe Trish can kill D.X. and approaches Punisher with a deal: Coy will provide whatever Punisher needs if the vigilante kills Hanrahan. Meanwhile, Trish fails to kill D.X., who takes her captive. Punisher gathers some supplies and gets a ride to Tiger Mountain, where he threatens to blow up Hanrahan and himself. D.X. calls Punisher's bluff and the two fight. Punisher is able to get far enough away to put on an aluminum-covered asbestos suit as one of General Coy's men, who's been ordered to kill Hanrahan and Punisher, drops Napalm on Tiger Mountain. Punisher and Trish survive, but Punisher leaves Trish to fend for herself in the Madripoor jungle.

PUNISHER: WAR ZONE #23 (January 1994)

"Bringing Down the House Pt. 2" (29 pages)

CREDITS: Larry Hama (writer), John Buscema (pencils), Val Mayerik, Art Nichols, Jimmy Palmiotti (inks), Michael Higgins (letters), Kevin Tinsley, Ericka Moran (colors), Tim Tuohy (asst editor), Don Daley (editor), Michael Golden (c art)
FEATURE CHARACTER: Punisher (last in PWJ #61, '93, next in Pun #86, '94)
SUPPORTING CAST: Microchip, Mickey Fondozzi (both last in PWJ #61, '93, next in Pun #86, '94)
VILLAINS: August Dragon Clan, Flynn Cullen & the Black Cullens, Bruce Lam, Vlad Slozchk, Vito Vaducci, Buck Wrango, "Tiger" Tanner Wilson, Turk, Pike, Tony Rhee, Jackie-Dee, Bruce & all their men inc Binky & Reilly (all last in PWJ #61, '93, die), Rapido (last in PWJ #61, '93, next in Pun Ann #7, '94)
OTHER CHARACTERS: ATF agents, FBI agents, police, bystanders
LOCATIONS/ITEMS: New York inc Manhattan Tower (destroyed) / Punisher's machine pistol, Excalibur fine wines truck w/Semtex explosives & dead man's switch detonator; Microchip's ConEd van & detonator; mobsters' various guns

SYNOPSIS: Armed with his dead man's switch set to destroy Manhattan Tower, Punisher opens fire on the gathered killers. When Binky fires back at the Punisher, Jackie-Dee kills Binky, not wanting to risk Punisher letting go of the switch and killing everyone present. Listening in, the law enforcement agencies evacuate, believing Punisher will destroy the building. As Punisher continues to kill his attackers, Microchip detonates explosives beneath Manhattan Tower, which cuts the Tower's power. Punisher continues his killing spree in the darkness, eventually taking Rapido hostage. Punisher uses Rapido's gun arm to kill more attackers, then uses Rapido as a diversion to kill the remaining survivors until Tanner is the only one left. Tanner promises not to shoot Punisher if the vigilante lets Tanner go. Punisher releases the dead man's switch and Manhattan Tower explodes.

NOTE: Cover labeled "Suicide Run: 2" & is foil-embossed. Features black and white negative cover image frontispiece (1 page) & title/credits page (1 page) w/black and white cover image. Followed by Pun #86, '94 preview (1 page). Story continued from PWJ #61, '93 & continues in Pun #86, '94.

2ND STORY: "The Punisher's Conditioning Techniques" (5 pages)
CREDITS: Roger Salick (writer), Val Mayerik (art), Richard Starkings (letters), Glynis Oliver (colors), Tim Tuohy (asst editor), Don Daley (editor)
FEATURE CHARACTER: Punisher
VILLAINS: Crooks
LOCATIONS/ITEMS: Microchip's warehouse / post of bamboo & foam padding, heavy bag, bar bells & weights, trash, automated attacker

dummies with bats & pipes, board wrapped in rope, tire iron, Punisher's gi
SYNOPSIS: Punisher reviews his conditioning techniques, including repeatedly hitting and being hit by hard objects to build endurance, weight training, controlled falling and landing, reflex training, street brawling, meditation and martial arts.

PUNISHER: WAR ZONE #24 (February 1994)

"Shhh! Pt. 5" (20 pages)

CREDITS: Larry Hama (writer), John Buscema (pencils), Val Mayerik, Art Nichols (inks), Joe Andreani (colors), Michael Higgins (letters), Tim Tuohy (asst editor), Don Daley (editor), Michael Golden (c art)
FEATURE CHARACTER: Punisher (also as Frank Castle in fb between Pun #1, '98 fb & Pun #100, '95 fb; between Pun #86-87, '94)
SUPPORTING CAST: Maria Castle, Lisa Castle, Frank Castle, Jr. (all in fb between Pun:Xmas #1, '07 fb & Pun #100, '95 fb)
VILLAINS: Lt. Blackwell (last in PWJ #62, '94, next in Pun #87, '94), Tommy Cullen (between Pun #86-87, '94) & his men: Liam & Eamon
OTHER CHARACTERS: Sheriff Harry Bendix (Laastekist sheriff) & his deputies inc Mose & Reed, Amy Bendix (Harry's daughter) (all 1st, next in Pun #87, '94), Marge (Cider Press employee, 1st, next in PWJ #68, '94), Outlaw (last in Pun #86, '94, next in PWJ #63, '94), VIGIL inc Capt. Nails (last in PWJ #62, '94, next in Pun #87, '94) & Crosby (dies); Punisher's "corpse" (last in PWJ #62, '94, next bts in PWJ #67, '94), Carson (next in Pun #88, '94), Wills (both last in Pun #86, '94), Dr. Grosz (medical examiner), Chuckie (weapons dealer), bystanders, opossum; Sinclair (mentioned, Outlaw's contact)
LOCATIONS/ITEMS: Castle home, hospital (both in fb), New York inc Medical Examiner's morgue security annex & Manhattan Tower (wreckage); Bendix home inc Amy's tree house / Grosz's bone saw, VIGIL helicopter, Crosby's revolver, Blackwell's gun, Eamon's Uzi, Tommy's handgun
FLASHBACK: Frank hides a present for Maria, swearing Lisa to secrecy. Later, Frank's family visits him after an appendectomy.
SYNOPSIS: During Punisher's autopsy, Dr. Grosz discovers the body was dressed post-mortem, because the wounds don't match the suit's damage. Fearing ridicule for declaring Punisher dead when he isn't, Carson and Wills consider covering up their mistake. At the Manhattan Tower wreckage, Blackwell and Nails receive word about a fire at the morgue and decide to investigate. Meanwhile, Outlaw buys some weapons. Punisher crawls out of the sewers and meets the young Amy Bendix. Carson and Wills hear about the morgue fire and realize Grosz is responsible. Punisher secretly rides under Amy's ride home. At the morgue, Carson and Wills take umbrage to Nails issuing an APB on Punisher, and learn their surveillance saw Outlaw following Cullen. Later, Amy finds Punisher hiding in her tree house. Nails and Blackwell find the Cullens, who shoot at them. Amy accidentally reveals to her father, Sheriff Harry Bendix, that a man is in her tree house. Harry accuses Punisher of molesting Amy.
NOTE: Cover labeled "Suicide Run: 5." Features title/credits page (1 page) w/black and white cover image. Followed by Pun #87, '94 preview (1 page). Story continued from PWJ #62, '94 & continues in Pun #87, '94. PWJ #67, '94 reveals the autopsy on Punisher's "corpse" was finished by Joseph Highland.

PUNISHER: WAR ZONE #25 (March 1994)

"Last Dance in Laastekist Pt. 8" (29 pages)

CREDITS: Larry Hama (writer), John Buscema (pencils), Val Mayerik, Art Nichols (inks), Joe Andreani (colors), Michael Higgins (letters), Freddy Mendez (asst editor), Don Daley (editor)
FEATURE CHARACTER: Punisher (also in rfb, also as Frank Castle in fb between PWJ #1, '88 fb & Pun #17, '97 fb; last in PWJ #63, '94, next in Pun #88, '94)
SUPPORTING CAST: Maria Castle, Lisa Castle, Frank Castle, Jr. (all in fb between PWJ #1, '88 fb & Pun #17, '97 fb), Lynn Michaels (last in PWJ #63, '94, next in Pun #88, '94)
VILLAINS: Lt. Blackwell (last in PWJ #63, '94, next in Pun #88, '94), August Dragon Clan inc Danny (also as Punisher), Derek & Shannon (prev 3 die); the Righteous Ones, Mr. Vaducci (mobster, Vito's brother) & his sons: Matthew, Peter (both die), Paul & John (prev 5 last in PWJ #63, '94)
OTHER CHARACTERS: Sheriff Harry Bendix & his deputies inc Mose (dies), Amy Bendix (all last in PWJ #63, '94, next in PWJ #68, '94), Payback (last in PWJ #63, '94, next in Pun #88, '94), air traffic controller (voice only), police (some die)
LOCATIONS/ITEMS: Laastekist inc sheriff's office & Bendix house (destroyed) w/Amy's tree house; Central Park (in rfb & fb) / Punisher's Kevlar vest, CS grenades, Col python magnum, pr-24 baton, Glock 9mm, 12-gauge pump-action shotgun & spray paint; Lynn's van & gun; Vaducci's Lear jet, guns, infrared scanner & bazooka; Payback's Uzi, Blackwell's gun, Bendix's shotgun, Dragons Clan's guns, police guns
FLASHBACKS: In Central Park, the Castle family has a picnic (1) before they're killed (PWJ #1, '88 fb).
SYNOPSIS: Bendix refuses to free Punisher, even after the Dragon Clan kill his deputies. Meanwhile, Lynn Michaels and Payback travel to Laastekist. Elsewhere, the Vaducci's plane makes a denied landing at the airfield. They shoot it out with the police and head for Laastekist. Bendix frees Punisher and arms him, and after spray painting his skull symbol on his vest Punisher knocks Bendix out to keep the sheriff safe. Punisher kills some members of the Dragon Clan and steals their car. Amy sneaks out of her tree house while her captors are distracted by Punisher's arrival. Punisher uses one of the Dragon Clan as a decoy to lure Amy's captors out of the house, and kills them. Blackwell takes Amy hostage. The Vaduccis arrive and Punisher kills two of them. Lynn and Payback arrive and the Vaduccis retreat. Punisher confronts Blackwell in Amy's tree house and prepares to kill him, but Amy begs Punisher not to kill Blackwell. Punisher drops his gun, but before Blackwell shoot Punisher, Bendix shoots Blackwell. Bendix thanks Punisher for keeping Amy safe and Punisher leaves.
NOTE: Cover labeled "Suicide Run: 8." Features title/credits page (1 page) w/reversed cover image. Story continued from PWJ #63, '94 & continues in Pun #88, '94. Mr. Vaducci is called "Vito" here; that was his brother, who was killed in PWZ #23, '94.

2ND STORY: "The Condemned" (10 pages)
CREDITS: Chuck Dixon (writer), Bill Marimon (pencils), Matt Banning (inks), Jim Novak (letters), Sue McTiegue (colors), Tim Tuohy (asst editor), Don Daley (editor)

FEATURE CHARACTER: Punisher (last in PunTheNam, '94, next in PWJ #64/2, '94)
VILLAINS: Mobsters inc Jules, Sid & Vic, crack dealers (all die)
LOCATIONS/ITEMS: Bronx inc derelict building w/crack house / Punisher's assault rifle & crane; mobsters' guns, crack dealers' guns
SYNOPSIS: Punisher attacks a mob execution and chases the surviving mobsters into a crack house, where crack dealers attack the mobsters. As the mobsters and dealers shoot each other, Punisher uses a nearby crane to level the building, killing everyone inside.

PUNISHER: WAR ZONE #26 (April 1994)

"Pirates" (22 pages)

CREDITS: Chuck Dixon (writer), John Buscema (art), Jim Novak (letters), Kevin Tinsley (colors), Freddy Mendez (asst editor), Don Daley (editor), Rafael Kayanan (c pencils), Tom Palmer (c inks)
FEATURE CHARACTER: Punisher (also as Cliff Callador, last in PWJ #64/2, '94)
SUPPORTING CAST: Microchip (last in PunHol #2/5, '94)
VILLAINS: Ernesto Villamos (Puerto Dulce crime lord, 1st) & his men, Carmelita Villamos (Ernesto's sister, 1st), Javier Callador (Ernesto's gun runner, also as Cliff Callador, dies) & his man (dies), criminals (some die)
OTHER CHARACTERS: Puerto Dulce citizens, police (some die) & revolutionaries (some die); airplane passengers, bartender, bystanders
LOCATIONS/ITEMS: Manatee Shoals, FL inc Hotel Fiesta w/Javier's room; Puerto Dulce inc airport & Villamos estate; bar / Punisher's gun, Javier's gun & passport; Microchip's computer, bartender's shotgun, police guns, revolutionaries' assault rifles
SYNOPSIS: Looking for a gunrunner from the Caribbean, Punisher gets into a bar fight in Florida. The brawl ends when Punisher shoots some of the participants. Punisher pays the bartender ten thousand dollars and he points Punisher to the Hotel Fiesta. Later at the hotel, Microchip poses as an interested buyer. Punisher interrogates and kills a seller, learning Javier Callador is the gun runner. Punisher kills Callador, steals his passport but spares the woman Javier was with. Punisher uses Javier's fake passport to pose as "Cliff Callador" and travels to Puerto Dulce to find Callador's supplier. Punisher arrives to find Puerto Dulce in a civil war. He's picked up and brought to Ernest Villamos, Puerto Dulce's crime lord. Punisher is surprised to see that Ernesto's sister is the woman he spared in Florida.
NOTE: PWZ #27, '94 reveals Carmelita's name.

PUNISHER: WAR ZONE #27 (May 1994)

"Boss Sugar" (22 pages)

CREDITS: Chuck Dixon (writer), John Buscema (art), Jim Novak (letters), Kevin Tinsley (colors), Freddy Mendez (asst editor), Don Daley (editor), Rafael Kayanan (c art)
FEATURE CHARACTER: Punisher (also as Cliff Callador & Johnny Tower)
SUPPORTING CAST: Microchip
VILLAINS: Ernesto Villamos & his men, Carmelita Villamos, work camp Sinco guards & prisoners inc Comadreja (1st)
OTHER CHARACTERS: Mike "Ice" Phillips (last in PWJ #53, '93), boarding house staff & patrons, Puerto Dulce citizens, police (some die) & revolutionaries (some die), cockroach (dies)
LOCATIONS/ITEMS: Puerto Dulce inc Villamos estate & work camp Sinco (sugar plantation); boarding house / Punisher's gun & ballistic knife; Microchip's binoculars, Ernesto's men's clubs, revolutionaries' guns, work camp Sinco machetes & cage
SYNOPSIS: Carmelita Villamos reveals Punisher is not Callador, but rather the man who killed him. Ernesto's men attacks and knock out Punisher. The vigilante wakes up on a prison sugar plantation and is immediately put to work. Days later, Microchip is worried about Punisher's lack of communication. Microchip contacts Ice Phillips and hires him to rescue Punisher. Later, Punisher stops a worker from killing another and is attacked by the plantation guards for his trouble. Ice Phillips meets with Microchip. Ernesto notes the revolutionaries are making progress in the Puerto Dulce civil war. Punisher is told that if he fights against other prisoners, the winner will be set free. Ice Phillips meets Microchip in Puerto Dulce, but they find themselves in the middle of a battle between the Puerto Dulce police and the revolutionaries. At the plantation, Punisher prepares to fight.
NOTE: PWZ #28, '94 names work camp Sinco.

PUNISHER: WAR ZONE #28 (June 1994)

"Sweet Revenge" (22 pages)

CREDITS: Chuck Dixon (writer), John Buscema (art), Jim Novak (letters), Kevin Tinsley (colors), Freddy Mendez (asst editor), Don Daley (editor), Rafael Kayanan (c pencils)
FEATURE CHARACTER: Punisher
SUPPORTING CAST: Microchip
VILLAINS: Ernesto Villamos & his men, Carmelita Villamos, work camp Sinco guards (some die) & prisoners (some die) inc Comadreja (dies)
OTHER CHARACTERS: Ice Phillips, Carmelita's maids, Puerto Dulce citizens, police (some die) & revolutionaries (some die), alligators, snakes
LOCATIONS/ITEMS: Puerto Dulce inc Villamos estate, bar, airport, jungle & work camp Sinco / Punisher's gun & RPG; Ice's Carbine, Microchip's boat, Ernesto's jet (destroyed), police guns, revolutionaries' guns, work camp Sinco machetes, guns, boats & helicopter (destroyed)
SYNOPSIS: Punisher kills his opponents while the head guard makes a fortune in bets. Microchip learns that Punisher is being held at work camp Sinco while the revolutionaries take over the city. Ernesto tells his sister to pack a bag because they're abandoning Puerto Dulce; the revolutionaries are going to win the civil war. Ice Phillips and Microchip infiltrate work camp Sinco and rescue Punisher, but the guards chase

them. Microchip gives Punisher an RPG and Punisher shoots down the guards' helicopter. The guards chase them through the jungle until Punisher kills the head guard. The guards retreat and Punisher, Microchip and Ice Phillips continue on their way. Ernesto and Carmelita travel to Ernesto's jet, but revolutionaries destroy the jet before the crime lord can leave. Punisher evades some revolutionaries only to be surrounded by alligators.

PUNISHER: WAR ZONE #29 (July 1994)

"The Swine" (22 pages)

CREDITS: Chuck Dixon (writer), John Buscema (art), Jim Novak (letters), Kevin Tinsley (colors), Freddy Mendez (asst editor), Don Daley (editor), Rafael Kayanan (c art), Michael Golden (c colors)
FEATURE CHARACTER: Punisher
SUPPORTING CAST: Microchip
VILLAINS: Ernesto Villamos & his men, Carmelita Villamos, Carson (con man, 1st) & his men
OTHER CHARACTERS: Ice Phillips, Puerto Dulce citizens inc Mr. Gacho (dies) & his family (die), police (some die) & revolutionaries (some die), pig, alligators (some die)
LOCATIONS/ITEMS: Puerto Dulce inc Rancho Florida (airstrip), marina & jungle / Ice's gun & Carbine; Ernesto's gun & yacht (destroyed), Ernesto's men's guns, Carson & his men's guns, police guns, revolutionaries' guns & boat (destroyed)
SYNOPSIS: With too many alligators to kill, Punisher, Microchip and Ice Phillips climb a tree to escape. Ernesto and Carmelita prepare to escape on Ernesto's yacht, but revolutionaries destroy the yacht. When the alligators fall asleep, Punisher and the others escape. They walk through the jungle until they find a pig. They follow the pig, thinking it will lead them to its farm, which may have a vehicle. Ernesto hires one of his former employees to get them out of Puerto Dulce; it only costs a hundred thousand dollars and a Mercedes. The pig brings Punisher to some relaxing policemen. A firefight ensues ending with the policemen's deaths. Microchip checks their map and they make their way to an airstrip in the policemen's truck. Ernesto and Carmelita travel to the airstrip. At the airstrip, Rancho Florida, con man Carson takes people's money with the promise of flying them out of the country, but kills them instead.

PUNISHER: WAR ZONE #30 (August 1994)

"Part 5: Ring of FIRE" (22 pages)

CREDITS: Chuck Dixon (writer), John Buscema (pencils), Tom Palmer (co-inks, c inks, c colors), Klaus Janson, Art Nichols (co-inks), Jim Novak (letters), Kevin Tinsley (colors), Freddy Mendez (asst editor), Don Daley (editor), Raphael Kayanan (c pencils)
FEATURE CHARACTER: Punisher (next in Pun #89, '94)
SUPPORTING CAST: Microchip (next in Pun #89, '94)
VILLAINS: Ernesto Villamos & his man, Carmelita Villamos, Carson & his men (all die)
OTHER CHARACTERS: Ice Phillips, Puerto Dulce citizens (some die) & revolutionaries (some die)
LOCATIONS/ITEMS: Puerto Dulce inc Rancho Florida, sugar field & jungle / Punisher's machine gun & gas tank; Ice's Carbine, Carson's plane & gun, Carson's men's guns, Ernesto's gun, Carmelita's revolver, citizens' machetes, revolutionaries' guns
SYNOPSIS: as Punisher, Microchip and Ice Phillips drive to Rancho Florida, Ernesto and Carmelita pose as villagers so the revolutionaries won't attack them. Punisher fights off attacking revolutionaries, but their truck is destroyed. Ernesto and Carmelita are discovered, so they kill the villagers and continue on. At Rancho Florida, Carson takes their money, but tells them there's no room on his plane. Carmelita kills Carson's men to make room on the plane. Carson agrees to fly them to America, but Punisher has already taken their plane while they weren't watching. Ernesto kills Carson. To avoid being taken by the revolutionaries, Ernesto and Carmelita kills each other. As the plane takes off, Punisher regrets not being able to kill Ernesto.

PUNISHER: WAR ZONE ANNUAL #2 (1994)

"Hurts So Good" (31 pages)

CREDITS: Chuck Dixon (writer), Dale Eaglesham (pencils), Al Williamson (inks), Bill Oakley (letters), Christie Scheele (colors), Freddy Mendez (asst editor), Don Daley (editor)
FEATURE CHARACTER: Punisher (also in rfb, last in Pun:SS #4/2, '94)
SUPPORTING CAST: Mickey Fondozzi (also in rfb; last in PWJ #60, '93, next in PWZ #31, '94)
VILLAINS: Kiki (gangster) & his men inc Chorizo & Lupo; Rango (gun dealer) & his men; mobsters inc Telly; gangsters (all die); Thorn (also in rfb as Sal Carbone; last in PWZ #6, '92)
OTHER CHARACTERS: Newark Rescue Mission volunteers, gas station attendant, bartender, homeless people, bystanders (1 dies)
LOCATIONS/ITEMS: New York inc Kiki's hideout, warehouse, bar & highway; New Jersey inc Pine Barrens (also in rfb) & Newark; gas station / Punisher's guns, Rango's assault rifles, guns, grenades, shotgun & Cadillac; Mickey's gun, Kiki's gun, Kiki's men's guns, gangsters' guns
FLASHBACK: Punisher and Mickey take pictures of Sal Carbone dying under ice (PWZ #3, '92).
SYNOPSIS: At the Pine Barrens, the amnesiac Thorn interrupts a gun sale, kills the sellers and buyers and takes their Cadillac. Beginning to remember fragments of his past, he drives to New York. Meanwhile, gangster Kiki is angry that his guns haven't arrived yet and orders his men to look for the Cadillac. Thorn arrives in New York and recognizes Mickey Fondozzi. Thorn attacks and Mickey recognizes Thorn as Sal Carbone. Thorn lets Mickey escape and follows him. Kiki learns his Cadillac is in the neighborhood. Punisher meets Mickey in a bar, where Thorn attacks them. Kiki finds the Cadillac, grabs some guns and attacks Thorn. While Thorn is distracted, Punisher tries to run over Thorn with a taxi. The taxi crashes and Thorn shoots Punisher. Kiki arrives only for Thorn to kill him. Punisher gets up and pushes Thorn onto the highway. Thorn lands on a truck. Later, Thorn wakes up in Newark, New Jersey.
NOTE: Includes table of contents/credits page (1 page) w/ art taken from 1st story, page 19, panel 1, which is preceded by Thorn pin-up (1

page) by Dale Eaglesham (pencils) & Scott Koblish (inks). An editorial caption states this story takes place between Pun #85, '93 & PWJ #61, '93.

2ND STORY: "Second Chance" (16 pages)
CREDITS: Ralph Macchio (writer), Dave Ross (pencils), Tim Dzon (inks), Phil Felix (letters), Kevin Somers (colors), Freddy Mendez (asst editor), Don Daley (editor)
FEATURE CHARACTER: Punisher (also in photo & rfb)
SUPPORTING CAST: Microchip (last in Pun:SS #4/2, '94, next in Pun:BSS #3/2, '94)
VILLAINS: Roc (also in rfb, last in PWZ #11, '93, dies), Delgado (gun runner) & his men
OTHER CHARACTERS: Maria Castle, Lisa Castle, Frank Castle, Jr. (all in rfb), criminals (in photos)
LOCATIONS/ITEMS: New York inc Central Park (in rfb), Punisher's safehouse & docks w/Pier 13 Barnarus MFG Co. warehouse / Punisher's RSG sniper shotgun, MP5, knife, explosives & remote detonator; Roc's audio recorder, Delgado's guns
FLASHBACK: The Castle family is killed (PWJ #3, '89 fb). Punisher battles Roc (PWZ #11, '93).
SYNOPSIS: Microchip interrupts Punisher's workout and reminds the vigilante that Roc almost killed Punisher until Microchip shot Roc. Punisher leaves to ambush a gunrunning operation, but is upset when police sirens make the gunrunners leave before he can kill them. Roc confronts Punisher, revealing that he ruined Punisher's ambush, and has been ruining several of Punisher's recent operations. Wanting a rematch, Roc attacks Punisher. Roc knocks the vigilante around until Punisher breaks Roc's knee. Roc continues to attack, so Punisher breaks his neck. Roc continues to attack, so Punisher drags him into the river. Thinking Roc drowned Punisher climbs onto the pier, but Roc attacks again. Punisher jabs Roc's neck, wraps him in explosives and blow Roc up.

3RD STORY: "Domino Theory" (6 pages)
CREDITS: Steven Grant (writer), Alberto Saichann (art), Jade Moede (letters), John Kalisz (colors), Freddy Mendez (asst editor), Don Daley (editor)
FEATURE CHARACTER: Punisher (next in Pun:BSS #3, '94, Pun #93, '94)
VILLAINS: Stansfield Cuppia (mob boss) & his men inc Donny; Mrs. Cuppia (Stansfield's wife) & her men inc Duran (all die)
OTHER CHAARCTERS: International Hotel staff & patrons, cats; Hanley (mentioned, rival mob boss)
LOCATIONS/ITEMS: New York inc International Hotel w/Stansfield's suite / Punisher's sniper rifle, Mrs. Cuppia's revolver, Mrs. Cuppia's men's knives
SYNOPSIS: Mrs. Cuppia has her mob boss husband killed in a plot to take over the mob. She then kills her men so no one can prove she did it, and plans to blame rival mob boss Hanley. As she celebrates, Punisher shoots and kills her.

PUNISHER: WAR ZONE #31 (September 1994)

"River of Blood Part One: Scorched Earth" (22 pages)

CREDITS: Chuck Dixon (writer), Joe Kubert (art), Jim Novak (letters), Joe Rosas (colors), Freddy Mendez (asst editor), Don Daley (editor)
FEATURE CHARACTER: Punisher (last in Pun #93, '94)
SUPPORTING CAST: Microchip (last in Pun:BSS #3/2, '94), Mickey Fondozzi (between PWJ #60-61, '93)
VILLAINS: Vikady (Russian drug supplier), Taz (Vikady's associate), Randy Kwoc (Vietnamese mobster, also in photo) (all 1st) & his men (some die), crack dealers (die), smugglers (die)
OTHER CHARACTERS: Dragunov (Russian vigilante, 1st), police (some die), bystanders, smugglers' mules (die)
LOCATIONS/ITEMS: Hindu Kush, New York inc airport, Kwoc estate, Vikady's hideout & Punisher's safe house / Punisher's assault rifle, machine gun, gun, knife & taxi; Dragunov's rocket launcher, dragunov & gun; Vikady's machine guns, Taz's Gatling gun, Kwoc's men's guns, smugglers' rifles, police guns
SYNOPSIS: In the Hindu Kush, Dragunov, a vigilante, kills some smugglers. He asks the survivors where Vikady is, then kills the rest. In New York, police prepare to arrest Vikady, a drug supplier, but Vikady ambushes and kills the police officers. Meanwhile, Punisher kills some crack dealers. The survivor says that Randy Kwoc is getting ready to buy a large amount of heroin from a foreigner. Punisher kills the survivor. While Microchip researches Randy Kwoc, Punisher learns from Mickey Fondozzi Kwoc's supplier is Russian, and where Kwoc will buy the heroin. Punisher watches Kwoc's estate for days until Vikady arrives. Punisher prepares to kill everyone, but is surprised to see someone else attack first. Punisher joins in killing Kwoc's men and meets Dragunov when the shooting stops. Vikady and Kwoc escape.
NOTE: Includes title/credits page (1 page).

PUNISHER: WAR ZONE #32 (October 1994)

"River of Blood Part Two: Comrades" (22 pages)

CREDITS: Chuck Dixon (writer), Joe Kubert (art), Jim Novak (letters), Joe Rosas (colors), Freddy Mendez (asst editor), Don Daley (editor)
FEATURE CHARACTER: Punisher
SUPPORTING CAST: Microchip
VILLAINS: Vikady (also in Dragunov's dream), Taz, Randy Kwoc & his men (some die, others as corpses), Russian mobsters inc Katrinka & interrogator (both 1st), mob boss (1st) & his men
OTHER CHARACTERS: Dragunov (also in own dream), police, clothing store patrons & staff, Josef's Restaurant patrons, alley cat; Vikady's victims (in Dragunov's dream)
LOCATIONS/ITEMS: New York inc clothing store, Josef's Restaurant, Kwoc estate, mob hideout, Punisher's safe house, Dragunov's motel room & hotel w/Vikady's room / Punisher's machine gun, guns, Battle Van & taxi; Dragunov's dragunov & gun; Microchip's computer, Katrinka's gun, interrogator's drill, Kwoc's men's guns
SYNOPSIS: Punisher and Dragunov join forces to kill the rest of Kwoc's men. Realizing that Vikady escaped, Dragunov runs of in a rage. Punisher escapes as the police arrive. As Microchip researches Vikady, Vikady meets with mobsters to sell the heroin that he was going to sell to Kwoc. Meanwhile, Dragunov dreams of killing Vikady. When Vikady goes shopping, Microchip notices he's spent traveler's checks purchased in Moscow. Punisher searches for Dragunov in a Russian restaurant. Unfortunately, when he mentions Dragunov, he's immediately attacked

and knocked out. Vikady returns to his hotel room to find Randy Kwoc waiting to kill him. Punisher wakes up tied to a chair. The Russian mob begins to interrogate Punisher about Dragunov.
NOTE: Includes title/credits page (1 page). PWZ #33, '94 reveals Katrinka's name.

PUNISHER: WAR ZONE #33 (November 1994)

"River of Blood Part Three: Capital Crimes" (22 pages)

CREDITS: Chuck Dixon (writer), Joe Kubert (art, co-c colors), Jim Novak (letters), Joe Rosas (colors), Freddy Mendez (asst editor), Don Daley (editor), John Marks (co-c colors)
FEATURE CHARACTER: Punisher
SUPPORTING CAST: Microchip
VILLAINS: Vikady, Taz, Russian mobsters (most die) inc Katrinka & interrogator (dies), mob boss (dies) & his men (die)
OTHER CHARACTERS: Dragunov, Randy Kwoc & his men (both as corpses), police, bystanders, sea gulls
LOCATIONS/ITEMS: New York inc Verrazano Narrows, Josef's Restaurant, Punisher's safe house, mob hideout & hotel w/Vikady's room / Punisher's ballistic knife, listening device & taxi; Dragunov's dragunov & gun; Katrinka's gun, interrogator's drill, Russian mobsters' guns, Kwoc's men's guns, mobsters' guns, police guns
SYNOPSIS: The Russian mob begins to torture Punisher for information about Dragunov, but they're interrupted when Dragunov arrives. Dragunov kills all but one of the Russian mobsters, leaving Katrinka alive. Meanwhile, police arrive at Vikady's hotel room to find Randy Kwoc and his men dead. Katrinka tells Punisher and Dragunov that Vikady wanted to sell them heroin, but the Russian mob wasn't interested. Punisher and Dragunov leave and wait outside until Katrinka calls Vikady. Listening to the phone call with a listening device, they learn Vikady is meeting with other mobsters. Punisher and Dragunov attack the meeting and kill the mobsters, but Vikady escapes again. Punisher calls Microchip and arranges for transport to Russia.
NOTE: Includes title/credits page (1 page).

PUNISHER: WAR ZONE #34 (December 1994)

"River of Blood Part Four: Dead Men's Eyes" (22 pages)

CREDITS: Chuck Dixon (writer), Joe Kubert (art), Jim Novak (letters), Joe Rosas (colors), Freddy Mendez (asst editor), Don Daley (editor)
FEATURE CHARACTER: Punisher
SUPPORTING CAST: Microchip
VILLAINS: Vikady & his mercenaries, Taz, Russian criminal (dies), carjackers (die) inc Yuri (dies), Eastern European warlords, Russian Mafia informant
OTHER CHARACTERS: Dragunov, Svetlanya (Dragunov's assistant), Dr. Manfred Bhukurov (nuclear scientist, dies), Assyrian Mafia (Dragunov's associates), Kursk restaurant patrons & staff, Kamtex personnel inc Stephan & Michael (both corpses), policeman, bystanders, horses
LOCATIONS/ITEMS: Russia inc beach, Assyrian Mafia hideout & train station; Kursk inc hotel & restaurant; Ukraine inc restaurant & Kamtex nuclear facility / Punisher's assault rifle, Dragunov's dragunov & van; Bhukurov's nuclear codes, Svetlanya's gun, Assyrians' assault rifles, mercenaries' guns, carjackers' guns, nuclear bomb
SYNOPSIS: In Russia, Dragunov introduces Punisher to the Assyrian Mafia. The vigilantes explain they're searching for Vikady and ask for help. The Assyrians agree, but only if Dragunov and Punisher kill a criminal for them. When the criminal is dead, the Assyrians arrange a meeting with a policeman, who points the vigilantes toward a Mafia informant, who tells them Vikady is looking for Dr. Manfred Bhukurov, Kamtex Industries and a physics package. Meanwhile, Vikady gets some nuclear codes from Dr. Bhukurov, then kills the doctor. Dragunov brings Punisher across the country. Punisher meets with Microchip, who says Vikady is looking to acquire a nuclear bomb. Meanwhile, Vikady steals a nuclear bomb from Kamtex Industries and puts it for sale on the black market.
NOTE: Includes title/credits page (1 page).

PUNISHER: WAR ZONE #35 (January 1995)

"River of Blood Part Five: Open Wounds" (22 pages)

CREDITS: Chuck Dixon (writer), Joe Kubert (art, co-c colors), Jim Novak (letters), Joe Rosas (colors), Freddy Mendez (asst editor), Don Daley (editor), John-Marc Gorb (co-c colors)
FEATURE CHARACTER: Punisher
SUPPORTING CAST: Microchip
VILLAINS: Vikady, Taz (both also in photo), Serbian Army (some die), Bosnian Muslims (some die)
OTHER CHARACTERS: Dragunov, Josip (1st) & his men (freedom fighters) inc Mitar (1st), United Nations agents, CNN reporters, bystanders (some die)
LOCATIONS/ITEMS: Sarajevo inc Josip's hideout, rail yard, sewers & hotel w/Vikady's room / Punisher's assault rifle, Dragunov's dragunov, Mitar's rifle, Josip's knife, Josip's men's guns, United Nations agents' assault rifles, Serbian Army's guns & mortars
SYNOPSIS: Punisher, Microchip and Dragunov meet with some freedom fighters in war-torn Sarajevo. Punisher explains the Serbian Army bought a nuclear bomb from Vikady, and they plan to detonate it in Sarajevo. Josip and his freedom fighters agree to help. They make their way through the city, avoiding battles as they can. Eventually, they capture, interrogate and kill some Serbian Army soldiers, learning the bomb will be detonated within twenty-four hours, but not where. Vikady and Taz arrive in Serbia. Vikady arrives in Serbia; Punisher, Dragunov and the freedom fighters eventually find him in a hotel. They prepare to attack Vikady, but are stopped by United Nations agents.
NOTE: Includes title/credits page (1 page).

PUNISHER: WAR ZONE #36 (February 1995)

"River of Blood Part Six: Children of the Gun" (22 pages)

CREDITS: Chuck Dixon (writer), Joe Kubert (art), Jim Novak (letters), Joe Rosas (colors), Freddy Mendez (asst editor), Don Daley (editor)
FEATURE CHARACTER: Punisher (next in PWZ #38, '95)
SUPPORTING CAST: Microchip (next in PunHol #3/2, '95)
VILLAINS: Vikady, Taz (both die), Serbian Army (some die)
OTHER CHARACTERS: Dragunov, Josip & his men inc Mitar, United Nations agents, bystanders, cat
LOCATIONS/ITEMS: Sarajevo inc hotel & scrap yard / Punisher's assault rifle, gun & grenades; Vikady's transmitter, Mitar's rifle, Josip's assault rifle, Josip's men's guns, United Nations agents' assault rifles, nuclear bomb
SYNOPSIS: Punisher distracts the United Nations agents with a couple of hand grenades, making sure not to kill any of the agents. Vikady and Taz escape with the nuclear bomb. Punisher and Dragunov search for Vikady while Microchip and the freedom fighters search for Vikady's truck with the bomb. Microchip spots the truck going in to a scrap yard while Punisher evades UN agents. Microchip searches the scrap yard while Punisher finds Vikady. Punisher tries to get closer to Vikady. Josip finds the bomb, but Microchip can't disarm it; he needs the transmitter to turn it off. Freedom fighter Mitar provides cover fire so Punisher and Dragunov can get to Vikady. Vikady refuses to hand over the transmitter, threatening to detonate the device. Mitar shoots Vikady and the bomb is disabled.
NOTE: Includes title/credits page (1 page).

PUNISHER: WAR ZONE #37 (March 1995)

"Something Like Love" (21 pages)

CREDITS: Chuck Dixon (writer), Mark Texeira (art), Jim Novak (letters), Jim Starlin & Electric Prism (colors), Freddy Mendez (asst editor), Don Daley (editor), Paul Mounts (c colors)
FEATURE CHARACTER: Punisher (last in Pun:Blood, '91, next in Pun #49, '91)
SUPPORTING CAST: Microchip (last in Pun:Blood, '91, next in Pun #50, '91)
VILLAINS: Darrel, Louis, Mario & Money (all robbers, die), 2 crank dealers (1 as corpse)
OTHER CHARACTERS: Max (also in pfb, 1st chr app before Pun #54, '91), Empire Check Cashing owner (Max's former owner, also in pfb, dies), dog seller (in pfb), Nicodemus Santelli (pizzeria owner, mentioned, killed by robbers, see NOTE)
LOCATIONS/ITEMS: Bronx (also in pfb) inc Empire Check Cashing & Punisher's safe house / Punisher's shotgun, ballistic knife & Battle Van; Microchip's first aid kit, robbers' guns & axe
FLASHBACK: Max is bought on the street and trained to be an attack dog (p).
SYNOPSIS: Punisher interrogates a crank dealer about a group of robbers who hit a pizzeria and killed the owner, Nicodemus Santelli. Meanwhile, the group robs Empire Check Cashing and kills the owner, unwittingly releasing an attack dog. The dog chases the robbers into the street where Punisher finds them. Punisher and the dog chase and kill the robbers one by one, until a roof collapses and separately traps the dog and Punisher. Punisher is able to kill one of the robbers with his ballistic knife, then knocks the last robber down so the dog can kill him. Punisher takes the dog to his safe house and patches his wounds. Microchip names him Max.
NOTE: Includes title/credits page (1 page). As a teenager, Frank Castle delivered pizzas for Santelli.

PUNISHER: WAR ZONE #38 (April 1995)

"Dark Judgment Part 1" (22 pages)

CREDITS: Steven Grant (writer), John Hebert (pencils), Fred Fredericks (inks), Jim Novak (letters), Karl Bollers (colors), Freddy Mendez (asst editor), Don Daley (editor)
FEATURE CHARACTER: Punisher (also as computer repairman, also in fb between Pun:AG, '88 fb & Pun Ann #4, '91; last in PWZ #36, '95)
SUPPORTING CAST: Lisa Castle, Frank Castle, Jr. (both in fb between Pun:AG, '88 fb & Pun Ann #4, '91)
VILLAINS: Full Moon Killer (Judge DuPrey, 1st), Mr. Shockett (mobster, 1st) & his men (some die) inc Eddie (dies), Mr. Brazo (rival mobster, 1st) & his men
OTHER CHARACTERS: Jean Sutherland (reporter, 1st), Carson (FBI agent, 1st), Mr. Harrigan (defendant) & his lawyer, Brazo's secretary, postal worker, reporters, bystanders (1 dies), Peela (dog, dies)
LOCATIONS/ITEMS: Castle family home (in fb), New York inc post office, library, newspaper office, court house, Punisher's motel room, Shockett estate & Brazo estate w/interrogation room / Punisher's computer, shotgun, machine gun, revolver & guns; Full Moon Killer's cane sword, Carson's revolver, Shockett's machine pistol, Shockett's men's guns, Brazo's men's guns
FLASHBACK: Frank Castle plays with his children.
SYNOPSIS: A group of men attacks and subdues Punisher. They take him to Mr. Shockett, a mobster, who tells Punisher about the Full Moon Killer and tasks Punisher with killing the Killer. Shockett leaves. Punisher kills Shockett's men and follows Shockett home. Rival mobster Mr. Brazo has men watching the Shockett estate, and when they see Punisher leaving they abduct one of Shockett's men, Eddie. Later, Brazo interrogates Eddie, who says Punisher works for Shockett. Punisher gets some supplies and investigates the Full Moon Killer. Unsatisfied with the library's information, he poses as a computer repairman and hacks a newspaper's computer for better information. Later, FBI agent Carson is upset the judge threw out his case. Punisher bumps into him and steals Carson's ID, which he uses to get the FBI's information on the Full Moon Killer. Carson finds and ambushes Punisher, but Brazo's men intervene and abduct Carson. Elsewhere, the Full Moon Killer kills again.
NOTE: PWZ #39, '95 names Full Moon Killer & reveals he's a judge, PWZ #40, '95 reveals his real name.

PUNISHER: WAR ZONE #39 (May 1995)

"Dark Judgment Part 2" (22 pages)

CREDITS: Steven Grant (writer), John Hebert (pencils), Fred Fredericks (inks), Jim Novak (letters), Karl Bollers (colors), Freddy Mendez (asst editor), Don Daley (editor), Bobbie Chase (group editor), Elman Brown (c inks), Paul Mounts (c colors)
FEATURE CHARACTER: Punisher
VILLAINS: Full Moon Killer, Mr. Shockett & his men (some die), Mr. Brazo (dies) & his men (some die), criminals
OTHER CHARACTERS: Jean Sutherland, Carson, Mr. Hanson (Punisher's lawyer) & his aide, police, bystanders, Shockett's dogs
LOCATIONS/ITEMS: New York inc Sutherland's apartment, court house, Shockett estate & warehouse, Brazo estate w/interrogation room / Punisher's binoculars, assault rifle, guns & knife; Full Moon Killer's cane sword, Brazo's gun, Brazo's men's guns, Shockett's men's guns, police guns

SYNOPSIS: Punisher infiltrates Shockett's home and demands to know why the mobster wants Punisher to kill the Full Moon Killer. Shockett claims the killer is rival mobster Brazo. Before Punisher can question Shockett further, Shockett's men attack and Shockett escapes. Meanwhile, Brazo interrogates Carson. When Brazo learns Carson is an FBI agent, he yells at his men and orders Carson killed. Punisher arrives at Brazo's estate as Carson is dragged out and saves Carson. Reporter Jean Sutherland arrives and drives away with Punisher and Carson. Punisher dresses Carson's wounds at Jean's apartment and renews his search for the Full Moon Killer. Brazo finds where Shockett is hiding and attacks. Shockett accidentally kills Brazo. Punisher checks for areas where the Full Moon Killer hasn't yet struck and finds him. Punisher prepares to kill the Killer, but police stop him. The next day at Punisher's arraignment, Punisher recognizes his judge as the Full Moon Killer.

PUNISHER: WAR ZONE #40 (May 1995)

"Dark Judgment the Conclusion" (22 pages)

CREDITS: Steven Grant (writer), John Hebert (pencils), Fred Fredericks (inks), Jim Novak (letters), Karl Bollers (colors), Freddy Mendez (asst editor), Don Daley (editor), Bobbie Chase (group editor)
FEATURE CHARACTER: Punisher (next in PunHol #3, '95, GR/W/Pun, '94, PWJ #61, '93, PWZ #23, '94)
VILLAINS: Full Moon Killer, Mr. Shockett (both die) & his men, mob bosses, jail inmates
OTHER CHARACTERS: Jean Sutherland, Carson, Carl (DuPrey's doorman), DuPrey's secretary & helicopter pilot (dies), police, reporters
LOCATIONS/ITEMS: New York inc Sutherland's apartment, jail, newspaper office, DuPrey estate, court house w/DuPrey's office / Punisher's assault rifle & lock picks; Full Moon Killer's cane sword, yacht & helicopter; Carson's revolver, Shockett's man's sniper rifle, police guns

SYNOPSIS: Shockett meets with the city's mob bosses, who chastise Shockett for killing Brazo. They tell Shockett to take over Brazo's territory and no retaliation will be taken as long as nothing changes from how Brazo had things. Shockett realizes that Brazo had Judge DuPrey, the Full Moon Killer, in his pocket, and that Punisher is going to kill DuPrey. Carson escorts Punisher out of the police station for transport to a Federal facility, but one of Shockett's men tries to kill Punisher. Punisher steals Carson's revolver, kills the assassin and escapes. Punisher bursts into DuPrey's office, but he's already gone. Jean Sutherland learns Punisher is hunting DuPrey. Shockett meets with DuPrey to make sure things don't change. DuPrey kills Shockett. As DuPrey leaves, Jean approaches him for an interview. Carson tries to arrest DuPrey, but DuPrey knocks him out. DuPrey tries to escape by helicopter, but Punisher kills him.

PUNISHER: WAR ZONE #41 (July 1995)

"Dead and Deader" (22 pages)

CREDITS: Chuck Dixon (writer), Rod Whigham (pencils), Mike Witherby (inks), Vickie Williams (letters), Tom Ziuko (colors), Chris Cooper (editor), Bobbie Chase (group editor), Jae Lee (c art)
FEATURE CHARACTER: Punisher (also in rfb, last in SM:PoT #4, '95, next in Pun #104, '95)
SUPPORTING CAST: Mickey Fondozzi (between Pun #103-104, '95)
VILLAINS: Bullseye, Stone Cold (both last in PWJ #79, '95, next in Pun #104, '95), Kingpin (last in DD #342, '95, next in Pun #104, '95), Arranger (last in W/Pun #3, '93), Mr. Dandy (Kingpin's employee), Salvador Borosco (Bolivian cocaine supplier, dies) & his men (die) inc Guzman & Luis (both die)
OTHER CHARACTERS: Payback (last in PWJ #78, '95, dies), reporter (on TV), Kevin & Shanna Dreyer (both off-panel), Steven & Lisa Dreyer (prev 4 corpses), police; Maria Castle, Lisa Castle, Frank Castle, Jr. (prev 3 in rfb)
LOCATIONS/ITEMS: New York inc Sal's condo, Kingpin's exercise room, Punisher's motel room, Mickey's trailer, police station & Central Park (also in rfb) / Punisher's assault rifle, gun & listening device; Payback's machine gun, grenade & gun; Stone Cold's assault rifle & gun; Bullseye's machine gun, Sal's machine guns, Sal's men's guns, Phalanx armor
FLASHBACK: The Castle family is killed in Central Park (PWJ #1, '88 fb).

SYNOPSIS: Punisher prepares to kill Salvador Borosco, a cocaine supplier. Payback, thinking Punisher killed Microchip, suddenly bursts in and attacks Punisher. As Punisher and Payback battle, Sal sends his men to investigate the ruckus. Meanwhile, Wilson Fisk plans to take advantage of the chaos Punisher has caused in the criminal underworld and retake his position as Kingpin of crime. Elsewhere, Bullseye, in the Phalanx armor, takes Mickey Fondozzi hostage. Sal's men follow Punisher and Payback into Central Park. Payback escapes from Punisher to regroup, only for Stone Cold to kill him. Punisher follows the sound of Stone Cold's gunfire and fires at movement. He's stunned to find two dead civilians. Sal attacks Punisher, who in a daze kills Sal and his men. Later, Punisher contemplates suicide for killing two innocent bystanders, but instead decides to turn himself in to the police.

NOTE: Final issue of this volume. Cover labeled "Countdown 2." Story continued from PWJ #79, '95 where Stone Cold killed Microchip & continues in Pun #104, '95 where Kingpin stops Punisher from turning himself in to the police. Pun #1, '95 names the two dead civilians as Steven & Lisa Dreyer, reveals their children Kevin & Shanna were also killed and that Bullseye killed them, not Punisher.

PUNISHER #1 (November 1995)

"Condemned!" (23 pages)

CREDITS: John Ostrander (writer), Tom Lyle (pencils), Chris Ivy (inks), Richard Starkings & Comicraft (letters), John Kalisz & Malibu (colors), Chris Cooper (editor), Bobbie Chase (group editor)
FEATURE CHARACTER: Punisher (also in photo, rfb & pfb)
GUEST STARS: Avengers: Black Widow (Natasha Romanova, last in SMTU #4, '96, next in IHulk #440, '96), Giant-Man (Hank Pym, last in SMTU #4, '96, next in Thor #495, '96); Timothy "Dum Dum" Dugan (SHIELD Special Director, last in IHulk #434, '95, next in IHulk #437, '96), Doc Samson (Leonard Samson, Gamma powered psychologist, also in pfb, last in DE:Ω, '95, next in DocS #1, '96)
SUPPORTING CAST: Don Mario Geraci (mob Capo), Vinnie Barbarossa (Geraci lieutenant) (both 1st)
VILLAIN: Bullseye (also as a priest, last in PWJ #80, '95, chr next in DCvM #1, '96, next in Elektra #1, '96)
OTHER CHARACTERS: Mikel Fury (Nick Fury's son, last in DE:Ω, '95, next in Pun #7, '96), la Contessa Valentina de Fontaine (SHIELD Special Director, last in IHulk #434, '95, next in Cap #449, '96), Dr. Kemble (1st, next in Pun #4, '96, prison doctor, on Geraci's payroll), prison executioner (1st, next in Pun #3, '96), Judge Robert Braithwaite (1st), Molly Fitzgerald (Frank's public defender) (both in pfb), Geraci's men (as paramedics), prison warden & guards; Nick Fury LMD (see NOTE); Ghost Rider (both in rfb); Microchip, Frank Castle Jr., Lisa Castle, Maria Castle, Carlos Cruz, Kevin Dreyer, Lisa Dreyer, Shanna Dreyer, Steven Dreyer (prev 8 in Punisher's thoughts)
LOCATIONS/ITEMS: New York inc courtroom (in pfb), prison w/Frank's cell & execution chamber & San Genaro neighborhood w/Geraci warehouse / Bullseye's rifle & handgun; Vinnie's handgun & revolver; Geraci's cane, electric chair, body bag, stretcher, ambulance
FLASHBACKS: Punisher kills Nick Fury. Ghost Rider gives Punisher the penance stare (DE:Ω, '95). Frank Castle pleads guilty to the murder of the Dreyer family and Nick Fury. Doc Samson testifies that Punisher wasn't responsible for Fury's death due to mind control, but admits he was lucid for the Dreyers' deaths. Frank is found guilty and sentenced to the electric chair. Castle refuses to let his lawyer file for an appeal (p).
SYNOPSIS: SHIELD agents and the Avengers prepare to witness Frank Castle's execution as a priest gives Frank his last rites. The priest reveals he is Bullseye, admitting he killed the Dreyers, not Frank. The Punisher is executed and his body is taken away. Castle wakes up in a warehouse, where Don Mario Geraci introduces himself and his bodyguard, Vinnie. Geraci tells Punisher that he faked the execution because he wants him to take over the Geraci crime family. Mario tells Punisher his family doesn't deal in drugs or prostitution, and that he's dying and needs a successor. While touring Geraci's neighborhood, Mario is shot. Vinnie throws Punisher a gun, who quickly finds that Bullseye fired the shot. Instead of killing him, Punisher shoots Bullseye's hands as his punishment. Punisher accepts Geraci's offer.
NOTE: 1st issue to be published under the Marvel Edge group. Todd Klein designed the new cover logo. Pun #9, '96 reveals Mario Geraci hired Bullseye to force Punisher to accept his offer by wounding him. Pun #4, '96 reveals Punisher accepts Geraci's offer so he can take down the crime family from within. Fury/13 #1-2, '98 reveals the Nick Fury Punisher killed was actually an advanced LMD (Life Model Decoy, a robot designed to mimic specific people). The San Genaro neighborhood is named in Pun #3, '96.

PUNISHER #2 (December 1995)

"Family" (22 pages)

CREDITS: John Ostrander (writer), Tom Lyle (pencils), Chris Ivy (inks), Richard Starkings & Comicraft (letters), John Kalisz (colors), Chris Cooper (editor), Bobbie Chase (group editor)
FEATURE CHARACTER: Punisher (also in photo, next in DCvM #1, '96, DCvM #2-4, '96 bts)
SUPPORTING CAST: Leslie Geraci (Mario's granddaughter), Horace Halftree, Kim Sung Young (all Geraci lieutenants), Mary Rose Geraci (Mario's granddaughter, next in Pun #6, '96), Tom Nichols (Geraci family consigliere) (all 1st)
VILLAINS: Jigsaw (last in PWJ #61, '93), Joey Geraci (Mario's grandson), Yakuza clan Daichi Doku inc Sho Honikawa (clan Oyabun) (prev 3 1st), Hachiman (Yakuza "Hatchetman" assassin, bts, en route to USA), Geraci family inc Robert (1st) & Jerry
OTHER CHARACTERS: Judge Robert Braithwaite (dies); Frank Castle Jr., Lisa Castle, Maria Castle (prev 3 in photo)
LOCATIONS/ITEMS: Geraci Hudson River Estate inc dining room & Punisher's room, Honikawa's suite, Braithwaite's chambers / Geraci's helicopter (destroyed) & jeep; Geraci family's guns & baseball bats; Jigsaw's Punisher suit & Uzi
SYNOPSIS: Frank Castle is brought to the Geraci Estate, where the news of his takeover is not well-received. As Mario's injuries are treated, Vinnie introduces Frank to the rest of the family and promises to follow him until Frank betrays them. Elsewhere, hearing the Geraci family is weak, the Yakuza set their sights on Geraci's territory. Honikawa is reluctant to call in Hachiman to aid them, distrusting metahumans. Meanwhile, Geraci's men refuse to follow Frank given his past as the Punisher. Frank challenges them all to a fight to which Geraci agrees, but with no guns. Frank suits up and begins systematically taking down Geraci's men. Robert decides he's had enough and attempts to pull his gun, but Leslie shoots his hand as punishment for breaking the rules. Frank emerges victorious. In the city, Jigsaw, who is wearing a stitched together Punisher suit, guns down Judge Braithwaite for his role in Frank's death.

PUNISHER #3 (January 1996)

"Hatchet Job" (23 pages)

CREDITS: John Ostrander (writer), Tom Lyle (pencils), Chris Ivy (inks), Richard Starkings & Comicraft (letters), John Kalisz & Malibu (colors), Chris Cooper (editor), Bobbie Chase (group editor)
FEATURE CHARACTER: Punisher
SUPPORTING CAST: Leslie Geraci, Horace Halftree (both next in SM/Pun #1, '96), Vinnie Barbarossa, Don Mario Geraci, Tom Nichols, Kim Sung Young
VILLAINS: Jigsaw, Joey Geraci (next in SM/PUN #1, '96), Hachiman (1st full app, next in Pun #9, '96), Yakuza clan Daichi Doku (6 die) inc Tatsu & Sho Honikawa, Geraci family inc Robert
OTHER CHARACTERS: Augie & Stella Corto (deli owners), prison executioner (last in Pun #1, '95, dies), bystander
LOCATIONS/ITEMS: Corto Deli, Daichi Doku HQ, San Genaro, Sansone's Italian restaurant, Geraci Estate / Punisher's guns, bow & arrows; Kim's gun & Uzi; Leslie's gun & machine gun; Jigsaw's Punisher suit & gun; Vinnie's Rolls Royce, Yakuza's guns, Hachiman's hatchets

SYNOPSIS: The Punisher interrupts a Yakuza attempt to extort money from a Geraci business. He kills three and sends one back to his bosses with a message. Honikawa decides to try and recruit Geraci lieutenant Kim Young before Hachiman arrives. Later, while Frank restructures and learns about the business of being a don, the Yakuza approach Kim, but he guns them down in response. Honikawa sends out Hachiman, who draws the Geracis out by attacking their neighborhood. Punisher leads the response force, but their bullets can't penetrate Hachiman's force field. Noticing rain penetrates it, Punisher sends Leslie for a bow and arrows while he rescues a civilian from a Geraci man using her as a shield. Just before Hachiman kills Kim, Punisher hits his arm with an arrow, piercing his field. Punisher spares his life in exchange for Hachiman telling his bosses they should talk. In Punisher's debt, Hachiman leaves. Elsewhere, Jigsaw kills the man who flipped the switch on Punisher's electric chair.
NOTE: The cover is dated December while the indicia says January.

PUNISHER #4 (February 1996)

"Clash" (21 pages)

CREDITS: John Ostrander (writer), Tom Lyle (pencils), Chris Ivy (co-inks, c inks), Art Nichols (co-inks), Richard Starkings & Comicraft (letters), John Kalisz & Malibu (colors), Chris Cooper (editor), Bobbie Chase (group editor)
FEATURE CHARACTER: Punisher (next in SM/Pun #1-2, '96)
GUEST STAR: Daredevil (last in DD #351, '96, next in Goblin #6, '96)
SUPPORTING CAST: Don Mario Geraci, Kim Sung Young (both next in SM/Pun #1, '96), Tom Nichols (next in SM/Pun #2, '96), Vinnie Barbarossa
VILLAINS: Jigsaw (next in Pun #9, '96), Joey Geraci, Geraci family inc Robert
OTHER CHARACTERS: Dr. Kemble (last in Pun #1, '95, dies), bystander
LOCATIONS/ITEMS: Hell's Kitchen inc 41st police precinct; San Genaro, Sansone's Italian restaurant / Jigsaw's Punisher suit, Uzis & van; Daredevil's Billy clubs, Geraci family's guns, Punisher's gun

SYNOPSIS: Daredevil breaks up a fur theft by some of Geraci's men. After they are bailed out, Punisher demands to know who ordered the side job, and Geraci claims responsibility, confirming Frank's suspicions that Geraci wasn't really retired. Punisher quits, but the strain of aggravation weakens Geraci and he sends Vinnie to bring Punisher back. Elsewhere, Jigsaw attacks Dr. Kemble, who calls the Geracis for help. On the roof, Daredevil confronts Punisher, who explains he originally intended to take the Geraci family down from within but has discovered he's good at running a crime family. Geraci explains Kemble's predicament to Punisher, who reluctantly agrees to help as a matter of honor. Daredevil beats Punisher to Kemble's and battles Jigsaw to save the doctor. Learning Punisher is alive when he too arrives, Jigsaw is initially happy, then angry for being made a fool of, and he and Punisher and Jigsaw fight until Punisher defeats him. He leaves Jigsaw for the authorities and Daredevil gives Punisher a pass, having figured out what he's doing with the Geracis, but promises to keep an eye on him.
NOTE: Daredevil wears his original yellow and red costume, but is in his classic red costume on the cover.

PUNISHER #5 (March 1996)

"Firepower" (22 pages)

CREDITS: John Ostrander (writer), Pat Broderick (pencils), Ralph Cabrera (inks), Richard Starkings & Comicraft (letters), John Kalisz & Malibu (colors), Chris Cooper (editor), Bobbie Chase (group editor), Tom Lyle (c pencils), Chris Ivy (c inks)
FEATURE CHARACTER: Punisher
SUPPORTING CAST: Vinnie Barbarossa, Don Mario Geraci, Leslie Geraci, Tom Nichols (all last in SM/Pun #2, '96), Horace Halftree, Kim Sung Young (both last in SM/Pun #1, '96)
VILLAINS: Rosalie Carbone (last in DE:A, '95, dies) & her men (die), Firefox (Grigori Andreivitch, living arsenal hit man, last in FoS #4, '95), Hammerhead (metal-skulled mobster, last in SSWP #33, '95, next in SM #70, '96) & his men, Tombstone (Lonnie Lincoln, superstrong albino, last in SM/Pun #2, '96, next in Pun #9, '96) & his men, Kozorov (Mafiya cell leader, dies) & his men, other New York crime bosses (some die), Korzorov's enemies (die), Joey Geraci (last in SM/PUN #2, '96
LOCATIONS/ITEMS: Russian warehouse, New York inc conference room / Firefox's chain gun, Russian Uzis, Carbone's men's assault rifles, Tombstone's guns, Punisher's guns, Geraci lieutenants' guns, Rosalie's gun

SYNOPSIS: Firefox completes his latest job, then kills his employer and takes over his Mafiya cell. When he says he is looking to expand to America, one of his new men mentions the weakened Geraci territory. Firefox orders preparations made while he consolidates his position. The next night, a New York crime families' meeting protesting Punisher's new position is crashed by Rosalie Carbone, demanding vengeance against Punisher. As her men storm the place, Punisher gets Geraci out, teaming with Tombstone and holding Rosalie's men off. Punisher lures them away and heads for the roof where he finds Rosalie waiting. Punisher is blown off the roof just before his men storm it, blasting Rosalie's men. Rosalie finds Punisher hanging to the ledge and is about to kill him when Leslie shoots her. Leslie helps him up and explains knowing him poisoned Rosalie, and she suspects he'll try to do the same to her. However, since Rosalie's example to the male-dominated mob soured Leslie's own chances to become the true Geraci capo, she saved Punisher anyway.

PUNISHER #6 (April 1996)

"Hostage to the Devil" (22 pages)

CREDITS: John Ostrander (writer), Pat Broderick (pencils), Bruce Patterson (inks), Richard Starkings & Comicraft (letters), John Kalisz & Malibu (colors), Chris Cooper (editor), Bobbie Chase (group editor), Tom Lyle (c pencils), Christopher Ivy (c inks)
FEATURE CHARACTER: Punisher (next in Foxfire #3-4, OtEdge #5, DocS #3, all '96)
SUPPORTING CAST: Mary Rose Geraci (last in Pun #2, '95), Vinnie Barbarossa, Leslie Geraci, Tom Nichols (all next in OtEdge #5, '96), Don Mario Geraci (next in Pun #9, '96), Horace Halftree, Kim Sung Young
VILLAINS: Firefox (next in Pun #9, '96) & his men inc Vassily Vassilevitch (all die), Joey Geraci (next in OtEdge #5, '96), Geraci family & informants
OTHER CHARACTERS: Mario Barbarossa (Vinnie's son, last in SM/Pun #2, '96, dies), Father Dominic Geraci (priest & Geraci's grandson, 1st, next in Pun #10, '96)
LOCATIONS/ITEMS: Tomasi dance school, Church of St. Janisius, Hatch funeral home in Westchester, Sansone's Italian restaurant, Hoboken railroad bridge,

San Genaro warehouse / Punisher's Kevlar skull cap, wig, blood packet & guns; Kim's Uzi & handgun, Geraci family's limo & machine guns, Firefox's chain gun

SYNOPSIS: Firefox abducts Mary Rose and kills her bodyguards, including Vinnie's son, Mario. Elsewhere, Frank pays a visit to Father Dominic Geraci to introduce himself, but they're interrupted by Geraci's men, who take them to the funeral home where Mario's body is. They receive a video with Firefox's demands for money and the names of the people they control. Geraci is willing to pay up despite objections from his men and Vinnie begging for vengeance. Frank promises to save Mary Rose and let Vinnie get his revenge, and sends his people out to find out what they can about Firefox. Later, Geraci fakes a stroke in order to allow Frank to attend the drop. As expected, Firefox attempts to kill Frank after receiving his money, but Frank is prepared, surviving thanks to hidden armor. Halftree tails Firefox to a San Genaro warehouse. Punisher quietly rescues Mary Rose before sounding the attack. Punisher chases Firefox to the water before he dives in and disappears. Punisher explains he didn't kill him because he promised that to Vinnie, and Leslie hopes that won't prove a future mistake.

NOTE: Last issue to be published under the Marvel Edge group.

PUNISHER #7 (May 1996)

"He's Alive?!" (22 pages)

CREDITS: John Ostrander (writer), Tom Lyle (pencils), Mike Sellers (inks), Richard Starkings & Comicraft (letters), John Kalisz & Malibu (colors), Chris Cooper & Jaye Gardner (editors), Chris (c inks)
FEATURE CHARACTER: Punisher (also in photo)
GUEST STARS: George Washington "G.W." Bridge (SHIELD director, last in W '95/2, next in XFor #55, '96), Doc Samson (between IHulk #440-441, '96), Dum Dum Dugan (last in IHulk #439, '96, next in Av #396, '96)
SUPPORTING CAST: Vinnie Barbarossa, Leslie Geraci, Tom Nichols (all last in OtEdge #5, '96), Mary Rose Geraci (last in OtEdge #5, '96, next bts in Pun #9, '96), Horace Halftree, Kim Sung Young
VILLAINS: Joey Geraci (last in OtEdge #5, '96, next in Pun #10, '96), Geraci family
OTHER CHARACTERS: Contessa Val Fontaine (last in Cap #449, '96), Mikel Fury (last in Pun #1, '95, chr next in SecWs #24, '11 fb, next in SecWs #11, '10), other SHIELD agents inc Mandroids & Cobra, Delta, Tiger & Wolf Squads; Nick Fury LMD (bts, gone missing, last in IHulk #434, '95, next in Fury/13 #1, '98), Senator Breidermann (appoints Bridge); Frank Castle Jr., Lisa Castle (both in photo), Maria Castle (in photo & Punisher's thoughts), Microchip (in Punisher's thoughts)
LOCATIONS/ITEMS: Washington DC inc Sen. Breidermann's office; Geraci Estate inc Punisher's room / SHIELD Mandroid armors, blasters, hovercraft, jetpacks, mercy bullets & Helicarrier inc w/meeting room & artificial cloud cover; Vinnie's gun, Mikel Fury's blaster, Geraci family's guns, Punisher's guns
SYNOPSIS: Mikel Fury learns Frank Castle is still alive and that Nick Fury's body is no longer in its grave. Mikel gathers squads of SHIELD agents to take down Castle despite Val and Dugan's protests. Joey Geraci's plan to turn his family against Punisher by setting up a tryst with the underage Mary Rose fails when Castle rejects the girl. Leslie Geraci discovers her brother's plan and threatens him to stop his shenanigans. Mikel and his agents sneak onto the Geraci estate to find and kill Punisher, but Castle, anticipating the raid, gets the drop on Mikel. Punisher refuses to be taken by an unauthorized "goon squad" and the Geracis are shot in the melee. Enraged, Castle strikes at Mikel, who goads Punisher into trying to kill him to justify SHIELD's use of lethal force against Castle. G.W. Bridge, the newly appointed head of SHIELD, arrives, orders his troops to stand down and reveals SHIELD used mercy bullets on the Geracis. Bridge kicks Mikel out of SHIELD for pursuing a personal vendetta and asserts his authority over the attack squad.

PUNISHER #8 (June 1996)

"Vengeance Is Mine!" (22 pages)

CREDITS: John Ostrander (writer), Tom Lyle (pencils), Robert Jones (inks), Richard Starkings & Comicraft (letters), John Kalisz & Malibu (colors), Mike Marts (asst editor), Jaye Gardner (editor)
FEATURE CHARACTER: Punisher
SUPPORTING CAST: Vinnie Barbarossa, Leslie Geraci, Horace Halftree, Tom Nichols, Kim Sung Young
VILLAINS: Mortalis (Esteban Morales, ex-DEA agent turned vigilante, also disguised as Acme cleaning services employee), Colombian drug lords inc Antony & Pepe (all die); Geraci family inc Hughie & Robert
OTHER CHARACTERS: Congressman Wachlinger (dies), Maria Morales (Moralis' deceased wife, mentioned)
LOCATIONS/ITEMS: Geraci Estate, Manhattan inc Congressman Wachlinger's hotel, Mortalis' East Side apartment building, Sansone's Italian restaurant & Tortelli Towers w/ furnace room, hotel room & stairwell / Mortalis' body armor, guns & smoke bomb; Punisher's gas mask, grenades, gun & rifle; Geraci family's guns & transceivers; Colombian drug lords' firearms
SYNOPSIS: The vengeance-driven vigilante Mortalis kills Colombian drug lords meeting with his target, Congressman Wachlinger. The politician runs for protection to the Geraci family, who bankrolled his career in return for favors. Frank Castle orders Geraci mobsters to guard Wachlinger and when Mortalis strikes again, Punisher fights him but fails to stop him from escaping. Castle learns Mortalis is an ex-DEA agent whose identity the congressman sold to drug lords, resulting in the bombing deaths of his family. Familiar with the kinds of tactics used by obsessed vigilantes, Punisher tracks down Mortalis and tells him to end his quest to kill Wachlinger. Mortalis refuses and appeals to Castle's sense of justice, but Horace Halftree kills Mortalis. Punisher returns to the Geraci Estate and kills the politician himself, claiming that he decides who is important to the crime family.
NOTE: Wachlinger is watching "Wheel of Fortune" on TV. Tom Nichols is called "Robbins" here. Letters page changes its name to "Bullet Proofs."

PUNISHER #9 (July 1996)

"Tumbling Down" (22 pages)

CREDITS: John Ostrander (writer), Tom Lyle (pencils), Robert Jones (inks), Richard Starkings & Comicraft (letters), John Kalisz (colors), Jaye Gardner (editor)
FEATURE CHARACTER: Punisher (also in photo)
SUPPORTING CAST: Vinnie Barbarossa, Horace Halftree, Kim Sung Young (all die), Mary Rose Geraci (bts, shopping, last in Pun #7, '96), Leslie Geraci
VILLAINS: Jigsaw (last in Pun #4, '96), Tombstone (last in Pun #5, '96), Yakuza clan Daichi Doku, Hachiman (both last in Pun #8, '96), Firefox & his men (last in Pun #6, '96), Mario Geraci (last in Pun #6, '96, dies), Geraci family (dies), Tom Nichols
OTHER CHARACTERS: Frank Castle Jr., Lisa Castle, Maria Castle (all in photo)

LOCATIONS/ITEMS: Geraci Estate inc Mario's room; New York inc Little Italy, Verrazano Bridge & Little Korea w/restaurant / Jigsaw's Punisher suit, gun, assault rifle & missile launcher; Punisher's knife & guns; Kim's Firebird & gun; Daichi Doku's & Firefox's men's guns, Vinnie's gun, Mario's nasal cannula, Hachiman's axes, Halftree's gun

SYNOPSIS: Frank Castle muses about his role as capo for the Geracis and Leslie Geraci tells him his goal to get her family out of the rackets is untenable. Tombstone kills Vinnie Barbarossa, Hachiman slays Kim Sung Young and Firefox murders Horace Halftree as part of a united assault on the Geracis orchestrated by Don Mario Geraci himself. As the Don confesses his plot to Punisher, Jigsaw, the Daichi Doku and Firefox's men launch an attack on the Geraci Estate. Mario Geraci and many of his mobsters are killed and the house burns down in the assault, but Castle finds a secret hiding place and survives, vowing to save the Geraci kids who are away from the property.

NOTE: Punisher makes his War Journal II: Entry 1 here. Pun #10, '96 reveals Tom is working against the Geracis with Mario, who has decided making Punisher his replacement was a bad idea.

PUNISHER #10 (August 1996)

"Last Shot Fired" (22 pages)

CREDITS: John Ostrander (writer), Tom Lyle (pencils), Robert Jones (inks), Richard Starkings & Comicraft (letters), John Kalisz & Malibu (colors), Jaye Gardner (editor)
FEATURE CHARACTER: Punisher (also disguised as chauffeur)
SUPPORTING CAST: Leslie Geraci (paralyzed), Mary Rose Geraci
VILLAINS: Jigsaw (next bts in Alias #26, '03, next in DD #62, '04), Tombstone (next in SMTU #5, '96), Firefox (next in Hawk #7, '04) & his men, Joey Geraci (last in Pun #7, '96), Tom Nichols (dies), Yakuza clan Daichi Doku, Hachiman
OTHER CHARACTERS: Fr. Dominic Geraci (last in Pun #6, '96), doctor
LOCATIONS/ITEMS: Manhattan inc St. Vincent's Hospital, riverside property w/brick building & bridge pier & Norris Theater w/lobby / Jigsaw's Punisher suit & gun; Punisher's assault rifle, sleeping gas & guns; Daichi Doku's & Firefox's men's guns; Hachiman's axes, Tombstone's limousine; Leslie's spinal brace, crane w/wrecking ball

SYNOPSIS: Frank Castle ambushes Tombstone in a limousine and forces him to divulge the location of Geraci children by chaining him to a wrecking ball and slamming him into a building before dropping him in the river. Punisher raids the theater where Jigsaw, Firefox and Hachiman hold Leslie, Mary Rose, Dominic, and Joey Geraci captive. When Jigsaw threatens to kill Leslie, Castle hesitates, leaving himself open to a shot from Firefox, but Hachiman slices off Firefox's arm, saving Punisher as repayment for Castle's sparing his life. Jigsaw takes Leslie up to the theater's fly loft and drops her, forcing Punisher to grab her and leave himself exposed. Leslie willingly lets go to save Castle, who shoots Jigsaw. Later, Punisher sneaks into Leslie's hospital and discovers she has severe spinal damage. Castle closes a chapter on his life and wonders about his future.

NOTE: Punisher makes his War Journal II: Entries 2-3 here. Tom Nichols is called "Tom Robbins" here.

PUNISHER #11 (September 1996)

"Manhattan Onslaught" (22 pages)

CREDITS: John Ostrander (writer), Tom Lyle (pencils), Robert Jones (inks), Richard Starkings & Comicraft (letters), John Kalisz & American Color (colors), Jaye Gardner (editor)
FEATURE CHARACTER: Punisher
GUEST STARS: G.W. Bridge (last in Cable #34, '96), Dum Dum Dugan (last in Cable #34, '96, chr next in Av Ann '99 fb, next in SM:DMH, '97)
VILLAINS: Onslaught (psionic merging of Professor X & Magneto's dark urges, bts, controlling Sentinels, last in Cable #35, '96, next in XMan #19, '96), Sentinels (mutant hunting robots, some last in UXM #336, '96, some next in XMan #19, '96), Junkyard Dogs (scavenger thieves) inc Rhashid Hammer Jones (leader) & Bulldog
OTHER CHARACTERS: Contessa Val Fontaine (last in Cable #34, '96, next in Cable #37, '96), other SHIELD agents inc Paraglide Troopers w/Alpha Squad leader, bystanders

LOCATIONS/ITEMS: Manhattan inc Hudson River, Junkyard Dogs HQ / SHIELD Helicarrier (destroyed), HAWK (High Altitude Wing Kite) attachments & blasters; Junkyard Dogs' grappling hooks, shotguns, assault rifles, guns, jet skis & motorboats; Punisher's guns

SYNOPSIS: Onslaught's Sentinels knock the SHIELD Helicarrier from the sky and into the Hudson River. Punisher is surprised to find himself running toward the crash to help. In Jersey, the Junkyard Dogs see the crash and decide to claim it for themselves as salvage. Dugan alerts Bridge to the Dogs' approach before he collapses. Bridge gives the evacuation order and sets the Helicarrier's auto-destruct. The Dogs storm the Helicarrier and pin down the SHIELD agents until Punisher arrives and scatters them. With Punisher's help, the SHIELD agents complete the evacuation. The scavengers discover the auto-destruct sequence and get out just before the Helicarrier explodes. SHIELD commandeers the Dogs' base and arrests the thieves when they return. Before Punisher can leave, Bridge reminds him he still owes SHIELD for Fury's death and tasks him with bringing down the New Mutant Liberation Front.

NOTE: Cover labeled "Onslaught Impact 2." Punisher makes his War Journal II: Entry 22 here.

PUNISHER #12 (October 1996)

"Capitol Offenses" (22 pages)

CREDITS: John Ostrander (writer), Tom Lyle (pencils), Robert Jones (inks), Richard Starkings & Comicraft (letters), Matt Webb & American Color (colors), Jaye Gardner & Mark Bernardo (editors)
FEATURE CHARACTER: Punisher (also in pfb)
GUEST STARS: G.W. Bridge (in pfb, next bts in Pun #16, '97), X-Cutioner (Carl Denti, mutant hunting FBI agent, also in pfb, last in GenX #17, '96)
VILLAINS: Deadeye (Mark Randall, New Mutant Liberation Front terrorist, also in pfb, 1st, dies), Simon Trask (Humanity's Last Stand leader, also in fb2; last in Mag #4, '97, next in Pun #15, '97)
OTHER CHARACTERS: Rev. William Conover (televangelist, head of Glory Day Ministry, also in fb1, last in X/ Brood #2, '96), Kymberly "Kym" Taylor (rookie SHIELD agent, in pfb, 1st), Senator Dalmato (1st, see NOTE), his

Congressional Committee & campaign aide, SHIELD agents inc Bainbridge, 2 C-SPAN TV cameramen, US Capitol security officer (all in pfb), National Park Service police, bystanders

LOCATIONS/ITEMS: Avengers Mansion (in pfb), Washington, DC inc US Capitol (in pfb) & Lincoln Memorial (also in pfb) / Kym's gun, security officer's revolver, Avengers monitor system w/sequencer X07 (all in pfb); Punisher's pistols, Deadeye's plasma eye-blast apparatus, surveillance drones ('gnats') & teleportation device (prev 4 also in pfb); X-Cutioner's Shi'ar omnium mesh body armor, Shi'ar battle lance & teleporter; NPS police revolvers

FLASHBACKS: Televangelist William Conover preaches mutant/human brotherhood (1). A shadowed Simon Trask records a video message declaring a death sentence on Conover on behalf of the radical New Mutant Liberation Front (2). In the aftermath of the battle against Onslaught, SHIELD occupies Avengers Mansion and G.W. Bridge asks Frank Castle to join one of his agents in protecting Conover from the NMLF to prevent anti-mutant hysteria from escalating. In Washington, DC, Conover testifies before a Congressional Committee investigating mutant activity and FBI agent Carl Denti and SHIELD's Kymberly Taylor report for duty to protect him. NMLF assassin Deadeye teleports in and attempts to kill Conover but Punisher and the two agents force him to retreat. Uninformed of her partnership with Castle and angry about his supposed slaying of Nick Fury, Taylor arrests Punisher but is ordered to cooperate with him. Deadeye appears again, and as Taylor gets Conover to safety, Castle lures him to the Lincoln Memorial. Denti sneaks off to assume his secret identity (p).

SYNOPSIS: Out of ammunition, Punisher finds himself at the mercy of Deadeye, but X-Cutioner suddenly kills the mutant assassin.

NOTE: Cover labeled "Total X-Tinction Part 1 of 4." Punisher makes his War Journal II: Entry 31 inc subs A-B. Conover's name is misspelled "Connover" throughout this story arc. Deadeye's real name is revealed in OHMU HC #8, '09. Dalmato bears a resemblance to real-life US Senator Al D'Amato. Gardner is listed as an editor in the credits, Bernardo is "Bullet Proofs."

PUNISHER #13 (November 1996)

"Friend or Foe?" (22 pages)

CREDITS: John Ostrander (writer), Tom Lyle (pencils), Robert Jones (inks), Richard Starkings & Comicraft (letters), Matt Webb & American Color (colors), Dan Hosek (asst editor), Mark Bernardo (editor)
FEATURE CHARACTER: Punisher
GUEST STAR: X-Cutioner
VILLAINS: New Mutant Liberation Front (anti-mutant fringe group posing as mutant terrorists): Blastfurnace (robot, 1st), Corpus Derelicti (Michael Black, cyborg, dies, replaced in Pun #16, '97), Deadeye (as corpse, replaced in Pun #14, '96)
OTHER CHARACTERS: Rev. Conover, Kym Taylor, homeless men inc Corker (dies) & Cully, Washington, DC coroner & police

LOCATIONS/ITEMS: Washington, DC inc alley, Gianni's Flower Shop, Glory Day Mission, Lincoln Memorial & police station w/ morgue & FBI HQ w/X-Cutioner's basement base / X-Cutioner's Shi'ar omnium mesh body armor, Shi'ar battle lance, teleporter & computer equipment; Blastfurnace's teleporter & wrist & helmet flame throwers; Corpus Derelicti's drones & energy field; Punisher's knife & pistol; police revolvers, SHIELD scanner, Kym's guns

SYNOPSIS: X-Cutioner proposes an alliance with Frank Castle and suggests an autopsy for Deadeye, before returning to his base and resuming his Carl Denti identity. Before Deadeye's body can be examined at the morgue, Blastfurnace, a New Mutant Liberation Front robot, incinerates it and teleports away. The next day, Denti, Punisher and Kym Taylor speculate about Blastfurnace's actions and X-Cutioner's motivations. Castle and Kym accuse each other of a secret alliance with the mutant killer. When Rev. Conover insists on serving the homeless at his mission, the three are forced to guard him in a public place. NMLF cyborg Corpus Derelicti raids the mission and Conover convinces Punisher to fight him without guns to protect the homeless men. As Denti gets the televangelist to safety, Taylor shoots off Corpus Derelicti's arm, forcing Blastfurnace to appear and burn the cyborg to ashes. The mission catches fire and the robot emerges from the conflagration, ready to kill Conover.

NOTE: Cover labeled "Total X-Tinction Part 2 of 5." Punisher makes his War Journal II: Entries 32-33 here. Corpus Derelicti's real name is revealed in OHMU HC #8, '09. Rev. Conover and Punisher both quote from the New Testament – Corinthians 7:22 and Philemon 1:16, respectively.

PUNISHER #14 (December 1996)

"Ashes, Ashes, All Fall Down" (22 pages)

CREDITS: John Ostrander (writer), Darick Robertson (pencils), Jeff Albrecht (inks), Richard Starkings & Comicraft's Kolja Fuchs (letters), Matt Webb, Joe Andreani & American Color (colors), Dan Hosek (asst editor), Mark Bernado (editor)
FEATURE CHARACTER: Punisher
GUEST STAR: X-Cutioner
VILLAINS: New Mutant Liberation Front: Burnout (Kristine Calverly, speedster, 1st), Blastfurnace (destroyed, replaced in Pun #15, '97), Deadeye (Jay Burnell, terrorist, 1st)
OTHER CHARACTERS: Rev. Conover, Kym Taylor, train engineer & fireman (both die), Washington, DC firefighters & police (see NOTE)

LOCATIONS/ITEMS: Tennessee countryside, Washington, DC inc Glory Day Mission / X-Cutioner's Shi'ar omnium mesh body armor, Shi'ar battle lance & teleporter; Blastfurnace's teleporter & wrist & helmet flame throwers; Burnout's wrist-mounted blades, Deadeye's plasma eye-blast apparatus, Punisher's .45 caliber automatic pistols, Kym's gun, SHIELD motorcycle w/sidecar, dynamite, train

SYNOPSIS: As Frank Castle and Kym Taylor face off against Blastfurnace, Carl Denti secretly assumes his X-Cutioner identity, enters the fray, then teleports away when Punisher destroys the superheated Blastfurnace with a torrent of water. Denti rejoins his partners and Taylor secretly confiscates a fragment of the demolished robot. After Rev. Conover insists on rejoining his flock at his home base, his three guardians accompany him on a specially requisitioned train bound for Oklahoma. On the way, Conover suspects that Punisher is guarding him because he

needs to unburden his troubled soul to the preacher. Conover tells Castle that killing is not his only recourse in punishing the wicked. Suddenly Burnout, the New Mutant Liberation Front speedster, attacks the train, slays its operators and slices Punisher's abdomen. Taylor evacuates Conover and as Burnout pursues them, a new Deadeye blows up the bridge as the train approaches it with Castle and Denti aboard.
NOTE: Cover labeled "Total X-Tinction Part 3 of 5." Punisher makes his War Journal II: Entries 34, 34.1, 34.2 & 34.3 here. Burnout's and Deadeye's real names are revealed in OHMU HC #8, '09. Washington, DC firefighters are erroneously shown as the New York Fire Department.

PUNISHER #15 (January 1997)

"Unmasked" (22 pages)

CREDITS: John Ostrander (writer), Tom Lyle (pencils), Robert Jones (inks), Richard Starkings & Comicraft's Kolja Fuchs (letters), Matt Webb & American Color (colors), Dan Hosek (asst editor), Mark Bernado (editor)
FEATURE CHARACTER: Punisher
GUEST STAR: X-Cutioner
VILLAINS: New Mutant Liberation Front (revealed as anti-mutant fringe group, Humanity's Last Stand): Blastfurnace (1st, replaces previous robot), Blindspot (Kylie Kopeikin, generates light flashes, 1st), Thermal (Carol Peterson, generates blasts of heat & cold, 1st), Simon Trask (last in Pun #12, '96 fb), Burnout, Deadeye (Burnell)
OTHER CHARACTERS: Rev. Conover, Kym Taylor, Mully & Sculder (FBI agents, both die, see NOTE), other FBI agent; Amos "Fred" Duncan (mentioned, previous X-Cutioner), Shaw Industries (mentioned, manufacturer of Blastfurnace parts)
LOCATIONS/ITEMS: New Mutant Liberation Front base beneath Humanity's Last Stand compound in East Suffolk, OK; Orton Hollow, TN inc FBI office, restaurant & water tower; Washington, DC inc FBI HQ w/lab / X-Cutioner's Shi'ar omnium mesh body armor, Shi'ar battle lance & teleporter, Thermal's heat & cold blasters; Blastfurnace's wrist & helmet flame throwers; Blindspot's light flashes, Burnout's wrist-mounted blades, Deadeye's plasma eye-blast apparatus, fragments of 1st Blastfurnace's armor; NMLF brainwashing device & teleporters; Punisher's pistols, SHIELD jetpack & motorcycle w/sidecar, Kim's gun, train
SYNOPSIS: Frank Castle and Carl Denti jump from the train and Denti teleports away before Punisher's eyes. X-Cutioner arrives on the scene too late to stop Burnout from subduing Kym Taylor and kidnapping Rev. Conover. Castle and Denti regroup at a local FBI office and learn that a second Blastfurnace robot destroyed the remains of his predecessor at an FBI lab in Washington. When Punisher tells Denti he knows his secret identity and suspects him of being in league with the New Mutant Liberation Front, the FBI agent reveals that Castle himself inspired his war against killer mutants. Punisher theorizes that the NMLF aren't mutants at all, but rather fanatics powered by drugs and suits who are out to escalate anti-mutant hysteria. Seeking to lure the NMLF into a trap, Denti calls a press conference to claim he knows the group's secret and makes himself a target. NMLF leader Simon Trask takes the bait and sends his followers to seize Denti. Castle and Taylor fight the NMLF, who succeed in teleporting away with Denti, just as Punisher planned.
NOTE: Cover labeled "Total X-Tinction Part 4 of 5." Punisher makes his War Journal II: Entries 34, 34.1, 34.2, 34.3 & 34.4 here, apparently expanding on entries made last issue. Blindspot's real name is revealed in OHMU HC #8, '09. Thermal's real name is revealed in Pun #17, '97. Mully and Sculder resemble Fox Mulder and Dana Scully, the main characters of the TV series, "The X-Files."

PUNISHER #16 (February 1997)

"Dead to Rights" (22 pages)

CREDITS: John Ostrander (writer), Tom Lyle (pencils), Robert Jones (inks), Richard Starkings & Comicraft (letters), Matt Webb & American Color (colors), Dan Hosek (asst editor), Mark Bernado (editor)
FEATURE CHARACTER: Punisher (next in Pun #17, '97 fb, UXM #341, '97)
GUEST STARS: X-Cutioner (next in Gam #1, '99), G.W. Bridge (bts, provides weapons & transport, last in Pun #12, '96 fb, next in TMU #1, '97), Peter Parker (aka Spider-Man, web-slinging crime fighter, last in SenSM #15, '97, next in SpSM #242, '97)
VILLAINS: Humanity's Last Stand/New Mutant Liberation Front: Blindspot, Burnout (Calverly), Deadeye (Burnell) (all die), Blastfurnace (destroyed), Burnout (Megan O'Toole, speedster), Corpus Derelicti (Adam Fisher, cyborg, dies), Thermal, Simon Trask, HLS agents & scientists
OTHER CHARACTERS: Joseph "Robbie" Robertson (Daily Bugle city editor), Ben Urich (Daily Bugle reporter) (both last in SM:HL #2, '97, next in SMU #16, '97), J. Jonah Jameson (Daily Bugle editor, last in SM #76, '97, next in SpSM #242, '97), Trish Tilby (reporter, last in GR #82, '97, next in Venom:OT #2, '97), SHIELD (bts, on standby alert), Rev. Conover, Kym Taylor, Humanity's Last Stand followers; Graydon Creed (mentioned, see NOTE)
LOCATIONS/ITEMS: Daily Bugle's Manhattan newsroom, FBI office in Orton Hollow, Tennessee; Humanity's Last Stand compound in East Suffolk, Oklahoma inc communications room & New Mutant Liberation Front's underground base; X-Cutioner's base in Washington, DC / X-Cutioner's Shi'ar omnium mesh body armor, Shi'ar battle lance, teleporter, ultrasound generator & computer equipment; Blastfurnace's wrist & helmet flame throwers; Punisher's grenades, knife, missile launcher & pistols; Trask's detonator, explosives & revolver; Burnout's wrist-mounted blades, Deadeye's plasma eye-blast apparatus, Humanity's Last Stand's fuel tanks, NMLF brainwashing device, SHIELD blaster; Kym's guns w/mercy slugs, Thermal's heat & cold blasters
SYNOPSIS: Frank Castle contacts reporters Trish Tilby and Ben Urich to let them know the New Mutant Liberation Front is run by the anti-mutant group, Humanity's Last Stand. Urich tells Punisher that anti-mutant presidential candidate Graydon Creed has been assassinated, which pushes the nation to the brink of a human/mutant war. Creed's death makes Rev. Conover's death less essential to Simon Trask's plans and Trask orders Burnout to take the captive Carl Denti away and kill him. Denti assaults Burnout and teleports away. Suffering from withdrawal from the drugs that grant her power, Burnout dies, and Trask orders the NMLF to find and slay Denti. As X-Cutioner, Denti retrieves Castle and Kym Taylor and teleports them back to HLS's compound. As Taylor evacuates the compound, Punisher and X-Cutioner raid the NMLF base beneath it. X-Cutioner teleports Conover to safety and Castle vanquishes the NMLF. Sensing defeat, Trask seeks to kill Punisher and become a martyr by rigging the base to explode. X-Cutioner rescues Taylor just as the facility is destroyed. Hours later, Tilby files a news report about Trask's plot and fears that both he and Castle died in the explosion.
NOTE: Cover labeled "Total X-Tinction Part 5 of 5." Burnout's and Corpus Derelicti's real names are revealed in OHMU HC #8, '09. Graydon Creed was assassinated in XFac #130, '97.

PUNISHER #17 (March 1997)

"Dead Man Walking" (22 pages)

CREDITS: John Ostrander (writer), Tom Lyle (pencils), Robert Jones (inks), Richard Starkings & Comicraft (letters), Matt Webb & American Color (colors), Dan Hosek (asst editor), Mark Bernardo (editor)
FEATURE CHARACTER: Punisher (also in photos & rfb; also as Frank Castle in fb1 between PWZ #25, '94 fb & Pun #4, '99 fb; also in fb2 between Pun #1, '86 fb & Pun:AG, '88 fb; also in fb4 between Pun #16, '97 & UXM #341, '97)
SUPPORTING CAST: Maria Castle, Lisa Castle, Frank Castle, Jr., (all in photo & rfb; in fb1 between PWZ #25, '94 fb & Pun #4, '99 fb)
GUEST STARS: Black Widow (last in DD #361, '97, next in Tb #1, '97), Daredevil (last in DD #362, '97, next in SS #128, '97), Spider-Man (also in fb3 between MTU #21, '74 & ASM #132, '74; last in SenSM #18, '97, next in SM:DMH, '97), G.W. Bridge (last in XFor #64, '97, next in XFor #66, '97)
VILLAINS: Thermal (also in rfb & pfb), Simon Trask (also in rfb; in pfb, next in UXM #500, '08), Estefan (Maria Montoya's boyfriend, 1st), Bruno Costa (in fb1 during PWJ #3, '89 fb), Matt Skinner (in fb1 to 1st chr app before PWJ #3, '89 fb), Rocco Venturi (mobster, 1st, in fb1 before bts in MP #2, '75 fb, in fb3 between bts in MP #2, '75 fb & Pun #1, '98), mobsters (in fb3)
OTHER CHARACTERS: Haskell "Hask" Salaki (US marshal, 1st) & his US deputy marshals: Mose Jessup, Mamacita, Corey Mandelbaum, Jimmy Pascal & Basia Sokjtewicz; Mr. Goodenough (intelligence agent), General Parcelli (US Army officer), Maria Montoya (abused woman), Julio Montoya (Maria's son) (all 1st), Ben Urich (last in SMU #16, '97, next in UXM #346, '97), Kym Taylor, other SHIELD agents; Estefan's friends; Blindspot (in rfb); X-Cutioner (on cover)
LOCATIONS/ITEMS: Humanity's Last Stand compound in East Suffolk, OK inc New Mutant Liberation Front's underground base (in pfb); Manhattan inc Central Park (in fb1), Midtown (also in fb3) w/Jones' Jewelry store & Tom's Restaurant (both in fb3), Avengers Mansion (now temporary SHIELD HQ), Daily Bugle, NYU Medical Center, Haskell Salaki's conference room & office & Alphabet City w/St. Jude's Church / Thermal's heat & cold blasters, Trask's explosives w/detonator (all in pfb); mobsters' handguns (in fb3), Punisher's pistols (in fb2), Daredevil's billy club, Mamacita's computer, Corey's laptop, Jimmy's knife, Sentinel head, Kym's gun
FLASHBACKS: Mobsters observe the Castle family picnicking in Central Park (1). The Castle family is killed (PWJ #3, '89 fb). Punisher goes to war on organized crime (2). Spider-Man stops mobsters from murdering Rocco Venturi, one of the Castle family killers (3). Simon Trask kills Blindspot and prepares to detonate a bomb (Pun #16, '97). Thermal freezes Trask's hand, Trask shoots Thermal and Punisher subdues Trask and carries Thermal out of the exploding Humanity's Last Stand compound (4).
SYNOPSIS: U.S. marshal Haskell Salaki and his deputies are assigned to find Frank Castle, who is believed to have survived the explosion of the Humanity's Last Stand compound six weeks earlier. They try to gather clues from Daredevil, Spider-Man and Kym Taylor, who blames herself for Punisher's apparent death. Salaki learns that New Mutant Liberation Front member Thermal survived the explosion and has emerged from a coma in a New York hospital. Thermal tells Salaki and his deputies that Punisher rescued her from the blast, confirming that the vigilante is still alive. In New York's Alphabet City, Julio Montoya enlists the aid of a bearded man based at the abandoned St. Jude's Church who has gained a reputation for punishing bad men. The man threatens Estefan, the boyfriend of Julio's mother, Maria, to stop abusing her, and when Maria arrives at the church to express her appreciation, her savior, Castle himself, claims not to know his own identity.
NOTE: Cover pays homage to DC's Superman #75, '93 "Death of Superman" cover. Lisa Castle is called "Christie" here. Rocco Venturi is revealed as one of the Castle family's killers here. Spider-Man sings a song based on the 1960s Spider-Man TV cartoon theme song. "Bullet Proofs" features LOC from Paul Dale Roberts, creator of the comic, The Legendary Dark Silhouette.

PUNISHER #18 (April 1997)

"Double Cross" (22 pages)

CREDITS: John Ostrander (writer), Tom Lyle (pencils), Robert Jones (inks), Richard Starkings & Comicraft (letters), Matt Webb & American Color (colors), Dan Hosek (asst editor), Mark Bernado (editor)
FEATURE CHARACTER: Punisher (also as Frank Castiglione in fb2 between bts in PWJ #25, '90 fb & Pun #1, '98 fb; also as Pvt. Castiglione in fb1 between Pun #59, '92 fb & Pun:AG, '88 fb; next in HFH #9, SM #89, SpSM #255, KZ #16 fb, KZ #15-16, SM:Made, all '98, Pun #1, '98 fb, Pun #3, '99 fb, Pun #4, '99 fb, Pun #1, '98)
VILLAINS: Street Demons (gang) inc Javier (leader), Chen & Raoul (all die); Hector Marin & Mr. Edgy (gun dealers, both die), Estefan (next in HFH #8, '98 fb), murderers (in fb2), Mr. Edgy's men
OTHER CHARACTERS: Julio Montoya, Maria Montoya, Haskell Salaki & his US deputy marshals: Mose Jessup, Corey Mandelbaum (all next in HFH #8, '98 fb), Jimmy Pascal, Basia Sokjtewicz (both next in HFH #9, '98 fb); Sister Margaret (Maggie Murdock, nun, Daredevil's mother, last in DD #349, '96, next in DD #375, '98), Dr. Ciliberti (hospital physician), US soldier (in fb1), victim (in fb2); Maria Castle, Frank Castle, Jr., Lisa Castle, Leslie Geraci, Jigsaw (prev 5 in rfbs), Rev. Conover (voice in Punisher's thoughts), Daredevil (in Sister Maggie's thoughts)
LOCATIONS/ITEMS: Vietnam (in fb1), East Buffalo, OK inc Cooper Community Hospital; Manhattan inc Alphabet City w/Montoyas' apartment, St. Jude's Church & abandoned bus barn on Avenue C / Punisher's automatic rifle, knife & pistol; Hector's revolver, Mr. Edgy's & Street Demons' guns, Sentinel head, Sister Maggie's cross; military rifles (in fb1), knife (in fb2)
FLASHBACKS: The Castle family is killed (PWJ #3, '89 fb). Pvt. Castiglione serves in Vietnam (1). Jigsaw drops Leslie Geraci from a theater fly loft (Pun #10, '96). As a boy, Frank Castiglione witnesses a murder (2).
SYNOPSIS: Haskell Salaki and his deputies learn that the amnesiac Frank Castle briefly appeared at a hospital following the explosion of the Humanity's Last Stand compound. In Alphabet City, Hector Marin gives the unrecognized Punisher a tip that the Street Demons gang is planning to buy guns from a Mr. Edgy. Castle returns to St. Jude's Church, where he encounters Sister Maggie, a nun who senses that he's a fallen angel seeking atonement and redemption. Punisher assaults Edgy and his men and takes their weapons before the Street Demons can claim them. The gang is forced to buy their firearms from Marin, who kills his rival Edgy and offers to take the Street Demons to the man who stole their guns. Upset that Maria and Julio Montoya arranged for Castle to threaten him, Estefan returns and beats the mother and child. Julio goes to St. Jude's for help and is forced to hide when Marin and the Street Demons raid the church looking for Punisher. Castle is forced to kill all the gangsters and sets out to find Estefan.
NOTE: Includes a b&w preview of Cable #42, '97 (3 pages). Story continued in HFH #8-9, '98 where Punisher surrenders to the US marshals, & SM #89, '98, where he regains his memory. Series continued in Pun #1, '98, where he kills himself, returning with angelic weapons.

PUNISHER #1 (November 1998)

"Purgatory Part 1: The Harvest" (22 pages)

CREDITS: Christopher Golden, Tom Sniegoski (writer), Bernie Wrightson (pencils, c pencils), Jimmy Palmiotti (inks, editor), Richard Starkings & Comicraft's Emerson Miranda (letters), & Eric Eng Wong (recap design), Brian Haberlin (colors), Nanci Dakesian (managing editor), Joe Quesada (editor), Joe Jusko (c paints), Jae Lee (variant c art)
FEATURE CHARACTER: Punisher (also in rfb, also as Frank Castiglione in fb6 between Pun #18, '96 fb & PWJ #18, '90 fb, also as Pvt. Castiglione in fb1 between PunBl, '91 fb & Pun #100, '95 fb, also as Frank Castle in fb7 during PunTheNam, '94 fb, also as Frank Castle in fb2 between Pun Ann #4, '91 & Pun:OM #1, '93, also as Frank Castle in fb5 between Pun:XMas #1, '07 fb & PWZ #24, '94 fb, also in fb3 between SM:Made, '98 & Pun #3, '99 fb)

SUPPORTING CAST: Maria Castle (in fb2 during Pun Ann #4, '91), Lisa Castle, Frank Castle, Jr. (both in fb2 between Pun Ann #4, '91 & PWZ #21, '93 fb)
GUEST STAR: Hellstorm (Daimon Hellstrom, Son of Satan, last in W #114, '97)
VILLAINS: Olivier (demon, "Frank Costa," 1st as Olivier, also in fb4 to 1st chr app before Pun #2, '98 fb, also bts in fb1; last in MSA Mag #1, '76 fb, chr last in Pun #4, '99 fb, see NOTE), his demons (bts in fb1) & his Stalkers (1st as Stalkers, see NOTE): Luis Allegre, Byron Hannigan, Leon Kolsky, Matt Skinner (prev 4 last in MSA Mag #1, '76 fb), Rocco Venturi (last in Pun #17, '97 fb); Tony Mellace (Lucy's abusive husband, 1st), drug dealers (die) inc Nelso & Diego
OTHER CHARACTERS: Gadriel (fallen angel, 1st but chr last in Pun #3, '99 fb), Esphares & Tariel (fallen angels, both die), Lucy Mellace (Punisher's childhood friend, 1st, also in fb5), Justin Randall (child, 1st, next in Pun #4, '99), his mother & his stepfather (both bts, in other room), Costa's mother, doctor (both in fb4), baseball player (in fb6), Eddie Dobbs (junkie), firefighters inc Ashley & Kaminski; Milton's patrons
LOCATIONS/ITEMS: Brooklyn (also in fb3) inc Justin's apartment, drug lab, abandoned Church of St. Tarcissius, hospital, Mellace apartment & Milton's (magic club); Heaven, Hell (both in fb4) / lab equipment, Punisher's guns & gun (in fb3) & angelic weapons (1st); drug dealers' guns & rocket launcher; Stalkers' blades, angel feather
FLASHBACKS: Frank Castiglione fights in Vietnam (1). Frank spends time with his family (2). Frank becomes the Punisher (Pun:YO #4, '95). Punisher prepares to kill himself (3). Olivier is cast from both Heaven and Hell. As punishment for his crimes, Olivier is born on Earth in the stillborn body of Frank Costa (4). After the war, Frank is friends with Lucy (5). Young Frank Castiglione plays baseball (6). Frank Castle re-enlists with the Marines (7). Punisher kills a criminal (MPr #2, '75 fb).
SYNOPSIS: Scared people leave gifts and offerings to the Punisher in the alley where he killed himself, hoping the urban legend will return to help. Meanwhile, Punisher raids a drug lab with new mystical weapons. He kills everyone inside and leaves the burning building, but the flames don't harm him. Elsewhere, two fallen angels, Esphares and Tariel, pray for forgiveness until the demon Olivier and his Stalkers attack. Tariel escapes to warn other angels as Olivier eats Esphares' angelic essence. Punisher stops Tony Mellace from beating his wife Lucy, who recognizes Punisher as a childhood friend. Punisher returns to the alley where he committed suicide and sees his family. He follows them to the dying Tariel. The angel tasks Punisher with stopping Olivier, and sends him to Milton's to find Gadriel. Gadriel reveals he brought Frank back from the dead, and that he was the Castle family's guardian angel. Punisher prepares to kill Gadriel.
NOTE: Includes recap page (2 pages) featuring Punisher & Ka-Zar. Letters page changes its name to "The Punisher." This issue reveals that Frank Costa from MSA Mag #1, '76 is actually the demon Olivier. Pun #4, '99 reveals the Stalkers are the rest of the Costa family.

PUNISHER #2 (December 1998)

"Purgatory Part 2: The Mark of Cain" (22 pages)

CREDITS: Christopher Golden, Tom Sniegoski (writer), Bernie Wrightson (pencils, c pencils), Jimmy Palmiotti (inks, editor), Richard Starkings & Comicraft's Emerson Miranda (letters) & Eric Eng Wong (recap design), Avalon (colors), Nanci Dakesian (managing editor), Joe Quesada (editor), Joe Jusko (c paints)
FEATURE CHARACTER: Punisher
GUEST STAR: Hellstorm (next in Pun #4, '99)
VILLAINS: Olivier (also as Frank Costa in fb between Pun #1, '98 fb & Pun #3, '99 fb), his demons & His Stalkers: Luis Allegre, Byron Hannigan, Leon Kolsky, Matt Skinner, Rocco Venturi; Vito & Tony (Frank Costa's friends, in fb), Tony Mellace (next in Pun #4, '99)
OTHER CHARACTERS: Gadriel, Lucy Mellace, Mrs. Ortega (custodian), Hafaza (angel's head), Malah & Zulum (Hellstorm's steeds), Milton's patrons, firefighters, paramedics, police; Frank Sinatra (voice only on record)
LOCATIONS/ITEMS: Milton's, Flatiron building inc Olivier's apartment, St. Mark's hospital / Hellstorm's trident & chariot; Punisher's angelic weapons, Olivier's tub of blood
FLASHBACK: Frank Costa is left as a lookout as his friends leave to kill someone. When their mark tries to escape, Costa shoots him, awakening his memories of his true demonic form.
SYNOPSIS: Gadriel tries to explain the need for Punisher's mission to stop Olivier, but Punisher refuses to stop shooting him despite the ineffectiveness. Gadriel is forced to pause their discussion when he senses Hellstorm in trouble nearby. Meanwhile at the Flatiron building, a focal point for arcane energy, one of Olivier's stalkers updates him on the attack on Hellstorm and gives him an angel's head to feed on. Gadriel tries to help Hellstorm against Olivier's demons, but they find themselves overwhelmed until Punisher joins the fight. When the demons are defeated, Hellstorm returns to his realm, believing the fight to be a distraction to allow Olivier to conquer his realm. Lucy sits over Tony's hospital bed wondering if she has the guts to take the opening Punisher gave her. Olivier learns of Punisher's involvement in his affairs. Gadriel interrogates one of Olivier's Stalkers until he identifies himself as someone Punisher killed. Gadriel fries the Stalker before he says more, leaving Punisher to wonder about Gadriel's intentions.
NOTE: Includes recap page (2 pages) featuring Punisher & Gadriel.

PUNISHER #3 (January 1999)

"Purgatory Part 3: A Gathering of Angels" (22 pages)

CREDITS: Christopher Golden, Tom Sniegoski (writer), Bernie Wrightson (pencils, c pencils), Jimmy Palmiotti (inks, editor), Richard Starkings & Comicraft's Emerson Miranda (letters), Elizabeth Lewis & Snakebite (colors), Nanci Dakesian (managing editor), Joe Quesada (editor), Joe Jusko (c paints)
FEATURE CHARACTER: Punisher (also as Sgt. Castle in fb1 between Pun #77, '93 fb & TheNam #52, '91, also in fb2 between Pun #1, '98 fb & Pun #1, '98, also in Pun #4, '99 fb)
VILLAINS: Olivier (also in fb1 as Frank Costa between Pun #2, '98 fb & Pun:YO #3, '95), his demons & his Stalkers: Bruno Costa (last in Pun:YO #3, '95, chr last in MSA Mag #1, '76 fb), Luis Allegre, Byron Hannigan, Leon Kolsky, Matt Skinner, Rocco Venturi
OTHER CHARACTERS: Armaros, Azazel (both former Grigori warriors), Ezekeel (patron saint of addiction), Sariel (former commander of the Grigori) (all die), Gadriel (also in fb2 to 1st chr app before Pun #1, '98), Lucy Mellace, Satannish demons; Frank Castle Jr., Lisa Castle, Maria Castle (prev 3 in Olivier's image), Costa's victim (in fb1)
LOCATIONS/ITEMS: Gadriel's brownstone, Satannish's realm, Costa's office (in fb1), cemetery, Olivier's apartment / Stalker's knives & spears; demon swords, shields & spears; Punisher's angelic weapons, Bruno's energy axe, Olivier's tub of blood
FLASHBACKS: Frank Costa performs blood rituals to restore his power. He focuses on Frank Castle to become his ultimate weapon and provide him with all the blood he'll need to be strong enough to conquer all of hell (1). Punisher kills himself. Gadriel uses his essence to restore Punisher to life. Punisher wanders until he finds one of his safe houses. He dons his uniform, draws his new angelic weapons, and remembers he's the Punisher (2).
SYNOPSIS: Gadriel tells Punisher he was heaven's weapons master and developed what Punisher now uses, but was demoted to a guardian angel after teaching humans how to make their own weapons. When he let Castle's family die he succumbed to booze and women, and now he's trying to atone for his mistakes. He brings Punisher to his brownstone to meet his other fallen brethren. Olivier's Stalkers attack. Meanwhile, Olivier oversees the conquest of Satannish's realm while musing about Punisher's fate. Elsewhere, Lucy visits Frank's grave and ponders her life. At Gadriel's, the fight is joined by Bruno Costa. He taunts Punisher that he and his fellow Stalkers killed Frank's family and knocks Punisher out. Punisher and Gadriel wake up in Olivier's apartment where Olivier reveals he's responsible for the Castle family deaths. wake up in Olivier's apartment where Olivier reveals he was responsible for the Castle family deaths.

PUNISHER #4 (February 1999)

"Purgatory Part 4: The Hour of Judgment" (21 pages)

CREDITS: Christopher Golden, Tom Sniegoski (writer), Bernie Wrightson (pencils, c pencils), Jimmy Palmiotti (inks, editor), Richard Starkings & Comicraft's Emerson Miranda (letters), Elizabeth Lewis & Prenevost (colors), Nanci Dakesian (managing editor), Joe Quesada (editor), Joe Jusko (c paints)
FEATURE CHARACTER: Punisher (also in rfb, also as Frank Castle in fb1 between Pun #17, '97 fb & PWJ #1, '88 fb, also as Frank Castle in fb2 between DE:A, '95 fb & PWJ #1, '88 fb, also as Frank Castle in fb3 between Pun Ann #4, '91 & PWJ #3, '89 fb, also in fb4 between MSA Mag #1, '76 fb & Pun #1, '86 fb; also in fb5 during Pun #3, '99 fb; next in W/Pun #1, '99)
SUPPORTING CAST: Maria Castle, Lisa Castle, Frank Castle, Jr. (all in rfb, in fb1 between Pun #17, '97 fb & PWJ #1, '88 fb, in fb2 between DE:A, '95 fb & PWJ #1, '88 fb, in fb3 between Pun Ann #4, '91 & PWJ #3, '89 fb)
GUEST STARS: Hellstorm (last in Pun #2, '98, chr next in Tb Ann '00 fb, next in FF Ann '99), Dr. Strange (last in HR:R #4, '97, next in MTU #8, '98)
VILLAINS: Olivier (also as Frank Costa in fb4 between MSA Mag #1, '76 fb & bts in Pun #1, '98 fb; next bts in Nc #1, '04, next in Nc #3, '05), his demons (others in fb5) & his Stalkers: Bruno Costa (also in fb2 between DE:A, '95 fb & PWJ #1, '88 fb, also in fb3 between Pun Ann #4, '91 & PWJ #3, '89 fb), Byron Hannigan, Matt Skinner (both also in fb2 between Pun/Cap #3, '92 fb & PWJ #1, '88 fb, also in fb3 between Pun Ann #4, '91 & PWJ #3, '89 fb), Leon Kolsky (also in fb2 between DE:A, '95 fb & PWJ #1, '88 fb) (prev 4 also in rfb), Luis Allegre, Rocco Venturi; Forest Hunt (in rfb, in fb2 between DE:A, '95 fb & PWJ #1, '88 fb), Tony Mellace (last in Pun #2, '98), tentacled Hell-beast, robber, criminals
OTHER CHARACTERS: Justin Randall (last in Pun #1, '98), Lucy Mellace (next in W/Pun #1, '99), Gadriel (also in rfb & Olivier's image), deli worker, bystanders (others in rfb); Gadriel's dates (in Olivier's image)
LOCATIONS/ITEMS: Flatiron Building inc Olivier's apt., Central Park (rfb), Costa's office (fb1), Hell, Brooklyn inc deli & Mellace apt. / Punisher's gun & angelic weapons inc sword; mobster's guns (rfb), Bruno's hammer & axe; Stalker's knives, Gadriel's energy sword, criminals' guns
FLASHBACKS: The Castle family picnics in Central Park (1) and stumble across a mob execution (2). The mobsters see the Castle family (MPr #2, '75 fb) and shoot them (3). Punisher kills Frank Costa. In hell, Olivier emerges from Costa's skin (4). Olivier's demons influence Punisher to kill himself (5). Gadriel revives Punisher (Pun #3, '98 fb).
SYNOPSIS: Olivier explains that he orchestrated the events surrounding the Castle family murders, and ever since Frank Castle became the Punisher, everyone he's killed has only fueled Olivier's power. Gadriel admits that in addition to not protecting the Castle family, he had recently given up on Frank Castle and allowed Olivier to influence Punisher into committing suicide. Enraged, Punisher breaks free and attacks Olivier. Olivier's Stalkers, actually the Costa family that murdered Frank's family, intervene. The battle rages until a gateway to Hell bursts open. Punisher forces Olivier into the portal. Tentacles from within ensnare Olivier and rip him apart. Gadriel sacrifices himself so the tentacles don't grab Punisher. As the gateway closes Punisher forgives Gadriel. Outside, Hellstorm and Dr. Strange confer that an eye should be kept on Punisher. Later, Punisher stops a deli from being robbed. Lucy calls the police to enforce the restraining order on her husband. Punisher stops a drive-by shooting and notes that his mission has changed from vengeance to redemption.
NOTE: The assassin Audrey killed Frank Costa in MSA Mag #1, '76 fb; he apparently survived only to be killed again by Punisher here.

WOLVERINE/PUNISHER: REVELATION #1 (June 1999)

"The Punisher & Wolverine: Revelation Chapter One - - Ladies in Waiting" (22 pages)

CREDITS: Tom Sniegoski, Christopher Golden (writers), Pat Lee (pencils, co-colors), Alvin Lee (inks), Richard Starkings & Comicraft (letters), Angelo Tsang (co-colors), Nanci Dakesian (managing editor), Joe Quesada, Jimmy Palmiotti (editors)
FEATURE CHARACTER: Punisher
VILLAINS: "Wolverine" (Skrull imposter posing as Wolverine, also in fb between XMU #24, '99 & W/Pun #2, '99 fb; last in XMU #24, '99, chr last & also in W/Pun #2, '99 fb, see NOTE), Revelation (death aura emitting Morlock, 1st but chr last in W/Pun #2, '99 fb), Failsafes (bio-androids programmed to retrieve or kill Revelation if she awakens, 3 destroyed), gang members (some die)
OTHER CHARACTERS: Caley Blair (museum curator, 1st but chr last in W/Pun #2, '99 fb, dies, also in 1st chr app in fb before W/Pun #2, '99 fb, next in W/Pun #2, '99 fb as corpse), Lucy Santini Mellace (last in Pun #4, '99), Council of Thrones (angels, 1st) inc Arcturus & Ephesus; construction workers inc Karl Geesey, Tom Stanley, & Harry Wessel; museum visitors (in fb), doorman, paramedics, bystanders
LOCATIONS/ITEMS: New York inc the Bronx w/Lucy's apartment, Manhattan inc Cadbury Station excavation site, Emerald Room (restaurant) & Museum of Cultural History (in fb); Morlock tunnels inc Soteira's lab; Logan's X-Mansion quarters, Dobbs Ferry, NY inc Council of Thrones' house / Punisher's angelic weapons, Logan's motorcycle, gang members' guns, exhibits of Japanese armor & swords inc wakizashi forged by Inouye Shinkai circa 1670-1680 AD, Revelation's stasis chamber
FLASHBACK: Logan meets Caley at the Museum of Cultural History and impresses her with his knowledge of ancient Japanese weaponry.
SYNOPSIS: Frank Castle walks Lucy home until a drive-by shooting interrupts their conversation. Punisher uses his angelic weapons to subdue the shooters and tells them to wait for the police. At Lucy's apartment Frank is suddenly teleported away. In the subway, some construction workers fall through the floor into a subterranean chamber. Logan goes on a date with Caley Blair, a museum curator. Caley gets a page about the workers. Punisher appears in the presence of the Council of Thrones, angels who demand he swear allegiance to them. Punisher refuses and leaves. Logan and Caley arrive at the excavation. As Logan helps the workers out, Caley accidentally frees a young woman that causes her to instantly become ill. Androids attack Logan as he tries to get Caley topside. Logan destroys them but Caley dies. Frank returns to the city to see people falling over sick, including Lucy. Wolverine swears to avenge Caley.
NOTE: UXM #375, '99 reveals that the Wolverine appearing here is a Skrull sleeper agent. W/Pun #3, '99 reveals Arcturus & Ephesus' names. W/Pun #2, '99 reveals the lab is Soteira's.

WOLVERINE/PUNISHER: REVELATION #2 (July 1999)

"Wolverine & the Punisher: Revelation Chapter Two - - Ascension" (22 pages)

CREDITS: Tom Sniegoski, Christopher Golden (writers), Pat Lee (pencils, co-colors), Alvin Lee (inks), Richard Starkings & Comicraft (letters), Angelo Tsang (co-colors), Nanci Dakesian (managing editor), Joe Quesada, Jimmy Palmiotti (editors)
FEATURE CHARACTER: Punisher
VILLAINS: "Wolverine" (Skrull, also as demon in Revelation's hallucination, also in fb4 between W/Pun #1, '99 fb & W/Pun #1, '99, also in fb3 during W/Pun #2, '99), Revelation (also in Punisher's vision & as hologram, also in fb2 during W/Pun #3, '99 fb, also in fb1 between W/Pun #3, '99 fb & W/Pun #1, '99), Failsafes
OTHER CHARACTERS: Caley Blair (in fb3 between W/Pun #1, '99 fb & W/Pun #1, '99, also as corpse in fb4 after W/Pun #2, '99), Lucy Santini Mellace (next in W/Pun #4, '99), Soteira (Morlock scientist, 1st, in fb2 before W/Pun #3, '99 fb, as hologram in fb1 after W/Pun #3, '99 fb), Revelation's parents (both corpses as holograms in fb2), Council of Thrones inc Arcturus & Ephesus; commuters (some in Punisher's vision), police, paramedics, bystanders inc Davey & his mother, rats (corpses, one also as demon in Revelation's hallucination)
LOCATIONS/ITEMS: New York inc subway station (also in Frank's vision), Morlock tunnels inc Soteira's lab, Lucy's apartment, Cadbury Station excavation site & Caley's apartment (in fb3) / Punisher's angelic weapons, Revelation's stasis chamber (also in fb1)
FLASHBACKS: Soteira records a hologram explaining that after failing to cure Revelation, she placed her in cryogenic stasis and developed the Failsafes to prevent her accidental awakening (1). After she accidentally killed her parents, Revelation is placed in Soteira's care (2). Logan shares a romantic morning with Caley (3). Logan howls over Caley's corpse (4).
SYNOPSIS: As people fall ill throughout New York, Punisher has a vision of Revelation as the cause. The Council of Thrones appear and tell Punisher to stop Revelation. In the sewers, Wolverine finds a holographic recording and learns Revelation is a Morlock with an uncontrollable death aura power. Meanwhile, Revelation hallucinates that she's passing through a horde of demons on her way to heaven. Punisher descends into the sewers and battles the Failsafe androids. Wolverine finds Revelation, who blasts him through a wall. Punisher finds Wolverine, who turns feral and attacks Punisher. The vigilante shoots Wolverine in the face to calm him down. Wolverine regains his senses and tells Punisher they need to help Revelation; it's not her fault she can't control her power. Before Punisher can ask Wolverine how they could help her, more Failsafes attack them.
NOTE: This issue reveals that when Punisher drops one of his angelic weapons it disappears, presumably returning to his heavenly arsenal.

WOLVERINE/PUNISHER: REVELATION #3 (August 1999)

"Wolverine & the Punisher: Revelation Chapter Three - - One Shot at Heaven" (22 pages)

CREDITS: Tom Sniegoski, Christopher Golden (writers), Pat Lee (pencils), Sigmund Torre (background pencil assist), Alvin Lee (inks), Richard Starkings & Comicraft (letters), Angelo Tsang (colors), Nanci Dakesian (managing editor), Joe Quesada, Jimmy Palmiotti (editors)
FEATURE CHARACTER: Punisher (also in Council's scrying mirror & as demon in Revelation's mind)
GUEST STAR: Daredevil (last in FF #23, '99, next in Thor Ann '00)
VILLAINS: "Wolverine" (Skrull, also in Council's scrying mirror & as demon in Revelation's mind), Revelation (also in fb1 to 1st chr app before W/Pun #2, '99 fb, also in fb2 during W/Pun #2, '99 fb), Failsafes (one destroyed, one as image in Council's scrying mirror) inc Failsafe Omega
OTHER CHARACTERS: Soteira (in fb2 during W/Pun:Rev #2, '99 fb), Revelation's parents (both die in fb1 to

1st chr app before W/Pun #2, '99 fb), Council of Thrones inc Arcturus & Ephesus; CDC workers inc Joe & Sharon; Morlocks (in fb1), Soteira's assistant (in fb2), rat (corpse), Dark Beast (Earth-295 version of Beast (Henry McCoy), mentioned, Soteira stole Omega's warhead from him)
LOCATIONS/ITEMS: Manhattan inc Morlock tunnels w/Revelation's childhood home (in fb5) & subway station, Dobbs Ferry, NY inc Council of Thrones' house / Daredevil's billy club, CDC mobile command center & HAZMAT suits, Punisher's angelic weapons, Failsafes' guns, Council's scrying mirror, Failsafe Omega's warhead (bts, inside Omega)
FLASHBACKS: Revelation's powers manifest themselves and kill her parents (1). Soteira places Revelation in cryogenic stasis (2).
SYNOPSIS: As CDC workers attempt to contain the spreading illness, Wolverine and Punisher battle the Failsafes. They destroy them all, but Punisher is impaled through the chest during the battle. Punisher is surprised he's not dead, but notices the wound is not healing. Wolverine and Punisher find Revelation and Punisher accidentally buries her in ceiling rubble with a warning shot. Revelation bursts free. See them as demons she attacks and escapes. Punisher notices that his chest wound is finally healing, but he's now sick from Revelation's power. Watching from afar, the Council of Thrones wonders how Punisher can be affected by Revelation if he wields heavenly power. More Failsafes activate their final solution, Failsafe Omega, who is equipped with a nuclear warhead. As they chase Revelation, Punisher worries that the only way to stop Revelation is to kill her. More Failsafes attack and Punisher follows Omega while Wolverine faces the others. The Council worries that Revelation could affect them too.

WOLVERINE/PUNISHER: REVELATION #4 (September 1999)

"Wolverine & the Punisher: Revelation Chapter Four - - So This is Hell" (22 pages)

CREDITS: Tom Sniegoski, Christopher Golden (writers), Pat Lee (pencils, co-colors), Sigmund Torre (background pencil assist), Alvin Lee (inks), Richard Starkings & Comicraft (letters), Angelo Tsang (co-colors), Nanci Dakesian (managing editor), Joe Quesada, Jimmy Palmiotti (editors)
FEATURE CHARACTER: Punisher (next in Pun #1, '00)
GUEST STAR: Storm (last in CoC2 #2, '99, chr last in CM #6, '00 fb, next in UXM #372, '99)
VILLAINS: "Wolverine" (Skrull, next in W #141, '99), Revelation (dies, also in image in Council's scrying mirror), Failsafes (all destroyed)
OTHER CHARACTERS: Lucy Santini Mellace (last in W/Pun #2, '99), Council of Thrones inc Arcturus & Ephesus; Denny & Matt (radio DJs, voices only), Revelation's parents (both in heavenly image), doctors, nurses inc Angie; bystanders
LOCATIONS/ITEMS: Manhattan inc subway station, hospital, Morlock tunnels & Central Park; Dobbs Ferry inc Council's home, Salem Center inc X-Mansion w/surrounding grounds / Punisher's gun w/scope, heavenly image sphere & energy sword; Failsafes' guns & warhead; defibrillator, scrying mirror (destroyed)
SYNOPSIS: The Council of Thrones argue about involving themselves directly in stopping Revelation. Wolverine destroys the Failsafes. Ephesus arrives and fails to convince Wolverine to let Punisher deal with Revelation alone. Failsafe Omega attacks Revelation. Punisher shoots Failsafe Omega in the head, but Revelation still thinks Punisher's a demon and attacks. As Wolverine arrives, Punisher pulls a heavenly sphere from his coat that ends Revelation's hallucinations. Failsafe Omega attacks again and arms his warhead. Wolverine and Punisher rip Omega apart. Punisher cuts out the warhead and shoves it into his jacket where it detonates harmlessly inside his heavenly arsenal. Revelation dies in Punisher's arms. The Council of Thrones arrives to take Revelation to heaven and declare Punisher worthy of his angelic powers if he still wants them. A week later, Frank talks with Lucy about Revelation's death. At the Xavier Institute, Logan broods until Storm convinces him to move on.
NOTE: Pun #1, '00 reveals Punisher declines the Council of Throne's offer and lost his angelic powers.

SPIDER-MAN VS PUNISHER (July 2000)

"No One Here Gets Out Alive" (22 pages)

CREDITS: Joseph Harris (writer), Michael Lopez (pencils), Jason Minor (inks), Dave Sharpe (letters), Mark Bernardo (colors), Ruben Diaz (asst editor), Ralph Macchio (editor)
FEATURE CHARACTERS: Spider-Man (also in rfb), Punisher
SUPPORTING CAST: J. Jonah Jameson, Joe Robertson
VILLAINS: Jackal (Miles Warren), the Grinder (John Gary, kidnapper, torturer & killer, dies)
OTHER CHARACTERS: Black Widow, Chameleon, Dr. Doom, Dr. Octopus, Ghost Rider, Green Goblin, Hammerhead, Human Torch, Kingpin, Kraven the Hunter, Lizard, Morbius, Mysterio, Rhino, Sandman, Shocker, Tarantula, Vulture, Harry Osborn, May Parker, George Stacey, Flash Thompson, Mary Jane Watson, Gwen Stacey (in rfb & Spider-Man's hallucination) (all in Spider-Man's thoughts); Bill (radio news announcer) & his helicopter pilot, police, bystanders; pigeons, rats
LOCATIONS/ITEMS: New York inc Brooklyn Bridge (also in rfb), Empire State Building, Flatiron Building & Daily Bugle w/Jameson's office / Punisher's shotgun, knife, rocket launcher, gas grenade, assault rifle & gun; news helicopter
FLASHBACK: On the Brooklyn Bridge, Gwen Stacey dies when Spider-Man fails to save her (ASM #121, '73).
SYNOPSIS: Punisher hunts down, tortures and kills the Grinder. Jackal introduces himself to Punisher and offers to help with the vigilante's war on crime. Later, Spider-Man mourns the death of Gwen Stacey until Punisher fires a rocket at him. Spider-Man recovers and searches for the shooter. Punisher ambushes Spider-Man with a gas grenade, causing Spider-Man to hallucinate. Punisher prepares to kill Spider-Man, but Spider-Man escapes by falling off the roof they're on. At the Daily Bugle, J. Jonah Jameson tells Joe Robertson to find Peter Parker to take pictures of Spider-Man battling Punisher, to take the photographer's mind off Gwen Stacey's death. Punisher follows the still groggy Spider-Man to the Empire State Building and attacks him. Spider-Man instinctively dodges when Punisher shoots at him, but the bullet accidentally hits a news helicopter. Punisher is surprised when Spider-Man exposes himself to attack by saving the people inside the crashing helicopter. Punisher apologizes to Spider-Man for thinking he's a killer and leaves. Elsewhere, Jackal plots his revenge against Spider-Man.
NOTE: An alternate retelling of ASM #129, '74 where Jackal claws Spider-Man instead of Punisher gassing Spider-Man and Punisher realizing Spider-Man's not a villain when Spider-Man points out Jackal is a killer instead of Spider-Man rescuing people from a falling helicopter. Punisher makes his War Journal entry #4 here.

"Welcome Back, Frank" (22 pages)

CREDITS: Garth Ennis (writer), Steve Dillon (pencils), Jimmy Palmiotti (inks, editor), Richard Starkings & Comicraft's Wes Abbott (letters), Chris Sotomayor (colors), Nanci Dakesian (managing editor), Joe Quesada (editor), Tim Bradstreet (c art), Dan Jurgens (variant c pencils), Jerry Ordway (variant c inks)
FEATURE CHARACTER: Punisher (also as John Smith)
SUPPORTING CAST: Nathaniel Bumpo (overweight), "Spacker" Dave (pierced), Joan "the Mouse" (quiet) (all Punisher's neighbors, 1st)
VILLAINS: Ma Gnucci's gang inc Bobbie Gnucci, Carlo Gnucci, Bruno (all die) & Sal (bts, getting police report); drug customer (dies), Mike (drug addict's friend, bts on phone), corrupt morgue employee
OTHER CHARACTERS: "Sticky" Eddie Gnucci (corpse), Gnucci drug dealers (corpses), Carlo Gnucci's date, bystanders; Maria Castle, Frank Castle Jr., Lisa Castle, angels (prev 4 mentioned, Frank glimpsed them in heaven)
LOCATIONS/ITEMS: Manhattan inc Empire State Building, World Trade Center, warehouse, hospital morgue & Punisher's tenement w/his apartment / Punisher's armory inc computer, grenades, punching knife, shotgun, Uzi & gas canister w/gasoline; Gnucci gang's guns, narcotics & briefcase w/money
SYNOPSIS: In a room full of dead drug dealers, Punisher offers to let their customer live if he reforms. When he tries to sell the drugs himself, Punisher kills him and burns the building down. Frank Castle stops by the tenement he's staying at under the name "John Smith." His neighbors greet him and he restocks his weapons. At the morgue, Bobby Gnucci mourns his brother Eddie until Punisher arrives and slaughters him and his men as a message to the Gnucci crime family: the Punisher is back. To further illustrate his point, Punisher follows Carlo Gnucci to the Empire State Building and tosses him from the top. As Carlo lands, Punisher thinks to himself about declining the angels' offer. They showed him his family in heaven and cast him back to Earth as punishment for disobeying them.
NOTE: Letters page features "In Defence of the Punisher" by Garth Ennis.

"Badaboom, Badabing" (22 pages)

CREDITS: Garth Ennis (writer), Steve Dillon (pencils, variant c art), Jimmy Palmiotti (inks, editor), Richard Starkings & Comicraft's Wes Abbott (letters), Chris Sotomayor (colors), Nanci Dakesian (managing editor), Joe Quesada (editor), Tim Bradstreet (c art)
FEATURE CHARACTER: Punisher (also in symbolic image)
SUPPORTING CAST: Detective Martin Soap (Punisher task force head, 1st but chr last in Pun #32, '03 fb), Joan, Mr. Bumpo, Spacker Dave
VILLAINS: Ma Gnucci (Isabella Carmela Magdelena Gnucci, Gnucci crime family head, voice only, 1st, next in Pun #4, '00), the Holy (Father Hector Redondo, insane priest, 1st), Eddie Lau, Harry "Heck" Thornton, "Tall" Joe Small (prev 3 hitmen, die), Joe Malizia (Gnucci family consigliere, dies), Mikey (Joe Malizia's driver, dies), gang member (dies)
OTHER CHARACTERS: Buddy "Bud" Plugg (behavioral psychologist, 1st), New York City Mayor & Police Commissioner (both voice only), police inc a Captain & Lieutenant, Little Italy restaurant patrons, pizza delivery man, police, prostitute, subway passengers, bystanders
LOCATIONS/ITEMS: New York inc Catholic Cathedral, Fifth Avenue, Little Italy w/restaurant, Long Island Expressway, police precinct inc Det. Soap's office, subway station & World Trade Center / Punisher's knife, S.U.V. & Uzi; Joan's cookies, police Punisher files, the Holy's ax
SYNOPSIS: The Gnucci crime family blackmails the mayor and police commissioner into hunting down the Punisher. In a Little Italy restaurant, Punisher secretly watches Gnucci family Consigliere Joe Malizia hire three hitmen to kill the Punisher. The unlucky Det. Soap is assigned to head the Punisher Task Force. Punisher hunts down the three hitmen and kills them. Det. Soap investigates the scene of Carlo Gnucci's death where he meets the rest of the Punisher Task Force: Bud Plugg, behavioral psychologist. After Joan gives Frank some cookies, Punisher abducts Malizia. As they speed down the Long Island Expressway, Punisher has Malizia call Ma Gnucci. He warns her that he's coming for her and kicks Malizia out while going over a hundred miles an hour. At a Catholic Cathedral, a gang member confesses various crimes to the priest, Father Redondo. The priest snaps and murders the criminal with an axe, then collapses and begs for forgiveness for killing again.
NOTE: Includes Spider-Man anti-drug comic "Fast Lane Part 4 of 4: Back on Target." See ASM Ann '01 in the ASM Index TPB for details. Ma Gnucci's full name revealed in PWZ #2, '09.

"The Devil by the Horns" (22 pages)

CREDITS: Garth Ennis (writer), Steve Dillon (pencils), Jimmy Palmiotti (inks, editor), Richard Starkings & Comicraft's Wes Abbott (letters), Chris Sotomayor (colors), Nanci Dakesian (managing editor), Joe Quesada (editor), Tim Bradstreet (c art)
FEATURE CHARACTER: Punisher
GUEST STAR: Daredevil (also in newspaper photo as Matt Murdock, last in BW #3, '01, next in DD:N #1, '00)
SUPPORTING CAST: Joan, Mr. Bumpo, Spacker Dave (all next in Pun #5, '00), Det. Martin Soap
VILLAINS: Ma Gnucci's soldiers inc "Big" Tony, Joey, Johnny (all die), Dino Gnucci (in newspaper photo, dies off-panel), the Holy, gang member
OTHER CHARACTERS: Bud Plugg (dies), Ken Ellis (bts, wrote newspaper article, last in Goblin #12, '96), Mrs. Pearse

(elderly church cleaning lady, 1st), police officer (in newspaper photo), gang member (corpse), toilet delivery men

LOCATIONS/ITEMS: New York inc Catholic Cathedral & vacant building / Punisher's van, 7.62 mm rifle, flamethrower, ultrasonic siren, chains & gun; copy of Daily Bugle, Gnucci soldiers' guns, police Punisher files

SYNOPSIS: Punisher lures several Gnucci soldiers into a vacant building, sets most of them on fire with a flamethrower and tricks the rest into killing themselves by shooting the abandoned flamethrower. Det. Soap reads Bud Plugg's unhelpful psychoanalysis on the Punisher and suggests that instead he go through the Punisher files and determine his methodology. Frank Castle plots to assassinate Dino Gnucci, Ma Gnucci's brother. Unfortunately, Nelson and Murdock are representing Dino in his current trial and Daredevil usually follows them. Det. Soap looks to Bud Plugg for some advice, but finds that Plugg has hung himself. After the first day of Dino's trial Punisher stakes out the jail where Dino is being held until Daredevil appears. Punisher quickly subdues him with an ultrasonic siren. Daredevil awakens chained and with a gun in his hand. Punisher offers him a choice: kill him and Dino lives, don't and Dino dies. Punisher kills Dino with his sniper rifle and tells Daredevil there wasn't a firing pin in the gun. Meanwhile, the Holy prepares to kill another criminal.

NOTE: Issue came bagged w/MKn/MB Genesis Edition, a sketchbook preview of MKn & MB.

PUNISHER #4 (July 2000)

"Wild Kingdom" (22 pages)

CREDITS: Garth Ennis (writer), Steve Dillon (pencils), Jimmy Palmiotti (inks), Richard Starkings & Comicraft's Wes Abbott (letters), Chris Sotomayor (colors), Nanci Dakesian (managing editor), Joe Quesada (editor), Tim Bradstreet (c art)
FEATURE CHARACTER: Punisher (next in Pun #6, '00 fb)
SUPPORTING CAST: Lt. Molly Elizabeth Chrysanthem Olga Von Richthofen (police officer assigned to capture Ma Gnucci, 1st), Det. Soap
VILLAINS: Ma Gnucci (1st full app, last voice only in Pun #2, '00), 3 of her soldiers (die), the Holy, gangster corpse
OTHER CHARACTERS: Ken Ellis (bts, wrote Daily Bugle article, next bts in Pun #9, '00), police (some in newspaper photo), Police Captain, piranhas, polar bears, python snake, zoo patrons, Dino Gnucci (corpse in newspaper photo)
LOCATIONS/ITEMS: New York inc Central Park Zoo, police precinct w/Det. Soap's office / Bud Plugg's suicide note, Ma Gnucci's limo, Punisher's pistol, Gnucci soldier's sub-machine guns, copy of Daily Bugle

SYNOPSIS: Det. Soap reads Bud Plugg's suicide note and is ridiculed by his fellow officers. Punisher is shot while following Ma Gnucci and learning her routine. He's chased into the nearby zoo where he kills one pursuer with piranhas and another with a python. He steals their weapons. Lt. Molly Von Richthofen, the sole Gnucci Family Task Force member, suggests to Det. Soap that they team up to solve both their cases. Punisher is chased into the polar bear habitat. He escapes while the bears maul Ma Gnucci. Father Redondo buries another corpse and cries for a sign that he's doing the right thing. A newspaper article on Punisher hits him in the face. Det. Soap and Lt. Von Richthofen arrive at the zoo and learn that despite her injuries, Ma Gnucci still alive.

NOTE: Lt. Richthofen's middle names revealed in PWZ #4, '09.

PUNISHER #5 (August 2000)

"Even Worse Things" (22 pages)

CREDITS: Garth Ennis (writer), Steve Dillon (pencils), Jimmy Palmiotti (inks), Richard Starkings & Comicraft's Wes Abbott (letters), Chris Sotomayor (colors), Nanci Dakesian (managing editor), Joe Quesada (editor), Tim Bradstreet (c art)
FEATURE CHARACTER: Punisher (also as "Mr. Smith")
SUPPORTING CAST: Joan, Spacker Dave (both last in Pun #3, '00, next in Pun #7, '00), Mr. Bumpo (last in Pun #3, '00, next in Pun #9, '00), Det. Soap, Lt. Von Richthofen
VILLAINS: Elite (high society vigilante), Mr. Payback (corporate targeting vigilante) (both 1st), the Holy (next in Pun #7, '00), Ma Gnucci, her cousin Stevie (dies) & her soldiers (2 die), inc Benny & Billy; crack dealers inc Stevie; mugger
OTHER CHARACTERS: Kevin (Lucky's Bar owner, 1st, next in Pun #8, '00), Al Grummet (lives across the street from Punisher, 1st), Mrs. Pearse (last in Pun #3, '00, next in Pun #7, '00), Maureen Bennett & her dog Mr. Fluffikins (dies), Worldwide Investment Corporation inc Mr. Chairman & Mark (most die), Mr. Clyde (cocaine addicted wife beater, corpse), baseball pitcher (on TV), Lucky's Bar cook, construction workers, bystanders
LOCATIONS/ITEMS: New York inc Catholic Cathedral, Ma Gnucci's hospital room & Lucky's Bar / Gnucci soldier's gun, Joan's pie

SYNOPSIS: Quadruple amputee Ma Gnucci orders a hit contract for ten million dollars on the Punisher. Joan gives Frank Castle her pie. At Lucky's Bar, Det. Soap and Lt. Von Richthofen plan to use the Punisher and Ma Gnucci against each other. The Holy murders another person in his confession booth. Mr. Payback slaughters the Worldwide Investment Corporation board for knowingly building faulty airplane parts and putting three thousand people out of work. Elite murders drug dealers trying to sell narcotics in his upscale neighborhood, then kills a dog for pooping on the sidewalk. Punisher kills a mugger. Hearing about the ten million dollars, Al Grummet sells the Punisher's address to Ma Gnucci.

NOTE: Maureen Bennett, Benny & Billy named in Pun #6, '00.

PUNISHER #6 (September 2000)

"Spit Out of Luck" (22 pages)

CREDITS: Garth Ennis (writer), Steve Dillon (pencils), Jimmy Palmiotti (inks), Richard Starkings & Comicraft's Wes Abbott (letters), Chris Sotomayor (colors), Nanci Dakesian (managing editor), Joe Quesada (editor), Tim Bradstreet (c art)
FEATURE CHARACTER: Punisher (also in fb between Pun #4-5, '00)
SUPPORTING CAST: Det. Soap, Lt. Von Richthofen (both also in pfb)
VILLAINS: Ma Gnucci, her soldiers (several die) inc Benny & Billy (prev 2 1st) & Johnny, Mikey, & Vinnie (prev 3 die); Elite, Mr. Payback (both also in photo), Worldwide Investment Corporation CEO (dies), 4 drug dealers (die)
OTHER CHARACTERS: Tim (Elite's son, 1st, voice only, next in PWZ #1, '09 fb), Al Grummet (also off-panel in fb), Channel 15 anchor (on TV), reporters & interviewees (both in pfb), Worldwide Investment Corporation

employee & helicopter pilot (both die)

LOCATIONS/ITEMS: Elite's house, Ma Gnucci's hospital room & mansion, Punisher's tenement / Punisher's 60 mm machine gun, 45 mm handgun, duffel bag & plastique; Mr. Payback's rocket launcher, Gnucci soldier's guns, Worldwide Investment Corporation helicopter

FLASHBACKS: Reporters interview people about vigilantism (p). Punisher staggers back home after surviving the zoo encounter with Ma Gnucci.

SYNOPSIS: Al Grummet sells Punisher's address to Ma Gnucci for ten thousand dollars. Ma orders her men to investigate the location. Mr. Payback kills the Worldwide Investment Corporation CEO. Elite kills more drug dealers. Frank decides he's getting too well known at his apartment and decides to leave after he kills Ma Gnucci. Ma's men spot him when he leaves. Det. Soap and Lt. Von Richthofen see an army of Gnucci soldiers leave Ma's mansion and decide to wait at the mansion for Punisher's inevitable arrival. The Gnucci army attacks Punisher. He fights back and kills them all, but passes out from the wounds he receives.

NOTE: Al Grummet's name is spelled "Grummett" here.

PUNISHER #7 (October 2000)

"Bring out your Dead" (22 pages)

CREDITS: Garth Ennis (writer), Steve Dillon (pencils), Jimmy Palmiotti (inks), Richard Starkings & Comicraft's Wes Abbott (letters), Chris Sotomayor (colors), Nanci Dakesian (managing editor), Joe Quesada (editor), Tim Bradstreet (c art)

FEATURE CHARACTER: Punisher (also as "Mr. Smith")

SUPPORTING CAST: Joan, Spacker Dave (both last in Pun #5, '00), Det. Soap, Lt. Von Richthofen

VILLAINS: Elite, Mr. Payback, the Holy (all next in Pun #9, '00), Ma Gnucci & her 2 soldiers (Benny & Billy, also posing as police)

OTHER CHARACTERS: Mrs. Pearse (last in Pun #5, '00, next in Pun #9, '00), Robert Leonard (Chairman of Wall Street Investors Association & co-owner of Metropolitan Trading Incorporated, on TV, dies), the Holy's victim (corpse), police, police captain (bts, ordered Soap to investigate the Holy), coroners, hot dog vendor, news reporter

LOCATIONS/ITEMS: New York inc Lucky's Bar & Punisher's tenement w/his apartment & armory room / Punisher's armory inc grenades, machine guns & shotguns; Billy & Benny's fake NYPD badges, Elite's grenade, Mr. Payback's handgun

SYNOPSIS: The Punisher awakens and staggers back to his apartment before the police arrive. Det. Soap and Lt. Von Richthofen are told to investigate corpses with crosses on their foreheads. Ma Gnucci orders the last two of her men to find out which apartment in the tenement is Punisher's. Det. Soap questions Father Redondo about the killings, but doesn't notice that Redondo knows more people have been killed than have been reported. Joan follows a blood trail into Punisher's apartment and finds his arsenal. Elite destroys a hot dog vendor's cart for setting up in his neighborhood. Joan and Spacker Dave tend to Punisher's wounds. Mr. Payback kills a Wall Street tycoon on national TV, declaring his fight for the common man on camera. Posing as police, Ma Gnucci's two men question Joan and get nowhere, but Spacker Dave confesses instantly.

PUNISHER #8 (November 2000)

"Desperate Measures" (22 pages)

CREDITS: Garth Ennis (writer), Steve Dillon (pencils), Jimmy Palmiotti (inks), Richard Starkings & Comicraft's Wes Abbott (letters), Chris Sotomayor (colors), Kelly Lamy (asst editor), Nanci Dakesian (editor), Tim Bradstreet (c art)

FEATURE CHARACTER: Punisher (also in rfb)

SUPPORTING CAST: Det. Soap, Lt. Von Richthofen, Spacker Dave, Joan

VILLAINS: Ma Gnucci (also in rfb) & her soldiers inc Benny & Billy (others in rfb); the Russian (Russian mercenary, 1st but chr last in Pun #9, '00 fb)

OTHER CHARACTER: Kevin (last in Pun #5, '00), Bravo Force (Special Ops team, all but 1 die), mob doctor; Carlo Gnucci, polar bears (both in rfb)

LOCATIONS/ITEMS: Punisher's tenement inc Joan's apartment; Kazakhstan inc the Russian's hideout; Lucky's Bar, Empire State Building (rfb) / Punisher's pistol & ballistic knife; Gnucci soldiers' pliers

FLASHBACKS: Punisher throws Carlo Gnucci off the Empire State Building (Pun #1, '00), sets Gnucci soldiers on fire (Pun #3, '00) and slaughters the rest (Pun #6, '00). Polar bears maul Ma Gnucci (Pun #4, '00).

SYNOPSIS: Ma Gnucci's men begin to torture Spacker Dave by pulling out his piercings to learn which apartment is Punisher's as Ma calls a hitman. At Lucky's Bar, Det. Soap and Lt. Von Richthofen work on their respective cases. Joan helps Punisher up and he kills Ma's men. Soap is depressed to learn Von Richthofen is a lesbian. A mob doctor operates on Punisher and Spacker Dave. Punisher pays the doctor ten thousand dollars and tells Joan that his real name is Frank. In Kazakhstan, military commando team Bravo Force fails to apprehend international fugitive the Russian. The Russian kills all but one, so he can report back to his commanders to leave him alone, or he will come find them. The Russian answers a phone call from Ma Gnucci and agrees to come to America.

NOTE: Joe Quesada continues to answers LOCs in the letters page, despite being promoted to Editor in Chief.

PUNISHER #9 (December 2000)

"From Russia with Love" (22 pages)

CREDITS: Garth Ennis (writer), Steve Dillon (pencils), Jimmy Palmiotti (inks), Richard Starkings & Comicraft's Wes Abbott (letters), Chris Sotomayor (colors), Kelly Lamy (asst editor), Nanci Dakesian (editor), Tim Bradstreet (c art)

FEATURE CHARACTER: Punisher (also in photo)

SUPPORTING CAST: Mr. Bumpo (last in Pun #5, '00), Spacker Dave, Joan (all next in Pun #11, '01), Det. Soap, Lt. Richthofen

VILLAINS: Ma Gnucci & her soldiers (one dies), the Russian (also in photo, also in fb to chr 1st app before Pun #8, '00), Elite, Mr. Payback, the Holy, other mob bosses (voices only)

OTHER CHARACTERS: Ken Ellis (bts, wrote Daily Bugle article, last bts in Pun #4, '00, next in Cable&Dp #24, '06), Kevin (next in Pun #1, '01), Mrs. Pearse (last in Pun #7, '00), Dougie (Mr. Payback's dog), Lucky's Bar patrons, news reporter (on TV), Elite's wife (voice only), the Berensteins (bts, guests at Elite's house), the Russian's victims inc military commander (in fb)

LOCATIONS/ITEMS: Catholic Cathedral, Elite's house, Punisher's tenement, Lucky's Bar, Ma Gnucci's mansion, Mr. Payback's hideout, Shamrock bar (in fb) / Russian's bazooka, chainsaw, & machine gun; Punisher's guns, copy of Daily Bugle

FLASHBACK: The Russian attacks a tank with a chainsaw, fires a rocket launcher into a bar, kills soldiers with a shovel and throws a military officer out of a helicopter.

SYNOPSIS: As other mob bosses refuse to help Ma Gnucci against the Punisher, the Russian finally arrives. Frank Castle packs up to leave his apartment behind, but learns that all of his neighbors now know he's the Punisher. Despite taking three weeks to arrive, Ma hires the Russian to kill the Punisher. Frank tells Spacker Dave it's dangerous for people to know he's the Punisher and that he's leaving. Det. Soap and Lt. Von Richthofen spot the Russian leaving Ma's mansion. The news reports on the recent rise of vigilantism, inspiring the Holy, Mr. Payback and Elite to seek each other out. Having done some research, Lt. Von Richthofen tells Det. Soap that the Russian is a war criminal that's wanted by most countries. They decide to let Punisher take care of him. In an attempt to get him to stay, Joan tells Frank that she's felt safe since learning he's the Punisher. She wants to leave the city but is afraid. He tells her to just go as the Russian arrives outside.

NOTE: Joe Quesada answers LOCs in the letters page.

PUNISHER #10   (January 2001)

"Glutton for Punishment" (22 pages)

CREDITS: Garth Ennis (writer), Steve Dillon (pencils), Jimmy Palmiotti (inks), Richard Starkings & Comicraft's Wes Abbott (letters), Chris Sotomayor (colors), Kelly Lamy (asst editor), Nanci Dakesian (editor), Tim Bradstreet (c art)
FEATURE CHARACTER: Punisher
SUPPORTING CAST: Det. Soap, Lt. Richthofen
VILLAINS: Ma Gnucci & one of her soldiers, the Russian, Vigilante Squad: Elite, Mr. Payback, the Holy; convenience store robber (dies)
OTHER CHARACTERS: New York City Mayor, Police Commissioner (both bts, on phone w/Ma Gnucci)
LOCATIONS/ITEMS: Catholic Cathedral, Punisher's tenement, Ma Gnucci's mansion / Punisher's knife & pistol; Elite's gun, the Holy's ax

SYNOPSIS: The Russian attacks Frank Castle, catching him off guard and tossing him through walls. Ma Gnucci calls the Mayor and the Police Commissioner, warning them to keep the police from responding to any emergency calls coming from the Punisher's apartment or she will release photographs of the two of them in sexual exploits to the media. The Russian smashes Punisher with a toilet. Lt. Von Richthofen yells at Det. Soap for being a whiner. Punisher stabs the Russian in the gut, but it doesn't slow him down. Mr. Payback tracks down Elite and proposes they work together. Punisher sets the Russian on fire. Mr. Payback easily finds the Holy and the three decide to look for the Punisher. The Russian stops Frank from grabbing a hidden gun and announces it's time for round two.

NOTE: The Vigilante Squad is named in Pun #11, '01.

PUNISHER #11   (February 2001)

"Any Which Way You Can" (22 pages)

CREDITS: Garth Ennis (writer), Steve Dillon (pencils), Jimmy Palmiotti (inks), Richard Starkings & Comicraft's Wes Abbott (letters), Chris Sotomayor (colors), Kelly Lamy (asst editor), Nanci Dakesian, Stuart Moore (editors), Tim Bradstreet (c art)
FEATURE CHARACTER: Punisher
SUPPORTING CAST: Mr. Bumpo, Joan, Spacker Dave (all last in Pun #9, '00), Det. Soap, Lt. Richthofen
VILLAINS: The Russian (next in Pun #1, '01), Ma Gnucci & her soldiers (one dies); Vigilante Squad: Elite, Mr. Payback, the Holy
LOCATIONS/ITEMS: Catholic cathedral, Punisher's tenement, Ma Gnucci's mansion / Lt. Richthofen's gun, the Holy's ax

SYNOPSIS: The Russian tosses Frank Castle through the wall an into Mr. Bumpo's apartment. Frank blinds the Russian, trips him and smothers him with the obese Mr. Bumpo. Twenty minutes later, Frank decides to continue smother the Russian for another ten minutes. Mr. Payback, Elite and the Holy quickly descend into squabbling instead of planning. Mr. Payback wants to attack corporations while Elite wants to establish curfews in ethnic neighborhoods. The Holy loses his temper. Frank tells his neighbors he won't be coming back and leaves for Ma Gnucci's mansion. As Ma waits for word from the Russian, Lt. Von Richthofen gets excited when the Punisher arrives. The Holy tells Mr. Payback and Elite that they just need to kill all criminals and names their group the Vigilante Squad. Punisher screams for Ma Gnucci and presents the Russian's severed head. The remaining Gnucci soldiers throw down their guns and leave. Ma is outraged but Punisher is pleased.

NOTE: Ma Gnucci's soldier is reading "The Bridges of Madison County." Joe Quesada answers LOCs in letters page.

PUNISHER #12   (March 2001)

"Go Frank Go" (22 pages)

CREDITS: Garth Ennis (writer), Steve Dillon (pencils, variant c art), Jimmy Palmiotti (inks), Richard Starkings & Comicraft's Wes Abbott (letters), Chris Sotomayor (colors), Kelly Lamy (asst editor), Nanci Dakesian, Stuart Moore (editors), Tim Bradstreet (c art)
FEATURE CHARACTER: Punisher (next in Dp #54-55, '01, MKn #1-4, '00, MaxS #1, '00 fb, MKn #5-11, '00-'01, MKn #14-15, '01, Pun #1, '01)
SUPPORTING CAST: Det. Soap (promoted to Police Commissioner, next in Pun #1, '01), Lt. Richthofen (next bts in Pun #1, '01), Joan (next in Pun #19, '03), Spacker Dave (next bts in Pun #1, '01), Mr. Bumpo
VILLAINS: Ma Gnucci (next in PWZ #3, '09 as corpse), Vigilante Squad: Elite, Mr. Payback, the Holy (all die)
OTHER CHARACTERS: Miss Willing (Soap's secretary, voice only), Maria Lopez (mentioned, cleaning lady accidentally killed by Mr. Payback), fireman, police officer, pigeon

LOCATIONS/ITEMS: New York inc Catholic Cathedral, Ma Gnucci's mansion, Police Commissioner's office & Punisher's tenement w/Joan, Mr. Bumpo, Spacker Dave's & Punisher's apartments / Punisher's gas canisters, grenade, money & Uzi; Lt. Richthofen's postcard

SYNOPSIS: Punisher sets fire to Ma Gnucci's mansion and kills Ma Gnucci. Det. Soap and Lt. Von Richthofen, depressed there's no one left for them to arrest. Punisher strikes a deal with them: they give him all their information on his imitation vigilantes and he gives them Ma's photographs of the Mayor and Police Commissioner in compromising sexual positions. A month later, Mr. Bumpo, Spacker Dave, and Joan find piles of money left for them from Frank. Joan's stack has a note telling her to "Just go." Police Commissioner Soap revels in his new position as Molly Von Richthofen enjoys an extended vacation before resuming a campaign for the Mayor's office. Punisher investigates Hector Redondo to find the Vigilante Squad in his church. They're overjoyed to see him, but he calls the Holy a lunatic and Elite a Nazi and tells Mr. Payback he's accidentally killed four people due to his poor planning. Punisher kills the Vigilante Squad.

PUNISHER #1 (August 2001)

"Well Come on Everybody and Let's Get Together Tonight" (22 pages)

CREDITS: Garth Ennis (writer), Steve Dillon (pencils), Jimmy Palmiotti (inks), Richard Starkings & Comicraft's Wes Abbott (letters), Chris Sotomayor (colors), Kelly Lamy (asst editor), Nanci Dakesian & Stuart Moore (editors), Tim Bradstreet (c art)
FEATURE CHARACTER: Punisher (also in photo)
SUPPORTING CAST: Det. Soap (last in Pun #12, '01), Lt. Richthofen (bts, says she's never leaving the Caribbean, last in Pun #12, '01), Spacker Dave (bts, started spacking movement, last in Pun #12, '01, next in PWZ #1, '09), Spacker Dave (bts, started spacking movement, last in Pun #12, '01, next in Pun #33, '03)
VILLAINS: Joe Grizzi (mobster) & his underlings; caged kidnappers, mugger (all die), the Russian (last in Pun #11, '01), General Kreigkopf's scientists (bts, monitoring the Russian's vital signs)
OTHER CHARACTERS: Kevin (last in Pun #9, '00), Soap's mother (barfly, 1st but chr last in Pun #32, '03 fb), Puff Daddy (musician, bts, attended party in new fur coat), New York Mayor (bts, assigned Det. Soap to Punisher Task Force), Grizzi's daughter (bts, kidnapped & suffocated), reporter, spacker (both on TV), Lucky's Bar patrons & staff; mugger's victim, police
LOCATIONS/ITEMS: New York inc police precinct w/Det. Soap's office, Grizzi's Restaurant (mailbox #3318), Grizzi's warehouse w/dock, Lucky's Bar & Empire State Building / Punisher's bomb, Uzi & stolen forklift; Det. Soap's Punisher files & gun; mugger's knife, Grizzi's cage
SYNOPSIS: Punisher kills a mugger but doesn't realize he's being stalked. Demoted from Commissioner for being photographed with a prostitute, Det. Soap returns to the Punisher Task Force. Punisher blows up Joe Grizzi and his underlings before interrupting Det. Soap's suicide. Punisher asks Soap to be his inside man at the precinct before killing more of Grizzi's men. Punisher finds that Grizzi had been holding those who kidnapped his daughter. They ask Punisher to release them, but he points out they killed Grizzi's daughter, then kills them. Soap gets drunk at Lucky's Bar and leaves with a woman; he doesn't realize she's his mother. Punisher is knocked out and wakes up on top of the Empire State Building with the Russian. He's now a cyborg transvestite and explains a secret agency revived him with stolen SHIELD technology and was granted permission by the US government to kill Punisher. The Russian throws Punisher off the Empire State Building.

PUNISHER #2 (August 2001)

"Does Whatever a Spider Can" (22 pages)

CREDITS: Garth Ennis (writer), Steve Dillon (pencils, variant c art), Jimmy Palmiotti (inks), Richard Starkings & Comicraft's Wes Abbott (letters), Chris Sotomayor (colors), Kelly Lamy (asst editor), Nanci Dakesian, Stuart Moore (editors), Tim Bradstreet (c art)
FEATURE CHARACTER: Punisher
GUEST STAR: Spider-Man (last in DD #20/2, '01, next in Av #31, '00)
SUPPORTING CAST: Det. Soap (next in Pun #10, '02)
VILLAINS: General Kreigkopf (former US Army general discharged for crippling a Lance Corporal, 1st) & his scientists (1st but last bts in Pun #1, '01), the Russian
OTHER CHARACTERS: Kevin (next in Pun #11, '02), Soap's mother (next in Pun #10, '02), reporter (on TV), Lucky's Bar patrons & staff; subway train driver, fireman, police, bystanders
LOCATIONS/ITEMS: New York inc Empire State Building, Lucky's Bar & Soap's mother's bedroom; Gen. Kreigkopf's Grand Nixon Island HQ/ Gen. Kreigkopf's scientists' tracking equipment, subway train
SYNOPSIS: Spider-Man catches the falling Punisher and returns him to the Empire State Building where the Russian attacks Spider-Man. He tosses Spider-Man away and chases Punisher. Det. Soap wakes up at his "date's" house, still unaware that he has slept with his own mother. Spider-Man returns only for the Russian to throw him away again. The Russian's employer, disgraced Gen. Kreigkopf, views the Russian's progress from afar. Spider-Man returns again and the Russian knocks him out. Punisher uses Spider-Man as a shield against the Russian's blows until he figures out how to uses Spider-Man's web-shooters. He squirts web fluid into the Russian's mouth and pushes him off the Empire State Building. The Russian falls through the street and is hit by a subway train. Punisher later meets with Det. Soap, who agrees to help Punisher.
NOTE: Pun #3, '01 reveals Kreigkopf's base to be on Grand Nixon Island.

PUNISHER #3 (September 2001)

"American Ugly" (20 pages)

CREDITS: Garth Ennis (writer), Steve Dillon (pencils), Jimmy Palmiotti (inks), Richard Starkings, Comicraft's Wes Abbott (letters), Chris Sotomayor (colors), Kelly Lamy (assist editor), Nanci Dakesian, Stuart Moore (editors), Tim Bradstreet (c art)
FEATURE CHARACTER: Punisher
VILLAINS: General Kreigkopf (also in Punisher's thoughts), his scientists & his mercenaries (some also in Punisher's thoughts, many die) inc Rodriguez (dies) & Terry Saint (exiled Royal Air Force pilot, 1st); Hackett (mercenary pilot, 1st), the Russian
OTHER CHARACTERS: Colonel Jean Romilly (French military, 1st), George W. Bush (US President, gave Kreigkopf permission to set the Russian loose in New York, next in Pun #5, '01, see NOTE), NYPD's deputy

commissioner, bystanders

LOCATIONS/ITEMS: New York, Grand Nixon Island (also in Punisher's thoughts) inc Kreigkopf's HQ, bar & jungle / Punisher's knife, gun & stolen Uzi; Hackett's plane, Col. Romilly's plane, Gen. Kreigkopf's scientists' equipment, mercenaries' guns

SYNOPSIS: Punisher interrogates the NYPD's deputy commissioner and learns that Gen. Kreigkopf is controlling the Russian. When Punisher asks who gave Kreigkopf permission to set the Russian loose in New York, he's surprised at the answer. On Grand Nixon Island, Col. Romilly thanks Gen. Kreigkopf for allowing France to use the island for refueling during France's nuclear tests. Punisher charters a plane to Grand Nixon Island and asks Hackett, the pilot, about Kreigkopf; he claims to not have heard of him. While Kreigkopf's scientists repair the Russian, Hackett betrays Punisher to Kreigkopf's mercenaries. Punisher shoots his way out and escapes into the surrounding jungle.

NOTE: Pun #5, '01 reveals Kreigkopf got permission from the President.

PUNISHER #4 (October 2001)

"Dirty Work" (22 pages)

CREDITS: Garth Ennis (writer), Steve Dillon (pencils, variant c art), Jimmy Palmiotti (inks), Richard Starkings & Comicraft's Wes Abbott (letters), Chris Sotomayor (colors), Kelly Lamy (assoc managing editor), Nanci Dakesian (managing editor), Stuart Moore (editor), Tim Bradstreet (c art)
FEATURE CHARACTER: Punisher
VILLAINS: General Kreigkopf, his scientists & his mercenaries (many die) inc a Major, a Captain & Terry Saint (prev 3 die); Hackett (dies), the Russian
OTHER CHARACTERS: Col. Jean Romilly
LOCATIONS/ITEMS: Grand Nixon Island inc bar, airfield & jungles / Punisher's traps, knife & stolen assault rifle w/grenade launcher; mercenaries' guns, Ogre One Zero (Kreigkopf's 747 jet, destroyed)

SYNOPSIS: As Punisher picks off Kreigkopf's mercenaries one by one, Hackett is hired to fly Kreigkopf's 747. Punisher kills more mercenaries but captures one, a former Rangers Major. Meanwhile, Kreigkopf loads his 747 with two hundred mercenaries and the Russian. Punisher learns from the Major that Kreigkopf plans to crash the 747 full of mercenaries into a meeting of European leaders in Brussels who plan to send a Rapid Reaction Force to Grand Nixon Island; when the Russian kills them Grand Nixon will be left alone. As the 747 prepares to leave, Punisher destroys it with a grenade launcher. The Russian survives. Gen. Kreigkopf decides to use Romilly's nuclear test on Brussels and sends his mercenaries against the Punisher.

PUNISHER #5 (December 2001)

"No Limits" (22 pages)

CREDITS: Garth Ennis (writer), Steve Dillon (pencils), Jimmy Palmiotti (inks), Richard Starkings & Comicraft's Saida Temofonte (letters), Chris Sotomayor (colors), Kelly Lamy (assoc managing editor), Nanci Dakesian (managing editor), Stuart Moore (editor), Tim Bradstreet (c art)
FEATURE CHARACTER: Punisher
VILLAINS: General Kreigkopf, his scientists & mercenaries; the Russian (all die)
OTHER CHARACTERS: George W. Bush (1st but last bts in Pun #3, '01, next in Cap Ann '01), Jean Romilly (also in newspaper photo, promoted to General)
LOCATIONS/ITEMS: Grand Nixon Island (destroyed) inc airfield; Washington, DC inc Oval Office / Punisher's gun, stolen Uzi & stolen assault rifle w/grenade launcher (both destroyed); Col. Romilly's plane & stolen Uzi,Kreigkopf's nuclear warhead, mercenaries' guns

SYNOPSIS: Col. Romilly protests to no avail at Gen. Kreigkopf's plan as the Russian loads Romilly's plane with the nuclear warhead. Punisher makes his way through the mercenaries and shoots Kreigkopf. Punisher boards Romilly's plane as it takes off, but so does the Russian. Punisher kills the mercenaries on board and convinces Romilly to prep the warhead and fly straight up. The Russian attacks, but Punisher hooks the warhead to his jaw and opens the plane's back hatch. Grand Nixon Island is destroyed and Punisher convinces Romilly not to arrest him; Grand Nixon is destroyed and Brussels has been saved from nuclear Armageddon, Romilly will be a hero. Two weeks later, Punisher breaks into the Oval Office and confronts the US President, warning the President that he knows the President authorized the Russian being let loose in New York and warning the President not to try to kill him again.

PUNISHER #6 (January 2002)

"Do Not Fall in New York City" (22 pages)

CREDITS: Garth Ennis (writer), Steve Dillon (pencils), Jimmy Palmiotti (inks), Richard Starkings & Comicraft's Wes Abbott (letters), Chris Sotomayor (colors), Kelly Lamy (assoc managing editor), Nanci Dakesian (managing editor), Stuart Moore (editor), Tim Bradstreet (c art)
FEATURE CHARACTER: Punisher (also voice only as Lt. Castle in fb between PWJ #4, '89 fb & Pun/Cap #3, '92 fb; next in Tb #57, '01, Tb #58, '01 bts)
VILLAINS: Joe Perrett (murdered his ex-wife and kids, also in photos & voice only as Sgt. Perrett in fb)
OTHER CHARACTERS: David (tourist), his wife, Michael & Rebecca (their kids), policeman, reporter (both on TV), diner waitress (dies), cook & patrons; bystanders inc homeless man w/AIDS
LOCATIONS/ITEMS: New York inc diner & Brooklyn Bridge / Punisher's gun, Joe's gun, copy of Daily Bugle
FLASHBACK: In Vietnam, Lt. Castle and Sgt. Perrett talk about the Statue of Liberty (voice only).

SYNOPSIS: Punisher combs the city looking for Joe Perrett, a fellow military veteran who saved Frank's life in Vietnam, but is now wanted for the murder of his ex-wife and children following a custody dispute. Frank seeks to kill Joe before he is captured by the police and dragged through a lengthy trial and media spectacle. Joe sits dazed at a diner thinking someone else killed another family until the waitress rudely asks him to leave. Joe kills her and stumbles out, believing someone else pulled the trigger. On the Brooklyn Bridge trying to see the Statue of Liberty, Joe pulls his gun on a tourist family. He prepares to kill them until he remembers what he did and lets them escape. Punisher arrives and shoots Joe, holding up his former friend in his arms as he dies.

NOTE: Letters page features "A Note from the Writer" by Garth Ennis explaining the story's inspiration and tributes New York City; and "A Note from the Editor" by Stuart Moore.

PUNISHER #7 (February 2002)

(Untitled, 22 pages)

CREDITS: Steve Dillon (writer, pencils), Jimmy Palmiotti (inks), Chris Sotomayor (colors), Kelly Lamy (assoc managing editor), Nanci Dakesian (managing editor), Stuart Moore (editor), Tim Bradstreet (c art)
FEATURE CHARACTER: Punisher
VILLAINS: Paul Rosso (mob boss, also in newspaper photo, dies) & his mobsters (many die); drug dealer (dies)
OTHER CHARACTERS: 2 teenage boys (one dies), 2 police officers, Henry's Bar patrons, bystanders
LOCATIONS/ITEMS: New York inc Ace Imports building, basketball court, Casey's warehouse (destroyed) & Harry's Bar and Restaurant / Punisher's knife, gun, & rifle; drug dealer's narcotics bag, mobsters' guns, teen's gun, policeman's gun, Rosso's bomb, copy of Daily Bugle

SYNOPSIS: Punisher marches into mob boss Paul Rosso's hideout, killing his men, but Rosso escapes. Punisher later interrogates another mobster, who tells him Rosso is at Casey's warehouse. Punisher investigates, only to find a bomb waiting for him. He escapes, kills his informant and interrogates other mobsters into giving up Rosso's location. As Punisher heads to Russo's hideout, he spots a couple of teenage boys buying narcotics from a drug dealer. Punisher kills the dealer and scares the boys away. Punisher later spots Paul Rosso walking out of his hideout and kills him with a sniper rifle from a nearby rooftop. Nearby, the police have killed one of the teenagers for pulling a gun, and are arresting the other boy.

NOTE: This issue is part of 'Nuff Said month, a line-wide stunt where most of Marvel's books were published without dialogue. A 5-page feature in the back of this issue prints Steve Dillon's mock script ending with a self-portrait. Followed by "Heroes," a pin-up (1 page) featuring firemen responding to the 9/11 World Trade Center attacks by Garth Ennis (writer), Steve Dillon (pencils), Jimmy Palmiotti (inks) & Matt Hollingsworth (colors).

PUNISHER #8 (March 2002)

"When Frank Sleeps" (23 pages)

CREDITS: Ron Zimmerman (writer), Mike Lilly (pencils), Rodney Ramos (inks), Richard Starkings & Comicraft's Wes Abbott (letters), Avalon Studios' Steve Oliff (colors), Kelly Lamy (assoc managing editor), Nanci Dakesian (managing editor), Stuart Moore (editor), Timothy Bradstreet (c art)
FEATURE CHARACTER: Punisher (also in own dream)
OTHER CHARACTERS: Lisa Castle, Barbara Castle, Frank Castle Jr. (all in Punisher's thoughts), Mr. Fantastic, Nick Fury, Dum Dum Dugan, Al Capone & his enforcers inc Albert Anselmi, Frank Nitti, Jack Guzik, John Scalise, Ralph Capone, "Rocco", Stu Shezlow, Sylvester Barton; Capone's prostitutes, Hymie Weiss & Bugs Moran (all rival crime lords), Baritone crime family inc Pauly; Petey McCormick (taxi driver), bar patrons, mobsters (all in Punisher's dream)
LOCATIONS/ITEMS: New York inc Baritone Family complex & Baxter Building, Chicago inc Al Capone's office & Metropole Hotel (all in Punisher's dream), Punisher's motel room / Punisher's Uzis, tommy gun & borrowed unstable molecule clothes; Mr. Fantastic's time machine & time trigger; mobster's tommy guns & switchblade; Capone's baseball bat (all in Punisher's dream), Punisher's assault rifle

SYNOPSIS: The Baritone crime family talk about Al Capone being the originator of organized crime until Punisher kills them. Punisher finds Nick Fury in a bar and asks for a favor. Fury takes Punisher to the Baxter Building where Mr. Fantastic uses his time machine to send Frank back in time to 1920's Chicago. Frank heads straight to Al Capone's business office, killing his guards out to prove his worth. Capone hires Frank, sending him out to kill rival crime lords to prove his loyalty. After Frank kills all of Capone's competition, Frank is invited to a dinner for Capone's lieutenants. Capone has several of his men tied up, including Frank, and kills them with a baseball bat for various offenses committed against him. Frank breaks free and activates Mr. Fantastic's time trigger to summon the time portal. He kills Capone, but Capone's men gun him down before he can escape. As he dies Frank feels content, but he then awakens from his dream, having slept peacefully.

PUNISHER #9 (April 2002)

"You Talkin' to Me?" (22 pages)

CREDITS: Tom Peyer (writer), Manuel Gutierrez (art), Richard Starkings & Comicraft's Wes Abbott (letters), Avalon's Steve Oliff (colors), Kelly Lamy (assoc managing editor), Nanci Dakesian (managing editor), Stuart Moore (editor), Tim Bradstreet (c art)
FEATURE CHARACTER: Punisher (also as Philly)
VILLAINS: Medallion (taxi fleet owner), Amber, Jared (both Medallion's employees, next in Pun #11, '02), Hopkins (Medallion's blind butler/chauffeur), Mr. Badwrench (Medallion's mechanic/weaponeer), Tjinder (Medallion's cabbie) (all 1st), Johnny Gorto (mobster, dies)
OTHER CHARACTERS: Phillip "Philly" Dylan (Gorto's cabbie), Artis Lee (Daily Bugle political cartoonist) (both 1st), bystanders, Thing actor, Thor actor, Wasp actor (prev 3 voice only, in recordings, see NOTE)
LOCATIONS/ITEMS: New York inc Medallion's mansion w/ parlor, Tjinder's home & East River / Punisher's taxi, gun & chain; Tjinder's taxi w/ rocket launcher & missile; Gorto's gun, Mr. Badwrench's prosthetic wrench hand

SYNOPSIS: Posing as taxi driver Philly, whom he has locked in the trunk, Punisher picks up mobster Gorto in his cab, while ignoring a black man who tries to hail him. Punisher shoots Gorto in the face. Meanwhile, eager to foreclose on his loan on Philly's taxi medallion, Medallion orders Amber and Jared to recruit Tjinder to kill Philly before he can pay off the debt; they later coerce Tjinder into accepting the hit job. As Punisher dumps Gorto's body in the East River, Philly explains that he was using Gorto as a screen to protect himself from Medallion. Mr. Badwrench arrives at Medallion's mansion where Medallion insists he undress and explains that he intends to start a Taxi War, which will result in millions of dollars in profit for his fleet. Meanwhile, Punisher is curious why anyone would want to kill Philly, and the cabbie says that he knew other cabbies who were recently murdered. Just then, Tjinder's cab appears in Punisher's rear-view mirror, firing a missile from the cab's rocket launcher. The missile strikes Punisher's taxi.

NOTE: Mr. Badwrench's prosthetic wrench hand is considered a part of him, and will not be listed in Items in his future appearances. It is likely that the voices in Philly's cab recordings are performances by voice actors, rather than those of the real heroes. Artis Lee is named in Pun #10, '02. Amber & Jared are named in Pun #11, '02.

PUNISHER #10 (May 2002)

"This Makes It Personal!" (22 pages)

CREDITS: Tom Peyer (writer), Manuel Gutierrez (art), Richard Starkings & Comicraft's James Betancourt (letters), Avalon's Steve Oliff (colors), Kelly Lamy (assoc managing editor), Nanci Dakesian (managing editor), Stuart Moore (editor), Tim Bradstreet (c art)
FEATURE CHARACTER: Punisher (also in political cartoon)
SUPPORTING CAST: Det. Soap (last in Pun #2, '01)
VILLAINS: Mr. Badwrench (next in Pun #12, '02), Radio Annie (Medallion's dispatcher, 1st, also on monitor), Tjinder (dies), Medallion, Hopkins
OTHER CHARACTERS: Artis Lee (also in political cartoon, next in Pun #12, '02), Joe Robertson (last in TWoS #11, 20'02, next in PPSM #39, '02), Soap's mother (last in Pun #2, '01), Phillip "Philly" Dylan (dies), Bobby (Badwrench's assistant, dies), police inc Kendra, firefighters, cab driver

LOCATIONS/ITEMS: New York inc Daily Bugle, 15th police precinct w/Soap's office, Medallion's Uptown Taxis fleet office, Mr. Badwrench's Long Island City garage / Medallion's humvee limo & wrist radio; Punisher's gun, Philly's cab (destroyed, also in political cartoon), Tjinder's cab w/rocket launcher (destroyed), Badwrench's Cabattoir (cab w/remote control steering wheel sword)

SYNOPSIS: Punisher survives the cab's destruction and kills Tjinder, but Philly dies. The next morning at the Daily Bugle, Artis Lee prepares that day's political cartoon, showing Punisher driving the cab that ignored him, an act he ascribes to racism. Soap's mom drops him off at the police station. Lt. Soap is shocked to find Punisher waiting for him in his office. Punisher gives him a list of the recently murdered cab drivers, and asks for information linking them. Soap calls a friend on the force, but she hangs up on him. Later, Punisher applies for a cabbie position at Medallion's fleet office, and Radio Annie recognizes and hires him. Medallion arrives at Badwrench's garage and informs him that Punisher is investigating the recent murders. Medallion is concerned that Badwrench's assistant Bobby will overhear their discussion, so Badwrench kills Bobby as a demonstration of what his new Cabattoir can do. Radio Annie calls Medallion to report that he has hired Punisher as a cabbie, just as he ordered.

PUNISHER #11 (June 2002)

"Cabattoir" (22 pages)

CREDITS: Tom Peyer (writer), Manuel Gutierrez (art), Richard Starkings & Comicraft's Wes Abbot (letters), Avalon's Steve Oliff (colors), Kelly Lamy (assoc managing editor), Nanci Dakesian (managing editor), Stuart Moore (editor), Tim Bradstreet (c art)
FEATURE CHARACTER: Punisher
SUPPORTING CAST: Det. Soap
VILLAINS: Amber, Jared (both last in Pun #9, '02, die), Hopkins, Medallion
OTHER CHARACTERS: Kevin (last in Pun #2, '01) & his customer, Manilow (Soap's sister, 1st), Soap's mother (next bts in Pun #32, '03), Punisher's cab passenger, Happy Nappy's security guard (dies) & other workers, bystanders, She-Hulk actor (voice only)

LOCATIONS/ITEMS: New York City, Medallion's mansion, Lucky's Bar, Queens inc Happy Nappy Diaper Service, Punisher's armory / Medallion's taxi computer desk, Cabattoir (Punisher's cab), Amber & Jared's cab & guns, Punisher's gun, Cabattoir's blade-release remote control

SYNOPSIS: Medallion plays solitaire instead of plotting to kill Punisher. Driving a cab, Punisher picks up a fare and notices he's being tailed. Medallion's hitmen Amber and Jared pursue and talk about how to work the Cabattoir that Punisher is driving, unaware of whom they're following. Soap's mother drinks at Lucky's Bar until she recognizes a young woman looking through the window, and she runs out the back. The woman enters and shows Kevin a picture of her mother. When Kevin realizes that the woman is Soap's sister, he sets up a meeting between the two. Meanwhile, Punisher lures Amber and Jared to Happy Nappy Diaper Service. When they storm into the building, Punisher knocks them into a vat of dirty diapers and they tell him their boss is Mr. Badwrench. He secretly switches cabs with them, and when they hit the remote control, the Cabattoir's blades kill them. Later, while Punisher arms himself, Kevin introduces Soap and Manilow, and they fall for each other.

NOTE: It is likely that the She-Hulk voice in Punisher's cab recording is a performance by a voice actor. The movie that Jared refers to here is "The Long Goodbye," '73.

PUNISHER #12 (July 2002)

"Yo! There Shall Be an Ending!" (22 pages)

CREDITS: Tom Peyer (writer), Manuel Gutierrez (art), Richard Starkings & Comicraft's Wes Abbot (letters), Avalon's Andy Troy (colors), Kelly Lamy (assoc managing editor), Nanci Dakesian (managing editor), Stuart Moore (editor), Tim Bradstreet (c art)
FEATURE CHARACTER: Punisher
SUPPORTING CAST: Det. Soap
VILLAINS: Mr. Badwrench, Medallion, Dr. Morphine (1st) (all die), Hopkins, Medallion's cabbies
OTHER CHARACTERS: Artis Lee (last in Pun #10, '02), Kevin, Manilow, bystanders
LOCATIONS/ITEMS: New York City, Mr. Badwrench's Long Island City garage, Medallion's mansion, Soap's bedroom, Lucky's Bar, Port Authority bus terminal, Henry Hudson Parkway / taxi tank w/flamethrower, Dr.

Morphine's tranquilizer, Medallion's cabs (some destroyed), Punisher's gun
SYNOPSIS: Punisher rips Mr. Badwrench's arm out. Badwrench tells Punisher about Medallion and his Taxi War plan, and Punisher kills him. As Punisher readies Badwrench's taxi tank Medallion calls Badwrench and says he's changed plans; he's teamed with Dr. Morphine and will release a plague on New York. When he realizes that he has been revealing his plans to Punisher, he panics and Morphine sedates him. Det. Soap wakes up in bed with Manilow, and grows despondent when he realizes he has cheated on his true love. While Medallion's cabbies attack Punisher's tank on the streets, Soap wallows in self-pity at Lucky's Bar. Kevin berates him as Manilow catches a bus leaving town. Punisher leads his pursuers to the Henry Hudson Parkway, until the overpass takes them above Medallion's mansion. Punisher sends the tank flying off the overpass and crashing through a skylight, where it lands on top of Medallion and Dr. Morphine. Hopkins enters the room and Punisher raises his gun.
NOTE: Medallion's mansion's address is Mario Cuomo Tower, West 163rd.

2ND STORY: "The Call of Duty" (5 pages)
NOTE: Part 3 of a 5-part preview of Call:B #1, '02, each part of which was printed in five of Marvel's July 2002 releases. Also printed in IHulk #40, Task #4, Tb #64, UltMTU #16 and BW #2, all '02

PUNISHER #13 (August 2002)

"A Good Clean Fight" (22 pages)

CREDITS: Garth Ennis (writer), Steve Dillon (art), Richard Starkings & Comicraft's Wes Abbot (letters), Avalon's Steve Oliff (colors), Kelly Lamy (assoc managing editor), Nanci Dakesian (managing editor), Stuart Moore (editor), Tim Bradstreet (c art)
FEATURE CHARACTER: Punisher (also in pfb)
SUPPORTING CAST: Det. Soap (in pfb)
VILLAINS: John "Bubba" Prong (recent parolee, in pfb, 1st), Thomas Casino (old school godfather, also in photo, 1st but chr last in Pun #17, '02), F.A.R.C. (terrorist guerrillas, many die) inc Carlos, Hector & Miguel
OTHER CHARACTERS: Kevin, Lucky's Bar patrons (both in pfb), Soap's D.E.A. source (bts in pfb, gave Soap information), Guitterez (Punisher's Colombian guide, 1st)
LOCATIONS/ITEMS: Colombian rain forest inc terrorist camp; Lucky's Bar (in pfb) / Punisher's binoculars, remote controlled bomb, mortar w/sarin-filled rounds, target rifle, assault rifle & hypodermic syringe & dart with sarin antidote, Guitterez' gun, terrorists' guns & helicopter w/machine gun mount (destroyed), net w/trip wire
FLASHBACK: In order to prevent a mob war that could kill hundreds of innocents, Punisher agrees to consider rescuing Tommy Casino from Colombian terrorists. Afterwards, Soap gets drunk with a recent parolee who invites him to try something new (p).
SYNOPSIS: In the Colombian rain forest, Punisher injects himself with sarin antidote, shoots Tommy Casino with a dart filled with the same, and launches sarin gas into the guerrilla camp Casino is being held in. As Casino's captors die around him, Punisher announces he's been rescued. Punisher meets his guide Guitterez, who asks for his money. Punisher reminds him he'll get paid once they reach the airport. While crossing a rope bridge a guerilla squad attacks, but Punisher quickly kills them all. While taking a break, Casino learns that Punisher is paying Guitterez and says they should talk privately. Later, Casino carelessly sets off a tripwire. Meanwhile, Carlos and Miguel approach their trap, eager to discover if they've captured any rival guerilas. Punisher, trapped in a net with Guitterez and Casino, shoots them when they approach. Now they can only wait for the well-worn net to eventually break under their weight.
NOTE: John "Bubba" Prong's full name is revealed in Pun #14, '02.

PUNISHER #14 (September 2002)

"Killing La Vida Loca" (22 pages)

CREDITS: Garth Ennis (writer), Steve Dillon (art), Richard Starkings, Comicraft's Wes Abbot (letters), Avalon's Matt Milla (colors), Stuart Moore (editor), Tim Bradstreet (c art)
FEATURE CHARACTER: Punisher (also in pfb, next in MKnDS #1, '02)
SUPPORTING CAST: Det. Soap (also in dfb, promoted to Lieutenant)
VILLAINS: John "Bubba" Prong, Thomas Casino, Guitterez (both also in pfb), Casino's fellow mob bosses from New York, Philadelphia, New Jersey & Boston, mobsters (all die), Pacheco (crime boss) & his men, guerillas (in pfb, some die)
OTHER CHARACTERS: Kevin, Bubba's victims (partial corpses), reporter (on TV), press (off-panel in dfb), bystanders, anaconda (in pfb)
LOCATIONS/ITEMS: Colombian town inc Pacheco's bar & Guitterez' motel room; Colombian rain forest (in fb), Lucky's Bar, Bubba's apartment, Italian restaurant w/basement / Punisher's machete, knife, pistol & assault rifle; guerillas' guns & net(both in fb), Pacheco's men's guns, Bubba's axe, Soap's gun
FLASHBACKS: Having escaped from the net, Punisher, Guitterez and Casino encounter a band of guerilas seeking revenge. Punisher kills the rebel leader and feeds him to a snake. They escape by leaping into a river (p). Soap appears before the press after being promoted for killing Prong (d).
SYNOPSIS: Guitterez leads Punisher and Tommy Casino to Pacheco's Bar. Det. Soap wakes up in Bubba's apartment, stunned to find himself in bed with him. Having sold out to Casino, Guitterez betrays Punisher and turns him over to Pacheco, the local crime boss. Soap finds several severed heads and hands in Bubba's refrigerator. He turns to find Bubba wielding an axe. Pacheco is dejected to discover the guerilas will only pay two thousand for Castle, and that Casino was going for ten million. Punisher says he knows where to find Casino, but when Pacheco releases him, Punisher breaks his jaw and leaves. Punisher tracks down Casino and recaptures him, after killing Guitterez. Later, Punisher meets Lt. Soap at Lucky's Bar, who says he's still on the Punisher Task Force despite his promotion. Casino meets with the other Northeastern mob bosses and proposes they band together to kill the Punisher. Punisher calls Casino, rhetorically asking if he ever wondered why Castle wanted all the mob bosses in one place. In horror, Casino watches Punisher descend the stairs, brandishing an assault rifle.

PUNISHER #15 (October 2002)

"The Exclusive" (22 pages)

CREDITS: Garth Ennis (writer), Darick Robertson (pencils), Nelson DeCastro (inks), Richard Starkings & Comicraft's Wes Abbot (letters), Avalon's Matt Milla (colors), Kelly Lamy (assoc managing editor), Nanci Dakesian (managing editor), Stuart Moore (editor), Tim Bradstreet (c art)
FEATURE CHARACTER: Punisher (next in MKn #1-6, '02, JLA/Av #1, '03, MKnDS #4/2, '02)
SUPPORTING CAST: Lt. Soap
VILLAINS: Chuck Self (Daily Bugle investigative journalist), "Brothers Dim" (Self's two hired thugs), Russian mobsters, Deek Baker (drug dealer) & his street gang, Bobby Bogart (child molester), Fat Musso & his gang, Russian drug dealers, other Mafia thugs (all die)
OTHER CHARACTERS: Kevin (next in Pun #23, '03)
LOCATIONS/ITEMS: New York inc Lucky's Bar; I-278, Westchester inc Fat Musso's farmhouse w/barn / Punisher's Uzi, gun & grenade; Self's car & cassette recorder; street gang's guns & jeep (destroyed); Mafia thugs' guns & rocket launcher; Soap's handcuffs, mobsters' guns, Fat Musso's woodchipper
SYNOPSIS: Daily Bugle journalist Chuck Self blackmails Punisher into taking him along for a night so he can write an expose, or else he'll expose Lt. Soap's relationship with Frank Castle. Chuck handcuffs himself to Frank. If Self doesn't send hourly texts, his thugs will kill Soap. Punisher kills some Russian drug dealers, but Chuck is shot in the hand. Punisher kills Deek Baker and his men give chase. During the pursuit Self is shot in the rear and Punisher tricks him into running over Bobby Bogart. Baker's men follow them to Westchester where Fat Musso's summit meeting has descended into chaos; Punisher had started rumors that Musso intended to ambush his fellow mobsters. When they land, Chuck bites off his tongue and Baker's men are killed. Punisher fights back but has to dodge a fired rocket and Self lands in a wood chipper. Punisher races back to Lucky's Bar and kills the thugs holding Soap, still handcuffed to Chuck's corpse.

PUNISHER #16 (November 2002)

"Vertical Challenge" (22 pages)

CREDITS: Garth Ennis (writer), Darick Robertson (art), Richard Starkings, Comicraft's Wes Abbot (letters), Avalon's Matt Milla (colors), Stuart Moore (editor), Tim Bradstreet (c art)
FEATURE CHARACTER: Punisher (also on video monitor)
GUEST STARS: Wolverine (also on video monitor, last in NX #122, '02), Spider-Man (last in DD #35, '02, chr last in DD #65, '04 fb, next in Order #5, '02)
SUPPORTING CAST: Lt. Soap (next bts in Pun #19, '03)
VILLAINS: "Big Pete" Grigio (Mafia soldier) & other Mafia thugs, Paulie Grigio (Pete's brother), Tony Casino (Tommy Casino's brother, in shadow, 1st but chr last in Pun #17, '02 fb) & his gang of little people, bullies (inc Danny)
OTHER CHARACTERS: Garden of Eden stripper, bartender & customers, rats, Soap's mother (in photo)
LOCATIONS/ITEMS: New York inc Little Anthony's (restaurant), Dillon's (bar), Garden of Eden Gentlemen's Club, Soap's office & bootlegger tunnels; Tony Casino's Red Hook warehouse w/night watchman's office / Punisher's shotgun, lighter, stolen baseball bat & gasoline; bullies' beer bottle & axe; Tony's tranquilizer gas
SYNOPSIS: Intending to kill "Big Pete" Grigio, Punisher charges into Little Anthony's only to find the floor littered with severed legs. Meanwhile in Dillon's, Wolverine gets into a bar fight. While the fight rages, two mysterious figures knock out Danny with tranquilizer gas. Wolverine hears a chainsaw and notices a blood trail leading from two severed legs to a trapdoor. Later, Grigio wakes up chained to a bed with his legs amputated. Lt. Soap tells Punisher about several recent chainsaw attacks on low-level mobsters, but clues indicate the victims are still alive. Punisher stakes out a strip club and enters when he hears an attack, but arrives too late. He follows a trail into bootlegger tunnels beneath the city, eventually running into Wolverine, who assumes Punisher is responsible for the chainsaw mutilations and attacks. Punisher's shotgun blows Logan's face off, and when he pours gasoline over Wolverine, the mysterious assailants stop the fight, reveal themselves as little people, and declare the mob will die as soon as they're cut down to size.
NOTE: Tony Casino's name revealed in Pun #17, '02.

PUNISHER #17 (December 2002)

"Aim Low" (22 pages)

CREDITS: Garth Ennis (writer), Darick Robertson (art), Richard Starkings, Comicraft's Wes Abbot (letters), Avalon's Matt Milla (colors), Stuart Moore (editor), Tim Bradstreet (c art)
FEATURE CHARACTER: Punisher
GUEST STAR: Wolverine (next in NX #123, '02)
VILLAINS: Tony Casino (also in fb to 1st chr app before Pun #16, '02) & his gang of little people, Paulie Grigio, "Big Pete" Grigio & other Mafia thugs (all die), Tommy Casino (in fb to 1st chr app before Pun #13, '02) & his friends (in fb)
OTHER CHARACTERS: Dogs (in fb)
LOCATIONS/ITEMS: Casino's Red Hook warehouse w infirmary; public restroom, mob hideout, pit, football field (prev 4 in fb) / Punisher's gun, grenade, stolen baseball bat & borrowed steamroller; Casino's men's pistols & Uzis; Tony's chainsaw
FLASHBACK: As a child, Tony learns how to hate when he is tortured and humiliated by Tommy & his friends.
SYNOPSIS: The gang of little people overwhelms Punisher and Wolverine. Tony Casino, Tommy Casino's brother, reveals himself as the leader and explains that he's taking over Tommy's position in organized crime. By amputating the legs of the Grigio brothers and their friends, he's simultaneously taking vengeance on his brother's friends for the years they spent torturing him and building a race of slaves. Punisher taunts Wolverine until the mutant breaks free. As Wolverine skewers the gang Punisher escapes. Wolverine follows, but Punisher shoots Wolverine in the crotch to keep him out of his way. As Punisher slaughters the gang of little people, Casino tries to chop off Wolverine's legs with a chainsaw. Punisher's attack distracts Casino and Wolverine cuts Tony off at the knees. Casino crawls down a manhole, but Punisher kills him by dropping a grenade down the hatch. Unable to cope with his new life, Paulie kills himself. The injured Wolverine continues to threaten Castle, but Punisher runs a steamroller over him. Before leaving the warehouse, Punisher visits the infirmary to kill Pete and his men.

PUNISHER #18 (December 2002)

"Downtown" (22 pages)

CREDITS: Garth Ennis (writer), Steve Dillon (art), Richard Starkings & Comicraft's Wes Abbot (letters), Avalon's Matt Milla (colors), Kelly Lamy (assoc managing editor), Nanci Dakesian (managing editor), Joe Quesada (editor), Tim Bradstreet (c art)
FEATURE CHARACTER: Punisher (also in pfb)
VILLAINS: Pat Morrison (I.R.A. informant, also in photo, dies), Bobby Colbert (Red Hand Commando), other Red Hand Commandoes (some die), Fallis (I.R.A. drug dealer), street criminals (many die), I.R.A. & Irish Protestant terrorists
OTHER CHARACTERS: Yorkie Mitchell (British intelligence agent, in pfb, 1st, see NOTE), cab driver, police, bystanders (in fb)
LOCATIONS/ITEMS: Belfast inc McMichael's pub, Redborn bar & warehouse w/ office; London pub (in pfb) / Punisher's pistol & assault rifle; I.R.A. Molotov cocktails, guns, crowbars & clubs; police billy clubs
FLASHBACK: On the trail of cocaine stolen from drug dealer Jonny Peron, Punisher meets Yorkie Mitchell in a London pub. Mitchell points him in the direction of Belfast and gives him a primer on the various I.R.A. factions (p).
SYNOPSIS: Punisher meets with Yorkie's contact, I.R.A. informant Pat Morrison, in McMichael's. Morrison takes Punisher to a warehouse where he has a weapons stash, and gives him a pistol and assault rifle. After killing Morrison as a favor to Yorkie, Punisher blitzes Belfast, until he turns up the name of Fallis. He corners Fallis, and the drug dealer admits taking Peron's drugs, but before he can reveal the cocaine's location, Colbert and his gang appear, eager to talk to Fallis themselves. Punisher leads Fallis to safety, but his interrogation is interrupted when a gang war breaks out nearby between the I.R.A. and Irish Protestants. Castle spots Colbert watching the melee in glee and captures him. He questions Colbert and Fallis together. Fallis reveals that he transported the drugs into England, and will use the money from the sale to finance his war against the Protestants. When Colbert announces he would have done the same, Punisher shoots both men in the legs and leaves in disgust.
NOTE: This is Yorkie's only Earth-616 appearance, but he next appears in Pun #8, '04 on Earth-200111.

PUNISHER #19 (January 2003)

"Of Mice and Men" (22 pages)

CREDITS: Garth Ennis (writer), Steve Dillon (art), Richard Starkings & Comicraft's Wes Abbot (letters), Avalon's Matt Milla (colors), Kelly Lamy (assoc managing editor), Nanci Dakesian (managing editor), Joe Quesada (editor), Tim Bradstreet (c art)
FEATURE CHARACTER: Punisher
SUPPORTING CAST: Joan (last in Pun #12, '01), Lt. Soap (bts, provided tip to Punisher, last in Pun #16, '02) (both also in Punisher's thoughts)
VILLAINS: Josef (Russian mobster) & his gang inc Boris, Rudi & Yuri (all die), Stalin (Josef's rottweiler), East Coast & Canadian mobsters, Russian mobsters inc Piotr (prev 3 dead)
OTHER CHARACTERS: Nathaniel Bumpo, Ma Gnucci, the Russian, Spacker Dave (all in Punisher's thoughts), Frankie (Joan's dog), ducks (some die)
LOCATIONS/ITEMS: Joan's Vermont cabin & nearby woods w/clearing / Punisher's assault rifle & grenade; Joan's garden claw, pen knife, needle & thread; Yuri's pistol, Josef's machete, mobsters' guns
SYNOPSIS: After being injured in a crossfire between the Mafia and the Russian mob, Punisher passes out near Joan the Mouse's cabin in the Vermont woods. When he wakes up he tells Joan that mobsters are chasing him, but he's in no shape to fight or leave. She refuses to call the police for protection so he sends her to the scene of the firefight and bring back the biggest gun she can carry. Meanwhile, Josef and his gang search for the culprit that killed his men. When Joan returns with an assault rifle, one of Josef's men breaks into the cabin and is surprised to see Punisher. Castle kills him and takes his pistol. That night, Josef and his gang stage a midnight assault on the cabin, but Punisher kills the mobsters with his rifle. Josef enters the cabin and is trapped when he falls through a booby trapped hole in the floor. Punisher approaches him ominously with a pen knife. Later, Castle buries the bodies and bids Joan goodbye.

PUNISHER #20 (February 2003)

"Brotherhood, Part One" (22 pages)

CREDITS: Garth Ennis (writer), Steve Dillon (art), Richard Starkings & Comicraft's Wes Abbot (letters), Avalon's Matt Milla (colors), Kelly Lamy (assoc managing editor), Joe Quesada (editor), Tim Bradstreet (c art)
FEATURE CHARACTER: Punisher
SUPPORTING CAST: Lt. Soap (last bts in Pun #19, '03, next in Pun #23, '03)
VILLAINS: Lt. Tom Leary, Cecil, Carl, Joey, Robbie (prev 3 next in Pun #22, '03) (all crooked police detectives), Big Pete (mob underboss, dies), Bobby Cestone (bts as Big Pete's boss, next in Pun #22, '03), drug dealers (many die)
OTHER CHARACTERS: Andy Seifert (also in answering machine recording), Mike Pearse (both police detectives), Becky Pearse (Mike's wife), Phil Fonseca (police & Punisher's informant) (all 1st), police
LOCATIONS/ITEMS: New York inc pool hall, police station, Fonseca's Rodeo Bar office, Leary's home & Pearse's home / Punisher's Uzi, pistol & binoculars; police guns, drug dealers' guns
SYNOPSIS: Punisher secretly watches the aftermath of a police drug raid, and notices Det. Seifert surreptitiously swipe a cocaine packet. Castle overhears Seifert discuss the value of Fonseca's tips with his partner. Later at the station, Det. Pearse cautions Seifert not to associate with Leary and his men, whom he suspects of being dirty. Lt. Soap turns over Seifert and Pearse's files to Punisher, but warns him that if he takes out the detectives, their relationship is over. At the Rodeo Bar, Fonseca tells Punisher that he is close to learning the source of the cocaine, and that Seifert has recently been pressuring him for the same information. That evening, Castle follows Seifert to Leary's house, and watches the detective turns over the cocaine packet to Big Pete. When Pete leaves, Punisher abducts him, intent on gaining information before killing the

dealer. Late that night, Pearse makes multiple unsuccessful attempts to reach Seifert. When Becky enters the room and sees he's been drinking, she scolds him. He loses his temper and punches her. From the hedges outside, Punisher watches.

NOTE: Fonseca's first name is revealed in Pun #21, '03. Cestone's bts role as Big Pete's boss is revealed in Pun #22, '03.

PUNISHER #21 (March 2003)

"Brotherhood, Part Two" (22 pages)

CREDITS: Garth Ennis (writer), Steve Dillon (art), Richard Starkings & Comicraft's Albert Deschesne (letters), Avalon's Matt Milla (colors), Kelly Lamy (assoc managing editor), Nanci Dakesian (managing editor), Joe Quesada (editor), Tim Bradstreet (c art)
FEATURE CHARACTER: Punisher
VILLAINS: Lt. Tom Leary, Carl, drug dealers (die)
OTHER CHARACTERS: Father Billy (Pearse's priest), Phil Fonseca (dies), Becky Pearse, Mike Pearse, Andy Seifert, truck driver, police, bar customers, bystanders, Bobby Cestone (in photo)
LOCATIONS/ITEMS: New York inc Pearse's home, drug lab (destroyed), police station w/Leary's office, Father Billy's office & O'Neill's bar / Punisher's Uzi, gasoline & grenade; drug dealers, police & Pearse's guns
SYNOPSIS: Pearse promises Becky he'll never strike her again. Meanwhile, Punisher escalates his attack on the drug dealers, wiping out a lab. Pearse and Seifert arrive soon after, and Seifert is horrified to discover the lab in flames. He confides to Pearse that he owes a large gambling debt to Cestone, and was planning on using the proceeds from selling the cocaine through Lt. Leary to settle his debt. Later, Leary agrees to give Seifert more time to get the promised cocaine. After interrogating Fonseca about Leary, Punisher tricks the snitch into getting run over by a delivery truck. Meanwhile, Pearse confesses to his priest and lifelong friend Father Billy that he has been beating his wife again. He blames the pressures of his job, but Father Billy refuses to absolve him. That night, Punisher watches Seifert drown his sorrows at O'Neill's, and concludes he's following the wrong detective. Pearse drinks whiskey at home until Becky walks in. Moments later, she crawls from the house spitting blood. In the den, Pearse tries to kill himself, but doesn't have the courage.

PUNISHER #22 (April 2003)

"Brotherhood, Conclusion" (22 pages)

CREDITS: Garth Ennis (writer), Steve Dillon (art), Richard Starkings (letters), Avalon's Matt Milla (colors), Kelly Lamy (assoc managing editor), Nanci Dakesian (managing editor), Joe Quesada (editor), Tim Bradstreet (c art)
FEATURE CHARACTER: Punisher
VILLAINS: Bobby Cestone (1st but last bts in Pun #20, '03) & his thugs inc Philly & Stack; Lt. Tom Leary, Cecil, Carl, Joey, Robbie (prev 3 last in Pun #20, '03) (all die)
OTHER CHARACTERS: Mike Pearse, Andy Seifert (both die), Father Billy, Becky Pearse, women's shelter staff & residents, bar customers, police (some as pallbearers), funeral attendees
LOCATIONS/ITEMS: New York inc women's shelter, O'Neill's bar, Pearse's home, cemetery & Ace Café (Cestone's front) w/office / Punisher's shotgun, Pearse, Leary, Carl, Cecil, Joey, Robbie & Cestone's men's guns
SYNOPSIS: Pearse screams for Becky at the women's shelter until Punisher arrives and forces the detective to leave. At O'Neill's, Castle watches Pearse make amends with Seifert. Pearse wants to use his life savings to settle Seifert's debt. Pearse asks Father Billy to help him count the money but Billy misinterprets, thinking the money is an effort to buy absolution from the church for beating Becky. Later, Pearse leaves Seifert outside the Ace Café while he meets Cestone. Cestone reveals that he knows about Seifert's narcotics pipeline, and his men usher Leary and Pearse into the office. Leary and Pearse are surprised to see each other. When Cestone laughs over the size of Pearse's life savings, the detective shoots and kills him. He quickly kills Cestone's men, but is shot and pinned down by Leary and his team. Outside, Stack attacks Seifert, but Punisher kills him and tells Seifert to help Pearse. Everyone but Punisher dies in a violent firefight. Later, Punisher watches from a hilltop as Seifert and Pearse, hailed as heroes for uncovering Leary's corruption, are laid to rest.

PUNISHER #23 (May 2003)

"Squid" (22 pages)

CREDITS: Garth Ennis (writer), Steve Dillon (art), Dave Sharpe (letters), Matt Milla (colors), Kelly Lamy (assoc managing editor), Nanci Dakesian (managing editor), Joe Quesada (editor), Tim Bradstreet (c art)
FEATURE CHARACTER: Punisher
SUPPORTING CAST: Lt. Soap (last in Pun #20, '03, next in Pun #27, '03)
VILLAINS: Sid Saggio (low-level mobster & squid enthusiast) & his friends inc Mel & Jimmy (all also as ghosts), Saggio's hired thugs (all die), giant squid
OTHER CHARACTERS: Kevin (last in Pun #15, '02, next in Pun #27, '03), Lucky's Bar patron, bystanders
LOCATIONS/ITEMS: Flatbush inc Paulie's Bar w/men's room; Lucky's Bar, Saggio's home, Gravesend Bay inc warehouse (destroyed) & pier / Saggio's friends & hired thugs' guns; Punisher's shotgun & stun grenades; Saggio's razor, Uzi, scuba gear & bomb w/ remote control
SYNOPSIS: During their weekly poker game, Saggio's friends ridicule him over his dream of finding a live giant squid. While he's in the restroom Punisher kills his friends. Saggio crawls out a window and runs away. The ghosts of his friends accuse him of cowardice and hound his every move over the next several days. He eventually asks what they want and they reply vengeance against Punisher. At Lucky's Bar, Lt. Soap tells Castle that Saggio has assembled a task force to kill Punisher, and has named a time and place. Later, Punisher raids a warehouse and kills all but one of the men inside. The lone survivor reveals that they were under instructions to ambush Punisher and call Saggio later. Punisher reasons that it's a trap and leaves just as Saggio detonates a bomb, destroying the warehouse. Saggio finds Punisher lying stunned on the pier and prepares to kill him, but is grabbed by a giant tentacle. Saggio has finally found his giant squid, but it kills him.

NOTE: Seggio reads "The Search for the Giant Squid," a book by Richard Ellis.

PUNISHER #24 (June 2003)

"Hidden, Part One" (22 pages)

CREDITS: Garth Ennis (writer), Tom Mandrake (art), Dave Sharpe (letters), Matt Milla (colors), Kelly Lamy (assoc managing editor), Nanci Dakesian (managing editor), Joe Quesada (editor), Tim Bradstreet (c art)
FEATURE CHARACTER: Punisher
VILLAINS: Man Down Below (cannibal, voice only, also as Baby in fb to 1st chr app before Pun #25, '03 fb, chr last in Pun #26, '03 fb) & his homeless army (some die) inc Ronnie; Monk Macchio's crew (die)
OTHER CHARACTERS: Mommy (Baby's 400-pound mother, in fb), Jen Cooke (social worker), Paul (Jen's friend) (all 1st), Craig, Pete (both boys in Baby's neighborhood, bts in fb, taunted Baby), homeless people (some die, some as corpses), homeless subway conductor, bystanders (some also in fb), rats, roaches
LOCATIONS/ITEMS: Mommy's home (in fb), New York City inc subway, underground tunnels & soup kitchen / Punisher's pistol, Jen's mace
FLASHBACK: After being shunned by other boys in the neighborhood, Baby runs home crying. Mommy holds him tight and soothes him.
SYNOPSIS: While New Yorkers ignore the homeless people around them, from deep in the underground tunnels, a plaintive cry rises from a mound of corpses, "Mommeee!" Punisher chases Monk Macchio's crew into the subway and kills two of them, but the third escapes down a subway tunnel. Meanwhile, Jen and Paul serve meals at a soup kitchen. Ronnie berates the other homeless people for accepting the food. Jen questions Ronnie, who reveals that the Man Down Below feeds them. Suspicious, Jen has Ronnie take her to the Man Down Below. In the tunnels, Punisher pursues the third mobster into the path of an onrushing train. In the subway entrance, Paul declines to accompany Jen into the tunnels. When several of Ronnie's friends surround her she uses mace but it's useless; they're already blind. She screams. The nearby Punisher kills Ronnie and the others. He offers to walk her to safety, but other crazed homeless people surround them and attack. While Punisher fights the small army Jen runs away. She falls through a manhole and lands on the mound of corpses.
NOTE: Jen's last name is revealed in Pun #27, '06.

PUNISHER #25 (June 2003)

"Hidden, Part Two" (22 pages)

CREDITS: Garth Ennis (writer), Tom Mandrake (art), Dave Sharpe (letters), Matt Milla (colors), Kelly Lamy (assoc managing editor), Nanci Dakesian (managing editor), Joe Quesada (editor), Tim Bradstreet (c art)
FEATURE CHARACTER: Punisher
VILLAINS: Man Down Below (1st full app, also as Baby in fb between Pun #24, '03 fb & Pun #26, '03 fb) & his homeless army (many die) inc Big Nappy
OTHER CHARACTERS: Mommy (dies in fb), Jen Cooke, Paul, homeless people (as corpses), fly
LOCATIONS/ITEMS: Mommy's home (in fb), New York City inc subway, underground tunnels & Punisher's armory townhouse / Punisher's pistol, knife, shotgun, grenades & flamethrower (off panel); Jen's rock, chicken bone (in fb)
FLASHBACK: After telling Baby a bedtime story, Mommy chokes on a chicken bone and falls on Baby, trapping the boy under her weight. Baby struggles to get out from under Mommy.
SYNOPSIS: As Jen tries to descend the mound of corpses she finds Paul, whose throat has been slashed. Jen tells the terrified Paul that she must leave for help, but stops when the Man Down Below crawls from beneath the mound. He berates his followers for bringing him someone who has friends. Meanwhile, the homeless army nearly overwhelms Punisher, until he unleashes a grenade. Shrapnel cuts Punisher's ankle, hobbling him. He leaps aboard a subway train, but Big Nappy follows him. When the train reaches its stop, the doors open and Big Nappy falls to the platform, with Punisher's knife in his throat. Punisher returns to his armory where he collects his weapons. Later, Jen slips quietly down the subway tunnel. When she hears a noise she hoists a rock over her head, but discovers it's Punisher. Castle advises her to find a hospital, but she follows him, arguing that the homeless people aren't responsible for their actions. Castle reminds her that their victims are still dead, no matter the motive, and warns her to stay out of his way.

PUNISHER #26 (July 2003)

"Hidden, Part Three" (22 pages)

CREDITS: Garth Ennis (writer), Tom Mandrake (art), Dave Sharpe (letters), Matt Milla (colors), Kelly Lamy (assoc managing editor), Nanci Dakesian (managing editor), Joe Quesada (editor), Tim Bradstreet (c art)
FEATURE CHARACTER: Punisher (next in W #183, '03)
VILLAIN: Man Down Below (dies, also as Baby in fb between Pun #25, '03 fb & Pun #24, '03) & his homeless army (many die)
OTHER CHARACTERS: Mommy (corpse), police inc Henry, bystanders (all in fb), Jen Cooke, Paul (corpse), homeless people (mountain of corpses, destroyed), cab driver
LOCATIONS/ITEMS: Mommy's home w/bedroom (in fb), New York City inc subway, underground tunnels & Man Down Below's chamber / Punisher's shotgun, bandolier, M18 claymore mine, flamethrower (destroyed), flare, & rope
FLASHBACKS: Police arrive at Mommy's home after no one has heard from her in two weeks. They find Mommy's decomposing corpse with Baby underneath. Paramedics remove Baby and discover that the boy ate part of Mommy to survive.
SYNOPSIS: Punisher and Jen move deeper into the tunnels. When he notices they're being followed, Punisher sets up a mine that kills a gang of the Man Down Below's army. Punisher and Jen find the Man Down Below's mountain of corpses. Jen is horrified to see its enormity and finds that Paul died while she was gone. Punisher leaves to end the Man Down Below's atrocities. A pair of hands reach from beneath the pile and grabs Paul's ankles, scaring Jen. Punisher finds the rest of the Man Down Below's army and tells them to leave; he kills those that don't. Jen tries to kill the Man Down Below, but he embraces her tightly. Punisher returns and, at Jen's suggestion, burns the corpses with his flamethrower. Frantic, the Man Down Below releases Jen and lunges for Frank, who immolates him and wedges his fuel tank into him. The tank explodes in the flames, destroying the corpses and killing the Man Down Below. Frank puts a shaken Jen in a cab and sends her to the nearest hospital.
NOTE: This is Jen Cooke's last Earth-616 app to date, but her Earth-200111 counterpart next appears in Pun #26, '06 fb.

PUNISHER #27 (July 2003)

"Elektra" (22 pages)

CREDITS: Garth Ennis (writer), Tom Mandrake (art), Dave Sharpe (letters), Matt Milla (colors), Kelly Lamy (assoc managing editor), Nanci Dakesian (managing editor), Joe Quesada (editor), Tim Bradstreet (c art)
FEATURE CHARACTER: Punisher (next in W #186, '03, AgentX #2, '02, SM:GetK #1/2 fb, '02)
GUEST STAR: Elektra (Elektra Natchios, assassin, also as prostitute, also in photo, last in Elek:G&E #4, '02, next in Elektra #11, '02)
SUPPORTING CAST: Lt. Soap (next in Pun #32, '03)
VILLAINS: Figsy Goleano (strip club owner/heroin dealer, dies), Anthony Balbo (mobster, dies) & his friends (as corpses), 3 Dell'Orro brothers, Jimmy the Gun, the Dutchman, Don Alberto Luigi Pariani (prev 6 criminals, as corpses), Skinny Vic Strega (mobster, dies) & his henchmen (die)
OTHER CHARACTERS: Kevin (last in Pun #23, '03, next in Pun #32, '03), Lucky's Bar patrons, Elektra's victims (in photos)
LOCATIONS/ITEMS: New York inc Gino's Place (strip club) w/Goleano's office, Punisher's apartment, Dante's (restaurant), Lucky's Bar, Dell'Orros' house w/swimming pool, warehouse, restaurant kitchen, Pariani's mansion w/bathroom, Remington (hotel) w/penthouse suite & henchmen's room / Punisher's sniper rifle, shotgun, submachine gun, handgun & assault rifle; Elektra's sai & katana, Strega's henchmen's guns
SYNOPSIS: Punisher prepares to snipe a crooked strip club owner through his office window, but Elektra fatally skewers the owner and vanishes. The next night, Punisher heads to a gangster's birthday party but finds the gangster and all the guests dismembered, again the work of Elektra. Punisher meets with Lt. Soap at Lucky's Bar, who shakingly gives him a police dossier on Elektra. Over the next four days, Punisher finds every criminal he targets already killed by Elektra. Figuring Elektra is slaying his quarry as a precursor to her eliminating him, Punisher targets a mobster at a hotel penthouse with the intention of confronting her if she appears. Elektra does, disguised as a prostitute hired by the mobster, and rips out the crook's heart. As Punisher enters the penthouse and Elektra begins to explain her actions, the mobster's henchmen arrive. Punisher kills them all, and Elektra finally tells him that the sole reason for her killing spree of Punisher's targets was simple boredom. Impressed, Frank asks her out to dinner.

PUNISHER #28 (August 2003)

"Streets of Laredo Part One" (22 pages)

CREDITS: Garth Ennis (writer), Cam Kennedy (pencils), Avalon Studios (inks, colors), Virtual Calligraphy's Cory Petit (letters), Kelly Lamy (assoc managing editor), Nanci Dakesian (managing editor), Joe Quesada (editor), Tim Bradstreet (c art)
FEATURE CHARACTER: Punisher (also as "John Smith," also in pfb)
VILLAINS: Rich the Snitch (in pfb, die off-panel), Rachel (militia leader & arms dealer, 1st) & her militia (some in pfb, all in pfb die) inc Spit, gang-bangers (all in pfb, all die)
OTHER CHARACTERS: Kim Wells (hotel owner), Steve Southall (sheriff), Gerry (deputy) (all 1st), Bob (car rental owner), police (bts in pfb), bar patrons, US Army soldier
LOCATIONS/ITEMS: Branding, TX inc airport, Bob's Rentals (car rental), hotel w/Frank's room, Larry's (bar) & Monastery Hill w/Rachel's camp; New York (in pfb) inc Bensonhurst w/public bathroom, vacant lot (133rd St. & Lexington Ave.) & Rich's apartment / Punisher's rifle (in pfb), rental truck & duffel bag; New York arms shipment (in pfb) inc M-16 assault rifles, Mossberg pump-action shotguns, M-203 grenade launchers, grenades & M-60 machine gun; rocket launcher (in pfb, destroyed), arms dealers' guns (some in pfb), Spit's Beretta 92 handgun, billiard balls, Army trucks; Texas arms shipment: M-16s w/1,000 rounds of ammunition each & magazines, 50 M-203s w/100 anti-personnel rounds each, 24 M-60s w/5,000 rounds of linked ammunition each, 300 M-18A1 Claymore mines, 200 M-67 fragmentation grenades, 200 M-34 white phosphorus grenades, 200 ANM14 TH3 incendiary grenades, 50 1-pound Semtex bricks
FLASHBACK: Punisher coerces the location of an upcoming cocaine transaction from Rich the Snitch. Upon arrival, he discovers the deal actually involves military weaponry. He is spotted and a firefight ensues, but a stray rocket detonates the shipment and kills the dealers and buyers. Punisher interrogates Rich for the arms dealers' central location, and kills the Snitch (p).
SYNOPSIS: Frank Castle arrives in Branding, Texas, and checks into the local hotel, unaware that local sheriff Steve Southall is watching him. Frank agrees to a liaison with the hotel owner, Kim Wells. Afterwards, Kim gives Frank background on the town and on a militia based in its outskirts. Frank goes to a pool hall Kim mentioned and finds a trio of the militia's members inside, led by a man named Spit. Frank shoots a billiard ball into Spit's crotch, then takes his gun, which Frank notices still has US Army markings, and shoos the others out. Outside, Southall approaches Frank and politely asks Frank's intentions, but subtly warns him against causing trouble. At the militia's compound, their leader, Rachel, takes custody of a shipment of weaponry sold to her by corrupt US Army soldiers. She admonishes and dismisses Spit for not filing the Army markings off his gun before Frank took it, then ponders Frank's intentions.
NOTE: Gerry's name is revealed in Pun #29, '03. Branding's population is 989.

PUNISHER #29 (September 2003)

"Streets of Laredo Part Two" (22 pages)

CREDITS: Garth Ennis (writer), Cam Kennedy (pencils), Avalon Studios (inks, colors), Virtual Calligraphy's Cory Petit (letters), Kelly Lamy (assoc managing editor), Nanci Dakesian (managing editor), Joe Quesada (editor), Tim Bradstreet (c art)
FEATURE CHARACTER: Punisher (also in photo)
VILLAINS: Preacher (Rev. Henry McCarthy, socially conservative preacher, 1st); Rachel & her militia inc Clark (Rachel's son) (Clark & one other militia member dies)
OTHER CHARACTERS: Gerry, Steve Southall, Kim Wells, Branding residents; Fakir Auda-Sayed, Freddie Clegg, Leon Michael Daley, Harvey Oscar Dyer, Terry Fitts-Gleason, Duval Griffin, Carlotta Guiterrez, Benny "BJ" Jorgenson, Tsukada Kosugi, Miku Mederos, Johnny Molini, Joey "The Fork" Moscone, Tariq Mukhtar, Joe "The Hook" Ottman, Detroit Phillips, Frank Thring, 3 others (prev 20 criminals, all in mugshots on cover, all either listed as killed by the Punisher or incarcerated)
LOCATIONS/ITEMS: Branding, TX inc Kim's hotel w/Frank's room, Larry's & sheriff's office; Monastery Hill militia camp / Punisher's pool cue, militia's guns, Rachel's brass knuckles, Preacher's car, Bowie knife, printout of Punisher's FBI file
SYNOPSIS: Preacher, Branding's self-appointed voice of decency, asks to know Frank Castle's intentions in Branding, but Frank refuses. Rachel's son Clark leaves the militia camp, and a militia member utters an anti-gay slur. Rachel baits the man into a fight and beats him to death for speaking ill of her son. Clark meets with his new boyfriend, Sheriff Steve Southall, and suggests they run away together, but Steve insists on staying in Branding despite any local negative opinions about his sexuality. Southall tells Clark he has to investigate Rachel's militia. Spit returns to the pool hall with a new group. Frank beats all of them handily and runs them off. Steve and Clark's date is cut short when Gerry radios Steve and tells him he has identified Frank. Following another night with Kim, Frank asks Kim about Preacher. Steve arrives at his office and is stunned to see Frank's massive FBI file. That night, while trying to call Steve on a pay phone, Clark is repeatedly run over with a car and killed.
NOTE: Pun #31, '03 reveals Preacher to be Clark's killer. Freddie Clegg's appearance on the cover is an homage to Terence Stamp's namesake character in the 1965 film, "The Collector." Joey "The Fork" Moscone is modeled after artist Joe Jusko. Tariq Mukhtar is modeled after Sudanese footballer Tariq Mukhtar Saeed. Frank Thring is modeled and named after an Australian actor.

PUNISHER #30 (October 2003)

"Streets of Laredo Part Three" (22 pages)

CREDITS: Garth Ennis (writer), Cam Kennedy (pencils), Avalon Studios (inks, colors), Virtual Calligraphy's Cory Petit (letters), Kelly Lamy (assoc managing editor), Nanci Dakesian (managing editor), Joe Quesada (editor), Tim Bradstreet (c art)
FEATURE CHARACTER: Punisher
VILLAINS: Preacher; Rachel & her militia (some die) inc Clark (as corpse) & Spit
OTHER CHARACTERS: Gerry, Steve Southall, Kim Wells, Branding residents, Joe Conner (mentioned, law enforcement ally of Steve's)
LOCATIONS/ITEMS: Monastery Hill militia camp (destroyed) w/underground armory, Branding, TX inc sheriff's office, Kim's hotel / Steve's police car (destroyed), rifle & handgun; Gerry's shotgun; militia's vehicles (one destroyed) & weapons (some destroyed) inc assault rifles, grenade launchers, rocket launchers, hand grenades, knives & Semtex; Punisher's handguns
SYNOPSIS: Rachel swears vengeance against the entirety of Branding for Clark's death. Gerry arrives to see Steve Southall arming himself for the arrival of Rachel's militia and offers condolences for his loss. Having never shot at a human being, Gerry declines to help with the militia's impending reprisal. Steve understands and sends him home, then visits Frank Castle at Kim Wells' hotel. Frank refuses to help Steve, but asks Steve to let him handle Rachel and her men alone. Steve leaves, and delivers a mouth-closing rebuttal to the Preacher's latest tirade against him. Steve roadblocks the road out of Monastery Hill and, when Rachel and her men arrive, asks her to let the law seek justice for Clark. Rachel refuses and a firefight ensues. Punisher attacks the camp and kills the militia members guarding it. As Steve fights a losing battle against Rachel and her men, Punisher locates the militia's underground weapons cache. Rachel shoots Steve, sending him over a cliff, but he continues to fight despite his grievous injuries. Meanwhile, Punisher blows up the camp and leaves.
NOTE: Steve sings "Streets of Laredo" while waiting for Rachel.

PUNISHER #31 (November 2003)

"Streets of Laredo Conclusion" (22 pages)

CREDITS: Garth Ennis (writer), Cam Kennedy (pencils), Avalon Studios (inks, colors), Virtual Calligraphy's Cory Petit (letters), Kelly Lamy (assoc managing editor), Nanci Dakesian (managing editor), Joe Quesada (editor), Tim Bradstreet (c art)
FEATURE CHARACTER: Punisher (also in photo)
VILLAINS: Preacher; Rachel (dies) & her militia (die) inc Spit
OTHER CHARACTERS: Steve Southall (dies), Gerry, Kim Wells, Branding residents
LOCATIONS/ITEMS: Branding, TX inc sheriff's office, Larry's, liquor store, Kim's hotel, hardware store & Preacher's church; Monastery Hill inc remains of militia camp / Punisher's belt-fed machine gun, handgun, pool cue, meathook, rental truck & tow chain; militia's wrecked vehicles & guns; Rachel's handgun & hatchet
SYNOPSIS: Punisher finds a bloodied Steve Southall lashed to a wall, cuts him down and tells Steve his injuries are fatal. Steve accepts his impending death and asks that Frank avenge him. Rachel and her men inspect the remains of their camp, then leave for Branding. Gerry arrives to see Steve. Punisher tells him that, despite his earlier cowardice, he can still help by finding Clark's killer. At the pool hall, Punisher kills Spit and tells the other militia members present that he will wait for them in front of the town hall at high noon. Although

outnumbered, Punisher slaughters the entire group except Rachel, who escapes into a hardware store. Punisher follows, but Rachel ambushes him with a hatchet. Punisher finishes the fight quickly by impaling Rachel through the neck with a meathook. Later, Gerry confronts Preacher with his findings that he killed Clark. Preacher is steadfast that his actions restored the town's morality. Soon after, Frank leaves Branding and bids Gerry goodbye before driving off with Preacher gagged and bound to a tow chain behind his rental truck.

PUNISHER #32 (November 2003)

"Soap" (22 pages)

CREDITS: Garth Ennis (writer), Steve Dillon (pencils), Avalon's Matt Milla (inks, colors), Virtual Calligraphy's Cory Petit (letters), Kelly Lamy (assoc managing editor), Nanci Dakesian (managing editor), Joe Quesada (editor), Tim Bradstreet (c art)
FEATURE CHARACTER: Punisher (in pfb, also in rfb & Soap's thoughts)
SUPPORTING CAST: Lt. Soap (also in rfb, also in pfb, also in fb to 1st chr app before Pun #1, '01)
VILLAINS: Mobsters (in pfb, all die)
OTHER CHARACTERS: Father Halifax (head of Dunmore Orphanage), Det. "Pints" O'Riordan (drunken policeman, dies), Bobby Pankowicz (school bully), police academy Commandant & graduates, judge, doctor, lawyers, nurses (all in fb), Soap's mother (bts, dumped Soap, last in Pun #11, '02, also in photo, in fb to 1st chr app before Pun #1, '01), Kevin (last in Pun #27, '03), Lucky's Bar patrons inc a transvestite; Ma Gnucci's soldiers (in rfb), John "Bubba" Prong (in Soap's thoughts)
LOCATIONS/ITEMS: NJ inc Dunmore Orphanage & hospital; police academy inc dorms; court room, Soap's office (all in fb), Joe's bar (in pfb), Lucky's Bar / Punisher's guns & shotgun; Soap's revolver, mobsters' guns (all in pfb), Halifax's cane (in fb)
FLASHBACKS: The newly born Martin Soap is dropped on his head. He grows up in the Dunmore Orphanage, where the other boys pick on him and he's passed up for adoption many times. In his one bit of good luck, Father Halifax deems Soap a plain child and decides not to molest him. At age ten, Soap runs away from the orphanage and hitches a ride with the drunken Det. "Pints" O'Riordan, who inspires Soap to become a policeman before returning Soap to the orphanage. "Pints" later drives off a bridge. In high school, Soap is bullied by Bobby Pankowicz, who believes cops are kings of the world and can take what they want. Soap graduates from police academy, but his bad luck keeps his cases from reaching convictions for various reasons (1). Punisher kills Ma Gnucci's soldiers (Pun #1, '00). Soap is assigned to the Punisher Task Force (Pun #2, '00). Soap follows Punisher on one of his missions, wanting to see the vigilante act on the information he gives him. Soap is horrified by the carnage and is almost killed by an escaping mobster. Punisher blasts the mobster's head all over Soap's face (p).
SYNOPSIS: At Lucky's Bar, Lt. Soap laments his unlucky life as Kevin continues to give him free drinks. Soap feels his luck is about to change when he strikes up a conversation with a woman at the bar, unaware "she" is a transvestite.
NOTE: Soap notes here that since he began helping Punisher, he's helped Castle commit 417 murders.

PUNISHER #33 (December 2003)

"Confederacy of Dunces Part 1" (22 pages)

CREDITS: Garth Ennis (writer), John McCrea (pencils), Crimelab Studios, Danny Miki (inks), Virtual Calligraphy's Cory Petit (letters), Avalon Studios (colors), Kelly Lamy (assoc managing editor), Nanci Dakesian (managing editor), Joe Quesada (editor), Tim Bradstreet (c art)
FEATURE CHARACTER: Punisher (also in photo & rfb)
GUEST STARS: Daredevil (also in photo, last in DD #46, '03, chr last in DD #65, '04 fb), Spider-Man (also in photo, last in PPSM #50, '03, chr last in Dline #2, '02), Wolverine (last in XMU #45, '03) (all also in rfb), Bruce Banner (bts, abducted & being auctioned, last in Hulk:Nm #6, '04)
SUPPORTING CAST: Spacker Dave (last in Pun #12, '01), Lt. Soap (next in Pun #35, '04)
VILLAINS: Mickey Clooney, Irish mob, snitches (all die), Inskipp (top snitch, 1st, next in Pun #37, '03)
OTHER CHARACTERS: Kevin (next in Pun #35, '04), Lucky's Bar patrons; the Russian (in Punisher's thoughts & rfb); Joan, Ma Gnucci, Mr. Bumpo (prev 3 in Punisher's thoughts); Captain America, Iron Man, Marvel Girl, Thing, Thor (prev 5 in photos)
LOCATIONS/ITEMS: Lucky's Bar, Big Man Chan's, Garth's Diner, Irish bar, Red Hook warehouse, Empire State Building (in rfb) / Punisher's shotgun, grenade, gas can & guns; Irish mob's Uzis & guns; Spacker Dave's record card
FLASHBACKS: Punisher flattens Wolverine (Pun #17, '02). Punisher uses Spider-Man as a shield against the Russian (Pun #2, '01). Punisher forces Daredevil into a moral dilemma (Pun #3, '00).
SYNOPSIS: Daredevil convinces Spider-Man and Wolverine to work with him in bringing the Punisher to the authorities. Meanwhile, Punisher chases Mickey Clooney and ends up battling the Irish mob. He learns about an upcoming auction from a dying mobster. At Lucky's Bar, Soap confirms for Punisher that he's heard all the major gangs are gathering for the auction, but doesn't know much else. Punisher works through a dozen snitches until he finds one with a location and a time for the auction. Punisher resupplies his armament and confronts the man who had been following him all night: Spacker Dave. Dave reveals he's taken up super-spotting and is hoping Punisher will have a team-up with other heroes, so he can check them off his record card. Punisher tells Dave not to follow him and meets Inskipp, another snitch, in a diner, only for Daredevil, Spider-Man and Wolverine to confront him. Unfazed, Punisher says he feels like having a cheeseburger.
NOTE: Danny Miki is credited only on the cover. The auction's prize is revealed to be a man in Pun #34, '03; that man is revealed to be Bruce Banner in Pun #36, '04.

PUNISHER #34 (December 2003)

"Confederacy of Dunces, Part 2" (22 pages)

CREDITS: Garth Ennis (writer), John McCrea (pencils), Crimelab Studios, Danny Miki (inks), Virtual Calligraphy's Cory Petit (letters), Avalon Studios (colors), Kelly Lamy (assoc managing editor), Nanci Dakesian (managing editor), Joe Quesada (editor), Tim Bradstreet (c art)
FEATURE CHARACTERS: Punisher
GUEST STARS: Bruce Banner (in shadows), Daredevil, Spider-Man, Wolverine
SUPPORTING CAST: Spacker Dave (next in Pun #36, '04)
VILLAINS: Bonedog Posse (Bedford-Stuyvesant gang), Bob Lee Andersen ("King of the Angels," meth dealer), George Bironne (New Jersey mobster), Pope Emil (Harlem criminal), "Iron Joe" Safonov (Russian expatriate mobster), Roger "Big Man" Chan (Chinatown racketeer) & his men inc Karl (all die)
OTHER CHARACTERS: Cab driver, diner waitress, female slaves
LOCATIONS/ITEMS: Punisher's safehouse, Garth's Diner, Chinatown inc Big Man Chan's w/bathroom, fire escape & meeting room / Daredevil's billy club, Spacker Dave's record card; Punisher's knife & shotgun; Big Man Chan's videotape, Big Man Chan's men's MAC-10 machine pistols
SYNOPSIS: Punisher orders a cheeseburger. Spacker Dave arrives and asks Daredevil to sign his record card. The waitress asks Spider-Man if he's going to order anything. Punisher provokes Wolverine into a berserker rage and escapes during the confusion. After Daredevil and Spider-Man calm Wolverine down, they consider a new plan over cheeseburgers. Punisher crashes Big Man Chan's auction, frees Chan's female slaves and slaughters all the criminal attendees. He makes off with the auction item, an unconscious man in the back of a van. Punisher returns to his safehouse and watches a videotape that was shown at the auction. He's shocked by what the unconscious man can do.
NOTE: Danny Miki is credited only on the cover. Spacker Dave refers to the 1979 science fiction horror film, "Alien." Big Man Chan's is near the corner of Bowery & Canal Street.

PUNISHER #35 (January 2004)

"Confederacy of Dunces, Part 3" (22 pages)

CREDITS: Garth Ennis (writer), John McCrea (pencils), Crimelab Studios, Danny Miki (inks), Virtual Calligraphy's Cory Petit (letters), Avalon Studios (colors), Kelly Lamy (assoc managing editor), Nanci Dakesian (managing editor), Joe Quesada (editor), Tim Bradstreet (c art)
FEATURE CHARACTERS: Punisher
GUEST STARS: Daredevil, Spider-Man, Wolverine, Bruce Banner (has amnesia)
SUPPORTING CAST: Lt. Soap (also in own fantasy, last in Pun #33, '03)
VILLAIN: Tim McKinney (ex-convict, dies)
OTHER CHARACTERS: Kevin (also in Soap's fantasy, last in Pun #33, '03), Lucky's Bar patrons (some in Soap's fantasy), Soap's female fans (in Soap's fantasy), John Barry's Café bartender, Girl Scouts, bystanders, dog
LOCATIONS/ITEMS: Punisher's safehouse, Manhattan inc Lucky's Bar & dock; Hell's Kitchen inc booby-trapped building, leather store, John Barry's Café & Pub & Tony Carroll's Crazy Cat collectibles store / Punisher's explosive-laden stew w/Immodium, Claymore mines, handcuffs, knife, note, .45-caliber pistol, pressure pads, rocket launcher & ultrasonic trigger; Daredevil's billy club
SYNOPSIS: Punisher tends to the amnesiac man he found in the van, telling the man he'll keep him safe from the men after him. Punisher feeds the man stew and locks him in his safehouse. Lt. Soap waits for Lucky's Bar to open. Girl Scouts beat him up when he only wants to buy one box of cookies. Kevin laughs at him as he opens up. Daredevil, Spider-Man and Wolverine discuss their failure with Punisher. Soap dreams of personal glory. Seeking to buy himself some time until his secret weapon is ready, Punisher goes to Hell's Kitchen and tortures and kills a criminal whose screams draw Daredevil's attention. When the three heroes arrive, Punisher fires a rocket launcher at Wolverine and lures Spider-Man into a booby-trapped building, trapping him with Claymore mines. He prepares to use an ultrasonic siren that subdued Daredevil in the past, but Daredevil attacks before he can.
NOTE: Danny Miki is credited only on the cover. John Barry's Café & Pub has Killian's Red on tap. The stew Punisher feeds Banner is revealed to be loaded with plastique in Pun #37, '04.

PUNISHER #36 (January 2004)

"Confederacy of Dunces Part 4" (22 pages)

CREDITS: Garth Ennis (writer), John McCrea (pencils), Crimelab Studios, Danny Miki (inks), Virtual Calligraphy's Cory Petit (letters), Avalon Studios (colors), Kelly Lamy (assoc managing editor), Nanci Dakesian (managing editor), Joe Quesada (editor), Tim Bradstreet (c art)
FEATURE CHARACTER: Punisher
GUEST STARS: Hulk (also in Pun #37, '04 fb), Daredevil, Spider-Man, Wolverine
SUPPORTING CAST: Spacker Dave (last in Pun #34, '03), Lt. Soap
OTHER CHARACTERS: Kevin, dock workers
LOCATIONS/ITEMS: Punisher's safehouse, Manhattan inc Lucky's Bar bathroom & docks; Hell's Kitchen inc booby-trapped building, Daredevil's brownstone, Nelson & Murdock law offices & sewers / Punisher's stew, Claymore mines & pressure pads; Daredevil's billy club, Soap's revolver
SYNOPSIS: Punisher charges Daredevil and knocks him out a window, causing Daredevil to dislocate his shoulders. Punisher leaves while Daredevil convinces Spider-Man that Punisher wouldn't kill him, and that the Claymore mines aren't armed. Punisher returns to his safehouse. The amnesiac man complains the stew tastes funny, but that's all Punisher will feed him. Spider-Man relocates Daredevil's shoulder, and the two tend to Wolverine at Daredevil's brownstone. At Lucky's Bar, Kevin stops Lt. Soap from committing suicide and ridicules him. Angered, Soap threatens to kill Kevin and announces he's going to arrest Punisher. A week later, Punisher calls Matt Murdock, knowing he's Daredevil from

the media, and arranges for the heroes to find him. Punisher beats up the amnesiac man until the man starts turning green. Punisher meets the heroes and warns them a final time to back off. They refuse, and Punisher dives into the sewer and out of the way of his secret weapon: the incredible Hulk.

NOTE: Danny Miki is credited only on the cover.

PUNISHER #37 (February 2004)

"Confederacy of Dunces Part 5" (17 pages)
"Epilogue" (5 pages)

CREDITS: Garth Ennis (writer), John McCrea (pencils), Crimelab Studios, Danny Miki (inks), Virtual Calligraphy's Cory Petit (letters), Avalon Studios (colors), Kelly Lamy (assoc managing editor), Nanci Dakesian (managing editor), Joe Quesada (editor), Tim Bradstreet (c art)
FEATURE CHARACTER: Punisher (also in photo, also in DD #65, '04 fb & CM #2, '08, next in W/Pun #1-5, '04, Pun:Silent, '05, Pun:RedX, '04, MTU #8 & 10, '05, MKSM #15, '05, DDvPun #1-6, '05-06, U #3-4, '06, DocS #2, '06, PunvBull #2-5, '05-06, DoD #5, '06, Pun:BV, '06, DD #84-85, '06, ASM #533, '06, DD #86-87, '06, MK #9-10, '07, CW #4, '06, Pun:XMas, '07, PWJ #1, '07, see NOTE)
GUEST STARS: Daredevil (next in DD #46, '03), Hulk (also in fb during Pun #36, '04; next in IHulk #33, '01 fb), Spider-Man (also in photo, chr next in SM:BBRead, '06 fb, next in PPSM #51, '03), Wolverine (next in W #187, '03), Iron Man (last in MDS #4, '03, next bts in Hood #6, '02, next in IM #59, '02)
SUPPORTING CAST: Lt. Soap, Spacker Dave
VILLAIN: Inskipp (dies)
OTHER CHARACTERS: Captain America, Thing (both in photos), police (voice only), bystanders, duck (dies)
LOCATIONS/ITEMS: Red Hook, Brooklyn inc sewer; Boston Commons, Punisher's safehouse (in fb), Spacker Dave's hospital room, Manhattan inc Empire State Building / Punisher's note (in fb) & detonator; Soap's revolver, Spacker Dave's record card
FLASHBACK: Hulk finds Punisher's note.
SYNOPSIS: Hulk attacks Daredevil, Spider-Man and Wolverine, while elsewhere Lt. Soap roughs up Inskipp to get Punisher's location. Daredevil ends up in the sewer, where Punisher confronts him, while Hulk's punch sends Wolverine flying; he lands in Boston. As Spider-Man dodges Hulk's fists, Punisher tells Daredevil some small-time criminals saw Hulk revert to Banner in Los Angeles, knocked him out and drugged him, intending to auction Hulk off as a weapon. Spacker Dave watches the fight and checks off his record card, until Hulk runs over him. Informing Daredevil he's been feeding Banner explosives, Punisher stops Hulk by detonating them, then reiterates to Daredevil to leave him alone. Later, Soap tries to arrest Punisher, shooting him when the vigilante doesn't listen, but Punisher's Kevlar vest stops the bullet. Punisher tells Soap that when things aren't getting any better, he should "Just go." Subsequently: Dave is a quadriplegic; Soap quits the force and uses an asset that hadn't previously occurred to him to become a porn star; and Punisher tosses Inskipp off the Empire State Building to celebrate the anniversary of his return to New York City.
NOTE: Danny Miki is credited only on the cover. The indicia mistakenly lists the publication date as February 2003. Punisher's note says "You are the Hulk. You like to smash." Series continued in Pun #1, '04, which is published under the MAX imprint and takes place on Earth-200111. Punisher's next Earth-616 ongoing series will start with PWJ #1, '07.

BORN #1 (August 2003)

"The First Day" (22 pages)

CREDITS: Garth Ennis (writer), Darick Robertson (pencils), Tom Palmer (inks), Virtual Calligraphy's Rus Wooton (letters), Paul Mounts (colors), Nick Lowe (asst editor), Kelly Lamy (assoc managing editor), Nanci Dakesian (managing editor) Joe Quesada (editor), Wieslaw Walkuski (c art)
FEATURE CHARACTER: Captain Frank David Castle (1st but chr last in Pun #58, '08 fb, see NOTE)
VILLAINS: The Darkness (voice in Castle's mind, 1st, next in Born #3, '03, see NOTE), North Vietnamese resupply squadron (all die), North Vietnamese sniper (bts)
OTHER CHARACTERS: U.S. Marines (many die) inc Private First Class Stephen Albert "Stevie" Goodwin (last bts in Pun #56, '08 fb), James "Angel" Morris (last bts in Pun #57, '08 fb), Colonel Ottman (Firebase Valley Forge Commanding Officer, next in Born #3, '03), Tedrow, McDonald (all 1st), General Padden (dies), Captain Garand (mentioned, noted as killed), oxen
LOCATIONS/ITEMS: Vietnam inc Firebase Valley Forge & jungle / North Vietnamese AK-47 machine guns, rpg's & mortars; sniper warning sign, U.S. Military cargo plane (destroyed), helicopters, helmets, machine guns & mortars
SYNOPSIS: Captain Frank Castle leads his Marine platoon on patrol through the Vietnam jungle, ambushing and destroying a North Vietnam Army resupply squad. Private Stevie Goodwin is horrified by the bloodthirsty behavior of some of his fellow soldiers, but believes Captain Castle is the reason he will survive the war. Later at Firebase Valley Forge, Castle reports to Colonel Ottman and warns him that the North Vietnamese may be preparing for an offensive. The drunken Ottman disregards Castle and tells Castle to give the visiting General Padden a tour of the base. Castle explains to Gen. Padden that the base is undersupplied and understaffed, and there are no officers left willing to maintain order or discipline. Castle requests reinforcements and resupply, and warns of a possible enemy offensive. When Padden reveals he's going to close the base, Castle kills the General by walking him into enemy sniper range. That night, a voice tempts Frank with a war he can fight forever.
NOTE: 1st Punisher issue to be published under the MAX imprint; set on Earth-200111, which 1st appeared in Fury #1, '01. It is a world with few superhumans and no sliding timescale but, as Microchip's fb in Pun #3, '04 demonstrates, the major events in Punisher's life are otherwise broadly similar to those that occurred on Earth-616. The Darkness, named in Pun #3, '04, remains unexplained. It could be the Devil, Frank going insane or his inner demons, or something else entirely. The Darkness' corruption of Castle is similar to the Earth-616 demon Olivier's corruption of Castle, from Pun #1-4, '98-99, who focused on Castle during wartime and later used the Costa crime family to kill his family, but on Earth-200111 the Drago crime family is responsible for their deaths, as revealed in Pun:Cell, '05. Pun #56, '08 reveals PFC Goodwin's full name & rank. Born #2, '03 reveals Angel's nickname & Pun #57, '08 reveals his full name. McDonald is named in Born #2, '03. North Vietnamese soldiers are called "Vietcong" throughout the mini-series.

BORN #2 (September 2003)

"The Second Day" (22 pages)

CREDITS: Garth Ennis (writer), Darick Robertson (pencils), Tom Palmer (inks), Virtual Calligraphy (letters), Paul Mounts (colors), Nick Lowe (asst editor), Kelly Lamy (assoc managing editor), Nanci Dakesian (managing editor) Joe Quesada (editor), Wieslaw Walkuski (c art)
FEATURE CHARACTER: Capt. Frank Castle
VILLAINS: North Vietnamese snipers (all die), Coltrane (drug dealing Marine, 1st), Garcia (Marine, Coltrane's associate, 1st), McDonald (rapes a prisoner, dies)
OTHER CHARACTERS: U.S. Marines (some die) inc PFC Goodwin, Angel & Tedrow (dies)
LOCATIONS/ITEMS: Vietnam inc Firebase Valley Forge & jungle / U.S. military's Hueys & machine guns; North Vietnamese sniper rifles, Angel's heroin, Garcia's straight razor, Castle's M60
SYNOPSIS: Private Goodwin stops Angel from shooting up heroin so that they can go on patrol. Coltrane, one of Firebase Valley Forge's narcotics dealers, threatens Goodwin for costing him money, but leaves Goodwin alone when Captain Castle walks over. Castle leads them out on patrol, but North Vietnamese snipers soon ambush them. The platoon panics as they are picked off, but Castle single-handily guns each of the snipers down from their perches in the trees. When the Marines find a survivor, McDonald rapes her. Castle shoots her in the head and tells his platoon that rape is not allowed. When McDonald washes his face in a nearby stream, Castle drowns him. Goodwin spies the murder from behind a tree nearby. That night, Castle tells Goodwin he knows Goodwin saw McDonald's murder. Goodwin asks why Castle did it. Castle says he wanted to punish McDonald. Castle tells Goodwin that he doesn't have to fear Castle, but Goodwin privately does anyway.
NOTE: Followed by 3-page preview of SuPo #2, '03.

BORN #3 (October 2003)

"The Third Day" (22 pages)

CREDITS: Garth Ennis (writer), Darick Robertson (pencils), Tom Palmer (inks), Virtual Calligraphy (letters), Paul Mounts (colors), Nick Lowe (asst editor), Kelly Lamy (assoc managing editor), Nanci Dakesian (managing editor) Joe Quesada (editor), Wieslaw Walkuski (c art)
FEATURE CHARACTER: Capt. Frank Castle
VILLAINS: North Vietnamese soldiers (some die), the Darkness (last in Born #1, '03), Coltrane, Garcia
OTHER CHARACTERS: U.S. Marines inc Col. Ottman (last in Born #1, '03), PFC Goodwin & Angel; Vietnamese city residents & rural villagers (many die), corpse (skeletal remains)
LOCATIONS/ITEMS: Vietnam inc Firebase Valley Forge, city bridge, jungle & villages / North Vietnamese machine guns, U.S. Military bomber planes, fighter jets, flare gun & flare, grenade, Huey helicopters, machine guns, missiles & plastique explosives, Castle's M60
SYNOPSIS: Captain Castle tells Colonel Ottman that they need to be prepared for an offensive by the North Vietnamese, warning him that an incoming storm will provide cover for the enemy to attack. Ottman brushes Castle off, saying that the war is all but over and they'll be leaving soon. Castle considers killing Ottman and taking control of Firebase Valley Forge. Instead, Castle checks on Private Goodwin, who is shocked when he learns Castle has a wife, a child and another on the way. Goodwin leaves when he sees Angel heading into Coltrane's tent. Goodwin knocks Coltrane unconscious and leads Angel away, telling him not to take a smack habit home with him. Angel argues with Goodwin about how different life will be like for them after the war. Their conversation is cut short when the base is attacked. Castle calls for an illumination flare, which reveals hundreds of North Vietnamese soldiers attacking Firebase Valley Forge.

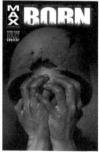

BORN #4 (November 2003)

"The Last Day" (22 pages)

CREDITS: Garth Ennis (writer), Darick Robertson (pencils), Tom Palmer (inks), Virtual Calligraphy's Rus Wooten (letters), Paul Mounts (colors), Nick Lowe (asst editor), Kelly Lamy (assoc managing editor), Nanci Dakesian (managing editor) Joe Quesada (editor), Wieslaw Walkuski (c art)
FEATURE CHARACTER: Capt. Frank Castle (also in Punmax #12, '11 fb; next as Frank Castle in Punmax #13, '11 fb, Pun #75, '09 fb, Punmax #13, '11 fb, Punmax #18, '11 fb, Punmax #20, '12 fb, Punmax #13-16, '11 fbs, Pun #75/4, '09 fb, Pun #75/2, '09, Pun #50, '07 fb, Pun #1, '04 fb, Punmax #20, '12 fb, bts in Pun:Tyger '06 fb, Punmax #21, '12 fb, Pun #75/2, '09, Pun #4, '04 fb, Punmax #21, '12 fb, next as Punisher in Punmax #16, '11 fb, Pun:Tyger '06, Pun #52, '08 fb, Punmax #20, '12 fb, Pun:Cell '05, Punmax #21, '12 fb, Punmax #20, '12 fb, Pun #47, '07 fb, Pun #43, '07 fb, Pun #75/4, '09 fb, Pun #1, '04)
SUPPORTING CAST: Maria Elizabeth Castle (Frank's wife), Lisa Castle (Frank's daughter), Frank David Castle Jr. (Frank's son) (all 1st but chr last in Punmax #12, '11 fb, chr next in Punmax #13, '11 fb; see NOTE)
VILLAINS: North Vietnamese soldiers, Coltrane, Garcia (all die), the Darkness
OTHER CHARACTERS: U.S. Marines (many die) inc Col. Ottman, PFC Goodwin, Angel (all die); other U.S. soldiers inc Tusker leader (John Chadwick, tank pilot, voice only, 1st, next bts in Pun #56, '08 fb), Sgt. William J. Torrance (1st, next bts in Pun #59, '08 fb) & a lieutenant; stewardesses (in Goodwin's fantasy), airport commuters
LOCATIONS/ITEMS: Vietnam inc Firebase Valley Forge; U.S. airport / Castle's M60, shovel, crutches & sling; North Vietnamese flamethrowers, machine guns, bayonets & machetes; U.S. Military bomber plane, cannons, bombs, Huey helicopters & machine guns; freedom bird (commercial airliner, also in Goodwin's fantasy)
SYNOPSIS: The North Vietnamese Army slowly overwhelms Firebase Valley Forge, despite Captain Castle mowing them down with his M60. Castle orders his men to fall back, but Marines are dying all around them. Colonel Ottman kills himself. During the chaos Coltrane attacks Goodwin, and Castle kills the drug dealer. US fighter jets drop napalm on the base. Castle runs out of ammunition and resorts to hand-to-hand combat. Goodwin dies on a bayonet. As Castle is swarmed the voice returns, promising Castle's survival and a never ending war, but warns that

there will be a price. Castle accepts. When reinforcements arrive the next morning, they only find a bloodied Castle standing among hundreds of corpses. Sometime later at the airport, Frank is welcomed into his waiting family's arms. As Frank tells Maria that he's never going away again, the voice reminds Frank of the price for his survival. Frank hugs his family and tells them to hold on tight.
NOTE: All natives of Earth-200111, Maria's, Lisa's & Frank Jr.'s full names are confirmed in Pun #1, '04. Pun #56, '08 reveals Tusker leader's real name. Torrance is named in Pun #59, '08.

PUNISHER #1 (March 2004)

"In the Beginning Part One" (22 pages)

CREDITS: Garth Ennis (writer), Lewis Larosa (pencils), Tom Palmer (inks), Virtual Calligraphy's Randy Gentile (letters), Dean White (colors), John Miesegaes (asst editor), Axel Alonso (editor), Tim Bradstreet (c art)
FEATURE CHARACTER: Punisher (also in fb as Frank Castle between Pun #50, '07 fb & Punmax #16, '11 fb)
SUPPORTING CAST: Maria Castle, Lisa Castle, Frank Castle, Jr. (all in fb between Pun #50, '07 fb & Punmax #16, '11 fb), Microchip (David Linus Lieberman, Punisher's former partner, 1st but chr last in Pun #3, '04 fb; see NOTE), Kathryn O'Brien (member of Bethel's CIA task force, 1st but chr last in Pun #40, '07 fb)
VILLAINS: Don Massimo Giovanni Cesare (elderly mobster, 1st but chr last bts in Pun #20, '05 fb, dies), Cesare family members (many die) inc Dominic, John, Peter & Sean Gorrini (prev 4 die), Annabella Gorrini (bts, at party, next in Pun #43, '07), Larry Barrucci (bts, at party)
OTHER CHARACTERS: Robert Bethel (CIA task force leader, 1st), William Roth (member of Bethel's CIA task force, 1st), other CIA operatives, bystanders, watchdog (corpse)
LOCATIONS/ITEMS: Cesare Estate, New York inc Hotel Claude w/Bethel's suite, Punisher's safehouse w/armory & cemetery w/Castle family grave / Punisher's weapons inc M60 machine gun, assault rifle, grenade launcher, shotguns, guns & Claymore mines; mobsters guns, O'Brien's binoculars
FLASHBACK: 1976: In Central Park, Lisa Castle's guts spill out of her belly, Maria Castle has a hole in her chest where her heart was, and Frank Castle Jr.'s brains fall out into his father's hands.
SYNOPSIS: Frank Castle visits his family's grave before returning to his safehouse where he gathers weapons for an upcoming mission as the Punisher. He is unaware that he is being watched by two CIA operatives, O'Brien and Roth. That night, Punisher crashes Don Massimo Cesare's birthday party and kills the hundred year old Mafia boss in front of the entire Cesare family. As the Mafioso chase Punisher outside, he guns them down with his M60. When they try to flank him, they trip the Claymore mines he set earlier. At the Hotel Claude in New York, CIA agent Bethel and his team hack into NASA satellite surveillance to watch Punisher in action. Impressed with Punisher's performance, Bethel asks his newest operative and Punisher expert Microchip when they can move forward. Microchip says he will be able to take down Punisher soon.
NOTE: Dominic, John, Peter & Sean Gorrini are named in Pun #43, '07. Cesare's middle name revealed in Pun #2, '04. Roth's 1st name revealed in Pun #3, '04. Bethel's 1st name revealed in Pun #6, '04. O'Brien's 1st name revealed in Pun #21, '05. Gorrini revealed as bts in Pun #43, '07. Larry Barrucci revealed as bts in Pun #2, '04. The Microchip appearing here is an Earth-200111 native. The Castle family tombstone reads "Maria Elizabeth Castle 1948 - 1976, Lisa Castle 1967 - 1976, Frank David Castle 1971 - 1976."

PUNISHER #2 (March 2004)

"In the Beginning Part Two" (22 pages)

CREDITS: Garth Ennis (writer), Lewis Larosa (pencils), Tom Palmer (inks), Virtual Calligraphy's Randy Gentile (letters), Dean White (colors), John Miesegaes (asst editor), Axel Alonso (editor), Tim Bradstreet (c art)
FEATURE CHARACTER: Punisher (also in Microchip's thoughts)
SUPPORTING CAST: Microchip, Kathryn O'Brien
VILLAINS: Nicolas "Nicky" Cavella (mob boss), Carmine "Pittsy" Gazzera, Ink (both Nicky's psychotic mob enforcers) (all 1st but chr last in Pun #20, '05 fb), Laurence "Larry" Barrucci (mob boss, 1st), Cesare family members (many die) inc Lenny (dies) & Jackie; Herbie (pimp, dies)
OTHER CHARACTERS: Robert Bethel, William Roth, other CIA operatives, Alpha Team (military unit, 1st, next in Pun #4, '04), funeral attendees inc priest, reporter (voice only on TV), Dennis (news anchor, bts), prostitutes inc Nadine, waitress, dead criminals (in Microchip's thoughts)
LOCATIONS/ITEMS: New York inc Hotel Claude w/Bethel's suite, cemetery, restaurant & Punisher's safehouse / Punisher's rocket launcher, guns & Uzi; Microchip's binoculars & shotgun; O'Brien's sub-machine gun
SYNOPSIS: Punisher fires a rocket into Don Cesare's funeral, killing several Mafia Captains. Bethel's CIA team decides to attack Punisher tonight. Punisher learns from Nadine, one of Herbie's prostitutes, that crime has slowed since his attack on the Cesare family. Punisher notices one of the prostitutes is underage, kills Herbie and tells Nadine to send the girl home. Larry Barrucci, recently promoted Cesare family Captain, meets with Nicky Cavella, an exiled Cesare family member known for his ruthlessness. Nicky agrees to aid Larry in killing Punisher, but warns that he'll want a leadership position in the family. That night, Microchip approaches Punisher outside the vigilante's safehouse. Microchip knocks Punisher over by shooting him in the chest with a shotgun. Microchip shoots the Uzi out of Punisher's hand, then shoots Punisher in the face.
NOTE: Nicky, Pittsy & Larry's full names revealed in Pun #6, '04. Jackie is named in Pun #3, '04. Microchip notes that he worked with Punisher for ten years and helped him kill over 800 people.

PUNISHER #3 (April 2004)

"In the Beginning Part 3" (22 pages)

CREDITS: Garth Ennis (writer), Lewis Larosa (pencils), Tom Palmer (inks), Virtual Calligraphy's Randy Gentile (letters), Dean White (colors), John Miesegaes (asst editor), Axel Alonso (editor), Tim Bradstreet (c art)
FEATURE CHARACTER: Punisher (also in rfb as Capt. Castle)
SUPPORTING CAST: Microchip (also in fb to chr 1st app before Pun #1, '04), Kathryn O'Brien
VILLAINS: Nicky Cavella, Pittsy Gazzera, Ink, Larry Barrucci, Jackie (dies)
OTHER CHARACTERS: Robert Bethel, William Roth, other CIA operatives, Walter Krause (Punisher's neighbor, 1st, also in pfb), Channel 8 reporter (hand only in pfb), Channel 8 news anchor (on TV), Microchip's son (corpse in fb), morgue doctor (in fb), pool hall patrons; North Vietnamese soldiers (in rfb), Maria Castle, Lisa Castle, Frank Castle Jr. (prev 3 in photos)
LOCATIONS/ITEMS: New York inc hospital w/Jackie's room, Hotel Claude w/Bethel's suite, Walter Krause's apartment & pool hall; morgue (in fb) / Capt. Castle's assault rifle (in rfb), Punisher's restraints, Pittsy's pillow, Roth's gun
FLASHBACKS: Walter Krause tells reporters he saw Punisher's abduction (p). In Vietnam, Capt. Frank Castle succumbs to the Darkness inside him (Born #4, '03). Microchip mourns his son's death.
SYNOPSIS: At the hospital, senior Cesare family member Jackie tells Larry Barrucci to send Nicky Cavella back to Boston. Pittsy and Ink kill Jackie while Nicky watches the news report that the police have captured Punisher. Suspicious, Nicky tells Larry to call his contact in the police to find out what's going on. As Microchip talks with the captured Frank Castle, Bethel sends Roth to tell Walter Krause, an eyewitness to Punisher's capture, not to talk to the media anymore. Learning the police are covering for the CIA, Nicky decides to talk with Krause. O'Brien eavesdrops on Punisher and is attracted to his voice. At Krause's apartment, Nicky abducts Roth and begins to interrogate him about the CIA's Punisher operation. When Roth doesn't check in, Bethel sends O'Brien to check on Roth. Microchip offers Frank a way to stop being the Punisher.

PUNISHER #4 (May 2004)

"In the Beginning Part 4" (22 pages)

CREDITS: Garth Ennis (writer), Lewis Larosa (pencils), Tom Palmer (inks), Virtual Calligraphy's David Sharpe (letters), Dean White (colors), John Miesegaes (asst editor), Axel Alonso (editor), Tim Bradstreet (c art)
FEATURE CHARACTER: Punisher (also as Frank Castle in fb between Pun #75/2, '09 & Punmax #21, '12 fb)
SUPPORTING CAST: Kathryn O'Brien, Microchip
VILLAINS: Nicky Cavella, Pittsy Gazzera, Ink, Larry Barrucci
OTHER CHARACTERS: William Roth (also in photo), Robert Bethel, other CIA operatives (1 dies), Alpha Team (last in Pun #2, '04, dies), Bob Barrett (Frank Castle's neighbor, in fb), Carrie Barrett (Bob's estranged wife, mentioned in fb, staying with her mother in Jersey), Frank's other neighbors (in fb), Walter Krause, Hotel Claude staff & patrons
LOCATIONS/ITEMS: New York inc Hotel Claude w/Bethel's suite & Walter Krause's apartment; Castle family home (in fb) / Punisher's restraints, alpha Team's sub-machine guns, Larry & Nicky's guns, Pittsy's shotgun
FLASHBACK: 1976: As Frank Castle packs up his dead family's belongings, his neighbor Bob Garrett tells Frank that he's having an affair and has split up with his wife. Maddened by Bob's callous disregard for his wife, Frank warns Bob to run. When Bob doesn't, Frank beats Bob senseless, only stopping when other neighbors restrain him.
SYNOPSIS: Microchip tells Frank Castle he can hunt terrorists for the CIA instead of wasting his time with Mafioso. Having interrogated Roth, Nicky Cavella drives to the Hotel Claude. Frank turns down Microchip's offer, refusing to work for a corrupt government. At Walter Krause's apartment, O'Brien finds a castrated Roth. She calls Bethel to warn him that Cavella is on his way to kill Punisher. Bethel sends his Alpha Team after Cavella, but Ink sabotages the elevator the military unit is in, sending them to their deaths. Frank tells Microchip that he warned Bob Garrett before he punished Bob, and asks where Bethel gets his funding from? Nicky knocks on Bethel's door and Pittsy shoots the agent who answers in the face. Nicky shoots Bethel in the knees and bursts into Punisher's interrogation room.

PUNISHER #5 (June 2004)

"In the Beginning Part 5" (22 pages)

CREDITS: Garth Ennis (writer), Lewis Larosa (pencils), Tom Palmer (inks), Virtual Calligraphy's Cory Petit (letters), Dean White (colors), John Miesegaes (asst editor), Axel Alonso (editor), Tim Bradstreet (c art)
FEATURE CHARACTER: Punisher
SUPPORTING CAST: Kathryn O'Brien (next in Pun #19, '05), Microchip
VILLAINS: Ink (dies), Nicky Cavella, Pittsy Gazzera, Larry Barrucci, Cesare family soldiers, mob doctor
OTHER CHARACTERS: William Roth (next in Pun #21, '05), Robert Bethel, other CIA operatives inc Archer (voice only, on phone); paramedics, police
LOCATIONS/ITEMS: New York inc Hotel Claude w/Bethel's suite; Larry Barrucci's house, Microchip's Brooklyn safehouse / Punisher's restraints & assault rifle; Cesare soldier's guns, Ink's grenade, Nicky's gun, Microchip's cell phone w/CIA tracer, O'Brien's sub-machine gun, Pittsy's shotgun
SYNOPSIS: Nicky shoots Microchip in the chest and puts his gun against Frank Castle's head. Frank bites Nicky's fingers. O'Brien arrives and kills Ink, and Nicky shoots O'Brien. A wounded Microchip frees Frank from his restraints. Frank attacks Nicky and rips out Pittsy's eye. The mobsters escape. Frank takes Microchip and they drive to Microchip's safehouse. O'Brien quits Bethel's CIA team, and he orders her sent back to prison. Microchip reveals that Bethel gets funding by selling heroin from Afghanistan. His suspicions confirmed, Frank accuses Microchip of joining the enemy. Frank calls Larry Barrucci's home and taunts Nicky to come and finish him. Frank shows Microchip that Bethel put a tracer on him, and warns Microchip to run. Microchip decides to stay and help Frank against the arriving mob and CIA.
NOTE: Microchip notes he hasn't seen Punisher since 1996.

PUNISHER #6 (July 2004)

"In the Beginning Part 6: Conclusion" (22 pages)

CREDITS: Garth Ennis (writer), Lewis Larosa (pencils), Tom Palmer (inks), Virtual Calligraphy's Randy Gentile (letters), Dean White (colors), John Miesegaes (asst editor), Axel Alonso (editor), Tim Bradstreet (c art)
FEATURE CHARACTER: Punisher (also off-panel in Pun #43, '07 fb)
SUPPORTING CAST: Microchip (dies)
VILLAINS: Nicky Cavella (next in Pun #19, '05), Larry Barrucci (both also in Pun #43, '07 fb), Pittsy Gazzera (both die), Cesare family soldiers (die)
OTHER CHARACTERS: Robert Bethel (dies), other CIA operatives, Officer Laura Miller (dies), Officer Stephen Gein (dies off-panel), helicopter pilots inc Gundog
LOCATIONS/ITEMS: Brooklyn inc Microchip's safehouse / Punisher's assault rifle, Pittsy's knife & shotgun; Nicky's binoculars & gun; Microchip's assault rifle, Larry's gun, Cesare family soldier's guns, helicopter w/machine guns
SYNOPSIS: Nicky and Larry watch as Punisher guns down their henchmen as they attack Microchip's safehouse. Pittsy slips out of the trunk of a one of the attacking cars and sneaks into the warehouse. He cuts open Microchip's abdomen and attacks Punisher. Bethel arrives at the scene in a helicopter. Pittsy shoots out one of Punisher's ribs. When Bethel fires at Microchip's safehouse, the helicopter pilots throw him out. Punisher throws Pittsy out a window, impaling Pittsy on a fence. Punisher resumes firing on the mobsters. Nicky forces Larry to charge the Punisher, escaping while Punisher guns down Larry. Pittsy attacks Punisher again, so Punisher shoots Pittsy's face off. Nicky kills two police officers and steals their car. Bethel dies in the street. Punisher tells Microchip he should have run when he had the chance, and blows Microchip's head off.

PUNISHER #7 (August 2004)

"Kitchen Irish Part One" (22 pages)

CREDITS: Garth Ennis (writer), Leandro Fernández (art), Virtual Calligraphy's Randy Gentile (letters), Dean White (colors), John Miesegaes (asst editor), Axel Alonso (editor), Tim Bradstreet (c art)
FEATURE CHARACTER: Punisher
VILLAINS: Finn Cooley (faceless former IRA bomber), Michael Morrison (guns & narcotic dealer), Peter Cooley (Finn's nephew) (all 1st but chr last in Pun #10, '04 fb), Westies inc Tommy Toner (leader, 1st but chr last in Pun #10, '04 fb), Maginty (Irish crime lord, 1st) & his men
OTHER CHARACTERS: Napper French (former IRA clean-up man), Billy (Napper's grandson) (both 1st), coffee shop waitress (dies) & patrons (most die), police inc a Captain & crime scene unit; reporter, cameraman, firefighters, paramedics, bystanders (some die), dog (dies)
LOCATIONS/ITEMS: Hell's Kitchen inc Kerry Castle & coffee shop (both destroyed); marina, playground / Punisher's sniper rifle & binoculars; Maginty's men's van & machine guns; Cooley's bomb
SYNOPSIS: Punisher is eating lunch in a coffee shop when the Kerry Castle bar across the street explodes. Other people's bodies shield him from serious injury, but when he sees the carnage around him he realizes he doesn't know what to do. He plugs a man's open chest with his hand until paramedics arrive. Punisher overhears police discussing evidence that the IRA set the bomb. Elsewhere, the bombers, Finn Cooley, Michael Morrison and Peter Cooley, discuss how a radio detonator accidentally triggered the bomb early; they intended for it to explode during a meeting of Hell's Kitchen's Irish mobs. Punisher watches the crime scene for the bar's owner, Tommy Toner, to arrive so he can abduct Toner and kill his men. Maginty beats Punisher to it. Later, Maginty asks Napper French, who used to dispose of bodies, if he could dismantle a living person. Napper refuses, claiming retirement, but Maginty's men take Napper's grandson Billy as motivation.

PUNISHER #8 (August 2004)

"Kitchen Irish Part Two" (22 pages)

CREDITS: Garth Ennis (writer), Leandro Fernández (art), Virtual Calligraphy's Randy Gentile (letters), Dean White (colors), John Miesegaes (asst editor), Axel Alonso (editor), Tim Bradstreet (c art)
FEATURE CHARACTER: Punisher
VILLAINS: Finn Cooley, Peter Cooley, Michael Morrison (all also in photos), River Rats (pirates) inc Polly, Eamon (sibling leaders, both 1st but chr last in Pun #10, '04 fb), Bunk & Danni; Maginty & his men; Tommy Toner
OTHER CHARACTERS: Lieutenant-Colonel Yorkie Mitchell (MI6 agent, 1st, see NOTE), Lance-Corporal Andy Lorimer (Yorkie's associate, 1st), Napper French, Billy, pleasure cruisers inc David; O'Malley's patrons, diner patrons, police, firefighters, bystanders
LOCATIONS/ITEMS: Hell's Kitchen inc Maginty's apartment, O'Malley's pub & diner / Maginty's knife, handcuffs & bag of tools; River Rats' Uzis, shotgun & knives; pleasure cruisers' yacht & pearl necklace; Punisher's shotgun
SYNOPSIS: At a diner, Punisher spots Yorkie and his associate Andy. They ask for Punisher's help in stopping the Kerry Castle's bombers, Finn and Peter Cooley. Yorkie lays out Finn's past crimes with the IRA before he was released from prison during the Good Friday Agreement. Peter killed Andy's father. They believe the Cooleys are in America to contact Michael Morrison. Despite them being on an unsanctioned MI6 mission on American soil, Punisher agrees to help. Meanwhile, Maginty has Napper go to work taking Tommy apart. Elsewhere, the River Rats, a pirate group, robs a yacht. Finn mails Tommy's left hand to the Westies and orders another part taken off Tommy. Finn. Peter and Michael have a drink at O'Malley's. They're surprised that none of the other Irish gangs arrived for the meeting they called. Someone recognizes Finn and calls a toast in his honor, but the festivities stop when Punisher enters.
NOTE: The Yorkie appearing here is an Earth-200111 native; his rank is revealed in Pun #42, '07. The Good Friday Agreement, or Belfast Agreement, was a major political development in the Northern Ireland peace process between the region's political parties and the British government.

PUNISHER #9 (September 2004)

"Kitchen Irish Part Three" (22 pages)

CREDITS: Garth Ennis (writer), Leandro Fernández (art), Virtual Calligraphy's Randy Gentile (letters), Dean White (colors), John Miesegaes (asst editor), Axel Alonso (editor), Tim Bradstreet (c art)
FEATURE CHARACTER: Punisher
VILLAINS: Brenda Toner (Tommy's wife, 1st, but chr last in Pun #10, '04 fb), River Rats (most die) inc Danni (dies), Polly, Eamon & Bunk; Finn Cooley, Peter Cooley, Michael Morrison, Maginty & his men, Tommy Toner, Westies inc Gerry
OTHER CHARACTERS: Yorkie Mitchell, Lance-Corporal Andy Lorimer, Yorkie Mitchell, Napper French, Billy, O'Malley's patrons
LOCATIONS/ITEMS: Hell's Kitchen inc O'Malley's pub, River Rats' house, Punisher's safe house, Toner house, Maginty's apartment / Punisher's shotgun, grenade & butterfly knife; Yorkie & Andy's submachine guns; River Rats' guns, Brenda's rifle

SYNOPSIS: O'Malley's pub clears out at Punisher's request. Just as Punisher approaches Finn, the River Rats arrive for Finn's meeting. Punisher opens fire on the River Rats and Finn. Peter and Michael run out the back where Yorkie and Andy wait. Finn and Michael escape by taking a hostage, but Peter is injured and captured. Polly, Eamon and Bunk are the only River Rats to get out alive. Punisher and Yorkie begin to torture Peter for information, despite Andy's misgivings about their methods. Michael fails to convince Finn that Punisher is bad news and they need to leave town. Brenda Toner receives her husband Tommy Toner's hand that Maginty mailed her and prepares to take the Westies to war for Nesbitt's money. Napper continues to take parts off Tommy. Peter tells Punisher that Nesbitt willed ten million dollars to the local Irish mobs. Tommy was going to bring the gangs together and split the money. Finn wants all of the money for the struggle back home and set the bomb to get the other mobs out of the way.

PUNISHER #10 (October 2004)

"Kitchen Irish Part Four" (22 pages)

CREDITS: Garth Ennis (writer), Leandro Fernández (art), Virtual Calligraphy's Randy Gentile (letters), Dean White (colors), Cory Sedlmeier (asst editor), Axel Alonso (editor), Tim Bradstreet (c art)
FEATURE CHARACTER: Punisher (also poses as Maginty on the phone)
VILLAINS: Finn Cooley, Peter Cooley, Michael Morrison, Tommy Toner (dies) (all also in fb to 1st chr app before Pun #7, '04), Brenda Toner (also in fb to 1st chr app before Pun #9, '04 fb), River Rats inc Polly, Eamon (both also in fb to 1st chr app before Pun #8, '04) & Bunk; Maginty & his men, Westies (also in fb, some die) inc Gerry; Old Man Nesbitt (in fb)
OTHER CHARACTERS: Yorkie Mitchell, Lance-Corporal Andy Lorimer, Napper French, Billy, Patty Feeny (Pot O'Gold bartender); Nesbitt's lawyer, pub patrons (both in fb)
LOCATIONS/ITEMS: Hell's Kitchen inc Punisher's safe house, Pot o' Gold, River Rats' house & Maginty's apartment; pub, hospital room (both in fb) / Punisher's rifle & grenade launcher; River Rats' guns & Uzis; Westies' guns, Napper's butcher knife, Yorkie's M-60 chain gun, Maginty's machete, Maginty's men's submachine guns, Intrepid (aircraft carrier turned museum)

FLASHBACK: Original Westie Old Man Nesbitt hates everyone. New Westie Tommy Toner idolizes Nesbitt. Finn Cooley buys guns from Nesbitt. Young Polly and Eamon hate their great-uncle Nesbitt. When Nesbitt is dying he makes out his will. When Nesbitt dies, Finn receives a letter with a code to be shared with the other Irish gangs. Nesbitt claims he wants his legacy to be saving Hell's Kitchen by splitting his ten million dollars between the gangs so they'll leave Hell's Kitchen.

SYNOPSIS: Peter tells Punisher that Nesbitt sent each of the Irish mobs different codes that had to be combined to find Nesbitt's money. Punisher doubts Nesbitt's intentions. Elsewhere, the Westies receive more pieces of Tommy. Brenda decides he's dead and takes over the Westies, determined to get the money. Punisher reasons the other gangs will follow the Westies' lead and decides to set them up. Posing as Maginty, Punisher calls the Westies and sets up a meeting to trade Tommy for their code. Brenda decides it's a good chance to kill Maginty. Finn and Michael watch the Westies leave and follow. The River Rats hear about the meeting and prepare their own assault. Meanwhile, Maginty shows Billy his grandfather at work, and tells Napper he only needs one more piece of Tommy for a meeting he just heard of. Everyone converges at the Intrepid where Punisher and Yorkie ambush the Westies. Unseen, Maginty prepares to get the drop on Punisher.

PUNISHER #11 (November 2004)

"Kitchen Irish Part Five" (22 pages)

CREDITS: Garth Ennis (writer), Leandro Fernández (art), Virtual Calligraphy's Randy Gentile (letters), Dean White (colors), Cory Sedlmeier (asst editor), Axel Alonso (editor), Tim Bradstreet (c art)
FEATURE CHARACTER: Punisher
VILLAINS: Finn Cooley, Peter Cooley, Brenda Toner, River Rats inc Bunk (dies), Polly & Eamon; Michael Morrison, Maginty & his men (1 dies); Westies (die) inc Gerry (dies)
OTHER CHARACTERS: Tommy Toner (corpse, head only), Yorkie Mitchell, Lance-Corporal Andy Lorimer, Napper French, police
LOCATIONS/ITEMS: West Side Highway, Hell's Kitchen inc Maginty's apartment, Punisher's safe house & Pot O'Gold club / Punisher's assault rifle w/attached grenade launcher, guns, grenades, stun grenades & assault rifle; Napper's tools, knives & fire extinguisher; Maginty's machete & van; Maginty's men's guns, Westies' guns, River Rats' Uzis, Brenda's revolver, Yorkie's M-60 chain gun, Andy's Uzi, police helicopter, Intrepid

SYNOPSIS: The police arrive, forcing Punisher, Yorkie and Andy to escape. Maginty's ambush on Punisher goes afoul when one of Maginty's men tips off their position. Punisher fires at them before making his escape. Maginty uses Tommy's head to make one final play for a wounded Brenda's part of the code, but she refuses and he takes off as the police move in. Brenda escapes and runs into Finn. The Rats spot Punisher leaving, but Andy opens fire on them first, hitting Eamon and covering their departure. Maginty returns home only Napper to knock him out. Finn patches up Brenda and proposes a partnership since they can't beat each other. Polly takes care of Eamon's wound while their crew abandons them. Yorkie tries to convince the captured Peter that Finn doesn't care about the struggle back home; he only wants the money to fix his face. Realizing the futility of it, Yorkie tells Peter that Andy will kill Peter when everyone else is dead. Maginty wakes up tied to his bed with Napper above him sharpening his tools.

PUNISHER #12 (December 2004)

"Kitchen Irish Part Six" (22 pages)

CREDITS: Garth Ennis (writer), Leandro Fernández (art), Virtual Calligraphy's Randy Gentile (letters), Dean White (colors), Cory Sedlmeier (asst editor), Axel Alonso (editor), Tim Bradstreet (c art)
FEATURE CHARACTER: Punisher
VILLAINS: Finn Cooley, Peter Cooley, Michael Morrison, Brenda Toner, River Rats inc Eamon & Polly; Maginty & his men (all die)
OTHER CHARACTERS: Yorkie Mitchell (next bts in Pun #37, '06), Lance-Corporal Andy Lorimer, Napper French (dies); Old Man Nesbitt (in Maginty's thoughts)
LOCATIONS/ITEMS: Hell's Kitchen inc Maginty's apartment & Pot O' Gold / Punisher's stun grenade & knife; Yorkie's submachine gun & gun; Andy's submachine gun, Nesbitt's code sheets & trunk w/plastique; Capitan Piluso (Nesbitt's cargo ship, destroyed), Maginty's man's shotgun, Napper's knife, Finn's grenade, Maginty & Polly's guns
SYNOPSIS: Napper cuts off Maginty's fingers before Maginty's men walk in and kill Napper. Maginty meets with Finn Cooley, Brenda and the Westies and the remaining River Rats who all agree to pool their resources. They combine their codes and learn Nesbitt's money is in a docked cargo ship. Punisher, Yorkie and Andy follow. As Finn, Brenda, Maginty and the River Rats search the cargo ship, Eamon spots Punisher's crew. Punisher kills Maginty's guards and attempts to get the drop on the gang leaders. During the resulting firefight, Maginty stumbles upon a trunk. While Yorkie helps Punisher retreat, the gang leaders open the trunk and discover it's a bomb. The ship explodes. Andy helps Yorkie and Punisher out of the water. Later, Andy gets his revenge on Peter, but finds it doesn't fill the hole left by his father's death. Yorkie points to the Punisher as an example, a man who's had thirty years of revenge.

PUNISHER #13 (January 2005)

"Mother Russia Part One" (22 pages)

CREDITS: Garth Ennis (writer), Dougie Braithwaite (pencils), Bill Reinhold (inks), Virtual Calligraphy's Randy Gentile (letters), Raul Treviño (colors), Cory Sedlmeier (asst editor), Axel Alonso (editor), Tim Bradstreet (c art)
FEATURE CHARACTER: Punisher
GUEST STAR: Colonel Nick Fury (former SHIELD Director, last in Fury #6, '02, see NOTE)
VILLAINS: Gen. John Archer, Gen. Jake Farmington, Gen. Don Kent, Gen. Bradley Landers, Gen. Kurt Perino, Gen. Bobby Van Abst, Gen. Paul Vertraeus, Gen. Joe Vraciu (all corrupt U.S. Generals, 1st), William Rawlins (corrupt CIA agent, 1st but chr last in Pun #40, '07 fb), Leon Rastovich (Russian mobster, also in photo, dies), his mother (dies) & his men (die)
OTHER CHARACTERS: Alexandr Baranovich Formichenko (Russian WWII veteran), bartender (both 1st, next in Pun #18, '05), U.S. military, waitress
LOCATIONS/ITEMS: Brighton Beach inc bar & Leon's mother's house; New York inc restaurant; Rhode Island Air Force base inc Generals' office; Rawlins' Saudi Arabian base / Punisher's knife, shotgun, grenade & gun; Leon's mother's meat cleaver, Leon's men's guns, Fury's file w/ user names & passwords to DEA, FBI, INS, Customs & Eastern seaboard police department computer systems, U.S. military jet
SYNOPSIS: In a Brighton Beach bar, Alexandr, a Russian war veteran, speaks poorly of the recently released from prison Leon Rastovich. The bartender kicks the veteran out and some thugs follow. Punisher forcefully tells the bartender that the veteran is protected and interrogates and kills the thugs, learning that Leon is at his mother's house. Eight Army and Air Force Generals argue with Colonel Nick Fury over who he's planning to use for an upcoming mission. Punisher kills Rastovitch, his mother and his men. Col. Fury approaches Punisher in the street and reveals he got Rastovitch released from prison early to get Punisher's attention. Fury offers Punisher access to computer systems for DEA, FBI, Customs, INS, Coast Guard and every major police department on the Eastern seaboard in return for one job. If the mission is completed successfully, Fury regains full control of SHIELD. Not trusting Punisher, the Generals call Rawlins in Saudi Arabia and tell him to activate his terrorist team.
NOTE: Pun #14, '05 reveals Gen. Van Abst's 1st name. Pun #56, '08 reveals Gen. Perino's full name and Gen. Farmington's & Gen. Vraciu's 1st names. Pun #59, '08 reveals Gen. Archer's, Gen. Kent's, Gen. Landers' & Gen. Vertraeus' full names and Gen. Farmington's, Gen. Van Abst's & Gen. Vraciu's last names. Pun #59, '08 reveals Rawlins' 1st name. Pun #14, '05 reveals the Air Force base is in Rhode Island. The Col. Fury here is a native to Earth-200111.

PUNISHER #14 (January 2005)

"Mother Russia Part Two" (22 pages)

CREDITS: Garth Ennis (writer), Dougie Braithwaite (pencils), Bill Reinhold (inks), Virtual Calligraphy's Randy Gentile (letters), Raul Treviño (colors), Cory Sedlmeier (asst editor), Axel Alonso (editor), Tim Bradstreet (c art)
FEATURE CHARACTER: Frank Castle (also as missile silo guard, also in pfb)
GUEST STAR: Col. Nick Fury
VILLAINS: William Rawlins (next in Pun #19, '05), Russian military (many die), Gen. Archer, Gen. Farmington, Gen. Kent, Gen. Landers, Gen. Perino, Gen. Van Abst, Gen. Vertraeus, Gen. Vraciu
OTHER CHARACTERS: Captain Martin Vanheim (Delta Force, also as missile silo guard, 1st, also in pfb), Evgeny Stenkov (Russian scientist, created Barbarossa, in photo), Galina Stenkov (Evgeny's 6 year old daughter, in photo), U.S. military, bar patrons, bartender, airport staff & commuters

LOCATIONS/ITEMS: Rhode Island inc Air Force base (also in pfb) inc briefing room (in pfb) & situation room; Siberia inc Gory Byrranga, Suhdek w/bar & missile silo; Saudi Arabia inc airport / Punisher's & Vanheim's machine guns & HALO gear w/parachutes; Punisher's vodka bottle, Vanheim's knife, nuclear plant guards' uniforms, ID swipe cards & Skoda; American Airlines Flight 2205, Gulf South Flight 29

FLASHBACK: Col. Nick Fury tells Frank Castle the mission is in Russia and briefs him on it: Evgeny Stenkov created Barbarossa, a super-virus that can strip a human's flesh down to the skeleton within minutes. Eight Army and Air Force Generals offered Evgeny asylum in the USA in exchange for the virus, so he killed his assistant, destroyed his work records and injected his daughter Galina with the only remaining sample of Barbarossa for transport. The Russians captured Evgeny, but he died from a heart attack during interrogation. The virus didn't kill Galina because she was also injected with the antidote, which will kill the virus within forty eight hours. Castle must rescue Galina so the USA can extract the virus, but the Generals have insisted that Captain Martin Vanheim of Delta Force accompany him (p).

SYNOPSIS: Castle and Vanheim parachute into Siberia. With the mission officially started, Col. Fury excuses himself and the Generals congratulate each other in their back-up plan with Rawlins. Vanheim sees some off duty missile silo guards in a tavern, so Castle starts a fight, steals a bottle of vodka, kills two guards and steals their uniforms. Castle and Vanheim break into the missile silo. Meanwhile, Rawlins puts his terrorist team on a plane headed to Moscow.

PUNISHER #15 (February 2005)

"Mother Russia Part Three" (22 pages)

CREDITS: Garth Ennis (writer), Dougie Braithwaite (pencils), Bill Reinhold (inks), Virtual Calligraphy's Randy Gentile (letters), Raul Treviño (colors), Cory Sedlmeier (asst editor), Axel Alonso (editor), Tim Bradstreet (c art)
FEATURE CHARACTER: Frank Castle
GUEST STAR: Col. Nick Fury
VILLAINS: The Man of Stone (General Nikolai Alexandrovich Zakharov, 1st but chr last in Pun #39, '06 fb), the Mongolian (Man of Stone's assassin, 1st), Colonel Semyon Lugansky, Major Yeremin (both missile silo commanding officers, 1st), Russian scientists & military (some as corpses, many die), Gen. Archer, Gen. Farmington, Gen. Kent, Gen. Landers, Gen. Perino, Gen. Van Abst, Gen. Vertraeus, Gen. Vraciu
OTHER CHARACTERS: Galina Stenkov (1st), Capt. Vanheim, U.S. military, bar patron, Fury's prostitutes
LOCATIONS/ITEMS: Siberian missile silo, Fury's hotel room, Col. Lugansky's office, RI Air Force base w/ situation room / Punisher's machine guns, rocket launcher & plastique; Russian military's T-54 tank & machine guns; Vanheim's machine guns

SYNOPSIS: As Frank Castle and Martin Vanheim storm the missile silo, a scientist scolds Galina Stenkov for being scared. Castle kills the scientist and tells Galina not to be afraid. The Generals watch the mission via satellite and are impressed with Castle's efficiency. Castle promises to keep Galina safe and makes her promise to keep her eyes closed as he walks her through the hallways filled with dead guards and scientists to meet Vanheim. As they near the exit, Vanheim is surprised to see men repairing a tank and starts a firefight. Castle scolds Vanheim after they escape. General Zakharov arrives at Colonel Lugansky's office looking for an update on obtaining Barbarossa from Galina's blood. During the meeting they learn the silo she's being held in is under attack. Vanheim accesses the silo's computer systems as Castle attacks the military at the exit. Gen. Zakharov interviews participants in Castle's bar fight and determines that Americans are attacking the silo, not terrorists as Lugansky believes. Worried, the Generals call Col. Fury, who tells them to calm down.

PUNISHER #16 (March 2005)

"Mother Russia Part Four" (22 pages)

CREDITS: Garth Ennis (writer), Dougie Braithwaite (pencils), Bill Reinhold (inks), Virtual Calligraphy's Randy Gentile (letters), Raul Treviño (colors), Cory Sedlmeier (asst editor), Axel Alonso (editor), Tim Bradstreet (c art)
FEATURE CHARACTER: Frank Castle
GUEST STAR: Col. Nick Fury
VILLAINS: Gen. Archer, Gen. Farmington, Gen. Kent, Gen. Landers, Gen. Perino, Gen. Van Abst, Gen. Vertraeus, Gen. Vraciu, Gen. Zakharov, the Mongolian, Col. Lugansky, Maj. Yeremin, Russian military (many die) inc a Captain; Rawlins' terrorist team (1st)
OTHER CHARACTERS: Gulf South Flight 29 pilots, stewardesses & commuters (1 dies) (all 3 1st); Capt. Vanheim, Galina Stenkov, U.S. military
LOCATIONS/ITEMS: Siberian missile silo, Col. Lugansky's office, RI Air Force base w/situation room / Punisher's explosives, machine gun & assault rifle; Russian military's assault rifles, Gulf South Flight 29, pilot's gun

SYNOPSIS: The Russian military fail to gain access to the missile silo when they trip Frank Castle's booby traps. Gen. Zakharov explains to Colonel Lugansky why he thinks the attackers are American: They aren't terrorists because they haven't detonated the missiles, they aren't responding to radio hails to make demands because they know their linguistic analysts can pinpoint their origin, and the only reason they're stalling is to escape with Galina. Rawlins' terrorist team takes control of Gulf South Flight 29. Castle stops another Russian military access attempt, but doesn't notice Zakharov's associate, the Mongolian, sneak inside. Col. Fury reassures the Generals that Castle has the situation under control. The Mongolian attacks and knocks out Vanheim. Galina calls for Frank. The terrorists broadcast their intention to attack Moscow and the Russian military grants authority to shoot down the plane. The Mongolian defeats Castle. Seventeen minutes have passed, so Gen. Zakharov tells Lugansky he can now send his men into the silo.

PUNISHER #17 (April 2005)

"Mother Russia Part Five" (22 pages)

CREDITS: Garth Ennis (writer), Dougie Braithwaite (pencils), Bill Reinhold (inks), Virtual Calligraphy's Randy Gentile (letters), Raul Treviño (colors), Cory Sedlmeier (asst editor), Axel Alonso (editor), Tim Bradstreet (c art)
FEATURE CHARACTER: Frank Castle
GUEST STAR: Col. Nick Fury
VILLAINS: Gen. Archer, Gen. Farmington, Gen. Kent, Gen. Landers, Gen. Perino, Gen. Van Abst, Gen. Vertraeus, Gen. Vraciu, Gen. Zakharov, the Mongolian (dies), Col. Lugansky, Maj. Yeremin, Russian military (many die) inc a Captain; Rawlins' terrorist team (bts, dies)
OTHER CHARACTERS: Gulf South Flight 29 pilots, stewardesses & commuters (all bts, die); Capt. Vanheim, Galina Stenkov, U.S. military; Lisa Castle (in Punisher's hallucination)
LOCATIONS/ITEMS: Siberian missile silo, Col. Lugansky's office, RI Air Force base w/situation room, Central Park (Punisher's hallucination) / Punisher's machine gun & assault rifle; Vanheim's syringes w/stabilizer; Galina's gun, folder w/Russian go-codes, Fury's belt, Gulf South Flight 29 (destroyed)
SYNOPSIS: Gulf South Flight 29 is shot down. Gen. Zakharov learns of the terrorists, but quickly dismisses them as a feint by the Americans. The Mongolian slaps Galina. Frank Castle stands up and catches the Mongolian's kick, then smashes him against the walls until he's dead. As the Generals celebrate their ruse, Col. Fury returns to ask what they've done. Galina asks Frank if she can help with the approaching Russian military, but he tells her never to play with guns. As Castle battles the military, Vanheim awakens and apologizes to Galina. The Generals admit to Fury that they arranged for the terrorist team to attack Moscow. Fury mercilessly beats Gen. Van Abst with his belt, cursing them all for killing the flight's passengers. Castle stops Vanheim from killing Galina. Vanheim tells Castle that Plan B is to take a blood sample if they can't escape with Galina, and that Fury knows nothing about Plan B. Castle gives Vanheim nuclear go-codes and tells him to target major Russian cities. They contact Col. Lugansky, demanding a safe escape or they'll decimate Russia.

PUNISHER #18 (May 2005)

"Mother Russia Part Six" (22 pages)

CREDITS: Garth Ennis (writer), Dougie Braithwaite (pencils), Bill Reinhold (inks), Virtual Calligraphy's Randy Gentile (letters), Raul Treviño (colors), Cory Sedlmeier (asst editor), Axel Alonso (editor), Tim Bradstreet (c art)
FEATURE CHARACTER: Punisher
GUEST STAR: Col. Nick Fury (next in Pun #55, '08)
VILLAINS: Gen. Archer, Gen. Kent, Gen. Landers, Gen. Vertraeus, Gen. Vraciu (all next in bts Pun #50, '07), Gen. Farmington, Gen. Perino, Gen. Van Abst, Gen. Zakharov (next in Pun #37, '06), Col. Lugansky (dies), Maj. Yeremin, Russian military
OTHER CHARACTERS: Alexandr Baranovich Forminchenko, bartender (both last in Pun #13, '05), Vladimir Putin (Russian President, bts, on phone), Capt. Vanheim (dies), Galina Stenkov, NORAD (bts, on phone), U.S. military inc a lieutenant & Silverfish crew
LOCATIONS/ITEMS: Siberia inc missile silo, RI Air Force base inc situation room; Col. Lugansky's office, Brighton Beach bar / Punisher's parachute, assault rifle, knife & vodka bottle; Vanheim's parachute & assault rifle; Zakharov's gun, nuclear missile, Silverfish (U.S. military plane)
SYNOPSIS: Col. Fury tells the panicking Generals to calm down. Vanheim destroys the computer console to avoid outside rebooting. Gen. Zakharov tells Col. Lugansky to calm down; the Americans won't start a nuclear war. A missile launches bound for Moscow. Fury tells NORAD to stand down and commends Castle on his ingenuity. Gen. Zakharov tells President Putin not to worry; the situation is under control. When Lugansky tries to relieve Zakharov of command, Zakharov kills Lugansky. The missile's engines stop and the warhead deactivates. As it falls to Earth, Castle and Vanheim parachute out with Galina. Zakharov deduces the Americans escaped in the missile and compliments their resourcefulness. Vanheim lost his pack in the fall; they now only have one coat. Castle draws straws to see who returns with Galina and who freezes to death in Siberia. Days later, the Generals are upset that Castle wouldn't let Barbarossa be extracted from Galina; it's now destroyed. Fury convinces them not to arrest Castle and arranges custody for Galina. With no Barbarossa, the promised system access is gone and Fury doesn't get SHIELD back. Castle delivers the vodka he acquired at the Brighton Beach bar for Alexandr.

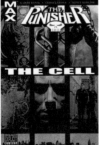

PUNISHER: THE CELL (July 2005)

"The Cell" (48 pages)

CREDITS: Garth Ennis (writer), Lewis LaRosa (pencils), Scott Koblish (inks), Virtual Calligraphy's Randy Gentile (letters), Raul Treviño (colors), Cory Sedlmeier (asst editor), Axel Alonso (editor), Tim Bradstreet (c art)
FEATURE CHARACTER: Punisher (also disguised as Capt. Leonard, also in pfb; last in Punmax #20, '12 fb, next in Punmax #21, '12 fb)
VILLAINS: Don Francesco Drago (Drago family boss, 1st but chr last in Pun #75/2, '09 fb, also in fb3 after Pun #75/2, '09 fb), Paulie & Philly Germaine (twins, Drago's bodyguards, 1st but chr last in Pun #75/2, '09 fb, also in fb3 after Pun #75/2, '09 fb, also in fb2), Enzo Gaucci (Drago family soldier, 1st but chr last in Pun #75/2, '09 fb, also in fb3 after Pun #75/2, '09 fb, also in fb1), George Apostolo (Drago family consigliere, 1st but chr last in Pun #75/2, '09 fb) (all die), Angelo Drago (Drago's cousin, bts in fb1, sent Gaucci to kill rival's wife), Tommy Drago (Drago's brother, bts in fb3, ordered assassination on Drago, 1st, next in Pun #75/2, '09 fb), Denny Welsh (ex-con, dies in pfb), Riker's Penitentiary inmates (several die) inc Squeaky Pete (dies), Ty Curtis (dies) & Aryan Nation leader (Capt. Leonard's lover)
OTHER CHARACTERS: Knowles (Punisher's cellmate, corpse), Angelo's rival's wife, doctor, nurse (prev 3 in fb1), prostitute (corpse, in fb2), bystanders (in fb3), Kreiger (mentioned, head found in dryer), Riker's Penitentiary security guards & medical staff
LOCATIONS/ITEMS: Riker's Penitentiary inc Drago's cell, Punisher's solitary confinement cell & general population cell; New York (in pfb) inc Central Park (3); Phoenix hospital (1), hospital bathroom (2) / Punisher's gun (in pfb), Leonard's nightstick & nametag; Germaine twins' guns (in fb3) & knives; Gaucci's assault rifle (in fb2), Thompson (in fb3) & knife; Riker's security's assault rifles, Drago's lounge chair

FLASHBACKS: Punisher tortures ex-con Denny Welsh for information about Riker's Penitentiary then kills him (p). On orders from Angelo Drago, Enzo murders a rival's wife while she's in labor (1). Philly Germaine murders a prostitute and Paulie later violates the corpse (2). Summer, 1976: Wanting Tommy Drago to take over the family, Gaucci tries to assassinate Don Francesco Drago in Central Park. A firefight ensues between Gaucci and the Germaine twins. Drago survives (3).

SYNOPSIS: Having turned himself over to the authorities, Punisher is incarcerated at Riker's Penitentiary. Security chief Captain Leonard tells Punisher that Drago and his men run the prison. Leonard reports to Drago, who tells him to keep Punisher in solitary confinement while he forms a plan. When Punisher is transferred into the general population, he foments a riot by framing Leonard and the Aryan Nation for killing an inmate. Leonard taunts Punisher when the riot breaks, but Punisher steals Leonard's uniform and assault rifle. Inmates scatter from Punisher's path as he makes his way to Drago's cell. Drago's men try to figure out why Punisher is coming for them but can't. Punisher shoots them all in the knees and tells Drago that his consigliere Apostolo tried to assassinate him, and his soldier Enzo was the shooter, in Central Park, 1976. When they realize what that means, Punisher begins to kill them. He stabs Enzo in the gut and heart for his daughter's and wife's wounds then beats the Germaine twins' brains out for his son's. Drago kills Apostolo for his betrayal. Punisher tells Drago he won't stop killing mobsters because they impose their wills on others and don't care what happens to anyone else. As Drago dies, Punisher announces he'll escape Riker's and continue his war on crime.

NOTE: On Earth-616, the Costa family was responsible for the Castle family deaths. Punisher killed Tommy Drago in Florida sometime before the pfb. Pun #1, '04 refers to the events of this story as "long ago."

PUNISHER #19 (June 2005)

"Up is Down and Black is White Part One" (22 pages)

CREDITS: Garth Ennis (writer), Leandro Fernandez (pencils), Scott Hanna (inks), Virtual Calligraphy's Randy Gentile (letters), Dan Brown (colors), Cory Sedlmeier (asst editor), Axel Alonso (editor), Tim Bradstreet (c art)
FEATURE CHARACTER: Punisher (also in photo, next in Pun #21, '05)
SUPPORTING CAST: Maria Castle, Lisa Castle, Frank Castle Jr. (all corpses, skeletal remains, chr last in Pun #75/4, '09 fb, also in dfb), Kathryn O'Brien (last in Pun #5, '04, next in Pun #21, '05)
VILLAINS: Gen. Farmington, Gen. Perino, Gen. Van Abst (all next bts in Pun #50, '07), Nicky Cavella (last in Pun #6, '04, also in dfb), William Rawlins (last in Pun #14, '05, next in Pun #21, '05), Teresa Gazzera (Pittsy's younger sister, 1st, also off-panel in dfb), Joey Picardi, Tony Pizzo, Fat Mike, Max, Pete (prev 5 recently promoted mob bosses, 1st), Horace "Spoonie" Moore (drug dealer, dies) & his men (die), prison inmates inc Marcie
OTHER CHARACTERS: Big Joe McClusky (drug dealer) & his men, prison guard (all corpses), Morocco Coffee staff & patrons, diner staff & patrons, news anchor (on TV)
LOCATIONS/ITEMS: New York inc Morocco Coffee, Giorgio's Café & diner; Queens inc pool hall; cemetery inc Castle family grave; prison inc O'Brien's showers & cell / Punisher's shotgun & gun; Moore & his men's guns, inmate's knife, Nicky's video camera
FLASHBACK: Nicky Cavella urinates on the Castle family's disinterred corpses (d).
SYNOPSIS: Nicky Cavella digs up the Castle family and sets up a video camera. In a prison shower room, O'Brien fights off other attacking inmates. The Generals from Punisher's Russian mission hire Rawlins to kill Punisher. Punisher kills two gangs of drug dealers. Later, Nicky Cavella calls a meeting of the remaining mob Captains that are left from Punisher's slaughter a year ago. Nicky points out they're not making the money they used to and people no longer respect them. He tells them he can take care of their problems by killing the Punisher, but he demands to made mob boss when he does. He tells them to watch tonight's news before they decide. The prison inmates frame O'Brien for killing a guard. The news shows footage of Nicky desecrating the Castle family's corpses. Punisher says nothing.
NOTE: Tony Pizzo's surname is revealed in & the other four mob bosses are named in Pun #20, '05. Giorgio's Café is named in Pun #22, '05. Gen. Farmington's daughter is on the board of Morocco Coffee. O'Brien is reading "Sunset and Sawdust" by Joe R. Lansdale.

PUNISHER #20 (June 2005)

"Up is Down and Black is White Part Two" (22 pages)

CREDITS: Garth Ennis (writer), Leandro Fernandez (pencils), Scott Hanna (inks), Virtual Calligraphy's Randy Gentile (letters), Dan Brown (colors), Cory Sedlmeier (asst editor), Axel Alonso (editor), Tim Bradstreet (c art)
FEATURE CHARACTER: Punisher (only on cover)
VILLAINS: Nicky Cavella (also in fb to 1st chr app before Pun #2, '04), Pittsy Gazzera, Ink (both in fb to 1st chr app before Pun #2, '04), Massimo Cesare (bts in fb to 1st chr app before Pun #1, '04, sends Nicky to Boston), Johnny Cavella (Nicky's father, in fb, dies), Auntie Mo (Nicky's paternal aunt, in fb, dies), Jimmy Cavella (Nicky's paternal uncle, bts in fb, dies), David Kai (mob boss, in fb) & his 2 sons (in fb, die), Cavella family Captains inc Jackie & soldiers (in fb), Joey Picardi (dies), Tony Pizzo, Fat Mike, Max, Pete (both next in Pun #22, '05), Teresa Gazzera
OTHER CHARACTERS: Wong Kai (David Kai's youngest son, as David's meal), Joanie Cavella (Nicky's mother), Nicky's sister (all corpses), Ronnie Gavigan (bar owner, owes Cavellas $25,000), bystanders, dog (all in fb), subway commuters
LOCATIONS/ITEMS: Cavella Estate inc bedroom, basement & surrounding woods; New York (also in fb) inc David Kai's restaurant, Café di Gavriago (all in fb), Giorgio's Café w/bathroom, Empire State Building & Hudson River / Nicky's guns, Pittsy's meat cleaver, Kai's son's guns (all in fb), Teresa's knife
FLASHBACK: In the woods, eight years old Nicky Cavella shoots his father in the face and blames it on his uncle Jimmy. Nicky's Auntie Mo takes control of the family and orders Jimmy killed. Mo congratulates Nicky on killing his mother, sister and father and sticking to their plan of taking what they feel to be rightfully theirs. Mo brings young Nicky to a meeting with her Captains, who don't think Nicky being there is a good idea. Mo insists and the meeting continues. Years later, Mo celebrates with Nicky on his birthday, then tells Nicky to kill the captured Ronnie Gavigan, who owes the Cavellas twenty five thousand dollars. On the day Nicky is made a soldier, Nicky kills Mo during their celebration. Fifteen years ago, Nicky intimidates mob rival David Kai by surreptitiously feeding Kai's pre-teen son Wong to David, then killing David's two other sons. Kai starts a war and Don Massimo Cesare sends Nicky to Boston.
SYNOPSIS: Nicky Cavella waits while the mob bosses discuss his offer to kill the Punisher. Joey Picardi tells him privately that he'll never agree to it, so Teresa kills him and dumps his body in the Hudson. When Joey doesn't return, the other mob bosses agree to Nicky's terms.

PUNISHER #21 (July 2005)

"Up is Down and Black is White Part Three" (22 pages)

CREDITS: Garth Ennis (writer), Leandro Fernandez (pencils), Scott Hanna (inks), Virtual Calligraphy's Randy Gentile (letters), Dan Brown (colors), Cory Sedlmeier (asst editor), Axel Alonso (editor), Tim Bradstreet (c art)
FEATURE CHARACTER: Punisher (also in photo, also in Pun #43, '07 fb)
SUPPORTING CAST: Kathryn O'Brien (last in Pun #19, '05)
VILLAINS: Nicky Cavella (also in rfb), William Rawlins (also in photo, last in Pun #19, '05), Nikolai Kaganovitch (dies) & his men (1 survives, rest die), 2 youth gangs (bts, killed by Punisher), drug dealers (die), Tony Pizzo (also in photo), Fat Mike, Teresa Gazzera
OTHER CHARACTERS: William Roth (last in Pun #5, '04), Ronald Kai (racketeer, corpse, in dfb), reporters, cameramen (both in dfb), police (other in dfb) inc a Detective, Police Commissioner (bts, on phone), news anchor (on TV), club patrons & staff inc bouncer, strippers, paramedics; Pizzo's mother (in photo), Maria Castle, Lisa Castle, Frank Castle Jr. (prev 3 skeletal remains, in photo & rfb)
LOCATIONS/ITEMS: Punisher's safehouse, Roth's Jersey City apartment, Brighton Beach inc night club; New York inc Giorgio's Café; Kai's Chinatown stronghold (in dfb) / Punisher's assault rifles, M60, guns, rocket launcher, grenades, shotguns & machete; drug dealers' assault rifles & Uzis; Kaganovitch's man's gun
FLASHBACKS: After a Punisher attack, police keep reporters away from Ronald Kai's stronghold (d). Nicky Cavella urinates on the Castle family's disinterred corpses (Pun #19, '05 fb).
SYNOPSIS: Kathryn O'Brien pounds on William Roth's door until he lets her in. She tells him she broke out of prison after she was framed for killing a guard and asks him to make her a new identity. She's shocked by a newspaper headline about Punisher's desecrated family. Punisher storms a night club and kills Nikolai Kaganovitch and his crew. As Roth puts together an identity for O'Brien, he notices that her ex-husband Rawlins is staying at the Mandarin. She asks Roth for a gun. Police find a survivor in Kaganovitch's crew with a message: Bury Punisher's family. Nicky Cavella watches the news, which reports that Punisher has left several other similar messages across New York. Rawlins, who knows Nicky from his time in Boston, arrives. Punisher slaughters a gang of drug dealers.

PUNISHER #22 (August 2005)

"Up is Down and Black is White Part Four" (22 pages)

CREDITS: Garth Ennis (writer), Leandro Fernandez (pencils), Scott Hanna (inks), Virtual Calligraphy's Randy Gentile (letters), Dan Brown (colors), Cory Sedlmeier (asst editor), Axel Alonso (editor), Tim Bradstreet (c art)
FEATURE CHARACTER: Punisher (also in own dream)
SUPPORTING CAST: Kathryn O'Brien
VILLAINS: Nicky Cavella, William Rawlins, Teresa Gazzera, Tony Pizzo, Fat Mike, Max, Pete (both last in Pun #20, '05) & their men, 2 thieves
OTHER CHARACTERS: Maria Castle, Lisa Castle, Frank Castle Jr., corpses (all in Punisher's dream), William Roth, New York City Mayor & his advisors inc Peter & Jonathan, Police Commissioner, District Attorney, reporters inc Amanda & Tim, cameramen, bystanders, birds
LOCATIONS/ITEMS: New York (also as ruins in Punisher's dream) inc Giorgio's Café, Mayor's office & jewelry store / Punisher's M60 & shotgun; O'Brien's binoculars, Rawlins' sniper rifle
SYNOPSIS: Two thieves decide not to rob a jewelry store after discussing Punisher's current rampage. Punisher wakes from a dream where he slaughters all of New York, criminal and innocent alike. Rawlins offers to kill the Punisher for Nicky Cavella. At first Nicky isn't interested, but Rawlins convinces him to team up. O'Brien and Roth spy on Rawlins and Cavella from afar. O'Brien tells Roth that she's planning to kill Rawlins. The Mayor, Police Commissioner and District Attorney discuss their options and decide to re-bury the Castle family. Nicky gets dressed and accepts Rawlins' offer. The District Attorney announces the Castle family will be buried as soon as possible. Satisfied, Punisher decides attack Cavella, knowing the mobster will be ready for him. Deducing he's at Tony Pizzo's Giorgio's Café, Punisher attacks. Rawlins prepares to snipe Punisher, but O'Brien knocks him out and shoots Cavella.

PUNISHER #23 (September 2005)

"Up is Down and Black is White Part Five" (22 pages)

CREDITS: Garth Ennis (writer), Leandro Fernandez (pencils), Scott Hanna (inks), Virtual Calligraphy's Randy Gentile (letters), Dan Brown (colors), Cory Sedlmeier (asst editor), Axel Alonso (editor), Tim Bradstreet (c art)
FEATURE CHARACTER: Punisher
SUPPORTING CAST: Kathryn O'Brien
VILLAINS: Nicky Cavella, William Rawlins, Teresa Gazzera, Tony Pizzo, Fat Mike, Max, Pete & their men (many die)
OTHER CHARACTER: William Roth (also off-panel in Pun #59, '08 fb)
LOCATIONS/ITEMS: New York inc Giorgio's Café; Roth's Jersey City apartment inc kitchen & bedroom / Punisher's shotgun; Teresa's shotgun & knife; Roth's gun & first aid kit; Rawlins' sniper rifle, O'Brien's gun, Nicky's bullet proof vest; gangster's guns
SYNOPSIS: Teresa shoots Punisher in the chest with a shotgun, stunning him. O'Brien shoots some more mobsters and tosses Rawlins into Roth's trunk. They pull the car around, pick up Punisher and escape. Nicky Cavella checks his bullet proof vest as he and Teresa follow Roth's car. Punisher begins to interrogate Rawlins. As they watch Roth's apartment Teresa makes a pass at Nicky, but he misunderstands and calls for reinforcements. Punisher learns that the Generals from his Russian mission sent Rawlins to kill him. Roth tells Punisher to get Rawlins' confession on video, then blackmail the Generals with it to leave him alone. O'Brien tends to Punisher's wounds and asks if he's up for a little fun. Teresa tries to kiss Nicky, but he's visibly disgusted and shoves her away. As Punisher and O'Brien have some fun, Nicky learns that reinforcements aren't coming. Nicky leaves to raise reinforcements in person. Against Nicky's orders, Teresa attacks Punisher.
NOTE: O'Brien reveals she was born in December, 1967. Punisher took out one of Rawlins' eyes off-panel during his interrogation.

PUNISHER #24 (October 2005)

"Up is Down and Black is White Conclusion" (22 pages)

CREDITS: Garth Ennis (writer), Leandro Fernandez (pencils), Scott Hanna (inks), Virtual Calligraphy's Randy Gentile (letters), Dan Brown (colors), Cory Sedlmeier (asst editor), Axel Alonso (editor), Tim Bradstreet (c art)
FEATURE CHARACTER: Punisher (also off-panel in Pun #59, '08 fb)
SUPPORTING CAST: Kathryn O'Brien (also voice only in Pun #59, '08 fb; next in Pun #37, '06)
VILLAINS: William Rawlins (also in Pun #59, '08 fb; next in Pun #37, '06), Nicky Cavella (dies off-panel), Teresa Gazzera (dies), Tony Pizzo (next in Pun #45, '07), Fat Mike, Max, Pete & their men
OTHER CHARACTERS: William Roth (also off-panel in Pun #59, '08 fb, dies), bystanders, birds
LOCATIONS/ITEMS: Jersey City inc Roth's apartment w/bedroom & kitchen; New York inc Giorgio's Café; woods / Punisher's gun, Roth's gun, camcorder & first aid kit; Teresa's knife, O'Brien's gun, Nicky's gun
SYNOPSIS: Teresa stabs Punisher and attacks O'Brien. O'Brien bites off Teresa's nose and shoots Teresa in the face. Nicky Cavella demands that the mob bosses send some men to kill the Punisher. They refuse. When Nicky threatens them, they remind him he has no men; there's nothing he can force them to do. Nicky storms off. O'Brien tends to Punisher's wounds and they record Rawlins' confession. Punisher and O'Brien leave to make a copy when they see Nicky outside looking for Teresa. Nicky grabs a child hostage, but lets the kid go when Punisher tells him his options. O'Brien races back to the apartment to get Roth, but finds him dead and Rawlins gone. Later, Punisher takes Cavella into the woods and shoots him in the gut. Nicky will painfully die from blood poisoning in a few days. Punisher leaves as Nicky screams.
NOTE: Rawlins' confession is seen in Pun #59, '08.

PUNISHER #25 (November 2005)

"The Slavers Part 1" (22 pages)

CREDITS: Garth Ennis (writer), Leandro Fernandez (pencils), Scott Koblish (inks), Virtual Calligraphy's Randy Gentile (letters), Dan Brown (colors), Cory Sedlmeier (asst editor), Axel Alonso (editor), Tim Bradstreet (c art)
FEATURE CHARACTER: Punisher
VILLAINS: Cristu Bulat (soldier turned sex slaver), Vera Konstantin (Cristu's business manager) (both 1st but chr last in Pun #26, '05 fb), Detective Stu Westin (dirty cop, 1st), Antony Pavla (drug lord, dies) & his men (die)
OTHER CHARACTERS: Captain Tom Price, Officer Marcie Miller, Officer Russ Parker (all 1st), Viorica (escaped sex slave, 1st but chr last in Pun #26, '05 fb), other police, captured suspects
LOCATIONS/ITEMS: Bock Nite Club, Cristu's office, 15th Precinct, Punisher's safe house, Price's precinct inc Price's office / Punisher's sniper rifle & guns; Pavla's men's guns & knife; Viorica's gun, Miller & Parker's guns
SYNOPSIS: Punisher's latest hit is interrupted when a young woman shoots at his targets, Pavla and his men. Pavla's men chase the woman into a blind alley. Punisher kills Pavla and stops his men from raping the woman by killing them. She begs Punisher for help to get revenge for the death of her baby. Before Punisher can consider, police officers Miller and Parker respond to the crime scene. Punisher knocks them down and leaves with the young woman. Elsewhere, having heard about the evening's events, Cristu and Vera decide to proactively protect their business interests and use their man inside the police department, Detective Stu Westin. Punisher takes the woman to his safehouse. Westin approaches Miller and Parker's police Captain and convinces him it would be a career-making move to declare war on Punisher, now that he's "attacked" police officers. Punisher learns the woman's name is Viorica as she begins her story.
NOTE: Cristu's surname revealed in Pun #27, '06. Vera's surname revealed in Pun #28, '06.

PUNISHER #26 (December 2005)

"The Slavers Part 2" (22 pages)

CREDITS: Garth Ennis (writer), Leandro Fernandez (pencils), Scott Koblish (inks), Virtual Calligraphy's Randy Gentile (letters), Dan Brown (colors), Cory Sedlmeier (asst. editor), Axel Alonso (editor), Tim Bradstreet (c art)
FEATURE CHARACTER: Punisher
VILLAINS: Tiberiu Bulat (Cristu's father, 1st but chr last in Pun #29, '06 fb), Cristu Bulat (also in fb between Pun #29, '06 fb & Pun #25, '05) (both also in Viorica's thoughts), Vera Konstantin (also in fb between Pun #29, '06 fb & Pun #25, '05) & his men, Det. Westin, gang members (die), Pavla's men (die)
OTHER CHARACTERS: Jen Cooke (social worker, 1st in fb, see NOTE), Viorica (also in fb to 1st chr app before Pun #25, '05), Anna (Viorica's baby, in fb, also as corpse in photo), Officer Ernie Mosstow (1st), Shelley Marks (mentioned, Marcie's friend in 15th precinct), Capt. Price, Marcie Miller, Russ Parker, sex slaves, brothel clients, reporters, cameramen, police, bystanders (fb)
LOCATIONS/ITEMS: Punisher's safe house, abandoned plant, police precinct, Bock Nite Club, Jamaica Bay subway tunnel, Cooke's office (in fb), Queens brothel (also in fb) / Tiberiu's sub-machine gun, Miller & Parker's neck brace, cast, sling & crutches; Punisher's gun, Pavla's men's shotgun, Mosstow's gun
FLASHBACK: Cristu runs the sex slave business and Vera manages the girls through fear and dominance. Viorica is allowed to see her baby once a week to keep her motivated. Viorica escapes with Anna and calls a social worker, Jen Cooke, who Viorica heard will help. Vera learns who Jen is, takes Anna and sends Jen a photo of Anna's corpse.
SYNOPSIS: Viorica tells Punisher that when she was fifteen she was abducted from her village, raped, beaten, and forced into sex slavery. When she became pregnant, she was selected to be one of the girls to go to America. Meanwhile, Tiberiu deals with a rival drug dealer by gouging his eyes out before breaking his neck. Cristu, uncomfortable with his father personally conducting business, tries to stop him from killing the dealer's associates so they can send a message, but Tiberiu ignores him and guns them all down. Cristu leaves and calls Vera, telling her he's considering killing Tiberiu to protect their business. Viorica explains that after her daughter died, she saw Pavla in the street and went crazy. She says America is supposed to be a land of promise, but it's a nightmare. Miller and Parker are forced to appear in a press conference where

Price declares war on Punisher. Punisher attacks the remnants of Pavla's men to learn where the brothel is. He abducts two brothel clients to get inside, but a police officer spots them. Punisher evades the officer.
NOTE: Cooke, Mosstow & Tiberiu are named in Pun #27, '06. The Jen Cooke appearing here is an Earth-200111 native.

PUNISHER #27 (January 2006)

"The Slavers Part 3" (22 pages)

CREDITS: Garth Ennis (writer), Leandro Fernandez (pencils), Scott Koblish (inks), Virtual Calligraphy's Randy Gentile (letters), Dan Brown (colors), Cory Sedlmeier (asst editor), Axel Alonso (editor), Tim Bradstreet (c art)
FEATURE CHARACTER: Punisher
VILLAINS: Cristu Bulat (also in fb to 1st chr app before Pun #29, '06 fb), Det. Westin (next in Pun #29, '06), Tiberiu Bulat (also in fb to 1st chr app before Pun #25, '05) & his militia (in fb), Vera Konstantin (bts, on phone w/ Cristu), pimp
OTHER CHARACTERS: Viorica (next in Pun #30, '06), Jen Cooke, Capt. Price, Marcie Miller, Russ Parker, Ernie Mosstow (also in photo, next in Pun #29, '06 fb), police, reporters (1 on TV) inc Judy; Old Bar bartender & patrons; lecture attendees; 'Lana, Katalina, 'Maja (prev 3 sex slaves, in photo)
LOCATIONS/ITEMS: Tiberiu's house, Old Bar, Price's precinct inc Price's office & locker room; Viorica's motel room, lecture hall, Cooke's office & apartment inc bathroom; Eastern Europe badlands (in fb) / Punisher's knife, Tiberiu's revolver, police nightsticks, Cooke's files
FLASHBACK: Tiberiu's militia raids villages in Europe until Cristu decides there's more profit in slavery. They begin abducting the healthy young women in their raids.
SYNOPSIS: Punisher realizes he won't find the information he needs through his usual sources and resorts to plan B. The news reports that Punisher beat up Officer Ernie Mosstow, the officer Punisher evaded the previous night. Cristu fails to convince his father Tiberiu to stay away from Punisher. Realizing Tiberiu will never stop drawing unwanted attention to their operation, Cristu tells Vera to kill Tiberiu. Miller and Parker talk with Mosstow, who admits that Det. Westin made him say Punisher injured him, when Punisher didn't. Meanwhile, Captain Price tells Westin that Punisher has more fans in the department than he thought, and the press is now breathing down their necks for results. Mosstow calls Westin about Miller and Parker. Punisher brings Viorica food before seeing Jen Cooke, who is giving a lecture about human trafficking. Miller and Parker find themselves attacked by fellow officers. Punisher manages to convince Jen to hand over her files on the slavers.

PUNISHER #28 (February 2006)

"The Slavers Part 4" (22 pages)

CREDITS: Garth Ennis (writer), Leandro Fernandez (pencils), Scott Koblish (inks), Virtual Calligraphy's Randy Gentile (letters), Dan Brown (colors), Cory Sedlmeier (asst editor), Axel Alonso (editor), Tim Bradstreet (c art)
FEATURE CHARACTER: Punisher
VILLAINS: Cristu Bulat & his men (die), Tiberiu Bulat, Vera Konstantin, gang members (die)
OTHER CHARACTERS: Marcie Miller (also in Pun #29, '06 fb), Russ Parker (also bts in Pun #29, '06 fb), Jen Cooke, store clerk, sex slaves, bystanders
LOCATIONS/ITEMS: Tiberiu's house inc kitchen & bedroom; book store, bar, Indian Lake brothel, Vera's office / Punisher's human anatomy book, Hummer, tranquilizer, shotgun, knife & syringe w/adrenaline; Tiberiu's revolver & teapot of boiling water; gang members' guns, shotgun & Uzi; Cristu's men's guns
SYNOPSIS: Punisher picks up a book on human anatomy. Gang members attack Tiberiu in his house to kill him for killing their brothers, but he easily kills all but one and interrogates the survivor to find out who told them where to find him. Miller and Parker realize their fellow officers attacked them because they talked to Mosstow and decide to do their own investigating. Punisher drives to the Bulats' Indian Lake brothel. Vera tells Cristu that Tiberiu survived the attack. Punisher watches as Cristu's reinforcements arrive. That night, Punisher drugs their dinner. As they lie unconscious Punisher kills everyone in the house but Cristu and the girls. Punisher calls Jen Cooke, who knows a shelter where they can stay. Miller and Parker approach Jen once she's back in town. In the woods, Punisher wakes up Cristu to interrogate him. Punisher tells Cristu he can still survive if he talks quickly. Cristu sees that he's been disemboweled.
NOTE: Mosstow is spelled "Mostow" here.

PUNISHER #29 (March 2006)

"The Slavers Part 5" (22 pages)

CREDITS: Garth Ennis (writer), Leandro Fernandez (pencils), Scott Koblish (inks), Virtual Calligraphy's Randy Gentile (letters), Dan Brown (colors), Cory Sedlmeier (asst editor), Axel Alonso (editor), Tim Bradstreet (c art)
FEATURE CHARACTER: Punisher
VILLAINS: Cristu Bulat (bts, died at noon, also in fb2 between Pun #27, '06 fb & Pun #26, '05 fb) & his men (in fb2), Vera Konstantin (dies, also in fb2 to 1st chr app before Pun #26, '05 fb), Det. Westin (last in Pun #27, '06), Tiberiu Bulat & his men (some die)
OTHER CHARACTERS: Ernie Mosstow (bts, attempted suicide, also in fb1), Marcie Miller (also in fb1 during Pun #28, '06), Russ Parker, Jen Cooke, sex slaves (in fb2), diner cook & waitress, police, bystanders
LOCATIONS/ITEMS: Indian Lake brothel, Cooke's apartment, Vera's office, diner (on Atlantic Ave.), 15th Precinct / Punisher's gun & assault rifle; Tiberiu's men's assault rifles & Uzis; Tiberiu's assault rifle, Miller's gun, Vera's safe & files
FLASHBACKS: Miller beats a confession out of Mosstow (1). Vera has Cristu's men rape the girls to establish dominance and better control them (2).
SYNOPSIS: Tiberiu attacks the Indian Lake brothel, but Cristu and the girls are missing and everyone inside is dead. Punisher attacks Tiberiu and his men, but is unprepared for the former soldiers' collected response. Punisher escapes and calls Jen Cooke, warning her that Tiberiu can

find her address and will likely come for her. Miller and Parker have Cooke arrange a meeting with him. Tiberiu tells Vera he knows about her involvement in the attack on him. He leaves two of his men with her to wait for Cristu. Punisher meets Jen and the officers. They tell him that Detective Westin has been working with the Bulats, but they can't prove it. The officers agree sit on their discoveries while Punisher kills the Bulats, if he can find some evidence on Westin for them. Punisher gets the Bulats' file on Westin as he tortures Vera. She begs for her life, but he reminds her that he's dominant and can do whatever he wants. As Punisher kills Vera, he realizes for the first time in a long time, he feels genuine hate.

NOTE: Mosstow is spelled "Mostow" here. Cristu's body won't be found until Pun #44, '07.

PUNISHER #30 (April 2006)

"The Slavers Conclusion" (22 pages)

CREDITS: Garth Ennis (writer), Leandro Fernandez (pencils), Scott Koblish (inks), Virtual Calligraphy's Randy Gentile (letters), Dan Brown (colors), Cory Sedlmeier (asst editor), Axel Alonso (editor), Tim Bradstreet (c art)
FEATURE CHARACTER: Punisher (next in Pun #31 fb, Pun #32-36, Pun #31, all '06)
VILLAINS: Tiberiu Bulat & his men, human trafficker (all die); Det. Westin (disappears)
OTHER CHARACTERS: Viorica (last in Pun #27, '06), Jen Cooke, Marcie Miller, Russ Parker, diner staff & patrons, flight attendants, commuters, bystanders, sex slaves (in photos)
LOCATIONS/ITEMS: Viorica's motel room, brothel, sewer, Cooke's motel room & office; JFK airport, diner / Punisher's explosives, detonator, shotgun, video camera, gasoline & lighter; Tiberiu's knife, Cooke's files, Vera's file

SYNOPSIS: Punisher brings Viorica more food. Miller and Parker wait for Punisher's call, but Miller hates working alongside Punisher. Knowing where the Bulats' new brothel is from Vera's files, Punisher attacks. He sets an explosion and kills Tiberiu's wounded men as he chases Tiberiu through the house. When Tiberiu uses one of the girls as a human shield, Punisher calls Tiberiu a coward. Tiberiu flies into a rage, and Punisher easily knocks him out. Miller visits Jen to learn more about the slave trade. They're interrupted when Punisher sends more girls to Jen. Punisher lures Detective Westin to him. He tells Westin to deliver a package to the Bulats' contacts in Moldova and have passports made for the freed girls, in return he'll give Westin Vera's file. Punisher films as he sets Tiberiu on fire, and tells the camera to stay away. Westin disappears in Moldova. Parker is demoted. Miller quits the force and works for Jen Cooke. Of the seven girls Punisher rescued, two are dead, one disappeared and another is a prostitute and the other three are well enough. Viorica is a waitress, trying to live whatever life they left her with.

PUNISHER: THE TYGER #1 (February 2006)

"The Tyger" (48 pages)

CREDITS: Garth Ennis (writer), John Severin (art), Virtual Calligraphy's Randy Gentile (letters), Paul Mounts (colors), Cory Sedlmeier (assoc editor), Axel Alonso (editor), Tim Bradstreet (c art)
FEATURE CHARACTER: Punisher (also as Frank Castle in fb2 to 1st chr app; also as Frank Castle in fb1 before Punmax #20, '12 fb, also as Lt. Castle in fb3 between Punmax #21, '12 fb & Punmax #20, '12 fb, also as Capt. Castle in fb4 between Pun #56, '08 fb & Pun #52, '08 fb, also bts as Frank Castle in fb5 between Pun #75/4, '09 fb & Punmax #21, '12 fb; last in Punmax #16, '11 fb, next in Pun #52, '08 fb)
VILLAINS: New York's foremost crime family inc boss, underboss, a half-dozen captains & consiglieri (all die); Rosa family (in fb1) inc Albert Rosa (boss, dies off-panel) & Vincent Rosa (dies)
OTHER CHARACTERS: Mr. Castle (Frank's father, WWII veteran, 1st, also in fb2, next in Punmax #20, '12 fb), Mrs. Castle (Frank's mother, 1st, next bts in Punmax #21, '12 fb), Michael Castle (mentioned, Frank's stillborn brother, would have been 3 years old), Father David (w Frank's poetry class inc Joseph; Sal Buvoli (Marine Pvt., corpse as Sgt. in fb3), Lauren Buvoli (Frank's friend & Sal's sister, commits suicide), Tony Buvoli (Sal's father), Angie Buvoli (Sal's mother, voice only), Sue Carmenelli (Lauren's friend, commits suicide), Tim Donegan (neighborhood kid), Kate Donegan (mentioned, Tim's sister, impregnated by Vincent Rosa), Terry Cooley (mentioned, paralyzed in construction accident), Henry Tulley (mentioned, went with Mr. Castle to see Albert Rosa), 3-Star General (bts in fb4, captured), Marines (in fb3, some as corpses), museum patrons & guard; Brooklyn Navy Yard security, construction workers, paramedics, police, bully (all in fb1), bystanders (others in fb1, others voice only in fb5), doctors (voice only in fb5), tiger (in fb4, others in fb2, also in Frank's thoughts)
LOCATIONS/ITEMS: Brooklyn inc Navy Yard, Castle home, Buvoli home, Father David's church, Carmine's Ristorante, Maxie's Diner & Washington Cemetery; New York inc American Museum of Natural History, Vietnam (all in fb1), Bronx Zoo (in fb2), Ferrara's Ristorante / Mr. Castle's gun, Sal's gasoline, Lt. Castle's rifle, helicopters (all in fb1), Punisher's sniper rifle
FLASHBACKS: Brooklyn, 1960: Ten year old Frank Castle sees a man burned alive at the Brooklyn Navy Yard. He later goes to Father David's poetry class with Lauren Buvoli. Afterward, they see Lauren's friend Sue Carmenelli commit suicide. He overhears his parents wonder if Vincent Rosa got Sue pregnant. Frank asks Lauren if she knows Vincent, but she changes the subject and they continue on to the museum. Later, Frank saves Tim Donegan from a bully and asks Tim what happened between Tim's sister Kate and Vincent Rosa. Frank begins to realize that Vincent is getting girls pregnant and several of them are killing themselves, and worries about Lauren. After she runs out of poetry class Frank follows her home, but he's too late; she's already slit her wrists. Later, Frank overhears his mother say that the Rosa family imposes their wills on others and don't care what happens to anyone else. That night Frank takes his father's gun and follows Vincent Rosa, only to see Lauren's brother Sal ambush Vincent. Sal drags Vincent into Washington Cemetery and sets Vincent on fire (1). Frank and his father visit the Bronx Zoo (2). In Lt. Castle's first week in Vietnam, he sees that Sgt. Buvoli has died in combat (3). During Capt. Castle's second tour, on a mission to silence a captured three-star General, he sees a wild tiger (4). Frank survives his family's murder. Doctors tell Frank his children didn't suffer, but he knows his daughter died because the doctors tried to save his wife instead (5).
SYNOPSIS: Winter, 1976: Frank Castle realizes that people will blame Vietnam for what he's about to do. As he slaughters New York's foremost crime family he admits to himself they'll be right, but they won't know the full story. With his opening salvo in his war on crime fired, Frank Castle walks away as the Punisher.
NOTE: Frank's poetry class discusses "the Tyger" by William Blake. It was rumored in Born #1, '03 that Frank assassinated a General; he's on a mission to do just that here. Punmax #16, '11 fb reveals Nick Fury gave Frank the names of New York's foremost crime family.

PUNISHER #31 (May 2006)

"Barracuda Part One" (22 pages)

CREDITS: Garth Ennis (writer), Goran Parlov (art), Virtual Calligraphy's Randy Gentile (letters), Giulia Brusco (colors), Cory Sedlmeier (assoc editor), Axel Alonso (editor), Tim Bradstreet (c art)
FEATURE CHARACTER: Punisher (also as Lt. Joseph D. Carson, also in fb1 between Pun #30, '06 & Pun #32, '06; during Pun #36, '06)
VILLAINS: Harry Ebbing (Dynaco CEO), Dermot Leary (formerly O'Leary, Dynaco board member), Enrique (drug dealer, dies) (all 1st but chr last in Pun #32, '06 fb), Barracuda (mercenary, 1st but chr last in Barracuda #2, '07 fb), Sgt. Billy Lacurda (crooked cop, also in fb2), Alice Ebbing (Harry's wife, 1st) (all in fb1)
OTHER CHARACTERS: Si Stephens (former Dynaco board member), Enrique's men (corpses) (both 1st but chr last in Pun #32, '06 fb), Barracuda's crack whore (1st), reporters (others in fb2) inc Brett David & John (both on TV); police (others in fb2) inc Captain Art Carlin (63rd precinct CO, on TV); Dynaco board members & party guests, diner staff & patrons, criminals, fire fighters, taxi driver, bystanders (all in fb1), Dynaco investors (corpses, during Pun #36, '06), sharks, seagulls
LOCATIONS/ITEMS: New York inc Enrique's apartment, diner & 63rd police precinct w/holding cells; Dynaco building inc Harry's office (all in fb1); Gulf of Mexico / Punisher's shotgun, knife, white phosphorous grenades, fake police badge & ID; Enrique's cocaine (destroyed) & Uzi; Alice's cocaine, Barracuda's crack pipe, Lacurda's revolver, police guns (all in fb1), Barracuda (Barracuda's boat, also in fb1)
FLASHBACKS: Punisher kills a cocaine dealer and is surprised to find a naked man tied up in the bathroom. As Punisher destroys the cocaine the man asks for protection. Punisher tells him to talk to the arriving police and leaves. In Miami at a Dynaco company celebration, Dermot Leary tells CEO Harry Ebbing that Si Stephens was going to tell the FBI about their upcoming deal. Dermot had his cocaine supplier Enrique take care of Si, but the Punisher killed Enrique and now Stephens is in police custody. Harry calls in a favor to clean up the mess. Punisher sees on the news that Si is being held at the sixty-third police precinct, and watches the crooked Billy Lacurda enter the building. Suspecting mob involvement, Punisher poses as a police lieutenant and enters the sixty-third precinct in time to stop Lacurda from killing Stephens. Punisher sets a small fire to cover their escape. Ebbing learns that Si is now with Punisher and contacts Barracuda, the only man he knows that may be able to handle the Punisher (1). Famous police officer Billy Lacurda is disgraced when his mob connections are revealed (2).
SYNOPSIS: In the Gulf of Mexico, Punisher watches as sharks eat the Dynaco investors.
NOTE: Pun #32, '06 names the Dynaco company and reveals Dermot's former and current surnames.

PUNISHER #32 (June 2006)

"Barracuda Part Two" (22 pages)

CREDITS: Garth Ennis (writer), Goran Parlov (art), Virtual Calligraphy's Randy Gentile (letters), Giulia Brusco (colors), Cory Sedlmeier (assoc editor), Axel Alonso (editor), Tim Bradstreet (c art)
FEATURE CHARACTER: Punisher (also as Antony Delfini)
VILLAINS: Harry Ebbing, Dermot Leary, Enrique & his men (all in fb to 1st chr app before Pun #31, '06), Barracuda (also in symbolic image), Horace (drug dealer, 1st) & his men (die); Alice Ebbing
OTHER CHARACTERS: Si Stephens (also in fb to 1st chr app before Pun #31, '06), Barracuda's crack whore, snake (both die), Dynaco board members (also in fb) & their wives, strippers (in fb), Frank's Favorite Diner staff & patrons, airport employees & commuters, bystanders
LOCATIONS/ITEMS: Dynaco building, strip club, restaurant (all in fb), New York inc "Frank's Favorite Diner," Punisher's safehouse & airport; ski lodge inc Alice's room / Dermot's cocaine, Enrique's Uzi & his men's guns (all in fb), Punisher's fake driver's license, assault rifles, Uzis & rocket launcher; Barracuda's M60 & crack pipe; commercial jet, Barracuda
FLASHBACK: Harry Ebbing is hired as CEO for Dynaco, an energy company, and streamlines the company by firing ninety percent of the employees and turns the remaining board members into a team that works and celebrates together. Dynaco becomes successful when they base their accounts on expected profits instead of actual profits. Harry takes board member Dermot O'Leary on as a protégé and convinces Dermot to change his last name to Leary. Dermot proposes a plan to surreptitiously cut power to Florida, creating an energy demand that will generate profit for Dynaco. Si Stephens objects and threatens to tell the FBI. Dermot sends his cocaine supplier Enrique to kill Stephens.
SYNOPSIS: Barracuda's prostitute smokes too much crack and runs outside only for a snake to bite her. Barracuda kills the snake, sees the woman is already dead, and leaves. At a Dynaco celebration, Harry's wife Alice seduces Dermot. Si Stephens tells Punisher that Dynaco is planning to cut power to Florida. Barracuda finds Horace, a drug dealer who owes the mercenary money, kills Horace's men and throws Horace into his car's trunk. Si admits that after his ordeal he won't tell the FBI about Dynaco's plan. Punisher takes a commercial flight to Florida to make Ebbing rethink Dynaco's strategy.

PUNISHER #33 (July 2006)

"Barracuda Part Three" (22 pages)

CREDITS: Garth Ennis (writer), Goran Parlov (art), Virtual Calligraphy's Randy Gentile (letters), Giulia Brusco (colors), Cory Sedlmeier (assoc editor), Axel Alonso (editor), Tim Bradstreet (c art)
FEATURE CHARACTER: Punisher
VILLAINS: Barracuda, Harry Ebbing, Dermot Leary, Alice Ebbing, Horace
OTHER CHARACTERS: Si Stephens, taxi driver (dies), Chromium bartender & patrons, airport commuters, bystanders, sharks
LOCATIONS/ITEMS: Miami inc airport, Chromium (bar), beach & Dynaco building w/Harry's office; Barracuda's shack, Gulf of Mexico / Barracuda's rope, harpoons, hatchet, barbed wire & butterfly knife; Punisher's knife, Dynaco jet, Barracuda
SYNOPSIS: Harry Ebbing calls Barracuda and stops the mercenary from taking a commercial flight to New York; he's learned the Punisher is coming to Miami. Already at the airport, Barracuda sees Punisher and follows the vigilante. Barracuda runs Punisher's taxi off the road and Punisher is knocked unconscious. Alice Ebbing and Dermot Leary continue their affair. Punisher wakes up in

Barracuda's trunk and attacks Barracuda when the trunk is opened. Punisher stabs Barracuda's eye and cuts off some of his fingers. Alice proposes that she and Dermot steal Harry's money and run away together. Punisher fails to strangle Barracuda with barbed wire and the mercenary overpowers Punisher. Harry doesn't notice that Dermot is acting nervously when the CEO reveals that Si Stephens is back; Si told Harry that the Punisher was heading for Miami. Barracuda sails out into the ocean with his two prisoners, cuts Horace's throat and tosses the drug dealer into the water. With Horace's blood attracting sharks, Barracuda throws Punisher into the water.

PUNISHER #34 (August 2006)

"Barracuda Part 4" (22 pages)

CREDITS: Garth Ennis (writer), Goran Parlov (art), Virtual Calligraphy's Randy Gentile (letters), Giulia Brusco (colors), Cory Sedlmeier (assoc editor), Axel Alonso (editor), Tim Bradstreet (c art)
FEATURE CHARACTER: Punisher
VILLAINS: Barracuda, Harry Ebbing, Dermot Leary, Alice Ebbing, Horace (dies)
OTHER CHARACTERS: Si Stephens, diner waitress & patrons, sharks
LOCATIONS/ITEMS: Dynaco building inc Harry's office & Alice's room; diner, Barracuda's shack, Gulf of Mexico / Barracuda's rope, shotgun & machete; Barracuda
SYNOPSIS: As a shark bites off Horace's legs Punisher surfaces for air. Barracuda shoots at Punisher, forcing the vigilante to dive back underwater. Punisher is surprised to see that Horace is still alive. Si Stephens apologizes to Harry Ebbing and Harry forgives Si. Dermot Leary is upset that Harry is letting Si back into the team, but Harry shuts Dermot up by smacking him. Punisher uses Horace as a decoy by positioning the shark between himself and Barracuda. Barracuda thinks Punisher is eaten instead of Horace. Barracuda sails away and Punisher grabs the boat unseen. Harry tells Dermot and Si that Barracuda is coming to work as security for him, and that he met Barracuda in prison when he was convicted of insider trading. Punisher passes out in front of Barracuda's shack. Alice and Dermot continue their affair and agree to move forward with their plan, unaware that Barracuda is outside the room with a machete.

PUNISHER #35 (September 2006)

"Barracuda Part 5" (22 pages)

CREDITS: Garth Ennis (writer), Goran Parlov (art), Virtual Calligraphy's Randy Gentile (letters), Giulia Brusco (colors), Cory Sedlmeier (assoc editor), Alex Alonso (editor), Tim Bradstreet (c art)
FEATURE CHARACTER: Punisher
VILLAINS: Barracuda, Harry Ebbing, Dermot Leary, Alice Ebbing
OTHER CHARACTERS: Si Stephens (dies), Harry's secretary (1st), Dynaco board members, security, yacht Captain & investors, diner staff & patrons, reporters, cameramen, seagulls
LOCATIONS/ITEMS: Miami inc diner & Dynaco building w/Harry's office, Alice's room & bathroom; Barracuda's shack, Gulf of Mexico / Barracuda's fingers (destroyed), scuba gear, machete, assault rifles, rocket launchers & grenades; Evelyn (Harry's rented yacht), Dynaco helicopters, Barracuda
SYNOPSIS: Barracuda lets Dermot Leary and Alice Ebbing know he's there. They offer to pay Barracuda whatever he wants so they aren't killed and Harry doesn't find out about their affair. Punisher wakes up and stumbles into Barracuda's shack. While eating pancakes, Barracuda asks what the plan they were talking about is. Alice explains they're going to release proof to the media that Dynaco will black out Florida, Harry will be held responsible and Dermot will ensure Dynaco won't suffer any repercussions. Punisher gets some weapons from Barracuda's shack and feeds Barracuda's severed fingers to seagulls. Harry is surprised when Barracuda tells him Alice hasn't been cheating because Harry usually has Alice followed and she cheats all the time. Si Stephens walks in on Alice and Dermot and in a fit of rage, Dermot kills Si. Dermot and Alice call Barracuda to dispose of the corpse. The Dynaco investors meeting begins on a rented yacht where Alice tells Dermot they're going to have to kill Barracuda; he knows too much. Punisher swims away from the rented yacht and follows in Barracuda's boat. Harry is surprised to see reporters waiting to talk to him.

PUNISHER #36 (October 2006)

"Barracuda Part 6" (22 pages)

CREDITS: Garth Ennis (writer), Goran Parlov (art), Virtual Calligraphy's Randy Gentile (letters), Giulia Brusco (colors), Daniel Ketchum (asst editor), Cory Sedlmeier (assoc editor), Axel Alonso (editor), Tim Bradstreet (c art)
FEATURE CHARACTER: Punisher (also in Pun #31, '06)
VILLAINS: Harry Ebbing, Dermot Leary, Alice Ebbing (all die), Barracuda (next in Barracuda #1, '07)
OTHER CHARACTERS: Dynaco investors (some also in Pun #31, '06), board members, security, yacht Captain (all die) & helicopter pilot; Evelyn bartender (dies), Harry's secretary, reporters, cameramen, fish, sharks; Mandy Schuster (mentioned, in Dynaco's legal team)
LOCATIONS/ITEMS: Dynaco building, Gulf of Mexico / Punisher's bombs & shotgun; Dermot's wrench, Dynaco security's guns, Dynaco helicopter, Barracuda, Evelyn
SYNOPSIS: Harry Ebbing runs from reporters asking about the planned Florida power blackout and escapes by helicopter. The Dynaco investors see this on the news and demand to talk to Dermot Leary. Alice Ebbing distracts Barracuda while Dermot smashes Barracuda's head with a wrench. Dermot doesn't approve of how Alice distracted Barracuda and drags her back in the boat after they dump Barracuda overboard. Alice answers Dermot's phone when Harry calls and tells Harry about the affair they're currently actively engaged in. Dermot finds a bomb on the boat and Harry jumps out of the helicopter. Dermot assures the Dynaco investors that Harry was acting alone and Dynaco won't be held responsible, but a second bomb detonates and stops the boat. Harry calls and demands to talk to Ebbing. Dermot answers and makes it clear that Punisher can't kill a corporation, and even if Dynaco had blacked out Florida no one would care; anyone that matters would have made money from it. Barracuda returns and announces the first bomb is armed, so Punisher detonates it. A shark bites Alice in half and Punisher shoots Dermot and Barracuda. Punisher watches as sharks eat the Dynaco investors and leaves.

PUNISHER #37 (November 2006)

"Man of Stone Part One" (22 pages)

CREDITS: Garth Ennis (writer), Leandro Fernández (art), Virtual Calligraphy's Randy Gentile (letters), Dan Brown (colors), Daniel Ketchum (asst editor), Axel Alonso (editor), Tim Bradstreet (c art)
FEATURE CHARACTER: Punisher (also in Pun #43, '07 fb)
SUPPORTING CAST: Kathryn O'Brien (last in Pun #24, '05)
VILLAINS: John James Toomey (crack dealer, 1st but chr last in Pun #47, '07 fb, also in Pun #43, '07 fb) & his men (1 also in Pun #43, '07 fb) inc Earl (1st, also in Pun #43, '07 fb) & Dingo (all die), Gen. Zakharov (last in Pun #18, '05), Captain Viktor L. Dolnovich (Zakharov's enforcer) & his Black Sea Marines (both 1st), William Rawlins (last in Pun #24, '05), Alex Rastovich (Russian mobster, dies, see NOTE), Mohamad Sahar (Taliban member, dies), other Taliban member (both 1st but chr last in Pun #40, '07 fb) & his 2 bodyguards
OTHER CHARACTERS: Yorkie Mitchell (bts, commanding Special Air Service unit, last in Pun #12, '04) & his SAS unit inc Gaz & Johnny, Sahar's 12 years old wife, Afghan bystanders, seagulls; Jawan Arefi, Walli Homayoun, Abdul Tallosh (prev 3 mentioned, Taliban members, killed by O'Brien)
LOCATIONS/ITEMS: Russian tavern, Toomey's safehouse, Coney Island inc boardwalk, Cyclone & Ferris Wheel; Afghanistan inc Kabul & Sahar's estate / Punisher's razor & gun; Toomey & his men's guns, Dolnovich's knife, O'Brien's gun w/silencer, bodyguards' AK-47s, SAS units' guns & zip tie restraint
SYNOPSIS: Rawlins meets with a Russian to sell some information and is shocked to see the buyer is General Zakharov. Elsewhere, Punisher has allowed crack dealer John James Toomey to capture him. Toomey decides to claim a Russian bounty on Punisher, rather than kill the vigilante. Punisher frees himself and kills Toomey and his men. After brief torture, Rawlins reveals he put together the terrorist team that attacked Moscow to cover for the Punisher's Suhdek missile silo attack. To stop Zakharov from killing him, Rawlins offers a way to use O'Brien to lure the Punisher to them, so Zakharov can finally bring proof to Moscow about America's involvement in the Suhdek missile silo attack. In Afghanistan, O'Brien kills another Taliban member that raped her ten years ago. Punisher confronts Leon Rastovich, the Russian who put a bounty on Punisher for killing his cousin Leon. Leon reveals he was forced to drop the bounty by someone who is looking for O'Brien in Afghanistan. O'Brien prepares to kill her next target, but a British SAS unit stops her.
NOTE: Dolnovich's 1st name & middle initial are revealed in Pun #41, '07. Gaz & Johnny are named in Pun #38, '06. Alex's bounty on Punisher is fifty thousand dollars; his cousin Leon was killed by Punisher in Pun #13, '05.

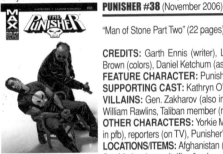

PUNISHER #38 (November 2006)

"Man of Stone Part Two" (22 pages)

CREDITS: Garth Ennis (writer), Leandro Fernández (art), Virtual Calligraphy's Randy Gentile (letters), Dan Brown (colors), Daniel Ketchum (asst editor), Axel Alonso (editor), Tim Bradstreet (c art)
FEATURE CHARACTER: Punisher
SUPPORTING CAST: Kathryn O'Brien (also in pfb)
VILLAINS: Gen. Zakharov (also in photo), Capt. Dolnovich (both also on TV) & his Black Sea Marines (8 die), William Rawlins, Taliban member (next in Pun #42, '07) & his 2 bodyguards (all in pfb)
OTHER CHARACTERS: Yorkie Mitchell (also in pfb) & his SAS unit inc Gaz & Johnny, Afghan bystanders (both in pfb), reporters (on TV), Punisher's military contacts (mentioned, Punisher called them, see NOTE)
LOCATIONS/ITEMS: Afghanistan (also in pfb) inc Kabul & SAS camp (both in pfb); Punisher's safehouse / Black Sea Marines' assault rifles & sub-machine guns, SAS unit's sub-machine guns, zip tie restraint & guns, bodyguards' AK-47s (all in pfb), Yorkie's gun & knife (both also in pfb); Punisher's assault rifles, grenades, sub-machine gun, guns & fake passport
FLASHBACK: Captain Dolnovich, his Black Sea Marines and Rawlins attack the SAS unit holding O'Brien. A firefight ensues and O'Brien spots Rawlins. The Russians retreat after taking losses. Zakharov threatens to kill Rawlins unless he comes up with a new plan. At the SAS camp, Yorkie Mitchell receives orders to kill O'Brien, and to kill Rawlins if seen again. Rawlins suggests that since they now can't use O'Brien as bait for the Punisher, they use Zakharov. If Zakharov allows himself to be spotted and filmed in Kabul, stating that he's looking for a comrade from Suhdek, Punisher will come to Afghanistan. Zakharov decides it's worth the risk of Moscow discovering he's in Afghanistan when he's not supposed to be. Yorkie prepares to execute O'Brien in the middle of nowhere when his phone rings (p).
SYNOPSIS: After calling several of his military contacts looking for a lead on O'Brien and having no luck, Punisher recalls a report about SAS involvement in Afghanistan and contacts Yorkie. After a brief argument, Yorkie agrees to free O'Brien and drives her into Kabul with a plan to make it look like she escaped. Punisher checks the news and learns Zakharov is in Kabul. Punisher prepares to leave for Afghanistan, realizing he's heading into a trap.
NOTE: Punisher's military contacts, of which there are at least twenty seven, include a Sergeant who is now a Colonel and a Captain who now runs the sniper school at Fort Bragg, both Vietnam veterans.

PUNISHER #39 (December 2006)

"Man of Stone Part Three" (22 pages)

CREDITS: Garth Ennis (writer), Leandro Fernández (art), Virtual Calligraphy's Randy Gentile (letters), Dan Brown (colors), Daniel Ketchum (asst editor), Axel Alonso (editor), Tim Bradstreet (c art)
FEATURE CHARACTER: Punisher (also as Patrick Hicks in pfb; next in Pun #54, '08 fb)
SUPPORTING CAST: Kathryn O'Brien (also in pfb; chr next in Pun #54, '08 fb)
VILLAINS: Gen. Zakharov (also in fb to 1st chr app before Pun #15, '05), Capt. Dolnovich, William Rawlins (all in pfb), Russian Marines inc a Captain (in fb)
OTHER CHARACTERS: Yorkie Mitchell (in pfb, next in Pun #42, '07) & his SAS unit inc Gaz & Johnny (in pfb), Robert Varick (writer, in pfb, 1st), plane passengers (in pfb), Mujahedeen & their families (both in fb, die), donkey (in pfb), dogs
LOCATIONS/ITEMS: Afghanistan (also in pfb) inc Zakharov's hangar, SAS camp, US Army ammunition depot & Kabul w/Kabul International Airport & Kabul Hilton (all in pfb), village north of Kandahar (in fb) / Zakharov's gunship & helicopter; US Army assault rifles, M60s, grenades & stinger launcher; Antonov (cargo plane), Yorkie's note (all in pfb), Russian helicopters & assault rifles, Mujahedeen AK-47s, rifles & rocket launchers (prev 5 in fb)

FLASHBACKS: On a cargo plane to Afghanistan, Punisher meets Robert Varick, who wrote a book about Zakharov. Outside Kabul, Yorkie leaves O'Brien with the jeep and a note for Punisher, giving her a time a place to meet with Punisher. Zakharov checks over his incoming weapons and supplies. Rawlins asks Zakharov for a job. Varick tells Punisher Zakharov's history and reveals he wants to gather enough evidence to have Zakharov indicted as a war criminal. Zakharov refuses Rawlins' request, knowing Rawlins would eventually betray him. Punisher advises Varick to go home and meets O'Brien at the Kabul Hilton. They use a key-code supplied by Yorkie to access a US army weapons depot and stock up before heading to the mountains for a tactical position (p). 1987: General Zakharov leads Russian Marines into the mountains north of Kandahar to stop Mujahedeen fighters from interdicting Russian supply lines. The Russian Marines slaughter the fighters' families and other villagers until the Mujahedeen open fire, revealing their position. During the ensuing firefight the Mujahedeen are killed and Zakharov doesn't move despite the flying artillery, earning his nickname "Man of Stone." He will do the same in six more villages.

SYNOPSIS: While making camp, Punisher and O'Brien begin to keep each other warm through physical activity.

PUNISHER #40 (January 2007)

"Man of Stone Part Four" (22 pages)

CREDITS: Garth Ennis (writer), Leandro Fernández (art), Virtual Calligraphy's Randy Gentile (letters), Dan Brown (colors), Daniel Ketchum (asst editor), Axel Alonso (editor), Tim Bradstreet (c art)
FEATURE CHARACTER: Punisher
SUPPORTING CAST: Kathryn O'Brien (also in fb to 1st chr app before Pun #1, '04; chr last in Pun #54, '08 fb)
VILLAINS: Mohamad Sahar, Taliban member (both in fb to 1st chr app before Pun #37, '06), other Taliban member (in fb, 1st, next in Pun #42, '07), Jawan Arefi, Walli Homayoun, Abdul Tallosh (prev 3 in fb), Gen. Zakharov, Capt. Dolnovich & his Black Sea Marines (die), William Rawlins (also in fb to 1st chr app before Pun #13, '05), Russian military pilots (some die)
OTHER CHARACTERS: Robert Varick (dies), Huey pilot (bts, ordered Rawlins' cargo dropped) & gunner (both in fb)
LOCATIONS/ITEMS: Afghanistan (also in fb) inc Zakharov's hangar & Hazar (mountain village) / Taliban's AK-47s & stinger launcher, Rawlins' heroin & knife, Huey w/machine gun (all in fb), Punisher's assault rifle & Claymore mines; O'Brien's assault rifle, cover blanket & stinger launcher; Zakharov's helicopter w/MOAB fuel-air missile & gunship w/rocket launchers (destroyed); Black Sea Marines' assault rifles, Dolnovich's machete

FLASHBACK: 1996: On their honeymoon, Rawlins tosses O'Brien out of a helicopter when attacked by the Taliban. He had stolen heroin from the Taliban and they want it back. O'Brien lands in a river and the pursuing Taliban capture and rape her.

SYNOPSIS: Zakharov has Robert Varick captured and killed. Meanwhile, Punisher and O'Brien set up their trap for Zakharov while O'Brien fills Punisher in on her history with Rawlins. When she starts to talk about her other failed relationships, Punisher makes it clear he's not interested in any long term commitments. Zakharov and his men move into the mountains, destroying Punisher's jeep when they spot it. They find Punisher waiting for them. When Punisher runs to the mountains for cover, O'Brien fires a stinger missile at Zakharov's gunship, destroying it. Punisher and O'Brien lay down suppressing fire to herd the Black Sea Marines into the mountains for cover. The Black Sea Marines retreat, only to be blown up by Claymore mines Punisher and O'Brien had set up earlier. Zakharov contacts Punisher and demands he surrender in a nearby village, or he'll bomb the village. Punisher and O'Brien begin the trek to the village, hoping they can come up with a plan on the way. Later, Zakharov finds an unarmed Punisher waiting in the village.

PUNISHER #41 (January 2007)

"Man of Stone Part Five" (22 pages)

CREDITS: Garth Ennis (writer), Leandro Fernández (art), Virtual Calligraphy's Randy Gentile (letters), Dan Brown, Giulia Brusco (colors), Daniel Ketchum (asst editor), Axel Alonso (editor), Tim Bradstreet (c art)
FEATURE CHARACTER: Punisher
SUPPORTING CAST: Kathryn O'Brien (dies)
VILLAINS: Gen. Zakharov, Capt. Dolnovich, William Rawlins, Russian military pilot (dies)
OTHER CHARACTERS: Russian & Afghan soldiers (skeletal corpses), Dolnovich's wife & son (in photo), Hazar residents
LOCATIONS/ITEMS: Afghanistan inc Hazar / Punisher's razor, Zakharov's helicopter w/MOAB fuel-air missile (destroyed), gun & zip tie restraint; Dolnovich's M60, machete & wallet; Rawlins' knife, landmine

SYNOPSIS: Zakharov orders Rawlins to search Punisher before binding the vigilante and taking him onto their helicopter. O'Brien grabs onto the helicopter's landing gear unseen as it lifts off. Rawlins demands to know where O'Brien is and threatens to cut Punisher's eye. Dolnovich throws Rawlins aside. O'Brien disables the helicopter's missile launcher. Punisher uses a razor blade he hid under his skin to cut himself free and grabs Dolnovich's M60. Punisher fires at Zakharov but hits the pilots. Punisher and O'Brien safely jump away, but Rawlins tackles Zakharov and breaks the General's neck, paralyzing him. The helicopter crashes and explodes. Dolnovich fails to kill Rawlins when Rawlins slices open Dolnovich's throat. O'Brien wonders what she'll do with her life once Rawlins is dead. Punisher reminds her he'll have nothing to do with it. An explosion rips O'Brien in half; she accidentally stepped on a landmine. Kathryn tells Frank there are two things he can do for her, one of which is kill Rawlins. Rawlins tells Dolnovich he's going to kill Dolnovich's wife and son. Frank holds Kathryn until she dies.

PUNISHER #42 (February 2007)

"Man of Stone Conclusion" (22 pages)

CREDITS: Garth Ennis (writer), Leandro Fernández (art), Virtual Calligraphy's Randy Gentile (letters), Dan Brown (colors), Daniel Ketchum (asst editor), Axel Alonso (editor), Tim Bradstreet (c art)
FEATURE CHARACTER: Punisher
VILLAINS: Gen. Zakharov, Capt. Dolnovich, William Rawlins, Taliban member (last in Pun #38, '06) & his 2 bodyguards, other Taliban member (last in Pun #40, '07 fb) (all die)
OTHER CHARACTERS: Yorkie Mitchell (last in Pun #39, '06, next in Pun #50, '07) & his SAS unit inc Gaz & Johnny, Russian & Afghan soldiers (both skeletal corpses), Kabul airport commuters & security
LOCATIONS/ITEMS: Afghanistan inc SAS camp & Kabul w/Kabul International Airport w/bathroom / Punisher's AK-47 & machete, SAS unit's helicopters & assault rifles; Rawlins' knife, Yorkie's Johnnie Walker, bodyguards'

AK-47s, airport security's assault rifles, wrecked helicopters, jets & tanks

SYNOPSIS: Punisher finds Dolnovich and the paralyzed Zakharov as Rawlins makes his way across the Afghani desert. Zakharov tells Punisher he has a week before Rawlins is unreachable; Rawlins took Dolnovich's papers and will fly to Moscow in seven days. Dolnovich dies and Punisher puts Zakharov out of his misery by smashing the General's head in. Punisher walks the desert for four days before finding an SAS unit and getting himself arrested. Punisher is taken to Yorkie, who reveals he's been relieved of command for letting O'Brien escape. Yorkie gives Punisher the file with the names of the remaining Taliban members O'Brien was planning to kill. They talk about old times over Scotch before Punisher says goodbye. Punisher kills the Taliban members before tracking down Rawlins. With O'Brien's first request done, being with her so she didn't take her last breath alone, Punisher corners Rawlins in a Kabul International Airport bathroom to complete her other request. Rawlins tries to cut Punisher's throat, but Punisher chops off Rawlins' hand. Rawlins asks to see O'Brien, hoping to make a deal with her. Punisher tells Rawlins that she's dead, just as Frank was starting to like her. Rawlins realizes he's going to die.

NOTE: Yorkie mentions he met Frank when Castle saved him from torture by North Vietnamese soldiers.

PUNISHER #43 (March 2007)

"Widowmaker Part 1" (22 pages)

CREDITS: Garth Ennis (writer), Lan Medina (pencils), Bill Reinhold (inks), Virtual Calligraphy's Randy Gentile (letters), Raul Treviño (colors), Daniel Ketchum (asst editor), Axel Alonso (editor), Tim Bradstreet (c art)

FEATURE CHARACTER: Punisher (also in photo, also bts in fb2 between Pun #47, '07 fb & fb4, also off-panel in fb4 between fb2 & Pun #75/4, '09 fb, also in fb5 during Pun #1, '04, also off-panel in fb3 during Pun #6, '04, also in fb1 during Pun #37, '06)

VILLAINS: Annabella Gorrini (Massimo Cesare's granddaughter, last bts in Pun #1, '04), Lorraine Zucca (also in fb2), Barbara "Barbi" Barrucci, Bonnie De Angelo, Shauna Toomey (all mob widows, also in photos, 1st but chr last in Pun #47, '07 fb); Nicky Cavella, Larry Barrucci (both in fb3 during Pun #6, '04), John James Toomey & his man (both in fb1 during Pun #37, '06), Artie De Angelo & other mobsters (in fb4), Cesare family members (in fb5), Paulie Zucca (off-panel) & Joe Consiglio's other mafia family members (both in fb2)

OTHER CHARACTERS: Jennifer "Jenny" Cesare (Annabella's sister & mob widow, 1st but chr last in Pun #47, '07 fb), John Richey (child porn distributor, corpse); nightclub bartender & patrons, taxi driver, doctor, nurses (both in fb2)

LOCATIONS/ITEMS: Gorrini estate, New York inc nightclub, Jenny's safehouse & Jenny's date's apartment / Toomey's gun, Barrucci's gun, Cavella's gun, Punisher's M60, gun (all in rfb) & pistol, Jenny's gun, Shauna's razor

FLASHBACKS: Punisher shoots John James Toomey (1). After Punisher attacked Joe Consiglio's card game, Lorraine Zucca rushes to the hospital bedside of her husband Paulie, who was shot in the face (2). Punisher shoots Larry Barrucci while Nicky Cavella escapes (3). Punisher uses a flamethrower to set Artie De Angelo and other mobsters on fire (4). Punisher slaughters the Cesare family (5).

SYNOPSIS: Punisher kills a child porn distributor. Meanwhile, five widows of mobsters, Annabella Gorrini, Barbi Barrucci, Bonnie De Angelo, Lorraine Zucca and Shauna Toomey, meet to plot revenge against the Punisher, who killed their husbands. Barbi questions why Shauna is present. In a nightclub, a woman picks up a man for casual sex. Shauna cuts off Barbi's necklace with a razor, declaring her husband was John James Toomey and that she has as much right to be present as the others. Annabella tells the others that Shauna took care of a problem for them a while back, but they can't bear to say the problem's name out loud. At the man's apartment, the woman is unsatisfied with his performance and beats his face bloody. Annabella announces they can't rely on the mob; they have to kill the Punisher themselves. Later, the woman removes makeup covering old scars and a padded bra and plots revenge against the mob widows.

NOTE: John Richey is named in Pun #44, '07. Jenny Cesare is named in Pun #44, '07.

PUNISHER #44 (March 2007)

"Widowmaker Part Two" (22 pages)

CREDITS: Garth Ennis (writer), Lan Medina (pencils), Bill Reinhold (inks), Virtual Calligraphy's Randy Gentile (letters), Raul Treviño (colors), Daniel Ketchum (asst editor), Axel Alonso (editor), Tim Bradstreet (c art)

FEATURE CHARACTER: Punisher (also in photo)

VILLAINS: Annabella Gorrini, Barbi Barrucci, Bonnie De Angelo, Lorraine Zucca, Shauna Toomey; Carl & Ann Larsen (married child pornographers, both die), teenage school shooter (in pfb, dies), Bone (gun dealer, bts, supplying mob widows with weapons)

OTHER CHARACTERS: Jenny Cesare, Detective Paul Budiansky (1st, also in pfb, next in Pun #46, '07), Gina Budiansky (Paul's wife, nurse, 1st, next in Pun #47, '07), Ms. Gordon (police psychologist & writer), Pete Baron (former high school classmate of Jenny Cesare), school students & teachers (some as corpses), reporters, cameramen, bystanders (prev 4 in pfb), police (bts, en route to Larsen home, others in pfb), Carl & Ann's 3 children (2 boys & a girl), restaurant staff & patrons; Cristu Bulat (mentioned, corpse found near Indian Lake)

LOCATIONS/ITEMS: Larsen home inc basement; Gorrini estate, Budiansky home, New York inc Ms. Gordon's office, restaurant & school (in fb) / Punisher's pistol w/silencer, Shauna's guns inc MP5Ks & 12 gauge shotgun; Annabella's Punisher FBI file, Budiansky's gun, teenager's guns (both in fb)

FLASHBACK: Detective Paul Budiansky defies his police captain's orders and enters a school where an armed teenager is shooting and killing students and teachers before tactical arrives. Det. Budiansky kills the shooter (p).

SYNOPSIS: Punisher confronts Ann and Carl Larsen at their doorstep, revealing he knows they film pornography with their children. Punisher kills the parents in the basement while the children wait in the living room. Punisher calls social services and leaves. Det. Paul Budiansky meets with police psychologist Ms. Gordon. The mob widows look over the Punisher's FBI file until Annabella deduces that Barbi is illiterate. Shauna suggests Barbi can help them in a different fashion by giving their gun supplier a bonus. Ms. Gordon suggests the school shooting incident traumatized Paul, but the Detective states he's only been sent to her as a form of retribution by his police captain for disobeying orders. Jenny Cesare is recognized by a former high school classmate Pete Baron. She denies her identity and sends Pete away. Paul confesses to his wife Gina that he identifies with the Punisher. The mob widows decide to trap Punisher by setting up a fake human slavery racket and using Bonnie as bait. Jenny Cesare eavesdrops and plots against the widows.

PUNISHER #45 (May 2007)

"Widowmaker Part Three" (22 pages)

CREDITS: Garth Ennis (writer), Lan Medina (pencils), Bill Reinhold (inks), Virtual Calligraphy's Randy Gentile (letters), Raul Treviño (colors), Daniel Ketchum (asst editor), Axel Alonso (editor), Tim Bradstreet (c art)
FEATURE CHARACTER: Punisher
VILLAINS: Annabella Gorrini, Barbi Barrucci, Bonnie De Angelo, Lorraine Zucca, Shauna Toomey, Tony Pizzo (last in Pun #24, '05, dies) (all also in pfb) & his men inc Joey (die), Pat Migliorato (Reno crimelord, dies)
OTHER CHARACTERS: Jenny Cesare (in pfb); Angie Denunzio (mentioned, Tony Pizzo's girlfriend), Tim Gallo (mentioned, Angie's cousin)
LOCATIONS/ITEMS: Gorrini estate, New York inc Girgio's Café & Tony's motel room (all in pfb), Bronx inc Shauna's vacant house; forest / Punisher's rocket launcher, Claymore mines & M4 Carbine w/attached M203 grenade launcher; Tony's men's assault rifles, shotguns & Uzis; Shauna's guns inc MP5Ks & 12 gauge shotgun; Jenny's listening device (in pfb), Bonnie's bulletproof vests (also in pfb)
FLASHBACK: Jenny Cesare eavesdrops as the mob widows send Barbi to seduce rising mobster Tony Pizzo to find out about any upcoming events that the Punisher will likely attack. She learns that the remaining mafia in New York plan to make Pat Migliorato, a crime lord from Reno, the new mafia boss and when they're bringing him in. Later, the widows sneak Bonnie, disguised as a prostitute, into the trunk of Pizzo's car and cover her with bullet proof vests so she won't be killed n the inevitable crossfire. Jenny watches nearby (p).
SYNOPSIS: In the woods, Punisher ambushes Pat Migliorato's convoy, killing Migliorato, Tony Pizzo and his men. Bonnie emerges from the trunks of Tony's car and tells Punisher she was meant to be the entertainment for Migliorato's meeting. She explains that she's a victim of a sex slave operation. She guides Punisher to a house in the Bronx, but he begins to doubt the details of her story. Inside the house, the other four widows prepare to kill Punisher.
NOTE: Includes recap/credits page (1 page).

PUNISHER #46 (June 2007)

"Widowmaker Part Four" (22 pages)

CREDITS: Garth Ennis (writer), Lan Medina (pencils), Bill Reinhold (inks), Virtual Calligraphy's Randy Gentile (letters), Raul Treviño (colors), Daniel Ketchum (asst editor), Axel Alonso (editor), Tim Bradstreet (c art)
FEATURE CHARACTER: Punisher
VILLAINS: Bonnie De Angelo (dies), Annabella Gorrini, Barbi Barrucci, Lorraine Zucca, Shauna Toomey (all also in photos)
OTHER CHARACTERS: Jenny Cesare, Captain Carling (police captain, 1st, next in Pun #48, '07), Det. Budiansky (last in Pun #44, '07), police inc Detective Woods & Bobby
LOCATIONS/ITEMS: Bronx inc Shauna's abandoned house; Gorrini estate, Jenny's safehouse / Punisher's M4 Carbine w/attached M203 grenade launcher & gun; Jenny's gun & combat knife; Shauna's guns inc MP5Ks & 12 gauge shotgun
SYNOPSIS: Punisher decides too late not to attack the house in the Bronx; Shauna shoots him through the chest. Before Shauna can fire again, Bonnie starts kicking Punisher. Jenny Cesare arrives, disembowels Bonnie and picks up Punisher's machine gun. Jenny fires at the house, forcing the other widows to flee. Jenny escapes with Punisher as the police arrive. Det. Budiansky interrogates the widows and is suspicious of the widows' story about buying a house from Mrs. Toomey, but his captain releases the widows without waiting for Budiansky's background check to come through. At her safehouse, Jenny tends to Punisher's wounds, saying she's his biggest fan. Budiansky's captain is mortified when the detective tells the captain who he released. At the Gorrini estate, Annabella reveals she recognized her sister Jenny as the one who killed Bonnie. Shauna is outraged and insists she killed Jenny years ago. Punisher asks Jenny why she's helping him. Jenny thanks Punisher for killing her husband.
NOTE: Includes recap/credits page (1 page).

PUNISHER #47 (July 2007)

"Widowmaker Part Five" (22 pages)

CREDITS: Garth Ennis (writer), Lan Medina (pencils), Bill Reinhold (inks), Virtual Calligraphy's Randy Gentile (letters), Raul Treviño (colors), Daniel Ketchum (asst editor), Axel Alonso (editor), Tim Bradstreet (c art)
FEATURE CHARACTER: Punisher (also in fb between Punmax #20, '12 fb & Pun #43, '07 fb bts)
VILLAINS: Barbi Barrucci, Lorraine Zucca, Shauna Toomey (all also in fb to 1st chr app before Pun #43, '07), Annabella Gorrini (also in fb to 1st chr app before bts in Pun #1, '04) (all also in photos), Bonnie De Angelo (in fb to 1st chr app before Pun #37, '06), John James Toomey (in fb to 1st chr app before Pun #43, '07), Curtis Pinner (Toomey's thug, 1st, also in fb), Ronald (Curtis' partner, in fb, dies), Tim Buccato (Jenny's husband, in fb, dies), Dominic Gorrini (Annabella's husband, in fb), other mobsters (some as wedding guests, some as corpses) inc Jenny's various boyfriends (in fb)
OTHER CHARACTERS: Jenny Cesare (also as Jenny Buccato in fb to 1st chr app before Pun #43, '07), Gina Budiansky (last in Pun #44, '07), Det. Budiansky, police inc Bobby (bts, on phone), Jenny's wedding guests inc Jenny's father (Massimo Cesare's son) (in fb), seagulls (in fb); Stan (mentioned, Budiansky's partner, on vacation), Doctor Pomeroy (mentioned, Gina's boss)
LOCATIONS/ITEMS: Cancun, Galveston, Buccato home, wedding chapel, restaurants, bar (all in fb), Gorrini estate (also in fb), Budiansky home, Jenny's safehouse, Curtis' tenement / Punisher's shotgun, mobsters' guns, Shauna's coffee pot (all in fb)
FLASHBACK: Jenny enjoys the life of a Cesare woman, receiving jewelry and having flings with men in Cancun. Later, Jenny marries Tim Buccato, an up and coming Cesare family enforcer. On their wedding night, he beats and rapes her. He later starts bringing other men home to rape her while he watches. Jenny's sister Annabella continually reassures Jenny that things will improve. Annabella meets Shauna when their husbands start doing business together. Later, Punisher kills Tim in one of his assaults on the mafia. That night, Jenny learns that she has breast cancer. Believing that Tim infected her with his evil, Jenny tells Annabella she's sick of the mafia and will go to the FBI with what she knows. Shauna smashes Jenny with a coffee pot and tells Annabella the only way to keep Jenny quiet is to kill her. Shauna has her husband's

men Curtis and Ronald dispose of Jenny, but they crash their car and Ronald dies. Curtis throws Jenny out off a bridge. She lands on a train and wakes up in Galveston.

SYNOPSIS: Jenny tells Punisher that the mob widows are just as bad as the mob, and she plans to kill them. Shauna admits to the other widows she didn't kill Jenny herself; she had Curtis, one of her husband's men do it. Budiansky learns the dead woman in the Bronx is another mob widow. Shauna learns from Curtis that he didn't make sure Jenny was dead. Jenny tells Punisher that after her mastectomy and reconstructive surgery she learned self defense and how to handle weapons, and admits she occasionally picks up men and injures them when they can't satisfy her.

NOTE: Includes recap/credits page (1 page). Tim Buccato's surname is revealed in Pun #49, '07. Curtis' surname is revealed in Pun #48, '07.

PUNISHER #48 (August 2007)

"Widowmaker Part Six" (22 pages)

CREDITS: Garth Ennis (writer), Lan Medina (pencils), Bill Reinhold (inks), Virtual Calligraphy's Randy Gentile (letters), Raul Treviño (colors), Daniel Ketchum (asst editor), Axel Alonso (editor), Tim Bradstreet (c art)
FEATURE CHARACTER: Punisher
VILLAINS: Annabella Gorrini, Barbi Barrucci, Lorraine Zucca, Shauna Toomey (all also in photos), Curtis Pinner (dies)
OTHER CHARACTERS: Jenny Cesare (also as Punisher), Captain Carling (last in Pun #46, '07), Det. Budiansky, Gina Budiansky, police inc Lt. Miller & Bobby; hospital staff & patients, bystanders
LOCATIONS/ITEMS: Gorrini estate, Budiansky home, New York inc Jenny's safehouse & hospital / Jenny's gun, Budiansky's guns, Curtis' gun
SYNOPSIS: Det. Paul Budiansky questions Annabella, Barbi and Lorraine, who deny having known Bonnie. Budiansky tells them he knows they tried to kill the Punisher, and when he verifies that they did know Bonnie he'll return to arrest them. Punisher wakes up to see Jenny preparing to kill the widows. Shauna Toomey has Curtis follow Budiansky as she meets with the other widows. When they tell Shauna that Budiansky mentioned the Punisher, Shauna orders Curtis to kill the detective. Paul visits Gina at the hospital where Curtis shoots at them, wounding Gina. Paul kills Curtis, using almost all of his bullets. Gina survives but will need several months of therapy to recover. Captain Carling suspends Budiansky from active duty. Seeing on the news that Budiansky survived, the widows decide to leave the country. Barbi points out that Jenny is still looking for them. Paul learns that Curtis was an associate of John James Toomey and grabs his gun. Jenny Cesare dons Frank's skull shirt and leaves to kill the widows.

NOTE: Includes recap/credits page (1 page).

PUNISHER #49 (September 2007)

"Widowmaker Part Conclusion" (22 pages)

CREDITS: Garth Ennis (writer), Lan Medina (pencils), Bill Reinhold (inks), Virtual Calligraphy's Randy Gentile (letters), Raul Treviño (colors), Daniel Ketchum (asst editor), Axel Alonso (editor), Tim Bradstreet (c art)
FEATURE CHARACTER: Punisher (also in rfb, next in Pun Ann #1, '07)
VILLAINS: Annabella Gorrini, Barbi Barrucci, Lorraine Zucca, Shauna Toomey (all also in photos, die)
OTHER CHARACTERS: Jenny Cesare (also as Punisher, dies), Det. Budiansky (also on TV), Gina Budiansky, Captain Carling (voice only), Curtis Pinner (corpse on TV), police, paramedics, bystanders; Kathryn O'Brien (in rfb)
LOCATIONS/ITEMS: Gorrini estate, New York inc Jenny's safehouse, hospital; Afghanistan (in rfb) / Jenny's gun, handcuffs, rope & baseball bat; Budiansky's gun, Shauna's gun
FLASHBACK: Punisher stays with Kathryn O'Brien so she doesn't take her last breath alone (Pun #41, '07).
SYNOPSIS: Wearing Punisher's shirt, Jenny Cesare arrives at the Gorrini estate as the widows are packing to flee the country. Jenny shoots Barbi through the abdomen, shoots Lorraine in the chest and shoots Shauna in the face. She shoots Lorraine again and leaves with Annabella. Det. Budiansky arrives only for Jenny to run him off the road. He sees her license plate before noticing the dead widows. Frank Castle awakens handcuffed to the bed and sees a nude Jenny berating a bound Annabella for her complicity with the mafia. Jenny beats Annabella's face with a baseball bat until it's a pulpy mess. Budiansky gets Jenny's address from her license plate. With her vengeance complete, Jenny has sex with Frank then kills herself while on top of him. Frank frees himself and cleans up Jenny's body. Budiansky, determined to kill Annabella, confronts the departing Punisher. Frank asks Paul if he really wants to be like the Punisher. Later, Paul sits at his wife's hospital bed, telling her to get better so they can spend their lives together. Punisher watches as paramedics carry away Jenny's body, mourning the sad, strange creature she had become.

NOTE: Includes recap/credits page (1 page). Jenny's license plate number is KLD 723.

PUNISHER MAX ANNUAL #1 (November 2007)

"The Hunted" (36 pages)

CREDITS: Mike Benson (writer), Laurence Campbell (art), Virtual Calligraphy's Cory Petit (letters), Lee Loughridge (colors), Daniel Ketchum (asst editor), Axel Alonso (editor)
FEATURE CHARACTER: Punisher (also in pfb, next in Pun:FoN #1, '08, Pun #50, '07)
VILLAINS: Eddie Gands, Tommy "Mad-Dog" Schultz (crime lord enforcers, both also in pfb) & their crew (in pfb), Omar Gonzales (crime lord, also in pfb) & his guards inc Angel (all die), Marcello & his bodyguards (Eddie Gands' rival crime gang), Lorenzo (veterinarian & crime doctor)
OTHER CHARACTERS: Maggie Mae patrons inc Martha, slum tenant (voice only, dies) (all in pfb), Cathy (Eddie's abused ex-girlfriend, voice only), Samba bar patrons, 2 police officers, police dispatcher (voice only), drug addicts, strippers inc "Sugar" (Bunny), subway passengers, taxi driver, bystanders, rats, Eddie's parents (in photo), Omar's brother-in-law (mentioned, slumlord, Omar paid his debts to acquire slum tenement)

LOCATIONS/ITEMS: Lorenzo's Alphabet City Veterinary Clinic, Cathy's apartment building, Eddie's apartment, subway station, tenement (destroyed), Maggie Mae's bar (both in pfb), Omar's office (also in pfb) / Punisher's gun (also in pfb) & Eddie's gas (in pfb) & gun, Eddie's crew member's knife (in pfb), Omar's cocaine

FLASHBACK: Crimelord Omar Gonzalez sends Eddie Gands and his crew to burn down a recently-acquired slum tenement to drive out the remaining residents who refuse to leave. Eddie sets the building on fire by soaking rats in gas and lighting them, but a woman is trapped inside and is burned to death. Afterward, Eddie and his crew get drunk at a bar. When they leave Punisher attacks them. Only Eddie and a wounded Tommy "Mad-Dog" Schultz escape (p).

SYNOPSIS: Eddie takes Tommy to crime doctor Lorenzo, who operates on Tommy but declares he won't survive his wounds. Eddie heads back to Omar Gonzalez's office and asks Omar to hide him from the Punisher. Punisher attacks Omar's office and kills Omar and his guards. Only Eddie escapes. Eddie fails to seek shelter with his old girlfriend Cathy and with rival gang leader Marcello, but everyone turns him down. Eddie returns home, packs his bag and leaves, but spots Punisher following him. Punisher methodically chases Eddie throughout the city. Eddie tries to turn himself in to a couple of police officers by telling them he's a murderer being chased by the Punisher. The officers dismiss Eddie and drive away. Punisher arrives and shoots Eddie in the face.

PUNISHER #50 (October 2007)

"Long Cold Dark Part One" (34 pages)

CREDITS: Garth Ennis (writer), Howard Chaykin (art), Virtual Calligraphy's Cory Petit (letters), Studio F's Edgar Delgado (colors), Daniel Ketchum (asst editor), Axel Alonso (editor), Tim Bradstreet (c art)
FEATURE CHARACTER: Punisher (also in own dream, also as Frank Castle in fb between Pun #75/4, '09 fb & Pun #1, '04 fb)
SUPPORTING CAST: Maria Castle, Frank Castle, Jr., Lisa Castle (all in fb between Pun #75/4, '09 fb & Pun #1, '04 fb, also in Punisher's dream)
VILLAINS: Gen. Archer, Gen. Kent, Gen. Landers, Gen. Vertraeus, Gen. Vraciu (all last in Pun #18, '05), Gen. Farmington, Gen. Perino, Gen. Van Abst (prev 3 last in Pun #19, '05) (all bts, hired Barracuda to kill Punisher), Barracuda (also in rfb, also in pfb; last in Barracuda #5, '07), gangsters inc Powder Joe Perona (die)

OTHER CHARACTERS: Yorkie Mitchell (also in pfb, last in Pun #42, '07, dies), Angie Mitchell (Yorkie's wife, corpse, dies in pfb) (both also in photos), Sarah O'Brien (Frank & O'Brien's daughter, 1st), Jessie Castle (Frank Jr.'s wife), John Castle (Frank Jr.'s son), Tony (Lisa's husband), Tony & Lisa's son (prev 4 in Frank's dream, see NOTE), La Jollans inc preschoolers & daycare caregivers (one dies bts), police, Kathryn O'Brien (in rfb), Yorkie's fellow soldiers (in photos), 24 of Punisher's victims (corpses, bts, buried in Pocono Mountains)
LOCATIONS/ITEMS: Yorkie's home (also in pfb); New York inc Punisher's apartment, Castle family home (in Punisher's dream), Sheep's Meadow (in fb), Barracuda's tenement & hotel w/17th floor penthouse; Pocono Mountains inc Punisher's private land; La Jolla, CA inc La Jolla Daycare / Yorkie's gun (also in pfb), Barb's letter (see NOTE); Barracuda's gun, M-60, timed Claymore mines, shotgun & zip-line; Punisher's AK-47 assault rifle, M-16 rifle w/attached M-203 grenade launcher, Colt M1911 handgun & satchel charge; gangsters' guns, SWAT officer's rifle
FLASHBACKS: Kathryn O'Brien hikes through the mountains of Afghanistan (Pun #39, '06). Barracuda shoots Yorkie and prepares to shoot Angie (p). As the Castle family dies, Frank cradles his son.
SYNOPSIS: Barracuda raids Yorkie Mitchell's home in England for leverage against Frank Castle. Finding what he needs, Barracuda kills Yorkie. After waking from an idyllic dream wherein his family is still alive, Frank Castle travels to his private land in the Poconos for target practice. In La Jolla, Barracuda visits a daycare center from which a bloodcurdling scream erupts shortly thereafter. Weeks later, Punisher sets up an attack on a massive gathering of criminal bosses at a luxury hotel. The gangsters and Punisher soon realize that none of those present invited them. Barracuda arrives and guns the gangsters down. From his hiding place in the ceiling, Punisher notices explosive charges and breaks cover just as the charges detonate. Through the gunfire, Punisher grabs one of the gangsters as a human shield and attempts escape through the service entrance, but a Claymore mine outside vaporizes the hostage and severely injures Punisher. Barracuda knocks Punisher out, then zip-lines the pair of them away as the police arrive. Punisher awakens tied up in a tenement room, where Barracuda explains that a third party him a list of Punisher's known contacts, which led him to Yorkie and a letter written to Yorkie by Kathryn O'Brien's sister containing the leverage Barracuda needed against Punisher. Barracuda produces his leverage: the infant daughter Frank conceived with O'Brien.
NOTE: Lisa and Frank Jr.'s spouses and children are figments of Frank's imagination. Pun #51, '07 reveals Sarah's name and that Barracuda killed the daycare worker for trying to stop him. Barb is Kathryn O'Brien's sister; her first name is revealed in Pun #52, '08. Pun #55, '08 reveals the eight Generals sent Barracuda the list of Punisher's known contacts.

PUNISHER #51 (December 2007)

"Long Cold Dark Part Two" (21 pages)

CREDITS: Garth Ennis (writer), Goran Parlov (art), Virtual Calligraphy's Cory Petit (letters), Lee Loughridge (colors), Daniel Ketchum (asst editor), Axel Alonso (editor), Tim Bradstreet (c art)
FEATURE CHARACTER: Punisher (also in dfb)
VILLAIN: Barracuda (also in dfb)
OTHER CHARACTERS: Sarah O'Brien (also in dfb), Dr. John (street surgeon, dies), Barb, Mark (Barb's husband) (prev 2 in photo), police (2 in dfb, 2 in photo) inc Capt. Hoefker & Det. Lamb, radio newscaster (voice only), doctor; Maria Castle, Frank Castle, Jr., Lisa Castle (prev 3 in Frank's thoughts), Yorkie Mitchell (in rfb),
LOCATIONS/ITEMS: New York inc tenement w/Barracuda's room (also in dfb), hospital w/Punisher's room, Dr. John's basement apartment & Punisher's chair / Barracuda's knife (also in dfb) & chair (in dfb); Punisher's bandages, cast, duffel bag of weapons & SUV; Dr. John's antiseptic & syringes; officers' guns & handcuffs
FLASHBACKS: Punisher breaks free and viciously beats Barracuda, but Barracuda stabs him in the side and smashes Punisher through the window with a chair, causing him to fall onto a passing police car (d). Yorkie Mitchell tells Barracuda that he is a joke compared to Frank (Pun #50, '07).
SYNOPSIS: Barracuda taunts Frank Castle and threatens his daughter with a knife. Hours later, Frank awakens in a hospital where two detectives question him. Frank tells the detectives that Barracuda will come and kill everyone in the hospital to get to him, but the detectives refuse to listen. Frank's doctor sends the detectives away. Barracuda sees a street surgeon for treatment of a bite wound Punisher gave him, but kills the man when he inadvertently disparages him. Out of concern for his patients, the doctor frees Frank and injects himself with a sedative to

stage Frank's "escape." Frank sedates one of the two responding police officers and handcuffs the other, then staggers back to his apartment. Upon waking, Frank reads a news story about the baby's abduction and learns her name is Sarah. He then packs an arsenal of weapons into his SUV and drives to California.
NOTE: Includes recap/credits page (1 page).

PUNISHER #52 (January 2008)

"Long Cold Dark Part Three" (22 pages)

CREDITS: Garth Ennis (writer), Goran Parlov (art), Virtual Calligraphy's Cory Petit (letters), Lee Loughridge (colors), Daniel Ketchum (asst editor), Axel Alonso (editor), Tim Bradstreet (c art)
FEATURE CHARACTER: Punisher (also in rfb, also as Frank Castle in fb1 between Pun:Tyger #1, '06 fb & Punmax #22, '12 fb, also in fb2 between Pun:Tyger #1, '06 & Punmax #20, '12 fb)
VILLAIN: Barracuda (also in rfb)
OTHER CHARACTERS: Sarah O'Brien, Barb (1st actual app, also in photo, next in Pun #54, '08), Mark, Barb & Mark's son & daughter (both 1st), Stephen Elkins (in photo), Stephen's mother, motorist, pilot, mall patrons, police, mall employee (voice only), soldiers (in fb1, some as corpses), Maria Castle, Lisa Castle (both in photo), Kathryn O'Brien (as corpse in rfb, also in photo)
LOCATIONS/ITEMS: Gas station, sky over California, Vietnam (in fb1), cemetery (in fb2), La Jolla, CA inc shopping mall & Barb & Mark's house w/living room & garage / Punisher's SUV, rifle & family photo (both in fb1), 2 disposable cellphones, binoculars, multitool & handgun; Stephen's mother's flyers, commuter plane, Army helicopters (in fb1, one as wreckage), Barracuda's binoculars & handgun
FLASHBACKS: During his third tour in Vietnam, Frank and his platoon find a wrecked helicopter with its crew bound and beheaded nearby. While transporting the corpses, Frank looks at a photo of his daughter and pregnant wife (1). Now the Punisher, Frank visits his family's grave (2). Punisher holds the dying Kathryn O'Brien (Pun #41, '07). Barracuda clings to the side of his boat (Pun #36, '06). Barracuda admits to a tied-up Punisher that Frank beat him (Pun #50, '07).
SYNOPSIS: A desperate mother shows a flyer of her missing son to Frank Castle as he refuels on the way to California. Meanwhile, a charter pilot flies Barracuda and Sarah to California. In La Jolla, Kathryn O'Brien's sister Barb fears that Sarah is already dead and goes to a local mall to clear her head. There, Frank calls in a bomb threat and drops a prepaid cellphone with his phone number attached into Barb's purse during the evacuation. As Barracuda and Sarah arrive in California and drive past Barb's house, Barb hides in her garage and calls Frank. Barb tells Frank that Kathryn made her promise never to identify him as the father. The next morning, Barb takes her family out of the house for a few days at Frank's request. Correctly deducing that Barracuda is surveilling the house, Punisher breaks into the house that night and Barracuda follows him inside, carrying a blanketed bundle. Punisher asks Barracuda if the mercenary has contacted the third party again; Barracuda says no. Punisher is satisfied that whoever it is doesn't know about Sarah, but Barracuda suddenly shoots the bundle at point-blank range.
NOTE: Includes recap/credits page (1 page). Barracuda sings Herb Wiedoeft's "Stagger Lee."

PUNISHER #53 (February 2008)

"Long Cold Dark Part Four" (22 pages)

CREDITS: Garth Ennis (writer), Goran Parlov (art), Virtual Calligraphy's Cory Petit (letters), Lee Loughridge (colors), Daniel Ketchum (asst editor), Axel Alonso (editor), Tim Bradstreet (c art)
FEATURE CHARACTER: Punisher
VILLAIN: Barracuda (also in own thoughts)
OTHER CHARACTERS: Sarah O'Brien, police; Barracuda's father (voice only, in Barracuda's thoughts)
LOCATIONS/ITEMS: La Jolla, CA inc Barb & Mark's house, beach, parking lot & nearby forest / Punisher's handgun, SUV (destroyed), jumper cables, chains, M-60 & multitool; Barracuda's handgun, Claymore mine & arsenal w/M-60
SYNOPSIS: Punisher immediately senses something is amiss with Barracuda's quick execution of his "daughter," which was actually a bundled baby doll, and quickly shoots Barracuda. After stomping Barracuda in the head repeatedly, Punisher chains Barracuda and clips jumper cables from his car battery to his groin in order to torture Sarah's location out of him. With Barracuda chained in the back of his car, Punisher drives to where Barracuda parked his car with Sarah inside. He finds Sarah safe, but with a Claymore wired to her car seat. As he attempts to disconnect the mine, Barracuda recalls being tortured by his father at a young age, which enrages him enough to break out of the chains and the back of Frank's SUV. Using each other's weaponry and each other's vehicles for cover, Punisher and Barracuda exchange gunfire until Punisher blows up his own SUV. Punisher takes Sarah into the nearby forest to finish disarming the mine, but a burned and maddened Barracuda arrives and viciously beats Frank.
NOTE: Includes recap/credits page (1 page). Punisher mentions he was in Khe Sanh in the spring of 1968.

PUNISHER #54 (March 2008)

"Long Cold Dark Conclusion" (22 pages)

CREDITS: Garth Ennis (writer), Goran Parlov (art), Virtual Calligraphy's Cory Petit (letters), Lee Loughridge (colors), Daniel Ketchum (asst editor), Axel Alonso (editor), Tim Bradstreet (c art)
FEATURE CHARACTER: Punisher (also in rfb, also in fb2 between Pun #39-40, '06-07)
SUPPORTING CAST: Kathryn O'Brien (also in rfb & in Punisher's thoughts; in fb2 between Pun #39-40, '06-07)
VILLAIN: Barracuda (also in fb1 to 1st chr app before Barracuda #2, '07 fb, also in Barracuda #2, '07 fb; dies)
OTHER CHARACTERS: Barracuda's prison cellmate, African villagers, gangsters, prostitutes (all die), Army recruiter & soldiers, orphanage worker, bartender, schoolchildren, police, paramedics (all in fb1), Sarah O'Brien, Barb (last in Pun #52, '08), Yorkie Mitchell (in rfb)
LOCATIONS/ITEMS: Army recruiting office, African jungle inc village, schoolyard, orphanage, bar, prison cell

(all in fb1), Afghani desert (in fb2 & rfb), motel room (in Punisher's thoughts), La Jolla, CA inc North Torrey Pines Elementary School w/football field & maintenance shed, motel w/Punisher's room, Barb & Mark's house / Army helicopters, cocaine, police officers' guns, soldier's assault rifles, Barracuda's shank, shotgun (all in fb1) & assault rifles (1 in fb1); Punisher's multitool, axe & rented SUV

FLASHBACKS: As a boy, Barracuda gouges out a school bully's eyes and castrates an orphanage worker who attempts to molest him. As an adult, Barracuda enlists in the Army and is stationed in Africa where his platoon massacres a village. Following his military service, Barracuda slaughters a bar filled with gangsters and prostitutes. In prison, Barracuda kills his cellmate (1). Yorkie Mitchell warns Barracuda that going after Frank is suicidal (Pun #50, '07). In Afghanistan, Punisher notices Kathryn O'Brien admiring the sunrise as they eat breakfast (2). Punisher and O'Brien trek through the Afghani desert (Pun #40, '07).

SYNOPSIS: As Barracuda pounds on him, Punisher reaches his multitool and tears Barracuda's nose off. With Barracuda disoriented and in pain, Punisher flees with Sarah. Barracuda collects himself, re-loads his weapon and follows Punisher into an elementary school. Punisher ambushes Barracuda with an axe, chopping off his arms and burying the axe in Barracuda's chest. Barracuda tries to say something, but Punisher liquefies the mercenary's head with his own rifle. Punisher, concerned with Sarah's welfare, takes her to a motel and finishes disconnecting the Claymore attached to her carrier. Frank spends a day with Sarah, enjoying his moment to be a parent rather than the Punisher, then calls Barb to arrange a meeting. At Barb's house, Frank gives a sleeping Sarah to her and, concerned for her long-term safety, advises Barb to never tell her who her father is. He offers Barb money, but Barb says Kathryn gave them some already. Barb asks what Kathryn was like. Frank tells her of a morning where he caught her enjoying a sunrise in Afghanistan, which was the moment Frank started to like Kathryn. After a day-and-a-half spent sleeping and recovering, Frank drives back to New York.

NOTE: Includes recap/credits page (1 page).

PUNISHER: FORCE OF NATURE #1 (April 2008)

"Force of Nature" (34 pages)

CREDITS: Duane Swierczynski (writer), Michael Lacombe (art), Virtual Calligraphy's Cory Petit (letters), Stephane Peru (colors), Daniel Ketchum (asst editor), Axel Alonso (editor), Mike Deodato (c art), Dean White (c colors)

FEATURE CHARACTER: Punisher (also in pfb, last in Pun Ann #1, '07, next in Pun #50, '07)

VILLAINS: Dwight Carter (Russian mob money launderer, also in pfb), Jackie Lutz (pimp), Ian Resnick (narcotics supplier) (all in pfb in photo), Russian mobsters, criminals (all in pfb) (all die)

OTHER CHARACTERS: Jackie's prostitute, tuna bird (both in pfb), bystanders, seagulls (both also in pfb), coast guard, whale; Richie Rys (mentioned), Dwight's credit man

LOCATIONS/ITEMS: Atlantic Ocean (also in pfb), Russian mob's warehouse, East Coast marina (both in pfb) & beach / Travellin's Dwight (Dwight's Mortenson), Dwight's inflatable lifeboat, flare gun & oars; Russian mobster's guns, Punisher's gun, flamethrower, rope, gasoline, match, Uzis, listening device, salt pills, prescribed Promethazine, Ephedrine (all in pfb), harpoon & speedboat (both also in pfb).

FLASHBACK: Punisher doesn't think much of it when a criminal tells him about Dwight Carter, but when a prostitute mentions Dwight, Punisher starts to investigate him by torturing various criminals. Punisher learns that Dwight is associated with the Russian mob, but no one knows what plan he's working on. Later, Punisher waits while Dwight meets with his friends Jackie Lutz and Ian Resnick for a celebratory boat trip. The boat's engine explodes and Jackie immediately blames the Punisher. The boat sinks and they escape on a small inflatable lifeboat. They take pills to ease their stomachs, but Punisher replaced the drugs with salt pills, making them sicker. They discover the flare gun doesn't work and their emergency rations are missing. Growing desperate and looking for a reason why the Punisher may be looking for them, the three admit they each have separate deals with the Russian mob. Jackie reveals he's supplying prostitutes to the Russians. The others accuse him of selling them out to the Punisher and kill Jackie. Dwight tells Ian he's been building an untraceable credit card network and confronts Ian on the amount of cocaine he's been buying. Punisher deduces the Russians are building a one-stop shop for chargeable prostitutes and drugs. Dwight kills Ian in self defense. When Dwight dumps Ian's body, Punisher fires his harpoon.

SYNOPSIS: Punisher harpoons Dwight and drags him toward shore until he hits a whale. Dwight tries to strangle Punisher with the harpoon line, but Punisher kills Dwight. On shore, Punisher prepares to mail Dwight's head to the Russian mob.

NOTE: Followed by "Cover Process" (1 page) featuring the pencil sketch, final line art and final colored art for the cover. Punisher's prescription is from Dr. D. Swierczynski and is made out to Steve Peru.

PUNISHER #55 (May 2008)

"Valley Forge, Valley Forge Part One" (22 pages)

CREDITS: Garth Ennis (writer), Goran Parlov (art), Virtual Calligraphy's Cory Petit (letters), Lee Loughridge (colors), Daniel Ketchum (asst editor), Axel Alonso (editor), Tim Bradstreet (c art)

FEATURE CHARACTER: Punisher (also in rfb)

GUEST STAR: Col. Nick Fury (last in Pun #18, '05, also in rfb)

VILLAINS: Gen. Farmington, Gen. Perino, Gen. Van Abst (all also in rfb), Gen. Archer, Gen. Kent, Gen. Landers, Gen. Vertraeus, Gen. Vraciu (all last bts in Pun #50, '07)

OTHER CHARACTERS: Colonel George Howe (Delta Force commander, 1st but chr last in Pun #56, '08 fb), Lt. Geller (Perino's aide, 1st), Roy (Howe's aide), Michael Goodwin (author, 1st bts in fb2 between Pun #59, '08 fb bts & Pun #56, '08 fb bts), Col. Ottman, Tusker Leader (Lt. John Chadwick, tank commander) (both as transcribed voices in fb1 before & during Born #4, '03), Tusker Three Bravo (tank radio operator, as transcribed voice in fb1), bartender, bar patrons, US soldiers (on TV, some as corpses), William Rawlins, Galina Stenkov (both in rfb), Martin Vanheim (in rfb & in photo), Howe's daughter (in photo)

LOCATIONS/ITEMS: New York inc bar, Punisher's apartment & William Roth's kitchen; Siberia, Rhode Island Air Force base (prev 3 in rfb), Iraq inc Baghdad (on TV), Ft. Bragg inc Howe's office / golf course / Fury's intelligence file on the Generals & belt; Gulf South Flight 29, Russian missiles (prev 3 in rfb), Perino's box of Cuban cigars, "Valley Forge, Valley Forge" (see NOTE)

FLASHBACKS: Russian missiles destroy a Saudi airliner (Pun #17, '05). Fury beats Van Abst with his belt (Pun #17, '05). William Rawlins is interrogated and videotaped (Pun #24, '05). Frank, cradling Galina Stenkov, leaves Martin Vanheim to die of exposure in Siberia (Pun #18, '05), then confronts the Generals alongside Fury (Pun #18, '05). October, 1971: Col. Ottman radios a nearby tank division for aid during the

NVA invasion of Firebase Valley Forge. The tank division abruptly loses contact with Valley Forge (1). Michael Goodwin begins his book with a summary of the aftermath of the Valley Forge massacre, from which Frank Castle emerged the sole survivor. He then depicts his upbringing with his older brother Stevie, then summarizes Stevie's letters from Vietnam, wherein Stevie describes the pitiful condition of Valley Forge. He then writes about the letter Stevie wrote in May, 1971 about the Marine Captain newly assigned to Valley Forge, Frank Castle (2).

SYNOPSIS: Frank Castle meets Nick Fury at a bar, where Fury ruminates on his wavering faith in his government. Fury gives Frank an envelope and, after Frank leaves, instigates a bar fight. On a golf course, the Generals lament Barracuda's failure to kill Punisher. The Generals are now assured that, armed with Rawlins' taped confession, Punisher has targeted them and he must be eliminated. Kurt Perino and Jake Farmington reveal to the others their idea to dispatch a team of Delta Force troops against Punisher, since the vigilante would refuse to kill American soldiers. Lt. Geller, Perino's lackey, meets with Col. George Howe, Delta Force's commander, who tells him, despite the fact that Frank may have been complicit in the death of Martin Vanheim, who was engaged to Howe's daughter, that he intends to capture Frank for dishonoring the military by using his Special Forces skills to commit countless acts of murder. Geller tells Howe that Perino wants Castle and a tape of sensitive material that he possesses. As Howe takes Geller to meet the team he intends to dispatch against Frank, Punisher examines the contents of Fury's envelope: photos and information on the Generals.

NOTE: Includes recap/credits page (1 page). Part of this story arc is devoted to prose excerpts from Michael Goodwin's book "Valley Forge, Valley Forge: The Slaughter of a U.S. Marine Garrison and the Birth of the Punisher." Michael's brother Stevie Goodwin served with Frank Castle at Firebase Valley Forge in Vietnam, as seen in Born #1-4, '03. Pun #56, '08 reveals Tusker Leader's real name, Howe's first name and Geller's last name. Pun #56, '08 reveals Howe is stationed at Ft. Bragg. Pun #60, '08 reveals why Howe volunteered to bring in the Punisher.

PUNISHER #56 (June 2008)

"Valley Forge, Valley Forge Part Two" (22 pages)

CREDITS: Garth Ennis (writer), Goran Parlov (art), Virtual Calligraphy's Cory Petit (letters), Lee Loughridge (colors), Daniel Ketchum (asst editor), Axel Alonso (editor), Tim Bradstreet (c art)

FEATURE CHARACTER: Punisher (also in fb2 as Capt. Castle between Punmax #19, '12 fb & Pun:Tyger #1, '06 fb, see NOTE)

GUEST STAR: Col. Nick Fury (bts, reading "Valley Forge, Valley Forge")

VILLAINS: Gen. Archer, Gen. Farmington, Gen. Kent, Gen. Landers, Gen. Perino, Gen. Van Abst , Gen. Vertraeus, Gen. Vraciu; NVA soldiers (in fb1, die)

OTHER CHARACTERS: Col. George Howe (also in fb1 to 1st chr app before Pun #55, '08); Lt. "Woody" Wood & his Delta Force team (all 1st, 3 referred to as Tom, Bill, & Steve, see NOTE): Lt. Stanaway, Sgt. Melinger, Sgt. Giroux, Sgt. Winburn, Sgt. McGee, Sgt. Rents, Cpl. McDonough; Lt. Geller, John Chadwick (as transcribed voice in fb3 after Born #4, '03), Michael Goodwin (bts in fb2 between Pun #55, '08 & Pun #57, '08, also as transcribed voice in 1st chr app in fb3 before Pun #55, '08), country club members, Capt. Castle's Long Range Reconnaissance Patrol team (in fb1), Sgt. Walt Mayne (Chadwick's senior NCO), Elizabeth Chadwick (Chadwick's wife), Vince (2nd Lt. assigned to Chadwick's division) & his tank crew inc Tusker Three Bravo (prev 4 mentioned), Arnag Chalikian (Armenian criminal, mentioned, killed by Punisher along with several of his henchmen prior to Pun #56, '08)

LOCATIONS/ITEMS: Laos inc village (in fb1), Delta Force HQ inc recreation room, country club lounge, New York inc Arnag Chalikian's bar / NVA machetes, assault rifles & tiger cage LRRP team's assault rifles & knife; severed hands & feet (all in fb1), Steve & Woody's guns, Steve's equipment belts & handcuffs; Howe's tracer & laptop computer; "Valley Forge, Valley Forge"

FLASHBACKS: Laos, Summer 1969: George Howe is kept by NVA forces in a tiger cage with the severed hands and feet of his fellow soldiers until a Marine LRRP team kills Howe's captors and rescues him (1). Michael Goodwin writes his interview with John Chadwick into his book as its third chapter (2). Goodwin interviews Chadwick for his book at Chadwick's Big Sur home. Chadwick tells Goodwin of his time commanding his M48 squad, then mentions the call one of his tanks received from Valley Forge at a time when Chadwick's tank was damaged by a mine. After reading the transcript of Valley Forge's last transmission, Chadwick somberly explains that the inexperienced tank commander that received the call insisted on checking with Chadwick before calling in air support for Valley Forge, but the base was silent by the time Chadwick ordered it himself. Chadwick admits he was unaware that anyone survived the massacre, let alone that the only survivor was the Punisher. He then details his post-war life and his pride that all of his men made it home (3).

SYNOPSIS: En route to their meeting with the Delta Force team, George Howe tells Lt. Geller about his imprisonment by the NVA in Laos and his subsequent rescue by a Marine recon team. Howe introduces Geller to Lt. Wood and his team, who explain their intended approach to hunting Frank Castle down. The Generals receive a call from Howe, assuring them that the manhunt for Frank has commenced. Wood and one of his men Steve, inspect the site of Frank's latest massacre, a bar owned by the Armenian mob. While searching the neighborhood for Castle, Punisher catches Steve unaware and questions the two of them as to their identity. Wood identifies them as military, and Punisher shoves Steve towards Wood before fleeing into a building. Punisher beats Steve unconscious, but Wood catches the vigilante at gunpoint on the roof. Wood suddenly falls through the weakened ceiling, and Punisher handcuffs him to the exposed plumbing before leaving. Wood reports to Howe that Castle escaped, but Steve was able to slip a tracer into Frank's coat during the altercation.

NOTE: Includes recap/credits page (1 page). Frank is not identified to have been the leader of the LRRP team that rescues Howe here, until Pun #60, '08. Though all but one of Wood's teammates' first names are revealed over the course of this story, which first name belongs to which team member is not specified. Steve, Bill and Tom's first names are identified in this issue; Jess, Joey and Mac's are revealed in Pun #57, '08.

PUNISHER #57 (July 2008)

"Valley Forge, Valley Forge Part Three" (22 pages)

CREDITS: Garth Ennis (writer), Goran Parlov (art), Virtual Calligraphy's Cory Petit (letters), Lee Loughridge (colors), Daniel Ketchum (asst editor), Axel Alonso (editor), Tim Bradstreet (c art)

FEATURE CHARACTER: Punisher

GUEST STAR: Col. Nick Fury (bts, reading "Valley Forge, Valley Forge")

VILLAINS: Gen. Archer, Gen. Farmington, Gen. Kent, Gen. Landers, Gen. Perino, Gen. Van Abst , Gen. Vertraeus, Gen. Vraciu

OTHER CHARACTERS: Col. George Howe; Lt. "Woody" Wood & his Delta Force team (5 referred to as Steve, Jess, Joey, Mac, & Tom): Lt. Stanaway, Sgt. Melinger, Sgt. Giroux, Sgt. Winburn, Sgt. McGee, Sgt. Rents, Cpl. McDonough; Lt. Geller, reporters inc Peter, NYPD captain, Michael Goodwin (bts in fb1 between Pun #56, '08 fb & Pun #59, '08 fb, also as transcribed voice in fb2 between Pun #56, '08 fb & Pun #59, '08 fb), Evelyn Morris (ex-actress, brother of James "Angel" Morris, as transcribed voice in fb2), 2 escorts (hired by Evelyn to protect Goodwin, mentioned in fb1)

LOCATIONS/ITEMS: New York inc Punisher's safehouse w/sewer tunnel, Delta Force's warehouse hideout, diner & Holy Cross Cemetery / Punisher's guns, baseball bat, grenade, crate of M-24 flash-bang grenades, smoke & tear gas charges w/detonator; Wood's team's assault rifles, SUV, gas masks, gas grenades & tasers; Howe's tracer & laptop computer; Wood's laptop computer, "Valley Forge, Valley Forge"

FLASHBACKS: Michael Goodwin writes his interview with Evelyn Morris into his book as its sixth chapter (1). Goodwin interviews Evelyn at her apartment in the Bronx, wherein she tells Goodwin about her brother's problems with drugs and how it led him to being drafted. She then tells him how happy her father was that he found friendship with Michael's brother. Evelyn intimates to Goodwin that she believes the military deliberately targets the disenfranchised for recruitment, and that she holds Frank Castle at least partially responsible for her brother's death (2).

SYNOPSIS: With Howe coordinating by radio, Wood leads his team on an assault of Frank Castle's safehouse. Punisher has prepared for them, however, and fights them off before dropping a fragmentation grenade into a box of flash-bang grenades to cover his escape into a sewer tunnel. The next morning, Howe debriefs Wood and his team, some of who are no longer in fighting shape, and plan their next move. Geller appears and announces the Generals' arrival. Perino is initially congenial towards Howe, but becomes enraged when he learns Frank escaped. Howe responds by offering to step down from the assignment and work with whoever they intend to set against Frank instead of him. The Generals back down. Wood reports that the tracer they placed on Frank is again active. At a diner, Punisher watches a news report about the NYPD investigation into the attack on his home while playing with the tracer. That night, Wood's team continues the hunt for Frank. They trace him to a cemetery, where he has wired a monument with explosives and has demanded to speak with Wood's commander.

NOTE: Includes recap/credits page (1 page). As seen in Born #1-4, '03, James "Angel" Morris served with Frank at Firebase Valley Forge and was a close friend of Stevie Goodwin. James was killed in Born #4, '03.

PUNISHER #58 (August 2008)

"Valley Forge, Valley Forge Part Four" (22 pages)

CREDITS: Garth Ennis (writer), Goran Parlov (art), Virtual Calligraphy's Cory Petit (letters), Lee Loughridge (colors), Daniel Ketchum (asst editor), Axel Alonso (editor), Tim Bradstreet (c art)

FEATURE CHARACTER: Punisher (also as Capt. Castle in fb4 between Punmax #21, '12 fb & Born #1, '03)

GUEST STAR: Nick Fury (bts, reading "Valley Forge, Valley Forge")

VILLAINS: Gen. Archer, Gen. Farmington, Gen. Kent, Gen. Landers, Gen. Perino, Gen. Van Abst , Gen. Vertraeus, Gen. Vraciu

OTHER CHARACTERS: Col. George Howe (also in photo); Lt. "Woody" Wood & his Delta Force team (3 unspecified members next in Pun #60, '08): Lt. Stanaway, Sgt. Melinger, Sgt. Giroux, Sgt. Winburn, Sgt. McGee, Sgt. Rents, Cpl. McDonough; Lt. Geller (next in Pun #60, '08), bartenders, waiters, US soldiers (in fb1, 4, & 9-11), Michael Goodwin (in 1st chr app in fb2 before Pun #56, '08), Stevie Goodwin (in 1st chr app in fb2 before fb8, also in fb3 between fb8 & Born #1, '03, also in fb8 between fb2&3), John Chadwick (in 1st chr app in fb5 before Pun #55, '08 fb), James "Angel" Morris (in 1st chr apps in fb7&8 before Born #1, '03), Sgt. William J. "Bill" Torrance (in 1st chr app in fb11 before bts in Pun #59, '08 fb)

LOCATIONS/ITEMS: New York inc Holy Cross Cemetery & Delta Force hideout; bistro, Vietnam (in fb1, 3-6 & 8-12) inc Firebase Valley Forge (in fb1, 3-4, 6, 8 & 12); Goodwin home (in fb2) / Punisher's smoke & gas charges, detonator, grenade & gas mask; Wood's team's guns, gas masks, taser & handcuffs; Huey helicopters (in fb1, 6, & 11, one as wreckage in fb12), US soldiers' guns (in fb3-4, 9, & 11), Chadwick's M24 tank (in fb5), F4 Phantom fighter-bomber (in fb10), Howe's gas mask & thermal imager; "Valley Forge, Valley Forge"

FLASHBACKS: During the Vietnam War: a helicopter flies over Firebase Valley Forge (1). Christmas 1969: Stevie Goodwin plays with his younger brother Michael (2). September 1971: Stevie nears the end of his tour (3). 1971: Capt. Castle loads his rifle (4). 1970: John Chadwick's tank division takes a break (5). Barely maintained Huey helicopters at Valley Forge await resupply (6). James Morris is photographed six months before his compulsory services (7). Stevie and Angel pose near the sign at Valley Forge reading "Danger: Sniper at Work, Dawn to Dusk" (8). The NVA attacks an unidentified US base (9). A soldier cheers as an F4 Phantom drops napalm (10). Bill Torrance boards his helicopter (11). The site where Valley Forge once stood now lies in overgrown ruins (12).

SYNOPSIS: George Howe arrives at the cemetery, where Punisher tells the Colonel that the Generals are corrupt and of their illicit activities. Howe refuses to listen, but Punisher continues telling him about Operation: Barbarossa and of Rawlins' confession. The Generals don't want him, they want his taped evidence. Howe promises Punisher that he will be treated fairly during his capture, but Punisher scoffs at the idea and detonates the charges, which are actually smoke and tear gas bombs. Punisher attempts escape, but despite injuring several of Howe's men, is subdued and captured. At Delta Force's hideout, Howe calls Perino and tells him that Frank Castle has been captured. Perino is angry that the tape is still missing, which Howe finds interesting. After telling his men to keep Geller out, Howe enters the room where Punisher is being held and sends the guard away. Howe tells Frank that he is starting to believe him about the Generals' primary target being the tape, then asks him to trust him, one soldier to another.

NOTE: Includes recap/credits page (1 page). This issues excerpt from Goodwin's book consists of a photo section from which this issue's flashbacks are derived. As revealed next issue, Bill Torrance was one of the soldiers who found Frank amidst the carnage at Valley Forge. Torrance's middle initial is also revealed next issue.

PUNISHER #59 (September 2008)

"Valley Forge, Valley Forge Part Five" (22 pages)

CREDITS: Garth Ennis (writer), Goran Parlov (art), Virtual Calligraphy's Cory Petit (letters), Lee Loughridge (colors), Daniel Ketchum (asst editor), Axel Alonso (editor), Tim Bradstreet (c art)

FEATURE CHARACTER: Punisher (also off-panel in fb1 during Pun #24, '05)

GUEST STAR: Nick Fury (bts, reading "Valley Forge, Valley Forge")

SUPPORTING CAST: Kathryn O'Brien (voice only in fb1 during Pun #24, '05)

VILLAINS: William Rawlins (in fb1 during Pun #24, '05), Gen. Archer, Gen. Farmington, Gen. Kent, Gen. Landers, Gen. Perino, Gen. Van Abst , Gen. Vertraeus, Gen. Vraciu

OTHER CHARACTERS: Col. George Howe; Lt. "Woody" Wood & 4 unspecified members of his Delta Force team; Michael Goodwin (bts in fb2 between Pun #57, '08 fb & Pun #60, '08 fb, also as transcribed voice in fb3 between Pun #57, '08 fb & Pun #55, '08 fb), Bill Torrance (in fb3 between Pun #58, '08 fb & Born #4, '03), Ron (Howe's friend), Chairman of the Joint Chiefs (prev 2 bts on phone)

LOCATIONS/ITEMS: New York inc Grand Central Station & Delta Force hideout; restaurant, William Roth's kitchen (in fb3&4) / Punisher's weapons inc .45 handgun; Rawlins tape w/attached C4 charge, Wood's SUV, Wood's team's guns, Howe's laptop computer & notebook; "Valley Forge, Valley Forge"

FLASHBACKS: Punisher, Kathryn O'Brien and William Roth videotape William Rawlins confessing his misdeeds and those of the Generals, detailing how the Generals had him assemble a Saudi terrorist cell to act as their personal suicide hit squad. In 2005, the Generals ordered Rawlins to have his cell hijack a civilian airliner and send it against the Kremlin as a tactical diversion. The hijack was meant to distract the Russian government while Frank Castle and Martin Vanheim were sent to retrieve Galina Stenkov and the inert Barbarossa sample in her blood (1). Michael Goodwin writes his interview with Bill Torrance into his book as its tenth chapter (2). Goodwin interviews Torrance, who tells him of his boyhood patriotism and how his experiences in Vietnam severely disillusioned him. Torrance tells Goodwin that he signed up for another tour in an attempt to do the good he couldn't in his first. He then tells him about seeing Frank Castle amidst the field of corpses at Valley Forge. That and his overall wartime experience robbed him of his idealism and patriotism (3).

SYNOPSIS: Col. Howe and Lt. Wood retrieve the Rawlins tape from the train station locker where Punisher left it. On the road back to their hideout, Howe and Wood discuss whether turning the tape and Frank Castle over to the Generals would be the right thing to do. At the hideout, Howe watches the Rawlins tape and takes notes. While dining with the Generals, Van Abst confronts Perino as to why he enlisted the aid of Howe, a soldier known for his outstanding moral character. Perino assures him that, if Howe refuses to do anything against Frank except due process, they will kill Castle themselves. Howe tells Wood to take his team home and to take Geller and all of Punisher's weapons except his handgun with him. Afterwards, Howe watches the rest of the Rawlins tape. Howe calls the Chairman of the Joint Chiefs, inquires about Rawlins' claim that he left intel about the Generals in his care, and advises him to destroy it. Howe then tells the captive Punisher that he will not expose the Rawlins tape for fear of destroying the American military's reputation. Punisher asks Howe where that now leaves them.

NOTE: Includes recap/credits page (1 page). Torrance says during his interview with Goodwin that he felt Capt. Castle had been speaking to someone, which Goodwin suggests may have been the birth of a split personality or the Devil.

PUNISHER #60 (October 2008)

"Valley Forge, Valley Forge Conclusion" (22 pages)

CREDITS: Garth Ennis (writer), Goran Parlov (art), Virtual Calligraphy's Cory Petit (letters), Lee Loughridge (colors), Daniel Ketchum (asst editor), Axel Alonso (editor), Tim Bradstreet (c art)

FEATURE CHARACTER: Punisher (also in rfb as Capt. Castle; next in Pun:LBB #1, '08)

GUEST STAR: Nick Fury

VILLAINS: Gen. Archer, Gen. Farmington, Gen. Kent, Gen. Landers, Gen. Perino, Gen. Van Abst , Gen. Vertraeus, Gen. Vraciu (all die)

OTHER CHARACTERS: Col. George Howe (also in rfb); Lt. "Woody" Wood & his Delta Force team (3 unspecified members last in Pun #58, '08): Lt. Stanaway, Sgt. Melinger, Sgt. Giroux, Sgt. Winburn, Sgt. McGee, Sgt. Rents, Cpl. McDonough; Lt. Geller (also in rfb, last in Pun #58, '08), Michael Goodwin (bts in fb1 after Pun #59, '08), bartenders, bar patrons, newscaster (on TV), US soldiers (all on TV), Capt. Castle's LRRP team (in rfb), NVA soldiers (as corpses in rfb), Stevie Goodwin, James "Angel" Morris (both in rfb)

LOCATIONS/ITEMS: Laotian village, Howe's Ft. Bragg office, Firebase Valley Forge (all in rfb), New York inc Delta Force hideout; bar / Punisher's .45 handgun, C-130 transport plane w/bathroom, Geller's file on Punisher, Generals' cars & guns, NVA tiger cage, LRRP team's assault rifles & knife (prev 3 in rfb), "Valley Forge, Valley Forge"

FLASHBACKS: Laos, 1969: Capt. Castle's LRRP team rescues Howe (Pun #56, '08). Geller meets with Howe in his office (Pun #55, '08). Michael Goodwin writes his book's thirteenth chapter, where he details the multiple contributing factors to the failure of Vietnam, the loss of his brother, and how those experiences shaped Frank Castle into the Punisher. Goodwin closes the book with a poem incorporating the book's title, then with a short epilogue (1). Stevie Goodwin and James Morris pose for a photo near the danger sign at Valley Forge (Pun #58, '08).

SYNOPSIS: George Howe has a long conversation with the captive Frank Castle regarding his motivations in his personal war against the Generals. On the transport plane back to Ft. Bragg, Geller looks at Frank's dossier, and after Wood confirms that Castle belonged to the Marine equivalent of Army Special Forces, Geller experiences a shocking revelation. Howe tells Frank that he realizes now that his mission to capture him was born not of duty or justice, but of profit. Outside, the Generals arrive with intention of killing Castle. Howe emerges, tells Perino he is done, and walks away. Aboard the plane, Geller leaves a frantic voicemail on Perino's phone, saying that he now realizes that Howe has played him and the Generals all along. Geller correctly surmised that Howe volunteered to capture Frank to protect him from the Generals, since Castle led the team that rescued Howe in Laos. At a bar, Nick Fury finishes reading his copy of "Valley Forge, Valley Forge," and, seeing news reports of the wars in Iraq and Afghanistan, ruminates that nothing has changed. Punisher, set free by Howe prior to the Generals' arrival, kills the Generals and walks away.

NOTE: Includes recap/credits page (1 page). Followed by preview of Pun #61, '08 (8 pages).

PUNISHER MAX SPECIAL: LITTLE BLACK BOOK #1 (August 2008)

"Little Black Book" (32 pages)

CREDITS: Victor Gischler (writer), Jefté Palo (art), Virtual Calligraphy's Cory Petit (letters), Lee Loughridge (colors), Daniel Ketchum (asst editor), Axel Alonso (editor), Dave Johnson (c art)

FEATURE CHARACTER: Punisher (also as Vette's bodyguard, also in pfb, next in Pun #61, '08)

VILLAINS: Carlos Ramirez (crooked businessman, dies) & his guards (most die), convicted criminals turned rap artists & their crews (most die)

OTHER CHARACTERS: Vette (high-class prostitute, also in fb & pfb), Karl (Vette's bodyguard, bts, in Vette's trunk), Vette's father (dog trainer, dies in fb), shepherd/wolf half-breed dog (in fb), Carlos' party guests; Fidel Castro (mentioned, Ramirez worked in his death squads), 2 drug gang leaders, police captain, his wife & daughter (prev 4 mentioned, killed by Ramirez)

LOCATIONS/ITEMS: Carlos' compound inc main gate, guard outposts & Carlos' bedroom; cemetery (in fb), Vette's bedroom (in pfb) / Vette's little black book (Blackberry, also in pfb, destroyed) & handgun; Punisher's fake moustache, Carlos' guards' machine guns, shotguns & handguns

FLASHBACKS: Punisher seduces Vette to get her little black book, a Blackberry with her client list and their contact information. Vette thought she could convince Punisher to work for her. Punisher tells Vette if she helps kill Carlos Ramirez he'll return her Blackberry. She agrees to help when he tells her that Ramirez killed a police Captain and his family (p). A shepherd wolf half-breed kills Vette's dog training father.

SYNOPSIS: Punisher, posing as Vette's bodyguard, drives Vette into Carlos Ramirez' compound. A guard recognizes Punisher, so Punisher kills him. Inside the compound, Vette walks Punisher through a party Carlos is throwing to celebrate signing a new rap artist to his record label, but Carlos is upstairs waiting for Vette. Upstairs, another guard recognizes Punisher, so Punisher kills him. Vette enters Carlos' bedroom for their appointment, but Carlos stops their activities when he hears gunshots. Punisher bursts into the room and shoots Carlos in the face. Vette gets dressed and follows Punisher as he kills his way through Carlos' men. Punisher resorts to combat when he runs out of bullets and Vette runs away. Vette tries to steal a car, but the people inside ignore her threats and begin to rape her. Punisher kills Vette's attackers bare handed and returns Vette's phone as promised. Vette destroys her little black book, realizing that she doesn't want her old life back.

PUNISHER #61 (October 2008)

"Girls in White Dresses Part One: Quinceañera" (22 pages)

CREDITS: Greg Hurwitz (writer), Laurence Campbell (art), Virtual Calligraphy's Cory Petit (letters), Lee Loughridge (colors), Daniel Ketchum (asst editor), Axel Alonso (editor), Dave Johnson (c art)
FEATURE CHARACTER: Punisher
VILLAINS: Drug cartel enforcers (1 dies), purse snatchers
OTHER CHARACTERS: Gabriela Nuñez (15-year-old girl), Angelica Nuñez (Gabriela's sister, chr next in Pun #63, '08 fb), Mrs. Nuñez (Gabriela's mother, next in Pun #63, '08), Tierra Rota coroner (all 1st), Angel Nuñez (Gabriela's father, dies), girl's corpse (another in pfb, others in Punisher's thoughts), Tierra Rota citizens (some also in pfb), police officer (dies in pfb), quinceañera guests, bartender, New York bystanders; Barney the dinosaur, Cap'n Crunch, football player, reporters (prev 4 on TV); Maria Castle, Lisa Castle, Frank Castle, Jr. (prev 3 in Punisher's thoughts)
LOCATIONS/ITEMS: Tierra Rota, Mexico inc church, school & La Casa restaurant; New York inc bar / Angel's broken bottle & knife; drug cartel's vans & guns; Punisher's gun & shotgun, bag of gold
FLASHBACK: Women and girls begin disappearing in Tierra Rota. Eventually, the girls return as naked, sewn up corpses. A policeman, whose sister was abducted, investigates but is killed (p).
SYNOPSIS: In Tierra Rota, Mexico, Gabriela Nuñez's quinceañera is interrupted when hooded men abduct her in front of Angelica, her little sister. A corpse with missing eyes and the back sewn up is left in Gabriela's place. In New York on the anniversary of the Castle family deaths, Punisher finds himself being followed. Punisher lures the man into an alley and confronts the man, who tells Punisher his town is under siege. He offers Punisher gold to come to Tierra Rota to save their women because the police and federales are useless. Punisher refuses, saying he's not a hitman or mercenary, and the man leaves. Back in Mexico, the kidnappers come for more women. Gabriela's father Angel decides to take a stand. He confronts the kidnappers but is quickly killed. In New York, stories about the violence in Tierra Rota haunt Punisher. Punisher arrives in Tierra Rota in time to save Angelica from being the next abductee.
NOTE: Includes recap/credits page (1 page). The man who comes to hire Punisher remains unnamed, but is identified as Tierra Rota's coroner in Pun #62, '08.

PUNISHER #62 (November 2008)

"Girls in White Dresses Part 2: Another Day in Paradise" (22 pages)

CREDITS: Greg Hurwitz (writer), Laurence Campbell (art), Virtual Calligraphy's Cory Petit (letters), Lee Loughridge (colors), Daniel Ketchum, Sebastian Girner (asst editor), Axel Alonso (editor), Dave Johnson (c art)
FEATURE CHARACTER: Punisher (also in Pun #63, '08 fb)
VILLAINS: Jigsaw (as the Heavy, see NOTE), El Jefe, Ramón Estrada, Ramón's half-brother (all 1st, also in Pun #63, '08 fb) & their drug cartel enforcers (1 as corpse), Skeleton (drug addict, dies), drug dealers
OTHER CHARACTERS: Angelica Nuñez (corpse, chr last in Pun #63, '08 fb), Tierra Rota's coroner, enslaved women (2 as bodies), Tierra Rota citizens, squirrel; Maria Castle, Lisa Castle, Frank Castle, Jr. (prev 3 in Punisher's thoughts)
LOCATIONS/ITEMS: Tierra Rota, Mexico inc motel w/Punisher's room, coroner's office, dealer's house, meat freezer, cartel's factory & clearing house / Punisher's shotgun, guns, grenades, chains & hooks; drug cartel's vans, shotguns & kitty litter; the Heavy's gasmask, bag of gold
SYNOPSIS: Punisher returns the town's gold and begins his investigation. The vigilante learns the dead women have been using latex gloves and have kitty litter on them. The man who hired Punisher is the town's coroner and takes Punisher to the morgue, where the vigilante performs an autopsy and discovers the lungs have been removed along with the eyes. Punisher deduces the women are being used as drug lab laborers. Punisher interrogates Skeleton, a local drug addict, and learns who the local drug dealers are. Punisher abducts the various dealers and hangs them up like meat. Skeleton tells the drug cartel leaders that he told Punisher who their dealers are. They kill Skeleton and the Heavy tells them that when dealing with the Punisher, they must be very careful. After beating information out of the dealers, Punisher heads to their exchange point where the sound of gunfire draws his attention. Punisher shoots through a window, behind which he finds Angelica's body with two bullet holes in it.
NOTE: Includes recap/credits page (1 page). The Heavy is revealed to be Jigsaw in Pun #64, '08; he is an Earth-200111 native.

PUNISHER #63 (December 2008)

"She is Dead" (22 pages)

CREDITS: Greg Hurwitz (writer), Laurence Campbell (art), Virtual Calligraphy's Cory Petit (letters), Lee Loughridge (colors), Daniel Ketchum, Sebastian Girner (asst editor), Axel Alonso (editor), Dave Johnson (c art)
FEATURE CHARACTER: Punisher (also in fb during Pun #62, '08)
VILLAINS: Jigsaw (as the Heavy), El Jefe, Ramón Estrada, Ramón's half-brother (all also in fb during Pun #62, '08) & their drug cartel enforcers, framer (also in fb, dies), 2 prostitutes (1st)
OTHER CHARACTERS: Angelica Nuñez (corpse, also in Punisher's thoughts, also in fb between Pun #61-62, '08), Mrs. Nuñez (last in Pun #61, '08), Tierra Rota coroner, innkeeper, enslaved women, 2 prostitutes (1st), Tierra Rota citizens; Maria Castle, Lisa Castle, Frank Castle, Jr. (prev 3 in Punisher's thoughts)
LOCATIONS/ITEMS: Tierra Rota, Mexico inc cemetery, motel w/Punisher's room, clearing house & cartel's factory / Punisher's guns, knife & shovel; cartel's trucks & cocaine, .22-caliber bullet, firecrackers (in fb)

FLASHBACK: A man is hired to make Punisher think he's killed an innocent. He's provided with Angelica's corpse, and he puts the body in the drug cartel's clearing house. He waits for Punisher to arrive and sets off firecrackers, making Punisher think guns are being fired. The man watches Punisher leave the clearing house with Angelica's corpse.

SYNOPSIS: A man races into Tierra Rota and announces that Punisher killed Angelica. Punisher carries Angelica's body into the cemetery where her mother blames Punisher for Angelica's death. Punisher returns to his motel room where he's haunted by thoughts of Angelica. Because an innocent is dead by his hand, Punisher prepares to punish himself through suicide. At the factory, the drug cartel celebrates Punisher's withdrawal and get back to business. Punisher sees Angelica pull a bullet from her chest, so he exhumes Angelica's corpse and performs an autopsy on her. He finds a .22-caliber bullet in her and not one of his .45-caliber bullets. Punisher finds the man who alerted the town to Angelica's death and interrogates him. After he admits to framing Punisher and tells the vigilante about the Heavy, Punisher kills him. Later, Punisher waits to attack one of the cartel leaders.

NOTE: Includes recap/credits page (1 page).

PUNISHER #64 (January 2009)

"Girls in White Dresses Part 4: Satan Dust" (22 pages)

CREDITS: Greg Hurwitz (writer), Laurence Campbell (art), Virtual Calligraphy's Cory Petit (letters), Lee Loughridge (colors), Daniel Ketchum, Sebastian Girner (asst editor), Axel Alonso (editor), Dave Johnson (c art)
FEATURE CHARACTER: Punisher (also in rfb)
VILLAINS: Jigsaw (also as the Heavy), El Jefe, Ramón Estrada, Ramón's half-brother (dies) & their drug cartel enforcers inc Joaquin (1 dies), 2 prostitutes (die)
OTHER CHARACTERS: Tierra Rota coroner, enslaved women, shark; Angelica Nuñez (in rfb)
LOCATIONS/ITEMS: Ramón's half-brother's mansion, cartel's factory, cartel's compound Tierra Rota's morgue / Punisher's shotgun & gun; drug cartel's cocaine, jeep w/machine gun & assault rifles; Ramón's gun & Ferrari; dealer's shotgun, the Heavy's gasmask, .22-caliber bullet
FLASHBACK: Punisher carries Angelica to Tierra Rota (Pun #63, '08).

SYNOPSIS: Punisher attacks Ramón's half-brother inside the drug lord's mansion. Unfortunately, the prostitutes with the drug lord attack Punisher while the drug lord grabs Punisher's shotgun. Punisher shoots a shark tank and lets the pet shark devour the drug lord. At the factory, the other bosses are alerted to the attack and the Heavy tells them Punisher's coming. Punisher brings the boss' head to the coroner, reassures Punisher that he knows Angelica's death was an accident. Punisher shows the coroner the bullet that proves he didn't kill Angelica. Later, Punisher attacks the drug cartel's compound. Ramón manages to escape and the Heavy orders the cartel enforcers to kill their slaves and move their operation. One of the women overhears, kills one of the enforcers and warns the other women. When Ramón arrives he sees the Heavy, who tells Ramón that the car Ramón left behind has a GPS that will lead Punisher right to them. The Heavy says he's moving the operation and punches Ramón. The Heavy removes his gas mask, revealing his scarred, jigsaw face underneath.
NOTE: Includes recap/credits page (1 page).

PUNISHER #65 (February 2009)

"Girls in White Dresses Part 5: Jigsaw" (24 pages)

CREDITS: Greg Hurwitz (writer), Laurence Campbell (art), Virtual Calligraphy's Cory Petit (letters), Lee Loughridge (colors), Daniel Ketchum, Sebastian Girner (asst editor), Axel Alonso (editor), Dave Johnson (c art)
FEATURE CHARACTER: Punisher (next in Pun:XMas #1, '09)
VILLAINS: Jigsaw, El Jefe, Ramón Estrada & their drug cartel enforcers (all die)
OTHER CHARACTERS: Tierra Rota coroner, enslaved women inc Mija, Myrna & Alexa (some die), Tierra Rota citizens; Angelica Nuñez (in Punisher's thoughts)
LOCATIONS/ITEMS: Tierra Rota, Mexico inc motel & cartel's factory; Times Square / Punisher's guns, assault rifle, grenades & knife; drug cartel's knives, shotguns, handguns, crane & shipping crate; Jigsaw's gun, El Jefe's shotgun, Ramón's Ferrari, enslaved women's shovel & chain

SYNOPSIS: Punisher returns to his motel room for his weapons. Outside, the coroner tells Punisher a policeman came forward with information about the drug cartel; it's mainly an export business to America, overseen by the Heavy. Punisher asks if anyone has seen the Heavy's face and leaves. At the factory, the cartel's enforcers begin to kill the women. One woman flees into a building, protecting a little girl. Punisher arrives, kills the woman's attacker and massacres the other enforcers until he finds Jigsaw. Jigsaw retreats to his office where his associates abandon him. Punisher attacks and after a brief battle, Jigsaw falls out of the office and onto a passing freight train. The remaining cartel enforcers attack, but Punisher drops a shipping container on them. El Jefe abandons Ramón and escapes. Ramón takes a hostage, only for Punisher to ignore his threats and kill him. The women return to Tierra Rota. When el Jefe arrives in Tierra Rota, a group of women beat him to death. Later, Punisher returns to New York.
NOTE: Includes recap/credits page (1 page).

PUNISHER MAX X-MAS SPECIAL #1 (February 2009)

"And on Earth Peace, Good Will toward Men" (34 pages)

CREDITS: Jason Aaron (writer), Roland Boschi (art), Virtual Calligraphy's Cory Petit (letters), Daniel Brown (colors), Sebastian Girner (asst editor), Axel Alonso (editor), Chris Bachalo (c art)
FEATURE CHARACTER: Punisher (also as Santa Claus, also off-panel as Frank Castle in fb2 between Punmax #20, '12 fb & Punmax #21, '12 fb, also off-panel as Lt. Castle in fb1 between Punmax #20, '12 fb & Punmax #21, '12 fb, also in dfb; next in Pun #66, '09)
SUPPORTING CAST: Maria Castle (off-panel in fb2 between Punmax #20, '12 fb & Punmax #21, '12 fb), Lisa Castle (in fb2 between bts in Punmax #20, '12 fb

& Punmax #21, '12 fb)

VILLAINS: Johnny Castellano (Chicago mob boss) & his men inc Sammy, Joey & Frank; Mrs. Castellano (Johnny's pregnant wife), Maranzano (rival mob boss), his hit squad inc Danny & his men inc Jackie (bts, on phone) & Johnny; Shepherd (pimp) & his crew inc Rory; Three Wise Hitmen (all die)

OTHER CHARACTERS: U.S. Marine medic, pregnant Vietnamese woman (both in fb1), doctor (in fb2), newborn infants (die), news anchor (on TV), baby Castellano, priest, bartender, hospital staff, taxi driver, prostitutes, bystanders, horses; Castellano's daughter (mentioned, got pregnant) & her boyfriend (mentioned, left Castellano's daughter when she got pregnant, castrated), elves (on cover)

LOCATIONS/ITEMS: Chicago, IL inc Dulohery's Saloon, DCW Waste Management office, Maranzano's estate, church, hospital inc nursery & Ragweed racetrack inc horse stable / Punisher's assault rifle knife, guns & note; hit squad's assault rifles & Uzi; Maranzano's golf club & money; Maranzano's men's guns, Castellano's men's guns, Shepherd's revolver, Three Wise Hitmen's guns

FLASHBACKS: In Vietnam, Lt. Castle assists with a birth (1). Frank Castle witnesses his daughter's birth (2). Punisher kills Maranzano and his men (1).

SYNOPSIS: A priest walks into a bar on Christmas Eve and drunkenly laments to Santa Claus that no one believes in Christmas and berates some nearby mobsters. The bartender kicks the priest out. The mobsters get a phone call telling them that mob boss Johnny Castellano is at the hospital; his wife will give birth soon. Santa Claus murders the mobsters, revealing himself as Punisher. Meanwhile, a hit squad storms the nearby hospital and slaughters all the infants in the nursery. Punisher hears the gunshots. The hit squad learns that Mrs. Castellano hasn't given birth yet. Punisher arrives, kills the hit squad and leaves with the Castellanos. Learning his hit squad failed, rival mob boss Maranzano hires Three Wise Hitmen to kill Castellano and Punisher. Shepherd learns from one of his prostitutes that Punisher is at a nearby racetrack. The hitmen overhear Johnny calling his men for help. Everyone converges at the stable where Punisher kills all but Shepherd, who Mrs. Castellano kills. Punisher delivers the baby and kills the Castellanos. On Christmas Day, Punisher drops off the baby at the priest's church with money and instructions to "Give this child something to believe in."

PUNISHER: FRANK CASTLE MAX #66 (March 2009)

"Six Hours to Kill Chapter One: The Weak End" (21 pages)

CREDITS: Duane Swierczynski (writer), Michel Lacombe (art), Virtual Calligraphy's Cory Petit (letters), Val Staples (colors), Sebastian Girner (asst editor), Axel Alonso (editor), Dave Johnson (c art)
FEATURE CHARACTER: Punisher
VILLAINS: Room 101 (black bag operations unit): Benjamin "Benji" Gard, Deirdre "Dre" Gard (sibling criminal entrepreneurs, 1st but chr last in Pun #68, '09 fb), Lieutenant-Commander Walter Rose (Vietnam veteran & Room 101's front man, 1st but chr last in Pun #67, '09 fb), Louis (hitman, 1st, dies), Joe "Don" Corliss (Mayor of Philadelphia, 1st), Charles Corliss (Mayor's cousin, runs Juvenile Learning Center, bts, avoiding reporters), Juvenile Learning Center guards (child traffickers, die)
OTHER CHARACTERS: Bobby (Mayor's driver), Zach (Mayor's aide, voice only on phone), reporter (voice only on radio), children; Jonathan Lynn Cavalier (Lizard King lawyer), bystanders (both in photo)

LOCATIONS/ITEMS: Philadelphia, PA inc Juvenile Learning Center, Louis' workshop & PNB building w/Room 101's apartment / Punisher's guns, garrote, Humvee, knife, assault rifle & Uzis; Juvenile Learning Center guards' guns & cattle prods; Louis' gas mask, knockout gas, syringe w/poison & file on Cavalier

SYNOPSIS: 10:05 PM: Punisher attacks a Philadelphia child trafficking ring run out of a Juvenile Learning Center, killing all the guards present. He calls in an anonymous tip and leaves the facility. 10:22 PM: Punisher finds someone waiting for him in his van. Punisher passes out when exposed to knockout gas. 11:45 PM: In their PNB building apartment, reassures Dre that everything is going according to plan. 12:10 AM: Punisher wakes up in Louis' workspace secured to a table. Louis injects Punisher with a poison that will kill him in six hours. 12:25 AM: The Philadelphia Mayor learns about Punisher's attack on the Juvenile Learning Center that his cousin runs. 12:38 AM: Louis offers Punisher a solution: kill Philadelphia crime lord Jon Cavalier and Punisher will receive the poison's antidote. Punisher agrees to the terms and Louis frees him only for Punisher to immediately kill Louis. Not afraid to die and doubting the existence of the antidote, Punisher decides to make the best of his final six hours.

NOTE: Includes title/recap/credits page (1 page). Series changes its name to Punisher: Frank Castle MAX to distinguish itself from the returning Earth-616 Punisher series. Room 101 is named in and Benji and Dre's surnames are revealed in Pun #68, '09. Pun #67, '09 reveals the Mayor's full name and Walter's name and rank. Benji's & Jon's full 1st names are revealed in Pun #69, '09. When talking about Dre and himself, Benji paraphrases a line from Jim Morrison's poem "The Celebration of the Lizard."

PUNISHER: FRANK CASTLE MAX #67 (April 2009)

"Six Hours to Kill Chapter Two: Field Day" (22 pages)

CREDITS: Duane Swierczynski (writer), Michel Lacombe (art), Virtual Calligraphy's Cory Petit (letters), Val Staples (colors), Sebastian Girner (asst editor), Axel Alonso (editor), Dave Johnson (c art)
FEATURE CHARACTER: Punisher
VILLAINS: Room 101: Benji Gard, Deirdre Gard, Walter Rose (also in fb between Pun #68, '09 & Pun #66, '09), Charles Corliss (1st but last bts in Pun #66, '09), Joe Corliss (also in photo), Jon Cavalier (Philadelphia crime lord & lawyer, 1st, also in photo), Mikhal Stadnycki (Russian mob captain, also in photo, dies) & his men, Mikhal's nephew (1st, next in Pun #69, '09), Baz L'Salle (real estate profiteer, dies), Shenice (Baz's girlfriend), Jeffro Carter (sexual predator, also in photo, dies, see NOTE), Saugherty (mercenary contractor, 1st) & his mercenaries (disguised as police), North Vietnamese soldier (in fb)
OTHER CHARACTERS: Louis (corpse), Club Trouble bouncer, Jeffro's dates, police, paramedics, party guests, bystanders

LOCATIONS/ITEMS: "Hanoi Hilton" (Hỏa Lò Prison in Vietnam, in fb), Philadelphia, PA inc the Bellevue-Stratford, Little Odessa nightclub, Juvenile Learning Center, Baz's house, Club Trouble & Louis' workshop / Punisher's Humvee, files, gun, knife, stun grenades, rifle, ballistic knife & machete; mercenaries' shotguns & fake police badges; Baz's gun, shotgun & shovel; Shenice's frying pan, Mikhal's gun

FLASHBACK: Walter is interrogated and tortured through beatings and shock treatment at "Hanoi Hilton."

SYNOPSIS: 12:45 AM: Unable to reach Louis, Dre decides to take Walter and investigate. 12:51 AM: Punisher looks through his Philadelphia file and picks his first target: Russian mob captain Mikhail Stadnycki. 1:11 AM: Punisher lures Mikhail out of the Little Odessa nightclub by defacing Mikhail's car then shoots Mikhail. 1:14 AM: The Mayor visits his cousin, who admits to running a child slavery operation out of the Juvenile Learning Center. Fearing further scandal on top of the one already plaguing his office, the Mayor hires mercenaries to kill the Punisher by dawn. 1:40 AM: Punisher kills Baz L'Salle, a crooked real estate developer. 1:45 AM: Jon Cavalier learns he's being implicated in the Juvenile Learning Center child slavery operation. 2:02 AM: Punisher kills sexual predator Jeffro Carter. 2:06 AM: Dre and Walter find Louis' body, discovering that his Blackberry is missing. Having run out of targets worth his time, Punisher decides to look into Cavalier. Cavalier has a faux pleasant chat at the party with Benji, wondering when Benji will kill him. 3:13 AM: Disguised as policemen, a group of mercenaries prepare to kill the Punisher.

NOTE: Includes title/recap/credits page (1 page). Jeffro's brother Dwight Carter was killed by Punisher in Pun:FoN #1, '08.

PUNISHER: FRANK CASTLE MAX #68 (May 2009)

"Six Hours to Kill Chapter Three: Hour Game" (22 pages)

CREDITS: Duane Swierczynski (writer), Michel Lacombe (art), Virtual Calligraphy's Cory Petit (letters), Val Staples (colors), Sebastian Girner (asst editor), Axel Alonso (editor), Dave Johnson (c art)
FEATURE CHARACTER: Punisher (also as Perelli in Walter's delusion)
VILLAINS: Room 101: Benji Gard, Deirdre Gard (both also in fb2 to 1st chr app before Pun #66, '09), Walter Rose (also in photo, also in fb1 to 1st chr app before Pun #67, '09 fb); Joe Corliss (next in Pun #70, '09), Jon Cavalier (also in photo) & his men (die), Saugherty & his mercenaries (disguised as police, some die), Perelli (traitorous American soldier), North Vietnamese soldiers (1 also in Walter's delusion) (both in fb1)
OTHER CHARACTERS: Morozzi (Cavalier's associate, voice only), PNB building doorman (corpse), Philadelphia councilmen (in fb2), police SWAT team, party guests; college students, Benji's victims, Benji's attack dog (prev 3 in fb2); Cavalier's wife & 2 children (in photo); Perelli (mentioned, betrayed Walter to North Vietnamese Army)

LOCATIONS/ITEMS: World Trade Center, Hindu Kush, Bryn Mawr college, Gard house in Wayne, PA; public relations firm board room in Center City, PA (all in fb2), "Hanoi Hilton" (in fb1), Philadelphia, PA inc the Bellevue-Stratford, subway station, PNB building w/Room 101's apartment & Cavalier's office; Mayor's estate in Chestnut Hill, PA / Punisher's Humvee (destroyed), Uzis & stun grenade; mercenaries' shotguns & fake police badges; Cavalier's men's guns & silencers; SWAT assault rifles

FLASHBACKS: North Vietnamese soldiers begin to interrogate Walter (1). In September, 2001, the teenage Benji and Dre decide their future will involving profiting from terrorism. A few years later while Benji is serving in the Hindu Kush and making contacts, Dre sells drugs in college and later to city councilmen. When Benji returns home, he and Dre plan their future business enterprises as a black bag operations unit, using Lieutenant-Commander Walter Rose as their front man (2).

SYNOPSIS: 3:15 AM: Punisher ducks just as the mercenaries shoot at him. Realizing they aren't real police, Punisher fires back. The vigilante escapes, but his Humvee is destroyed. 3:29 AM: Dre lets Benji know that Louis is dead and that Punisher has Louis' Blackberry. Cavalier orders Dre captured and interrogated. 3:33 AM: With his arsenal destroyed in the Humvee and his reflexes dulled by the poison, Punisher decides to find Cavalier with the time he has left, but a SWAT team attacks him. Punisher escapes. The mercenaries tell the Mayor they need two-hundred thousand dollars to hire the Killaz to kill the Punisher. 3:46 AM: Dre and Walter return home to find masked men waiting for them. Walter brutally kills them. 3:48 AM: Benji tries to call Dre, but she's busy thanking Walter for his performance. Benji calls the Killaz to hire them, but learns they've already been hired to kill Punisher. 3:49 AM: In Cavalier's office, Punisher cross-references contacts in Cavalier's rolodex with contacts in Louis' phone and finds Benji and Dre in both. 3:58 AM: Punisher breaks into Dre's apartment, but Walter hallucinates that Punisher is Perelli, the man who betrayed Walter in Vietnam.

NOTE: Includes title/recap/credits page (1 page). Perelli is named in Pun #69, '09.

PUNISHER: FRANK CASTLE MAX #69 (June 2009)

"Six Hours to Kill Chapter Four: Minute Men" (22 pages)

CREDITS: Duane Swierczynski (writer), Michel Lacombe (art), Virtual Calligraphy's Cory Petit (letters), Val Staples (colors), Sebastian Girner (asst editor), Axel Alonso (editor), Dave Johnson (c art)
FEATURE CHARACTER: Punisher (also as Perelli in Walter's delusion)
VILLAINS: Room 101: Benji Gard, Deirdre Gard, Walter Rose; Jon Cavalier (bts), Broad Street Killaz (thugs for hire, some die), Mikhail's nephew (last in Pun #67, '09), Mikhail's men, Saugherty & his mercenary
OTHER CHARACTERS: Alice (CBS-10 reporter), Ricky Hickey (CBS-10 cameraman & Alice's lover) (both 1st), FBI agents inc Andy, party guests
LOCATIONS/ITEMS: Philadelphia, PA inc the Bellevue-Stratford, Alice's apartment, diner, parking garage, Interesting Times Pub & PNB Building w/Room 101's apartment / Punisher's gun, knife & wood spike; Mikhail's nephew's gun & rocket launcher; Mikhail's men's guns, Killaz' guns, FBI assault rifles

SYNOPSIS: 4:14 AM: Walter battles Punisher. Dre stops Walter from killing Punisher long enough to tempt Punisher with the antidote if he reconsiders doing their job and maybe partnering with them. Punisher refuses. 4:20 AM: The Killaz search for Punisher. 4:24 AM: Walter prepares to kill Punisher, but Punisher barks at Walter in Vietnamese. Walter freezes long enough for Punisher to stab Walter in the leg with a piece of wood and escapes. 4:26 AM: Dre calls and tells Benji that Punisher tried to kill her and escaped, but the vigilante left his gun behind. Benji tells Dre not to touch the gun and calls a reporter, telling her that Cavalier ran the child slavery operation and hired the Killaz to kill Punisher. 4:37 AM: On the street, Punisher uses his environment to stay ahead of the Killaz. 4:45 AM: Mikhail's nephew stumbles across Punisher, looking for revenge for his uncle. Punisher escapes by leaping into a bar where he passes out. 4:49 AM: Dre and Walter prepare for the next part of Benji's plan. 4:52 AM: The FBI finds the unconscious Punisher, unaware Mikhail's nephew has a rocket launcher pointed at them and the Killaz are closing in.

NOTE: Includes title/recap/credits page (1 page). Pun #70, '09 reveals Andy's name and the station Alice & Ricky work for.

PUNISHER: FRANK CASTLE MAX #70 (July 2009)

"Six Hours to Kill Chapter Five: No More Second Chances" (22 pages)

CREDITS: Duane Swierczynski (writer), Michel Lacombe (art), Virtual Calligraphy's Cory Petit (letters), Val Staples (colors), Sebastian Girner (asst editor), Axel Alonso (editor), Dave Johnson (c art)
FEATURE CHARACTER: Punisher (next in Pun:NK #1, '09)
VILLAINS: Room 101: Benji Gard, Deirdre Gard, Walter Rose; Mikhail's nephew, Mikhail's men, Broad Street Killaz (all die), Joe Corliss (last in Pun #68, '09), Jon Cavalier, Saugherty & his mercenary
OTHER CHARACTERS: Alice, Ricky Hickey, FBI Agents (some die) inc Andy, bartender, reporters, cameramen, bystanders
LOCATIONS/ITEMS: Philadelphia, PA inc Interesting Times Pub, parking garage, bar & Cavalier's office / Punisher's gun, Molotov cocktails & syringe w/sugar water; FBI assault rifles & guns; Killaz's shotguns & guns; Dre's knockout gas, gas mask & syringe w/antidote; Mikhail's nephew's rocket launcher, Walter's gun, Benji's gun, Saugherty's gun
SYNOPSIS: 4:53 AM: Mikhail's nephew fires a rocket into the bar Punisher and the FBI are in. After the explosion, Punisher grabs an assault rifle and kills Mikhail's nephew. 4:59 AM: A firefight breaks out between the Killaz and the FBI agents. Determined to save the remaining two FBI agents, Punisher convinces them to use Molotov cocktails so they can escape. 5:20 AM: The FBI agents arrest Punisher, but Dre and Walter arrive, use knockout gas on the FBI agents and escape with Punisher. 6:12 AM: Punisher wakes up. Dre offers Punisher the antidote if he'll join them. Punisher closes his eyes and waits for death. 6:15 AM: Walter tries to stop Dre from giving Punisher the antidote and Dre kills Walter. 6:20 AM: Punisher wakes up, angry that he's still alive. Punisher frees himself and kills Dre. 6:40 AM: Benji prepares to kill Cavalier in the lawyer's office with Punisher's gun. Punisher arrives and kills Benji. Punisher stabs Cavalier with a syringe, telling the lawyer he'll die in sixty minutes and promises the antidote if Cavalier dismantles his criminal empire and confesses his crimes to the press. 7:01 AM: Cavalier goes before the press, indicting the Mayor and his mercenaries. 7:35 AM: Punisher steals a news van and leaves Philadelphia, knowing Cavalier won't die from the injected sugar water.
NOTE: Includes title/recap/credits page (1 page). Issue is dedicated to the memory of colorist Stéphane Peru.

PUNISHER MAX: NAKED KILL #1 (August 2009)

Untitled (32 pages)

CREDITS: Jonathan Maberry (writer), Laurence Campbell (art), Virtual Calligraphy's Joe Caramagna (letters), Lee Loughridge (colors), Sebastian Girner (asst editor), Axel Alonso (editor), Tim Bradstreet (c art)
FEATURE CHARACTER: Punisher (also as R. Kirsch, next in Pun #71, '09)
VILLAINS: Mickey Fane (security systems businessman & torture snuff porn entrepreneur), Eleventhree (well-endowed torture snuff porn star & Mickey's nephew, also in recording), Polly Hu (Mickey's slave master), Daedalus Tower guards inc Jason Pinter, Mischa Wheat, Ed, Frost, Goldy, Homler, Keith & Lafferty; Dirtbox (Dennis Tafoya, torture snuff porn distributor), other torture snuff porn distributors, torture snuff porn film crew (all die)
OTHER CHARACTERS: Mickey's enslaved girls (1 in recording, some die), Fane's secretary (voice only), Fane's clients, doctor, taxi drivers
LOCATIONS/ITEMS: Distributors' house, Daedalus Tower inc custodial closet, Fane's office, armory & film set; hospital, Fane's other office / Punisher's Uzis, knife & Pain-Eeze gel caps (used as fake poison); Daedalus security's assault rifles, handguns, shotguns, Uzis, glass, handcuffs, pencils, rag, scrub brush & book (see NOTE); Hu's riding crop, hair stick & handgun; Fane's helicopter
SYNOPSIS: Punisher kills some torture snuff porn film distributors. The surviving distributor, Dirtbox, offers to take Punisher to where the films are made in exchange for his life. Punisher agrees, but feeds Dirtbox a poison that, without the antidote, will kill Dirtbox in four hours to keep Dirtbox honest. Dirtbox doesn't know the pills are only painkillers. They arrive at Daedalus Tower, Mickey Fane's high-security, eight-story building designed by Fane. Inside, Fane gives his clients a tour to sell them his security systems as Dirtbox gets Punisher a job as a janitor. With Fane's elaborate security measures, Punisher is unable to bring in weapons or get to the top floor filming area without floor captains authorizing the elevator access. Punisher uses whatever he can as a weapon to kill each floor's captain until they reach the seventh floor and find a weapons cache. Punisher kills Dirtbox and opens fire on the film set, killing everyone but the girls. Fane locks the building down and escapes. The girls help Punisher make a human ladder by handcuffing corpses together, and they climb eight stories down outside the building. Punisher takes the girls to the hospital and goes to Fane's other office to kill Fane.
NOTE: Includes credits page (1 page). Punisher uses Maberry's book "Patient Zero" as a weapon.

PUNISHER: FRANK CASTLE MAX #71 (August 2009)

"Welcome to the Bayou" (22 pages)

CREDITS: Victor Gischler (writer), Goran Parlov (art), Virtual Calligraphy's Cory Petit (letters), Lee Loughridge (colors), Sebastian Girner (asst editor), Axel Alonso (editor), Dave Johnson (c art)
FEATURE CHARACTER: Frank Castle
VILLAINS: Big Daddy Geautreaux, Roy Geautreaux, female Geautreaux (all 1st), Earl Geautreaux (off-panel), Jay Geautreaux (bts, carving up Billy) (cannibalistic family), Nigel (thug, bts, in trunk of Frank's car)
OTHER CHARACTERS: Billy, blonde (both next in Pun #73, '09), Kyle (dies), redhead (all college students on spring break, 1st), General Lee (12-foot alligator, 1st, next in Pun #73, '09), Fluffy (Roy's rat)
LOCATIONS/ITEMS: Louisiana inc Geautreaux's Gas, house, shack, river house & swamp / bucket of catfish heads, jar of rat corpses, jar of eyes, alligator skulls, cage
SYNOPSIS: Frank Castle drives through Louisiana to New Orleans with a special delivery in the trunk of his car. A group of college students on spring break speed past him, but he catches up to them at a rundown gas station. Frank notices the gas station attendant leering at the college girls, but decides to keep his schedule and continues on his trip. Down the road, Castle wonders why the students haven't passed him yet. He stops and waits ten minutes, then another ten. He returns to the gas station to find it closed and investigates at the house behind the station. He finds a flirtatious woman who surreptitiously leads Frank back to his car. Meanwhile in the swamp, the girls are tortured in a cage by the Geautreaux family. When the tied-up Kyle yells for the girls to be left alone, Big Daddy unleashes General Lee, a twelve-foot alligator who eats Kyle. Big Daddy mentions that Billy is being prepared for the barbeque as the package in Castle's trunk starts making noise.
NOTE: Nigel is named in Pun #74, '09.

PUNISHER: FRANK CASTLE MAX #72 (September 2009)

"Welcome to the Bayou Part 2" (22 pages)

CREDITS: Victor Gischler (writer), Goran Parlov (art), Virtual Calligraphy's Cory Petit (letters), Lee Loughridge (colors), Sebastian Girner (asst editor), Axel Alonso (editor), Dave Johnson (c art)
FEATURE CHARACTER: Frank Castle
VILLAINS: Roy Geautreaux (dies), Earl Geautreaux (1st full app), Big Daddy Geautreaux, female Geautreaux, several other Geautreaux family members (many die), Nigel (1st but last bts in Pun #71, '09)
OTHER CHARACTER: Redhead
LOCATIONS/ITEMS: Louisiana inc Geautreaux's Gas, house, shack, river house & swamp / Franks' gun & revolver; female Geautreaux's axe
SYNOPSIS: Frank Castle leaves the gas station, grabs a gun and circles back on foot. Finding the woman already gone, Frank heads into the swamp and finds a shack where the gas station attendant has the redhead tied up. Castle kills the attendant and frees the redhead, only for the woman to attack with an axe. Frank quickly disarms her, but she yells for Big Daddy. Castle finds himself surrounded by a dozen Geautreaux. Frank kills the attackers, but Earl arrives and defeats Castle in a fist fight. Meanwhile, Nigel frees himself from the trunk of Frank's car. He grabs a map and a revolver from Castle's glove box and plots to kill the Punisher.
NOTE: Includes recap/credits page (1 page). Followed by MvPro #1, '09 preview (6 pages).

PUNISHER: FRANK CASTLE MAX #73 (October 2009)

"Welcome to the Bayou Part 3" (22 pages)

CREDITS: Victor Gischler (writer), Goran Parlov (art), Virtual Calligraphy's Cory Petit (letters), Lee Loughridge (colors), Sebastian Girner (asst editor), Axel Alonso (editor), Dave Johnson (c art)
FEATURE CHARACTER: Frank Castle
VILLAINS: Earl Geautreaux (dies), Junior Geautreaux (1st in shadows), Big Daddy Geautreaux, female Geautreaux, several other Geautreaux family members, Nigel
OTHER CHARACTERS: General Lee (dies), Billy (corpse, eaten), blonde (all last in Pun #71, '09), redhead, other alligators
LOCATIONS/ITEMS: Louisiana inc Geautreaux's Gas, river house & swamp / Frank's revolver, Earl's knife, Big Daddy's revolver, Billy's barbeque spit, Geautreaux rifle, alligator skulls, cage
SYNOPSIS: Frank Castle wakes up to find himself tied up and the college girls back in the cage. The flirtatious woman tells Frank he's the guest of honor at the Geautreaux family barbeque. Castle sees they're cooking Billy to eat. The woman taunts Frank and the family begins their party while Castle can only watch. Meanwhile, Nigel finds the closed gas station. He breaks in and steals some bottled water, only for Earl to grab him by the neck. Big Daddy declines to eat Nigel, but instead suggests they hunt him for sport. Nigel later wakes up to see the party still raging. Earl feels restless, so he wrestles and kills General Lee and drags the blonde college girl into his shack. After everyone falls asleep, Nigel frees himself, grabs Earl's knife and prepares to kill Frank. Castle grabs Nigel with his legs and threatens to kill Nigel unless Nigel frees Frank. Nigel agrees, only for Earl to catch them. Castle kills Earl by impaling him on Billy's barbeque spit. Frank and Nigel flee into the swamp as the Geautreaux family wakes up. Big Daddy calls for Junior, warning him Frank and Nigel are headed his way.
NOTE: Includes recap/credits page (1 page).

PUNISHER: FRANK CASTLE MAX #74 (November 2009)

(untitled, 35 pages)

CREDITS: Victor Gischler (writer), Goran Parlov (art), Virtual Calligraphy's Cory Petit (letters), Lee Loughridge (colors), Sebastian Girner (asst editor), Axel Alonso (editor), Dave Johnson (c art)
FEATURE CHARACTER: Frank Castle
VILLAINS: Big Daddy Geautreaux, Junior Geautreaux, female Geautreaux, several other Geautreaux family members (all die), Nigel
OTHER CHARACTERS: Redhead, alligator, moccasin; Benny (Nigel's cousin, mentioned, has information Frank needs)
LOCATIONS/ITEMS: Louisiana inc Junior's shack & swamp / Frank's revolver, Junior's meat cleaver, lantern, opossum pelts & rabbit doll; Geautreaux rifles & shotguns; alligator skull
SYNOPSIS: Frank Castle and Nigel make their way through the swamp as the Geautreaux family searches for them. Frank and Nigel find a shack where they grab some clothes. When Nigel picks up a rabbit doll, Junior smashes through the wall to retrieve it. Castle throws a lantern at Junior; when it smashes Junior and the shack catch on fire. Frank and Nigel escape. Castle says they have to attack the Geautreaux if they want to survive, Nigel just wants to run. Frank says he can't let Nigel run; he grabbed him in the first place because Nigel owes his cousin Benny money, and Castle wants to trade Nigel for information Benny has. Wanting to survive, Nigel agrees to help and throws a moccasin into one of the Geautreaux boats. Frank and Nigel use the boat to get further ahead of their pursuers. Junior finds his rabbit doll and sits in his burning shack. Castle and Nigel abandon their boat as a decoy and ambush the Geautreaux family when they come looking for the pair. Big Daddy tries to reason with Frank, but Castle just shoots Big Daddy in the face. With the crisis over, Frank tells Nigel they're going to continue on to New Orleans to see Benny, but Junior arrives and attacks Nigel, breaking his arm and poking out an eye. Castle cuts Junior's throat, understanding that Junior was only upset about his home being torn down. Frank lets Nigel leave, wondering if he'll survive in the swamp. Castle frees the redhead college girl who asks if her friends are all right; she doesn't remember what happened to them. The Geautreaux woman suddenly attacks and Frank breaks her neck. The redhead mentions she didn't like that woman as she and Castle leave.
NOTE: Includes recap/credits page (1 page). Followed by Pun #75, '09 preview (7 pages).

PUNISHER: FRANK CASTLE MAX #75 (December 2009)

"Dolls" (10 pages)

CREDITS: Tom Piccirilli (writer), Laurence Campbell (art), Virtual Calligraphy's Cory Petit (letters), Lee Loughridge (colors), Sebastian Girner (asst editor), Axel Alonso (editor), Dave Johnson (c art), Steve Dillon (variant c art)
FEATURE CHARACTER: Punisher (also in fb as Frank Castle during Punmax #13, '11 fb; next in Pun #75/3, '09)
SUPPORTING CAST: Maria Castle, Lisa Castle, Frank Castle Jr. (all in fb during Punmax #13, '11 fb)
VILLAIN: Maxwell Hawthorne (harbormaster syndicate bagman, dies)
OTHER CHARACTERS: Becky & her father, Hawthorne's birthday party guests, Sally Stylish salesman, bystanders
LOCATIONS/ITEMS: New York inc Hawthorne's brownstone / Punisher's sniper rifle, Becky's Sally Stylish doll, Lisa's Sally Stylish doll (in fb)
FLASHBACK: The Castle family goes on a stroll while Lisa plays with her Sally Stylish doll.
SYNOPSIS: Punisher prepares to kill Maxwell Hawthorne, but a lost girl, Becky, interrupts him. Punisher pauses his mission to help Becky find her father. While they search, Punisher buys Becky a Sally Stylish doll, which he recalls his daughter Lisa had years ago. They find Becky's father, and Punisher uses him to steady his shot to kill Hawthorne. Punisher warns the father to never let Becky out of his sight.
NOTE: Includes titles/credits page (1 page).

2ND STORY: "Gateway" (8 pages)
CREDITS: Gregg Hurwitz (writer), Das Pastoras (art, colors), Virtual Calligraphy's Cory Petit (letters), Sebastian Girner (asst editor), Axel Alonso (editor)
FEATURE CHARACTER: Frank Castle (last in Punmax #16, '11 fb, also in Punmax #16, '11 fb, Pun #75/4, '09 fb, Pun #50, '07 fb, Pun #1, '04 fb, Punmax #20, '12 fb, Pun:Tyger #1, '06 fb bts & Punmax #21, '12 fb, next in Pun #4, '04 fb)
SUPPORTING CAST: Maria Castle, Lisa Castle, Frank Castle Jr. (all during Punmax #16, '11 fb)
VILLAINS: Don Francesco Drago (also in photo), Enzo Gaucci (both in chr 1st app before Pun:Cell #1, '05 fb), Paulie & Philly Germaine (both last in Punmax #16, '11 fb, next in Pun:Cell #1, '05 fb), George Apostolo (in chr 1st app before Pun:Cell #1, '05), Tommy Drago (1st full app, chr last bts in Pun:Cell #1, '05 fb), Gateway (mafia information courier, dies)
OTHER CHARACTERS: Gateway's wife & 2 children, U.S. Marine (served w/Castle in Vietnam), bystanders
LOCATIONS/ITEMS: Gateway's home, Tommy Drago's home, Central Park, Frank's hospital room, Castle home / Enzo's Thompson, Frank's shotgun & guns
SYNOPSIS: Gateway meets with Drago family consigliere George Apostolo and brings Tommy Drago's order to kill Francesco Drago to Enzo Gaucci. In Central Park, the Castle family is caught in the crossfire when Enzo attacks Francesco and the Germaine twins. Later, a fellow Marine visits Frank in the hospital, telling him Gateway passed on the information that led to the Castle family deaths. Frank returns home where a half-eaten family breakfast is still on the table. Castle grabs his shotgun, travels to Gateway's home and kills the information courier.

3RD STORY: "Ghoul" (6 pages)
CREDITS: Duane Swierczynski (writer), Tomm Coker (art), Virtual Calligraphy's Cory Petit (letters), Dan Freedman (colors), Sebastian Girner (asst editor), Axel Alonso (editor)
FEATURE CHARACTER: Punisher

OTHER CHARACTERS: Sgt. Hickey (officer in charge of evidence locker after Castle family deaths)

LOCATIONS/ITEMS: New York inc Hickey's apartment / Punisher's shears, Frank Jr.'s shirt & toy police car

SYNOPSIS: Sgt. Hickey sells the shirt Frank Castle Jr. was wearing the day he was killed on an auction site for a five figure sum. He leaves to meet someone selling the Castle family picnic blanket, but is ambushed. Hickey wakes up in his apartment where Punisher cuts off one of his fingers. Punisher tells Hickey to buy back all of the items he's sold over the years and document their destruction, or Hickey will lose his arm next. Punisher leaves a bag of money to pay for the items. Later, Hickey prepares to destroy Frank Jr.'s toy police car.

4TH STORY: "Father's Day" (7 pages)

CREDITS: Peter Milligan (writer), Goran Parlov (art), Virtual Calligraphy's Cory Petit (letters), Lee Loughridge (colors), Sebastian Girner (asst editor), Axel Alonso (editor)

FEATURE CHARACTER: Punisher (also in rfb, also in fb2 as Frank Castle between Punmax #16, '11 fb & Pun:Tyger #1, '06 fb bts, also in Punmax #16, '11 fb, Pun #75/2, '09, Pun #50, '07 fb, Pun #1, '04 fb & Punmax #20, '12 fb; also in fb1 between Pun #43, '07 fb & Pun #1, '04)

SUPPORTING CAST: Maria Castle, Lisa Castle, Frank Castle Jr. (all in fb2 between Punmax #16, '11 fb & Pun #19, '05, also in Punmax #16, '11 fb, Pun #75/2, '09, Pun #50, '07 fb, Pun #1, '04 fb & Punmax #20, '12 fb; die)

VILLAIN: The Russian (in fb1)

OTHER CHARACTERS: Barracuda, Microchip, the Mongolian, Tibieru Bulat, Jenny Cesare, Teresa Gazzera, Annabella Gorrini, Kathryn O'Brien, Sarah O'Brien, Westies, Riker's Penitentiary inmates, seagulls, sharks

LOCATIONS/ITEMS: Punisher's motel room, Central Park (in fb) / Lisa's letter (in fb2), Punisher's shotgun & sutures

FLASHBACKS: Punisher wires a cemetery monument with explosives (Pun #57, '08), battles Barracuda to save Sarah O'Brien (Pun #54, '08), watches Jenny Cesare kill herself (Pun #49, '07), stays with Kathryn O'Brien as she dies (Pun #41, '07), shoots Barracuda (Pun #36, '06), sets Tibieru Bulat on fire (Pun #30, '06), battles Teresa Gazzera (Pun #24, '05), kills the Mongolian (Pun #17, '05), ambushes the Westies (Pun #10, '04), kills Microchip (Pun #6, '04), and stalks the mobsters that killed his family in Riker's Penitentiary (Pun:Cell #1, '05). Punisher fights the Russian (1). In Central Park, Frank Castle is shot while his family is killed (2).

SYNOPSIS: In a motel room, Punisher sews his wounds closed while he recalls a letter his daughter Lisa wrote to him entitled "I feel safe when you are with me" on the day she was killed.

NOTE: The Russian appearing here is an Earth-200111 native.

5TH STORY: "Smallest Bit of This" (9 pages)

CREDITS: Charlie Huston (writer), Ken Lashley (pencils), Rob Stull (inks), Virtual calligraphy's Cory Petit (letters), Edgar Delgado (colors), Sebastian Girner (asst editor), Axel Alonso (editor)

FEATURE CHARACTER: Punisher (also in own thoughts, next in Pun:Get #1, Pun:Bf #1, Pun:Happy #1, Pun:Hot #1, Pun:Tiny #1, Punmax #1, all '10)

VILLAIN: Mobster

OTHER CHARACTERS: Frank Castle Jr. & his 3 children, Maria Castle, Lisa Castle (all in Punisher's thoughts), mobsters (corpses)

LOCATIONS/ITEMS: Central Park (in Punisher's thoughts), bar / Punisher's knife, mobster's knife, gun

SYNOPSIS: Surrounded by dead mobsters in a burning bar, Punisher and the only surviving mobster, both armed with knives, scramble for a gun. As they struggle, Punisher imagines his family surviving the attack in Central Park and growing old. When the mobster stabs Punisher, the vigilante imagines dying along with his family. When Punisher kills the mobster, he imagines his family surviving alone. Punisher is satisfied when he emerges victorious.

NOTE: Followed by Punmax #1, '10 preview (8 pages). Series continued in Punmax #1, '10.

PUNISHERMAX #1 (January 2010)

"Kingpin Part One" (22 pages)

CREDITS: Jason Aaron (writer), Steve Dillon (art), Virtual Calligraphy's Cory Petit (letters), Matt Hollingsworth (colors), Sebastian Girner (asst editor), Axel Alonso (editor), Dave Johnson (c art)

FEATURE CHARACTER: Punisher (last in Pun:Tiny #1, '10, also in dfb)

VILLAINS: Don Rigoletto (mob boss, 1st but chr last bts in Punmax #6, '10 fb) & his soldier (also in dfb, dies), Wilson Fisk (Rigoletto's bodyguard, 1st but chr last in Punmax #2, '10, see NOTE), Don Cesare, Don Pizzo, Don Macari, Don Totti (prev 4 mob bosses), Jackie (mob boss, 1st, next in Punmax #4, '10), Joey D'Amico (Jackie's captain, dies), other mob captains & soldiers (most die)

OTHER CHARACTERS: Vanessa Fisk (Wilson's wife), Richard Fisk (Wilson's son) (both 1st, see NOTE), prostitute

LOCATIONS/ITEMS: Punisher's safe house, Hell's Kitchen inc Fisk home; Poconos inc Rigoletto's house / Punisher's gun, hacksaw, pliers, salt, knives, scalpel & assault rifle; Fisk's gun, mob captains' guns

FLASHBACK: Punisher kills the interrogated mobster when he reveals Rigoletto is holding a meeting tonight (d).

SYNOPSIS: Punisher interrogates a mobster by cutting pieces off of him. Later, Don Rigoletto holds a meeting to discuss what the mob can do about the Punisher. He proposes they set up a new boss of bosses called the Kingpin to lure the Punisher into a trap. When Jackie's captain Joey objects, Rigoletto's bodyguard Wilson Fisk attacks Joey and pops Joey's eyes out. When Joey is brought outside to be killed, Punisher arrives and attacks the meeting. Fisk gets Rigoletto to safety as Punisher kills the other mobsters. Later, Wilson spends time with his wife and son until Rigoletto calls Fisk and tells him the Kingpin plan has been agreed to by the other mob bosses.

NOTE: The Wilson, Vanessa and Richard Fisk appearing here are Earth-200111 natives. Punmax #2, '10 reveals Macari & Totti's names.

PUNISHERMAX #2 (February 2010)

"Kingpin Part Two" (22 pages)

CREDITS: Jason Aaron (writer), Steve Dillon (art), Virtual Calligraphy's Cory Petit (letters), Matt Hollingsworth (colors), Sebastian Girner (asst editor), Axel Alonso (editor), Dave Johnson (c art)
FEATURE CHARACTER: Punisher
VILLAINS: Don Rigoletto (also in fb to 1st chr app before bts in Punmax #6, '10 fb) & his bodyguard (in fb), Wilson Fisk (also in fb to 1st chr app before Punmax #1, '10), Attica prison inmates inc Big Lucky (in fb), criminals (others in fb, some die)
OTHER CHARACTERS: Vanessa Fisk, Richard Fisk (next in Punmax #4, '10), Dave (computer hacker, dies), Fisk's father, Big Lucky's wife (both off-panel in fb, die), realtor, police (voice only), prostitutes (die), homeless men (in fb), strippers, bystanders, rats (in fb); Fisk's mother (mentioned, committed suicide)
LOCATIONS/ITEMS: New York inc "Kingpin's" office, Dave's Computer Repair, pool hall & strip club; Hell's Kitchen inc Fisk home; Punisher's safe house, golf course, Attica prison, Big Lucky's house, Rigoletto's office (prev 3 in fb) / Punisher's police radio, grenade, guns, Uzis & assault rifles; Fisk's knife, cheese, camera (prev 3 in fb) & gun (also in fb)
FLASHBACK: After his father killed his dog, young Wilson Fisk has rats chew off his father's face then kills his father. Years later in Attica prison, Big Lucky rapes Wilson. When Fisk is released, he finds Big Lucky's wife and hires a dozen homeless men to rape her. Wilson sends photos of the event to Big Lucky, who breaks out of prison. Fisk kills Big Lucky and his wife. Later, Don Rigoletto hires Wilson to be his bodyguard.
SYNOPSIS: Wilson Fisk says goodbye to his family and begins the process of setting up the "Kingpin of crime" identity by renting office space. Punisher listens to the police radio. Fisk hires some prostitutes to entertain the Kingpin. Punisher hears about the Kingpin from the prostitutes. Fisk hires men to work for the Kingpin, checks in with Rigoletto then kills the prostitutes. Later, Fisk hires a computer hacker to establish a social security number and tax history for the Kingpin. Punisher kills some criminals, who tell him the Kingpin is coming to New York to kill the Punisher. The hacker creates a history of a millionaire spice merchant who likes to visit the Japanese countryside. Fisk kills the hacker and leaves.
NOTE: Includes recap page (1 page).

PUNISHERMAX #3 (March 2010)

"Kingpin Part Three" (22 pages)

CREDITS: Jason Aaron (writer), Steve Dillon (art), Virtual Calligraphy's Cory Petit (letters), Matt Hollingsworth (colors), Sebastian Girner (asst editor), Axel Alonso (editor), Dave Johnson (c art)
FEATURE CHARACTER: Punisher
VILLAINS: Don Rigoletto (bts, calls Fisk), Wilson Fisk (also in photo), the Mennonite (assassin, 1st), Mamma Cesare (dies) & her men, Russian mobsters, rapist
OTHER CHARACTERS: Vanessa Fisk, the Mennonite's wife, 2 sons (both 1st, next in Punmax #5, '10) & horse, Mennonites, bystanders
LOCATIONS/ITEMS: Coney Island inc bar; Fisk home, Cesare estate, the Mennonite's home / Punisher's gun, the Mennonite's guns, knives, handcuffs & shovel; Kingpin's gun, Mamma's shotgun
SYNOPSIS: The Mennonite, a former assassin, worries for his sick wife and chastises his sons when they find his old weapons. Wilson Fisk establishes a truce with the Russian mob when he provides as a gift the man who raped the Russian mob boss's sister. Vanessa calls Wilson to warn him that Mamma Cesare knows that Fisk is positioning himself as the Kingpin. Meanwhile, Punisher travels to the Cesare estate to see if Mamma Cesare knows anything about the Kingpin. Fisk underestimates Mamma Cesare and she tries to kill him. Punisher arrives and kills Mamma Cesare, but Fisk escapes. Wilson returns home and tells Vanessa he's the new Kingpin. The Mennonite receives word from Rigoletto and leaves for New York.
NOTE: Includes recap page (1 page). Followed by FF #575, '10 preview (6 pages).

PUNISHERMAX #4 (April 2010)

"Kingpin Part Four" (22 pages)

CREDITS: Jason Aaron (writer), Steve Dillon (art), Virtual Calligraphy's Cory Petit (letters), Matt Hollingsworth (colors), Sebastian Girner (asst editor), Axel Alonso (editor), Dave Johnson (c art)
FEATURE CHARACTER: Punisher
VILLAINS: Don Rigoletto & his men, Wilson Fisk & his men, the Mennonite, Don Alfano & his bodyguard, Don Garafolo, Don Labruzzo, Don Tartamella (prev 5 die), Don Marzano (bts, calls Rigoletto)
OTHER CHARACTERS: Vanessa Fisk, Richard Fisk (last in Punmax #2, '10), Vo Dai manicurist (dies), prostitute, bystanders, the Mennonite's horses
LOCATIONS/ITEMS: New York inc Rigoletto's office & Vo Dai Nail Spa; Hell's Kitchen inc Fisk home; Jackie's house / Punisher's boot knife, taser, chains & gun, the Mennonite's sledgehammer & axe
SYNOPSIS: Don Rigoletto hires the Mennonite to kill Punisher. Wilson Fisk moves his family to a motel room until his plan to be Kingpin is finalized, but is interrupted when Punisher arrives. Punisher prepares to kill Fisk, but the Mennonite attacks and breaks Punisher hand with a sledgehammer. Punisher and Mennonite battle as Fisk escapes. Meanwhile, Fisk's men simultaneously kill the various New York mob bosses. Jackie calls Rigoletto, telling him that all of their money has been taken by Fisk just as Fisk arrives at Rigoletto's office. As Punisher continues to battle Mennonite, Jackie is killed and Fisk kills Rigoletto's men.
NOTE: Includes recap page (1 page).

PUNISHERMAX #5 (May 2010)

"Kingpin Conclusion" (22 pages)

CREDITS: Jason Aaron (writer), Steve Dillon (art), Virtual Calligraphy's Cory Petit (letters), Matt Hollingsworth (colors), Sebastian Girner (asst editor), Axel Alonso (editor), Dave Johnson (c art)
FEATURE CHARACTER: Punisher (also in photo)
VILLAINS: Don Rigoletto & his men (all die), Wilson Fisk (becomes Kingpin), the Mennonite (dies), Bullseye (Shelton Pendergrass, assassin, 1st but chr last in Punmax #6, '10 fb, see NOTE)
OTHER CHARACTERS: Vanessa Fisk (next in Punmax #8, '10), Richard Fisk (dies, next off-panel in Punmax #18, '11 as corpse), the Mennonite's wife, 2 sons (both last in Punmax #3, '10) & horses (die), Barbara (Kingpin's secretary); Maria Castle, Lisa castle, Frank Castle, Jr. (prev 3 in photo)
LOCATIONS/ITEMS: Kingpin's penthouse & office; Fisk's motel room, Punisher's safe house, the Mennonite's home / Punisher's Claymore mines & electrified gun rack w/shotguns & assault rifles; Fisk's gun, Rigoletto's knife, Rigoletto's men's guns
SYNOPSIS: Wilson Fisk returns to his motel room to find Don Rigoletto inside holding his family hostage. Punisher lures the Mennonite to his safe house and sets off a Claymore mine. Mennonite survives when his horses take the brunt of the blast. The two renew their battle. Fisk apologizes to his son and shoots Rigoletto's men. Rigoletto kills Richard Fisk. Tired of fighting, the Mennonite grabs one of Punisher's guns but is electrocuted. Punisher drops a safe on Mennonite's head, killing him. Fisk kills Rigoletto and tells Vanessa they will have another son. The Mennonite's sons wait for their father to return. Wilson Fisk becomes New York's Kingpin of crime, but already has an appointment waiting for him: the assassin Bullseye.
NOTE: Includes recap page (1 page). The Bullseye appearing here is an Earth-20111 native; his real name is revealed in Punmax #7, '10.

PUNISHER MAX: GET CASTLE #1 (March 2010)

"Get Castle!" (32 pages)

CREDITS: Rob Williams (writer), Laurence Campbell (art), Virtual Calligraphy's Cory Petit (letters), Lee Loughridge (colors), Sebastian Girner (asst editor), Axel Alonso (editor), Tim Bradstreet (c art)
FEATURE CHARACTER: Punisher (also in own dream, last in Pun #75/5, '09, next in Pun:Bf #1, '10)
VILLAINS: Major Tommy Bresslaw (SAS drug dealer) & his Special Air Service unit inc SSgt. McBride & Capt. Woodward; Kevin (drug dealer), Donna (Kevin's girlfriend) (all die), captive terrorist
OTHER CHARACTERS: Corporal Daniel Mitchell (Yorkie Mitchell's son, also in photo & Punisher's dream, dies), Half Moon bartender & patrons, train passengers, cows; Maria Castle, Lisa Castle, Frank Castle, Jr., Yorkie Mitchell (in photo) (prev 4 in Punisher's dream); Harvin (mentioned, criminal's partner), Aleisha (4 years old), Laverneus (2 years old), Macy (6 months old) (prev 3 mentioned, criminal's children)
LOCATIONS/ITEMS: New York inc Brooklyn Bridge & Hudson River; Bronx inc Punisher's safehouse; Wales inc Brecon Beacons, Hereford train station, Half Moon tavern, farm, Kevin's apartment & Donna's apartment / Punisher's gun, Claymore mines, sniper rifle, rocket launcher, binoculars & van; SAS assault rifles, guns & Chinook (destroyed); CIA jet
SYNOPSIS: Punisher kills a criminal, but is concerned that he paused before pulling the trigger. In Wales, Major Tommy Bresslaw of the SAS kills Corporal Daniel Mitchell, Yorkie Mitchell's son, and stages it as a suicide. Punisher checks one of his safehouses and gets a letter from Yorkie, sent three weeks before Yorkie's death. The letter warns Punisher of corruption in the SAS that Yorkie's son Daniel was investigating. Punisher takes a CIA prisoner plane to Wales, enters a bar and asks for Daniel's murderer. Outside the bar Punisher is threatened, but local girl Donna picks Punisher up and takes him to her boyfriend Kevin's apartment. Punisher interrogates Kevin and learns the SAS killed Daniel. Donna hides Punisher in a farm. SAS troops attack the farm, but Punisher kills the troops. Major Bresslaw is upset, but one of his troops is in contact with Donna, and knows that Punisher is going to Kevin's apartment. Punisher tortures Kevin, who admits that Daniel was killed because Daniel was going to shut down Major Bresslaw's drug operation. Punisher dresses Kevin in a Punisher shirt as a decoy. When the SAS troops arrive they kill Kevin. Punisher calls for a meeting with Bresslaw. When Bresslaw arrives with his SAS troops, Punisher kills them. Bresslaw asks why Punisher is doing this. Punisher says he needed a vacation, then kills Bresslaw. Later, Punisher kills Donna without hesitation.
NOTE: Includes title/credits page (1 page). Daniel Mitchell calls himself "Tom Mitchell." Followed by Hulk #19, '10 preview (6 pages).

PUNISHER MAX: BUTTERFLY #1 (May 2010)

"Butterfly" (34 pages)

CREDITS: Valerie D'Orazio (writer), Laurence Campbell (art), Virtual Calligraphy's Cory Petit (letters), Lee Loughridge (colors), Sebastian Girner (asst editor), Axel Alonso (editor)
FEATURE CHARACTER: Punisher (also in rfb; last in Pun:Get #1, '10, next in Pun:Happy #1, '10)
VILLAINS: Butterfly (assassin, also in fb2, fb4, fb6, fb5, fb8, fb7, fb3 & fb1) & her father (child molester, in fb2 & fb4), Riolo family hitmen (all die), Mort (Butterfly's boss, in fb8)
OTHER CHARACTERS: Elliot (Roman Books editor, also in Butterfly's hallucination, in fb7, fb3 & fb1, dies), Chuck (Elliot's assistant, also in fb3 & fb1, dies), Celeste (Butterfly's girlfriend, dies), Ms. Murrell (elderly woman) & her cats, Butterfly's mother, sister, brother (prev 3 in fb2 & fb4) & goldfish (in fb4, dies), Trevor (Butterfly's boyfriend, in fb6, dies), Butterfly's maids (die), funeral attendees (in fb4), bystanders; Don Massimo Cesare, Cesare family members (both in rfb)
LOCATIONS/ITEMS: New York inc Elliot's office (also in fb1 & fb3), Butterfly's apartment, Murrell home & café; Mexico inc Butterfly's estate; Bed-Stuy inc Butterfly's motel room; Butterfly's childhood home (in fb2 & fb4), Cesare estate (in fb5 & rfb), Trevor's apartment (in fb6), restaurant (in fb7), Mort's office (in fb8) / Punisher's M60 (in rfb) & gun; Butterfly's sniper rifle (in fb5), knives, guns, silencers & computer; Riolo family hitmen's knife, gun & assault rifle; Trevor's rope & scissors (both in fb6)

FLASHBACKS: Roman Books editor Elliot works with Butterfly on her book (1). As a young girl, Butterfly's father molests her (2). Elliot begins to work with Butterfly on her book (3). Butterfly's father kills her goldfish then kills himself (4). Butterfly prepares to kill a Riolo family mobster at Don Cesare's one hundredth birthday party, but before she can (5) Punisher slaughters the mobsters (Pun #1, '04). As a young woman, Butterfly and her boyfriend experiment with bondage. When he doesn't pay attention to her safe word, she kills him (6). Elliot agrees to publish a book written by Butterfly (7). Mort, Butterfly's boss, yells at her for keeping a journal and destroys it. In retaliation, she decides to write a book (8).

SYNOPSIS: Riolo family hitmen kill the Roman Books staff to stop them from publishing a book written by the assassin Butterfly. Hearing of the murders, Butterfly prepares to leave the country with her girlfriend. On the train, Butterfly hallucinates Elliot's ghost and her girlfriend is killed. Butterfly hides out in Mexico and continues to write her book with Elliot's ghost, who tells her chapter thirteen, where she witnessed Punisher slaughtering the Cesare crime family, needs work. Riolo family hitmen attack Butterfly, but she kills them. In a Bed-Stuy motel, Butterfly finishes her book and e-mails it to various news outlets. After waiting to see what happens, Punisher arrives. Butterfly realizes the importance of chapter thirteen as Punisher kills her.

NOTE: Includes title/credits page (1 page).

PUNISHERMAX #6 (June 2010)

"Bullseye Part One" (22 pages)

CREDITS: Jason Aaron (writer), Steve Dillon (art), Virtual Calligraphy's Cory Petit (letters), Matt Hollingsworth (colors), Sebastian Girner (asst editor), Axel Alonso (editor), Dave Johnson (c art)
FEATURE CHARACTER: Punisher
VILLAINS: Kingpin & his men, Bullseye (also in fb to 1st chr app before Punmax #5, '10), Don Rigoletto (bts, calls Bullseye, in fb between Punmax #2, '10 fb & Punmax #1, '10), Mr. Lawrence (Ponzi scheme mastermind, in fb, dies) & his men (die) inc Igus (dies)
OTHER CHARACTERS: Dr. William Bayer (Vietnam veteran, 1st), Channel 9 news anchor (on TV), bystanders
LOCATIONS/ITEMS: New York inc Fisk Tower w/Kingpin's office; Punisher's safe house, Lawrence's safe house (in fb) / Punisher's sniper rifle, Bullseye's gun (in fb) & sniper rifle; Kingpin's men's guns, Lawrence's men's guns
FLASHBACK: Two months ago, after a year of tracking him, Bullseye kills Ponzi scheme mastermind Mr. Lawrence by posing as a pizza deliveryman. Don Rigoletto hires Bullseye to kill the Punisher.

SYNOPSIS: Kingpin hires Bullseye to kill Punisher. Elsewhere, Dr. Bayer tends to Punisher's broken hands, reminding him he's not a young man anymore and doesn't heal as fast as he used to. When Dr. Bayer starts talking about their days together in Vietnam, Punisher kicks the doctor out. Later, Punisher tries to kills Kingpin through his office window, but the glass is bulletproof. Bullseye ambushes and shoots Punisher, but only wounds the vigilante.

NOTE: Includes recap page (1 page). Punmax #7, '10 reveals Dr. Bayer's 1st name.

PUNISHERMAX #7 (July 2010)

"Bullseye Part Two" (22 pages)

CREDITS: Jason Aaron (writer), Steve Dillon (art), Virtual Calligraphy's Cory Petit (letters), Matt Hollingsworth (colors), Sebastian Girner (asst editor), Axel Alonso (editor), Dave Johnson (c art)
FEATURE CHARACTER: Punisher (also in photo)
VILLAINS: Kingpin, Bullseye, Sgt. Wendell Dulohery (corrupt policeman, 1st) (all also in photo)
OTHER CHARACTERS: Dr. Bayer, Punisher's arms dealer (dies), father (dies), mother, their son & daughter (prev 4 1st), reporters inc Regina Nierman (on TV), prostitutes inc Janelle, bystanders; Barracuda, Jigsaw, Finn Cooley, Yorkie Mitchell, Gen. Zakharov (prev 5 in photos)
LOCATIONS/ITEMS: New York inc Fisk Tower w/Kingpin's basement & office; Queens inc Bayer home; cemetery inc castle family grave; Punisher's safe house & abandoned safe house; former Castle home (see NOTE) / Punisher's shotgun & knife; Bullseye's baseball bat, gun w/silencer & copy of "Valley Forge, valley forge"

SYNOPSIS: Bullseye tortures and interrogates Punisher's arms dealer to learn what the Punisher's personality is like. Meanwhile, Sgt. Dulohery tells Kingpin what he's learned of Bullseye: Shelton Pendergrass, a former military lawyer with no combat experience, is now an assassin who's never failed to kill a target. Meanwhile, Dr. Bayer tends to Punisher's wounds. Punisher tells Bayer that he can't remember what Maria's voice sounds like. Sgt. Dulohery takes Bullseye to Punisher's abandoned safe house. Bullseye demands that Kingpin buy it and moves in. Not wanting his senses dulled, Punisher throws away his pain medication. Bullseye continues to research Punisher by reading "Valley Forge, Valley Forge" and wearing Punisher's shirt. Later, Bullseye kills Dr. Bayer. Punisher hears of Bayer's death on the news and attacks Sgt. Dulohery, asking him about Kingpin. Bullseye attacks a man and abducts his family.

NOTE: Includes recap page (1 page). Punmax #22, '12 reveals Sgt. Dulohery's 1st name. Bullseye's victims' home, #106, is revealed to be the former Castle family home in Punmax #13, '11.

PUNISHERMAX #8 (August 2010)

"Bullseye Part Three" (22 pages)

CREDITS: Jason Aaron (writer), Steve Dillon (art), Virtual Calligraphy's Cory Petit (letters), Matt Hollingsworth (colors), Sebastian Girner (asst editor), Axel Alonso (editor), Dave Johnson (c art)
FEATURE CHARACTER: Punisher
VILLAINS: Kingpin & his men, Bullseye (also in photo), Sgt. Dulohery (dies)
OTHER CHARACTERS: Vanessa Fisk (last in Punmax #5, '10), Dr. Bayer (bts, corpse found), father (corpse), mother, their son & daughter (prev 3 die), Channel 9 news anchor (on TV), Fisk Tower staff; Richard Fisk (in photo); Fancy Dan, Ox (both mentioned, Kingpin's enforcers)
LOCATIONS/ITEMS: New York inc Central Park & Fisk Tower w/Kingpin's penthouse; Punisher's safe house, former Castle family home / Punisher's pliers, wrenches, hacksaw, hammer, shears, nail gun & gun; Kingpin's men's machine guns

SYNOPSIS: Bullseye holds a family hostage and announces they're going to the park. Kingpin ignores his wife's depression. Punisher interrogates Sgt. Dulohery about the Kingpin, cutting off body parts when Dulohery doesn't answer. Bullseye loads the family into the trunk of their car. Vanessa angrily interrupts Kingpin's meeting. Punisher asks Dulohery about Bullseye and how to infiltrate Fisk Tower, then takes a break. Bullseye takes the family to the park. Vanessa sleeps with Kingpin. Punisher hears on the news that the police have ruled Dr. Bayer's death a suicide. On Bullseye's command, Kingpin's men approach the captive family. Punisher punches his TV. Kingpin's men kill the captive family in Central Park. Vanessa shoots Kingpin. Punisher kills Sgt. Dulohery. Bullseye is confused; the family's death doesn't mean anything to him. Kingpin takes Vanessa's gun and kicks her out of bed.
NOTE: Includes recap page (1 page).

PUNISHERMAX #9 (September 2010)

"Bullseye Part Four" (22 pages)

CREDITS: Jason Aaron (writer), Steve Dillon (art), Virtual calligraphy's Cory Petit (letters), Matt Hollingsworth (colors), Sebastian Girner (asst editor), Axel Alonso (editor), Dave Johnson (c art)
FEATURE CHARACTER: Punisher (also in photos)
VILLAINS: Kingpin & his men (some die), Bullseye
OTHER CHARACTERS: Vanessa Fisk (next in Punmax #17, '11), Punisher's arms dealer (dies), police inc Bobby, bystanders; Maria Castle, Lisa Castle, Frank Castle, Jr., US Marine (prev 4 in photos)
LOCATIONS/ITEMS: New York inc Fisk Tower; Punisher's safe houses, Vanessa's motel room / Punisher's assault rifles, explosives, rocket launcher, gun & chemical munitions; police guns
SYNOPSIS: Kingpin chastises Bullseye for murdering four families in Central Park and tries to fire him as Bullseye and Kingpin's men enter Punisher's abandoned safe house. Just then, Punisher attacks Bullseye. Kingpin rehires Bullseye. Bullseye locks himself in a safe room as Punisher kills Kingpin's men. Bullseye asks what Punisher's favorite color is and retreats. When Punisher leaves, two policemen try to arrest him for Sgt. Dulohery's death. Punisher shoots them in the legs. Bullseye enters Fisk Tower as Vanessa is being kicked out. He tells her that despite her anger, not to kill Kingpin. Once she does, nothing will be able to fill her life except more killing. Bullseye gives Kingpin a map of Punisher's safe houses, which police later raid. Punisher picks up his order from one of his arms dealers. When the dealer says he can't work with Punisher anymore for fear of Kingpin, Punisher kills him. Bullseye continues to research Punisher as Punisher inspects his new chemical munitions.
NOTE: Includes recap page (1 page).

PUNISHER MAX: HAPPY ENDING #1 (October 2010)

"Happy Ending" (32 pages)

CREDITS: Peter Milligan (writer), Juan Jose Ryp (art), Virtual Calligraphy's Cory Petit (letters), Morry Hollowell, Andres Mossa (colors), Sebastian Girner (asst editor), Axel Alonso (editor)
FEATURE CHARACTER: Punisher (last in Pun:Bf #1, '10, next in Pun:Hot #1, '10)
VILLAINS: Luigi Bassi (mobster) & his men in JD (all die)
OTHER CHARACTERS: Joseph Bonner (accountant), Jenny Bonner (Joseph's wife) (both also in photo), Happy Ending Massage security (1 dies), patrons & prostitutes inc Gi-Gi; taxi driver, bystanders
LOCATIONS/ITEMS: New York inc Bonner home, Happy Ending Massage, Gi-Gi's apartment & Mulligan & Alfonso Accountants office / Punisher's assault rifle & gun; Bassi's gun, Bassi's men's guns, Gi-Gi's disc
SYNOPSIS: Joseph Bonner gets into another argument with his wife Jenny about a subject he can't remember and leaves. He finds a card for the Happy Ending Massage parlor in his wallet. As he stands outside trying to decide if he should go in, Gi-Gi, a parlor employee, grabs Joseph and kisses him. Suddenly, gunfire erupts around them; Punisher is attacking Luigi Bassi, a mobster at the parlor. Joseph and Gi-Gi escape as Bassi's men are killed. Gi-Gi steals a car, drives to her apartment and sends Joseph in to retrieve a disc she's holding; the information on the disc can be used to blackmail Bassi. In the apartment, one of Bassi's men, waiting for Gi-Gi, attacks Joseph. Joseph knocks out the mobster and gets the disc. They go to Joseph's accounting office to use a computer to see what's on the disc. Punisher finds Joseph's wallet at Gi-Gi's apartment. Gi-Gi suddenly threatens to kill Joseph. Before she can, Bassi and his men arrive and shoot at both of them. Joseph tells Gi-Gi to run as he shoots at Bassi's men. Punisher arrives, kills Bassi and his men and tells Joseph to go back to his life. Joseph returns home, but realizes he can't go back to his old unsatisfying life after the night's excitement. He packs a bag, leaves his wife and drives away.
NOTE: Includes title/credits page (1 page).

PUNISHER MAX: HOT RODS OF DEATH #1 (November 2010)

"Getting Mad" (32 pages)

CREDITS: Charlie Huston (writer), Shawn Martinbrough (art), Virtual Calligraphy's Cory Petit (letters), Felix Serrano (colors), Sebastian Girner (asst editor), Axel Alonso (editor), Tim Bradstreet (c art)
FEATURE CHARACTER: Punisher (also in pfb; next in Pun:Tiny #1, '10)
VILLAINS: Pike (mercenary) & his Marauders (road gang) (all also in pfb, die), Roxxon executives
OTHER CHARACTERS: "Mad" Billy Finn (Vietnam veteran, in pfb & photo, dies); Roland Hugh (town owner), George Leung, Tony Leung (both brothers, uranium prospectors), Bonita Suarez (runs general store), Zed Suarez (moonshiner), Tess Suarez (mechanic), Juniper Vetch (runs cafe) (prev 7 also in pfb), Carter Vetch (Juniper's husband, mentioned, dead), other town members (also in pfb), vultures (in pfb); snake (in photo)
LOCATIONS/ITEMS: New York (in pfb), American Southwest (also in pfb) inc cave (in pfb) & town / Punisher's car (also in pfb), motorcycle & axe; Pike's car (also in pfb), explosives (in pfb) & gun; Pike's Marauders' motorcycles & cars; Finn's motorcycle, Tess' truck (both in pfb), Roland's Molotov cocktails, George & Tony's uranium (both also in pfb), Roxxon helicopter

FLASHBACK: Three days ago, Punisher meets with Vietnam veteran "Mad" Billy Finn, who explains that oil executives are trying to destroy the town he lives in because uranium has been discovered there. Punisher follows Finn to the Southwest, but before they can reach the town Pike's Marauders attack them in the street. Punisher wakes up spiked to the desert ground next to the dead Finn. Pike tells him the scorpions will kill him before the sun sets. Tess Suarez later frees Punisher and brings him to a cave where Punisher organizes the town residents to fight back against Pike's Marauders. The next day, Punisher drives into town and attacks Pike's Marauders (p).

SYNOPSIS: Punisher battles Pike's Marauders. When the Marauders fight back, the town attacks and kills the Marauders. Later, Roxxon executives arrive to claim the destroyed town, only to be shot with uranium pellets. The executives flee before being exposed to more. Punisher chains Pike to his motorcycle and drives away.

NOTE: Lee Loughridge is credited for colors on the cover; Felix Serrano is credited in the interior.

PUNISHER MAX: TINY UGLY WORLD #1 (December 2010)

"Tiny Ugly World Chapter One: Personal Jesus" (7 pages)
"Chapter Two: The Little Things" (3 pages)
"Chapter Three: Recon" (4 pages)
"Chapter Four: The Little Shop of Horrors" (6 pages)
"Chapter Five: The It Girl" (2 pages)
"Chapter Six: A Desperate Plea for Love and Understanding" (10 pages)

CREDITS: David Lapham (writer), Dalibor Talajic (art), Virtual Calligraphy's Cory Petit (letters), Matt Hollingsworth (colors), Sebastian Girner (asst editor), Axel Alonso (editor), Tim Bradstreet (c art)
FEATURE CHARACTER: Punisher (next in Punmax #1, '10)
VILLAINS: Bobby Boorsteen (sadist, also in own fantasy & fb), Anthony Marrano (mobster), his girlfriend & his meth dealers; Carlo Carillo, Sammy Bruno, Al Faratto (prev 3 mobsters) (all die)
OTHER CHARACTERS: DMV patrons (also in fb) inc Monica Smithson (also in Boorsteen's fantasy), Boorsteen's mother (in fb, dies), Boorsteen's neighbor/girlfriend (in fb), restaurant staff & patrons, police; Manny (in Boorsteen's thoughts & mentioned, Marrano's girlfriend's son, died in meth explosion), Boorsteen's aunt (mentioned, looked after Boorsteen after mother's suicide, died from cancer)
LOCATIONS/ITEMS: New York inc DMV (also in fb), restaurant & apartment building w/Boorsteen's apartment (also in Boorsteen's fantasy & fb) & Marrano's apartment; New Jersey inc Carmine's / Punisher's assault rifle & gun; Boorsteen's genitals (also in fb), medical journal & surgical tools; Boorsteen's mother's knife (in fb), meth dealers' guns
FLASHBACKS: After Bobby Boorsteen sleeps with his mother, she cuts off Bobby's genitals and kills herself. Bobby gets a job at the DMV and eventually dates a girl, but she runs away horrified when she learns Bobby keeps his genitals in a jar.
SYNOPSIS: Punisher kills some meth dealers and tortures their boss Anthony Marrano for the location of an upcoming mob meeting. Punisher leaves Marrano to die, but neighbor Bobby Boorsteen drags Marrano into his apartment and clamps Marrano's wounds. Boorsteen refuses to tell the police anything useful, reminding them he called them about a meth explosion six months ago that killed a child and they didn't do anything. Boorsteen practices removing body parts from Marrano. Boorsteen meets Monica Smithson at the DMV and fantasizes about dismembering her, but can't build up the courage. He goes to the mob meeting to practice on another mobster, but Punisher kills them all. Boorsteen yells at Punisher for not leaving any survivors for him to work with. Punisher kills Boorsteen.
NOTE: Includes credits page (1 page).

PUNISHERMAX #10 (April 2011)

"Bullseye Part Five" (22 pages)

CREDITS: Jason Aaron (writer), Steve Dillon (art), Virtual Calligraphy's Cory Petit (letters), Matt Hollingsworth (colors), Sebastian Girner (editor), Axel Alonso (exec editor), Dave Johnson (c art)
FEATURE CHARACTER: Punisher (also in photos)
VILLAINS: Kingpin & his men, Bullseye
OTHER CHARACTERS: Police, reporters, bystanders; Maria Castle, Lisa Castle, Frank Castle, Jr. (prev 3 in photo)
LOCATIONS/ITEMS: New York inc Times Square, Fisk Tower & police station / Punisher's assault rifles, guns, grenades, Semtex, taser, chemical munitions, explosives, gas mask & van; Kingpin's men's guns
SYNOPSIS: The police publicly declare war on the Punisher. Kingpin decides that Bullseye is completely insane and orders his men to kill Bullseye. Punisher parks his van in Times Square with a "Death to America" note left near it. In a daze, Bullseye kills Kingpin's men while trying to figure out the Punisher. A policeman finds Punisher's van with a chemical bomb inside. Kingpin attacks Bullseye. With police diverted to the "terrorist attack" at Times Square, Punisher attacks Fisk Tower. Bullseye breaks Kingpin's fingers, realizes something about the Punisher and declares he can kill Frank Castle. Punisher begins to slaughter Kingpin's men.
NOTE: Includes recap page (1 page).

PUNISHERMAX #11 (May 2011)

"Bullseye Conclusion" (22 pages)

CREDITS: Jason Aaron (writer), Steve Dillon (art), Virtual Calligraphy's Cory Petit (letters), Matt Hollingsworth (colors), Sebastian Girner (editor), Dave Johnson (c art)
FEATURE CHARACTER: Punisher
VILLAINS: Kingpin (next in Punmax #15, '11) & his men (several die), Bullseye (next in Punmax #18, '11)
OTHER CHARACTERS: Police
LOCATIONS/ITEMS: Fisk Tower / Punisher's assault rifle, chemical weapons & gas mask; Bullseye's gun, Kingpin's men's guns, Fisk Tower construction equipment inc sledgehammer, axes, nail gun, hacksaw, wrenches & hammers
SYNOPSIS: Bullseye attacks Punisher. Meanwhile, Kingpin retreats to his office and tells the police to ignore

Times Square and instead arrest Punisher at Fisk Tower. Punisher fights Bullseye off and continues to kill Kingpin's men. Punisher eventually finds Kingpin on the roof and prepares to kill Kingpin, but Bullseye stops him. As they fight, Bullseye tells Punisher what he figured out about that day in Central Park, which shocks Punisher. Kingpin shoots out the skylight Bullseye and Punisher are on, and the two fall a story down in front of the arriving police. Bullseye smiles.
NOTE: Includes recap page (1 page).

PUNISHERMAX #12 (June 2011)

"Frank Part One" (22 pages)

CREDITS: Jason Aaron (writer), Steve Dillon (art), Virtual Calligraphy's Cory Petit (letters), Matt Hollingsworth (colors), Sebastian Girner (editor), Dave Johnson (c art)
FEATURE CHARACTER: Punisher (also as Capt. Castle in fb during Born #4, '03)
SUPPORTING CAST: Maria Castle, Lisa Castle (both in fb between Punmax #21, '12 fb & Born #4, '03), Frank Castle, Jr. (in fb between bts in Punmax #21, '12 fb & Born #4, '03)
VILLAINS: Insane US Marine (in fb, dies), prison inmates inc Dee
OTHER CHARACTERS: US Marines (some die), field hospital medics (some die), Military Police, airport commuters (all in fb), prison security
LOCATIONS/ITEMS: Da Nang inc field hospital; airport (all in fb), prison inc infirmary w/Punisher's room / Military Police's guns, insane Marine's scalpel (all in fb), inmates' shivs
FLASHBACK: In Da Nang, Frank Castle recovers from his injuries sustained at Firebase Valley Forge. Another recovering Marine warns Frank that he won't be able to handle being out of war and in the real world. Frank may know how to field strip an M16, but he's forgotten how to hold a child. The Marine warns Frank that he'll likely kill himself. Later, Frank awakens to see the Marine has killed everyone in the field hospital. Military Police arrive and kill the insane Marine. Later, Frank meets his family at the airport.
SYNOPSIS: In prison, Punisher heals in the infirmary while the inmates consider killing him. However, even the Punisher laid up in traction is still too terrifying for the prisoners to attempt it.
NOTE: Includes recap page (1 page). Followed by Hulk #34, '11 preview (5 pages).

PUNISHERMAX #13 (July 2011)

"Frank Part Two" (22 pages)

CREDITS: Jason Aaron (writer), Steve Dillon (art), Virtual Calligraphy's Cory Petit (letters), Matt Hollingsworth (colors), Sebastian Girner (editor), Dave Johnson (c art)
FEATURE CHARACTER: Punisher (also in photo, also as Frank Castle in fb2 between Punmax #21, '12 fb & Punmax #19, '12 fb, also as Frank Castle in fb1 between Born #4, '03 & Punmax #14, '11 fb, also in Pun #75, '09 fb, Punmax #18, '11 fb & Punmax #20, '12 fb)
GUEST STAR: Nick Fury (in fb1 between Punmax #22, '12 fb & Punmax #14, '11 fb)
SUPPORTING CAST: Maria Castle (in fb1 between Born #4, '03 & Punmax #14, '11 fb, also in Pun #75, '09 fb & Punmax #18, '11 fb), Lisa Castle (in fb1 between Born #4, '03 & Punmax #15, '11 fb, also in Pun #75, '09 fb), Frank Castle, Jr. (in fb1 between Born #4, '03 & Punmax #15, '11 fb, also in Pun #75, '09 fb & Punmax #20, '12 fb)
VILLAINS: North Vietnamese army soldier (in fb2), Todd (meat inspector, in fb1, 1st), prison inmates inc Big Jesus (Estaban, 1st)
OTHER CHARACTERS: Castle family neighbors, meat packing plant owner & employees inc Teresa (1st) (all in fb1), prison security inc McIlhaney; US Marines (in photos)
LOCATIONS/ITEMS: Castle home, meat packing plant (both on fb1), Vietnam (in fb2, prison inc Central Punitive Segregation Unit w/cell 17 (Punisher's cell) & cell 18 (Big Jesus' cell) / Castle's gun & Purple Hearts (all in fb1), Big Jesus' shiv, prison security's nightsticks
FLASHBACKS: Frank returns home but finds himself emotionally distant from his family. Eventually, a friend of Frank's father hires Frank to work in a meat packing plant. Frank notices Todd, the meat inspector and owner's son, is a bully. Frank feels someone needs to teach Todd a lesson, but refuses to be the one who does. That night, Frank locks up his medals and tries to begin living a normal life with his family. Later at work, Todd harasses Teresa, a fellow employee. Teresa pushes Todd away and his hand accidentally lands in a meat grinder. Frank does nothing, despite being next to the shut off switch. Frank returns home, unaware Nick Fury is watching him (1). Castle battles in Vietnam (2).
SYNOPSIS: Punisher is transferred to the Central Punitive Segregation Unit, but his legs give out and the inmates see how weak he is. To get close to Punisher, Big Jesus attacks a guard and is transferred to the cell next to Punisher.
NOTE: Includes recap page (1 page). Punmax #14, '11 reveals Todd & Teresa's names. Punmax #14, '11 reveals Big Jesus' real name.

PUNISHERMAX #14 (August 2011)

"Frank Part Three" (22 pages)

CREDITS: Jason Aaron (writer), Steve Dillon (art), Virtual Calligraphy's Cory Petit (letters), Matt Hollingsworth (colors), Sebastian Girner (editor), Dave Johnson (c art)
FEATURE CHARACTER: Punisher (also as Frank Castle in fb between Punmax #13, '11 fb & Punmax #15, '11 fb)
GUEST STAR: Nick Fury (also in fb between Punmax #13, '11 fb & Punmax #15, '11 fb, last in Pun #60, '08, next in Punmax #22, '12)
SUPPORTING CAST: Maria Castle (in fb between Punmax #13, '11 fb & Punmax #15, '11 fb)
VILLAINS: Don Margello (mob boss) & his men, Westies (rival mobsters, die), Todd (all in fb), prison inmates inc Big Jesus
OTHER CHARACTERS: Teresa (corpse), meat packing plant employees, Fat Sal's bartender & patrons (all in

fb); Dean Martin (in photo)

LOCATIONS/ITEMS: Castle home, meat packing plant, Fat Sal's (all in fb), prison inc Central Punitive Segregation Unit w/cell 17 & 18 / Castle's meat cleaver & bottle; mobsters' shotgun & guns (all in fb); Big Jesus' shiv, inmates' shivs

FLASHBACK: Maria asks Frank about Todd's accident at work, but Frank refuses to talk about it. Maria tells Frank that if he's going to leave again he should just tell her. Later, Todd returns to work and Teresa is killed. Frank prepares to kill Todd, but quits his job instead. Frank gets a job washing dishes. One night Frank notices mobsters preparing to kill Don Margello, who's eating in the restaurant. Frank kills the attacking mobsters and Margello shows Frank his gratitude with cash. Frank later throws the money away. Outside, Nick Fury offers Frank a job. Frank refuses and leaves. On the street, Don Margello drives up next to Frank with an offer.

SYNOPSIS: Big Jesus taunts Punisher through the cell walls. Nick Fury visits Punisher to tell the vigilante he can't get him out and he'll likely die in prison. Big Jesus prepares a shiv. When prison guards enter Big Jesus' cell to beat him up, Big Jesus attacks them.

NOTE: Includes recap page (1 page). Followed by Cap #1, '11 preview (5 pages). Punmax #15, '11 reveals Don Margello's name.

PUNISHERMAX #15 September 2011)

"Frank Part Four" (20 pages)

CREDITS: Jason Aaron (writer), Steve Dillon (art), Virtual Calligraphy's Cory Petit (letters), Matt Hollingsworth (colors), Sebastian Girner (editor), Dave Johnson (c art)

FEATURE CHARACTER: Punisher (also as Frank Castle in fb between Punmax #14, '11 fb & Punmax #16, '11 fb)

GUEST STAR: Nick Fury (in fb between Punmax #14, '11 fb & Punmax #16, '11 fb)

SUPPORTING CAST: Maria Castle (in fb between Punmax #14, '11 fb & Punmax #16, '11 fb), Lisa Castle, Frank Castle, Jr. (both in fb between Punmax #13, '11 fb & Punmax #16, '11 fb)

VILLAINS: Don Margello & his men inc Jimmy (all in fb, die), Kingpin (last in Punmax #11, '11, next in Punmax #17, '11) & his men (1 as prison security), prison inmates (some die) inc Big Jesus (bts, leading riot)

OTHER CHARACTERS: Fury's Team A (in fb), prostitutes (another in fb), prison security (some die); Francesco Drago (mentioned in fb, Margello wants Castle to kill him)

LOCATIONS/ITEMS: New York (also in fb) inc Margello's office (in fb) & Fisk Tower w/Kingpin's penthouse; Castle family home (in fb), prison inc Central Punitive Segregation Unit w/cell 17 / Castle's sniper rifle, Team A's guns w/silencers (all in fb), Kingpin's man's grenade, inmates' shivs, security's nightsticks

FLASHBACK: Don Margello offers Frank a job: assassinate Francesco Drago. Frank refuses. Margello stops in front of Frank's house, tells Frank he doesn't like being told "no" and tells Frank to think about his offer. Inside, Maria asks Frank what's wrong, but Frank refuses to tell her. When Maria leaves, Frank Jr. asks Frank if he killed people in Vietnam. Frank says that he did, but doesn't kill people any more if he can help it. Later, Frank notices Margello's men watching his home. Frank calls Margello, accepts the Don's offer and requests a sniper rifle to complete the job. Later, Frank prepares to kill Margello, but Nick Fury stops him. Fury tells Frank he can't live a normal life, and if he wants to keep his family safe he should work for Fury. As a gesture of good faith, Fury orders his men to kill Margello. When the mobsters are dead, Frank leaves. Frank considers Fury's offers through the night, and in the morning asks Maris if she wants to go on a picnic in the park.

SYNOPSIS: Kingpin waits for confirmation of Punisher's death. As Big Jesus incites a prison riot, one of Kingpin's men poses as a guard and throws a grenade into Punisher's cell.

NOTE: Includes recap page (1 page).

PUNISHERMAX #16 (October 2011)

"Frank Conclusion" (20 pages)

CREDITS: Jason Aaron (writer), Steve Dillon (art), Virtual Calligraphy's Cory Petit (letters), Matt Hollingsworth (colors), Sebastian Girner (editor), Dave Johnson (c art)

FEATURE CHARACTER: Punisher (also as Frank Castle in fb1 between Punmax #15, '11 fb & Punmax #20, '12 fb, also in Pun #75/4, '09 fb, Pun #75/2, '09, Pun #50, '07 fb & Pun #1, '04 fb, also in fb2 between Punmax #21, '12 fb & Pun:Tyger #1, '06)

GUEST STAR: Nick Fury (in fb between Punmax #15, '11 fb & Punmax #21, '12 fb)

SUPPORTING CAST: Maria Castle, Lisa Castle, Frank Castle, Jr. (all in fb between Punmax #15, '11 fb & Punmax #20, '12 fb, also in Pun #75/4, '09 fb, Pun #75/2, '09, Pun #50, '07 fb & Pun #1, '04 fb)

VILLAINS: Paulie & Philly Germaine (in fb1 to 1st chr app before Pun #75/2, '09 fb), Todd (in fb, dies), Kingpin's man (as prison security, dies), prison inmates (several die) inc Big Jesus (dies off-panel)

OTHER CHARACTERS: Meat packing plant employees, bystanders (all in fb), police

LOCATIONS/ITEMS: Central Park (in fb), Castle home (also in fb), prison inc central Punitive Segregation Unit w/cell 17 / castle's gun, knives, hacksaw & rope (all in fb); Kingpin's man's grenade & revolver; Big Jesus' shiv

FLASHBACKS: Frank brings his family to Central Park for a picnic. As his children play, Frank tells Maria that he can't live this life anymore, wants a divorce and is leaving. Maria starts to cry in anger, but is stopped short when she's shot in the chest. Frank looks around to see his children gunned down as he is also shot (1). After his family's funeral, Frank sits in his empty house until Nick Fury arrives. Fury gives Frank some names, tells Frank to do what he has to do, tells Frank he can protect him but only so much, and offers a fresh start whenever Frank is ready. Later, Frank murders Todd at the meat packing plant (2).

SYNOPSIS: Punisher uses his mattress to shield himself from the grenade's explosion, kills Kingpin's man and uses his gun to kill some rioting inmates. Big Jesus explains he caused the riot to help Punisher escape; Kingpin killed Big Jesus' brother and Big Jesus wants revenge. Punisher escapes with Big Jesus but kills him. With nowhere else to go, Punisher travels to his family's home, which is now empty and in foreclosure.

NOTE: Includes recap page (1 page). Followed by Castle preview (5 pages). The names Fury gives Frank are of New York's foremost crime family; Punisher acts on this information in Pun:Tyger #1, '01.

PUNISHERMAX #17 (November 2011)

"Homeless Part One" (20 pages)

CREDITS: Jason Aaron (writer), Steve Dillon (art), Virtual Calligraphy's Cory Petit (letters), Matt Hollingsworth (colors), Sebastian Girner (editor), Dave Johnson (c art)
FEATURE CHARACTER: Punisher
VILLAINS: Kingpin (last in Punmax #15, '11) & his men (some die) inc Mad Dog (dies), Vanessa Fisk (last in Punmax #9, '11), the Hand (ninja assassins, 1st, next in Punmax #22, '12, see NOTE) inc Elektra (1st, see NOTE), drug dealers (some die)
OTHER CHARACTERS: Bar patrons, prostitutes
LOCATIONS/ITEMS: New York inc Big Apple Souvenirs, Fisk Tower & bar; Castle family home / Punisher's binoculars, Elektra's sais, Mad Dog's gun, drug dealer's gun, souvenir Punisher t-shirt
SYNOPSIS: Punisher kills some drug dealers and takes their guns. He passes a souvenir shop and steals a Punisher shirt. Kingpin hires the Hand, a ninja assassin group, to protect him from the Punisher. Kingpin is angry when Elektra, a woman, is revealed as his bodyguard. When Elektra kills Kingpin's men, he agrees to hire her. Punisher spies on Fisk Tower. Kingpin realizes he's scared of Elektra. Punisher returns to his family's home. Vanessa Fisk meets with the Hand, who assures her the Kingpin will be dead soon.
NOTE: Includes recap/credits page (1 page). The Hand & Elektra appearing here are Earth-200111 natives.

2ND STORY: "Moment of Truth" (8 pages)
NOTE: Reprinted from Moment, '02.

PUNISHERMAX #18 (December 2011)

"Homeless Part Two" (20 pages)

CREDITS: Jason Aaron (writer), Steve Dillon (art), Virtual Calligraphy's Cory Petit (letters), Matt Hollingsworth (colors), Sebastian Girner (editor), Dave Johnson (c art)
FEATURE CHARACTER: Punisher (also as Frank Castle in fb between Punmax #13, '11 fb & Punmax #20, '12 fb)
SUPPORTING CAST: Maria Castle (in fb during Punmax #13, '11 fb)
VILLAINS: Kingpin (also in photo) & his men (some die), Bullseye (last in Punmax #11, '11, dies), Vanessa Fisk, Elektra, drug dealers (die)
OTHER CHARACTERS: Richard Fisk (corpse, off-panel, last in Punmax #5, '10), Attica nurse, prostitutes
LOCATIONS/ITEMS: Castle family home (also in fb), Fisk Tower, Vanessa's apartment, Attica prison inc infirmary; cemetery inc Richard Fisk's grave / Punisher's guns, revolvers, Uzi, shotgun, assault rifle & shovel; Elektra's sais
FLASHBACK: Frank and Maria spend a vigorous evening together.
SYNOPSIS: In Attica, Punisher forces a nurse to show him where Bullseye is being held. Finding him in a coma, Punisher kills the still smiling Bullseye. Kingpin enjoys his time with some prostitutes until Elektra kicks the women out. Punisher continues his war on crime and decides he needs to make the Kingpin come to him. Kingpin holds a meeting and demands to know why Punisher isn't dead yet. They tell him that criminals are scared of the Punisher again, and not scared of the Kingpin. Elektra and Kingpin angrily kill Kingpin's men, then have sex. Later, Elektra meets with Vanessa. As Punisher digs up Kingpin's son's corpse, Elektra and Vanessa sleep together.
NOTE: Includes recap/credits page (1 page). Richard's tombstone reads "Richard Fisk, Beloved Son, 2001-2009."

PUNISHERMAX #19 (January 2012)

"Homeless Part Three" (20 pages)

CREDITS: Jason Aaron (writer), Steve Dillon (art), Virtual Calligraphy's Cory Petit (letters), Matt Hollingsworth (colors), Sebastian Girner (editor), Dave Johnson (c art)
FEATURE CHARACTER: Punisher (also as Frank Castle in fb2 between Punmax #13, '11 fb & Pun #56, '08 fb, also in fb1 between Punmax #17-18, '11)
VILLAINS: Kingpin & his men (1 dies), Vanessa Fisk, Elektra, Vietnamese guerrilla fighter (in fb2, dies), criminals (some die, others in fb1)
OTHER CHARACTERS: Richard Fisk (corpse), Kingpin's man's wife & son, police (in fb1), bystanders, criminals' dogs (die)
LOCATIONS/ITEMS: New York inc Fisk Tower, Vanessa's apartment, subway & bar; cemetery inc Richard Fisk's grave / Castle's knife (in fb), Punisher's guns & assault rifle; Elektra's sais, criminals' guns & knives; police guns
FLASHBACKS: Punisher continues to kill criminals, build his arsenal and evade the police (1). In Vietnam, Castle battles a Vietnamese guerrilla fighter who refuses to die. Castle beats his head into paste before he finally stops moving (2).
SYNOPSIS: Punisher drags Richard Fisk's body to the Castle family home. Vanessa calls the Kingpin to tell him Punisher dug up their son. Scared of Punisher, Kingpin does nothing. Later, Elektra shows Kingpin that one of his men has been stealing from the Kingpin. When the man confesses, Elektra has the man's family brought into the room. Angry that his own men are more scared of the Punisher than the Kingpin, Kingpin kills the man in front of his family. Later, Kingpin sneaks out of Fisk Tower. Elektra calls Vanessa to tell her Kingpin is missing. Vanessa turns around to see her son's body and the Punisher waiting for her.
NOTE: Includes recap/credits page (1 page). Followed by Av:XSanc #1, '12 preview (6 pages).

PUNISHERMAX #20 (February 2012)

"Homeless Part Four" (20 pages)

CREDITS: Jason Aaron (writer), Steve Dillon (art), Virtual Calligraphy's Cory Petit (letters), Matt Hollingsworth (colors), Sebastian Girner (editor), Dave Johnson (c art)
FEATURE CHARACTER: Punisher (also as Frank Castle in fb5 between Pun:Tyger #1, '06 fb & Punmax #21, '12 fb, also as Frank Castle in fb3 between Punmax #21, '12 fb & off-panel in Pun:XMas #1, '09 fb, also as Pvt. Castle in fb1 between Pun:Tyger #1, '06 fb & Pun:XMas #1, '09 fb, also as Frank Castle in fb6 between Punmax #18, '11 fb & Punmax #13, '11 fb, also as Frank Castle in fb7 between Punmax #16, '11 fb & Pun #75/4, '09 fb, also in fb between Pun #52, '08 fb & Pun:Cell #1, fb, also in fb4 between Punmax #21, '12 fb & Pun #47, '07 fb)
SUPPORTING CAST: Maria Castle (in fb3 between Punmax #21, '12 fb & off-panel in Pun:XMas #1, '09 fb), Lisa Castle (bts, being born, in fb3 to 1st chr app before Pun:XMas #1, '09 fb), Frank Castle, Jr. (in fb6 during Punmax #13, '11 fb) (all in fb7 between Punmax #16, '11 fb & Pun #75/4, '09 fb)
VILLAINS: Kingpin & his men, Vanessa Fisk, Elektra (next in Punmax #22, '12), female prison inmates (in fb2, 1 dies)
OTHER CHARACTERS: Mr. Castle (in fb5 between Pun:Tyger #1, '06 fb & Punmax #21, '12 fb), Flo (prostitute, in fb4), US Marines (in fb1), North Vietnamese Army soldier (corpse, in fb1), doctor, nurse (both in fb3), bystanders (die)
LOCATIONS/ITEMS: Vietnam (in fb1), women's prison (in fb2), hospital (in fb3), motel room (in fb4), shooting range (in fb5), river (in fb6), Central Park (in fb7), New York inc Vanessa's apartment; cemetery inc Richard Fisk's grave; Castle family home / Pvt. Castle's assault rifle (in fb1), Punisher's sniper rifle (in fb2) & gun; Elektra's sais, throwing stars & smoke grenade; Mr. Castle's gun (in fb5), Kingpin's gun, Kingpin's men's guns
FLASHBACKS: July 17, 1969: In Vietnam, Frank Castle kills his first man, a North Vietnamese Army soldier (1). August, 1978: Punisher kills his first woman, a prison inmate who drowned her children (2). Franks passes out as Maria gives birth to Lisa (3). Punisher pays a prostitute for services rendered (4). Frank's father teaches him how to shoot a gun (5). Frank tells his son he won't teach him how to shoot a gun (6). In Central Park, Frank wants to die with his family (7).
SYNOPSIS: Vanessa tries to call Kingpin, but he doesn't answer. Punisher prepares to kill Vanessa, but the lights suddenly go out. Elektra attacks Punisher. Meanwhile, Kingpin visits his son's empty grave, expecting to see Punisher there. As Punisher and Elektra fight, Kingpin tours his old neighborhood. When two people confront him, Kingpin kills them. Elektra stabs Punisher, and he shoots Elektra in the chest. Elektra calls Kingpin, who tells Punisher's he's waiting for him at his family's home.
NOTE: Includes recap/credits page (1 page).

PUNISHERMAX #21 (March 2012)

"Homeless Conclusion" (20 pages)

CREDITS: Jason Aaron (writer), Steve Dillon (art), Virtual Calligraphy's Cory Petit (letters), Matt Hollingsworth (colors), Sebastian Girner (editor), Dave Johnson (c art)
FEATURE CHARACTER: Punisher (also as Frank Castle off-panel in fb9 & in fb3 during Punmax #20, '12 fb, also as Frank Castle in fb5, fb1, off-panel in fb8 & in fb11 between off-panel in Pun:XMas #1, '09 fb & Pun:Tyger #1, '06 fb, also as Lt. Castle in fb2 between off-panel in Pun:XMas #1, '09 fb & Punmax #13, '11 fb, also as Capt. Castle fb10 between Punmax #22, '12 fb & Pun #58, '08 fb, also as Frank Castle in fb4 between bts in Pun:Tyger #1, '06 fb & Pun #75/2, '09, also as Frank Castle in fb6 between Pun #4, '04 fb & Punmax #16, '11 fb, also in fb7 between Pun:Cell #1, '05 & Punmax #20, '12 fb; dies)
GUEST STAR: Nick Fury (in fb7 between Punmax #16, '11 fb & Fury #1, '01 fb)
SUPPORTING CAST: Maria Castle (in fb9 & fb3 to 1st chr app before Punmax #20, '12 fb, in fb1 & fb11 between off-panel in Pun:XMas #1, '09 fb & Punmax #12, '11 fb), Lisa Castle (in rfb, as infant in fb1 & fb11 between Pun:XMas #1, '09 fb & Punmax #12, '11 fb), Frank Castle, Jr. (in rfb, bts, born, in fb10 to 1st chr app before Punmax #12, '11 fb)
VILLAINS: Kingpin (dies) & his men (some die), Vanessa Fisk (becomes Kingpin)
OTHER CHARACTERS: Mr. Castle (in fb5 after Punmax #20, '12 fb), Mrs. Castle (bts, dies, in fb2 after Pun:Tyger #1, '06 fb), doctor (in fb4), nurses (in fb5, another in fb4), mortician (in fb6), US Marines (in fb2 & fb10) inc a Drill Sgt. (in fb8), Barracuda, Bullseye, Sarah O'Brien (prev 3 in rfb)
LOCATIONS/ITEMS: Castle family home (also in fb1 & fb11), Vietnam (in fb2 & fb10), hospital (in fb4, another in fb5), funeral home (in fb6), movie theater (in fb9), New York (also in fb7) inc Fisk Tower & Central Park (in rfb) / Punisher's gun & hammer; Kingpin's gun
FLASHBACKS: In front of their new home, Frank Castle tells Maria he enlisted in the Marine Corps (1). In Vietnam, Castle learns his mother has died (2). Maria tells Frank that she's pregnant (3). In the hospital, Frank demands to know who in his family died in Central Park (4). Considering enlisting in the Marine Corps, Frank visits his dying father (5). Frank buys caskets for his family (6). Now that the Drago mobsters are dead, Nick Fury asks Punisher if his war on crime will end (7). Frank goes through basic training (8), looks at his dead family (Punmax #16, '11), dates Maria (9), learns he now has a son (10), learns he has a daughter (Pun #50, '07) and defeats Bullseye (Punmax #11, '11). As Frank leaves for basic training, Maria bids him farewell (11).
SYNOPSIS: Punisher, barely walking after his fight with Elektra, arrives at his family's home. Kingpin's men ambush him, but Punisher kills them all. Kingpin attacks, and after a fight, Punisher sticks a hammer in Kingpin's head. Kingpin stumbles to Fisk Tower, but Vanessa is already inside and has taken his place. Punisher shoots Kingpin in the head, killing him. Punisher stumbles back to his family's home, collapses and dies in the street, alone.
NOTE: Includes recap/credits page (1 page).

PUNISHERMAX #22 (April 2012)

"War's End" (20 pages)

CREDITS: Jason Aaron (writer), Steve Dillon (art), Virtual Calligraphy's Cory Petit (letters), Matt Hollingsworth (colors), Sebastian Girner (editor), Dave Johnson (c art)
FEATURE CHARACTER: Punisher (corpse, also as Frank Castle in fb between Pun #52, '08 fb & Punmax #21, '12 fb)
GUEST STAR: Nick Fury (also in fb between Fury:PM #6, '06 & Punmax #13, '11 fb; last in Punmax #14, '11)
VILLAINS: Kingpin (dies) & her men inc Bobby & Paulie (both off-panel, die), Elektra (last in Punmax #20, '12, dies), the Hand (last in Punmax #17, '11), gang members (some die), North Vietnamese Army (in fb)
OTHER CHARACTERS: Wilson Fisk (ashen remains), Punisher vigilante mobs, coroner, mortician, bartender, reporters inc Walter (on TV), police inc Bobby, FBI agents, bystanders; Lincoln Bernard (mentioned, Ponzi scheme mastermind, killed by Punisher vigilante mob)
LOCATIONS/ITEMS: Castle family home (destroyed), cemetery inc Castle family grave; Fisk Tower, morgue, funeral home, bar / Castle's assault rifle, NVA assault rifles (both in fb), Fury's gun (also in fb), Punisher's rifle, flame thrower, shotgun & War Journal (destroyed)
FLASHBACK: In Vietnam, Frank Castle fights alongside Nick Fury against the North Vietnamese Army.
SYNOPSIS: Nick Fury witnesses Frank Castle's autopsy until some police officers arrive. One officer accuses Punisher of being insane and professes Wilson Fisk's innocence. Fury kicks him out. Fury berates the other officers for letting Punisher do their job for them for thirty-plus years and leaves. Fury goes to the Castle family home to find FBI agents reading Frank War Journal. Fury kicks the agents out and sets the house on fire. Meanwhile, Vanessa Fisk flushes Wilson Fisk's ashes down the toilet. Elsewhere, Elektra is paralyzed. The Hand kills her. Fury has a beer with Frank and is the only person to attend Frank's burial. Fury yells at some reporters then kills Vanessa Fisk. Fury has a drink in Frank's memory but is distracted by the news. Vigilante mobs have risen up throughout the city, attacking mobsters and gang members. Fury is pleased that Frank has left a legacy behind that's worth something.
NOTE: Followed by an afterward (by Jason Aaron)/credits page (1 page). The Castle family tombstone reads "Frank Castle 1947-2012, Maria Elizabeth Castle 1948-1976, Lisa Castle 1967-1976, Frank David Castle 1971-1976."

While the ongoing Punisher MAX series was initially intended to continue 616 Punisher's adventures, it ultimately proved to be chronicling an alternate reality (Earth-200111) Punisher in a world with fewer superhumans and no sliding timescale. Meanwhile, though he lacked an ongoing series between Feb '04's Pun #37 and PWJ #1, '07, 616 Punisher appeared in miniseries and specials, indexed below:

WOLVERINE/PUNISHER #1 (May 2004)

"Part One: Napoleon" (22 pages)

CREDITS: Peter Milligan (writer), Lee Weeks (pencils), Tom Palmer (inks), Virtual Calligraphy's Randy Gentile (letters), Dean White (colors), John Miesegaes (asst editor), Axel Alonso (editor), Mike Deodato, Jr. (c art), Hermes Tadeo (c colors)
FEATURE CHARACTERS: Punisher (last in Pun #37, '04, also in fb between Bull:GH #3, '05 fb & ASM #161, '76, also in recording), Wolverine (last in W #19, '04)
VILLAINS: Atheist (Gerald O'Higgins, former terrorist), Demon (Van Daemon, socialite-turned-murderer) (both 1st but chr last in W/Pun #2, '04 fb), Lady (Victoria, wife of a criminal, 1st), Gottlieb (Neo-Nazi, ruler of Erewhon ruling council, 1st, also in fb & pfb, see NOTE), Erewhon ruling council (1st), Napoleon (Oswald Zinn, bank robbery mastermind & member of Erewhon ruling council, 1st, also in fb, next in W/Pun #3, '04), his men (in fb, die) inc Billy, Berkeley Cell (also disguised as Jimmy Carter, Bill Clinton, Richard Nixon & Ronald Reagan) inc Roy & Val, Dallas Cell & San Bernadino Boys (both bts, killed by Punisher) & his bodyguards (in fb); Immortals (hitmen, in fb, die), Harvey Long (contract killer, 1st, also in photo, also in pfb), Erewhon residents (asylum seeking criminals)
OTHER CHARACTERS: Books (Waverly Jones, accountant, 1st), bartender, butler, security guards, gallery attendees, guides, party guests, skiers (prev 7 in fb), waitress (in pfb), bystanders (in fb, 1 dies, others in pfb), birds; Jimmy (mentioned, Lady's criminal husband)
LOCATIONS/ITEMS: Los Angeles, CA inc First National Bank & abandoned building; mansion, ski lodge, art gallery, Zinn estate, Fanelli Wholesale warehouse, hotel inc bar, train station (all in fb), maximum security prison, bar (both in pfb), Central American jungle inc Erewhon (both in fb) w/ruling council chamber / Napoleon's men's Uzis & guns; Punisher's shotguns, gun (all in fb) & assault rifle, Atheist's assault rifle, Books' assault rifle, Demon's Uzi, Lady's gun
FLASHBACKS: Ten years ago, Oswald Zinn, aka Napoleon, masterminds bank robberies for his men to carry out. In Los Angeles, Punisher is present when Napoleon's men's rob First National Bank. Following them to an abandoned building, he witnesses them argue whether to betray Napoleon and take all the money for themselves. Interrupting, Punisher kills two of them and interrogates the other two for information on Napoleon's operation. Learning Punisher is systematically destroying his network, killing his men and coming to kill him, Napoleon hires the Immortals to assassinate Punisher, but the vigilante easily kills the mercenaries. Napoleon goes into hiding and considers plastic surgery and sex change operations so Punisher won't find him. Gottlieb offers Napoleon another option: Erewhon, a mythic sanctuary for criminals. Napoleon travels to South America and discovers Erewhon is nothing but four shacks (1). Mercenary Harvey Long escapes from prison. Gottlieb invites Harvey to live in Erewhon (p).
SYNOPSIS: Erewhon's ruling council announces to the Erewhon residents that their chance to kill Punisher is coming soon. As Atheist, Demon and Lady discuss who should be allowed to kill Punisher, the vigilante chases Harvey Long through the surrounding jungle. Napoleon explains to the ruling council that even though Punisher has killed their other bait to lure the vigilante to Erewhon, Harvey Long is protected. In the jungle, Punisher is stopped from killing Harvey Long by Wolverine.
NOTE: W/Pun #2, '04 reveals Lady's name. W/Pun #3, '04 reveals Books' name & Atheist's first name. Gottlieb claims that Adolf Hitler is his father in W/Pun #4, '04; it remains unrevealed if he means this literally or metaphorically. He also claims Erewhon was founded shortly after WWII, despite Erewhon only consisting of four shacks ten years ago.

WOLVERINE/PUNISHER #2 (June 2004)

"Part Two: The Lady, the Atheist, and the Demon" (22 pages)

CREDITS: Peter Milligan (writer), Lee Weeks (pencils), Tom Palmer (inks), Virtual Calligraphy's Randy Gentile (letters), Dean White (colors), John Miesegaes (asst editor), Axel Alonso (editor), Gary Frank (c art), Edgar Delgado (c colors)
FEATURE CHARACTERS: Punisher (also in Atheist's thoughts), Wolverine
VILLAINS: Atheist (also in fb1 to 1st chr app before W/Pun #1, '04 fb), Demon (also in fb2 to 1st chr app before W/Pun #1, '04 fb), Harvey Long (dies), Lady, Napoleon, Gottlieb, Erewhon residents (1 dies)
OTHER CHARACTERS: Founding Father (Adolf Hitler clone, corpse, in shadows, 1st, see NOTE), Books; Irish soldier, Atheist's target, mobsters, bystanders (prev 4 in fb1), Demon's wife & children (both in fb2)
LOCATIONS/ITEMS: Northern Ireland, restaurant, Atheist's apartment, bar (all in fb1), Van Daemon estate (in fb2), Central American jungle inc Erewhon w/bar, hotel, ruling council's chamber & Founding Father's chamber / British tank, Atheist's machine gun, shotgun (all in fb1), gun (also in fb1) & assault rifle; Demon's axe (in fb2), Punisher's assault rifle (destroyed), gun & knife; Erewhon resident's machete
FLASHBACKS: Twenty years ago, Atheist is a Northern Irish terrorist who earns money for the cause by working as a mercenary for American crime families. Ten years ago, he becomes blasé to life and loses faith in himself, rendering him unable to perform mercenary work (1). Van Daemon is a socialite who is rumored to be running for the Senate until one night he decides to chop up his family with an axe, earning the nickname "the Demon" (2).
SYNOPSIS: Wolverine tells Punisher that he can't kill Harvey Long until the mercenary has gone to court and testified against his employers. Punisher attacks Wolverine and Harvey escapes to Erewhon, where he warns people that Punisher is coming. Wolverine follows Long's scent to Erewhon and they split up to search for Harvey. An Erewhon resident fails to kill Punisher. The vigilante recognizes the man as a criminal and kills him. Meanwhile, Lady asks Wolverine to help her escape from Erewhon. She leaves as Punisher arrives and Wolverine suggests that they stay the night. Later, Atheist argues that he should be allowed to kill Punisher so he can find something to believe in again. Demon argues that if he kills what he hates the most, Punisher for chasing him to Erewhon, then he might understand why he killed what he loved most, his family. The discussion is interrupted when they learn Wolverine is helping Lady escape Erewhon. Gottlieb sends Atheist to kill Lady for breaking the rules, then privately presents Harvey's severed head to the Founding Father as an offering.
NOTE: Founding Father is named in W/Pun #3, '04 and revealed to be Adolf Hitler's corpse in W/Pun #4, '04. YM #24, '53 fb reveals that the Human Torch burned Hitler to death, and SVTU #17, '80 fb reveals that Arnim Zola created a clone brain for Hitler to transfer his consciousness into at that moment, along with other clone bodies as backups. Task #3, '11 reveals that Nazi scientist Horst Gorscht continued to cultivate other Hitler clones in Bolivia. This mummified corpse is likely one of these Hitler clones.

WOLVERINE/PUNISHER #3 (July 2004)

"Part Three: Who Are All Those People and Why Are They Shooting At Me?" (22 pages)

CREDITS: Peter Milligan (writer), Lee Weeks (pencils), Tom Palmer (inks), Virtual Calligraphy's Randy Gentile (letters), Dean White (colors), John Miesegaes (asst editor), Axel Alonso (editor), Chris Brunner (c art), Edgar Delgado (c colors)
FEATURE CHARACTERS: Punisher, Wolverine
VILLAINS: Lady (dies), Atheist, Demon, Napoleon, Gottlieb, Erewhon ruling council (last in W/Pun #1, '04), Erewhon residents (some die) inc Pocketbook Bob
OTHER CHARACTERS: Founding Father (in shadows), Books
LOCATIONS/ITEMS: Central American jungle inc Erewhon w/hotel (destroyed) w/Punisher's room, underground tunnels & Founding Father's chamber / Punisher's assault rifle, machine gun & guns; Atheist's assault rifle, Uzi, gun, shillelagh, crossbow, snare & net; Demon's Flat Lock percussion pistol, Erewhon residents' assault rifles
SYNOPSIS: Books sneaks into Punisher's hotel room, but fails to steal the vigilante's guns when Punisher wakes up. Books' life is spared when the Erewhon residents attack the hotel in an attempt to kill Punisher. In the jungle, Wolverine hears the gunfire and Lady admits it was an ambush for Punisher. Wolverine starts to go back when Atheist and his backup abduct Lady and shoot Wolverine. Lady pleads for her life only for Atheist to shoot her. Wolverine flies into a rage and kills Atheist's men. Punisher recognizes one of his attackers as a criminal he lost track of years ago. As Wolverine fights Atheist, the hotel collapses on top of Punisher. Atheist escapes and Wolverine stays with Lady as she dies. Demon stops Punisher from freeing himself from the hotel rubble and prepares to kill the vigilante. Wolverine races towards Erewhon, but trips Atheist's snare and becomes trapped. Atheist tells Wolverine that killing someone who heals himself may restore his faith in himself. Books escapes to Erewhon's secret underground tunnels and finds the ruling council waiting for him in the Founding Father's chamber. They offer Books the great honor of kissing the Father's posterior.

WOLVERINE/PUNISHER #4 (August 2004)

"Part Four: The Founding Father" (22 pages)

CREDITS: Peter Milligan (writer), Lee Weeks (pencils), Tom Palmer (inks), Virtual Calligraphy's Randy Gentile (letters), Dean White (colors), John Miesegaes (asst editor), Axel Alonso (editor), Clayton Crain (c art)
FEATURE CHARACTERS: Punisher, Wolverine
VILLAINS: Demon (dies), Atheist, Napoleon, Gottlieb, Erewhon ruling council (1 dies), Erewhon residents (some die)
OTHER CHARACTERS: Founding Father, Books
LOCATIONS/ITEMS: Central American jungle inc Erewhon w/hotel ruins, underground tunnels, ruling council chamber & Founding Father's chamber / Punisher's assault rifle, machine gun & propane tank; Atheist's crossbow & snare; Erewhon residents' assault rifles, machine guns, noose & guns; Demon's Flat Lock percussion pistol, Gottlieb's gun

SYNOPSIS: In the jungle, Atheist shoots Wolverine through the head with an arrow. In Erewhon, Demon frees Punisher from the rubble and threatens to kill him. Wolverine frees himself and attacks Atheist, but his damaged brain is still healing and he falls into a seizure. Atheist escapes. Punisher guesses that Demon really wants to punish himself for killing his family. Demon gives Punisher his gun and Punisher kills Demon. Wolverine recovers and attacks Atheist. Punisher attacks the Erewhon residents as the ruling council watches from afar. Gottlieb mentions he never expected Punisher to be killed, but rather he wanted Punisher to thin out the Erewhon population. Wolverine finds Punisher and shows the vigilante the underground tunnels. A council member objects to Gottlieb's plan, so Gottlieb kills him. Unable to find Punisher, the Erewhon residents attack Books. To save himself, Books reveals Gottlieb's plan to the residents and leads them to the council. Wolverine and Punisher find the Founding Father's chamber and recognize the Founding Father as Adolf Hitler's corpse. The council confronts them and Gottlieb claims Erewhon was created after WWII. As the Erewhon residents storm the underground tunnels, Atheist wakes up to find himself trapped in his own snares.

WOLVERINE/PUNISHER #5 (September 2004)

"Conclusion: It's a Jungle Out There" (22 pages)

CREDITS: Peter Milligan (writer), Lee Weeks (pencils), Tom Palmer (inks), Virtual Calligraphy's Randy Gentile (letters), Dean White (colors), John Miesegaes (asst editor), Axel Alonso (editor), Greg Land (c pencils), Matt Ryan (c inks)
FEATURE CHARACTERS: Punisher (chr next in Pun:Silent #1, '06, next in Pun:RedX #1, '04), Wolverine (chr next in RamW/4, '09, next in AX #1, '04)
VILLAINS: Napoleon, Gottlieb, Erewhon ruling council (all), Erewhon residents (some die), Atheist
OTHER CHARACTERS: Founding Father (destroyed), Books
LOCATIONS/ITEMS: Central American jungle inc Erewhon w/arena, underground tunnels & Founding Father's chamber / Punisher's assault rifle, Erewhon residents' machine guns, scythe, knife, torches & rubble; Napoleon's Luger & knife; Books' machine gun & shotgun; Atheist's snare, Erewhon ruling council's machine guns & tranquilizers

SYNOPSIS: The Erewhon residents attack the ruling council. Gottlieb tries to calm them down by giving them Punisher to kill, but they don't care and attack the council. Hitler's corpse catches fire and Gottlieb instinctively rushes towards the corpse and is set ablaze himself. Punisher and Wolverine are overpowered during the melee. In the jungle, Atheist frees himself from his own snares by dislocating his shoulder. Punisher and Wolverine awaken chained in an arena, still groggy from tranquilizers. Napoleon gives Punisher a knife to even the odds and tells them to kill each other. Punisher throws the knife and kills Napoleon. That night, Books frees them, gives them weapons and reveals he lives in Erewhon is because he likes it there, not because he's a criminal. As Punisher and Wolverine trek through the jungle, Books tells the Erewhon residents why he freed Punisher: They need the fear of Punisher in the real world to give their lives context; without Punisher they're just a bunch of criminals. Punisher vows to return to Erewhon and eradicate it.

PUNISHER: RED X-MAS #1 (February 2005)

"Red Xmas" (34 pages)

CREDITS: Jimmy Palmiotti (co-writer, inks), Justin Gray (co-writer), Mark Texeira (pencils, c art), Virtual Calligraphy's Randy Gentile (letters), Raúl Treviño (colors), Cory Sedlmeier (asst editor), Axel Alonso (editor)
FEATURE CHARACTER: Punisher (also as Santa Claus, also in Pun:Silent, '06, next in SpSM #1000, '11, MTU #8 & 10, '05, MKSM #15, '05, DDvPun #1, '05)
VILLAINS: Suspiria (legendary Italian assassin, also in photo, 1st but chr last in Pun:BV, '06 fb, next in Pun:BV, '06) & her assistant (also as Suspiria, dies), Napolitano family New York heads inc Albert, Dominick, Donnie & Eddie (die) & their wives inc Regina (Suspiria's cousin, dies) & Angelina; Dominick's men inc Brian, Charlie, Paul & Ralph (die)
OTHER CHARACTERS: Michael Brogan (reporter, also on TV, dies), Tony (Michael's cameraman), paramedics (on TV), police (some on TV), bystanders (some on TV, some die), the Juice Box strippers, Grand Hyatt doorman, canary; Camorra family heads (mentioned, killed by Suspiria)
LOCATIONS/ITEMS: New York inc the Juice Box (mob strip club), Times Square, Tiffany's & Co, JFK International Airport, Grand Hyatt w/ Regina's room & Punisher's apartment w/bathroom; Rinaldi funeral parlor in Gravesend, Brooklyn; Piazza Aprile in Taormina, Sicily / Punisher's sub-machine gun, grenades, knives, sniper rifle, gun & assault rifles; Suspiria's heat tracker, assault rifle, knife, handgun & Learjet; Suspiria's assistant's wig & sniper rifle; Dominick's men's guns, Regina's gun, Napolitano wives' valuables

SYNOPSIS: Disguised as Santa Claus asking for donations, Punisher kills the Napolitano family heads. At the funeral, Regina meets with the other new widows and proposes they run the family themselves and hire Regina's cousin Suspiria, the legendary Italian assassin, to kill

Punisher. Two and a half million dollars and forty-eight hours later, Suspiria arrives at JFK International Airport. On New Year's Eve, Punisher attacks the Juice Box strip club and kills Dominick, the last Napolitano head, who was in Miami when the other heads were killed. During the New Year's Eve countdown, Suspiria kills random celebrators every few minutes and threatens to blow up Times Square, demanding Punisher's presence. Punisher sees Times Square on the news. With a sniper rifle, Punisher kills the shooter, who turns out to be a decoy, which gives away his position to the real Suspiria. The assassin follows the vigilante to his apartment and attacks, but Punisher eventually defeats Suspiria and interrogates her. Suspiria sells the names of her employers for a kiss. Punisher gets Regina's attention by throwing Suspiria onto Regina's car. Regina assembles the widows in her hotel room where Punisher kills Regina. Punisher offers the other widows a stay of execution if they leave the country and make substantial donations to the Santa outside Tiffany's for the families of the Times Square victims.

DAREDEVIL VS. PUNISHER #1 (September 2005)

"Good Deeds, Bad Seeds" (22 pages)

CREDITS: David Lapham (writer, art), Chris Eliopoulos (letters), Studio F (colors), Warren Simons (editor)
FEATURE CHARACTERS: Daredevil (last in MTU #10, '05, chr last in FNSM #2, '06), Punisher
VILLAINS: Hammerhead (last in MKSM #11, '05, chr last in S #5, '06 fb) & his henchmen (one as corpse), Jackal (Professor Miles Warren or clone thereof; cloning expert, also in Punisher's thoughts, possibly last in MaxC:O, '95, see NOTE), Hector Nino (criminal, dies) & his henchmen (some die), knife-wielding junkie (dies), purse snatcher (in shadow)
OTHER CHARACTERS: Mr. Bastelli (diner owner), Martin "Marty" Bastelli (Bastelli's son, busboy), Mary Bastelli (Bastelli's daughter, waitress) (all 1st), Vinnie (abusive husband) & his wife (both voices only), purse snatcher's victim (in shadow), homeless man (corpse), prostitute & her customer, Bastelli's Diner patrons, police, park visitors, bystanders, birds (one as corpse, another in rfb), maggots; dog; Maria Castle, Lisa Castle, Frank Castle Jr. (prev 3 in rfb)
LOCATIONS/ITEMS: New York inc Central Park, Fisherman's Club (restaurant), abandoned loft, Mellville Building (Hammerhead's residence), Times Square, Bastelli's Diner & Sticks (pool hall) / Punisher's sniper rifle, gun, smoke grenade & binoculars; henchmen's guns, junkie's knife, Daredevil's billy club (see NOTE)
FLASHBACK: Frank Castle's family is killed (MP #2, '75 fb).
SYNOPSIS: Punisher observes Hammerhead and Jackal leaving a restaurant from his sniper's nest and prepares to shoot them, but Daredevil attacks and ruins his shot. Hearing police sirens, Punisher distracts Daredevil with a smoke grenade and escapes. A week later, Hammerhead puts a ten-million dollar bounty on the Punisher. Frank Castle plans to blow up the Mellville Building, Hammerhead's new home, but he spots Daredevil lying in wait. His plan foiled, Frank takes a walk through Times Square and snaps the neck of a junkie who attacks him for the reward. He stops into Bastelli's Diner, where he notices that the owner and his son, Martin, have been beaten. Frank is surprised by the owner's daughter, Mary, who resembles his late wife Maria. Two collectors arrive and take money from Mr. Bastelli, but Mary, seeing Frank's gun, subtly convinces him not to intervene. Frank leaves by the back door, where Martin, at Frank's asking, identifies the man who has been extorting his father as Hector Nino. Martin secretly follows as Punisher goes to the pool hall Nino frequents and kills everyone inside, including Nino. Punisher finds Martin vomiting outside and sends him home.
NOTE: Daredevil's billy club will be considered his standard equipment for this miniseries. Miles Warren apparently died in MaxC:O, '95; the Jackal here, who displays an unusual physiognomy and sensitivity to cold, may be a defective clone.

DAREDEVIL VS. PUNISHER #2 (September 2005)

"The Big Squeeze" (23 pages)

CREDITS: David Lapham (writer, art), Virtual Calligraphy's Mike Sellers (letters), Edgar Delgado (colors), Warren Simons (editor)
FEATURE CHARACTERS: Daredevil, Punisher
SUPPORTING CAST: Franklin P. "Foggy" Nelson (Matt Murdock's law partner, last in MTU #9, '05, chr last in SM/BCat #4, '06, next in DD #76, '05)
VILLAINS: Bushwacker (Carl Burbank, cyborg assassin, arm only, last in SH #5), Hammerhead & his henchmen (some die) inc Mr. Ahmet, Swedish Dan (both die), Jimmy Sweets (1st) & Schmidlin; Jackal
OTHER CHARACTERS: Mrs. Bastelli (Bastelli's wife, 1st), Mr. Bastelli (both next in DDvPun #4), Martin Bastelli (also as young boy in photo), Mary Bastelli, Rajan Kumar (Fresh Market owner, dies), Frida (Martin & Mary's aunt), Tommy (Martin's friend); party attendees inc Jennifer Tillman & Benjamin "Ben" Bradford (Jennifer's boyfriend), Melanie (prostitute, 1st), Fresh Market customers, police inc Sgt. Joe Horton (1st), paramedics, crime scene technician, partygoers, waiter, TV reporters, TV cameramen, bystanders, Hammerhead's guard dogs; Gina (mentioned, Mary's friend), Tommy's friend (mentioned, sold Martin his gun)
LOCATIONS/ITEMS: New York inc Fresh Market (grocery store), 43rd St. Subway Station, Bastelli's Diner w/upstairs apartment w/Martin's bedroom; Mellville Building w/Hammerhead's penthouse, Nelson & Murdock law offices inc Matt's office, party house & Blue View Hotel w/ Melanie's room / Punisher's handgun, smoke grenade & Uzis; Martin's gun, Sweets' gun, henchmen's guns, Spider-Man T-shirt
SYNOPSIS: Jimmy Sweets and Swedish Dan, two of Hammerhead's men, fatally beat a grocery store owner for failing to notify them that the Punisher was in his store. Daredevil is present as the police, led by Sgt. Joe Horton, process the crime scene. Elsewhere, Punisher stalks Sweets and Dan with the intention of killing them, but the two lead him into an armed ambush. Punisher kills all of his assailants except for Sweets, who flees for his life. At the Bastellis' apartment, Martin shows Mary a gun he purchased, but Mary demands that Martin get rid of it. During a banquet at Hammerhead's penthouse, Jackal kills one of the men for being an informant for the Punisher. Later, Daredevil fights his way into the Mellville Building and warns Hammerhead to stay away from Punisher. After Daredevil leaves, Punisher fires six rounds into a bulletproof window at Jackal, alarming the villains. Martin attempts to chat up a girl at a party, but her boyfriend beats and humiliates Martin. Punisher finds Sweets hiding out in a flophouse with Melanie, a prostitute. Daredevil arrives to stop Punisher from killing Sweets, but a third party arrives and ignites a flamethrower into the room.
NOTE: Ben's last name is revealed next issue. Bushwacker's real name is revealed in NAvF #1, '05. Joe's first name is revealed in DDvPun #4, '05, his last name in DDvPun #5, '05, and his rank next issue.

DAREDEVIL VS. PUNISHER #3 (October 2005)

"Victory, Now!" (22 pages)

CREDITS: David Lapham (writer, art), Virtual Calligraphy's Chris Eliopoulos (letters), Edgar Delgado (colors), Warren Simons (editor)
FEATURE CHARACTERS: Daredevil, Punisher
VILLAINS: Bushwacker (next in PWJ #5, '07), Hammerhead & his henchman, Jimmy Sweets, Jackal
OTHER CHARACTERS: Martin Bastelli, Mary Bastelli, Melanie (dies), Gina, police inc Joe Horton, club patrons inc jealous man & his girlfriend, club bouncer, prostitutes, soldiers, bystanders (some die)
LOCATIONS/ITEMS: New York inc Blue View Hotel w/Melanie's room, Mellville Building inc Hammerhead's penthouse, Bastellis' apartment inc Martin's bedroom, Paradiso Dance Club inc men's restroom & adjoining alleyway & hospital inc Sweets' room; Aberdeen Proving Grounds inc security checkpoint & armory; warehouse / Punisher's rocket launcher, fireworks, Battle Van, helicopter, machine gun, assault rifles, gun & stolen aerial bomb; Bushwacker's jet fuel, jealous club patron's knife, Martin's gun
SYNOPSIS: Bushwacker engulfs Melanie's apartment in flames, severely burning Melanie and Sweets. Daredevil carries Melanie out of the apartment, but she dies. Bushwacker chases Punisher out onto the fire escape, but Daredevil distracts him with his billy club. As Bushwacker begins firing on Daredevil, Punisher shoots Bushwacker with a rocket launcher, the explosion from which Hammerhead and Jackal can see from their penthouse. Mary Bastelli invites Martin to a club to cheer him up, but the club's environment proves too stimulating for Martin. Outside, Martin sees a clubgoer threatening his girlfriend and scares him off with a warning shot from his gun. The club crowd cheers for Martin's act of chivalry. Daredevil intimidates the hospitalized Sweets into informing on Hammerhead. Punisher lights an array of fireworks near the Mellville Building as a distraction for Bushwacker, then flees when he arrives. As Daredevil arrives and battles Bushwacker, Punisher flies a bomb he stole from a military base to the Mellville Building and blows a hole through the roof. Punisher finds only one of Hammerhead's henchmen inside, who tells him Daredevil and the police hauled Hammerhead's entire gang to prison earlier that day.

DAREDEVIL VS. PUNISHER #4 (November 2005)

"Over the Line" (22 pages)

CREDITS: David Lapham (writer, art), Virtual Calligraphy's Mike Sellers (letters), Edgar Delgado (colors), Warren Simons (editor)
FEATURE CHARACTERS: Daredevil, Punisher
VILLAINS: Hammerhead (next in DD #81, '06), Jackal (next in DDvPun #6, '06), Salamanca inmates inc Leonard (Hammerhead's cellmate) & Vinnie Vicucci (bts, told his wife "Fletcher's starring on Broadway tonight"), Thomas Wynn (crooked Assistant District Attorney, also in photo, dies off-panel), mobsters inc Sid (2 die in Sid)
OTHER CHARACTERS: Mr. Bastelli, Mrs. Bastelli (both last in DDvPun #2, '05), Martin Bastelli, Mary Bastelli, Joe Horton, Paulie (parking valet, dies off-panel), Eugene (transvestite prostitute), Vinnie Vicucci's wife & infant son, prostitute & her customer, prison visitors, bar patrons, 3 homeless men (1st), Donald Fletcher (judge) & his wife (both bts, Daredevil stopped their murder), 2 junkies (bts, hired to kill Fletcher, stopped by Daredevil), Levi Sachs (Hammerhead's lawyer, bts, Jackal had him killed), Mickey (Paulie's associate, bts on phone, dies off-panel)
LOCATIONS/ITEMS: Salamanca Federal Prison inc Hammerhead's cell, visitors' room & parking lot; New York inc parking garage, Mrs. Vicucci's apartment, Criminal Courts Building w/Wynn's office, police station rooftop, bar & Bastelli's Diner w/kitchen & upstairs apartment / Punisher's binoculars, Battle Van, assault rifle & gun; Martin's gun
SYNOPSIS: At Salamanca Prison, Jackal visits Hammerhead in his cell to inform him that he has assumed control of their joint empire, which he can more securely run in prison outside the Punisher's reach. Meanwhile, Punisher determines the prison's security is impenetrable. Daredevil visits one of the prison's visitors, whose husband has enlisted her to deliver coded messages on behalf of the Jackal, and informs her that her last message nearly led to a judge's assassination. The next day, Matt Murdock tells ADA Thomas Wynn that Jackal is circumventing the prison's security measures. Wynn eventually agrees to look into it but Punisher kills him that night. Daredevil is outraged, certain that Wynn was not corrupt. New extortionists arrive at Bastelli's Diner and beat Mr. Bastelli. Martin kills them with his gun. Daredevil hunts Punisher down and the two come to blows. Punisher accidentally shoots a homeless man during the melee. Enraged, Daredevil knocks Punisher out. Horton tries unsuccessfully to get Bastelli to reveal the whereabouts of Martin, whom they sent into hiding with his aunt. After Horton leaves, a trio of men who have been watching the Bastellis' home knock on their door.

DAREDEVIL VS. PUNISHER #5 (December 2005)

"The Unraveling!" (22 pages)

CREDITS: David Lapham (writer, art), Virtual Calligraphy's Joe Caramagna (letters), Edgar Delgado (colors), Warren Simons (editor)
FEATURE CHARACTERS: Daredevil, Punisher (also in rfb)
VILLAINS: Assassins (one as a janitor) inc Mike (some die inc Mike)
OTHER CHARACTERS: Mr. Bastelli (under sheet as corpse), Mrs. Bastelli (bts, taken to hospital), Martin Bastelli, Mary Bastelli, police inc Joe Horton & Sam, paramedics inc Charlie, crime scene technicians, 3 homeless men, newscaster (on TV), patients, nurses, doctors; Maria Castle (in rfb)
LOCATIONS/ITEMS: New York inc Bastelli's Diner w/Bastellis' upstairs apartment w/Martin's room & fire escape; Mercy General Hospital inc emergency room, vagrant's room & Mary's room; Sheep Meadow (in rfb) / Punisher's Battle Van, gun, Uzi, grenade & knife; ambulance, assassins' guns, police SWAT van & helicopters
FLASHBACK: Frank Castle hovers over his dying wife (MP #2, '75 fb).
SYNOPSIS: Punisher awakens in the street to see two homeless men stealing his boots. They flee and a remorseful Punisher drives away. Joe Horton rushes to the Bastellis' home to learn that Mr. Bastelli was killed, Mary was raped and Mrs. Bastelli was severely injured. Meanwhile,

Daredevil carries the homeless man Punisher shot to a hospital, where he encounters Horton who is there to watch over Mary and her mother. Horton tells Daredevil evidence was discovered proving Wynn to be corrupt. A disguised Frank Castle goes to the hospital and finds the man he shot. Thankful that he will live, Frank visits Mary. As a shaken Martin Bastelli arrives, Matt Murdock notices and subdues a would-be assassin approaching Mary's room. Frank ushers Martin outside, but they are separated when a number of assassins appear and attack. After Frank and Daredevil defeat the attackers, Punisher finds Martin at home, where he went to bring Mary a memento of home. More assassins arrive and Punisher fights them off, but a large number of police surround the building. Punisher and Martin attempt to flee via the fire escape but find Daredevil waiting for them.

DAREDEVIL VS. PUNISHER #6 (January 2006)

"The Second Chance..." (22 pages)

CREDITS: David Lapham (writer, art), Virtual Calligraphy's Joe Caramagna (letters), Edgar Delgado (colors), Warren Simons (editor)
FEATURE CHARACTERS: Daredevil (also in Thing #3, '06, next in SMU #12/2, '06), Punisher (also in photo & rfb, next in U #3-4, '06, DocS #2, '06, PunvBull #2, '06)
VILLAINS: Jackal (last in DDvPun #4, '05, possibly next in ASM #659/2, '11; see NOTE), assassins inc Harry, Tommy & Sal (2 as corpses inc Harry, others die), Salamanca inmates inc Toby (Jackal's cellmate), crooked Salamanca medic (dies)
OTHER CHARACTERS: Martin Bastelli (dies), Mary Bastelli, Mrs. Bastelli (all also in photo), Jill (on TV), Ted (voice only) (both Channel 4 news reporters), Jimmy (Jill's cameraman, off-panel), police inc Joe Horton, nurse, prison guards & medics; Maria Castle, Lisa Castle, Frank Castle Jr., Luis Allegre, Bruno Costa, Byron Hannigan, Leon Kolsky, Matt Skinner, Rocco Venturi, mafia informant (corpse) (prev 10 in rfb); Mr. Bastelli (in photo)
LOCATIONS/ITEMS: New York inc Sheep's Meadow (in rfb), Matt Murdock's office, Bastellis' Diner w/Bastellis' upstairs apartment & Mercy General Hospital w/Mary & Mrs. Bastelli's rooms; Salamanca Federal Prison inc Jackal's cell & infirmary / Punisher's Uzi, police guns, tactical armor & helicopter; assassins' guns, gangsters' guns, Salamanca medic's poison, Mary's letter
FLASHBACK: Frank Castle and his family stumble upon a mob execution during a family picnic and are all shot (MP #2, '75 fb).
SYNOPSIS: As the NYPD and a crew of assassins seeking the bounty on the Punisher converge on the Bastellis' home, Daredevil and the Punisher fight as Martin Bastelli watches. The NYPD and the assassins exchange fire as the fight rages. In Salamanca, a pampered Jackal watches the siege of the Bastellis' building on TV. Martin points a gun at Daredevil, demanding that he leave Punisher alone. Punisher and Daredevil, both injured from the fight, tell Martin to drop the gun, but the assassins arrive and open fire. In the ensuing firefight between Punisher, the assassins and an NYPD SWAT team, Martin is killed. The SWAT team kills the remaining assassins and arrest Punisher. Days later, Mary Bastelli writes Frank Castle one of several letters she has sent him since regaining consciousness. She tells him about Martin and that, while permanently paraplegic, her mother survived her injuries. As Frank reads the letter in Salamanca's infirmary, a prison medic in the Jackal's employ tries to give Frank poisoned medication, but Frank makes the medic swallow them as the guards turn a blind eye. Now that Frank and the Jackal are in the same prison, Frank vows to kill him.
NOTE: The Jackal in ASM #659/2, '11 looks noticeably different from the one here; given Warren's cloning proclivity, the ASM #659/2 Jackal may well be a different clone or the real Miles Warren.

PUNISHER: SILENT NIGHT #1 (February 2006)

"Silent Night" (36 pages)

CREDITS: Andy Diggle (writer), Kyle Hotz (art), Virtual Calligraphy's Randy Gentile (letters), José Villarrubia (colors), Cory Sedlmeier (asst editor), Axel Alonso (editor), Mike Deodato, Jr. (c art)
FEATURE CHARACTER: Punisher (also as Santa Claus, last in W/Pun #5, '04, also & next in Pun:RedX #1, '05)
VILLAINS: Junior Calvani (also in pfb) & his men (1 in pfb), Timothy "Tiny Tim" Torino (mob snitch & mall Santa, also in pfb), Gerardo Falsetti (mob snitch & former Calvani consigliere, also in pfb) & his men (2 in pfb) inc Nate (all die), Calvani senior (dies), Calvani family, San Quentin inmate (prev 3 in pfb)
OTHER CHARACTERS: St. Nicholas Orphanage orphans & priest, bystanders, reindeer
LOCATIONS/ITEMS: San Quentin, cemetery, Junior's office, upstate NY mall (all in pfb), New York inc Hellgate Wharf & mall; St. Nicholas Orphanage inc chapel / San Quentin inmate's sharpened toothbrush (in pfb), Punisher's M4, knife, fake Hepcat Events ID, shotgun, Claymore mines & detonator; Junior's men's crates of cocaine, gun & assault rifles; Junior's Mercedes & knife; Falsetti's carving knife
FLASHBACK: Calvani senior is killed in San Quentin prison after his consigliere, Gerardo Falsetti, turned state's evidence on him. Junior promises retribution and goes deep underground to run the Calvani family. Years later, Falsetti, looking to give something back to the orphanage he grew up in, hires "Tiny" Tim Torino to play Santa for the orphans (p).
SYNOPSIS: Punisher pauses on killing his latest targets when he recognizes them as Junior Calvani's men. Seeing an opportunity, Punisher spares the weakest amongst them and interrogates him for Junior's location. He reveals Junior found the consigliere and is going to kill Falsetti at an orphanage upstate on Christmas Eve. Punisher throws him into the river and dumps their supply of cocaine. Punisher learns from "Tiny" Tim that Junior is coming out of hiding to kill Falsetti personally. Punisher forces Tim to come with him so he can't warn Junior. Posing as Santa and his little helper, Punisher and Tim enter the orphanage. Punisher orders some of the children to build snowmen. Punisher kills the guard at the back gate and at dinner, handcuffs Falsetti to the fireplace as bait. As Junior's men storm the grounds, Punisher leads the children and priest to the chapel, leaving a shotgun behind for defense. Punisher kills Junior's men with Claymore mines hidden in the snowmen. As Punisher kills Junior, Tim frees Falsetti. Knowing Tim sold him out, Falsetti kills Tim. The former consigliere fails to escape when he runs into Punisher. Falsetti begs for Christmas mercy, but Punisher refuses.

PUNISHER VS. BULLSEYE #1 (January 2006)

"The Man's Got Style" (22 pages)

CREDITS: Daniel Way (writer), Steve Dillon (art), Virtual Calligraphy's Rus Wooton (letters), Avalon's Dan Kemp (colors), Cory Sedlmeier (asst editor), Axel Alonso (editor), Mike Deodato Jr. (c pencils), Rain Beredo (c inks)
FEATURE CHARACTERS: Punisher (in fb between ASM #202, '80 & ASM Ann #15, '81), Bullseye (last in Bull:GH #5, '05)
VILLAINS: Nico Patrillo, Alphonso "Fonzie" Patrillo (Nico's uncle, also in fb, next in PunvBull #4, '06) (both 1st), Rocco Patrillo (Alphonso's brother, bts, dies in fb), mobsters inc Richie & Sammy (some dead in pfb, others die in fb), Leo Rossi (mobster, bts, hired Bullseye to kill Patrillos, next in PunvBull #5, '06)
OTHER CHARACTERS: Rosalo Patrillo (Nico's grandmother, 1st, next in PunvBull #5, '06), Nick Katzenbaum (Nico's lawyer, dies), delivery man, Stately Oaks residents, Nick's wife (bts, killed by Bullseye), bystanders; Alphonso's date & bodyguards, disco dancers & staff, Diana Ross (bts, seen at Disco) (prev 5 in fb)
LOCATIONS/ITEMS: Alphonso's Westport, CT home, Stately Oaks Retirement Village w/ basement & Rosalo's room, Richie's Brooklyn party site (in fb), New York City (also in fb) inc skyscraper observation deck, subway station & disco w/ coat room (both in fb) / Punisher & Alphonso's guns (in fb), Nico's flashlight, Bullseye's gun (bts)
FLASHBACK: Punisher stages an attack at a disco and kills several mobsters, sending mob leader Alphonso Patrillo into hiding as a transvestite.
SYNOPSIS: After Richie's bachelor party is massacred, Nico Patrillo seeks advice from his Uncle Fonzie. Fonzie, maintaining his years-long disguise as a woman, instructs Nico to issue a bounty on Punisher's head. Fonzie explains that this will serve two purposes: buy them time in their gang war with the rival Rossi family, and lead to the deaths of either the Rossis or Punisher. Nico leaves Fonzie's home by way of an underground tunnel which terminates in the basement of his grandmother's retirement home. He visits with his grandmother, who assures him that she loves him, despite his stupidity. Later, Katzenbaum calls Bullseye and reports that he's received an offer on the Punisher's head. After receiving the good news, Bullseye shoots and kills Katzenbaum from his perch on a skyscraper observation platform.
NOTE: Followed by PunvBull #2, '06 preview (1 page), featuring Punisher, Bullseye & Nico Patrillo. Nico believes that Punisher is responsible for the bachelor party massacre, but the culprit is actually Bullseye, as revealed in PunvBull #5, '06, hoping to goad the Patrillos into going after Punisher. Bullseye is revealed to be working for Rossi in PunvBull #5, '06.

PUNISHER VS. BULLSEYE #2 (February 2006)

"The Drop" (22 pages)

CREDITS: Daniel Way (writer), Steve Dillon (art), Virtual Calligraphy's Rus Wooton (letters), Avalon's Dan Kemp (colors), Cory Sedlmeier (asst editor), Axel Alonso (editor)
FEATURE CHARACTERS: Punisher, Bullseye (also as deliveryman)
VILLAINS: Nico Patrillo & his men inc Bobby
OTHER CHARACTERS: Mary (Java Junction waitress, 1st, next in PunvBull #5, '06), Java Junction diners, bystanders; Alphonso Patrillo (on cover)
LOCATIONS/ITEMS: Nico's apartment, Manhattan inc Java Junction, Luigi's Steakhouse & nearby rooftops w/ storage shed / Punisher's guns & binoculars; Bullseye's balloons & bomb w/ remote control detonator; Nico's gun
SYNOPSIS: Bullseye interrupts Nico's shower to announce that he is taking the bounty on Punisher. While staking out the Rossi gang's steakhouse, Bullseye discovers Punisher's weapons cache atop a nearby building. He eats lunch at Java Junction and flirts with a waitress, getting her phone number. That night, Punisher is on the rooftop overlooking Luigi's, and discovers his weapons have been replaced by Bullseye's balloons. He sees Bullseye atop a higher building nearby. Bullseye mouths the word "Duck!" and hits him with a paper airplane, before setting off a bomb near Punisher's perch. Later, Bullseye meets Nico at Java Junction. He knows Punisher is watching them, because he used his lunch ticket as the paper airplane.
NOTE: Includes recap page (1 page). Mary's name is revealed in PunvBull #5, '06.

PUNISHER VS. BULLSEYE #3 (March 2006)

"Massacre on 34th Street" (22 pages)

CREDITS: Daniel Way (writer), Steve Dillon (art), Virtual Calligraphy's Joe Caramagna (letters), Avalon's Dan Kemp (colors), Cory Sedlmeier (asst editor), Axel Alonso (editor), Leinil Francis Yu (c pencils), Dave McCaig (c inks)
FEATURE CHARACTERS: Punisher, Bullseye
VILLAINS: Nico Patrillo & his men (die) inc Bobby (dies), Tony DiFazzio & his gang (many die)
OTHER CHARACTERS: Debbie (Java Junction waitress), Java Junction diners, car owner, bus driver (dies) & passengers, police inc policewoman (1st), bystanders
LOCATIONS/ITEMS: Manhattan inc Java Junction with kitchen & Mulberry Street pool hall w/ basement / Punisher's gun, Bullseye's gun, Nico's men's guns, DiFazzio's men's guns, police guns & helicopter
SYNOPSIS: Bullseye goads Punisher into attacking by shooting the restaurant's customers. He helps Nico escape but leaves Nico's men behind to be killed by Punisher. Castle follows Bullseye through the back of the restaurant into an alley, where the assassin hijacks a public bus. Punisher chases him in a stolen car, and Bullseye crashes the bus into Tony DiFazzio's pool hall. While Punisher wipes out DiFazzio's gang, police respond to the carnage in the streets. They board the bus and mistakenly believe the bus driver committed suicide by ramming the bus into the building. They begin to treat the wounded passengers--including Bullseye. Police surround the pool hall, and when Punisher seeks to escape through a basement window, he is confronted by a policewoman, her gun trained on him.
NOTE: Includes recap page (1 page). The story's title is a play on the movie "Miracle on 34th Street," '47.

PUNISHER VS. BULLSEYE #4 (April 2006)

"Two of a Kind" (22 pages)

CREDITS: Daniel Way (writer), Steve Dillon (art), Virtual Calligraphy's Joe Caramagna (letters), Avalon's Dan Kemp (colors), Cory Sedlmeier (assoc editor), Axel Alonso (editor), Mark Texeira (c art), Paul Mounts (c colors)
FEATURE CHARACTERS: Punisher, Bullseye
VILLAINS: Alphonso Patrillo (last in PunvBull #1, '06), Nico Patrillo, Nico's captains inc Mikey & Lonnie (some voice only, die)
OTHER CHARACTERS: Policewoman (dies), paramedics (dead), Trevon (neighborhood boy) & his friend
LOCATIONS/ITEMS: New York City including espresso shop, Vinnie's Used Cars & Lonnie's construction site w/office; Alphonso's Westport, CT home / Punisher's guns & handcuffs; Bullseye's knife, hypodermic needles, rocket launcher w/rocket, gun & motorcycle; police helicopters, policewoman's gun
SYNOPSIS: Punisher stares down the policewoman and turns away. She prepares to shoot, but suddenly falls to the ground, killed by a hypodermic needle thrown by Bullseye from a nearby ambulance. Over the next few days, Punisher kills several of Nico's captains in his search for Bullseye. Punisher gets the drop on Lonnie and interrogates him, but the questioning is cut short when Bullseye strikes Lonnie's office with a rocket launcher, and Castle narrowly escapes. Bullseye donates his rocket launcher to Trevon, who is fascinated by the weapon. Punisher attacks Bullseye and they fight. Castle gets the upper hand, but Trevon forces him to stand down by aiming the rocket launcher at him. While Punisher tries to talk Trevon into giving up the launcher, Bullseye escapes on his motorcycle. Meanwhile, at Alphonso's home, a depressed Alphonso asks his nephew how their lives went wrong. Nico, now also wearing a dress, admits he doesn't understand either.
NOTE: Includes recap page (1 page).

PUNISHER VS. BULLSEYE #5 (May 2006)

"Profit and Loss" (22 pages)

CREDITS: Daniel Way (writer), Steve Dillon (art), Virtual Calligraphy's Joe Caramagna (letters), Avalon's Dan Kemp (colors), Cory Sedlmeier (assoc editor), Axel Alonso (editor), Paul Gulacy (c pencils), Jason Keith (c inks)
FEATURE CHARACTERS: Punisher (also in pfb, next in DoD #4-5, '06, Pun:BV #1, '06), Bullseye (also voice only as "Tommy" in dfb, next in DD #79, '06)
VILLAINS: Alphonso Patrillo, Nico Patrillo (both die), Leo Rossi (1st but last bts in PunvBull #1, '06) & his men
OTHER CHARACTERS: Mary (last in PunvBull #2, '06), Louis (Mary's children's babysitter) (both die), Mary's son & daughter (all also in pfb)
LOCATIONS/ITEMS: Alphonso's Westport, CT home, construction site w/office (also in pfb), Stately Oaks Retirement Village with basement & Rosalo Patrillo's room, Leo Rossi's office, Java Junction, Mary's home (both in fb) / Punisher's guns, rocket launcher & bomb w/remote control (also in pfb), Bullseye's gun & botox dart
FLASHBACKS: Posing as "Tommy," Bullseye calls Mary and asks her out, telling her he will send a car to pick her up (d). Bullseye calls Louis and advises him that he needs to tell Mary how much he loves her. He tells Louis where Mary will be that night (d). Punisher places a bomb in the construction site office (p).
SYNOPSIS: Bullseye calls Nico and alerts him that he will kill Punisher when the vigilante attacks a Rossi family meeting that night. That night, Punisher is awaiting the supposed Rossi meeting, and is surprised when Mary arrives, who herself is surprised when Louis arrives. When Louis mentions "Tommy," Punisher knows he guessed right, and that Bullseye is watching them from the office overlooking the site. Punisher prepares to detonate his bomb, but when Louis tells Mary that Tommy is watching the children, the vigilante realizes the children are in the office with Bullseye. Murdering Mary and Louis, Bullseye paralyzes Punisher with a botox dart. He tells Castle that he's meeting Nico later in Westport. Bullseye arrives at Alphonso's and picks up his bounty. To prove he's killed Castle, he shows them Punisher's tunic. As he disappears through the trap door, he informs them that he shot up the bachelor party, not Punisher. The Patrillos look out their window and see Castle, just as he fires a rocket at the house. Bullseye emerges from the tunnel in Stately Oaks and visits Rosalo. The next morning, he collects his million-dollar bounty from Rossi for wiping out the Patrillo family.
NOTE: This issue includes a letters page w/LOC by science fiction writer Paul Di Filippo. Alphonso's home is located at 116 East Willow. Bullseye mistakenly refers to Nico Patrillo as Nico Rossi. This issue reveals that Bullseye has been secretly working for Leo Rossi for the entire series.

PUNISHER: BLOODY VALENTINE #1 (April 2006)

"Bloody Valentine" (34 pages)

CREDITS: Jimmy Palmiotti (co-writer, inks), Justin Gray (co-writer), Paul Gulacy (pencils), Virtual Calligraphy's Randy Gentile (letters), Paul Mounts (colors), Cory Sedlmeier (asst editor), Axel Alonso (editor)
FEATURE CHARACTER: Punisher (also as Frank Castle in rfb, also as Joe Delfini, next in DD #84-85, '06, ASM #533, '06, DD #86-87, '06, MK #9-10, '07, CW #4, '06, Pun:XMas #1, '07)
VILLAINS: Vincent Carraciola (crime lord, also in fb) & his men; Herman "the German" Zeufrieden (arms supplier, Carraciola's partner & child abductor) & his arms dealers, casino security inc Pete (all die)
OTHER CHARACTERS: Suspiria (also as Mrs. Delfini, also in fb to 1st chr app before Pun:RedX #1, '04; last in Pun:RedX #1, '04), her assistants inc Karen; her pilot (bts, wakes up Suspiria), daughter (bts, sold to a family in Hamburg, Germany, also in photo, also in fb) & her husband (dies in fb), Cyber (Suspiria's dog, dies), U.S. Senator (bts, hired Suspiria to find his missing son; casino staff & patrons, abducted children inc a Senator's son; Maria Castle, Lisa Castle, Frank Castle Jr., Luis Allegre, Klosky, Skinner (prev 6 in rfb)
LOCATIONS/ITEMS: Warehouse (destroyed) in Red Hook, Brooklyn; Piazza Aprile (destroyed) in Taormina, Sicily; beach in Basilicata, Italy, Rome inc church, Aeroporto di Villanovia & Grand Hotel Palazzo Della Fonte w/Suspiria's room, Carraciola's room & casino / Punisher's NTW20

anti-materiel rifle, zip line, knife, assault rifle, gun & bomb; Suspiria's gun (also in fb), Learjet, parachutes, boat, knife & grenade; Suspiria's assistants' sub-machine gun, knife & Uzi; Carraciola's men's shotguns, assault rifles, sub-machine guns, guns & rocket launcher; arms dealers' Lamborghini, crowbar, knife & Spider-Man ornament; casino security's Uzis & guns; Herman's jet airliner

FLASHBACKS: While picnicking in Central Park, mobsters kill Frank Castle's wife and children (MP #2, '75 fb). While vacationing in the French Riviera, Vincent Carraciola kills Suspiria's husband and abducts her daughter.

SYNOPSIS: Punisher prepares to kill some arms dealers, but is surprised to see Suspiria enter the dealers' warehouse. As Suspiria kills the dealers, Punisher stops one that escapes. Suspiria demands to interrogate the dealer. Punisher agrees when she points out she spent nine months learning to walk again after their last encounter. Punisher blows up the warehouse and Suspiria kills the dealer, promising to take Punisher to the arms supplier. As he flies to Italy with her, Suspiria explains a U.S. Senator hired her to rescue his kidnapped son from Herman Zeufrieden, the arms supplier. They parachute into Suspiria's estate, which is surrounded by Vincent's men. Suspiria's assistants trace Carraciola's location and lure the mercenaries inside before blowing up the estate. Suspiria explains to Punisher that Vincent used her daughter to blackmail Suspiria into working for him, but while Suspiria was in rehab Carraciola thought she found a new employer and decided to kill her. Punisher and Suspiria infiltrate the casino where Carraciola is playing cards. They find Vincent, who reveals that when he thought Suspiria was dead, he gave Suspiria's daughter to Herman. Suspiria kills Vincent and escapes with Punisher. Later, they kill Herman and rescue the children he abducted, including the Senator's son. The next day, Suspiria tells Punisher she's been pardoned for her crimes in exchange for working for the Italian government. She starts after she retrieves her daughter from the family in Hamburg, Germany that Herman sold her daughter to. Before heading their separate ways, they make plans for one more night together.

PUNISHER: X-MAS SPECIAL #1 (January 2007)

"The List" (34 pages)

CREDITS: Stuart Moore (writer), C.P. Smith (art), Virtual Calligraphy's Joe Caramagna (letters), Dean White (colors), Michael O'Connor (asst editor), Axel Alonso (editor)

FEATURE CHARACTER: Punisher (also off-panel as Frank Castle in fb between PunHol #2, '93 fb & Pun #1, '98 fb; next in PWJ #1, '07)

SUPPORTING CAST: Maria Castle (in fb between PunHol #2, '93 fb & PWZ #24, '94 fb), Lisa Castle, Frank Castle Jr. (both in fb between Pun Ann #4, '91 & PWZ #24, '94 fb)

VILLAINS: Jimmy Nouveau (James Novinski, mob underboss, also in photo, dies) & his men (die)

OTHER CHARACTERS: Wendy Jay (Jimmy Nouveau's girlfriend, also in photo, dies), Adam Jay (Wendy's dead son, in photo), Robert "Red" Sanchez (policeman), Michael Hanlon (Red's dead partner, in photo), Captain Terrence Raymond (bts, spoke to press), bus driver (voice only), Pink Puddytat Lounge dancers & patrons, police, "Mouse" Moconi (mobster, in photo), Patrice Fabry, Mario Rastellini, Jimmy Patino, Willard "Ratman" Solari, John "Country" Gloria, Colby "Frenchman" French, Anthony Spiccoli, Mick "Spider" Ellis (prev 8 on Punisher's naughty list)

LOCATIONS/ITEMS: Brooklyn inc Punisher's safehouse, Morhan's Bar & Grill, Wendy's apartment, bus station & Pink Puddytat Lounge w/ Jimmy Nouveau's office / Punisher's gun, sub-machine gun & naughty & nice list; Pink Puddytat Lounge coaster, Jimmy Nouveau's business records

FLASHBACK: The Castle family celebrates Christmas.

SYNOPSIS: Punisher puts together a naughty list and decides to kill mob underboss Jimmy Nouveau. At Morhan's Bar & Grill, police officer Robert Sanchez, feeling guilty over the death of his police partner and young boy Adam Jay in a shootout with Jimmy Nouveau, gets drunk. Sanchez walks outside to kill himself, but Punisher stops and questions him about the shooting. Sanchez doesn't know anything and returns to the bar. Punisher puts Sanchez on his nice list and, posing as a police detective, questions Wendy Jay, Adam's mother. Wendy tells Punisher that Jimmy Nouveau dropped a coaster to the Pink Puddytat Lounge. Punisher puts Wendy on his nice list. At the Pink Puddytat Lounge, Punisher kills Jimmy's men. Punisher tells Jimmy that he'll be crossed off the naughty list if the mobster cooperates. Jimmy gives Punisher his business records. Punisher kills Jimmy and crosses him off the naughty list. Punisher returns to Morhan's and tells Sanchez a recent ballistics report determined Sanchez didn't kill his partner or Adam. Punisher looks through Jimmy's records and discovers Wendy was Jimmy's girlfriend. Punisher confronts Wendy at the bus station. Overcome with grief, Wendy tries to kill herself by running in front of a bus. Punisher puts her out of her misery and checks to see who is next on his naughty list.

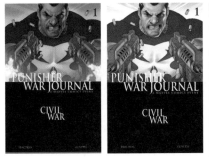

PUNISHER WAR JOURNAL #1 (January 2007)

"How I Won the War, Part 1: Bring On the Bad Guys" (32 pages)

CREDITS: Matt Fraction (writer), Ariel Olivetti (art), Virtual Calligraphy's Joe Caramagna (letters), Dean White (colors), Warren Simons (asst editor), Axel Alonso (editor)

FEATURE CHARACTER: Punisher (also in photo, also & next in CW #5, '06)

GUEST STARS: Captain America (during CW #5, '06), Spider-Man (during & also in CW #5, '06)

SUPPORTING CAST: G.W. Bridge (last in Cable&DP #27, '06), Stuart Clarke (engineer & reformed villain Rampage, last in IM #20, '99, last bts in NAv #3, '05)

VILLAINS: Jack O'Lantern (Steven Mark Levins, during & also in CW #5, '06, dies, next in GR #8, '07), Jester (Jody Putt, during & also in CW #5, '06, dies, next in Tb:RM #1, '08), Stilt-Man (Wilbur Day, scientist, last in ASM #533, '06, dies, next in PWJ #4, '07), Tinkerer (Phineas Mason, criminal inventor, last in MKSM #12, '05, next in W:O #12, '07), Fulvio Morsella (child pornographer, dies), mugger

OTHER CHARACTERS: Jasper Sitwell (SHIELD agent, last in SecWar #5, '05, last bts in HoM #6, '05, next in PWJ #5, '07), SHIELD medics, scientist & agents inc "cape-killers;" muggers' 2 victims inc Craig; Stamford residents, FBI agent, bystanders, dog; Stamford Sluggers (baseball team, in photo)

LOCATIONS/ITEMS: New York inc Stuart's warehouse base, DiPasquale's Italian restaurant, mosque, Queens, sewer tunnel, smugglers' tunnel, tanning parlor & Secret Avengers underground hideout; Stamford, Connecticut; New Rochelle, NY hardware store / Spider-Man's

armored costume version 2.0 (see NOTE); Punisher's Battle Van, binoculars, light anti-tank weapon & .38-caliber pistol; Bridge's gun & SHIELD badge; Clarke's mechanical battle suit, mini-Iron Man robots & Stark tech detector; SHIELD night vision goggles & rifles; SHIELD Helicarrier Pericles III inc morgue; awl used as a weapon, copy of Daily Bugle, Tinkerer's van; Stilt-Man's hydraulic suit w/wrist-mounted machine guns (designed by Tinkerer)

SYNOPSIS: Jasper Sitwell reactivates G.W. Bridge to arrest Frank Castle. As Punisher prepares to kill a child pornographer, a reformed Stilt-Man arrives to apprehend the man. Punisher slays Stilt-Man with a rocket and kills the pornographer. While flushing out Punisher's ordinance storage units, Bridge discovers a secret tunnel and a SHIELD unit finds Punisher inside. Punisher subdues the SHIELD agents, takes their rifles and leaves town. He arrives at a vigil in Stamford, Connecticut, where the Tinkerer mourns the death of his grandson. Tinkerer admits that he is the source of Stilt-Man's new hardware and tells Punisher that Raft escapee Stuart Clarke has been supplying villains with high-tech weapons. Punisher finds Clarke and fights off an army of his mini-Iron Man robots. Clarke gives Punisher information about villains using tech supplied by Tony Stark and hands Punisher a tracking device for Stark tech. The device pinpoints super-humans underground and Punisher heads into the sewers to investigate. Seeing the Jester and Jack O'Lantern beating on Spider-Man, Punisher shoots Jack O'Lantern in the head and fires several bullets into Jester's torso. Castle carries the injured Spider-Man to the secret underground hideout of the "Secret Avengers," outlaw opponents of the Superhuman Registration Act, led by Captain America. Bridge resigns from SHIELD to go after Punisher outside the law.

NOTE: Cover labeled "Civil War." Unlike the first volume of Punisher War Journal, this volume was the only ongoing Punisher series set on Earth-616 during its publication run. The Stamford vigil is for victims of an explosion in CW #1, '06, the catalyst for the enacting of the Superhuman Registration Act that sparked a super-hero Civil War. The costume Spider-Man wears is an armored suit designed by Tony Stark and introduced in ASM #530, '06. Punisher thinks of Billy Joel's song, "Scenes from an Italian Restaurant." This issue reveals that Bridge is Muslim and Jasper Sitwell wears Old Spice aftershave.

PUNISHER WAR JOURNAL #2 (February 2007)

"How I Won the War, Part 2: Dead Soldiers" (22 pages)

CREDITS: Matt Fraction (writer), Ariel Olivetti (art), Virtual Calligraphy's Joe Caramagna (letters), Dean White (colors), Warren Simons (asst editor), Axel Alonso (editor)

FEATURE CHARACTER: Punisher (also in CW #6, '06, ASM #537, '07 & PWJ #3, '07, see NOTE)

GUEST STARS: Young Avengers: Hawkeye (Kate Bishop, archer, last in CW #5, '06, also & next in CW #6, '06), Hulkling (Dorrek VIII, aka Teddy Altman, Kree/Skrull hybrid shapeshifter, last in CW #5, next in CW #6, '06), Patriot (Elijah "Eli" Bradley, grandson of black "Captain America" Isaiah Bradley, last in CW #5, '06, also in SenSM #34, '06,also & next in CW #6, '06), Vision ("Jonas," android, last in CW #5, '06, also in SenSM #34, '06,ASM #537, '07 & CW #6, '06); Luke Cage (Carl Lucas, steel-skinned mercenary hero, last in CW #5, '06, also in SenSM #34, '06, ASM #537, '06, CW #6, '06 & PWJ #3, '07, next in CW #6, '06), Firebird (Bonita Juarez, radiation-powered social worker), Hercules (Heracles, ancient Greek demigod) (prev 3 during & also in CW #6, '06), Captain America (last in CW #5, '06, also CW:WarC #1, '07, BP #23, '07, SenSM #34, '06, BP #24, '07, CW #6, '06 & ASM #537, '07), Diamondback (Rachel Leighton, last in CW #5, '06, also in CW #6, '06, next in Av:In #8, '08 fb), Falcon (last in CW:WarC #1, '07, also in BP #24, CW #6, '06, next in BP #25, '07), Human Torch (Jonathan "Johnny" Storm, flame generator, last in FF #542, '06, also in ASM #537, '07 & CW #6, '06, also & next in PWJ #3, '07), Invisible Woman (Susan "Sue" Richards, during & also in CW #6, '06, also & next in PWJ #3, '07), Living Lightning (Miguel Santos, transforms self into electricity, last & also in CW #6, next in CW:FL #11, '07), Molten Man (Mark Raxton, covered w/gold liquid metal alloy, last in SenSM #31, '06, next in ASM #581, '09), Pulsar (Monica Rambeau, former harbor patrol officer, last in CW #5, '06, also in BP #24-25, '07 & CW #6, '06, also & next in PWJ #3, '07), Spider-Man (last in CW #5, '06, also in ASM #536, '06, SenSM #32-34, '06, IM #14, '07, FNSM #14-16, '07, ASM #537, '07, CW #6, '06 & PWJ #3, '07, next in CW #6, '06), Ultragirl (Tsu-Zana, aka Suzy Sherman, mutant human/Kree hybrid, last in ASM #537, '07, next in Av:In #1, '07)

SUPPORTING CAST: G.W. Bridge, Stuart Clarke

VILLAINS: Goldbug (Matthew Gilden, criminal w/gold-coated exo-skeleton, last in HFH #1, '06, also & next in CW #6, '06, dies), Plunderer (David Kivlin, also & next in CW #6, '06, dies, see NOTE), Scarecrow (Ebenezer Laughton, murderous contortionist, last in SenSM #31, '06, next in NAv Ann #2, '08), Veranke (Skrull Queen posing as Spider-Woman, last in CW #6, '06, next in BP #25, '07, see NOTE), criminals

OTHER CHARACTERS: Bridge's men inc Bill, SHIELD agents inc "cape-killers"

LOCATIONS/ITEMS: New York inc Stuart's warehouse base, Madison's, the Remington, sewer & Secret Avengers underground hideout / Punisher's automatic rifles, blasters, faux-white phosphorus grenade, zip line & rig w/anti-mobility glue; Clarke's armored chest plate, black-box suit, gadgets, headset, mechanical battle suit & mini-Iron Man robots; SHIELD Battle Van & rifles; Bridge's men's firearms, criminals' guns

SYNOPSIS: Punisher and Captain America talk about the Punisher's joining the Secret Avengers while Cap's allies eavesdrop. Cap agrees to let Punisher join but lays down the ground rules against killing. As G.W. Bridge stakes out Stuart Clarke's apartment, Cap and Punisher conduct tactical strikes and obtain the codes for the Ryker's Island portal to the Negative Zone prison. After fighting Scarecrow, they escape from a trap set by Molten Man and SHIELD troops. Castle visits Clarke to pick up a black-box suit Clarke designed for use in infiltrating the Baxter Building. After Punisher leaves, Bridge meets Clarke. Castle returns to the Secret Avengers' hideout and interrupts a meeting in which Cap welcomes villains Goldbug and Plunderer to the team. Punisher kills the two criminals. Cap punches Punisher, calling him a murderous piece of trash. Punisher tells Cap to punish him for disobeying his order not to kill.

NOTE: Cover labeled "Civil War." Indicia dated December, 2006. Portions of PWJ #2-3, '07 overlap. MCP #6/2, '08 reveals the Plunderer appearing here is a lookalike employed by the real Plunderer, Edgar Parnival Plunder, to be his American representative; OHMU:U #1, '10 reveals the lookalike's name. NAv #40, '08 reveals the Skrull Queen Veranke is posing as Spider-Woman.

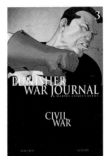

PUNISHER WAR JOURNAL #3 (March 2007)

"How I Won the War, Part 3: Mutually Assured Destruction" (22 pages)

CREDITS: Matt Fraction (writer), Ariel Olivetti (art), Virtual Calligraphy's Joe Caramagna (letters), Dean White (colors), Warren Simons (asst editor), Axel Alonso (editor)
FEATURE CHARACTER: Punisher (also as Frank Castiglione in fb between Pun:Int, '89 fb & Pun:RBN, '89 fb; also in CW #6, '06, PWJ #2, '07 & CW #7, '07)
GUEST STARS: Captain America, Pulsar (both also in CW #6, '06 & PWJ #2, '07, next in BP #25, '07), Luke Cage, Vision (both also in CW #6, '06 & PWJ #2, '07, next in CW #6, '06), Human Torch, Invisible Woman (both also in CW #6, '06, next in BP #25, '07), Spider-Man (during & also in CW #6, '06, next in ASM #538, '07), Patriot (last & also in CW #6, '06, next in BP #25, '07)
SUPPORTING CAST: G.W. Bridge (also in Cable&DP #33-34, '06-07, next in PWJ #5, '07), Stuart Clarke (next in PWJ #6, '07 fb)
VILLAIN: Rhino (Aleksei Mikhailovich Sytsevich, super-strong Russian criminal, last in SenSM #34, '07)
OTHER CHARACTERS: "Captain America" (in fb, see NOTE), U.S. Marines (in fb), Bridge's men, elevator attendant, office workers
LOCATIONS/ITEMS: Camp Lejeune, NC inc barracks & mess hall (in fb), New York inc Clarke's warehouse base, mosque, Secret Avengers underground hideout, SHIELD armory, waterfront warehouse & office building w/elevator / SHIELD firearms & missiles; Clarke's armored chest plate, golf club & mini-Iron Man robots; Bridge's men's firearms, Satan Claw (strength-enhancing gauntlet)
FLASHBACK: A man dressed as Captain America trains Frank Castiglione and other U.S. Marines at Camp Lejeune. After Frank refuses to strike the trainer out of respect for the uniform, his fellow Marines beat him up.
SYNOPSIS: Punisher tries to justify his murderous actions as the enraged Captain America regrets their alliance. Cap pummels Punisher, but Castle refuses to fight back. Cap labels Punisher insane and the Secret Avengers decide to let him go. G.W. Bridge warns Stuart Clarke that Punisher will turn on him and orders his men to take Clarke out. Clarke escapes ungracefully with the help of a chest plate he designed. Some time later, after being unconscious for days from a severe beating, Punisher awakens in Clarke's presence in a SHIELD armory, where weapons and intelligence data give Punisher the tools he needs to go after super-villains. Punisher sets fire to the waterfront warehouse that Rhino is living in to draw him out, and defeats Rhino with a Satan Claw. Punisher tells the villain to spread the word that Punisher is back. Bridge prays for strength in his mission.
NOTE: Cover labeled "Civil War." The Captain America appearing in flashback here is an unidentified man employed by the military.

PUNISHER WAR JOURNAL #4 (April 2007)

"Small Wake for a Tall Man" (22 pages)

CREDITS: Matt Fraction (writer), Mike Deodato (art), Virtual Calligraphy's Joe Caramagna (letters), Rain Beredo (colors), Michael O'Connor (asst editor), Axel Alonso (editor)
FEATURE CHARACTER: Punisher (also disguised as a bartender)
GUEST STARS: Spider-Man (also in rfb, also in fb during DD #27, '67; last in CW #7, '07, next in ASM #538, '07), Daredevil (in rfb & fb during DD #27, '67)
VILLAINS: Absorbing Man (Carl "Crusher" Creel, last in MHol, '06, next bts in SH #17, '07, next in AntM #12, '07), Answer (Aaron Nicholson, last in CW:WarC #1, '07, next bts in SH #17, '07, next in NAv #35, '07 fb), Armada (David Breyer, last in CW:WarC #1, '07, next bts in SH #17, '07), Armadillo (Antonio Rodriguez, last in U #5, '06, next bts in SH #17, '07, next in CW #7, '07), Cat Burglar (also in rfb, last as Prowler in PPSSM #48, '80, next bts in SH #17, '07), Chameleon (Dmitri Smerdyakov, last in SenSM #31, '06, next bts in SH #17, '07, next in SVTU #2, '07), Dragon Man (last in I♥M:Web #1, '06, next bts in SH #17, '07, next in AntM #9, '07), Eel (Edward Lavell, last in Tb #108, '07, next bts in SH #17, '07, next in Cap #28, '07), Grizzly (Maxwell Markham, last in SH #6, '06, next bts in SH #17, '07, next in PWJ #14, '08), Masked Marauder (Frank Farnum, also in rfb, last in PPSSM #28, '79, next bts in SH #17, '07), Princess Python (Zelda Dubois, also in rfb, last in Dlk #9, '00, last bts in DoD #5, '06, next bts in SH #17, '07, next in PWJ #16, '08) & Pythagoras (her python, 1st, next bts in SH #17, '07, next in PWJ #16, '08), Professor Power (Prof. Anthony Power, last in XFac Ann #9, '94, next bts in SH #17, '07, next in Nomad #1, '09), Rhino (next bts in SH #17, '07, next in FallSon:SM, '07), Ringer (Keith Kraft, last in SH #59, '94, next bts in SH #17, '07, next in Av:In #26, '09), Shocker (Herman Schultz, also in rfb, last in ASM #533, '06, next in SH #17, '07), Xandu (last in SecDef #8, '93, next bts in SH #17, '07), a Doombot (reprogrammed by Armada)
OTHER CHARACTERS: Gibbon (Martin Blank, last in SH #6, '06 fb, next bts in SH #17, '07, next in PWJ #16, '08), Prowler (also as Hobie Brown in fb to 1st chr app before ASM #78, '69 fb; last in MsM #6, '06, next bts in SH #17, '07, next in SVTU #1, '07), Puma (Thomas Fireheart, last in SenSM #34, '07, next bts in SH #17, '07, chr next in SVTU #2, '07 fb, next in SVTU #1, '07), Will O' the Wisp (Jackson Arvad, last in SenSM #31, '06, next bts in SH #17, '07), Robert Farrell (Rocket Racer, last in PPSM #55, '03, next bts in SH #17, '07, next in SVTU #1, '07), Stilt-Man (corpse, also in rfb, also in fb during DD #27, '67; last in PWJ #1, '07), Emma Johnson Farrell (Rocket Racer's mother, bts, doing well, last in SMU #14, '96, next in SVTU #1, '07); Daredevil, Hulk; Avengers: Wasp, Yellowjacket; Circus of Crime: Benny (Princess Python's python), Clown, Ringmaster; bystanders (prev 8 in rfb); Dr. Octopus (arms only), Sandman (both only on cover)
LOCATIONS/ITEMS: New York (also in fb & rfb) inc Cuts (bar, destroyed) / Stilt-Man's hydraulic suit, Punisher's poison, kerosene & note
FLASHBACKS: Stilt-Man battles Daredevil and Spider-Man (DD #27, '67). Daredevil saves window washer Hobie Brown when Stilt-Man knocks him down (1). As Stilt-Man fights Spider-Man, Daredevil battles the Masked Marauder (DD #27, '67). The Circus of Crime attacks Wasp and Yellowjacket's wedding (Av #60, '69). Spider-Man fights the Cat Burglar (ASM #30, '65). Spider-Man fights Shocker (ASM #46, '67). Princess Python attacks Hulk with her python (IHulk #217, '77).
SYNOPSIS: Villains and former criminals gather in a bar for Stilt-Man's wake. When Princess Python, Stilt-Man's widow, arrives, they start telling stories about their glory days over drinks. At first the hero Prowler attacks Cat Burglar for stealing his identity, but they soon put aside past differences. Will O' the Wisp catches up with Bob Farrell, the Rocket Racer. When Armadillo accidentally spills his drink on Rhino, a drunken brawl breaks out. Everyone fights until Spider-Man arrives for the wake, who is disappointed to see the villains brawling. He tells Puma to take Prowler away and tells the others to be careful; the world isn't as fun as it used to be. When Spider-Man leaves Masked Marauder berates the others for letting a hero lecture them. Cat Burglar and others begin to vomit blood and Masked Marauder realizes the bartender poisoned them. He finds a note from the Punisher as the bar catches fire. Punisher walks away as the bar explodes.

NOTE: This issue reveals Stilt-Man and Princess Python were married. Pythagoras is named in PWJ #16, '08. SH #17, '07 reveals the villains were rushed to the hospital, had their stomachs pumped and were treated for burns. It remains unrevealed if Armada, Cat Burglar, Masked Marauder, Prowler, Will O' the Wisp or Xandu survived.

PUNISHER WAR JOURNAL #5 (May 2007)

"NYC Red" (22 pages)

CREDITS: Matt Fraction (writer), Ariel Olivetti (art, colors), Virtual Calligraphy's Joe Caramagna (letters), Michael O'Connor (asst editor), Axel Alonso (editor)
FEATURE CHARACTER: Punisher (next in PWJ #6-9, '07 fbs)
SUPPORTING CAST: G.W. Bridge (last in PWJ #3, '07)
VILLAIN: Bushwacker (last in DDvPun #3, '05, next in NAv #35, '07 fb)
OTHER CHARACTERS: Jasper Sitwell (voice only, last in PWJ #1, '07), Ian Amsterdam (NYPD Auxiliary volunteer, 1st, also in fb, next in PWJ #11, '07), other NYPD Auxiliary volunteers (in fb), New York police (also in fb) inc Phil James (Emergency Service Unit officer, 1st), Bob Ranks (patrol sergeant, 1st) & Jerry; G.W. Bridge's men, Bushwacker's hostage, EMT, press photographers, tourists, TV news reporters, cameraman, bystanders (also in fb); Sharon Carter (SHIELD agent), Captain America, US marshal (prev 3 in rfb)
LOCATIONS/ITEMS: New York inc Westin Hotel (in fb), apartment building, firehouse, police station, subway entrance & Times Square / Ian's badge & pistol; G.W. Bridge's gun & transceiver; NYPD police cars, vans, barricades & firearms; SHIELD Helicarrier
FLASHBACKS: Ian Amsterdam joins the NYPD Auxiliary but is let go after his family is killed in the tragedy in Stamford, Connecticut (1). Captain America is killed (Cap #25, '07).
SYNOPSIS: Bushwacker takes a hostage in Times Square and NYPD Auxiliary volunteer Ian Amsterdam tries to arrest him. G.W. Bridge arrives and tells Ian to stand down, but Ian refuses. Bridge calls for backup, talks to responding police and learns he's been federally deputized by Jasper Sitwell. A SWAT team arrives, but Ian still refuses to stand down. Bushwacker demands to see the Punisher. Bridge learns that Ian was let go from the auxiliary force and is not currently an officer of any kind. Frank Castle arrives and concludes that the whole set-up is a ruse by Bridge to lure him into the open. When Bushwacker gets out of control, Bridge is forced to shoot him. As Punisher leaves, everyone in Times Square sees TV news coverage of Captain America's assassination.
NOTE: Includes recap page (1 page). Ian's badge number is 2828; his surname is revealed in OHMU HC #6, '09. Billboards advertise the Broadway productions of "Aida," "Beauty and the Beast" and "The Lion King."

PUNISHER WAR JOURNAL #6 (June 2007)

"Goin' Out West" (22 pages)

CREDITS: Matt Fraction (writer), Ariel Olivetti (art, colors), Virtual Calligraphy's Joe Caramagna (letters), Michael O'Connor (asst editor), Axel Alonso (editor)
FEATURE CHARACTER: Punisher (also in fb1 between PWJ #5, '07 & PWJ #7, '07 fb, also in fb2 during PWJ #9, '07 fb)
SUPPORTING CAST: G.W. Bridge (in fb1, next in PWJ #8, '07 fb), Stuart Clarke (in fb1 between PWJ #3, '07 & PWJ #7, '07 fb)
VILLAINS: Hate-Monger (white supremacist, also in newspaper, 1st but chr last in PWJ #9, '07 fb, also in fb1 to 1st chr app before PWJ #7, '07 fb) & his cyborg coyotes, National Force (Texas-based white supremacist militia, 1st in fb1 between PWJ #7, '07 fb, off-panel in fb2 during PWJ #9, '07 fb, see NOTE)
OTHER CHARACTERS: Jasper Sitwell (in fb1 between PWJ #5, '07 & PWJ #8, '07 fb), Tatiana "Tati" Arocha (photojournalist, 1st, see NOTE), Carla (911 dispatcher, 1st) & her mother (bts, on phone w/Carla), 911 callers (voices only), police, police dogs, Mexicans, newspaper deliveryman, waitress, SHIELD agents inc cape-killers (all in fb1)
LOCATIONS/ITEMS: California/Mexico border inc Mexican lay up colony; 911 call center, Connie's Country Cooking diner, New York City inc Brooklyn Bridge, East River & SHIELD armory (all in fb1), Sonoran Desert / SHIELD Helicarrier Pericles III, SHIELD helicopters, SHIELD agents' guns, jetpacks, scuba gear & spearguns; National Force's air cars, flamethrowers & gas masks; police cars & helicopter; Tati's camera, Crónicas newspaper, Punisher's van, stolen SHIELD equipment crates w/rebreathers (all in fb1), automatic firearms, bandolier (both in fb2) & his Captain America-inspired uniform (also in fb2)
FLASHBACKS: Dressed in Nazi costumes reminiscent of Captain America's uniform, white supremacists Hate-Monger and the National Force slaughter a group of Mexicans planning to cross over into the U.S. Reporter Tatiana Arocha takes pictures of the event. G.W. Bridge and Jasper Sitwell track Punisher and Stuart Clarke's location and deploy a squad of cape-killers to pursue them. A chase ensues, and Punisher and Clarke escape by driving off the Brooklyn Bridge and surfacing undetected. They go to a diner, where they see a newspaper report about Hate-Monger. Castle resolves to go to Mexico by stolen car and shoot Hate-Monger in the face (1). Sporting his Cap-based uniform, Punisher opens fire on the Hate-Monger's men (2).
SYNOPSIS: Stripped of his new uniform, Castle is tied to a stake and Hate-Monger tells him he's going to die.
NOTE: Cover labeled "The Initiative." Includes recap page (1 page). Tatiana and National Force are named in PWJ #7, '07. This National Force is not to be confused with the neo-fascist group of the same name introduced in Cap #231, '79.

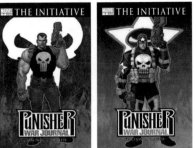

PUNISHER WAR JOURNAL #7 (July 2007)

"Blood and Sand" (22 pages)

CREDITS: Matt Fraction (writer), Ariel Olivetti (art, colors), Virtual Calligraphy's Joe Caramagna (letters), Michael O'Connor (asst editor), Axel Alonso (editor)
FEATURE CHARACTER: Punisher (also in fb & dfb between PWJ #6, '07 fb & PWJ #8, '07 fb)
SUPPORTING CAST: Stuart Clarke (also in fb & dfb between PWJ #6, '07 fb & PWJ #8, '07 fb)
VILLAINS: Hate-Monger (also in fb1 between PWJ #6, '07 fb & PWJ #9, '07 fb) & his cyborg coyotes, National Force (chr last in PWJ #9, '07 fb, also in fb1 between PWJ #6, '07 fb & PWJ #8, '07 fb) inc Tank
OTHER CHARACTERS: Carla (corpse), US Customs & Border Protection officer (1st), Tati Arocha, bartender, bull (all in fb1), Rose (mentioned, Carla's co-worker)
LOCATIONS/ITEMS: Sonoran Desert inc trailer park w/Carla's trailer, US customs office, Westerner Bar & motel w/Tati Arocha's room, National Force base w/bullpen (all in fb1) & National Force outpost / Tati's camera, Crónicas newspaper, Punisher's wood board (all in fb1) & Captain America-inspired uniform; National Force rifles
FLASHBACKS: Punisher and Stuart Clarke arrive in the Southwest, where photojournalist Tati Arocha questions a US Border Protection officer in her investigation into the story behind the recent killings of Mexicans. Frank Castle poses as a white supremacist and insinuates himself into the Hate Monger's gang while Clarke tracks down Tati. After finding a slain dispatcher who had received a tip about the slaying, Tati rushes back to her motel, where she encounters Clarke. She says she thought he was dead and kisses him. Castle passes an initiation into the National Force by defeating a bull (1). Stuart applies a Nazi symbol tattoo to Frank's arm (d).
SYNOPSIS: Hate-Monger puts Frank Castle's Cap-inspired uniform back on him and gives him a nativist, racist speech. The villain prepares to have his National Force execute Castle, who calls himself Captain America.
NOTE: Cover labeled "The Initiative." Includes recap page (1 page) & UltFF #42, '07 sneak peak (4 pages). The dfb occurs during the fb.

PUNISHER WAR JOURNAL #8 (August 2007)

"Sunset" (22 pages)

CREDITS: Matt Fraction (writer), Ariel Olivetti (art, colors), Virtual Calligraphy's Joe Caramagna (letters), Aubrey Sitterson (asst editor), Axel Alonso (editor)
FEATURE CHARACTER: Punisher (also in fb between PWJ #7, '07 fb & PWJ #9, '07 fb)
GUEST STARS: Maria Hill (SHIELD deputy director, in fb between BP #26, '07 & FallSon:W, '07), Tony Stark (SHIELD Director, in fb between CW:In, '07 & MAv #1, '07 fb, see NOTE)
SUPPORTING CAST: G.W. Bridge (bts, arrives at National Force's base, last in PWJ #6, '07 fb, chr last in PWJ #9, '07 fb, also in fb between PWJ #6, '07 fb & PWJ #9, '07 fb), Stuart Clarke (in fb between PWJ #7, '07 fb & PWJ #9, '07 fb)
VILLAINS: National Force inc Tank (also in fb between PWJ #7, '07 fb & PWJ #9, '09 fb), Hate-Monger
OTHER CHARACTERS: Jasper Sitwell (in fb between PWJ #6, '07 fb & PWJ #24, '08), US Customs & Border Protection officer (in fb, next in PWJ #10, '07), Tati Arocha, bystanders, motel employee (all in fb)
LOCATIONS/ITEMS: Newark, NJ's Turnpike Motel (in fb), Sonoran Desert inc customs office, hotel w/Stuart Clarke's room (both in fb) & National Force outpost / SHIELD Helicarrier w/meeting room, Tank's pistol, Crónicas newspaper, Punisher's ammunition belt, GPS device, grenades, night vision goggles (all in fb) & Captain America-inspired uniform (also in fb); G.W. Bridge's laptop computer (in fb) & laser sight; National Force's firearms & flamethrowers; Hate-Monger's Luger P-08
FLASHBACK: SHIELD Director Tony Stark fires G.W. Bridge for failing to capture Frank Castle. Punisher returns to Stuart Clarke's hotel room in the Sonoran Desert and finds him there with Tati Arocha, whom he learns is Clarke's girlfriend. Castle says the National Force is going on another raid and has Clarke and Tati help him whip up a new mask and uniform that incorporate elements of Captain America's costume. In a Newark motel, G.W. Bridge offers a reward via the Internet for information leading to Castle's capture. The Border Protection officer Tati questioned reveals to National Force interrogators that Tati is looking into the Force. That night, Frank, Stuart and Tati go into the desert, and after Punisher leaves the others to rendezvous undercover with Hate-Monger, National Force members grab Tati and Clarke flees.
SYNOPSIS: Hate-Monger beats Frank Castle, and as he's about to shoot his victim, a National Force member points out that someone else is present.
NOTE: Cover labeled "The Initiative." Includes recap page (1 page) and promo for Annihilation Conquest titles, '07 (4 pages). Tony Stark took the SHIELD directorship in CW #7, '07.

PUNISHER WAR JOURNAL #9 (September 2007)

"Duel" (22 pages)

CREDITS: Matt Fraction (writer), Ariel Olivetti (art, colors), Virtual Calligraphy's Joe Caramagna (letters), Aubrey Sitterson (asst editor), Axel Alonso (editor)
FEATURE CHARACTER: Punisher (also in fb between PWJ #8, '07 fb & PWJ #6, '07, also in PWJ #6, '07 fb & PWJ #15, '08 fb)
SUPPORTING CAST: G.W. Bridge (also in fb between PWJ #8, '07 fb & bts in PWJ #8, '07), Stuart Clarke (in fb between PWJ #8, '07 fb & PWJ #10, '07)
VILLAINS: Hate-Monger (also in fb between PWJ #7, '07 fb & PWJ #6, '07), National Force inc Tank (also in fb between PWJ #8, '07 fb & PWJ #7, '07 & also in PWJ #6, '07 fb)
OTHER CHARACTERS: Tati Arocha (in fb, also in PWJ #15, '08 fb, dies), US Border Patrol officers (in fb)

LOCATIONS/ITEMS: Manhattan, Newark, NJ's Turnpike Motel, Phoenix airport (in fb), Sonoran Desert inc National Force outpost (also in fb), Mexican border crossing & Stuart Clarke's hotel room (both in fb) / Stuart's revolvers, National Force aircraft, vehicles & Nazi flags (all in fb), National Force firearms, flamethrowers & gas masks (prev 3 also in fb); Punisher's automatic firearms (in fb) & Captain America-inspired uniform (also in fb); G.W. Bridge's laptop computer, SHIELD badge w/ID (both in fb) & assault rifle; Hate-Monger's H-ray generator (in fb) & Luger P-08

FLASHBACK: The National Force takes Frank Castle to their desert outpost. Meanwhile, Stuart Clarke answers G.W. Bridge's online reward ad and calls Bridge to verify that Bridge is still looking for Frank. Hate-Monger tells Castle of his plan to spread hatred by setting up a series of H-ray generators like the one at the outpost. Exposure to H-rays makes people want to kill, and it begins to affect Castle. Bridge flies from New Jersey to Phoenix and then drives into Mexico. At the National Force outpost, Hate-Monger tells Castle to kill the captured Tati Arocha as an initiation assignment. Consumed by hate, Castle complies as Force members cheer. Bridge meets with Clarke, who tells Bridge about the National Force and their plans for another raid. That night, the National Force heads out on their mission and Castle dons his new costume and clears his head. He mows through a bunch of the white supremacists, but he's overpowered and subdued.

SYNOPSIS: A sniper opens fire and several of Hate Monger's men are hit. The shooter reveals himself as G.W. Bridge, who says he's arrived to arrest Frank Castle.

NOTE: Cover labeled "The Initiative." Includes recap page (1 page).

PUNISHER WAR JOURNAL #10 (October 2007)

"Sunset" (22 pages)

CREDITS: Matt Fraction (writer), Ariel Olivetti (art, colors), Virtual Calligraphy's Joe Caramagna (letters), Aubrey Sitterson (asst editor), Axel Alonso (editor)
FEATURE CHARACTER: Punisher
GUEST STAR: Tony Stark (bts, on phone, last in FallSon:Cap, '07, next in FallSon:IM, '07)
SUPPORTING CAST: Stuart Clarke (next in PWJ #12, '07), G.W. Bridge
VILLAINS: Hate-Monger (dies), National Force inc Tank (dies)
OTHER CHARACTERS: US Customs & Border Protection officer (last in PWJ #8, '07 fb, dies) & his wife (bts, on phone), Tati Arocha (corpse), SHIELD agent (bts, on phone)
LOCATIONS/ITEMS: Sonoran Desert inc customs office & National Force outpost / Punisher's Captain America-inspired uniform, automatic rifle, knife & explosives; Hate-Monger's H-ray generator & Luger P-08; National Force firearms, flamethrowers, gas masks, Nazi flags & vehicles; G.W. Bridge's assault rifle, Stuart's revolver, SHIELD paperwork

SYNOPSIS: Stuart Clarke sets off explosions at the National Force outpost, forcing Hate-Monger and his men to abandon Frank Castle to G.W. Bridge. Bridge frees Frank Castle. At the National Force compound, Stuart finds Tati's body and starts shooting National Force members. He swears to find out who killed her and make them pay. Punisher finds Hate-Monger in the compound, destroys the H-ray generator and shoots Hate-Monger in the face. After contacting SHIELD to have them bring a mop-up squad, Bridge kills Force member Tank. Stuart finds Punisher defacing Hate-Monger's uniform. Bridge lets Punisher and Clarke go and decides to refuse an anticipated offer by Tony Stark to rejoin SHIELD. Accompanied by Castle, Clarke begins a revenge spree to kill those involved in Tati Arocha's murder by killing the US Border Protection officer, unaware of Castle's involvement.

NOTE: Cover labeled "The Initiative." Includes recap page (1 page).

PUNISHER WAR JOURNAL #11 (November 2007)

"Heroes and Villains" (22 pages)

CREDITS: Matt Fraction (writer), Leandro Fernandez (pencils), Francisco Paronzini (inks), Virtual Calligraphy's Joe Caramagna (letters), Val Staples (colors), Aubrey Sitterson (editor), Axel Alonso (exec editor), Ariel Olivetti (c art)
FEATURE CHARACTER: Punisher (also in newspaper)
GUEST STARS: Iron Man (last in FF #544, '07 fb, last bts in MsM #14, '07, next in WWHulk:X #1, '07 fb), Winter Soldier (James Buchanan "Bucky" Barnes, Captain America's former partner & ex-Soviet agent, between Cap #26-27, '07)
SUPPORTING CAST: G.W. Bridge (next in PWJ #13, '08), Lynn Michaels (SHIELD agent posing as psychologist, last in PWJ #80, '95, next in PWJ #18, '08, see NOTE)
VILLAIN: Jigsaw (last in NAv #3, '05, chr last in NAv #42, '08 fb, next in NAv #35, '07 fb)
OTHER CHARACTERS: Ian Amsterdam (last in PWJ #5, '07, next in PWJ #18, '08), alligator
LOCATIONS/ITEMS: Florida Everglades, Washington, DC inc Thomas Jefferson Memorial, Washington Monument & Tidal Basin; New York City inc Russo Psychiatric Home w/office & shooting range / Punisher's Captain America-inspired uniform, duffle bag & key; G.W. Bridge's houseboat & pistols; Ian's pistol, Winter Soldier's pistol

SYNOPSIS: Iron Man visits G.W. Bridge on his houseboat in the Everglades. Bridge talks about his hatred for Frank Castle, admits to a spiritual crisis, and confesses that he let Punisher go. Stark offers him a job and Bridge asks for his crew. Winter Soldier meets with Punisher in Washington, DC to ask him what inspired him to don a Captain America-like uniform. They fight, and Punisher gives Winter Soldier the costume and the keys to a dead drop containing Cap's mask, which Castle admits to grabbing after Cap's arrest. At an unusual psychiatric hospital in New York, Jigsaw and a female psychologist mold the troubled Ian Amsterdam into a killing machine with psychotropic drugs, electroshock and counseling.

NOTE: Cover labeled "The Initiative." Includes recap page (1 page). PWJ #23, '08 reveals the psychologist is SHIELD agent Lynn Michaels.

PUNISHER WAR JOURNAL #12 (December 2007)

"World War Frank" (34 pages)

CREDITS: Matt Fraction (writer), Ariel Olivetti (art, colors), Virtual Calligraphy's Rus Wooton (letters), Aubrey Sitterson (editor), Axel Alonso (exec editor)
FEATURE CHARACTER: Punisher (also in symbolic image)
SUPPORTING CAST: Stuart Clarke (last in PWJ #10, '07)
VILLAINS: Mung the Inconceivable (Sakaar native, last in IHulk #108, '07, dies) & his insectoid army (some die)
OTHER CHARACTERS: Hulk (in symbolic image), Venom, police (both in Stuart's thoughts), little girl, her parents (residents of 171 Fulton St.) & her maternal grandfather (mentioned, died from emphysema), Mr. Kitty (little girl's cat), stranded New Yorkers

LOCATIONS/ITEMS: New York inc 107 Fulton St. home, Stuart's workshop, abandoned building & Staten Island Ferry terminal / Punisher's chainsaws, gun & shotgun; Mung's swords & axe; Mung's insectoid army's swords, axes & spears; Stuart Clarke's van & hidden arsenal inc sword-shooting gun, electro-blasters & Venomech System armor (full-body, high-impact synthiote of liquid smart-armor suit); Staten Island Ferry
SYNOPSIS: In an evacuated New York due to Hulk's rampage, a little girl locates her cat only for Mung the Inconceivable's insectoid army to attack her. Punisher arrives armed with chainsaws and kills the creatures. Punisher and Stuart Clarke take the girl to her home where her parents explain they didn't leave when the city was evacuated because her grandfather was too sick. Now that he's passed away, they want to leave the city. Stuart takes Punisher to his workshop where they gather weapons. After fighting their way back to the family's home, Punisher and Clarke plot a course to safety. Once outside, the insectoid army attacks them, and Mung confronts Punisher. To get the family to safety, Punisher challenges Mung to a duel in one hour. Seeking shelter in an abandoned building, Punisher finds other stranded New Yorkers. Agreeing to lead them to safety as well, Punisher and Clarke decide that the Staten Island Ferry is the most efficient way out of the city. Equipping himself with Clarke's self-repairing Venomech System, Punisher battles Mung while Clarke leads everyone to the Ferry. Punisher kills Mung but learns the little girl's cat ran away again. Punisher promises to find Mr. Kitty.
NOTE: Cover labeled "World War Hulk." Includes recap page (1 page).

PUNISHER WAR JOURNAL #13 (January 2008)

"Hunter/Hunted, Part 1" (22 pages)

CREDITS: Matt Fraction (writer), Cory Walker (art), Virtual Calligraphy's Joe Caramagna (letters), Dave Stewart (colors), Aubrey Sitterson (editor), Axel Alonso (exec editor), Ariel Olivetti (c art)
FEATURE CHARACTER: Punisher
GUEST STARS: Spider-Man (last in SenSM Ann #1, '07, next in SenSM #38, '07), Domino (Neena Thurman, mutant w/luck enhancing abilities, last in Cable&Dp #43, '07 fb, next in PWJ #19, '08)
SUPPORTING CAST: G.W. Bridge (last in PWJ #11, '07)
VILLAINS: Bushmaster (Quincy McIver, cyborg w/snake-like body, last in Tb #107, '06), Kraven the Hunter (Alyosha Kravinoff, last in Beyond #6, '07), Rhino (last in NW #2, '07 fb), Tiger Shark (Todd Arliss, insane amphibious renegade, last in FallSon:Av, '07), Vulture (Adrian Toomes, winged inventor, last in SH #17, '07), 2 bank robbers, 3 Turkish criminals
OTHER CHARACTERS: Frog-Man (Eugene Patilio, inept hero, last in SpecSM #185, '92), Aragorn (winged steed of Vatican's Black Knight, last in BP #5, '05, see NOTE), Jim Maclemore (security guard, dies), Manny (barista), bank teller & customers, police inc detectives, SHIELD agents, Turkish street vendor, bystanders, cat, dog
LOCATIONS/ITEMS: Maras, Turkey, New York inc bank, crackhouse, docks, rooftop & alley / Punisher's missile launcher, pistol & rifle; Kraven's blow dart gun, darts, cages, strength-enhancing elixir & electromagnetic collars w/detonator; bank robbers' pistol, rifle & ski masks; Turkish criminals' pistols, Tiger Shark's water tank, Bella Anna (Kraven's ship)
SYNOPSIS: Rhino robs a bank and accidentally kills the security guard. Punisher kills Rhino's accomplices and fires missiles at Rhino, but the nearby Spider-Man protects the belligerent villain from Punisher's murderous tactics. In Turkey, an injured Domino fails to escape from her pursuers when she breaks her ankle. G.W. Bridge and his SHIELD agents rescuer her, and he recruits her in putting the team back together to arrest the Punisher. Spider-Man webs up Punisher and tries to calm down Rhino, but Al Kraven suddenly shoots Spider-Man and Rhino with tranquilizer darts in front of the webbed-up Punisher. Kraven escapes with Rhino and Spider-Man tells Punisher to stay away from Kraven. Later, Rhino awakens on a ship in a cell next to Vulture, Tiger Shark, Frog-Man, Bushmaster and Aragorn.
NOTE: Includes recap/title page (1 page). The team to which Bridge refers is the Six Pack, a group of mercenaries originally known as the Wild Pack and introduced in XFor #8, '92. The Aragorn shown here should not be confused with Dane Whitman's winged horse of the same name.

PUNISHER WAR JOURNAL #14 (February 2008)

"Hunter/Hunted, Part 2" (22 pages)

CREDITS: Matt Fraction (writer), Scott Wegener (art), Virtual Calligraphy's Joe Caramagna (letters), Shannon Blanchard (colors), Aubrey Sitterson (editor), Axel Alonso (exec editor), Ariel Olivetti (c art)
FEATURE CHARACTER: Punisher
GUEST STAR: Gargoyle (Isaac Christians, bio-mystical energy manipulator, last in Av:In #3, '07)
SUPPORTING CAST: G.W. Bridge, Stuart Clarke
VILLAINS: la Contessa Valentina Allegra de Fontaine (Skrull, last in Cap #26, '07, next in PWJ #19, '08, see NOTE), Grizzly (last in PWJ #4, '07, last bts in SH #17, '07), Kangaroo (Brian Hibbs, marsupial-suited crook, last in CW:WarC #1, '07, next in WoSM #1/3, '09), Man-Bull (William "Bill" Taurens, horned criminal, last in U #3, '06), Mandrill (Jerome Beechman, simian pheromone manipulator, last in NAv #35, '07 fb), Mongoose (genetically

engineered mongoose, last in SH #17, '07), Bushmaster, Kraven the Hunter, Rhino, Tiger Shark, Vulture, AIM robots
OTHER CHARACTER: Aragorn (dies), Frog-Man (bts, in cell)
LOCATIONS/ITEMS: New York inc docks, New York Public Library & Kraven's properties; Paris inc Eiffel Tower / Punisher's binoculars, pistols, rifle & van; Kraven's blow dart gun, dart, cages, electromagnetic collars, microphone, skull cup & test tube; Contessa's blaster & HAWK (High-Altitude Wing Kite) attachment; AIM robots' throwing stars, Stuart's flash drive, Bella Anna
SYNOPSIS: Intending to keep his captives as a menagerie, Kraven shows them what will happen if they displease him by blowing Aragorn to bits. Stuart Clarke acquires information on every property in the city owned by Kraven. Punisher and Stuart check each one, finally coming to a ship at the docks. In their cells, Vulture shows Rhino that Kraven broke Vulture's hands, leaving him unable to tamper with their explosive collars. Kraven feeds his prisoners Aragorn meat. In Paris, G.W. Bridge recruits la Contessa Valentina de Fontaine as she completes a mission. Punisher sneaks aboard Kraven's ship and finds his caged captives, who are starting to act animalistic. Punisher frees Rhino when Kraven arrives, but Kraven subdues Punisher and Rhino with tranquilizer darts. Punisher awakens in chains and Kraven tells him he's removed the humanity from the captives and set them free on the ship, which is sinking. The savage Tiger Shark approaches Punisher.
NOTE: Includes recap/title page (1 page). The Contessa who appears in this series is revealed as a Skrull in SecInvPro, '08.

PUNISHER WAR JOURNAL #15 (March 2008)

"Hunter/Hunted, Part 3" (22 pages)

CREDITS: Matt Fraction (writer), Scott Wegener (art), Virtual Calligraphy's Joe Caramagna (letters), Shannon Blanchard (colors), Aubrey Sitterson (editor), Axel Alonso (exec editor), Ariel Olivetti (c art)
FEATURE CHARACTER: Punisher (also in fb during PWJ #9, '07 fb; next in MChan #3, '08 fb, Et #1, '08, PWJ Ann #1, '09)
GUEST STARS: Gargoyle (next in Av:In #8, '08 fb), Silver Sable (Silver Sablinova, Symkarian head of Silver Sable International, last in S&F #4, '06, next in PWJ #19, '08)
SUPPORTING CAST: G.W. Bridge (next in PWJ #19, '08), Stuart Clarke (chr next in PWJ Ann #1, '09, next in PWJ #17, '08)
VILLAINS: Bushmaster (next in W #73, '09), Grizzly (next in ASM #573/2, '08), Kraven the Hunter (next in ASM:Swing #1, '08), Man-Bull (next in DR:LL #2, '09), Mandrill (next in NAv #46, '08), Rhino (chr next in PWJ Ann #1, '09, next bts in PWJ #22, '08), Swarm (Fritz von Meyer, Nazi scientist's disembodied mind controlling killer bee colony, last in SenSM #30, '06, next in Tb #122, '08), Tiger Shark (next in Tb:RM #1, '08), Vulture (next bts in PWJ #26, '09)
OTHER CHARACTERS: Frog-Man (next in Av:In #20, '09), Tati Arocha (in fb during PWJ #9, '07 fb), Jim Maclemore & his wife (both mentioned), Kraven's saber-toothed cat, SHIELD agents
LOCATIONS/ITEMS: Kraven's Savage Land lair, museum, New York docks / Punisher's pistol & van; Kraven's blow dart gun, dart, brazier, chair, electromagnetic collar, knife, spear, strength-enhancing elixir & teleportation device; Silver Sable's glass cutter, infrared goggles, rope & suction cups; G.W. Bridge's pistol, Rhino's letter, SHIELD agents' firearms, "Washington Diamond," Bella Anna
FLASHBACK: Punisher grabs Tati Arocha by the throat.
SYNOPSIS: Aboard Kraven's sinking ship, Punisher defeats Tiger Shark. Meanwhile, Kraven wounds Frog-Man and Bushmaster. Grizzly knocks a horn off Man-Bull and Frank Castle uses the horn to attack Mandrill. After being injured in an encounter with Gargoyle and Swarm, Punisher fights Kraven. G.W. Bridge sets Silver Sable up in a museum diamond heist and blackmails her into working for the team he's assembling. Rhino helps Punisher defeat Kraven, forcing the villain to teleport back to the Savage Land. Rhino convinces Punisher that the death of the guard he killed was an accident. Punisher decides not to kill him. After swimming back to shore, Rhino writes an apology letter to the guard's widow with Vulture's help. Castle reports back to Stuart Clarke and tells him they have to go to the Savage Land to get Kraven.
NOTE: Includes recap/title page (1 page). Rhino uses the pseudonym Ryan O'Smith, a play on his name, in his letter to Maclemore's widow.

PUNISHER WAR JOURNAL #16 (April 2008)

"The Survivors Guild" (22 pages)

CREDITS: Matt Fraction (writer), Howard Chaykin (art), Virtual Calligraphy's Joe Caramagna (letters), Edgar Delgado (colors), Aubrey Sitterson (editor), Alex Maleev (c art)
FEATURE CHARACTER: Punisher
VILLAINS: Gibbon (also as Martin Siamang, last in PWJ #4, '07, last bts in NW #3, '07, next in MApes #1, '08), Princess Python (last in PWJ #4, '07, last bts in SH #17, '07, next in MApes #1, '08), Pythagoras (last in PWJ #4, '07, last bts in SH #17, '07, dies) & her new snake (1st), Tinkerer (last in W:O #15, '07, next in InvIM #4, '08), Joseph Allen "Joey" Grady (pawn shop owner, 1st, next in PWJ #18, '08, see NOTE), other Punisher victims inc Bruce & Ramon; pimp
OTHER CHARACTERS: Prostitutes inc Sasha, pawn shop owner, pet store clerk, bystanders
LOCATIONS/ITEMS: New York City inc stores (see NOTE), computer repair shop, meeting room, pet store, Joey's pawn shop & Martin Blank's apartment / Punisher's pistol, Gibbon's bandages, goggles, revolver & forged documents; pimp's knife, Tinkerer's wheelchair
SYNOPSIS: A badly burned and bandaged Martin Blank, the Gibbon, attends a Survivors Guild meeting, a group of Punisher victims. Blank goes home to his wife, Princess Python, who was blinded in the bar Punisher blew up, and discovers that her pet snake Pythagoras has died. Tinkerer stops by to give Blank forged papers for a new identity, which Blank intends to use to pull a gun to kill Punisher. On the way home from another Survivors Guild meeting, Blank starts to interfere with a pimp beating a prostitute but runs home, where he removes the bandages from his face. Blank buys a gun, but his wife finds the gun and throws it in the trash. Blank takes her dead snake and incinerates it before fetching his gun from a dumpster. He buys a new snake, then sees the pimp he previously encountered. Punisher kills the pimp. When Martin comes face-to-face with Punisher, Blank loses his nerve and gives Punisher his gun. Punisher lets Martin go. Blank gives his wife the new snake and re-applies bandages to his face.
NOTE: Includes recap/title page (1 page). Punisher injured many of the Survivors Guild villains in PWJ #4, '07. Joey's name and status as a villain is revealed in PWJ #18, '08. A storefront sign for Shinsky Zota & Morlax is an inside reference to the Enclave -- Wladyslav Shinski, Carlo Zota and Maris Morlak -- introduced in FF #66, '67.

"How I Survived the Good Ol' Days" (22 pages)

CREDITS: Matt Fraction (writer), Howard Chaykin (art), Virtual Calligraphy's Joe Caramagna (letters), Edgar Delgado, Jesus Aburto (colors), Aubrey Sitterson (editor), Alex Maleev (c art)

FEATURE CHARACTER: Punisher (next in ASM #577, '09, Run #25-26, '07, Run #30, '08, PWJ #19, '08)

GUEST STARS: Champions: Ghost Rider (Johnny Blaze, stunt cyclist/demonic being, in fb4 during G&Ch #1, '11), Hercules (Heracles, ancient Greek demigod), Iceman (Bobby Drake, mutant ice creator) (both in rfb), Angel (Warren Worthington III, winged mutant), Black Widow (all in fb1 between Ch #7, '76 & G&Ch #1, '11); Tony Stark (in rfb as Iron Man; in fb10 between IM #87, '04 fb & Av/Tb #1, '04)

SUPPORTING CAST: Stuart Clarke (also in rfbs; also in fb2 to 1st chr app before Ch #5, '76; also in fb1 between Ch #7, '76 & G&Ch #1, '11; also in fbs4-3 between G&Ch #1, '11 & Ch #8, '76; also in fb5 between Ch #8, '76 & PPSSM #18, '78 fb; also in fb6 between PPSSM #18, '78 & WM #5, '92; also in fb7 between WM #21, '93 & IM #19, '99 fb, also in fbs8-10 between IM #20, '99 & bts in NAv #1, '05; last in PWJ #15, '08, chr last in PWJ Ann #1, '09, next in PWJ #19, '08)

VILLAINS: Sunset Bain (head of Baintronics, weapons supplier, also in fb6 between IM #20, '99 & Task #1, '02; last in Task #4, '02, next in MCP #10/2, '08), Parnell Jacobs (also as War Machine in rfb; also in fb5 during IM #19, '99 fb; last in IM #20, '99, next in WarM #1, '08)

OTHER CHARACTERS: Beast, Wonder Man (both in rfb), partiers (in fb3), shoppers (in fb4), attorney, judge (both in fb10), SHIELD agents (in fb9, one dies), policeman (in fb9), bystanders

LOCATIONS/ITEMS: Los Angeles (in fb1 & rfb) inc mall (in fb4) & nightclub (in fb3); Baintronics Inc. (in fb6); Stuart's lab (in fbs 2, 6 & 7); courtroom (in fb8), New York inc Stuart's bedroom, Golden Cup Diner, Punisher's safehouse, Ramona's Restaurant, St. Mark's Church & warehouse in Greenpoint, Brooklyn / Black Widow's "Widow's line" (in fb1), Ghost Rider's motorcycle (in fb1) & chain (in fb4); Rampage's exoskeleton suit (in rfbs & fbs 1, 2 & 4), SHIELD firearms (in fb9), War Machine armor w/helmet (also in rfb & fb7), Stuart's crutches, wheelchair (both in fb5), attaché case (in fb8), lab equipment (in fbs 2, 6 & 7) & revolver; Punisher's laptop computer, van & firearms inc pistol

FLASHBACKS: Rampage fights the Champions (1). Stuart Clarke works on his exoskeleton (2), enjoys his bizarre celebrity status (3) and fights Ghost Rider as Rampage (4). Rampage blows up (Ch #8, '76). A paralyzed Clarke sits in a wheelchair (5). Clarke heals and gets to work inventing again (6). Rampage fights Beast and Wonder Man (WM #6, '92). Parnell Jacobs brings Clarke a War Machine armor he found (7). As War Machine, Jacobs fights Iron Man (IM #19, '99). After firing Clarke, Sunset Bain yells at him as he packs his things and leaves (8). Clarke kills a SHIELD agent (9). At Clarke's trial, Tony Stark testifies that Clarke is crazy (10).

SYNOPSIS: Sunset Bain meets with Stuart Clarke to ask for his help. She says Parnell Jacobs, a former associate who is now out of prison, is hunting her. Clarke gets a call for help from Jacobs, who claims Bain is hunting him. Clarke arranges to meet Jacobs then goes home with Sunset for a good time. Bain shows Clarke that she has a War Machine helmet and that Parnell is after it. Clarke meets Jacobs, shows Stuart most of a War Machine armor he's been hiding and says that Sunset seeks to have it. When Parnell asks if Sunset has the missing helmet, Clarke shoots Jacobs and takes the armor back to Bain. After more fun with Stuart, Sunset suddenly strikes Clarke and takes the armor and helmet to sell it on the black market. Clarke tells Punisher that Bain is at a local restaurant. Punisher shoots Sunset and drives off with Clarke.

NOTE: Includes recap/title page (1 page). The Golden Cup Diner is on West 77th St. in Manhattan. The Brooklyn warehouse is at Kingsland and North Henry.

"Jigsaw, Part 1 of 6" (22 pages)

CREDITS: Matt Fraction (writer), Howard Chaykin (art), Virtual Calligraphy's Joe Caramagna (letters), Edgar Delgado, Jesus Aburto (colors), Aubrey Sitterson (editor), Alex Maleev (c art)

FEATURE CHARACTER: Punisher (only on cover, in rfb as Frank Castle)

SUPPORTING CAST: Lynn Michaels (as psychologist, also as Punisher, last in PWJ #11, '07)

VILLAINS: Jigsaw (also as Punisher, also as Billy Russo in rfb & in fb between Pun:YO #4, '95 & ASM #161, '76 fb; last in NAv Ann #2, '08, chr last in NAv #46, '08, next in PWJ #20, '08), Ian Amsterdam (also as Punisher, last in PWJ #11, '07), Francis MacNeil Grady, Michael Patrick "Mikey" Grady (both crooked NYPD officers, also in pfb, die), Joey Grady (also in pfb; last in PWJ #16, '08, dies), Billy Russo's criminal associates (in fb)

OTHER CHARACTERS: Maria Castle, Lisa Castle, Frank Castle Jr., Bruno Costa & Maggia (all in rfb), bystanders, NYPD officers inc Lenny & O'Malley

LOCATIONS/ITEMS: New York City inc Central Park (in rfb), hospital room (in fb), Joey's pawn shop & NYPD 23rd precinct house w/evidence locker; Harbor Post construction site in Jersey City, NJ / Jigsaw's knife, shotgun & van; Ian's & Lynn's firearms, Francis & Mikey's pistols, confiscated firearms & cash; Maggia pistols (in rfb)

FLASHBACKS: The Grady brothers reap the benefits of fencing guns (p). Frank Castle's family is gunned down in Central Park (PWJ #1, '88 fb). Punisher throws Billy Russo through a window (Pun:YO #4, '95). Russo recovers in the hospital.

SYNOPSIS: Jigsaw tortures Joey, a pawn shop owner whose police officer brothers smuggle guns from an NYPD evidence locker to sell on the black market through his store. The two crooked cops prepare to make a drop but instead of their brother they encounter Ian Amsterdam and his psychologist, both dressed as the Punisher. The ersatz Punishers attack the police officers. As he changes into a negative Punisher costume, Jigsaw tells Joey that he and his brothers sold the Costas the guns that killed Punisher's family and blames the Gradys for creating the Punisher, and by extension for Punisher ruining Jigsaw's face. Ian and his psychologist kill the Grady officers. Identifying himself as the Punisher, Ian calls the police to report the incident and tells them that his victims were fencing firearms. Jigsaw kills the pawn shop owner.

NOTE: Includes recap/title page (1 page). Joey is said to be 38 years old here.

PUNISHER WAR JOURNAL #19 (July 2008)

"Jigsaw, Part 2 of 6" (22 pages)

CREDITS: Matt Fraction, Rick Remender (writers), Howard Chaykin (art), Virtual Calligraphy's Joe Caramagna (letters), Edgar Delgado, Jesus Aburto (colors), Aubrey Sitterson (editor), Alex Maleev (c art)
FEATURE CHARACTER: Frank Castle (also in photos as Punisher)
GUEST STARS: Domino (last in PWJ #13, '08), Silver Sable (last in PWJ #15, '08)
SUPPORTING CAST: Lynn Michaels (posing as Diamonelle, a masseuse, also as psychologist, also as Punisher, see NOTE), Stuart Clarke (last in PWJ #17, '08), G.W. Bridge (last in PWJ #15, '08)
VILLAINS: Contessa Val Fontaine (last in PWJ #14, '08), Jigsaw (also as Punisher) & his men, Ian Amsterdam (also as Punisher)

OTHER CHARACTERS: Smitty (Frank's apartment building doorman, all die), Mr. Chow (grocer) (all die), Gage (Mr. Chow's nephew) & his mother, Chico, Merv (both NewsStand store employees, 1st), restaurant employees & patrons (some die), police (some on TV, off-panel), vagabonds, bystanders; Spider-Man, J. Jonah Jameson, Francis Grady, Michael Grady (both corpses) (prev 4 in photos); Hood (Parker Robbins, crime kingpin, mentioned, Jigsaw cleared his fencing operation with him), Francone family (mentioned, killed by Ian the previous night)
LOCATIONS/ITEMS: New York inc police station (on TV), Diamonelle's apartment, Mr. Chow's grocery, Frank's apartment, Jigsaw's meat locker base, Stuart's apartment, NewsStand store & restaurant / Frank's gun, magazines & groceries inc Tiger Ball; Ian's assault rifle, grenades, motorcycle & ankle jet-packs; Diamonelle's masseuse table, police guns, copy of DB
SYNOPSIS: Going about his routine, Frank gets a message from Diamonelle, buys his groceries from Mr. Chow, picks up his NewsStand store magazine subscriptions and returns to his apartment to read the newspaper, learning there is a Punisher imposter killing people. Now the city's main gun fencer, Jigsaw chastises Ian for leaving a witness alive that may be able to identify Ian as a fake Punisher. Jigsaw and the psychologist send Ian out to kill three people: a drug trafficker, a pimp and a prostitute. Later, Frank learns Mr. Chow was killed. Returning to his apartment, Castle finds his doorman dead. A disguised Ian shoots at Frank and runs away. Castle realizes Diamonelle will be killed next and chases Ian, who kills bystanders to distract Frank. Reaching Diamonelle first, Frank escapes to Stuart Clarke's apartment. Stuart tells Frank the police are looking for Punisher, believing he killed two officers. Castle realizes Jigsaw framed him. Meanwhile, G.W. Bridge questions the NewsStand store employees in his search for Punisher.
NOTE: Includes recap/title page (1 page). Followed by Et #1, '08 preview (5 pages). PWJ #22, '08 reveals Diamonelle to be Ian's psychologist. Chico is named in PWJ #20, '08. Frank Castle subscribes to "Edge Weapons Enthusiast," "Modern Urban Camouflage," "Patriot's Militia Monthly," "Bone and Joint" and various adult magazines at the NewsStand store.

PUNISHER WAR JOURNAL #20 (August 2008)

"Jigsaw, Part 3 of 6" (22 pages)

CREDITS: Matt Fraction, Rick Remender (writers), Howard Chaykin (art), Virtual Calligraphy's Joe Caramagna (letters), Edgar Delgado (colors), Aubrey Sitterson (editor), Alex Maleev (c art)
FEATURE CHARACTER: Punisher (also in photo)
GUEST STARS: Domino, Silver Sable
SUPPORTING CAST: G.W. Bridge (last in PWJ #15, '08), Lynn Michaels (as Diamonelle, next in PWJ #22, '08), Stuart Clarke (next in PWJ #22, '08)
VILLAINS: Lady Gorgon (telepathic leader of the Hand, a demonic clan of ninja assassins), Illumination (energy-wielding assassin), Silhouette (cold assassin) (all 1st, see NOTE), Jigsaw (also in photo, also as Punisher, next in PWJ #22, '08) & his men (some also as Punisher), Ian Amsterdam (also as Punisher), Contessa Val Fontaine, Hand ninjas (some die, others last in DD #115, '09, others next in DD #116, '09)

OTHER CHARACTERS: Chico, Merv
LOCATIONS/ITEMS: New York inc Groovy Goodies, Jigsaw's meat locker base & NewsStand store / Punisher's armament chest, shotgun & pistols inc P32; Hand ninjas' blow dart guns, darts, bows, arrows, crescent-moon spear, katanas, knife, mace & nunchakus; Stuart's rifle, Lady Gorgon's katana, SHIELD Helicarrier
SYNOPSIS: Jigsaw hires the Hand to kill the Punisher and despite the demands of their leader, Lady Gorgon, for an exclusive contract, Jigsaw declares an open bounty on Punisher's head. G.W. Bridge and his team figure out that a Punisher imposter is responsible for the recent killings and that Jigsaw is trying to frame Punisher. When Punisher forces NewsStand employees Chico and Merv to tell him about their encounter with Bridge, they tell him about Jigsaw's bounty. Later, Hand ninjas attack Punisher, Stuart Clarke and Diamonelle. Punisher orders his associates to get to safety while he leads the ninjas on a chase. Wounded, Castle encounters Lady Gorgon and her associates, Illumination and Silhouette.
NOTE: Includes 1 page recap/title page (1 page). PWJ #21, '08 reveals Lady Gorgon's name, and OHMU HC #5, '08 reveals Illumination's and Silhouette's.

PUNISHER WAR JOURNAL #21 (September 2008)

"Jigsaw, Part 4 of 6" (22 pages)

CREDITS: Matt Fraction, Rick Remender (writers), Howard Chaykin (art), Virtual Calligraphy's Joe Caramagna (letters), Edgar Delgado, Jesus Aburto (colors), Daniel Ketchum (asst editor), Axel Alonso (exec editor), Alex Maleev (c art)
FEATURE CHARACTER: Punisher
GUEST STARS: Domino, Silver Sable
SUPPORTING CAST: G.W. Bridge
VILLAINS: Lady Gorgon (next in FC #18, '10), Ian Amsterdam (also as Punisher, next in PWJ #23, '08), Contessa Val Fontaine, Illumination, Silhouette
OTHER CHARACTERS: Stephen Colbert (political satirist, on Colbert '08 presidential campaign poster), Kenneth William Duncan (vagabond, dies), other vagabonds, SHIELD agents

LOCATIONS/ITEMS: New York inc Tremont Ave. & Wall St. subway stations / Punisher's pistol, SHIELD flight harnesses & rifles; Lady Gorgon's katana, Silver Sable's rifle, Val de Fontaine's pistols w/heat seekers

SYNOPSIS: As Lady Gorgon, Illumination and Silhouette prepare to kill Punisher, Silver Sable, Domino and Contessa Val Fontaine interrupt them. The wounded Punisher flees as the ladies fight. The Hand leader follows and attacks Punisher. Silver Sable enters the fray and her intervention allows Punisher to retrieve his pistol and shoot Lady Gorgon in the head. Domino and Val dispatch Lady Gorgon's associates and find the wounded Silver Sable. Punisher stumbles into a subway train and passes out. When he awakens, he sees Ian dressed as the Punisher and engages in a brutal fistfight with him. Ian overpowers Punisher and tries to decapitate Castle in a closing subway train door, but G.W. Bridge and his SHIELD agents arrive and shoot Ian.

NOTE: Includes recap/title page (1 page). Duncan is named in Pun #18, '10.

PUNISHER WAR JOURNAL #22 (October 2008)

"Jigsaw, Part 5 of 6" (22 pages)

CREDITS: Matt Fraction, Rick Remender (writers), Howard Chaykin (art), Virtual Calligraphy's Joe Caramagna (letters), Edgar Delgado, Jesus Aburto (colors), Axel Alonso (exec editor), Daniel Ketchum (asst editor), Alex Maleev (c art)
FEATURE CHARACTER: Punisher
GUEST STARS: Domino, Silver Sable
SUPPORTING CAST: G.W. Bridge (also in fb to chr 1st app before XFor #8, '92 fb), Lynn Michaels (as Diamonelle, last in PWJ #20, '08), Stuart Clarke
VILLAINS: Wrecking Crew: Bulldozer, Piledriver, Thunderball, Wrecker (all last in NAv #46, '08); Jigsaw (also as Punisher, last in PWJ #20, '08), Rhino (bts, on phone, last in PWJ #15, '08, chr last in PWJ Ann #1, '09), Contessa Val Fontaine

OTHER CHARACTERS: US soldiers (in fb), SHIELD agents, hospital nurse & orderly

LOCATIONS/ITEMS: New York inc Brooklyn Bridge, safe house & Brooklyn's Fort Hamilton Veterans Affairs Hospital / Stuart's padded vest, tools & firearms inc automatic rifle & pistol; SHIELD armored van & prisoner transport vehicle; G.W. Bridge's pistol, Jigsaw's high-tech rocket launcher, Thunderball's ball & chain, Wrecker's crowbar

FLASHBACK: Army soldier G.W. Bridge goes on a recon mission.

SYNOPSIS: Dedicated to Frank Castle and his mission to eradicate deadly criminals, Stuart Clarke prepares to free Punisher from SHIELD custody. G.W. Bridge and his team release Punisher from a hospital and prepare to transport him to prison. Diamonelle tries to stop Clarke and tells him that Castle confessed about killing Tati Arocha, but Stuart refuses to believe her and dismisses her traitorous behavior. Diamonelle shoots Clarke, declaring that it's her mission to deal with criminals like him, revealing herself as Ian Amsterdam's Punisher-like psychologist. In the transport vehicle, Bridge lectures the Punisher about the meaninglessness of his mission and tries to convince Castle to give it up. As the vehicle crosses the Brooklyn Bridge, Jigsaw blasts it with a rocket launcher and his new hired hands, the Wrecking Crew, attack. As Thunderball assaults the accompanying armored van carrying Domino, Silver Sable and Contessa Val Fontaine, Bridge frees Castle of his restraints and prepares to fight back.

NOTE: Includes recap/title page (1 page).

PUNISHER WAR JOURNAL #23 (November 2008)

"Jigsaw, Part 6 of 6" (22 pages)

CREDITS: Matt Fraction, Rick Remender (writers), Howard Chaykin (art), Virtual Calligraphy's Joe Caramagna (letters), Edgar Delgado, Jesus Aburto (colors), Daniel Ketchum (asst editor), Axel Alonso (exec editor), Alex Maleev (c art), Kaare Andrews (variant c art)
FEATURE CHARACTER: Punisher
GUEST STARS: Domino (next in XFor #8, '08), Silver Sable (next in Hulk #17, '10)
SUPPORTING CAST: G.W. Bridge, Lynn Michaels, Stuart Clarke
VILLAINS: Wrecking Crew: Bulldozer, Piledriver, Wrecker (all next in SecInv #6, '08), Thunderball (next in SecInv #4, '08); Contessa Val Fontaine (next in SecInv #8, '09 fb), Jigsaw (also as Punisher, next in NAv #50, '09), Ian Amsterdam (last in PWJ #21, '08), Rhino (next in PWJ #26, '09)

OTHER CHARACTERS: SHIELD agents, clinic patients

LOCATIONS/ITEMS: Brooklyn Bridge, clinic, Raft inc Punisher's cell; SHIELD Facility 832 inc Ian Amsterdam's & Jigsaw's cells / G.W. Bridge's pistol & wheelchair, SHIELD armored van, prisoner transport vehicle & rifle; Domino's stolen tractor trailer, Contessa's communicator, Jigsaw's knives, Thunderball's ball & chain, Wrecker's crowbar

SYNOPSIS: Domino rams Piledriver with a tractor trailer. G.W. Bridge tries to defend Punisher but is assaulted by Wrecker. Summoned by Stuart Clarke, the Rhino arrives and subdues Wrecker while Punisher decks Thunderball with Wrecker's crowbar. With the score settled between Rhino and Castle, Rhino takes the defeated Wrecking Crew away. Armed with the crowbar, Punisher beats the tar out of Jigsaw but stops short of killing him and turns himself over to Bridge and SHIELD. Missing three fingers from Diamonelle's assault, Clarke considers becoming Rampage again. At a SHIELD facility, Bridge thanks agent Lynn Michaels for her infiltration into Jigsaw's organization as Ian's psychologist and her neutralization of Clarke as Diamonelle. Michaels apologizes to Ian for the turmoil he's been put through and takes him to shoot Jigsaw. SHIELD agents arrest Michaels.

NOTE: Includes recap/title page (1 page). Ian's SHIELD prison ID is 1351-KL.

PUNISHER WAR JOURNAL #24 (December 2008)

"Secret Invasion: Part 1 of 2" (22 pages)

CREDITS: Matt Fraction, Rick Remender (writers), Howard Chaykin (art), Virtual Calligraphy's Joe Caramagna (letters), Edgar Delgado (colors), Daniel Ketchum, Sebastian Girner (assist editors), Axel Alonso (exec editor), Alex Maleev (c art)
FEATURE CHARACTER: Punisher (also in rfb)
SUPPORTING CAST: G.W. Bridge
VILLAINS: Rampage (Stuart Clarke), Skrulls (one in photo, several die, some as skulls) inc "Hammerhead/ Kingpin" Super-Skrull (1st); SHIELD Grey Box Facility inmate
OTHER CHARACTERS: Jasper Sitwell (last in PWJ #8, '07 fb, next in SecWs #4, '09), other SHIELD agents (some in photo), reporter (on TV), bystanders; Tatiana Arocha, National Force (both in rfb)
LOCATIONS/ITEMS: New York inc Rampage's workshop, DVD Repair building, SHIELD Grey Box Facility 17, SHIELD Temporary Field HQ, String Works building / Punisher's rocket launcher, grenades, guns & Humvee; Stuart Clarke's DVD, updated Rampage armor & energy rifle; G.W. Bridge's blaster & gun; SHIELD Guardbots, SHIELD agents' tanks & blasters; Skrull ships, blasters & axes
FLASHBACK: Frank Castle kills Tatiana Arocha (PWJ #9, '07 fb).
SYNOPSIS: Stuart Clarke works on a glove to replace the fingers he lost until a DVD is delivered through his mail slot. Stuart watches the DVD and vomits when he sees footage of Frank Castle killing his girlfriend Tatiana Arocha. Punisher bides his time as an inmate in SHIELD Grey Box Facility 17 until the power suddenly shuts off. Punisher escapes the prison to see alien ships attacking New York. Stuart finishes working on his new Rampage armor and tests his weaponry on the invading Skrulls. Jasper Sitwell informs G. W. Bridge of the Punisher's escape and orders Bridge to capture the Punisher; the vigilante is using guerrilla tactics against the Skrulls and may endanger civilians. Bridge finds Punisher slaughtering Skrulls. Punisher saves Bridge from an explosion and the two join forces against a Hammerhead/Kingpin Super-Skrull. Before the Super-Skrull can kill Punisher and Bridge, Rampage blasts the Skrull and asks Punisher what happened to Tatiana in Mexico.
NOTE: Includes recap/title page (1 page).

PUNISHER WAR JOURNAL #25 (January 2009)

"Secret Invasion: Part 2 of 2" (32 pages)

CREDITS: Matt Fraction, Rick Remender (writers), Howard Chaykin (art), Virtual Calligraphy's Joe Caramagna (letters), Edgar Delgado (colors), Daniel Ketchum, Sebastian Girner (assist editors), Axel Alonso (exec editor), Alex Maleev (c art)
FEATURE CHARACTER: Punisher (next in W #73, AT:WPun #1-6, GR #32, all '09)
SUPPORTING CAST: G.W. Bridge (next in Pun #6, '09)
VILLAINS: Rampage (Stuart Clarke, becomes Jigsaw, next bts in FC #17, '10), Skrulls (some die) inc "Hammerhead/Kingpin" Super-Skrull (dies)
OTHER CHARACTERS: SHIELD agents, construction crew, hospital staff
LOCATIONS/ITEMS: New York inc department store, apartment building & hospital / Punisher's gun, G.W. Bridge's gun & blaster; Skrull sniper blaster & rocket launcher, Rampage's armor
SYNOPSIS: With the Super-Skrull briefly downed, Rampage angrily confronts Punisher over the death of his girlfriend, threatening to kill Castle. The Super-Skrull revives and attacks, forcing G. W. Bridge, Punisher and Rampage to work together to kill the Super-Skrull. When the fight is brought outside, a Skrull sniper begins shooting at the trio, injuring Bridge in the process. Discovering the sniper's location, Rampage agrees to put his vendetta against Punisher aside long enough to take out the sniper. As Rampage kills the sniper, Bridge informs Punisher of Rampage's murderous past, prompting the Punisher to restart the fight with Rampage. The two fiercely battle and Punisher electrifies Rampage's face until Skrulls in the street blast them. Bridge kills the Skrulls in the street and tends to the injured Rampage as the Punisher escapes. Later, as reconstruction begins following the Skrull invasion, Bridge visits Stuart Clarke in the hospital, where the jigsaw-faced Clarke announces that he has big plans for the future.
NOTE: Cover labeled "Secret Invasion." Includes recap/title page (1 page).

PUNISHER WAR JOURNAL ANNUAL #1 (January 2009)

"If I Die Before I Wake" (34 pages)

CREDITS: Simon Spurrier (writer), Werther Dell'Edera (pencils), Antonio Fuso (inks), Virtual Calligraphy's Joe Caramagna (letters), Lee Loughridge (colors), Daniel Ketchum, Sebastian Girner (asst editors), Axel Alonso (editor), David Wilkins (c art)
FEATURE CHARACTER: Punisher (last in Et #1, '08, next in PWJ #16, '08)
SUPPORTING CAST: Stuart Clarke (also as Sweetums in Punisher's hallucination, chr last in PWJ #15, '08, chr next in PWJ #17, '08)
VILLAINS: Captain Pepper (club owner, kidnapper & drug dealer, also as Man in the Moon, Little Red Riding Hood, Gingerbread Man, a princess, a clown & a unicorn in Punisher's hallucination) & his men (some also as Cheshire Cat, Tweedle Dee, Tweedle Dum, White Rabbit, Caterpillar, Queen of Hearts, Mad Hatter, Humpty Dumpty, teddy bears & trees in Punisher's hallucination, some die), Mister Jingle, Mister Jangle (both eat dreams and regurgitate them as hallucinogenic drugs, also as a lollipop, elf & monkey in Punisher's hallucination), Rhino (chr last in PWJ #15, '08, chr next bts in PWJ #22, '08)
OTHER CHARACTERS: Sally Warne (kidnapped girl, also as Big Bad Wolf in Punisher's hallucination) & her parents, Captain Pepper's Helter Skelter Club patrons (also as Mr. Hyde, clowns, dolls, fairies, a snake-man & a whale in Punisher's hallucination), police (also as toy soldiers in Punisher's hallucination); criminals (in Stuart's hallucination), John Lennon (on poster)

LOCATIONS/ITEMS: New York inc Captain Pepper's Helter Skelter Club w/dance hall, bathroom, Fab 4 floor, Thrillin' Third floor & Captain Pepper's office / Punisher's explosives (also as magic apples in Punisher's hallucination), assault rifle w/attached grenade launcher, shotgun, gun, knives, glider & rope; Stuart's mini-Galactus recon robot (also as Tinkerbell in Punisher's hallucination) & gun; Captain Pepper's blaster & hallucinogen; Captain Pepper's men's Uzis, guns & knives; police shotguns & guns

SYNOPSIS: As Captain Pepper opens his Helter Skelter Club, Punisher blasts his way into the club to rescue Sally Warne, a girl Captain Pepper kidnapped. Stuart Clarke activates his Galactus recon robot. Punisher fights his way through Captain Pepper's men and runs into a drunken Rhino. The vigilante throws Rhino out a window, who lands on a police car. Captain Pepper's men gas Punisher with a hallucinogen, and the vigilante starts seeing everything as cartoons. Captain Pepper taunts Punisher, telling he he's living a child's dream through his hallucinations. Stuart tells Punisher what he's really seeing through the recon robot. Punisher finds Captain Pepper, but is blasted and captured. Captain Pepper tells Punisher he creates hallucinogens from people's dreams through his creatures Mr. Jingle and Mr. Jangle, and kidnapped Sally as bait for Punisher. Captain Pepper wants to make hallucinogens from Punisher's dreams. As police surround the club, Mr. Jingle and Mr. Jangle begin eating Punisher's dreams. Stuart arrives and frees Punisher, but Captain Pepper releases the Punisher hallucinogen. Stuart and the club patrons begin hallucinating murderous nightmares, but Punisher's head clears. Punisher escapes with Sally, reunites her with her parents and blows up the club.

PUNISHER WAR JOURNAL #26 (February 2009)

(untitled, 22 pages)

CREDITS: Matt Fraction (writer), Andy MacDonald (art), Virtual Calligraphy's Joe Caramagna (letters), Nick Filardi (colors), Sebastian Girner (asst editor), Axel Alonso (exec editor), Dave Wilkins (c art)
FEATURE CHARACTER: Punisher (next in PWZ #1, '09)
VILLAINS: Stilt-Man (Michael "Mikey" Watts, car thief, 1st, next in X:TS&P #4/3, '11), Travis Butler (murderer, dies), William "Bill" Anthony (thief), Roger "Rocky" Ramsey (drug dealer) (all also in pfb), Sal (criminal), Rhino (last in PWJ #23, '08, next in ASM #610, '10), Tinkerer (bts, provided the Stilt-Man suit, last in W:O #36, '09, last bts in MsM #37, '09, next in MK #2, '09), Vulture (bts, asked Rhino to feed his pigeons, last in PWJ #15, '08, next in ASM #594, '09)
OTHER CHARACTERS: Vulture's pigeons, homeless men, police (off-panel in pfb)
LOCATIONS/ITEMS: New York inc Cuts Too (formerly Cuts), Rhino's apartment building & police station (in pfb) / Punisher's directional microphone & Gatling gun; Travis' gun, Vulture's bird food, Stilt-Man hydraulic suit
FLASHBACK: Roger, William, Travis and Michael each have their mug shots taken (p).
SYNOPSIS: On Christmas, Punisher waits on a rooftop across the street from Cuts Too, formerly the villain's bar Cuts that he blew up. He's waiting to hear if the people inside acquired a Stilt-Man suit; if they did he plans to kill them. Inside the bar, Travis worries that the Punisher will blow up the bar again. Sal assures him that the Punisher never strikes the same place twice. Mikey shows Travis, Bill, Rocky and Sal that he has the Stilt-Man suit. They argue over who will be the new Stilt-Man until Travis demands that he's Stilt-Man at gunpoint. Sal steals Travis' gun and kicks him out of the bar. The others don't notice when Travis is shot in the street and vote for Mikey to be Stilt-Man. As Mikey tries out the suit, Punisher prepares to kill them. Rhino arrives to feed Vulture's pigeons and stops Punisher, requesting that the vigilante spare the idiot criminals on Christmas. Punisher remembers that he only punishes the guilty, not the stupid.
NOTE: Includes recap/credits page (1 page). Series continued in Pun #1, '09.

PUNISHER: WAR ZONE #1 (February 2009)

"The Resurrection of Ma Gnucci, Part One" (22 pages)

CREDITS: Garth Ennis (writer), Steve Dillon (art), Virtual Calligraphy's Cory Petit (letters), Matt Hollingsworth (colors), Sebastian Girner, Daniel Ketchum (asst editors), Axel Alonso (editor), John Romita, Jr. (variant c pencils), Klaus Janson (variant c inks), Dean White (variant c colors)
FEATURE CHARACTER: Punisher (also in rfb)
SUPPORTING CAST: Lt. Molly Von Richthofen (also as "Det. Clinton," last bts in Pun #1, '01)
VILLAINS: Andy (Charlie's friend, dies), Elite (Tim, son of the original Elite, last voice only in Pun #6, '00, 1st full app, also in fb1-2), Pete Alceno (Mafia boss, 1st), Alceno family members & associates, Joey Alceno (Pete Alceno's son, in fb3), Ma

Gnucci lookalike (see NOTE) & her bodyguards
OTHER CHARACTERS: Charles B. "Charlie" Schitti (Alceno soldier, Punisher's informant, 1st, also in fb3), Ollie (Tim's coke-addicted friend, in fb1), Shannon (model, Molly's polyamorous girlfriend, 1st), David McTaggart (Shannon's boyfriend, 1st, next in PWZ #3, '09), vagrant (in fb1, dies), Joey's girlfriend, zoo patrons, chimpanzee, vulture (prev 4 in fb3), Shannon's neighbor & his poodle (both next in PWZ #6, '09), bartender, bar patrons; Elite (Tim's father, in rfb), 3 drug dealers (in rfb); Ma Gnucci (in Punisher's thoughts)
LOCATIONS/ITEMS: New York (also in fb1) inc zoo (in fb2), beach, Elite's bedroom, Shannon's brownstone w/bedroom, bar & Alceno's home w/backyard / Punisher's shotgun, SUV, assault rifle, & rocket launcher; Tim's sportscar; original Elite's gun, war journal & hidden guns; Charlie's revolver (in fb2), Andy's shotgun, Molly's gun, Ma lookalike's wheelchair, bodyguards' guns
FLASHBACKS: Tim accidentally hits a vagrant with his car, then runs him over again, fearing prosecution (1). Elite kills a car full of drug dealers (Pun #5, '00). Punisher kills the Elite (Pun #12, '01). Tim finds one of his father's weapon caches which contains his war journal (2). While guarding Joey Alceno and his girlfriend at a zoo, Charlie Schitti sees Joey try to kick an inadvertently freed chimpanzee, which grabs Joey's genitals. Charlie is unable to bring himself to follow Joey's order to shoot the ape; it tears Joey's genitals off and flings them into another cage, where they are eaten by a vulture (3).
SYNOPSIS: Charlie Schitti, an out-of-favor Mafia soldier, is led along a beach by his friend, Andy, who has been ordered to execute him.

Schitti is saved when the Punisher kills Andy. The new Elite, the original's son, writes his first entry in his computer war journal, where he details his father's activities and how he considers the Punisher the antithesis of everything his father fought to defend. On the road back to the city, Schitti tells Punisher about the zoo incident that Pete Alceno, his boss, holds him responsible for his son's inability to provide an heir. Molly Von Richthofen leaves for work from the home of her polyamorous girlfriend, Shannon, upset that Shannon has a date that night with her boyfriend, David. Punisher tells Charlie that he intends to use him as an informant to assure that the Gnucci family is well and truly gone, and that he will kill Alceno and his crew to prevent reprisals against him. That night, Molly watches David leave Shannon's house and physically intimidates him into staying away from Shannon's neighborhood. Punisher prepares to attack a backyard barbecue at Pete Alceno's house but stops short when he sees the arrival of Ma Gnucci.

NOTE: PWZ #3, '09 reveals David's name and Charlie's full first name and middle initial. Any appearance in this miniseries of Ma Gnucci, who was killed in Pun #12, '01, is attributed in PWZ #3, '09 to a group of lookalikes surgically modified by the new Elite as part of his plan to avenge Punisher's murder of his father.

PUNISHER: WAR ZONE #2 (February 2009)

"The Resurrection of Ma Gnucci, Part Two" (22 pages)

CREDITS: Garth Ennis (writer), Steve Dillon (art), Virtual Calligraphy's Cory Petit (letters), Matt Hollingsworth (colors), Sebastian Girner, Daniel Ketchum (asst editors), Axel Alonso (editor)
FEATURE CHARACTER: Punisher (also in Elite's dream)
SUPPORTING CAST: Lt. Molly Von Richthofen
VILLAINS: Elite, 2 Ma Gnucci lookalikes (one dies, one in pfb, lookalike in pfb 1st, next in PWZ #4, '09 fb) & their bodyguards (2 die, another 2 in pfb, bodyguards in pfb both 1st, next in PWZ #4, '09 fb), Pete Alceno (dies), Alceno family members & associates (die) inc Mike Alceno; Tommy Bones (mob boss, bts in pfb, next in PWZ #4, '09 fb)
OTHER CHARACTERS: Charlie Schitti (also in pfb), Shannon, bystanders, police, firefighters, restaurant patrons, bar patrons, 2 bartenders, TV announcer (voice only), pedestrians (1 in pfb); looters, gangsters, Middle Eastern men, vagrants, well-to-do suburbanites, poodle (headless corpse) (prev 6 in Elite's dream)
LOCATIONS/ITEMS: New York (also in Elite's dream) inc Elite's bedroom, Alceno's home, outdoor cafe, Wonder! Wimmin (lesbian bar), Paddy's Bar, Mercuccio's (Bones' restaurant, bts, see NOTE) & cemetery / Punisher's Uzi (in Elite's dream), assault rifle & knife; Mike's gun, Charlie's shovel, Ma lookalike's wheelchair (in pfb), propane tanks (destroyed)
FLASHBACK: Charlie sees "Ma Gnucci" being wheeled into Tommy Bones' restaurant (p).
SYNOPSIS: The Elite experiences a nightmare in which racial minorities and vagrants pillage his neighborhood and the Punisher kills his upper-class neighbors. Meanwhile, Punisher blows up "Ma Gnucci" then opens fire on Pete Alceno and his cohorts, killing them all and blowing up the house by shooting a pair of propane tanks. Molly Von Richthofen arrives at the request of a trio of inept detectives to identify "Ma," and Molly refutes the possibility that the corpse is the same woman she saw die years ago. The next day at a cafe, Punisher kills an Alceno family member before the mob can kill Charlie. Molly meets with Shannon at a bar where she sees another woman flirting with her. Molly learns David told Shannon that he attributed Molly's attack on him to six men and that the attack made him sexually dysfunctional. Molly retires to the restroom, where she punches the woman that flirted with Shannon, then suggests that she and Shannon go somewhere else. At another bar, Charlie tells Punisher he saw "Ma" appear at another mob-run business, and Punisher takes Charlie to Ma's grave and forces him to exhume her.
NOTE: Includes recap page (1 page). The name and business type of Bones' "place" are identified in PWZ #4, '09.

PUNISHER: WAR ZONE #3 (February 2009)

"The Resurrection of Ma Gnucci, Part Three" (22 pages)

CREDITS: Garth Ennis (writer), Steve Dillon (art), Virtual Calligraphy's Cory Petit (letters), Matt Hollingsworth (colors), Sebastian Girner, Daniel Ketchum (asst editors), Axel Alonso (editor)
FEATURE CHARACTER: Punisher
SUPPORTING CAST: Lt. Molly Von Richthofen
VILLAINS: Elite, his 12 assassins (die) & physicians; Ma Gnucci lookalikes
OTHER CHARACTERS: Ma Gnucci (as skeletal remains, last in Pun #12, '01), David McTaggart (last in PWZ #1, '09), Charlie Schitti, Shannon, restaurant patrons & staff, police inc a Captain & crime scene technician
LOCATIONS/ITEMS: New York inc cemetery, restaurant & Elite's mansion inc medical lab / Punisher's gun & grenade; Elite's tranquilizer rifle w/drugged dart, first aid kit, forceps & sutures; assassins' guns, Elite's tranquilizer rifle w/drugged dart, first aid kit, forceps & sutures, Charlie's shovel
SYNOPSIS: Just as Charlie Schitti unearths Ma Gnucci's remains, Punisher sees a van observing them and hauls Charlie out of the grave just as an explosive planted in Ma's coffin detonates. A gang of assassins attack, but Punisher eventually kills them all. On a date, Molly Von Richthofen and Shannon find David drinking alone. David is stunned silent when he recognizes Molly, but Molly doesn't mention their previous encounter. Molly is called away just as Shannon suggests David discuss his "attack," and Molly leaves him with a threat of further bodily harm written on a business card she verbally identifies as a psychiatrist's phone number. Elite, perched upon a tree with a rifle, shoots a drugged dart at Punisher but hits Charlie instead. Punisher fires back, severing two of the Elite's fingers. Seeing the police arriving, Punisher drags Charlie away. Molly is present as her fellow officers process the cemetery, and learns to her chagrin that she is now once again the sole member of Punisher task force. A forensics scientist gives her Elite's fingers and Charlie's wallet. At his mansion, Elite stitches his wounds and tells his group of Ma Gnucci lookalikes that they must now earn their keep.
NOTE: Includes recap page (1 page).

PUNISHER: WAR ZONE #4 (February 2009)

"The Resurrection of Ma Gnucci, Part Four" (22 pages)

CREDITS: Garth Ennis (writer), Steve Dillon (art), Virtual Calligraphy's Cory Petit (letters), Matt Hollingsworth (colors), Sebastian Girner (asst editor), Axel Alonso (editor)
FEATURE CHARACTER: Punisher (also as bleeding-toothed skull in Charlie's hallucination)
SUPPORTING CAST: Lt. Molly Von Richthofen (also in own daydream)
VILLAINS: Elite & his 2 henchmen, Joey Balls (maître d' & gangster, dies), Tommy Bones (1st but last bts in PWZ #2, '09 fb, also in pfb, dies) & his henchmen (die, 2 in pfb), Alceno family assassins (also in Molly's daydream) inc Vito, Sammy & Mo; 2 Ma Gnucci lookalikes (one last in PWZ #2, '09 fb, one also in pfb), one lookalike's 2 bodyguards (last in PWZ #2, '09 fb, one also in pfb), Ricky Caruna (mobster, 1st), Bruno Benati (mobster, bts, playing golf)
OTHER CHARACTERS: Charlie Schitti, Shannon (bts on phone, also in Molly's daydream, next in PWZ #6, '09), police (one bts on phone, others in Molly's daydream), restaurant patrons, deli owner, pedestrians; David McTaggart, Molly's parents, minister, funeral attendees (prev 4 in Molly's daydream); Frankie T, the Salvatores, Ricky Caruna's cousins (prev 3 mentioned, mobsters)
LOCATIONS/ITEMS: New York inc Mercuccio's w/upstairs rooms (also in pfb), Charlie's house w/kitchen & bathroom, deli & Goddess (Caruna's stripclub); cemetery (in Molly's daydream) / Punisher's SUV, gun & silencer; Elite's limo w/caltrops & machinegun; Ma lookalikes' wheelchairs (one also in pfb) & limos; Molly's gun, assassins' guns, Charlie's pumpkin, henchmen's assault rifles
FLASHBACK: A Ma Gnucci lookalike meets with Tommy Bones and tells him that she has come back from Hell to wreak vengeance on the Mafia families that turned their backs on her and that they have one way to make amends: deliver the Punisher (p).
SYNOPSIS: Punisher drives to Tommy Bones' restaurant, Mercuccio's, with a drug-addled Charlie Schitti in tow. Punisher enters the restaurant, forces the maître d' to lead him to the upstairs rooms, and kills all of Bones' men. Molly Von Richthofen arrives outside Charlie's house to find it inhabited by a gang of assassins ordered by Pete Alceno to kill Charlie. At Mercuccio's, Bones tells Punisher of his meeting with "Ma Gnucci" before Punisher kills him. Molly enters Charlie's house and hides in the bathroom, but one of the assassins goes to use the bathroom before she can summon backup, forcing her to hide in the shower. Punisher leaves Mercuccio's and finds Schitti stealing a pumpkin, for which he has taken a disturbing fancy. He pays the deli owner and asks Schitti who else "Ma" might meet. On Schitti's information, he and Punisher arrive at a Mafia-owned stripclub to find "Ma" leaving. Punisher follows her limo, but sees another limo with another "Ma" inside. Molly considers confronting the assassins, but a daydream of her impending funeral discourages her. The second limo releases caltrops that burst Punisher's tires. Elite emerges from the trunk, and he and his henchmen open fire on Punisher's car.
NOTE: Includes recap page (1 page). Mo is named next issue.

PUNISHER: WAR ZONE #5 (March 2009)

"The Resurrection of Ma Gnucci, Part Five" (22 pages)

CREDITS: Garth Ennis (writer), Steve Dillon (art), Virtual Calligraphy's Cory Petit (letters), Matt Hollingsworth (colors), Sebastian Girner (asst editor), Axel Alonso (editor)
FEATURE CHARACTER: Punisher (also in rfb)
SUPPORTING CAST: Lt. Molly Von Richthofen
VILLAINS: Elite (Tim) & his 2 henchmen (both die); Alceno assassins (die) inc Vito, Sammy, & Mo; 2 Ma Gnucci lookalikes (one dies in pfb), Charlie's house w/bathroom / Punisher's SUV, shotgun (both & their 2 bodyguards (one dies), mobsters inc Sammy's cousin (Sammy's cousin & one other die)
OTHER CHARACTERS: Charlie Schitti, police, subway commuters; Elite (Tim's father, as corpse in rfb); Ma Gnucci, demons (both on cover)
LOCATIONS/ITEMS: New York inc warehouse & Charlie's house w/bathroom / Punisher's SUV, shotgun (both destroyed), gun, needle & thread; Elite's machine gun & limo (destroyed); Molly's gun & handcuffs; henchmen's assault rifles, shotguns & guns; Charlie's pumpkin, Ma lookalike's wheelchair, mobsters' guns, "Asian Rampage" (adult magazine)
FLASHBACK: Punisher kills the original Elite (Pun #12, '01).
SYNOPSIS: Punisher shields Charlie Schitti from the Elite's barrage and is wounded. He knees his SUV's accelerator, running over one of the Elite's men. Punisher recognizes Elite's mask during the ensuing firefight, and escapes. At Charlie's house, Molly Von Richthofen stays huddled in Charlie's shower. Elite escapes after he kills the Ma Gnucci lookalike in his limo. On a subway car, Elite barks orders to his men on his phone. He becomes embarrassed when he realizes the other passengers can hear him. At Charlie's house, Punisher uses Charlie and his pumpkin as a distraction, then enters through the back and kills the assassins. Molly appears and holds Punisher and Charlie at gunpoint. Elsewhere, as a Ma lookalike orders a gang of mobsters to capture Punisher, one of the mobsters tells "Ma" that his cousin's crew is staking out Charlie's house, and one of "Ma's" bodyguards whispers that Charlie's house is close to where the Elite's shootout with Punisher happened. The mobster's cousin and a friend go to Charlie's, and Molly shoots them. Punisher convinces Molly that mob reinforcements are coming, so she agrees to a temporary alliance. They send Charlie to the basement, just as a mob army arrives.
NOTE: Includes recap page (1 page). Followed by AoAtlas #1, '09 preview (6 pages).

PUNISHER: WAR ZONE #6 (March 2009)

"The Resurrection of Ma Gnucci, Conclusion" (22 pages)

CREDITS: Garth Ennis (writer), Steve Dillon (art), Virtual Calligraphy's Cory Petit (letters), Matt Hollingsworth (colors), Sebastian Girner (asst editor), Axel Alonso (editor)
FEATURE CHARACTER: Punisher (also in photo, next in Pun #1, '09)
SUPPORTING CAST: Lt. Molly Von Richthofen (also in photo)
VILLAINS: Elite (Tim) & his 2 henchmen, Ma Gnucci lookalikes, mobsters (all die)
OTHER CHARACTERS: Charlie Schitti, Shannon (last bts in PWZ #4, '09), Shannon's neighbor & his poodle (dies) (both last in PWZ #1, '09), SWAT officers, TV camera crew, TV news helicopter pilot (voice only), Princeton University operator (bts, on phone); Elite (Tim's father, in photo)
LOCATIONS/ITEMS: New York inc Charlie's house w/basement & kitchen, Shannon's brownstone, Elite's

mansion w/bedroom; Punisher's apartment; forest / Punisher's machine gun, shotgun & gun w/silencer; Molly's shotgun & guns; TV news helicopter & camera; SWAT officers' guns & armor; henchman's assault rifle, mobsters' guns, Charlie's pumpkin, copy of New York Globe

SYNOPSIS: Punisher and Molly Von Richthofen engage the encroaching mobsters in a massive firefight, while Charlie Schitti spends time with his pumpkin in the basement and Elite watches from across the street with one of his henchmen and a Ma Gnucci lookalike. During the battle, Molly's clothes catch on fire and Punisher tears them off, leaving her only in her bra and panties. A TV news crew and a SWAT team arrive, and the news crew records footage of the scantily clad Molly shooting it out alongside Punisher. With all of the mobsters killed, Punisher hides in the basement, leaving Molly to deal with her fellow officers. The next day, a furious Shannon, having seen a front-page photo of Molly and Punisher's shootout, breaks up with Molly, who shoots her neighbor's poodle on the way out of Shannon's home. Charlie relocates to a solitary life camping in the outdoors. Punisher researches the new Elite and determines he is the original Elite's son. He goes to Elite's mansion and finds that Elite's henchmen have killed all the Ma Gnucci lookalikes. He kills the henchmen, then finds Elite writing in his war journal and kills him too.

NOTE: Includes recap page (1 page).

PUNISHER #1 (March 2009)

"Living in Darkness" (22 pages)

CREDITS: Rick Remender (writer), Jerome Opena (art), Virtual Calligraphy's Joe Caramagna (letters), Dan Brown (colors), Anthony Dial (production), Sebastian Girner (asst editor), Axel Alonso (editor), Mike McKone (c art)
FEATURE CHARACTER: Punisher
SUPPORTING CAST: Henry Russo (tech genius & hacker, 1st but chr last in Pun:ItB #5, '11 fb, see NOTE)
VILLAINS: Norman Osborn (HAMMER Director, last in MsM #38, '09, chr last in DR:Hawk #5, '10), Sentry (Robert "Bob" Reynolds, former "Golden Guardian of Good," last in Time #4, '09, next in MsM #40, '09)
OTHER CHARACTERS: Subway passengers, bystanders, seagulls
LOCATIONS/ITEMS: New York inc abandoned factory, alley, Bellevue Hospital & subway stations / Punisher's fake bomb, acid, remote detonator, explosives, handcuffs, pistol, Skrull rifle w/mount & sight & Battle Van; Stark Industries billboard, subway train
SYNOPSIS: Punisher fires a sniper bullet at Norman Osborn as the HAMMER Director addresses a crowd in Manhattan. The assassination fails when Sentry intercepts the bullet and pursues Punisher. The vigilante leads the Avenger on a cat-and-mouse chase and sustains an abdominal injury in the process. Punisher activates his remote detonator and says a bomb will destroy Bellevue Hospital in five seconds. Sentry flies off to find the bomb, only to discover the bomb is a fake. By the time Sentry returns, Punisher is gone. Castle continues to elude Sentry with the help of a mystery man who calls him on his cell phone. Punisher finally passes out from his wound at the feet of his assistant.

NOTE: Cover labeled "Dark Reign." Cover is an homage to ASM #129, '74's cover. Includes letters page w/message from Rick Remender. Punisher quotes from "The Art of War" by ancient Chinese military general, Sun-Tzu. Osborn was appointed director of HAMMER, the agency that replaced SHIELD following the Skrull invasion, in SecInv #8, '09. Sentry joined Osborn's Avengers in DAv #1, '09. Pun #2, '09 reveals Henry's 1st name; his surname becomes apparent when he's revealed as Jigsaw's son in Pun #9, '09 & is confirmed in Pun #11, '10.

2ND STORY: "Punisher Saga" (13 pages)
CREDITS: Ronald Byrd (writer), Spring Hoteling (design), Alex Starbuck (asst editor), Jeff Youngquist (editor)
NOTE: A recap of Punisher's history. Followed by "The Punisher Reading Chronology (1 page) and AoAtlas #1, '09 preview (5 pages).

PUNISHER #2 (April 2009)

"Living in Darkness, Part 2" (22 pages)

CREDITS: Rick Remender (writer), Jerome Opena (art), Virtual Calligraphy's Joe Caramagna (letters), Dan Brown (colors), Sebastian Girner (asst editor), Axel Alonso (editor), Mike McKone (c art)
FEATURE CHARACTER: Punisher (also in photo, next in Dp:SK #1-5, '09, MK #26-30, '09)
SUPPORTING CAST: Henry Russo (next in Dp:SK #2, '09)
VILLAINS: Norman Osborn (also in rfb; also in MsM #39-41, MsM #43-46, Tb #128 fb, AoAtlas #3-

5, DR:Elek #2-5, Tb #128-129, Dp #7-8, Tb #130, Dp #9, Tb #131, SKK #5, DR:LL #1 fb, Dp #10, Dp #12, DR:LL #2-3 fb, DR:Hood #2, DR:LL #3, all '09, W:MrX #1, '10, Tb #133, '09, DR:MM #1, '09 & DR:Z #1, '09, next in Pun #5, '09), Hood (Parker Robbins, criminal w/mystical cloak, last in DR:Hood #2, '09, see NOTE), arms dealers (die) inc Jamar (dies), Siberian arms buyers (die), pawn shop security (die), human traffickers (die)
OTHER CHARACTERS: Ken Ellis (newspaper reporter, bts, writes column about rising crime, last in Cable&DP #28, '06, last bts in CW:FSDB, '07), Matt Herring, Brian LeTendre, Jeremy Santiago (prev 3 newspaper reporters, bts, write columns about Punisher's activities), Ken (TV news host), kidnapped women (1 as corpse), pawn shop owner; Sentry, bystanders (both in rfb), drug dealers (in photo)
LOCATIONS/ITEMS: New York inc TV studio, Norman Osborn's home, Henry's apartment w/bathroom & pawn shop w/hidden arsenal /

Punisher's automatic rifle, Battle Van, camera, blasters, explosives & pistol; arms dealers' nuclear weapon, automatic rifles & pistol; pawn scanner, shop panic button & palm print reader; Henry's computer equipment, Hood's cloak, human trafficker's assault rifles, newspapers inc the DB; AIM mask, Ant-Man's helmet, Blacklash's helmet & whip, Black Widow's Widow's Bite, Dr. Octopus' tentacle, Green Goblin's pumpkin bombs, Hawkeye's bow & arrows, Iron Man's glove, Rocket Racer's rocketboard, Taskmaster's shield, Titanium Man's glove, Skrull ice rifle & blasters, crescent guns

FLASHBACK: Sentry saves Norman Osborn from Punisher's sniper bullet (Pun #1, '09).

SYNOPSIS: Frank Castle awakens to discover that his wounds have been patched by his savior, Henry. Henry shows Punisher a televised interview with Norman Osborn, who brands Castle a terrorist. Henry tells Punisher that he's tracked Osborn's subsidiaries to drug running, prostitution, third-world slavery, black ops and arms dealing. He tells Castle to take Osborn down by exposing these operations. Punisher asks Henry if he's ready to be an accessory to murder. That night, Punisher heads to a pawn shop that Henry identifies as a front for arms dealing. Castle kills the guards and finds an exotic weapons armory he can use in his crusade. Over time, Punisher raids a human trafficking operation, and busts up a nuclear arms deal involving terrorists and takes photos to document the incidents. He returns to Henry, who vomits upon seeing Castle's pictures of slaughter. Later, Osborn reviews Punisher's exploits and enlists the Hood to deal with Castle.

NOTE: Cover labeled "Dark Reign." Cover is an homage to Pun #3, '86's cover. Includes recap page (1 page). Letters page includes LOC from comics writer Brandon Barrows. Hood is a member of Osborn's cabal, formed in SecInv #8, '09 & SecInv:DR #1, '09. Dormammu is the source of Hood's power, revealed in NAv #46, '08; while considered bts is all Hood's appearances, he is only listed when he actively participates in events. This issue reveals Henry is a fan of the bands Angst, Bad Brains, Black Flag, Descendents, GBH, Meat Puppets & T.S.O.L.

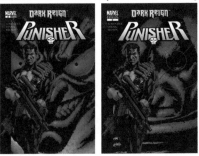

PUNISHER #3 (May 2009)

"Living in Darkness, Part 3" (22 pages)

CREDITS: Rick Remender (writer), Jerome Opena (art), Virtual Calligraphy's Joe Caramagna (letters), Dan Brown (colors), Sebastian Girner (asst editor), Axel Alonso (editor), Mike McKone (c art)

FEATURE CHARACTER: Punisher

GUEST STAR: Wolverine (in fb during NAv #31, '07)

SUPPORTING CAST: Henry Russo (last in Dp:SK #4, '09)

VILLAINS: Hood, his street operations captains (some die) & ersatz SWAT officers; Microchip (last in PWJ #79, '95, see NOTE), Yagyu Kojiro (Hand operative, in fb), Shaolin Scientist Squad (Chinese scientists versed in martial arts, 1st, next in Pun #6, '09)

OTHER CHARACTERS: 10 organ donors (corpses), wolves

LOCATIONS/ITEMS: New York inc Henry's apartment, warehouse, Hood's Bushwick, Brooklyn base w/operations room & Chinatown inc elevator shaft, sewers & organ-harvesting lab w/rooftop, stairwell & vent shaft / Punisher's pistol, rifle & transceiver; Hood's cloak, knife & pistol; SWAT flak vests, gas masks, hand grenades & rifles; Yagyu Kojiro's sword (in fb), Henry's computer, bio vats

FLASHBACK: Wolverine cuts out a Hand operative's eyes. The ninja then gets new eyes, courtesy of an organ harvesting-operation.

SYNOPSIS: The Hood tortures and murders his captains for their failure in stopping Punisher from shutting down some of his street operations. Henry tells Castle of an organ harvesting operation in Chinatown. Hood consults with a mysterious ally who knows about Punisher's methods. They determine Punisher is working with someone who has extensive experience in hacking computer systems. When Punisher goes to shut the organ harvesting operation down, he discovers it's a set up. Guided remotely by Henry, Castle flees the lab's Shaolin Scientist Squad and is chased into the sewers by a SWAT team. Henry warns Punisher that the SWAT team is fake just before they open fire on the vigilante.

NOTE: Cover labeled "Dark Reign." Includes recap page (1 page). Letters page includes LOC from comics writer Brandon Barrows. Microchip's identity is revealed in Pun #4, '09. The Hood quotes from Nietzsche's book, "Ecce Homo."

PUNISHER #4 (June 2009)

"Living in Darkness, Part 4" (22 pages)

CREDITS: Rick Remender (writer), Jerome Opena (art), Virtual Calligraphy's Joe Caramagna (letters), Dan Brown (colors), Sebastian Girner (asst editor), Axel Alonso (editor), Mike McKone (c art)

FEATURE CHARACTER: Punisher

SUPPORTING CAST: Henry Russo

VILLAINS: Hood (also in photo), his gang: Squid (Don Callahan, criminal w/ tentacles), Answer (both last in DR:Hood #1, '09, next in DR:MrN #1, '09), Grizzly (last in AoAtlas #2, '09), Tombstone (last in Dp:SK #1, '09, next in ASM #626, '10), his ersatz SWAT officers inc Aaron (die) & his men inc Jaten (little man in devil costume, 1st), Microchip

OTHER CHARACTERS: Prostitutes inc Millie (1st), casino employees & customers inc Steve, bystanders

LOCATIONS/ITEMS: New York inc Henry's apartment, Chinatown inc restaurants & sewers & Bushwick, Brooklyn inc Hood's base w/ bunker & casino / Punisher's knife, rifles, timed explosive, transceiver, noose, U-Move rental truck & white phosphorus bombs; Henry's bomb, computers & surgical stapler; Hood's cloak & pistol; SWAT flak jackets, gas masks & rifles; Microchip's computer, Ant-Man's helmet, Blacklash's whip, Black Widow's Widow Bite, Dr. Octopus' tentacle, Hawkeye's bow & arrows, Taskmaster's shield, Skrull ice rifle, crescent guns, Satan Claw

SYNOPSIS: Punisher evades and attacks the fake SWAT team, killing them one by one. Realizing that Punisher is receiving transmissions from an assistant, Hood's mysterious ally hacks into Henry's computer and discovers his location. As Punisher kills the rest of the fake SWAT team, Hood sends Grizzly to kill Henry, but Henry sets a booby trap that blows up his apartment with Grizzly in it. Henry reconnoiters with Punisher and tells him he's tracked Hood's base & warns Castle about Hood's power. Punisher arms himself with the various super-hero paraphernalia he recently purloined from a pawn shop armory. Hood touches base with his ally, Microchip, who is deliberately leading Punisher into a trap.

NOTE: Cover labeled "Dark Reign." Cover is a homage to Pun #1, '87's cover. Includes recap page (1 page). The Hood's SWAT officers are revealed as divided into Alpha, Bravo and Charlie teams. The few super villains in this issue are part of a larger gang organized by the Hood in

NAv #35, '07. Hood makes indirect references to Smokey the Bear, the Chicago Bears and the 1997 film, "The Edge." Punisher recites a line from Lynyrd Skynyrd's song, "Sweet Home Alabama."

PUNISHER #5 (July 2009)

"Living in Darkness, Part 5" (23 pages)

CREDITS: Rick Remender (writer), Jerome Opena (art), Virtual Calligraphy's Joe Caramagna (letters, production), Dan Brown (colors), Sebastian Girner (asst editor), Axel Alonso (editor), Mike McKone (c art), Morry Hollowell (c colors)
FEATURE CHARACTER: Punisher
SUPPORTING CAST: Henry Russo
VILLAINS: Bird-Man (Achille DiBacco, former Ani-Man), Cheetah (Esteban Carracus, cat-like bandit), Cyclone (Andre Gerard, wind-generating scientist), Firebrand (Gary Gilbert, fire-projecting eco-terrorist), Hijacker (Howard Mitchell, gas-wielding businessman), Letha (Hellen Feliciano, cybernetically enhanced wrestler), Mind-Wave (Erik Gelden, telepathic bank plunderer), Mirage (Desmond Charne, holography technician), Turner D. Century (Clifford F. Michaels, nostalgia-obsessed criminal) (all last in Cap #320, '86), Basilisk (Basil Elks, burglar w/eye beams, last in FF #289, '86), Black Abbott (telepathic/telekinetic cult leader, last in MTU #148, '84, last bts in Cap #394/2, '91), Blue Streak (Don Thomas, criminal w/rocket-powered roller skates, last in Cap #318, '86), Death Adder (Roland Burroughs, mute serpent-like assassin, last in Cap #319, '86, last bts in Cap #426, '94), Human Fly (Richard "Rick" Deacon, criminal w/fly DNA, last in ASM #276, '86), Lascivious (Davida Devito, cybernetically enhanced wrestler, 1st as Lascivious, last in Thing #33, '86 as Titania), Megatak (Gregory Nettles, living computer program, former industrial spy, last in Thor #358, '85), Miracle Man (Joshua Ayres, hypnotist, bts, resurrected, hidden from view, last in Thing #24, '85), Wraith (Brian DeWolff, vigilante, former policeman, last in Morb #19, '93) (all resurrected, last as corpses); Dormammu (mystic-powered ruler of Dark Dimension), Hood, his gang: Brothers Grimm (Barton & Percy Grimes, magically armed twins) & their crow, Razor-Fist (Douglas Scott, blade-handed assassin) (both last in DR:Hood #5, '09, next in NAv #55, '09), Grizzly (next in Tb #139, '10), Mr. Hyde (Calvin Zabo, chemically bulked-up medical research scientist, last in Av:In #13, '08, next in NAv #56, '09) & his men (some die) inc Black Stream operatives (die) inc Brandon (dies); Norman Osborn (last in Pun #2, '09), Jaten, Microchip
OTHER CHARACTERS: Millie (next in Pun #7, '09), 5 Action News TV reporter, casino employees & customers, prostitute, Team Awesome Pizza! deliveryman
LOCATIONS/ITEMS: New York inc Norman Osborn's bathroom, Hood's home inc basement chamber & Bushwick, Brooklyn inc Hood's base w/escape tunnel (bts), bunker, casino & elevator / Punisher's C4 explosive, motorcycle, pistol, rental truck, assault rifle & transceiver; Henry's computer, Hood's cloak, Microchip's computer, Hood's men's assault rifles, Ant-Man's helmet, Pym Particles, Skrull ice rifle & blaster
SYNOPSIS: A pizza is delivered to the Hood's base. When one of the Hood's Black Stream operatives eat the pizza, Punisher uses Pym Particles to enlarge himself inside the operative's head, killing the operative. Punisher kills the other operatives and encounters Microchip, who tells him that Hood resurrected him and has the power to bring his son back to life. Microchip invites Punisher to join the Hood so Castle's family can be resurrected too. Punisher refuses and battles the Brothers Grimm, Mr. Hyde, Grizzly and Razorfist. Punisher defeats the Hood's gang with his exotic weaponry and blows up the base. A news report of the explosion and exposure of the Hood's underground operation irks Norman Osborn, who's maintained a public front that New York is safe. Seeking to eliminate Punisher, Hood summons Dormammu, who mystically resurrects several deceased villains.
NOTE: Cover labeled "Dark Reign." Cover is an homage to DD #183, '82's cover. Includes recap page (1 page). Hood learned that Dormammu is the being behind his mystical cloak in NAv #46, '08. Most of the resurrected villains shown here died at the hands of serial criminal killer Scourge, many in Cap #319, '86. A car radio plays the song "It's Tricky" by Run-DMC.

PUNISHER #6 (August 2009)

"Dead End" (22 pages)

CREDITS: Rick Remender (writer), Tan Eng Huat (art), Virtual Calligraphy's Joe Caramagna (letters), Lee Loughridge (colors), Sebastian Girner (asst editor), Axel Alonso (editor), Mike McKone, Morry Hollowell (c art)
FEATURE CHARACTER: Punisher (also in photos, next in Pun Ann #1, '09)
GUEST STAR: G.W. Bridge (last in PWJ #25, '09)
SUPPORTING CAST: Henry Russo (next in Pun Ann #1, '09)
VILLAINS: Hood, Black Abbott, Cheetah, Miracle Man, Norman Osborn (all next in Pun #8, '09), Bird-Man, Lascivious, Letha (prev 3 next in Pun Ann #1, '09), Blue Streak (next in Pun #9, '09), Shaolin Scientist Squad (last in Pun #3, '09, some die, next in FC #17, '10), Wraith (off panel, attending meeting), Oscorp guards (some die) & Black Stream technicians, Jaten (next in Pun:ItB #1, '11), Basilisk, Cyclone, Death Adder, Firebrand, Hijacker, Human Fly, Megatak, Microchip, Mind-Wave, Mirage, Turner D. Century
OTHER CHARACTERS: Sandy Bridge (G.W. Bridge's wife, corpse), Tyler (G.W. Bridge's stepson, see NOTE) (both 1st), Scourge (serial criminal killer, in Hood's conjured image), radio news reporter (voice only), Oscorp receptionist, TV news reporter, grocery clerk & customers
LOCATIONS/ITEMS: New York inc G.W. Bridge's home, grocery store, Hood's basement chamber & Oscorp Textiles factory inc access tunnel, reception area & secret weapons facility / Punisher's explosives, knife, laser cutter, pistols, rental truck & scuba gear; Hood's cloak & Punisher file; Oscorp guards' garrote & guns; Henry's computer, Ant-Man's helmet, Blacklash's whip, Dr. Octopus' tentacle, Hawkeye's bow & arrows, Iron Man's glove, Rocket Racer's rocketboard w/energy cell from Titanium Man's glove, Taskmaster's shield, crescent gun
SYNOPSIS: The Hood tells the resurrected villains that Frank Castle, as the Scourge of the Underworld, was the man who murdered them and they must kill Punisher or the spell that gives them life for thirty days will not be extended. Meanwhile, Punisher breaks into an Oscorp textiles factory, actually a weapons facility, and battles Black Stream technicians, Oscorp guards and the Shaolin Scientist Squad. With his adversaries killed, Punisher destroys the Oscorp facility. The villains plot to band together to bring down Punisher, but Death Adder and Basilisk leave with a separate plan of their own. Henry leaks information about the textiles factory's destruction and its actual purpose to the press. G.W. Bridge returns home, only to find his wife killed and his stepson taken captive by Death Adder and Basilisk, who demand to know Castle's whereabouts.
NOTE: Cover labeled "Dark Reign." Includes recap page (1 page). Followed by 12 pages with bios by Madison Carter and creator commentary

about Basilisk, Cheetah, Cyclone, Death Adder, Firebrand, Hijacker, Human Fly, Lascivious, Letha, Megatak, Mirage and Turner D. Century. This issue reveals that Punisher prefers Miller High Life beer and G.W. Bridge has a family; Pun #9, '09 reveals that Bridge met his wife and stepson after the recent Skrull invasion. Tyler's name is revealed in Pun #8, '09.

PUNISHER ANNUAL #1 (November 2009)

"Remote Control" (32 pages)

CREDITS: Rick Remender (writer), Jason Pearson (art), Virtual Calligraphy's Joe Caramagna (letters), Dave Stewart (colors), Sebastian Girner (asst editor), Axel Alonso (editor)
FEATURE CHARACTER: Punisher (also as FBI agent, next in AVenom #1-3, '09-10, Pun #7, '09)
GUEST STAR: Spider-Man (between ASM #591-592, '09)
SUPPORTING CAST: Henry Russo (next in AVenom #2, '10)
VILLAINS: Lascivious, Letha (both also in photos, between Pun #6-7, '09), Bird-Man (last in Pun #6, '09, next in Pun #8, '09)
OTHER CHARACTERS: Military veterans (die) inc Dan (dies), Veterans Hospital staff inc a psychologist (dies), police inc Brianna, Delcorum employees (corpses) & patron, constructions workers, bystanders, pigeons
LOCATIONS/ITEMS: New York inc Veterans Hospital, Delcorum (boutique shop) & construction site / Punisher's motorcycle, Battle Van, Uzi, shotgun, knife & assault rifle (destroyed); Blacklash's whip, Boomerang's boomerang, Daredevil's billy club, Dr. Octopus' tentacle, Green Goblin's pumpkin bombs, Iron Man's glove, Pym Particles, Letha's car & calling card
SYNOPSIS: Letha and Lascivious murder a group of military veterans and their therapist. Later, Punisher poses as an FBI agent to investigate the crime scene and sees the calling card left behind. He calls Henry Russo, who tells Punisher the cards were printed at Delcorum, a boutique shop. Punisher finds Letha and Lascivious at the shop. Letha's powers don't work on Punisher, because he's already filled with hate. Punisher detonates a pumpkin bomb in Lascivious' mouth and electrocutes Letha with Blacklash's whip. Spider-Man arrives and stops Punisher from killing Letha. Letha entrances Spider-Man into attacking Punisher and escapes with Lascivious. Spider-Man fights through Letha's power and tosses Punisher away so he doesn't kill the vigilante. Punisher uses Daredevil's billy club to slow his fall, and lands on Letha's car. Spider-Man returns and stops Punisher from killing the villainesses, but Punisher is able to knock Letha out, breaking her control on Spider-Man. Punisher blasts Spider-Man with Iron Man's glove. Lascivious uses her power to make the returning Spider-Man love Punisher. With the vigilante distracted, Bird-Man flies Letha and Lascivious away. Punisher traps Spider-Man in one of Dr. Octopus' tentacles and continues his search for the villainesses.
NOTE: Includes recap page (1 page). The variant covers for this issue and Pun #8-10, '09 combine to form one larger image.

PUNISHER #7 (September 2009)

(untitled, 22 pages)

CREDITS: Rick Remender (writer), Tan Eng Huat (art), Virtual Calligraphy's Joe Caramagna (letters), Lee Loughridge (colors), Sebastian Girner (asst editor), Axel Alonso (editor), Mike McKone (c art)
FEATURE CHARACTER: Punisher
SUPPORTING CAST: Henry Russo (last in AVenom #3, '10), G.W. Bridge
VILLAINS: Firebrand (next in Pun #10, '09), Hijacker (next in Pun #9, '09), Lascivious, Letha (both last in Pun Ann #1, '09), Black Stream operatives (die), Wraith (dies), Basilisk, Cyclone, Death Adder, Human Fly, Megatak, Microchip, Mind-Wave, Mirage
OTHER CHARACTERS: Frank Castle Jr., Lisa Castle, Maria Castle, Hood (all in Punisher's dream), Millie (last in Pun #5, '09), Tina (prostitute, deceased), Sandy Bridge (corpse), Tyler, pigeons
LOCATIONS/ITEMS: Frank Castle's home, alley, Catholic church w/confessional (all in Punisher's dream), New York inc Bar With No Name (see NOTE), munitions plant, rooftops & shady motel / Punisher's rental truck, Henry's computer, Microchip's computer, Black Stream rifles & tank, Blacklash's whip, Hawkeye's bow & arrows, Taskmaster's shield, crescent guns
SYNOPSIS: Frank Castle naps and has a nightmare about the Hood resurrecting his family. He gets impatient for an assignment requiring a kill and upsets Henry. Meanwhile, Microchip programs Megatak to search cyberspace for Henry. Mirage, Cyclone, Mind-Wave and Firebrand get into an argument of the sexes with Letha and Lascivious, who uses her new mind-control power to humiliate Mirage. Death Adder and Basilisk take G.W. Bridge and his family to the Bar With No Name and threaten G.W.'s son to get Bridge to agree to help them catch Punisher. Castle tracks down Wraith and kills him. Henry leads Punisher to a shady motel where the Human Fly has succumbed to his cannibalistic urges and is eating a prostitute. Black Stream operatives attack Human Fly, but he kills them and abducts another prostitute. Punisher arrives and attacks Human Fly.
NOTE: Includes recap page (1 page). Megatak notes his current incarnation as version 4.5. The Bar With No Name shown here is in New York and is not to be confused with the Bar With No Name in Ohio where some of the resurrected villains were killed by Scourge, seen in Cap #319, '86.

PUNISHER #8 (October 2009)

(untitled, 22 pages)

CREDITS: Rick Remender (writer), Tan Eng Huat (art), Virtual Calligraphy's Joe Caramagna (letters, production), Lee Loughridge (colors), Sebastian Girner (asst editor), Axel Alonso (editor), Mike McKone (c art), Jim Cheung, Steve Dillon, Tom Raney (variant c art)
FEATURE CHARACTER: Punisher
GUEST STAR: G.W. Bridge
SUPPORTING CAST: Henry Russo
VILLAINS: Black Abbott (also as Dr. Druid), Cheetah (also as Beast) (both last in Pun #6, '09), Bird-Man (last in Pun Ann #1, '09, next in IM #20, '10), Hood (last in Pun #6, '09, next in Pun #10, '09), Norman Osborn (last in Pun #6, '09, next in DR:Z #1, '09), Cyclone (next in Pun #10, '09), Miracle Man (prev 2 as Black Knight & Thor, see NOTE), Lascivious, Letha (prev 2 also as Captain Marvel (Rambeau) & She-Hulk, see NOTE), Mind-Wave (also as Iron Man), Mirage (also

as Captain America, next in Pun:ItB #2, '11), Basilisk, Death Adder, Human Fly, Megatak, Microchip

OTHER CHARACTERS: Beast, Black Bolt, Black Panther (Shuri), Luke Cage, Cyclops, Daredevil, Deadpool, Emma Frost, Nick Fury, Molly Hayes, Hulk, Human Torch (Storm), Invisible Woman, Iron Man, Ms. Marvel, Nova, Pixie, Psylocke, Punisher, Red Hulk, Ronin, Sentry, Spider-Man, Spider-Woman, Storm, Sub-Mariner, Thing, Thor, War Machine, Wolverine, X-23 (all on variant cover only), Millie (dies), Sandy Bridge (bts, deceased, at Bar With No Name), Tyler

LOCATIONS/ITEMS: New York inc alley, Bar With No Name, Henry's apartment, Norman Osborn's office & shady motel / Punisher's blaster, spiked brass knuckles, dagger, hand grenades, motorcycle, pistols, rental truck, rifles & transceiver; Hood's cloak & video communicator; G.W. Bridge's laser cutter, Henry's computer, Letha's transceiver, Black Stream tank, Blacklash's whip, Dr. Octopus' arm, Taskmaster's shield, crescent guns

SYNOPSIS: Human Fly kills a prostitute before Punisher's eyes and an angry Punisher fights the villain. When he has Human Fly on the ropes, Punisher faces a group of ersatz Avengers from the past. Punisher defends himself against the "heroes" and reveals them to be resurrected criminals in disguise. Punisher captures Mirage and disperses Mind-Wave, Letha, Lascivious and Black Abbott with a grenade. At the Bar With No Name, Death Adder and Basilisk force the captive G.W. Bridge to give them a distress signal code that will lure Punisher to them. Henry intercepts the signal and tells Punisher about Bridge's location. Norman Osborn yells at the Hood about the villains' conspicuous attack and Hood gets upset. After Mirage tells Punisher about the Hood's resurrection of villains, Punisher sends the criminal back to his teammates with a grenade in his mouth. Letha removes the grenade and the villains go after Punisher. Microchip finds Henry's location and sends Megatak after the hacker.

NOTE: Includes recap page (1 page). Variant cover celebrates 70 years of Marvel Comics, as do all ongoing Marvel series this month. Letters page includes LOC from comics writer Brandon Barrows. Although the identities of all the villains disguised as Avengers are known, for some of the imposters it is unclear exactly who is who. For the most part, the villains are disguised as Avengers from Av #279-285, '87. "Iron Man" is shown with the "Silver Centurion" armor introduced in IM #200, '85 and "Thor" is shown wearing the armor introduced in Thor #378, '87.

PUNISHER #9 (November 2009)

"Dead End" (22 pages)

CREDITS: Rick Remender (writer), Tan Eng Huat (art), Virtual Calligraphy's Joe Caramagna (letters, production), Lee Loughridge (colors), Sebastian Girner (asst editor), Axel Alonso (editor), Mike McKone, Morry Hollowell (c art), Tom Raney (variant c art)
FEATURE CHARACTER: Punisher
GUEST STAR: G.W. Bridge
SUPPORTING CAST: Henry Russo (also in fb to 1st chr app before off-panel in Pun:ItB #1, '11 fb)
VILLAINS: Blue Streak (last in Pun #6, '09, dies), Hijacker (last in Pun #7, '09), Jigsaw (in fb between Pun:YO #4, '95 & Pun:ItB #1, '11 fb), Basilisk, Death Adder, Human Fly, Lascivious, Letha, Megatak, Microchip

OTHER CHARACTERS: Sandy (Henry's mother, in fb, 1st, next in Pun:ItB #1, '11), kittens (in fb, die), Sandy Bridge (bts, deceased, at Bar With No Name), Hood (as illusion), Tyler, bystanders, homeless men, 2 police detectives

LOCATIONS/ITEMS: Henry's boyhood home inc bathroom & Henry's bedroom (in fb); New York inc Bar With No Name, Midtown & cemetery w/Castle family graves / Punisher's rental truck, rifle, transceiver & downloaded war journal; Jigsaw's revolver (in fb), Basilisk's transceiver, Blue Streak's wrist-mounted knives, G.W. Bridge's laser pen, Henry's computer, Hijacker's horror gas, Microchip's computer, Rocket Racer's rocketboard w/energy cell from Titanium Man's glove, Black Stream tank, Blacklash's whip, Dr. Octopus' arm, Taskmaster's shield, Pym Particles, Skrull blaster

FLASHBACK: Jigsaw forces his son Henry to drown kittens in a bathroom sink.

SYNOPSIS: Henry flees from Megatak's assault, but is chased by Blue Streak. Meanwhile, Microchip hacks Henry's communications signal and tells Punisher that Henry is dead and that he's downloaded Punisher's war journal. As Microchip taunts Punisher, Henry manages to kill Blue Streak. After seeing what he's done, Henry becomes ill. As Punisher defeats Fly, Letha, Lascivious, and Hijacker, G.W. Bridge frees himself and attacks Basilisk and Death Adder. Punisher arrives in the tank he commandeered from Hijacker and helps Bridge battle his captors. Meanwhile, police discover the Castle family bodies have been exhumed.

NOTE: Includes recap page (1 page). Letters page features an interview with Rick Remender from marvel.com. This issue reveals Henry is a fan of the bands Adolescents, Agent Orange, Black Flag, Graphics, New Shapes & Tator.

PUNISHER #10 (December 2009)

"Dead End" (22 pages)

CREDITS: Rick Remender (writer), Tan Eng Huat (art), Virtual Calligraphy's Joe Caramagna (letters, production), Lee Loughridge (colors), Sebastian Girner (asst editor), Axel Alonso (editor), Mike McKone (c art), Morry Hollowell (c colors), Tom Raney (variant c art)
FEATURE CHARACTER: Punisher (also as Frank Castle in fb between Pun #100, '95 fb & Pun Ann #4, '91; next in Hulk #14-15, '09, FoH:RH #2, '10 fb, Hulk #15-17, '09-10, DrV #4, '10, Girl #1/3, '10, DRL:Pun #1, '09)
SUPPORTING CAST: Maria Castle (also in fb between Pun #100, '95 fb & Pun Ann #4, '91), Lisa Castle, Frank Castle Jr. (both also in fb between Pun #100, '95 fb & Pun:RBN, '89 fb) (all corpses, last in Pun:YO #1, '94, last bts in MSA Mag #1, '76 fb), Henry Russo (next in DRL:Pun, '09), G.W. Bridge (dies, next as corpse in Pun:ItB #1, '11)
VILLAINS: Basilisk (next in IM #20, '10), Firebrand (last in Pun #7, '09, dies), Hood (next in MAv #24, '09), Microchip (next in Pun:ItB #1, '11), Cyclone (dies), Death Adder
OTHER CHARACTER: Microchip Jr. (corpse, last in Pun #9, '88)
LOCATIONS/ITEMS: Kitchen of Castle family's home (in fb), New York inc public restroom & Hood's basement chamber / Punisher's knife, pistol & rental truck; Hood's cloak, dagger & pistols; G.W. Bridge's pistol, Microchip's pistol, Taskmaster's shield

FLASHBACK: The Castle family has dinner at home.

SYNOPSIS: Punisher and G.W. Bridge defend themselves against Basilisk and Death Adder but the villains subdue them. Punisher awakens in Hood's basement chamber before Hood, Microchip, Firebrand, Cyclone and a group of caskets containing the corpses of Castle's family and Microchip's son. Hood tells Castle that if he kills the captive Bridge his loved ones will be brought back to life. Punisher declines, but Microchip kills Bridge and the corpses are resurrected. Disgusted at the thought of his family benefitting from villainous means and refusing to believe it's really them, Castle forces Firebrand to incinerate the reanimated bodies. When Firebrand does, Punisher kills him and Microchip frantically fails to extinguish his son's burning corpse. Punisher attacks Hood. When Hood has Punisher on the ropes, Castle forces the villain to let him go by pointing out Hood's family will die if he fails to retrieve an envelope scheduled to be sent to Wilson Fisk. As Punisher leaves, Hood tells him Henry is Jigsaw's son. Later, Castle parts ways with Henry, unsure that Jigsaw's son can be trusted.

NOTE: Includes recap page (1 page).

DARK REIGN: THE LIST – PUNISHER #1 (December 2009)

"A Good Lie" (23 pages)

CREDITS: Rick Remender (writer), John Romita, Jr. (pencils), Klaus Janson (inks), Virtual Calligraphy's Joe Caramagna (letters), Dean White (colors), Sebastian Girner (asst editor), Axel Alonso (editor), Frank Cho (variant c art), Steve Dillon (2nd printing c art)
FEATURE CHARACTER: Punisher (dies, also & next in DRL:Pun #1, '0)
GUEST STAR: Man-Thing (last in DrV #5, '10, next in SM:BiQ #1, '10)
SUPPORTING CAST: Henry Russo (between Pun #10-11, '09-'10)
VILLAINS: Iron Patriot (Norman Osborn, last in DRL:SecWs #1, '09, also bts in Pun #11, '10, next in DRL:Hulk #1, '09), "Wolverine" (Daken, Wolverine's son, last in NAv Ann #3, '10, also in Pun #11, '10, next in DRL:Hulk #1, '09), HAMMER agents (some next in Pun #11, '10) & glider troops (some also in Pun #11, '10)
OTHER CHARACTERS: Bystanders
LOCATIONS/ITEMS: New York inc alleys, pier, rooftop & sewers / Punisher's computer, knife, pistol, rifles, timed explosive & U-Move rental truck; HAMMER blasters, computers, gliders, headsets, Helicarriers, hydraulic lift platform, missiles & pumpkin bombs; Henry's headset, Iron Patriot armor, Rocket Racer's rocketboard w/energy cell from Titanium Man's glove, Blacklash's whip, Pym Particles, Taskmaster's shield, crescent guns
SYNOPSIS: Henry Russo tries to contact Frank Castle to warn him that Norman Osborn and HAMMER are on a mission to kill the Punisher. As HAMMER agents find Punisher's location, Castle wakes up for breakfast. After a missile attack fails to kill Frank Castle, Norman Osborn sends Daken and glider troops to exterminate the vigilante. Punisher escapes using Pym Particles, and when he enlarges Henry finally finds him. Henry tries to warn Punisher that Osborn is trying to kill him, but Castle knocks him out. HAMMER glider troops arrive and force Punisher into the sewers, where Daken attacks the vigilante. Punisher bites off Daken's lip and blasts him in the torso before escaping. Daken heals and follows, moving the battle from the sewers to a rooftop where Punisher is cornered between HAMMER troops and Daken. As Daken uses his claws to chop off Punisher's arms, Frank Castle welcomes death, ready to see his wife again. Daken decapitates Castle and tosses the body parts into an alley.
NOTE: Includes recap page (1 page). Followed by Pun #11, '10 preview (11 pages), Pun:RIP variant cover gallery by Tom Raney & Scott Hanna (4 pages) and Punisher reading chronology (1 page). Issue includes a quotation from author James Thurber. The HAMMER gliders and pumpkin bombs shown here are based on technology developed and used by Norman Osborn in his Green Goblin identity. Daken joined Osborn's "Dark Avengers" in DAv #1, '09.

PUNISHER #11 (January 2010)

(untitled, 23 pages)

CREDITS: Rick Remender (writer), Tony Moore (art), Virtual Calligraphy's Joe Caramagna (letters), Dan Brown (colors), Sebastian Girner (asst editor), Axel Alonso (editor), David Wilkins (c art)
FEATURE CHARACTER: Punisher (also in DRL:Pun #1, '09, resurrected)
GUEST STARS: Legion of Monsters: Living Mummy (N'Kantu, millennia-old African chieftain, last in LoM:S #1/2, '07), Man-Thing (Theodore "Ted" Sallis, plant-matter creature, last in DAv #10, '09, next in Pun #13, '10), Manphibian (aquatic alien, last in NFHC #6, '06), Morbius (Dr. Michael Morbius, pseudo-vampiric scientist), Werewolf (Jacob "Jack Russell" Russoff, werewolf by night) (both last in MZ4 #4, '09) (all also in pfb)
SUPPORTING CAST: Henry Russo (last in DRL:Pun #1, '09, next in Pun #14, '10)
VILLAINS: "Wolverine" (Daken, during DRL:Pun #1, '09); HAMMER agents inc Cross & Jaken (Cross & Jaken die); Hunter of Monster Special Force (monster extermination squad) inc Capt. Yamato Takahishi (field leader) (all 1st, some also in pfb); Robert Hellsgaard (armored monster hunter, Special Force's leader, voice & obscured video image only, 1st but chr last in Pun #14, '10 fb), Norman Osborn (bts, orders HAMMER to collect Punisher's remains, during DRL:Pun #1, '09)
OTHER CHARACTERS: Molten Man-Thing (lava creature, village preacher, see NOTE), Two-Headed Thing (subterranean shapeshifter) (both last in FFU #7, '94), Grottu (giant ant, last in FF/IM:Big #1, '06, chr last in FFU #7, '95), Rommbu (Fourth Galaxy invader, last in MM:MOTP #1, '05), Orrgo (telepathic alien conqueror, last in NFHC #6, '06), monsters (some die, some also in pfb) inc Moloids (inc one wearing a Devo t-shirt, 1st), Kakaranatharian (dragon, see NOTE), alien of Manoo's species (race last in MM:WMD #1, '05), ape (see NOTE), "Martian" (see NOTE), Groot (see NOTE), giant insects, crustaceans; Tragg (rat creature, in pfb, last in MM:MOTP #1, '05) & offspring (as corpses in pfb), Devil Dinosaur, Titanno, Fin Fang Foom, Monster "at the window" (prev 4 pictured in stain-glass window)
LOCATIONS/ITEMS: Monster Island, New York inc sewers & Monster Metropolis (monster village in Morlock tunnels) w/Morbius' laboratory, central market & church / Punisher's power-supply backpack & mechanical components (see NOTE) & "synaptic glue" pills; Special Force's armor,

katanas, rifles, rocket-darts, wrist-blasters & flight packs; Henry's hoverboard, HAMMER Helicarrier; HAMMER agents' guns, grenades, & gliders
FLASHBACK: The Legion of Monsters defend the denizens of Monster Island from the Hunter of Monster Special Force and take them to refuge in the Morlock tunnels (p).
SYNOPSIS: On Monster Island, a high-tech samurai team slaughters a group of monsters, then report to their unseen leader. In New York, Henry Russo awakens to see Daken behead the Punisher. Henry flees from the HAMMER agents besieging the area. Two HAMMER agents are assigned to collect Frank Castle's remains, but a group of Moloids gather them first. The agents pursue, but Man-Thing kills them. Frank awakens in Michael Morbius' lab, who has rebuilt Castle as a Frankenstein's Monster-like creature. In a state of madness due to waking before Morbius could complete work on his brain, Frank rampages his way out of the lab and into a subterranean village inhabited by various monsters. Despite Morbius and his allies' attempts to stop him, Frank smashes a swath of destruction through the village until the village minister, Molten Man-Thing, captures him. Frank is brought back to the lab, where Morbius gives him pills that will maintain his normal brain function. Morbius asks Frank to help defend the refugee monsters against the samurai that have been hunting them. Frank refuses and leaves.
NOTE: Cover labeled "FrankenCastle." Includes recap/credits page (1 page). Punisher's mechanical parts will be considered his standard equipment for his appearances in his "Franken-Castle" state. Though cover labeled "FrankenCastle" through Pun #16, '10 and, beginning with FC #17, '10, the series changes its name to "Franken-Castle," Punisher never assumes this name in-story. Pun #13, '10 reveals Hellsgaard's surname. Pun #14, '10 reveals Hellsgaard's first name and Yamato's given name. Monster Metropolis is named next issue. The human-sized Molten Man-Thing is an appendage standing atop the submerged giant-sized creature's head, and not a separate individual. The Kakaranatharian may be the race's most famous representative, Fin Fang Foom, last in GSAv #1/9, '08, but as several of the species are on Earth, it may be one of the others, last seen in IM #275, '91. The ape may be Erik Gorbo, the Monster Ape, last in Cap #136, '71. The Martian is one of Zetora's species, last in JIM #58, '60. The treelike alien Groot from Planet X returned to space, as seen in AnniC:SL #1, '07; however, his species reproduce identical offspring via budding, and are all called Groot. The one here was presumably spawned before the "main" Groot left Earth following NFHC #6, '06.

PUNISHER #12 (February 2010)

(untitled, 22 pages)

CREDITS: Rick Remender (writer), Tony Moore (art), Virtual Calligraphy's Joe Caramagna (letters), Dan Brown (colors), Sebastian Girner (asst editor), Axel Alonso (editor), Mike McKone (c art), Morry Hollowell (c colors)
FEATURE CHARACTER: Punisher
GUEST STARS: Legion of Monsters (all also as statues and in painting): Manphibian (next in Pun #15, '10), Living Mummy, Morbius, Werewolf
VILLAINS: Robert Hellsgaard (1st full app); Hunter of Monster Special Force (some die) inc Capt. Yamato
OTHER CHARACTERS: Molten Man-Thing, Manphibian's children (corpses); refugee monsters (some die) inc Melgorno (cyclopean creature), Monster (alien fugitive, last in ST #95/2, '62), Cyclops (Olympian monster, last in ToS #10, '60), Moloids (inc Devo t-shirt wearer, dies), Sporr (mutated amoeba, last in ToS #11, '60), Monstro (mutated octopus, last in ToS #8, '60), Thing that Crawled by Night (plant creature, last in ToS #26, '62), Ape Man ("Salty" Gruner, transformed convict, last in ST #85, '61), Uboongi (goatlike alien, race last in ST #100/3, '62), Mighty Oak (sentient tree, last in ST #100/4, '62), Space Beast (cowardly alien invaders, race last in ToS #29, '62), the Stranger "who walked through walls" (supernatural being, last in TTA #26, '61), Kakaranatharian, headless soldier, giant insects, gate guardians, werewolves, amoeboid; rat, Morbius' insects; Dracula, Frankenstein's Monster, Ghost Rider, Hellstorm, Satana (prev 5 as statues & in painting), Titanno, Monster "at the window" (both in stain-glass window)
LOCATIONS/ITEMS: Alps inc Hellsgaard's castle w/torture chamber; Monster Metropolis inc Punisher's hovel, central market, Morbius' lab w/ safe room, Hall of Monsters (Legion's HQ & museum) & church / Punisher's synaptic glue pills, Special Force's armor, rocket launchers, restraint chair & rifles; Hellsgaard's armor, museum weapons collection inc Exorcist Gun, Wakefield Falchion, Blade's Cathari swords, Skull of Daimon, Libros del Malditos (book), Stephen Loss' Ruinsaw, Fur Journal & Pus-knives; Bloodstone (gem that empowers user), Uncle Freddie's Canned Worms can, Moloid child's candy
SYNOPSIS: The Hunter of Monster Special Force drag Manphibian before Robert Hellsgaard. Manphibian refuses to reveal the refugees' location, until Hellsgaard shows him the corpses of his many children. In a sewer hovel, Punisher takes a pill to maintain his brain functions; he plans to commit suicide while he can still think. He prepares to eat a rat as his last meal, but a Moloid arrives and offers him a candy bar as a friendship token. Frank accepts and the two sit in his room, eating candy. In Morbius' lab, Morbius and Jack Russell argue philosophical differences. After Jack leaves, Morbius briefly contemplates locking away the Bloodstone he secretly carries. The Living Mummy visits Frank, gives him more pills, and takes Frank on a tour of the refugee city, culminating with a visit to a museum honoring the Legion of Monsters. Morbius and the Molten Man-Thing debate whether the Bloodstone is affecting Morbius' judgment, but their discussion is cut short by a mass assault by the Special Force. Morbius attempts to hide the Bloodstone, but Hellsgaard finds him before he can. The Moloid who befriended Frank tries to warn him of the attack but is killed before Frank's eyes.
NOTE: Cover labeled "FrankenCastle." Includes recap/credits page (1 page). The Hall of Monsters is named in FC #17, '10. Next issue reveals that the Molten Man-Thing found the Bloodstone in his volcanic home and entrusted it to Morbius. The location of Hellsgaard's castle is revealed in Pun #14, '10. The story opens with a quote from Frederich Nietzsche: "He who fights with monsters might take care lest he thereby become a monster."

PUNISHER #13 (March 2010)

(untitled, 22 pages)

CREDITS: Rick Remender (writer), Tony Moore (pencils), Mike Hawthorne (inks), Virtual Calligraphy's Joe Caramagna (letters), Dan Brown (colors), Sebastian Girner (asst editor), Axel Alonso (editor), Mike McKone (c art), Morry Hollowell (c colors)
FEATURE CHARACTER: Punisher
GUEST STARS: Legion of Monsters: Man-Thing (last in Pun #11, '10, next in Dp:Merc #6, '10), Morbius (next in Pun #15, '10), Living Mummy, Werewolf
VILLAINS: Robert Hellsgaard (next in Pun #15, '10); Hunter of Monster Special Force (some die, some as corpses) inc Capt. Yamato (dies)
OTHER CHARACTERS: Giganto (Deviant mutate, last in MHol '05, next in F.F. #4, '11), Molten Man-Thing, Helene (werewolf, mentioned by Jack, killed along with her pack by the Special Force in Montreal), refugee monsters (some as corpses) inc Moloids (one as corpse), Dracula, Ghost Rider (both in painting)
LOCATIONS/ITEMS: New York inc Monster Metropolis w/adjoining tunnels, Morbius' laboratory, central market, & Hall of Monsters / Punisher's katana, rifle, grenade & burrower shell launcher; Special Force's armor, katanas, rifles, wrist blasters, flight packs & helicopter; Hellsgaard's armor w/solar beam projector, museum weapon collection, Bloodstone
SYNOPSIS: As Punisher slaughters his way through the Hunter of Monster Special Force, Robert Hellsgaard captures Morbius and the Bloodstone. Jack Russell faces an entire platoon of the Special Force single-handedly. Close to defeat despite thinning his foes' numbers, Jack is saved by Punisher, who kills the Special Force with a grenade. Captain Yamato arrives and engages Frank in a brutal fight that takes them throughout Monster Metropolis. Thinking Castle finished, Yamato fires on the Man-Thing, but Frank arises and shoots Yamato with shells that burrow into his body. Yamato nevertheless escapes, and Castle helps a healing Man-Thing to his feet. Hellsgaard and the surviving Special Force board their helicopter with Morbius and the Bloodstone. Giganto erupts through the street, but fails to prevent the villains' escape. Frank hurls the Man-Thing towards the fleeing Yamato. Man-Thing incinerates Yamato as Hellsgaard watches. Later, the Molten Man-Thing reveals that he gave Morbius the Bloodstone and implored him to share his burden with the Legion. Castle mentions he knows someone who can help them find Hellsgaard, then vows to show him the face of a true monster.
NOTE: Cover labeled "FrankenCastle." Includes recap/credits page (1 page).

PUNISHER #14 (April 2010)

(untitled, 22 pages)

CREDITS: Rick Remender (writer), Tony Moore (art), Dan Brereton (painted flashback art), Virtual Calligraphy's Joe Caramagna (letters), Dan Brown (colors), Sebastian Girner (editor), Axel Alonso (consulting editor), Mike McKone (c art), Morry Hollowell (c colors)
FEATURE CHARACTER: Punisher
GUEST STARS: Ulysses Bloodstone (nigh-immortal monster hunter, in fb2 between MUni #7, '98 fb & RH #8/2, '78 fb), Legion of Monsters: Living Mummy (next in FC #17, '10), Werewolf by Night (next in ASM #622, '10)
SUPPORTING CAST: Henry Russo (last in Pun #11, '10)
VILLAINS: Dracula (Vlad Tepes, vampire lord, in fb2 between DracL #9/5, '74 & Inv #9, '76 fb), Robert Hellsgaard (in fb1-3 to 1st chr app before Pun #11, '10, also in photo), Hunter of Monster Special Force inc Capt. Yamato (in fb3 to 1st chr app before Pun #11, '10)
OTHER CHARACTERS: Elisa Hellsgaard (Hellsgaard's daughter), Gerhardt Hellsgaard (both hand only, corpses), Nadja Hellsgaard (Hellsgaard's wife, dies), villagers of Lenskirch (corpses), werewolf (dies), coachman & his horse, refugee monster (all in fb1), prison guards (in fb2), vampires (in fb2&3, some die), atomic super-monsters (in fb3, one dies), Morlocks (in fb3, some die), Nikola Tesla (inventor, bts, met with Hellsgaard prior to fb1, chr 1st, bts next in Cap:ME #1, '94)
LOCATIONS/ITEMS: Morbius' laboratory; Lenskirch, Germany (in fb1) inc Hellsgaard's house w/Elisa & Gerhardt's bedroom, prison w/ Hellsgaard's cell (in fb2), Bloodstone's castle w/Hellsgaard's laboratory (in fb2&3), Tokyo (in fb3) inc Tokyo Tower, sewers & subway tunnel / Hellsgaard's copy of a Frederich Nietzsche book, journal, crossbow, arrows (all in fb2), arrows (in fb2), armor & limbo portal machinery (both in fb2&3); silver tableware, guards' rifles, Ulysses Bloodstone's sword, Bloodstone (prev 4 in fb2), Special Force's armor, rifles & katanas (prev 3 in fb3), Henry's laptop computer
FLASHBACKS: 1898: Robert Hellsgaard returns from a meeting with Nikola Tesla to find the people of his village either dead or turned into werewolves, including his entire family. He kills all the werewolves, including his wife, but, since the werewolves revert to human form upon death, Hellsgaard is imprisoned for the villagers' murders (1). 1910: Ulysses Bloodstone breaks Hellsgaard out of prison and enlists him as an ally in his war against Earth's monsters. Years later, Hellsgaard develops a suit of armor intended to aid their endeavors, and a portal into the Limbo dimension with which to imprison their adversaries. Dracula leads a vampire attack on the castle, and Hellsgaard dons the armor to fend them off. Dracula tears the coolant hose away from the armor, boiling Hellsgaard in the suit's life-support fluids, and shoves him through the portal into limbo (2). 1978: Dr. Yamato Takahishi and his team of scientists, seeking a solution to the escalating monster invasions of Japan, travel to Hellsgaard's castle to seek technology that can combat the monsters. They inadvertently free Hellsgaard and pledge fealty to him. Hellsgaard arms Yamato and his team, who become the Hunter of Monster Special Force. At first content to hunt monsters, Hellsgaard and the Special Force eventually turn their attentions to mutants and the merely disfigured (3).
SYNOPSIS: Henry Russo briefs Punisher, Jack Russell, and the Living Mummy on Robert Hellsgaard's history. While they are unsure as to the exact reason for which Hellsgaard wanted the Bloodstone, Frank nevertheless is steadfast in his plan to stop him.
NOTE: Cover labeled "FrankenCastle." Includes recap/credits page (1 page). The limbo that Hellsgaard ends up in is the demonic realm limbo (aka Otherplace) ruled by Belasco, rather than the similarly named realm outside time, Limbo, ruled by Immortus.

PUNISHER #15 (May 2010)

(untitled, 22 pages)

CREDITS: Rick Remender (writer), Roland Boschi (art), Virtual Calligraphy's Joe Caramagna (letters), Dan Brown, Lee Loughridge (colors), Sebastian Girner (editor), Axel Alonso (consulting editor), Mike McKone (c art), Morry Hollowell (c colors)
FEATURE CHARACTER: Punisher
GUEST STARS: Legion of Monsters: Manphibian (last in Pun #12, '10), Morbius
SUPPORTING CAST: Henry Russo (next in FC #17, '10)
VILLAINS: Robert Hellsgaard (last in Pun #13, '10); Hunter of Monster Special Force inc Akio (all die); undead soldiers

OTHER CHARACTERS: Maria Castle, Lisa Castle, Frank Castle Jr. (all as reanimated corpses in Frank's dream), Firebrand (in Punisher's dream), dragon (dies), Makoto (Special Force Hunter, mentioned)
LOCATIONS/ITEMS: Punisher's hovel & staging room, Hellsgaard's castle w/torture chamber / Punisher's guns, submachinegun, shotgun, swords & mine; Hellsgaard's armor w/flamethrower & rotary saw whip; Special Force's rifles, flight packs, armor & artillery cannon, Bloodstone
SYNOPSIS: Punisher dreams of incinerating his re-animated family, declaring that they belong dead. Henry Russo wakes Punisher and acknowledges that Frank has accepted his help despite his parentage but questions why they are helping the refugee monsters. Castle boards a dragon and replies that he is repaying a debt. As a bound, tortured Morbius watches, Robert Hellsgaard inserts the Bloodstone into his armor, increasing his power to a point that his humanity will soon be restored. Outside, Frank attacks the castle astride the dragon, killing many of Hellsgaard's forces, but the dragon is struck dead during the battle. Hellsgaard uses the Bloodstone to raise an army of undead soldiers and sets them against Castle, but he fights through them. The Special Force tries to kill Punisher with an artillery cannon, but that only lets the surviving undead in to kill them. As the Special Force falls victim to the undead and a mine trap set by Frank, Castle frees Morbius and Manphibian, but Hellsgaard subdues Punisher, then turns his flamethrower on the vigilante.
NOTE: Cover labeled "FrankenCastle." Includes recap/credits page (1 page). Frank's dream partially mirrors events in Pun #10, '09.

PUNISHER #16 (June 2010)

(untitled, 22 pages)

CREDITS: Rick Remender (writer), Tony Moore (art), Virtual Calligraphy's Joe Caramagna (letters), Dan Brown (colors), Sebastian Girner (editor), Axel Alonso (consulting editor), Mike McKone (c art), Morry Hollowell (c colors), David Taylor (variant c art)
FEATURE CHARACTER: Punisher (next in DpTU #894, '10, FC #17, '10)
GUEST STARS: Legion of Monsters: Manphibian (next in FC #17, '10), Morbius (next in ASM #622, '10)
VILLAINS: Robert Hellsgaard, Hunter of Monster Special Force (next in FC #17, '10, some die)
LOCATIONS/ITEMS: Hellsgaard's castle inc laboratory; limbo (Otherplace) / Punisher's synaptic glue pills, Hellsgaard's armor w/bola launcher, rotary cannon & chainsaw; Special Force's armor, harpoon-chain launchers & rifles; portal machinery

SYNOPSIS: As Manphibian awakens, Robert Hellsgaard and his soldiers bind Punisher with chains. Manphibian attacks, but Hellsgaard shoots Manphibian in the head as Frank watches. Hellsgaard activates his limbo portal then tosses Manphibian and Castle's pill bottle through it. By wrenching out the stitches holding his right shoulder together, Frank muscles himself free and goes through the portal, dragging Hellsgaard through with him using the chains used to bind him. As Morbius awakens and faces the remaining Special Force soldiers, Hellsgaard and Castle viciously beat one another, but Punisher is unable to gain the upper hand. Frank finds his pill bottle near Manphibian as Hellsgaard advances, but as Castle recovers Hellsgaard becomes uncertain and Punisher takes the opportunity to gain the upper hand. Manphibian, who survived the shot due to his alien anatomy, tears Hellsgaard out of his armor and prepares to kill him. Frank stops Manphibian, warning the alien against walking a path of revenge. Morbius arrives through the portal and retrieves Castle and Manphibian. The portal then closes, leaving Hellsgaard trapped in limbo once again.
NOTE: Cover labeled "FrankenCastle." Includes recap/credits page (1 page). Series title changes to "Franken-Castle" next issue. The story closes with a quote from psychiatrist Milton R. Sapirstein: "There is nobody as enslaved as the fanatic. The person in whom one impulse, one value, has assumed ascendancy over all others."

FRANKEN-CASTLE #17 (August 2010)

"Missing Pieces" (22 pages)

CREDITS: Rick Remender (writer), Roland Boschi (art), Virtual Calligraphy's Cory Petit (letters), Dan Brown (colors), Sebastian Girner (editor), Axel Alonso (consulting editor), Dale Eaglesham (variant c art)
FEATURE CHARACTER: Punisher (also as statue & in painting)
GUEST STARS: Legion of Monsters: Living Mummy (last in Pun #12, '10, next in FC #21, '10), Morbius (last in MZ4 #5, '10, next in FC #21, '10) (both also as statues & in painting), Manphibian (also in painting, last in Pun #16, '10, next in FC #21, '10)
SUPPORTING CAST: Henry Russo (last in Pun #15, '10)

VILLAINS: Tanya Adrian (assassin, 1st, next in Pun:ItB #1, '11, see NOTE), Jigsaw (Russo, last in NAv #61, '10, next in Pun:ItB #1, '11), Jigsaw (Clarke, last in PWJ #25, '09, next in Pun:ItB #1, '11) (both bts, sent Tanya, see NOTE), Hunter of Monster Special Force (last in Pun #16, '10), 3 Shaolin Scientist Squad members (Squad last in Pun #6, '09, die)

OTHER CHARACTERS: Googam (last in FFF #2, '08), refugee monsters inc Moloids, Captain America (see NOTE), newscaster, revelers (prev 3 on TV), Dracula, Hellstorm, Man-Thing, Satana, Werewolf (prev 5 as statues & in painting), Ghost Rider (in painting), Basilisk, Daken, Death Adder, Fly, Hood, Jigsaw, Lady Gorgon, Microchip (prev 8 in photos)

LOCATIONS/ITEMS: New York inc cemetery, Monster Metropolis w/Morbius' laboratory w/safe room, Punisher & Henry's hideout, central market & Hall of Monsters w/underground holding cells / Punisher's shotgun, motorcycle, gun, submachineguns, minigun, synaptic glue pills & life support equipment; Henry's computer workstation, Lady Gorgon's motorcycle & sniper rifle; Shaolin Scientist's shuriken, Bloodstone

SYNOPSIS: Unable to fully heal the injuries Punisher suffered at Robert Hellsgaard's hands, Morbius reluctantly implants the Bloodstone within the vigilante. A month later, Castle awakens in his lair, where Henry cautions him about overexertion and berates him for Frank's behavior towards Henry despite his genuine desire to aid Castle. Frank silences Henry by apologizing, then tells him line up work. While walking through Monster Metropolis, Manphibian asks Castle for advice regarding the Special Force soldiers they captured. Punisher hands Manphibian a gun and walks away, but Manphibian opts not to kill the soldiers. Frank travels to the cemetery where his family is buried to insure the reports that Microchip re-interred their remains were true. As Castle visits his family's gravesite, the Shaolin Scientist Squad attack him. Punisher kills two of them and interrogates the third, but a leather-clad woman kills the Squad member and escapes. Henry is unable to track her, and Frank returns to the tunnels. Henry tells Castle that evidence points to Lady Gorgon having set the trap to restore her standing with the Hand. Punisher makes her the first target of a hit list containing all of his recent enemies.

NOTE: Includes recap/credits page (1 page). Tanya is teased to be Maria Castle in Pun:ItB #1, '11, revealed to be working for the Jigsaws in Pun:ItB #3, '11 & named in Pun:ItB #4, '11. Captain America returned in Cap:Re #6, '10 and made his public return in Siege #3, '10. Henry listens to TSOL's "Abolish Government/Silent Majority" & is revealed to be a fan of 7 Seconds & Bad Brains here.

FRANKEN-CASTLE #18 (August 2010)

(untitled, 22 pages)

CREDITS: Rick Remender (writer), Jefté Palo (art), Virtual Calligraphy's Joe Caramagna (letters), Dan Brown (colors), Sebastian Girner (editor), Axel Alonso (consulting editor), Mike McKone (c art), Morry Hollowell (c colors)

FEATURE CHARACTER: Punisher (next in DW #88, '10)

SUPPORTING CAST: Henry Russo (next in DW #88, '10)

VILLAINS: Lady Gorgon (last in PWJ #21, '08, dies) & her ninjas (all die), Hand inc Kazu Yoshiokya (leader of the Hand's Kabukicho Clan)

OTHER CHARACTERS: Kenneth William Duncan (see NOTE), Mary Duncan (Duncan's wife), Christina Duncan (Duncan's daughter) (all in photos), Tokyo residents

LOCATIONS/ITEMS: Tokyo inc Lady Gorgon's building w/Gorgon's office & helipad, Hand's District w/ Yoshiokya's dojo; Punisher & Henry's Monster Metropolis hideout / Punisher's assault rifle, machete & motorcycle (destroyed); Hand ninja's bows, arrows, swords, & spears; Gorgon's ninja's swords, shuriken & spears; Gorgon's helicopter, Izanami-no-Mikoto (sword wielded by Hand founder and Yoshiokya's great-uncle Kagenobu Yoshiokya)

SYNOPSIS: In Tokyo, Lady Gorgon inspects a sword once used by the Hand's founder that she intends to present to clan leader Kazu Yoshiokya in order to regain the Hand's favor. One of her henchmen arrives with a letter addressed to her, containing photos and information on the vagrant she killed during her last encounter with the Punisher. The lights go out, and Gorgon uses the light-emitting jewel of the sword to see all of her men killed. She flees to the rooftop helipad, where she finds more of her men dead. Punisher appears and Gorgon dispatches more of her men against him. Frank kills them all, then throws Gorgon off the roof. Gorgon saves herself and lands on a car, then psychically compels the driver to drive into a group of pedestrians. Castle drives his motorcycle into the car, stopping it. Gorgon flees as Frank rescues the driver. She arrives at Kazu Yoshiokya's dojo, who tells her to kill Castle if she seeks reinstatement. Despite leading Frank into an ambush, Castle emerges victorious. Yoshiokya kills Gorgon for her failure as Punisher watches. Frank tells Henry to cross Gorgon off his list, then to call up his file on Daken.

NOTE: Includes recap/credits page (1 page), which states the story takes place before DD #505, '10. Kagenobu Yoshioka's last name is spelled "Yoshiokya" in this story, whereas it was spelled "Yoshioka" in his appearances in Elek:Hand #1-5, '05. Whether or not this is a modern re-spelling of the name, given the spelling of his great-nephew Kazu Yoshiokya's last name, is unclear. Lady Gorgon killed Duncan in PWJ #21, '08.

FRANKEN-CASTLE #19 (September 2010)

(untitled, 22 pages)

CREDITS: Rick Remender (writer), Tony Moore (art), Virtual Calligraphy's Joe Caramagna (letters), Dan Brown (colors), Sebastian Girner (editor), Axel Alonso (consulting editor), Simone Bianchi (c art), Simone Peruzzi (c colors)

FEATURE CHARACTER: Punisher (next in DW #89, '10)

GUEST STAR: Wolverine (last in W:O #50, '10, next in DW #89, '10)

SUPPORTING CAST: Henry Russo (between DW #88-89, '10)

VILLAIN: Daken (between DW #88-89, '10)

OTHER CHARACTERS: Commuters, subway driver

LOCATIONS/ITEMS: Tokyo inc subway tunnels, subway station & construction site; Punisher & Henry's Monster Metropolis hideout / Punisher's grenade, sniper rifle, synaptic glue pills, assault rifle & handgun; Henry's computer workstation, wrecked car, subway voltage rail, cargo cable, powered saw, sharpened pipes & rebar; Bloodstone

SYNOPSIS: Daken hunts Punisher through the subway tunnels but falls prey to a spike trap. While he is impaled on improvised spikes, Frank drops a live grenade into the pit, blowing Daken up. Castle attempts to snipe Daken as he crawls out, but Punisher's brain begins to lose cohesion before he can fire. As Daken falls victim to another trap wherein a wrecked car is swung into him, Henry Russo tries to convince Frank to swallow one of his pills and abort the mission. Castle refuses. Daken attacks Punisher and tries to get the Bloodstone out of the vigilante's chest. Frank mangles Daken's arm and hurls him into a train station. Daken makes another try for the Bloodstone, but Castle electrocutes Daken

with the track's voltage rail. Daken flees to a construction site in order to heal his injuries, but Frank catches up and kicks him into an array of rebar, impaling him again. Maddened by his injuries, Daken lunges for Castle, but Punisher shoves a power saw into his chest. Frank attempts to entomb Daken in a bed of concrete, but Wolverine, refusing to let Castle kill his son, appears and stabs Punisher from behind.
NOTE: Cover labeled "Chapter 2: Punishment." Includes recap/credits page (1 page). Story continued from DW #89, '10, where Punisher attacked Daken at a Tokyo restaurant and battled him in the subway tunnels, and continues in DW #89, '10. Story begins with a quote from John Milton: "He that studieth revenge keepeth his own wounds green, which otherwise would heal and do well."

FRANKEN-CASTLE #20 (November 2010)

(untitled, 22 pages)

CREDITS: Rick Remender (writer), Tony Moore (pgs 1, 7-9 & 12-22 art), Paco Diaz (pgs 2-6 art), John Lucas (pgs 10-11 art), Virtual Calligraphy's Cory Petit (letters), Dan Brown (colors), Sebastian Girner (editor), Axel Alonso (consulting editor), Simone Bianchi (c art), Simone Peruzzi (c colors)
FEATURE CHARACTER: Punisher
GUEST STAR: Wolverine (last in DW #89, '10, chr next in W #5/2, '11, next in W:RTH, '10)
SUPPORTING CAST: Henry Russo (last in DW #89, '10)
VILLAIN: Daken (between DW #89-90, '10)
OTHER CHARACTERS: Police (some die, see NOTE)
LOCATIONS/ITEMS: Tokyo; Punisher & Henry's hideout / Punisher's rifle & thermite grenade; police officers' Special Unit armor, riot shields, guns, Special Unit van & helicopters (one destroyed); dump truck, bus, downed power lines, Bloodstone
SYNOPSIS: Daken plants the Bloodstone into his chest, then attacks a responding Tokyo Special Unit team. Punisher runs Daken over with a dump truck and smashes him into a bus, but Daken survives and, empowered by the Bloodstone, handily defeats Frank and the Special Unit team. More police arrive and fire on Daken, who is shocked when fleshy tumors appear around the wounds. Wolverine arrives and recharges Castle with a downed power cable, then argues with Frank about whether Daken should be killed. Daken commandeers a police helicopter, but Castle and Wolverine attack the helicopter and force it to crash atop a building. Punisher shoves a thermite grenade into Daken's chest, which causes his enhanced healing factor to overcompensate and blanket the entire roof with excess flesh. Frank explains to Wolverine that he saw the Bloodstone overamplifying Daken's healing factor and decided to exploit that. Wolverine carves the Bloodstone out of Daken and reimplants it in Castle. Wolverine maintains his stance against killing Daken and promises to lock his son away, but Daken has cut himself free of his excess flesh and escaped. Punisher also vanishes, leaving Wolverine alone atop the building.
NOTE: Cover labeled "Chapter 4: Punishment." Includes recap/credits page (1 page). Story continued from DW #89, '10, where Wolverine stopped Punisher from killing Daken, and Daken cut out the Bloodstone from Punisher's chest. Depicted as SWAT, the police sent to stop Punisher and Daken are presumably one of the Japanese equivalent units - either kidotai (riot police), Tokyo's Special Investigation Team (SIT) or the counter-terrorist Special Unit (aka Special Assault Team/SAT).

FRANKEN-CASTLE #21 (November 2010)

(untitled, 22 pages)

CREDITS: Rick Remender (writer), Dan Brereton (painted art), Virtual Calligraphy's Joe Caramagna (letters), Sebastian Girner (editor), Axel Alonso (consulting editor)
FEATURE CHARACTER: Punisher (also in painting, next in FC #21/2, '10)
GUEST STARS: Elsa Bloodstone (monster hunter, Ulysses Bloodstone's daughter, last in Girl #2/5, '10, next in LoM #1, '11); Legion of Monsters: Living Mummy (last in FC #17, '10, next in ToT #1/4, '10), Man-Thing (last in DpTU #894, '10, next in Tb #144, '10) (both also as statues), Manphibian (last in FC #17, '10, next in LoM #1, '11), Morbius (last in FC #17, '10, next in ASM #642, '10), Werewolf (last in DpTU #894, '10, next in ToT #1/3, '10)
SUPPORTING CAST: Henry Russo (next in Pun:itB #1, '11)
OTHER CHARACTERS: Tricephalous, Vandoom's Monster (both last in JLA/Av #1, '03), Gigantus (last in Wlk&IW #7, '92), Fin Fang Foom (last in AoH #3, '10, next in AX #36, '11), Monster Island monsters (2 die, some as skeletal remains), Dracula, Ghost Rider, Hellstorm (prev 3 as statues)
LOCATIONS/ITEMS: Monster Island inc Punisher's cave; Monster Metropolis inc Hall of Monsters & Punisher & Henry's hideout / Punisher's boat, knife & gun; Henry's computer workstation, Elsa's rifles, Living Mummy's wrappings, Bloodstone
SYNOPSIS: Following his missions in Tokyo, Punisher lands his sailboat on Monster Island per Henry Russo's suggestion. Henry asks Frank to lay low and heal, then call for pickup once he is fully healed. Castle is unaware that the Legion of Monsters has decided to maroon Frank on Monster Island until the Bloodstone has finished healing him. Weeks pass, and Castle, fully restored to human form by the Bloodstone, has made himself a life on Monster Island by protecting the weaker monsters and hunting those who prey on them, but the Bloodstone begins to affect his mind. The Legion decides to retrieve Frank and the Bloodstone, and have enlisted the aid of Elsa Bloodstone to do so. Elsa and the Legion travel to Monster Island, but, despite the Legion's attempt to reason with Castle, the overzealous Elsa begins firing on Frank, causing Castle to believe the Legion has come to kill him. Frank fights Elsa and the Legion, who eventually convince Castle that the Bloodstone has blurred his sense of who deserves punishment. Frank tears the Bloodstone from his chest, drops it in front of them, and walks away.
NOTE: Includes recap/credits page (1 page).

2ND STORY: (untitled, 8 pages)
CREDITS: Rick Remender (writer), Andrea Mutti (art), Virtual Calligraphy's Joe Caramagna (letters), Luca Malisan (colors), Sebastian Girner (editor), Axel Alonso (consulting editor)
FEATURE CHARACTER: Punisher (next in Pun:ItB #1)
VILLAINS: Bumps, G-Dey (gangsters, both die) & their new recruits

OTHER CHARACTERS: Det. Sakai (police officer, mentioned, killed by Bumps), bystanders
LOCATIONS/ITEMS: Bushwick, NY inc G-Dey's apartment / Punisher's assault rifle & note, G-Dey's Glock handgun, Bumps' .357 Magnum handgun
SYNOPSIS: Gangsters Bumps and G-Dey go to G-Dey's apartment, discussing Bumps' recent murder of a police officer. G-Dey opens the door to find the Punisher waiting for them. The vigilante orders the pair to disarm themselves and sit, then identifies Bumps' weapon as the same caliber used to kill the officer. Punisher tells G-Dey he can leave if he kills Bumps, and G-Dey complies. Punisher then backs G-Dey against his window, orders him to string a note around his neck, then shoots him, forcing him to fall through the window onto a parked car. G-Dey and Bumps' fellow gangsters find G-Dey's body and Punisher's note: a picture of the Punisher insignia and the word "BACK."
NOTE: Series continues in Pun:ItB #1-5, '11.

PUNISHER: IN THE BLOOD #1 (January 2011)

"In The Blood Part One" (22 pages)

CREDITS: Rick Remender (writer), Roland Boschi (art), Virtual Calligraphy's Joe Caramagna (letters), Dan Brown (colors), Sebastian Girner (editor), Axel Alonso (exec editor), Francesco Mattina (c art)
FEATURE CHARACTER: Punisher (also in photos)
SUPPORTING CAST: Henry Russo (also off-panel in fb between Pun #9, '09 fb & Pun:ItB #5, '11 fb)
VILLAINS: Jigsaw (Russo, also in photos, also in fb between Pun #9, '09 fb & Pun:ItB #5, '11 fb), Jigsaw (Clarke) (both last bts in FC #17, '10), Tanya Adrian (last in FC #17, '10), Jaten (also in pfb, last in Pun #6, '09, dies), Microchip (also in photos, last in Pun #10, '09), 400 Temple prison inmates (die)
OTHER CHARACTERS: G.W. Bridge (corpse, last in Pun #10, '09), Sandy (last in Pun #9, '09 fb), Warden Jasta (Temple prison warden, voice only), Temple prison guards & staff, CNN reporter (on TV), Alphabet City residents (some as corpses), police (in pfb), Moloids, birds
LOCATIONS/ITEMS: The Temple (Maximum Security Prison, destroyed), Microchip's hideout, Alphabet City, Punisher's hideout, South Bronx inc Sandy's apartment / Punisher's broomstick, glider, knife, assault rifle, gun, machine guns & motorcycle; Henry's computers & 7-inch records; Tanya's gasoline & match; Microchip's computers, Russo's pistol
FLASHBACKS: Jaten is arrested (p). Jigsaw abuses a young Henry Russo.
SYNOPSIS: Punisher infiltrates Temple prison and interrogates Hood's henchman Jaten, who tells the vigilante where Microchip is. Punisher calls the prison warden and tells him he has time to evacuate the staff and guards but not enough to evacuate the prisoners. Punisher detonates his bomb, destroying the prison and killing the inmates, and escapes. Meanwhile, Microchip rants at G.W. Bridge's rotting corpse until Jigsaw abducts Microchip. Punisher returns to his hideout in time to see Henry open a birthday present. Henry tells Punisher that he's learned Jigsaw is still alive and Frank vows to kill him. Henry receives a phone call from his mother asking him to come over immediately. Henry believes she's asking for help with her alcoholism and tells Frank that he has to leave. Frank warns Henry he can't just leave whenever he wants, and tells Henry never to come back. At Microchip's hideout, Punisher finds a woman in leather burning the place. She taunts him and leaves. Henry arrives at his mother's apartment to find her drunk and two Jigsaws, Russo and Clarke, waiting for him.
NOTE: Includes recap page (1 page). Henry is a fan of Dead Kennedys & Circle Jerks, revealed here. Followed by BP #513, '11 preview (6 pages).

PUNISHER: IN THE BLOOD #2 (February 2011)

"In The Blood Part Two" (22 pages)

CREDITS: Rick Remender (writer), Roland Boschi (art), Virtual Calligraphy's Joe Caramagna (letters), Dan Brown (colors), Sebastian Girner (editor), Axel Alonso (exec editor), Nic Klein (c art)
FEATURE CHARACTER: Punisher (also in dfb)
SUPPORTING CAST: Henry Russo
VILLAINS: Jigsaw (Russo), Jigsaw (Clarke) & their henchmen, Tanya Adrian, Mirage (also as Venom, last in Pun #8, '10, dies), Microchip (next in Pun:ItB #4, '11), Tiny T & Louche (both drug manufacturers, die), Aryan Resistance members inc Aaron & his girlfriend; human traffickers (many as corpses), other criminals (1 in dfb, many die) inc dog-fight trainer, Hype dealer & Italian mobster
OTHER CHARACTERS: Sandy (next in Pun:ItB #4, '09), Microchip Jr. (in photo), Murio's patrons, sex shop manager, prostitutes, bystanders, dogs
LOCATIONS/ITEMS: Jigsaw's base inc Microchip's cell; New York inc dog fighting arena, human traffickers' base, Sex Shop & Tiny T & Louche's drug lab; South Bronx inc Sandy's apartment; Bushwick inc Murio's / Punisher's knife, Uzi, rocket launcher, grenade & shotgun; Tanya's gun & motorcycle; Henry's pistol, Tiny T & Louche's machine guns; Hype vial
FLASHBACK: Punisher interrogates a criminal for Microchip's location (d).
SYNOPSIS: Russo and Clarke tell Henry they know he works for the Punisher, but warn that Frank has turned against all of his partners and has turned now turned on Henry, and will be coming for him soon. Three days later, tortured at the thought of who the leather-clad woman is, Punisher continues to tear through the underworld, interrogating criminals as to the whereabouts of Microchip. The Jigsaws take Henry on a tour of their criminal base. Henry denounces the criminal enterprises, but Clarke shows Henry footage of Punisher rampaging through town and Russo says Punisher is hunting for Henry. Later, Clarke takes a meal to the captured Microchip and the two contrast their time as Frank's technical assistant. Clarke begins to tell Microchip what the Jigsaws' plan is for Punisher, but Russo stops him. Meanwhile, Punisher interrogates the super-villain Mirage and almost learns Microchip's location, but the burned leather-clad woman kills Mirage before Punisher's eyes. She teases Punisher that she's his dead wife Maria and flees.
NOTE: Includes recap/title/credits page (1 page).

PUNISHER: IN THE BLOOD #3 (March 2011)

(untitled, 22 pages)

CREDITS: Rick Remender (writer), Michele Bertilorenzi (art), Dan Brown (colors), Sebastian Girner (editor), Axel Alonso (exec editor), Jean-Sébastien Rossbach (c art)
FEATURE CHARACTER: Punisher (also in photo)
SUPPORTING CAST: Henry Russo
VILLAINS: Jigsaw (Russo), Jigsaw (Clarke) & their henchmen (several die), Tanya Adrian, Dimitri Sidorov (Russian mob boss, dies), Russian mobsters (several die), criminals (several die)
OTHER CHARACTERS: Maria Castle, Lisa Castle, Frank Castle Jr. (all in Punisher's hallucination), Russian sweatshop workers, aquarium fish, moth
LOCATIONS/ITEMS: Jigsaw's hideout, Punisher's hideout, New York inc Russian mob bar, slaughterhouse & sweatshop / Punisher's motorcycle, nun-chuck bomb, pistol & shotgun; Russian mobster's ax, baseball bats, chains, crowbar, golf putter, knife, pistol & sledgehammer; Russo's narcotics & needle; Clarke's switchblade, Jigsaw's henchmen's pistols, meat slicing machine, Captain America pinball machine
SYNOPSIS: Punisher continues his rampage through the criminal underworld, searching for Microchip and the woman he believes to be his resurrected wife. Meanwhile, the Jigsaws fool around with "Maria." Later, Punisher interrogates Russian mobsters, killing them until only the boss Dimitri Sidorov is left. Punisher pins Dimitri to a meat slicer and asks again for the location of the mystery man who has Microchip and his wife. Soon after, Punisher invades the Jigsaws' base. He kills several of the Jigsaws' henchmen before finding Henry Russo. Punisher believes that Henry wants revenge against him for his father and Henry believes that Frank is there to kill him. Henry sets off a booby-trap in the floor, electrocuting Punisher and knocking him unconscious. The Jigsaws arrive, taunt Punisher and announce the next part of their plan can now begin.
NOTE: Includes recap page (1 page). Only credits given are those on cover.

PUNISHER: IN THE BLOOD #4 (April 2011)

(untitled, 22 pages)

CREDITS: Rick Remender (writer), Roland Boschi (art), Virtual Calligraphy's Joe Caramagna (letters), Dan Brown (colors), Sebastian Girner (editor), Axel Alonso (exec editor), Jean-Sébastien Rossbach (c art)
FEATURE CHARACTER: Punisher
SUPPORTING CAST: Henry Russo
VILLAINS: Jigsaw (Russo), Jigsaw (Clarke, dies), Tanya Adrian (also in photos, dies), Microchip (dies)
LOCATIONS/ITEMS: Jigsaw's hideout inc Punisher & Microchip's cell / Punisher's steak knife & garrote; Russo's butterfly knife & pistol; Clarke's razor, Tanya's flamethrower
SYNOPSIS: In a prison cell inside the Jigsaws' base, Punisher watches in anger and disgust on a monitor screen as Russo and Clarke have sex with "Maria." Later, the Jigsaws taunt Punisher and open a wall in Punisher's cell, revealing a chained up Microchip on the other side, with a steak and a steak knife in between the two of them. As Microchip tries to reason with Punisher, Frank uses a hidden garrote to grab the steak and uses the knife to picks his locks. Punisher stands up and kills Microchip with the knife. Russo leaves Henry to meet with Clarke and the Jigsaws argue with each other. Henry hacks the computer system and frees Punisher, telling him the Jigsaws fooled them into acting against each other. Henry remotely guides Punisher through the compound, but Frank runs into "Maria." Punisher surrenders to the woman, but as she sets Punisher on fire, Henry finds her file and tells Punisher she's not really Maria but Tanya Adrian, an assassin Frank set on fire years ago. Clarke confronts Henry as Punisher kills Tanya. Russo arrives and kills Clarke for attacking Henry. Russo announces he needs a new partner, one with a jigsaw face.
NOTE: Includes credits page (1 page).

PUNISHER: IN THE BLOOD #5 (May 2011)

(untitled, 23 pages)

CREDITS: Rick Remender (writer), Roland Boschi (art), Virtual Calligraphy's Joe Caramagna (letters), Dan Brown (colors), Sebastian Girner (editor), Jean-Sébastien Rossbach (c art)
FEATURE CHARACTER: Punisher (next in IHulk #615/2, '10, ChW #4, '11, Sland #1 & 3, '10, Sland:SM #1, '10 fb, Sland #4-5, '10-11, HFH #4-5, '11, Pun #1, '11)
SUPPORTING CAST: Henry Russo (also in fb between off-panel in Pun:ItB #1, '11 fb & Pun #1, '09)
VILLAIN: Jigsaw (also in fb between Pun:ItB #1, '11 fb & bts in ASM #161, '76)
OTHER CHARACTER: Sandy (last in Pun:itB #2, '11)
LOCATIONS/ITEMS: Jigsaw's hideout, South Bronx inc Sandy's apartment / Punisher's grenade & steak knife; Henry's bike & record albums; Jigsaw's knife & pistol
FLASHBACK: A young Henry begs Jigsaw to stop beating him.
SYNOPSIS: Jigsaw begins to cut Henry, but can't bring himself to harm his son. Henry stabs Jigsaw and escapes, but his path is blocked by flames and he heads to the roof. Jigsaw recovers and confronts Henry, but Punisher arrives and interrupts. Jigsaw rants at Punisher for using his son Henry and prepares to shoot Punisher, but Henry stops him. Punisher attacks Jigsaw and bashes his face for using his memory of Maria against him. Jigsaw fights back until Punisher sets off a grenade between them. The blast weakens the roof and Henry falls through a hole, barely catching the side. Henry asks Jigsaw for help, but Russo decides to attack Punisher again instead. Henry pulls himself up and attacks Jigsaw, who falls through the hole. Henry tries to save Jigsaw, but Russo refuses and falls into the burning building. Punisher grabs Henry and jumps off the roof before the building explodes. Frank tells Henry to leave and never come back. Weeks later, Henry tells his now sober mother he has a job training abused women how to use computers. Henry thanks his mother for the birthday gift she sent, but she tells him she didn't know where he was, she couldn't have sent him anything. Henry realizes the gift was from Frank Castle.
NOTE: Includes recap/credits page (1 page).

PUNISHER #1 (September 2011)

"Punisher: One" (20 pages)

CREDITS: Greg Rucka (writer), Marco Checchetto (art), Virtual Calligraphy's Joe Caramagna (letters), Matt Hollingsworth (colors), Rachel Pinnelas (asst editor), Stephen Wacker (editor), Bryan Hitch (c pencils), Paul Neary (c inks), Paul Mounts (c colors)

FEATURE CHARACTER: Punisher

SUPPORTING CAST: Det. Walter Bolt (NYPD detective, 1st but chr last in Pun #1/2, '11), Det. Oscar "Ozzy" Clemons (NYPD detective, 1st but chr last in Pun #7, '12 fb), Sgt. Rachel Cole (Marine sergeant, becomes Mrs. Rachel Alves, also in photo, 1st)

VILLAINS: The Exchange (criminal organization, 1st, several die) inc Liam Malloy & Tommy (dies); Owl's henchmen (die)

OTHER CHARACTERS: Dr. Daniel Alves (Rachel's husband, also in photo, dies), Alves-Cole wedding guests (some also in photos, most die), Sway (weapons dealer, also in photo, corpse), police, subway passengers, prostitutes, Clemons' dog (1st, next in Pun #5, '12); Moon Knight (in photo)

LOCATIONS/ITEMS: New York inc Statue of Liberty, One Police Plaza, Chez Pinnelas & Punisher's safehouse; South Bronx, Gravesend, Brooklyn inc bar / Punisher's motorcycle, laptop, shotgun, machine gun, pistol & knife; Malloy's machine gun & pistol; Bolt's gun, Clemons' revolver, Exchange's machine guns, Owl's henchman's B&T MP9

SYNOPSIS: At Sgt. Rachel Cole and Dr. Daniel Alves' wedding, a firefight breaks out between Exchange agents and Owl's men. Owl's men are killed, but many wedding guests are caught in the crossfire and killed as well. Rachel is shot and passes out. Det. Oscar Clemons meets his new partner, Det. Walter Bolt, and they investigate the scene. Bolt thinks it was a gang hit, but Clemons realizes the killings were collateral damage. Later, Bolt receives a message and delivers all information he has regarding the wedding to Punisher. In the South Bronx, Clemons and Bolt look for weapons dealer Sway, hoping to learn who he's sold weapons to recently. They only find his corpse. In Gravesend, Brooklyn, the Exchange agents celebrate a successful attack on the Owl's men. The lights suddenly go out and Punisher kills everyone but the leader. Punisher lets the Exchange agent escape.

NOTE: Includes recap/credits page (1 page). Pun #2, '11 reveals Cole's rank, Clemons' nickname & Liam Malloy's name. Pun #5, '12 reveals the Exchange is comprised of former AIM, Hydra and Hive agents. Bolt notes himself as Detective First here, but Clemons notes Bolt as Detective Third in Pun #5, '12.

2ND STORY: "Interview, Ref: #110401-C" (8 pages)

CREDITS: Greg Rucka (writer), Marco Checchetto (art), Virtual Calligraphy's Joe Caramagna (letters), Matt Hollingsworth (colors), Rachel Pinnelas (asst editor), Stephen Wacker (editor)

FEATURE CHARACTER: Punisher (in fb between Girl #1/3, '10 & DRL:Pun, '09)

SUPPORTING CAST: Officer Walter Bolt (also in fb, 1st chr app, next in Pun #1, '11)

VILLAINS: Hernando Torres (drug runner) & his men, Newark gang members (all in fb, die)

OTHER CHARACTERS: Officer Scott Moffat (Bolt's police partner, dies), PS 137 students & teacher, tourists (all in fb), Det. Robert Seever (police interviewer)

LOCATIONS/ITEMS: New York inc Cloisters (in fb) & One Police Plaza interview room / Torres' machine gun & pistol; Bolt's gun, Moffat's gun, Newark gang's machine guns (all in fb)

FLASHBACK: Officers Bolt and Moffat are on routine surveillance of drug runner Hernando Torres, who meets with a Newark criminal gang at the Cloisters museum. Worried that touring students from PS 137 might be hurt from an impending scuffle, Bolt considers revealing himself as a police officer. Suddenly, Punisher arrives and pulls a fire alarm to evacuate the building. A firefight erupts between the criminals and Officer Moffat is killed in the crossfire. Losing his own gun, Punisher kills the gangsters with both Bolt's and Moffat's firearms.

SYNOPSIS: Det. Robert Seever interviews Bolt about Moffat's death. Bolt omits Punisher's presence from the events and takes credit for Punisher's actions. Impressed by "Bolt's" quick thinking and heroism, Seever is convinced that Bolt will be promoted to detective.

NOTE: Includes title/credits page (1 page). Pun #2, '11 reveals the location as the Cloisters and notes the flashback happened "last spring." Letters page changes its name to "Let's Be Frank" & has editorial by Stephen Wacker. Followed by Ults #1, '11 preview (6 pages).

PUNISHER #2 (October 2011)

(untitled, 20 pages)

CREDITS: Greg Rucka (writer), Marco Checchetto (art), Virtual Calligraphy's Joe Caramagna (letters), Matt Hollingsworth (colors), Rachel Pinnelas (asst editor), Stephen Wacker (editor), Bryan Hitch (c pencils), Paul Neary (c inks), Paul Mounts (c colors)

FEATURE CHARACTER: Punisher

SUPPORTING CAST: Rachel Alves, Det. Bolt, Det. Clemons

VILLAINS: The Exchange inc Stephanie Gerard (Exchange head, 1st), Christian Poulsen (Exchange division manager, 1st) (both next in Pun #5, '12), Dove (Exchange division manager, 1st), Liam Malloy (dies); Vulture (Jimmy Natale, mutated criminal, last in ASM #644, '10); Shark (South Bronx gang leader, dies) & his gang members (die)

OTHER CHARACTERS: Norah Winters (Daily Bugle reporter, last in Osborn #5, '11), prostitutes (some also in photos), Liam's Exchange agents (corpses), doctors, bystanders; Ben Urich (mentioned, keeps assigning Norah to TV assignments)
LOCATIONS/ITEMS: New York inc McClaine's Travel Tours, custom glass shop, Ozai Studio 1-hour photo studio & St. Vincent's Hospital w/ Rachel's room; Gravesend, Brooklyn; South Bronx inc 161st Street & Shark's club / Punisher's night vision goggles, sniper rifle, gun & car; Shark's "Pain" brass knuckles & revolver; Dove's shotgun, Norah's notebook
SYNOPSIS: Exchange agent Liam Malloy runs for his life, unaware Punisher is following him. Liam looks for asylum but everyone turns him down. Meanwhile, Exchange agents Stephanie and Christian, realizing that Liam will lead Punisher straight to them and the Exchange, hire the Vulture to take care of their problem. The next day, Detectives Bolt and Clemons investigate the crime scene in Gravesend, Brooklyn where Norah Winters meets them. Clemons refuses to answer her questions, but tells her that if she wants to keep reporting and not be on TV anymore, she should cut her hair extremely short. Bolt learns that Rachel Cole has regained consciousness. Liam tries to lay low in Shark's club, but Shark throws him out. Punisher attacks and kills Shark and his gang. At St. Vincent's Hospital, Clemons and Bolt attempt to question Rachel Cole. She corrects them; her name is Rachel Alves, and remembers that her entire family was killed. She flies into an uncontrollable panic and doctors sedate her. Punisher follows Malloy to 161st St. and watches as Dove kills Malloy for his failures. She reveals they know Punisher is present as the Vulture attacks the vigilante.
NOTE: Includes recap/credits page (1 page). Pun #5, '12 reveals Gerard & Poulsen's surnames. Pun #8, '12 reveals Poulsen is a former SHIELD agent.

PUNISHER #3 (November 2011)

(untitled, 20 pages)

CREDITS: Greg Rucka (writer), Marco Checchetto (art), Virtual Calligraphy's Joe Caramagna (letters), Matt Hollingsworth (colors), Rachel Pinnelas (asst editor), Stephen Wacker (editor), Bryan Hitch (c pencils), Paul Neary (c inks), Paul Mounts (c colors)
FEATURE CHARACTER: Punisher
SUPPORTING CAST: Rachel Alves, Det. Bolt, Det. Clemons
VILLAINS: The Exchange inc Dove (next in Pun #5, '12); Vulture (dies)
OTHER CHARACTERS: Liam Malloy (corpse), Norah Winters, Hair by Alonso stylist, doctor, nurse, bystanders
LOCATIONS/ITEMS: New York inc Hair by Alonso & St. Vincent's Hospital w/Rachel's room; South Bronx inc 161st Street / Punisher's gun & knife; Dove's shotgun, Exchange's machine guns, Bolt's gun, Clemons' revolver
SYNOPSIS: Vulture attacks Punisher. Doves yells for Vulture to stop playing with Punisher and to just kill him. Vulture grabs Punisher and flies into the sky. At St. Vincent's Hospital, Rachel Alves regains consciousness. In the sky, Punisher stabs Vulture. Det. Bolt and Det. Clemons respond to shots fired at 161st Street and find Liam Malloy's corpse. Vulture vomits acid on Punisher, but the vigilante continues to fight. Norah Winters gets a haircut, but leaves before the stylist can finish when she learns Punisher is fighting the Vulture in midair. Vulture claws at Punisher's eye and Punisher stabs Vulture in the heart. As Bolt and Clemons rush to follow Punisher, Vulture lands on a building and Punisher lands in a dumpster.
NOTE: Includes recap/credits page (1 page).

2ND STORY: "Periphery" (8 pages)
NOTE: Reprinted from A Moment of Silence, '02.

PUNISHER #4 (December 2011)

(untitled, 20 pages)

CREDITS: Greg Rucka (writer), Marco Checchetto (art), Virtual Calligraphy's Joe Caramagna (letters), Matt Hollingsworth (colors), Rachel Pinnelas (asst editor), Stephen Wacker (editor), Bryan Hitch (c pencils), Paul Neary (c inks), Paul Mounts (c colors)
FEATURE CHARACTER: Punisher (also as Frank Castle in Norah's thoughts, also in pfb; next in SI:NYC #1, '11)
SUPPORTING CAST: Rachel Alves (also as Sgt. Cole in Norah's thoughts), Det. Bolt, Det. Clemons
VILLAINS: Gang members (all die)
OTHER CHARACTERS: Vulture (corpse), Ben Urich (last in Osborn #5, '11, next in Fear:SM #1, '11), Carlie Cooper (forensic pathologist, last in ASM #661, '11, next in ASM #663, '11), Norah Winters (also in pfb, next in Fear:SM #1, '11), Lion's Head Pub waiter & patrons, gang victim, police, bystanders; Maria Castle, Lisa Castle, Frank Castle Jr., Marines, criminals (prev 5 in Norah's thoughts), Spider-Man (on poster)
LOCATIONS/ITEMS: New York inc Punisher's safehouse (in pfb), Lion's Head Pub, 150th Street Animal Hospital & St. Vincent's Hospital w/ Rachel's room; Norah's apartment, South Bronx / Punisher's gun, M60, assault rifles, machine guns, grenades, rocket launcher (all in pfb) & gun (also in pfb); gang member's revolver, Norah's notebook
FLASHBACK: Norah Winters finds Punisher in a dumpster and takes him to the vigilante's safehouse (p).
SYNOPSIS: Norah Winters attempts to write a story on the Punisher, but takes a break to meet Ben Urich at the Lion's Head Pub. He's disappointed in her haircut and says he can't put her on TV anymore. She asks him for advice in a story she's writing. He tells her that not every truth is a story, some stories only serve to help the writer and not the public, and some stories don't need to be told. Punisher bandages himself and abandons his safe house. In the South Bronx, Carlie Cooper processes the Vulture's remains and Clemons learns Punisher survived the fight. Meanwhile, Punisher has broken into the 150th Street Animal Hospital to use their supplies to suture his wounds, but is interrupted by an attempted murder outside. Punisher kills the gang members and has the victim help him stitch his wounds. Norah meets with Rachel Alves and begins writing her story on Rachel. Clemons finds Norah at the Lion's Head Pub and reveals he knows she helped Punisher, but she refuses to answer his questions. Punisher leaves the Animal Hospital money to cover the medical supplies he used.
NOTE: Includes recap/credits page (1 page). Clemons calls Bolt "Clem" here.

PUNISHER #5 (January 2012)

(untitled, 21 pages)

CREDITS: Greg Rucka (writer), Marco Checchetto (art), Virtual Calligraphy's Joe Caramagna (letters), Matt Hollingsworth (colors), Ellie Pyle, Rachel Pinnelas (asst editors), Stephen Wacker (editor)
FEATURE CHARACTER: Punisher
SUPPORTING CAST: Det. Bolt, Det. Clemons (both next in Pun #7, '12), Rachel Alves
VILLAINS: The Exchange inc Stephanie Gerard (next in Pun #8, '12), Christian Poulsen (both last in Pun #2, '11), Dove (last in Pun #3, '11)
OTHER CHARACTERS: Norah Winters (last in SI:DF #1, '11), Carlie Cooper (bts, processing crime scene, last in ASM #675, '12), Mr. Creel (Exchange division manager, corpse) & his 4 operatives (corpses), Hope (Det. Bolt's girlfriend), her parents & guests, Rachel's physical therapist, rehabilitation center patrons, Lion's Head Pub bartender & patrons, police, child, Clemons' dog (last in Pun #1, '11)
LOCATIONS/ITEMS: New York inc Lion Head's Pub, rehabilitation center & Midas Building w/meeting room & Gerard's office; Far Rockaway, Queens inc Punisher's hideout; Creel estate / Punisher's gun, Clemons' revolver, Rachel's gun, Norah's notebook, police shotguns
SYNOPSIS: In Far Rockaway, a child finds a shack, unaware Punisher is using it for a hideout. Meanwhile, police storm the Creel estate only to find Creel and his associates dead inside. Det. Clemons tells Det. Bolt he thinks Punisher is responsible. Elsewhere, Rachel Alves finishes a physical therapy session and grabs her gun. At the Midas Building, Stephanie Gerard heads an Exchange meeting, tells the group Creel and his division managers were killed by Punisher, assigns Dove to take over Creel's responsibilities and tells Christian Poulsen to take care of Punisher. The child talks with Punisher, assuming him to be a soldier on a mission. Rachel meets Norah Winters at the Lion's Head Pub for drinks and sneaks a look at Norah's notebook. Bolt calls Clemons to wish him a happy Thanksgiving and receives a request of information from Punisher. While Punisher is out, the child brings pie for Thanksgiving and discovers he's the Punisher. The child leaves in disgust.
NOTE: Includes recap/credits page (1 page). Variant cover is an homage to NM #87, '90. Followed by Av:XSanc

#1, '12 preview (6 pages).

PUNISHER #6 (February 2012)

"The Exchange" (20 pages)

CREDITS: Greg Rucka (writer), Matthew Southworth, Matthew Clark (art), Virtual Calligraphy's Joe Caramagna (letters), Matt Hollingsworth (colors), Ellie Pyle (asst editor), Stephen Wacker (editor), Bryan Hitch (c pencils), Paul Neary (c inks), Paul Mounts (c colors)
FEATURE CHARACTER: Punisher (next in Pun #8, '12)
SUPPORTING CAST: Rachel Alves (also as bellman, next in Pun #8, '12)
VILLAINS: The Exchange inc Christian Poulsen (bts, called meeting, next in Pun #8, '12), Mr. Dawson (Exchange division manager, dies), other managers (die) & guards (die) inc Alec & Reggie (both die)
OTHER CHARACTERS: Norah Winters, Mundi (Exchange division manager, corpse),Restaurant Mosaic patrons & staff, ski resort patrons & staff inc bellmen, Doberman pinschers, Daredevil, Bruiser (both in photo)
LOCATIONS/ITEMS: Brooklyn inc Restaurant Mosaic; Greenwich Village inc Norah's apartment; North Creek, NY inc Hudson River Valley & ski resort w/chalet & Dawson's lodge / Punisher's guns, Battle Van, shotguns, assault rifles, knife, grenades, Ketamine, sausages, female canine urine & silencer; Exchange guard's guns & shotguns; Norah's notebook, Rachel's machine pistol w/silencer
SYNOPSIS: Punisher learns of an upcoming Exchange meeting from a dead Exchange division manager's phone. Elsewhere, Rachel Alves learns of an Exchange agent's license plate number from Norah Winters' notebook. In North Creek, NY, Punisher prepares for an assault on the Exchange meeting. Meanwhile, Rachel follows the Exchange agent's car to a ski resort in North Creek. Exchange guards patrol the Hudson River Valley surrounding the ski resort. Rachel pays a bellman for his uniform. The guards' Doberman pinschers are distracted by sausages. Rachel brings Exchange division manager Dawson his luggage. The Doberman pinschers fall asleep. Rachel kills Dawson by crushing his trachea. Punisher attacks the Exchange guards. Rachel prepares to attack the Exchange meeting. More Exchange guards respond to the passed-out Dobermans. Rachel shoots out the ski resort lights. Punisher kills more guards. Rachel attacks the Exchange meeting. Punisher hears gunfire in the ski resort and breaks in. Rachel steps over dead Exchange division managers and confront the arriving Punisher.
NOTE: Includes recap page (1 page). Dawson's license plate number is L99 2BW.

PUNISHER #7 (March 2012)

"The String" (20 pages)

CREDITS: Greg Rucka (writer), Michael Lark (pencils, c art), Stefano Gaudiano (inks), Virtual Calligraphy's Joe Caramagna (letters), Matt Hollingsworth (colors), Ellie Pyle (asst editor), Stephen Wacker (editor), Brian Thies (special thanks)
FEATURE CHARACTER: Punisher (in fb1 during Pun #10, '88 & DD #257, '88)
GUEST STAR: Daredevil (in fb1 during Pun #10, '88 & DD #257, '88, in fb2 between DD #257-258, '88)
SUPPORTING CAST: Det. Clemons (also in fb1-2 to 1st chr app before Pun #1, '11), Det. Bolt (both last in Pun #5, '12)
VILLAIN: Alfred Coppersmith (in fb1 during Pun #10, '88 & DD #257, '88, in fb2 after DD #257, '88, dies off-panel)
OTHER CHARACTERS: Caitlin Leigh (Clemons' previous partner, in fb1-2), Cindy (Coppersmith's neighbor, in fb1 after Pun #10, '88), police (others in fb) inc Captain Rangel & Sheriff Kyle Schmidt, the Exchange managers & guards (corpses), Punisher's

victims (in photos), Carlie Cooper (mentioned, possibly seeing Bolt romantically)

LOCATIONS/ITEMS: New York (also in fb) inc Coppersmith's apartment building, police holding cell (both in fb), George Washington Bridge & One Police Plaza w/Clemons' office; Diner, North Creek, NY inc ski resort / Punisher's gun, Daredevil's billy club, Coppersmith's gun, Clemons' revolver (all in fb) & knife (also in fb); Exchange guard's assault rifle

FLASHBACKS: Det. Clemons and his partner Caitlin Leigh investigate Alfred Coppersmith, who killed four people by poisoning aspirin, in anger for losing his job to automated machinery. They find Punisher and Daredevil battling over Coppersmith; Daredevil wants Coppersmith arrested and Punisher wants to kill Coppersmith. Punisher escapes and Daredevil leaves Coppersmith for the police. Clemons retrieves Punisher's knife from Coppersmith's apartment (1). Matthew Murdock, Coppersmith's lawyer, has convinced Coppersmith to enter a plea (2).

SYNOPSIS: Det. Clemons studies the pattern of Punisher's killings until Captain Rangel tells him to investigate a multiple homicide at an upstate ski resort. Det. Bolt drives and is surprised when Clemons mentions a possible relationship between Bolt and Carlie Cooper. Bolt asks Clemons why he wants to arrest Punisher when the vigilante is doing the police's work for them. Clemons tells Bolt about Alfred Coppersmith, but his case was thrown out and Coppersmith went free when Coppersmith withdrew his plea; the Coppersmith evidence was tainted by Punisher's presence, raising the possibility that Punisher planted evidence. Coppersmith was found dead in his apartment the next day. At the ski resort, Clemons tells Bolt he knows Bolt has been passing information to the Punisher and tells Bolt to stop it. While investigating the ski resort crime scene, Clemons notices a discarded bellman uniform and realizes there was another person involved in the killing. Clemons announces that Punisher has a partner.

NOTE: Includes recap page (1 page). Clemons notes that Punisher has killed 41 criminals since the Alves-Cole wedding (Pun #1, '11).

PUNISHER #8 (April 2012)

(untitled, 20 pages)

CREDITS: Greg Rucka (writer), Marco Checchetto (art), Joe Caramagna (letters), Matt Hollingsworth (colors), Ellie Pyle (asst editor), Stephen Wacker (editor)

FEATURE CHARACTER: Punisher

SUPPORTING CAST: Rachel Alves (also in photo, last in Pun #6, '12), Det. Bolt, Det. Clemons

VILLAINS: The Exchange: Stephanie Gerard (last in Pun #5, '12), Christian Poulsen (last bts in Pun #6, '12)

OTHER CHARACTERS: The Exchange managers & guards (all corpses), 727 Varick security guards; Dr. Robert Alves (photo), Ms. Daughtry (Exchange division manager, mentioned, all Exchange deposits now sent to her)

LOCATIONS/ITEMS: Hudson River Valley inc ski resort; Astoria, Queens inc U-Store-It complex w/abandoned SHIELD facility; New York inc Punisher's gas station safehouse, 727 Varick, 19th floor, Suite A & 728 Varick / Punisher's gun, assault rifle, bow, telescope, car & van; Rachel's machine pistol w/silencer & shotgun; Christian's gun, Nick Fury breath sample & security drones; Stephanie's wrist blaster, Exchange laptop computers, Stark repulsor battery

SYNOPSIS: In the ski resort, surrounded by Exchange manager corpses, Punisher and Rachel Alves confront each other. They separately take the managers' laptop computers. Punisher tells Rachel to stay out of his way and leaves. In Astoria, Queens, Stephanie Gerard meets Christian Poulsen and chastises him for his managers being killed by Punisher. Christian tells her the managers were bait for Punisher; if Punisher didn't kill someone the vigilante would have known he was walking into a trap. Christian leads Stephanie into an abandoned SHIELD facility, where Stephanie gives Christian one more week to kill Punisher. Frank Castle uses the acquired laptop to learn an Exchange address. Meanwhile, detectives Clemons and Bolt question Rachel about a possible partnership between her and Punisher. Later, Punisher stakes out the Exchange address as Rachel breaks in. Christian, thinking Rachel is Punisher, attacks Rachel with remote controlled security drones. As he taunts "Punisher," Punisher steps out of the shadows and approaches Christian from behind.

NOTE: Includes recap/credits page (1 page). Christian's authorization code is "Indigo, Two-Two-Nine, Victor, Eight-Six, Delta."

PUNISHER #9 (May 2012)

(untitled, 20 pages)

CREDITS: Greg Rucka (writer), Mirko Colak (art), Virtual Calligraphy's Joe Caramagna (letters), Matt Hollingsworth (colors), Ellie Pyle (asst editor), Stephen Wacker (editor)Bryan Hitch (c pencils), Paul Neary (c inks), Paul Mounts (c colors)

FEATURE CHARACTER: Punisher

SUPPORTING CAST: Rachel Alves, Det. Bolt, Det. Clemons

VILLAINS: Black Spectre (criminal organization, last in DD #6, '12, some die), Christian Poulsen

OTHER CHARACTERS: Daredevil (mentioned, has Omega Drive, see NOTE); police, bystanders

LOCATIONS/ITEMS: New York inc 727 Varick, 19th floor, Suite A & 728 Varick; Long Island city inc 24-Hour Diner / Punisher's gun, knife, first aid kit & Battle Van; Rachel's machine pistol w/silencer & SR 25 rifle w/Acog sight; Poulsen's security drones, combustion nullification field & water micron stream gun; Black Spectre helicopter & guns, Omega Drive (mentioned, Fantastic Four communication device)

SYNOPSIS: Christian Poulsen realizes that the "Punisher" he's taunting is actually a woman. Punisher announces his presence and fires his gun at Christian, but the gun misfires. Poulsen reveals he has a SHIELD-issue combustion nullification field, and guns won't work around him. Christian shoots Punisher with a micron stream of water that cuts Punisher's arm. Across the street, Rachel Alves sees a helicopter approaching. Punisher stabs Poulsen and the room explodes. Black Spectre agents abduct Christian and tell him Daredevil has the Omega Drive. As the Black Spectre agents get Poulsen aboard their helicopter, Punisher attacks them. Rachel shoots the agents from across the street, leaving one alive. Punisher interrogates the survivor about the Omega Drive. Twenty minutes later, detectives Bolt and Clemons arrive at the scene, not noticing Rachel getting into Punisher's van. Later at a diner, Rachel introduces herself to Punisher. Impressed, Punisher takes Rachel on as an apprentice and partner.

NOTE: Includes recap/credits page (1 page). Daredevil acquired the Omega Drive in DD #6, '12. Story continued in "The Omega Effect" crossover between AvSM #6, '12, Pun #10, '12 & DD #11, '12.

PUNISHER SUMMER SPECIAL #1 (August 1991)

"Bombs 'R' Us" (20 pages)

CREDITS: Pat Mills, Tony Skinner (writers), Val Mayerik (pencils), Armando Gil (inks), Pat Brosseau (letters), Ed Lazellari (colors), Kevin Kobasic (designer, managing editor), Don Daley (editor), Roderick Delgado (c pencils), Micheal Bair (c inks)
FEATURE CHARACTER: Punisher (last in Dlk #7, '92)
VILLAINS: Colonel de Sade (war veteran & killer, 1st) & his men (die), Joe Toto (mobster, dies), & his men (die)
OTHER CHARACTERS: Covert and International Security Exhibition exhibitors, security guards & attendees inc Senor Bellini; Midcity Bank patrons, employees & security; police, bystanders, Toto's guard dogs
LOCATIONS/ITEMS: Toto Estate, exhibit center, New York inc Midcity Bank, Herb's Plants & de Sade's warehouse / Punisher's micro-locator chip, rocket launcher, fake ID, MSRG Excalibur Anti-Riot gun, motorcycle & credit card knife; de Sade's leg irons, barbed wire projector, straightjacket, OS gas grenade launcher, knife, revolver & riot tank w/turret gun, electrified hull, low friction plastic confetti & electrified water jet; de Sade's men's assault rifles, bank security's revolvers, police revolvers, exhibitors' electro-shock batons, photic driver, SAP gloves, nunchakus & angled batons
SYNOPSIS: Punisher waits until mobster Joe Toto eats dinner, then fires a rocket which homes in on the locator chip hidden in Toto's food, blowing him up. Later, Punisher goes to the Covert & International Security Exhibition to buy some new weapons. He runs into Colonel de Sade, who he knows from the war and doesn't trust. Punisher follows de Sade for four days until de Sade robs a bank and tortures its patrons. Punisher attacks de Sade as the robber escapes, but Punisher is quickly overpowered. Punisher wakes up in de Sade's warehouse when de Sade begins torturing him. Punisher breaks free and kills de Sade's men. Punisher traps de Sade in barbed wire and sets him on fire. Punisher leaves as the police approach.
NOTE: Includes interior covers by Jimmy Palmiotti, table of contents/credits page (1 page) by Darren Auck & back cover pin-up by Roderick Delgado. Logo & story title designs by Juan Martinez.

2ND **STORY:** "Crossed Purposes" (10 pages)
CREDITS: Peter David (writer), Mark Texeira (pencils), Micheal Bair (inks), Phil Felix (letters), Greg Wright (colors), Kevin Kobasic (managing editor), Don Daley (editor)
FEATURE CHARACTER: Punisher (also as "Frank Knight," next in 4th story)
VILLAINS: Simon Bartlett (mobster) & his men inc Lonni (all die), Joel Bartlett (Simon's son, mobster) & his men (1 dies)
OTHER CHARACTERS: Joel's wife, son & daughter, Aldo's Ristorante waitresses
LOCATIONS/ITEMS: New York inc Aldo's Ristorante (destroyed); Bartlett estate / Punisher's Super Redhawk .44, ash broom & broken bottle; Joel's men's rocket launcher, revolver & Uzi; Lonni's fire poker
SYNOPSIS: At Aldo's Ristorante, Punisher plans to kill mobster Simon Bartlett, but Simon's son Joel beats Punisher to it when Joel's men fire a rocket into the restaurant. Having excused himself before the explosion, Joel returns to drag Punisher out of the wreckage and takes the vigilante to his home, where Joel introduces his wife and children to Punisher. Simon's bodyguard Lonni, injured in the explosion, arrives and attacks the vigilante. Punisher kills Lonni and spares Joel, telling the mobster to change his business practices.
NOTE: Punisher makes his War Journal Entry #974 here. Followed by Pun #53-59, '91 preview (2 pages).

3RD **STORY:** "Independence Day" (8 pages)
CREDITS: Dan Slott (writer), Mike Harris (pencils), Jimmy Palmiotti (inks), Bill Oakley (letters), Joe Rosas (colors), Kevin Kobasic (managing editor), Don Daley (editor)
FEATURE CHARACTER: Punisher (also on wanted poster, chr next in PWJ #48, '92 fb, next in PWJ #37, '91)
VILLAINS: Ray Hammond (killer, also on wanted poster, dies), other criminals
OTHER CHARACTERS: Detective McIntyre (widower) & his wife (in photo), other police officers, Don Daley (on wanted poster)
LOCATIONS/ITEMS: New York inc police station & factory / McIntyre's gun, Hammond's knife & severed finger
SYNOPSIS: July 4: The recently widowed Detective McIntyre searches for Ray Hammond, his wife's killer, eventually finding him at a factory. They fight and Ray eventually overpowers McIntyre. Punisher arrives and Ray runs off. July 8: McIntyre receives a package marked "D.O.A." from the Punisher; inside is Ray's finger.
NOTE: Followed by Punisher/Nick Fury: Rules of the Game GN preview (2 pages); advertised as by Greg Wright (co-writer) & Jim Lee (co-writer & art) at 64 pages with a late '91 release date.

4TH **STORY:** "Wish Granted" (5 pages)
CREDITS: Will Murray (writer), Rodney Ramos (art), Pat Brosseau (letters), Santiago Oliveras (colors), Kevin Kobasic (managing editor), Don Daley (editor)
FEATURE CHARACTER: Punisher (next in 3rd story)
VILLAINS: Adbul, Rafik, Shaboof (terrorists from Bombadad, die)
OTHER CHARACTERS: Wizzyland patrons (some die), staff (some die) inc Marvin Mouse actor (dies) & security guard (dies); Federal Express deliveryman (dies), bus driver (voice only), bystanders
LOCATIONS/ITEMS: New York inc terrorists' dorm room, Wizzyland amusement park / Punisher's Uzis, terrorists' Uzis, Wizzyland security guard's gun
SYNOPSIS: June 18: Bombadad terrorists Abdul, Rafik and Shaboof plan to attack America on Flag Day, America's biggest holiday. They're not worried because American police can't kill them and American prisons are comfortable. They take the bus to Wizzyland and kill a Federal Express deliveryman on the way, mistaking him for a Federal employee. At Wizzyland, they kill patrons and employees. A security guards warns them to stop shooting, but they kill the security guard. Punisher kills the terrorists.

PUNISHER SUMMER SPECIAL #2 (August 1992)

"Rough Cut" (34 pages)

CREDITS: Pat Mills (writer), Mike McKone (pencils), Mark McKenna (inks), Mick Gray (background inks), Richard Starkings (letters), Kevin Tinsley (colors), Tim Tuohy, Kevin Kobasic (managing editors), Don Daley (editor), Simon Bisley (c art)
FEATURE CHARACTER: Punisher (also in rfb; last in PWZ #11, '93)
VILLAINS: Colonel de Sade (also in rfb, pfb & dfb) & his men inc Dee; Alison (de Sade's assistant) (all die)
OTHER CHARACTERS: Center for Urban Survival members inc Gus; Severalls security guard (dies), police (in pfb), models inc Majorette Sindy (in dfb, dies), Sheryl Majors, Sherry Brown & Lulu Flynn; bystanders; Midcity Bank patron (in rfb)
LOCATIONS/ITEMS: Severalls Maximum Security Hospital, New York inc Center for Urban Survival, Punisher's safehouse, de Sade's studio & fuel storage warehouse / Punisher's Tanto knife, throwing knives, ATC Kukri sword, Buck Titanium folding knife, revolver, Battle Van, binoculars, chains & Uzi; de Sade's Atemi whips, cameras, van, gun, train, grain silo, fork lift, shipping crate, knife (in dfb) & barbed wire projector (in rfb); de Sade's men's guns, bottle & baseball bat; Gus' knife, Severalls guard's gun, police fire extinguisher (in pfb)
FLASHBACKS: Colonel de Sade tortures a bank patron. Punisher traps de Sade in barbed wire and sets the killer on fire (PunSS #1, '91). Police rescue de Sade (p). De Sade records a message for Punisher and films himself murdering Majorette Sindy (d).
SYNOPSIS: De Sade films himself murdering a Severalls Maximum Security Hospital security guard. At the Center for Urban Survival, a sparring session gets out of hand when Punisher almost kills Gus. Punisher takes a shower, then gets a video message from Colonel De Sade. Punisher finds de Sade's studio, where de Sade's assistant Alison is recruiting models for de Sade's future movies. Punisher kills de Sade's men and shows the models de Sade's video. The models attack Alison, but Punisher stops the models and lets Alison escape. Punisher follows Alison to de Sade's warehouse, where de Sade prepares to kill Alison in his next movie because she didn't recruit any new models. Punisher kills de Sade's men, battles de Sade and saves models from various death-traps. De Sade threatens to kill Alison; Punisher lets him and blows up de Sade.
NOTE: Includes interior covers by Jimmy Palmiotti, table of contents/credits page (1 page) w/art taken from page 8, panel 6 & back cover pin-up by Chris Sprouse (pencils) & Joe Rubinstein (inks). De Sade refers to the movies "Citizen Kane," "Raging Bull" and the "Rocky" series, and quotes from "White Heat."

2ND STORY: "High Risk" (4 pages)
CREDITS: Chuck Dixon (writer), Flint Henry (pencils), Terry Austin (inks), Dave Sharpe (letters), Marie Javins (colors), Tim Tuohy, Kevin Kobasic (managing editors), Don Daley (editor)
FEATURE CHARACTER: Punisher (also as "Mr. Villa")
VILLAINS: Bloods (street gang, die)
OTHER CHARACTER: Hudson Varney (insurance salesman)
LOCATIONS/ITEMS: Compton, Los Angeles, CA inc Punisher's rented house / Punisher's guns, shotgun & grenades; Bloods' Uzis
SYNOPSIS: Hudson Varney, insurance salesman, tries to sell Punisher health insurance during a firefight between Punisher and the street gang, Bloods. Realizing that Punisher's line of work will disqualify him from health coverage, Hudson offers Punisher some homeowner's insurance.

3RD STORY: "The Local" (8 pages)
CREDITS: Chuck Dixon (writer), John Hinklenton (art), Steve Dutro (letters), Ed Lazellari (colors), Tim Tuohy, Kevin Kobasic (managing editors), Don Daley (editor)
FEATURE CHARACTER: Punisher (next in MK #35-37, '92, Pun #63, '92)
VILLAINS: Thugs (die)
OTHER CHARACTERS: Subway commuters (some die)
LOCATIONS/ITEMS: New York subway / Punisher's gun, commuter's gun, thug's gun
SYNOPSIS: On the subway, thugs harass an elderly couple. The woman shoots and kills two thugs, Punisher kills the rest.
NOTE: Followed by PWJ #50, '93 preview (1 page).

PUNISHER SUMMER SPECIAL #3 (August 1993)

"Dead Man Coming Through" (26 pages)

CREDITS: Pat Mills, Tony Skinner (writers), Tony Harris (pencils), Wade von Grawbadger (inks), Richard Starkings (letters), Matt Hollingsworth (colors), Tim Tuohy (asst editor), Don Daley (editor), Brian Stelfreeze (c art)
FEATURE CHARACTER: Punisher (last in Pun #80, '93)
VILLAINS: Surprise Boys (murderous paintball team) inc Earl Dreller (real estate agent), Ripley & Vasquez; Boff Johnson (refurbishes weapons) (all die)
OTHER CHARACTERS: Bodybaggers (paintball team, 2 die) inc Darryl (dies) & Ripper; college student (paintball enthusiast, dies) & his 4 friends (college students, bts, killed), 2 paintball game marshals (corpses), Killing Fields owner
LOCATIONS/ITEMS: New York inc Boff's workspace w/spiked floor, Paintball Wizard Amusement Park & Killing Fields paintball arena / Punisher's MP5 & paintball gun; Surprise Boys' converted paintball guns w/ball bearings & Napalm; Boff's Uzi, crossbow, revolver & files; Bodybaggers' paintball guns, Earl's riot gun, college student's paintball gun
SYNOPSIS: Paintball team the Surprise Boys kills their opponents with ball bearings loaded into their paint guns instead of paintballs. Punisher reads about the killings in the paper and interrogates Boff Johnson, someone capable of converting the paint guns. Boff fails to kill Punisher and dies. Punisher goes through Boff's files and learns Boff converted paint guns for Earl Dreller, a real estate agent. At the Killing Fields paintball

arena, the Surprise Boys begin killing their opponents, Bodybaggers. Punisher intervenes, but Bodybaggers leader Ripper doesn't believe the Surprise Boys are murderous until Napalm is fired at him. Teaming up with Punisher, Ripper attacks the Surprise Boys with Punisher's gun while Punisher attacks with his bare hands. Punisher grabs the Napalm paintball gun and kills all the Surprise Boys but Earl. Earl throws a tantrum, complaining that the police, FBI, CIA and Marines wouldn't take him. Punisher kills Earl with his own converted paintball gun and leaves.
NOTE: Includes interior covers by Jimmy Palmiotti, table of contents/credits page (1 page) w/art taken from page 6, panel 6 & back cover pin-up by Brian Stelfreeze.

2ND STORY: "Faster, Faster" (14 pages)
CREDITS: Chuck Dixon (writer), Joe Phillips (art), Phil Felix (letters), Kevin Tinsley, Ericka Moran (colors), Tim Tuohy (asst editor), Don Daley (editor)
FEATURE CHARACTER: Punisher
SUPPORTING CAST: Microchip (bts, converted Punisher's station wagon, last in PWJ #56, '93, next in PWZ #17, '93)
VILLAINS: Mickey Fondozzi (child pornographer, dies), carjackers (die)
OTHER CHARACTERS: Woman & her daughter, bystanders
LOCATIONS/ITEMS: Long Island / Punisher's converted station wagon & gun; Mickey's portfolio, carjacker's Uzi, daughter's Polly doll
SYNOPSIS: Punisher kills child pornographer Mickey Fondozzi. As Punisher drives away, he sees a group steal a woman's car; her daughter yells that Polly is still in the car. Punisher follows the carjackers, engaging them in a firefight and eventually running them off the road. Punisher learns that Polly is only a doll and not a baby, and kills the carjackers.
NOTE: The Mickey Fondozzi appearing here should not be confused with former member of the Carbone crime family Mickey Fondozzi.

3RD STORY: "Idyll" (6 pages)
CREDITS: Steven Grant (writer), Brian Stelfreeze (pencils), Joel Thomas (inks), Ed Lazellari (colors), Tim Tuohy (asst editor), Don Daley (editor)
FEATURE CHARACTER: Frank Castle (also in pfb; next in PWZ #17, '93)
VILLAINS: 2 bank robbers (also in pfb, die)
OTHER CHARACTERS: National Bank Southeast security guard (dies), patrons (some die) & tellers (all in pfb)
LOCATIONS/ITEMS: National Bank Southeast, airport (both in pfb), ocean / Punisher's motorcycle & Uzi (both in pfb) & glider; bank robbers' guns, plane (both in pfb), scarf (also in pfb), boat & knife
FLASHBACK: A man and woman rob a bank, gleefully killing the guard and patrons. Frank Castle follows them but they escape in a plane. The woman leaves her scarf behind as a calling card (p).
SYNOPSIS: In a hang glider over the ocean, Frank Castle catches up to the bank robbers' boat. Frank jumps into the boat and knocks the pair into the ocean. Castle kills the man, but the woman stabs Frank. The woman surfaces only to be killed by her boat. Castle returns her scarf and swims away.
NOTE: Story is silent w/no dialogue or sound effects. Followed by Punisher Gallery pin-up page (1 page) featuring Punisher & woman by Wade von Grawbadger.

PUNISHER SUMMER SPECIAL #4 (July 1994)

"Soiled Legacy" (26 pages)

CREDITS: Don Lomax (writer), Alberto Saichann (art), Steve Dutro (letters), John Kalisz & Comicolor (colors), Freddy Mendez (asst editor), Don Daley (editor), John Romita, Jr. (c pencils), Klaus Janson (c inks), John Cebollero (c colors)
FEATURE CHARACTER: Punisher (last in Pun #92, '94)
SUPPORTING CAST: Microchip (bts, organized passage to Kenya, last in Pun #90, '94)
VILLAINS: Warlord (dies) & his poachers (some die), smugglers (some die)
OTHER CHARACTERS: Kito Tamri (Tasvo Wildlife Reserve Conservation agent), Kenyans, bystanders, zebra (corpse), elephants (some as corpses), alligator, birds, cat, lions, oxen, rats, rhino, snake, vultures
LOCATIONS/ITEMS: New York inc harbor & smuggler's warehouse/security office; Kenya / Punisher's cleats, Uzi, guns, knives, shotgun, grenades, rented plane & jeep; smugglers' Uzis, assault rifles & Liberian freighter; poachers' jeep w/mounted machine guns; warlord's assault rifle, elephant tusks, Bengal tiger pelts, giant panda pelts, gorilla skins
SYNOPSIS: Punisher sneaks aboard a docked freighter and kills several smugglers. Inside the ship, Punisher sees someone else, Kito Tamri, is already confronting the smugglers. Punisher watches as Kito defeats some smugglers, and intervenes when reinforcements arrive. Punisher kills the attackers, but leaves one alive for interrogation. Kito asks the smuggler who ordered the smuggled shipment of endangered animal pelts. When the smuggler refuses to answer Kito's questions, Punisher kills the smuggler. Microchip arranges passage to Kenya for Punisher and Kito. Kito explains that poachers are killing animals for pelts and tusks, driving certain species into extinction. Punisher and Kito find a warlord and his poachers and attack. The poachers are killed in a firefight, but the warlord runs away. Punisher follows the warlord into the jungle, where a rhino kills the warlord. Punisher wishes Kito luck and returns to New York.
NOTE: Includes interior covers by Jimmy Palmiotti, table of contents/credits page (1 page) w/art taken from page 23, panel 3 & back cover pin-up by Greg Luzniak (pencils), Dan Panosian (inks) & John Cebollero (colors). Followed by Punisher Armory pin-up (1 page) by Eliot R. Brown (writer, art) & John Wellington (colors) featuring 2 Colt Cobalt Commanders w/ammunition: 1 standard Full Metal Jacket, 2 Remington 45 ACP in +P power, 2 Federal ACP Match, 2 Federal Premium 45 ACP & 1 Remington Shot Cartridge in .45.

2ND STORY: "Killing an Afternoon" (19 pages)
CREDITS: Chuck Dixon (writer), Greg Luzniak (pencils), Matt Banning (inks), Jim Novak (letters), John Kalisz & Comicolor (colors), Freddy Mendez (asst editor), Don Daley (editor)
FEATURE CHARACTER: Frank Castle (also as "Ted Bishop," next in PWZ Ann #2, '94)
SUPPORTING CAST: Microchip (next in PWZ Ann #2/2, '94), Mickey Fondozzi (last in Pun #86, '94, next in PWJ #62, '94)
VILLAINS: Jimmy Flynn (Tommy Flynn's brother, see NOTE), Danny, Willy (Jimmy's men, both die), Phat (gangster, dies) & his men (die)

OTHER CHARACTERS: Minh's Pizza employee, dentist, Vanni (dentist's patient) & his mother, bystanders
LOCATIONS/ITEMS: New York inc dentist's office, Minh's Pizza w/Phat's hideout / dentist's Nitrous Oxide, bone chisel, elevator, retractor, vertical condenser, drill, scalpel & Novocaine; Microchip's converted Mercedes w/tear gas & explosives; Phat's revolver, Phat's men's assault rifle & guns; Jimmy's gun, Danny's gun, Willy's gun, Spider-Man t-shirt
SYNOPSIS: Frank Castle goes to the dentist to have an abscessed tooth removed. Jimmy Flynn, upset over his brother's death, attacks the dentist and knocks out Frank with Nitrous Oxide. Meanwhile, Mickey Fondozzi calls Microchip asking for Frank to meet at Minh's Pizza. Jimmy tortures Castle with the dentist's tools. At Minh's Pizza, Phat and his gangsters ambush Microchip. Mickey says he owes Phat money and was hoping Frank could help him. Microchip tells the gangsters the money is in the trunk of his car. Frank bits Jimmy's finger and steals a scalpel when Jimmy is distracted by customers. Microchip and Mickey escapes when Microchip's car shoots gas at Phat and his men. Castle kills Jimmy's men and knocks out Jimmy. Microchip's car explodes, killing the gangsters. Frank tells Jimmy he didn't kill his brother and shoots out Jimmy's knee caps. Microchip picks up Castle, who isn't happy to see the Mercedes has been destroyed.
NOTE: Tommy Flynn died in PWJ #42, '92; Jimmy blames Punisher for Tommy's death, Punisher was present but Kim Rhee killed Tommy. Followed by preview (1 page) for PWJ #65-69, PWZ #26-30, Pun #89-92, PWZ #31-36, Pun #94-95 & PWJ #70-75, all '94.

PUNISHER BACK TO SCHOOL SPECIAL #1 (November 1992)

"The Sinner" (4 pages)

CREDITS: Chuck Dixon (writer), Mark Nelson (art), Willie Schubert (letters), Greg Wright (colors), Tim Tuohy (asst editor), Don Daley (editor), Bill Sienkiewicz (c art), George Roussos (c colors)
FEATURE CHARACTER: Punisher (also in own thoughts, last in Dhold #5, '93)
OTHER CHARACTERS: Maria Castle, Lisa Castle, Frank Castle, Jr., Bruno Costa, Klosky, Skinner (all in rfb), Jigsaw, criminals (both in Punisher's thoughts), cemetery grave diggers
LOCATIONS/ITEMS: Central Park (in rfb), cemetery / Punisher's roses, grave diggers' shovel & crane
FLASHBACK: The Castle family is killed in Central Park (MP #2, '75 fb).
SYNOPSIS: Punisher visits his family's grave and places a rose on their tombstone. He wants to be with them, but can't be until his work is finished.
NOTE: Includes table of contents/credits page (1 page). Story preceded by pin-up (1 page) by Shawn McManus featuring Punisher.

2ND STORY: "Mott Haven 10454" (33 pages)
CREDITS: Chuck Dixon (writer), Walter McDaniel (pencils), J.J. Birch, Kevin Kobasic, Greg Luzniak (inks), Ken Lopez (letters), Kevin Tinsley (colors), Tim Tuohy (asst editor), Don Daley (editor)
FEATURE CHARACTER: Punisher (also as "Frank Bergen")
VILLAINS: Parnell (gun supplier, dies) & his men (die), janitor (gun dealer, dies), Tino (dies) & his friends (steroid-using students, some die), 3 teenage thieves (die), bullies (1 dies)
OTHER CHARACTERS: Henry James High School students inc Chester (dies), Angelo & Nicky; Sal's Gas Station employee & patron, basketball coach, teacher, Angelo's mother & 2 brothers
LOCATIONS/ITEMS: Brooklyn inc Sal's Gas Station, Punisher's apartment, Angelo's home & Henry James High School w/gym, coach's office, cafeteria, bathroom, locker room, showers & library / Punisher's shotgun, Uzi, knife & books; thieves' revolvers & shotgun; Parnell's Sig Sauer & money; Angelo & Chester's revolver, Tino's revolver, Tino's friends' steroids, thug's Uzis, janitor's revolver
SYNOPSIS: Punisher kills some teenagers trying to rob a gas station. At Henry James High School, students Chester and Angelo are excited about the gun they just bought. Punisher poses as an assistant basketball coach to discover where the guns are coming from. He makes an example out of the back-talking Tino by making him do push-ups so the other students listen to him. Later, some bullies try to steal Chester's jacket, and Angelo shoots the bullies. Punisher attacks Parnell, a gun supplier, who denies selling guns to kids. Punisher kills Parnell. Chester asks Angelo for the gun, but Angelo refuses to give it up. As Punisher interrogates students in the bathroom, bullies try to make Angelo give up his seat in the cafeteria. Angelo refuses, and Angelo and the bullies shoot at each other. The bullies and Chester are killed. Later, Tino and his friends attack Punisher in the locker room. Punisher fights them off, killing some, only for the janitor, the school's gun supplier, to attack. Punisher kills the janitor.

3RD STORY: "Child's Play" (10 pages)
CREDITS: Tom Brevoort, Mike Kanterovich (writers), Alex Morrissey (pencils), Jeff Albrecht (inks), Richard Starkings (letters), Kevin Tinsley (colors), Tim Tuohy (asst editor), Don Daley (editor)
FEATURE CHARACTER: Punisher
VILLAINS: Gangsters (die)
OTHER CHARACTERS: Alfred (young Punisher fan) & his mother, Barney, Yaz (both Al's friends), Guy Luigi (station manager), Les (reporter) (both on TV), policeman, cat; Don Daley (on "Tome" magazine cover, noted as man of the year), Spider-Man, Vulture (both in photo), Mrs. Wynorski (mentioned, Al's teacher)
LOCATIONS/ITEMS: New York inc a park & Al's home w/his bedroom / Punisher's Uzi, gun & blaster; gangsters' guns, revolver, assault rifle & grenade; Barney & Yaz's toy guns
SYNOPSIS: Al, a Punisher fan, watches TV while his mother runs errands. His friends Barney and Yaz arrive and they play in the park; Al as Punisher and the others as criminals. A policeman tells them to stop fooling around and Al heads for home. On his way, he happens across a gun fight between Punisher and some criminals. Punisher kills the criminals, but a loose grenade almost kills Al. The boy goes home shaken, and doesn't cheer up until his mother brings him a newspaper with a Spider-Man story.
NOTE: Al is watching "Lug Nuts" on TV featuring truck drivers Guido & Ernesto. The news notes that Punisher killed 37 criminals this week, including the ones appearing here.

4TH STORY: "Back to School" (6 pages)
CREDITS: Barry Dutter (writer), John Ridgway (art), Phil Felix (letters), Ed Lazellari (colors), Tim Tuohy (asst editor), Don Daley (editor)
FEATURE CHARACTER: Punisher (next in Pun #73, '92)
VILLAINS: Mr. Asintra (mobster) & his men (all die)
OTHER CHARACTERS: Tommy, Bruce (school kids), other students, bystanders, Joey Scirroco (mentioned, works for Mr. Asintra)
LOCATIONS/ITEMS: New York inc school & Asintra's apartment / Punisher's Uzi & Battle Van; Asintra's man's gun
SYNOPSIS: Tommy and Bruce skip school so they can start working for mobster Mr. Asintra. Asintra gives them twenty dollars each to run drugs, but the Punisher arrives and kills Asintra and his men. Punisher threatens to kill Tommy and Bruce for working for mobsters, but they give Punisher their pay and swear to go back to school. The kids sneak back into school and wonder if the Punisher was serious about watching them, then see him outside.

PUNISHER BACK TO SCHOOL SPECIAL #2 (October 1993)

"No Pain" (26 pages)

CREDITS: Mike Lackey (writer), Ernie Stiner (pencils), Frank Percy (inks), Richard Starkings (letters), Joe Andreani (colors), Tim Tuohy (asst editor), Don Daley (editor), Bill Sienkiewicz (c art)
FEATURE CHARACTER: Punisher (also in pfb, last in Pun Ann #6/3, '93)
SUPPORTING CAST: Microchip (last in PWJ #57, '93, last bts in PWJ #59, '93, next in Pun #83, '93)
VILLAINS: Razor Emmanuel (Razor's Gym owner & steroid dealer, dies) & his employees inc Atlas, Herk, Tisa (prev 3 die) & Vince; Dr. Robert Motz (Razor's partner)
OTHER CHARACTERS: Razor's Gym patrons inc Eric (policeman), criminal (corpse, in pfb), Dr. Motz's patients, bystander
LOCATIONS/ITEMS: Punisher's safehouse, Motz home, Hell's Kitchen inc Razor's Gym / Punisher's Uzi (in pfb), assault rifle, gun, lock picks & thermite; steroids (also in pfb) inc Zap & Bangers and Mash; Microchip's computer, Atlas' shotgun, Herk's shotgun, Razor's razors
FLASHBACK: Punisher finds steroids on a dead criminal (p).
SYNOPSIS: Frank Castle works out at Razor's Gym to learn who the local steroid supplier is. Vince, a gym employee, suddenly flies into a rage and attacks Frank. Castle knocks Vince out. Razor Emmanuel, the gym's owner, is impressed and hires Frank. Later, Microchip explains to Punisher how steroids are bad for people. Castle shows up for work at the gym. Atlas, Herk and Tisa train him how to sell steroids, and he's surprised to learn some police officers use steroids. That night, Punisher attacks Dr. Motz, the doctor who supplies to steroids to Razor's Gym, and scare shim into setting up a free clinic for steroid users. Punisher returns to the gym to destroy Razor's steroid supply, but Atlas and Herk catch him. Punisher kills them and battles Tisa. After drowning Tisa in the sauna, Punisher kills Razor with his own razors. Punisher checks on Dr. Motz, and threatens to kill the doctor if he stops helping people for free.
NOTE: Includes table of contents/credits page (1 page).

2ND STORY: "Stage Fright" (8 pages)
CREDITS: Mike Lackey (writer), Kevin Kobasic (pencils), Joe Rubenstein (inks), Dave Sharpe (letters), Kevin Tinsley (colors), Tim Tuohy (asst editor), Don Daley (editor)
FEATURE CHARACTER: Punisher (also as WARG performer)
VILLAINS: WARG (murderous heavy metal band, die) inc Spew (lead singer, dies)
OTHER CHARACTERS: WARG fans & victims
LOCATIONS/ITEMS: New York inc stadium / Punisher's knife & motorcycle; WARG's instruments, cage, swords, Uzi, axe & guillotine
SYNOPSIS: Punisher sneaks backstage to a WARG concert. He's heard the band's violent stage show is real; they don't use special effects, they actually murder people on stage. He verifies WARG kills people, disguises himself as a band member, and kills WARG on stage. When Punisher kills the lead singer, he's disappointed to learn WARG lip-synchs.

3RD STORY: "Lost Lands" (9 pages)
CREDITS: Chuck Dixon (writer), Dave Eaglesham (pencils), Pat Redding (inks), Steve Dutro (letters), Christie Scheele (colors), Tim Tuohy (asst editor), Don Daley (editor)
FEATURE CHARACTER: Punisher
VILLAINS: Smiler & his homeless army inc Fuzz (dies) & Billy; drug dealer (dies)
LOCATIONS/ITEMS: New York / Punisher's gun & knife; Smiler's knife, Fuzz's revolver, homeless army's bats, chains & pipes
SYNOPSIS: A drug dealer stumbles across an army of homeless people. Smiler, the army's leader, orders Billy to kill the stranger. Billy can't bring himself to do it, so Fuzz kills the dealer instead. Punisher arrives and verifies the dealer he was chasing is now dead. Smiler order Fuzz to kill Punisher, but the vigilante easily kills the homeless man. Punisher challenges Smiler's authority, and Smiler is too cowardly to stand up to the vigilante. Punisher leaves as the homeless army turns on and attacks Smiler. Billy asks Punisher to save them; Punisher tells Billy to save himself.
NOTE: Followed by Punisher Gallery pin-up (1 page) by David Cullen (pencils), Jon Holdredge (inks) & John Kalisz (colors) featuring Punisher and 4 thugs in the swamp.

4TH STORY: "Sorry, My Mistake" (8 pages)
CREDITS: Dan Slott (writer), Neil Hansen (art), Richard Starkings (letters), Kevin Tinsley (colors), Tim Tuohy (asst editor), Don Daley (editor)
FEATURE CHARACTER: Frank Castle (next in Pun #82, '93)

VILLAINS: Corrupt policemen inc Barnes (paid by mob), Galan (steals narcotics from evidence locker) & Marsh (uses excessive force on minority suspects); criminals (1 dies)
OTHER CHARACTERS: Policemen inc Dunphy, Sarge & Washington
LOCATIONS/ITEMS: New York inc police station / Punisher's concealed gun & car; Washington's revolver, policeman's revolver
SYNOPSIS: At a police station, Frank Castle identifies a murderer from a police lineup, then shoots the man. He battles his way out of the station through corrupt cops, and apologizes to the one honest officer he punches. Once outside, a policeman tries to arrest Frank for illegally parking. When the policeman realizes Frank is legally parked, the officer apologizes, "Sorry. My mistake" and lets Frank go.
NOTE: Followed by Punisher Gallery (2 pages) by Alex Morrissey (pencils), Jon Holdredge (inks) & Sue McTiegue (colors); 1st pin-up features Punisher jumping off a plane's wings at 2 assassins, 2nd pin-up features Punisher and 2 thugs in the sewer.

PUNISHER BACK TO SCHOOL SPECIAL #3 (October 1994)

"Brain Drain High" (25 pages)

CREDITS: Don Lomax (writer, co-inks), Dave Hoover (pencils, co-inks, c art), Jade Moede (letters), Mike Thomas (colors), Freddy Mendez (asst editor), Don Daley (editor)
FEATURE CHARACTER: Punisher (also as gorilla in hallucination, also as Frank Castle in fb between Pun:OM #1, '93 & PunTheNam, '94 fb; last in PWZ Ann #2/3, '94)
VILLAINS: Mr. Mohr (school principal & drug boss, dies), drug dealers (some also students, some die), North Vietnamese Army (in fb, die), drug supplier
OTHER CHARACTERS: Sheila Stump (head of school cafeteria), U.S. Marines (in fb, also as monsters in hallucination) inc Junior; students inc Cindy & Gary; corpses (some as skeletal remains, in fb), cafeteria workers, paramedics, homeless man
LOCATIONS/ITEMS: Laos (in fb), New York inc warehouse & high school w/cafeteria & bell tower / NVA guns & assault rifle; U.S. Marines' assault rifles, Castle's assault rifle (all in fb), Punisher's machine guns, explosives & confiscated guns; drug dealers' Uzi, guns, assault rifles & car; Mohr's shotgun, student's Spider-Man t-shirt
FLASHBACKS: In Laos, Castle and his unit are confused when North Vietnamese soldiers suddenly run around screaming, shooting into the air. Castle finds the enemy soldiers' hideout to find they killed themselves. They restock their water supply and move on. Later, Castle hallucinates. He makes himself calm down and stops fellow Marine Junior from killing himself. The hallucinations eventually wear off.
SYNOPSIS: Punisher poses as a high school cafeteria worker to discover who is selling drugs in school. While he's there, he confiscates guns from students. Suddenly, students start freaking out; the food has been drugged. Punisher follows one student and stops him from killing himself. Sheila Stump, cafeteria head, tells Punisher which students drugged the food. Punisher follows the students until they meet with their supplier. Punisher kills the students, breaks the supplier's hands and forces the supplier to take him to his boss. Punisher is surprised to see the drug boss is the school principal, and kills the principal.
NOTE: Includes table of contents/credits page (1 page).

2ND STORY: "Ahead of the Game" (22 pages)
CREDITS: Don Lomax (writer, inks), Paul Martin (pencils), Jade Moede (letters), Ashley Posella (colors), Freddy Mendez (asst editor), Don Daley (editor)
FEATURE CHARACTER: Punisher
SUPPORTING CAST: Microchip (last in PWZ Ann #2/2, '94, next in PWZ #31, '94)
VILLAINS: Flames inc Sabah (Larry, leader), Headhunters (both street gangs), Cosgrove, Pinker, Snyde (prev 3 lawyers, die), Victor Lu (assassin, dies, corpse also as Punisher)
OTHER CHARACTERS: Sgt. Teel ("Ol' Sarge," retired private investigator), Mi Teel (Teel's wife), 12 severed heads, decapitated corpse, Steadfast Delivery employee, construction workers, bystanders inc lynch mob
LOCATIONS/ITEMS: New York inc Punisher's safehouse, Cosgrove, Pinker & Snyde's law offices, Little Malaysia inc Teel's apartment & construction site / Punisher's machine pistols, knife & guns; Cosgrove, Pinker & Snyde's Uzi, shotgun & assault rifle; bystanders' clubs & bats; Microchip's computer, Teel's gun, Sabah's shotgun, Flames' guns, Headhunters' guns, Victor's machete
SYNOPSIS: In Little Malaysia, Punisher investigates a serial killer who beheads his victims. Ol' Sarge confronts Punisher, thinking the vigilante is responsible for the killings. Before Punisher can explain his position, a lynch mob attacks them both. Ol' Sarge is knocked out and Punisher escapes with Ol' Sarge. At his apartment, the retired Sgt. Teel explains to Punisher that two local gangs, the Flames and the Headhunters, are blaming each other for the killings, but he thinks a single killer is responsible. Hysteria is making people move out of town. Punisher asks how people can afford to move, and Teel reveals three lawyers are buying property from the fleeing families. Teel arranges a meeting where both gangs deny responsibility. Later, Microchip investigates the lawyers and discovers they're making payments to a known assassin, Victor Lu, two days before each killing. Punisher kills Lu and sends the severed heads to the lawyers. The lawyers meet Punisher at a construction site and Punisher kills them.

3RD STORY: "The Lesson" (6 pages)
CREDITS: Mike Lackey (writer), Aaron Guzman (co-plot, pencils), Chip Wallace (inks), Michael Higgins (letters), Ashley Posella (colors), Freddy Mendez (asst editor), Don Daley (editor)
FEATURE CHARACTER: Punisher (in pfb, also as homeless man, next in Pun #93, '94)
VILLAINS: Dee Dee Ray Walker (paralyzed gang member, also in pfb) & his gang inc 2E Chill, Johnnie Greene (both die), 'Berto, Bunche-Man, Sergio & Thomas (prev 6 in pfb)
OTHER CHARACTERS: Students, teacher, bystanders (in pfb)
LOCATIONS/ITEMS: New York (also in pfb) inc train station (in pfb) & school / Punisher's gun, 2E Chill's knife, Bunche-Man's bat (all in pfb), Dee Dee Ray Walker's wheelchair
FLASHBACK: Dee Dee Ray and his gang attack a homeless man for fun. The homeless man fights back, revealing himself as the Punisher. Punisher kills some of the gang members as others escape. Dee Dee Ray Walker is left behind and Punisher shoots him, leaving Dee Dee for dead (p).
SYNOPSIS: Dee Dee Ray Walker, now a paraplegic, speaks to students about staying in school.

PUNISHER HOLIDAY SPECIAL #1 (January 1993)

"Red Christmas" (32 pages)

CREDITS: Steven Grant (writer), John Herbert (pencils), Rod Ramos (inks), Kenny Lopez (letters), John Kalisz (colors), Tim Tuohy (asst editor), Don Daley (editor), Bill Wylie (c pencils), Steve Geiger (c inks)
FEATURE CHARACTER: Punisher (also as bust, last in Pun #75/3, '93, next in MHol, '92/4, PWZ #37, '95, PWZ #12, '93)
VILLAINS: Little Tony Caruso (mobster & Big Tony's son) & his men, Rudy Kessler (Little Tony's business manager & Pleasant Valley mall owner, dies) & his mall security guards (many die) inc Cody, Martz & Tully (prev 3 die); drug dealer
OTHER CHARACTERS: Sandy Welck (teenage runaway), Stuart Welck (Sandy's father), Mrs. Welck (Sandy's mother), Salvation Army Santa Claus, 2 concerned citizens, Pleasant Valley mall shoppers, police, Big Tony Caruso (Little Tony's father, in photo & Little Tony's thoughts, mentioned, killed by Punisher)
LOCATIONS/ITEMS: Welck home, Caruso estate inc dining room & Little Tony's bedroom; New York inc Pleasant Valley Mall w/Rod's Pizza, Tower Records, Bob's Glasses kiosk, Tom's Pets, Liquor & Wines, Hardware by Hayner, McClane Shoes, Allison Jewelers & arcade / Punisher's Uzi, knife, gun, matches, grenades & binoculars; mall security's tear gas, shotgun & guns; mall Christmas tree w/ornaments, Santa Claus & reindeer display & display car (destroyed); Martz's power saw
SYNOPSIS: Big Tony Caruso has been killed by the Punisher, so Little Tony Caruso orders his business manager Rudy Kessler to have the Punisher killed. Elsewhere, Punisher stops two concerned citizens from killing a drug dealer. The dealer tells Punisher that Little Tony Caruso is planning to rob Pleasant Valley Mall on Christmas Eve; Punisher spares the dealer's life. Punisher sneaks into the place Christmas time at closing time, unaware Kessler and his security guards are watching. When no one robs the place Punisher realizes he's walked into a trap. Punisher attacks the security guards and blows up a display car and hides. Punisher runs into Sandy Welck, a teenage runaway, who shows the vigilante how to move through the mall's crawl spaces. Punisher systematically kills the security guards, but Kessler takes Sandy hostage. Punisher kills Rudy, and the next day delivers Kessler's head to Little Tony as a Christmas present. Meanwhile, Sandy returns home and has her father arrested.
NOTE: Cover is foil enhanced.

2ND STORY: "Armed Salvation" (8 pages)
CREDITS: Eric Fein (writer), J.J. Birch (art), Jim Novak (letters), Christie Scheele (colors), Tim Tuohy (asst editor), Don Daley (editor)
FEATURE CHARACTER: Punisher (last in Cage #4, '92, next in MHol, '91/3, PWJ #38, '92 fb)
VILLAINS: "King" Louie Bonetti (mobster, bts, ordered Bailey killed) & his men (die) inc Frankie, Freddie & Nickie (prev 3 die)
OTHER CHARACTERS: John Bailey (in witness protection for testifying against King Louie), Eileen Bailey (John's wife), Jason Bailey (John's son), Caitlin Bailey (John's daughter), Murphy (Jason's dog)
LOCATIONS/ITEMS: Lube, ME inc Bailey home / Punisher's binoculars, Battle Van, garrote & knives; King Louie's men's van, assault rifle & guns w/silencers
SYNOPSIS: King Louie Bonetti's men prepare to kill John Bailey for testifying against Bonetti. While preparing for Christmas dinner, Jason doesn't understand why his father John made the family move away from his friends. Knowing the witness protection program won't protect the Bailey family, Punisher kills Bonetti's men, but one escapes. The mobster attempts to kill Jason, but Punisher kills the mobster first. Punisher explains to Jason he should be proud of his father for standing up for what's right. Jason tells his father he loves him.

PUNISHER HOLIDAY SPECIAL #2 (January 1994)

"The Killing Season!" (16 pages)

CREDITS: George Caragonne (plot), Eric Fein (script), J.J. Birch (art), Steve Dutro (letters), Joe Andreani (colors), Don Daley (editor), Bill Sienkiewicz (c art)
FEATURE CHARACTER: Punisher (also as Santa Claus, also as Lt. Castle in fb1 between TheNam #53, '91 & PWJ #4, '89 fb, also as Frank Castle in fb2 between Pun Ann #4, '91 & Pun:XMas #1, '07 fb off-panel; last in SSol #8, '93)
SUPPORTING CAST: Microchip (last in PWZ #21, '93, next in PunHol #2/5, '94), Maria Castle (in fb2 between Pun Ann #4, '91 & Pun:Xmas #1, '07 fb)
VILLAINS: Vincent Tortufo (mob boss) & his men (all die), North Vietnamese Army (bts in fb1, killed Marines), purse snatcher (in fb2), Freddie (thief)
OTHER CHARACTERS: U.S. Marines (in fb1, die), the Farrels (Microchip's friends), Sid & Pete (police officers), Freddie's son, bystanders (in fb2)
LOCATIONS/ITEMS: Vietnam (in fb1), New York (also in fb2) inc Punisher's safehouse; Queens inc Tortufo estate; Farrel home / 2nd Lt. Castle's assault rifle & jeep; Marines' assault rifles (all in fb1), Frank's gun (in fb2), Punisher's M60, Uzis & Battle Van; Tortufo's steels Christmas tree & gifts; Freddie's stolen TV
FLASHBACKS: Lt. Castle's unit wants a Christmas tree for their camp, so Castle leaves to get one. When he returns, he finds his unit has been slaughtered by the North Vietnamese Army (1). While Frank is Christmas shopping, a purse snatcher steals Maria's purse. Frank pulls his gun to shoot the thief, but Maria stops him. (2).
SYNOPSIS: Microchip invites Punisher to a Christmas party, but the vigilante refuses to go. Punisher finds Freddy stealing a TV, but Freddy's son begs Punisher not to hurt his dad. Punisher lets Freddy go and continues on to the Tortufo estate, where mobster Vincent is having a Christmas part for his men. Dressed as Santa Claus, Punisher enters the party and kills Tortufo and his men. Punisher takes Tortufo's presents and, still dressed as Santa, arrives at Microchip's Christmas party. Microchip is happy to see Frank, but his friends are confused by receiving gun holsters for Christmas.

2ND STORY: "The Silences" (10 pages)
CREDITS: Steven Grant (writer), Gerry DeCaire (pencils), Pam Eklund (inks), Jim Novak (letters), Sue McTiegue (colors), Don Daley (editor)
FEATURE CHARACTER: Punisher
VILLAINS: Daddy Parish, Calvin Parish, Calvin Parish, Jr., Joseph Parish, Luther Paris, Peter Parish (all bank robbers & kidnappers, die)
OTHER CHARACTERS: Lizabeth Hanek (bank teller, also in pfb), reporter, police (both in pfb), Forest Ranger
LOCATIONS/ITEMS: Oregon (also in pfb) inc bank (in pfb) / Punisher's rope & gun; Daddy's rifle & knife; Calvin, Calvin Jr., Joseph & Peter's knives, Forest Ranger's helicopter
FLASHBACKS: The Parish family robs a bank and takes Lizabeth Hanek, a bank teller, hostage (p).
SYNOPSIS: Punisher tracks the Parish family through the snow-covered Oregon wilderness, eventually finding them. Punisher attacks the Parish family, but is quickly overpowered. Punisher fires his gun into the air, causing an avalanche. Punisher covers Lizabeth while the Parish family is buried. Later, a Forest Ranger finds Lizabeth alive, but only Punisher's boot prints can be seen.

3RD STORY: "Silent Night Part 1: Slay Ride" (6 pages)
CREDITS: Dan Abnett, Andy Lanning (writers), John Ridgway (art), Ed Lazellari (colors), Don Daley (editor)
FEATURE CHARACTER: Punisher (also as Santa Claus)
VILLAINS: Mobsters (die) inc 2 as Salvation Army Santa Claus'
OTHER CHARACTERS: Bystanders
LOCATIONS/ITEMS: New York inc shopping mall / Punisher's gun, mobsters' guns & helicopter; Santa's gun & gas grenade bell
SYNOPSIS: Punisher sees a mobster giving a package to a Salvation Army Santa Claus. Punisher kills the mobster, but the Santa escapes. Punisher chases the Santa through a shopping mall, eventually killing him. Punisher dons the Santa suit and retrieves the package.
NOTE: Story is silent w/no dialogue or sound effects.

4TH STORY: "Silent Night Part 2: Let it Snow" (5 pages)
CREDITS: Dan Abnett, Andy Lanning (writers), John Czop (pencils), Ken Branch (inks), Ericka Moran (colors), Dan Daley (editor)
FEATURE CHARACTER: Punisher (also as waiter, next in Tstrike #3, '93, Pun #85, '93)
VILLAINS: Mobsters (boss dies)
OTHER CHARACTERS: Party guests, wait staff, homeless people
LOCATIONS/ITEMS: New York inc banquet hall / Punisher's catering van, mobsters' Uzis
SYNOPSIS: Disguised as a waiter, Punisher infiltrates a mob Christmas party. Punisher kills the mob boss and escapes in a catering van. Punisher happens across some homeless people and gives them all the food inside the catering van.
NOTE: Story is silent w/no dialogue or sound effects.

5TH STORY: "Silent Night Part 3: Last on the List" (3 pages)
CREDITS: Dan Abnett, Andy Lanning (writers), Mike Harris (pencils), Jimmy Palmiotti (inks), Christie Scheele (colors), Don Daley (editor)
FEATURE CHARACTER: Microchip (last in PunHol #1, '94, next in SM/Pun/Sabre, '93)
VILLAIN: Mugger
OTHER CHARACTERS: Store employees, shoppers
LOCATIONS/ITEMS: New York inc electronics store, clothing store, book store & shoe store / Microchip's shopping list & gifts; robber's rifle
SYNOPSIS: Microchip goes Christmas shopping. A mugger tries to steal from Microchip, but he easily defeats the mugger. Microchip finds gifts for everyone except Punisher, who he can't think of anything to buy for.
NOTE: Story is silent w/no dialogue or sound effects. Microchip's list shows he's shopping for Don, Dan, Andy, Mike, Jimmy, Christine, Ed, Tim & Frank.

PUNISHER HOLIDAY SPECIAL #3 (January 1995)

"The Cold Land" (21 pages)

CREDITS: Chuck Dixon (writer), Dale Eaglesham (pencils), Pat Redding (inks), Bill Oakley (letters), Christie Scheele (colors), Freddy Mendez (asst editor), Don Daley (editor), Dan Green (c inks), Michael Golden (c colors)
FEATURE CHARACTER: Punisher (last in PWZ #40, '95)
SUPPORTING CAST: Microchip (bts, prepped Punisher's grenades, last in PWZ #36, '95)
VILLAINS: Nicky (mobster & informant, dies), Orestes Stephano (St. Louis mob boss, bts, ordered Nicky killed) & his men (die)
OTHER CHARACTERS: Kenny (Nicky's son), Nicky's wife (dies), Federal Marshals (die), gas station attendant, police, commuters
LOCATIONS/ITEMS: Kansas inc Federal safehouse & gas station / Punisher's rented car (destroyed), gun, knife, sniper rifle & assault rifle w/attached grenade launcher, 40mm. grenades w/Semtex & kinked steel wire; Stephano's men's jeeps, shotgun, guns & assault rifles; Federal marshals' car, rifle, guns, shotguns & revolver
SYNOPSIS: In Kansas, Punisher prepares to kill Nicky, a mobster who turned state's evidence against Orestes Stephano, another mobster. Nicky and his family are in the witness protection program to protect them against Stephano's men, and Punisher is surprised to see Stephano's men attack the Federal safehouse. Stephano's men kill the Federal Marshals and Nicky's wife. Punisher arrives in time to kill Stephano's men and save Nicky's son Kenny. Punisher drives Kenny away, but when he stops for gas, more of Stephano's men attack them, trying to kill Kenny. Punisher escapes with Kenny, only for the mobsters to run him off the road. Punisher kills the mobsters and walks Kenny to a police barricade. Kenny doesn't want to leave Punisher, but Punisher tells Kenny he was the one who killed his father Nicky. Kenny goes with the police.
NOTE: Includes table of contents/credits page (1 page) by Frank Teran. Followed by Punisher's Arsenal pin-up (1 page) by Eliot R. Brown (writer, art) & John Wellington (colors) featuring a Galil Squad Automatic Rifle w/removed folding stock, folding bipod & match grade 7.65 NATO standard rounds and Punisher War Journal Equipment Page (1 page) by Eliot R. Brown (writer, art) & John Wellington (colors) featuring a Boston Whaler converted into a gunboat w/2 Johnson 75 motors & Kevlar ENG-ARM engine armor, and the Battle Van.

2ND STORY: "X-Mas Stalkings" (30 pages)
CREDITS: Mike Lackey (writer), Phil Gosier (pencils), Frank Percy (inks), Vickie Williams (letters), Philip Lynch (colors), Freddy Mendez (asst editor), Don Daley (editor)
FEATURE CHARACTER: Punisher (also as Santa Claus, next in GR/W/Pun, '94)
SUPPORTING CAST: Microchip (next in PWJ #61, '93)
VILLAINS: Charlie Quinn (stalker, also in pfb), Santa Snatcher (thief targeting Salvation Army Santa Claus') (both die)
OTHER CHARACTERS: Terri Rampling (stalker victim, also in photo, also in pfb), Sean Rampling (Terri's brother, dies), Salvation Army Santa Claus, police (1 dies, others in pfb), bystanders, fish
LOCATIONS/ITEMS: Whitehall, NC inc grocery store, movie theater, police station & Terri's home (all in pfb); New York inc Punisher's safehouse, Quinn's apartment & Sean's video store (also in pfb); Quinn's upstate home / Punisher's Battle Van, machine guns, tear gas grenade & guns; Quinn's knife & gun, Microchip's computer, Terri's homing device & Sean activator, police guns
FLASHBACK: Charlie Quinn stalks Terri Rampling. She thinks Charlie killed her boyfriend but can't prove it. The police don't do anything for Terri until Quinn breaks into her house. Charlie is arrested and Terri moves to New York. Eventually, Quinn finds Terri and starts stalking her again (p).
SYNOPSIS: Terri and her brother Sean create a fake disturbance in front of a Salvation Army Santa Claus. The Santa turns out to be Punisher, who attacks Sean. Terri stops Punisher and explains they need Punisher's help: Charlie Quinn is stalking Terri and they want Punisher to kill Quinn. Microchip looks up Charlie's history and learns he's independently wealthy since he killed his mother. Punisher goes to Charlie's apartment, but Quinn isn't there. Meanwhile, Charlie attacks Terri at Sean's video store and kills Sean. Before he dies, Sean activates a tracking unit Microchip placed on Terri. Punisher receives the signal, but pauses to kill the Santa Snatcher, the thief stealing from Santas, the reason Punisher was dressed as Santa in the first place. Charlie leaves with Terri and kills a policeman. Punisher arrives at the video store, only to be blamed for killing the officer. As Charlie forces Terri to dress in lingerie, Punisher follows the signal and attacks Quinn. Terri stops Punisher from killing Charlie, but Quinn takes her hostage. Terri sets Charlie on fire and to spare Teri the guilt of murder, Punisher shoots and kills Quinn.
NOTE: Followed by Punisher's Arsenal (1 page) by Eliot R. Brown (writer, art) & John Wellington (colors) featuring 2 Springfield Armory knock-offs of the Ithica Gun Company's collapsible rifle-shotgun w/rimfire .22 ammunition.

PUNISHER: P.O.V. #1 (1991)

"Book One: Foresight" (48 pages)

CREDITS: Jim Starlin (writer), Bernie Wrightson (art), Bill Oakley (letters), Bill Wray (colors), Suzanne Dell'Orto (asst editor), Nel Yomtov (titles, editor), Carl Potts (exec editor), Ruben Diaz, Greg Wright (special thanks)
FEATURE CHARACTER: Punisher (last in PWJ #30, '91)
GUEST STAR: Nick Fury (voice only, last in Av #337, '91)
SUPPORTING CAST: Microchip (last in PWJ #30, '91)
VILLAINS: Kingpin (last in WoSM Ann #6, '90) & his men (some die) inc Chief (1st), Derrick "Deke" Wainscroft, Barry "Zonkers" Powell (also in Deke's hallucination, dies) (both political terrorists, also in photo, 1st), Daemian Wainscroft (Wainscroft Chemical owner & Deke's father, 1st), Chester Goudal (delusional vigilante, 1st), Buzz Conners (drug smuggler, dies) & his men (die); Sergio Valez (crack dealer, dies) & his men (die); Barry Willis (gun dealer, also in photo, dies); prison inmates
OTHER CHARACTERS: Geraldo Rivera (on TV, last in ASM #304, '88, next in Blaze #3, '94), Carol Nelson (pregnant woman, 1st), prostitute (1st), Deke's other victim (1st), Mrs. Goudal (Chester's mother, also as monster in Chester's hallucination, dies), Jess Moondoggy (science-fiction writer & former political terrorist), Lance Jefferson (stock broker, dies), Betty (Jefferson's maid, dies), Peter Malcolm (mutilated corpse), Charles Baker (president of Gotham Federal) & his secretary (voice only), Wainscroft Chemical scientists inc Nelson (dies) & anti-bacteriological team (some die), police inc Det. Holiday (1st), Kingpin's secretary, Guido's Pizza employees & patrons; bar patrons, reporters (on TV), prison guard, bystanders (some die), dog (dies), giant mutated rat (1 dies, another as corpse), pigeons
LOCATIONS/ITEMS: New York inc Willis' warehouse (destroyed), Deke & Zonkers' safehouse (destroyed), Gotham Federal Midtown branch (destroyed), Gotham Federal Building w/Baker's office, Wainscroft Chemical w/laboratory & infirmary w/Deke's room, Fisk Tower w/Kingpin's office, Washington Square Park, Punisher's safehouse, Jess' apartment, Malcolm's Park Ave. apartment, Jefferson's penthouse, Deke's construction site hideout, Guido's Pizza, bar & sewers; Queens inc Goudal home; Wainscroft estate, prison / Punisher's Uzi, knife, sniper rifle, grappling wire, listening device & Battle Van w/missile launchers; Chester's knives, steaks, axe, crossbow, rifle, hammer, revolver, gun, cross, crucifix, acid bombs & shotgun w/dimes; Microchip's computers, Deke & Zonkers' plastique, Kingpin's tracking device, Sergio's men's assault rifle, Wainscroft's men's guns, prison guard's rifle, SS-8 serum (alters DNA to survive environment)
SYNOPSIS: Political terrorists Deke and Zonkers are released from prison on early parole. They decide to rob some convenience stores to get some money. Later, Punisher sees Deke and Zonkers buy some plastique from Barry Willis. Unaware of who they are, Punisher lets them go. When crack dealer Sergio Valez arrives to buy some guns from Willis, Punisher blows everyone up. Deke and Zonkers blackmail Gotham Federal bank for a hundred thousand dollars by blowing up the Gotham Federal midtown branch. Two banks later, Punisher decides to go after Deke and Zonkers. In Queens, Chester Goudal plans to kill all of the monsters he sees. Zonkers prepares a new bomb for another bank, but the bomb explodes. Horribly burned, Deke grabs Zonkers' head and stumbles into the sewers. Meanwhile, Punisher searches for Deke. At Wainscroft Chemical, an experimental serum becomes volatile, so Daemian Wainscroft orders it dumped into the sewers, which engulfs Deke. An anti-bacteriological team is sent to gather samples of life exposed to the serum and find Deke. Punisher finds Deke's destroyed safehouse. Daemian recognizes his son Deke and declares Deke a specimen to be studied. Two weeks later, Punisher kills drug smuggler Buzz Conners. Now insane, Deke breaks out of Wainscroft Chemicals and attacks a pregnant woman in the street, draining her blood. Hearing of the "vampire killer" on the news, Chester begins his mission by killing his mother. Daemian makes a deal with the Kingpin to capture Deke, who continues to steal women's blood and kill rich people. Punisher learns from Det. Holiday that Deke is attacking women as Chester searches for the "vampire." Punisher listens to Daemian's phone calls hoping to learn where Deke is and is surprised to hear Nick Fury's voice. Later, Punisher finds Deke attacking a prostitute, but Deke quickly overpowers the vigilante.
NOTE: Published in the prestige format w/square bound spine. Includes title/credits page (interior front cover), faux "Mad Scientist kit" ad

(interior back cover) by Eliot R. Brown & back cover pin-up (photo) by Eliot R. Brown. Cover logo designed by Ken Lopez. Pun:POV #2, '91 names the SS-8 serum & reveals Deke's hideout to be in a construction site. Pun:POV #3, '91 reveals Zonkers' severed head is fused to Deke's chest; it is considered present whenever Deke appears. Deke and Zonkers' safehouse is at 355 Park Avenue. Punisher's Battle Van is called "Battle Wagon" here.

PUNISHER: P.O.V. #2 (1991)

"Book Two: Extrospection" (48 pages)

CREDITS: Jim Starlin (writer), Bernie Wrightson (art), Bill Oakley (letters), Bill Wray (colors), Suzanne Dell'Orto (asst editor), Nel Yomtov (titles, editor), Carl Potts (exec editor), Ruben Diaz, Greg Wright (special thanks)
FEATURE CHARACTER: Punisher (also in own dream)
GUEST STAR: Nick Fury
SUPPORTING CAST: Microchip (voice only)
VILLAINS: Kingpin & his men (some die) inc Charlie Marx, Karl (both also as monsters in Chester's hallucination, die) & Chief; Deke Wainscroft, Daemian Wainscroft, Chester Goudal
OTHER CHARACTERS: Network Nina (psychic SHIELD agent, last in NF:AoS #29, '91), Carol Nelson (voice only), Dr. Hughes (Carol's obstetrician, 1st), prostitute (also as monster in Chester's hallucination, dies), homeless woman (dies), Chester's victim (dies), UPS deliveryman (dies), police inc Det. Holiday; paramedics; Maria Castle, Lisa Castle, Frank Castle, Jr. (prev 3 in Punisher's dream), Zonkers (in Deke's hallucination)
LOCATIONS/ITEMS: New York inc Nelson home, Dr. Hughes' office, prostitute's apartment, Fisk Tower w/Kingpin's office, 28th & Park construction site w/Deke's hideout; Wainscroft estate inc study / Punisher's Uzi, knife, pipe, grappling hook gun, listening device & Battle Van; Chester's stake, hammer, crossbow, knife, axe & shotgun w/dimes; Kingpin's tracking device, Kingpin's men's Uzis & revolvers; Chief's gun, Deke's sledgehammer, SHIELD listening device
SYNOPSIS: Punisher dreams of his family and wakes to see Deke battling Kingpin's men. Deke escapes and Punisher forms a temporary alliance with Kingpin. Deke attacks a homeless woman. Chester arrives, kills the homeless woman and two of Kingpin's men. Punisher leaves, unaware Kingpin's men planted a listening device on Punisher's van. Carol Nelson, the pregnant woman Deke attacked, calls her doctor and arranges an appointment; she's suddenly not feeling well. As Punisher spies on a meeting between Nick Fury and Daemian and learns the serum that Deke was exposed to altered his DNA to adapt and survive whatever environment he is in. Fury points out that a construction site owned by Daemian is in the center of the "vampire" attacks on women. Kingpin's men hear the same information through their listening device. Chester kills one of Deke's victims, thinking he's tainted by the "vampire's" blood. Punisher attacks Deke in his construction site hideout. Chester kills another of Deke's victims. Kingpin's men join Punisher's attack on Deke. Though shot, stabbed, beaten about the head and tossed off the building, Deke' doesn't die. Chester waits for Carol Nelson to come home. Punisher and Chief interrogate Daemian and learn the serum was being worked on for the government. Daemian escapes when the police arrive. Once Deke is dealt with, Fury plans to commandeer Daemian and his research. Meanwhile, Deke drives upstate.
NOTE: Published in the prestige format w/square bound spine. Includes title/credits page (interior front cover), faux "U.S. Government Surplus" ad (interior back cover) by Eliot R. Brown & back cover pin-up (photo) by Eliot R. Brown.

PUNISHER: P.O.V. #3 (1991)

"Book Three: Introspection" (48 pages)

CREDITS: Jim Starlin (writer), Bernie Wrightson (art), Bill Oakley (letters), Bill Wray (colors), Suzanne Dell'Orto (asst editor), Nel Yomtov (titles, editor), Carl Potts (exec editor), Ruben Diaz, Greg Wright (special thanks)
FEATURE CHARACTER: Punisher
GUEST STAR: Nick Fury
SUPPORTING CAST: Microchip
VILLAINS: Kingpin (also as Punisher's shooting target) & his men (some die) inc Chief; Deke Wainscroft, Daemian Wainscroft, Chester Goudal, corrupt police Captain
OTHER CHARACTERS: Alexander Pierce (SHIELD agent, last in Pun Ann #4/2, '91), Network Nina, Carol's baby (monstrous newborn, 1st, arm only), Carol Nelson, Dr. Hughes (both die), nurses (some die), police (1 also as monster in Chester's hallucination, dies) inc Capt. Baker (1st), Officer Green & Det. Holiday; Deke's victim; Lisa Castle (in Punisher's thoughts), Zonkers (in Deke's hallucination)
LOCATIONS/ITEMS: New York inc Fisk Tower w/Kingpin's office & Memorial Hospital w/Carol's room; Punisher's NJ safehouse inc shooting range; Catskill Mountains inc Wainscroft summer home & Saugerties w/police station / Punisher's Uzi, flame thrower, rocket launcher, knife, axe, log & shooting targets; Chester's rifle, crossbow, knives, revolver, stakes, hammer, cross, crucifix, acid bombs & shotgun w/dimes; police revolvers, rifles, assault rifles & helicopter; Kingpin's men's assault rifles & net gun; Chief's knife, Microchip's computers, Pierce's stun gun, SHIELD Vibranium/Titanium manacles
SYNOPSIS: As Microchip searches for reports of Deke's activities, Deke arrives at the Wainscroft summer home in the Catskill Mountains. A woman is attacked in Saugerties and the police file a report. Kingpin, Nick Fury and Punisher hear of it through different means. Later in the Catskill Mountains, Punisher and Kingpin's men team up to search for Deke. Chester calls the hospital and learns where Carol Nelson is. Punisher finds Deke and sees that Zonkers' head is fused to Deke's chest; Deke is feeding Zonkers blood. Punisher fires a rocket at Deke. Carol goes into labor. Kingpin's men fire a net at Deke, but accidentally trap Punisher instead. Chester arrives at the hospital. Chief frees Punisher and they attack Deke. Carol dies and Dr. Hughes tries to save her baby. Chester kills a policeman. Punisher sets Deke on fire, but Deke survives. Carol's baby erupts from Carol's corpse and kills Dr. Hughes and his nursing staff. Deke attacks Punisher. Chester makes his way to Carol's baby. Punisher bashes Deke's head, which slows Deke down. Nick Fury, SHIELD agents and the police arrive and, knock out Punisher. Chester follows Carol's baby into the sewers. SHIELD takes custody of Deke, the police arrest Punisher and Kingpin's men are let go. Det. Holiday finds the carnage Carol's baby left behind.
NOTE: Published in the prestige format w/square bound spine. Includes title/credits page (interior front cover) & back cover pin-up (photo) by Eliot R. Brown.

PUNISHER: P.O.V. #4 (1991)

"Book Four: Hindsight" (48 pages)

CREDITS: Jim Starlin (writer), Bernie Wrightson (art), Bill Oakley (letters), Bill Wray (colors), Suzanne Dell'Orto (asst editor), Nel Yomtov (titles, editor), Carl Potts (exec editor), Ruben Diaz, Greg Wright (special thanks)
FEATURE CHARACTER: Punisher (also as monster in Chester's hallucination, next in PWJ #31, '91)
GUEST STAR: Nick Fury (next in InfG #1, '91)
SUPPORTING CAST: Microchip (next in PWJ #31, '91)
VILLAIN: Kingpin (next in Sleep #5, '91)
OTHER CHARACTERS: Network Nina (next in NF:AoS #30, '91), Alexander Pierce (next in DD #298, '91), la Contessa Valentina de Fontaine (last in NF:AoS #27, '91, chr last in Pun/Cap #2, '92, next in InfG #1, '91), Carol's baby (dies), SHIELD agents (some die) & scientist; police inc Capt. Baker & Det. Holiday; SWAT team (dies), subway commuters; Lisa Castle, Frank Castle, Jr. (both in Punisher's thoughts)
LOCATIONS/ITEMS: New York inc Memorial Hospital, Hudson River, sewers & Fisk Tower w/Kingpin's office; Pacific Ocean inc 2-acre island w/ SHIELD facility; Catskill Mountains / Punisher's assault rifle, knife & Battle Van; Chester's acid bombs, axe & shotgun w/dimes; police assault rifles & helicopter; SHIELD sonic motion detector, assault rifles & helicopter; Baker's revolver, subway train (also as monster in Chester's hallucination)
SYNOPSIS: Daemian inspects Deke and declares he's brain damaged and will never recover. Nick Fury learns that Carol Nelson went into labor and Daemian suggests that since she was attacked by Deke, she should be quarantined. Det. Holiday sends a SWAT team into the sewers. The police taunt Punisher as they fly him into New York by helicopter. The SWAT team finds Carol's baby. Fury learns that Carol is dead and Fury sends a SHIELD team into the sewers. Punisher escapes police custody and dives into the Hudson River. As Chester searches for Carol's baby in the sewers, Fury arrives at the hospital and Punisher meets Microchip. Chester finds the corpses of the SWAT team. Punisher runs into the SHIELD agents in the sewers. They attack but Punisher escapes. Fury authorizes lethal force against Carol's baby and Daemian threatens to go to Fury's superiors if they kill the baby. Punisher finds the corpses of the SHIELD agents. Carol's baby attacks Chester, then retreats. Punisher finds Carol's baby, but can't bring himself to kill it. As he tries to decide what to do, Chester arrives and shoots the baby. Punisher attacks Chester in a rage. Carol's baby defends Punisher and Chester escapes. Punisher stays with the baby until it dies, then chases Chester into the path of an oncoming subway train. Punisher meets with Microchip. Kingpin calls Punisher and they end their temporary alliance. Later, Nick Fury visits Daemian at his SHIELD research facility on a Pacific island. Daemian is angered to learn that Fury is indefinitely detaining Daemian on the island.
NOTE: Published in the prestige format w/square bound spine. Includes title/credits page (interior front cover) & back cover pin-up (photo) by Eliot R. Brown.

PUNISHER/CAPTAIN AMERICA: BLOOD & GLORY #1 (October 1992)

"We the People…" (47 pages)

CREDITS: D.G. Chichester, Margaret Clark (writers), Klaus Janson (art), Jim Novak (letters), John Wellington (colors), Cindy Emmert (design), Pat Garrahy (asst editor), Ralph Macchio (editor), Howard Mackie (special thanks)
FEATURE CHARACTERS: Captain America (also in photo, last in AFlt #100, '91), Punisher (last in DD #293, '91)
VILLAINS: Roger Mollech (U.S. Attorney General), Angela Stone (Mollech's aide), Col. Max Kalee & his men inc Theopolous, Lt. Malev, Cain & Kane (both next in Pun/ Cap #3, '92); Gen. Miguel Alfredo Navatilas (Mediusuela dictator) (all 1st) & his men inc Carlos & Manuel; Dr. Slickster (drug & arms dealer) & his helicopter pilot, Bull (Slickster's bodyguard) (prev 3 die), Die Hards (street gang, die) inc Bruce & Julie (both die), assassin (dies)
OTHER CHARACTERS: Charles Foster (White House reporter), Maureen O'Boyle ("A Current Affair" host), Eugene Somma (White House Press Secretary) (all on TV), George Bush (U.S. President, bts, concerned w/Navatilas' pattern of aggression, last in Av #333, '91, next bts in Pun/Cap #3, '92), Ernest Braun (Smithsonian scientist), "Rocking Horse" Royoko (WWII veteran & warehouse supervisor), flight controller (voice only), file clerk (dies), bartender, bar patrons, Mass Transit Authority employees inc Charley, reporters inc Tony, cameramen, bystanders
LOCATIONS/ITEMS: New York inc Die Hards' apartment & Astor Place subway station, Washington, DC inc Capitol Building, Smithsonian Museum, Mollech's office & White House w/press room; Mediusuela inc Navatilas estate; Texas shipyards, Andrews Air Force base, government warehouse, bar, Angela's motel room / Punisher's explosives, rifle, tripwire, gun, chain & knife; Captain America's magnifying device & parachute; Dr. Slickster's crate of guns, suitcase of cocaine, bazooka & helicopter; Kalee & his men's crates of defective weapons, helicopters, assault rifles & gun; Die Hards' guns, file clerk's gun
SYNOPSIS: In Texas, Captain America ambushes Dr. Slickster's gun sale to Gen. Navatilas' men. Manuel, one of the buyers, grabs a weapon to use on Cap, but it blows up when he fires it. Cap demands to know why Dr. Slickster warned Manuel not to use it, but is interrupted when Col. Kalee and his men arrive. Kalee arrests the buyers and sellers and thanks Cap for his help. Disturbed by the looks between the troops and criminals, Cap secretly grabs a piece of the destroyed weapon. In Washington, DC, reporters question Attorney General Roger Mollech about his aggressive attacks on Navatilas' alleged drug trafficking and how they could affect foreign policy. In New York, the not arrested Dr. Slickster sells cocaine to the street gang Die Hards. Punisher blows up the apartment and chases Dr. Slickster to the roof where a helicopter takes Dr. Slickster away. Punisher crashes the helicopter into the Astor Place subway entrance and pursues Dr. Slickster onto a train. Punisher kills Dr. Slickster and escapes. Disturbed by Dr. Slickster's military terminology, Punisher decides to investigate. In Medisuela, Mollech's aide Angela Stone assures Gen. Navatilas that despite interruptions in Texas and New York, their system of selling confiscated drugs to buy weapons for Navatilas is still working. At the Smithsonian, Cap learns that the destroyed weapon was engineered to explode after use. Cap investigates the other seized weapons, finds they're in Kalee's possession and verifies they will explode after use as well. Unfortunately, he's spotted by Kalee's men. Punisher's investigation leads him to Stone posing as a whistleblower. After a file clerk fakes an assassination attempt on Angela, Stone tells Punisher there's corruption in the government led by Captain America. In Washington, DC, Punisher shoots Cap.
NOTE: Published in the prestige format w/square bound spine. Cover is embossed. Includes credits page (interior front cover) & frontispiece/title page featuring the White House, homeless people & the Will Rogers quote "Diplomacy is the art of saying 'Nice Doggie,' until you can find a rock."

PUNISHER/CAPTAIN AMERICA: BLOOD & GLORY #2 (November 1992)

"Eternal Vigilance" (47 pages)

CREDITS: D.G. Chichester, Margaret Clark (writers), Klaus Janson (art), John Workman (letters), Sam Otis (colors), Cindy Emmert (design), Pat Garrahy (assoc editor), Ralph Macchio (editor), John Wellington (c colors), Eliot Brown (special thanks)
FEATURE CHARACTERS: Captain America (also in photo, also as "Mr. Stevens"), Punisher
GUEST STARS: Avengers: Hawkeye (last in Av #333, '91, next in AWC Ann #6, '91), Iron Man (last in NF:AoS #27, '91, last bts in Av #332, '91, next in IM:LD #1, '08 fb), She-Hulk (last in AFlt #101, '91, next in SH #27, '91), Thor (last in Av Ann #20/4, '91, next in Namor #13, '91), Vision (last in AFlt #101, '91, next in Av Ann #20, '91); Nick Fury (last in Av #333, '91, next bts in W #41, '91, next in W #42, '91), Dum Dum Dugan (last in NF:AoS #27, '91, next in MCP #93/4, '92)
VILLAINS: Roger Mollech, Angela Stone, Col. Kalee & his men (some die) inc Theopolous (dies) & Lt. Malev; Gen. Navatilas & his men inc Col. Veneno (1st)
OTHER CHARACTERS: Edwin Jarvis (last in Av #333, next bts in IM Ann #12, next in Namor Ann #1, all '91), la Contessa Valentina de Fontaine (last in NF:AoS #27, '91, next in Pun:POV #4, '91), Booch (civil servant), Ms. White (weapons dealer's agent, dies), diner cook & patrons inc Edwards (Vietnam veteran); reporters (some on TV) inc Walter; cameramen, Medisuela citizens (1 dies), funeral attendees, warehouse employees, doctors, nurses, guard dogs, cats, horses
LOCATIONS/ITEMS: Washington, DC inc Walter Reed Memorial hospital & National Cathedral; Medisuela inc beach & Navatilas estate; Michigan diner, weapons dealer's warehouse / Punisher's motorcycle, gun, wire cutters, war quoit, Congolese hunga-munga & Asanda throwing knife; Captain America's motorcycle & magnifying device; Kalee's men's motorcycles & caltrops; Theopolous' knife & truck; Mollech's yacht & raft; Navatilas' men's defective weapons, bomb & chains; Stone's drill
SYNOPSIS: Nick Fury controls the situation as Captain America is rushed into surgery. Cap warns Fury of the conspiracy and tells Nick to let him die. Soon after, a funeral is held for Captain America with the Avengers as his pallbearers. In Michigan, Punisher meets with Booch, who tells him about the DEA-confiscated drugs disappearing from impound and ending up back on the streets, coordinated by someone in the government. Meanwhile, Punisher is implicated in Cap's death. Mollech and Stone meet with Navatilas to reaffirm the proceeds from the drug sales will fund his weapons, so long as he uses them against his neighboring countries that the US opposes. They secretly plan to double-cross Navatilas with faulty weapons and take over his country. Punisher leaves the diner. Kalee's man Theopolous stabs Booch and chases Punisher. Cap, in disguise, tends to Booch. Punisher battles Theopolous and his men, but is overtaken. Cap arrives and helps Punisher defeat the men. Punisher apologizes for "killing" Cap, and Cap recruits Punisher to help him find who's responsible for the government corruption. In Medisuela, Mollech attends Navatilas' party, eventually taking part in a human sacrifice. Cap and Punisher investigate a weapons dealer, first posing as buyers and later breaking in. They find evidence that the U.S. Department of Defense purposefully sold sabotaged weapons to Navatilas. Later, Stone interrogates and kills the person Cap and Punisher spoke with, learning that Cap and Punisher are still alive. In Medisuela, Captain America confirms the defective weapons are being used by the Medisuelan Army, but finds a bomb. Cap tosses Punisher his shield for protection as the bomb explodes. Navatilas' men capture Cap while Punisher lays unconscious in the jungle.
NOTE: Published in the prestige format w/square bound spine. Includes credits page (interior front cover) & frontispiece/title page featuring a soldier w/a folded American flag & the Rostand quote "Kill one man and you are a murderer. Kill millions and you are a conqueror. Kill all and you are a god."

PUNISHER/CAPTAIN AMERICA: BLOOD & GLORY #3 (December 1992)

"Establish the Blessings of Liberty" (47 pages)

CREDITS: D.G. Chichester, Margaret Clark (writers), Klaus Janson (art), John Workman (letters), Judy Johnson, Sherilyn Van Valkenburgh (colors), Cindy Emmert (design), Pat Garrahy (assoc editor), Ralph Macchio (editor)
FEATURE CHARACTERS: Captain America (also in rfb; next in Namor #13, '91), Punisher (also as Capt. Castle in fb1 between Pun #6, '02 fb voice only & Pun Ann #4, '91, also as Frank Castle in fb2 during DE:A, '95 fb; next in Namor #16, '91)
GUEST STAR: Terror (absorbs abilities & sensations from stolen body parts, last in CMass #7, '90, next in TInc #1, '92)
SUPPORTING CAST: Maria Castle, Lisa Castle, Frank Castle Jr. (all in fb2 between PWJ #3, '89 fb & DE:A, '95 fb)
VILLAINS: Angela Stone, Col. Kalee & his men inc Lt. Malev, Cain & Kane (both last in Pun/Cap #1, '92) (all die), Gen. Navatilas (dies) & his men (many die) inc Col. Veneno, Enrico (both die); Roger Mollech (also in pfb); Bruno Costa, Byron Hannigan, Leon Klosky, Matt Skinner, Forest Hunt (prev 5 in fb2 between PWJ #3, '89 fb & DE:A, '95 fb)
OTHER CHARACTERS: George Bush (bts, denies Medisuela invasion, last bts in Pun/Cap #1, '92, next in Av #336, '91 fb), U.S. Congressmen (in pfb), U.S. soldiers (some die, others in rfb, others in fb, 1 dies), air traffic controller (voice only), Arlington guards, Medisuela citizens; Dr. Abraham Erskine, Project: Rebirth scientist, Army doctor & recruits (prev 4 in rfb)
LOCATIONS/ITEMS: Medisuela inc jungle, Navatilas estate & church; Dallas/Fort Worth International airport, Arlington National Cemetery / Punisher's Asanda throwing knife, assault rifle, gun & Vietnam Combat Infantry Badge; Navatilas' men's defective assault rifles, machetes, chains & bag of rice; Veneno's gun, Malev & his men's Apache helicopters & guns; Malev's knife, Mollech's plane & suitcase of money, Arlington guard's rifle
FLASHBACKS: Mollech recommends an invasion of Medisuela to Congress (p). When Steve Rogers volunteers for military service he is declared 4F (ToS #63, '65). Dr. Erskine uses the Super Soldier Serum to transform Steve into Captain America (CapC #1, '41). On a reconnaissance mission in Vietnam, one of Captain Castle's men triggers a land mine and dies (1). The Castle family plays with a kite and encounters the Costa family in Central Park (2).
SYNOPSIS: In Medisuela, Navatilas' men search for Captain America's shield as a trophy. They find it, but attached to a still-alive Punisher, who kills them. Meanwhile, Cap is tortured. Punisher throws Cap's shield with a bomb attached to the torturers. When the bomb explodes, Cap frees himself and defeats Navatilas' men. The Medisuelan Army attacks, but they're defeated when their weapons explode in their faces. Cap and Punisher search for Navatilas. Later, Terror arrives at the battlefield and takes the eyes of one of the dying men. In Washington, DC, Mollech is angry that the President denied his

recommended invasion of Medisuela. Stone orders Kalee's team to invade anyway, which will force the President to either admit to rogue forces within the U.S. government, or to commit to the invasion. Terror tells Gen. Navatilas that his men are dead and Captain America and Punisher are still alive, but withholds information about the sabotaged weapons for more money. Navatilas demands the information, but Terror kills his men and leaves Navatilas with the advice to accept his fate. As Cap and Punisher prepare for battle, Kalee and his men invade Medisuela. Punisher and Cap return fire, with Cap engaging Kalee directly while Cain and Kane find Navatilas and kill him. As Punisher kills Cain and Kane, Cap defeats Kalee but fails to stop Kalee from biting into a suicide pill. Later, Terror offers to use his talents on Navatilas to find out what he knows as a favor to be eventually repaid. Punisher refuses, but Cap accepts. Cap and Punisher intercept Mollech and Stone in Dallas as they attempt to flee the country. Punisher kills Stone but stops Cap from killing Mollech. At Arlington National Cemetery, Cap tells Punisher his attempted murder will be overlooked. Punisher gives Cap his Vietnam Combat Infantry Badge. The two soldiers salute each other and depart.

NOTE: Published in the prestige format w/square bound spine. Cover uses the art from pages 29-30. Includes credits page (interior front cover) & frontispiece/title page featuring American soldiers raising the American flag at Iwo Jima & the George Bernard Shaw quote "Liberty means responsibility—that's why most men dread it."

PUNISHER: GHOSTS OF INNOCENTS #1 (January 1993)

(untitled, 48 pages)

CREDITS: Jim Starlin (writer), Tom Grindberg (art), Phil Felix (letters), Steve Oliff (colors), Keith Wilson (logo design), Reneé Witterstaetter (editor)
FEATURE CHARACTER: Punisher (last in Pun #70, '92)
SUPPORTING CAST: Microchip (last in Pun #70, '92)
VILLAINS: Kingpin (last in Pun #70, '92) & his men (some die) inc Snake (Roger Lewis, low-level thug, also in photo), Ralphy (Snake's partner, dies), Rock Baker (Snake's boss) (prev 3 1st), drug dealers (some die)
OTHER CHARACTERS: Benny (Snake's victim), school children (also in Punisher's thoughts as ghosts), bus driver (all die), police, bystanders; Maria Castle, Lisa Castle, Frank Castle Jr., Bruno Costa, Byron Hannigan, Leon Klosky, Matt Skinner (prev 7 in rfb); Rita Baker (mentioned, Rock's wife & Snake's lover)
LOCATIONS/ITEMS: New York inc Central Park (in rfb), abandoned Rusty Belt factory (destroyed), Punisher's safehouse, docks & Fisk Tower w/Kingpin's office / Punisher's hang glider, Battle Van, plastique explosives, Uzis, M60, assault rifle w/attached grenade launcher, grenades & guns; Snake's baseball bat & Uzi; drug dealers' Uzis, shotguns & guns; Kingpin's helicopter, Kingpin's men's assault rifles & guns; police revolvers
FLASHBACK: The Castle family is killed in Central Park (MP #2, '75 fb).
SYNOPSIS: Snake kills a man who owes their boss money and learns he and his partner Ralphy are on guard duty for a drug buy at a factory the next morning. Punisher ambushes the buy and blows up the factory, scattering the dealers. Snake takes a school bus hostage to escape, but Punisher gives chase. Punisher boards the bus and attempts to take Snake down, but Snake kills the bus driver and Snake escapes as the bus goes over railroad tracks and is hit by an oncoming train, killing everyone except Punisher. Punisher hobbles away and is picked up by Microchip. Observing footage Micro took of the buy, Punisher is able to identify Snake as one of Kingpin's low-level thugs. Believing Snake will take the money he retrieved to Kingpin, and haunted by the ghosts of the school children, Punisher decides to go after Snake despite possibly having a concussion. Microchip tries to remind Punisher that killing Kingpin will only create a void that will be filled by violence as others try to take his place. Using his knowledge of Kingpin's tower, Punisher walks in the front door and works his way upstairs, killing Kingpin's men along the way. Kingpin doesn't intend to give Punisher what he wants, and has Rock contact Travis Air and the police. The "ghosts" force Punisher to press on despite numerous new injuries until he finally penetrates Kingpin's office. Seeing Kingpin fleeing via helicopter, Punisher professes he did his best before collapsing as the police storm the office.
NOTE: Published in the prestige format w/square bound spine. Back cover image is taken from page 43, panel 3.

PUNISHER: GHOSTS OF INNOCENTS #2 (January 1993)

(untitled, 48 pages)

CREDITS: Jim Starlin (writer), Tom Grindberg (art), Phil Felix (letters), Marie Javins (colors), Joe Kaufman (design), Keith Wilson (logo design), Reneé Witterstaetter (editor)
FEATURE CHARACTER: Punisher (also in own thoughts, next in Pun #53, '92)
SUPPORTING CAST: Microchip (next in Pun #53, '92)
VILLAINS: Kingpin (next in TM:BB, '95) & his men (some die) inc Snake, Bellevue Hospital orderly (both die) & Rock Baker; Ramon Garcia Perez (Columbian drug lord) & his men (both die)
OTHER CHARACTERS: Maria Castle, Lisa Castle, Frank Castle Jr., school children (all in Punisher's thoughts as ghosts), Rita Baker, Bellevue Hospital doctors, nurses & orderlies; police
LOCATIONS/ITEMS: New York inc Bellevue Hospital, Fisk Tower inc Kingpin's office & meeting room, Punisher's safehouse, Kingpin's warehouse & Brooklyn rail yard; Catskill Mountains inc safehouse / Punisher's sniper rifle, assault rifle, Battle Van & helicopter; Snake's Uzi, Kingpin's men's guns, Bellevue gurney w/restraints, electro-shock machine & pillow
FLASHBACK: The train hits the school bus, killing the children inside (Pun:GI #1, '93).
SYNOPSIS: Punisher begs the ghosts for forgiveness when he sees his family coming towards him. Punisher goes to embrace them, but Maria informs him he's not quite dead yet. Punisher is determined to stay where he is until he does finally die, ready to be with his family. Meanwhile, doctors tend to Punisher and decide to take the vigilante out of his coma with electroshock therapy. An orderly, secretly working for the Kingpin, plans to use an "accident" to kill Punisher, but is thwarted when the doctor administers the treatment himself. Punisher is taken out of his coma and the orderly tries again later by snuffing him with a pillow. Punisher frees himself and fights back. Stealing the orderly's uniform and sneaking out, Punisher apologizes to Maria but states his work isn't done. Punisher sends a bullet into Kingpin's office to get his attention and demands Snake. Microchip tries to remind Punisher Kingpin has to be kept alive, but Punisher threatens to take down the whole organization if he has to. He begins systematically attacking Kingpin's interests. Snake, meanwhile, enjoys living it up with Rock's wife at a house in the Catskills. Eventually, Kingpin relents to Punisher's demands and has Snake dumped in the train yards with an Uzi. Punisher hunts Snake until he leaves Snake wounded on the tracks. Punisher keeps Snake there until a train runs Snake over. Punisher offers it as the best justice he can give the ghosts, and they disappear. Punisher realizes they will haunt him for a long time to come.
NOTE: Published in the prestige format w/square bound spine. Back cover image is taken from page 34, panel 2.

PUNISHER: THE ORIGIN OF MICROCHIP #1 (July 1993)

"Over the Edge" (24 pages)

CREDITS: Mike Baron, Carl Potts (writers), Louis Williams (pencils), Art Nichols (co-inks, c inks), Joe Rubinstein (co-inks), Michael Higgins (letters), John Kalisz (colors), Don Daley (editor), Dougie Braithwaite (c pencils)
FEATURE CHARACTERS: Frank Castle (last in PunTheNam, '94 fb, also in Pun:Int, '89 fb, PunTheNam, '94 fb, Pun:BSS #3, '94 fb, PunTheNam, '94 fb, Pun #77, '93 fb, TheNam #52-53, '91, PunHol #2, '94 fb, Pun #1, '86 fb, PWJ #4, '89 fb, voice only in Pun #6, '02 fb, Pun #3, '99 fb, Pun/Cap #3, '92 fb, Pun Ann #4, '91 & Pun #1, '98 fb; next in PWZ #21, '93 fb, Pun Ann #4, '91, PunHol #2, '94, fb, Pun:XMas #1, '07 fb, Pun #1, '98 fb, PWZ #24, '94 fb, Pun #100, '95 fb, Pun #10, '09 fb, Pun Ann #4, '91, Pun:RBN, '89 fb, MP #2, '75 fb, PWJ #1, '88 fb, PWZ #25, '94 fb, Pun #17, '97 fb, Pun #4, '99 fb, PWJ #1, '88 fb, Pun Ann #4, '91, PWJ #1, '88 fb, PunBl, '91 fb, DE:A, '95 fb, Pun/Cap #3, '92 fb, DE:A, '95 fb, Pun #1, '98 fb, PWJ #1, '88 fb, MP #2, '75 fb, Pun Ann #4, '91, Pun #4, '99 fb, PWJ #1, '88 fb, Pun/Cap #3, '92 fb, Pun Ann #4, '91, PWJ #1, '88 fb, MP #2, '75 fb, PWJ #1, '88 fb, PWJ #3, '89 fb, Pun #1, '86 fb, Pun:YO #1, '94, Pun:AG, '88 fb, Pun:YO #2, '95, Pun Ann #4, '91, MSA Mag #1, '76 fb, Pun:YO #2-4, '95, MSA Mag #1, '76 fb, Pun #4, '99 fb, Pun #17, '97 fb, Pun:AG, '88 fb, PunBl, '91 & fb, ASM #202, '80 fb), David Linus Lieberman (State University computer science student, 1st chr app, also in dfb)
SUPPORTING CAST: Janice O'Reilly (State University English lit student & Linus' girlfriend, 1st)
VILLAINS: Professor Thomas Halliday (crooked economics professor, also in dfb), Mark Johnson (Linus' roommate, thief), Roger Wong (arms dealer), Mr. Melchior (head of Bank International) & his men (also in dfb) inc Gunther & Lothar (all 1st), North Vietnamese Army (many die), crazed lunatic
OTHER CHARACTERS: U.S. soldiers inc drill instructors, Military Police & Castle's unit inc a Lt.; military draftees, recruitment doctor, Vietnamese villagers (some as corpses), State University students, Zurich citizens, bartender, bodyguard (Frank's co-worker), actress, reporters; Maria Castle, Lisa Castle, Frank Castle Jr. (prev 3 in photo)
LOCATIONS/ITEMS: State University inc Linus' dorm room, classroom, student union & Halliday's office; Southeast Asia inc village & military prison; Zurich inc Bank International w/Melchior's office; New York inc recruitment center & private security firm office; Milwaukee, WI recruitment center; Fort Dix, Halliday home, bar / Frank's M16, gun & knife; Linus' computer & black box; Halliday's gun & computer; Melchior's men's shotgun & machine gun, Gunther's handgun, Roger's M60, U.S. soldier's assault rifles, North Vietnamese assault rifles, crazed lunatic's knife
FLASHBACK: Melchior's men find and attack Halliday and Linus.
SYNOPSIS: Frank Castle and Roger Wong go through basic training. At State University, Linus Lieberman meets Janice O'Reilly. Three months later, Mark Johnson begs Linus to alter Mark's grades electronically. Thinking about it, Linus attends Prof. Halliday's class, where he antagonizes the professor over his socialist views. That night, Linus has some fun with his girlfriend Janice and later alters Mark's grades. Days later, Halliday confronts Linus over the altered grades, and blackmails Linus into helping steal money from mob-run banks. In Vietnam, two days into his first tour, Frank finds a tortured village. His unit ambushes and kills the responsible North Vietnamese Army soldiers. Roger secretly sells the villagers weapons to defend themselves. Linus learns Mark stole his possessions and Janice is pregnant. Linus helps Halliday steal and proposes to Janice, but she turns him down. In Zurich, Bank International head Mr. Melchior orders his men to deal with the missing money. In Southeast Asia, Roger is arrested for his black market weapons operation. Two weeks later, Frank is put on recruitment duty in New York. Linus is drafted. Three weeks later, Linus reports to the Milwaukee recruitment center. Frank rejects Linus due to his poor physical condition. Years later, Frank works for a private security firm.
NOTE: PunTheNam, '94 reveals this is Frank Castle's second Marine enlistment, the first time was under his birth name Castiglione. Linus attends State University on the John J. Beckwith Science scholarship. Lothar is named next issue.

PUNISHER: THE ORIGIN OF MICROCHIP #2 (August 1993)

"Over the Edge Part 2" (24 pages)

CREDITS: Mike Baron, Carl Potts (writer), Louis Williams (pencils), Art Nichols (inks, c inks), John Kalisz, Kevin Tinsley (colors), Don Daley (editor), Dougie Braithwaite (c pencils)
FEATURE CHARACTERS: Punisher (also as Citadel, also in Kill:EY #3, '93, ASM #129, '74 & ASM #134-135, '74, next in GSSM #4, '75), David Linus Lieberman (also as Brad McMillan, becomes Microchip, also in dfb, next bts in Pun #3, '87, next in Pun #4, '87)
SUPPORTING CAST: Janice O'Reilly (becomes Janice Frohike), Louis Frohike (Linus & Janice's son, also in photo, 1st chr app before Pun #4, '87) (both also in dfb)
VILLAINS: Mr. Melchior & his men inc Gunther & Lothar; Prof. Halliday, Roger Wong, Ethiopian gangsters, terrorist, drug lord, mobster (all die), Peter Bagget (real estate swindler)
OTHER CHARACTERS: Mr. Frohike (Janice's husband, insurance salesman), Janice's daughter (both in dfb), Mrs. Halliday (corpse), Halliday's daughter (corpse), other child (bts, dead), Cocker Spaniel (corpse) & fish (die), Jesus (Microchip's supplier), Cleese (Microchip's client), motel employee (voice only), flight attendant (voice only), Microchip's landlady, San Francisco police, taxi driver, trucker, bystanders
LOCATIONS/ITEMS: Halliday home, state park, Linus & Jan's apartment, Cleveland, OH inc motel; Minneapolis, MN inc Microchip's rented house; San Francisco, CA inc Microchip's apartment; Albany, NY inc park; New York inc Brooklyn Bridge & Microchip's warehouse; Washington, DC inc park; Zurich inc Punisher's rented apartment & Bank International w/Melchior's office / Punisher's assault rifle, assault rifle w/attached grenade launcher, sniper rifle, M60, machine gun, gun, knife, binoculars, motorcycle, explosives & van; Microchip's computers, binoculars & gun; Melchior's men's machine gun, assault rifles & gun; Halliday's computer, Bagget's garrote, Ethiopian gangsters' assault rifles
FLASHBACK: Microchip finds Janice in Albany and learns his son's name is Louis.
SYNOPSIS: Melchior's men kill Halliday and his family while Linus escapes. The next night, Linus explains the situation and tells Janice to leave town. She curses him for endangering her and ruining her life. Linus goes on the run and changes his identity. He sets up a hacking business and calls himself Microchip, but he has to relocate often. Punisher fights in his war on crime. Microchip continues to do odd hacking jobs and relocate. Elsewhere, Punisher gets half of his latest gun shipment from Roger. Five years after going on the run and now in New York, Microchip

trades Leonardo, his potent computer virus that remotely erases hard drives, for equipment. Despite his precautions, smart college kids tend to track Microchip down, including his son Louis. While giving Punisher the rest of his gun shipment, Ethiopian gangsters kill Roger, who previously cheated them. Punisher escapes. A week later, Punisher contacts and recruits Microchip. A week later in Zurich, Microchip steals money from the mob-run Bank International electronically, but leaves an obvious trail so Melchior can find him. Punisher ambushes and kills Melchior's men, then kills Melchior. Microchip agrees to work with Punisher permanently. When they return to Microchip's warehouse, they find Microchip's son waiting for them.

NOTE: Frank recalls vetoing Linus' Marines application in Albany, NY, despite that happening in Milwaukee, WI.

WOLVERINE AND THE PUNISHER: DAMAGING EVIDENCE #1 (October 1993)

"Damaging Evidence Part 1 of 3" (21 pages)

CREDITS: Carl Potts (writer), Gary Erskine (art), Richard Starkings w/John Gaushell (letters), Marie Javins (colors), Greg Wright, Rob Tokar (editors)
FEATURE CHARACTERS: Punisher (also in photo, also in pfb, last in Pun #48, '91), Wolverine (last in MTU #19, '06)
SUPPORTING CAST: Microchip (in pfb, last in Pun #48, '91)
VILLAINS: Kingpin (last in DD #291, '91, last bts in Av #327, '90), Arranger (Kingpin's aide, 1st, see NOTE), Damage (Kingpin's cyborg killer, last in PWJ #20, '90), Sniper (Rich von Burian, Kingpin's hitman, last in PWJ #21, '90), Mr. Phillips (Kingpin's hitman, dies), Kingpin's employees (some die) inc Dr. Daltry (scientist), Loomis, Mr. Moore & 1 as Punisher (prev 3 die), Reavers: Donald Pierce (last in W #39, '91, next in W/Pun #3, '93), Bonebreaker (voice only), Murray Reese (both last in W #39, '91, next in UXM #281, '91), Pretty Boy (voice only, last in UXM #269, '90, next in UXM #281, '91)
OTHER CHARACTERS: Mrs. Moore (Moore's wife), Sean Moore (Moore's son), reporter (voice only on TV), news vendor, taxi driver, police, bystanders, Punisher's horse, Conchita Ortiz (mentioned, see NOTE)
LOCATIONS/ITEMS: Mexico inc Kingpin's drug ranch w/Moore home; Australia inc Reavers' base w/Pierce's lab; New York inc Punisher's safehouse (also in pfb), Dr. Daltry's private clinic, Fisk Tower w/gym & communications room & JFK International airport w/newsstand; Hong Kong / Punisher's gun, truck & Battle Van; Damage's gun & shoulder cannon; "Punisher's" Uzi & grenade; Kingpin's bench press & computerized chess set; Kingpin's employees' shotguns, guns & helicopter; Sniper's sniper rifle & knife; Phillips' gun, Moore's shotgun, Reese's machine gun
FLASHBACK: Microchip asks Punisher if the anniversary of Conchita's death is the reason Punisher has been targeting Kingpin's operations lately.
SYNOPSIS: In Mexico, Punisher attacks Kingpin's drug ranch. During the resulting firefight, Sniper arrives via helicopter but doesn't recognize Punisher. Punisher kills Kingpin employee Mr. Moore while the Moore family watches. Moore's wife stops her son Sean from shooting Punisher while Sniper's helicopter crashes. Punisher escapes. In New York, Arranger tells Kingpin that his Damage project is incapable of completion with their current technology. Kingpin decides to buy the needed technology from the Reavers and kill Punisher in one deal. In Hong Kong, Wolverine battles Reese of the Reavers and overhears Pierce mention a contract to kill Punisher on Reese's radio. Meanwhile, Pierce offers his technology to Kingpin for free if Punisher is killed within ten days, or else the cost jumps to ten million dollars. Three days later, Arranger oversees a test of Damage's new cybernetics by sending in a fake Punisher. Damage easily kills the "Punisher," but is upset to learn he didn't kill the real thing. Arranger tells Damage Punisher will be his prey if he undergoes one more procedure. Later, Wolverine doubts reports about Punisher killing bystanders during a gang raid. Punisher hears the same reports and investigates the crime scene, unaware he's being targeted.
NOTE: Indicia reads "Wolverine and the Punisher: Damaging Evidence" in this issue, but reads "The Punisher and Wolverine: Damaging Evidence" in the next two issues. W/Pun #2-3, '93 have editorial captions stating this story takes place before UXM #248-281, '89-91 & DD #296-300, '91-92. The Arranger appearing here is a blonde woman, not Kingpin's normal Arranger, a bald man. Punisher's lover Conchita Ortiz was killed in Pun #17, '89.

WOLVERINE AND THE PUNISHER: DAMAGING EVIDENCE #2 (November 1993)

"Damaging Evidence Part 2 of 3" (21 pages)

CREDITS: Carl Potts (writers), Gary Erskine (art), Richard Starkings w/John Gaushell (letters), Marie Javins (colors), Greg Wright, Rob Tokar (editors)
FEATURE CHARACTERS: Punisher (also as Det. Fort), Wolverine (also in photo)
SUPPORTING CAST: Microchip (bts, out buying supplies, next in Pun Ann #4/3, '91)
VILLAINS: Kingpin, Damage (also as Punisher, also in photo), Arranger, Sniper, Kingpin's crack dealers (die)
OTHER CHARACTERS: Mr. Moore, Mrs. Moore, Sean Moore (all in rfb), delivery man (dies), reporter (voice only on TV), bystanders (some die) inc John (dies), police
LOCATIONS/ITEMS: New York inc Punisher's safehouse, apartment building, crack dens & toxic waste plant & Fisk Tower w/Kingpin's office & communications room / Punisher's assault rifle, fake police ID & Battle Van; Damage's assault rifle, shoulder cannon, flamethrower & Battle Van; Sniper's binoculars, knife, Old Spice, van, tranquilizer & sniper rifle w/drugged dart; Kingpin's electronic chess set, crack dealers' guns
FLASHBACKS: Sean Moore and his mother watch Mr. Moore die (W/Pun #1, '93).
SYNOPSIS: Sniper watches as Punisher, disguised as a detective, investigates the crime scene. Punisher finds no clues and leaves. Wolverine arrives and notes that Punisher's scent is curiously fresh for an eighteen hour old event. Sniper asks Kingpin for permission to kill Punisher, wanting revenge against the vigilante. Kingpin instead puts Sniper in charge of shadowing Damage, who will kill Punisher. Later, Punisher attacks a crack den while Damage, disguised as Punisher, watches. Punisher later learns that the family upstairs from the crack den was killed. Punisher wonders if he's having blackouts. Wolverine arrives at the crime scene and Sniper alerts Kingpin. After Kingpin sends a delivery, Sniper hits Wolverine with tranquilizer and stashes him in a van. Punisher attacks another crack den, resulting in a bystander being hit by a stray bullet. Wolverine wakes up and hotwires the van. Punisher escapes as Damage, as Punisher, arrives and opens fire on the other bystanders. Wolverine attacks Damage and their battles take them to a nearby toxic waste plant.
NOTE: Includes Siege of Darkness preview (14 pages), a crossover between the Midnight Sons books.

"Damaging Evidence Part 3 of 3" (23 pages)

CREDITS: Carl Potts (writer), Gary Erskine (art), Richard Starkings w/John Gaushell (letters), Pat Garrahy, Marie Javins, Chris Matthys (colors), Greg Wright, Rob Tokar (editors)
FEATURE CHARACTERS: Punisher (next in DC #4, '91), Wolverine (next in UXM #278, '91)
VILLAINS: Kingpin (next in DD Ann #7/2, '91), Donald Pierce (last in W/Pun #1, '93, next in UXM #281, '91), Damage (also as Punisher, destroyed), Sniper (dies), Arranger
OTHER CHARACTERS: Mr. Moore, Mrs. Moore, Sean Moore (all in rfb), bystanders (some die)
LOCATIONS/ITEMS: New York inc toxic waste plant, cemetery & Fisk Tower / Punisher's gun, knife & Battle Van; Sniper's sniper rifle, binoculars & gun; Kingpin's electronic chess set, check, sealed container & note; Damage's grenade launcher
FLASHBACK: Sean Moore and his mother watch Mr. Moore die (W/Pun #1, '93).
SYNOPSIS: Wolverine battles Damage, slicing away his limbs and cutting him open to little effect. Wolverine rips out Damage's grenade launcher and fires it inside Damage's chest, but Damage keeps fighting and stabs Wolverine with his severed limb. Stuck to Damage, Wolverine drowns him in chemical waste. Convinced Damage is dead, Sniper goes to the funeral of the upstairs family killed during Punisher's raid, knowing Punisher will be there. Sniper begins killing the funeral attendees until Punisher shoots him. Sniper takes a hostage, but Punisher gets in close enough to stab him. As he dies, Sniper tells Punisher to go to the toxic waste plant. Punisher frees Wolverine from Damage's arm, but Damage wakes up and attacks. Punisher kicks Damage into the chemical waste and sets the chemicals on fire. Arranger suggests that Kingpin send Damage's head to the Reavers and claim he's the Punisher, but Kingpin instead sends the head along with a check for fifty million dollars as compensation to have Damage rebuilt. Pierce agrees, though he's shocked when he learns Wolverine was involved in Damage's defeat.

"Family Business" (22 pages)

CREDITS: Dan Abnett, Andy Lanning (writers), Dale Eaglesham (pencils), Scott Koblish (inks), Bill Oakley (letters), Marie Javins & Electric Crayon (colors), Freddy Mendez (asst editor), Don Daley (editor), Vince Evans (c paint), Cindy Emmert (c design)
FEATURE CHARACTER: Frank Castle (last in Pun #1, '86 fb, also in Pun:AG, '88 fb)
SUPPORTING CAST: Maria Castle, Lisa Castle, Frank Castle Jr. (all corpses, last in PWJ #3, '89 fb, next bts in MP #2, '75 fb)
VILLAINS: Forest Hunt (during PWJ #3, '89 fb, dies), Maurice Howles (mob hitman) & his partner (both 1st)
OTHER CHARACTERS: Miles Warren (Empire State University professor, last in SpSM Mag #2, '68, next in ASM Ann '96 fb), Det. Johnny Laviano (1st chr fb), Det. Stan Witts (Laviano's police partner, 1st), Mike McTeer (washed up reporter, 1st), police inc Weiss (1st), Renaldi & Keever (bts, obtained Castle's military history); Bob (Buchan's Bar bartender), Buchan's Bar patrons, paramedics; Mrs. Weiss (Officer Weiss' wife, bts, abducted by hitmen), Dr. Treaks (mentioned, Warren is covering his shift while on vacation), Eddie, Steeler Gus, Toecap, Coombs (prev 4 mentioned, in Castle's unit)
LOCATIONS/ITEMS: New York inc Central Park, Buchan's Bar & Mount Sinai hospital w/Frank's room / Castle family's body bags, paramedic's sedative, McTeer's Jack Daniel's whiskey, hitmen's pistols, police revolver, Mrs. Weiss' wedding ring
SYNOPSIS: In Central Park, gunfire awakens drunken reporter Mike McTeer. Thinking the sounds are firecrackers, he stumbles across the bullet riddled Castle family and Forest Hunt. Later, Det. Laviano meets his partner Det. Witts at the scene. Witts tells Laviano the family and Hunt have been declared dead, and the only witness is McTeer. As Laviano angrily interviews McTeer, Frank Castle leaps out of his body bag and attacks the police. Frank has to be sedated twice before he finally falls on his wife's body. At Mount Sinai hospital, McTeer overhears the police discuss Castle's military history and leaves thinking he's stumbled across a Pulitzer. Laviano learns from Miles Warren that Forest Hunt is also still alive. Laviano demands that Frank not be told about Hunt's survival, not wanting to turn Castle into a vigilante. As McTeer begins to write his story, Hunt dies before Laviano can question him. Two mob hitmen infiltrate the hospital, convince the guard to let them through and prepare to kill Frank Castle.
NOTE: Includes credits page (1 page) w/Dale Eaglesham's pencils of cover as frontispiece & recap page (1 page). Maurice is named next issue. Witts notes that Frank received the Bronze Star, Silver Star and four Purple Hearts. Laviano notes Frank has the Presidential Medal of Honor coming.

"Post Mortem" (22 pages)

CREDITS: Dan Abnett, Andy Lanning (writers), Dale Eaglesham (pencils), Scott Koblish (inks), Bill Oakley (letters), Justin Gabrie, Colin Jorgensen (colors), Freddy Mendez (asst editor), Don Daley (editor), Vince Evans (c paint), Cindy Emmert (c design)
FEATURE CHARACTER: Frank Castle (also in Pun Ann #4, '91 & MSA Mag #1, '76 fb)
GUEST STAR: Peter Parker (last in ASM #83, '70, next in Cap #130, '70)
VILLAINS: Captain Howard "Howie" Furniss (corrupt policeman, 1st), Maurice Howles & his partner (dies)
OTHER CHARACTERS: Betty Brant, Joe Robertson (both last in ASM #83, '70, next in ASM Ann '96 fb), J. Jonah Jameson (bts, meets w/McTeer, last in ASM #83, '70, next in ASM #86, '70), Det. Laviano (also in Pun Ann #4, '91, next in MSA Mag #1, '76 fb), Det. Witts, Mike McTeer, Jenny McTeer (Mike McTeer's wife, 1st bts, calls for

Mike), police inc Weiss (dies); Daily Bugle employees, diner patrons; Maria Castle, Lisa Castle, Frank Castle Jr. (prev 3 in photos)

LOCATIONS/ITEMS: Castle home, New York inc diner, Daily Bugle w/Robertson's office, Mount Sinai hospital w/Frank's room & police station w/Captain Furniss' office & Det. Laviano's office / Frank's Johnnie Walker scotch, wheelchair, Marine uniform & service pistol; Brant's memo pad, hitmen's pistols, Laviano & Witt's revolvers, Peter Parker's camera

SYNOPSIS: Frank Castle attacks the hitmen. Frank uses one as a human shield and the hitman dies. The other hitman tries to shoot his way out, killing a policeman, but Castle captures him. Laviano stops Frank from killing the hitman. Later, Castle identifies from mug shots members of the Costa family as his family's killers. Laviano ecstatically tells his Captain that Frank wants to testify. At the Daily Bugle, McTeer convinces Joe Robertson to give him a chance at writing a piece on Castle and borrows a camera from Peter Parker. McTeer visits Castle, explains who he is and convinces Frank to let him write his story by lying about Mrs. McTeer being dead. Laviano learns from his Captain that the department won't be pressing charges against the Costas. When McTeer hears this, he takes Castle to the Daily Bugle to speak directly to J. Jonah Jameson. While McTeer waits, McTeer's wife calls the Bugle. Realizing McTeer lied and that he's out of options, Frank Castle heads home and prepares to commit suicide.

NOTE: Includes credits page (1 page) w/Dale Eaglesham's pencils of cover as frontispiece & recap page (1 page). Janey is named next issue.

PUNISHER: YEAR ONE #3 (February 1995)

"In Memoriam" (22 pages)

CREDITS: Dan Abnett, Andy Lanning (writers), Dale Eaglesham (pencils), Scott Koblish (inks), Susan Crespi, Jim Novak, Bill Oakley (letters), Justin Gabrie, Colin Jorgensen (colors), Freddy Mendez (asst editor), Don Daley (editor), Vince Evans (c paint), Cindy Emmert (c design)
FEATURE CHARACTER: Frank Castle
VILLAINS: Bruno Costa (last in Pun Ann #4, '91, next in MSA Mag #1, '76 fb), Frank Costa (last in Pun #3, '99 fb, next in MSA Mag #1, '76 fb), Billy "the Beaut" Russo (Costa family hitman, chr 1st app), Maurice Howles (dies), Costa network mobsters inc Rico "the Beard" Colicos (also in photo), Flynn Mulligan, Vargas (in photo, mentioned, Atlantic City money launderer), Dupont & Luff (both mentioned, in protection racket); Costa family guards, Captain Furniss (bts, assigns Laviano & Witts to look into aggression against Costa family)
OTHER CHARACTERS: Det. Laviano (last in MSA Mag #1, '76 fb), Det. Witts, Mike McTeer (dies), Janey McTeer (voice only) (both also in photo), Mt. Sinai hospital nurses & staff, bar patrons & bartender, police, taxi driver, Frank's neighbors; Maria Castle (in photo)
LOCATIONS/ITEMS: Castle family home (destroyed), Alphabet City inc bar; Queens inc laundromat; Little Italy inc Aldo's; Brooklyn inc McTeer's brownstone; New York inc Mt. Sinai hospital w/Maurice's room & police station w/Laviano's office; Punta Verde, FL inc Costa estate / Frank's Marine uniform & service pistol; Russo's gun w/silencer, Maurice's wheelchair, Costa guard's assault rifle, mobster's knife, Peter Parker's camera
SYNOPSIS: McTeer hears gunfire as he arrives at the Castle home. He rushes inside to find Frank still alive, unable to kill himself. Castle attacks McTeer for lying to him; McTeer admits to using Frank because he needed a bestselling story to redeem himself. Having tried Laviano and McTeer's ways and failing, Frank decides to take his own initiative against the Costa family. Using McTeer's ties to the press, Castle and McTeer track down and interrogate various Costa family associates. Laviano's Captain orders him to look into the recent aggression against the Costa family, but Laviano ignores the order. In Costa Verde, Frank Costa tells his brother Bruno not to worry; he knows just the man to take care of the problem. In Brooklyn, Frank and McTeer go over the Costa information they've acquired and plan to learn more tomorrow. At Mt. Sinai, Costa's hitman kills Maurice Howles. Feeling good about his life, McTeer calls his wife. As he waits for her to answer, Costa's hitman kills McTeer. Castle returns home, but notices Maria's flowers have been trampled. The house suddenly explodes.
NOTE: Includes credits page (1 page) w/Dale Eaglesham's pencils of cover as frontispiece & recap page (1 page). Billy Russo is identified next issue.

PUNISHER: YEAR ONE #4 (March 1995)

"Fire With Fire" (23 pages)

CREDITS: Dan Abnett, Andy Lanning (writers), Dale Eaglesham (pencils), Scott Koblish (inks), Bill Oakley (letters), Colin Jorgensen (colors), Freddy Mendez (asst editor), Don Daley (editor), Vince Evans (c paint), Cindy Emmert (c design), Peter Sanderson (thanks), Louise Stephenson (special thanks)
FEATURE CHARACTER: Frank Castle (becomes Punisher, next in MSA Mag #1, '76 fb, Pun #4, '99 fb, Pun #17, '97 fb, PunBl, '91 & fb, ASM #202, '80 fb, Pun:OM #2, '93, Kill:EY #3, '93, ASM #129, '74)
VILLAINS: Billy Russo (becomes Jigsaw, next in PWJ #18, '08 fb), 25 other mobsters (die) inc Lonny (dies)
OTHER CHARACTERS: Det. Laviano (next in Pun Ann #4, '91), Det. Witts, Mike McTeer (corpse), the Mechanic (Vietnam veteran, bts, provides Castle w/ordnance), Ace bar patrons, Salvagno's chef & waiters, firefighters, police, McTeer's neighbors, bystanders, pigeons
LOCATIONS/ITEMS: Castle family home (wreckage), Long Island inc Laviano home, Brooklyn inc McTeer's brownstone; New York inc Punisher's hideout, Salvagno's & Ace bar / Punisher's service pistol, armored vest, camouflage paint, Claymore mines, shotgun, grenade, guns, handcuffs & reel-to-reel tape recorder; Russo's gun, mobsters' guns
SYNOPSIS: Detectives Laviano and Witts laments Frank Castle's death, unaware Frank survived his home's explosion. Castle races to McTeer's brownstone and finds his corpse. Later, Frank confronts Laviano at the detective's home, demanding information on the hitman who set the bomb at his home. Laviano mentions that he often carelessly leaves his briefcase in his car. Castle tells Laviano that Frank Castle died in Central Park with his family. In his hideout, Frank Castle records his first journal entry and prepares himself to punish criminals that the law can't or won't. Punisher sneaks into Salvagno's while inside, Billy Russo celebrates another successful job. Punisher evacuates the staff and brutally attacks the mobsters. Punisher kills everyone except Billy Russo. Punisher tells Russo that he's the one thing Russo's kind hoped would never exist. Russo tries to bribe Punisher, but the vigilante tosses Russo through a plate glass window and onto the street below, giving Russo a Jigsaw face. Later, Laviano and Witts celebrate at a bar, where Laviano toasts Frank for starting his war on crime.
NOTE: Includes credits page (1 page) w/Dale Eaglesham's pencils of cover as frontispiece & recap page (1 page). Dedicated to Gerry Conway

and to the memory of Ross Andru. These events occur "six weeks" before MSA Mag #1, '76. Punisher makes his War Journal "First Entry" here. A movie theater is playing "Love Story."

SPIDER-MAN/PUNISHER: FAMILY PLOT #1 (February 1996)

"Family Plot Part One: The Fall" (39 pages)

CREDITS: Tom Lyle (writer, c pencils), Shawn McManus, Mike Harris, Dick Giordano (co-pencils), Mike Manley (co-pencils, co-inks), Randy Emberlin, Brett Breeding, Chris Ivy, Al Milgrom, Arne Starr (co-inks), Janice Chiang (letters), Mark Bernardo & Malibu (colors), Tom Brevoort (editor), Scott Hanna (c inks)
FEATURE CHARACTERS: Spider-Man (Ben Reilly, last in SMHol '95/5), Punisher (last in Pun #4, '96)
SUPPORTING CAST: Don Mario Geraci, Vinnie Barbarossa (both last in Pun #4, '96), Kim Sung Young (between Pun #4-5, '96), Leslie Geraci (last in Pun #3, '96), Horace Halftree (last in Pun #3, '96, next in Pun #5, '96)
VILLAINS: Tombstone (Lonnie Thompson Lincoln, mob enforcer, last in WoSM #120, '95), Grover Dill (Tombstone's idea man, 1st, dies), Joey Geraci, (last in Pun #4, '96), Steve Marlowe (1st), Jeff Phelps (dies) (both Tombstone gang members), Geraci family, purse snatcher
OTHER CHARACTERS: Mario Barbarossa (Vinnie's son), Kathy Somers (Daily Grind employee), Steve "Stevie" Marlowe, Jr. (Kathy's son) (all 1st), Carmine (Punisher's "snitch"), Vince Williams (chief of police, off-panel, dies), Gianelli (city councilman, mentioned, Tombstone hit victim), Daily Grind customers, police (inc "a cop on the take," others bts), purse snatcher's victim, prostitutes & potential client, bystanders
LOCATIONS/ITEMS: New York inc San Genaro neighborhood, The Daily Grind coffee house, Geraci estate, Kathy Somers' apartment, Tombstone's penthouse (destroyed), Steve Marlowe's apartment / Spider-Man's spider-tracers, web-shooters & tranquilizer spider-stinger; Punisher's automatic pistols w/silencer, grappling rope & binoculars; Marlowe, Phelps, Don Geraci & Mario Barbarossa's guns; Stevie's key to his father's apartment, Tombstone's sphere electrocution device & sphere bomb
SYNOPSIS: Spider-Man interrupts a gang hit on Don Geraci in which Vinnie Barbarossa is wounded. Angry that Spidey is interfering in "family business" Vinnie's son Mario attacks him, allowing the gunmen to flee. Back at his Daily Grind job, Ben Reilly meets co-worker Kathy Somers' son Stevie and ex-husband Steve Marlowe who triggers his spider-sense. At the Geraci estate, the family votes that the Punisher must kill Spider-Man. Joey Geraci frets that his alliance with the family's enemies was not supposed to include a hit on the Don. Meanwhile, Tombstone berates his men, Jeff Phelps and Steve Marlowe, for botching the hit. He kills Phelps, then sends Marlowe to kill Police Chief Williams. Spidey tails Marlowe from his home, while Punisher searches for Spidey, discovering Mario following him. Threatened by Frank, Mario admits Don Geraci sent him to spy. Punisher finds and attacks Spidey, inadvertently allowing Marlowe to kill Williams. Marlowe escapes when Spidey and Punisher vie over him, returning to Tombstone. Soon after, Spidey and Punisher break in. During the fight, Grover Dill is killed, leaving Tombstone without his mob takeover mastermind. Punisher declares his intent to kill Marlowe for being in on the Geraci hit. Marlowe lobs Tombstone's sphere bomb at the heroes and helps his boss escape. The bomb explodes, destroying the penthouse.

SPIDER-MAN/PUNISHER: FAMILY PLOT #2 (February 1996)

"Family Plot Part Two: Redemption" (39 pages)

CREDITS: Tom Lyle (writer), Joe Bennett (pencils, c art), Mike Witherby, Tom Webrzyn (inks), Bill Oakley/NJQ (letters), Chris Matthys & Malibu (colors), Chris Cooper (editor)
FEATURE CHARACTERS: Spider-Man (also in symbolic image, also in rfb as Ben Reilly, also in pfb; next in SpSM #231, '96), Punisher (also in rfb, also in pfb; next in Pun #5, '96)
SUPPORTING CAST: Don Mario Geraci, Leslie Geraci, Vinnie Barbarossa (all next in Pun #5, '96), Tom Nichols (between Pun #4-5, '96)
VILLAINS: Tombstone (also in rfb, next in Pun #5, '96) & his men inc John, Gordy (both die), Shawn & Benny (1 other dies), Joey Geraci (next in Pun #5, '96), Steve Marlowe (also in rfb, dies), Geraci family
OTHER CHARACTERS: Rudolph "Rudy" Giuliani (New York mayor, 1st, next bts in Pun #10, '01), Mario Barbarossa (next in Pun #6, '96), Kathy Somers (also in rfb), Grover Dill (corpse), Stevie Marlowe, police (some die), ambulance crew (bts, in ambulance), bystanders, dog, birds
LOCATIONS/ITEMS: New York inc Tombstone's penthouse (also in rfb, destroyed), Geraci estate, Kathy Somers' apartment w/Stevie's bedroom, Steve Marlowe's apartment, Gracie Mansion (Mayor's residence), Fritz Lang Hotel, The Daily Grind coffee house (also in rfb) / Spider-Man's web-shooters, spider-tracer & spider-stingers; Punisher's automatic pistol & rocket launcher; Marlowe, John, Tombstone & his other men's guns; Stevie's key to his father's apartment & Spider-Man pin
FLASHBACKS: Ben Reilly meets Steve Marlowe. Spidey captures Marlowe but Punisher intervenes and Marlowe escapes. Marlowe tosses a sphere bomb (all SM/Pun #1, '96). Spidey and Punisher jump from the penthouse (p).
SYNOPSIS: As they fall, Spider-Man uses his webbing to save Punisher and himself. With the penthouse destroyed, Marlowe offers his apartment to Tombstone. Meanwhile, Stevie sneaks out, leaving his mother's apartment for his father's place. He walks in on Tombstone killing his henchman Gordy. Tombstone holds Stevie hostage while Marlowe and two others set out to murder the mayor. Arriving at Marlowe's place, Punisher trails the hitmen while Spidey breaks in to save Stevie. As Tombstone's men storm the mayor's residence, Punisher intervenes and kills all but Marlowe. Kathy Somers, finding Stevie missing, comes to Marlowe's apartment, just as Spidey attacks Tombstone. Punisher arrives with Marlowe, who tries to save his family, but Tombstone shoots and kills Marlowe. Punisher shoots Tombstone with a rocket launcher, apparently killing him. Later, Ben Reilly tells Stevie his dad became a good man by sacrificing himself and that Stevie should remember the good over the bad. At the Geraci estate, Punisher argues that he couldn't honorably kill Spidey since the web-slinger saved his life from the penthouse explosion. Mario, witnessing this while spying, vouches for Frank. Punisher later wonders if bonding with the Geraci family betrays his real family.
NOTE: Stevie has a Thor comic book on his bedroom floor.

PUNISHER KILLS THE MARVEL UNIVERSE
(November 1995) (46 pages)

CREDITS: Garth Ennis (writer), Douglas Braithwaite (pencils), Martin Griffith, Michael Halbleib, Sean Hardy, Donald C. Hudson, John Livesay, Robin Riggs (inks), Bill Oakley (letters), Shannon Blanchard, Tom Smith (colors), Marc McLaurin (editor)
FEATURE CHARACTER: Punisher (also in pfb)
SUPPORTING CAST: Microchip
GUEST STARS: Daredevil (also in pfb), Hulk, Spider-Man (also as floating head in Kesselring's narrative), Alpha Flight: Puck, Sasquatch; Shaman, Avengers: Captain America, Hawkeye, Thor, Vision (also as floating head in Kesselring's narrative); X-Men: Beast, Cable, Cannonball, Colossus, Cyclops (also as floating head in Kesselring's narrative), Gambit, Iceman, Jean Grey, Jubilee, Rogue, Sunspot, Strong Guy, Storm, Wolverine (all die)
VILLAINS: Kesselring (disfigured millionaire, dies) & Kesselring's associates inc Mrs. McEneany, Mr. Krieg, Mr. Marseille, Mrs. Pierce, Ms. Dunn; Apocalypse, Dr. Doom & his Doombots, Juggernaut, Kingpin & his bodyguards, Magneto, Mr. Sinister, Omega Red, Sabretooth, Sauron, Venom (also as floating head in Kesselring's narrative), White Queen (prev 13 all die), Brood, Skrulls, Hell's Kitchen bullies (in pfb only)
OTHER CHARACTERS: Dunn (Castle's partner), Latverian citizens, SHIELD agents, TV reporter, police, bystanders, deer (stuffed, on wall only), Black Panther, Ghost Rider, Green Goblin, Human Torch, Invisible Woman, Iron Man, Nick Fury, Psylocke, Thing (prev 9 head's only, in Kesselring's narrative only)
LOCATIONS/ITEMS: Central Park, Hell's Kitchen, Latveria inc Dr. Doom's castle, Kesselring's mansion, the Moon, courthouse, prison / Dr. Doom's lasers, microwave guns, nuclear bomb, robots & smart weapons, Matt Murdock's books, Punisher's helicopter, machine guns, tracking device & tracer bullet; SHIELD prison transport spaceship, judge, trial audience
FLASHBACK: A young Frank Castle saves a young Matt Murdock from being bullied by neighborhood kids, warning Matt to stick up for himself.
SYNOPSIS: In an alternative universe the Avengers and X-Men accidentally kill Frank Castle's family while battling an alien invasion in Central Park. Frank Castle arrives on the scene to find his family's corpses. When Cyclops attempts to apologize for their deaths, Frank kills Cyclops and several X-Men and Avengers before being apprehended. He is sentenced to life in prison, but is freed by a mysterious disfigured man named Kesselring, who brings Castle to his mansion and introduces him to several others who have been injured carelessly during superhero battles. Kesselring offers to arm Frank if he will begin a war against superpowered people. Castle agrees, and calling himself the Punisher, he kills every costumed hero and villain over the next 5 years using weaponry stolen from the Kingpin and Magneto's bases. With only Daredevil left to kill, Kesselring and his group attempt to celebrate with the Punisher. Punisher mocks their depravity, and start to leave, warning he's done working for them. When Kesselring tries to stop him, Punisher kills him and warns the other members of Kesselring's group to disband. Punisher later confronts Daredevil in Hell's Kitchen. Daredevil tries to get Frank to end his vendetta, but Frank fatally wounds Daredevil, then unmasks the vigilante to discover his victim is his childhood friend Matt Murdock. As Murdock dies, Frank turns the gun on himself, his crusade finished.
NOTE: This story is set on alternate Earth-95126. Jubilee's costume resembles Kitty Pryde's first X-Men costume. Kesselring calls Mrs. McEneany "him."

PUNISHER: THE END (June 2004)

"The End" (48 pages)

CREDITS: Garth Ennis (writer), Richard Corben (art), Comicraft's Richard Starkings & James Betancourt (letters), Lee Loughridge (colors), John Miesegaes (asst editor), Axel Alonso (editor)
FEATURE CHARACTER: Punisher (Frank Castle)
VILLAINS: The Coven (Senators and captains of industry, secret world leaders since WWII, caused nuclear armageddon), New York bunker scientist & security; Paris Peters (arsonist) (all die)
OTHER CHARACTERS: US President, Secretary of State (both voice only in dfb), Sing-Sing Warden, Charlie (Warden's assistant), Sing-Sing guards inc Ferris (all die), Sing-Sing inmates (corpses), bystanders (skeletal corpses); New York Governor (bts, on phone w/Warden, ordered prisoners killed); William Teacher (designed nuclear bunkers, mentioned, told Punisher New York bunker location & access code), Maskey, Vicks (both Sing-Sing guards, mentioned, deserted posts to be with family), Kenning (Sing-Sing guard, mentioned, tries to open prison fallout shelter, killed by Punisher), Leary, Young (both Sing-Sing guards, mentioned, tried to eat Kenning, killed by Punisher)
LOCATIONS/ITEMS: Sing-Sing Maximum Security Prison inc Warden's office, & D-Block w/Punisher's cell; New York (ruins) inc East River & subway tunnels w/nuclear bunker w/lab, security break room & comms / Punisher's assault rifle & Geiger counter; Warden's Johnnie Walker scotch & gun; bunker scientist's adrenaline & scalpel; bunker security's gun, machine guns & assault rifles; prison security's assault rifles
FLASHBACK: In the Washington, DC bunker, the President of the United States rapes the Secretary of State (d).
SYNOPSIS: As war looms, Sing-Sing Prison's Warden orders the inmates killed. However the Punisher kills the guards when they come for him. A year later, having survived in the prison's fallout shelter, Punisher and Paris Peters enter a nuclear war-ravaged world. Checking his Geiger counter Punisher realizes radiation poisoning will kill them within days. As they trek thirty miles to New York, Punisher explains to Peters that America's "War on Terror" led to war with China. They reach New York's ruins without seeing anything living and enter a bunker under the old World Trade Center site. The entry code Punisher tries is invalid, triggering gas, and they wake inside the bunker under armed guard, to be informed they'll be dead within hours. Killing the guards, Punisher confronts the Coven, surviving billionaires and politicians who secretly ran the world. Punisher explains William Teacher, the bunker's designer who the Coven framed, gave Punisher the access code in prison. The Coven tells Punisher only their New York bunker survived, but they can repopulate Earth via frozen human embryos when radiation levels become tolerable. Punisher kills the Coven, then Paris Peters, the last criminal. His war finally done, Frank Castle, the last man on Earth, walks to Central Park to be reunited with his family.
NOTE: Part of Marvel's "The End" series, set in alternate futures depicting possible final stories of prominent characters. This story is set on Earth-40616.

ABBREVIATION KEY

Below are the abbreviations used in this Index. A comprehensive list can be found at http://www.marvel.com/universe/index.

1st – in chronologies this usually refers to the first appearance. When it means another first, such as the first time a character is mentioned, a clarification (1st mention) is included.
Ann – Annual
app – appearance
bts – a behind the scenes appearance, where a character was not seen, but nonetheless impacted on the story in some way.
chr – chronologically. Differentiates between the real last and next appearances, and revised last and next appearances created by flashbacks and other continuity inserts.
dfb – during flashback. A flashback set within the issue it is presented in.
fb – flashback. An appearance set in a time frame earlier than the rest of a given issue's story.
HC – hardcover
inc – including
LOC – letter of comment
pfb – prior flashback. A flashback set just before the events in the main story.
prev – previous
rfb – reminder flashback. A flashback that reshows past events with no new content.
Spec – Special
TPB – trade paperback

AFlt – Alpha Flight
AnniC:SL – Annihilation: Conquest - Starlord
AntM – Irredeemable Ant-Man
AoAtlas – Agents of Atlas
AoH – Age of Heroes

ASM – Amazing Spider-Man
ASM:Swing – Amazing Spider-Man: Swing Shift (Free Comic Book Day)
AT:W/Pun – Astonishing Tales: Wolverine/Punisher (digital comic)
Av – Avengers
Av/Tb – Avengers/Thunderbolts
Av:In – Avengers: the Initiative
Av:XSanc – Avengers: X-Sanction
AVenom – Amazing Spider-Man Presents: Anti-Venom - New Ways to Live
AvS – Avengers Spotlight
AvSM – Avenging Spider-Man
AWC – Avengers West Coast
AX – Astonishing X-Men
Barracuda – Punisher Presents: Barracuda
BCat – Black Cat
BP – Black Panther
Bull:GH – Bullseye: Greatest Hits
BW – Black Widow
C&D – Cloak and Dagger
Cable&Dp – Cable & Deadpool
Cap – Captain America
Cap:ME – Captain America: the Medusa Effect
Cap:Re – Captain America: Reborn
CapC – Captain America Comics
CD – ClanDestine
Ch – Champions
ChW – Chaos War
CM – Captain Marvel
CMass – Critical Mass
CoC2 – Contest of Champions II
CPun – Classic Punisher
CW – Civil War
CW:BDR – Civil War: Battle Damage Report
CW:FL – Civil War: Front Line
CW:FSDB – Civil War: Fallen Son Daily Bugle Special
CW:In – Civil War: the Initiative
CW:WarC – Civil War: War Crimes
DAv – Dark Avengers
Daz – Dazzler

DC – Damage Control
DC2 – Damage Control vol. 2
DCvM – DC versus Marvel
DD – Daredevil
DD:N – Daredevil: Ninja
DDvPun – Daredevil vs. Punisher
DE:A – Double Edge: Alpha
DE:Ω – Double Edge: Omega
Dhawk – Darkhawk
Dhold – Darkhold: Pages From the Book of Sins
Dline – Deadline
Dlk – Deathlok
DocS – Doc Samson
DoD – Daughters of the Dragon
Dp – Deadpool
Dp:Merc – Deadpool: Merc with a Mouth
Dp:SK – Deadpool: Suicide Kings
DpTU – Deadpool Team-Up
DR:Elek – Dark Reign: Elektra
DR:Hawk – Dark Reign: Hawkeye
DR:Hood – Dark Reign: the Hood
DR:LL – Dark Reign: Lethal Legion
DR:MM – Dark Reign: Made Men (digital comic)
DR:MrN – Dark Reign: Mr. Negative
DR:Z – Dark Reign: Zodiac
DracL – Dracula Lives!
DRL:Hulk – Dark Reign: the List - Hulk
DRL:Pun – Dark Reign: the List - Punisher
DRL:SecWs – Dark Reign: the List - Secret Warriors
DrS – Doctor Strange
DrV – Doctor Voodoo: Avenger of the Supernatural
DW – Dark Wolverine
Elek:G&E – Elektra: Glimpse & Echo
Elek:Hand – Elektra: the Hand
Et – Eternals
F.F. – FF
FallSon:Cap – Fallen Son: the Death of Captain America - Captain America

FallSon:IM – Fallen Son: the Death of Captain America - Iron Man

FallSon:SM – Fallen Son: the Death of Captain America - Spider-Man

FallSon:W – Fallen Son: the Death of Captain America - Wolverine

FC – Franken-Castle

Fear:SM – Fear Itself: Spider-Man

FF – Fantastic Four

FF/IM:Big – Fantastic Four/Iron Man: Big in Japan

FFF – Fin Fang Four (digital comic)

FFU – Fantastic Four Unlimited

FNSM – Friendly Neighborhood Spider-Man

FoH:RH – Fall of the Hulks: Red Hulk

FoS – Fury of SHIELD

Fury/13 – Fury/Agent 13

Fury:PM – Fury: Peacemaker

G&Ch – Gambit and the Champions: From the Marvel Vault

Gam – Gambit

GenX – Generation X

Girl – Girl Comics

Goblin – Green Goblin

GotG – Guardians of the Galaxy

GR – Ghost Rider

GR/W/Pun – Ghost Rider/Wolverine/Punisher

GSSM – Giant-Size Spider-Man

Hawk – Hawkeye

HFH – Heroes for Hire

HoM – House of M

Hulk:Nm – Hulk: Nightmerica

I♥M:Web – I ♥ Marvel: Web of Romance

IHulk – Incredible Hulk

IM – Iron Man

IM:LD – Iron Man: Legacy of Doom

ImpSVS – Impossible Man Summer Vacation Spectacular

InfG – Infinity Gauntlet

Inv – Invaders

InvIM – Invincible Iron Man

JIM – Journey Into Mystery

JLA/Av – JLA/Avengers

KConan – King Conan

Kill:EY – Killpower: the Early Years

KZ – Ka-Zar

LoM – Legion of Monsters

LoM:S – Legion of Monsters: Satana

Mag – Magneto

MApes – Marvel Apes

MAv – Mighty Avengers

MaxC:A – Spider-Man: Maximum Clonage Alpha

MaxC:O – Spider-Man: Maximum Clonage Omega

MaxS – Maximum Security

MChan – Marvels Channel: Monsters, Myths & Marvels (digital comic)

MCP – Marvel Comics Presents

MDS – Marvel Double-Shot

MEnc – Marvel Encyclopedia

MGN:RMA – Marvel Graphic Novel: Rick Mason, the Agent

MHol – Marvel Holiday Special

MK – Moon Knight

MK:Div – Moon Knight: Divided We Fall

MKn – Marvel Knights

MKnDS – Marvel Knights Double-Shot

MKSM – Marvel Knights Spider-Man

MM:MOTP – Marvel Monsters: Monsters on the Prowl

MM:WMD – Marvel Monsters: Where Monsters Dwell

Morb – Morbius, the Living Vampire

Motor – Motormouth

MP – Marvel Preview

MPr – Marvel Premiere

MSA – Marvel Super Action

MSA Mag – Marvel Super Action Magazine

MsM – Ms. Marvel

MSUn – Midnight Sons Unlimited

MTU – Marvel Team-Up

MUni – Marvel Universe

MvPro – Marvels Project

MWOFiles – Marvel Westerns: Outlaw Files

MZ4 – Marvel Zombies 4

NAv – New Avengers

NAvF – New Avengers: Most Wanted Files

NF:AoS – Nick Fury: Agent of SHIELD

NFHC – Nick Fury's Howling Commandos

Ns – Nightstalkers

NThr – Night Thrasher

NW – New Warriors

NX – New X-Men

OHMU – Official Handbook of the Marvel Universe

OHMU:U – Official Handbook of the Marvel Universe: Update

OtEdge – Over the Edge

PP – Power Pack

PPSM – Peter Parker: Spider-Man

PPSSM – Peter Parker, the Spectacular Spider-Man

Pun – Punisher

Pun 2099 – Punisher 2099

Pun/BW – Punisher/Black Widow: Spinning Doomsday's Web

Pun/Cap – Punisher/Captain America: Blood & Glory

Pun:AG – Punisher: Assassin's Guild

Pun:Anniv – Punisher Anniversary Magazine

Pun:Bf – Punisher MAX: Butterfly

Pun:Blood – Punisher: Blood on the Moors

Pun:BSS – Punisher: Back to School Special

Pun:BV – Punisher: Bloody Valentine

Pun:Cell – Punisher: the Cell

Pun:Easy – Punisher: Die Hard in the Big Easy

Pun:EQ – Punisher: Empty Quarter

Pun:FoN – Punisher: Force of Nature

Pun:Get – Punisher MAX: Get Castle

Pun:GF – Punisher: G-Force
Pun:GI – Punisher: the Ghosts of Innocents
Pun:Happy – Punisher MAX: Happy Ending
Pun:Hot – Punisher MAX: Hot Rods of Death
Pun:Int – Punisher: Intruder
Pun:ItB – Punisher: In the Blood
Pun:KG – Punisher: Kingdom Gone
Pun:LBB – Punisher MAX: Little Black Book
Pun:NE – Punisher: No Escape
Pun:NK – Punisher MAX: Naked Kill
Pun:OM – Punisher: the Origin of Microchip
Pun:POV – Punisher: POV
Pun:Prize – Punisher: the Prize
Pun:RBN – Punisher: Return to Big Nothing
Pun:RedX – Punisher: Red X-Mas
Pun:Silent – Punisher: Silent Night
Pun:Tiny – Punisher MAX: Tiny Ugly World
Pun:Tyger – Punisher: the Tyger
Pun:XMas – Punisher: X-Mas
Pun:YO – Punisher: Year One
PunArm – Punisher Armory
PunBl – Punisher Bloodlines
PunHol – Punisher Holiday Special
Punmax – Punishermax
PunSS – Punisher Summer Special
PunTheNam – Punisher Invades the 'Nam
PunvBull – Punisher vs. Bullseye
PWJ – Punisher War Journal
PWZ – Punisher War Zone
Q – Quasar
RamW – Rampaging Wolverine
RH – Rampaging Hulk
Run – Runaways
Sabre – Sabretooth
SecDef – Secret Defenders
SecInv – Secret Invasion
SecInvPro – Secret Invasion

Prologue (digital comic)
SecWar – Secret War
SecWs – Secret Warriors
SenSM – Sensational Spider-Man
SH – She-Hulk
Shadow – Shadowmasters
SI:DF – Spider-Island: Deadly Foes
SI:NYC – Spider-Island: I Love New York City
SKK – Skrull Kill Krew
Sland – Shadowland
Sland:SM – Shadowland: Spider-Man
Sleep – Sleepwalker
SM – Spider-Man
SM/BCat – Spider-Man/Black Cat
SM/Pun – Spider-Man/Punisher: Family Plot
SM/Pun/Sabre – Spider-Man/Punisher/Sabretooth: Designer Genes
SM:BBRead – Spider-Man: Black & Blue & Read All Over
SM:BiQ – Spider-Man: Back in Quack
SM:DMH – Spider-Man: Dead Man's Hand
SM:GetK – Spider-Man: Get Kraven
SM:HL – Spider-Man: Hobgoblin Lives
SM:Made – Spider-Man: Made Men
SM:PoT – Spider-Man: the Power of Terror
SMTU – Spider-Man Team-Up
SMU – Spider-Man Unlimited
SpSM – Spectacular Spider-Man
SS – Silver Surfer
SSol – Super Soldiers
SSwConan – Savage Sword of Conan
SSWP – Silver Sable & the Wild Pack
ST – Strange Tales
SuPo – Supreme Power
SVTU – Super-Villain Team-Up
SW – Spider-Woman
SW:O – Spider-Woman: Origin

Task – Taskmaster
Tb – Thunderbolts
Tb:RM – Thunderbolts: Reason in Madness
TheNam – The 'Nam
Time – Timestorm: 2009-2099
TInc – Terror, Inc.
TM:BB – Tales of the Marvels: Blockbuster
TMU – Tales of the Marvel Universe
ToS – Tales of Suspense
ToT – Tomb of Terror
Tstrike – Thunderstrike
TTA – Tales to Astonish
TWoS – Tangled Web of Spider-Man
U – Underworld
UltFF – Ultimate Fantastic Four
UltMTU – Ultimate Marvel Team-Up
Ults – Ultimates
UXM – Uncanny X-Men
Venom:FP – Venom: Funeral Pyre
Venom:OT – Venom: On Trial
W – Wolverine
W/Pun – Wolverine/Punisher
W:Kill – Wolverine: Killing
W:MrX – Wolverine: Mr. X
W:O – Wolverine: Origins
W:RTH – Wolverine: Road to Hell
WarM – War Machine
WI? – What If?
Wlk&IW – Warlock and the Infinity Watch
WM – Wonder Man
WoSM – Web of Spider-Man
WWHulk:X – World War Hulk: X-Men
X – X-Men
X/Brood – X-Men/Brood
X:TS&P – X-Men: To Serve and Protect
X23 – X-23
XFac – X-Factor
XFor – X-Force
XMan – X-Man
XMU – X-Men Unlimited